lonely planet

Mediterranean Europe

Janet Austin
Carolyn Bain
Neal Bedford
Verity Campbell
Joyce Connolly
Fionn Davenport
Matt Fletcher
Susan Forsythe
Kate Galbraith
Jeremy Gray

Paul Hellander
Mark Honan
Patrick Horton
Keti Japaridze
John King
Sarah Mathers
John Noble
Tim Nollen
Jeanne Oliver
Daniel Robinson
Miles Roddis

David Rowson
Andrea
 Schulte-Peevers
Rachel Suddart
Bryn Thomas
Julia Wilkinson
David Willett
Nicola Williams
Neil Wilson
Pat Yale

LONELY PLANET PUBLICATIONS
Melbourne • Oakland • London • Paris

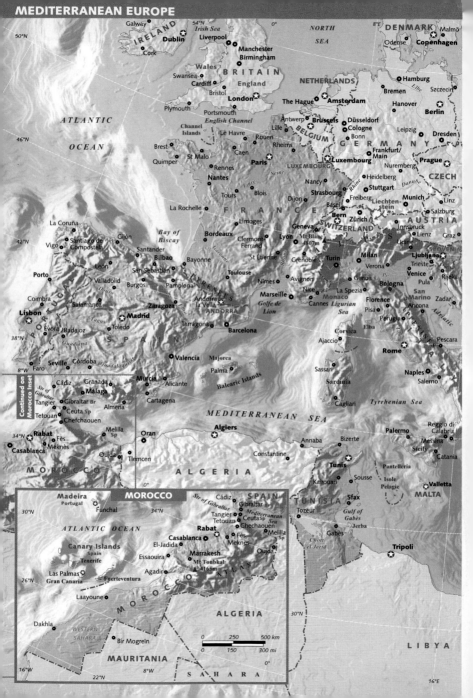

MEDITERRANEAN EUROPE

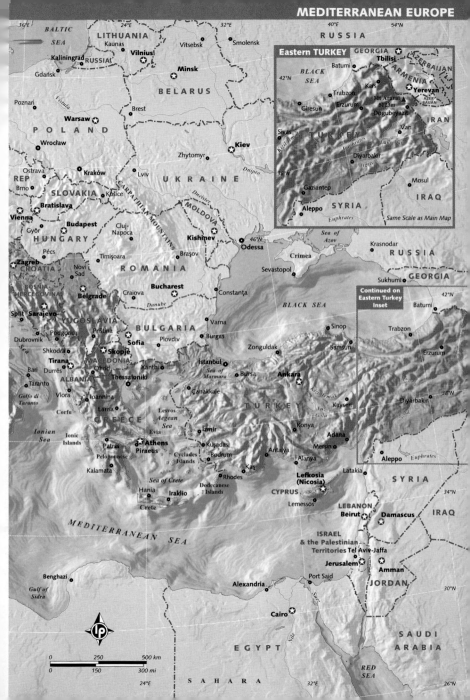

Mediterranean Europe
5th edition – January 2001
First published – January 1993

Published by
Lonely Planet Publications Pty Ltd ABN 36 005 607 983
90 Maribyrnong St, Footscray, Victoria 3011, Australia

Lonely Planet Offices
Australia Locked Bag 1, Footscray, Victoria 3011
USA 150 Linden St, Oakland, CA 94607
UK 10a Spring Place, London NW5 3BH
France 1 rue du Dahomey, 75011 Paris

Photographs
All of the images in this guide are available for licensing from
Lonely Planet Images.
email: lpi@lonelyplanet.com.au

Front cover photograph
The crystalline waters at Le Vieux Castillon, Castillon du Gard, Gard,
France (Chris Sanders, Stone)

ISBN 1 86450 154 5

text & maps © Lonely Planet 2001
photos © photographers as indicated 2001

Printed by The Bookmaker International Ltd
Printed in China

Although the authors and Lonely Planet try to make the information as accurate as possible, we accept no responsibility for any loss, injury or inconvenience sustained by anyone using this book.

Contents – Text

CROATIA 123

FRANCE 203

GREECE 343

ITALY 425

Contents – Maps

8 Contents – Maps

The Authors

Janet Austin
Janet worked on the Italy chapter. Her taste for travel was fostered at an early age with two childhood ocean voyages from Australia to the UK. She was lured back in her teenage years by a love for all things European and the London punk rock explosion, remaining for over 10 years. Janet edits Lonely Planet's travel literature series, Journeys, which allows her to vicariously clock up some kilometres while sitting in front of a computer screen. She is married and lives in Melbourne with two grey cats.

Carolyn Bain
Carolyn worked on the Greece chapter. She was born in Melbourne, Australia (the third-largest Greek city in the world) and first visited Greece as a teenager (on a package tour from Scandinavia, no less). She was therefore eminently qualified to ferry-hop around two dozen Greek islands in search of the perfect beach, best calamari and any unattached shipping magnates. Due to an unfortunate shortage of shipping magnates, she returned to her job as an editor at Lonely Planet's Melbourne office.

Neal Bedford
Neal worked on the Spain chapter. Born in Papakura, New Zealand, Neal gave up an exciting career in accounting after university to experience the mundane life of a traveller. With the urge to move, travel led him through a number of countries and jobs, ranging from an au pair in Vienna, lifeguard in the USA, fruit picker in Israel and lettuce washer at rock concerts. Deciding to give his life some direction, he well and truly got his foot stuck in the door by landing the lucrative job of packing books in Lonely Planet's London office. One thing led to another and he managed to cross over to the mystic world of authoring. Neal currently resides in London, but the need to move will probably soon kick in and force him to try his luck somewhere else.

Verity Campbell
Verity worked on the Turkey chapter. Born with a ticket in her hand, Verity was on a mission to have a full passport by the age of seven. Struggling to fight the travel bug, she went to Uni and studied Landscape Architecture. It was in vain – a year later she quit her graduate job and wrestled Tony Wheeler to the ground to land a job at Lonely Planet (Melbourne). She jumped (literally) at the chance to return to Turkey where she lived in 1990-91. Lured by Turkish Delight and misdemeanours, İstanbul nightlife and with a belly to dance she all too willingly abandoned her hairy companion Max.

Joyce Connolly

Joyce Connolly worked on the Morocco chapter. Born in Edinburgh, Scotland, she has been on the move since an early age, including time in Germany and the Netherlands where she developed an appreciation of fine beers. Fuelled by the travel bug, she studied to become a professional tourist but instead stumbled into publishing in Oxford. In 1995 she set off to Australia in pursuit of Jason Donovan who obligingly moved in round the corner from her in Bondi, then moved to Melbourne to woo LP; she became an editor and was entrusted with updating the Gippsland chapter of the *Victoria* guide. Since then she's flown the editorial coop to update the Zimbabwe chapter of *Southern Africa* and *Morocco*. She's now based in the UK.

Fionn Davenport

Fionn worked on the Italy chapter. He was born in and spent most of his youth in Dublin – that is, when his family wasn't moving him to Buenos Aires or Geneva or New York. Infected with the travel disease, he became a nomad in his own right after graduating from Trinity College, moving first to Paris and then to New York, where he spent five years as a travel editor and sometime writer. The call of home was too much to resist, however, so armed with his portable computer, his record collection and an empty wallet he returned to Dublin and decided to continue where he left off in New York. Only it was quieter, wetter and a hell of a lot smaller. When he's not DJing in pubs and clubs throughout the city he's writing and updating travel guides. He has worked on Lonely Planet guides to *Spain*, *Dublin*, *Ireland*, *Sicily*, *England* and *Britain*.

Matt Fletcher

Matt worked on the Morocco chapter. After travelling on and off since leaving Art College, Matt got the inspiration for a writing career while travelling down through Southern Africa. A brief incarnation as a staff writer on an adventure sports magazine soon passed on and Matt has been freelancing ever since, travelling and trekking in the UK, Europe and East Africa. Matt is a contributor to Lonely Planet's *Walking in Spain* and *Walking in Australia*, *Kenya* and *East Africa* guides. When not working he plays at playing football and studies libel law.

Kate Galbraith

Kate updated the Albania and Macedonia chapters (and flew home to run the London marathon in between). Born in Washington, DC, Kate first heard the call of the Balkans in 1996, when she spent the summer before her final year at Harvard University working for a local news agency in Sarajevo. Two years later she updated the Bosnia-Hercegovina chapter for *Eastern Europe 5*, subsequent LP

sojourns include Latvia and Micronesia. Kate recently finished a Masters degree at the London School of Economics in Eastern European political economy. She currently works for Economist.com, the website of *The Economist* magazine, in New York and London.

Jeremy Gray

Jeremy worked on the France chapter. A Louisiana native, he studied literature and business in Texas before moving to Germany on a scholarship in 1984. Infatuated with Europe, he chucked his MBA plans and stayed on to teach English, translate and best of all, file plumbing orders for the US Air Force. In the meantime he grew to appreciate many things French, such as the wonderful way the *pâtisseries* wrap takeaway cakes like baby gifts. A master's degree in international relations from Canterbury led Jeremy back to Germany, where he spent the 1990s chasing politicians and CEOs for news agencies, newspapers and television. While freelancing for the *Financial Times* he discovered Lonely Planet, and since 1998 has contributed to or written *Germany*, *The Netherlands* and city guides for *Munich* and *Montreal*. He now lives in Amsterdam.

Paul Hellander

Paul worked on the France chapter. He has never really stopped travelling since he first looked at a map in his native England. He graduated from Birmingham University with a degree in Greek before heading for Australia. He taught Modern Greek and trained interpreters and translators for thirteen years before throwing it all away for a life as a travel writer. Paul has contributed to over 20 LP titles including guides to *Greece*, *Cyprus*, *Israel*, *Eastern Europe*, *Singapore* and *Central America*. When not travelling, he lives in Adelaide, South Australia. He was last spotted heading once more for Greece to write a guide to *Rhodes & the Dodecanese*.

Mark Honan

Mark worked on the Getting Around chapter. After a university degree in philosophy opened up a glittering career as an office clerk, Mark decided that there was more to life than data entry. He set off on a two-year trip round the world, armed with a backpack and an intent to sell travel stories and pictures upon his return. Astonishingly, this barely-formed plan succeeded and Mark has since contributed regularly to magazine travel pages. He started writing for Lonely Planet in 1991 and has worked on guides to *Vienna*, *Austria*, *Switzerland*, *India*, *Mexico*, *Central America* and *Solomon Islands* – next up are *Vienna* and *Austria* again.

Patrick Horton

Patrick updated the Yugoslavia chapter. Patrick, a writer and photographer, was born with restless feet. He travelled extensively in his native Britain before hitting the around-the-world trail as a Thatcher refugee in 1985. Since bringing his old British bikes out to Australia, he now calls Melbourne home. He prefers the more arcane areas of travel such as North Korea, Eritrea or Tonga, or riding a motorcycle over the Himalaya. Patrick lives with his long-suffering partner Christine, another ardent traveller he met in Paris. Patrick has had photographs published in many Lonely Planet guides and contributed to Lonely Planet's *Australia* guide.

Keti Japaridze

Keti worked on the Bosnia-Hercegovina chapter. Born in Tbilisi, Georgia, Keti is an art historian by profession. The writing of the Georgia section of the Lonely Planet guide to *Georgia, Armenia & Azerbaijan* with her husband David introduced her to the world of travel writing, a development unlikely to have occurred when her country was part of the USSR. She was fascinated to compare the culture and recent history of Bosnia-Hercegovina, another former communist republic in the south-east of Europe, with that of her homeland, and impressed by the sense of a country bursting with vitality again after the terrible years of war.

John Noble & Susan Forsyth

John and Susan worked on the Spain chapter. John comes from the Ribblesdale, England, Susan from Melbourne, Australia. After studies, John worked in Fleet Street journalism and Susan taught secondary and adult students. But travel distracted them both and one year they found themselves simultaneously in Sri Lanka _ Susan working as a volunteer teacher and John carrying out his first commission for Lonely Planet. They married three years later and have since been kept extremely busy rearing two children, Isabella and Jack, as well as coauthoring heaps of Lonely Planet titles such as *Mexico*, *Spain*, *Andalucía*, *Indonesia*, *Russia*, *Ukraine & Belarus* and *Baltic States*. Current home base is an Andalucian hill village.

Jeanne Oliver

Jeanne Oliver updated the Croatia and Slovenia chapters. Born in New Jersey, she spent her childhood mulling over the *New York Times* travel section and plotting her future voyages. After a BA in English and a stint at the *Village Voice* newspaper, Jeanne got a law degree. Her legal practice was interrupted by ever-more-frequent trips to far-flung destinations and eventually she set off on a round-the-world trip that landed her in Paris. A job in the tourist business led to freelance writing assignments for magazines and guidebooks. She started working for Lonely Planet in 1996 and has written the first editions of *Croatia*, *Crete* and *Crete Condensed* guides as well as updating chapters in *Greece*, *Mediterranean Europe* and *Eastern Europe*.

Daniel Robinson

Daniel worked on the France chapter. He was raised in the USA (the San Francisco Bay Area and Glen Ellyn, Illinois) and Israel. His passion for shoestring travel was kindled at age 17 with a trip to Cyprus, and since then he has spent several years on the road exploring some of the more remote parts of Asia, the Middle East and Europe.

Daniel's work for Lonely Planet has included the 1st editions of the award-winning *Vietnam* and (with Tony Wheeler) *Cambodia*, and all four editions of *France*. Daniel has a BA in Near Eastern Studies from Princeton University and is currently finishing up an MA in Israeli history at Tel Aviv University.

Miles Roddis

Miles worked on the Andorra, France and Spain chapters. Miles and his partner Ingrid live in a shoe-box sized apartment in the Barrio del Carmen, the oldest and most vibrant quarter of Valencia, Spain. His involvement with France began when, 15 and spotty, he noisily threw up the night's red wine in a Paris cafe. Undeterred, he mainlined in French at university, became seriously hooked and later bought an equally tiny place in a hamlet in the Jura that will never feature in any guidebook. Miles has contributed to Lonely Planet's *Africa on a Shoestring*, *West Africa*, *Read This First: Africa*, *Lonely Planet Unpacked*, *France*, *Spain*, *Walking in Britain*, *Walking in France* and *Walking in Spain*.

David Rowson

David worked on the Bosnia-Hercegovina chapter. Brought up in the suburbs of London, David graduated in English Literature and then hit on the time-honoured idea of teaching English as a good way to get out and see something of the world. This profession has taken him to Spain, Egypt and Georgia. He was recently surprised to realise that he had spent a quarter of his life in Tbilisi, which came in handy when he wrote the Georgia section of the *Georgia, Armenia & Azerbaijan* guide with his wife Keti. He is now adapting to life in Kingston upon Thames again, but doesn't rule out future moves.

Andrea Schulte-Peevers

Andrea worked on the Spain chapter. She is a Los Angeles-based writer, editor and translator who caught the travel bug early and had been to all continents but Antarctica by the age of 18. After finishing high school in Germany, she decided the world was too big to stay in one place and moved first to London, then to Los Angeles. Armed with a degree from UCLA, she managed to turn her wanderlust into a professional career as a travel writer and may still chase penguins around the South Pole one of these days. Since joining the LP team in 1995 Andrea has updated and/or authored the guides to *Los Angeles*, *Berlin*, *Germany*, *California & Nevada* and *Spain*.

Rachel Suddart

Rachel updated the Cyprus Chapter. Born and raised in Cumbria, she escaped to the city to study English at Manchester University. After being eyeballed by the sphinx at the age of 15, she knew she wanted more and funded her subsequent travels by pulling endless pints, waiting tables and soldering circuit boards. Despite her dire navigational skills she has travelled round many countries and hopes to continue until she's too old to carry her ever-expanding rucksack.

In January 2000, she got her first taste of Lonely Planet authorship by taking part in a BBC documentary. She currently lives in London where she thrives on paperback fiction, soap operas and copious amounts of salad cream.

Bryn Thomas

Bryn worked on the Facts for the Visitor and Getting There & Away chapters. Born in Zimbabwe, where he grew up on a farm, Bryn contracted an incurable case of wanderlust during camping holidays by the Indian Ocean in Mozambique. An anthropology degree at Durham University in England earned him a job polishing the leaves of pot plants in London. He also has been a ski-lift operator, encyclopedia seller, and an English teacher in Cairo, Singapore and Tokyo.

Travel on six continents has included a 2500km Andean cycling trip. Bryn's first guide, the *Trans-Siberia Handbook*, was shortlisted for the Thomas Cook Guidebook of the Year awards. He is also coauthor of Lonely Planet's *Britain*, *India* and *Goa*, and has contributed to *Walking in Britain*.

Julia Wilkinson & John King

Julia and John worked on the Portugal chapter. After leaving university, Julia set off from England for a jaunt round the world and immediately got sidetracked in Hong Kong, where she stayed for some 20 years, exploring Asia as a freelance travel writer and photographer. A frequent PATA award winner, she has contributed to numerous international publications. She is also author of Lonely Planet's *Lisbon* guide and coauthor, with her husband John King, of LP's *Portugal* and *South-West France*.

John grew up in the USA, and in earlier incarnations has been a physics teacher and an environmental consultant. In 1984 he headed off to China and ended up living there for half a year. He and Julia met in Lhasa. John took up travel writing with the 1st edition of LP's *Karakoram Highway*. He has also coauthored LP's *Pakistan*; *Central Asia*; *Russia, Ukraine & Belarus*; *Czech & Slovak Republics*; and the *Prague* city guide.

David Willett

David worked on the Greece and Tunisia chapters. He is a freelance journalist based near Bellingen on the north coast of New South Wales, Australia. He grew up in Hampshire, England, and wound up in Australia in 1980 after stints working on newspapers in Iran (1975-78) and Bahrain. He spent two years working as a sub-editor on the Melbourne *Sun* before trading a steady job for a warmer climate. Between jobs, David has travelled extensively in Europe, the Middle East and Asia. He is also the author of Lonely Planet's guide to *Tunisia* and coordinating author of *Greece*. He has contributed to various other guides, including *Africa, Australia, New South Wales, Indonesia* and *South-East Asia*.

Nicola Williams

Nicola worked on the France chapter. Since her first trip to Romania in 1991 with 10 Welsh policemen as part of an international aid convoy, her work as a journalist has taken her to most corners of Eastern Europe. Following 12 months in Latvia as features editor of the *Baltic Times* newspaper, she moved to Lithuania to bus it around the Baltics as editor-in-chief of the *In Your Pocket* city-guide series. In 1996 she traded in Lithuanian *cepelinai* for Lyonnais *andouillette*.

Nicola has authored or updated several Lonely Planet titles, including *Romania & Moldova, Estonia, Latvia & Lithuania* and *Russia, Ukraine & Belarus*.

Neil Wilson

Neil updated the Malta chapter. After working as a geologist in Australia and the North Sea and doing geological research at Oxford University, Neil gave up the rock business for the more precarious life of a freelance writer and photographer. Since 1988 he has travelled in five continents and written some 27 travel and walking guides for various publishers. He has worked on Lonely Planet's *Georgia, Armenia & Azerbaijan, Malta, Czech & Slovak Republics, Prague* and *Slovenia* guides. Although he was born in Glasgow, Neil defected to the east at the age of 18 and still lives in Edinburgh.

Pat Yale

Pat Yale worked on the Turkey chapter. Pat first went to Turkey in 1974 in an old van that didn't look as if it would make it past Dover. After graduating she spent several years selling holidays before throwing away sensible careerdom to head overland from Egypt to Zimbabwe. Returning home, she mixed teaching with extensive travelling in Europe, Asia, and Central and South America. A full-time writer now, she has worked on Lonely Planet *Britain, Ireland, London, Dublin, Middle East* and assorted other titles. She currently lives in an old pasha's house in Göreme, Cappadocia.

This Book

This Book

Many people have helped to create this 5th edition of *Mediterranean Europe*. Among the major contributors to past editions were Mark Armstrong, Mark Balla, Tom Brosnahan, Stefano Cavedoni, Colin Clement, Adrienne Costanzo, Geoff Crowther, Rob van Driesum, Richard Everist, Steve Fallon, Hugh Finlay, Kate Galbraith, Helen Gillman, Rosemary Hall, Charlotte Hindle, Frances Linzee Gordon, Jeanne Oliver, Corinne Simcock, Damien Simonis, David Stanley, Robert Strauss, Dorinda Talbot, Gary Walsh, Sally Webb and Tony Wheeler.

Mediterranean Europe is part of Lonely Planet's Europe series, which includes *Eastern Europe*, *Central Europe*, *Scandinavian & Baltic Europe*, *Western Europe* and *Europe on a Shoestring*. Lonely Planet also publishes phrasebooks to these regions.

FROM THE PUBLISHER

The editing of this edition of *Mediterranean Europe* was coordinated by Susannah Farfor and the cartography by Rachel Imeson. They were assisted by Susie Ashworth, Yvonne Bischofberger, Lisa Borg, Simon Bracken, Yvonne Byron, Csanád Csutoros, Hunor Csutoros, Tony Davidson, Paul Dawson, Janine Eberle, Tony Fankhauser, Liz Filleul, Quentin Frayne, Cris Gibcus, Mark Griffiths, Ann Jeffree, Birgit Jordan, Russell Kerr, Joelene Kowalski, Craig MacKenzie, Sarah Mathers, Fiona Meiers, Sally Morgan, Shelley Muir, Tim Nollen, Darren O'Connell, Brett Pascoe, Adrian Persoglia, Agustín Poó y Balbontin, Tim Ryder, Jacqui Saunders, Chris Thomas, Ray Thompson, Tim Uden, Natasha Velleley, Celia Wood, Chris Wyness and Sara Yorke.

THANKS

Many thanks to the travellers who used the last edition and wrote to us with helpful hints, advice and interesting anecdotes. Your names appear in the back of this book.

Foreword

ABOUT LONELY PLANET GUIDEBOOKS

The story begins with a classic travel adventure: Tony and Maureen Wheeler's 1972 journey across Europe and Asia to Australia. Useful information about the overland trail did not exist at that time, so Tony and Maureen published the first Lonely Planet guidebook to meet a growing need.

From a kitchen table, then from a tiny office in Melbourne (Australia), Lonely Planet has become the largest independent travel publisher in the world, an international company with offices in Melbourne, Oakland (USA), London (UK) and Paris (France).

Today Lonely Planet guidebooks cover the globe. There is an ever-growing list of books and there's information in a variety of forms and media. Some things haven't changed. The main aim is still to help make it possible for adventurous travellers to get out there – to explore and better understand the world.

At Lonely Planet we believe travellers can make a positive contribution to the countries they visit – If they respect their host communities and spend their money wisely. Since 1986 a percentage of the income from each book has been donated to aid projects and human rights campaigns.

Updates Lonely Planet thoroughly updates each guidebook as often as possible. This usually means there are around two years between editions, although for more unusual or more stable destinations the gap can be longer. Check the imprint page (following the colour map at the beginning of the book) for publication dates.

Between editions up-to-date information is available in two free newsletters – the paper *Planet Talk* and email *Comet* (to subscribe, contact any Lonely Planet office) – and on our Web site at www.lonelyplanet.com. The *Upgrades* section of the Web site covers a number of important and volatile destinations and is regularly updated by Lonely Planet authors. *Scoop* covers news and current affairs relevant to travellers. And, lastly, the *Thorn Tree* bulletin board and *Postcards* section of the site carry unverified, but fascinating, reports from travellers.

Correspondence The process of creating new editions begins with the letters, postcards and emails received from travellers. This correspondence often includes suggestions, criticisms and comments about the current editions. Interesting excerpts are immediately passed on via newsletters and the Web site, and everything goes to our authors to be verified when they're researching on the road. We're keen to get more feedback from organisations or individuals who represent communities visited by travellers.

Lonely Planet gathers information for everyone who's curious about the planet – and especially for those who explore it first-hand. Through guidebooks, phrasebooks, activity guides, maps, literature, newsletters, image library, TV series and Web site we act as an information exchange for a worldwide community of travellers.

Research Authors aim to gather sufficient practical information to enable travellers to make informed choices and to make the mechanics of a journey run smoothly. They also research historical and cultural background to help enrich the travel experience and allow travellers to understand and respond appropriately to cultural and environmental issues.

Authors don't stay in every hotel because that would mean spending a couple of months in each medium-sized city and, no, they don't eat at every restaurant because that would mean stretching belts beyond capacity. They do visit hotels and restaurants to check standards and prices, but feedback based on readers' direct experiences can be very helpful.

Many of our authors work undercover, others aren't so secretive. None of them accept freebies in exchange for positive write-ups. And none of our guidebooks contain any advertising.

Production Authors submit their raw manuscripts and maps to offices in Australia, USA, UK or France. Editors and cartographers – all experienced travellers themselves – then begin the process of assembling the pieces. When the book finally hits the shops, some things are already out of date, we start getting feedback from readers and the process begins again …

WARNING & REQUEST

Things change – prices go up, schedules change, good places go bad and bad places go bankrupt – nothing stays the same. So, if you find things better or worse, recently opened or long since closed, please tell us and help make the next edition even more accurate and useful. We genuinely value all the feedback we receive. Julie Young coordinates a well travelled team that reads and acknowledges every letter, postcard and email and ensures that every morsel of information finds its way to the appropriate authors, editors and cartographers for verification.

Everyone who writes to us will find their name in the next edition of the appropriate guidebook. They will also receive the latest issue of *Planet Talk*, our quarterly printed newsletter, or *Comet*, our monthly email newsletter. Subscriptions to both newsletters are free. The very best contributions will be rewarded with a free guidebook.

Excerpts from your correspondence may appear in new editions of Lonely Planet guidebooks, the Lonely Planet Web site, *Planet Talk* or *Comet*, so please let us know if you *don't* want your letter published or your name acknowledged.

Send all correspondence to the Lonely Planet office closest to you:

Australia: Locked Bag 1, Footscray, Victoria 3011
USA: 150 Linden St, Oakland, CA 94607
UK: 10A Spring Place, London NW5 3BH
France: 1 rue du Dahomey, 75011 Paris

Or email us at: talk2us@lonelyplanet.com.au

For news, views and updates see our Web site: www.lonelyplanet.com

HOW TO USE A LONELY PLANET GUIDEBOOK

The best way to use a Lonely Planet guidebook is any way you choose. At Lonely Planet we believe the most memorable travel experiences are often those that are unexpected, and the finest discoveries are those you make yourself. Guidebooks are not intended to be used as if they provide a detailed set of infallible instructions!

Contents All Lonely Planet guidebooks follow roughly the same format. The Facts about the Destination chapters or sections give background information ranging from history to weather. Facts for the Visitor gives practical information on issues like visas and health. Getting There & Away gives a brief starting point for researching travel to and from the destination. Getting Around gives an overview of the transport options when you arrive.

The peculiar demands of each destination determine how subsequent chapters are broken up, but some things remain constant. We always start with background, then proceed to sights, places to stay, places to eat, entertainment, getting there and away, and getting around information – in that order.

Heading Hierarchy Lonely Planet headings are used in a strict hierarchical structure that can be visualised as a set of Russian dolls. Each heading (and its following text) is encompassed by any preceding heading that is higher on the hierarchical ladder.

Entry Points We do not assume guidebooks will be read from beginning to end, but that people will dip into them. The traditional entry points are the list of contents and the index. In addition, however, some books have a complete list of maps and an index map illustrating map coverage.

There may also be a colour map that shows highlights. These highlights are dealt with in greater detail in the Facts for the Visitor chapter, along with planning questions and suggested itineraries. Each chapter covering a geographical region usually begins with a locator map and another list of highlights. Once you find something of interest in a list of highlights, turn to the index.

Maps Maps play a crucial role in Lonely Planet guidebooks and include a huge amount of information. A legend is printed on the back page. We seek to have complete consistency between maps and text, and to have every important place in the text captured on a map. Map key numbers usually start in the top left corner.

Although inclusion in a guidebook usually implies a recommendation we cannot list every good place. Exclusion does not necessarily imply criticism. In fact there are a number of reasons why we might exclude a place – sometimes it is simply inappropriate to encourage an influx of travellers.

Introduction

Mediterranean Europe evokes images of beautiful beaches, the brilliant blue of the Mediterranean Sea, spectacular landscapes dotted with olive and citrus groves, outdoor cafes, wonderful food, friendly local people, exuberant festivals and a relaxed way of life. It *is* all this – and even more.

This book offers an insight into the many different countries of the region, their peoples and cultures, and provides practical information to help you get the most out of your time and money. It covers the area from Portugal and Morocco in the west to Cyprus and Turkey in the east. Although Portugal is not on the Mediterranean, and Morocco, Tunisia and most of Turkey are not part of Europe, these countries have been included because of their proximity and accessibility as well as their historical ties to the region.

Given the exceptional diversity of the countries and cultures in Mediterranean Europe, the choice of things to see and do is almost limitless. Some of Europe's earliest and most powerful civilisations flourished around the Mediterranean, and traces of them remain in the many archaeological sites and in the monuments, architecture, art, writings and music they created. There are countless churches, galleries and museums with works of art ranging from the Renaissance masters to 20th-century innovators. The region features architectural masterpieces as diverse as the Parthenon in Athens, Chartres' cathedral in France, the Hagia Sofia in Istanbul, St Peter's Basilica in Rome, the Alhambra in Granada and Gaudí's extraordinary creations in Barcelona.

When museums and churches begin to overwhelm you, turn to the many outdoor pursuits Mediterranean Europe has to offer. There is skiing or trekking in the Alps, Apennines, Pyrenees and Atlas Mountains; island-hopping in Greece; or you can simply laze on a beach anywhere along the coast. The food of the Mediterranean region is one of its principal delights, not to mention the wine of Burgundy, Tuscany and elsewhere. There are even places where you can escape from other travellers, as relatively few tourists have made their way to Albania or to many parts of eastern Turkey and southern Italy.

Mediterranean Europe includes much practical information on how to get there and how to get around once you've arrived, whether it's by road, rail or ferry. There are extensive details on what to see, when to see it and how much it all costs. The thousands of recommendations about places to stay range from *domatia* (rooms to rent) in Greece to cheap hotels in the medinas (old towns) of Morocco. Restaurant recommendations include outdoor cafes in France, trattorias in Italy and *gostilne* in Slovenia. If shopping appeals, the Mediterranean area offers outlets ranging from chic boutiques in Paris and Istanbul's Grand Bazaar to flea markets.

It's 3000km from the Strait of Gibraltar to the Turkish coast – a huge region with a huge number of attractions waiting to be enjoyed. To experience them, all you have to do is go.

Facts for the Visitor

HIGHLIGHTS
The Top 10
There is so much to see and do in Mediterranean Europe that compiling a top 10 is next to impossible. But we asked the authors involved in this book to list their personal highlights. The results are as follows:

1. Paris
2. Rome
3. The Alps
4. Florence & Tuscany
5. Greek Island-hopping
6. Epiros in north-west Greece
7. Istanbul
8. Venice
9. Cappadocia
10. Morocco's High Atlas Mountains

Other nominations included the Dalmatian coast, Barcelona, Umbria, Provence, the Pyrenees, Corsica, Andalucía, Seville, Lisbon, the wine cellars of Oporto, and camel trekking in the Sahara.

The Bottom 10
The writers were also asked to list the 10 worst 'attractions' of the region:

1. Spain's Costa del Sol
2. The Greek island of Kos
3. Albufeira on Portugal's Algarve
4. Disneyland Paris
5. Palma de Mallorca
6. Bullfights in Spain
7. Milan
8. Monte Carlo's casino
9. Agios Nikolaos on Crete
10. France's far northern coast

PLANNING
When to Go
Any time can be a good time to visit Mediterranean Europe, depending on what you want to do. Summer lasts roughly from June to September in the northern half of Europe and offers the most pleasant climate for outdoor pursuits. Along the Mediterranean coast, on the Iberian Peninsula and in southern Italy and Greece, where the summers tend to be hotter and longer, you can extend that period by one or even two months either way, when temperatures may also be more agreeable. The best time to visit most of Tunisia and Morocco is spring and autumn.

You won't be the only tourist during the summer months in Mediterranean Europe – everyone in France, Spain and Italy, for instance, goes on holiday in August. Prices can be high, accommodation fully booked and the sights packed. You'll find much better deals – and far fewer crowds – in the shoulder seasons either side of summer; in April and May, for instance, flowers are in bloom and the weather can be surprisingly mild, and Indian summers are common in Mediterranean Europe in September and October.

On the other hand, if you're keen on winter sports, resorts in the Alps and the Pyrenees begin operating in November or early December and move into full swing after the New Year, closing down again when the snows begin to melt in March or April.

The Climate and When to Go sections under Facts for the Visitor in the individual country chapters explain what to expect and when to expect it, and the Climate Charts in Appendix I in the back of the book will help you compare the weather in different destinations. The temperate climate along the Atlantic seaboard is relatively wet all year, with moderate extremes in temperature; the Mediterranean coast is hotter and drier, with most rainfall occurring during the mild winter; and the continental climate in eastern France and the Alps has greater extremes in weather between summer and winter.

What Kind of Trip
Travelling Companions If you decide to travel with others, keep in mind that travel can put relationships to the test like few other experiences can. Many a long-term friendship has collapsed under the strain of constant negotiations about where to stay and eat, what to see and where to go next. But many friendships also become closer than ever before. You won't find out until you try, but make sure you agree on itineraries and routines beforehand and try to remain flexible

about everything even in the heat of an August afternoon in Rome or Madrid. Travelling with someone else also has financial benefits as a single room is more expensive per person than a double in most countries.

If travel is a good way of testing established friendships, it's also a great way of making new ones. Hostels and camping grounds are good places to meet fellow travellers, so even if you're travelling alone, you need never be lonely.

The Getting Around chapter has information on organised tours.

Move or Stay? 'If this is Tuesday, it must be Barcelona.' Though often ridiculed, the mad dash that crams six countries into a month does have its merits. If you've never visited Mediterranean Europe before, you won't know which areas you'll like, and a quick 'scouting' tour will give an overview of the options. A rail pass that offers unlimited travel within a set period of time is the best way to do this.

But if you know where you want to go, or find a place you like, the best advice is to stay put for a while, discover some lesser known sights, make a few local friends and settle in. It's also cheaper in the long run.

For information on working in Mediterranean Europe, see the Work section later in this chapter.

Maps

Good maps are easy to come by once you're in Europe, but you might want to buy a few beforehand to plan and track your route. The maps in this book will help you get an idea of where you might want to go and will be a useful first reference when you arrive in a city. Proper road maps are essential if you're driving or cycling.

For some European cities Lonely Planet now has detailed city maps. Michelin maps are also good and, because of their soft covers, they fold up easily so you can stick them in your pocket. As a rule, maps published by European automobile associations (the AA in Britain, the ADAC and AvD in Germany etc) are excellent and sometimes free if membership of your local association gives you reciprocal rights. Tourist offices are often another good source for (usually free and fairly basic) maps.

What to Bring

It's very easy to find almost anything you need in Mediterranean Europe and, since you'll probably buy things as you go along, it's better to start with too little rather than too much.

A backpack is still the most popular method of carrying gear as it is convenient, especially for walking. On the down side, a backpack doesn't offer too much protection for your valuables, the straps tend to get caught on things and some airlines may refuse to accept responsibility if the pack is damaged or tampered with.

Travelpacks, a combination backpack/shoulder bag, are very popular. The backpack straps zip away inside the pack when they are not needed, so you almost have the best of both worlds. Some packs have sophisticated shoulder-strap adjustment systems and can be used comfortably even on long hikes. Backpacks or travelpacks can be made reasonably theft-proof with small padlocks. Another alternative is a large, soft zip bag with a wide shoulder strap so it can be carried with relative ease. Forget suitcases unless you're travelling in style, but if you do take one, make sure it has wheels to allow you to drag it along behind you.

As for clothing, the climate will have a bearing on what you take along. Remember that insulation works on the principle of trapped air, so several layers of thin clothing are warmer than a single thick one (and will be easier to dry). You'll also be much more flexible if the weather suddenly turns warm. Be prepared for rain at any time of year.

Bearing in mind that you can buy virtually anything on the spot, a minimum packing list could include:

- underwear, socks and swimming gear
- a pair of jeans and maybe a pair of shorts or skirt
- a few T-shirts and shirts
- a warm sweater
- a solid pair of walking shoes
- sandals or thongs for showers
- a coat or jacket
- a raincoat, waterproof jacket or umbrella
- a medical kit and sewing kit
- a padlock
- a Swiss Army knife
- soap and towel
- toothpaste, toothbrush and other toiletries

World Heritage List

Unesco keeps a list of 'cultural and natural treasures of the world's heritage', including the following places in Mediterranean Europe:

ALBANIA
Ancient ruins of Butrint

CROATIA
Dubrovnik's old city
Plitvice Lakes National Park

Poreč's Euphrasian Basilica
Split's historic centre with

Diocletian's Palace
Trogir's old town

CYPRUS
Ancient capital of Paphos

Painted churches of Troodos
Massif

Choirokoitia

FRANCE
Amiens Cathedral
Arc-et-Senans' royal saltworks
Arles' Roman and
  Romanesque monuments
Avignon's historic centre
Bourges Cathedral
Carcassonne
Canal du Midi
Chambord's chateau and
  estate
Chartres Cathedral
Corsica's Cape Girolata, Cape
  Porto, Les Calanche and
  Scandola Natural Reserve

Fontainebleau Palace and
  Park
Fontenay's Cistercian abbey
Lascaux and other caves in
  the Vézère Valley
Lyon's historic centre
Mont Saint Michel and its bay
Place Stanislas, Place de la
  Carrière and Place d'Alliance
  in Nancy
Pont du Gard Roman aque-
  duct near Nîmes
Roman theatre and triumphal
  arch at Orange

Notre Dame and banks of the
  Seine in Paris
Abbey of St Rémi and Tau
  Palace at Reims
St Émilion
Church of Saint Savin sur
  Gartempe
Santiago de Compostela
  routes
Grande Île section of Stras-
  bourg
Chateau of Versailles and
  gardens
Vézelay's basilica

GREECE
The Acropolis in Athens
Mount Athos
Temple of Apollo Epicurios at
  Bassae
Monasteries of Daphni,
  Hossios, Luckas and Nea
  Moni at Chios
Delos

Delphi archaeological site
Epidaurus archaeological site
Meteora
Mycenae and Tyrins' archaeo-
  logical sites
Mystras
Olympia's archaeological site
Hora, the Monastery of Saint

John and the Monastery of
  the Apocalypse on Patmos
Medieval city of Rhodes
Pythagorio and Hereon at
  Samos
Thessaloniki's early Christian
  and Byzantine monuments
Vergina's archaeological site

ITALY
Agrigento archaeological area
Alberobello's trulli
Aquileia archaeological area
  and the patriarchal Basilica
Caserta's Royal Palace with
  the park, aqueduct of
  Vanvitelli and the San
  Leucio complex

Castel del Monte
Cilento and Vallo di Diano
  National Park with the
  archaeological sites of
  Paestum and Velia, and the
  Certosa di Padula
Cinque Terre, Portvenere and
  islands

Costiera Amalfitana
Crespi d'Adda
The Renaissance city of
  Ferrara
The historic centre of Florence
The sassi (traditional stone
  houses) of Matera
Milan's Church of Santa

World Heritage List

Maria delle Grazie and convent including The Last Supper by Leonardo da Vinci
Modena's cathedral, Torre Civica and Piazza Grande
The historic centre of Naples
Padua's botanical garden
Pienza's historic centre
Pisa's Piazza del Duomo

Archaeological areas of Pompei and Herculaneum
Ravenna's Early Christian monuments and mosaics
Rome's historic centre
The historic centre of San Gimignano
Residences of the royal house of Savoy
Siena's historic centre

Su Nuraxi fortress at Barumini
Urbino's historic centre
Valle Camonica's rock carvings
Vatican City
Venice and its lagoon
Villa Adriana (Tivoli)
Villa Romana del Casale
Vincenza and its Palladian villas

MACEDONIA
Ohrid and its lake

MALTA
Hypogeum prehistoric temples at Paola

Megalithic temples
Valetta

MOROCCO
Kasbah of Aït Benhaddou
The medina at Fès
The medina at Marrakesh

Meknès
The medina at Tetouan
Volubilis archaeological site

PORTUGAL
Monastery of Alcobaça
The central zone of Angra do Heroism in the Azores
Batalha Monastery
Côa Valley's prehistoric

rock-art sites
Évora's historic centre
Lisbon's Monastery of the Hieronymites and Tower of Belém

Madeira's Laurisilva
Oporto's historic centre
The cultural landscape of Sintra
Convent of Christ in Tomar

SLOVENIA
Škocjan Caves

SPAIN
Alcalá de Henares university and historic area
Altamira Cave
Churches of the kingdom of Asturias
The old town section of Ávila
Güell park and palace, Casa Mila, palace of the Música Catalana and Sant Pau hospital, Barcelona
Burgos Cathedral
The old town section of Cáceres
Historic centre of Córdoba

Cuenca's walled city
Doñana National Park
Garajonay National Park
Rock art on the Iberian Peninsula
La Alhambra, El Generalife summer palace and Albaicín Moorish quarter of Granada
Biodiversity and culture of Ibiza
El Escorial near Madrid
Las Médulas
Archaeological ensemble of Mérida
Poblet Monastery

Salamanca's old town
Royal Monastery of Santa María de Guadeloupe
San Cristóbal de la Laguna
Santiago de Compostela's old town and route
The old town and aqueduct of Segovia
Sevilla's cathedral, Alcázar Archivo de Indias
Mudejar architecture of Teruel
Toledo's historic centre
Valencia's La Lonja de la Seda (silk exchange)

World Heritage List

TUNISIA

Carthage archaeological site	The amphitheatre at El Jem	The walled city of Kairouan
Dougga	Carthaginian site and necrop-	The medina at Sousse
Ichkeul National Park	olis of Kerkouane	Tunis' medina

TURKEY

Divrigi's Great Mosque and	Walled city of Hattuşaş	Safranbolu and its traditional
hospital	Hierapolis-Pamukkale	timber houses
Göreme National park and	Istanbul's historic areas	Archaeological site at Troy
Cappadocia	Nemrut Dag	Xanthos-Letoön

YUGOSLAVIA

Durmitor National Park	Stari Ras and Sopoćani	Studenica Monastery
Kotor and its gulf	Monastery	

A padlock is useful to lock your bag to a luggage rack in a bus or train; it may also be needed to secure your hostel locker. A Swiss Army knife comes in handy for all sorts of things. *Any* pocketknife is fine, but make sure it includes such essentials as scissors, a bottle opener and strong corkscrew! Soap, toothpaste and toilet paper are readily obtainable, but you'll need your own supply of paper in many public toilets and those at camping grounds. Tampons are available at pharmacies and supermarkets in all but the most remote places. Condoms, both locally made and imported, are widely available in Mediterranean Europe.

A tent and sleeping bag are vital if you want to save money by camping. Even if you're not camping, a sleeping bag is still very useful. Get one that can be used as a quilt. A sleeping sheet with pillow cover (case) is necessary if you plan to stay in hostels you may have to hire or purchase one if you don't bring your own. In any case, a sheet that fits into your sleeping bag is easier to wash than the bag itself. Make one yourself out of old sheets (include a built-in pillow cover) or buy one from your hostel association.

Other optional items include a compass, a torch (flashlight), a pocket calculator for currency conversions, an alarm clock, an adapter plug for electrical appliances (such as a cup or immersion water heater to save on expensive tea and coffee), a universal bath/sink plug (a film canister sometimes works), portable short-wave radio, sunglasses, a few clothes pegs and premoistened towelettes or a large cotton handkerchief that you can soak in fountains and use to cool off while touring cities in the hot summer months. During city sightseeing, a small daypack is better than a shoulder bag at deterring thieves (see Theft in the Dangers & Annoyances section of this chapter).

Also, consider using plastic carry bags or bin liners inside your backpack to keep things separate but also dry if the pack gets soaked.

RESPONSIBLE TOURISM

As a visitor, you have a responsibility to the local people and to the environment. For guidelines on how to avoid offending the people you meet, read the following Appearances & Conduct section. When it comes to the environment, the key rules are to preserve natural resources and to leave the countryside as you find it. Those alpine flowers look much better on the mountainside than squashed in your pocket (many species are protected anyway).

Wherever you are, littering is irresponsible and offensive. Mountain areas have fragile ecosystems, so stick to prepared paths whenever possible, and always carry your rubbish away with you. Don't use detergents or toothpaste in or near watercourses, even if they are biodegradable. If you just gotta go when you're out in the wilderness somewhere, bury human waste in holes at least 15cm deep and at least 100m from any watercourse.

Recycling is an important issue in many Mediterranean countries, and you will be encouraged to follow suit. Traffic congestion on the roads is a major problem, and visitors will do themselves and residents a favour if they forgo driving and use public transport.

Appearances & Conduct

Most Mediterranean countries attach a great deal of importance to appearance, so your clothes may well have some bearing on how you're treated, especially in Spain, Portugal, Italy and Greece.

By all means dress casually, but keep your clothes clean and ensure sufficient body cover (trousers or a knee-length dress) if your sightseeing includes churches, monasteries, mosques or synagogues. Wearing shorts away from the beach is not very common among men in Mediterranean Europe. Also keep in mind that in most Muslim countries, such as Morocco, Western women *or* men in shorts or sleeveless shirts are virtually in their underwear in the eyes of the more conservative locals. Many nightclubs and fancy restaurants refuse entry to anyone wearing jeans, or a tracksuit and sneakers (trainers); men might consider packing a tie as well, just in case.

On the beach, nude bathing is generally limited to restricted areas, but topless bathing is common in many parts of Mediterranean Europe. Nevertheless, women should be wary of sunbathing topless in more conservative countries or untouristed areas. If nobody else seems to be doing it, you should not do it either.

You'll soon notice that Europeans shake hands and even kiss when they greet one another. Don't worry about the latter with those you don't know well, but get into the habit of shaking hands with virtually everyone you meet. In some parts of Mediterranean Europe, it's also customary to greet the proprietor when entering a shop, cafe or quiet bar, and to say goodbye when you leave.

VISAS & DOCUMENTS
Passport

Your most important travel document is your passport, which should remain valid until well after you return home. If it's just about to expire, renew it before you go. This may not be easy to do overseas, and some countries insist that your passport remains valid for a specified period (usually three months beyond the date of your departure from that country).

Applying for or renewing a passport can take anything from an hour to several months, so don't leave it till the last minute. Bureaucratic wheels usually turn faster if you do everything in person rather than relying on the post or agents, but check first what you need to take with you: photos of a certain size, birth certificate, population register extract, signed statements, exact payment in cash etc.

Australian citizens can apply at a post office or the passport office in their state capital; Britons can pick up application forms from major post offices, and the passport is issued by the regional passport office; Canadians can apply at regional passport offices; New Zealanders can apply at any district office of the Department of Internal Affairs; US citizens must apply in person (but may usually renew by mail) at a US Passport Agency office or at some courthouses and post offices.

Once you start travelling, carry your passport at all times and guard it carefully. Camping grounds and hotels sometimes insist that you hand over your passport for the duration of your stay, which is very inconvenient, but a driving licence or Camping Card International usually solves the problem.

Citizens of the European Union (EU) and those from certain other European countries (eg, Switzerland) don't need a valid passport to travel to another EU country or even some non-EU countries; a national identity card is sufficient. If you want to exercise this option, check with your travel agent or the embassies of the countries you plan to visit.

Visas

A visa is a stamp in your passport or on a separate piece of paper permitting you to enter the country in question and stay for a specified period of time. Often you can get the visa at the border or at the airport on arrival, but not always – check first with the embassies or consulates of the countries you plan to visit. It's seldom possible on trains.

There's a wide variety of visas, including tourist, transit and business ones. Transit visas are usually cheaper than tourist or business visas, but they only allow a very short stay (one or two days) and can be difficult to extend. Most readers of this book, however, will have very little to do with visas. With a

Visa Requirements

	Aust	Can	Ire	NZ	UK	USA	SA
Albania	–	+	–	–	–	–	✓
Andorra	–	–	–	–	–	–	–
Bosnia-Hercegovina	✓	–	–	✓	–	–	✓
Croatia	–	–	–	–	–	–	✓
Cyprus	–	–	–	–	–	–	+
France	–	–	–	–	–	–	✓
Greece	–	–	–	–	–	–	✓
Italy	–	–	–	–	–	–	✓
Macedonia	✓	✓	–	–	–	✓	✓
Malta	–	–	–	–	–	–	–
Morocco	–	–	–	–	–	–	✓
Portugal	✓	*	–	*	–	*	✓
Slovenia	–	–	–	–	–	–	✓
Spain	–	–	–	–	–	–	✓
Tunisia	✓	–	–	✓	–	–	✓
Turkey	–	–	✓	–	✓	–	+
Yugoslavia	✓	✓	✓	✓	✓	✓	✓

✓ tourist visa required
+ 30-day maximum stay without visa
* 60-day maximum stay without visa

valid passport you'll be able to visit most of the countries around the Mediterranean for up to three months (sometimes even six), provided you have some sort of onward or return ticket and/or 'sufficient means of support' (ie, money).

In line with the Schengen Agreement there are no longer passport controls at the borders between Germany, France, Spain, Portugal, the Benelux countries (Belgium, Netherlands and Luxembourg), Italy and Austria. A national identity card should suffice, but it's always safest to carry your passport. The other EU countries (Britain, Denmark, Finland, Greece, Ireland and Sweden) are not yet full members of Schengen and still maintain low-key border controls over traffic from other EU countries.

Border procedures between EU and non-EU countries can still be thorough, but citizens of Canada, Israel, Japan, New Zealand, Norway, Switzerland and the USA do not need visas for tourist visits to any Schengen country. Australians don't need visas for most Schengen countries, Portugal being a major exception.

All non-EU citizens visiting a Schengen country and intending to stay for longer than three days or to visit another Schengen country from there are supposed to obtain an official entry stamp in their passport either at the point of entry or from the local police within 72 hours. But in general registering at a hotel will be sufficient.

For those who do require visas, it's important to remember that these will have a 'use-by' date, and you'll be refused entry after that period has elapsed. Your visa may not be checked when entering these countries overland, but major problems can arise if it is requested during your stay or on departure and you can't produce it.

Visa requirements can change, and you should always check with the individual embassies or a reputable travel agent before travelling.

It's generally easier to get your visas as you go along, rather than arranging them all beforehand. Carry spare passport photos (you may need from one to four every time you apply for a visa).

Travel Insurance

A travel-insurance policy to cover theft, loss and medical problems is a good idea. The policies handled by STA Travel and other student-travel organisations are usually good value. Some policies offer lower and higher medical expense options; the higher ones are chiefly for countries like the USA that have extremely high medical costs. There is a wide variety of policies available so check the small print.

Some policies specifically exclude 'dangerous activities', which can include scuba diving, motorcycling and even trekking. Some even exclude entire countries like Bosnia and Yugoslavia. A locally acquired motorcycle licence is not valid under some policies.

You may prefer a policy that pays doctors or hospitals directly rather than you having to pay on the spot and claim later. If you have to claim later make sure you keep all documentation. Some policies ask you to call back (reverse charges) to a centre in your home country where an immediate assessment of your problem is made.

Check that the policy covers ambulances or an emergency flight home.

Driving Licence & Permits

Many non-European driving licences are valid in Europe, but it's still a good idea to bring along an International Driving Permit (IDP), which can make life much simpler, especially when hiring cars and motorcycles. Basically a multilingual translation of the vehicle class and personal details noted on your local driving licence, an IDP is not valid unless accompanied by your original licence. An IDP can be obtained for a small fee from your local automobile association – bring along a passport photo and a valid licence.

Camping Card International

The Camping Card International (CCI; formerly the Camping Carnet) is a camping ground ID that can be used instead of a passport when checking into a camp site and includes third party insurance. As a result, many camping grounds offer a small discount if you sign in with one. CCIs are issued by automobile associations, camping federations and, sometimes, on the spot at camping grounds. In the UK, the AA issues them to its members for UK£4.50.

Hostel Cards

A hostelling card is useful – if not always mandatory – for those staying at hostels. Some hostels in Mediterranean Europe don't require that you be a hostelling-association member, but they often charge less if you have a card. Many hostels will issue one on the spot or after a few stays, though this might cost a bit more than getting it in your home country. See Hostels in the Accommodation section later in this chapter.

Student & Youth Cards

The most useful of these is the International Student Identity Card (ISIC), a plastic ID-style card with your photograph, which provides discounts on many forms of transport (including airlines and local public transport), cheap or free admission to museums and sights, and inexpensive meals in some student cafeterias and restaurants.

If you're aged under 26 but not a student, you can apply for a GO25 card issued by the Federation of International Youth Travel Organisations (FIYTO) or the Euro<26 card. Both go under different names in various countries and give much the same discounts and benefits as an ISIC. All these cards are issued by student unions, hostelling organisations or youth-oriented travel agencies.

Seniors Cards

Museums and other sights, public swimming pools and spas, and transport companies frequently offer discounts to retired people/old age pensioners/those over 60 (slightly younger for women). Make sure you bring proof of age; that suave *signore* in Italy or that polite Parisian *mademoiselle* is not going to believe you're a day over 39.

European nationals aged 60 and over can get a Railplus (formerly Rail Europe Senior) Card. For more information see Cheap Tickets under Train in the Getting Around chapter.

International Health Certificate

You'll need this yellow booklet only if you're arriving in Europe from certain parts of Asia, Africa and South America, where diseases such as yellow fever are prevalent. See Immunisations in the Health section for more information on jabs.

Copies

All important documents (passport data page and visa page, credit cards, travel insurance policy, air/bus/train tickets, driving licence etc) should be photocopied before you leave home. Leave one copy with someone at home and keep the other with you.

While you're on the road add the serial numbers of your travellers cheques (cross them off as you cash them) to the photocopies of your impotant documents and keep all this emergency material separate from your passport, cheques and cash. Add some emergency money (eg, US$50 to US$100 in cash) to this separate stash as well. If you do lose your passport, notify the police immediately to get a statement, and contact your nearest consulate.

It's also a good idea to store details of your vital travel documents in Lonely Planet's free online Travel Vault in case you lose the photocopies or can't be bothered with them. Your password-protected Travel Vault is accessible online anywhere in the world – create it at www.ekno.lonelyplanet.com.

EMBASSIES & CONSULATES

See the listings in the individual country chapters for information on embassies and consulates.

Getting Help from Your Embassy

As a tourist, it's important to realise what your own embassy – the embassy of the country of which you are a citizen – can and cannot do.

Generally speaking, it won't be much help in emergencies if the trouble you're in is remotely your fault. Remember that you are bound by the laws of the country you are in. Your embassy will not be sympathetic if you end up in jail after committing a crime locally, even if such actions are legal in your own country.

In genuine emergencies you might get some assistance, but only if other channels have been exhausted. For example, if you need to get home urgently, a free ticket home is exceedingly unlikely as the embassy would expect you to have insurance. If you have all your money and documents stolen, it might assist with getting a new passport, but a loan for onward travel is almost always out of the question.

CUSTOMS

Duty-free goods are no longer sold to those travelling from one EU country to another. For goods purchased at airports or on ferries *outside* the EU, the usual allowances apply for tobacco (200 cigarettes, 50 cigars or 250g of loose tobacco), alcohol (1L of spirits or 2L of liquor with less than 22% alcohol by volume; 2L of wine) and perfume (50g of perfume and 0.25L of toilet water).

Do not confuse these with *duty-paid* items (including alcohol and tobacco) bought at normal shops and supermarkets in another EU country, where certain goods might be more expensive. (Cigarettes in France, for example, are half the price they are in the UK.) Then the allowances are more than generous: 800 cigarettes, 200 cigars or 1kg of loose tobacco; 10L of spirits (more than 22% alcohol by volume), 20L of fortified wine or aperitif, 90L of wine or 110L of beer; unlimited quantities of perfume.

MONEY
Exchanging Money

By the year 2002, the EU will have a single currency called the euro (see boxed text 'The Euro'). Until then francs, lire, pesetas, escudos and drachmas remain in place or share equal status with the euro in the EU countries covered in this guide.

In general, US dollars, Deutschmarks, pounds sterling, and French and Swiss francs are the most easily exchanged currencies in Europe, followed by Italian lire and Dutch guilders, but you may well decide that other currencies suit your purposes better. You lose out through commissions and customer exchange rates every time you change money, so if you only visit Portugal, for example, you may be better off buying escudos straight away if your bank at home can provide them.

The importation and exportation of certain currencies (eg, Moroccan dirham, Tunisian dinar and Cypriot pounds) is restricted or banned entirely so get rid of any local currency before you leave the country. Try not to have too many leftover Portuguese escudos or Maltese lire, and definitely get rid of any Yugoslav dinar as it is impossible to change them back into hard currency. More and more banks and *bureaux de change* will now exchange Croatian kuna and Slovenian tolar but usually in neighbouring countries just over the border.

The Euro

Don't be surprised if you come across two sets of prices for goods and services in Western Europe. Since 1 January 1999 Europe's new currency – the euro – has been legal tender here along with the local monetary unit.

While Britain, Denmark, Sweden and Greece have not yet joined, the other 11 EU countries (Austria, Belgium, Finland, France, Germany, Ireland, Italy, Luxembourg, Netherlands, Portugal, Spain) are all counting down the days when venerable currencies like the franc and escudo will be no longer be legal tender – 1 July 2002, to be precise. Between now and that date the countries in Euroland operate two currencies – running their old currencies alongside the euro.

No actual coins or banknotes will be issued until 1 January 2002; until then, the euro is, in effect, 'paperless'. Prices are quoted in euros, but there aren't actually any euros in circulation. Companies use the new currency for their accounting, banks offer euro accounts and travellers cheques in euros, credit-card companies bill in euros. Essentially, the euro is used any time it is not necessary to hand over hard cash.

This can lead to confusion – a restaurant might list prices in both francs and euros or escudos and euros. Check your bill carefully – the total might have the amount in francs or escudos, your credit card may bill you in the euro equivalent. In practice, however, the total is usually listed in both currencies. Things could be more complicated during the first half of 2002 when countries can use both their old currencies and the newly issued euro notes and coins.

The euro has the same value in all member countries of the EU; the E5 note in France is the same E5 note you will use in Italy and Portugal. The official exchange rates were set on 1 January 1999.

Coins and notes have already been designed. There are seven euro notes (five, 10, 20, 50, 100, 200 and 500 euros), and eight euro coins (one and two euros, then one, two, five, 10, 20 and 50 cents). Each country is permitted to design coins with one side standard for all euro coins and the other bearing a national emblem.

Rates of exchange of the euro and foreign currencies against local currencies are given in the country chapters.

country	unit		euro	country	unit		euro
Australia	A$1	=	€0.64	Canada	C$1	=	€0.75
France	1FF	=	€0.15	Germany	DM1	=	€0.51
Ireland	IR£1	=	€1.27	Italy	L1000	=	€0.52
Japan	¥100	=	€1.02	Netherlands	f1	=	€0.45
New Zealand	NZ$1	=	€0.50	Spain	100 ptas	=	€0.60
South Africa	R1	=	€0.16	UK	UK£1	=	€1.66
USA	US$1	=	€1.11				

Most airports, central train stations, some fancy hotels and many border posts have banking facilities outside working hours, sometimes open on a 24-hour basis. Post offices in Europe often perform banking tasks, tend to have longer opening hours, and outnumber banks in remote places. Be aware that while they always exchange cash, they might not be prepared to change travellers cheques unless they're denominated in the local currency.

The best exchange rates are usually at banks. *Bureaux de change* usually, but not always by any means, offer worse rates or charge higher commissions. Hotels are almost always the worst places to change money. American Express and Thomas Cook offices usually do not charge commissions for changing their own cheques, but they may offer a less favourable exchange rate than banks.

Cash Nothing beats cash for convenience, or risk. If you lose it, it's gone forever and very few travel insurers will come to your rescue. Those that will, limit the amount to somewhere around US$300. For tips on carrying your money safely, see Theft in the

Dangers & Annoyances section later in this chapter.

It's still a good idea, though, to bring some local currency in cash, if only to tide you over until you get to an exchange facility or find an automatic teller machine (ATM). The equivalent of, say, US$50 or US$100 should usually be enough. Some extra cash in an easily exchanged currency (eg, US dollars or Deutschmarks) is also a good idea.

Travellers Cheques The main idea of carrying travellers cheques rather than cash is the protection they offer from theft, though they are losing their popularity as more travellers – including those on tight budgets – deposit their money in their bank at home and withdraw it as they go along through ATMs.

American Express, Visa and Thomas Cook travellers cheques are widely accepted and have efficient replacement policies. If you're going to remote places, it's worth sticking to American Express since small local banks may not always accept other brands.

When you change cheques, don't look at just the exchange rate; ask about fees and commissions as well. There may be a service fee per cheque, a flat transaction fee or a percentage of the total amount irrespective of the number of cheques. Some banks charge fees (often exorbitant) to cash cheques and not cash; others do the reverse.

Plastic Cards & ATMs If you're not familiar with the options, ask your bank to explain the workings and relative merits of credit, credit/debit, debit, charge and cash cards.

A major advantage of credit cards is that they allow you to pay for expensive items (eg, airline tickets) without you having to carry great wads of cash around. They also allow you to withdraw cash at selected banks or from the many ATMs that are linked up internationally. However, if an ATM in Europe swallows a card that was issued outside Europe, it can be a major headache. Also, some credit cards aren't hooked up to ATM networks unless you specifically ask your bank to do this.

Cash cards, which you use at home to withdraw money directly from your bank account or savings account, can be used throughout Europe at ATMs linked to international networks like Cirrus and Maestro.

Credit and credit/debit cards like Visa and MasterCard are widely accepted. MasterCard is linked to Europe's extensive Eurocard system, and Visa (sometimes called Carte Bleue) is particularly strong in France and Spain. However, these cards often have a credit limit that is too low to cover major expenses like long-term car rental or airline tickets and can be difficult to replace if lost abroad. Also, when you get a cash advance against your Visa or MasterCard credit card account, your issuer charges a transaction fee and/or finance charge. With some issuers, the fees can reach as high as US$10 *plus* interest per transaction so it's best to check with your card issuer before leaving home and compare rates.

Charge cards like American Express and Diners Club have offices in the major cities of most countries that will replace a lost card within 24 hours. However, charge cards are not widely accepted off the beaten track.

The best advice is not to put all your eggs in one basket. If you want to rely heavily on bits of plastic, go for two different cards – an American Express or Diners Club, for instance, along with a Visa or MasterCard. Better still is a combination of credit or cash card and travellers cheques so you have something to fall back on if an ATM swallows your card or the banks in the area are closed.

A word of warning – fraudulent shopkeepers have been known to quickly make several charge slip imprints with your credit card when you're not looking, and then simply copy your signature from the one that you authorise. Try not to let your card out of sight, and always check your statements upon your return.

International Transfers Telegraphic transfers are not very expensive but, despite their name, can be quite slow. Be sure to specify the name of the bank and the name and address of the branch where you'd like to pick it up.

It's quicker and easier to have money wired via an American Express office (US$60 for US$1000). Western Union's Money Transfer system (available at post offices in some countries) and Thomas Cook's MoneyGram service are also popular.

Guaranteed Cheques Guaranteed personal cheques are another way of carrying money or obtaining cash. Eurocheques, available if you have a European bank account, are guaranteed up to a certain limit. When cashing them (eg, at post offices), you will be asked to show your Eurocheque card bearing your signature and registration number, and perhaps a passport or ID card. Your Eurocheque card should be kept separately from the cheques. Many hotels and merchants refuse to accept Eurocheques because of the relatively large commissions.

Costs

The secret to budget travel in Mediterranean Europe is cheap accommodation. Europe has a highly developed network of camping grounds and hostels, some of them quite luxurious, and they're great places to meet people.

Other money-saving strategies include preparing your own meals and avoiding alcohol; using a student card (see Visas & Documents earlier in this chapter) and buying any of the various rail and public transport passes (see the Getting Around chapter). Also remember that the more time you spend in any one place, the lower your daily expenses are likely to be as you get to know your way around.

Including transport, but not private motorised transport, your daily expenses could work out to around US$35 to US$40 a day if you're operating on a rock-bottom budget. This means camping or staying in hostels, eating economically and using a transport pass. In Greece, Portugal, Spain and especially Turkey, you could probably get the daily cost down below that.

Travelling on a moderate budget, you should be able to manage on about US$40 to US$50 in the cheaper countries and US$60 to US$80 a day elsewhere in the region. This would allow you to stay at cheap hotels or guesthouses. You could afford meals in economical restaurants and even a few beers. Again Greece and Portugal would be somewhat cheaper, while France and Italy would be pricier.

A general warning about all the prices listed in this book – they're likely to change, usually moving upward, but if last season was particularly slow they may remain the same or even come down. Nevertheless, relative price levels should stay fairly constant – if hotel A costs twice as much as hotel B, it's likely to stay that way.

Tipping

In many European countries it's common (and the law in France) for a service charge to be added to restaurant bills, in which case no tipping is necessary. In others, simply rounding up the bill is sufficient. See the individual country chapters for details.

Taxes & Refunds

Value-added tax (VAT) is a kind of sales tax which applies to most goods and services throughout many European countries; it's 19.6% in France, 20% in Italy and Slovenia, 18% in Greece and 16% in Spain. In most countries, visitors can claim back the VAT on purchases that are being taken out of the country. Those actually *residing* in one EU country are not entitled to a refund on VAT paid on goods bought in another EU country. Thus an American citizen living in London is not entitled to a VAT rebate on items bought in Paris while an EU passport holder residing in New York is.

The procedure for making the claim is fairly straightforward, though it may vary somewhat from country to country, and there are minimum-purchase amounts imposed. First of all make sure the shop offers duty-free sales (often identified with a sign reading 'Tax-Free for Tourists'). When making your purchase, ask the shop attendant for a VAT-refund voucher (sometimes called a Tax-Free Shopping Cheque) filled in with the correct amount and the date. This can either be refunded directly at international airports on departure or stamped at ferry ports or border crossings and mailed back for refund.

POST & COMMUNICATIONS
Post

From major European centres, airmail typically takes about five days to North America and a week to Australasian destinations, though mail from the UK can be much faster and from Greece much slower. Postage costs vary from country to country, as does post office efficiency – the Italian post office is notoriously unreliable.

You can collect mail from poste restante sections at major post offices. Ask people writing to you to print your name clearly and underline your surname. When collecting mail, your passport may be required for identification and you may have to pay a small fee. If an expected letter is not awaiting you, ask to check under your given name; letters commonly get misfiled. Post offices usually hold mail for about a month, but sometimes less. Unless the sender specifies otherwise, mail will always be sent to the city's main post office.

You can also have mail (but not parcels) sent to you at American Express offices so long as you have an American Express card or are carrying American Express travellers cheques. When you buy the cheques, ask for a booklet listing all the American Express offices worldwide.

Telephone

You can ring abroad from almost any phone box in Europe. Public telephones accepting stored value phonecards (available from post offices, telephone centres, newsstands or retail outlets) are virtually the norm now; in some countries, France, for example, coin-operated phones are almost impossible to find.

There's a wide range of local and international phonecards. Lonely Planet's eKno global communication service provides low cost international calls, a range of innovative messaging services, an online travel vault where you can securely store all your important documents, free email and travel information, all in one easy service. You can join online at www.ekno.lonelyplanet.com, where you can also find the best local access numbers to connect to the 24-hour customer service centre to join or find out more. Once you have joined always check the eKno website for the latest access numbers for each country and updates on new features.

For local calls you're usually better off with a local phonecard. Without a phonecard, you can ring from a booth inside a post office or telephone centre and settle your bill at the counter. Reverse-charge (collect) calls are often possible, but not always. From many countries, however, the Country Direct system lets you phone home by billing the long-distance carrier you use at home. The numbers can often be dialled from public phones without even inserting a phone card.

Area codes for individual cities are provided in the country chapters. For country codes, see Appendix II – Telephones at the end of the book.

Fax

You can send faxes and telexes from most main post offices.

Email & Internet Access

Travelling with a portable computer is a great way to stay in touch with life back home but, unless you know what you're doing, it's fraught with potential problems. A good investment is a universal AC adapter for your appliance, so you can plug it in anywhere without frying the innards if the power supply voltage varies. You'll also need a plug adapter for each country you visit, often easiest bought before you leave home.

Secondly, your PC-card modem may or may not work once you leave your home country – and you won't know for sure until you try. The safest option is to buy a reputable 'global' or 'world' modem before you leave home, or buy a local PC-card modem if you're spending an extended time in any one country. Keep in mind that the telephone socket in each country you visit will probably be different from that at home, so ensure that you have at least a US RJ-11 telephone adapter that works with your modem. You can almost always find an adapter that will convert from RJ-11 to the local variety. For more information on travelling with a portable computer, see www.teleadapt.com or www.warrior.com.

Major Internet service providers (ISPs) such as AOL (www.aol.com), CompuServe (www.compuserve.com) and IBM Net (www.ibm.net) have dial-in nodes throughout Europe; it's best to download a list of the dial-in numbers before you leave home. If you access your Internet email account at home through a smaller ISP or your office or school network, your best option is either to open an account with a global ISP, like those mentioned above, or to rely on cybercafes and other public access points to collect your mail.

If you do intend to rely on cybercafes, you'll need to carry three pieces of information with you so you can access your Internet mail account: your incoming (POP or IMAP) mail server name, your account name, and your password. Your ISP or network supervisor will give you these. Armed with this information, you should be able to access your Internet mail account from any Net-connected machine in the world, provided it runs some kind of email software (remember that Netscape and Internet Explorer both have mail modules). It pays to become familiar with the process for doing this before you leave home. A final option to collect mail through cybercafes is to open a free eKno Web-based email account online at www.eKno.lonelyplanet.com. You can then access your mail from anywhere in the world from any Internet-connected machine running a standard Web browser.

You'll find cybercafes throughout Europe – check the country chapters in this book, and see www.netcafeguide.com for an up-to-date list. You may also find public Internet access in post offices, libraries, hostels, hotels, universities and so on.

INTERNET RESOURCES

The World Wide Web is a rich resource for travellers. You can research your trip, hunt down bargain air fares, book hotels, check on weather conditions or chat with locals and other travellers about the best places to visit (or avoid!).

Airline Information What airlines fly where, when and for how much.
www.travelocity.com

Airline Tickets Name the price you're willing to pay for an airline seat and if an airline has an empty seat for which it would rather get something than nothing, US-based Priceline lets you know.
www.priceline.com

Currency Conversions Exchange rates of hundreds of currencies worldwide.
www.xe.net/ucc

Lonely Planet There's no better place to start your Web explorations than the Lonely Planet Web site. Here you'll find succinct summaries on travelling to most places on earth, postcards from other travellers and the Thorn Tree bulletin board, where you can ask questions before you go or dispense advice when you get back. You can also find travel news and updates to many of our most popular guidebooks, and the subWWWay section links you to the most useful travel resources elsewhere on the Web.
www.lonelyplanet.com

Rail Information Train fares and schedules on the most popular routes in Europe, including information on rail and youth passes.
www.raileurope.com

Tourist Offices Lists tourist offices at home and around the world for most countries.
www.mbnet.mb.ca/lucas/travel

NEWSPAPERS & MAGAZINES

In larger towns and cities you can buy the excellent *International Herald Tribune* on the day of publication, as well as the colourful but superficial *USA Today*. Among other English-language newspapers widely available are the *Guardian*, the *Financial Times* and *The Times*. The *European* weekly newspaper is also readily available, as are *Newsweek*, *Time* and the *Economist*.

RADIO & TV
Radio

You can pick up a mixture of the BBC World Service and BBC for Europe on medium wave at 648kHz AM and on short wave at 6195kHz, 9410kHz, 11955kHz, 12095kHz (a good daytime frequency) and 15575kHz, depending on the time of day. BBC Radio 4 broadcasts on long wave at 198kHz.

The Voice of America (VOA) can usually be found at various times of the day on 7170kHz, 9535kHz, 9680kHz, 9760kHz, 9770kHz, 11805kHz, 15135kHz, 15205kHz, 15255kHz, 15410kHz and 15580kHz. There are also numerous English-language broadcasts (or even BBC World Service and VOA re-broadcasts) on local AM and FM radio stations.

TV

Cable and satellite TV have spread across Europe with much more gusto than radio. Sky TV can be found in many upmarket hotels throughout Mediterranean Europe, as can CNN, BBC Prime and other networks. You can also pick up many cross-border TV stations, including British stations close to the Channel.

VIDEO SYSTEMS

If you want to record or buy video tapes to play back home, you won't get a picture if the image registration systems are different. Europe generally uses PAL (SECAM in France), which is incompatible with the North American and Japanese NTSC system. Australia also uses PAL.

PHOTOGRAPHY

Mediterranean Europe is extremely photogenic, but the weather and where you'll be travelling will dictate what film to use. In places like northern France where the sky can often be overcast, photographers should bring high-speed film (200 or 400 ASA), but for most of the sunny Mediterranean, slower film is the answer.

Read Lonely Planet's *Travel Photography: a Guide to Taking Better Pictures.*

Film and camera equipment are available everywhere in the region, but obviously shops in the larger towns and cities will have a wider selection. Avoid buying film at tourist sites in Europe (eg, at the kiosks below the Leaning Tower of Pisa or at the entrance to the Acropolis). It may have been stored badly or have reached its sell-by date. It will certainly be more expensive.

TIME
Most of the countries covered in this book are on Central European Time (GMT/UTC plus one hour), the same time used from Spain to Poland. Morocco is on GMT/UTC (all year) while Greece, Turkey and Cyprus are on East European Time (GMT plus two hours).

Clocks are advanced for daylight-saving time in most countries on the last Sunday in March and set back one hour on the last Sunday in September. At that time Central European Time is GMT/UTC plus two hours and East European Time (GMT plus two hours).

ELECTRICITY
Voltages & Cycles
Most of Europe runs on 220V, 50Hz AC. The exceptions are the UK and Malta, which have 240V, and Spain and Andorra, which usually have 220V but sometimes 125V depending on the network (some houses have both). Some old buildings and hotels in Italy, including Rome, might also have 125V. All EU countries were supposed to have been standardised at 230V by now, but like everything else in the EU, this is taking longer than anticipated.

Check the voltage and cycle (usually 50Hz) used in your home country. Most appliances set up for 220V will handle 240V without modifications (and vice versa); the same goes for 110V and 125V combinations. It's always preferable to adjust your appliance to the exact voltage if you can (some modern battery chargers and radios will do this automatically). Just don't mix 110/125V with 220/240V without a transformer (which will be built into an adjustable appliance).

Several countries outside Europe (such as the USA and Canada) use 60Hz AC, which will affect the speed of electric motors even after the voltage has been adjusted to European values, so CD and tape players (where motor speed is all-important) will be useless. But things like electric razors, hair dryers, irons and radios will be fine.

Plugs & Sockets
Cyprus and Malta use a design like the one in the UK and Ireland: three flat pins (two for current and one for earth). The rest of Mediterranean Europe uses the 'europlug' with two round pins. Many europlugs and some sockets don't have provision for earth, since most local home appliances are double-insulated. When provided, earth usually consists of two contact points along the edge, although Italy and Greece use a third round pin. In Greece the standard two-pin plug still fits the sockets, but this is not always so in Italy.

If your plugs are of a different design, you'll need an adapter. Get one before you leave, since the adapters available in Europe usually go the other way. If you find yourself without one, however, a specialist electrical-supply shop should be able to help.

HEALTH
Travel health depends on your predeparture preparations, your daily health care while travelling and how you handle any medical problem that does develop.

Predeparture Planning
Immunisations Jabs are not really necessary for Mediterranean Europe, but they may be an entry requirement if you're coming from an infected area – yellow fever is the most likely requirement. If you're going to Europe with stopovers in Asia, Africa or South America, check with your travel agent or with the embassies of the countries you plan to visit.

There are, however, a few routine vaccinations that are recommended whether you're travelling or not, and this Health section assumes that you've had them: polio (usually administered during childhood), tetanus and diphtheria (usually administered together during childhood, with a booster shot every 10 years) and measles. See your physician or nearest health agency about these. You might also consider having an immunoglobulin or hepatitis A (Havrix) vaccine before extensive travels in southern Europe; a tetanus booster;

an immunisation against hepatitis B before travelling to Malta; or a rabies (pre-exposure) vaccination.

All vaccinations should be recorded on an International Health Certificate (see that entry under Visas & Documents earlier in this chapter). Don't leave this till the last minute, as the vaccinations may have to be staggered over a period of time.

Health Insurance Make sure that you have adequate health insurance. See Travel Insurance under Visas & Documents earlier in this chapter for details.

Other Preparations Make sure you're healthy before you start travelling. If you are going on a long trip make sure your teeth are OK. If you wear glasses take a spare pair and your prescription.

If you require a particular medication take an adequate supply, as it may not be available locally. Take part of the packaging showing the generic name, rather than the brand, which will make getting replacements easier. To avoid any problems, it's a good idea to have a legible prescription or letter from your doctor to show that you legally use the medication.

Basic Rules

Food Salads and fruit should be safe throughout Europe. Ice cream is usually OK, but beware if it has melted and been refrozen. Take great care with fish or shellfish (cooked mussels that haven't opened properly can be dangerous, for instance), and avoid under-cooked meat.

If a place looks clean and well run, and if the vendor also looks clean and healthy, then the food is probably safe. In general, places that are packed with travellers or locals will be fine. Be careful with food that has been cooked and left to go cold.

Water Tap water is almost always safe to drink in Europe, but be wary of water taken directly from rivers or lakes unless you can be sure that there are no people or cattle upstream. Run-off from fertilised fields is also a concern. Tap water is usually *not* safe to drink in North Africa or Turkey (though probably OK in Istanbul), so stick to bottled water and avoid ice cubes and even fruit

---

Medical Kit Check List

Following is a list of items you should consider including in your medical kit – consult your pharmacist for brands available in your country.

☐ **Aspirin or paracetamol (acetaminophen in the USA)** – for pain or fever

☐ **Antihistamine** – for allergies, eg, hay fever; to ease the itch from insect bites or stings; and to prevent motion sickness

☐ **Cold and flu tablets, throat lozenges and nasal decongestant**

☐ **Multivitamins** – consider for long trips, when dietary vitamin intake may be inadequate

☐ **Antibiotics** – consider including these if you're travelling well off the beaten track; see your doctor, as they must be prescribed, and carry the prescription with you

☐ **Loperamide or diphenoxylate** –'blockers' for diarrhoea

☐ **Prochlorperazine or metaclopramide** – for nausea and vomiting

☐ **Rehydration mixture** – to prevent dehydration, which may occur, for example, during bouts of diarrhoea; particularly important when travelling with children

☐ **Insect repellent, sunscreen, lip balm and eye drops**

☐ **Calamine lotion, sting relief spray or aloe vera** – to ease irritation from sunburn and insect bites or stings

☐ **Antifungal cream or powder** – for fungal skin infections and thrush

☐ **Antiseptic (such as povidone-iodine)** – for cuts and grazes

☐ **Bandages, Band-Aids (plasters) and other wound dressings**

☐ **Water purification tablets or iodine**

☐ **Scissors, tweezers and a thermometer** – note that mercury thermometers are prohibited by airlines

---

juice, as water may have been added to it. In these areas, use purified water rather than tap water to brush your teeth.

Dairy products are fine throughout Europe, but should be treated with suspicion in North Africa and Turkey because milk is often unpasteurised. Boiled milk is fine if it is kept hygienically, and yogurt is always good.

Water Purification If you're going to spend some time in North Africa or Turkey, or are planning extended hikes where you have to rely on water from rivers or streams, you'll need to know about water purification. The simplest way of purifying water is to boil it thoroughly. Vigorous boiling should be satisfactory though at high altitude water boils at a lower temperature, so germs are less likely to be killed. Boil it for longer in this situation.

Consider purchasing a water filter for a long trip. There are two main kinds of filter. Total filters take out all parasites, bacteria and viruses, and make water safe to drink. They are often expensive, but they can be more cost-effective than buying bottled water. Simple filters (which can even be a nylon mesh bag) take out dirt and larger foreign bodies from the water so that chemical solutions work much more effectively; if water is dirty, chemical solutions may not work at all.

It's very important when buying a filter to read the specifications so that you know exactly what it removes from the water and what it doesn't. Simple filtering will not remove all dangerous organisms so if you cannot boil water it should be treated chemically. Chlorine tablets (Puritabs, Steritabs or other brand names) will kill many pathogens, but not some parasites like giardia and amoebic cysts. Iodine is more effective in purifying water and is available in tablet form (eg, Potable Aqua). Follow the directions carefully and remember that too much iodine can be harmful.

Medical Problems & Treatment

Local pharmacies or neighbourhood medical centres are good places to visit if you have a small medical problem and can explain what the problem is. Hospital casualty wards will help if it's more serious. Major hospitals and emergency numbers are mentioned in the various country chapters of this book and sometimes indicated on the maps. Tourist offices and hotels can put you on to a doctor or dentist, and your embassy or consulate will probably know one who speaks your language.

Environmental Hazards

Altitude Sickness Lack of oxygen at high altitudes (over 2500m) affects most people to some extent. The effect may be mild or severe and occurs because less oxygen reaches the muscles and the brain, requiring the heart and lungs to compensate by working harder. Symptoms of Acute Mountain Sickness (AMS) usually develop during the first 24 hours at high altitude but may be delayed up to three weeks. Mild symptoms include headache, lethargy, dizziness, difficulty sleeping and loss of appetite. AMS may become more severe without warning and can be fatal. Severe symptoms include breathlessness, a dry, irritating cough (which may progress to the production of pink, frothy sputum), severe headache, lack of coordination and balance, confusion, irrational behaviour, vomiting, drowsiness and unconsciousness. There is no hard-and-fast rule as to what is too high; AMS has been fatal at 3000m, although 3500m to 4500m is the usual range.

Treat mild symptoms by resting at the same altitude until recovery, usually a day or two. Paracetamol or aspirin can be taken for headaches. If symptoms persist or become worse, however, immediate descent is necessary; even 500m can help. Drug treatments should never be used to avoid descent or to enable further ascent.

Heat Exhaustion Dehydration and salt deficiency can cause heat exhaustion. Take time to acclimatise to high temperatures, drink sufficient liquids and do not do anything too physically demanding.

Salt deficiency is characterised by fatigue, lethargy, headaches, giddiness and muscle cramps; salt tablets may help, but adding extra salt to your food is better.

Heat Stroke This serious, occasionally fatal, condition can occur if the body's heat-regulating mechanism breaks down and the body temperature rises to dangerous levels. Long, continuous periods of exposure to high temperatures and insufficient fluids can leave you vulnerable to heatstroke.

The symptoms are feeling unwell, not sweating very much (or at all) and a high body temperature (39° to 41°C or 102° to 106°F). Where sweating has ceased, the skin becomes flushed and red. Severe, throbbing headaches and lack of coordination will also occur, and the sufferer may be confused or aggressive. Eventually the victim will become delirious or convulse. Hospitalisation is essential, but in the interim get victims out of the sun, remove their clothing, cover them with a wet sheet or towel and then fan continually. Give fluids if they are conscious.

Hypothermia Too much cold can be just as dangerous as too much heat. Be prepared for cold, wet or windy conditions even if you're just out walking or hitching.

Hypothermia occurs when the body loses heat faster than it can produce it and the core temperature of the body falls. It is surprisingly easy to progress from very cold to dangerously cold due to a combination of wind, wet clothing, fatigue and hunger, even if the air temperature is above freezing. It is best to dress in layers; silk, wool and some of the new artificial fibres are all good insulating materials. A hat is important, as a lot of heat is lost through the head. A strong, waterproof outer layer (and a 'space' blanket for emergencies) is essential. Carry basic supplies, including food containing simple sugars to generate heat quickly and fluid to drink.

Symptoms of hypothermia are exhaustion, numb skin (particularly toes and fingers), shivering, slurred speech, irrational or violent behaviour, lethargy, stumbling, dizzy spells, muscle cramps and violent bursts of energy. Irrationality may take the form of sufferers claiming they are warm and trying to take off their clothes.

To treat mild hypothermia, first get the person out of the wind and/or rain, remove their clothing if it's wet and replace it with dry, warm clothing. Give them hot liquids – not alcohol – and some high-kilojoule, easily digestible food. Do not rub victims; instead, allow them to slowly warm themselves. This should be enough to treat the early stages of hypothermia. The early recognition and treatment of mild hypothermia is the only way to prevent severe hypothermia, which is a critical condition.

Jet Lag Jet lag is experienced when a person travels by air across more than three time zones (each time zone usually represents a one-hour time difference). It occurs because many of the functions of the human body (such as temperature, pulse rate and emptying of the bladder and bowels) are regulated by internal 24-hour cycles. When we travel long distances rapidly, our bodies take time to adjust to the 'new time'

of our destination, and we may experience fatigue, disorientation, insomnia, anxiety, impaired concentration and loss of appetite. These effects will usually be gone within three days of arrival, but to minimise the impact of jet lag:

- Rest for a couple of days prior to departure.
- Try to select flight schedules that minimise sleep deprivation; arriving late in the day means you can go to sleep soon after you arrive. For very long flights, try to organise a stopover.
- Avoid excessive eating (which bloats the stomach) and alcohol (which causes dehydration) during the flight. Instead, drink plenty of noncarbonated, nonalcoholic drinks such as fruit juice or water.
- Avoid smoking.
- Make yourself comfortable by wearing loose-fitting clothes and perhaps bringing an eye mask and ear plugs to help you sleep.
- Try to sleep at the appropriate time for the time zone you are travelling to.

Motion Sickness Eating lightly before and during a trip will reduce the chances of motion sickness. If you are prone to motion sickness try to find a place that minimises movement – near the wing on aircraft, close to midships on boats, near the centre on buses. Fresh air usually helps; reading and cigarette smoke don't. Commercial motion-sickness preparations, which can cause drowsiness, have to be taken before the trip commences. Ginger (available in capsule form) and peppermint (including mint-flavoured sweets) are natural preventatives.

Prickly Heat Prickly heat is an itchy rash caused by excessive perspiration trapped under the skin. It usually strikes people who have just arrived in a hot climate. Keeping cool, bathing often, drying the skin and using a mild talcum or prickly heat powder or resorting to air-conditioning may help.

Sunburn In the tropics, the desert or at high altitude you can get sunburnt surprisingly quickly, even through cloud. Use a sunscreen, a hat, and a barrier cream for your nose and lips. Calamine lotion or a commercial after-sun preparation are good for mild sunburn. Protect your eyes with good quality sunglasses, particularly if you will be near water, sand or snow.

Infectious Diseases

Diarrhoea Simple things like a change of water, food or climate can all cause a mild bout of diarrhoea, but a few rushed toilet trips with no other symptoms is not indicative of a major problem.

Dehydration is the main danger with any diarrhoea, particularly in children or the elderly as dehydration can occur quite quickly. Under all circumstances, fluid replacement is the most important thing to remember. Weak black tea with a little sugar, soda water, or soft drinks allowed to go flat and diluted 50% with clean water are all good. With severe diarrhoea a rehydrating solution is preferable to replace minerals and salts lost. Commercially available oral rehydration salts (ORS) are very useful; add them to boiled or bottled water. In an emergency you can make up a solution of six teaspoons of sugar and half a teaspoon of salt to a litre of boiled or bottled water. You need to drink at least the same volume of fluid that you are losing in bowel movements and vomiting. Urine is the best guide to the adequacy of replacement – if you have small amounts of concentrated urine, you need to drink more. Keep drinking small amounts often. Stick to a bland diet as you recover.

Lomotil or Imodium can be used to bring relief from the symptoms, but they do not actually cure the problem. Only use these drugs if you do not have access to toilets (eg, if you *must* travel). For children under 12 years Lomotil and Imodium are not recommended. Do not use these drugs if the person has a high fever or is severely dehydrated.

Viral Gastroenteritis This is caused not by bacteria but, as the name suggests, by a virus. It is characterised by stomach cramps, diarrhoea and sometimes by vomiting and/or a slight fever. All you can do is rest and drink lots of fluids.

Fungal Infections Fungal infections occur more commonly in hot weather and are usually found on the scalp, between the toes (athlete's foot) or fingers, in the groin and on the body (ringworm). You get ringworm (which is a fungal infection, not a worm) from infected animals or other people. Moisture encourages these infections.

To prevent fungal infections wear loose, comfortable clothes, avoid artificial fibres, wash frequently and dry yourself carefully. If you do get an infection, wash the infected area at least daily with a disinfectant or medicated soap and water, and rinse and dry well. Apply an antifungal cream or powder like tolnaftate. Try to expose the infected area to air or sunlight as much as possible and wash all towels and underwear in hot water, change them often and let them dry in the sun.

Hepatitis Hepatitis is a general term for inflammation of the liver. It is a common disease worldwide. The symptoms are fever, chills, headache, fatigue, feelings of weakness, and aches and pains, followed by loss of appetite, nausea, vomiting, abdominal pain, dark urine, light-coloured faeces, jaundiced (yellow) skin and the whites of the eyes may turn yellow. **Hepatitis A** is transmitted by contaminated food and drinking water. You should seek medical advice, but there is not much you can do apart from resting, drinking lots of fluids, eating lightly and avoiding fatty foods. People who have had hepatitis should avoid alcohol for some time after the illness, as the liver needs time to recover.

There are almost 300 million chronic carriers of **hepatitis B** in the world. It is spread through contact with infected blood, blood products or body fluids, for example through sexual contact, unsterilised needles and blood transfusions, or contact with blood via small breaks in the skin. Other risk situations include having a shave, getting a tattoo or having your body pierced with contaminated equipment. The symptoms of type B may be more severe and may lead to long-term problems. Hepatitis C and D are spread in the same way as hepatitis B and can also lead to long-term complications.

HIV & AIDS Infection with the human immunodeficiency virus (HIV) may lead to acquired immune deficiency syndrome (AIDS), which is a fatal disease. Any exposure to blood, blood products or body fluids may put the individual at risk. The disease is often transmitted through sexual contact or dirty needles – vaccinations, acupuncture, tattooing and body piercing can be potentially as dangerous as intravenous drug use. HIV/AIDS can also be spread through infected blood transfusions: some developing countries cannot afford to screen blood used for transfusions.

Sexually Transmitted Diseases

HIV/AIDS and hepatitis B can be transmitted through sexual contact – see the relevant sections earlier for more details. Other STDs include gonorrhoea, herpes and syphilis; sores, blisters or rashes around the genitals and discharges or pain when urinating are common symptoms. In some STDs, such as wart virus or chlamydia, symptoms may be less marked or not observed at all, especially in women. Chlamydia infection can cause infertility in men and women before any symptoms have been noticed. Syphilis symptoms eventually disappear completely but the disease continues and can cause severe problems in later years. While abstinence from sexual contact is the only 100% effective prevention, using condoms is also effective. The treatment of gonorrhoea and syphilis is with antibiotics. The different sexually transmitted diseases each require specific antibiotics.

Cuts, Bites & Stings

Cuts & Scratches Wash well and treat any cut with an antiseptic such as povidone-iodine. Where possible avoid bandages and Band-Aids, which can keep wounds wet.

Bedbugs & Lice Bedbugs live in various places, but particularly in dirty mattresses and bedding, evidenced by spots of blood on bedclothes or on the wall. Bedbugs leave itchy bites in neat rows. Calamine lotion or a sting relief spray may help.

All lice cause itching and discomfort. They make themselves at home in your hair (head lice), your clothing (body lice) or in your pubic hair (crabs). You catch lice through direct contact with infected people or by sharing combs, clothing and the like. Powder or shampoo treatment will kill the lice and infected clothing should then be washed in very hot, soapy water and left in the sun to dry.

Insect Bites & Stings Bee and wasp stings are usually painful rather than dangerous. However, in people who are allergic to them severe breathing difficulties may occur and require urgent medical care. Calamine lotion or a sting relief spray will give relief and ice packs will reduce the pain and swelling.

Mosquitoes can be a nuisance in southern Europe, but can almost drive you insane during the summer months in northern Europe,

particularly around lakes and rivers. They also cause sleepless nights in a swampy country like the Camargue delta in southern France. Fortunately, mosquito-borne diseases like malaria are for the most part unknown in Europe. Most people get used to mosquito bites after a few days as their bodies adjust, and the itching and swelling will become less severe. An antihistamine cream may help alleviate the symptoms. For some people, a daily dose of vitamin B will keep mosquitoes at bay.

Ticks You should always check all over your body if you have been walking through a potentially tick-infested area as ticks can cause skin infections and other more serious diseases. If a tick is found attached, press down around the tick's head with tweezers, grab the head and gently pull upwards. Avoid pulling the rear of the body as this may squeeze the tick's gut contents through the attached mouth parts into the skin, increasing the risk of infection and disease. Smearing chemicals on the tick will not make it let go and is not recommended.

Lyme disease is a tick-transmitted infection that may be acquired in parts of southern Europe. The illness usually begins with a spreading rash at the site of the tick bite and is accompanied by fever, headache, extreme fatigue, aching joints and muscles, and mild neck stiffness. If untreated, these symptoms usually resolve over several weeks but over subsequent weeks or months disorders of the nervous system, heart and joints may develop. Treatment works best early in the illness. Medical help should be sought.

Rabies Rabies is a fatal viral infection but is rare in most countries in Europe. Rabies is nonexistent in Portugal, Monaco and Malta. Many animals can be infected (such as dogs, cats, foxes and bats) and it is their saliva which is infectious. Any bite, scratch or even lick from a warm-blooded, furry animal should be cleaned immediately and thoroughly. Scrub with soap and running water, and then apply alcohol or iodine solution. Medical help should be sought promptly to receive a course of injections to prevent the onset of symptoms and death.

Snakes To minimise your chances of being bitten always wear boots, socks and long trousers when walking through undergrowth where snakes may be present. Don't put your hands into holes and crevices, and be careful when collecting firewood.

Snake bites do not cause instantaneous death, and antivenenes are usually available. Immediately wrap the bitten limb tightly, as you would for a sprained ankle, and then attach a splint to immobilise it. Keep the victim still and seek medical help, if possible with the dead snake for identification. Don't attempt to catch the snake if there is a possibility of being bitten again. Tourniquets and sucking out the poison are now comprehensively discredited.

Women's Health

Antibiotic use, synthetic underwear, sweating and contraceptive pills can lead to fungal vaginal infections, especially when travelling in hot climates. Fungal infections are characterised by a rash, itch and discharge and can be treated with a vinegar or lemon-juice douche, or with yogurt. Nystatin, miconazole or clotrimazole pessaries or vaginal cream are the usual treatment. Maintaining good personal hygiene and wearing loose-fitting clothes and cotton underwear may help prevent these infections.

Sexually transmitted diseases are a major cause of vaginal problems. Symptoms include a smelly discharge, painful intercourse and sometimes a burning sensation when urinating. Medical attention should be sought and male sexual partners must also be treated. For more details see the section on Sexually Transmitted Diseases earlier. Besides abstinence, the best thing is to practise safer sex using condoms.

WOMEN TRAVELLERS

Women are more likely to experience problems in rural Spain, southern Italy (especially Sicily), Morocco, Turkey and Tunisia, where many men still think that staring at or calling out to a passing woman is to pay her a flattering compliment. Slightly conservative dress can help to deter lascivious gazes and wolf whistles and sunglasses may prevent unwanted eye contact. Marriage is highly respected in the region, and a wedding ring (on the left ring finger) sometimes helps, along with talk about 'my husband'.

In Muslim countries, a Western woman without a male companion will have a trying time coping with constant attention from males. The average Muslim woman is still bound to very strict codes of behaviour and dress, so it's not surprising that her Western counterpart is seen as being free from moral or sexual constraints. Although head cover is not compulsory in these countries, it's a good idea to wear a headscarf if you're visiting mosques and so on. Hitching alone in these areas is definitely asking for trouble.

GAY & LESBIAN TRAVELLERS

This book lists contact addresses and gay and lesbian venues in the individual country chapters; look in the Facts for the Visitor and Entertainment sections.

The *Spartacus International Gay Guide* (Bruno Gmünder, US$39.95) is a good male-only international directory of gay entertainment venues in Europe and elsewhere. It's best when used in conjunction with listings in local gay papers, usually distributed for free at gay bars and clubs. For lesbians, *Women's Travel in Your Pocket* (Ferrari Publications, UK£8.99) is a good international guide.

DISABLED TRAVELLERS

If you have a physical disability, get in touch with your national support organisation (preferably the 'travel officer' if there is one) and ask about the countries you plan to visit. They often have complete libraries devoted to travel, and they can put you in touch with travel agents who specialise in tours for the disabled.

The British-based Royal Association for Disability & Rehabilitation (RADAR) publishes a useful guide entitled *European Holidays & Travel Abroad: A Guide for Disabled People* (published in even-numbered years; UK£5), which gives a good overview of facilities available to disabled travellers in Europe, and one to places farther afield called *Long-Haul Holidays* (in odd-numbered years). Contact RADAR (☎ 020-7250 3222, fax 7250 0212) at 12 City Forum, 250 City Rd, London EC1V 8AF.

SENIOR TRAVELLERS

Senior citizens are entitled to many discounts in Europe on things like public transport and museum admission fees, provided they show proof of their age. In some cases they might need a special pass. The minimum qualifying age is generally 60 or 65 for men and slightly younger for women.

In your home country, a lower age may already entitle you to all sorts of interesting travel packages and discounts (eg, on car hire) through organisations and travel agents that cater for senior travellers. Start hunting at your local senior citizens advice bureau. European nationals aged 60 and over can get a Railplus (formerly Rail Europe Senior) Card, which entitles the holder to reduced fares. For more information see Cheap Tickets under Train in the Getting Around chapter.

TRAVEL WITH CHILDREN

Successful travel with young children requires planning and effort. Don't try to overdo things; even for adults, packing too much into the time available can cause problems. And make sure the activities include the kids as well – balance that day at the Louvre with a day at Disneyland Paris. Include children in the trip planning; if they've helped to work out where you will be going, they will be much more interested when they get there. Lonely Planet's *Travel with Children* by Maureen Wheeler is a good source of information.

Most car-rental firms in Europe have children's safety seats for hire at a nominal cost, but it's essential that you book them in advance. The same goes for highchairs and cots (cribs); they're standard in most restaurants and hotels, but numbers are limited. The choice of baby food, formulas, soy and cow's milk, disposable nappies (diapers) and the like is as great in the supermarkets of most European countries as it is at home, but the opening hours might be different. Run out of nappies on Saturday afternoon and you're in for a messy weekend.

DANGERS & ANNOYANCES

On the whole, you should experience few problems travelling in Mediterranean Europe – even alone – as the region is well developed and relatively safe. But do exercise common sense.

Whatever you do, don't leave friends and relatives back home worrying about how to get in touch with you in case of emergency. Work out a list of places where they can contact you. Better still, phone home now and then or email.

Theft

Theft is definitely a problem in Mediterranean Europe, and nowadays you also have to be wary of other travellers. The most important things to guard are your passport, papers, tickets and money – in that order. It's always best to carry these next to your skin or in a sturdy leather pouch on your belt. Train station lockers or luggage storage counters are useful places to store your bags (but *never* valuables) while you get your bearings in a new town. Be very suspicious about people who offer to help you operate your locker. Carry your own padlock for hostel lockers.

You can lessen the risks further by being careful of snatch thieves. Cameras or shoulder bags are an open invitation for these people, who sometimes operate from motorcycles or scooters and expertly slash the strap before you have a chance to react. A small daypack is better, but watch your rear. Be very careful at cafes and bars; loop the strap around your leg while seated.

Pickpockets are most active in dense crowds, especially in busy train stations and on public transport during peak hours. A common ploy is for one person to distract you while another zips through your pockets. Beware of gangs of kids – both dishevelled-looking *and* well dressed – waving newspapers and demanding attention. In the blink of an eye, a wallet or camera can go missing.

Be careful even in hotels; don't leave valuables lying around in your room. Parked cars are prime targets for petty criminals in most cities, and cars with foreign number plates and/or rental-agency stickers in particular. Remove the stickers (or cover them with local football club stickers or something similar), leave a local newspaper on the seat and generally try to make it look like a local car. Don't ever leave valuables in the car, and remove all luggage overnight, even if it's in a parking garage. In some places, freeway service centres have become unsafe territory: in the time it takes to drink a cup of coffee or use the toilet, your car can be broken into and cleared out.

Another ploy is for muggers to pull up alongside your car and point to the wheel; when you get out to have a look, you become one more robbery statistic. While driving in cities, beware of snatch thieves when you pull up at the lights – keep doors locked and windows rolled up high. In case of theft or loss, always report the incident to the police and ask for a statement. Otherwise your travel-insurance company won't pay up.

Drugs

Always treat drugs with a great deal of caution. There are a lot of drugs available in Mediterranean Europe, but that doesn't mean they are legal. Even a little harmless hashish can cause a great deal of trouble in some places.

Don't even think about bringing drugs home with you either. With what they may consider 'suspect' stamps in your passport (eg, Morocco), energetic customs officials could well decide to take a closer look.

ACTIVITIES

Mediterranean Europe offers countless opportunities to indulge in more active pursuits than sightseeing.

For more local information, see the individual country chapters.

Windsurfing & Surfing

After swimming and fishing, windsurfing could well be the most popular of the many water sports on offer in Europe. It's easy to rent sailboards in many tourist centres, and courses are usually available for beginners.

Believe it or not, you can also go surfing in Europe. While the calm Mediterranean is not the best place for the sport, there can be excellent surf (and an accompanying surfer scene) along the Atlantic coast of France and Portugal, and along the north and south-west coasts of Spain. The Atlantic seaboard of Morocco, too, has some excellent waves and deserted beaches.

Boating

The Mediterranean itself is not the only body of water with opportunities for boating. The region's many lakes, rivers and other coastlines offer a variety of boating options unmatched anywhere in the world. You can kayak down rapids in Slovenia, charter a yacht in the Aegean, row on a peaceful Alpine lake, rent a sailing boat on the Côte d'Azur, cruise the canals of France – the possibilities are endless.

Hiking

Keen hikers can spend a lifetime exploring Europe's many exciting trails. Probably the most spectacular are in the Alps and Italian Dolomites which are crisscrossed with well-marked trails, and food and accommodation are available along the way in season. The equally sensational Pyrenees are less developed, which can add to the experience as you often rely on remote mountain villages for rest and sustenance. Hiking areas that are less well known but nothing short of stunning can be found in Corsica, Sardinia, Crete, Croatia and northern Portugal while the High Atlas Mountains in Morocco offer a mind-blowing experience through tumbledown Berber villages in untamed country. The Picos de Europa range in Spain is also rewarding.

Cycling

Along with hiking, cycling is the best way to really get close to the scenery and the people, while keeping yourself fit in the process. It's also a good way to get around many cities and towns.

Much of Europe is ideally suited to cycling. In the north-west, the flat terrain ensures that bicycles are a popular form of everyday transport, though strong headwinds often spoil the fun. In the rest of the continent, hills and mountains can make for heavy going, but this is offset by the dense concentration of things to see. Cycling is a great way to explore many of the Mediterranean islands, though the heat can get to you after a while (make sure you drink enough fluids).

Popular cycling areas include the coastal areas of Sardinia (around Alghero) and Apulia, and the hills of Tuscany and Umbria in Italy, anywhere in the Alps (for those fit enough), and the south of France.

If you are arriving from outside Europe, you can often bring your own bicycle along on the plane (see Bicycle in the Getting Around chapter). Alternatively, this book lists many places where you can hire one.

See the introductory Getting Around chapter for more information on bicycle touring, and the Getting Around sections in the individual country chapters for rental agencies and tips on places to visit.

Skiing

Skiing is quite expensive due to the costs of ski lifts, accommodation and the inevitable après-ski drinking sessions. Equipment hire (or even purchase), on the other hand, can be relatively cheap if you follow the tips in this book, and the hassle of bringing your own skis may not be worth it. As a rule, a skiing holiday in Europe will work out twice as expensive as a summer holiday of the same length. Cross-country skiing costs less than downhill since you don't rely as much on ski lifts.

The skiing season generally lasts from early December to late March, though at higher altitudes it may extend an extra month either way. Snow conditions can vary greatly from one year to the next and from region to region, but January and February tend to be the best (and busiest) months.

Ski resorts in the French Alps offer great skiing and facilities but are also among the most expensive in Europe. Prices in the French Pyrenees and Italian Alps and Apennines are slightly cheaper (with upmarket exceptions like Cortina d'Ampezzo), and can work out to be relatively cheap with the right package. Cheaper still are the Julian Alps in Slovenia, which are luring skiers away from the flashier resorts just across the border in Austria and Italy.

Possibly the cheapest skiing in Europe can be found in the Pyrenees in Spain and Andorra, and in the Sierra Nevada mountain range in the south of Spain. Greece also boasts a growing ski industry, and skiing there is good value.

COURSES

If your interests are more cerebral, you can enrol in courses on anything from language to alternative medicine. Language courses are available to foreigners through universities or private schools, and are justifiably popular since the best way to learn a language is in the country where it's spoken. But you can also take courses in art, literature, architecture, drama, music, cooking, alternative energy, photography and organic farming, among other subjects.

The individual country chapters in this book give pointers on where to start looking. In general, the best sources of information are the cultural institutes maintained by many European countries around the world; failing that, try their national tourist offices or embassies. Student-exchange organisations, student-travel agencies, and organisations like the YMCA/YWCA and Hostelling International (HI) can also put you on the right

track. Ask about special holiday packages that include a course.

WORK

European countries aren't keen on handing out jobs to foreigners when unemployment rates are what they are in some areas. Officially, an EU citizen is allowed to work in any other EU country, but the paperwork isn't always straightforward for long-term employment. Other country/nationality combinations require special work permits that can be almost impossible to arrange, especially for temporary work. That doesn't prevent enterprising travellers from topping up their funds occasionally by working in the hotel or restaurant trades at beach or ski resorts or teaching a little English, and they don't always have to do this illegally either.

The UK, for example, issues special 'working holiday' visas to Commonwealth citizens aged between 17 and 27 valid for two years. In France you can get a visa for work as an au pair if you are going to follow a recognised course of study (eg, a French-language course) and complete all the paperwork before leaving your country. Your national student-exchange organisation may be able to arrange temporary work permits to several countries through special programs. For more details on working as a foreigner, see Work in the Facts for the Visitor sections of the individual country chapters.

If one of your parents or a grandparent was born in an EU country, you may have certain rights you never knew about. Get in touch with that country's embassy and ask about dual citizenship and work permits – if you go for citizenship, also ask about any obligations, such as military service and residency. Ireland is particularly easy-going about granting citizenship to people with an Irish parent or grandparent, and with an Irish passport, the EU is your oyster. Be aware that your home country may not recognise dual citizenship.

If you do find a temporary job, the pay may be less than that offered to local people. The one big exception is teaching English, but these jobs are hard to come by, at least officially. Other typical tourist jobs (picking grapes in France, washing dishes in Alpine resorts) often come with board and lodging, and the pay is little more than pocket money, but you'll have a good time partying with other travellers.

Work Your Way Around the World by Susan Griffith gives good, practical advice on a wide range of issues. Its publisher, Vacation Work, has many other useful titles, including *Summer Jobs Abroad*, edited by David Woodworth. Check the Web site at www.vacationwork.co.uk. *Working Holidays*, published by the Central Bureau for Educational Visits & Exchanges in London, is another good source.

If you play an instrument or have other artistic talents, you could try working the streets. As every Peruvian pipe player (and his fifth cousin) knows, busking is fairly common in major cities of Mediterranean Europe, especially in France, Spain and Italy. Beware though: many countries require municipal permits that can be hard to obtain. Talk to other buskers first.

Selling goods on the street, apart from at flea markets, is generally frowned upon and can be tantamount to vagrancy. It's also a hard way to make money if you're not selling something special. Most countries require permits for this sort of thing. It's fairly common, though officially illegal, in Spain.

ACCOMMODATION

The cheapest places to stay in Europe are camping grounds, followed by hostels and accommodation in student dormitories. Cheap hotels are virtually unknown in the northern half of Europe, but guesthouses, pensions and private rooms often offer good value. Self-catering flats and cottages are worth considering with a group, especially if you plan to stay somewhere for a while.

See the Facts for the Visitor sections in the individual country chapters for an overview of the local accommodation options. During peak holiday periods, accommodation can be hard to find, and unless you're camping, it's advisable to book ahead. Even camping grounds can fill up, especially in or around big cities.

Reservations

Cheap hotels in popular destinations (eg, Paris, Rome and Madrid), especially the well-run ones in desirable or central neighbourhoods, fill up quickly. It's a good idea to make reservations as many weeks ahead as possible – at least for the first night or two. A three-minute international phone call to reserve a room (followed, if necessary, by written confirmation and/or deposit) is a lot cheaper than wasting your first day in a city looking for a place to stay.

If you arrive in a country by air and without a reservation, there is often an airport accommodation-booking desk, although it rarely covers the lower strata of hotels. Tourist offices often have extensive accommodation lists, and the more helpful ones will go out of their way to find you something suitable. In most countries the fee for this service is very low and if accommodation is tight it can save you a lot of running around. This is also an easy way to get around any language problems. Agencies offering private rooms can be good value. Staying with a local family doesn't always mean that you'll lack privacy, but you'll probably have less freedom than in a hotel.

Sometimes people will come up to you on the street offering a private room or a hostel bed. This can be good or bad, there's no hard-and-fast rule – just make sure it's not way out in a dingy suburb somewhere and that you negotiate a clear price. As always, be careful when someone offers to carry your luggage; they might carry it off altogether.

Camping

Camping is immensely popular in Mediterranean Europe (especially among German and Dutch tourists) and provides the cheapest accommodation. There's usually a charge per tent or site, per person and per vehicle. National tourist offices should have booklets or brochures listing camping grounds for their country. See Visas & Documents earlier in this chapter for information on the Camping Card International.

In large cities, most camping grounds will be some distance from the centre. For this reason, camping is most popular with people who have their own transport. If you're on foot, the money you save by camping can quickly be eaten up by the bus or train fares spent on commuting to and from a town centre. You may also need a tent, sleeping bag and cooking equipment, though not always. Many camping grounds hire bungalows or cottages accommodating from two to eight people.

Camping other than on designated camping grounds is difficult because the population density of Europe makes it hard to find a suitable spot to pitch a tent away from prying eyes. It is also illegal without permission from the local authorities (the police or local council office) or from the owner of the land (don't be shy about asking – you may be pleasantly surprised by the response).

In some countries (eg, France), free camping is illegal on all but private land, and in Greece it's illegal altogether. This doesn't prevent hikers from occasionally pitching their tent for the night, and they'll usually get away with it if they have only a small tent, are discreet, stay only one or two nights, take the tent down during the day and do not light a campfire or leave rubbish. At worst, they'll be woken up by the police and asked to move on.

Hostels

Hostels offer the cheapest (secure) roof over your head in Europe, and you don't have to be a youngster to use them. Most hostels are part of the national youth hostel association (YHA), which is affiliated with what was formerly called the IYHF (International Youth Hostel Federation) and has been renamed Hostelling International (HI) in order to attract a wider clientele and move away from the emphasis on youth. The situation remains slightly confused, however. Some countries, such as the USA and Canada, immediately adopted the new name, but many European countries will take a few years to change their logos. In practice it makes no difference – IYHF and HI are the same thing and the domestic YHA almost always belongs to the parent group.

Technically, you're supposed to be a YHA or HI member to use affiliated hostels, but you can often stay by paying an extra charge and this will usually be set against future membership. Stay enough nights as a nonmember and you're automatically a member.

To join the HI, ask at any hostel or contact your local or national hostelling office. There's a useful Web site at www.iyhf .org/index.html with links to most HI sites. The offices for English-speaking countries appear below. Otherwise, check the individual country chapters for addresses.

Australia Australian Youth Hostels Association (☎ 02-9565 1699, fax 9565 1325, ✉ yha@yha .org.au), Level 3, 10 Mallett St, Camperdown, NSW 2050

Canada Hostelling International Canada (☎ 613-237-7884, fax 237-7868, ✉ info@hostellingintl .ca), 205 St Catherine St, Suite 400, Ottawa, Ontario K2P IC3

England & Wales Youth Hostels Association (☎ 01727-855215, fax 844126, ✉ customer services@yha.org.uk), Trevelyan House, 8 St Stephen's Hill, St Albans, Herts AL1 2DY

Ireland An Óige (Irish Youth Hostel Association; ☎ 01-830 4555, fax 830 5808, ✉ mailbox@ anoige.ie), 61 Mountjoy St, Dublin 7

New Zealand Youth Hostels Association of New Zealand (☎ 03-379 9970, fax 365 4476, ✉ info@yha.org.nz), 193 Cashel St, 3rd floor, Union House, Christchurch

Northern Ireland Hostelling International Northern Ireland (☎ 0128-9031 5435, fax 9043 9699, ✉ info@hini.org.uk), 22-32 Donegall Rd, Belfast BT12 5JN

Scotland Scottish Youth Hostels Association (☎ 01786-891400, fax 891333, ✉ info@syha .org.uk), 7 Glebe Crescent, Stirling FK8 2JA

South Africa Hostelling International South Africa (☎ 021-424 2511, fax 424 4119, ✉ info@hisa.org.za), PO Box 4402, St George's House, 73 St George's Mall, Cape Town 8001

USA Hostelling International/American Youth Hostels (☎ 202-783 6161, fax 783 6171, ✉ hi ayhserv@hiayh.org), 733 15th St NW, Suite 840, Washington DC 20005

At a hostel, you get a bed for the night, plus use of communal facilities, which often include a kitchen where you can prepare your own meals. You are usually required to have a sleeping sheet – simply using your sleeping bag is not permitted. If you don't have your own approved sleeping sheet, you can usually hire or buy one. Hostels vary widely in character, but the growing number of travellers and the increased competition from other forms of accommodation, particularly private 'backpacker hostels', have prompted many hostels to improve their facilities and cut back on rules and regulations. Increasingly, hostels are open all day, curfews are disappearing and the 'warden' with a sergeant-major mentality is an endangered species. In some places you'll even find hostels with single and double rooms.

There are many hostel guides with listings available, including the *HI Europe* (£7.50). Many hostels accept reservations by phone or fax, but usually not during peak periods, and they'll often book the next hostel you're heading to for a small fee. You can also book hostels through national hostel offices. Popular hostels can be heavily booked in summer and limits may even be placed on how many nights you can stay.

University Accommodation

Some university towns rent out student accommodation during holiday periods. This is very popular in France (see the France chapter for details). Accommodation will sometimes be in single rooms (more commonly in doubles or triples) and may have cooking facilities. Inquire at the college or university, at student information services or at local tourist offices.

Guesthouses & Hotels

There's a huge range of accommodation above the hostel level. In some countries private accommodation may go under the name of pension, guesthouse, *chambre d'hôte*, *domatia* and so on. Although the majority of guesthouses are simple affairs, there are more expensive ones where you will find attached bathrooms and other luxuries.

Above this level are hotels which, at the bottom of the bracket, may be no more expensive than guesthouses, but at the other extreme extend to luxury five-star properties with price tags to match. Although categorisation depends on the country, the hotels recommended in this book will generally range from no stars to one or two stars. You'll often find inexpensive hotels clustered around the bus and train station areas – always good places to start hunting.

Check your hotel room and the bathroom before you agree to take it, and make sure you know what it's going to cost; discounts are often available for groups or for longer stays. Ask about breakfast; sometimes it's included but at other times it may be obligatory and you'll have to pay extra for it. If the sheets don't look clean, ask to have them changed right away. Check where the fire exits are.

If you think a hotel room is too expensive, ask if there's anything cheaper. (Often hotel owners may have tried to steer you into more expensive rooms.) In southern Europe in particular, hotel owners may be open to a little bargaining if times are slack. In France it is now common practice for business hotels (usually rated higher than two stars) to slash their rates by up to 40% on Friday and Saturday nights when business is slow. Save your big hotel splurge for the weekend here.

FOOD

Few regions in the world offer such a variety of cuisines in such a small area as Mediterranean Europe. Dishes are completely different from one country (and even region) to the next, and sampling the local food can be one of the most enjoyable aspects of travel. The Facts for the Visitor sections in the individual country chapters contain details of local cuisines, and the Places to Eat sections list many suggestions.

Restaurant prices vary enormously. The cheapest places for a decent meal are often the self-service restaurants in department stores. University restaurants are dirt cheap, but the food tends to be bland and you may not be allowed in if you're not a local student. Kiosks often sell cheap snacks that can be as much a part of the national cuisine as the fancy dishes.

Self-catering – buying your ingredients at a shop or market and preparing them yourself – can be a cheap and wholesome way of eating. Even if you don't cook, a lunch on a park bench with a half a loaf of fresh bread, some local cheese and salami and a tomato or two, washed down with a bottle of local wine makes a nice change from restaurant food.

If you have dietary restrictions you're a vegetarian or you keep kosher, for example, tourist organisations may be able to advise you or provide lists of suitable restaurants. We list some vegetarian and kosher restaurants in this book.

In general, vegetarians have no need to worry about going hungry in Mediterranean Europe; many restaurants have one or two vegetarian dishes, and southern European menus in particular tend to contain many vegetable dishes and salads.

Getting There & Away

Step one of your trip is actually getting to Mediterranean Europe and, in these days of severe competition among airlines, there are plenty of opportunities to find cheap tickets to a variety of gateway cities.

Forget shipping – only a handful of ships still carry passengers across the Atlantic; they don't sail often and are very expensive, even compared with full-fare air tickets. Some travellers still arrive or leave overland – the options being Africa, the Middle East and Asia via Russia on the Trans-Siberian railway from China.

AIR
Always remember to reconfirm your onward or return bookings by the specified time – at least 72 hours before departure on international flights. Otherwise there's a real risk that you'll turn up at the airport only to find that you've missed your flight because it was rescheduled, or that you've been reclassified as a 'no show' and 'bumped' (see the Air Travel Glossary in this chapter).

Buying Tickets
An air ticket alone can gouge a great slice out of anyone's budget, but you can reduce the cost by finding discounted fares. Stiff competition has resulted in widespread discounting – good news for travellers! The only people likely to be paying full fare these days are travellers flying in 1st or business class. Passengers flying in economy can usually manage some sort of discount. But unless you buy carefully and flexibly, it is still possible to end up paying exorbitant amounts for a journey.

For long-term travel there are plenty of discount tickets which are valid for 12 months, allowing multiple stopovers with open dates. For short-term travel cheaper fares are available by travelling mid-week, staying away at least one Saturday night or taking advantage of short-lived promotional offers.

When you're looking for bargain air fares, go to a travel agent rather than directly to the airline. From time to time, airlines do have promotional fares and special offers, but generally they only sell fares at the official listed price. One exception to this rule is the expanding number of 'no-frills' carriers operating in the United States and north-west Europe, which mostly sell direct to travellers. Unlike the 'full service' airlines, no-frills carriers often make one-way tickets available at around half the return fare, meaning that it is easy to put together a return ticket when you fly to one place but leave from another.

The other exception is booking on the Internet. Many airlines, full-service and no-frills, offer some excellent fares to Web surfers. They may sell seats by auction or simply cut prices to reflect the reduced cost of electronic selling. Many travel agents around the world have Web sites, which can make the Internet a quick and easy way to compare prices, a good start for when you're ready to start negotiating with your favourite travel agency. On-line ticket sales work well if you are doing a simple one-way or return trip on specified dates. However, on-line super-fast fare generators are no substitute for a travel agent who knows all about special deals, has strategies for avoiding stopovers and can offer advice on everything from which airline has the best vegetarian food to the best travel insurance to bundle with your ticket.

The days when some travel agents would routinely fleece travellers by running off with their money are, happily, almost over, though it's generally not advisable to send money (even cheques) through the post unless the agent is very well established. Paying by credit card generally offers protection, as most card issuers provide refunds if you can prove you didn't get what you paid for. Similar protection can be obtained by buying a ticket from a bonded agent, such as one covered by the Air Transport Operators Licence (ATOL) scheme in the UK. Agents who only accept cash should hand over the tickets straight away and not tell you to 'come back tomorrow'. After you've made a booking or paid your deposit, call the airline and confirm that the booking was made.

You may decide to pay more than the rock-bottom fare by opting for the safety of a better known travel agent. Firms such as STA

Air Travel Glossary

Cancellation Penalties If you have to cancel or change a discounted ticket, there are often heavy penalties involved; insurance can sometimes be taken out against these penalties. Some airlines impose penalties on regular tickets as well, particularly against 'no-show' passengers.

Courier Fares Businesses often need to send urgent documents or freight securely and quickly. Courier companies hire people to accompany the package through customs and, in return, offer a discount ticket which is sometimes a phenomenal bargain. However, you may have to surrender all your baggage allowance and take only carry-on luggage.

Full Fares Airlines traditionally offer 1st class (coded F), business class (coded J) and economy class (coded Y) tickets. These days there are so many promotional and discounted fares available that few passengers pay full economy fare.

Lost Tickets If you lose your airline ticket an airline will usually treat it like a travellers cheque and, after inquiries, issue you with another one. Legally, however, an airline is entitled to treat it like cash and if you lose it then it's gone forever. Take good care of your tickets.

Onward Tickets An entry requirement for many countries is that you have a ticket out of the country. If you're unsure of your next move, the easiest solution is to buy the cheapest onward ticket to a neighbouring country or a ticket from a reliable airline which can later be refunded if you do not use it.

Open-Jaw Tickets These are return tickets where you fly out to one place but return from another. If available, this can save you backtracking to your arrival point.

Overbooking Since every flight has some passengers who fail to show up, airlines often book more passengers than they have seats. Usually excess passengers make up for the no-shows, but occasionally somebody gets 'bumped' onto the next available flight. Guess who it is most likely to be? The passengers who check in late.

Promotional Fares These are officially discounted fares, available from travel agencies or direct from the airline.

Reconfirmation If you don't reconfirm your flight at least 72 hours prior to departure, the airline may delete your name from the passenger list. Ring to find out if your airline requires reconfirmation.

Restrictions Discounted tickets often have various restrictions on them – such as needing to be paid for in advance and incurring a penalty to be altered. Others are restrictions on the minimum and maximum period you must be away.

Round-the-World Tickets RTW tickets give you a limited period (usually a year) in which to circumnavigate the globe. You can go anywhere the carrying airlines go, as long as you don't backtrack. The number of stopovers or total number of separate flights is decided before you set off and they usually cost a bit more than a basic return flight.

Transferred Tickets Airline tickets cannot be transferred from one person to another. Travellers sometimes try to sell the return half of their ticket, but officials can ask you to prove that you are the person named on the ticket. On an international flight tickets are compared with passports.

Travel Periods Ticket prices vary with the time of year. There is a low (off-peak) season and a high (peak) season, and often a low-shoulder season and a high-shoulder season as well. Usually the fare depends on your outward flight – if you depart in the high season and return in the low season, you pay the high-season fare.

Travel, which has offices worldwide, Council Travel in the USA and usit CAMPUS (formerly Campus Travel) in the UK are not going to disappear overnight and they do offer good prices to most destinations.

If you purchase a ticket and later want to make changes to your route or get a refund, you need to contact the original travel agent. Airlines only issue refunds to the purchaser of a ticket – usually the travel agent who bought the ticket on your behalf. Many travellers change their routes halfway through their trips, so think carefully before you buy a ticket which is not easily refunded.

Student & Youth Fares Full-time students and people under 26 have access to better deals than other travellers. The better deals may not always be cheaper fares but can include more flexibility to change flights and/or routes. You have to show a document proving your date of birth or a valid International Student Identity Card (ISIC) when buying your ticket and boarding the plane. There are plenty of places around the world where nonstudents can get fake student cards, but if you get caught using a fake card you could have your ticket confiscated.

Frequent Flyers Most airlines offer frequent flyer deals that can earn you a free air ticket or other goodies. To qualify, you have to accumulate sufficient mileage with the same airline or airline alliance. Many airlines have 'blackout periods', or times when you cannot fly for free on your frequent-flyer points (Christmas and Chinese New Year, for example). The worst thing about frequent-flyer programs is that they tend to lock you into one airline, and that airline may not always have the cheapest fares or most convenient flight schedule.

Courier Flights Courier flights are a great bargain if you're lucky enough to find one. Air-freight companies expedite delivery of urgent items by sending them with you as your baggage allowance. You are permitted to bring along a carry-on bag, but that's all. In return, you get a steeply discounted ticket.

There are other restrictions: courier tickets are sold for a fixed date and schedule changes can be difficult to make. If you buy a return ticket, your schedule will be even more rigid. You need to clarify before you fly what restrictions apply to your ticket, and don't expect a refund once you've paid.

Booking a courier ticket takes some effort. They are not readily available and arrangements have to be made a month or more in advance. You won't find courier flights on all air routes either – just on the major ones.

Courier flights are occasionally advertised in the newspapers, or you could contact air-freight companies listed in the phone book. You may even have to go to the air-freight company to get an answer – the companies aren't always keen to give out information over the phone. *Travel Unlimited* (PO Box 1058, Allston, MA 02134, USA) is a monthly travel newsletter based in the USA that publishes many courier flight deals from destinations worldwide. A 12-month subscription to the newsletter costs US$25, or US$35 for readers outside the USA. Another possibility (at least for US residents) is to join the International Association of Air Travel Couriers (IAATC). The membership fee of $45 gets members a bimonthly update of air-courier offerings, access to a fax-on-demand service with daily updates of last minute specials and the bimonthly newsletter *The Shoestring Traveler*. For more information, contact IAATC (☎ 561-582-8320) or visit its Web site, www.courier.org. However, be aware that joining this organisation does not guarantee that you'll get a courier flight.

Second-hand Tickets You'll occasionally see advertisements on youth hostel bulletin boards and in newspapers for 'second-hand tickets'. That is, somebody purchased a return ticket or a ticket with multiple stopovers and now wants to sell the unused portion of the ticket. Unfortunately, these tickets, if used for international travel, are usually worthless, as the name on the ticket must match the name on the passport of the person checking in. Some people reason that the seller of the ticket can check you in with his or her passport, and then give you the boarding pass – wrong again! Usually the immigration people want to see your boarding pass, and if it doesn't match the name in your passport, then you won't be able to board your flight.

Travellers with Special Needs

Most international airlines can cater to people with special needs – travellers with disabilities, people with young children and even children travelling alone.

Travellers with special dietary preferences (vegetarian, kosher etc) can request appropriate meals with advance notice. If you are travelling in a wheelchair, most international airports can provide an escort from check-in desk to plane where needed, and ramps, lifts, toilets and phones are generally available.

Airlines usually allow babies up to two years of age to fly for 10% of the adult fare, although a few may allow them free of charge. Reputable international airlines usually provide nappies (diapers), tissues, talcum and all the other paraphernalia needed to keep babies clean, dry and half-happy. For children between the ages of two and 12, the fare on international flights is usually 50% of the regular fare or 67% of a discounted fare.

The USA

Discount travel agents in the USA are known as consolidators. San Francisco is the ticket consolidator capital of America, although some good deals can be found in Los Angeles, New York and other big cities. Consolidators can be found through the Yellow Pages or the major daily newspapers. Ticket Planet is a leading ticket consolidator and is recommended. Visit its Web site at www.ticketplanet.com.

The *New York Times, LA Times, Chicago Tribune* and *San Francisco Chronicle* all have weekly travel sections in which you'll find any number of travel agents' ads. Council Travel, America's largest student travel organisation, has around 60 offices in the USA; its head office (☎ 800-226-8624) is at 205 E 42 St, New York, NY 10017. Call to find out the office nearest you or visit its Web site at www.ciee.org. STA Travel (☎ 800-777-0112) has offices in major cities. Call for office locations or visit its Web site at www.statravel.com.

You should be able to fly from New York to London or Paris and back for US$400 to US$500 in the low season and US$550 to US$800 in the high season. Equivalent fares from the west coast are US$100 to US$300 higher.

On a stand-by basis, one-way fares can work out to be remarkably cheap. New York-based Airhitch (☎ 212-864 2000) can get you to/from Europe for US$185/235/265/215 each way from the east coast/midwest/west coast/southeast. Visit its Web site at www.airhitch.org.

Another option is a courier flight. A New York-London return ticket can cost as little as US$210 in the low season. See Courier Flights in the Buying a Ticket section earlier or try As You Like It Travel (☎ 212-216 0644) or Now Voyager Travel (☎ 212-431 1616), or visit their Web sites at www.asulikeit.com and www.nowvoyagertravel.com.

Canada

Canadian discount air ticket sellers are also known as consolidators and their air fares tend to be about 10% higher than those sold in the USA. The *Globe & Mail*, the *Toronto Star*, the *Montreal Gazette* and the *Vancouver Sun* carry travel agents ads and are a good place to look for cheap fares.

Travel CUTS (☎ 800-667-2887) is Canada's national student travel agency and has offices in all major cities. Its Web address is www.travelcuts.com.

Airhitch (see the USA section) has stand-by fares to/from Toronto, Montreal and Vancouver.

Australia

Cheap flights from Australia to Europe generally go via South-East Asian capitals, involving stopovers at Kuala Lumpur, Bangkok or Singapore. If a long stopover between connections is necessary, transit accommodation is sometimes included in the price of the ticket. If it's at your own expense, it may be worth considering a more expensive ticket.

Quite a few travel offices specialise in discount air tickets. Some travel agents, particularly smaller ones, advertise cheap air fares in the travel sections of weekend newspapers, such as the *Age* in Melbourne and the *Sydney Morning Herald*.

Two well-known agents for cheap fares are STA Travel and Flight Centre. STA Travel (☎ 03-9349 2411) has its main office at 224 Faraday St, Carlton, VIC 3053, and offices in all major cities and on many university campuses. Call ☎ 131 776 Australia-wide for the location of your nearest branch or visit its Web site at www.statravel.com.au. Flight Centre (☎ 131 600 Australia-wide) has a central office at 82 Elizabeth St, Sydney, and there are dozens of offices throughout Australia. Its Web address is www.flightcentre .com.au. The usit CAMPUS representative in Australia is Student Uni Travel (02-9232 8444, ✉ sydney@backpackers.net).

Flights from Australia to a European destination on Thai, Malaysian, Qantas and Singapore airlines start from about A$1700 (low season) up to A$2500. All have frequent promotional fares so it pays to check daily newspapers. Flights to/from Perth are a couple of hundred dollars cheaper. Another option for travellers wanting to go to Britain between November and February is to hook up with a charter flight returning to Britain. These low-season, one-way fares do have restrictions, but may work out to be considerably cheaper. Ask your travel agent for details.

New Zealand
As in Australia, STA and Flight Centres International are popular travel agents in New Zealand. The usit CAMPUS representative is usit Beyond (☎ 09-379 4224) with a useful Web site at www.usitbeyond.co.nz. The cheapest fares to Europe are routed through Asia. A discounted return flight to London from Auckland costs around NZ$2100. An RTW ticket with Air New Zealand or Lufthansa via the USA is around NZ$2400 in the low season.

The UK
Discount air travel is big business in London. Advertisements for many travel agents appear in the travel pages of the weekend broadsheets, such as the *Independent on Saturday* and the *Sunday Times*. Look out for the free magazines, such as *TNT*, which are widely available in London – often outside the main railway and underground stations.

For students or travellers under 26, popular travel agencies in the UK include STA Travel (☎ 020-7361 6144), which has an office at 86 Old Brompton Rd, London SW7 3LQ, and other offices in London and Manchester. Visit its Web site at www.statravel .co.uk. Usit CAMPUS (☎ 0870-240 1010), 52 Grosvenor Gardens, London SW1WOAG, has branches throughout the UK. The Web

address is www.usitcampus .com. Both of these agencies sell tickets to all travellers but cater especially to young people and students. Charter flights can work out as a cheaper alternative to scheduled flights, especially if you do not qualify for the under-26 and student discounts.

Other recommended travel agencies include: Trailfinders (☎ 020-7938 3939), 194 Kensington High St, London W8 7RG; Bridge the World (☎ 020-7734 7447), 4 Regent Place, London W1R 5FB; and Flightbookers (☎ 020-7757 2000), 177-178 Tottenham Court Rd, London W1P 9LF.

Continental Europe
Though London is the travel discount capital of Europe, there are several other cities in which you will find a range of good deals. Generally, there is not much variation in air fare prices for departures from the main European cities. All the major airlines are usually offering some sort of deal, and travel agents generally have a number of deals on offer, so shop around.

Across Europe many travel agencies have ties with STA Travel, where cheap tickets can be purchased and STA-issued tickets can be altered (usually for a US$25 fee). Outlets in major cities include: Voyages Wasteels (☎ 08 03 88 70 04 – this number can only be dialled from within France), 11 rue Dupuytren, 75006 Paris; STA Travel (☎ 030-311 0950), Goethestrasse 73, 10625 Berlin; Passaggi (☎ 06-474 0923), Stazione Termini FS, Galleria Di Tesla, Rome; and ISYTS (☎ 01-322 1267), 11 Nikis St, Upper Floor, Syntagma Square, Athens.

France has a network of student travel agencies which can supply discount tickets to travellers of all ages. OTU Voyages (☎ 01 44 41 38 50) has a central Paris office at 39 Ave Georges Bernanos, 5e, and another 42 offices around the country. Its Web address is www.otu.fr. Acceuil des Jeunes en France (☎ 01 42 77 87 80), 119 rue Saint Martin, 4e, is another popular discount travel agency. General travel agencies in Paris which offer some of the best services and deals include Voyageurs du Monde (☎ 01 42 86 16 00) at 55 rue Sainte Anne, 2e; and Nouvelles Frontières (☎ 08 03 33 33 33), 5 Ave de l'Opéra, 1er, Web address: www.nouvelles-frontieres.com.

Belgium, Switzerland, the Netherlands and Greece are also good places for buying discount air tickets. In Belgium, Acotra Student Travel Agency (☎ 02-512 86 07) at rue de la Madeline, Brussels, and WATS Reizen (☎ 03-226 16 26) at de Keyserlei 44, Antwerp, are both well-known agencies. In Switzerland, SSR Voyages (☎ 01-297 11 11) specialises in student, youth and budget fares. There is a branch at Leonhardstrasse 10, Zurich and in most major Swiss cities. Its Web address is www.ssr.ch.

In the Netherlands, NBBS Reizen is the official student travel agency. You can find them in Amsterdam (☎ 020-624 09 89) at Rokin 66 and there are several other agencies around the city. Another recommended travel agent in Amsterdam is Malibu Travel (☎ 020-626 32 30) at Prinsengracht 230.

In Athens, check the many travel agencies in the backstreets between Syntagma and Omonia Squares, or try Magic Bus (☎ 01-323 7471).

Africa

Nairobi and Johannesburg are probably the best places in Africa to buy tickets to Europe, thanks to the many bucket shops and the lively competition between them. Student Travel Centre (☎ 011-716 3945) in Johannesburg and the Africa Travel Centre (☎ 021-235 555) in Cape Town are worth trying for cheap tickets.

Several West African countries such as Senegal and The Gambia offer cheap charter flights to France and London. Charter fares to Morocco and Tunisia can be quite cheap if you're lucky enough to find a seat.

Asia

Singapore and Bangkok are the discount airfare capitals of Asia. Shop around and ask the advice of other travellers before handing over any money. STA has branches in Hong Kong, Tokyo, Singapore, Bangkok, Jakarta and Kuala Lumpur.

In India, tickets may be slightly cheaper from the bucket shops around Delhi's Connaught Place. Check with other travellers about their current reliability.

LAND

Bus

Eurolines, Europe's largest network of buses, has seven circular explorer routes, always starting and ending in London. For further details, see the Bus section in the Getting Around chapter.

Deutsche-Touring (☎ 069-790 30), Am Römerhof 17, Frankfurt

Eurolines Austria (☎ 01-712 04 53), Autobusbahnhof Wien-Mitte, Landstrasser Hauptstrasse, 1030 Vienna

Eurolines Nederland (☎ 020-560 87 87), Rokin 10, 1012 KR Amsterdam

Eurolines UK (☎ 08705-143219), 52 Grosvenor Gardens, London SW1, Britain

Train

UK The Channel Tunnel allows for a land link between Britain and France. Eurostar is the passenger train service which travels between London and Paris and London and Brussels; cars travel on the Eurotunnel vehicle service.

Eurostar The highly civilised Eurostar passenger train service takes three hours (not including the one-hour time change) to get from London's Waterloo station to the Gare du Nord in Paris. Passport and customs checks take place on board or very cursorily on arrival.

There's quite a wide range of tickets. Cheapest is the non-refundable Leisure Apex return which must include a Saturday night; booked at least 14 days in advance it costs £69/119 in standard/first class; booked at least seven days in advance it costs £85/160. Flexi Tickets can be refunded and cost £140/220. Regular one-way tickets cost £155/190.

The Youth Return ticket (£75) available to those under 26 can be booked at any time. Changes can be made only once in each direction and the ticket is non-refundable.

Children's return fares, available for those aged four to 11 years, are £58/90 in standard/first class. There are often special deals on offer (eg, day returns, weekend trips etc), so it pays to phone Eurostar or its agents for the latest information.

Eurostar tickets are available direct from Eurostar (☎ 0990-186 186 in the UK, or ☎ 08 36 35 35 39 in France), from some travel agents, at Waterloo station, from the international ticket offices at many of the UK's mainline train stations, and from Rail Europe

(☎ 0990-300 003) which also sells other European rail tickets. Eurostar's Web site is at www.eurostar.com.

You can take a bicycle on Eurostar as part of your luggage only if it is in a bike bag.

Eurotunnel The Eurotunnel vehicle service (☎ 0990-353 535 in the UK, or ☎ 03 21 00 61 00 in France) travels between terminals in Folkestone and Calais. Its Web address is www.eurotunnel.com. This train carries cars, motorcycles and bicycles along with their passengers/riders.

You can just drive into the terminal, buy your ticket and get on the next train but you'll almost always make a saving by buying your ticket in advance. Fares vary with the time of year and there are peak (6.30 am to 10 pm) and off-peak (10 pm to 6.30 am) periods. The one-way/return fare for a car with driver and all passengers is £169.50/369 or £134.50/269 off-peak. A five-day return costs £159 off-peak or £229 peak. A day return is £69, and for the same price you can get an overnight return as long as you leave after 12 noon on the 1st day and are back by 4 pm on the 2nd day.

A motorcycle and rider costs from £89 return. Bicycles can be taken but only on two trains per day and they must be booked 24 hours in advance on ☎ 01303-288680. The cost is £15 for bicycle and rider.

Trains run 24 hours a day, every day of the year, with up to four departures an hour during peak periods. During the 35-minute crossing, passengers can sit in their cars or walk around the air-conditioned, sound-proofed rail carriage. The entire process, including loading and unloading, should take about an hour.

Train-Boat-Train There are train-boat-train combos in association with Hoverspeed (☎ 0990-240 241) and others from London's Charing Cross station to Paris' Gare du Nord that take between seven and eight hours and cost £39/58 one way/return (or £49 for a five-day return). The Hoverspeed Web site is at www.hoverspeed.co.uk. It's obviously cheaper than Eurostar but takes a lot longer, and you've got to mess around transferring by bus between the train station and the ferry terminal on both sides.

Africa & Asia Morocco and most of Turkey lie outside Europe, but the rail systems of both countries are still covered by Inter-Rail (Zone F & Zone G respectively). The price of a cheap return train ticket from London to Morocco compares favourably with equivalent bus fares.

It *is* possible to get to Western Europe by rail from central and eastern Asia, though count on spending at least eight days doing it. You can choose from four different routes to Moscow: the Trans-Siberian (9297km from Vladivostok), the Trans-Mongolian (7860km from Beijing) and the Trans-Manchurian (9001km from Beijing), which all use the same tracks across Siberia but have different routes east of Lake Baikal; and the Trans-Kazakhstan, which runs between Moscow and Urumqi in north-western China. Prices vary enormously, depending on where you buy the ticket and what is included – advertised 2nd-class fares cost around US$330 from Beijing to Moscow. Web sites worth consulting for trans-sib erian packages include: www.monkeysh rine.com, www.trans-siberian.co.uk, www .regent-holidays.co.uk and www.finnsov.fi.

There are countless travel options between Moscow and the rest of Europe. Most people will opt for the train, usually to/from Berlin, Helsinki, Munich, Budapest or Vienna. The *Trans-Siberian Handbook* (Trailblazer) by Bryn Thomas is a comprehensive guide to the route, as is the *Trans-Siberian Rail Guide* (Compass Star) by Robert Strauss & Tamsin Turnbull. Lonely Planet's *Russia, Ukraine & Belarus* has a chapter on trans-Siberian travel.

Overland Trails

In the early 1980s, the overland trail to/from Asia lost much of its popularity as the Islamic regime in Iran made life difficult for most independent travellers, and the war in Afghanistan closed that country off to all but the foolhardy. Now that Iran seems to be rediscovering the merits of tourism, the Asia route has begun to pick up again, though unsettled conditions in Afghanistan, southern Pakistan and north-west India could prevent the trickle of travellers turning into a flood for the time being.

To reach North Africa you can either cross the Mediterranean by ferry or travel overland via Turkey, Syria, Jordan, Israel and Egypt. Owing to unrest in parts of the Sahara and Sudan, however, the main trans-Africa routes are more difficult than they were in the 1980s.

Travelling by private transport beyond Europe requires plenty of paperwork and other preparations. A detailed description is beyond the scope of this book, but the following Getting Around chapter tells you what's required within Europe.

SEA

Channel Ferries

Several different ferry companies compete on all the main Channel ferry routes. The resulting service is comprehensive but very complicated. The same ferry company can have a host of different prices for the same route depending upon the time of day or year, the validity of the ticket, or the length of your vehicle. Vehicle tickets include the driver and often up to five passengers free of charge. It is worth planning (and booking) ahead where possible as there may be special reductions on off-peak crossings and advance purchase tickets. On Channel routes, apart from one-day or short-term excursion returns, there is little price advantage in buying a return ticket as against two singles.

The shortest cross-Channel routes between England and France (Dover to Calais or Folkestone to Boulogne) are also the busiest, though there is now great competition from the Channel Tunnel. P&O Stena handle the short-hop Dover-Calais routes. P&O Ferries and Brittany Ferries also sail direct between England and northern Spain, taking 24 to 35 hours, and between France and Ireland.

Rail-pass holders are entitled to discounts or free travel on some lines (see the earlier Train section), and most ferry companies give discounts to disabled drivers.

Useful Web sites include Brittany Ferries: www.brittany-ferries.com; P&O European Ferries: www.poef.com; and P&O Stena Line: www.posl.com.

Mediterranean Ferries

There are many ferries across the Mediterranean between Africa and Europe. The ferry you take will depend on your travels in Africa, but options include: Spain-Morocco, Italy-Tunisia and France-Morocco and France-Tunisia. There are also ferries between Greece and Israel via Cyprus. Ferries are often filled to capacity in summer, especially to/from Tunisia, so book well in advance if you're taking a vehicle across. See the relevant country chapters.

Passenger Ships & Freighters

Regular, long-distance passenger ships disappeared with the advent of cheap air travel and were replaced by a small number of luxury cruise ships. Cunard's *Queen Elizabeth 2* sails between New York and Southampton 20 times a year; the trip takes six nights each way and costs around UK£1500 for the return trip, though there are also one-way and 'fly one-way' deals. The bible for passenger ships and sea travel is the *OAG Cruise & Ferry Guide* published by the UK-based Reed Travel Group (☎ 01582-600 111), but it costs UK£50 per issue so you may want to consult it at your library.

A more adventurous alternative is as a paying passenger on a freighter. Freighters are far more numerous than cruise ships and there are many more routes from which to choose. The previously mentioned *OAG Cruise & Ferry Guide* is the most comprehensive source of information, though *Travel by Cargo Ship* (Cadogan) is also a good source. Passenger freighters typically carry six to 12 passengers (more than 12 would require a doctor on board) and, though less luxurious than dedicated cruise ships, give you a real taste of life at sea. Schedules tend to be flexible and costs vary, but seem to hover around US$100 a day; vehicles can often be included for an additional fee.

DEPARTURE TAX

Some countries charge you a fee for the privilege of leaving from their airports. Some also charge port fees when departing by ship. Such fees are *usually* included in the price of your ticket, but it pays to check this when purchasing it. If not, you'll have to have the fee ready when leaving. Details of departure taxes are given at the end of the Getting There & Away sections of individual country chapters.

Getting Around

Travel within most of the EU, whether by air, rail or car, has been made easier following the Schengen Agreement, which abolished border controls between signed-up states. Britain and Ireland are the only EU countries currently outside the agreement.

AIR

Air travel is best viewed as a means to get you to the starting point of your itinerary rather than as your main means of travel, since it lacks the flexibility of ground transport. Using air travel for short hops can be extremely expensive, though for longer trips the air option might be cheaper than going by bus or train.

Since 1997 air travel within the EU has been deregulated. This 'open skies' policy allows greater flexibility in routing, wider competition and lower prices. Air travel is still dominated by the large state-run and private carriers, but these have been joined by several no-frills small airlines which sell budget tickets directly to the customer. They operate routes from the UK to most countries in Western Europe, though note they sometimes use smaller, less convenient airports.

Refer to the Air Travel Glossary in the previous Getting There & Away chapter for information on types of air tickets. London is a good centre for picking up cheap, restricted-validity tickets through bucket shops. Some airlines, such as the UK-based easyJet (Web site: www.easyjet.com), give discounts for tickets purchased via the Internet; its one-way fares from the UK to Barcelona, Madrid or Nice start at UK£50.

Amsterdam and Athens are other good places for bucket-shop tickets in Europe. From Athens, you can get good deals to elsewhere in Mediterranean Europe; typical one-way fares are UK£81 to Rome, UK£92 to Milan and UK£140 to Madrid. Depending on the season, there are cheap charter flights from London, Paris and Madrid to Morocco and Tunisia. For more information, see the individual country chapters.

So-called open-jaw returns, by which you can travel into one city and exit from another,

are worth considering, though they sometimes work out more expensive than simple returns. In the UK, Trailfinders (☎ 020-7937 5400) and STA Travel (☎ 020-7361 6161) can give you tailor-made versions of these tickets. Your chosen cities don't necessarily have to be in the same country. STA sells Young Europe Special (YES) flights, which allow travel around Europe using Lufthansa Airlines at UK£39, UK£59 or UK£79 per flight (minimum four flights, maximum 10). Britain is the starting point, and the offer is open to students under 31 years of age and anybody under 26.

If you are travelling alone, courier flights are a possibility. You get cheap passage in return for accompanying a package or documents through customs and delivering it to a representative at the destination airport. EU integration and electronic communications mean there's increasingly less call for couriers, but you might find something.

Getting between airports and city centres is no problem in Europe thanks to good public-transport networks.

BUS
International Buses

International bus travel tends to take second place to train travel. The bus has the edge in terms of cost, sometimes quite substantially, but is generally slower and less comfortable. Europe's biggest network of international buses is provided by a group of companies operating under the name Eurolines. Web site: www.eurolines.com.

Eurolines representatives include:

Eurolines France (☎ 08-36 69 52 52), Gare Routière Internationale, 28 Ave du Général de Gaulle, 75020 Paris
Eurolines Italy (☎ Florence: 055-35 71 10), Ciconvallazione Nonentana 574, Lato Stazione Tiburtina, Rome
Eurolines Peninsular (☎ 93-490 4000), Estació d'Autobuses de Sants, Calle Viriato, Barcelona

These companies may also be able to advise you on other bus companies and deals. See the bus section in the Getting There and

Away chapter for Eurolines offices in other European cities.

Eurolines return tickets are valid for six months, and youths under 26 and seniors over 60 pay less. Paris-Barcelona return costs 1000FF (adults) or 900FF (youths/seniors); Paris-Rome costs 860FF or 780FF. The service running between Paris and Tangier (1350FF return – no youth/senior discount) takes at least 9½ hours, including the ferry crossing. It doesn't run in winter.

Eurolines also offer passes, which are cheaper but not as extensive or as flexible as rail passes. They cover 48 European cities as far afield as Dublin, Glasgow, Stockholm, Tallinn, Bucharest, Rome and Madrid. All trips must be international (ie, you can't get on at Paris and get off at Lyon, even though both cities are included in the pass). The cost is UK£245 for 30 days (UK£195 for youths/senior citizens) or UK£283 for 60 days (UK£227). The passes are cheaper off-season.

Busabout (☎ 020-7950 1661), 258 Vauxhall Bridge Rd, Victoria, London SW1, England, operates buses that complete set circuits round Europe, stopping at major cities. You get unlimited travel per sector, and can 'hop-on, hop-off' at any scheduled stop, then resume with a later bus. Buses are often oversubscribed, so prebook each sector to avoid being stranded. Departures are every two days from April to October, or May to September for Spain and Portugal. The circuits cover all countries in continental Western Europe, and you can pay to 'add-on' Greece, Scandinavia or a London-Paris link. See the Web site (www.busabout.com) for further information.

Busabout's Consecutive Pass allows unlimited travel within the given time period. For 15/21 days the cost is UK£155/219 for adults or UK£139/199 for students and those under 26. Passes are also available for one, two or three months, or for the whole season (UK£659 for adults, UK£589 for students/youths). The Flexipass allows you to select travel days within the given time period. Ten or 15 days in two months costs UK£235 or UK£335; 21 days in three months costs UK£445 and 30 days in four months is UK£609. Student/youth prices are about 10% lower than these adult prices.

In conjunction with Eurolines, the Moroccan national bus line, CTM (Compagnie des Transports Marocains), operates buses from Spain, France, Belgium, Germany, Britain and northern Italy to most of the large Moroccan towns.

See the individual country chapters for more information about long-distance buses.

National Buses

Domestic buses provide a viable alternative to the rail network in most countries. Compared to trains they are slightly cheaper and, with the exception of Spain, Portugal and Greece, somewhat slower. Buses tend to be best for shorter hops such as getting around cities and reaching remote villages. They are often the only option in mountainous regions where railway tracks don't exist. Advance reservations are rarely necessary. On many city buses you usually buy your ticket in advance from a kiosk or machine and validate it on boarding.

See the individual country chapters and city sections for more details on local buses.

TRAIN

Trains are a popular way of getting around: they are comfortable, frequent and generally on time. The Channel Tunnel makes it possible to get from Britain to continental Europe using the Eurostar service (see the France Getting There & Away section). In some countries, such as Spain, Portugal and (to some extent) Italy, fares are reasonably low; in others, European rail passes make travel more affordable. Supplements and reservation costs are not covered by passes, and pass-holders must always carry their passport for identification purposes.

If you plan to travel extensively by train, it might be worth getting hold of the *Thomas Cook European Timetable*, which gives a complete listing of train schedules and indicates where supplements apply or where reservations are necessary. It is updated monthly and is available from Thomas Cook outlets in the UK, and in the USA from Forsyth Travel Library (☎ 800-367 7984). Check the Web sites: www.thomascook.com and www.forsyth.com. In Australia, contact Mercury Travel Books (☎ 02-9344 8877).

If you are planning to do a lot of train travel in one or a handful of countries – Spain and

Portugal, say – it might be worthwhile getting hold of the national timetables published by the state railways. The *European Planning & Rail Guide* is an informative annual magazine, primarily geared towards North American travellers. To get a copy, call the toll-free USA number ☎ 877-441 2387, or visit the Web site (www.budgeteuropetravel.com). It's free within the USA; send US$3 if you want it posted anywhere else.

Paris and Milan are important hubs for international rail connections in Mediterranean Europe; see the relevant city sections for details and budget ticket agents. Some approximate 2nd-class fares are Paris-Milan US$115 (under seven hours) and Rome-Madrid US$190 (31 hours).

Note that European trains sometimes split en route in order to service two destinations, so even if you're on the right train, make sure you're also in the correct carriage.

Express Trains
Fast trains or those that make few stops are identified by the symbols EC (Eurocity) or IC (InterCity). The French TGV and Spanish AVE are even faster. Supplements can apply on fast trains, and it is a good idea (sometimes obligatory) to make seat reservations at peak times and on certain lines.

Overnight Trains
Overnight trains will usually offer a choice of couchette or sleeper if you don't fancy sleeping in your seat with somebody else's elbow in your ear. Again, reservations are advisable as sleeping options are allocated on a first-come, first-served basis.

Couchette bunks are comfortable enough, if lacking a bit in privacy. There are four per compartment in 1st class or six in 2nd class. A bunk costs a fixed price of around US$28 for most international trains, irrespective of the length of the journey.

Sleepers are the most comfortable option, offering beds for one or two passengers in 1st class, and two or three passengers in 2nd class. Charges vary depending upon the journey, but they are significantly more expensive than couchettes. Most long-distance trains have a dining (buffet) car or an attendant who wheels a snack trolley through carriages. Food prices tend to be steep.

Security
Stories occasionally surface about train passengers being gassed or drugged and then robbed, though bag-snatching is more of a worry. Sensible security measures include not letting your bags out of your sight (especially when stopping at stations), chaining them to the luggage rack, and locking compartment doors overnight.

Rail Passes
Shop around, as pass prices can vary between different outlets. Once purchased, take care of your pass, as it cannot be replaced or refunded if lost or stolen. European passes get reductions on Eurostar through the Channel Tunnel and on certain ferries. In the USA, Rail Europe (☎ 800-438 7245) sells all sorts of rail passes. See the Web site (www.raileurope .com) for more information.

Eurail These passes can only be bought by residents of non-European countries, and are supposed to be purchased before arriving in Europe. However, Eurail passes *can* be purchased within Europe, so long as your passport proves you've been there for less than six months, but the outlets where you can do this are limited, and the passes will be more expensive than getting them outside Europe. If you've lived in Europe for more than six months, you are eligible for an Inter-Rail pass, which is a better buy.

Eurail passes are valid for unlimited travel on national railways and some private lines in Austria, Belgium, Denmark, Finland, France (including Monaco), Germany, Greece, Hungary, Ireland, Italy, Luxembourg, the Netherlands, Norway, Portugal, Spain, Sweden and Switzerland (including Liechtenstein), The UK is not covered.

Eurail is also valid on some ferries between Italy and Greece and between Sweden and Finland. Reductions are given on some other ferry routes and on river/lake steamer services in various countries.

Eurail passes offer reasonable value to people aged under 26. A Youthpass gives unlimited 2nd-class travel within a choice of five validity periods: 15/21 days (US$388/ 499) or one/two/three months (US$623/882/ 1089). The Youth Flexipass, also for 2nd class, is valid for freely chosen days within a two-month period: 10 days for US$458 or 15 days for US$599. Overnight journeys commencing after 7 pm count as the following day's travel. The traveller must fill out in ink the relevant box in the calendar before starting a day's travel.

For those aged over 26, the equivalent passes provide 1st-class travel. The standard Eurail pass costs US$554/718 for 15/21 days or US$890/1260/1558 for one/two/three months. The Flexipass costs US$654/862 for 10/15 days within two months. Two people travelling together can get a 'saver' version of either pass, saving about 15%. Eurail passes for children are also available.

Europass Also for non-Europeans, the Europass gives unlimited travel on freely chosen days within a two-month period. Youth (aged under 26) and adult (solo, or two sharing) versions are available, and purchasing requirements and sales outlets are as for Eurail passes. They are cheaper than Eurail passes as they cover only France, Germany, Italy, Spain and Switzerland. The youth/adult price is US$296/348 for a minimum five travel days, or US$620/728 for a maximum 15 days. 'Associate countries' can be added on to the basic pass. The charge to add any one/two countries is US$52/86 for youths or US$60/100 for adults. These associate countries are Austria (including Hungary), Belgium (including Luxembourg and the Netherlands), Greece (including ferries from Italy) and Portugal.

Inter-Rail Inter-Rail passes are available to European residents of at least six months standing (passport identification is required). Terms and conditions vary slightly from country to country, but in the country of origin there is a discount of around 50% on normal fares.

The Inter-Rail pass is split into zones. Zone A is Ireland and Britain (though if you buy your Zone A pass in Britain, you get only 30% off, or no discount at all with the 26+ version); B is Sweden, Norway and Finland; C is Denmark, Germany, Switzerland and Austria; D is the Czech Republic, Slovakia, Poland, Hungary and Croatia; E is France, Belgium, the Netherlands and Luxembourg; F is Spain, Portugal and Morocco; G is Italy, Greece, Turkey, Slovenia and Italy-Greece

ferries; and H is Bulgaria, Romania, Yugoslavia and Macedonia.

The normal Inter-Rail pass is for people under 26, though travellers over 26 can get the Inter-Rail 26+ version. The price for any one zone is UK£129 (UK£179 for 26+) for 22 days. Multizone passes are valid for one month: two zones cost UK£169 (UK£235), three zones UK£195 (UK£269) and the all-zone global pass is UK£219 (UK£309).

Euro Domino There is a Euro Domino pass for each of the countries covered in the Inter-Rail pass, and they're worth considering if you're homing in on a particular region. They're sold in Europe to European residents. Adults (travelling 1st or 2nd class) and youths under 26 can opt for three to eight days valid travel within one month. Examples of adult/youth prices for eight days in 2nd class are UK£108/48 for Greece and UK£196/122 for Spain.

National Rail Passes If you intend to travel extensively within one country, check which national rail passes are available. These can sometimes save you a lot of money; details can be found in the Getting Around sections in the individual country chapters. You need to plan ahead if you intend to take this option, as some passes can only be purchased prior to arrival in the country concerned. Some national flexi passes, near-equivalents to the Domino passes mentioned above, are only available to non-Europeans.

Cheap Tickets

European rail passes are only worth buying if you plan to do a reasonable amount of inter-country travelling within a short space of time. Some people tend to overdo it and spend every night they can on the train, ending up too tired to enjoy sightseeing the next day.

When weighing up options, consider the cost of other cheap ticket deals, including advance purchase reductions, one-off promotions or special circular-route tickets. Normal international tickets are valid for two months, and you can make as many stops as you like en route; make your intentions known when purchasing, and inform the train conductor how far you're going before they punch your ticket.

Travellers aged under 26 can pick up BIJ (Billet International de Jeunesse) tickets which can cut fares by up to about 30%. The BIJ Paris to Madrid return for UK£142 saves UK£36 on the normal fare, though on some other routes the reduction may be much less. Various agents issue BIJ tickets in Europe, eg, Voyages Wasteels (☎ 01 43 43 46 10), 2 Rue Michel Chasles, Paris. There are over 60 branches of Wasteels across France; visit its Web site at www.voyages-wasteels.fr. Rail Europe (☎ 08705-848 848), 179 Piccadilly, London, sells BIJ tickets, Eurail and Inter-Rail. Web site: www.raileurope.co.uk.

For a small fee, European residents aged 60 and over can get a Railplus (formerly Rail Europe Senior) Card as an add-on to their national rail senior pass. It entitles the holder to reduced European fares. The percentage saving varies according to the route – it's usually similar to the BIJ reduction.

CAR & MOTORCYCLE

Travelling with your own vehicle is the best way to get to remote places and it gives you the most flexibility. Unfortunately, the independence you enjoy does tend to isolate you from the local people. Also, cars are usually inconvenient in city centres, where it is generally worth ditching your vehicle and relying on public transport. Various car-carrying trains (motorail) can help you avoid long, tiring drives.

Paperwork & Preparations

Proof of ownership of a private vehicle should always be carried (Vehicle Registration Document for British-registered cars) when touring Europe. An EU driving licence is acceptable for driving throughout Europe. However, old-style green UK licences are no good for Spain or Italy. If you have any other type of licence it is advisable or necessary to obtain an International Driving Permit (IDP) from your motoring organisation (see Visas & Documents in the earlier Facts for the Visitor chapter). An IDP is recommended for Turkey even if you have a European licence.

Third party motor insurance is a minimum requirement in Europe. Most UK motor insurance policies automatically provide this for EU countries. Get your insurer to issue a Green Card (which may cost extra), an internationally

recognised proof of insurance, and check that it lists all the countries you intend to visit. You'll need this in the event of an accident outside the country where the vehicle is insured. Also ask your insurer for a European Accident Statement form, which can simplify things if the worst happens. Never sign statements you can't read or understand – insist on a translation and sign that only if it's acceptable.

If you want to insure a vehicle you've just purchased (see the following Purchase section) and have a good insurance record, you might be eligible for considerable discounts if you can show a letter to this effect from your insurance company back home.

Taking out a European motoring assistance policy is a good investment, such as the AA Five Star Service or the RAC European Motoring Assistance. Expect to pay about UK£54 for 14 days cover with a small discount for association members. Non-Europeans might find it cheaper to arrange international coverage with their national motoring organisation before leaving home. Ask your motoring organisation for details about free services offered by affiliated organisations around Europe (see Documents in the earlier Facts for the Visitor chapter).

Every vehicle travelling across an international border should display a sticker showing its country of registration (see the International Country Abbreviations appendix). A warning triangle, to be used in the event of breakdown, is compulsory almost everywhere. Recommended accessories are a first-aid kit (compulsory in Greece and several Central European countries), a spare bulb kit (compulsory in Croatia and Spain) and a fire extinguisher (compulsory in Greece and Turkey). Bail bonds are no longer required for Spain. In the UK, contact the RAC (☎ 0800-550055) or the AA (☎ 08705-500600) for more information.

Road Rules

Motoring organisations can supply members with country-by-country information on motoring regulations, or they may produce motoring guidebooks for general sale. Find useful motoring information on the RAC Web site at www.rac.co.uk.

With the exception of Malta and Cyprus, driving in Mediterranean Europe is on the right-hand side. Vehicles brought over from the UK or Ireland, where driving is on the left, should have their headlights adjusted to avoid blinding oncoming traffic at night (a simple solution on older headlight lenses is to cover up a triangular section of the lens with tape). Priority is usually given to traffic approaching from the right in countries that drive on the right-hand side.

Take care with speed limits, as they vary from country to country. You may be surprised at the apparent disregard for traffic regulations in some places (particularly in Italy and Greece), but as a visitor it is always best to be cautious. Many driving infringements are subject to an on-the-spot fine in most European countries. Always ask for a receipt.

European drink-driving laws are particularly strict. The blood-alcohol concentration (BAC) limit when driving is generally between 0.05% and 0.08%, though it is 0% in Gibraltar. See the introductory Getting Around sections in the country chapters for more details on traffic laws.

Roads

Conditions and types of roads vary across Europe, but it is possible to make some generalisations. The fastest routes are four or six-lane dual carriageways/highways (ie, two or three lanes either side) – called *autoroutes*, *autostrade* etc. These tend to skirt cities and plough through the countryside in straight lines, often avoiding the most scenic bits. Some of these roads incur tolls, which are often quite hefty (eg, in Italy, France and Spain), but there will always be an alternative route you can take. Motorways and other primary routes are generally in good condition.

Road surfaces on minor routes are not so reliable in some countries (eg, Morocco and Greece) although normally they will be more than adequate. These roads are narrower and progress is generally much slower. However, you can expect much better scenery and plenty of interesting villages along the way.

Rental

The big international firms will give you reliable service and a good standard of vehicle. Usually you will have the option of returning the car to a different outlet at the end of the rental period. Prebook for the lowest rates –

if you walk into an office and ask for a car on the spot, you will pay over the odds, even allowing for special weekend deals. Fly-drive combinations and other programs are worth looking into. You should be able to make advance reservations on line. Check the Web sites:

Avis	www.avis.com
Budget	www.budget.com
Europcar	www.europcar.com
Hertz	www.hertz.com

Brokers can cut hire costs. Holiday Autos (UK ☎ 08750-300400) has low rates and offices or representatives in over 20 countries. Its Web site is at www.holidayautos.com. In the USA call Kemwel Holiday Autos (☎ 800-576 1590). In the UK, a competitor with even lower prices is Autos Abroad (☎ 020-7287 6000). Web site: www.autosabroad.co.uk.

If you want to rent a car and haven't prebooked, look for national or local firms, which can often undercut the big companies by up to 40%. Nevertheless, you need to be wary of dodgy deals where they take your money and point you towards some clapped-out wreck, or where the rental agreement is bad news if you have an accident or the car is stolen – a cause for concern if you can't even read what you sign.

No matter where you rent, make sure you understand what is included in the price (unlimited or paid kilometres, tax, injury insurance, collision damage waiver etc) and what your liabilities are. We recommend taking the collision damage waiver, though you can probably skip the injury insurance if you and your passengers have decent travel insurance. Ask in advance if you can drive a rented car across borders from a country where hire prices are low into another where they're high.

The minimum rental age is usually 21 or even 23, and you'll probably need a credit card. Note that prices at airport rental offices are usually higher than at branches in the city centre.

Motorcycle and moped rental is common in some countries, such as Italy, Spain, Greece and the south of France. Sadly, it's also common to see inexperienced riders leap on rented bikes and very quickly fall off them again, leaving a layer or two of skin on the road in the process.

Purchase

The purchase of vehicles in some European countries is illegal for non-nationals or non-EU residents. Britain is probably the best place to buy: second-hand prices are good and, whether buying privately or from a dealer, the absence of language difficulties will help you establish exactly what you are getting and what guarantees you can expect in the event of a breakdown. Bear in mind that you will be getting a car with the steering wheel on the right in Britain. If you want left-hand drive and can afford to buy new, prices are usually reasonable in Greece, France, Germany, Belgium, Luxembourg and the Netherlands. Paperwork can be tricky wherever you buy, and many countries have compulsory roadworthiness checks on older vehicles.

Leasing

Leasing a vehicle has none of the hassles of purchasing and can work out considerably cheaper than hiring over longer periods. The Renault Eurodrive scheme provides new cars for non-EU residents for a period of between 17 and 170 days. Under this arrangement, a Renault Clio 1.2 for 30 days, for example, would cost 4710FF (if picked up/dropped off in France), including insurance and roadside assistance. Other companies with comparable leasing programs include Peugeot and Citroen. Check out the options before leaving home. In the USA, Kemwel Holiday Autos (see under Rental earlier) arranges European leasing deals.

Camper Van

A popular way to tour Europe is for three or four people to band together to buy or rent a camper van. London is the usual embarkation point. Look at the advertisements in London's free *TNT* magazine if you wish to form or join a group. *TNT* is also a good source for purchasing a van, as is the *Loot* newspaper and the Van Market in Market Rd, London N7 (near the Caledonian Rd tube station), where private vendors congregate on a daily basis. Some second-hand dealers offer a 'buy-back' scheme for when you return from the Continent, but we've received warnings that some dealers don't fully honour their refund commitments. Buying and re-selling privately should be more advantageous if you

have the time. A reader recommended Down Under Insurance (☎ 020-7402 9211) for European cover. Web site: www.downunderinsurance.co.uk.

Camper vans usually feature a fixed high-top or elevating roof and two to five bunk beds. Apart from the essential camping gas cooker, professional conversions may include a sink, fridge and built-in cupboards. You will need to spend at least UK£2000 (US$3000) for something reliable enough to get you around Europe for any length of time. Getting a mechanical check (from UK£30) is a good idea before you buy. Once on the road you should be able to keep budgets lower than backpackers using trains, but don't forget to set some money aside for emergency repairs.

The main advantage of going by camper van is flexibility: with transport, eating and sleeping requirements all taken care of in one unit, you are tied to nobody's timetable but your own. It's also easier to set up at night than if you rely on a car and tent.

A disadvantage of camper vans is that you are in a confined space for much of the time. Four adults in a small van can soon get on each other's nerves, particularly if the group has been formed at short notice. You might also become too self-contained, and miss out on experiences in the world outside your van.

Other negatives are that vans are not very manoeuvrable around town, and you'll often have to leave your gear unattended inside (many people bolt extra locks onto the van). They're also expensive to buy in spring and hard to sell in autumn.

Motorcycle Touring

Mediterranean Europe is made for motorcycle touring, with good-quality winding roads, stunning scenery and an active motorcycling scene.

The wearing of helmets for both rider and passenger is compulsory everywhere in Europe. Croatia, Portugal, Slovenia, Spain and Yugoslavia (plus Austria, Belgium, France, Germany, Luxembourg and some eastern nations) also require that motorcyclists use headlights during the day.

On ferries, motorcyclists rarely have to book ahead as they can generally be squeezed in. Take note of local custom about parking motorcycles on pavements (sidewalks).

Though this is illegal in some countries, the police usually turn a blind eye so long as the vehicle doesn't obstruct pedestrians.

Fuel

Fuel prices can vary enormously from one country to the next, and may bear little relation to the general cost of living. You can make significant savings by filling up in the cheapest country – prices are 80% higher in France than in Andorra. In between, in ascending price order, come Spain, Greece, Turkey, Portugal and Italy. Motoring organisations such as the RAC can supply more details.

Unleaded petrol is now widely available throughout Europe (except in Morocco) and is usually slightly cheaper than super (premium grade, the only 'leaded' choice in some countries). Diesel is usually significantly cheaper.

TAXI

Taxis in Europe are metered and rates are usually high. There might also be supplements (depending on the country) for things like luggage, the time of day, the location from which you boarded and for extra passengers. Good bus, rail and underground (subway/metro) railway networks make the taking of taxis all but unnecessary, but if you need one in a hurry they can usually be found idling near train stations or outside big hotels. Lower fares make taxis more viable in some countries, such as Spain, Greece and Portugal.

BICYCLE

A tour of Europe by bike may seem a daunting prospect, but one organisation that can help in the UK is the Cyclists' Touring Club (CTC; ☎ 01483-417 217, ✉ cycling@ctc.org.uk), Cotterell House, 69 Meadrow, Godalming, Surrey GU7 3HS. It can supply information to members on cycling conditions in Europe as well as detailed routes, itineraries and maps. Membership includes specialised insurance and costs UK£25 per annum, or UK£12.50 for people aged under 27 or over 65. Web site: www.ctc.org.uk.

A primary consideration on a cycling tour is to travel light, but you should take a few tools and spare parts, including a puncture repair kit and an extra inner tube. Panniers are essential to balance your possessions on either side of

the bike frame. A bike helmet is also a very good idea. Take a good lock and always use it when you leave your bike unattended.

Michelin maps indicate scenic routes, which can help you construct good cycling itineraries. Seasoned cyclists can average 80km a day, but there's no point in overdoing it. The slower you travel, the more local people you are likely to meet. If you get tired of pedalling or simply want to skip a boring transport section, you can put your feet up on the train. See the following Transporting a Bicycle section.

For more information about cycling, see Activities in the Facts for the Visitor chapter and in the individual country chapters.

Rental

It is not as easy to hire bikes in some parts of Mediterranean Europe as it is elsewhere on the Continent, but where available they are hired out on an hourly, half-day, daily or weekly basis. It is sometimes possible to return the bike to a different outlet so you don't have to retrace your route. Many train stations have bike-rental counters. See the country chapters for more details.

Purchase

For major cycling tours, it's best to have a bike you're familiar with, so consider bringing your own (see the following section) rather than buying on arrival. There are plenty of places to buy in Europe (shops sell new and second-hand bicycles or you can check local papers for private vendors), but you'll need a specialist bicycle shop for a machine capable of withstanding European touring. CTC can provide members with a leaflet on purchasing. European prices are quite high (certainly higher than in North America), but non-Europeans should be able to claim VAT on the purchase.

Transporting a Bicycle

If you want to bring your own bicycle to Europe, you should be able to take it along with you on the plane relatively easily. You can either take it apart and pack everything in a bike bag or box, or simply wheel it to the check-in desk, where it should be treated as a piece of luggage. You may have to remove the pedals and turn the handlebars sideways so that it takes up less space in the aircraft's hold; check all this with the airline well in advance, preferably before you pay for your ticket. If your bicycle and other luggage exceed your weight allowance, ask about alternatives or you may suddenly find yourself being charged a fortune for excess baggage.

Within Europe, bikes can usually be transported as luggage on slower trains, subject to a small supplementary fee. Fast trains can rarely accommodate bikes: they might need to be sent as registered luggage and may end up on a different train from the one you take. This is often the case in France and Spain. Eurostar (the train service through the Channel Tunnel) charges UK£20 to send a bike as registered luggage on its routes. You can also transport your bicycle with you on Eurotunnel through the Channel Tunnel. With a bit of tinkering and dismantling (eg, removing wheels), you might be able to get your bike into a bag or sack and take it on a train as hand luggage.

The European Bike Express is a coach service where cyclists can travel with their bicycles. It runs in the summer from north-east England to France, Italy and Spain, with pick-up/drop-off points en route. The maximum return fare is UK£169 (£10 off for CTC members); phone ☎ 01642-251 440 in the UK for details or visit its Web site at www.bike-express.co.uk.

HITCHING

Hitching is never entirely safe in any country in the world, and we don't recommend it. Travellers who decide to hitch should understand that they are taking a small but potentially serious risk. People who do choose to hitch will be safer if they travel in pairs and let someone know where they plan to go.

Hitching can be the most rewarding and frustrating way of getting around. Rewarding, because you get to meet and interact with local people and are forced into unplanned detours that may yield unexpected highlights off the beaten track. Frustrating, because you may get stuck on the side of the road to nowhere with nowhere (or nowhere cheap) to stay. Then it begins to rain...

That said, hitchers can end up making good time, but obviously your plans need to be flexible in case a trick of the light makes

you appear invisible to passing motorists. A man and woman travelling together is probably the best combination. Two or more men must expect some delays; two women together will make good time and should be relatively safe. A woman hitching on her own is taking a big risk, particularly in parts of southern Europe, Turkey and North Africa.

Don't try to hitch from city centres: take public transport to suburban exit routes. Hitching is usually illegal on motorways (freeways) – stand on the slip roads, or approach drivers at petrol stations and truck stops. Look presentable and cheerful and make a cardboard sign indicating your intended destination in the local language. Never hitch where drivers can't stop in good time or without causing an obstruction. At dusk, give up and think about finding somewhere to stay. If your itinerary includes a ferry crossing (from mainland France to Corsica, for instance), it's worth trying to score a ride before the ferry rather than after, since vehicle tickets sometimes include all passengers free of charge. This also applies to Eurotunnel, the vehicle-carrying train through the Channel Tunnel.

It is sometimes possible to arrange a lift in advance: scan student notice boards in colleges, or contact car-sharing agencies. Such agencies are particularly popular in France (eg, Allostop Provoya, Auto-Partage).

BOAT
Mediterranean Ferries

There are many ferries across the Mediterranean between southern Europe and North Africa, including: Spain to Morocco; Italy to Tunisia; and France to Algeria, Morocco and Tunisia. There are also ferries between Italy and Greece (eg, Brindisi or Bari to Corfu, Igoumenitsa or Patras), and between Greece and Israel. Ferries are often filled to capacity in summer, especially to/from Tunisia, so book well in advance if you're taking a vehicle across.

The Greek islands are connected to the mainland and each other by a spider's web of routings; Lonely Planet's *Greek Islands* gives details. Ferries also link other islands in the Mediterranean with mainland ports: Corsica with Nice, Marseille and Toulon in France and with Genoa, La Spezia, Piombino and

Livorno in Italy; Sicily and Sardinia with Genoa and Naples (among other Italian ports) and with Tunis; and Malta with Sicily and Naples. See the relevant country chapters in this book for more details.

ORGANISED TOURS

Tailor-made tours abound; see your travel agent or look in the small ads in newspaper travel pages. Specialists include Ramblers Holidays (☎ 01707-331 133) in Britain for hiking trips and CBT Tours (☎ 800-736-2453) in the USA for bicycle trips. Web sites are: www.ramblersholidays.co.uk and www.cbttours.com.

Young revellers can party on Europewide bus tours. Contiki and Top Deck offer camping or hotel-based bus tours for the 18 to 35 age group. The duration of Contiki's tours is 10 to 46 days, and prices start at around UK£25 per day including 'food fund'. Contiki (☎ 020-7290 6422) and Top Deck

(☎ 020-7370 4555) have London offices, as well as offices or representatives in Europe, North America, Australasia and South Africa. Check the Web sites: www.contiki.com and www.topdecktravel.co.uk.

For people aged over 50, Saga Holidays (☎ 0800-300 500), Saga Building, Middelburg Square, Folkestone, Kent CT20 1AZ, England, offers holidays ranging from cheap coach tours to luxury cruises (and has cheap travel insurance). In the USA, Saga Holidays (☎ 800-343 0273) is at 222 Berkeley St, Boston, MA 02116.

National tourist offices in most countries offer organised trips to points of interest. These may range from one-hour city tours to several-day circular excursions. They often work out more expensive than going it alone, but are sometimes worth it if you are pressed for time. A short city tour will give you a quick overview of the place and can be a good way to begin your visit.

Albania

Until 1990 a closed communist country, Albania caught world attention in November of that year as the last domino to tumble in Eastern Europe's sudden series of democratic revolutions. Long considered fair prey by every imperialist power, Albania chose a curious form of isolation, with everything centred on Josef Stalin. The Stalinist rule of Enver Hoxha, Albania's iron-fisted dictator from 1944 to his death in 1985, did save Albania from annexation by Yugoslavia after WWII, but few Albanians have positive feelings about him.

Albanians call their country the Republika e Shqipërisë, or 'Land of the Eagle'. Albania is Europe's last unknown, with enchanting classical ruins at Apollonia, Butrint and Durrës, the charming 'museum towns' of Gjirokastra and Berat, vibrant cities like Tirana, Shkodra, Korça and Durrës, colourful folklore and majestic landscapes of mountains, forests, lakes and sea.

Albania's first years of attempted democracy have been troubled. The country spiralled into violence and anarchy following the collapse of fraudulent pyramid schemes in late 1996, and while things have since improved, problems remain. Travellers to Albania should mingle curiosity with a healthy caution, but visiting this country, as it slowly opens up to the world, is a rare experience.

AT A GLANCE

Capital	Tirana
Population	3.2 million
Official Language	Albanian (Tosk)
Currency	1 lekë (L) = 100 qintars
Time	GMT/UTC+0100
Country Phone Code ☎	355

YUGOSLAVIA   YUGOSLAVIA

MACEDONIA

Durrës p87 ●   ✪ Tirana p82

GREECE

Facts about Albania

HISTORY

In the 2nd millennium BC, the Illyrians, ancestors of today's Albanians, occupied the western Balkans. The Greeks arrived in the 7th century BC to establish self-governing colonies at Epidamnos (now Durrës), Apollonia and Butrint. They traded peacefully with the Illyrians, who formed tribal states in the 4th century BC. The south became part of Greek Epirus.

In the second half of the 3rd century BC, an expanding Illyrian kingdom based at Shkodra came into conflict with Rome, which sent a fleet of 200 vessels against Queen Teuta (who ruled over the Illyrian Ardian kingdom) in 228 BC. A long war resulted in the extension of Roman control over the entire Balkans by 167 BC.

Like the Greeks, the Illyrians preserved their own language and traditions despite centuries of Roman rule. Under the Romans, Illyria enjoyed peace and prosperity, though the large agricultural estates were worked by slave labour. The main trade route between Rome and Constantinople, the Via Egnatia, ran from Durrës to Thessaloniki.

When the Roman Empire was divided in AD 395, Illyria fell within the Eastern Roman Empire, later known as Byzantium. Invasions by migrating peoples – Visigoths, Huns, Ostrogoths and Slavs – continued through the

WARNING

! For this edition of *Mediterranean Europe*, the Lonely Planet author decided for security reasons to visit only Tirana and Durrës. Other places described in this chapter have been given brief general descriptions, and any traveller wanting more travel information should make inquiries around Tirana.

However, it is essential that travellers check the current situation in Albania before they make their decision to go, as criminal activity remains prevalent throughout the country, and travel outside the major cities was not recommended at the time of writing. Travellers should check with their foreign office or their embassy in Tirana to monitor the current situation, as the political climate in Albania can change at flash-flood speed. In mid-2000, the US Department of State still warned against all travel to Albania, considering the overall security situation unstable.

Once in Albania, general caution can be observed by never travelling at night and avoiding the northern part of the country, where banditry is particularly widespread (see the Dangers & Annoyances section of this chapter). It is also wise to have someone, preferably Albanian, to accompany you – or, at least, to meet you at your first port of entry.

5th and 6th centuries and only in the south did the ethnic Illyrians survive.

In 1344 Albania was annexed by Serbia, but after the defeat of Serbia by the Turks in 1389 the whole region was open to Ottoman attack. The Venetians occupied some coastal towns, and from 1443 to 1468 the national hero Skënderbeg (George Kastrioti) led Albanian resistance to the Turks from his castle at Kruja. Skënderbeg won all 25 battles he fought against the Turks, and even Sultan Mehmet-Fatih, conqueror of Constantinople, could not take Kruja.

From 1479 to 1912 Albania, the most backward corner of Europe, was under Ottoman rule. In the 15th and 16th centuries thousands of Albanians fled to southern Italy to escape Turkish rule and over half of those who remained converted to Islam.

In 1878 the Albanian League at Prizren (in present-day Kosova) began a struggle for autonomy that was put down by the Turkish army in 1881. Uprisings between 1910 and 1912 culminated in a proclamation of independence and the formation of a provisional government led by Ismail Qemali at Vlora in 1912. These achievements were severely compromised when Kosova, nearly half of Albania, was given to Serbia in 1913. With the outbreak of WWI, Albania was occupied by the armies of Greece, Serbia, France, Italy and Austria-Hungary in succession.

In 1920 the capital was moved from Durrës to less vulnerable Tirana. Thousands of Albanian volunteers converged on Vlora and forced the occupying Italians to withdraw. Ahmet Zogu became the ruler of Albania and declared himself King Zog I in 1928, but his close collaboration with Italy backfired in April 1939 when Mussolini ordered an invasion of Albania. Zog fled to Britain and used gold looted from the Albanian treasury to rent a floor at London's Ritz Hotel.

On 8 November 1941 the Albanian Communist Party was founded with Enver Hoxha (pronounced Hodja) as first secretary, a position he held until his death in April 1985. The communists led the resistance against the Italians and, after 1943, against the Germans, ultimately tying down some 15 combined German-Italian divisions.

The Rise of Communism

After the fighting died down, the communists consolidated power. In January 1946 the People's Republic of Albania was proclaimed, with Enver Hoxha as president.

In September 1948, Albania broke off relations with Yugoslavia, which had hoped to incorporate the country into the Yugoslav Federation. Instead, Albania allied itself with Stalin's USSR and put into effect a series of Soviet-style economic plans.

Albania collaborated closely with the USSR until 1960, when a heavy-handed Khrushchev demanded a submarine base at Vlora. Albania broke off diplomatic relations with the USSR in 1961 and reoriented itself towards the People's Republic of China.

From 1966 to 1967 Albania experienced a Chinese-style cultural revolution. Administrative workers were suddenly transferred to

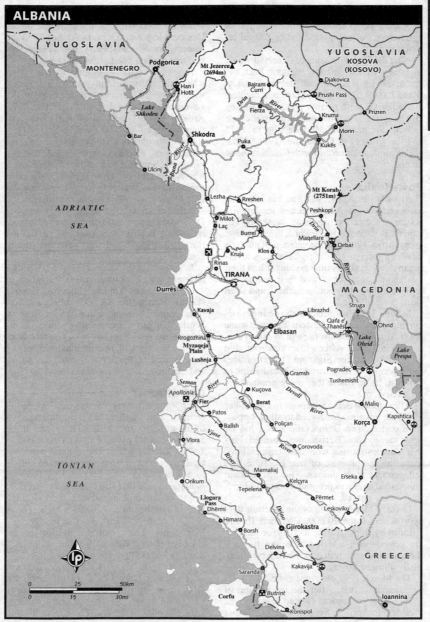

ALBANIA

YUGOSLAVIA

MONTENEGRO

Podgorica

Mt Jezerce
(2694m)

Bajram
Curri

YUGOSLAVIA
KOSOVA
(KOSOVO)

Djakovica

Han i
Hotit

Prushi Pass

Lake
Shkodra

Drin River

Fierza

Kruma

Prizren

Shkodra

Puka

Morin

Bar

Kukës

Ulcinj

Lezha

Reshen

Mt Korab
(2751m)

ADRIATIC

SEA

Milot

Laç

Burrel

Peshkopi

Drin

Maqellare

Debar

Kruja

Klos

Rinas

Burrel

TIRANA

Durrës

MACEDONIA

Kavaja

Librazhd

Struga

Qafa e'
Thanës

Ohrid

Rrogozhina

Elbasan

Lake
Ohrid

Myzaqeja
Plain

Lushnja

Lake
Prespa

Seman River

Apollonia

Gramsh

Pogradec

Fier

Kuçova

Devoll

Tushemisht

Patos

Berat

Osum

Maliq

Ballsh

Poliçan

River

Korça

Kapshtica

Vlora

Vjose

Çorovoda

IONIAN

SEA

Memaliaj

River

Erseka

Orikum

Kelçyra

Tepelena

Përmet

Leskoviku

Llogara
Pass

Dhërmi

Drino River

Himara

Gjirokastra

Borsh

Delvina

GREECE

Kakavija

Saranda

Corfu

Butrint

Ioannina

Konispol

0   25   50km
0   15   30mi

LP

remote areas and younger cadres were placed in leading positions. The collectivisation of agriculture was completed and organised religion banned.

After the Soviet invasion of Czechoslovakia in 1968, Albania left the Warsaw Pact and embarked on a self-reliant defence policy. Some 750,000 igloo-shaped concrete bunkers and pillboxes with narrow gun slits, built by Hoxha, serve as a reminder of this policy.

With the death of Mao Zedong in 1976 and the changes in China after 1978, Albania's unique relationship with China came to an end.

Post-Hoxha

Hoxha died in April 1985 and his longtime associate Ramiz Alia assumed leadership. Aware of the economic decay caused by Albania's isolation, Alia began a liberalisation program in 1986 and broadened Albania's ties with foreign countries. Travellers arriving in Albania at this time no longer had their guidebooks confiscated and their beards and long hair clipped by border barbers, and short skirts were allowed.

In June 1990, inspired by the changes occurring elsewhere in Eastern Europe, some 4500 Albanians took refuge in Western embassies in Tirana. After a brief confrontation with police and the Sigurimi (secret police) these people were allowed to board ships to Brindisi, Italy, where they were granted political asylum.

After student demonstrations in December 1990, the government agreed to allow opposition parties. The Democratic Party, led by heart surgeon Sali Berisha, was formed. Further demonstrations won new concessions, including the promise of free elections and independent trade unions. The government announced a reform program and party hardliners were purged.

In early March 1991, as the election date approached, some 20,000 Albanians fled to Brindisi by ship, creating a crisis for the Italian government, which had begun to view them as economic refugees. Most were eventually allowed to stay.

The March 1992 elections ended 47 years of communist rule. After the resignation of Ramiz Alia, parliament elected Sali Berisha president in April. In September 1992 former president Ramiz Alia was placed under house arrest after he wrote articles critical of the Democratic government. In August 1993 the leader of the Socialist Party, Fatos Nano, was also arrested on corruption charges.

A severe crisis developed in late 1996, when private pyramid investment schemes – widely thought to have been supported by the government – collapsed spectacularly. Around seventy percent of Albanians lost their savings – in total over US$1 billion – and nationwide disturbances and violence resulted. New elections were called, and the victorious Socialist Party under Fatos Nano – who had been freed from prison by the rampaging mob – was able to restore some degree of security and investor confidence.

Albania shuddered again in November 1998 when Azem Hajdan, a popular Democratic Party deputy, was assassinated, but the riots following his death were eventually contained.

In spring 1999, Albania faced a crisis of a different sort. This time, it was the influx of 450,000 refugees from neighbouring Kosova (Kosovo) during the NATO bombing and Serbian ethnic cleansing campaign in Kosova. While this put a tremendous strain on resources, the net effect has been positive. Substantial amounts of international aid money have poured in, the service sector has grown and inflation has decreased to almost nothing.

GEOGRAPHY

Over three-quarters of this 28,750-sq-km country (a bit smaller than Belgium) consists of mountains and hills. There are three zones: a coastal plain, a mountainous region and an interior plain. The coastal plain extends over 200km from north to south and up to 50km inland. The 2000m-high forested mountain spine that stretches along the entire length of Albania culminates at Mt Jezerce (2694m) in the north. Albania's highest peak is Mt Korab (2751m), on the border with Macedonia. The country is subject to destructive earthquakes, such as the one in 1979 that left 100,000 people homeless.

The longest river is the Drin (285km), which drains Lake Ohrid. In the north the Drin flows into the Buna, Albania's only navigable river, which connects shallow Lake Shkodra to the sea. The Ionian littoral, especially the 'Riviera of Flowers' from Vlora to Saranda, offers magnificent scenery. Forests cover 40% of the land, and the many olive trees, citrus plantations and vineyards give Albania a true Mediterranean air.

CLIMATE

Albania has a warm Mediterranean climate. The summers are hot, clear and dry, and the winters, when 40% of the rain falls, are cool, cloudy and moist. In winter the high interior plateau can be very cold as continental air masses move in. Along the coast the climate is moderated by sea winds. Gjirokastra and Shkodra receive twice as much rain as Korça, with November, December and April being the wettest months. The sun shines longest from May to September and July is the warmest month, but even April and October are quite pleasant.

ECOLOGY & ENVIRONMENT

Large parts of the country were subjected to ecological vandalism during the communist years, particularly near the Fier oil fields in central Albania. Albanians are turning their attention to cleaning up their act, but issues such as improving roads still take precedence.

GOVERNMENT & POLITICS

Albania has a parliamentary democracy with a president (currently Rexhep Meidani) and prime minister, Ilir Meta of the Socialist Party. The main opposition, the Democratic Party, is chaired by Sali Berisha, the former president and rival to Socialist Party leader (and former prime minister) Fatos Nano. Elections were due to be held late in 2000.

ECONOMY

Albania is rich in natural resources such as crude oil, natural gas, coal, copper, iron, nickel and timber and is the world's third-largest producer of chrome, accounting for about 10% of the world's supply. The Central Mountains yield minerals such as copper (in the north-east around Kukës), chromium (farther south near the Drin River), and iron nickel (closer to Lake Ohrid). The government is now preparing Albania's mining industry to be privatised through sales to foreigners.

There are textiles industries at Berat, Korça and Tirana. Oil was discovered in Albania in 1917 and the country at one point supplied all its own petroleum requirements. Oil and gas from Fier also enabled the production of chemical fertilisers.

There are several huge hydroelectric dams on the Drin River in the north. Albania obtains 80% of its electricity from such dams and by 1970 electricity had reached every village in the country.

After a period of neglect in the agricultural sector, farmers have begun the long task of rebuilding the rural infrastructure, and agriculture currently accounts for 52% of Albania's GDP, which was projected in 1999 at US$3.3 billion.

Albania remains heavily dependent on remittances coming from Albanian communities abroad, particularly in Greece and Italy. Albania is also angling for more international aid money, particularly in light of its generous intake of Kosovar Albanian refugees in 1998. Priority projects for aid money involve infrastructure improvement.

Despite many challenges, Albania's economy was projected to grow at 7% to 8% for the third straight year in 2000, making it one of the fastest-growing economies in Europe.

POPULATION & PEOPLE

The Albanians are a hardy Mediterranean people, physically different from the more Nordic Slavs. Although the Slavs and Greeks look down on the Albanians, the Albanians themselves have a sense of racial superiority based on their descent from the ancient Illyrians, who inhabited the region before the Romans. The country's name comes from the Albanoi, an ancient Illyrian tribe.

Approximately 3.2 million Albanians live in Albania. Harsh economic conditions in Albania have unleashed successive waves of emigration: to Serbia in the 15th century, to Greece and Italy in the 16th century, to the USA in the 19th and 20th centuries and to Greece, Italy and Switzerland today. The Arbereshi, longtime Albanian residents of 50 scattered villages in southern Italy, fled west in the 16th century to escape the Turks. As many as two million ethnic Albanians live in Turkey, emigrants from Serb-dominated Yugoslavia between 1912 and 1966. Since 1990 hundreds of thousands of Albanians have migrated to Western Europe (especially

Greece and Italy) to escape the economic hardships at home. Minorities inside Albania include Greeks (3% of the population) and Vlachs, Macedonians and Roma (comprising a further 2% of the population).

The Shkumbin River forms a boundary between the Gheg cultural region of the north and the Tosk region in the south. The people in these regions still vary in dialect, musical culture and traditional dress.

ARTS
Music
Polyphony, the blending of several independent vocal or instrumental parts, is a southern Albanian tradition that dates back to ancient Illyrian times. Peasant choirs perform in a variety of styles, and the songs, usually with epic-lyrical or historical themes, may be dramatic to the point of yodelling or slow and sober, with alternate male or female voices combining in harmonies of unexpected beauty. Instrumental polyphonic *kabas* are played by small Roma ensembles usually led by a clarinet. Improvisation gives way to dancing at colourful village weddings. One well-known group, which often tours outside Albania, is the Lela Family of Përmet.

An outstanding recording of traditional Albanian music is the CD *Albania, Vocal and Instrumental Polyphony* (LDX 274 897) in the series 'Le Chant du Monde' (Musée de l'Homme, Paris).

Literature
Prior to the adoption of a standardised orthography in 1909, very little literature was produced in Albania, though Albanians resident elsewhere in the Ottoman empire and in Italy did write works. Among these was the noted poet Naim Frashëri (1846-1900), who lived in Istanbul and wrote in Greek. Around the time of independence (1912), a group of romantic patriotic writers at Shkodra wrote epics and historical novels.

Perhaps the most interesting writer of the interwar period was Fan Noli (1880-1965). Educated as a priest in the USA, Fan Noli returned there to head the Albanian Orthodox Church in America after the Democratic government of Albania, in which he served as premier, was overthrown in 1924. Although many of his books are based on religious subjects, the introductions he wrote to his own translations of Cervantes, Ibsen, Omar Khay-yám and Shakespeare established him as Albania's foremost literary critic.

The poet Migjeni (1911-38) focused on social issues until his early death from tuberculosis. In his 1936 poem, *Vargjet e lira* (Free Verse), Migjeni seeks to dispel the magic of old myths and awaken the reader to present injustices.

Albania's best-known contemporary writer is Ismail Kadare, born in 1935, whose almost 20 novels have been translated into 20 languages. *Chronicle in Stone* (1971) relates wartime experiences in Kadare's birthplace, Gjirokastra, as seen through the eyes of a boy. *Broken April* (1990) deals with the blood vendettas of the northern highlands before the 1939 Italian invasion. Although Kadare lived in Tirana throughout the Hoxha years and even wrote a book, *The Great Winter* (1972), extolling Hoxha's defiance of Moscow, he sought political asylum in Paris in October 1990. A recent classic is *The Two-Arched Bridge* (1997), an ominous and beautiful 14th-century tale, told by a monk, of the troubled construction of a bridge during turbulent political times.

Cinema
A film worth checking out is *Lamerica*, a brilliant and stark look at Albanian postcommunist culture. Despite its title, it is about Albanians seeking to escape to Bari, Italy, in the immediate post-communist era. The title is a symbol for ordinary Albanians seeking a better and more materially fulfilling life in the West. Woven loosely around a plot concerning a couple of Italian scam artists, the essence of the film is the unquenchable dignity of ordinary Albanians in the face of adversity.

SOCIETY & CONDUCT
Traditional dress is still common in rural areas, especially on Sunday and holidays. Men wear embroidered white shirts and knee trousers, the Ghegs with a white felt skullcap and the Tosks with a flat-topped white fez. Women's clothing is brighter than that of the men. Along with the standard white blouses with wide sleeves, women from Christian areas wear red vests, while Muslim women

wear baggy pants tied at the ankles and coloured headscarves. Older Muslim women wear white scarves around the neck; white scarves may also be a sign of mourning.

The *Kanun* is an ancient social law outlining most aspects of social behaviour including the treatment of guests. This has meant that Albanians can be hospitable in the extreme and will often offer travellers lodging and food free of charge. Travellers must be wary of exploiting this tradition and while payment may well be acceptable in some cases, a small gift of a book or a memento from home will often suffice.

Be respectful when visiting mosques – remove your shoes and avoid visits during prayer times.

RELIGION
From 1967 to 1990 Albania was the only officially atheist state in Europe. Public religious services were banned and many churches were converted into theatres or cinemas. In mid-1990 this situation ended and in December of that year Nobel Prize-winner Mother Teresa of Calcutta, an ethnic Albanian from Macedonia, visited Albania and met President Alia. Traditionally, Albania has been 70% Sunni Muslim, 20% Albanian Orthodox (mostly in the south) and 10% Roman Catholic (mostly in the north). It's the only country in Europe with an Islamic majority.

LANGUAGE
Albanian (Shqipja) is an Indo-European dialect of ancient Illyrian, with many Latin, Slavonic and (modern) Greek words. The two main dialects of Albanian have diverged over the past 1000 years. In 1909 a standardised form of the Gheg dialect of Elbasan was adopted as the official language, but since WWII a modified version of the Tosk dialect of southern Albania has been used.

Outside the country, Albanians resident in former Yugoslavia speak Gheg, those in Greece speak Tosk, whereas in Italy they speak another dialect called Arberesh. With practice you can sometimes differentiate between the dialects by listening for the nasalised vowels of Gheg. In 1972, the Congress of Orthography at Tirana established a unified written language based on the two dialects which is now universally accepted.

You'll find that Italian is the most useful foreign language to know in Albania, and English is a strong second.

Many Albanian place names have two forms because the definite article is a suffix. In this book we use the form most commonly used in English, but Tirana actually means *the* Tiranë. On signs at archaeological sites, *p.e. sonë* means BC, and *e sonë* means AD. Public toilets may be marked *burra* for men and *gra* for women. Albanians, like Bulgarians, shake their heads to say yes and usually nod to say no.

See the Language chapter at the back of the book for pronunciation guidelines and useful words and phrases.

Facts for the Visitor

HIGHLIGHTS
The beauty and mystique of Albania's mountains and coastal region makes the country itself a highlight.

PLANNING
Maps
A topographical/road map of Albania is produced by Cartographia in Budapest and sold for 800 lekë in bookshops in Tirana.

TOURIST OFFICES
There are no tourist information offices in Albania, but hotel receptionists or travel agencies will sometimes give you directions. You can buy city maps of Tirana in bookshops and larger kiosks in the capital, but in most other towns they're unobtainable. In addition, many streets lack signs and the buildings have no numbers marked on them! Some streets don't seem to have any name at all. Most of the towns are small enough for you to get around without such things.

VISAS & DOCUMENTS
No visa is required from citizens of EU countries or from citizens of Australia, New Zealand and the United States. Travellers from other countries should check with an Albanian embassy for visa requirements. Citizens of most countries – even those entering visa-free – will be required to pay an 'entry tax' at the border. The entry tax for US citizens is

US$45, for UK citizens it's US$57, and for Australians it's US$40. It's generally equal to the visa fees charged to Albanian citizens for entering those respective countries.

Upon arrival you will fill in an arrival and departure card. Keep the departure card, which will be stamped, with your passport and present it when you leave.

EMBASSIES & CONSULATES
Albanian Embassies & Consulates
Listed below are some of the main addresses for Albanian embassies.

France (☎ 01-45 53 51 32) 13 rue de la Pompe, Paris 75016
Greece (☎ 01-723 4412, fax 723 1972) Karahristou 1, 114 21 Athens
UK (☎ 020-7730 5709, fax 7828-8869) 24 Buckingham Gate, 2nd Floor, London SW1 E6CB
USA (☎ 202-223 4942, fax 628 7342) 2100 S St NW, Washington DC 20008

Embassies & Consulates in Albania
The following embassies are in Tirana (area code ☎ 042):

Bulgaria (☎ 331 55, fax 38 937) Rruga Skënderbeg 12
Greece (☎ 342 90, fax 344 43) Rruga Frederik Shiroka
Macedonia (☎ 309 09, fax 325 14) Lekë Dukagjini 2
Turkey (☎ 333 99, fax 327 19) Rruga E Kavajës 31
UK (☎/fax 349 73) Rruga Skënderbeg
USA (☎ 278 52 or 335 20, fax 322 22) Rruga Elbasanit 103

MONEY
Currency
Albanian banknotes come in denominations of 100, 200, 500 and 1000 lekë. There are 5, 10, 20 and 50 lekë coins. Notes issued after 1997 are smaller and contain a sophisticated watermark to prevent forgery. In 1964 the currency was revalued 10 times; prices on occasion may still be quoted at the old rate.

Everything can be paid for with lekë; however, bear in mind that most hotel and transport prices in this chapter are quoted in US dollars or Deutschmarks.

Exchange Rates
Conversion rates for major currencies in mid-2000 are listed below:

country	unit		lekë
Australia	A$1	=	83.5 lekë
Canada	C$1	=	95.2 lekë
euro	€1	=	127.5 lekë
France	10FF	=	194.4 lekë
Germany	DM1	=	65.2 lekë
Japan	¥100	=	129.6 lekë
NZ	NZ$1	=	63.7 lekë
UK	UK£1	=	210.6 lekë
US	US$1	=	140.5 lekë

For the most recent currency rates of the Albanian lek, point your Web browser at www.xe.net/ucc/full.shtml.

Exchanging Money
Some banks will change US dollar travellers cheques into US dollars cash without any commission. Travellers cheques in small denominations may be used when paying bills at major hotels but cash is preferred everywhere. You'll find that credit cards are only accepted in the larger hotels and travel agencies, and a few places in Tirana and Durrës will offer credit card advances (usually for MasterCard). Unfortunately, there are no ATMs in Albania.

Every town has its free currency market, which usually operates on the street in front of the main post office or state bank. Look out for the men standing around with wads of money or pocket calculators in their hand. Such transactions are not dangerous and it all takes place quite openly, but be careful and make sure you count their money twice before tendering yours.

The advantages with changing money on the street are that you get a good rate and avoid the 1% commission some banks may charge. You also save time and don't have to worry about banking hours. Unlike the banks, private moneychangers never run out of currency notes.

In Albania US dollars are the favourite foreign currency, though Greek drachmas are also quite acceptable to many moneychangers. The import and export of Albanian currency is prohibited, but there's no reason to do either.

Tipping

Albania is a tip-conscious society. You should round up the bill in restaurants. However, with taxi drivers you will normally agree on a fare beforehand so an extra tip will not be considered necessary.

POST & COMMUNICATIONS
Post

There are no public mailboxes in Albania; you must hand in your letters at a post office in person. Leaving letters at hotel reception for mailing is unwise, although the Europapark (Rogner) Hotel in Tirana has a reliable postal service. Mail your parcels from the main post office in Tirana to reduce the amount of handling. Letters to the USA, Australia and Canada cost 90 lekë and within Europe, 50 lekë.

Mail that is sent to Poste Restante, Tirana, Albania should reach you OK. However, you should bear in mind that your letters and cards may be opened.

Telephone

Long-distance telephone calls made from main post offices are cheap, costing about 90 lekë a minute to Italy. Calls to the USA cost 230 lekë per minute. Phonecards are available from the post office in versions of 50 units (560 lekë), 100 units (980 lekë) and 200 units (1800 lekë). It's best not to buy the phonecards from the hawkers outside the post office.

Albania's country phone code is ☎ 355. Albania has one mobile/cellphone provider, Albanian Mobile Communications, which covers Albania's western coast from Shkodra to Tirana, as well as Fier and Vlora in the south and Kukës in the north.

The network may have been extended in 2000 to include Elbasan, Gjirokastra and Korça. Check with your home provider for possible roaming agreements. Local mobile/cellphone numbers are in the format ☎ 038 123 4567.

Albania's international access code is ☎ 00. Try dialling ☎ 14 for directory assistance.

Fax

Faxing can be done from the main post office in Tirana, or from major hotels, though they will charge more.

Email & Internet Access

Places to access the Internet abound in Tirana, and it won't be long before the craze hits Durrës.

INTERNET RESOURCES

Useful Web sites that you can access are www.albanian.com (the Albanian WWW Home Page) or www.tirana.al (a good info source on current events).

BOOKS

In her book, *Albania, The Search for the Eagle's Song,* June Emerson gives a picture of what it was like to visit Albania just before 1990. Untainted by hindsight, her book is an unwitting snapshot of a time that has vanished forever.

The Artful Albanian: The Memoirs of Enver Hoxha, edited by Jon Halliday, contains selected passages from the 3400 pages of Hoxha's six volumes of memoirs. Chapters like 'Decoding China' and 'Battling Khrushchev' give an insight into the mind of this controversial figure.

The Accursed Mountains: Journeys in Albania by Robert Carver is a lively, colourful narrative of one journalist's entertaining but occasionally harrowing journey through Albania in 1996.

Albania: From Anarchy to Balkan Identity (1997), by Miranda Vickers and James Pettifer, traces the history of Albania's isolation and its implications for the country's transition.

Lonely Planet's *Mediterranean Europe phrasebook* contains a helpful list of translated Albanian words and phrases.

An excellent source of rare and out-of-print books on Albania is Eastern Books (☎/fax 020-8871 0880, ✉ info@easternbooks.com), 81 Replingham Rd, Southfields, London SW18 5LU, England, UK. Check its Web page (www.easternbooks.com). Also try Oxus Books (☎/fax 020-8870 3854), 121 Astonville St, London SW18 5AQ, England, UK, which has a catalogue you can request.

NEWSPAPERS & MAGAZINES

A wide variety of newspapers are published in Tirana. The independent daily *Koha Jonë* is the paper with the widest readership.

The *Albanian Daily News* is a fairly dry English-language publication that has useful information on happenings around Albania. It's generally available from major hotels for 300 lekë, or you can read it online at www.AlbanianNews.com.

RADIO & TV

There are many TV channels available in Albania including the state TV service TVSH, the private station TVA and, among others, Eurosport, several Italian channels and a couple of French ones.

The BBC World Service can be picked up in and around Tirana on 103.9 FM.

TIME

Albania is one hour ahead of GMT/UTC, the same as Yugoslavia, Macedonia and Italy, but one hour behind Greece. Albania goes on summer time at the end of March, when clocks are turned forward an hour. At the end of September, they're turned back an hour.

TOILETS

Public toilets should be used in dire circumstances only! There are only a handful in the whole of Tirana. Use hotel or restaurant toilets whenever you can. The ones in the main hotels in Tirana are very clean and modern. Plan your 'rest' stops carefully when travelling in the country.

HEALTH

Health services are available to tourists for a small fee at state-run hospitals, but service and standards are not crash hot. Make sure your travel or health insurance covers treatment in Albania and will allow evacuation. Use the private clinics where available; there's a good one in Tirana.

WOMEN TRAVELLERS

While women are not likely to encounter any predictable dangers, it is recommended that you travel in pairs or with male companions, in order to avoid unwanted attention – particularly outside Tirana. Bear in mind that Albania is a predominantly Muslim country. Dress should be conservative.

GAY & LESBIAN TRAVELLERS

Homosexuality became legal in Albania early in 1995, however attitudes are still highly conservative.

DISABLED TRAVELLERS

Few special facilities exist for travellers in wheelchairs. However, there are toilets that cater for disabled people in the Tirana International Hotel and the Europapark (Rogner) Hotel in Tirana.

DANGERS & ANNOYANCES

Beware of pickpockets on crowded city buses and don't flash money around! Walking around the larger towns is generally safe during the day, but at night you must beware of falling into deep potholes in the unlit streets, and occasional gangs of youths. Be aware of theft generally, but don't believe the horror stories you hear about Albania in Greece and elsewhere.

Take special care if accosted by Roma women and children begging; avoid eye contact and head to the nearest hotel.

As Albania has been closed for so long, black travellers may encounter some curious stares. At worst, proprietors of small hotels may try to refuse service.

Corrupt police may attempt to extort money from you by claiming that something is wrong with your documentation, or they might try another pretext. Strongly resist paying them anything without an official receipt. Always keep at least a copy of your passport with you.

Be warned that there may be landmines near the northern border with Kosova around Bajram Curri.

You should also be aware of abysmal roads and chaotic driving conditions. Never drive at night. Banditry is prevalent, particularly in the northern part of the country and in the stretch in the south between Memaliaj and Gjirokastra. It's inadvisable to travel outside the main cities, but this is particularly true in the north. Note that 750,000 Kalashnikov rifles were looted by the residents of Albania during the post-pyramid scheme chaos.

Do not drink the tap water; plenty of bottled water is available.

BUSINESS HOURS

Most businesses open at 8.30 am, and some close for a siesta from noon to 4 pm, opening again from 4 to 7 pm. Banking hours are shorter (generally 8.30 am to 2 pm).

PUBLIC HOLIDAYS & SPECIAL EVENTS

Public holidays in Albania include New Year's Day (1 January), Easter Monday (March/April), Labour Day (1 May), Independence & Liberation Day (28 November) and Christmas Day (25 December).

Ramadan and Bajram, variable Muslim holidays, are also celebrated.

COURSES

The University of Tirana runs a summer school program in Albanian Language and Culture from mid-August to mid-September. The registration fee is US$100. For more information, contact fax 241 09 in Tirana or ✆ gezim_gurga@hotmail.com.

ACCOMMODATION

Accommodation is undergoing a rapid transformation in Albania, with the opening up of new custom-built private hotels to replace the dismal state hotels. Priced at about US$35 to US$50 per person per night and upwards (usually including breakfast), these are modern, well-appointed establishments.

Another positive development is the conversion of homes or villas into so-called private hotels. For budget travellers, these are without doubt the best way to go.

You can often find unofficial accommodation in private homes by asking around. However, for security reasons camping is inadvisable.

FOOD

Lunch is the main meal of the day though eating out in the evening is very common in Tirana. The quality of restaurants in the capital has improved greatly. In the country and other towns things are also getting much better, so you should have no problem getting a decent meal.

Albanian cuisine, like that of Serbia, has been strongly influenced by Turkey. Grilled meats like *shishqebap* (shish kebab), *romstek* (minced meat patties) and *qofte* (meat balls) are served all across the Balkan countries. Some local dishes include *çomlek* (meat and onion stew), *fërges* (a rich beef stew), *rosto me salcë kosi* (roast beef with sour cream) and *tavë kosi* (mutton with yoghurt). Lake Shkodra carp and Lake Ohrid

trout are the most common fish dishes. For dessert, try the ice cream *(akullore)*, which is very popular everywhere.

DRINKS

Albanians take their coffee both as *kafe turke* (Turkish coffee) and *kafe ekspres* (espresso). If you ask for *kafe surogato* you will get what is the closest to filter coffee. Avoid unbottled drinks as they may contain tap water.

Albanian white wine is better than the vinegary red. However, the red *Shesi e Zi* from either Librazhd or Berat is an excellent drop. Most of the beer consumed in Albania is imported from Macedonia or Greece, but draught Austrian or Italian beer is available in the posher joints in Tirana. *Raki* (a clear brandy distilled from grapes) is taken as an aperitif – always ask for homemade if possible (raki ë bërë në shtëpi). There's also *konjak* (cognac – the Skenderbed cognac makes a good gift on your trip home), *uzo* (a colourless aniseed-flavoured liqueur like Greek ouzo) and various fruit liqueurs. *Fërnet* is a medicinal aperitif containing herbal essences, made at Korça.

A good word to know is the favourite Albanian drinking toast – *gëzuar!*

ENTERTAINMENT

Check the local theatre for performances. These are usually advertised on painted boards either in front of the theatre or on main streets. Ask someone to direct you to the venue if it's not clear.

There's usually a disco or two to complement the zillions of cafes in a given town; ask around for what's hot.

SPECTATOR SPORTS

Football is played at local stadiums on weekend afternoons. As a foreigner, you may need someone to help you obtain tickets.

SHOPPING

Most hotels have tourist shops where you can buy Albanian handicrafts such as carpets, silk, ornaments (made from silver, copper and wood), embroidery, handmade shoes, shoulder bags, picture books, musical instruments, and records and cassettes of folk music. One of Albania's cleverest souvenirs is an ashtray made to resemble Hoxha's bunkers.

Getting There & Away

AIR

Rinas airport is 26km north-west of Tirana. Taxis ply the route to Tirana.

Ada Air arrives from Athens, Bari, Prishtina, Skopje, and Ioannina; Adria Airways from Ljubljana; Albanian Airlines from Bologna, Frankfurt, Istanbul, Prishtina, Rome and Zürich; Austrian Airlines from Vienna; Hemus Air from Sofia; Lufthansa from Frankfurt and Munich; Malev Hungarian Airlines from Budapest; Olympic Airways from Athens via Ioannina or Thessaloniki; Swissair from Zürich; and Turkish Airlines from Istanbul.

Some examples of return fares are US$308 from Rome flying with Albanian Airlines; US$220 from Athens with Olympic and Ada; US$322 from Budapest with Malev; US$155 from Prishtina with Ada Air (US$171 with Albanian Airlines); and US$250 from Istanbul with Turkish Airlines.

Before investing in any of the above fares, compare them with the price of a cheap flight to Athens or Thessaloniki, from where Albania is easily accessible by local bus with a change of bus at the border. However, be sure you feel comfortable with taking a bus around Albania. Another option is a charter flight to Corfu, from where you can take a ferry to Saranda in southern Albania.

Some useful airline phone numbers in Tirana are:

Ada Air	(☎ 561 11)
Adria Airways	(☎ 284 83)
Albanian Airlines	(☎ 351 62)
Alitalia	(☎ 300 23)
Austrian Airlines	(☎ 350 35)
Malev	(☎ 341 63)
Olympic Airways	(☎ 289 81)
Swissair	(☎ 350 28)
Turkish Airlines	(☎ 341 85)

LAND
Bus

Buses to Thessaloniki (US$20, 10 hours) and Athens (US$35, 24 hours) leave at 5.30 am each morning from in front of Skënderbeg Travel (☎ 321 71) in Tirana. They stop in El Basan and Korça. Skënderbeg in Thessaloniki can be reached at ☎ 031-38 367; in Athens ☎ 0152-987 39/40; in El Basan ☎ 0545-21 31; in Korça ☎ 0824-28 47; and in Durrës at ☎ 052-23 274.

Buses to Prishtina, the capital of Kosova, leave daily from beside the Tirana International Hotel at 6 pm. The 12-hour ride costs around US$24.

If you're Macedonia-bound, take the daily bus to Tetovo from the Axhensi bus office. From Tetovo you can take a frequent local bus to Skopje.

Buses for Istanbul and Sofia leave from Albtransport (☎ 230 26) on Rruga Mine Peza in Tirana. The Sofia bus (US$26 one-way, US$47 return, 15 hours) leaves 10 am on Wednesday. Two buses for Istanbul (US$40 one-way, US$70 return, 24 hours) depart at 10 am and 1 pm on Monday, and go through Sofia. The Albtransport office is open 8 am to 4 pm weekdays.

Car & Motorcycle

Bringing a car to Albania is still a risky business as car theft and banditry are problems. If you can find an Albanian driver, that will alleviate the security situation as the driver can help guard the car.

Travel is slow because of the dreadful condition of the roads and the arterial infrastructure, which cannot properly support the marked increase in vehicular traffic. Apart from an 8km stretch of 'freeway' between Tirana and Durrës there has been no visible improvement in the roads since the days of communism. See the Getting Around section later in this chapter for further information on local driving conditions.

The following highway border crossings are open to motorists, cyclists and pedestrians.

Yugoslavia/Kosova You can, in theory, cross at Han i Hotit (between Podgorica and Shkodra) and at Morin (between Prizren and Kukës). The Albanian government is planning to build a good road that starts in Durrës and links Tirana and Prishtina, crossing the border in Morin. Another border crossing is located at Prushi Pass, between the town of Kruma in Albania and the Kosovar town of Djakovica.

Macedonia Cross at Tushemisht (near Sveti Naum, 29km south of Ohrid), Qafa e Thanës (between Struga and Pogradec) and Maqellare (between Debar and Peshkopi).

Greece The border crossings are Kapshtica (between Florina and Korça) and Kakavija (between Ioannina and Gjirokastra). An EU-funded border crossing north of the Greek port of Igoumenitsa is under construction.

SEA

The Italian company Adriatica di Navigazione offers ferry services to Durrës from Bari (nine hours, 220km) daily and from Ancona (20 hours, 550km) four times a week.

Deck fares per passenger are US$60/80 from Bari/Ancona to Durrës; cabin fares cost more. Bicycles are carried free. From Ancona you can catch a ferry to Split, Croatia.

A ferry runs every Tuesday and Saturday from Trieste to Durrës (and returns on Wednesday and Sunday). The trip on deck costs US$37.

In Trieste ferry tickets are available from Agenzia Marittima 'Agemar' (☎ 040-363 737); in Bari the agent is 'Agestea' (☎ 080-5531 555, ✉ agestea.bari02@interbusiness .it), Via Liside 4; and in Ancona it's Maritime Agency Srl (☎ 071-204 915, ✉ tickets.adn@ maritime.it), Via XXIX Settembre 10. In Albania tickets are sold by any number of travel agencies in Durrës or Tirana.

The fastest ferry connection between Bari and Durrës are the two passenger catamarans operated by the line La Vikinga (US$100, 3½ hours). These high-speed vessels leave Durrës daily at 5.30 pm and 9.30 am and Bari at 11 am and 5 pm and travel at speeds of up to 90km/h. The Bari agent is at ☎ 080-523 2429.

From Vlora, Albania Travel & Tours (☎/fax 063-249 01 in Vlora) can arrange tickets for the ferry *Niobe 1*, which runs three times a week to Brindisi and three times a week to Otranto. The price to both is 60,000 lire (plus 10,000 lire in port taxes). There are two other ferries, the *Vlora 5* and the *Europa Skenderbeg,* which run to Brindisi; it shouldn't be a problem to find a travel agent to book your ticket at either end.

Travellers from Corfu are advised to look for the ticket vendors (from any of the three ferry companies) who hang around the New Harbour before the ferries depart. There are usually three ferries a day.

ORGANISED TOURS

Package tours to Albania, which trailed off after the 1997 civil disturbances, are now slowly coming back. The companies listed either do offer or plan to resume offering tours to Albania. As tourism in Albania has depleted, your tour may be individually arranged or you may have a small group size, which makes for a more immediate and authentic experience. The programs they offer vary quite a bit, so it's best to get a prospectus from all agencies.

Exodus (☎ 020-8675 5550, fax 8673 0779, ✉ sales@exodustravels.co.uk) 9 Weir Rd London SW12 0LT, UK
Intertrek BV (☎ 070-363 6416, fax 070-364 0269, ✉ omfp@infotrek.nl) Postbus 18760, NL-2502 ET Den Haag, Netherlands
Kutrubes Travel (☎ 800-876 8566, fax 617-426 3196, ✉ ktravel@world.std.com) 328 Tremont St, Boston, MA 02116 USA
Regent Holidays (☎ 0117-921 1711, fax 925 4866, ✉ regent@regentsholidays.co.uk) 15 John St, Bristol BS1 2HR, UK
Skënderbeg-Reisen GmbH (☎ 0234-308 686, fax 308 505, ✉ reisen@skenderbeg.de) Postfach 102204, D-44722 Bochum, Germany

DEPARTURE TAX

Airport departure tax is US$10, payable in dollars or lekë. A US$4 tariff is imposed on people leaving Albania by ferry, and there's a US$6 tariff on vehicles.

Getting Around

BUS

Most Albanians travel around their country in private minibuses or state-owned buses. These run fairly frequently throughout the day between Tirana and Durrës (38km) and other towns north and south. Buses to Tirana depart from towns all around Albania at the crack of dawn. Tickets are sold by a conductor on board, and the fares are low (eg, Tirana-Durrës is 60 lekë).

City buses operate in Tirana, Durrës and Shkodra (pay the conductor). Watch your possessions on crowded city buses.

ALBANIA

TRAIN

Before 1948, Albania had no railways, but the communists built up a limited north-south rail network based at the port of Durrës. Today, however, nobody who can afford other types of transport takes the train, even though train fares are about a third cheaper than bus fares. The reason will be obvious once you board – the decrepit carriages typically have broken windows and no toilets.

Daily passenger trains leave Tirana for Shkodra (3½ hours, 98km), Fier (4¼ hours), Ballsh (five hours), Vlora (5½ hours) and Pogradec (seven hours). Seven trains a day also make the 1½-hour trip between Tirana and Durrës.

CAR & MOTORCYCLE

Albania has only recently acquired an official road traffic code and most motorists have only learned to drive in the last five years. The road infrastructure is poor and the roads badly maintained, but the number of cars on the road is growing daily. There are petrol stations in the cities, but they are few and far between in the country.

Hazards include pedestrians who tend to use the roads as an extension of the footpaths; animals being herded along country roads; gaping potholes; a lack of road warnings and signs; and occasionally reckless drivers. Security is also an issue. Park your vehicle in a secure location, such as hotel grounds, or in a guarded parking lot. Store removables like hubcaps inside the car when parked. An immobiliser alarm is also a very good idea.

Banditry is prevalent in the northern part of the country, as well as on the road north from Gjirokastra. It's wise to check up on the current situation, and best not to drive in these areas at all. Never drive at night in any part of Albania.

Unleaded fuel may only be available closer to Tirana, so fill up when you can. A litre of unleaded petrol costs 110 lekë, while diesel costs close to 90 lekë.

No rental car companies currently operate in Albania, but Avis is planning to open up a rental car chain in Tirana. If you hire from Avis, it's worthwhile hiring an Albanian driver as well.

HITCHING

With buses so cheap, hitching will probably only be an emergency means of transport. You can afford to be selective about the rides you accept as everyone will take you if they possibly can.

You can get an indication of where a vehicle might be going from the letters on the licence plate: Berat (BR), Durrës (DR), Elbasan (EL), Fier (FR), Gjirokastra (GJ), Korça (KO), Kruja (KR), Lezha (LE), Pogradec (PG), Saranda (SR), Shkodra (SH), Tirana (TR) and Vlora (VL).

Lonely Planet does not recommend hitching as a form of transport.

LOCAL TRANSPORT

Shared minibuses run between cities. They usually cost about five times the bus fare but for foreigners they're still cheap. Because they're not expecting foreigners, you'll probably be charged the price for locals. If not, try bargaining it down. Pay the conductor once you leave the bus.

Tirana

☎ 042 • pop 440,000

Tirana (Tiranë), an energetic city of 444,000 people (compared with 30,000 before WWII), lies almost exactly midway between Rome and Istanbul. Mt Dajti (1612m) rises to the east. Founded by a Turkish pasha (military governor) in 1614, Tirana developed into a craft centre with a lively bazaar.

In 1920 the city was made the capital of Albania and in the 1930s the bulky Italianate government buildings went up. In the communist era, larger-than-life 'palaces of the people' blossomed in and around Skënderbeg Square and along Bulevardi Dëshmorët e Kombit (Martyrs of the Nation Boulevard). You'll also see Italian parks and a Turkish mosque, but the market area on the east side of Tirana is also worth exploring. The city is compact and can be explored on foot.

Orientation

Orientation is easy in Tirana, as the whole city revolves around central Skenderbeg Square. Running south from the square is Bulevardi Dëshmorët e Kombit which leads to the three-arched university building. Running north the same street leads to the train station. Coming from the airport (26km) you will enter the city along Rruga Durrësit. Buses from neighbouring countries will drop you off close to Skënderbeg Square. Most major services and hotels are within a few minutes' walk of Skënderbeg Square.

Information

Tourist Offices Tirana has no official tourist office, but there are a number of travel agencies. One helpful publication is *Tirana 2000: The Practical Guide of Tirana* (or, if they are ambitious, *Tirana 2001*, etc), available at bookshops and some of the larger kiosks for 300 lekë. This gives telephone numbers and addresses for everything from hospitals to banks to embassies, and has a handy map in the back. The new guide *Tirana In Your Pocket* is expected to be published in 2000.

Money A free currency market operates directly in front of the post office.

If you would prefer to avoid the swarms of men, the Europapark (Rogner) Hotel has a currency exchange booth (near the Swissair offices) that offers MasterCard advances, cashes travellers cheques for 1% commission and exchanges cash. It's open 10.30 am to 5 pm weekdays. American Bank of Albania, Rruga Ismail Qemali 27, is also a reliable, secure place to cash travellers cheques (2% commission). It's open 9.30 am to 3.30 pm weekdays. World Travel, the American Express representative on Mine Peza 2, cashes travellers cheques for 2% commission.

The Unioni Financiar Tiranë Exchange, just south of the post office, offers Western Union wire transfer services.

Post & Communications The post office (open 8 am to 7 pm weekdays) and telephone centre are adjacent on a street jutting west from Skenderbeg Square. Another telephone centre is on Bulevardi Dëshmorët e Kombit, about 100m past Skenderbeg Square on the right-hand side.

The international courier service DHL has two offices in Tirana, one at 6 Rruga Ded Gjo Luli (☎ 276 67 or 339 32), the other at Rruga Dëshmorët e 4 Shkurtit 7/1 (☎ 328 16).

Email & Internet Access Internet access is the latest rage in Tirana. One cybercafe is on the top floor in the Palace of Culture near Skënderbeg Square (380 lekë per hour); another, the Internet Centre, is on Rruga Brigada VIII 8/1, about 20m from the intersection with Deshmoret e 4 Shkurtit (300 lekë per hour).

Travel Agencies Albania Travel & Tours (☎ 329 83, fax 339 81), Rruga Durrësit 102, is a good place to arrange ferry tickets from Vlora and Durrës (see the Getting There & Away section earlier in this chapter), or to book private rooms. The office is open from 8 am to 7 pm weekdays, and 8 am to 2 pm on weekends.

Other travel agencies abound.

Newspapers & Magazines Foreign newspapers and magazines, including the *International Herald Tribune*, the *Financial Times* and the *Economist* are sold at most major hotels and at some central street kiosks. The International Bookshop, in the Palace of Culture on the right-hand side, gets these papers in the afternoon most days. It also has a selection of Penguin literary classics as well as maps of Tirana and Albania and an excellent selection of books about Albania. The shop is open 9 am to 9 pm daily.

Medical & Emergency Services Most foreigners use the ABC Health Foundation at 260 Rruga Quemal Stafa (☎ 341 05, ✉ ABC@maf.org); it's across the street from the 'New School' but watch carefully for the small sign. Staffed by western-trained doctors, the clinic offers a range of services including regular (US$60) and emergency (US$90) consultations. The fee goes down if you pay the US$120 12-month registration. Patients are seen by appointment 9 am to 1 pm weekdays.

The emergency phone number for an ambulance is ☎ 222 35 and for the police ☎ 19.

Things to See & Do

Most visits to Tirana begin at **Skënderbeg Square**, a great open space in the heart of the city. Beside the 15-storey Tirana International Hotel (the tallest building in Albania), situated on the northern side of the square, is

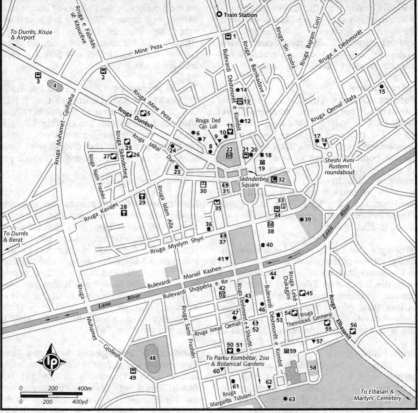

the **National Museum of History** (1981), the largest and finest museum in Albania. It's open 8 am to 1 pm Monday to Saturday (admission 300 lekë). A huge mosaic mural entitled *Albania* covers the facade of the museum building. Temporary exhibits are shown in the gallery on the side of the building facing the Tirana International Hotel (admission free).

To the east is another massive building, the **Palace of Culture**, which has a theatre, shops and art galleries. Construction of the palace began as a gift from the Soviet people in 1960 and was completed in 1966, after the 1961

Soviet-Albanian split. The entrance to the **National Library** is on the south side of the building. Opposite this is the cupola and minaret of the **Mosque of Ethem Bey** (1793), one of the most distinctive buildings in the city. Enter to see the beautifully painted dome. Tirana's **clock tower** (1830) stands beside the mosque.

In the middle of the square is an equestrian statue (1968) of Skënderbeg himself looking straight up Bulevardi Dëshmorët e Kombit (formerly Bulevardi Stalin and before that, Bulevardi Zog I), north towards the train station. Behind Skënderbeg's statue

TIRANA

the boulevard leads directly south to the three arches of **Tirana University** (1957). As you stroll down this tree-lined boulevard, you'll see Tirana's **art gallery** (closed Monday), a one-time stronghold of socialist realism, with a significant permanent collection that has been exhibited here since 1976.

Continue south on Bulevardi Dëshmorët e Kombit to the bridge over the Lana River. On the left just across the river you'll be able to see the sloping white-marble walls of the **former Enver Hoxha Museum** (1988). Just beyond, on the right, is the four-storey **former Central Committee building** (1955) of the Party of Labour, which now houses various ministries.

Follow Rruga Ismail Qemali, the street on the south side of the Central Committee building, a long block west to the **former residence of Enver Hoxha** (on the north-west corner of the intersection). Formerly it was forbidden to walk along these streets, since many other party leaders lived in the surrounding mansions. When the area was first opened to the general public in 1991, great crowds of Albanians flocked to see the style in which their 'proletarian' leaders lived.

On the left, farther south on Bulevardi Dëshmorët e Kombit, is the ultramodern **Palace of Congresses** (1986). Some 1800 objects from prehistoric times to the Middle Ages are on display. It's interesting to note how the simple artefacts of the Palaeolithic and Neolithic periods give way to the weapons and jewellery of the Copper and Bronze ages, with evidence of social differentiation. Although Greek and Roman relics are well represented, evidence of the parallel Illyrian culture is present throughout, illustrating that the ancestors of the present Albanians inhabited these lands since time immemorial.

Behind the museum is the **Qemal Stafa Stadium** (1946). The boulevard terminates at the university, with the Faculty of Music on the right.

Beyond the university is **Parku Kombëtar** (National Park), a large park with an open-air theatre (Teatri Veror) and an artificial lake. There's a superb view across the lake to the olive-coloured hills. Cross the dam retaining the lake to **Tirana Zoo**. Ask directions to the **botanical gardens** just west of the zoo. If you're keen, you can hire a rowing boat and paddle on the lake.

About 5km south-east on Rruga Elbasanit is the **Martyrs' Cemetery** (Varrezat e Dëshmorëve), where some 900 partisans who died during WWII are buried. Large crowds once gathered here each year on 16 October, Enver Hoxha's birthday, since this is where he and other leading revolutionaries such as Gog Nushi, Qemal Stafa and Hysni Kapo were formerly interred. (In May 1992 Hoxha's lead coffin was dug up and reburied in a common grave in a public cemetery on the other side of town.) The hill-top setting with a beautiful view over the city and mountains is subdued, and a great white figure of Mother Albania (1972) stands watch. Nearby, on the opposite side of the highway, is the **former palace of King Zog**, now a government guesthouse.

Places to Stay

Private Rooms Staying in private rented apartments or with local families is the best budget accommodation in Tirana. Newer private hotels are pleasant but high priced.

Albania Travel & Tours (see Travel Agencies earlier in the chapter) has private rooms for around 2500 lekë per person. It can also organise private rooms or hotels in Gjirokastra, Korça, Vlora and Durrës. Other travel agencies may also find you a private room if you ask around.

The tiny **Hotel Endri** (☎ 442 68 or 293 34, Apartment 30, Bldg 3, Rruga Vaso Pasha 37) is an excellent deal. The hotel, which consists of two rooms adjacent to manager Petrit Alikaj's apartment, is sparkling clean, new, and has very nice bathrooms with excellent showers. The price is US$20 a night. Handily, Petrit is also a taxi driver.

Hotels A pleasant private hotel is **Europa International Hotel** (☎/fax 274 03), which has modern singles/doubles for US$60/70, including breakfast and parking out front. Look for the sign on Rruga Myslym Shyri. Just off Rruga Durrësit is the nifty **Hotel California** (☎/fax 322 28, Rruga Mihal Duri 2/7). Clean rooms with mini-bar and TV cost US$50/70.

The high-rise **Tirana International Hotel** (☎ 341 85, fax 341 88, Skënderbeg Square) has well-appointed rooms for US$140/190, with breakfast. The hotel accepts MasterCard, American Express and Diner's Club.

To the right of the Tirana International Hotel is the smaller **Hotel Miniri** (☎ 309 30, fax 330 96, Rruga e Dibres 3). Adequate but unexciting rooms with phone and TV are US$60/100, with breakfast included.

The somewhat dour and ageing **Hotel Dajti** (☎ 510 35, fax 510 36, Bulevardi Dëshmorët e Kombit 6) was erected in the 1930s by the Italians. The 90 rooms with bath are US$50-60/80.

The big shots stay at **Hotel Europapark Tirana** (☎ 350 35, in the USA 1-800-650 8018, fax 35 050) on Bulevardi Dëshmorët e Kombit. The hotel, run by the Rogner group and locally known as the Rogner, has excellent rooms with good amenities, including a safety box. There's a swimming pool and tennis court in the back and a nice, spacious bar inside. Rooms are US$200/230 per night, including breakfast. MasterCard, Eurocard, American Express and Diners Club cards are accepted.

Places to Eat

There is no shortage of small restaurants, cafes and snack bars on and around Skënderbeg Square and Bulevardi Dëshmorët e Kombit. Generally, pizza will cost US$2.50 to US$3.50, while a main course in a restaurant will set you back US$5 to US$7.

If you fancy a cuppa and a sandwich – or even a pizza, nachos or fajitas – call into **Qendra Stefan**, a friendly, nonsmoking American-run place. Lunchtime specials are posted on a blackboard outside. It's near the fruit and vegetable market. Call ☎ 347 48 and they'll bicycle your order to you at no extra charge (though a tip would be appropriate). **Piazza Restaurant** is a tastefully designed and well-appointed establishment just north of Skënderbeg Square. The food and service are excellent and prices, for what you get, are reasonable.

One of Tirana's nicest restaurants is **Il Passatore** (Rruga Vaso Pasha 22/1), better known as Antonella's, which is convenient to Murphy's pub for the after-dinner wind-up. Food and service here are excellent, with delicious specials of fish or pasta and a diverse salad bar.

Check out the **Bar Artisti** cafeteria at the Institute of Art, which is good for a coffee and snack.

Among Tirana's innumerable pizza places, the two-floor *La Voglia*, on Rruga Desmoret e 4 Shkurtit near the river, serves a very good pizza (350 lekë or so) and has menus in English.

The *Ambassador* restaurant, tucked away on a small street behind the Italian embassy, is among Tirana's best for atmosphere. Try and sample a plateful of Albanian specialties (rice wrapped in grape leaves, burek, and more).

Entertainment

As soon as you arrive, check the *Palace of Culture* on Skënderbeg Square for opera or ballet. Performances begin at 7 pm (6 pm in winter); you can usually buy tickets half an hour before the show.

For more on events and exhibitions also check the leaflet *Buletini Informativ Kulturori Tiranes,* which has English, French, Italian and Albanian-language summaries of the current cultural events in town.

Tirana finally and inevitably has an Irish pub! *Murphy's*, on Rruga Abdyl Frashëri right next to the Tirana Fitness Centre, serves up Guinness on tap, Murphy's and a host of other brews, making it the before-and-after-dinner darling of the expat community. It's open until the last person leaves. The bathroom is clean.

Pop concerts and other musical events often take place in the *Qemal Stafa Stadium* next to the university. Look out for street banners bearing details of upcoming events. At the stadium there are also football matches held every Saturday and Sunday afternoon, except during July and August.

The *London Bar* (Bulevardi Dëshmorët e Kombit 51), near the Tirana International Hotel, Is also popular.

The buffed hang out at the trendy *Tirana Fitness Centre* (☎ 529 51, Rruga Abdyl Frashëri 7/1), across from the Croatian embassy, where you can socialise while you sweat (or soak in a sauna). Membership costs US$20 for the first month, plus US$35/50/70 for two/three/seven days a week use.

The biggest hit in Tirana is the new *Kinema Millennium* (☎ 486 47), on Rruga Kavajes near Skënderbed Square, which shows recent box-office hits for 200 or 300 lekë (earlier shows are cheaper).

Shopping

Tirana's public market, north of the Sheshi Avni Rustemi roundabout several blocks east of the clock tower, is largest on Thursday and Sunday. A few shops here sell folkloric objects such as carved wooden trays, small boxes, wall hangings and bone necklaces.

A good choice of souvenir shop is Suvenir Stella, on Bulevardi Dëshmorët e Kombit, just past the telephone office on that street. Souvenirs sold here include brass plates with the Albanian insignia and ashtrays cleverly modelled on Hoxha's bunkers.

Getting There & Away

Air For information about routes and fares of flights to/from Rinas airport see the Getting There & Away section earlier in this chapter.

Many of the airline offices are on Rruga Durrësit, just off Skënderbeg Square. Alitalia has an office on Skënderbeg Square behind the National Museum of History, and Swissair and Austrian Airlines are at Hotel Europapark. Olympic Airways, is in the Ve-Ve Business Centre on Deshmorët e Kombit behind the Tirana International Hotel, and Turkish Airways is in the Tirana International Hotel. See the Getting There & Away section earlier in this chapter for airline telephone numbers.

Bus Both private and state-owned buses operate between Tirana and most towns. There's no one central bus station in Tirana and pick-up venues may change, so check for the latest departure points. Minibuses to/from Durrës (100 lekë, one hour, 38km) leave from the block adjacent to the train station whenever they're full.

Buses to Berat (122km), Elbasan (54km), Fier (113km), Gjirokastra (232km), Kakavija (263km), Korça (181km), Lushnja (83km), Pogradec (140km), Saranda (284km) and Vlora (147km) leave from Southern Bus Station, on the west side of Selman Stërmasi Stadium. From about 6 am every day you can get buses to almost anywhere south and east from here: they leave when full throughout the day. As late as 5 pm you'll still find buses to Berat, Elbasan, Fier and perhaps farther.

Buses to Kruja (32km) leave from Rruga Mine Peza, at the beginning of the highway to Durrës.

North-bound buses to Lezha (69km), Shkodra (116km), Kukës (208km) and other places leave from a station out on the Durrës highway just beyond the Asllan Rusi Stadium.

Train The train station is at the northern end of Bulevardi Dëshmorët e Kombit. Seven trains a day go to Durrës (60 lekë, one hour, 36km). Trains also depart for Ballsh (four hours, twice daily), Elbasan (four hours, three daily), Pogradec (seven hours, twice daily), Shkodra (3½ hours, twice daily), Fier (4¼ hours, twice daily) and Vlora (5½ hours, twice daily).

Getting Around
To/From the Airport A taxi to/from the airport should cost about US$20 or 5000 drachmas – depending on what currency you have in your pocket.

Car & Motorcycle Some of the major hotels offer guarded parking; others have parking available out the front. Currently no organisation in Tirana rents out cars, but Avis had plans to start up a chain in 2000.

Taxi Taxi stands dot the city and charge 300 lekë for a ride inside Tirana (500 lekë at night). Work out the price in your head before getting in and make sure you reach an agreement with the driver before setting off. Radio Taxi (☎ 777 77), with 24-hour service, is particularly reliable. These local taxis are much cheaper than the Mercedes taxis parked at the large hotels.

The older private taxis are usually found around the market or at bus and train stations, and the shiny Mercedes tourist taxis park outside the Europapark Tirana (Rogner) and Tirana International Hotels (which quote fares in US dollars but also take lekë).

Around Tirana

DURRËS
☎ 052 • pop 85,000
Unlike Tirana, Durrës (Durazzo in Italian) is an ancient city. In 627 BC the Greeks founded Epidamnos (Durrës) whose name the Romans changed to Dyrrhachium. It was the largest port on the eastern Adriatic and the start of the Via Egnatia (an extension of the Via Appia to Constantinople). The famous Via Appia (Appian Way) to Rome began 150km south-west of Durrës at the town of Brindisi, Italy.

Durrës changed hands frequently before being taken by the Turks in 1501, under whom the port dwindled into insignificance. A slow revival began in the 17th century and from 1914 to 1920 Durrës was the capital of Albania. Landings here by Mussolini's troops on 7 April 1939 met fierce though brief resistance, and those who fell are regarded as the first martyrs in the War of National Liberation.

Today, Roman ruins and Byzantine fortifications embellish this major industrial city and commercial port, which lies 38km west of Tirana. Durrës is Albania's second-largest city, with 85,000 inhabitants. On a bay southeast of the city are long, sandy beaches where some tourist hotels and restaurants are concentrated. In 1991 the city saw desperate mobs attempting to escape by ship to Italy and there's now a heavy Italian military presence in the area. Car ferries from Italy dock on the east side of the port. The entry/exit point is even farther east. Look for road signs to the ferry quay when departing.

Information
The Savings Bank of Albania, across the bus parking lot from the train station, changes travellers cheques and offers MasterCard advances for a 1% commission. It's open until 2 pm weekdays.

The post office and phone centre are located one block west of the train and bus stations.

Things to See
Behind the archaeological museum which faces the waterfront promenade near the port (closed indefinitely) are the 6th-century **Byzantine city walls**, built after the Visigoth invasion of AD 481 and supplemented by round Venetian towers in the 14th century.

The impressive **Roman amphitheatre**, built between the 1st and 2nd centuries AD, is on the hillside just inside the walls. Much of the amphitheatre has now been excavated and you can see a small built-in 10th-century Byzantine church decorated with wall mosaics. Follow the road just inside the walls

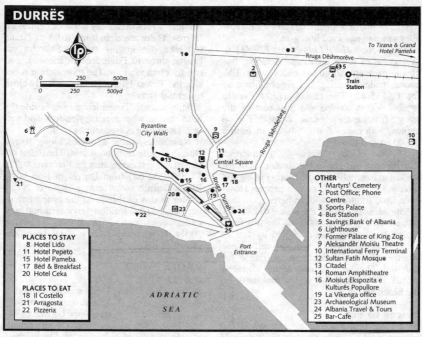

DURRËS

To Tirana & Grand Hotel Pameba

Rruga Dëshmorëve

Train Station

Byzantine City Walls

Central Square

Rruga Skënderbeg

Rruga Durrah

ADRIATIC SEA

Port Entrance

PLACES TO STAY
8 Hotel Lido
11 Hotel Pepeto
15 Hotel Pameba
17 Bëd & Breakfast
20 Hotel Ceka

PLACES TO EAT
18 Il Costello
21 Arragosta
22 Pizzeria

OTHER
1 Martyrs' Cemetery
2 Post Office; Phone Centre
3 Sports Palace
4 Bus Station
5 Savings Bank of Albania
6 Lighthouse
7 Former Palace of King Zog
9 Aleksandër Moisiu Theatre
10 International Ferry Terminal
12 Sultan Fatih Mosque
13 Citadel
14 Roman Amphitheatre
16 Moisiut Ekspozita e Kulturës Popullore
19 La Vikenga office
23 Archaeological Museum
24 Albania Travel & Tours
25 Bar-Cafe

down towards the port and you'll find the
Sultan Fatih Mosque (1502) and the **Moi-siut Ekspozita e Kulturës Popullore**, with
ethnographic displays housed in the former
home of actor Alexander Moisiu (1879-
1935). It's open in the morning only.

The **former palace of King Ahmet Zog** is
on the hill top west of the amphitheatre. The
soldiers guarding the palace will expect you
to buy a ticket from them to wander around.
In front is a statue of Skënderbeg and huge
radar disks set up by the Italian army. The
next hill beyond bears a **lighthouse** which
affords a splendid view of Albanian coastal
defences, Durrës and the entire coast.

As you're exploring the centre of the city,
stop to see the **Roman baths** directly behind
Aleksandër Moisiu Theatre, on the central
square. The large **mosque** on the square was
erected with Egyptian aid in 1993, to replace
one destroyed during the 1979 earthquake. At
the western end of Rruga Dëshmorevë is the
Martyrs' Cemetery, guarded by half-a-dozen
decrepit bunkers.

Places to Stay

Durrës has a handful of pleasant mid-priced
hotels (along with several seedy ones).
These hotels tend to fill up quickly, particularly in summer, so call ahead. The hotels
listed should have English-speaking staff,
unless otherwise noted. You should be able
to find a private room, but it might require
some persistence.

Albania Travel & Tours (☎ 242 76, ☎/fax
254 50), along Rruga Durrah near the waterfront, may be able to help arrange a private
room with advance notice; the office is open
8 am to 8 pm daily.

An excellent choice is the *bed & breakfast*
(☎ 243 43, ✉ ipmcrsp@icc.al.eu.org, Dom
Nikoll Kaçorri 5) in the gracious 19th-century
house of a personable Italian-Albanian couple,
Alma Tedeschini and her husband, Josef.
B&B in this former Austrian consulate costs a
bargain US$15; if you want lunch and dinner
it's just US$10 more. The place is a bit hard to
find: From the square fronting the mosque,
walk towards the restaurant Il Costello. Take

ALBANIA

the first right, then a quick left, then a quick right. The house is about 10m down a narrow alleyway and has a red iron gate.

The 13-room *Hotel Lido* (*☎/fax 279 41*), in the centre of town on Rruga A Goga, has clean, pleasant singles/doubles with TV, phone, fridge, heating and air-conditioning for US$35/42. The cheery *Hotel Pepeto* (*☎ 241 90, ☎/fax 263 46*), just east of the square fronting the mosque, is another good choice, with rooms for US$40/60, including breakfast and laundry.

The *Hotel Ceka* (*☎/fax 244 12*), on Rruga Currila on a hill above the former archaeological museum, has simple rooms but a good price – US$25 for one or two people. However, little English is spoken here.

The pleasant *Hotel Pameba* (*☎ 242 70, ☎/fax 241 49*), about 400m up the hill from the port entrance, was occupied by Italian soldiers at the time of writing; call to see whether the rooms are now available for tourists. The new *Grand Hotel Pameba* (*☎/fax 272 50*) is a few kilometres south on the beach by Golem.

Places to Eat

By far the best place to eat in town is the restaurant *Il Castello* (*☎ 268 87, Rruga H Troplini 3*), which has outstanding pastas (try the seafood pasta at 450 lekë), and a good selection of fish.

For a meal of fresh shrimp or fish on a patio overlooking the water, try *Arragosta*, out on the point about an 800m walk west from the town centre. A *pizzeria*, next to the Fish Restaurant on the waterfront on the way to Arragosta, is also a possibility.

Otherwise, if you happen to be along the beach south of Durrës, numerous restaurants offer seaside dining.

There is also a number of cafes along the main street, Rruga Durrah.

Entertainment

The niftiest place for a coffee or beer is the *bar-cafe* in the tower beside the port entrance. You can sip your beverage of choice while inside or atop the tower.

Alternatively, you could pay a visit to the *Aleksandër Moisiu Theatre* in the centre of Durrës and the *Sports Palace* on Rruga Dëshmorevë to see if anything is on.

Getting There & Away

Albania's 720km railway network centres on Durrës. There are eight trains a day to Tirana (60 lekë, 1½ hours), two to Shkodra via Lezha, three to Pogradec via Elbasan, and two to Vlora via Fier. The train station is beside the Tirana Highway, conveniently close to central Durrës.

Minibuses to Tirana leave from beside the train station whenever they're full, and service elsewhere is frequent as well.

Numerous travel agencies along Rruga Durrah handle ferry bookings. The ticket office of the fast catamaran *La Vikinga* (*☎ 225 55, fax 242 68*) from Durrës to Bari is on Rruga Durrah (see Getting There & Away earlier in this chapter). At the time of writing, a US$10.4 million ferry terminal was under construction in Durrës (opening 2001). If boarding a ferry at Durrës allow plenty of time.

KRUJA
☎ 0532

In the 12th century, Kruja was the capital of the Principality of Arberit, but this hill-top town attained its greatest fame between 1443 and 1468 when national hero George Kastrioti (1405-68), also known as Skënderbeg, made Kruja his seat.

At a young age, Kastrioti, son of an Albanian prince, was handed over as a hostage to the Turks, who converted him to Islam and gave him a military education at Edirne. There he became known as Iskënder (after Alexander the Great) and Sultan Murat II promoted him to the rank of bey (governor), thus the name Skënderbeg.

In 1443 the Turks suffered a defeat at the hands of the Hungarians at Niš, giving the nationally minded Skënderbeg the opportunity he had been waiting for to abandon Islam and the Ottoman army and rally his fellow Albanians against the Turks. Among the 13 Turkish invasions he subsequently repulsed was that led by Murat II himself in 1450. Pope Calixtus III named Skënderbeg 'captain general of the Holy See' and Venice formed an alliance with him. The Turks besieged Kruja four times. Though beaten back in 1450, 1466 and 1467, they took control of Kruja in 1478 (after Skënderbeg's death) and Albanian resistance was suppressed.

Kruja is 6.5km off the main road to Tirana, and was visited for its crucial historical importance and striking location 608m up on the side of a mountain.

Northern Albania

Visits to northern Albania should be avoided until the security situation has stabilised since banditry and violence plagues the area. Above all, never drive at night.

Visits to the north usually took in only the coastal strip, but a journey into the interior is well worthwhile for the marvellous scenery. Between Puka and Kukës the road winds through 60km of spectacular mountains.

Shkodra, the old Gheg capital near the lake of the same name, is a pleasant introduction to Albania for those arriving from Montenegro. South of here is Lezha and Skënderbeg's tomb.

SHKODRA
☎ 0224 • pop 81,000

Shkodra (also Shkodër and, in Italian, Scutari), the traditional centre of the Gheg cultural region, is one of the oldest cities in Europe. In 500 BC an Illyrian fortress already guarded the strategic crossing just west of the city where the Buna and Drin rivers meet and all traffic moving up the coast from Greece to Montenegro must pass. These rivers drain two of the Balkans' largest lakes: Shkodra, just north-west of the city, and Ohrid, far up the Drin River, beyond several massive hydro-electric dams. The route inland to Kosova also begins in Shkodra. North of Shkodra, line after line of cement bunkers point the way to the Han i Hotit border crossing into Montenegro (33km). Tirana is 116km south.

Queen Teuta's Illyrian kingdom was based here in the 3rd century BC. Despite wars with Rome in 228 and 219 BC, Shkodra was not taken by the Romans until 168 BC. Later the region passed to Byzantium before becoming the capital of the feudal realm of the Balshas in 1350. In 1396 the Venetians occupied Shkodra's Rozafa Fortress, which they held against Suleiman Pasha in 1473 but lost to Mehmet Pasha in 1479. The Turks lost 14,000 men in the first siege and 30,000 in the second.

As the Ottoman empire declined in the late 18th century, Shkodra became the centre of a semi-independent pashalik, which led to a blossoming of commerce and crafts. In 1913, Montenegro attempted to annex Shkodra (it succeeded in taking Ulcinj), but this was not recognised by the international community and the town changed hands often during WWI. Badly damaged by the 1979 earthquake, Shkodra was subsequently repaired and now, with a population of 81,000, is Albania's fourth-largest city.

Rozafa Fortress

Two kilometres south-west of Shkodra, near the southern end of Lake Shkodra, is the Rozafa Fortress, founded by the Illyrians in antiquity and rebuilt much later by the Venetians and Turks. From the highest point there's a marvellous view on all sides.

The fortress derived its name from a woman named Rozafa, who was allegedly walled into the ramparts as an offering to the gods so that the construction would stand. The story goes that Rozafa asked that two holes be left in the stonework so that she could continue to suckle her baby. Nursing women still come to the fortress to smear their breasts with milky water taken from a spring here.

KUKËS
☎ 10 (operator)

Kukës has perhaps the most beautiful location of any town in Albania, set high above Lake Fierza below the bald summit of Mt Gjalica (2486m). Old Kukës formerly stood at the junction of two important rivers, the White Drin from Kosova and the Black Drin from Lake Ohrid, but from 1962 the town was moved to its present location when it was decided that the 72-sq-km reservoir of the 'Light of the Party' hydroelectric dam would cover the old site.

Southern Albania

The south of the country is rich in historical and natural beauty. Apollonia and Butrint are renowned classical ruins, while Berat and Gjirokastra are museum towns and strongholds of Tosk tradition. Saranda, on the Ionian Sea, is an undeveloped resort town.

South-east of the vast, agricultural Myza-qeja plain, the land becomes extremely mountainous, with lovely valleys such as those of the Osum and Drino Rivers, where Berat and Gjirokastra are situated. The 124km of Ionian coast north from Saranda to Vlora are stunning, with 2000m mountains falling directly to the sea.

FIER & APOLLONIA
☎ 0642

Fier is a large town by the Gjanica River at a junction of road and rail routes, 89km south of Durrës. Albania's oil industry is centred at Fier, with a fertiliser plant, an oil refinery and a thermal power plant fuelled by natural gas. Fier has a pleasant riverside promenade as well as the imposing 13th-century Orthodox Monastery of St Mary, with wonderful icons inside, and a rich archaeological museum.

By far the most interesting sight in the vicinity is the ruins of ancient Apollonia (Pojan), 12km west of Fier, set on a hill top surrounded by impressive bunkers. Apollonia was founded by Corinthian Greeks in 588 BC and quickly grew into an important city-state, minting its own currency. Under the Romans the city became a great cultural centre with a famous school of philosophy.

Julius Caesar rewarded Apollonia with the title 'free city' for supporting him against Pompey the Great during a civil war in the 1st century BC, and sent his nephew Octavius, the future Emperor Augustus, to complete his studies there. After a series of military disasters, the population moved south to present-day Vlora (the ancient Avlon), and by the 5th century only a small village with its own bishop remained at Apollonia.

Only a small part of ancient Apollonia has so far been uncovered.

VLORA
☎ 063

Vlora (Vlorë), the main port of southern Albania, sits on lovely Vlora Bay just across an 80km strait from Otranto, Italy. Inexpensive ferries run between these towns three times a week, making Vlora a useful gateway to/from southern Italy (see Getting There & Away earlier in this chapter). This is probably the only real reason to come here as Vlora's own attractions don't warrant a special trip.

SARANDA
☎ 10 (operator)

Saranda (Sarandë) is a town on the Gulf of Saranda, between the mountains and the Ionian Sea, 61km south-west of Gjirokastra. An early Christian monastery dedicated to 40 saints (Santi Quaranta) gave Saranda its name. This southernmost harbour of Albania was once the ancient port of Onchesmos. Saranda's pebble beach is nothing special, although the setting of the town is quite appealing. Saranda's main attractions are its sunny climate and the nearby ruins of Butrint. It is also a useful entry and exit point for travellers arriving in Albania via Corfu in Greece.

Blue Eye Spring

The Blue Eye spring, 15km east of Saranda, to the left off the Gjirokastra road and before the ascent over the pass to the Drino valley, is definitely worth seeing. Its iridescent blue water gushes from the depths of the earth and feeds the Bistrica River. French divers have descended to 70m, but the spring's actual depth is still unknown.

BUTRINT

The ancient ruins of Butrint, 18km south of Saranda, are surprisingly extensive and interesting. Virgil claimed that the Trojans founded Buthroton (Butrint), but no evidence of this has been found. Although the site had been inhabited long before, Greeks from Corfu settled on the hill in Butrint in the 6th century BC. Within a century Butrint had become a fortified trading city with an acropolis. The lower town began to develop in the 3rd century BC and many large stone buildings existed when the Romans took over in 167 BC.

Butrint's prosperity continued throughout the Roman period and the Byzantines made it an ecclesiastical centre. Then the city declined; it was almost abandoned when Italian archaeologists arrived in 1927 and began carting off any relics of value to Italy until WWII interrupted their work. Some of these have been returned to Tirana's National Museum of History.

The government is planning to make Butrint into a national park, with a 25-sq-km zone around the site and a visitor's centre.

GJIROKASTRA
☎ 0726

This strikingly picturesque museum town, midway between Fier and Ioannina, is like an Albanian eagle perched on the mountainside with a mighty citadel for its head. The fortress surveys the Drino Valley above the three- and four-storey tower houses clinging to the slopes. Both buildings and streets are made of the same white-and-black stone. For defence purposes during blood feuds, these unique stone-roofed houses (*kulla*) were designed with no windows on the ground floor; this level was used for storage, and the living quarters above were reached by an exterior stairway.

The town's Greek name, Argyrokastro, is said to refer to a Princess Argyro, who chose to throw herself from a tower rather than fall into the hands of enemies. However, it's more likely to be derived from the Illyrian Argyres tribe which inhabited these parts.

Gjirokastra was well established by the 13th century, but the arrival of the Turks in 1417 brought on a decline. By the 17th century Gjirokastra was thriving again with a flourishing bazaar where embroidery, felt, silk and the still-famous white cheese were traded. Ali Pasha Tepelena took the town in the early 19th century and strengthened the citadel. Today, all new buildings must conform to a historical preservation plan.

BERAT
☎ 062

Berat, Albania's second most important museum town, is sometimes called the 'city of a thousand windows' for the many openings in the white-plastered, red-roofed houses on terraces overlooking the Osum River. Along a ridge high above the gorge is a 14th-century citadel that shelters small Orthodox churches. On the slope below this, all the way down to the river, is Mangalem, the old Muslim quarter. A seven-arched stone bridge (1780) leads to Gorica, the Christian quarter.

In the 3rd century BC an Illyrian fortress called Antipatria was built here on the site of an earlier settlement. The Byzantines strengthened the hill-top fortifications in the 5th and 6th centuries, as did the Bulgarians 400 years later. The Serbs, who occupied the citadel in 1345, renamed it Beligrad, or 'White City', which has become today's Berat. In 1450 the Ottoman Turks took Berat. The town revived in the 18th and 19th centuries as a Turkish crafts centre specialising in woodcarving. For a brief time in 1944, Berat was the capital of liberated Albania. Today, most of Albania's crude oil is extracted from wells just north-west of the city, but Berat itself is a textile town with a mill once known as Mao Zedong.

ELBASAN
☎ 0545 • pop 83,000

Elbasan is on the Shkumbin River, midway between Durrës and Pogradec and 54km south-east of Tirana. It has been prominent since 1974, when the Chinese built the mammoth 'Steel of the Party' steel mill. It also has a cement factory and burgeoning pollution, though the old town retains a certain charm. With 83,000 inhabitants, Elbasan is Albania's third-largest city, having more than doubled in size since 1970.

The Romans founded Skampa (Elbasan) in the 1st century AD as a stopping point on the Via Egnatia. Stout stone walls with 26 towers were added in the 4th century to protect against invading barbarians. The Byzantines continued this trend, also making Skampa the seat of a bishopric. In 1466, Sultan Mohammed II rebuilt the walls as a check against Skënderbeg at Kruja and renamed the town El Basan ('The Fortress' in Turkish). Elbasan was an important trade and handicrafts centre throughout the Turkish period.

Andorra

The principality of Andorra, nestled in the Pyrenees mountains between France and Spain, covers an area of just 464 sq km. Although tiny, this political anomaly is at the heart of some of Europe's most dramatic scenery. It's also a budget skiing venue and duty-free shopping haven. These activities, together with great summer walking, attract over eight million visitors a year and bring not only wealth but some unsightly development around the capital of Andorra la Vella.

From the middle ages until as recently as 1993, Andorra's sovereignty was invested in two 'princes': the Catholic bishop of the Spanish town of La Seu d'Urgell and the French president (who inherited the job from France's pre-Revolutionary kings). Nowadays, democratic Andorra is a 'parliamentary co-princedom', the bishop and president remaining joint but largely nominal heads of state. Andorra is a member of the United Nations and the Council of Europe, but not a full member of the EU.

Andorrans form only about a quarter of the total population of 66,000, and are outnumbered by Spaniards. The official language is Catalan, which is related to both Spanish and French. Most people speak a couple of these languages and sometimes all three, while younger people, especially in the capital and ski resorts, manage more than a smattering of English also.

AT A GLANCE

Capital	Andorra la Vella
Population	66,000
Official Language	Catalan
Currency	1 French franc (FF) = 100 centimes 1 peseta (pta) = 100 centimos
Time	GMT/UTC+0100
Country Phone Code	☎ 376

Andorra la Vella pp96-97

Facts for the Visitor

VISAS & DOCUMENTS

Visas aren't necessary; the authorities figure that if Spain or France let you in, that's good enough for them – but bring your passport or national ID card with you.

EMBASSIES & CONSULATES

Andorra has embassies in France and Spain, both of whom have reciprocal diplomatic missions in Andorra.

MONEY

Andorra uses the Spanish peseta (ptas) and the French franc (FF) and, like both countries, will use the euro from 2002. It's best to use pesetas – the exchange rate for francs in shops and restaurants is seldom in your favour. See the France and Spain chapters for exchange rates.

POST & COMMUNICATIONS
Post

Andorra has no postal system of its own; France and Spain each operate separate systems with their own Andorran stamps, which

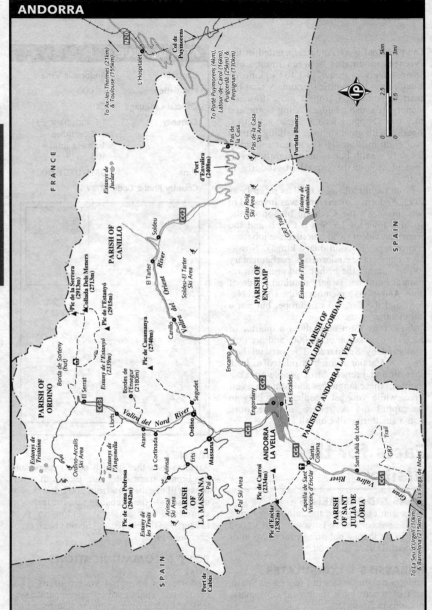

ANDORRA

are needed only for international mail, ie, letters within the country are delivered free. Regular French and Spanish stamps cannot be used in Andorra.

It's usually swifter to route international mail (except letters to Spain) through the French postal system.

Telephone

Andorra's country code is ☎ 376. The cheapest way to make an international call is to buy a *teletarja* (phonecard, sold for 500 ptas, 900 ptas and 1350 ptas at tourist offices and kiosks) and ring off-peak (9 pm to 7 am plus all day Sunday). At these times a three-minute call to Europe costs 210 ptas (306 ptas to the US or Australia). You can't make a reverse-charge (collect) call from Andorra.

Email & Internet Access

Log on at Punt Internet on the 5th floor of Carrer Bonaventura 39, very near the bus station (1000 ptas per hour). It is open 10 am to 1 pm and 3.30 to 9 pm weekdays, and 4 to 8 pm Saturday in August and September.

TIME

Andorra is one hour ahead of GMT/UTC in winter (two hours ahead from the last Sunday in March to the last Sunday in September).

BUSINESS HOURS

Shops in Andorra la Vella are generally open 9.30 am to 1 pm and 3.30 to 8 pm daily, except (usually) Sunday afternoon.

ACTIVITIES

Above the main valleys, you'll find attractive lake-dotted mountain country, good for skiing in winter and walking in summer. The largest and best ski resorts are Soldeu-El Tarter and Pas de la Casa/Grau Roig. The others – Ordino-Arcalís, Arinsal and Pal – are a bit cheaper but often colder and windier. Ski passes cost 2800 ptas to 4200 ptas a day, depending on location and season; downhill ski-gear is 1200 ptas to 1600 ptas a day, and snowboards are 2500 ptas to 3000 ptas.

Tourist offices have a useful English-language booklet, *Sport Activities*, describing numerous hiking and mountain-bike

routes. In summer, mountain bikes can be rented in some resorts for around 2800 ptas a day.

ACCOMMODATION

Tourist offices stock a comprehensive free brochure, *Hotels, Restaurants, Apartaments i Cámpings*. Be warned, however, that the prices it quotes are merely indicative.

There are no youth hostels and, outside Andorra la Vella, few budget options for independent travellers. In compensation, there are plenty of camping grounds, many beautifully situated. In high season (December to March and July/August), some hotels put prices up substantially and others don't take in independent travellers.

For walkers, Andorra has 26 off-the-beaten-track *refugis* (mountain refuges), all except one unstaffed and free. If you're trekking, invest 200 ptas in the *Mapa de Refugis i Grans Recorreguts*, which pinpoints and describes them all.

Getting There & Away

The only way to reach Andorra, unless you trek across the mountains, is by road.

FRANCE

Autocars Nadal (☎ 821138) has two buses a day (2750 ptas, four hours) on Monday, Wednesday, Friday and Sunday, linking Toulouse's Gare Routière (bus station) and Andorra la Vella.

By rail, take a train from Toulouse to either L'Hospitalet (2¼ to 2¾ hours, four daily) or Latour-de-Carol (2½ to 3¼ hours). Two daily connecting buses link Andorra la Vella with both L'Hospitalet (960 ptas) and Latour-de-Carol (1125 ptas). On Saturdays, up to five buses run from L'Hospitalet to Pas de la Casa, just inside Andorra.

SPAIN

Alsina Graells (☎ 827379) runs up to seven buses daily between Barcelona's Estació del Nord and Andorra la Vella's bus station (2435 ptas to 2715 ptas, four hours). Eurolines (☎ 860010) has four services daily (2800 ptas)

ANDORRA

between Andorra (departing from the car park of Hotel Diplomátic) and Barcelona's Sants bus station.

Samar/Andor-Inter (☎ 826289) operates three times weekly between Andorra and Madrid (4700 ptas, nine hours) via Zaragoza (2300 ptas).

La Hispano Andorrana (☎ 821372) has five to eight buses daily between La Seu d'Urgell, across the border, and Carrer Doctor Nequi in Andorra la Vella (345 ptas, 30 minutes).

Getting Around

BUS
Ask at a tourist office for a timetable of the eight bus routes, run by Cooperativa Interurbana (☎ 820412), which follow Andorra's three main highways.

Destinations from the Avinguda Príncep Benlloch stop in Andorra la Vella include Ordino (130 ptas, every half-hour), Arinsal (185 ptas, three daily), Soldeu (375 ptas,

hourly) and Pas de la Casa (620 ptas, daily at 9 am).

CAR & MOTORCYCLE
The speed limit is 40km/h in populated areas and 90km/h elsewhere. Two problems are the recklessness of local drivers on the tight, winding roads and Andorra la Vella's horrendous traffic jams. Bypass the worst of the latter by taking the ring road around the south side of town.

Petrol in Andorra is about 25% cheaper than in Spain or France.

Andorra la Vella

pop 23,300
Andorra la Vella (elevation 1029m) is squeezed into the Riu Gran Valira Valley and is mainly engaged in retailing electronic and luxury-goods. With the constant din of jackhammers and shopping-mall architecture, you might be in Hong Kong – but for the

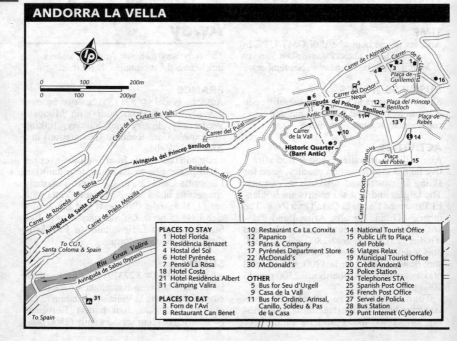

ANDORRA LA VELLA

PLACES TO STAY		10 Restaurant Ca La Conxita	14 National Tourist Office
1 Hotel Florida		12 Papanico	15 Public Lift to Plaça
2 Residència Benazet		13 Pans & Company	del Poble
3 Hostal del Sol		17 Pyrénées Department Store	16 Viatges Relax
6 Hotel Pyrénées		22 McDonald's	19 Municipal Tourist Office
7 Pensió La Rosa		30 McDonald's	20 Crèdit Andorrà
18 Hotel Costa			23 Police Station
21 Hotel Residència Albert		**OTHER**	24 Telephones STA
31 Càmping Valira		5 Bus for Seu d'Urgell	25 Spanish Post Office
		9 Casa de la Vall	26 French Post Office
PLACES TO EAT		11 Bus for Ordino, Arinsal,	27 Servei de Policía
3 Forn de l'Aví		Canillo, Soldeu & Pas	28 Bus Station
8 Restaurant Can Benet		de la Casa	29 Punt Internet (Cybercafe)

snowcapped peaks and an absence of noodle shops!

Orientation

Andorra la Vella is strung out along the main drag, whose name changes from Avinguda del Príncep Benlloch to Avinguda de Meritxell to Avinguda de Carlemany. The tiny historic quarter (Barri Antic) is split by this heavily trafficked artery. The town merges with the once-separate villages of Escaldes and Engordany to the east and Santa Coloma to the south-west.

Information

Tourist Offices The helpful municipal tourist office (☎ 827117) at Plaça de la Rotonda is open 9 am to 1 pm and 4 to 8 pm daily (to 7 pm on Sunday, continuously to 9 pm in July and August). It sells stamps and telephone cards.

The national tourist office (☎ 820214) is just off Plaça de Rebés. It's open 10 am (9 am from July to September) to 1 pm and 3

to 7 pm Monday to Saturday, plus Sunday morning.

Money Crèdit Andorrà, Avinguda Meritxell 80, has a 24-hour banknote exchange machine that accepts 15 currencies.

Banks, open 9 am to 1 pm and 3 to 5 pm weekdays and to noon Saturday, abound.

American Express is represented by Viatges Relax (☎ 822044), Carrer de Mossén Tremosa 2.

Post & Communications La Poste, the French post office, Carrer de Pere d'Urg 1, takes only French francs. Conversely, the Spanish post office, Correus i Telègrafs, Carrer de Joan Maragall 10, accepts only pesetas. Both are open 8.30 am to 2.30 pm weekdays and 9 am to noon Saturday.

You can make international calls from pay phones or from the Servei de Telecomunicacions d'Andorra (STA), Avinguda Meritxell 110, which also has a fax service. It's open 9 am to 9 pm daily.

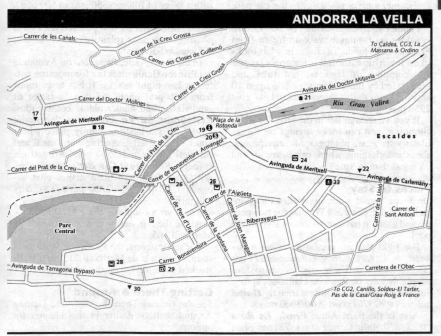

ANDORRA

Things to See & Do

The small **Barri Antic** (old quarter) was the heart of Andorra la Vella when the principality's capital was little more than a village. The narrow cobblestone streets around the **Casa de la Vall** are flanked by attractive stone houses.

Built in 1580 as a private home, the Casa de la Vall has served as Andorra's parliament building since 1702. Downstairs is **El Tribunal de Corts**, the country's only courtroom. Free guided tours (available in English) are given 9.30 am to 1 pm and 3 to 7 pm, Monday to Saturday (daily in August). In summer, book at least a week ahead (☎ 829129) to ensure a place – though individuals can often be squeezed in at the last minute.

The **Plaça del Poble**, a large public square just south of Plaça de Rebés occupies the roof of a modern government office building. Giving good views, it's a popular local gathering place, especially in the evening. The free public lift in the southeast corner whisks you away to the car park below.

Pamper yourself at **Caldea** (☎ 800995) in Escaldes, a 10-minute walk upstream from Plaça de la Rotonda. Enclosed in what looks like a futuristic cathedral is Europe's largest spa complex of lagoons, hot tubs and saunas, fed by thermal springs. It's open 10 am to 11 pm daily; three-hour tickets cost 2950 ptas.

If you've enough left in the kitty for some **shopping**, you can make savings on things like sports gear, photographic equipment, shoes and clothing, where prices are around 25% less than in Spain or France.

Places to Stay

Open year-round, *Camping Valira* on Avinguda de Salou charges 1575 ptas for two people and a tent. It has a small indoor swimming pool.

For 1400 ptas per person *Residència Benazet* (☎ 820698, Carrer la Llacuna 21) has large rooms with washbasin for up to four people. Nearby on Plaça de Guillemó, spruce singles/doubles with shower at friendly *Hostal del Sol* (☎ 823701) cost 2000/3900 ptas.

Also in the Barri Antic, *Pensió La Rosa* (☎ 821810, Antic Carrer Major 18) has plain singles/doubles for 2000/3500 ptas, plus triples, quads and a veritable dormitory sleeping six for 1500 ptas per person.

Hotel Costa (☎ 821439, 3rd floor, Avinguda de Meritxell 44) has basic but clean rooms for 1700/3000 ptas. *Hotel Residència Albert* (☎ 820156, Avinguda del Doctor Mitjavila 16) has recently had a face lift. Good value singles/doubles/triples, the majority with bathroom, cost 2700/4500/6000 ptas.

More upmarket, the delightful *Hotel Florida* (☎ 82 01 05, fax 86 19 25, @ aran@solucions.ad), one block from Plaça de Guillemó, has well-equipped singles/doubles for 5425/7850 ptas (6750/9500 ptas on weekends), including breakfast. At *Hotel Pyrénées* (☎ 86 00 06, fax 82 02 65, @ ph@mypic.ad), singles/doubles cost 5000/8250 ptas; you're required to take half-board in the high season.

Places to Eat

Pans & Company at Plaça de Rebés 2 and Avinguda de Meritxell 91 is good for baguettes with a range of fillings (350 ptas to 500 ptas). Just off Plaça de Guillemó, *Forn de l'Aví* has an excellent *menú* for 850 ptas and does good *platos combinados* (plentiful mixed dishes; 725 ptas to 850 ptas).

In the Barri Antic, *Papanico* on Avinguda del Príncep Benlloch is fun for morning coffee to late-night snacks. It has tasty *tapas* from 250 ptas each and does a range of sandwiches and hunky platos combinados. *Restaurant Ca La Conxita* (Placeta de Monjó 3) is a bustling family place where you can see staff preparing your meal and eat well for around 2500 ptas. Around the corner is *Restaurant Can Benet* (Antic Carrer Major 9) where main dishes cost between 1600 ptas and 2300 ptas, is equally delightful.

There are a couple of clone McDonald's – opposite the bus station and at Avinguda de Meritxell 105.

For self-caterers, the *Pyrénées* department store, Avinguda de Meritxell 21, has a well-stocked supermarket on the 2nd floor.

Getting There & Around

See the Getting There & Away and Getting Around sections earlier in this chapter for options.

Around Andorra la Vella

CANILLO & SOLDEU

Canillo, 11km east of Andorra la Vella, and Soldeu, a further 7km up the valley along the CG2, are as complementary as summer and winter.

In summer, Canillo offers canyon clambering, a *vía ferrata* climbing gully and climbing wall, the year-round Palau de Gel with ice rink and swimming pool, guided walks and endless possibilities for hiking (including an easy, signposted nature walk which follows the valley downstream from Soldeu). The helpful tourist office (☎ 851002) is on the main road at the east end of the village.

Particularly in winter, Soldeu and its smaller neighbour **El Tarter** come into their own as 23 lifts (including a cabin lift up from Canillo) connect 86km of runs with a vertical drop of 850m. The slopes, wooded in their lower reaches, are often warmer than Andorra's other more exposed ski areas and offer the Pyrenees' finest skiing and snowboarding. Lift passes for one/three days cost 3650/8580 ptas (low season) and 4200/10,050 ptas (high season).

Places to Stay

Year round, accommodation in Canillo is markedly less expensive than in Andorra La Vella. Of its five camping grounds, *Camping Santa Creu* (☎ 851462) is the greenest and quietest. *Hotel Casa Nostra* (☎ 851023) has simple rooms for 2500 ptas (3250 ptas with shower, 3750 ptas with full bathroom). *Hotel Pellissé* (☎ 851205, fax 85 18 75), just east of town, has quite decent singles/doubles for 2750/4400 ptas, while the *Hotel Canigó* (☎ 851024, fax 851824) provides comfortable singles/doubles at 3000/5000 ptas.

Places to Eat

On Soldeu's main drag, the cheerful *Hotel Bruxelles* restaurant does well-filled sandwiches (450 ptas to 575 ptas), whopping burgers and a tasty *menú* at 1175 ptas.

Entertainment

The music pounds on winter nights in Soldeu. *Pussy Cat* and its neighbour, *Fat Albert*, both

one block from the main drag, rock until far too late for impressive skiing next day. *Capital Discoteca* has free entry on Tuesday, Wednesday and weekends and is a busy dance hang-out.

Getting There & Around

Buses run from Andorra la Vella to El Tarter and Soldeu (375 ptas, 40 minutes, hourly) between 9 am to 8 pm. In winter there are free shuttle buses (just flash your ski pass) between Canillo and the two upper villages. These run approximately hourly (with a break from noon to 3 pm) until 11 pm.

All three villages are also on the bus route between Andorra la Vella and the French railheads of Latour-de-Carol and L'Hospitalet (see the main Getting There & Away section earlier in this chapter).

ORDINO & AROUND

Despite recent development, Ordino (population 1000), on highway CG3 8km north of Andorra la Vella, retains its Andorran character, with most building still in local stone. At 1000m it's a good starting point for summer activity holidays. The tourist office (☎ 737080), beside the CG3, is open 9 am to 1 pm and 3 to 7 pm daily (closed Sunday afternoon).

Things to See & Do

The **Museu d'Areny i Plandolit** (☎ 836908) is a 17th-century manor house with a richly furnished interior. Within the same grounds, is the far from nerdy **Museo Postal de Andorra**. It has an interesting 15-minute audiovisual program (available in English) and stamps by the thousand, issued by France and Spain specifically for Andorra (see Post & Communications earlier in this chapter). Admission to each museum costs 300 ptas. Both are open 9.30 am to 1.30 pm and 3 to 6.30 pm Tuesday to Saturday plus Sunday morning.

There are some excellent walking trails around Ordino. From the hamlet of **Segudet**, 500m east of Ordino, a path goes up through fir woods to the **Coll d'Ordino** (1980m), reached in about 1½ hours. **Pic de Casamanya** (2740m), with knock-me-down views is some two hours north of the col.

Other trails lead off from the tiny settlements beside the CG3 north of Ordino. A track (three hours one way) heads west from **Llorts** (1413m) up the Riu de l'Angonella Valley to a group of lakes, the **Estanys de l'Angonella** at about 2300m.

Just north of **El Serrat** (1600m), a secondary road leads 4km east to the **Borda de Sorteny** mountain refuge (1969m), from where trails lead into the high mountain area.

From **Arans** (1385m), a trail goes northeastwards to **Bordes de l'Ensegur** (2180m), where there's an old shepherd's hut.

Places to Stay & Eat

The cheapest option in the village is the cavernous *Hotel Casamanya* (☎ 835011), with singles/doubles for 4000/7000 ptas. *Bar Restaurant Quim* on the Plaça Major has a basic *menú* for 1350 ptas. Next door, *Restaurant Armengol* offers a *menú* for 1500 ptas and a good range of meat dishes.

Up the valley and some 200m north of Llorts, *Camping Els Pardassos* (☎ 850022) is one of Andorra's most beautiful camp sites. Open mid-June to mid-September, it charges 975 ptas for two people and a tent. Bring your own provisions. *Hotel Vilaró* (☎ 850225) 200m south of the village has rooms for 2200/2400 ptas.

Getting There & Away

Buses between Andorra la Vella and Ordino (130 ptas) run about every half-hour from 7 am to 9 pm daily. Buses to El Serrat (240 ptas) via Ordino leave Andorra la Vella at 1 and 8.30 pm. The valley is also served by four buses daily (10 in the ski season) linking Ordino and Arcalís.

ARINSAL

In winter, Arinsal, 10km north-west of Andorra la Vella, has good skiing and snow-boarding and a lively après-ski scene. There are 13 lifts (including a smart new cabin lift to hurtle you up from the village), 28km of pistes and a vertical drop of 1010m.

In summer, Arinsal is a good departure point for medium mountain walks. From Aparthotel Crest at Arinsal's northern extremity, a trail leads north-west then west to **Estany de les Truites** (2260m), a natural lake. The steepish walk up takes around 1½ hours. From here, it's about a further 1½ to two hours to bag **Pic de la Coma Pedrosa** (2964m), Andorra's highest point.

Places to Stay

Just above Estany de les Truites, *Refugi de Coma Pedrosa* (☎ 327955) is open June to late September, and charges 1100 ptas overnight. It does snacks and meals (dinner 1800 ptas).

The large, well equipped *Camping Xixerella* between Arinsal and Pal is open all year and has an outdoor swimming pool. Charges are 500 ptas to 600 ptas each per adult, tent and car.

In Arinsal, the recently renovated *Hostal Pobladó* (☎ 835122, fax 838 79, ✉ hospobl ado@andornet.ad) beside the new cabin lift is friendliness itself. With a lively bar (which offers Internet access on the side), its rooms cost 4400 ptas (6100 ptas with bathroom), including breakfast.

Places to Eat

As a change from the plentiful snack and sandwich joints, try *Refugi de la Fondue*, which does cheese or meat *fondue* dishes. *Restaurant el Moli* bills itself as Italian – and indeed offers the usual staple pastas and pizzas (both 900 ptas to 1200 ptas) – but also has more exotic fare such as pork stir fry (1575 ptas) and Thai green coconut chicken curry (1650 ptas). *Rocky Mountain* has a gringo menu with dishes such as T-bone steak and 'New York style cheesecake'.

Entertainment

In winter, Arinsal fairly throbs after sunset. In summer, it can be almost mournful. When the snow's around, call by *Surf* near the base of the cabin lift. A pub, dance venue and restaurant, it specialises in juicy Argentinian meat dishes (1250 ptas to 2200 ptas). *Quo Vadis* occasionally has live music.

Getting There & Away

Buses leave Andorra la Vella for Arinsal (185 ptas) via La Massana at 9.30 am, 1 and 6.15 pm. There are also more than 10 buses daily between La Massana and Arinsal. In winter, Skibus (325 ptas) runs five times daily between La Massana and Arinsal.

Bosnia-Hercegovina

Sandwiched between Croatia and Yugoslavia, the small mountainous country of Bosnia-Hercegovina has been a meeting point of east and west for nearly two millennia. Here the realm of Orthodox Byzantium mingled with Catholic Rome, and the 15th-century swell of Turkish power settled among the Slavs. This unique history created one of the most fascinating cultures in Europe, with a heterogeneous population of Croats, Serbs and Slavic converts to Islam.

In the 20th century Bosnia-Hercegovina had more than its share of strife. WWI was sparked in Sarajevo when a Serb nationalist assassinated an Austrian aristocrat, and much of the bitter partisan fighting of WWII took place in this region. Forty-five years of peace ensued, with Bosnia-Hercegovina the third-largest republic in Yugoslavia. This ended soon after Bosnia declared independence in October 1991. Six months later Bosnian Serb ultranationalists, assisted by Yugoslavia's federal army, began a campaign of ethnic cleansing intended to bring Bosnia-Hercegovina into Belgrade's orbit.

When the three-way war ended in 1995, it left the country physically devastated and ethnically divided. Out of a prewar population of four and a half million, over two million fled their former homes. Peace is currently enforced by 20,000 NATO troops, and a large international civilian presence is working to reintegrate and rebuild the country. Progress since peace has been substantial, but as a destination for visitors Bosnia-Hercegovina itself is unalterably changed.

Facts about Bosnia-Hercegovina

HISTORY

The ancient inhabitants of this region were Illyrians, followed by the Romans who settled around the mineral springs at Ilidža near Sarajevo. When the Roman Empire was divided in AD 395, the Drina River, today the border between Bosnia-Hercegovina and Yugoslavia,

---

AT A GLANCE

Capital	Sarajevo
Population	3.5 million
Official Language	Bosnian (Serbo-Croatian)
Currency	1 convertible mark (KM) = 100 convertible pfennigs
Time	GMT/UTC+0100
Country phone code	☎ 387

The Two 'Entities' of Bosnia-Hercegovina p104

Sarajevo p111

Mostar p118

Medugorje p120

---

became the line that divided the Western Roman Empire from Byzantium.

The Slavs arrived in the late 6th and early 7th centuries. In 960 the area became independent of Serbia, only to pass through the hands of other conquerors: Croatia, Byzantium, Duklja (modern-day Montenegro) and Hungary. The first Turkish raids came in 1383 and by 1463 Bosnia was a Turkish province with Sarajevo as its capital. Hercegovina is named after Herceg (Duke) Stjepan Vukčić, who ruled the southern portion of the present republic from his mountaintop castle

WARNING

! ● Landmines

Over one million landmines are estimated to be in Bosnia-Hercegovina. These were laid mostly in conflict zones. All of Sarajevo's suburbs are heavily mined, as are areas around Travnik and Mostar. The most frightening statistic is that only about half of Bosnia-Hercegovina's minefields are in known locations. The Mine Action Centre in Sarajevo (☎ 033-201 298/299, fax 667 311) runs valuable 1½-hour mine information briefings, which are open to visitors.

Unexploded ordinances (UXOs, mortars, grenades and shells) also pose a huge danger around former conflict areas.

The golden rule for mines and UXOs is to stick to asphalt surfaces. Abandoned-looking areas are avoided for a reason. Do not drive off the shoulder of roads, do not poke around in abandoned villages or damaged houses, do not get curious about shiny metal objects on the grass, and regard every centimetre of ground as suspicious.

at Blagaj near Mostar until the Turkish conquest in 1468.

During 400 years of Turkish rule, Bosnia-Hercegovina was completely assimilated and became the boundary between the Islamic and Christian worlds. Wars against Venice and Austria were frequent. Many inhabitants converted to Islam, and the region still forms a Muslim enclave deep within Christian Europe.

As the Ottoman Empire weakened in the 16th and 17th centuries, the Turks strengthened their hold on Bosnia-Hercegovina as an advance bulwark of their empire. The national revival movements of the mid-19th century led to a reawakening among the South Slavs, and in 1875-76 there were peasant uprisings against the Turks in Bosnia-Hercegovina and Bulgaria. In 1878 Turkey suffered a crushing defeat by Russia in a war over Bulgaria, and it was decided at the Congress of Berlin that same year that Austria-Hungary would occupy Bosnia-Hercegovina. However, the population desired autonomy and had to be brought under Habsburg rule by force.

Resentment against foreign occupation intensified in 1908 when Austria annexed Bosnia-Hercegovina outright. The assassination of the Habsburg heir Archduke Franz Ferdinand by a Bosnian Serb at Sarajevo on 28 June 1914 led Austria to declare war on Serbia one month later. When Russia supported Serbia, and Germany came to the aid of Austria, the world was soon at war.

Following WWI, Bosnia-Hercegovina was taken into the Serb-dominated Kingdom of the Serbs, Croats, and Slovenes (renamed Yugoslavia in 1929). In 1941 the Axis powers annexed Bosnia-Hercegovina to the fascist Croatian state, but the area's mountains quickly became a wartime partisan stronghold. A conference in 1943 in Jajce laid the ground for post-war Yugoslavia, and after the war Bosnia-Hercegovina was granted republic status within Yugoslavia.

In the republic's first free elections in November 1990, the communists were easily defeated by nationalist Serb and Croat parties and by a predominantly Muslim party favouring a multiethnic Bosnia-Hercegovina.

The Croat and Muslim parties united against the Serb nationalists, and independence from Yugoslavia was declared on 15 October 1991. Serb parliamentarians withdrew and set up a government of their own at Pale, the village 20km east of Sarajevo where the 1984 Winter Olympics took place. Bosnia-Hercegovina was recognised internationally and admitted to the UN, but this over-hasty recognition caused talks between the parties to break down.

The War

War broke out in April 1992, shortly after Bosnian Serb snipers in the Sarajevo Holiday Inn opened fire on unarmed civilians demonstrating for peace in Sarajevo, killing a dozen people.

The Serbs had inherited almost the entire arms stock of the Yugoslav National Army (JNA). As had been done in Croatia they began seizing territory with the support of some of the 50,000 JNA troops in Bosnia-Hercegovina. Sarajevo came under siege by Serb irregulars on 5 April 1992 and shelling by Serb artillery began soon after. Directed from nearby Pale, the brutal siege was to leave over 10,000 civilians dead and the city ravaged before it ended in summer 1995.

BOSNIA-HERCEGOVINA

Glina
CROATIA
Slavonski Brod
Vinkovci
VOJVODINA
Sava
River
Županja
Bosanski Novi
Prijedor
Orašje
Derventa
Brčko
Bijeljina
Drina River
Bihać
Doboj
Banja Luka
Tuzla
SERBIA
Zvornik
Bosna River
Jajce
Travnik
Zenica
Srebrenica
Knin
Kupres
Žepa
SARAJEVO
Ilidža
Pale
Višegrad
CROATIA
Konjić
Bjelašnica (2067m)
Jahorina (1913m)
Goražde
Šibenik
Jablanica
Neretva River
Foča
Split
YUGOSLAVIA
Brač
Mostar
Hvar
Međugorje
Blagaj
Počitelj
MONTENEGRO
Ploče
Neum
Nikšić
Korčula
Trebinje
Mljet
Dubrovnik
ADRIATIC SEA
Herceg-Novi
Podgorica

0 25 50km
0 15 30mi

BOSNIA-HERCEGOVINA

Serb forces began a campaign of 'ethnic cleansing', brutally expelling the Muslim population from northern and eastern Bosnia to create a 300km corridor joining Serb ethnic areas in the west of Bosnia and in Serbia proper. Villages were terrorised and looted, and homes were destroyed to prevent anyone from returning. Crowning their campaign of ethnic cleansing, the Serbs set up concentration camps for Muslims and Croats and initiated the mass atrocities which were a devastating feature of this war.

In August 1992 the UN Security Council authorised the use of force to ensure delivery of humanitarian relief supplies, and by September 7500 UN troops were in Bosnia-Hercegovina. However, this UN Protection Force (UNPROFOR) was notorious for its impotence, which was dramatically displayed in January 1993 when the vice-premier of Bosnia-Hercegovina, Hakija Turajlić, was pulled out of a UN armoured personnel carrier at a Serb checkpoint and killed in front of French peacekeepers.

By mid-1993, with Serb 'ethnic cleansing' almost complete, the UN proposed setting up 'safe areas' for Muslims around five Bosnian cities, including Sarajevo. The Serbs, confident that the West would not intervene, continued their siege of Sarajevo.

The Vance-Owen peace plan, which would have divided Bosnia-Hercegovina into 10 ethnically based provinces, was rejected by Serb leaders in 1993. Nonetheless, the plan's formulation seemed to confirm to all sides that Bosnia's fate lay in ethnic partition.

The Croats wanted their own slice of Bosnia-Hercegovina. The Croatian Community of Herceg-Bosna was set up in July 1992, and in March 1993 fighting erupted between Muslims and Croats. The Croats instigated a deadly mini-siege of the Muslim quarter of Mostar, which culminated in the destruction of Mostar's historic old bridge in 1993.

In May 1993 Croatian president Franjo Tudjman made a bid for a 'Greater Croatia' by making a separate deal with the Bosnian Serbs to carve up Bosnia-Hercegovina between themselves. This was foiled by the renewed strength of the Bosnian army, and fighting between Muslims and Croats intensified.

NATO finally began taking action against the Bosnian Serbs. After a Serb mortar attack on a Sarajevo market in February 1994 left 68 dead and 200 injured, NATO's threatened air strikes cowed the Bosnian Serbs into withdrawing their guns temporarily from around the city.

US fighters belatedly began enforcing the no-fly zone over Bosnia by shooting down four Serb aircraft in February 1994 (the first actual combat in NATO's 45-year history). Two months later NATO aircraft carried out their first air strikes against Bosnian Serb ground positions after the Serbs advanced on a UN 'protected area'. When a British plane was shot down, the NATO raids quickly ceased.

Meanwhile, at talks held in Washington in March 1994, the US pressured the Bosnian government to join the Bosnian Croats in a federation. Worried about Serb enclaves on its own soil, Croatia went on the offensive in May 1995 and rapidly overran Croatian Serb positions and towns in western Slavonia, within Croatia.

With Croatia now heavily involved, a pan-Balkan war seemed closer than ever. Again, Bosnian Serb tanks and artillery attacked Sarajevo, again UN peacekeepers requested NATO air strikes. When air strikes to protect Bosnian 'safe areas' were finally authorised,

the Serbs captured 300 UNPROFOR peacekeepers and chained them to potential targets to keep the planes away.

In July 1995 Bosnian Serbs attacked the safe area of Srebrenica, slaughtering an estimated 6000 Muslim men as they fled through the forest. This was the largest massacre in the war, and highlighted the futility of the UN presence.

Nonetheless, the twilight of Bosnian Serb military dominance was at hand. European leaders called loudly for strong action not just to try once more to defend the Bosnians but to defeat the Bosnian Serbs. Croatia renewed its own internal offensive, expelling Serbs from the Krajina region.

With Bosnian Serbs finally on the defensive and battered by two weeks of NATO air strikes in September 1995, US president Bill Clinton's proposal for new peace talks was accepted.

The Dayton Accord

The peace conference in Dayton, Ohio, USA, began in November 1995 and the final agreement was signed in Paris in December.

The Dayton agreement stated that the country would retain its prewar external boundaries, but would be composed of two parts or 'entities'. The Federation of Bosnia-Hercegovina (the Muslim and Croat portion)

THE TWO ENTITIES OF
BOSNIA-HERCEGOVINA

○ ZAGREB

☐ Muslim-Croat Federation

▨ Republika Srpska

● Prijedor   **Posavina Corridor**

● Bihać   Sanski Most ●   ● Banja Luka   Brčko ●

Tuzla

Travnik

CROATIA   SARAJEVO ○ ● Pale

● Goražde

● Split   Mostar ●

● Medugorje

ADRIATIC SEA   YUGOSLAVIA

0   50   100km
0   30   60mi   Dubrovnik

ALBANIA

would administer 51% of the country, including Sarajevo, and the Serb Republic of Bosnia-Hercegovina 49%. The latter is commonly referred to as the Republika Srpska (RS). Eastern and western portions of the RS would be linked together by the narrow Posavina Corridor in the north-east. Brčko, situated in the narrowest part of the corridor, was so contentious that its final fate was left up to international arbitration, whose eventual decision was to give it multiethnic status.

The agreement also emphasised the rights of refugees to return to their prewar homes. This was relevant for both the 1.2 million people who sought refuge in other countries (including Yugoslavia and Croatia), and the one million people who were displaced within Bosnia-Hercegovina during the ethnic cleansing process.

A NATO-led peace implementation force, IFOR, was installed as the military force behind the accords. IFOR's 60,000 international troops gave way in January 1997 to the 20,000-strong Stabilisation Force (SFOR), whose current mandate has no definite time limit.

The Dayton accords also emphasised the powers of the War Crimes Tribunal in the Hague, which had been established in 1993. NATO was given the authority to arrest indicted war criminals. Initially action on this was slow, but recently the momentum of arrests has increased. Thus far over 40 have been brought to the Hague, though the most-wanted war criminals, Bosnian Serb leader Radovan Karadžić and his military henchman Ratko Mladić, remain at large.

After Dayton

In early 1996 Bosnian, Serb and Croat forces withdrew to the agreed lines, and NATO-led IFOR took up positions between them. Karadžić stepped down from the RS presidency in July 1996, after the international community threatened to reintroduce sanctions against the Serbs if he did not quit public office. Seemingly unfazed, Karadžić continued to wield behind-the-scenes influence, even as his successor Biljana Plavsić took over as the RS president.

Bosnia-Hercegovina's first post-war national elections in September 1996 essentially shored up the existing leadership. Municipal elections scheduled for the same time were postponed for one year while the international community, which supervised the elections, ironed out the logistics of allowing people to vote in their prewar municipalities. When municipal elections finally took place in September 1997, exiled leaders were elected in several towns, notably Muslims in Serb-controlled Srebrenica and Prijedor and Serbs in Croat-controlled Drvar.

Meanwhile Plavsić, wooed by western support and ostensibly concerned about corruption, split from the hardline Karadžić during summer 1997. The RS itself seemed to be splintering along these lines, with the Pale-based eastern RS backing Karadžić and Plavsić's domain in Banja Luka-based western RS becoming more open. Banja Luka emerged triumphant from the struggle and took over from Pale as the RS capital in January 1998.

Western hopes were given a further boost in January 1998 when a new, relatively liberal Bosnian Serb prime minister, Milorad Dodik came to power. Dodik quickly pushed several measures through the RS parliament aimed at compliance with Dayton, including a common license plate (that would no longer be entity-specific), common passports and a new common currency called the convertible mark. A new national flag was approved just in time for the 1998 Winter Olympic Games.

Bosnia-Hercegovina today remains divided along ethnic lines. However, Muslim-Croat tensions have ebbed, and more people are now crossing between the RS and the Federation. Many of the country's towns are physically destroyed, although a US$5.1 billion reconstruction program is underway. A further hopeful sign was the selection of the first multiethnic team for the Sydney 2000 Olympics.

GEOGRAPHY

Bosnia-Hercegovina is a mountainous country of 51,129 sq km on the west side of the Balkan Peninsula, almost cut off from the sea by Croatia. Most of the country's rivers flow north into the Sava; only the Neretva cuts south from Jablanica through the Dinaric Alps to Ploče on the Adriatic Sea. Bosnia-Hercegovina contains over 30 mountain peaks from 1700m to 2386m high.

CLIMATE

Since Bosnia-Hercegovina is a mountainous country, it gets hot in summer but quite chilly in winter, and snowfall can last until April.

GOVERNMENT & POLITICS

The Dayton Accords stipulate that the central government be headed by a rotating three-person presidency, with one elected by the Serb Republic and the others, a Muslim and a Croat, by the Federation. The House of Peoples is selected from the legislatures of the two entities and a House of Representatives directly elected by each entity. Two-thirds of each house is from the Federation, one-third from the Serb Republic, and a Council of Ministers is responsible for carrying out government policies and decisions.

Despite ideals of a central government in Sarajevo, each individual division of Bosnia-Hercegovina maintains an essentially separate administration. Few of the ethnically joint institutions called for by the Dayton agreement are functioning, even between Muslims and Croats within the Federation.

In lieu of some local cooperation, Bosnia-Hercegovina is essentially ruled by the West, which has taken an increasingly firm hand in forcing the parties to come to decisions together. The international community's High Representative received stronger powers at a conference in Bonn in December 1997 and began dismissing obstructionist officials.

In the April 2000 local elections a multi-ethnic party made some gains, although voting on nationalist lines was still predominant.

ECONOMY

Bosnia-Hercegovina was one of the poorest regions of Yugoslavia, its economy driven by mining, hydroelectricity and timber. War brought virtually all activity to a halt. The situation is now gradually improving, though the unemployment rate remains very high.

The Republika Srpska, which initially received less international assistance, is significantly poorer than the Federation.

POPULATION & PEOPLE

Before the war, Bosnia-Hercegovina's population stood at around four million. In 1991 the largest cities were Sarajevo (525,980), Banja Luka (195,139), Zenica (145,577), Tuzla (131,861) and Mostar (126,067). The massive population shifts have changed the size of many cities, swelling the population of Banja Luka to 239,000 and initially shrinking Sarajevo and Mostar, though the former has recently been growing again and its population now stands at around 500,000.

Bosnia-Hercegovina's prewar population was incredibly mixed, but ethnic cleansing has concentrated Croats in Hercegovina (to the south), Muslims in Sarajevo and central Bosnia, and Serbs in areas adjacent to Yugoslavia.

Serbs, Croats and Bosnian Muslims are all South Slavs of the same ethnic stock. Physically the three peoples are indistinguishable.

ARTS

Bosnia's best known writer is Ivo Andrić (1892-1975), winner of the 1961 Nobel Prize for Literature. His novels *The Travnik Chronicles* and *Bridge on the Drina*, both written during WWII, are fictional histories which deal with the intermingling of Islamic and Orthodox societies in the small Bosnian towns of Travnik and Višegrad.

SOCIETY & CONDUCT

Removing your shoes is customary in Muslim households; the host family will provide slippers. Bosnians are incredibly friendly, but when the subject turns to politics, the best strategy is listening. In general, Bosnians are understandably less interested in talking about the war than many foreign visitors are.

RELIGION

Before the war, Bosnia-Hercegovina's population was 43% Muslim Slavs, 31% Orthodox Serbs and 17% Catholic Croats. Of the current population of approximately 3.5 million, around 42% are Muslim, 37% Serb, and 15% Croat. The current proportions are roughly the same despite the population shifts. In each part of Bosnia-Hercegovina, churches and mosques are being built (or rebuilt) at lightning speed. This phenomenon is more a symptom of nationalism than of religion, since most people are fairly secular.

LANGUAGE

Notwithstanding different dialects, the people of Bosnia-Hercegovina basically speak the same language. However, that language is referred to as 'Bosnian' in the Muslim part of the Federation, 'Croatian' in Croat-controlled parts, and 'Serbian' in the RS. The Federation uses the Latin alphabet but the RS uses Cyrillic. See the Croatian, Serbian & Bosnian section of the Language chapter at the back of the book for pronunciation guidelines and useful words and phrases.

Facts for the Visitor

HIGHLIGHTS

Sarajevo is a major historic site, which is now recovering its vibrancy. Beautifully situated Mostar deserves a visit for its cobbled old town. Driving or taking the bus through the ravaged but slowly recovering countryside of Bosnia-Hercegovina is an unforgettable experience.

SUGGESTED ITINERARIES

Two days
  Visit Sarajevo
One week
  Visit Sarajevo and Mostar
Two weeks
  Visit Sarajevo, Mostar, Travnik and Banja Luka

PLANNING

When to Go

The best time to visit is spring or summer. Don't worry about a seasonal crush of tourists just yet.

Maps

Freytag & Berndt produces a good 1:250,000 road map of Bosnia-Hercegovina.

WHAT TO BRING

It's a myth that Bosnia-Hercegovina suffers from shortages. Shops sell goods imported from the rest of Europe, for which you usually have to pay in cash.

VISAS & DOCUMENTS

No visas are required for citizens of the USA, Canada, Ireland, the UK and most other EU countries. Citizens of other countries can obtain a tourist visa in advance by sending a personal cheque or money order for US$35, their passport, a copy of a round-trip plane ticket, an invitation letter, and an application to the nearest embassy.

Tourists in Bosnia are required to register with the local police. A hotel or accommodation agency will do this for you, but foreigners staying in private houses must do this themselves (in Sarajevo, try the Ministry of Internal Affairs office, Zmaja od Bosne 9, room 3).

EMBASSIES & CONSULATES

Bosnian Embassies & Consulates

The following are some of the countries in which Bosnia-Hercegovina has embassies and/or consulates; check the Web page www.bosnianembassy.org/offices for further listings.

Australia (☎ 02-9257 5798, fax 9257 7855) 15 State Circle, Forrest ACT 2603
Croatia (☎/fax 01-48 19 420/424) Pavla Hatza 3, 41000 Zagreb
France (☎ 01-426 734 22, fax 01-405 385 22) 174 Rue de Courcelles, 75017 Paris
Germany
  Consulate: (☎ 0228 365 911, fax 365 837) Buergerstrasse 12, 53173 Bonn
  Consulate: (☎ 030-802 3026, fax 802 2501) Albertinenstrasse 7 14165 Berlin
Slovenia
  Consulate: (☎ 061-159 1249, fax 159 2527) Celovska 199, Ljubljana
UK (☎ 020-7255 3758, fax 7255 2760) 320 Regent St, London W1R 5AB
USA (☎ 202-833 3612, fax 337 1502) 2109 E St NW, Washington DC 20037
  Consulate: (☎ 212-751 9015/16, fax 751 9019) 866 UN Plaza, Suite 580, New York NY 10017

Embassies & Consulates in Bosnia-Hercegovina

These embassies are in Sarajevo (area code ☎ 033):

Austria (☎ 668 337, fax 668 339) Džidžikovac 7
Bulgaria (☎ 668 191, fax 668 182) Trampina 14/2
Canada (☎ 447 900, fax 447 901) Logavina 7
Croatia (☎ 444 330, fax 472 434) Mehmeda Spahe 20
Czech Republic (☎/fax 447 525) Potoklinica 6
France (☎ 668 149, fax 668 103) Mehmed-bega K.Lj 18
Germany (☎ 275 000, fax 443 176) Mejtaš Buka 11-13
Hungary (☎ 208 353, fax 205 303) Armaganuša 32

Macedonia (☎/fax 206 004) Splitska 6
Netherlands (☎ 668 422, fax 668 423) Obala
  Kulina bana 4/2
Slovenia (☎ 447 660, fax 447 659) Bentbaša 7
UK (☎ 444 429, fax 666 131) Tina Ujevića 8
USA (☎ 659 992 or 445 700, fax 659 722)
  Alipašina 43

MONEY
Currency
At the time of writing, the 'convertible mark',
Bosnia's common currency, was tied to the
Deutschmark at a rate of 1KM to DM1.
Deutschmarks were accepted everywhere,
except in official institutions such as post of-
fices. When the euro is introduced in 2002,
Bosnia-Hercegovina intends to tie the con-
vertible mark to the euro.

Croatian kuna are currently accepted in the
Croatian parts of Bosnia, as are Serbian dinars
in the RS, but this should change fairly soon.
You may receive these in change, but there is
no problem paying in KM anywhere, and a polite request for change in KM should suffice.

Exchange Rates
Conversion rates for major currencies in mid-
2000 are listed below:

country	unit		convertible mark
Australia	A$1	=	1.28KM
Canada	C$1	=	1.46KM
euro	€1	=	1.96KM
France	10FF	=	2.98KM
Germany	DM1	=	1KM
Japan	¥100	=	1.99KM
NZ	NZ$1	=	0.98KM
UK	UK£1	=	3.23KM
US	US$1	=	2.15KM

For the most recent currency rates, point your
Web browser at www.xe.net/ucc/full.shtml.

Exchanging Money
ATMs (Visa only) are limited to Sarajevo.
Travellers cheques can be exchanged at
banks in most cities, except Banja Luka;
however, commissions are generally 3% and
above, on top of poor exchange rates.

Credit Cards
The Sarajevo offices of some western airlines
(Swissair and Austrian Airlines) accept major

credit cards, along with a smattering of hotels
in Sarajevo and Hercegovina. A few banks
can give credit card advances, but otherwise
the rule is cash cash cash.

Costs
Costs in Bosnia-Hercegovina haven't changed
substantially in recent times. In fact, the economy is quite stable, even if this situation has
been artificially maintained.

Tipping
Tipping is customary at nice restaurants – just
leave 5KM or so on the table, or round up the
bill. Taxi fares can be treated the same way.

POST & COMMUNICATIONS
Post
Bosnia's postal system works, but poste
restante is unavailable except at the post office in west Mostar.

Telephone & Fax
To call Bosnia-Hercegovina from abroad,
dial the international access code ☎ 387 (the
country code for Bosnia-Hercegovina), the
area code (without the initial zero) and the
number. If you are calling the Republika
Srpska, you may have more luck dialling
through Yugoslavia (☎ 381, then city code).

To make an international call from Bosnia-
Hercegovina, it's cheapest to go to the post
office. Dial the international access number
(00), then the country code and number. A
three-minute call to the USA costs 6KM.

Phone cards, useful for local or short international calls, can be purchased at post
offices. Note, however, that cards issued in
Serb, Croat, and Muslim-controlled areas are
not interchangeable.

Some important telephone numbers are
☎ 901 for international operator, ☎ 988 for
local directory information, ☎ 92 for police,
☎ 93 for the fire department, and ☎ 94 for
emergency assistance.

Faxes can be sent from most post offices,
though machines may be slow and prices
consequently high.

Email & Internet Access
Although email access is quite limited in
Bosnia-Hercegovina, it can be accessed cheaply
and easily from the university in Sarajevo.

INTERNET RESOURCES

For general background on the country try http://geog.gmu.edu/projects/bosnia/ to take a 'Bosnia Virtual Fieldtrip'. You can always visit the Web site of the Office of the High Representative (www.ohr.int) to get detailed news updates.

BOOKS

Noel Malcolm's *Bosnia: A Short History* is a good country-specific supplement to Rebecca West's mammoth classic *Black Lamb & Grey Falcon*, which exhaustively describes her 1930s trip through Yugoslavia. For a detailed account of the recent war, try *The Death of Yugoslavia* by Laura Silber & Allan Little, or *The Fall of Yugoslavia* by Misha Glenny. Zoë Brân's *After Yugoslavia*, part of the Lonely Planet Journeys series, retraces the author's 1978 trip through the former Yugoslavia.

NEWSPAPERS & MAGAZINES

All parts of Bosnia-Hercegovina have different papers. Sarajevo's independent daily *Oslobođenje* functioned throughout the war. *Dani*, the popular and outrageous bi-weekly magazine, keeps the Sarajevo government on its toes with colourful covers and entertaining political satire.

RADIO & TV

Studio 99 is both a television and a radio station; the latter carries some Radio Free Europe broadcasting. Radio Zid has some Voice of America news. Serb Radio Television (SRT) is broadcast out of Banja Luka.

PHOTOGRAPHY & VIDEO

Kodak and Fuji film is available in larger cities from 10KM up to 14KM a roll. It is quite common to take photographs of war damage, but use prudence and sensitivity.

TIME

Bosnia-Hercegovina is on Central European Time, which is GMT/UTC plus one hour. Daylight savings time in late March sets clocks forward one hour, but in late October clocks are turned back one hour.

HEALTH

Clinics with western doctors serve only international organisations. Visiting a Bosnian doctor costs about 10KM to 30KM. Make sure that your medical insurance plan includes evacuation from Bosnia-Hercegovina.

DANGERS & ANNOYANCES

Always look into local political conditions before undertaking a journey. In the Republika Srpska anti-western sentiments have in the past been reputed to run higher than in the Federation, but it is unlikely that you will be made to feel at all unwelcome. Some areas of Bosnia-Hercegovina are heavily mined (see Warning boxed text earlier in this chapter).

PUBLIC HOLIDAYS

Bosnia-Hercegovina observes Independence Day (1 March), May Day (1 May) and the Day of the Republic (25 November).

ACCOMMODATION

The year-round presence of international officials on expense accounts has jump-started Bosnia-Hercegovina's hotel industry. Both Sarajevo and Mostar have some pleasant new hotels but in general, prices are much higher than the typical socialist-style buildings warrant.

Pansions (pensions) and private accommodation agencies have sprouted in Sarajevo, but elsewhere (except for Međugorje, where every house is a pansion) there are few. The situation is changing quickly, so inquire at the tourist office. Or ask locals at the market or shops.

Private accommodation is usually very pleasant. Likely as not, your hosts will ply you with coffee, pull out old pictures of Tito (depending on their politics), and regale you with tales of Bosnia-Hercegovina's past glory.

Most accommodation attracts a tax of 2KM to 5KM, which is included in the prices listed in this chapter.

FOOD & DRINKS

Bosnia's Turkish heritage is savoured in its grilled meats such as *bosanski lonac* (Bosnian stew of cabbage and meat). When confronted with the ubiquitous *burek* (a layered meat pie sold by weight), vegetarians can opt for *sirnica* (cheese pie) or *zeljanica* (spinach pie). *Ćevapčići*, another favourite, is lamb and beef rolls tucked into a half-loaf of spongy somun bread. For sugar-soaked desserts, try baklava

BOSNIA-HERCEGOVINA

or *tufahije*, an apple cake topped with walnuts and whipped cream.

Good wines from Hercegovina include Žilavka (white) and Blatina (red). These are best sampled in the region's wineries. A meal can always be washed down with a shot of *šlivovica* (plum brandy) or *loza* (grape brandy).

Getting There & Away

AIR

Airlines serving Sarajevo include Croatia Airlines, Crossair (the partner of Swissair), Lufthansa and Austrian Airlines. Air Bosna flies to Belgrade, Istanbul, Vienna and several destinations in Germany.

LAND

In the virtual absence of international train lines (there's just one from Ploče, Croatia to Sarajevo), buses are an excellent, safe way to enter Bosnia-Hercegovina, and to see the countryside. Stowing luggage costs up to 5KM, depending on the route. Buses usually run on time, although they are slow due to winding roads and occasional stops for drivers and passengers to eat and smoke.

Travelling by bus between Croatia and the Muslim-Croat Federation of Bosnia-Hercegovina is routine. Four daily buses travel between Sarajevo and Zagreb (417km) and Sarajevo and Split. The Sarajevo-Dubrovnik bus makes one trip each day via Mostar, and buses from Sarajevo go to Germany several times a week. The Republika Srpska is closely connected by bus to Yugoslavia. Buses run every hour between Banja Luka and Belgrade, and a different bus runs from the Serb-held Sarajevo suburb of Lukavica to Belgrade. Several buses a day travel between Zagreb and Banja Luka, though you must change buses at the border (the other bus will be waiting).

Getting Around

Trains are generally useless, as they run only from Sarajevo to Zenica and a few other small cities. The exception is the beautiful trip from Sarajevo down to Ploče on the Croatian coast. Trains from Banja Luka have a limited radius within the RS.

Within each entity (the Federation and the RS), Bosnia's bus network is quite comprehensive. Inter-entity travel has become less of a problem since the 1998 introduction of daily buses between Sarajevo and Banja Luka.

Plenty of car rental places have sprung up, particularly in Sarajevo, Mostar and Međugorje. License plates used to be badges of identity, but the new standardised plates mean there is no problem crossing from one entity to another.

As elsewhere in the Balkans, people drive like maniacs, passing even on sharp curves.

Bosnia

SARAJEVO
☎ 033 • pop 500,000 (est. 2000)

Sarajevo, in a valley beside the Miljacka River, is the capital of Bosnia-Hercegovina. Before the war, the city was also an ethnic microcosm of Yugoslavia. For hundreds of years it was where Muslims, Serbs, Croats, Turks, Jews and others peacefully coexisted.

From the mid-15th century until 1878, Turkish governors resided in Sarajevo. The city's name comes from *saraj*, Turkish for 'palace'. Sarajevo is one of the most Oriental cities in Europe, retaining the essence of its rich history in its mosques, markets and the picturesque old Turkish bazaar called Baščaršija.

When the Turks finally withdrew, half a century of Austro-Hungarian domination began, culminating in the assassination of Archduke Franz Ferdinand and his wife Sophie by a Serbian nationalist in 1914. In 1984 Sarajevo again attracted world attention by hosting the 14th Winter Olympic Games.

Sarajevo's heritage of six centuries was pounded into rubble by Bosnian Serb artillery during the siege of 1992 to 1995, when Sarajevo's only access to the outside world was via a 1km tunnel under the airport. Over 10,500 Sarajevans died and 50,000 were wounded by Bosnian Serb sniper fire and shelling. The endless new graveyards near Koševo stadium leave a silent record of the terrible years.

SARAJEVO

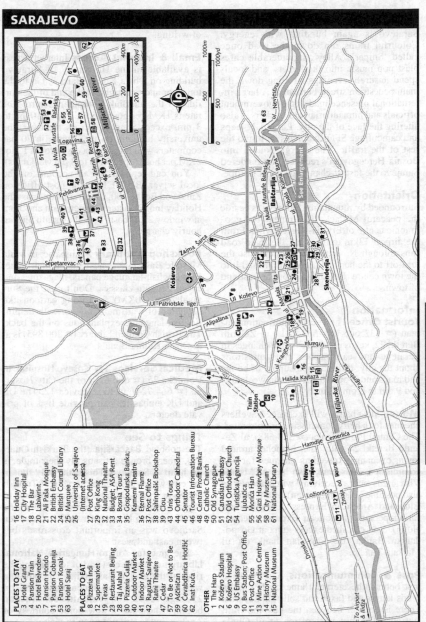

PLACES TO STAY
3 Hotel Grand
4 Pansion Train
18 The Bar
5 Hotel Belvedere
7 Pansion Hondo
31 Pansion Cobanija
51 Pansion Konak
63 Hotel Saraj

PLACES TO EAT
8 Pizzeria Indi
12 Supermarket
19 Texas
23 Restaurant Beijing
28 Taj Mahal
30 Pizzeria Galija
40 Outdoor Market
41 Indoor Market
42 Ragusa; Sarajevo
47 Cedar
57 To Be or Not to Be
59 Ćevabdžinica Hodžić
62 Inat Kuća

16 Holiday Inn
17 City Hospital
20 Labirint
21 Ali Paša Mosque
22 British Embassy
24 British Council Library
25 Marquee
26 University of Sarajevo
    (Internet access)
27 Post Office
29 King Kong
32 National Theatre
33 Budget; ASA Rent
35 Bosnia Tours
35 Gospodarska Banka;
    Kameni Theatre
36 Eternal Flame
37 Post Office
38 Sahinpašić Bookshop
39 Clou
43 Unis Tours
44 Orthodox Cathedral
45 Senator
46 Tourist Information Bureau
48 Central Profit Banka
49 Catholic Church
50 Old Synagogue
51 Canadian Embassy
52 Old Orthodox Church
54 Turistička Agencija
    Ljubačica
55 Morića Han
56 Gazi Husrevbey Mosque
58 City Museum
61 National Library

OTHER
1 The Harp
2 Koševo Stadium
6 Koševo Hospital
9 US Embassy
10 Bus Station; Post Office
11 Post Office
13 Mine Action Centre
14 History Museum
15 National Museum

Despite the highly visible scars of war, Sarajevo is again bursting with energy. Colourful trams run down the road once called 'Sniper's Alley', innumerable cafes blast pop music into the streets, and locals spend leisurely evenings strolling down the main pedestrian street, Ferhadija. A large international presence made up of government officials and humanitarian aid workers is also altering the face of the city. Large UN jeeps and camouflage SFOR vehicles melt into the rest of the traffic. The energy poured into Bosnia-Hercegovina's recovery has rendered Sarajevo the fastest-changing city in Europe.

Orientation
Surrounded by mountains, Sarajevo is beside the peaceful Miljacka River near the geographic centre of Bosnia-Hercegovina. From the airport 13km to the west, the main road runs through Novo Sarajevo, then past the turn-off to the bus and train stations and into the town centre. Baščaršija is on the east end of town.

Information
Tourist Office The Tourist Information Bureau (☎ 532 606, fax 532 281), ul Zelenih Beretki 22, keeps good tabs on the changes in Sarajevo and can answer most questions about the city. It has a good supply of books and maps and is open 8 am to 5 pm weekdays and 9 am to 5 pm Saturday.

Money Most banks will exchange travellers cheques for a hefty commission or poor rates. The Central Profit Banka (☎ 533 688), ul Zelenih Beretki 24 with other branches around town, exchanges travellers cheques for 3% commission. This bank also has ATMs for Visa cards only. Receiving wired money is also possible (1% commission), as are Diner's Club and American Express cash advances (bring personal American Express cheques along). You can shed excess kuna at Gospodarska Banka, the Croatian bank on ul Maršala Tita 56.

Post & Communications A post office just behind the eternal flame on Ferhadija sends letters and faxes and sells phonecards. There is another between the bus and train stations. The big post office at ul Obala Kulina Bana 8 was being restored at the time of writing.

Email & Internet Access Internet access is available in the University of Sarajevo building on Obala Kulina Bana 7. Go to the top floor and turn right: at the end of the corridor is the Interlink Computer Centre. The rate is 1KM per hour, and it's open 10 am to 3 pm, except Sunday. Across the river, the university building on ul Skenderija 70 has computers with Internet access in room 12 for 2KM per hour (open 9 am to 3 pm weekdays).

You can register for an account on the local server (BIHNET) at the post office on Zmaja od Bosne 100, four tram stops past the Holiday Inn. Register between 9 am and 3 pm at window 23. It costs 11KM a month plus an hourly charge.

Bookshop & Library Šahinpašić, ul Mula Mustafe Bašeskije 1, near the eternal flame, sells English-language papers, magazines and cheap Penguin classics. Don't miss the Survival Map (10KM), a striking cartoon-like depiction of wartime Sarajevo, with helpful English-language explanations on the back. The British Council Library (☎ 200 895) is at ul Obala Kulina Bana 4.

Medical Services Try Koševo Hospital, ul Bolnička 25 (☎ 666 620) or the City Hospital (☎ 664 724), ul Kranjčevića 12. The US and UK embassies can provide lists of private doctors.

Things to See
The cobbled **Baščaršija** (the Turkish Quarter), where bronze artisans ply their trade, is the heart of Sarajevo. This is the only spot in the city where most cafes serve real Turkish coffee in a *džežva* (brass pot), as opposed to espresso. **Morića Han**, now a cafe along Sarači, used to be a tavern and stable when Sarajevo was an important crossroads between east and west.

The graceful Austro-Hungarian **National Library** lies on the east end of town along the river at the end of Baščaršija. The building was destroyed by an incendiary shell on 25 August 1992, 100 years after construction began. It now has a new dome courtesy of Austria, but is still not open to visitors.

Austrian Archduke Franz Ferdinand and his wife Sophie paused at the National Library (then the town hall) on 28 June 1914, then rode west along the riverside in an open car to the second bridge. It was here that they were shot. A plaque bearing the footprints of the assassin, Gavrilo Princip, was ripped out of the pavement during the recent war because Princip was a Bosnian Serb. The one-room **City Museum** (under restoration at the time of writing), where ul Zelenih Beretki meets the river, now stands on 'Princip's corner'.

In the city centre, the **eternal flame** commemorates WWII. Places of worship for four different religions – Catholic, Orthodox, Muslim and Jewish – lie in close vicinity to one another, as Sarajevans still very proudly point out. These include the Catholic church on Ferhadija (which has an English-language service on Sunday); the old Orthodox Church on ul Mula Mustafe Bašeskije (which predates the yellow and brown Orthodox cathedral); the Gazi-Husrevbey Mosque (1531), built by masons from Dubrovnik; and the old Jewish synagogue along ul Mula Mustafe Bašeskije.

The three-year siege made Sarajevo itself a stunning sight. The road into the city from the airport (now Zmaja od Bosne) was dubbed **'Sniper's Alley'** during the war because Serb snipers in the surrounding hills picked off civilians crossing the road. The bright yellow **Holiday Inn** was the wartime home to international journalists, as the city's only functioning wartime hotel. The side facing Sniper's Alley was heavily damaged, but the hotel has since been given a massive facelift. Across from the Holiday Inn is the **National Museum**, which has interesting ethnology and archaeology collections. It's open 10 am to 2 pm Tuesday, Thursday and Sunday, and 11 am to 7 pm on Wednesday. A **History Museum** just up the road shows old photos of Bosnia-Hercegovina and has rotating exhibits, some of which pertain to the recent war. It's open 9 am to 2 pm weekdays, and 9 am to 1 pm on weekends (free).

A **treeline** still rings the city, demarcating the former front line. Residents cut down trees and burned benches for heat during the siege. Watch the pavement for **Sarajevo roses**, which are skeletal hand-like indentations where a shell exploded. Some of these are symbolically filled in with red rubber.

Special Events
In late August, internationally produced films are shown at the annual Sarajevo Film Festival (☎ 524 127, fax 664 547, ✉ sff@soros.org.ba). The Winter Festival in February and March features theatre and musical performances.

Places to Stay
Finding a room in Sarajevo is no longer difficult, since hotels and private rooms have sprung up to house visiting international officials. However, hotel prices remain very high, and reservations are wise. Private accommodation is a relative bargain at 40KM to 50KM per person, but some rooms may not be near the centre. Wherever you stay, be sure to ask about the water situation, since parts of the city have running water only during certain times of day.

Private Rooms Bosnia Tours (☎ 202 207 or 202 059, fax 202 206), ul Maršala Tita 54, near the eternal flame, has plenty of good rooms near the centre for 40KM a person (70KM for two people). If you don't like the room, staff will gladly show you another. The agency is closed Sunday.

Turistička Agencija Ljubačica (☎/fax 232 109), ul Mula Mustafe Bašeskije 65 in Baščaršija, has a handful of rooms near the centre and more rooms farther out. Prices are 30KM to 65KM, depending on location and room quality. If you arrive after 10 pm, call their mobile/cellphone ☎ 090 131 813.

Unis Tours (☎ 205 074, ☎/fax 209 089), Ferhadija 16, has rooms for rates between 40KM and 70KM.

Pansions The cheapest place in town is the bizarre **Pansion Train** (☎ 615 653, Halida Kajtaza 11), where beds in a stationary train sleeper car cost 33/40KM for a single/double. The rooms are cramped but clean, and as long as there aren't too many guests using the toilet and shower facilities it's a good bargain option. From the bus station, take the road to Hotel Grand. Turn left at the petrol station, and follow the big sign to the pansion.

The **Pansion Konak** (☎ 533 506, Mustafe Bašeskije 48) is located in the old town. Rooms cost 40/60KM.

Cosy **Pansion Hondo** (☎ 666 564, ☎/fax 469 375, ul Zaima Šarca 23) is a 20-minute walk uphill from the centre. Rooms cost 80/120KM, with breakfast included. Head straight up ul Pehlivanuša behind the cathedral. It will turn into ul Zaima Šarca.

Pansion Čobanija (☎ 441 749, ☎/fax 203 937, ul Čobanija 29), just past Pizzeria Galija on the south side of the river, has rooms with nice marbled private baths, cable TV, and a fax machine available for guests' use. Request an upstairs room, and enjoy the proximity to the large sitting room. Prices are 80/120KM.

Hotels At 150KM to 300KM a night, hotels are not cost-effective. *Hotel Saraj* (☎ 447 703/4, fax 472 691, ul Nevjestina 5) is the white building visible on the hill behind the National Library. Singles/doubles begin at 160/200KM. Rooms with a view of Sarajevo are more expensive, but all rooms are pleasant, with satellite TV and breakfast included. Another quality option is *Hotel Grand* (☎ 205 444, fax 205 866, ul Muhameda ef Pandže 7) behind the train station, which has rooms with breakfast for 164/260KM.

The aqua-green *Hotel Belvedere* (☎ 262 140/1, fax 206 470, ul Višnjik 2) near Koševo hospital has plain but comfortable rooms with satellite TV, phone and shower for 120/150KM, including breakfast.

Places to Eat

Sarajevo's restaurants are the domain of internationals, as Bosnians socialise over coffee and eat at home. Most restaurant menus are in English, and main meals usually cost 10KM to 15KM.

Ragusa (Ferhadija 10b) serves tasty Bosnian cuisine to diners relaxing at wood tables. Be sure to wash down dinner with a traditional shot of *rakija*. *To Be or Not to Be* (Čizmedžiluk 5) in Baščaršija has generous, colourful salads in a candlelit setting. Vegetarians can opt for an omelette or spaghetti, while others can enjoy classic Bosnian steaks.

Inat Kuća, on the opposite side of the river to the National Library, offers good food in a tasteful old Turkish setting, and has a story attached to it. When work began on the library, the authorities wanted to demolish the old house that stood in the way, but the owner insisted on having it moved piece by piece across the river and reconstructed, hence the name, which translates as 'Spite House'.

Sarajevo's roster of ethnic restaurants includes *Restaurant Beijing* (ul Maršala Tita 38d), which actually dares to offer tofu. Main meals are 13KM to 20KM. Spicy Indian dishes at *Taj Mahal* (ul Hamdije Kreševljakovića 6) are slightly less expensive. Or fill up on hearty burritos at *Texas* (ul Vladmira Perića 4) near the Bar. *Cedar* (Hadžiristićeva bb) is an upmarket Lebanese restaurant which sometimes has live music.

The most popular pizza spots include *Pizzeria Galija* (ul Čobanija 20) across the river, and *Pizzeria Indi*, at the corner of ul Gabelina and ul Koševo.

For a quick meal, ćevapi, burek and 'fast food' joints are ubiquitous, but *Ćevabdžinica Hodžić* (ul Bravadžiluk 34), near the National Library, is a ćevapi star. It's just up the street from *Aščinican* (ul Bravadžiluk 28), where you can choose what you want from an array of salads, vegetables and meats.

Self-Catering There is a sizable supermarket four tram stops beyond the Holiday Inn along Zmaja od Bosne. A year-round outdoor market, behind the cathedral on ul Mula Mustafe Bašeskije, has a good selection of fruits and vegetables. Its indoor counterpart, with dairy products and meats, is across the street in the sandy-coloured building.

Entertainment

Theatre The tourist office keeps a monthly list of concerts, ballets, and performances at the National Theatre on ul Zelenih Beretki; the Sarajevo Ratni Theatre (in the same building as Ragusa restaurant); and Kamerni Theatre, upstairs on ul Maršala Tita 56.

Nightclubs The king of Sarajevo's nightclub world is *Senator*, on ul Strossmayerova near the cathedral. It's open from 10 pm Saturday and has a 10KM cover. Other options are *Labiwrint* (ul Danijela Ozme 7) not far from the US Embassy, and the train station building, which is an occasional venue for dance parties.

Pubs & Jazz Clubs Sarajevo's best-known bar, formerly called the Internet Café, is now known simply as *The Bar* (ul Maršala Tita 7) and is near the intersection with ul Alipašina. It has live music some weekends and Czech

Budweiser on tap, which can be consumed for half-price at happy hour (5 to 8 pm Sunday). *The Harp (ul Patriotske lige)* is an Irish bar with Guinness and other native brews on tap. Head up ul Koševo, which turns into ul Patriotske lige. The pub is at the triangular intersection, a 25-minute walk from the centre. The crowded *Marquee (Obala Kulina Bana 5)* plays rock music.

For occasional live jazz, try *Clou (ul Mula Mustafe Bašeskija 5)*, open from 6 pm; and *King Kong (ul Hamdije Kreševljakovića 17)*.

Cinema Many cinemas play American films with subtitles. *Oslobođendje*, Sarajevo's daily paper, has daily cinema listings under the 'Kina' column.

Shopping

Metalworking craft shops line ul Kazandžiluk, at the end of Baščaršija. Turkish coffee sets and snazzy plates aside, the trendiest souvenirs are engraved shell cases (that's shell as in cartridge). Small ones sell for around 10KM. Bargaining is possible, indeed necessary, in these shops.

Getting There & Away

Four buses a day run to Sarajevo from Zagreb, four from Split and one from Dubrovnik. Two daily buses also go to and from Banja Luka. Buses run from the Serb-controlled Sarajevo suburb of Lukavica to various parts of the RS and Belgrade. Explain to a taxi driver that you want to go to the bus station in Lukavica, and he will take you to a spot on the RS border near the airport, where you can switch cabs or walk 150m to the bus station and buy a ticket.

Getting Around

An efficient but often crowded tram network runs east-west between Baščaršija and Ilidža. Tram 4 from Baščaršija peels off at the bus station; tram 1 goes between the bus station and Ilidža. Buy tickets (1KM) at kiosks near tram stations. Buses and trolleybuses also cost 1KM (punch your ticket on board); purchase bus tickets from the driver.

To/From the Airport In summer one under-utilised bus travels sporadically to and from the airport, about 13km west of the city

centre. Ask at the tourist office for departure times. A taxi should cost about 15KM.

Car Budget (☎/fax 206 640), ul Branilaca Sarajeva 21, also has an office at the airport (☎ 463 598); Diner's Club and American Express cards are accepted. ASA Rent has offices at ul Branilaca Sarajeva 20 (☎/fax 445 209/10) and at the airport (☎ 463 598).

Taxi Sarajevo's ubiquitous taxis all have meters that begin at 2KM and cost 1KM per kilometre. Call ☎ 970 for Radio Taxi.

AROUND SARAJEVO

Twenty-five kilometres south-east of Sarajevo, the deserted slopes of Mt Jahorina, the site of the 1984 Winter Olympics, still offer some of the best skiing in Europe at extremely cheap prices. Ask at the Tourist Information Bureau (see Tourist Office earlier) about ski trips. Buses leave from ul Franje Raćkog opposite the History Museum. Prices for accommodation are around 30KM to 70KM per night, ski rental is 15KM to 25KM, lift tickets 10KM, and lessons 15KM. Skiing on Jahorina is safe from mines.

TRAVNIK
☎ 030

Tucked into a narrow valley only 90km northwest of Sarajevo, Travnik served as the seat of Turkish viziers who ruled Bosnia from 1699 to 1851. The town grew into a diplomatic crossroads, and earned fame more recently as the birthplace of Bosnia's best-known writer Ivo Andrić.

Though wartime fighting between Muslims and Croats went on in the surrounding hills, it mostly spared the town itself. With its lovely medieval castle and pristine natural springs, the town, in Muslim hands today, is well worth a day trip from Sarajevo or a stop on the way to Banja Luka.

Orientation & Information

Travnik's main street, ul Bosanska, runs east to west. The bus station is on the west end of town, within sight of the post office.

Things to See

The **medieval fort** at the top of the hill is believed to date from the 15th century. Ask in the museum on the right of ul Bosanska about opening times or the key. The museum itself is worth a visit. For the castle, head up ul Hendek on the east side of town, turn right at the top of the steps and then take another right; you'll see the walkway across to the fort.

Near the base of ul Hendek lies the famous **Many Coloured Mosque** which allegedly contains hairs from Mohammed's beard. Just east of the mosque are the peaceful springs called **Plava Voda** (Blue Water), a favourite summer spot.

Back in town, the **Ivo Andrić Memorial Museum** on ul Mustafa Kundić marks the birthplace of the famed Bosnian author of *The Travnik Chronicles*. The museum contains Andrić texts in many languages, photographs of the 1961 Nobel Prize ceremonies, and a model 19th-century bedroom. Don't be fooled, though: the museum was reconstructed in 1974 and is not the original birth house. Ask at Restaurant Divan downstairs for someone with the key.

Places to Stay & Eat

The cheapest place to stay is the central *Pansion Oniks* (☎ 818 546) behind the cafe of the same name near the Many Coloured Mosque. Rooms cost 35/70KM for a single/double. *Hotel Orient* (☎/fax 511 420, ul Bosanska 29) is not far from the bus station, and rooms cost 82/104KM.

The much nicer *Hotel Slon* (☎/fax 811 008, ul Fatmić 11) hosted Princess Diana shortly before her death. The spacious, clean rooms have satellite TV, and cost 90/120KM. Reception may have ideas about private rooms.

The best food in town is at *Restaurant Divan*, on ul Mustafa Kundić, directly below the Ivo Andrić museum. Coming from the bus station, turn left on ul Zenjak and go one block. Patio seating is available in summer.

Getting There & Away

Buses go almost hourly to Sarajevo and two per day go to Banja Luka.

BANJA LUKA

☎ 051 (☎ 058 from Sarajevo) • pop 239,000
This important crossroads on the Vrbas River in north-western Bosnia is now known to the world as the capital of the Republika Srpska. Banja Luka was never much of a tourist centre

and in 1993 local Serbs made sure it never would be by blowing up all 16 of the city's mosques, complementing the damage previously done by WWII bombings and a 1969 earthquake. While not otherwise damaged during the recent war, the city is economically depressed and flooded with Serb refugees from the Bosnian Federation and the Croatian Krajina. Even as the RS leadership in Banja Luka opens slowly to the West, the city's transportation, banking and communication networks remain closely tied to Belgrade.

Orientation

Banja Luka is situated beside the river Vrbas in north-western Bosnia-Hercegovina, only 184km from Zagreb, 235km from Sarajevo and 316km from Belgrade. Many of Banja Luka's streets, including the main street Kralja Petra, have been renamed since the war and locals may not recognise the new names.

Information

Tourist Office The Turistički Savez (☎/fax 212 323, ☎ 218 022) at ul Kralja Petra 75 sells maps of Banja Luka and can give advice. Some English is spoken.

Money Cash advances on credit cards are unavailable and at the time of writing no banks could change travellers cheques. Currency can be exchanged at Vojvodjanska Banka, ul Kralja Petra 87, or Bank Kristal, Franje Jukića 4, near the town hall.

Post & Communications The main post office at ul Kralja Petra 93 has numerous telephone booths and sells phonecards. Getting through to Sarajevo is difficult.

Things to See

The large 16th-century **fort** along the Vrbas river is an interesting place to explore. Note the overgrown amphitheatre, whose benches were burned for fuel during the war.

War is the main theme of Banja Luka's sights. Atop the Šehitluci hill 5km south-east of town stands a huge white stone **WWII memorial**. This solitary and impressive slab affords a great view of the city.

In the city centre is the **presidential palace**, which has been the seat of government since January 1998. It faces the town hall. If you come across a bare patch of land in Banja Luka, most likely it used to be one of the city's 16 destroyed mosques. The most famous of these was **Ferhadija** (1580), built with the ransom money for an Austrian count. Ferhadija used to be across ul Kralja Petra from the tourist office.

Places to Stay
The 200-room *Hotel Bosna* (☎ *216 942 or 215 772, fax 44 536)* is situated smack in the centre of town. Functional rooms, all with phone, cable TV and bath tubs (a novelty in these parts) cost 150/180KM a single/double, breakfast included. Reserve a week in advance, as this hotel is residually full of international officials. Another good option is *Hotel Palace* (☎*/fax 218 723, Kralja Petra 1),* which has rooms for 110KM to 240KM. *Hotel Slavija* (☎ *211 806, ul Kralja Petra 85)* has shabby singles/doubles for 70/100KM.

Places to Eat
Restaurant Tropik Klub is tucked inside the castle walls in the former prison *(kazamat).* It serves excellent traditional food (mains from 11KM to 13KM) and has outdoor seating overlooking the Vrbas river in summer. The restaurant of the *Hotel Palace (Kralja Petra 1)* is very good value. The best place for fish is *Alas (Braće Mažar 47),* off the transit road between Zagreb and Sarajevo. *Lanaco* is a popular pizza joint, with live bands at weekends. Follow the signs off ul Kralja Petra into Stojanovića Park.

Getting There & Away
The train and bus stations lie roughly 3km north of the town centre; a taxi should cost 5KM. Buses (information ☎ 45 355) run twice a day to Zagreb, five times to Sarajevo, and no less than 23 times to Belgrade (seven hours).

Hercegovina

MOSTAR
☎ 036 • pop 120,000
Mostar, the main city in Hercegovina, is a beautiful medieval town set in the valley of the aqua-green Neretva River. Its name is derived from the 16th-century Turkish bridge that used to arc over the river; *mostar*

means keeper of the bridge. Sadly, the town was the scene of intense Muslim-Croat fighting during the recent war, which left many buildings destroyed or scarred. Even the bridge was destroyed by Croat shelling in November 1993. Once divided only by the Neretva River, Mostar is now segregated into Muslim and Croat sectors. Nonetheless, visitors are slowly drifting back to enjoy the old medieval buildings, cobbled streets and Turkish souvenir shops that give Mostar its charm.

Orientation
Mostar is a divided city. Though there are no physical barriers, Croats live on the west side of the Neretva River and Muslims on the east (though Muslims also control a small strip on the river's west bank). However, travellers can pass from one side to the other without any fuss.

Information
Tourist Offices The Atlas Travel Agency (☎/fax 318 771), in the same building as Hotel Ero, has useful suggestions and a rough map of the west side. In the tourist agency on the east side beside the bus station staff speak English and have information about accommodation and travel.

Money Hrvatska Banka, adjacent to Hotel Ero, changes travellers cheques to any currency except dinars for 1.5% commission.

Post & Communications The large, modern post office on the west side, around the corner from Hotel Ero, is the only place in Bosnia for poste restante mail; it's held for one month and pick-up is at window 12. Address mail to Poste Restante, 88000 Mostar (Zapadni), Bosnia-Hercegovina.

Email & Internet Access Inquire at the new Training Centre (Centar za Obuku; ☎ 580 058), ul Oneščukova 24 about 60m west of Stari Most, about public Internet access.

Things to See
Stari Most (old bridge) is still the heart of the old town, though it is now being rebuilt. Sadly the small Crooked Bridge, which spanned a Neretva tributary nearby and was

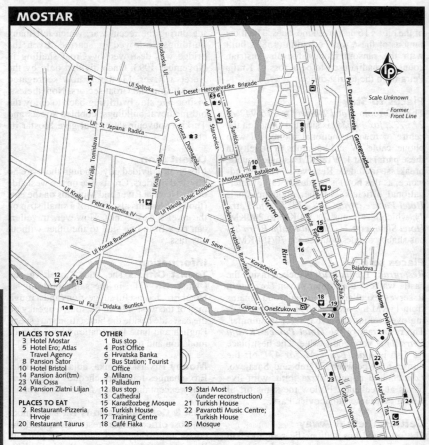

MOSTAR

UI Splitska

UI Deset Hercegivaške Brigade

UI Ante Starcevića

UI St Jepana Radića

UI Kneza Domagoja

UI Kralja Tvrtka

UI Kralja Tomislava

UI Kralja

Petra Krešimira IV

UI Kralja

UI Nikola Šubic Zrinski

Mostarskog Bataljona

UI Kneza Branimira

UI Sava

Bulevar Hrvatskih Branitelja

Neretva

River

Rudarska UI

Alekse Šantića

Put Dvadesetdevete Gercegovacke

UI Maršala Tita

UI Brace Fejića

Kovačevića

Bajatova

Kujundžiluk

Udarne Divizije

ul Fra Didaka Buntica

Gupca Onešukova

UI Cojka Vukovića

UI Maršala Tita

Scale Unknown

- - - - Former
Front Line

PLACES TO STAY
3 Hotel Mostar
5 Hotel Ero; Atlas
   Travel Agency
8 Pansion Šator
10 Hotel Bristol
14 Pansion âori(tm)
23 Vila Ossa
24 Pansion Zlatni Liljan

PLACES TO EAT
2 Restaurant-Pizzeria
   Hrvoje
20 Restaurant Taurus

OTHER
1 Bus stop
4 Post Office
6 Hrvatska Banka
7 Bus Station; Tourist
   Office
9 Milano
11 Palladium
12 Bus stop
13 Cathedral
15 Karadžozbeg Mosque
16 Turkish House
17 Training Centre
18 Café Fiaka

19 Stari Most
   (under reconstruction)
21 Turkish House
22 Pavarotti Music Centre;
   Turkish House
25 Mosque

BOSNIA-HERCEGOVINA

built a few years before Stari Most, was
swept away in floods on the last day of 1999.

The cobbled old town, called **Kujundžiluk**,
extends on both sides of Stari Most. It is still
pleasantly awash with small shops selling
Turkish-style souvenirs. Along the east side,
the most famous mosque in Mostar is the
Karadžozbeg Mosque (1557). The top of its
minaret was blown off in the recent war.
Nearby, the 350-year-old **Turkish House**, on
ul Bišcevića, has colourful Turkish-style rugs
and furniture. There is an even older Turkish
house, with a fascinating interior, at Gaše
Ilića 21 behind the Pavarotti Music Centre.

The dramatic **front line**, which now essentially divides the town between Muslims and
Croats, runs along the street behind Hotel
Ero, then jogs one street west to the main
boulevard.

Places to Stay

Mostar's three hotels are expensive, but a few
pleasant pansions offer relief. Many pansion
rooms have multiple beds. Reserve a week in
advance, because groups occasionally fill the
space. The nearest to the bus station is the
Pansion Šator (mobile/cellphone ☎ 090141
216, Maršala Tita 40), with just three double

rooms for 20KM per person. The 12-bed *Pansion Zlatni Liljan* (☎ 551 353, *ul Sehovina 8*) costs 20KM, with breakfast 25KM. Heading south past the Pavarotti Music Centre, swing left and follow the cobblestone road that starts by the mosque, then turn left again by the cemetery.

The 10-bed *Vila Ossa* (☎ 568 532, *Gojka Vokovića 40*) is on the other side of the river. The price for one/two people is 30/40KM, and 35/50KM with breakfast. *Pansion Ćorić* (☎ 331 077, fax 331 078, *ul Fra Didaka Buntića*) is about a 20-minute walk directly west of Stari Most. Beds cost 50KM including an excellent breakfast, and the friendly proprietors speak German but not English.

Hotel Ero (☎ 386 777, fax 386 700), on ul Ante Starčevića directly across the river from the bus station, has polished rooms with porches for 79/136KM for a single/double (American Express cards accepted). *Hotel Bristol* (☎ 580 092/3, fax 550 091), ul Mostarskog Bataljona on the river's west bank, has rooms for 64/97KM. At *Hotel Mostar* (☎ 322 679, fax 315 693, *Kneza Domagoja bb*) rooms are 72/124KM.

Places to Eat
Čevapi spots are everywhere, and restaurants with divine views of the river cluster along the western riverbank near Stari Most. Tables on a covered porch at *Restaurant Taurus* offer a lovely view of the spot where the Crooked Bridge used to stand; the food is hearty and traditional.

For a big salad or good pizza, try the *Restaurant-Pizzeria Hrvoje* at Kralja Tomislava in west Mostar.

Entertainment
Since it opened in December 1997, the large modern *Pavarotti Music Centre* (☎ 559 080, fax 552 081, *ul Maršala Tita 179*), has been the hub of Mostar's cultural activities, sponsoring music and dance courses for children. The reception desk keeps a monthly schedule of free public concerts and events, and the Centre's airy restaurant-cafe is always lively. *Café Fiaka*, across Stari Most in the old town, is a popular after-hours hangout for the Pavarotti crowd.

The youth of Mostar flock to the nightclubs. Try *Palladium*, off ul Kralja Tvrtka

near the west side roundabout, or *Milano* (ul Maršala Tita 75) on the east side.

Getting There & Away
Mostar lies on the route between Sarajevo and the coast. Six buses per day run to Sarajevo, two to Split, one to Dubrovnik and one to Zagreb. Two bus stops on the west side send buses to Međugorje and other parts of Hercegovina. There's also a daily train from Sarajevo to Ploče that stops in Mostar at 11 am (the Mostar-Ploče leg takes two and a half hours).

AROUND MOSTAR
About 15km south-east of Mostar is the village of **Blagaj**, well worth a day trip for its 16th century *tekke* (Dervish monastery), beautifully sited at the point where the river Buna gushes out of the mountainside. There's no charge to visit the tekke. Afterwards, you can sit by the waterside and eat excellent trout at one of the restaurants here. Buses run four times a day from Mostar bus station. From the stop in Blagaj the monastery is a 20-minute walk.

MEĐUGORJE
☎ 036
Međugorje is one of Europe's most remarkable sights. On 24 June 1981 six teenagers in this dirt-poor mountain village claimed they'd seen a miraculous apparition of the Virgin Mary, and Međugorje's instant economic boom began. A decade later Međugorje was awash with tour buses, souvenir stands, car rental offices, travel agencies, and pansions. The Catholic Church has not officially acknowledged the apparitions (the first in Europe since Lourdes, France in 1858 and Fatima, Portugal in 1917), but 'religious tourism' has developed as if this were a beach resort. Three of the original six still claim to see the vision daily, while the Virgin Mary only appears for the other three on special days.

After a wartime hiatus, the busloads of package pilgrims are returning with renewed fervour. Tourist facilities are fully intact, since the front line did not reach Međugorje – some locals attribute this to divine protection. Crowds are especially heavy around Easter, the anniversary of the first apparition (24 June), the Assumption of the Virgin

(15 August) and the Nativity of the Virgin (first Sunday after 8 September).

Orientation

Medugorje lies in the heart of Hercegovina, 125km and 129km from Split and Dubrovnik respectively and only 30 mountainous kilometres south from Mostar. Shops are clustered near the church. The streets have no names or numbers, but most tourist offices and hotels sell maps of Medugorje (10 kuna). Taxis cost a flat fee of US$4 to anywhere in town.

Information

Tourist Offices Tourist information centres are everywhere, but Globtour (☎/fax 651 393 or 651 593), 50m from the post office towards the church, is particularly helpful and staff speak English. Travel Agency Global (☎ 651 489, fax 651 501, ✆ global-medjugorje@ int.tel.hr) behind the central park is also worth trying. Both offices will arrange accommodation and charter buses for groups from Split or Dubrovnik.

Money Virtually any major currency will be accepted. However, using kuna will spare you the poor informal exchange rate. Hrvatska Banka, on the main street near the church, offers commission-free Visa cash advances and 1.5% commission to change travellers cheques.

Post & Communications International phone calls can be placed from the post office, which is right next to the bus stop.

Things to See

Completed in 1969 before the apparitions began, **St James' Church** is a hub of activity. An information office beside the church posts the daily schedule, as well as multilingual printouts of the Virgin's latest message.

Apparition Hill, where the Virgin was first spotted on 24 June 1981, is near the hamlet Podbrdo south-west of town. A blue cross marks the place where the Virgin was supposedly seen with a cross in the background, conveying a message of peace. It is a place for silence and prayer. To reach Apparition

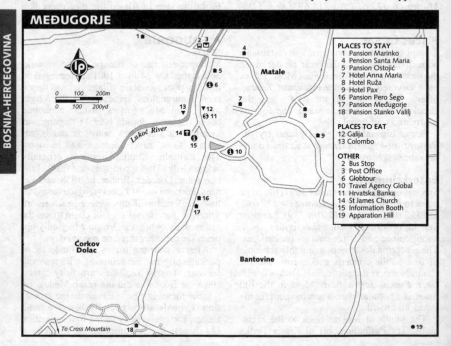

MEÐUGORJE

```
0    100   200m
0    100   200yd
```

Lukoć River

Matale

Čorkov Dolac

Bantovine

To Cross Mountain   18

PLACES TO STAY
1 Pansion Marinko
4 Pension Santa Maria
5 Pansion Ostojić
7 Hotel Anna Maria
8 Hotel Ruža
9 Hotel Pax
16 Pansion Pero Šego
17 Pansion Medugorje
18 Pansion Stanko Valilj

PLACES TO EAT
12 Galija
13 Colombo

OTHER
2 Bus Stop
3 Post Office
6 Globtour
10 Travel Agency Global
11 Hrvatska Banka
14 St James Church
15 Information Booth
19 Apparation Hill

Hill, take the road curving left (east) from the centre of town, and follow the signs to Podbrdo (3km away).

Cross Mountain (Mt Križevac) lies about 1.5km south-west of town. The 45-minute hike to the top leads to a white cross planted there in 1934 to commemorate the 1900th anniversary of Christ's death. Pilgrims stop to say the rosary at crosses along the trail. Wear sturdy shoes, as the path is extremely rocky. Candles are forbidden due to fire danger. After the hike, knock on the door of Pansion Stanko Vasilj, 300m from the base of Cross Mountain, and relax with a cool glass (1KM) of the town's best home-made wine.

Places to Stay
With 17,000 rooms, Međugorje has more accommodation than the rest of Bosnia combined. Reduced tourism means that beds are easy to find, except around major holidays. Larger pansions and hotels can fill unpredictably with large tour groups, so book in advance. Most pansion rooms look the same, though rooms around the church are the most expensive. Friendly proprietors usually offer the choice of B&B, half-board and full-board. Home-made meals are frequently complemented with a bottle of *domaći vino* (home-made wine). Tourist offices can also arrange accommodation, but this is more expensive than contacting the pansion directly. Tour groups can find reduced rates.

The city's few hotels are blander and more expensive than the pansions, and the rooms are not much better.

Pansions The 49-bed *Pansion Ostojić* (☎ 651 562, fax 651 095), near the post office, has rooms for 20/35/45KM with breakfast/half-board/full-board. Inquire in the Cafe Santa Fe in front of the pansion. Also cheap is *Pansion Marinko* (☎/fax 651 312) off a country road to the west of the bus station.

About 100m behind Ostojić, the white-washed *Pansion Santa Maria* (☎ 651 523, fax 651 723) charges 26.5/36.5/45.5KM. Make sure you reserve early, as it is often filled with groups.

The road to Cross Mountain yields some gems. *Pansion Pero Šego* costs 21.5/31.5KM for B&B/half-board. Farther on, the homy 25-bed *Pansion Međugorje* (☎ 651 315, fax 651 452) is a steal at 15/30/45KM a person for B&B/half-board/full-board. The *Pansion Stanko Vasilj*, 300m from Cross Mountain, charges 25/35/45KM.

Hotels Most hotels offer group rates, and all include breakfast in the service. *Hotel Anna Maria* (☎ 651 512, ☎/fax 651 023) has singles/doubles for 60/90KM. Rooms have satellite TV and phone. *Hotel Ruža* (☎ 643 118, fax 647 431) charges 38/76KM. Closest to Apparition Hill, the relatively ritzy *Hotel Pax* (☎/fax 651 604) costs 61.5/103KM and accepts MasterCard, American Express, Visa and Diner's Club cards.

Places to Eat
The half- or full-board option at the pansions includes a very hearty, meat-and-bread meal. Restaurants can be expensive. *Colombo*, near the church, is beloved for its pizzas and relatively low prices. For a platter of steaming fish, head across the street to *Galija*.

Getting There & Away
Most visitors come to Međugorje from Croatia. Two buses run daily from Split (3½ hours), one from Dubrovnik (three hours) and one from Zagreb (nine hours). Buses also go twice a week to and from Germany. Many international bus lines are run by Globtour; ask there for a schedule. A handful of buses run daily between Međugorje and Mostar. There's no posted schedule, so inquire at the post office about times.

BOSNIA-HERCEGOVINA

Croatia

Croatia (Hrvatska) extends in an arc from the Danube River in the east to Istria in the west and south along the Adriatic coast to Dubrovnik. Roman Catholic since the 9th century, and under Hungary since 1102, Croatia only united with Orthodox Serbia in 1918. Croatia's centuries-long resistance to Hungarian and Austrian domination was manifested in 1991 in its determined struggle for nationhood. Yet within Croatia, cultural differences remain between the Habsburg-influenced Central European interior and the formerly Venetian Mediterranean coast.

Traditionally, tourism has been focused along the Adriatic coast, with its unsurpassed combination of history, natural beauty, good climate, clear water and easy access. Seaside resorts are numerous, the swimming is good, and the atmosphere is relaxed – there are few rules about behaviour and few formalities. Since 1960 nudism has been promoted and Croatia is now *the* place to go in Europe to practise naturism.

When Yugoslavia split apart in 1991, no less than 80% of the country's tourist resorts ended up in Croatia. Publicity about the war brought tourism almost to a standstill but Croatia is slowly regaining its balance. In July and August, Istria and Krk are filled to capacity and much of Dalmatia is busy as well but outside the peak season all is quiet and, south of Krk in particular, you'll have some beautiful places all to yourself.

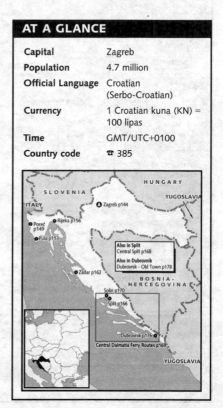

AT A GLANCE

Capital	Zagreb
Population	4.7 million
Official Language	Croatian (Serbo-Croatian)
Currency	1 Croatian kuna (KN) = 100 lipas
Time	GMT/UTC+0100
Country code	☎ 385

Facts about Croatia

HISTORY

In 229 BC the Romans began their conquest of the indigenous Illyrians by establishing a colony at Salona (near Split) in Dalmatia. Emperor Augustus extended the empire and created the provinces of Illyricum (Dalmatia and Bosnia) and Pannonia (Croatia). In AD 285, Emperor Diocletian decided to retire to his palace fortress in Split, today the greatest Roman ruin in Eastern Europe. When the empire was divided in 395, what is now Slovenia, Croatia and Bosnia-Hercegovina stayed with the Western Roman Empire, while present-day Serbia, Kosovo and Macedonia went to the Eastern Roman Empire, later known as the Byzantine Empire. Visigoth, Hun and Lombard invasions marked the fall of the Western Roman Empire in the 5th century.

Around 625, Slavic tribes migrated from present-day Poland. The Serbian tribe settled in the region that is now south-western Serbia and extended their influence southward and westward. The Croatian tribe moved into what is now Croatia and occupied two former Roman provinces: Dalmatian Croatia along the Adriatic and Pannonian Croatia to the north.

CROATIA

By the early part of the 9th century, both settlements had accepted Christianity but the northern Croats fell under Frankish domination while Dalmatian Croats came under the nominal control of the Byzantine Empire. The Dalmatian duke Tomislav united the two groups in 925 in a single kingdom that prospered for nearly 200 years.

Late in the 11th century, the throne fell vacant and a series of ensuing power struggles weakened central authority and split the kingdom. The northern Croats, unable to agree upon a ruler, united with Hungary in 1102 for protection against the Orthodox Byzantine Empire.

In 1242 a Tatar invasion devastated both Hungary and Croatia. In the 14th century the Turks began pushing into the Balkans, defeating the Serbs in 1389 and the Hungarians in 1526. Northern Croatia turned to the Habsburgs of Austria for protection against the Turks in 1527 and remained under their influence until 1918. To form a buffer against the Turks, in the 16th century the Austrians invited Serbs to settle the Vojna Krajina (military frontier) along the Bosnian border. The Serbs in the borderlands had an autonomous administration under Austrian control and these areas were not reincorporated into Croatia until 1881.

The Adriatic coast fell under Venetian influence as early as the 12th century although Hungary continued to struggle for control of the region. Some Dalmatian cities changed hands repeatedly until Venice imposed its rule on the Adriatic coast in the early 15th century and occupied it for nearly four centuries. Only the Republic of Ragusa (Dubrovnik) maintained its independence. The Adriatic coast was threatened but never conquered by the Turks and, after the naval Battle of Lepanto in 1571, when Spanish and Venetian forces wiped out the Turkish fleet, this threat receded.

After Venice was shattered by Napoleonic France in 1797, the French occupied southern Croatia, entering Ragusa (Dubrovnik) in 1808. Napoleon's merger of Dalmatia, Istria and Slovenia into the 'Illyrian provinces' in 1809 stimulated the concept of South Slav (Yugoslav) unity. After Napoleon's defeat at Waterloo in 1815, Austria-Hungary moved in to pick up the pieces along the coast.

A revival of Croatian cultural and political life began in 1835. In 1848 a liberal democratic revolution led by Josip Jelačić was suppressed, but serfdom was abolished. An 1868 reform transferred northern Croatia from Austria to Hungary, united the territory with Hungarian Slavonia and granted a degree of internal autonomy. Dalmatia remained under Austria. In the decade before the outbreak of WWI, some 50,000 Croats emigrated to the USA.

With the defeat of the Austro-Hungarian empire in WWI, Croatia became part of the Kingdom of Serbs, Croats & Slovenes (called Yugoslavia after 1929), which had a centralised government in Belgrade. This was strongly resisted by Croatian nationalists, who organised the Marseilles assassination of royal dictator, King Alexander I in 1934. Italy had been promised the Adriatic coast as an incentive to join the war against Austria-Hungary in 1915 and it held much of northern Dalmatia from 1918 to 1943.

After the German invasion of Yugoslavia in March 1941, a puppet government dominated by the fascist Ustaša movement was set up in Croatia and Bosnia-Hercegovina under Ante Pavelić (who fled to Argentina after the war). At first the Ustaša tried to expel all Serbs from Croatia to Serbia. But when the Germans stopped this because of the problems it was causing, the Ustaša launched an extermination campaign that surpassed even that of the Nazis in scale. Although the number of victims is controversial, estimates indicate that from 60,000 to 600,000 ethnic Serbs, Jews and Roma (gypsies) were murdered. The Ustaša program called for 'one-third of Serbs killed, one-third expelled and one-third converted to Catholicism'.

Not all Croats supported these policies, however. Josip Broz, known as Maršal Tito, was himself of Croat-Slovene parentage and tens of thousands of Croats fought bravely with his partisans. Massacres of Croats conducted by Serbian Četniks in southern Croatia and Bosnia forced almost all antifascist Croats into the communist ranks, where they joined the numerous Serbs trying to defend themselves from the Ustaša. In all, about a million people died violently in a war that was fought mostly in Croatia and Bosnia-Hercegovina.

Recent History

After the war, Marsal Tito became the prime minister of the new Yugoslav Federation and set up a state-planned economy modelled after Stalin's Soviet Union. Post-war Croatia was granted republic status within the Yugoslav Federation. During the 1960s, Croatia and Slovenia moved far ahead of the southern republics economically, leading to demands by reformers, intellectuals and students for greater autonomy. The 'Croatian Spring' of 1971 caused a backlash and purge of reformers, who were jailed or expelled from the Party. Increasing economic inertia was due to a cumbersome system of 'self-management' of state enterprises by employees. After Tito died in 1980 the paralysis spread to government and the federal presidency began rotating annually among the republics.

In 1989 severe repression of the Albanian majority in Yugoslavia's Kosovo province sparked renewed fears of Serbian hegemony and heralded the end of the Yugoslav Federation. With political changes sweeping Eastern Europe, many Croats felt the time had come to end more than four decades of communist rule and attain complete autonomy into the bargain. In the free elections of April 1990 Franjo Tudjman's Croatian Democratic

CROATIA

Union (Hrvatska Demokratska Zajednica) easily defeated the old Communist Party. On 22 December 1990 a new Croatian constitution was promulgated, changing the status of Serbs in Croatia to a national minority.

The constitution's failure to guarantee minority rights, and mass dismissals of Serbs from the public service, stimulated the 600,000-strong ethnic Serb community within Croatia to demand autonomy. A May 1991 referendum (boycotted by the Serbs) produced a 93% vote in favour of independence but, when Croatia declared independence on 25 June 1991, the Serbian enclave of Krajina proclaimed its independence from Croatia.

Heavy fighting broke out in Krajina (the area around Knin, north of Split), Baranja (the area north of the Drava River opposite Osijek) and Slavonia (the region west of the Danube). The 180,000-member, 2000-tank Yugoslav People's Army, dominated by Serbian communists, began to intervene on its own authority in support of Serbian irregulars under the pretext of halting ethnic violence. After European Community (EC) mediation, Croatia agreed to freeze its independence declaration for three months to avoid bloodshed.

In the three months following 25 June, a quarter of Croatia fell to Serbian militias and the federal army. In September the Croatian government ordered a blockade of 32 federal military installations in the republic, lifting morale and gaining much-needed military equipment. In response, the Yugoslav navy blockaded the Adriatic coast and laid siege to the strategic town of Vukovar on the Danube.

In early October 1991 the federal army and Montenegrin militia moved against Dubrovnik to protest against the ongoing blockade of their garrisons in Croatia. On 7 October the presidential palace in Zagreb was hit by rockets fired by Yugoslav air-force jets in an unsuccessful assassination attempt against President Tudjman. Heroic Vukovar finally fell on 19 November when the army culminated a bloody three-month siege by concentrating 600 tanks and 30,000 soldiers there. During six months of fighting in Croatia 10,000 people died, hundreds of thousands fled and tens of thousands of homes were deliberately destroyed.

Independence

When the three-month moratorium on independence expired on 8 October 1991, Croatia declared full independence. To fulfil a condition for EC recognition, in December the Croatian parliament belatedly amended its constitution to protect minority and human rights. In January 1992 the EC, succumbing to strong pressure from Germany, recognised Croatia. This was followed three months later by US recognition and in May 1992 Croatia was admitted to the United Nations.

In January 1993 the Croatian army suddenly launched an offensive in southern Krajina, pushing the Serbs back as much as 24km in some areas and recapturing strategic points. The Krajina Serbs vowed never to accept rule from Zagreb and in June 1993 they voted overwhelmingly to join the Bosnian Serbs (and eventually Greater Serbia).

The self-proclaimed 'Republic of Serbian Krajina' held elections in December 1993, which no international body recognised as legitimate or fair. Meanwhile, continued 'ethnic cleansing' left only about 900 Croats in Krajina out of an original population of 44,000. Although no further progress was made in implementing the Vance Peace Plan (negotiated by United Nations special envoy Cyrus Vance in December 1991), the Krajina Serbs signed a comprehensive ceasefire on 29 March 1994, which substantially reduced the violence in the region and established demilitarised 'zones of separation' between the parties.

While the world's attention turned to the grim events unfolding in Bosnia-Hercegovina, the Croatian government quietly began procuring arms from abroad. On 1 May 1995, the Croatian army and police entered and occupied western Slavonia, east of Zagreb, and seized control of the region within days. As the Croatian military consolidated its hold in western Slavonia, some 15,000 Serbs fled the region despite assurances from the Croatian government that they were safe from retribution.

Belgrade's silence throughout this campaign made it clear that the Krajina Serbs had lost the support of their Serbian sponsors, encouraging the Croats to forge ahead. At dawn on 4 August the military launched a massive assault on the rebel Serb capital of

Knin. Outnumbered by two to one, the Serb army fled towards northern Bosnia, along with 150,000 civilians whose roots in the Krajina stretched back centuries. The military operation ended in days, but was followed by months of terror. Widespread looting and burning of Serb villages, as well as attacks upon the few remaining elderly Serbs, seemed designed to ensure the permanence of this massive population shift.

The Dayton agreement signed in Paris in December 1995 recognised Croatia's traditional borders and provided for the return of eastern Slavonia, a transition that was completed in January 1998.

Although stability has returned to the country, a key provision of the agreement was the promise by the Croatian government to allow the return of Serbian refugees. Housing, local industry and agriculture in Slavonia and the Krajina were devastated by the war, however, making resettlement both costly and complicated. Although Serbian refugees face a tangle of bureaucratic obstacles, Croatia's new government is finally acceding to the international community's demands and refugees are slowly trickling back.

GEOGRAPHY

Croatia is half the size of present-day Yugoslavia in area (56,538 sq km) and population. The republic swings around like a boomerang from the Pannonian plains of Slavonia between the Sava, Drava and Danube rivers, across hilly central Croatia to the Istrian Peninsula, then south through Dalmatia along the rugged Adriatic coast.

The narrow Croatian coastal belt at the foot of the Dinaric Alps is only about 600km long as the crow flies, but it's so indented that the actual length is 1778km. If the 4012km of coastline around the offshore islands is added to the total, the length becomes 5790km. Most of the 'beaches' along this jagged coast consist of slabs of rock sprinkled with naturists. Don't come expecting to find sand, but the waters are sparkling clean, even around large towns.

Croatia's offshore islands are every bit as beautiful as those in Greece. There are 1185 islands and islets along the tectonically submerged Adriatic coastline, 66 of them inhabited. The largest are Cres, Krk, Mali Lošinj,

Pag and Rab in the north; Dugi Otok in the middle; and Brač, Hvar, Korčula, Mljet and Vis in the south. Most are barren and elongated from north-west to south-east, with high mountains that drop right into the sea.

CLIMATE

The climate varies from Mediterranean along the Adriatic coast to continental inland. The high coastal mountains help to shield the coast from cold northerly winds, making for an early spring and late autumn. In spring and early summer a sea breeze called the *maestral* keeps the temperature down along the coast. Winter winds include the cold *bura* from the north and the humid *široko* from the south.

The sunny coastal areas experience hot, dry summers and mild, rainy winters, while the interior regions are cold in winter and warm in summer. Because of a warm current flowing north up the Adriatic coast, sea temperatures never fall below 10°C in winter and are as high as 26°C in August. You can swim in the sea from mid-June until late September. The resorts south of Split are the warmest.

NATIONAL PARKS

When the Yugoslav Federation collapsed, seven of its finest national parks ended up in Croatia. Brijuni near Pula is the most carefully cultivated park, with well-preserved Mediterranean holm oak forests. The mountainous Risnjak National Park near Delnice, east of Rijeka, is named after one of its inhabitants – the *ris*, or lynx.

Dense forests of beech trees and black pine in Paklenica National Park near Zadar are home to a number of endemic insects, reptiles and birds, as well as the endangered griffon vulture. The abundant plant and animal life, including bears, wolves and deer, in Plitvice National Park between Zagreb and Zadar has put it onto Unesco's list of World Natural Heritage sites. Both Plitvice and Krka National Park near Šibenik feature a dramatic series of cascades.

The 101 stark and rocky islands of the Kornati Archipelago and National Park make it the largest in the Mediterranean. The island of Mljet near Korčula also contains a forested national park.

CROATIA

GOVERNMENT & POLITICS

Croatia is a parliamentary democracy with a powerful presidency. Croatia's first president was Franjo Tudjman who died in December 1999. Beleaguered by allegations of corruption and cronyism, Tudjman's party, the Croatian Democratic Union or HDZ, was resoundingly defeated in parliamentary elections that took place in January 2000.

The election of Ivica Račan as prime minister and Stipe Mesic as president was a rejection of the strongly nationalistic policies of the HDZ and has ushered in a rapprochement with the West. The new government has moved to end Croatia's international isolation by cooperating with the War Crimes Tribunal at the Hague, speeding the return of Serbian refugees and enacting legislation expanding minority rights. In May 2000, Croatia was admitted into NATO's Partnership for Peace, further cementing ties with the West.

ECONOMY

The years since independence have presented the government with some formidable challenges. As a new country, the government had to switch from a state-controlled to a privatised economy. It had to rebuild its infrastructure after a devastating war, rehouse returning refugees and find new markets for its products after losing markets in the southern regions of former Yugoslavia. Although the government has generally been pursuing a fiscally sound policy in order to earn support from the International Monetary Fund, the sale of state assets to politically connected insiders under Tudjman's regime made privatisation look more like highway robbery than economic reform.

In addition to dealing with the residue of a banking crisis that occurred in the late 1990s, the new government is pushing ahead with a more transparent approach to privatisation and attempting to improve exports by allowing the kuna to depreciate. Nevertheless, exports remain weak as demand for Croatian products in Italy, Germany, Austria and Russia has slowed. Keeping inflation in check (4.4% in 1999) by holding the lid on wage increases in the public sector and maintaining a tight fiscal policy should pull Croatia out of the economic doldrums by the middle of this decade and lead to stronger growth. Currently, a 3% growth rate is forecast for 2000 but the unemployment rate is high (16.5% in 1999) and the average wage is only about 3000KN (US$375) per month. The average Croatian has seen a steep decline in their standard of living since the country's independence.

Tourism is expected to spearhead the new economy in Croatia. In the past, one-third of Croatia's national income came from tourism, but between 1991 and 1995 tourist numbers fell dramatically. Just as tourism was beginning to rebound, the 1999 war in Kosovo again labelled the region as a war zone and tourists stayed away in droves. Investment in improving tourist infrastructure has started to pay off and, if the region remains peaceful, tourism should eventually return to prewar levels.

POPULATION & PEOPLE

Before the war, Croatia had a population of nearly five million, of which 78% were Croats and 12% were Serbs. Now it has a population of around 4.7 million, but with a constant flow of refugees in both directions, reliable statistics since the war have been very difficult to compile. It's estimated that only 5% of the Serbian population remains in Croatia. Small communities of Slavic Muslims, Hungarians, Slovenes, Italians, Czechs and Albanians complete the mosaic. The largest cities in Croatia are Zagreb (one million), Split (300,000), Rijeka (225,000), Osijek (175,000) and Zadar (150,000).

ARTS

The Art Pavilion in Zagreb is a good place to keep up with the latest developments in Croatian art.

Painting

Vlaho Bukovac (1855-1922) was the most notable Croatian painter in the late 19th century. Early 20th-century painters of note include Miroslav Kraljević (1885-1913) and Josip Račić (1885-1908). Post-war artists experimented with abstract expressionism but this period is best remembered for the naive art that was typified by Ivan Generalić (1914-1992). Recent trends have included minimalism, conceptual art and pop art.

Sculpture

The work of sculptor Ivan Meštrović (1883-1962) is seen in town squares all around Croatia. Besides creating public monuments, Meštrović designed imposing buildings such as the circular Historical Museum of Croatia in Zagreb. Both his sculpture and architecture display the powerful classical restraint he learnt from Rodin. Meštrović's studio in Zagreb and his retirement home at Split have been made into galleries of his work.

Music & Dance

Croatian folk music bears many influences. The *kolo*, a lively Slavic round dance in which men and women alternate in the circle, is accompanied by Roma-style violinists or players of the *tambura,* a three- or five-string mandolin popular throughout the country. The measured guitar-playing and rhythmic accordions of Dalmatia have a gentle Italian air.

A recommended recording available locally on CD is *Narodne Pjesme i Plesovi Sjeverne Hrvatske* (Northern Croatian Folk Songs and Dances) by the Croatian folkloric ensemble Lado. The 22 tracks on this album represent nine regions, with everything from haunting Balkan voices reminiscent of Bulgaria to lively Mediterranean dance rhythms.

SOCIETY & CONDUCT

As the Yugoslav years and the bitter struggle for independence recede into the past, the country's real personality is beginning to emerge. The long coastline that spent centuries under Italian domination is infused with a Mediterranean insouciance while the interior has a Central European sense of orderliness and propriety. The contrasting attitudes create a society that operates efficiently even though there seem to be few rules and the prevailing spirit is *'nema problema'* (no problem).

Croats take pride in keeping up appearances. Despite a fragile economy, money can usually be found to brighten up the town centre with a fresh coat of paint or to repair a historic building. Even as their bank accounts diminish, most people will cut out restaurants and movies to afford a shopping trip to Italy for some new clothes. The tidy streets and stylish clothes are rooted in the Croats' image

of themselves as Western Europeans, not Yugoslavs, a word that makes Croats wince. Dressing neatly will go a long way towards gaining a traveller acceptance.

RELIGION

Croats are overwhelmingly Roman Catholic, while virtually all Serbs belong to the Eastern Orthodox Church. In addition to various doctrinal differences, Orthodox Christians venerate icons, allow priests to marry and do not accept the authority of the Roman Catholic pope. Long suppressed under communism, Catholicism is undergoing a strong resurgence in Croatia and churches have strong attendances every Sunday. Muslims make up 1.2% of the population and Protestants 0.4%, with a tiny Jewish population in Zagreb.

LANGUAGE

Croatian is a South Slavic language, as are Serbian, Slovene, Macedonian and Bulgarian. Prior to 1991 both Croatian and Serbian were considered dialects of a single language known as Serbo-Croatian. As a result of the civil war in former Yugoslavia, the local languages are being revised, so spellings and idioms may change.

The most obvious difference between Serbian and Croatian is that Serbian is written in Cyrillic script and Croatian in Roman script. There are also a number of variations in vocabulary.

Geographical terms worth knowing are *aleja* (walkway), *cesta* (road), *donji* (lower), *gora* (hill), *grad* (town), *jezero* (lake), *krajina* (frontier), *luka* (harbour), *malo* (little), *novo* (new), *obala* (bank, shore), *otok* (island), *planina* (mountain), *polje* (valley), *prolaz* (strait), *put* (path), *rijeka* (river), *selo* (village), *šetalište* (way), *stanica* (station, stop), *stari* (old), *šuma* (forest), *sveti* (saint), *toplice* (spa), *trg* (square), *ul* (street), *veliko* (big), *vrata* (pass), *vrh* (peak) and *zaljev* (bay).

Two words everyone should know are *ima* (there is) and *nema* (there isn't). If you make just a small effort to learn a few words, you'll distinguish yourself from the packaged tourists and be greatly appreciated by the local people.

As a result of history, tourism and the number of returned 'guest workers' from

Germany, German is the most commonly spoken second language in Croatia. Many people in Istria speak Italian and English is popular among young people.

Lonely Planet's *Mediterranean Europe phrasebook* includes a useful chapter on the Serbian and Croatian languages, with translations of key words and phrases from each appearing side by side, providing a clear comparison of the languages. For a basic rundown on travellers' Croatian and Serbian, see the Language Guide at the end of this book.

Facts for the Visitor

HIGHLIGHTS
Museums & Galleries
Art museums and galleries are easier for a foreign visitor to enjoy than historical museums, which are usually captioned in Croatian only. In Zagreb, the Museum Mimara contains an outstanding collection of Spanish, Italian and Dutch paintings as well as an archaeological collection, exhibits of ancient art from Asia and collections of glass, textiles, sculpture and furniture. The Strossmayer Gallery, also in Zagreb, is worthwhile for its exhibits of Italian, Flemish, French and Croatian paintings.

The Meštrović Gallery in Split is worth a detour and in Zagreb the Meštrović Studio gives a fascinating insight into the life and work of this remarkable sculptor.

Beaches
Whether rocky, pebbly, gravelly or (rarely) sandy, Croatian beaches are often on the edge of a pine grove and slope into crystalline water that always seems to be the right temperature. The coastline is indented with wide bays and cosy coves where you just might be tempted to cast off your bathing suit along with the many naturists that flock to the Croatian shores each summer.

Historic Towns
All along the Adriatic coast are white-stone towns with narrow, winding streets enclosed by defensive walls. Each town has its own flavour. Hilly Rovinj looks out over the sea, while the peninsula of Korčula town burrows

into it. Zadar retains echoes of its original Roman street plan while Hvar and Trogir are traditional medieval towns. None can match the exquisite harmony of Dubrovnik, with its blend of elements of medieval and Renaissance architecture.

SUGGESTED ITINERARIES
Depending on the length of your stay, you might want to see and do the following things:

Two days
  Visit Dubrovnik.
One week
  Visit Zagreb, Split and Dubrovnik.
Two weeks
  Visit Zagreb and all of Dalmatia.
One month
  Visit all the areas covered in this chapter.

PLANNING
When to Go
May is a nice month to travel along the Adriatic coast, with good weather and few tourists. June and September are also good, but in the popular months of July and August all of Europe arrives and prices soar. September is perhaps the best month since it's not as hot as summer, though the sea remains warm, the crowds will have thinned out as children return to school, off-season accommodation rates apply and fruit such as figs and grapes will be abundant. In April and October it may be too cool for camping, but the weather should still be fine along the coast and private rooms will be plentiful and inexpensive.

Maps
Kümmerley & Frey's map *Croatia & Slovenia* (1:500,000) is detailed and depicts the latest borders. Most tourist offices in the country have local maps, but make sure the street names are up to date.

TOURIST OFFICES
Local Tourist Offices
The Croatian National Tourist Board (☎ 45 56 455, fax 45 57 827, ✉ info@htz.hr), Iberov trg 10, Importanne Gallerija, 10000 Zagreb, is a good source of information and has a useful Web site at www.htz.hr. There

are regional tourist offices that supervise tourist development, and municipal tourist offices that have free brochures and good information on local events. Some arrange private accommodation.

Tourist information is also dispensed by commercial travel agencies such as Atlas, Croatia Express, Generalturist, and Kompas, which also arrange private rooms, sightseeing tours etc. The agencies often sell local guidebooks, which are excellent value if you'll be staying for a while. Ask for the schedule for coastal ferries.

Tourist Offices Abroad
Croatian tourist offices abroad include:

UK (☎ 020-8563 7979) Croatian National Tourist Office, 2 Lanchesters, 162-64 Fulham Palace Rd, London W6 9ER

USA (☎ 212-279 8672) Croatian National Tourist Office, Suite 4003, 350 Fifth Ave, New York, NY 10118

EMBASSIES & CONSULATES
Visitors from Australia, Canada, New Zealand, the UK and the USA no longer require a visa for stays less than 90 days. For other nationalities, visas are issued free of charge at Croatian consulates. Croatian authorities require all foreigners to register with the local police when they first arrive in a new area of the country, but this is a routine matter that is normally handled by the hotel, hostel, camp site or agency securing private accommodation.

Croatian Embassies & Consulates
Croatian embassies and consulates abroad include:

Australia (☎ 02-6286 6988) 14 Jindalee Crescent, O'Malley, ACT 2601
 (☎ 03-9699 2633) 9-24 Albert Rd, South Melbourne, Vic 3205
 (☎ 02-9299 8899) Level 4, 379 Kent St, Sydney, NSW 2000
 (☎ 09-321 6044) 68 St George's Terrace, Perth, WA 6832
Canada (☎ 613-568 7820) 229 Chapel St, Ottawa, Ontario K1N 7Y6
 (☎ 905-277 9051) Suite 302, 918 Dundas St E, Mississauga, Ontario L4Y 2B8

New Zealand (☎ 09-836 5581) 131 Lincoln Rd, Henderson, Box 83200, Edmonton, Auckland
UK (☎ 0171-387 0022) 21 Conway St, London W1P 5HL
USA (☎ 202-588-5899) 2343 Massachusetts Ave NW, Washington, DC 20008

Embassies & Consulates in Croatia
The following addresses are in Zagreb (area code ☎ 01), unless otherwise noted:

Albania (☎ 48 10 679) Jurišiaeva 2a
Australia (☎ 48 36 600) Kršnjavoga 1
Bosnia-Hercegovina (☎ 46 83 762) Torbarova 9
Bulgaria (☎ 48 23 336) Novi Goljak 25
Canada (☎ 48 81 200) Prilaz Gjure Deželića 4
Czech Republic (☎ 61 77 246) Savska 41
Hungary (☎ 48 34 990) Krležin Gvozd 11a
Poland (☎ 48 34 579) Krležin Gvozd 3
Romania (☎ 24 30 137) Srebrnjak 150a
Slovakia (☎ 48 48 941) Prilaz Gjure Deželića 10
Slovenia (☎ 63 11 014) Savska 41
UK (☎ 45 55 310) Vlaška 121, Zagreb 21000
 (☎ 021-341 464) Obala hrvatskog narodnog preporoda 10, Split 21000
 (☎ 020-412 916) Petilovrijenci 2, Dubrovnik 20000
USA (☎ 45 55 500) Andrije Hebranga 2
Yugoslavia (☎ 46 80 552) Mesićeva 19

MONEY
Currency
In May 1994 the Croatian dinar was replaced by the kuna, which takes its name from the marten, a fox-like animal whose pelt was a means of exchange in the Middle Ages. Visitors are allowed to import or export Croatian banknotes up to a value of around 2000KN but there's no reason to do either. Like other Continental Europeans, Croats indicate decimals with commas and thousands with points.

Exchange Rates

country	unit		kuna
Australia	A$1	=	4.75KN
Canada	C$1	=	5.59KN
euro	€1	=	7.46KN
France	10FF	=	11.37KN
Germany	DM1	=	3.81KN
Japan	¥100	=	7.77KN
NZ	NZ$1	=	3.57KN
UK	UK£1	=	12.32KN
USA	US$1	=	8.32KN

CROATIA

Exchanging Money

There are numerous places to change money, all offering similar rates; ask at any travel agency for the location of the nearest exchange. Banks and exchange offices keep long hours. Exchange offices may deduct a commission of 1% to change cash or travellers cheques but some banks do not. Kuna can be converted into hard currency only at a bank and if you submit a receipt of a previous transaction. Hungarian currency is difficult to change in Croatia.

Credit Cards American Express, Master-Card, Visa and Diners Club cards are widely accepted. ATMs accepting MasterCard, Maestro, Cirrus, Plus and Visa are available in most bus and train stations, airports, all major cities and most small towns. Make sure you have a four-digit personal identification number (PIN).

Costs

Hotel prices, private accommodation and ferry fares were set in Deutschmarks at the time of research and thus were fairly constant, though payment is in kuna calculated at the daily official rate. Accommodation is more expensive than it should be for a country trying to lure more tourism, and real budget accommodation is in short supply. Transport, concert and theatre tickets, and meals are reasonably priced for Europe.

Accommodation takes the largest chunk of a travel budget and costs vary widely depending on the season. If you travel in March you'll have no trouble finding a private room for 90KN per person but prices climb upward to double that amount in July and August. Count on 25KN for a meal at a self-service restaurant and 35KN to 50KN for an average intercity bus fare. It's not that hard to survive on 200KN daily if you stay in hostels or private rooms and you'll pay less if you camp and self-cater, sticking to things like bread, cheese, tinned fish or meat, yoghurt and wine (cooking facilities are seldom provided).

Your daily expenses will come down a lot if you can find a private room to use as a base for exploring nearby areas. Coastal towns that lend themselves to this include Rovinj, Krk, Rab, Split, Korčula and Dubrovnik. You will also escape the 30% to 50% surcharge on private rooms rented for less than four nights.

Tipping

If you're served fairly and well at a restaurant, you should round up the bill as you're paying, but a service charge is always included. (Don't leave money on the table.) Bar bills and taxi fares can also be rounded up. Tour guides on day excursions expect to be tipped.

Taxes & Refunds

A 22% Value Added Tax is imposed upon most purchases and services and is included in the price. If your purchases exceed 500KN in one store you can claim a refund upon leaving the country. Ask the merchant for the paperwork.

POST & COMMUNICATIONS
Post

Mail sent to Poste Restante, 10000 Zagreb, Croatia, is held at the post office (open 24 hours) next to the Zagreb train station. A good coastal address to use is c/o Poste Restante, Main Post Office, 21000 Split, Croatia.

If you have an American Express card, most Atlas travel agencies will hold your mail. Consult American Express for a list of the cooperating agencies.

Telephone

To call Croatia from abroad, dial your international access code, ☎ 385 (the country code for Croatia), the area code (without the initial zero) and the local number. When calling from one region to another within Croatia, use the initial zero but do not use the area code when calling within the region.

To make a phone call from Croatia, go to the main post office – phone calls placed from hotel rooms are much more expensive. As there are no coins you'll need a phonecard to use public telephones.

Phonecards are sold according to units (impulsa) and you can buy cards of 50, 100, 200 and 500 units. These can be purchased at any post office and most tobacco shops and newspaper kiosks. Many new phone boxes have a button on the upper left with a flag symbol. Press the button and you get instructions in English. A three-minute call from

Croatia will cost around 20KN to the UK and the USA, 24KN to Australia and 16KN to other European countries. The international access code is ☎ 00. Some other useful numbers are ☎ 92 for the police, ☎ 93 for fire, ☎ 94 for emergency medical assistance and ☎ 901 to place an operator-assisted call.

Email & Internet Access

Cybercafes are becoming increasingly plentiful in Croatia; their locations are noted in each city entry. The going rate is about 20KN per hour and the connections are usually good. America Online has access numbers in Zagreb, Split, Rijeka and Dubrovnik.

INTERNET RESOURCES

All regions and many municipalities now have Web sites that range from collections of pretty pictures to detailed information on accommodation and activities. Very few hotels have Web sites or even email, however, making online booking unreliable. Most boat companies have Web sites with up to date information on schedules and fares. The Jadrolinija site at www.tel.hr/jadrolinija is indispensable if you'll be travelling by boat. Also check the Adriatica Web site at www.adriatica.it and SEM at www.sem.hr/. Croatia Airlines maintains a useful site at www.ctn.tel.hr/ctn/index-en.html, and www.akz.hr connects you to the Zagreb bus station with schedules and fares. The jazzy site at www.dalmatia.net has a grab bag of cultural, political, practical and entertainment information as well as links to other sites.

BOOKS

For a comprehensive account of the personalities and events surrounding the collapse of former Yugoslavia it would be hard to surpass *The Death of Yugoslavia* by Laura Silber & Allan Little, based on the 1995 BBC television series of the same name. Richard Holbrooke's *To End a War* is a riveting look at the people and events surrounding the Dayton peace agreement. *Café Europa* is a series of essays by a Croatian journalist, Slavenka Drakulić, which provides an inside look at life in the country since independence. Rebecca West's 1937 travel classic, *Black Lamb & Grey Falcon*, contains a long section on Croatia as part of her trip through

Yugoslavia. Robert Kaplan's *Balkan Ghosts* touches on Croatia's part in the tangled web of Balkan history.

For a more comprehensive guide to Croatia, pick up Lonely Planet's *Croatia*. There's also Zoë Brân's *After Yugoslavia*, part of the Lonely Planet Journeys series, which retraces the author's 1978 trip through the former Yugoslavia.

NEWSPAPERS & MAGAZINES

The most respected daily newspaper in Croatia is *Vjesnik* but the most daring is the satirical news weekly *Feral Tribune*. Its investigative articles and sly graphics keep Croatian politicians and businessmen edgy. The English-language *Croatia Weekly* covers social, political and cultural developments and can be counted on for a rosy view of Croatian life. American, British and French newspapers and magazines can be hard to find outside large cities.

RADIO & TV

The three national television stations in Croatia fill a lot of air time with foreign programming, usually American and always in the original language. For local news, residents of Zadar, Split, Vinkovci and Osijek turn to their regional stations. Croatian Radio broadcasts news in English four times daily (8 am, 10 am, 2 pm, 11 pm) on FM frequencies 88.9, 91.3 and 99.3.

TIME

Croatia is on Central European Time (GMT/UTC plus one hour). Daylight saving comes into effect at the end of March, when clocks are turned forward an hour. At the end of September they're turned back an hour.

LAUNDRY

Self-service laundrettes are virtually unknown outside of Zagreb. Most camping grounds have laundry facilities, hotels will wash clothes for a (hefty) fee or you could make arrangements with the proprietor if you're staying in private accommodation.

HEALTH

Everyone must pay to see a doctor at a public hospital (*bolnica*) or medical centre (*dom zdravcja*) but the charges are reasonable.

CROATIA

Travel insurance is important, especially if you have a serious accident and have to be hospitalised. Medical centres often have dentists on the staff, otherwise you can go to a private dental clinic (*zubna ordinacija*).

WOMEN TRAVELLERS

Women face no special danger in Croatia although women on their own may be harassed and followed in large coastal cities. Some of the local bars and cafes seem like private men's clubs; a woman by herself is likely to be greeted with sudden silence and cold stares. There are few rules about appropriate dress and topless sunbathing is commonplace.

GAY & LESBIAN TRAVELLERS

Homosexuality has been legal in Croatia since 1977 and is generally tolerated as long as it remains discreet. Public displays of affection between members of the same sex may meet with hostility, however, especially outside major cities. A small lesbian and gay community is developing in Zagreb but not to the extent of many Western European cities. The only organisation that addresses homosexual issues is the lesbian group, Kontra, which has a hotline (☎ 098-238 308) open every Wednesday from 5 to 9 pm. Check out the Web site www.gay-croatia.com for up to date information on gay venues.

DANGERS & ANNOYANCES

Landmines left over from the war in Croatia pose no threat to the average visitor but it's important to be aware that certain areas of the country are still dangerous. Although the government moved with lightning speed to remove mines from any area even remotely interesting to tourists, the former confrontation line between Croat and federal forces is still undergoing de-mining operations. Eastern Slavonia was heavily mined and, outside of the main city of Osijek, de-mining is not yet completed. Main roads from Zagreb to the coast that pass through Karlovac and Knin are completely safe but it would be unwise to stray into fields or abandoned villages. As a general rule, you should avoid any area along this route in which shattered roofs or artillery-pocked walls indicate that rebuilding and, possibly, de-mining has not yet

occurred. If a place is abandoned, there may be a reason.

Personal security and theft are not problems in Croatia. The police and military are well disciplined and it's highly unlikely you'll have any problems with them in any of the places covered in this chapter.

See Post & Communications for emergency telephone numbers.

BUSINESS HOURS

Banking hours are 7.30 am to 7 pm on weekdays and 8 am to noon on Saturday. Many shops are open 8 am to 7 pm on weekdays and until 2 pm on Saturday. Along the coast, life is more relaxed; shops and offices frequently close around 1 pm for an afternoon break. Croats are early risers and by 7 am there will be lots of people on the street and many places will already be open.

PUBLIC HOLIDAYS & SPECIAL EVENTS

Public holidays are New Year's Day (1 January), Easter Monday (March/April), Labour Day (1 May), Bleiburg and Way of the Cross Victims Day (15 May), Statehood Day (30 May), Day of Antifascist Struggle (22 June), Homeland Thanksgiving Day (5 August), Feast of the Assumption (15 August), All Saints' Day (1 November) and Christmas and Feast of St Stephen (25 and 26 December). Statehood Day marks the anniversary of the declaration of independence in 1991, while Day of Antifascist Struggle commemorates the outbreak of resistance in 1941.

In July and August there are summer festivals in Dubrovnik, Opatija, Split and Zagreb. Mardi Gras celebrations that mark the beginning of Lent have recently been revived in many towns with the attendant parades and festivities. The many traditional annual events held around Croatia are included under Special Events in the city and town sections.

ACTIVITIES
Kayaking

There are countless possibilities for anyone carrying a folding sea kayak, especially among the Elafiti Islands (take the daily ferry from Dubrovnik to Lopud) and the Kornati Islands (take the daily ferry from Zadar to Sali).

Hiking

Risnjak National Park at Crni Lug, 12km west of Delnice between Zagreb and Rijeka, is a good hiking area in summer. Buses run from Delnice to Crni Lug near the park entrance about three times daily, and there's a small park-operated *hotel* (☎ 051-836 133) at Crni Lug, with rooms at around 200KN per person including breakfast. Because of the likelihood of heavy snowfalls, hiking is only advisable from late spring to early autumn. It's a 9km, 2½ hour climb from the park entrance at Bijela Vodica to Veliki Risnjak (1528m).

The steep gorges and beech forests of Paklenica National Park, 40km north-east of Zadar, also offer excellent hiking. Starigrad, the main access town for the park, is well connected by hourly buses from Zadar. Hotels and private accommodation are available in Starigrad, as well as a camping ground, *Paklenica* (☎ 023-369 276), which is open May to September.

Scuba Diving

The clear waters and varied underwater life of the Adriatic have led to a flourishing dive industry along the coast. Most dive shops offer certification courses for about 2124KN and one dive with rented equipment for 227KN to 268KN. Cave diving is the real speciality in Croatia; night diving and wreck diving are also offered and there are coral reefs in some places but in rather deep water.

You must get a permit to dive but this is easy: go to the harbour captain in any port with your passport, certification card and 100KN. Permission is valid for a year in any dive spot in the country. In Hvar, try Divecentre Hvar (☎ 021-761 822) at Hotel Jadran, Jelsa, and DDA Hvar (☎ 021-742 490) at Hotel Amphora, Hvar. On Krk, there's Delphin (☎ 051-656 126), Emilia Geistlicha 48, Baška. On Rab, there's Mirko (☎ 051-721 154), Barbat 710, Rab, and Rab-Eko (☎ 051-776 272), Kampor, Rab.

ACCOMMODATION

Along the Croatian coast, accommodation is priced according to three seasons, which tend to vary from place to place. Generally April, May and October are the cheapest months, June and September are mid-priced, but count on paying top price for the peak season, which runs for a six-week period in July and August. Prices quoted in this chapter are for the peak period and do not include 'residence tax', which runs from about 4KN to 7.50KN depending on the location and the season. Deduct about 25% if you come in June, the beginning of July and September, about 35% for May and October and about 50% for all other times. Note that prices for rooms in Zagreb are pretty much constant all year.

Camping

Nearly 100 camping grounds are scattered along the Croatian coast. Most operate from mid-May to September only, although a few are open in April and October. In May and late September, call ahead to make sure the camping ground is open before beginning the long trek out. The opening and closing dates in travel brochures and this book are only approximate and even local tourist offices can be wrong.

Many camping grounds, especially in Istria, are gigantic 'autocamps' with restaurants, shops and row upon row of caravans. These camps are the most expensive since the per person charge includes charges for a car or caravan. Expect to pay 28KN to 56KN per person at one of these establishments but only 16KN to 20KN per person and an additional 8KN to 16KN for a tent at most other camping grounds.

Nudist camping grounds (marked FKK) are among the best because their secluded locations ensure peace and quiet. However, bear in mind that freelance camping is officially prohibited.

Hostels

The Croatian YHA (☎ 01-48 47 953, fax 48 41 269), Dežmanova 9, Zagreb, operates summer youth hostels in Dubrovnik and Zadar and year-round hostels at Zagreb and Pula available to members only. Membership costs 40KN for adults over 26 years, 30KN for those under 26 and 10KN for children up to 14. The Zagreb hostel has the highest prices.

You can check out the YHA Web site at www.nncomp.com/hfhs.

CROATIA

Private Rooms

Private rooms in local homes are the best form of accommodation in Croatia – the equivalent of small private guesthouses in other countries. Such rooms can be arranged by travel agencies, but they add a lot of taxes and commission to your bill, so you'll almost always do better dealing directly with proprietors you meet on the street or by knocking on the doors of houses with 'sobe' or 'zimmer' (meaning 'rooms') signs. This way you avoid the residence tax but you also forgo the agency's quality control.

In major towns 'sobe' ladies are out hunting for customers from May to September but they tend to fade away off season. If the price asked is too high, bargain. Be sure to clarify whether the price agreed upon is per person or for the room. Tell the proprietor in advance how long you plan to stay or they may try to add a surprise 'supplement' when you leave after a night or two. At the agencies, singles are expensive and scarce but, on the street, sobe prices are usually per person, which favours the single traveller. Showers are always included.

It may be worthwhile to take half-board. Most families on the coast have a garden, a vineyard and access to the sea. You could begin with a home-made aperitif and progress to a garden-fresh salad, home-grown potatoes and grilled fresh fish, washed down with your host's very own wine.

It makes little sense to price-shop from agency to agency since prices are fixed in advance. Whether you deal with the owner directly or book through an agency, you'll pay more for short stays. Agencies add a 30% surcharge for stays less than four nights and sometimes 50% or even 100% for a one-night stay although you may be able to get them to waive the surcharge if you arrive off season. Travel agencies have classified rooms as either category I, II or III, but this is changing to a star system. The most expensive rooms are three-star and include a private bathroom. In a two-star room, the bathroom is shared with one other room; in a one-star room, the bathroom is shared with two other rooms or with the owner. If you're travelling in a small group, it may be worthwhile to get a small apartment with cooking facilities, which are widely available along the coast.

Hotels

There are few cheap hotels in Croatia – prices generally average around 350KN a double in the summer along the coast, dropping to around 250KN in late spring or early autumn. Still, if you're only staying one night and the private room agency is going to levy a 50% surcharge, you might consider getting a hotel room. In the off season, when most rooms are empty, you could try bargaining for a more realistic rate. Many hotels close from October to April or May.

The system of rating hotels is in the process of changing. Many hotels are classified as two, three or four star but some hotels retain the old A, B and C ratings as they await renovation. Four-star hotels are the most luxurious, with features such as satellite TV, direct-dial phones and minibars in rooms that are often air-conditioned; there may also be a swimming pool or two, a fitness centre and a nightclub. The vast majority of hotels are three-star and come equipped with TV, telephones and a hotel restaurant. Two-star hotel rooms tend to have private bathrooms but no TV or telephone.

Most hotels along the coast are sprawling cement blocks built in the 1970s to warehouse package tourists. Although the rooms are large, clean and reasonably comfortable the decor is often so out of date it's kitschy. Every so often you'll run across faded but elegant older hotels that recall the days when the Austrian aristocracy took holidays on the Adriatic but most of these hotels are sliding into decay. Recently, entrepreneurs have started up small hotels that show some style and provide a more intimate, personal experience for travellers.

FOOD

A restaurant (*restauracija*) or pub may also be called a *gostionica* and a cafe is known as a *kavana*. Self-service cafeterias are quick, easy and inexpensive, though the quality of the food tends to vary quite a lot. If the samples behind glass look cold or dried out, ask them to dish out a fresh plate for you. Better restaurants aren't that much more expensive if you choose carefully. In most of them the vegetables, salads and bread cost extra and some deluxe restaurants add a 10% service charge (not mentioned on the menu). Fish dishes are often charged by weight, which makes it difficult to know how much a certain dish will cost but an average portion is about 250g. Ice-cream cones are priced by the scoop.

Breakfast can be difficult to find in Croatia, as all you can get easily is coffee. For eggs, toast and jam you'll have to go somewhere expensive, otherwise you can buy some bread, cheese and milk at a supermarket and picnic somewhere. Throughout the former Yugoslavia the breakfast of the people is *burek,* a greasy layered pie made with meat *(mesa)* or cheese *(sira)* and cut on a huge metal tray.

A load of fruit and vegetables from the local market can make a healthy, cheap picnic lunch. There are plenty of supermarkets in Croatia – cheese, bread, wine and milk are readily available and fairly cheap. The person behind the meat counter at supermarkets will make a big cheese or bologna sandwich for you upon request and you only pay the price of the ingredients.

Regional Dishes

The Adriatic coast excels in seafood, including scampi, *prstaci* (shellfish) and Dalmatian *brodet* (mixed fish stewed with rice), all cooked in olive oil and served with boiled vegetables or *tartufe* (mushrooms) in Istria. In the Croatian interior, watch for *manistra od bobića* (beans and fresh maize soup) or *štrukle* (cottage cheese rolls). A Zagreb speciality is *štrukli* (boiled cheesecake).

Italian pizza and pasta are a good option in Istria and Dalmatia, costing about half of what you'd pay in Western Europe.

DRINKS

It's customary to have a small glass of brandy before a meal and to accompany the food with one of Croatia's fine wines. Ask for the local regional wine. Croatia is also famous for its plum brandies *(šljivovica),* herbal brandies *(travarica),* cognacs *(vinjak)* and liqueurs such as maraschino, a cherry liqueur made in Zadar, or herbal *pelinkovac.* Italian-style espresso is popular in Croatia.

Zagreb's Ožujsko beer *(pivo)* is very good but Karlovačko beer from Karlovac is even better. You'll probably want to practise saying *živjeli!* (cheers!).

ENTERTAINMENT

Culture was heavily subsidised by the communists and admission to operas, operettas and concerts is still reasonable. The main theatres offering musical programs are listed in this chapter, so note the location and drop by some time during the day to see what's on and purchase tickets. In the interior cities, winter is the best time to enjoy the theatres and concert halls. The main season at the opera houses of Rijeka, Split and Zagreb runs from October to May. These close for holidays in summer and the cultural scene shifts to the many summer festivals. Ask at municipal tourist offices about cultural events in their area.

Discos operate in summer in the coastal resorts and all year in the interior cities but the best way to mix with the local population is to enjoy a leisurely coffee or ice cream in a cafe. With the first hint of mild weather, Croatians head for an outdoor terrace to drink, smoke and watch the passing parade.

Getting There & Away

AIR

Croatia Airlines (☎ 01-48 72 727), at ul Teslina 5 in Zagreb, has flights from Zagreb to Amsterdam, Berlin, Düsseldorf, Frankfurt, Istanbul, London, Ljubljana, Madrid, Manchester, Milan, Mostar, Munich, Paris, Prague, Rome, Sarajevo, Skopje, Tel Aviv, Vienna and Zürich. There's a daily Croatia Airlines bus that connects Zagreb airport with Rijeka (85KN). Call (☎ 051-330 207) to reserve. (Note that all batteries must be removed from checked luggage for all Croatia Airlines flights.)

LAND
Bus

Austria Eurolines Vienna runs a weekly bus from Vienna to Rijeka, Split and Zadar (330KN) and a twice daily bus (except Sunday) to Zagreb (190KN).

Benelux Budget Bus/Eurolines offers a weekly bus all year from Amsterdam to Zagreb (820KN, 26 hours) and another bus to

Rijeka and Split with an extra weekly bus to both destinations during summer. All buses change at Frankfurt. Reductions are available for children under 13, but not for students or seniors. Eurolines operates a twice-weekly service all year from Brussels to Zagreb, changing in Munich or Frankfurt, and another weekly bus to Rijeka and the Dalmatian coast, changing in Frankfurt. On all Dutch and Belgian services you will be charged DM5 per piece of luggage. An advance reservation (25KN) is recommended.

Germany Deutsche Touring GmbH runs buses from Berlin (720KN, four daily), Cologne, Dortmund, Frankfurt-am-Main, Mannheim, Munich (240KN, 576km, twice daily), Nuremberg, Stuttgart and other cities to Šibenik, Zadar, Split and Zagreb, and two buses a week to Dubrovnik. There's a weekly bus to Istria from Frankfurt and two buses a week from Munich. The Dalmatian coast is also served by daily buses from German cities and there's a twice weekly bus direct from Berlin to Rijeka and on to Zadar and Split. Baggage is DM5 extra per piece. Information is available at bus stations in the cities just mentioned.

Italy Regular daily buses connect Trieste with the Istrian coast and there is a daily bus from Venice to Pula (150KN, six hours).

Yugoslavia There are three buses each morning from Zagreb to Belgrade (180KN, six hours). At Bajakovo on the border, a Yugoslav bus takes you on to Belgrade. The border between Montenegro and Croatia is open to visitors, allowing Americans, Australians, Canadians and Brits to enter visa-free. For further information see the Dubrovnik Getting There & Away section of this chapter.

Train
Austria The *Ljubljana* express travels daily from Vienna to Rijeka (eight hours), via Ljubljana, and the EuroCity *Croatia* from Vienna to Zagreb (347KN, 6½ hours); both travel via Maribor, Slovenia.

Germany There are three daily trains from Munich to Zagreb (500KN, nine hours) via Salzburg and Ljubljana.

Hungary To go from Budapest to Zagreb (156KN to 168KN, 6½ hours) you have a choice of four trains daily; you can stop in Nagykanizsa, the first main junction inside Hungary (84KN). As well as the international express trains, there are unreserved local trains between Gyékényes (Hungary) and Koprivnica (20 minutes), between Varaždin and Nagykanizsa (1½ hours) and between Pećs and Osijek (68KN, 2½ hours).

Italy Between Venice and Zagreb (279KN, seven hours) there's an overnight direct train and a daily train via Trieste and Ljubljana.

Romania There's one daily train to Bucharest (580KN, 25 hours).

Yugoslavia Four trains daily connect Zagreb with Belgrade (128KN, 6½ hours).

Car & Motorcycle
The main highway entry/exit points between Croatia and Hungary are Goričan (between Nagykanizsa and Varaždin), Gola (23km east of Koprivnica), Terezino Polje (opposite Barcs) and Donji Miholjac (7km south of Harkány). There are 29 crossing points to/from Slovenia, too many to list here. There are 23 border crossings into Bosnia-Hercegovina and 10 into Yugoslavia, including the main Zagreb to Belgrade highway. Major destinations in Bosnia-Hercegovina, such as Sarajevo, Mostar and Međugorje, are accessible from Zagreb, Split and Dubrovnik.

SEA
Regular boats connect Croatia with Italy. The Croatian Jadrolinija line, the Italian Adriatica Navigazione and the Croatian companies Lošinjska Plovidba and SEM all serve the Adriatic coast. Three to six Jadrolinija ferries run a week, year-round, between Ancona and Split (311KN, 10 hours). They stop twice a week from June to September at Stari Grad on Hvar Island. Adriatica Navigazione connects Ancona and Split three times a week in summer for the same price and twice a week in winter, and SEM connects the two cities six times a week in winter and daily in July and August for 230KN. SEM also connects Ancona and Stari Grad on Hvar Island twice a week in July and August.

Other Jadrolinija lines from Ancona stop at Zadar year-round (288KN, seven hours, twice weekly), Šibenik (311KN, 8½ hours, twice weekly in summer), Vela Luka on Korčula Island (311KN, 17 hours, weekly in summer).

The Jadrolinija coastal line connects Bari and Rijeka weekly year-round, stopping at Dubrovnik, Mljet, Korčula, Stari Grad, Split and Zadar. The 33-hour trip costs 1475KN. There's also a Dubrovnik-Bari connection weekly in winter and three times a week in summer (311KN, nine hours).

Both Adriatica Navigazione and Lošinjska Plovidba connect Italy with the Istrian coast in summer. From May to September Adriatica Navigazione runs the *Marconi* between Trieste and Rovinj (L30,000, 3½ hours), stopping at the Brijuni Islands six times a week and stopping three times a week in July and August at Poreč (L27,000, 2¾ hours) and once a week in Pula (L45,000, 5½ hours). Lošinjska Plovidba's *Marina* connects Venice with Zadar (L90,000, 14½ hours) twice a week from late June to September, stopping at Pula and Mali Lošinj. Payment must be made in Italian lire and the prices include departure tax.

From May to September, Miatours in Zadar runs a fast boat between Zadar and Ancona (370KN off season, 420KN July to August, 3¼ hours).

Prices given are for deck passage in the summer season. Prices are about 20% less in the off season and there's a 20% reduction for the return portion of a return ticket on Jadrolinija ferries. A couchette on an overnight boat costs about an extra 100KN to 150KN.

DEPARTURE TAX

The airport departure tax is 94KN, which is included in the cost of the ticket. There is no port tax if you leave the country by boat.

Getting Around

AIR

Croatia Airlines has daily flights from Zagreb to Brač (1005KN, 65 minutes), Dubrovnik (876KN, one hour), Pula (700KN, 50 minutes), Split (897KN, 85 minutes) and Zadar (700KN, 40 minutes). Prices are somewhat lower off season and there are discounts for seniors and people under 26.

BUS

Bus services in Croatia are excellent. Prices can vary substantially between companies and depend on the route taken, but the prices in this book should give you an idea of costs. Because the price is per kilometre it's possible to pay more for a slow local bus than a fast express. Luggage stowed in the baggage compartment under the bus costs extra (6KN a piece, including insurance).

At large stations, bus tickets must be purchased at the office, not from drivers; try to book ahead to be sure of a seat. Lists of departures over the various windows at the bus stations tell you which one has tickets for your bus. Tickets for buses that arrive from somewhere else are usually purchased from the conductor. On Croatian bus schedules, *vozi svaki dan* means 'every day', and *ne vozi nedjeljom ni praznikom* means 'not Sunday and public holidays'.

TRAIN

Train travel is about 15% cheaper than bus travel and often more comfortable, though slower. Local trains usually have only unreserved 2nd-class seats but they're rarely crowded. Reservations may be required on express trains. 'Executive' trains have only 1st-class seats and are 40% more expensive than local trains. Most train stations have left-luggage offices charging about 10KN apiece (passport required). There are two daily trains from Zagreb to Zadar and Split, stopping at Knin where you can change to Šibenik. Other trains include Zagreb to Osijek (80 to 96KN, five hours, 288km), Koprivnica (31KN, 1½ hours, 92km, local), Varaždin (36KN, three hours, 110km, local), Ljubljana (87KN, three hours, 160km, local), Rijeka (55KN, five hours, 243km, local) and Pula (90KN, 6½ hours).

On posted timetables in Croatia the word for arrivals is *dolazak* and for departures it's *odlazak* or *polazak*. Other terms you may encounter include *poslovni* (executive train), *brzi* or *ubrazni* (fast train), *putnički* (local train), *rezerviranje mjesta obvezatno* (compulsory seat reservation), *presjedanje* (change of trains), *ne vozi nedjeljom i blag-danom* (no service Sunday and holidays) and *svakodnevno* (daily).

CAR & MOTORCYCLE
Motorists require vehicle registration papers and the green insurance card to enter Croatia. Two-way amateur radios built into cars are no problem but must be reported at the border.

Petrol is either leaded super, unleaded (*bezolovni*) or diesel. You have to pay tolls on the motorways around Zagreb, to use the Učka tunnel between Rijeka and Istria, the bridge to Krk Island, as well as the road from Rijeka to Delnice.

Along the coast, the spectacular Adriatic highway from Italy to Albania hugs the steep slopes of the coastal range, with abrupt drops to the sea and a curve a minute. You can drive as far south as Vitaljina, 56km southeast of Dubrovnik but the curves, potholes and reckless drivers make it a road to be reckoned with.

Motorists can turn to the Hrvatski Autoklub (HAK; Croatian Auto Club) for help or advice. Addresses of local HAK offices are provided throughout this chapter and the nationwide HAK road assistance (*vučna služba*) number is ☎ 987.

Unless otherwise posted, the speed limits for cars and motorcycles are 50km/h in built-up areas, 80km/h on main highways and 130km/h on motorways. Police systematically fine motorists exceeding these limits. On any of Croatia's winding two-lane highways, it's illegal to pass long military convoys or a whole line of cars caught behind a slow-moving truck. Drive defensively, as some local motorists lack discipline.

Rental
The large car-rental chains represented in Croatia are Avis, Budget, Europcar and Hertz, with Budget (offices in Opatija, Split and Zagreb) generally the cheapest and Hertz the most expensive. Throughout Croatia, Avis is allied with Autotehna, while Hertz is often represented by Kompas.

Independent local companies are often much less expensive than the international chains, but Avis, Budget, Europcar and Hertz have the big advantage of offering one-way rentals that allow you to drop the car off at any one of their many stations in Croatia free of charge.

Prices at local companies begin at around 305KN a day with unlimited kilometres. Shop around as deals vary widely and 'special' discounts and weekend rates are often available. Third-party public liability insurance is included by law, but make sure your quoted price includes full collision insurance, called collision damage waiver (CDW). Otherwise your responsibility for damage done to the vehicle is usually determined as a percentage of the car's value. Full CDW begins at 30KN a day extra (compulsory for those aged under 25), theft insurance is 15KN a day and personal accident insurance another 10KN a day.

The minimum age to rent a car is 21 and some companies require that you have had a licence for at least a year. If you're paying by cash, the amount of the cash deposit is usually based upon the type of car and the length of the rental.

Sometimes you can get a lower car-rental rate by booking the car from abroad. Tour companies in Western Europe often have fly-drive packages that include a flight to Croatia and a car (two-person minimum).

BOAT
Jadrolinija Ferries
Year-round big, white and blue international Jadrolinija car ferries operate along the Bari-Rijeka-Dubrovnik coastal route, stopping at Zadar, Split, and the islands Rab, Hvar, Korčula, and Mljet. Service is almost daily to the big cities during summer but is greatly reduced in winter. The most scenic section is Split to Dubrovnik, which all Jadrolinija ferries cover during the day. Rijeka to Split (13 hours) is usually an overnight trip in either direction.

Ferries are a lot more comfortable than buses, though considerably more expensive. From Rijeka to Dubrovnik the deck fare is 192KN, but it's at least 10% cheaper from October to May and there's a 20% reduction on the return portion of a return ticket. On certain boats there is a surcharge of 10% on weekends to and from Rijeka. With a through ticket, deck passengers can stop at any port for up to a week, provided they notify the purser beforehand and have their ticket validated. This is much cheaper than buying individual sector tickets but is only good for one stopover. Cabins should be booked a week ahead, but deck space is usually available on all sailings.

Deck passage on Jadrolinija is just that: reclining seats (*poltrone*) are about 26KN extra and four-berth cabins (if available) begin at 329KN (Rijeka to Dubrovnik). Cabins can be arranged at the reservation counter aboard ship, but advance bookings are recommended if you want to be sure of a place. Deck space is fine for passages during daylight hours and when you can stretch out a sleeping bag on the upper deck in good weather, but if it's rainy you could end up sitting in the smoky cafeteria, which stays open all night. You must buy tickets in advance at an agency or Jadrolinija office since they are not sold on board.

Other Ferries

Local ferries connect the bigger offshore islands with each other and the mainland. The most important routes are Baška on Krk Island to Lopar on Rab Island (25KN, up to five daily from May to September), Zadar to Preko on Ugljan Island (9KN, at least nine daily), Split to Stari Grad on Hvar Island (26KN, 1¾ hours, two or three daily), Split to Vela Luka on Korčula Island via Hvar (30KN, 2¾ hours, daily), Orebić to Korčula Island (8KN, 30 minutes, nine daily) and Dubrovnik to Sobra on Mljet Island (26KN, 2¼ hours, two daily). On most lines, service is increased from May to September.

Some of the ferries operate only a couple of times a day and, once the vehicular capacity is reached, remaining motorists must wait for the next service. In summer the lines of waiting cars can be long, so it's important for passengers to arrive early. Foot passengers and cyclists should have no problem getting on but you must buy tickets at an agency before boarding since they are not sold on board. You should bear in mind that taking a bicycle on these services will incur an extra charge.

HITCHING

Hitching is never entirely safe in any country in the world, and we don't recommend it.

Travellers who decide to hitch should understand that they are taking a small but potentially serious risk. People who do choose to hitch will be safer if they travel in pairs and let someone know where they are planning to go.

Hitchhiking in Croatia is undependable. You'll have better luck on the islands but in the interior you'll notice that cars are small and usually full. Tourists never stop. Unfortunately, the image many Croats have of this activity is based on violent movies like *The Hitcher*.

LOCAL TRANSPORT

Zagreb has a well-developed tram system as well as local buses but in the rest of the country you'll only find buses. In major cities such as Rijeka, Split, Zadar and Dubrovnik buses run about every 20 minutes, and less often on Sunday. Small medieval towns along the coast are generally closed to traffic and have infrequent links to outlying suburbs.

Taxis

Taxis are available in all cities and towns but must be called or boarded at a taxi stand; note that it's usually not possible to hail them in the street. Prices are high (meters start at 15KN) and are generally the same throughout the country.

ORGANISED TOURS

There are many group package tour companies based in London but Croatian-owned Dalmatian and Istrian Travel (☎ 020-8749 5255, fax 020-8740 4432), 21 Sawley Rd, London W12 OLG, offers independent packages with accommodation ranging from luxury hotels to camping and outdoor activities. A typical package that includes a return London-Dubrovnik air fare and a week's stay in private accommodation costs £320 high season.

An interesting alternative for sailing enthusiasts is Katarina Line (☎ 051-272 110) at Tita 75, Opatija, which offers week-long cruises from Opatija to Krk, Rab, Pag, Mali Lošinj and Cres or cruises from Split to Zadar that pass the Kornati Islands. Prices start at 2400KN a week and include half-board. See the Web site at www.katarina-line.hr.

Zagreb

☎ 01 • pop 810,000

As the political, economic and cultural capital of Croatia, Zagreb throbs with the energy you would expect from a major city. Spread up from the Sava River, Zagreb sits on the southern slopes of Medvednica, the Zagreb uplands. Medieval Zagreb developed from the 11th to the 13th centuries in the twin towns of Kaptol and Gradec. Kaptol grew around St Stephen's Cathedral and Gradec centred on St Mark's Church. Clerics established themselves in Kaptol as early as 1094, whereas Gradec was the craftspeople's quarter.

Much of medieval Zagreb remains today, although the stately 19th-century city between the old town and the train station is the present commercial centre. There are many fine parks, galleries and museums in both the upper and lower towns. Zagreb is Croatia's main centre for primitive or naive art.

Finding a place to stay at a reasonable price remains the biggest problem for a traveller in this calm and graceful city.

Orientation

As you come out of the train station, you'll see a series of parks and pavilions directly in front of you and the twin neo-Gothic towers of the cathedral in the distance. Trg Jelačića, beyond the northern end of the parks, is the main city square. The bus station is 1km east of the train station. Tram Nos 2 and 6 run from the bus station to the nearby train station, with No 6 continuing to Trg Jelačića.

Information

Tourist Offices The extremely helpful tourist office (☎ 48 14 051, fax 48 14 056, ✉ tic@zagreb-touristinfo.hr), Trg Jelačića 11, is open 8.30 am to 8 pm weekdays, 9 am to 5 pm Saturday and 10 am to 2 pm Sunday. Look for the free leaflets, *Zagreb Info A-Z, Zagreb Events & Performances* and *City Walks*.

The Croatian Auto Club (HAK) has an information centre (☎ 46 40 800) at Derenčinova 20.

Plitvice National Park maintains an information office (☎ 46 13 586) at Trg Tomislava 19. It also has information on other national parks around Croatia.

Jadrolinija (☎ 48 73 307), Zrinjevac 20, has information on coastal ferries.

Money There are ATMs at the bus and train stations and the airport as well as numerous locations around town. Exchange offices at the bus and train stations change money at the bank rate with 1% commission. Both the banks in the train station (open 7 am to 9 pm) and the bus station (open 6 am to 8 pm) accept travellers cheques. Croatia Express at the train station is open 24 hours and changes cash and travellers cheques.

The American Express representative in Zagreb is Atlas travel agency (☎ 48 13 933), Trg Zrinjskoga 17.

You can also change money (including travellers cheques) at A Tours in the bus station, open 6 am to 8 pm Monday to Friday and 8 am to 3 pm Saturday.

Post & Communications Any poste-restante mail is held (for one month) in the post office on the eastern side of the train station, which is open 24 hours. Have your letters addressed to Poste Restante, 10000 Zagreb, Croatia.

This post office is also the best place to make long-distance telephone calls.

Email & Internet Access Zagreb's flashiest cybercafe is Art Net Club (☎ 45 58 471) at Preradovićeva 25, which is open 9 am to 11 pm daily and hosts frequent concerts and performances. There's also Sublink (☎ 48 11 329, ✉ sublink@sublink.hr), Teslina 12, open noon to 10 pm Monday to Friday and 3 to 10 pm weekends.

Travel Agencies Dali Travel (☎ 48 47 472), Dežmanova 9, the travel branch of the Croatian YHA, can provide information on HI hostels throughout Croatia and make advance bookings.

It also sells ISIC student cards (40KN) to those who have proof of attendance at an educational institution. It's open 8 am to 4 pm weekdays.

Bookshops The Algoritam bookshop in the Hotel Dubrovnik off Trg Jelačića has a wide selection of English-language books and magazines available.

Laundry Predom, across the street from HAK on Draškovićeva 31, is open 7 am to 7 pm weekdays, and Saturday mornings. Petecin, Kaptol 11, is open 8 am to 8 pm Monday to Friday. Expect to pay about 3KN for underwear, 4KN for a shirt and 10KN for a skirt.

Left Luggage Left-luggage offices in the train station are open 24 hours. The left-luggage office in the bus station is open 5 am to 10 pm Monday to Saturday and 6 am to 10 pm Sunday. The price posted at the left-luggage office in the bus station is 1.20KN *per hour*, so be careful. At the train station you pay a fixed price of about 10KN per day.

Medical & Emergency Services If you need to see a doctor, your best bet is the Emergency Centar (☎ 46 10 011), Draškovićeva 19. It's open all the time and charges 200KN for an examination. The police station for foreigners with visa concerns is at Petrinjska 30.

Things to See

Kaptol Zagreb's colourful **Dolac vegetable market** is just up the steps from Trg Jelačića and continues north along Opatovina. It's open daily, with especially large gatherings on Friday and Saturday. The twin neo-Gothic spires of **St Stephen's Cathedral** (1899), now renamed the Cathedral of the Assumption of the Blessed Virgin Mary, are nearby. Elements from the medieval cathedral on this site, destroyed by an earthquake in 1880, can be seen inside, including 13th-century frescoes, Renaissance pews, marble altars and a baroque pulpit. The baroque **Archiepiscopal Palace** surrounds the cathedral, as do 16th-century fortifications constructed when Zagreb was threatened by the Turks.

Gradec From ul Radićeva 5, off Trg Jelačića, a pedestrian walkway called stube Ivana Zakmardija leads to the **Lotršćak Tower** and a funicular railway (1888), which connects the lower and upper towns (2KN). The tower has a sweeping 360° view of the city (closed Sunday). To the right is the baroque **St Catherine's Church**, with Jezuitski trg beyond. The **Galerija Klovićevi Dvori**, Jezuitski trg 4, is Zagreb's premier exhibition hall where superb art shows are staged (closed Monday). Farther north and to the right is the 13th-century **Stone Gate**, with a painting of the Virgin, which escaped the devastating fire of 1731.

The colourful painted-tile roof of the Gothic **St Mark's Church** on Markovićev trg marks the centre of Gradec. Inside are works by Ivan Meštrović, Croatia's most famous modern sculptor, but the church is only open for mass twice daily on weekdays and four times on Sunday. On the eastern side of St Mark's is the **Sabor** (1908), Croatia's National Assembly.

To the west of St Mark's is the 18th-century **Banski Dvori Palace**, the presidential palace with guards at the door in red ceremonial uniform. From April to September there is a guard-changing ceremony at noon on weekends.

At Mletačka 8 nearby is the former **Meštrović Studio**, now a museum that is open 9 am to 2 pm weekdays (10/5KN for adults/students and seniors). Other museums in this area include the **Historical Museum of Croatia** (10/5KN for temporary exhibitions), Matoševa 9; the **Gallery of Naive Art**, Ćirilometodska 3 (10/5KN); and the **Natural History Museum**, Demetrova 1 (15/7KN). More interesting is the recently renovated **City Museum**, Opatička 20 (20/10KN), with a scale model of old Gradec. Summaries in English and German are in each room of the museum, which is in the former Convent of St Claire (1650). Note that most of these museums are closed Monday.

Lower Town Zagreb really is a city of museums. There are four on the parks between the train station and Trg Jelačića. The yellow **exhibition pavilion** (1897) across the park from the station presents changing contemporary art exhibitions. The second building north, also in the park, houses the **Strossmayer Gallery** of the Academy of Arts & Sciences, with old master paintings. It's closed on Monday, but you can enter the interior courtyard to see the Baška Slab (1102) from the island of Krk, one of the oldest inscriptions in the Croatian language.

The **Archaeological Museum**, Trg Nikole Zrinjskog 19, has a fascinating and wide-ranging display of artefacts from prehistoric

ZAGREB

OTHER	
1 Polish Embassy	11 Petecin
2 City Museum	12 Komedija Theatre
3 Meštrović Studio	13 Galerija Klovićevo Dvori
4 Natural History Museum	14 Gallery of Naive Art
5 Saloon	15 Tolkien's House
6 Historical Museum	16 Lotršćak Tower
of Croatia	17 St Catherine's Church
7 Banski Dvori Palace	18 Dolac Vegetable Market
8 St Mark's Church	19 St Stephen's Cathedral
9 Sabor (Parliament)	20 Post Office; Telephone
10 Stone Gate	Centre
	24 Tourist Office
	25 Rokotvorine
	26 Nama Department
	Store
	27 British Council
	28 27 26 25
	29 Funicular Railway
	30 Croatian YHA;
	Dali Travel
	35 Academy of Music
	36 Oktogon
	37 Algoritam
	38 Sublink
	39 Hard Rock Café
	40 Jadrolinija
	41 Archaeological Museum
	42 Croatia Airlines
	43 Atlas Travel Agency
	44 US Embassy
	45 Art Net Club
	46 Kaz Kav
	47 Canadian Embassy
	48 Arts & Crafts Museum
	49 Croatian National
	Theatre
	50 Uni Rent
	51 Gallery of Modern Art
	52 Strossmayer Gallery
	53 Police Station
	54 Emergency Centar
	55 Predom
	58 Exhibition Pavilion
	59 Puppet Theatre
	60 Ethnographic Museum
	62 Museum Mimara
	63 National Library
	65 Plitvice National
	Park Office
	67 Pivnica Tomislav
	68 Evistas
	69 Post Office
	70 City Hall
	71 Vatroslav Lisinski
	Concert Hall

PLACES TO STAY	PLACES TO EAT
20 Hotel Jadran	21 Mimiće
28 Pansion Jägerhorn	22 Restaurante
56 Hotel Sheraton	Mexicana
57 Omladinski Hotel	31 Biovega
(Youth Hostel)	32 Market
66 Intercontinental Hotel	33 Delikatese
67 Central Hotel	34 Pizzicato

times through to the medieval era (20/10KN). Behind the museum is a garden of Roman sculpture that is turned into a pleasant open-air cafe in summer.

West of the Centre The **Museum Mimara** at Rooseveltov trg 5 (closed Sunday and Monday; 20/15KN) houses a diverse collection amassed by Ante Topić Mimara and donated to Croatia. Housed in a neo-Renaissance palace, the collection includes icons, glassware, sculpture, Oriental art and works by painters such as Rembrandt, Velasquez, Raphael and Degas. The **Gallery of Modern Art** at Hebrangova 1 has an excel-

lent collection of paintings by Croatian masters created from 1850 to 1950 when Croatian art was at its zenith.

On Trg Maršala Tita is the neo-baroque **Croatian National Theatre** (1895), with Ivan Meštrović's sculpture *Fountain of Life* (1905) in front. The **Ethnographic Museum** (closed Monday; 15/10KN) at Trg Mažuranića 14 has a large collection of Croatian folk costumes with English captions. To the south is the Art-Nouveau **National Library** (1907). The **Botanical Garden** on ul Mihanovićeva (free, closed Monday) is attractive for the plants and landscaping as well as its restful corners.

Organised Tours
Within Zagreb, the tourist office organises three-hour walking and minibus tours every Wednesday and Saturday morning leaving from the InterContinental, Sheraton and Esplanade Hotels for 100KN.

Special Events
In odd years in April there's the Zagreb Biennial of Contemporary Music, Croatia's most important music event since 1961. Zagreb also hosts a festival of animated films in even years in June. Croatia's largest international fairs are the Zagreb spring (mid-April) and autumn (mid-September) grand trade fairs. In July and August the Zagreb Summer Festival presents a cycle of concerts and theatre performances on open stages in the upper town.

Places to Stay
Budget accommodation is in short supply in Zagreb. An early arrival is recommended, since private room-finding agencies are an attractive alternative and usually refuse telephone bookings.

Camping There's a camping area outside *Motel Plitvice* (☎ 65 30 444), which is not in Plitvice at all but near the town of Lučko on the Obilazinica Hwy south-west of Zagreb. The motel sometimes runs a minibus from Savski Most. Call to find out if and when the service is operating. Otherwise, take tram No 7 or 14 to Savski Most and then the Lučko bus to Lučko village, from which the motel/camp site is about a 10-minute walk. The price is 30KN per person and 18KN per tent and there's a lake and a sports centre nearby.

Hostels The noisy 215-bed *Omladinski Hotel* (☎ 48 41 261, fax 48 41 269, Petrinjska 77) is actually a youth hostel and is near the train station. It's open all year and charges 149/204KN for a single/double without bath, and 202/274KN with bath, including tax. A few of the six-bed dormitories (80KN per person) may still be occupied by war refugees, but most rooms remain available. The 5KN YHA discount is only available to people under 27 sleeping in the dormitory. You must check out by 9 am and you can't occupy the room until 2 pm.

Studenthotel Cvjetno Naselje (☎ 61 91 239), off Slavonska avenija in the south of the city, charges 240/360KN, breakfast included. The rooms are good, each with private bath, and the staff are friendly. There's a self-service student restaurant here where a filling meal with a Coke will cost 30KN. Cvjetno Naselje is available to visitors only from mid-July to the end of September – the rest of the year it's a student dormitory. Take tram No 4, 5, 14, 16 or 17 south-west on Savska cesta to 'Vjesnik'.

In July and August head straight for *Studentski dom Stjepan Radić* (☎ 36 34 255, Jarunska ul 3), off Horvaćanska ul in the south of the city near Lake Jarun (tram No 5 or 17). Rooms in this huge student complex cost 150/300KN, and one of Zagreb's more popular discos, The Best, is across the street.

Private Rooms For private accommodation, your best bet is Evistas (☎ 48 39 546, fax 48 39 543, @ evistas@zg.tel.hr), Šenoina 28. Rooms with shared bath cost 182/254KN and apartments start at 365KN plus residence tax. Those under 25 can get rooms for 155/200KN. Prices are based upon a three-night stay; there's a 20% surcharge for staying only one night. The office is open 9 am to 8 pm Monday to Friday and 9.30 am to 5 pm Saturday. Otherwise, try Lacio (☎/fax 65 21 523), Trnsko 15e; Di Prom (☎ 65 50 039), Trnsko 25a; or Lina Gabino (☎ 39 21 27) at Bartolići 33 near Lake Jarun, which is the only agency open on Sunday.

Hotels The best deal for budget travellers is the new and friendly *Hotel Ilica* (☎ 37 77 622, fax 37 77 722, Ilica 102), two stops west from Trg Jelađića, which offers 12 quiet, pleasant rooms with TV and telephone for 299/399KN a single/double and 449KN for a double with two beds. Prices include breakfast.

The 110-room *Central Hotel* (☎ 484 11 22, fax 48 41 304, Branimirova 3), opposite the train station, is blandly modern and charges 327/474KN, including breakfast and tax. There are more expensive rooms available that have air-con.

The six-storey *Hotel Jadran* (☎ 45 53 777, fax 46 12 151, Vlaška 50), near the city centre, charges 360/436KN with TV, telephone and breakfast.

CROATIA

For a little more money, the new *Pansion Jägerhorn* (☎ *48 30 161, fax 43 00 92, Ilica 14*) offers comfortable, modern rooms with TV, telephone and air-con for 400/600KN and a three- or four-person, two-room apartment for 900KN.

For a memorable splurge, stay at the five-star *Hotel Esplanade* (☎ *45 66 666, fax 45 77 907,* ✉ *reservation@esplanade.tel.hr*), next to the train station. It charges 759/1400KN, plus tax and breakfast, and there's a 30% discount for weekend stays. This six-storey, 215-room hotel erected in 1924 is truly majestic and has one of the best restaurants in Zagreb.

Places to Eat

One of the most elegant places in town is undoubtedly the *Paviljon* in the yellow exhibition pavilion across the park from the train station. Main courses with an Italian flavour start at 70KN.

Pizza places are everywhere, but it would be hard to do better than the delicious, freshly made pizzas at *Pizzicato* (*Gundiliċeva 4*) near the Academy of Music. Prices start at 18KN and the menu is translated into English. For a change of pace, there's the *Restaurante Mexicana* (*Jurišiċeva 19*), which turns out decent *fajitas* for 59KN. The best restaurant for meaty Croatian specialties is *Baltazar* (*Nova Ves 4*). Vegetarians should head down to *Biovega* (*Ilica 72*), which offers a two-course vegetarian meal for 60KN. *Mimiċe* (*Jurišiċeva 21*) has been a local favourite for decades, turning out plates of fried fish that cost from 9KN for 10 sardines and a hunk of bread.

Delikatese (*Ilica 39*) is a good place to pick up cheese, fruit, bread, yoghurt and cold meat for a picnic. Next door is a *grocery store* that sells whole roasted chickens, an assortment of prepared salads and Pag cheese. Farther along Ilica at Britanski trg, there's a fruit and vegetable *market* open daily until 3 pm that sells farm fresh produce. Don't hesitate to bargain.

Entertainment

Zagreb is a happening city. Its theatres and concert halls present a great variety of programs throughout the year. Many (but not all) are listed in the monthly brochure *Zagreb Events & Performances*, which is usually available from the tourist office.

Cafes & Bars The liveliest scene in Zagreb is along Tkalčićeva, north of Trg Jelačića, where crowds spill out of cafes onto the street, drinks in hand. Farther up on Kozarska ul the city's young people cluster shoulder to shoulder. Trg Petra Preradoviċa, Zagreb's flower-market square, attracts street performers in mild weather and occasional bands.

Pivnica Tomislav (*Trg Tomislava 18*), facing the park in front of the train station, is a good local bar with inexpensive draught beer. *Rock Forum Café* (*Gajeva ul 13*) occupies the rear sculpture garden of the Archaeological Museum (open in summer only) and across the street is *Hard Rock Café*, full of 1950s and 1960s memorabilia. Farther back in the passageway from Hard Rock is *Art Café Thalia*, which really tries to live up to its name. A couple of other cafes and music shops share this lively complex at the corner of Teslina and Gajeva streets. Check out *BP Club* in the complex basement for jazz, blues and rock bands.

One of Zagreb's most pretentious cafes is Kazališna Kavana, known as *Kaz Kav*, on Trg Maršala Tita, opposite the Croatian National Theatre. *Models* cafe, next door to Kaz Kav, is owned by a former model and adorned with photos of famous faces. For a more offbeat experience, try *Tolkien's House* on the corner of Matoševa and Vranic, which is decorated in the style of JRR Tolkien's books.

Discos & Clubs *Kulušić* (*Hrvojeva 6*), near the Hotel Sheraton (open 8 am to 11 pm Monday to Wednesday and 10 pm to 4 am Thursday to Sunday), is a casual, funky rock club that offers occasional live bands, fashion shows and record promos as well as standard disco fare.

Sokol klub, across the street from the Ethnographic Museum on Trg Maršala Tita, is more polished and admits women free before midnight. Live rock concerts are presented every Sunday.

Saloon (*Tuškanac 1a*) is Zagreb's oldest and classiest disco and attracts a somewhat older crowd.

Gay & Lesbian Venues Zagreb's only exclusively gay club is *Badboy (Ksaver 210)* in the north of the city on the way to Miragoj cemetery. It's open 5 pm to 1 am during the week, but stays open until 4 am Friday, Saturday and Sunday and attracts gays and lesbians.

Cinemas There are 18 cinemas in Zagreb that show foreign movies in their original language with subtitles. *Kinoteca (Kordunska 1)* shows foreign art house movies on weekdays at 4.30, 6.30 and 8.30 pm.

Theatre It's worth making the rounds of the theatres in person to check their programs. Tickets are usually available, even for the best shows. A small office marked 'Kazalište Komedija' (look for the posters) also sells theatre tickets; it's in the Oktogon, a passage connecting Trg Petra Preradovićeva to Ilica 3.

The neobaroque *Croatian National Theatre* (☎ 48 28 532, Trg Maršala Tita 15) was established in 1895. It stages opera and ballet performances; the box office is open 10 am to 1 pm and 5 to 7.30 pm weekdays and from 10 am to 1 pm Saturday as well as for a half-hour before performances on Sunday. You have a choice of orchestra *(parket),* lodge *(lože)* or balcony *(balkon)* seats.

Komedija Theatre (☎ 48 14 556, Kaptol 9), near the cathedral, stages operettas and musicals.

The ticket office of *Vatroslav Lisinski Concert Hall* (☎ 61 21 166), just south of the train station, is open 9 am to 8 pm weekdays and until 2 pm Saturday.

Concerts also take place at the *Croatian Music Institute* (☎ 48 30 822, Gundulićeva 6a) off Ilica.

There are performances at the *Puppet Theatre (ul Baruna Trenka 3)* at 5 pm on Saturday and at noon Sunday.

Spectator Sports

Basketball is popular in Zagreb, and from October to April games take place in a variety of venues around town, usually on weekends. The tourist office has the schedule.

Soccer games are held on Sunday afternoon at the Maksimir Stadium, Maksimirska

128, on the eastern side of Zagreb (tram No 4, 7, 11 or 12 to Bukovačka). If you arrive too early for the game, Zagreb's zoo is just across the street.

Shopping

Ilica is Zagreb's main shopping street. You can get in touch with Croatian consumerism at the Nama department store on Ilica, near Trg Jelačića.

Croatia is the birthplace of the necktie (cravat); Kroata Cravata in the Oktogon has locally made silk neckties at prices that run from 145KN to 340KN. Rokotvorine, Trg Jelačića 7, sells traditional Croatian handicrafts such as red and white embroidered tablecloths, dolls and pottery.

Getting There & Away

Air For information about flights to/from Zagreb, see the Getting There & Away and Getting Around sections earlier in this chapter.

Bus Zagreb's big, modern bus station has a large, enclosed waiting room where you can stretch out while waiting for your bus (but there's no heating in winter). Buy most international tickets at window Nos 11 and 12.

Buses depart from Zagreb for most of Croatia, Slovenia and places beyond. Buy an advance ticket at the station if you're travelling far.

The following domestic buses depart from Zagreb: Dubrovnik (135KN to 165KN, 713km, eight daily), Krk (108KN, 229km, three daily), Ljubljana (71KN, 135km, five daily), Plitvice (35KN to 55KN, 140km, 19 daily), Poreč (95KN to 128KN, 264km, six daily), Pula (90KN to 110KN, 283km, 13 daily), Rab (105KN to 122KN, 211km, daily), Rijeka (68KN to 101KN, 173km, 21 daily), Rovinj (105KN to 130KN, 278km, eight daily), Split (90KN to 120KN, 478km, 27 daily), Varaždin (40KN, 77km, 20 daily), Mali Lošinj (154KN, 298km, daily) and Zadar (80KN to 95KN, 320km, 20 daily).

For international connections, see Getting There & Away at the beginning of this chapter.

Train Four trains daily run from Zagreb to Osijek (80KN, 4½ hours), eight to Koprivnica

CROATIA

(31KN, two hours), 13 to Varazdin (36KN, three hours), six to Ljubljana (87KN, 160km), five to Rijeka (55KN, five hours), two to Pula (145KN, 5½ hours) and three or four to Split (91KN, nine hours). Both daily trains to Zadar (53KN, 11 hours) stop at Knin. Reservations are required on fast InterCity (IC) trains and there's a supplement that costs from 5KN to 21KN on local lines and up to 50KN on international lines.

For international connections, see the Getting There & Away section at the beginning of this chapter.

Getting Around

Public transport is based on an efficient but overcrowded network of trams, although the city centre is compact enough to make them unnecessary. Tram Nos 3 and 8 don't run on weekends.

Buy tickets at newspaper kiosks for 5.50KN or from the driver for 6KN. You can use your ticket for transfers within 90 minutes but only in one direction.

A *dnevna karta* (day ticket), valid on all public transport until 4 am the next morning, is available for 15KN at most Vjesnik or Tisak news outlets.

To/From the Airport

The Croatia Airlines bus to Pleso airport, 17km south-east of Zagreb, leaves from the bus station every half-hour or hour from about 5.30 am to 7.30 pm, depending on flights, and returns from the airport on about the same schedule (20KN).

Car Of the major car rental companies, you could try Budget Rent-a-Car (☎ 45 54 936) and Europcar (☎ 65 54 003) at the airport, Avis Autotehna (☎ 48 36 006) at the Inter-Continental Hotel, and Hertz (☎ 48 46 777) at Kačićeva 9a, near the InterContinental Hotel. Bear in mind that local companies usually have lower rates. Try Uni Rent (☎ 49 22 382) at Gajeva 29.

Taxi Zagreb's taxis all have meters that begin at a whopping 15KN and then ring up 6KN per kilometre. On Sunday and nights from 10 pm to 5 am there's a 20% surcharge. Waiting time is 40KN an hour. The baggage surcharge is 2KN per suitcase.

Istria

Istria (Istra to Croatians), the heart-shaped 3600 sq km peninsula just south of Trieste, Italy, is named after the Illyrian Histri tribe conquered by the Romans in 177 BC.

The 430km Istrian Riviera basks in the Mediterranean landscapes and climate for which the Adriatic coast is famous. The long summer season from May to October attracts large crowds.

Over the years Istria has been a political basketball. Italy took Istria from Austria-Hungary in 1919, then had to give it to Yugoslavia in 1947. A large Italian community lives in Istria and Italian is widely spoken. Tito wanted Trieste (Trst) as part of Yugoslavia too, but in 1954 the Anglo-American occupiers returned the city to Italy so that it wouldn't fall into the hands of the 'communists'. Today the Koper-Piran strip belongs to Slovenia while the rest is held by Croatia. See Piran quickly, then move south to Rovinj, a perfect base from which to explore Poreč and Pula.

Getting There & Away

Bus Koper and Rijeka are the main entry/exit points, with buses to most towns on Istria's west coast every couple of hours. Train services in Istria are limited, so plan on getting around by bus.

Boat In Istria, travel agencies such as Kompas or Atlas should know the departure times and prices of all international boats although tickets may only be available on board. All boats connecting Istria with Italy or the Dalmatian coast depart from the ferry wharves and schedules are sometimes posted there. It's an exciting way to travel.

For further information on connections between Istria and Italy see the Getting There & Away section at the beginning of this chapter.

POREČ

☎ 052 • pop 17,000

Poreč (Parenzo in Italian), the Roman Parentium, sits on a low, narrow peninsula about halfway down the west coast of Istria. The ancient Dekumanus with its polished stones is still the main street. Even after the fall of

Rome, Poreč remained important as a centre of early Christianity, with a bishop and a famous basilica. The town is now the centre of a region packed with tourist resorts but vestiges of earlier times and a quiet, small-town atmosphere make it well worth a stop or at least a day trip from Rovinj. There are many places to swim in the clear water off the rocks north of the old town.

Orientation & Information

The bus station (with a left-luggage office open 5 am to 8.30 pm daily, except Sunday, when it closes at 5 pm) is directly opposite the small-boat harbour just outside the old town. Follow Obala Maršala Tita into the old town.

The tourist office (☎ 451 293, fax 451 665, ✉ istra@io.com) is at Zagrebačka 8. The Atlas travel agency (☎ 434 983) at Eufrazijeva 63 represents American Express. There's another office (☎ 432 273) at Boze Milanovića 11.

The telephone centre in the main post office, Trg Slobode 14, is open 7 am to 9 pm Monday to Saturday and 9 am to noon Sunday. You can change money at any travel agency in town and there's an ATM at Istarska Banka, A Negrija 6.

Things to See

The many historic sites in the old town include the ruins of two **Roman temples**, between Trg Marafor and the western end of the peninsula. Archaeology and history are featured in the four-floor **Regional Museum** (open daily year-round) in an old baroque palace at Dekumanus 9 (captions in German and Italian).

The main reason to visit Poreč, however, is to see the 6th-century **Euphrasian basilica**, a World Heritage site that features wonderfully preserved Byzantine gold mosaics. The sculpture and architecture are remarkable survivors of that distant period. Entry to the church is free and for a small fee you may

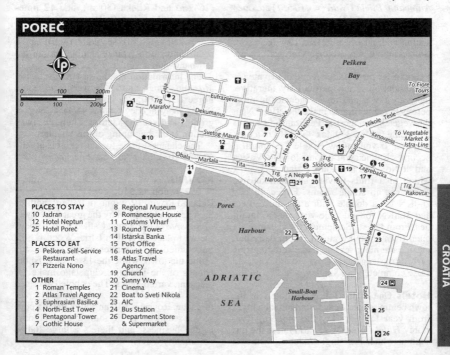

POREČ

PLACES TO STAY
10 Jadran
12 Hotel Neptun
25 Hotel Poreč

PLACES TO EAT
5 Peškera Self-Service Restaurant
17 Pizzeria Nono

OTHER
1 Roman Temples
2 Atlas Travel Agency
3 Euphrasian Basilica
4 North-East Tower
6 Pentagonal Tower
7 Gothic House
8 Regional Museum
9 Romanesque House
11 Customs Wharf
13 Round Tower
14 Istarska Banka
15 Post Office
16 Tourist Office
18 Atlas Travel Agency
19 Church
20 Sunny Way
21 Cinema
22 Boat to Sveti Nikola
23 AIC
24 Bus Station
26 Department Store & Supermarket

CROATIA

visit the 4th-century mosaic floor of the adjacent Early Christian basilica.

From May to mid-October there are passenger boats (12KN return) every half-hour to **Sveti Nikola**, the small island opposite Poreč Harbour, departing from the new wharf on Obala Maršala Tita.

Special Events

Annual events include the day-long Folk Festival (June) and the Musical Summer (May to September). Ask about these at the tourist office.

Places to Stay

Accommodation in Poreč is tight and the camping grounds are far from the town centre, so you might want to stop off only for the day on your way south or north.

Camping There are two camping grounds at Zelena Laguna, 6km south of Poreč. Both *Autocamp Zelena Laguna* (☎ 410 541) and *Autocamp Bijela Uvala* (☎ 410 551) are open from April to mid-October. Take the 'Plava Laguna' bus, which runs hourly from the bus station and get off at Zelena Laguna resort. Both camping grounds are a short walk away.

Private Rooms As the rental of private accommodation is not particularly lucrative, there are fewer and fewer agencies in prosperous Poreč willing to make the effort. Near the vegetable market at Partizanska there is Istra-Line (☎ 432 339, fax 432 116) in a pink building. If you follow Nikole Tesle until it becomes Kalčića you'll come to Mate Vašića and at No 6 is Fiore tours (☎/fax 431 397), which also finds private accommodation. There are no single rooms. Expect to pay 200KN for a double with a private shower and 168KN for a double with shared facilities. From June to September the agencies are open from around 8 am to 10 pm daily but, outside the main season, make sure to arrive early as most agencies close around noon and close completely on Sunday.

Hotels One of the following hotels in the town centre is open year-round but it changes from year to year. Try the modern, five-storey *Hotel Poreč* (☎ 451 811) near the bus station, which has singles/doubles with TV for 340/560KN. *Hotel Neptun* (☎ 452 711, fax 431 531, Obala M Tita 15) overlooks the harbour and has rooms for 360/600KN. *Jadran* (☎ 451 422) on Obala M Tita has simpler rooms for 284/488KN.

Places to Eat

The *Peškera Self-Service Restaurant*, just outside the north-western corner of the old city wall (open 9 am to 8 pm daily all year), offers good value and *Pizzeria Nono* (*Zagrebačka 4*) is a local favourite for its scrumptious pizzas.

There is a large supermarket and department store next to Hotel Poreč, near the bus station.

Getting There & Away

The nearest train station is at Pazin, 30km east (five buses daily from there).

Buses run once daily to Portorož (54km), and to Ljubljana (176km) in summer, twice daily to Trieste (89km), six times daily to Rovinj (38km), eight times daily to Zagreb (264km) and Rijeka (80km), and 12 times daily to Pula (56km). Between Poreč and Rovinj the bus runs along the Lim Channel, a drowned valley. To see it clearly, sit on the right-hand side if you're southbound, or the left-hand side if you're northbound.

For information on the fast motor vessel *Marconi,* which shuttles between Trieste and Poreč (L27,000, 2¾ hours), inquire at the Sunny Way agency (☎ 452 021), Alda Negrija 1, and see the Getting There & Away section at the beginning of this chapter.

The cheapest price for car rental is at AIC (☎ 434 103), Istarskog razvoda 11.

ROVINJ

☎ 052 • pop 12,910

Relaxed Rovinj (Rovigno in Italian), with its high peninsula topped by the great 57m tower of massive St Euphemia Cathedral, is perhaps the best place to visit in Istria. Wooded hills punctuated by low-rise luxury hotels surround the town, while the 13 green offshore islands of the Rovinj archipelago make for pleasant, varied views. The cobbled, inclined streets in the old town are charmingly picturesque. Rovinj is still an active fishing port, so you see local people going about their day-to-day business, and there's a large Italian community here.

Friendly Rovinj is just the place to rest before your island-hopping journey farther south.

Orientation & Information

The bus station is just south-east of the old town and there's an ATM next to the entrance. The tourist office (☎ 811 566, fax 816 007, ✆ tzg-rovinj@pu.tel.hr) is at Obala Pina Budicina 12, just off Trg Maršala Tita. The American Express representative is Atlas travel agency (☎ 811 241) in the Hotel Park, Ronjgova bb.

Phone calls can be made from the post office behind the bus station.

The left-luggage office at the bus station is open 6 am to 9 pm (ask at the ticket window).

Things to See

The **Cathedral of St Euphemia** (1736), which completely dominates the town from its hill-top location, is the largest baroque building in Istria, reflecting the period during the 18th century when Rovinj was the most populous town in Istria, an important fishing centre and the bulwark of the Venetian fleet.

Inside the cathedral, don't miss the tomb of St Euphemia (martyred in AD 304) behind the right-hand altar. The saint's remains were brought from Constantinople in 800. On the anniversary of her martyrdom (16 September) devotees congregate here. A copper statue of her tops the cathedral's mighty tower.

Take a wander along the winding narrow backstreets below the cathedral, such as **ul Grisia**, where local artists sell their work. Rovinj has developed into an important art centre and each year in mid-August Rovinj's painters stage a big open-air art show in town.

The **Regional Museum** on Trg Maršala Tita (open mornings, daily) contains an unexciting collection of paintings and a few Etruscan artefacts found in Istria. Captions are only in Croatian and Italian. The **Franciscan convent**, up the hill at E de Amicis 36, also has a small museum.

Better than either of these is the **Rovinj Aquarium** (1891) at Obala Giordano Paliaga 5. It exhibits a good collection of local marine life, from poisonous scorpion fish to colourful anemones. It's open daily but closed mid-October to Easter (10KN).

When you've seen enough of the town,

follow the waterfront southwards past the Park Hotel to **Punta Corrente Forest Park**, which was afforested in 1890 by Baron Hütterodt, an Austrian admiral who kept a villa on Crveni otok (Red Island). Here you can swim off the rocks, climb a cliff or just sit and admire the offshore islands.

Organised Tours

Delfin Agency (☎ 813 266), near the ferry dock for Crveni otok, runs half-day scenic cruises to the **Lim Channel** (80KN) or you can go with one of the independent operators at the end of Alzo Rismondo who run half-day and full-day boat trips around the region. There's an hourly ferry to Crveni otok (20KN return) and a frequent ferry to nearby **Katarina Island** (10KN) from the same landing. Get tickets on the boat or at the nearby kiosk. These boats operate from May to mid-October only.

Special Events

The city's annual events include the Rovinj-Pesaro Regata (early May), the 'Rovinj Summer' concert series (July and August) and the Rovinj Fair (August).

Places to Stay

Camping The camping ground closest to Rovinj is *Porton Biondi* (☎ 813 557), less than a kilometre from the town (on the Monsena bus). Five kilometres south-east of Rovinj is *Polari Camping* (☎ 813 441), open May to mid-October. Get there on the Villas Rubin bus.

Private Rooms The surcharge for a stay less than four nights is 50% and one-night guests are punished with a 100% surcharge. Lokva-Natale (☎ 813 365, fax 830 239, ✆ natale@pu.tel.hr), Via Carducci 4, opposite the bus station, has singles/doubles with private bath for 132/200KN and 108/160KN for two-star accommodation, as well as studios for 272KN. You could also try Futura Travel (☎ 817 281), M Benussi 2, or Integrale (☎ 814 022), Trg na Lokvi 3, which have rooms at the same price.

Hotels *Hotel Rovinj* (☎ 811 288) has a splendid location on Svetoga Križa overlooking the sea; it charges 324/520KN a

CROATIA

single/double for a four-night stay. The cheapest hotel is the 192-room **Hotel Monte Mulin** (☎ *811 512, fax 815 882*), on the wooded hillside overlooking the bay just beyond Hotel Park. It's about a 15-minute walk south of the bus station. Half-board is 260/400KN a room.

Places to Eat

Most of the fish and spaghetti places along the harbour cater to well-heeled tourists, but **Kantinon** (*obala Alzo Rismondo 18*) sells fresh grilled fish beginning at 20KN to a local crowd. **Veli Jože** (*Svetoga Križa 1*) is somewhat more expensive, but is a good place to try Istrian dishes in an interior crammed with knick-knacks or at tables outside. Picnickers can pick up supplies at the **supermarket** next to the bus station or in one of the kiosks selling burek near the vegetable market.

Getting There & Away

There's a bus from Rovinj to Pula (34km) every hour or so. There's up to eight daily to Poreč (38km), eight daily to Rijeka (84km), nine daily to Zagreb (278km), two daily to Koper (81km) and Split (509km), and one daily to Dubrovnik (744km) and Ljubljana (190km, summer only).

The closest train station is Kanfanar, 19km away on the Pula-Divača line.

Eurostar Travel (☎ 813 144), Obala Pina Budicina 1, has information about the *Marconi*, which shuttles between Rovinj and Trieste and may have tickets (which must be paid in Italian lire).

PULA
☎ 052 • pop 62,378

Pula (the ancient Polensium) is a large regional centre with some industry, a big naval base and a busy commercial harbour. The old town with its museums and well-preserved Roman ruins is certainly worth a visit, and nearby are rocky wooded peninsulas overlooking the clear Adriatic waters, which explains the many resort hotels and camping grounds.

Orientation

The bus station is on ul Carrarina in the centre of town. One block south is Giardini, the central hub, while the harbour is just north of the bus station. The train station is near the water about 1km north of town.

Information

Tourist Offices The Tourist Association of Pula (☎ 219 197, fax 211 855, ✉ tz-pula@pu.tel.hr), Forum 2, is open 9 am to 1 pm and 5 to 8 pm weekdays, and has maps, brochures and schedules of upcoming events.

Money You can change money in travel agencies and there is an automatic currency exchange at Kaptol Banka next to the bus station at Istarska 5. The most central ATM is at Riječka Banka on Giardini.

Post & Communications Long-distance telephone calls may be placed at the main post office at Danteov trg 4 (open until 8 pm daily). You can check email at Computer Club (☎ 217 720), Cankarova 4.

Travel Agencies The American Express representative is Atlas travel agency (☎ 214 172, fax 214 094, ✉ atl.pula@atlas.tel.hr), ul Starih Statuta 1, which also organises tours to the Brijuni Islands (200KN), Venice (390KN), the Istrian interior (215KN) and boat rides around the region (200KN). Jadroagent (☎ 211 878), Riva 14, sells ferry tickets.

Left Luggage The bus station has a left-luggage office open 4 am to 11 pm daily, except for two half-hour breaks. The train station's left-luggage service is open 9 am to 4 pm, but closed on Sunday.

Things to See

Pula's most imposing sight is the 1st-century **Roman amphitheatre** overlooking the harbour and north-east of the old town. Built entirely from local limestone, the amphitheatre was designed to host gladiatorial contests and could accommodate up to 20,000 spectators. The 30m-high outer wall is almost intact and contains two rows of 72 arches. Admission is 16KN. Around the end of July a Croatian film festival is held in the amphitheatre, and there are pop, jazz and classical events, often with major international stars, throughout summer.

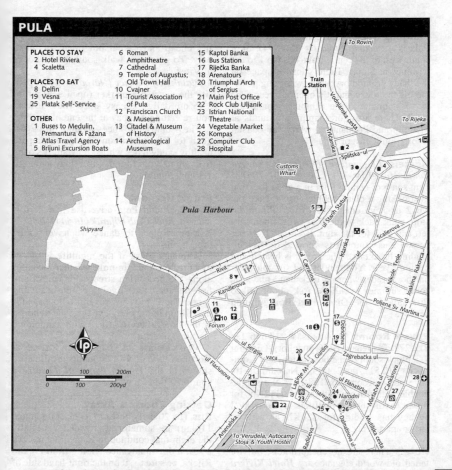

PULA

PLACES TO STAY
2 Hotel Riviera
4 Scaletta

PLACES TO EAT
8 Delfin
19 Vesna
25 Platak Self-Service

OTHER
1 Buses to Medulin,
   Premantura & Fažana
3 Atlas Travel Agency
5 Brijuni Excursion Boats

6 Roman
   Amphitheatre
7 Cathedral
9 Temple of Augustus;
   Old Town Hall
10 Cvajner
11 Tourist Association
   of Pula
12 Franciscan Church
   & Museum
13 Citadel & Museum
   of History
14 Archaeological
   Museum

15 Kaptol Banka
16 Bus Station
17 Riječka Banka
18 Arenatours
20 Triumphal Arch
   of Sergius
21 Main Post Office
22 Rock Club Uljanik
23 Istrian National
   Theatre
24 Vegetable Market
26 Kompas
27 Computer Club
28 Hospital

The **Archaeological Museum** is on the hill opposite the bus station. It's open daily in summer, and closed weekends in winter. General admission is 10KN.

Even if you don't get into the museum be sure to visit the large sculpture garden around it, and the **Roman Theatre** behind. The garden is entered through 2nd-century twin gates.

Along the street facing the bus station are **Roman walls** that mark old Pula's eastern boundary. Follow these walls south and continue down Giardini to the **Triumphal Arch of Sergius** (27 BC). The street beyond the arch

winds right around old Pula, changing names several times as it goes. Follow it to the ancient **Temple of Augustus** and the **old town hall** (1296). Above this square is the **Franciscan church** (1314), with a museum in the cloister (entry from around the other side) containing paintings, medieval frescoes and a Roman mosaic.

The **Museum of History** (open daily) is in the 17th-century Venetian citadel on a high hill in the centre of the old town. The meagre exhibits deal mostly with the maritime history of Pula, but the views of Pula from the citadel walls are good.

Places to Stay

Camping The closest camping ground to Pula is *Autocamp Stoja* (☎ *387 144*), 3km south-west of the centre (take bus No 1 to the terminus at Stoja). There's lots of space on the shady promontory, with swimming possible off the rocks and it's open all year. The two restaurants at the camping ground are good. There are more camping grounds at Medulin and Premantura, which are coastal resorts south-east of Pula.

Hostels *Ljetovalište Ferijalnog Saveza Youth Hostel* (☎ *391 133, fax 391 106*) is 3km south of central Pula in a great location overlooking a clean pebble beach. Take the No 2 or 7 Verudela bus to the 'Piramida' stop, walk back to the first street, then turn left and look for the sign. B&B is 71KN per person and camping is allowed (40KN including breakfast). The hostel is heated and open all year. You can sit and sip cold beer on the terrace, where a rock band plays on some summer evenings. Ask about Disco Piramida or the Disco Fort Bourguignon nearby.

Private Rooms Arenatours (☎ 218 696, fax 212 277, ✆ arenaturist1@pu.tel.hr), Giardini 4, a block south of the bus station, and Kompas (☎ 212 511, fax 211 592), Narodni trg 10, have private rooms for 108/184KN a single/double with private bath and 68/112KN for rooms with shared facilities. Atlas travel agency has studios for 320KN as well as larger apartments.

Hotels There are no cheap hotels, but for faded old-world elegance try *Hotel Riviera* (☎ *211 166, fax 211 166, Splitska ul 1*), overlooking the harbour. Erected in 1908, it offers large singles/doubles with high ceilings for 228/384KN with shared bath (256/432KN with private bath), breakfast included. For just a few extra kuna the brand new *Scaletta* (☎ *541 599, fax 541 026, Flavijeska 26*) offers beautifully decorated rooms with TV and telephone for 398/476KN including breakfast.

Places to Eat

Delfin (*Kandlerova 17*) has a pleasant terrace and an excellent selection of Istrian dishes, especially seafood. Locals rave about the home cooking at *Vodnjanka* (*Vitežića 4*). It's cheap and casual but open for lunch only. To get there, walk south on Radićeva to Vitežića.

Platak Self-Service (*Narodni trg 5*), opposite the vegetable market (open 9.30 am to 8.45 pm daily), is easy since you see what you're getting and pay at the end of the line.

The people at the cheese counter in *Vesna*, next to Kino Istra on Giardini, prepare healthy sandwiches while you wait. It's open 6.30 am to 8 pm Monday to Friday and until 1.30 pm Saturday.

Entertainment

Posters around Pula advertise live performances. *Rock Club Uljanik* (*Jurja Dobrile 2*) is a great place to dance whenever something's on.

Although most of the nightlife is out of town in Verudela, in mild weather the cafes along the pedestrian streets, Flanatička and Sergijevaca, are lively people-watching spots. The Forum has several outdoor cafes that fill up in the early evening; the trendiest is the cafe/gallery *Cvajner* with a stunning, art-filled interior.

Two cinemas on Giardini are *Zagreb* at No 1 and *Pula* at No 12. Quality art films are shown at the *Istrian National Theatre* a couple of times a week.

Getting There & Away

Bus The 20 daily buses to Rijeka (1½ hours, 110km) are sometimes crowded, especially the eight that continue to Zagreb, so reserve a seat a day in advance. Going from Pula to Rijeka, be sure to sit on the right-hand side of the bus for a stunning view of the Gulf of Kvarner.

Other buses from Pula include: 21 daily to Rovinj (42km); 12 to Poreč (56km); 14 to Zagreb (292km); four to Zadar (333km); three to Trieste (124km) and Split (514km); two each to Portorož (90km), Koper (104km) and Ljubljana (211km, summer only); and one to Dubrovnik (749km).

Train There are two daily trains to Ljubljana (90KN, four hours) and two to Zagreb (90KN, 6½ hours) but you must board a bus for part of the trip.

Boat The fast boat *Marina* connects Pula and Venice (L60,000), and Zadar (120KN) in summer. See the Getting There & Away section at the beginning of this chapter. The ferry to Mali Lošinj (34KN) and Zadar (66KN) runs once a week all year. Ask at Jadroagent or Kvarner Express on the harbour.

Getting Around

The only city buses of use to visitors are bus No 1, which runs to the camping ground at Stoja, and bus Nos 2 and 7 to Verudela, which pass the youth hostel. Frequency varies from every 15 minutes to every 30 minutes, with service from 5 am to 11.30 pm daily. Tickets are sold at newsstands for 8KN and are good for two trips.

AROUND PULA
Brijuni Islands

The Brijuni (Brioni in Italian) island group consists of two main pine-covered islands and 12 islets off the coast of Istria and just north-west of Pula. Each year from 1949 until his death in 1980, Maršal Tito spent six months at his summer residences on Brijuni in a style any western capitalist would have admired. In 1984 Brijuni was proclaimed a national park. Some 680 species of plants grow on the islands, including many exotic subtropical species which were planted at Tito's request.

You may only visit Brijuni National Park with a group. Instead of booking an excursion with one of the travel agencies in Pula, Rovinj or Poreč, which costs 200KN, you can take a public bus from Pula to Fažana (8km), then sign up for a tour (130KN) at the Brijuni Tourist Service (☎ 525 883) office near the wharf. It's best to book in advance, especially in summer.

Also check along the Pula waterfront for excursion boats to Brijuni. The five-hour boat trips from Pula to Brijuni may not actually visit the islands but only sail around them. Still, it makes a nice day out.

Gulf of Kvarner

The Gulf of Kvarner (Quarnero in Italian) stretches 100km south from Rijeka, between the Istrian Peninsula to the west and the Croatian littoral to the east. The many elongated islands are the peaks of a submerged branch of the Dinaric Alps, the range that follows the coast south all the way to Albania. Krk, Cres and Pag are among the largest islands in Croatia.

Rijeka, a bustling commercial port and communications hub at the northern end of the gulf, is well connected to Italy and Austria by road and rail. The railway built from Budapest to Rijeka in 1845 gave Hungary its first direct outlet to the sea. Big crowds frequent nearby Opatija, a one-time bathing resort of the Habsburg elite, and Krk Island, now linked to the mainland by bridge. Historic Rab, the jewel of the Gulf of Kvarner, is much harder to reach; with some difficulty it can be used as a stepping stone on the way south.

RIJEKA
☎ 051 • pop 167,964

Rijeka (Fiume in Italian), 126km south of Ljubljana, is such a transportation hub that it's almost impossible to avoid. The network of buses, trains and ferries that connect Istria and Dalmatia with Zagreb and points beyond all seem to pass through Rijeka. As Croatia's largest port, the city is full of boats, cargo, fumes, cranes and the kind of seediness that characterises most port cities.

Although Rijeka is hardly a 'must see' destination, the city does have a few saving graces, such as the pedestrian mall, Korzo, stately 19th-century buildings and a tree-lined promenade along the harbour. Because there is so little to interest tourists, accommodation, information and resources for visitors are scarce. The assumption seems to be that everyone will either leave the area as fast as possible or base themselves in Opatija.

Orientation

The bus station is on Trg Žabica, below the Capuchin Church in the centre of town. The train station is a seven-minute walk west of the bus station on ul Krešimirova. The Jadrolinija ferry wharf (no left-luggage section) is just a few minutes east of the bus station. Korzo runs east through the city centre towards the fast-moving Rječina River.

CROATIA

Information

Tourist Offices The Turistički Savez Općine Rijeka (☎ 335 882) is at Užarska 14. The Auto-Klub Rijeka (☎ 621 824), Preluk 6, assists motorists. Jadroagent (☎ 211 276, fax 335 172), Trg Ivana Koblera 2, is an excellent source of information on all ferry sailings from Croatia.

Money You can change money at Croatia Express on platform No 1 at the train station, from 8 am to 9 pm Monday to Friday and 9 am to 1 pm and 5 to 9 pm weekends. There's an ATM in the train station and an automatic currency exchange at Kaptol Banka, Trg Republike, as well as an exchange counter in the main post office. There's an exchange counter in the main post office, opposite the old city tower on Korzo.

Post & Communications The telephone centre is in the main post office on Korzo, opposite the old city tower. It's open 7 am to

9 pm Monday to Friday and until 2 pm weekends. You can check email at Multimedia Center Palach (☎ 215 063, @ otvoreni-krug@ri.tel.hr), on Krušna ul.

Left Luggage If the left-luggage office in the bus station (open 5.30 am to 10.30 pm daily) is full, there's a larger *garderoba* (cloakroom) in the train station (open 7.30 am to 9 pm).

Things to See

The **Modern Art Gallery** (closed Sunday and Monday) is at Dolac 1, upstairs in the scientific library across from Hotel Bonavia. The **Maritime Museum** and the **Museum of the Town of Rijeka** (both closed Sunday and Monday) are adjacent at Žrtava fašizma 18, above the city centre. The latter has photos, objects and memorabilia relating to Rijeka's history. Worth a visit if you have time is the 13th-century **Trsat Castle** (closed Monday), on a high ridge overlooking Rijeka, and the canyon of the Rječina River.

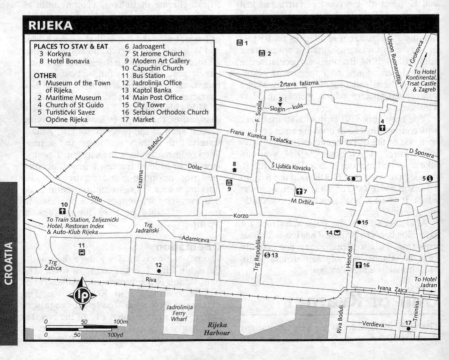

RIJEKA

PLACES TO STAY & EAT	
3 Korkyra	6 Jadroagent
8 Hotel Bonavia	7 St Jerome Church
	9 Modern Art Gallery
	10 Capuchin Church
OTHER	11 Bus Station
1 Museum of the Town	12 Jadrolinija Office
of Rijeka	13 Kaptol Banka
2 Maritime Museum	14 Main Post Office
4 Church of St Guido	15 City Tower
5 Turističvki Savez	16 Serbian Orthodox Church
Općine Rijeka	17 Market

Places to Stay

Currently there is no agency finding private accommodation. The cheapest place to stay is *Željeznički Hotel* (*☎/fax 551 246, Maja 34)*, which has basic singles/doubles for 125/200KN with shared shower and no breakfast. Take bus No 5 west from the town centre. The four-star *Hotel Bonavia* (*☎ 333 744, Dolac 4)* is central and has rooms with bath for 640/880KN. Cheaper alternatives include the B-category *Hotel Jadran* (*☎ 216 230, Šetalište XIII)* on the coast 3km southeast of town, and *Hotel Kontinental* (*☎ 372 008, Andrije Kašića Miočica)*, north-east of the town centre. Rooms with bath cost 284/380KN but for those prices you might as well pay more and stay in Opatija.

Places to Eat

Restoran Index (*ul Krešimirova 18)*, between the bus and train stations, has a good self-service section (*samoposluzi)*. *Korkyra* (*Slogin kula 5)* is one of the finest restaurants in the region and not excessively expensive considering the quality. It's cosy, has an appealingly casual ambience and serves up an assortment of specialties such as *brodetto* (fish stew), *bakalar* (codfish stew) and various pastas. If you come between 9 am and 1 pm you can get hot dishes for 20KN.

Getting There & Away

Bus There are 13 buses daily between Rijeka and Krk (31KN, 1½ hours), using the huge Krk Bridge. Buses to Krk are overcrowded and a seat reservation in no way guarantees you a seat. Don't worry – the bus from Rijeka to Krk empties fairly fast so you won't be standing for long.

Other buses depart from Rijeka for Baška, also on Krk Island (41KN, 76km, six daily), Dubrovnik (265KN, 639km, two daily), Koper (61KN, 86km), Ljubljana (128km, once daily), Mali Lošinj (76KN, 122km, four daily), Poreč (50KN, 91km, five daily), Pula (51KN, 110km, 17 daily), Rab (78KN, 115km, two daily), Rovinj (63KN, 105km, 10 daily), Split (167KN, 404km, 11 daily), Trieste (58KN, 70km, five daily), Zadar (100KN, 228km, 12 daily) and Zagreb (85KN, 3½ hours, 24 daily).

There's also a daily bus to Sarajevo (250KN), a bus to Vienna every Sunday evening and buses twice a week to Zürich (801km) and Berlin, as well as daily buses to Frankfurt, Munich (571km) and Stuttgart (786km). There's also a Friday bus to Paris and London. Luggage is DM5 per piece on all international services (Deutschmarks in cash required).

Train There's a train that runs on Friday and Sunday (daily in summer) to Budapest (340KN, nine hours) and an evening train to Munich (540KN) and Salzburg (365KN). Four trains daily run to Zagreb (50KN, five hours). There's also a daily direct train to Osijek (134KN, eight hours) and a daily train to Split that changes at Ogulin (67KN, 10 hours). Several of the seven daily services to Ljubljana (80KN, three hours) require a change of trains at the Slovenian border and again at Bifka or Bistrica. Reservations are compulsory on the *poslovni* (express) trains.

Car ITR Rent a Car (☎ 337 544), Riva 20, near the bus station, has rental cars from 250KN a day with unlimited kilometres. On a weekly basis it's 1453KN with unlimited kilometres.

Boat Jadrolinija (☎ 211 444), Riva 16, has tickets for the large coastal ferries that run all year between Rijeka and Dubrovnik. Southbound ferries depart from Rijeka at 6 pm daily.

Fares are 144KN to Split (13 hours), 176KN to Korčula (18 hours) and 192KN to Dubrovnik (17 to 24 hours). Fares are lower in winter. Berths to Dubrovnik are 352KN per person in a four-bed cabin, 448KN in a double room or 524KN in a double with private bath.

Miatours runs a fast boat on Wednesday in July and August from Rijeka to Zadar stopping at Dugi Otok, Ist and Silba Islands (240KN, 3½ hours). Ask at Jadroagent.

OPATIJA

☎ 051 • pop 9073

Opatija, just a few kilometres due west of Rijeka, was *the* fashionable seaside resort of the Austro-Hungarian empire until WWI. Many grand old hotels remain from this time and the elegant waterfront promenade stretches for 12km along the Gulf of Kvarner.

CROATIA

Although you get a passing glance of Opatija (literally 'abbey') from the Pula bus, the graceful architecture and stunning coastline make the town worth a stop for at least a day or two. West of Opatija rises Mt Učka (1396m), the highest point on the Istrian Peninsula.

Information

The tourist office (☎ 271 310, fax 271 699, ✉ tzgr.op@ri.tel.hr) is at Maršala Tita 101. Atlas travel agency (☎ 271 032) is at Maršala Tita 116.

The main post office, at Eugena Kumičića 2, behind the market (tržnica), opens from 8 am to 7 pm Monday to Saturday.

There's no left-luggage facility at Opatija bus station, which is on Trg Vladimira Gortana in the town centre, but Autotrans Agency at the station will usually watch luggage.

Places to Stay

Preluk Autokamp (☎ 621 913), beside the busy highway between Rijeka and Opatija, is open from May to September. City bus No 32 stops near the camping ground.

For private rooms, try Kompas (☎ 271 912) at Maršala Tita 110, Generalturist (☎ 271 613, fax 271 345) next to the Hotel Paris, and GIT (☎ 273 030, fax 271 967, ✉ gi-trade@ri.tel.hr) at No 65. All have rooms that start at 72KN per person for one-star accommodation plus a 50% surcharge for single-room occupancy.

There are no cheap hotels in Opatija, but the most reasonable are the elegant *Hotel Paris* (☎ 271 911, fax 711 823 Maršala Tita 198), which has rooms for 215/352KN a single/double, and the *Imperial* (☎ 271 677, fax 271 548, Maršala Tita 124), which charges 249/430KN.

Places to Eat

Maršala Tita is lined with decent restaurants offering pizza, grilled meat and fish. There's a *supermarket/deli* at Maršala Tita 80 and a *burek stand* down the stairs next to No 55 on Stubište Tomaševac.

Getting There & Away

Bus No 32 stops in front of the train station in Rijeka (11KN, 11km) and runs right along the Opatija Riviera, west from Rijeka, every 20 minutes until late in the evening.

KRK ISLAND

☎ 051 ● pop 16,402

Croatia's largest island, 409-sq-km Krk (Veglia in Italian) is very barren and rocky. In 1980 Krk was joined to the mainland by the enormous Krk Bridge, the largest concrete arch bridge in the world, with a span of some 390m. Since then, Krk has suffered from too-rapid development, from Rijeka airport and some industry at the northern end of Krk, to big tourist hotels in the middle and far south. Still, the main town (also called Krk) is rather picturesque and Baška has an impressive setting. You can easily stop at Krk town for a few hours of sightseeing, and then catch a bus to Baška and Krk's longest beach.

Krk Town

Tiny Krk town has a compact medieval centre that opens on to a scenic port. From the 12th to 15th centuries, Krk town and the surrounding region remained semi-independent under the Frankopan Dukes of Krk, an indigenous Croatian dynasty, at a time when much of the Adriatic was controlled by Venice. This history explains the various medieval sights in Krk town, the ducal seat.

Orientation & Information The bus from Baška and Rijeka stops by the harbour, a few minutes' walk from the old town of Krk. There's no left-luggage facility at Krk bus station. The Turistička Zajednica (☎/fax 221 414), Velika Placa 1, is in the city wall's Guard Tower. You can change money at any travel agency and there's an ATM accepting MasterCard and Cirrus in the shopping centre near the bus station.

Things to See The lovely 14th-century **Frankopan Castle** and 12th-century Romanesque **cathedral** are in the lower town near the harbour. In the upper part of Krk town are three old **monastic churches**. The narrow streets of Krk are worth exploring.

Places to Stay There is a range of accommodation options in and around Krk, but many places only open for the summer.

The closest camping ground is **Autocamp Ježevac** (☎ *221 081*) on the coast, a 10-minute walk south-west of Krk town. The rocky soil makes it nearly impossible to use tent pegs, but there are lots of stones to anchor your lines. There's good shade and places to swim.

Camping Bor (☎ *221 581*) is on a hill inland from Ježevac. **Politin FKK** (☎ *221 351*) is a naturist camp south-east of Krk, just beyond the large resort hotels.

Private rooms can be booked from Autotrans (☎ 221 111) at the bus station, Zlatni Otok (☎ 221 063) at the town entrance and Aurea (☎ 222 277) on the main road into town. Expect to pay from 140/160KN for a single/double.

Getting There & Away About 14 buses a day travel between Rijeka and Krk town (1½ hours), of which six continue on to Baška (one hour). One of the Rijeka buses is to/from Zagreb (229km). To go from Krk to the island of Mali Lošinj, change buses at Malinska for the Lošinj-bound bus that comes from Rijeka but check the times carefully as the connection only works once or twice a day.

Baška

Baška, at the southern end of Krk Island, is a popular resort with a 2km-long pebbly beach set below a high ridge. The swimming and scenery are better than at Krk and the old town has a lot of charm. This is a good base for hiking and you can pick up a map of hiking routes from the tourist office.

Orientation & Information The bus from Krk stops at the top of a hill on the edge of the old town, between the beach and the harbour. The main street is Zvonimirova, which has exchange offices, travel agencies and restaurants.

The tourist office (☎ 856 817) is at Zvonimirova 114, just down the street from the bus stop.

Places to Stay During July and August, it is essential to arrange accommodation well in advance as the town swarms with Austrian, German and Czech tourists. By late spring, hotels are booked solid for the summer season and accommodation is tight in the shoulder season as well.

There are two camping options at Baška. **Camping Zablaće** (☎ *856 909*), open from May to September, is on the beach south-west of the bus stop (look for the rows of caravans). In heavy rain you risk getting flooded here.

A better bet is **FKK Camp Bunculuka** (☎ *856 806*), open from May to September. A naturist camping ground over the hill east of the harbour (a 15-minute walk), it's quiet, shady and conveniently close to town.

For **private rooms** try Guliver (☎ 856 004) and Primaturist (☎ 856 971), both at Zvonimirova 98 in the centre; at Hotel Corinthia, try Kompas (☎ 856 460). Prices are the same as for Krk town. If you come in July or August, you may find it impossible to rent a room for less than four nights, impossible to rent a single room, impossible to rent a room near town or just plain impossible. Plan ahead.

The choice of hotels is not outstanding yet hotels are booked solid. The cheapest rooms are at the **Hotel Zvonimir** where you can find singles/doubles for 328/576KN. Next up in price is the **Corinthia II**, which has rooms for 380/688KN. Head of the pack is **Hotel Corinthia** (☎ *656 111, fax 856 584*), with rooms for 456/840KN. Prices are for half-board in high season. The hotels are all part of the same modern complex on the edge of town right next to the beach. Bookings for these places are made through the Hotel Corinthia.

Getting There & Away The ferry from Baška to Lopar on Rab Island (25KN) operates up to six times daily from June to September, but between October and May there's no service and you will be forced to backtrack to Rijeka to get farther south. To reach the Lopar ferry, follow the street closest to the water through the old town, heading south-east for less than 1km.

RAB ISLAND

Rab (Arbe in Italian), near the centre of the Kvarner Island group, is one of the most enticing islands in the Adriatic. The north-eastern side is barren and rocky, whereas the south-west is green with pine forests and dotted with sandy beaches and coves. High mountains protect Rab's interior from cold winds from the north and east.

CROATIA

Rab Town

☎ 051 • pop 592

Medieval Rab town is built on a narrow peninsula that encloses a sheltered harbour. The old stone buildings climb from the harbour to a cliff overlooking the sea. For hundreds of years Rab was an outpost of Venice until the Austrians took over in the 19th century. Today it is a favourite destination of German tourists, which is not surprising considering the beauty of the town and island. Rab would be the perfect stepping stone between Krk and Zadar if only the transport connections were more convenient.

Orientation The bus station is at the rear of a new commercial centre and around the corner from the Merkur department store, a five-minute walk from the old town. Narrow side-streets in the old town climb up from the main north-south streets Donja, Srednja and Gornja ul, or lower, middle and upper roads. The large Jadrolinija ferries tie up on the south-eastern tip of the peninsula (or will when the new port is built) and the small boat harbour is on the north-western side.

Information There are two tourist offices (☎ 771 111, 771 110, @ tzg-raba@ri.tel.hr). One is around the corner from the bus station opposite the Merkur department store and the other is on Arba Municipium, across from Café Revelin. There is a post office in the commercial centre open 7 am to 8 pm Monday to Saturday. The Atlas travel agency (☎ 724 585) is on Arba Municipium, opposite the post office.

Things to See Four tall church towers rise above the red-roofed mass of houses on Rab's high peninsula. If you follow Rade Končara north from the **Monastery of St Anthony** (1175), you soon reach the Romanesque **cathedral**, alongside a pleasant terrace with a view overlooking the sea.

Farther along, beyond a tall **Romanesque tower** and another convent, is a second terrace and **St Justine Church**, now a small museum of religious art. Just past the next chapel, keep an eye out for a small gate giving access to a park with the foundations of Rab's oldest church and the fourth tower (which you can climb).

Special Events Annual events to ask about include the Rab Fair (25 to 27 July) and the Rab Music Evenings (June to September).

Places to Stay Everything from camping to expensive hotels can be found in and around Rab town.

To sleep cheaply, carry your tent south along the waterfront for about 25 minutes to *Autocamp Padova* (☎ 724 355) at Banjol. Farther out of town at Kampor is a small camping ground with a large beach, *Halović* (☎ 776 087).

Several agencies rent out private rooms, including Turist Biro Mila (☎ 725 499) on the south-eastern corner of the bus station and Turist Biro Kristofor (☎ 725 543, fax 724 811, @ kristofor@ri.tel.hr), on the north-western corner. Prices are 100/120KN for a single/double in one-star accommodation and 120/160KN for rooms with private bathroom.

Hotel International (☎ 724 266, fax 724 206), on Obala kralja Petra Krešimira IV, facing the harbour, has the cheapest rooms at 268/440KN a single/double with bath and breakfast in peak season.

Places to Eat *Pizza Paradiso* (ul Radića 2) serves pizza for 40KN in a touristy but attractive enclosed terrace. For fast food, head to *Buffet Buza* on ul Ugalje near Arba Municipium, where you can eat a plate of fried squid for 20KN. There's a good *supermarket* in the basement at the Merkur department store for picnic supplies.

Getting There & Away All the local travel agencies have bus and ferry schedules posted in their offices.

The most reliable way to travel is on one of the two daily buses between Rab and Rijeka (78KN, 115km). In the tourist season there are two direct buses from Zagreb to Rab (105KN to 122KN, five hours, 211km). These services can fill up, so book ahead if possible.

There's no direct bus from Rab to Zadar but there are two daily buses that connect at Senj with Rijeka buses to Zadar (five hours). To avoid backtracking from Senj to Jablanac and also save some kuna, you can take a Zagreb-bound bus to the highway at Jablanac and catch the Rijeka bus as it heads to Zadar.

CROATIA

The citadel Kruja, Albania, perched on a ridge between towering mountains and the modern town.

Bullet casing coffee grinders, Bosnia

Street scene in Bosnia

Post Office, Sarajevo, Bosnia

St Blaise's Church, Dubrovnik, Croatia

A leisurely getaway, Cavtat, Dubrovnik

Dubrovnik, the crowning glory of Croatia's Dalmatian Coast

The timeless village of Pera, Republic of Cyprus

Remains of the Sanctuary of Apollon Ylatis, Cyprus

The late afternoon buses connect in about 20 minutes; otherwise you'll have to wait over an hour on the highway.

In addition to the summer ferry between Baška on Krk Island and Lopar on Rab Island, there will be a weekly Jadrolinija ferry from Rijeka when the new deep-water port is completed.

Dalmatia

Dalmatia (Dalmacija) occupies the central 375km of Croatia's Adriatic coast, from the Gulf of Kvarner in the north to the Bay of Kotor in the south, including offshore islands. The rugged Dinaric Alps form a 1500m-high barrier separating Dalmatia from Bosnia, with only two breaks: the Krka River canyon at Knin and the Neretva Valley at Mostar, both of which have railway lines.

After the last Ice Age, part of the coastal mountains were flooded, creating the same sort of long, high islands seen in the Gulf of Kvarner. The deep, protected passages that lie between these islands are a paradise for sailors and cruisers.

Historical relics abound in towns like Zadar, Trogir, Split, Hvar, Korčula and Dubrovnik, framed by the striking natural beauty of barren slopes, green valleys and clear water. The ferry trip from Split to Dubrovnik is one of the classic journeys of Eastern Europe. The vineyards of Dalmatia supply half of Croatia's wine. A warm current flowing north up the coast keeps the climate mild – dry in summer, damp in winter. Dalmatia is noticeably warmer than Istria or the Gulf of Kvarner and it's possible to swim in the sea right up until the end of September. This is the Mediterranean at its best.

ZADAR
☎ 023 • pop 76,300

Zadar (the ancient Zara), the main city of northern Dalmatia, occupies a long peninsula which separates the harbour on the east from the Zadarski Channel on the west. Its strategic position on the Adriatic coast made Zadar a desirable target for the Romans, the Byzantine Empire, the Venetian Empire, the Austro-Hungarian Empire and Italy. Although damaged by Allied bombing raids in 1943-44 and Yugoslav rockets in 1991, the resilient city has been rebuilt and restored, retaining much of its old flavour. The marble, traffic-free streets of the old town are replete with Roman ruins, medieval churches and several fascinating museums. Tremendous 16th-century fortifications still shield the city on the landward side with high walls running along the harbour. The tree-lined promenade along Obala kralja Petra Krešimira IV is perfect for a lazy stroll or a picnic and there are several small beaches east of the old town. More beaches lie to the west at Borik as well as on the islands of Ugljan and Dugi Otok, within easy reach of the town. Don't forget to sample Zadar's famous maraschino cherry liqueur.

Orientation
The train and bus stations are adjacent and a 15-minute walk south-east of the harbour and old town.

From the stations, Zrinsko-Frankopanska ul leads north-west past the main post office to the harbour. Buses marked 'Poluotok' run from the bus station to the harbour. Narodni trg is the heart of Zadar.

Information
The official tourist office is Turistička Zajednica (☎ 212 412, ✉ tzg-zadad@zd.tel.hr), Smiljanića 4, but you'll find more information at one of the travel agencies.

The American Express representative is Atlas travel agency (☎ 314 339), Branimirova Obala 12, across the footbridge over the harbour, just north-east of Narodni trg. Croatia Express (☎ 211 660, ✉ croatiae@zd.tel.hr) is on Široka ul next to an ATM. Croatia Airlines (☎ 314 272) is at Poljana Natka Nodila 7. You can change money at any travel agency, at the Jadrolinija office or in the post office. There is also an exchange office and an ATM at the bus station.

Telephone calls can be made from the main post office at Zrinsko-Frankopanska ul 8. It's open 7 am to 8 pm Monday to Saturday and until 2 pm Sunday. Computers and an Internet connection are available at Cybercafe (☎ 313 995, ✉ cyber@net.hr), Špire Brusine 8, Monday to Saturday.

The left-luggage at the train station is open 24 hours; at the bus station it is open 7 am to 9 pm Monday to Friday.

CROATIA

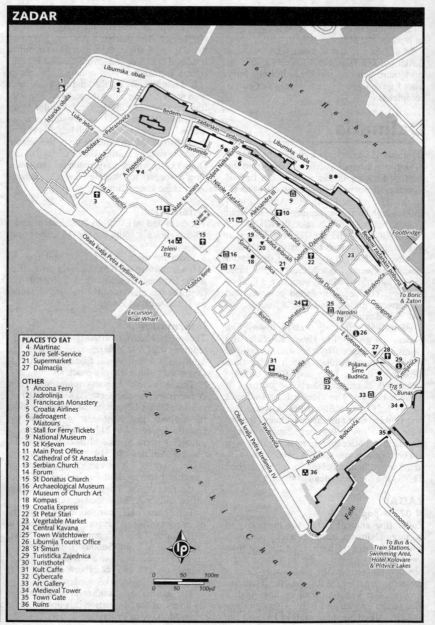

ZADAR

PLACES TO EAT
4 Martinac
20 Jure Self-Service
21 Supermarket
27 Dalmacija

OTHER
1 Ancona Ferry
2 Jadrolinija
3 Franciscan Monastery
5 Croatia Airlines
6 Jadroagent
7 Miatours
8 Stall for Ferry Tickets
9 National Museum
10 St Krševan
11 Main Post Office
12 Cathedral of St Anastasia
13 Serbian Church
14 Forum
15 St Donatus Church
16 Archaeological Museum
17 Museum of Church Art
18 Kompas
19 Croatia Express
22 St Petar Stari
23 Vegetable Market
24 Central Kavana
25 Town Watchtower
26 Liburnija Tourist Office
28 St Šimun
29 Turistička Zajednica
30 Turisthotel
31 Kult Caffe
32 Cybercafe
33 Art Gallery
34 Medieval Tower
35 Town Gate
36 Ruins

Things to See & Do
The main things to see are near the circular **St Donatus Church**, a 9th-century Byzantine structure built over the Roman forum. Slabs for the ancient forum are visible in the church and, on the north-western side, is a pillar from the Roman era. In summer, ask about musical evenings here (Renaissance and early baroque music). The outstanding **Museum of Church Art**, in the Benedictine monastery opposite, offers three floors of elaborate gold and silver reliquaries, religious paintings, icons and local lacework. It's open 10 am to 12.30 pm and 6 to 7.30 pm daily, except Sunday evening (20KN).

The 13th-century Romanesque **Cathedral of St Anastasia** nearby never really recovered from WWII destruction; the **Franciscan Monastery** a few blocks away is more cheerful. The large Romanesque cross in the treasury, behind the sacristy, is worth seeing.

Museums are open mornings and late afternoons but closed Sunday. The most interesting is the **Archaeological Museum** across from St Donatus, with an extensive collection of artefacts from the Neolithic period through the Roman occupation to the development of Croatian culture under the Byzantines. Some captions are in English and you are handed a leaflet in English when you buy your ticket (13KN).

Less interesting is the **National Museum** on Poljana Pape Aleksandra III, just inside the Sea Gate, featuring photos of Zadar from different periods, and old paintings and engravings of many coastal cities. The same admission ticket (5KN) will get you into the **art gallery** on Smiljanića. Notable churches include the 12th-century St Krševan church, St Simun with a 14th-century gold chest and St Petar Stari with Roman-Byzantine frescoes.

There's a swimming area with diving boards, a small park and a cafe on the coastal promenade off Zvonimira. Bordered by pine trees and small parks, the promenade takes you to a beach in front of the Hotel Kolovare and then winds on for about a kilometre along the coast.

Organised Tours
Any of the many travel agencies around town can supply information on tourist cruises to the beautiful Kornati Islands (250KN, including lunch and a swim in the sea or a salt lake). As this is about the only way to see these 101 barren, uninhabited islands, islets and cliffs it's worthwhile if you can spare the cash. There's also rafting on the Zrmanja River (185KN) and half-day excursions to the Krka waterfalls (160KN). Check with Miatours (☎/fax 212 788, ☒ miatrade@zd .tel.hr) at Vrata Sveti Krševana, or Kompas (☎/fax 433 380) on Široka.

Special Events
Major annual events include the town fair (July and August), the Dalmatian Song Festival (July and August), the musical evenings in St Donatus Church (August) and the Choral Festival (October).

Places to Stay
Most visitors head out to the 'tourist settlement' at Borik, 3km north-west of Zadar, on the Puntamika bus (6KN, every 20 minutes from the bus station). Here there are hotels, a hostel, a camp site and numerous 'sobe' signs; you can arrange a private room through an agency in town. If you arrive in the off season, try to arrange accommodation in advance, as hotels, hostels and camp sites will be closed.

Camping *Zaton (☎ 264 303)* is 16km north-west of Zadar on a sandy beach and should be open from May to September but call first. There are 12 buses marked Zaton leaving daily from the bus station. Nearer to Zadar is *Autocamp Borik (☎ 332 074)*, only steps away from Borik beach. You'll pay about 30KN per person.

Hostels Also near the beach at Borik is *Borik Youth Hostel (☎ 331 145, fax 331 190, Obala Kneza Trpimira 76)*, which is open from May to September. B&B costs 80KN and full board is 120KN.

Private Rooms Agencies finding private accommodation include Turisthotel (☎ 211 005, fax 312 750, ☒ turisthotel@zd.tel.hr) at Poljana Šime Budnića 1; Miatours (see Organised Tours earlier); Marlin Tours (☎/fax 313 194), around the corner from Atlas at Jeretova 3; or Liburnija tourist office (☎ 211 039) on Kotromanić. Expect to pay 120/200KN a single/double with private bath.

Hotels There are no budget hotels in town and only one regularly operating hotel, the ultra-modern *Hotel Kolovare* (☎ *203 200, fax 203 300,* ✉ *hotel-kolovare-zadar@zd.tel.hr, Bože Peričića 14),* with a pool and fitness centre. You'll pay 395/600KN a single/ double for fully renovated rooms with TV and air-con and 255/400KN for simpler, un-renovated rooms. Otherwise, head out to nearby Borik on the Puntamika bus. The two-star *Novi Park* (☎ *206 200), Barbara* (☎ *206 100)* and *Donat* (☎ *206 500),* all at Majstora Radovana 7, offer rooms with breakfast for 225/301KN.

Places to Eat

Dalmacija at the end of Kraljice Elizabete Kotromanić is a good place for pizza, spaghetti, fish and local specialities. The newly renovated *Jure* is a self-service restaurant in the passage off Nikole Matafara 9 that has hot dishes starting at 25KN. *Restaurant Martinac* (*Papavije 7)* has a se-cluded backyard terrace behind the restaur-ant that provides a relaxed ambience to sample delicious dishes such as risotto (35KN), fish (40KN to 45KN) and excellent clams. The restaurant of *Hotel Kolovare* has a wide assortment of meat, fish and pasta dishes at reasonable prices.

There's a *supermarket* on the corner of Široka and Sabora that keeps long hours and you'll find a number of *burek stands* around the vegetable market.

Entertainment

Central Kavana on Široka ul is a spacious cafe and hang-out with live music on week-ends. *Kult Caffe* on Stomarica draws a young crowd to listen to rap music indoors or relax on the large shady terrace outside. In summer the many cafes along Varoška and Klaića place their tables on the street; it's great for people-watching.

Getting There & Away

Air Zadar's airport, 12km east of the city, was destroyed in the war but has now been entirely rebuilt to receive charter flights and daily Croatia Airlines flights from Zagreb (700KN). There is no public transportation between the airport and the town centre; a taxi should cost around 100KN.

Bus & Train There are buses to Rijeka (97KN, 228km, 14 daily), Split (65KN, 158km, hourly), Mostar (168KN, 301km, nine daily), Dubrovnik (138KN, 393km, seven daily) and Sarajevo (208KN, once daily). There are two daily trains to Zagreb (53KN, 11 hours) that change at Knin. The bus to Zagreb (85KN, 320km) is quicker.

The Croatia Express travel agency (see In-formation earlier) sells bus tickets to many German cities, including Munich (400KN), Frankfurt (624KN), Cologne (760KN) and Berlin (800KN). For buses to Vienna (315KN, 13 hours, weekly), Trieste (94KN, seven hours, daily) and Amsterdam (1140KN, 24 hours, weekly), buy tickets at the bus station.

Boat From late June to September the fast boat *Marina* runs from Venice to Zadar twice a week and from Pula to Zadar four times a week, stopping at Mali Lošinj. There are weekly local ferries all year (three times a week in summer) between Mali Lošinj and Zadar (34KN, six hours) and between Pula and Zadar (66KN, eight hours). The Jadrolin-ija coastal ferry from Rijeka to Dubrovnik calls at Zadar twice a week (144KN).

For information on connections to Italy see the Getting There & Away section at the be-ginning of this chapter and contact Jadro-agent (☎ 211 447), on ul Natka Nodila, just inside the city walls. Jadrolinija (☎ 212 003) at Liburnska obala 7 on the harbour, has tick-ets for all local ferries.

On Tuesday and Thursday there's a ferry to Zaglav on Dugi Otok (13KN), which is a good day trip (on other days there's no con-nection to return to Zadar).

Miatours offers a daily boat to Sali on Dugi Otok (15KN) all year and a fast boat to Božava on Dugi Otok (50KN return), Silba (70KN return) and Rijeka (240KN, 2½ hours) on Wednesday in July and August.

AROUND ZADAR
Plitvice Lakes
☎ 053

Plitvice Lakes National Park lies midway be-tween Zagreb and Zadar. The 19.5 hectares of wooded hills enclose 16 turquoise lakes, which are linked by a series of waterfalls and cascades. The mineral-rich waters carve new paths through the rock, depositing tufa in continually changing formations. Wooden footbridges follow the lakes and streams over, under and across the rumbling water for an exhilaratingly damp 18km. Swimming is allowed in several lakes. Park admission is 60/80KN off season/in summer (students 40/48KN), but is valid for the entire stay. There is accommodation on site as well as private accommodation nearby. Check with the Plitvice Lakes National Park office in Zagreb (see Information under Zagreb earlier in this chapter).

Getting There & Away All buses to Zagreb stop at Plitvice (148km). It is possible to visit Plitvice for the day on the way to or from the coast but be aware that buses will not pick up passengers at Plitvice if they are full. Luggage can be left at the tourist information centre (☎ 751 048) at the first entrance to the park (open from 8 am to 10 pm daily).

SPLIT
☎ 021 • pop 189,390

Split (Spalato in Italian), the largest Croatian city on the Adriatic coast, is the heart of Dalmatia and lies on the southern side of a high peninsula sheltered from the open sea by many islands. Ferries to these islands are constantly coming and going. Within the ancient walls of Diocletian's Palace in the centre of town rises the majestic cathedral surrounded by a tangle of marble streets containing shops and businesses. The entire western end of the peninsula is a vast, wooded mountain park, while industry, shipyards, limestone quarries and the ugly commercial-military port are mercifully far enough away on the northern side of the peninsula. High coastal mountains set against the blue Adriatic provide a striking frame to the scene.

Split achieved fame when the Roman emperor Diocletian (AD 245-313), noted for his persecution of early Christians, had his retirement palace built here from 295 to 305. After his death the great stone palace continued to be used as a retreat by Roman rulers. When the nearby colony of Salona was abandoned in the 7th century, many of the Romanised inhabitants fled to Split and barricaded themselves behind the high palace walls, where their descendants live to this day.

Since 1945, Split has grown into a major industrial city with large apartment-block housing areas. However, much of old Split remains, which combined with its exuberant nature, makes it one of the more interesting cities in Europe. It's also the perfect base for excursions to many nearby attractions, so settle in for a few days.

Orientation
The bus, train and ferry terminals are adjacent on the eastern side of the harbour, a short walk from the old town. Obala hrvatskog narodnog preporoda, the waterfront promenade, is your best central reference point in Split.

Information
Tourist Office The Turistički Biro (☎/fax 342 142) is at Obala hrvatskog narodnog preporoda 12.

Money The American Express representative, Atlas travel agency (☎ 343 055) is at Trg Braće Radića. You can change money there or at any travel agency. There's also an ATM next to the Croatia Airlines office at Obala hrvatskog narodnog preporoda 9.

Post & Communications Poste-restante mail can be collected at window No 7 at the main post office, Kralja Tomislava 9. It's open 7 am to 8 pm weekdays and until 3 pm Saturday. The telephone centre here is open 7 am to 9 pm Monday to Saturday. Cyber Cafe at Kružićeva 3 offers an Internet connection and is open 9 am to 9 pm Monday to Friday and until 2 pm Saturday.

Bookshop Algoritam at Bajamontijeva 2 is a well-stocked English-language bookshop.

Left Luggage The garderoba kiosk at the bus station is open 4 am to 10 pm. The train station's left-luggage office is about 50m north of the station at Domagoja 6 and is open 7 am to 9 pm.

Things to See
The old town is a vast open-air museum and the new information signs before important sights explain a great deal of Split's history.

Diocletian's Palace, facing the harbour, is one of the most imposing Roman ruins in

CROATIA

SPLIT

Franciscan Monastery

Park Skojevaca

To Solin & Trogir

Sports Stadium

Poljud Harbour

Hrvatske mornarice

0   250   500m
0   250   500yd

Archaeological Museum

Lučićeva

Lovretska

Local Bus Station

Radničko Šetalište

Kaštelanska

Zrinsko-Frankopanska

Matoševa

Šetalište M Tartaglie

Ujevićeva Poljana
Plinarska

Svačićeva

Slačićeva

Istarska

Vukovarska

Marjan Hill

Prilaz Vladimira Nazora

Milićeva

Kniževa

Sinjskih

Zagrebačka

Kralja Tomislava

To Lisičina

Kneza Držislava

Slobode

Zoo

Jewish Cemetery

Senjska

Stairway to Marjan Hill

Obala preporoda

Hrvojeva

Vrzov dolac

Matice hrvatske

Marasovica

Kralja Zvonimira

Bačvice

Put Meja

To Meštrović Gallery

Obala kneza Branimira

Obala

Kneza Domagoja

Bus station

Bankinijeva

Šetalište

Matije Gupca

Vidia

Šetalište Ivana Meštrovića

Split Harbour

Yacht Harbour

Ferry Terminal

To Hotel Zenta

Bačvice

Beach

Put Firula

See Central Split Map

ADRIATIC SEA

CROATIA

existence. It was built as a strong rectangular fortress, with walls 215m by 180m long and reinforced by towers. The imperial residence, temples and mausoleum were south of the main street, connecting the east and west gates.

Enter through the central ground floor of the palace at Obala hrvatskog narodnog preporoda 22. On the left you'll see the excavated basement halls, which are empty but impressive. Continue through the passage to the **Peristyle**, a picturesque colonnaded square, with a neo-Romanesque cathedral tower rising above. The **vestibule**, an open dome above the ground-floor passageway at the southern end of the Peristyle, is overpowering. A lane off the Peristyle opposite the cathedral leads to the **Temple of Jupiter**, which is now a baptistery.

On the eastern side of the Peristyle is the **cathedral**, originally Diocletian's mausoleum. The only reminder of Diocletian in the cathedral is a sculpture of his head in a circular stone wreath below the dome directly above the baroque white-marble altar. The Romanesque wooden doors (1214) and stone pulpit are worth noting. You may climb the tower for a small fee.

The west palace gate opens onto medieval Narodni trg, dominated by the 15th-century Venetian Gothic **old town hall**. Trg Braće Radića, between Narodni trg and the harbour, contains the surviving north tower of the 15th-century Venetian garrison castle, which once extended to the water's edge. The east palace gate leads into the market area.

In the Middle Ages the nobility and rich merchants built residences within the old palace walls; the Papalic Palace at Papalićeva (also known as Žarkova) ul 5 is now the town museum. Go through the north palace gate to see the powerful **statue** (1929) by Ivan Meštrović of 10th-century Slavic religious leader Gregorius of Nin, who fought for the right to perform Mass in Croatian. Notice that his big toe has been polished to a shine; it's said that touching it brings good luck.

Museums & Galleries Most of Split's museums have been closed for the last 10 years awaiting money for renovation.

The **town museum** at Papalićeva ul 5, east of Narodni trg, has a well-displayed collection of artefacts, paintings, furniture and clothes from Split. Captions are in Croatian. It's open 10 am to 5 pm Tuesday to Friday, and until noon weekends, but it's closed Monday. The recently reopened **Ethnographic Museum** in Narodni trg has a mildly interesting collection of photos of Old Split, traditional costumes and memorabilia of important citizens, but captions are in Croatian.

If you're in the neighbourhood make a stop at the **archaeological museum**, Zrinjsko-Frankopanska 25, north of town (open mornings and late afternoons, closed Monday). First assembled in 1820, the only part of this valuable collection on display is in the garden outside, which shows various stone fragments from Solin.

The finest art museum in Split is the **Meštrović Gallery**, located at Šetalište Ivana Meštrovića 46 (closed Monday). You'll see a comprehensive, well-arranged collection of works by Ivan Meštrović, Croatia's premier modern sculptor, who built the gallery as his home in 1931-39. Although Meštrović intended to retire here, he emigrated to the United States soon after WWII. There are beaches on the southern side of the peninsula below the gallery. Bus

No 12 runs to the gallery from Trg Republike every 40 minutes.

From the Meštrović Gallery it's possible to hike straight up **Marjan Hill**. Go up ul Tonća Petrasova Marovića on the western side of the gallery and continue straight up the stairway to Put Meja ul. Turn left and walk west to Put Meja 76. The trail begins on the western side of this building. Marjan Hill offers trails through the forest, lookouts, old chapels and the local zoo.

Organised Tours

Atlas travel agency (see Information earlier) runs excursions to Krka waterfalls (220KN), organises rafting on the Cetina River (200KN), a canoe picnic on the Cetina River (220KN) as well as a fast boat to Bol beach on Brač every Sunday (95KN return).

Special Events

The Split Summer Festival (mid-July to mid-August) features opera, drama, ballet and concerts on open-air stages. There's also the Feast of St Dujo (7 May), a flower show (May) and the four-day Festival of Popular Music (end of June). The traditional February Carnival has recently been revived and from June to September a variety of evening entertainment is presented in the old town.

Places to Stay

Unfortunately, the closest camp site to Split is *Lisičina* (☎ 861 332), 20km south-east of Split, near Omiš.

In the summer, you may be met at the bus station by women offering zimmer. Otherwise, you'll need to head for the Turistički Biro, which offers singles/doubles for 78/92KN for one-star accommodation and 116/132KN for two-/three-star accommodation.

The 32-room *Slavija* (☎ 347 053, fax 591 558, Buvinova 3) has the cheapest rooms at 170/220KN a single/double without bath and 220/260KN with bath. Rooms are clean but basic. A more expensive alternative in the town centre is *Hotel Bellevue* (☎ 585 655, fax 363 383, Bana Jelačića 2) in an old but renovated building. Rooms are 375/490KN. The mid-range *Zenta* (☎ 357 229, Ivana Zajca 2) is east of the town centre, near the beach and the nightlife at Bačvice. Rooms cost 254/370KN.

CROATIA

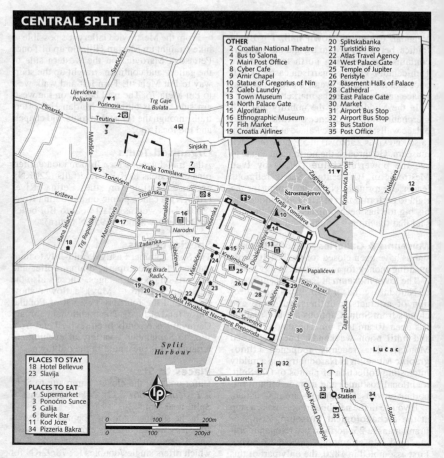

CENTRAL SPLIT

OTHER
2 Croatian National Theatre
4 Bus to Salona
7 Main Post Office
8 Cyber Cafe
9 Arnir Chapel
10 Statue of Gregorius of Nin
12 Galeb Laundry
13 Town Museum
14 North Palace Gate
15 Algotiam
16 Ethnographic Museum
17 Fish Market
19 Croatia Airlines
20 Splitskabanka
21 Turistički Biro
22 Atlas Travel Agency
24 West Palace Gate
25 Temple of Jupiter
26 Peristyle
27 Basement Halls of Palace
28 Cathedral
29 East Palace Gate
30 Market
31 Airport Bus Stop
32 Airport Bus Stop
33 Bus Station
35 Post Office

PLACES TO STAY
18 Hotel Bellevue
23 Slavija

PLACES TO EAT
1 Supermarket
3 Ponočno Sunce
5 Galija
6 Burek Bar
11 Kod Joze
34 Pizzeria Bakra

Split Harbour

Places to Eat

The best pizza in town is served at *Galija* on Tončićeva (daily until 11 pm), where they start at 22KN, but *Pizzeria Bakra* (*Radovanova 2*), off ul Sv Petra Starog and just down from the vegetable market, is not bad either. The vegetarian salad bar at *Ponočno Sunce* (*Teutina 15*) is good value at 40KN. It also serves pasta and grilled meat. For excellent Dalmatian specialties at a reasonable price, try *Kod Joze* (*Sredmanuška 4*).

There's a spiffy *Burek Bar* (*Domaldova 13*), just down from the main post office, and the vast *supermarket/delicatessen* at Svačićeva 1 has a wide selection of meat and cheese for sandwiches. The *vegetable market* has a wide array of fresh local produce.

Entertainment

In summer everyone starts the evening at one of the cafes along Obala hrvatskog narodnog preporoda and then heads to the *Bačvice* complex on the beach. This former public bath offers restaurants, cafes, discos and venues for live rock and salsa. During winter, opera and ballet are presented at the *Croatian National Theatre* on Trg Gaje Bulata. The best seats are about 60KN and tickets for the

CROATIA

same night are usually available. Erected in 1891, the theatre was fully restored in 1979 in the original style; it's worth attending a performance for the architecture alone.

Getting There & Away

Air Croatia Airlines (☎ 362 997) operates one-hour flights to/from Zagreb up to four times daily (897KN in peak season, 50% cheaper in the off season) and a daily flight to Zadar.

Bus Advance bus tickets with seat reservations are recommended. There are buses from the main bus station beside the harbour to Zadar (51KN to 78KN, 158km, 26 daily), Zagreb (86KN to 118KN, 478km, 26 daily), Rijeka (167KN, 404km, 14 daily), Ljubljana (188KN, 532km, one daily), Pula (215KN, 514km, three daily) and Dubrovnik (84KN, 235km, 12 daily). There are six daily buses from Split to Međugorje (50KN, 156km), 11 to Mostar (50KN, 179km) and six to Sarajevo (140KN, 271km).

Bus No 37 to Solin, Split airport and Trogir leaves from a local bus station on Domovinskog, 1km north-east of the city centre (see the Split map).

Croatia Express (☎ 338 525), near the bus station, sells tickets to many German cities, including Munich (400KN, 912km, daily) and Berlin (840KN, Saturday and Sunday). Agencija Touring (☎ 338 503) at the bus station also has many buses to Germany and a weekly bus to Amsterdam (900KN).

Train There are two trains daily between Split and Zagreb (60KN, eight hours), and Split and Šibenik (26KN, 90 minutes).

Boat Jadrolinija (☎ 338 333), in the large ferry terminal opposite the bus station, handles services to Hvar Island, which operate three or four times a week year-round. However, the local ferry is cheaper (23.30KN) and also calls at Vela Luka on Korčula Island (25KN) daily.

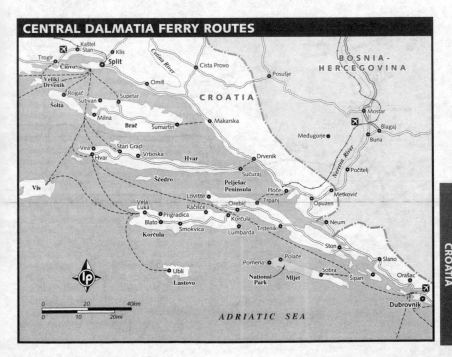

CENTRAL DALMATIA FERRY ROUTES

For information on connections to Italy see the Getting There & Away section at the beginning of this chapter and get the schedule and tickets from Jadroagent in the ferry terminal (open 8 am to 1.30 pm and 5 to 8 pm daily in the off season; it doesn't close in summer). There's also an SEM agency (☎ 338 292) in the terminal for tickets to Ancona.

Getting Around

The bus to Split airport (25KN) leaves from Obala Lazareta 3, about 90 minutes before flight times or you can take bus No 37 (two-zone ticket).

A one-zone ticket costs 6KN for one trip in Central Split if you buy it from the driver but 10KN for two trips and 50KN for 10 trips if you buy it from a kiosk. There's a kiosk that also distributes bus maps at the city bus stop.

SOLIN (SALONA)

The ruins of the ancient city of Solin (known as Salona by the Romans), among the vineyards at the foot of mountains 5km north-east of Split, are the most interesting archaeological site in Croatia. Today surrounded by noisy highways and industry, Salona was the capital of the Roman province of Dalmatia from the time Julius Caesar elevated it to the status of colony. Salona held out against the barbarians and was only evacuated in AD 614 when the inhabitants fled to Split and neighbouring islands in the face of Avar and Slav attacks.

Things to See

Manastirine, the fenced area behind the car park, was a burial place for early Christian martyrs before the legalisation of Christianity. Excavated remains of the cemetery and the 5th-century basilica are highlights, although this area was outside the ancient city itself. Overlooking Manastirine is **Tusculum**, an archaeological museum with interesting sculptures embedded in the walls and in the garden. The museum is open 9 am to 1 pm Monday to Saturday in the off season and until 6 pm in

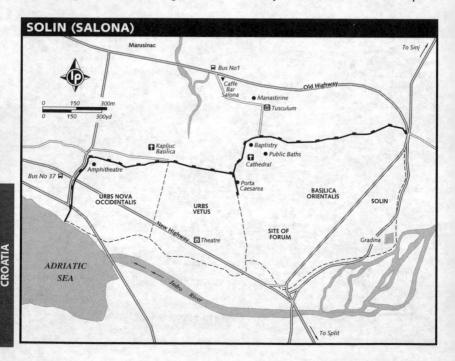

SOLIN (SALONA)

To Sinj

Marusinac

🚏 Bus No1

Caffe Bar Salona

Old Highway

● Manastirine

🏛 Tusculum

0   150   300m
0   150   300yd

🏛 Kapljuc Basilica

● Baptistry

🏛 ● Public Baths

Cathedral

🚏 Bus No 37

Amphitheatre

● Porta Caesarea

BASILICA ORIENTALIS

SOLIN

URBS NOVA OCCIDENTALIS

URBS VETUS

New Highway 🏛 Theatre

SITE OF FORUM

Gradina

ADRIATIC SEA

Jadro River

To Split

CROATIA

summer. There is a helpful map and some literature about the complex in the museum.

The Manastirine-Tusculum complex is part of an **archaeological reserve**. Admission is 10KN. A path bordered by cypresses runs south to the northern **city wall** of Salona. Notice the covered aqueduct along the inside base of the wall. The ruins you see in front of you as you stand on the wall were the Early-Christian cult centre, including the three-aisled 5th-century **cathedral** and small **baptistery** with inner columns. **Public baths** adjoin the cathedral on the east.

South-west of the cathedral is the 1st-century east city gate, **Porta Caesarea**, later engulfed by the growth of Salona in all directions. Grooves in the stone road left by ancient chariots can still be seen at this gate.

Walk west along the city wall for 500m to **Kapljuc Basilica** on the right, another martyrs' burial place. At the western end of Salona is the huge 2nd-century **amphitheatre**, destroyed in the 17th century by the Venetians to prevent it from being used as a refuge by Turkish raiders.

Getting There & Away

The ruins are easily accessible on Split city bus No 1 direct to Solin every half-hour from the city bus stop.

From the amphitheatre at Solin it's easy to continue to Trogir by catching a westbound bus No 37 from the nearby stop on the adjacent new highway. If, on the other hand, you want to return to Split, you can use the underpass to cross the highway and catch an eastbound bus No 37 (buy a four-zone ticket in Split if you plan to do this).

TROGIR
☎ 021 • pop 1600

Trogir (formerly Trau), a lovely medieval town on the coast just 20km west of Split, is well worth a stop if you're coming south from Zadar. A day trip to Trogir from Split can easily be combined with a visit to the Roman ruins of Solin (see the Solin section earlier in this chapter).

The old town of Trogir occupies a tiny island in the narrow channel between Čiovo Island and the mainland, and is just off the coastal highway. There are many sights on the 15-minute walk around this island.

Orientation

The heart of the old town is a few minutes' walk from the bus station. After crossing the small bridge near the station, go through the North Gate. Trogir's finest sights are around Narodni trg to the south-east.

Information

The tourist office (☎ 881 554) opposite the cathedral sells a map of the area. There's no left-luggage office in Trogir bus station, so you may end up toting your bags around town.

Things to See

The glory of the three-naved Venetian **Cathedral of St Lovro** on Narodni trg is the Romanesque portal of Adam and Eve (1240) by Master Radovan, which you can admire for free at any time. Enter the building through an obscure back door to see the perfect Renaissance Chapel of St Ivan and the choir stalls, pulpit, ciborium and treasury. You can even climb the cathedral tower, if it's open, for a delightful view. Also on Narodni trg is the **town hall**, with an excellent Gothic staircase and Renaissance loggia.

Getting There & Away

In Split bus No 37 leaves from the local bus station. If you're making a day trip to Trogir also buy your ticket back to Split, as the ticket window at Trogir bus station is often closed. Drivers also sell tickets if you're stuck. City bus No 37 runs between Trogir and Split (28km) every 20 minutes throughout the day, with a stop at Split airport en route. There's also a ferry once a week between Trogir and Split.

Southbound buses from Zadar (130km) will drop you off in Trogir. Getting buses north can be more difficult, as they often arrive full from Split.

HVAR ISLAND
☎ 021 • pop 11,459

Called the 'Croatian Madeira', Hvar is said to receive more sunshine than anywhere else in the country, 2724 hours each year. Yet the island is luxuriantly green, with brilliant patches of lavender, rosemary and heather. The fine weather is so reliable that hotels give a discount on cloudy days and a free stay if you ever see snow.

CROATIA

Hvar Town

Medieval Hvar lies between protective pine-covered slopes and the azure Adriatic, its Gothic palaces hidden among narrow back-streets below the 13th-century city walls. A long seaside promenade winds along the indented coast dotted with small, rocky beaches. The traffic-free marble avenues of Hvar have an air of Venice about them; under Venetian rule Hvar grew rich exporting wine, figs and fish.

Orientation & Information The barge from Split drops you off in the centre of old Hvar. The big Jadrolinija ferries call at Stari Grad, 20km east and are met by buses to Hvar town.

The tourist office (☎ 741 059) is in the arsenal building on the corner of Trg Sv Stjepana, but it is open limited hours off season. There's a left-luggage office, open 7 am to noon and 5 to 7 pm daily, in the bathroom next to the bus station.

The Atlas travel agency (☎ 741 670) faces the harbour. Public telephones are in the post office on the waterfront (open 7 am to 8 pm Monday to Friday and until 3 pm Saturday). A curious feature of Hvar is its lack of street names. You may stumble across a faded name on a plaque every so often but, in a small town where everyone knows everyone, street names seem superfluous to the residents.

Things to See The full flavour of medieval Hvar is best savoured on the backstreets of the old town. At each end of Hvar is a monastery with a prominent tower. The **Dominican monastery** at the head of the bay was destroyed by Turks in the 16th century and the local **archaeological museum** is now housed among the ruins. The museum is supposed to be open mornings during summer but if it is closed you'll still get a good view of the ruins from the road just above, which leads up to a stone cross on a hill top offering a picture-postcard view of Hvar.

At the south-eastern end of Hvar is the 15th-century Renaissance **Franciscan monastery**, with a fine collection of Venetian paintings in the church and adjacent museum, including *The Last Supper* by Matteo Ingoli (open morning and late afternoon Monday to Saturday).

Smack in the middle of Hvar is the imposing Gothic **arsenal**, its great arch visible from afar. The local commune's war galley was once kept here. Upstairs off the arsenal terrace is Hvar's prize, the first **municipal theatre** in Europe (1612), which was rebuilt in the 19th century. It's open morning and late afternoon Monday to Saturday, and Sunday morning, but hours differ (10KN).

On the hill top high above Hvar town is a **Venetian fortress** (1551) and it's well worth the climb for the sweeping panoramic views. Inside is a tiny collection of ancient amphora recovered from the sea bed. The fort was built to defend Hvar from the Turks, who sacked the town in 1539 and 1571.

The best beach in Hvar is in front of the Hotel Amphora, around the western corner of the cove, but most people take a launch to the naturist islands of Jerolim and Stipanska, just offshore.

Places to Stay Accommodation in Hvar is extremely tight in July and August. A prior reservation is highly recommended.

There's a camping site at *Jurjevac* (☎ 765 555) near Stari Grad and there are frequent buses to Jelsa, where you can pitch a tent at *Grebišće* (☎ 761 191) or *Mina* (☎ 761 227).

For private accommodation, try Mengola Travel (☎/fax 742 099, ✆ mengola-hvar@ st.tel.hr), a right-hand turn from Sv Stjepana along the harbour; or Pelegrini (☎/fax 742 250), next to where the Jadrolinija ferries tie up. Expect to pay from 92/140KN a single/double with private bathroom.

The cheapest hotels are *Dalmacija* (☎/fax 741 120) and the *Delfin* (☎/fax 741 168) on either side of the harbour, which charge 416/640KN with half-board. Both hotels open in mid-June. *Slavija* (☎ 741 820, fax 741 147) is usually open all year and charges only about 16KN more per person. Otherwise, splurge on the century-old *Hotel Palace* (☎ 741 966, fax 742 420), which charges 532/872KN for rooms with half-board. Prices drop 50% in the off season.

Places to Eat The pizzerias along the harbour offer the most predictable but inexpensive eating. For good quality fish, pasta and grilled meat, try *Hannibal* on the southern side of Trg Sv Stjepana and *Paradies Garden* up some stairs on the northern side of the cathedral. Expect to pay about 45KN to 65KN for a meal.

The *grocery store* on Trg Sv Stjepana is your best alternative to a restaurant.

Getting There & Away The Jadrolinija ferries between Rijeka and Dubrovnik stop in Stari Grad before continuing to Korčula. The Jadrolinija agency (☎ 741 132) beside the landing sells tickets.

The local ferry from Split calls at Stari Grad (26KN) three times daily (five in July and August) and connects Hvar town with Vela Luka on Korčula Island in the afternoon. See the Getting There & Away section of this chapter for information on international connections. Buses meet all ferries that dock at Stari Grad.

It's possible to visit Hvar on a (hectic) day trip from Split by catching the morning Jadrolinija ferry to Stari Grad, a bus to Hvar town, then the last ferry from Stari Grad directly back to Split.

KORČULA ISLAND
☎ 020 • pop 3000

Korčula is the largest island in an archipelago of 48 islets. Rich in vineyards and olive trees, the island was named Korkyra Melaina (Black Korčula) by the original Greek settlers because of its dense woods and plant life. The southern coast is dotted with quiet coves and small beaches linked to the interior by winding, scenic roads.

Korčula Town

The town of Korčula (Curzola in Italian), at the north-eastern tip of the island, hugs a small, hilly peninsula jutting into the Adriatic Sea. With its round defensive towers and compact cluster of red-roofed houses, Korčula is a typical medieval Dalmatian town. Korčula was controlled by Venice from the 14th to the 18th century and Venetian rule left its mark, especially on Cathedral Square. It's a peaceful little place, with grey-stone houses nestling between the deep-green hills and gunmetal-blue sea. There are rustling palms all around.

There's lots to see and do, so it's worth planning a relaxed four-night stay to avoid the 30% surcharge on private rooms. Day

trips are possible to Lumbarda, Vela Luka, Orebić on the Pelješac Peninsula and the islands of Badija and Mljet.

Orientation The big Jadrolinija car-ferry drops you off either in the west harbour next to the Hotel Korčula or the east harbour next to Marko Polo Tours. The old town lies between the two harbours. The passenger launch from Orebić is also convenient, terminating at the west harbour, but the car ferry from Orebić goes to Bon Repos in Dominče, several kilometres south-east of the centre.

Information The Turistička Agencija (☎/fax 711 710, **e** htp-korcula@du.tel.hr) is on the west harbour as you enter the old town. Atlas travel agency (☎ 711 231) is the local American Express representative and there's a Jadrolinija office (☎ 711 101) about 25m up from the west harbour.

The post office (with public telephones) is rather hidden next to the stairs up to the old town. There's Internet access at PC Centar 'Doom' (☎ 715 881, **e** buculin@du.tel.hr), Sveti Nikola 124, about 50m off the central square.

There's no ATM machine on the island but you can change money at the post office or any of the travel agencies. There's also Split-skabanka where you can change money or get a cash advance on your Visa card. There's no left-luggage office at the bus station.

Things to See Other than following the circuit of the former city walls or walking along the shore, sightseeing in Korčula centres on Cathedral Square. The Gothic **Cathedral of St Mark** features two paintings by Tintoretto (*Three Saints* on the altar and *Annunciation* to one side).

The **treasury** in the 14th-century Abbey Palace next to the cathedral is worth a look; even better is the **town museum** in the 15th-century Gabriellis Palace opposite. The exhibits of Greek pottery, Roman ceramics and home furnishings have English captions. It's said that Marco Polo was born in Korčula in 1254; for a small fee, you can climb the tower of what is believed to have been his house. There's also an **icon museum** in the old town. It isn't much of a museum, but visitors are let into the beautiful old **Church of All Saints**.

CROATIA

In the high summer season, water taxis at the eastern harbour collect passengers to visit various points on the island as well as **Badija Island**, which features a 15th-century Franciscan monastery (now a D-category hotel) and a naturist beach.

Organised Tours Marko Polo Tours (☎ 715 400, fax 715 800, ✆ marko-polo-tours@du.tel.hr) and Atlas travel agency both offer various day trips, but Marko Polo Tours is cheaper. You can go on a Fish Picnic (145KN), a tour to Mljet Island (145KN) or take a half-day boat trip around the surrounding islands (70KN).

Places to Stay Korčula offers quite a range of accommodation, though prices are high in July and August.

Autocamp Kalac (☎ 711 182) is behind Hotel Bon Repos in a dense pine grove near the beach.

Turistička Agencija and Marko Polo Tours arrange private rooms, charging 120/184KN for a single/double with private bath, except in peak season, when prices increase from 20% to 50%, depending on the period. You may get a better deal from the private operators who meet the boats, but check with the agencies first, since they're only steps from the harbour.

The B-category *Hotel Bon Repos* (☎ 711 102), overlooking a small beach outside town, and *Hotel Park* (☎ 726 004) in town, have the same rates - 330/480KN a single/double. You could also try the D-category *Badija* (☎ 711 115, fax 711 746) on Badija Island, which has a pool, beach, handball courts and other sports facilities. Rooms are 120/240KN with full board.

Places to Eat Just around the corner from Marco Polo's house, *Adio Mare* has a charming maritime decor and a variety of fresh fish. Restaurant-grill *Planjak*, between the supermarket and the Jadrolinija office in town, is popular with a local crowd, which appreciates the fresh, Dalmatian dishes as much as the low prices. A 20-minute walk outside town on the road to Lumbarda takes you to another local favourite, *Gastrionica Hajuk,* for delicious, inexpensive food. The shady terrace at *Hotel Korčula* is a nice place for a coffee.

Entertainment From May to September there's moreška sword dancing by the old town gate every Thursday at 9 pm. The clash of swords and the graceful movements of the dancers/fighters make an exciting show. Tickets (35KN) can be purchased from Atlas, the Turistička Agencija or Marko Polo Tours.

Getting There & Away Connections to Korčula are good. There's a daily bus service from Dubrovnik to Korčula (50KN, 113km) as well as a daily bus to Zagreb (165KN to 180KN) and two buses a week to Sarajevo (145KN).

Six daily buses link Korčula town to Vela Luka at the west end of the island (18KN, one hour). Buses to Lumbarda run hourly in the morning (7KN, 7km). No bus runs to Lumbarda on Sunday and services to Vela Luka are sharply reduced on weekends.

Boat Getting to Korčula is easy, as all the Jadrolinija ferries between Split and Dubrovnik tie up at a landing next to the old town. Most ferries tie up at the east harbour but some coastal ferries moor at the west harbour in front of Hotel Korčula. Once a week from June to September Jadrolinija runs a car-ferry between Korčula and Ancona, Italy (311KN, 17 hours), stopping at Split and Vis. Buy car-ferry tickets at the Jadrolinija office (☎ 715 410).

From Orebić, look for the passenger launch (8KN one-way, 15 minutes, four times daily year-round except weekends), which will drop you off at the Hotel Korčula right below the old town's towers. This is best if you're looking for a private room, but if you want to camp or stay at the hotel Bon Repos take the car-ferry to Dominče (6.80KN, 15 minutes) which stops near the hotel. The car-ferry is the only alternative on weekends. On Saturday, it connects with the bus from Lumbarda but on Sunday there is only one bus in the morning from Korčula to Orebić and one late afternoon bus returning.

Lumbarda

Just 15 minutes from Korčula town by bus, Lumbarda is a picturesque small settlement, known for its wine, near the south-eastern end of Korčula Island. A good ocean beach

(Plaža Pržina) is on the other side of the vineyards beyond the supermarket.

Bebić pension (☎ 712 183) and restaurant has a breathtaking view over the coast and serves good food. A double room or apartment is 200KN with bath and breakfast or 234KN per person with half-board.

The Turist Biro (☎/fax 712 005) arranges private accommodation and there are several small, inexpensive camp sites up the hill from the bus stop.

OREBIĆ

Orebić, on the south coast of the Pelješac Peninsula between Korčula and Ploče, offers better beaches than those found at Korčula, 2.5km across the water. The easy access by ferry from Korčula makes it the perfect place to go for the day. The best beach in Orebić is Trstenica cove, a 15-minute walk east along the shore from the port.

Getting There & Away

In Orebić the ferry terminal and the bus station are adjacent. Korčula buses to Dubrovnik, Zagreb and Sarajevo stop at Orebić. See Korčula for additional bus and ferry information.

MLJET ISLAND

☎ 020 • pop 1237

Created in 1960, **Mljet National Park** occupies the western third of the green island of Mljet (Meleda in Italian), between Korčula and Dubrovnik. The park centres around two salt-water lakes surrounded by pine-clad slopes. Most people visit on day trips from Korčula but it's possible to come by regular ferry from Dubrovnik, stay a few days and go hiking, cycling and boating.

Orientation

Tour boats from Korčula arrive at Pomena wharf at Mljet's western end, where a good map of the island is posted. Jadrolinija ferries arrive at Sobra on the eastern end and are met by a local bus for the 1½ hour ride to Pomena.

Things to See & Do

From Pomena it's a 15-minute walk to a jetty on **Veliko jezero**, the larger of the two lakes. Here the groups board a boat to a small lake islet and are served lunch at a 12th-century **Benedictine monastery**, now a restaurant.

Those who don't want to spend the rest of the afternoon swimming and sunbathing on the monastery island can catch an early boat back to the main island and spend a couple of hours walking along the lakeshore before catching the late-afternoon excursion boat back to Korčula. There's a small landing opposite the monastery where the boat operator drops off passengers upon request. It's not possible to walk right around the larger lake as there's no bridge over the channel connecting the lakes to the sea.

Mljet is good for cycling; the hotels rent out bicycles (60KN a half-day).

Organised Tours

See Korčula Organised Tours for agencies offering excursions to Mljet. The tour lasts from 8.30 am to 6 pm and includes the park entry fee of 50KN (25KN for children up to 18). The boat trip from Korčula to Pomena takes at least two hours, less by hydrofoil. Lunch isn't included in the tour price and meals at the hotels on Mljet are very expensive, so it's best to bring a picnic lunch.

Places to Stay

There's no camping in the national park but there's a small *camping ground* (☎ 745 071) in Ropa, about 1km from the park, open from June to September. The tourist office in Polače (☎ 744 086) arranges private accommodation at 200KN a double room in peak season but it is essential to make arrangements before arrival. Don't count on 'sobe' signs and in high season you'll have trouble renting for less than four nights. The only hotel is the luxury *Odisej* (☎ 744 022) in Pomena, with rooms at 317KN per person in July and August for half-board, and 50% less in the off season.

Getting There & Away

A regular ferry (26KN, daily except Sunday) leaves from Dubrovnik at 2 pm and goes to Sobra. The return ferry leaves from Sobra at 5.30 am, which means a very early morning departure by local bus from the national park. There are additional ferries in both directions in July and August. The big Jadrolinija coastal ferries also stop at Mljet twice a week in summer and once a week during the rest of the year.

CROATIA

DUBROVNIK

☎ 020 • pop 49,700

Founded 1300 years ago by refugees from Epidaurus in Greece, medieval Dubrovnik (Ragusa until 1918) was the most important independent city-state on the Adriatic after Venice. Until the Napoleonic invasion of 1806, it remained an independent republic of merchants and sailors.

Like Venice, Dubrovnik's fortunes now depend upon its tourist industry. Stari Grad, the perfectly preserved old town, is unique because of its marble-paved squares, steep cobbled streets, tall houses, convents, churches, palaces, fountains and museums, all cut from the same light-coloured stone. The intact city walls keep motorists at bay and the southerly position between Split and Albania has an agreeable climate and lush vegetation.

For those who watched the shelling of Dubrovnik on TV in late 1991, here's a bit of good news: the city is still there, as beautiful as ever, with few visible reminders of its trauma. The eight-month siege by the federal army from October 1991 to May 1992 tore through the town's distinctive honey-coloured clay roofs, however. Replacing them with matching tiles was extremely problematic and you'll notice a patchwork of colours as you walk around the city walls. The most severe blow to Dubrovnik was the catastrophic decline in tourism, which left its residents feeling abandoned and apprehensive. The city has made a striking comeback and in July and August the streets are again crowded with visitors. Whatever the time of year the magical interlay of light and stone is as enchanting as ever. Don't miss it.

Orientation

The Jadrolinija ferry terminal and the bus station are a few hundred metres apart at Gruž, several kilometres north-west of the old town. Most accommodation is on the leafy Lapad Peninsula, west of the bus station.

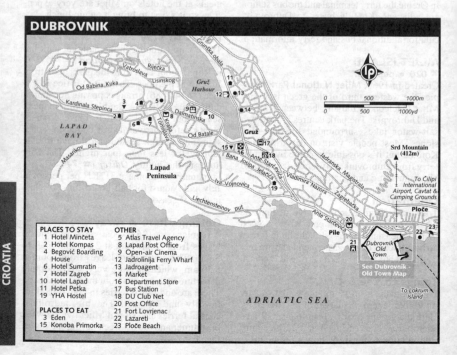

DUBROVNIK

PLACES TO STAY
1 Hotel Minčeta
2 Hotel Kompas
4 Begović Boarding House
6 Hotel Sumratin
7 Hotel Zagreb
10 Hotel Lapad
11 Hotel Petka
19 YHA Hostel

PLACES TO EAT
3 Eden
15 Konoba Primorka

OTHER
5 Atlas Travel Agency
8 Lapad Post Office
9 Open-air Cinema
12 Jadrolinija Ferry Wharf
13 Jadroagent
14 Market
16 Department Store
17 Bus Station
18 DU Club Net
20 Post Office
21 Fort Lovrjenac
22 Lazareti
23 Ploče Beach

CROATIA

Information

Tourist Offices The tourist office (☎ 426 354, fax 426 355, ✉ tzgd@du.tel.hr) is on Placa, opposite the Franciscan monastery in the old town. Look for the information booklet *Dubrovnik Riviera Guide* with tons of useful information. The American Express representative is the Atlas travel agency (☎ 442 222, 411 100) on Brsalje 17, outside Pile gate next to the old town, which holds mail. There's also an Atlas office in the harbour at Gruž (☎ 418 001), one in town at Lučarica 1 (☎ 442 528) and another in Lapad at Ćira Carića 3 (☎ 442 500).

Money You can change money at any travel agency or, if you arrive by bus, at the post office in the department store near the bus station. There are ATMs just south-east of the bus station at Dubrovačka Banka, Put Republike 9, for Visa and Plus, and at Zagrabačka Banka, Put Republike 5, for other cards. The same two banks also have ATMs on Gruž harbour near the Jadrolinija dock. There's also an ATM in the old town next to the Atlas office at Lučarica 1.

Post & Communications The main post office is at Ante Starčevića 2, a block from Pile Gate (open 8 am to 3 pm Monday to Friday), which is where you post international packages. There's also one in town on the corner of Široka and Od Puča that's open 8 am to 8 pm Monday to Friday and until 3 pm Saturday, as well as one in Lapad on the way to the Hotel Kompas. There's Internet access at DU Club Net (☎ 356 894), Put Republike 7, open 8 am to midnight daily.

Bookshops Algoritam on Placa has a good selection of English-language books and guidebooks.

Left Luggage Left-luggage at the bus station is open from 5 am to 10 pm. The bus service into town is fairly frequent.

Things to See & Do

You'll probably begin your visit at the city bus stop outside **Pile Gate**. As you enter the city, Placa or Stradun, Dubrovnik's wonderful pedestrian promenade, extends before you all the way to the clock tower at the other end of town. Just inside Pile Gate is the huge **Onofrio Fountain** (1438) and the **Franciscan monastery**, with the third-oldest functioning pharmacy (since 1391) in Europe by the cloister.

In front of the clock tower at the eastern end of Placa, you'll find the **Orlando Column** (1419) – a favourite meeting place. On opposite sides of Orlando are the 16th-century **Sponza Palace** (now the State Archives) and **St Blaise's Church**, a lovely Italian baroque building.

At the end of the broad street beside St Blaise, Pred Dvorom, is the baroque **cathedral** and, between the two churches, the Gothic **Rector's Palace** (1441), now a museum with furnished rooms, baroque paintings and historical exhibits. The elected rector was not permitted to leave the building during his one-month term without the permission of the senate. The narrow street opposite this palace opens onto Gundulićeva Poljana, a bustling morning market. Up the stairway at the southern end of the square is the imposing **Jesuit monastery** (1725).

Return to the cathedral and take the narrow street in front to the **aquarium** in Fort St John. Through an obscure entrance off the city walls, above the aquarium, is the **Maritime Museum**. If you're 'museumed out' you can safely give these two a miss.

By this time you'll be ready for a leisurely walk around the **city walls**. Built between the 13th and 16th centuries and still intact, these powerful walls are the finest in the world and Dubrovnik's main claim to fame. They enclose the entire city in a curtain of stone over 2km long and up to 25m high, with two round towers, 14 square towers, two corner fortifications and a large fortress. The views over the town and sea are great – this walk could be the high point of your visit (open from 10 am to 6.30 pm daily, admission 10KN).

Whichever way you go, you'll notice the large **Dominican monastery** in the northeastern corner of the city. Of all Dubrovnik's religious museums, the one in the Dominican monastery is the largest and most worth paying to enter.

Dubrovnik has many other sights, such as the unmarked **synagogue** at ul Žudioska 5, near the clock tower, which is the second

CROATIA

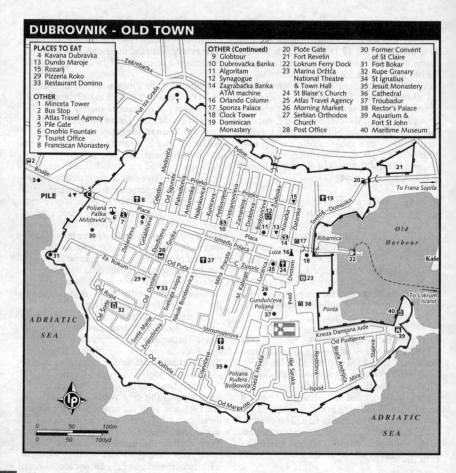

DUBROVNIK - OLD TOWN

PLACES TO EAT
4 Kavana Dubravka
13 Dundo Maroje
15 Rozarij
29 Pizzeria Roko
33 Restaurant Domino

OTHER
1 Mineta Tower
2 Bus Stop
3 Atlas Travel Agency
5 Pile Gate
6 Onofrio Fountain
7 Tourist Office
8 Franciscan Monastery

OTHER (Continued)
9 Globtour
10 Dubrovačka Banka
11 Algoritam
12 Synagogue
14 Zagrabačka Banka
   ATM machine
16 Orlando Column
17 Sponza Palace
18 Clock Tower
19 Dominican
   Monastery

20 Ploče Gate
21 Fort Revelin
22 Lokrum Ferry Dock
23 Marina Držíća
   National Theatre
   & Town Hall
24 St Blaise's Church
25 Atlas Travel Agency
26 Morning Market
27 Serbian Orthodox
   Church
28 Post Office

30 Former Convent
   of St Claire
31 Fort Bokar
32 Rupe Granary
34 St Ignatius
35 Jesuit Monastery
36 Cathedral
37 Troubadur
38 Rector's Palace
39 Aquarium &
   Fort St John
40 Maritime Museum

oldest synagogue in Europe (open 10 am to noon Tuesday and Friday). The uppermost streets of the old town below the north and south walls are pleasant to wander along.

Beaches The closest beach, Ploče, to the old city is just beyond the 17th-century **Lazareti** (former quarantine station) outside Ploče Gate. There are also hotel beaches on the **Lapad Peninsula**, which you can usually use without a problem.

An even better option is to take the ferry that shuttles hourly in summer to lush **Lokrum Island**, a national park with a rocky

nudist (FKK) beach, a botanical garden and the ruins of a medieval Benedictine monastery.

A day trip can be made from Dubrovnik to the resort town of **Cavtat**, just to the south-east. Bus No 10 runs often to Cavtat from Dubrovnik's bus station and there are three daily boats in summer (30KN). Like Dubrovnik, Cavtat was founded by Greeks from Epidaurus and there are several churches, museums and historic monuments as well as beaches. Don't miss the memorial chapel to the Račič family by Ivan Meštrović.

CROATIA

Special Events
The Dubrovnik Summer Festival from mid-July to mid-August is a major cultural event with over 100 performances at different venues in the old city. The Feast of St Blaise (3 February) and carnival (February) are also celebrated.

Places to Stay
Camping *Porto* (☎ 487 078) and *Matkovica* (☎ 486 096) are the sites closest to Dubrovnik, lying about 8km south of Dubrovnik near a quiet cove. The No 10 bus to Srebeno leaves you nearly at the gate. Otherwise, there's *Laguna* (☎ 488 960) and *Tigar* (☎ 486 980) about 5km farther in Plat, also reachable on bus No 10.

Hostels The *YHA hostel* (☎ 423 241, fax 412 592), up Vinka Sagrestana from Bana Josipa Jelačića 17, has been completely refurbished. A bed in a room for four with breakfast is 88KN. Lunch and dinner can be arranged but the hostel is on one of the liveliest streets in Lapad, full of bars, cafes and pizzerias.

Private Rooms The easiest way to find a place to stay is to accept the offer of a sobe from one of the women who may approach you at the ferry terminal. Their prices are lower than those charged by the room-finding agencies and, unless you arrive in July or August, they are open to bargaining.

Officially, there are no single rooms but in the off season you may be able to knock 20% off the price of a double room, which runs from 124KN for one-star rooms to 220KN for rooms with private facilities. Breakfast is an additional 26KN. Agencies that handle private accommodation include Atlas, Gulliver (☎ 419 109, fax 419 119) next to Jadroagent, and Globtour (☎ 428 144, fax 426 322) on Placa. The tourist office on Placa, opposite the Franciscan monastery, is another place to try.

Hotels Most hotels are in Lapad. The *Begović Boarding House* (☎ 435 191, Primorska 17), a couple of blocks west from Lapad post office (take bus No 6), has three rooms with shared bath at 75KN per person and three small apartments for 90KN per person. There's a nice terrace out the back with a good view.

Hotel Sumratin (☎ 436 333, fax 436 006) and *Hotel Zagreb* (☎ 436 146, fax 436 006) are near each other in a tranquil part of Lapad but Hotel Zagreb has more of a traditional European flavour. Prices are 248/400KN a single/double including breakfast at Hotel Sumratin and 272/440KN at Hotel Zagreb. *Hotel Minčeta* (☎ 447 100, fax 435 622) is far from town on the end of the Lapad Peninsula and offers slightly more expensive rates in summer. However, off-season rooms are as cheap as 100/200KN.

The renovated *Hotel Petka* (☎ 418 008, fax 418 058, Obala Stjepana Radića 38), opposite the Jadrolinija ferry landing, has 104 rooms at 260/440KN with breakfast. *Hotel Lapad* (☎ 413 576, fax 424 782, Lapadska Obala 37) is a better bet with 200 rooms, many equipped with air-conditioning and satellite TV. The hotel is a solid old limestone structure with simple but cheerful rooms and an outdoor swimming pool.

Places to Eat
You can get a decent meal at one of the touristy seafood or pasta places along ul Prijeko, a narrow street parallel to Placa, but you may prefer the quieter atmosphere at *Pizzeria Roko* on Za Rokum, which serves good pizzas starting at 22KN. The spaghetti with shrimp and squid risotto at *Dundo Maroje* on Kovačka are excellent.

Konoba Primorka (Nikole Tesle 8), just west of the department store in Gruž, has a good selection of seafood and national dishes at medium prices. In summer you dine below the trees on a lamp-lit terrace. The best dining in Lapad is at *Eden* (Kardinala Stepinca 54). The leafy terrace upstairs is an agreeable spot to enjoy meat, pasta or fish dishes that cost from 50KN to 80KN.

The cheapest way to fill up in Dubrovnik is to buy the makings of a picnic at a local supermarket, such as the one in the department store near the bus station.

Entertainment
Arsenal is Dubrovnik's latest disco next to the Pile Gate but *Esperanza*, next to the bus station, is a popular old stand-by. The open-air cinema on Kumičića in Lapad allows you to watch movies by starlight. *Club Nautika* (Brsalje 3), outside the Pile Gate, is an expensive

CROATIA

restaurant but you can enjoy the two open-air terraces overlooking the sea for the price of a coffee or a drink. *Troubadur* on Gunduličeva is a local favourite for live music, which occasionally includes jazz.

Ask at the tourist office about concerts and folk dancing.

Getting There & Away

Air Daily flights to/from Zagreb are operated by Croatia Airlines. The fare is about 700KN one-way in summer but less in the off season.

Bus Daily buses from Dubrovnik include three to Rijeka (266KN, 639km), seven to Zadar (152KN, 393km), 14 to Split (83KN, 235km), eight to Zagreb (135KN to 165KN, 713km), and one to Orebić (145KN, 113km) and Korčula. Services to Bosnia-Hercegovina include Mostar (80KN, 143km, two daily) and Sarajevo (161KN, 278km, daily). There's a bus to the Montenegrin border Monday, Wednesday and Friday (20KN, 30 minutes) from which a Montenegro bus takes you to Merceg-Novi (10KN, two hours) and on to Bar (65KN, five hours). For further information ask at Globtour on Placa. In a busy

summer season and on weekends, buses out of Dubrovnik can be crowded, so book a ticket well before the scheduled departure time.

Boat In addition to the Jadrolinija coastal ferry north to Hvar, Split, Zadar and Rijeka, there's a local ferry that leaves Dubrovnik for Sobra on Mljet Island (26KN, 2½ hours) at 2 pm daily, except Sunday, throughout the year. In summer there are two ferries a day. There are several ferries a day year-round to the outlying islands of Šipanska, Sugjuraj, Lopud and Koločep. Information on domestic ferries is available from Jadrolinija (☎ 418 000), Obala S Radića 40.

For information on international connections see the Getting There & Away section at the beginning of this chapter.

Getting Around

Čilipi international airport is 24km south-east of Dubrovnik. The Atlas airport buses (20KN) leave from the main bus station one hour and 20 minutes before flight times.

Dubrovnik's buses run frequently and on time. The fare is 10KN if you buy from the driver (exact change only), but only 7KN if you buy a ticket at a kiosk.

Cyprus

Cyprus, the Mediterranean's third-largest island, is the legendary birthplace of Aphrodite. Close to Greece, Turkey, Jordan, Israel and Egypt, it is a useful stepping stone for those travelling between east and west.

Cyprus presents an infinite variety of natural and architectural delights. Two high mountain ranges tower above a fertile plain. Landscapes are dotted with ancient Greek and Roman ruins, Orthodox monasteries and crusader castles.

There's an easy-going lifestyle on the island, the crime rate is low and the sun shines a lot. All of this makes Cyprus sound like a paradise, and perhaps it would be, were it not for the Turkish invasion of 1974 and subsequent partition of the island. Despite this, its people are friendly, relaxed and hospitable.

Facts about Cyprus

HISTORY

Cyprus' position in the eastern Mediterranean has meant that since ancient times it has been an important trading post, and consequently, has a rich history fraught with battles and conquest.

Inhabited since the Neolithic period, Cyprus has been colonised by the Mycenaeans, Phoenicians, Egyptians, Assyrians and Persians. In 295 BC, Ptolemy I, one of Alexander's generals who became king of Egypt, won control of the island. His dynasty ruled Cyprus until it was annexed by Rome in 58 BC.

As part of the Roman Empire, Cyprus enjoyed relative peace and prosperity. Later it came to be torn between the warring Byzantine and Islamic empires, and from the 7th to the 11th century it changed hands at least 11 times.

Richard the Lionheart conquered the island in 1191 during the Third Crusade, but when the Cypriots rebelled, he sold the island to the Knights Templar. They in turn sold it to Guy de Lusignan, the deposed king of Jerusalem, whose French dynasty ruled Cyprus for the next three centuries. This was

AT A GLANCE

Capital	Lefkosia (formerly Nicosia)
Population	926,000
Official Language	Greek, Turkish in North Cyprus
Currency	1 Cypriot pound (CY£) = 100 cents; 1 Turkish lira (TL) = 100 kurus
Time	GMT/UTC+0200
Country Phone Code	☎ 357 (North Cyprus ☎ 90 392)

North Nicosia (Lefkoşa) p199

Lefkosia p191

a period of prosperity but also oppression of Cypriot culture and Greek Orthodoxy.

By the late 14th century the Lusignanians were in decline and the Venetians took control in 1489. They strengthened the island's fortifications, but in 1570 the Turks attacked, killing some 2000 people, and began 300 years of Ottoman rule.

In 1878 the administration of Cyprus was ceded to Britain. This was done out of fear of

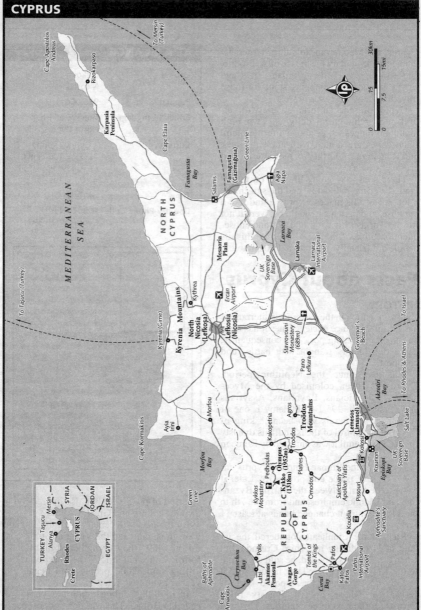

CYPRUS

To Mersin (Turkey)

Cape Apostolos Andreas

Rizokarpaso

Karpasia Peninsula

Cape Elaia

MEDITERRANEAN SEA

NORTH CYPRUS

Famagusta Bay

Famagusta (Gazimağusa)

Green Line

Salamis

Agia Napa

To Taşucu (Turkey)

Cape Kormakitis

Kythrea

Kyrenia Mountains

Kyrenia (Girne)

Ercan Airport

North Nicosia (Lefkoşa)

Lefkosia (Nicosia)

Mesaoria Plain

UK Sovereign Base

Larnaka Bay

Larnaka

Larnaka International Airport

Stavrovouni Monastery (689m)

Pano Lefkara

Governor's Beach

To Israel

Akrotiri Bay

To Rhodes & Athens

Morfou

Ayia Irini

Morfou Bay

Green Line

Agros

Kakopetria

Troödos Mountains

Olympus (1952m)

Troödos

Platres

Pedhoulas

Kykko (1318m)

Kykkos Monastery

Omodos

Lemesos (Limassol)

Kolossi

Kourion

UK Sovereign Base

Episkopi Bay

Salt Lake

R E P U B L I C   O F   C Y P R U S

Sanctuary of Apollon Ylatis

Pissouri

Koukila

Aphrodite's Sanctuary

Chrysochou Bay

Polis

Latsi

Akamas Peninsula

Avagas Gorge

Baths of Aphrodite

Cape Arnaouti

Tombs of the Kings

Pafos

Kato Pafos

Pafos International Airport

Coral Bay

TURKEY

Taşucu

Mersin

Alanya

SYRIA

JORDAN

ISRAEL

CYPRUS

Rhodes

Crete

EGYPT

30km

15mi

0   15

0   7.5

Russia's expansionist policy, with Britain promising in return to aid Turkey in the event of a Russian attack.

In 1925 Cyprus became a UK crown colony. By now, Cypriots were deeply frustrated by their lack of self-determination, and the first stirring of the *enosis* movement (which wanted union with Greece) were felt. This led to intercommunal riots between Greeks and Turks. The latter (18% of the population) opposed enosis, believing that it would lead to even greater oppression. By the late 1940s, the Cypriot Orthodox Church openly supported enosis, and a 1951 plebiscite showed that 96% of Greek Cypriots were also in favour.

In 1954 Britain prepared a new constitution for Cyprus which was accepted by the Turkish population, but not the extremist National Organisation of Cypriot Freedom Fighters (EOKA) which wanted enosis and began guerilla activities against the British administration, causing much suffering and many deaths.

In August 1960 the UK granted independence to Cyprus. Archbishop Makarios became president, with a Turk, Fasal Kükük, as vice president. In December 1963 Makarios proposed constitutional amendments which would have given the Greeks greater control. The Turkish government rejected these and threatened military intervention, but was restrained by international pressure. Intercommunal violence increased significantly and in 1964 the United Nations sent in a peace-keeping force.

In 1967 a military junta seized power in Greece and the demands for enosis ceased – nobody wanted union with such a repressive regime. However, on 15 July 1974, Greece overthrew Makarios in a coup d'etat. When he escaped assassination and fled the country, Greece put ex-guerilla leader Nicos Samson in power. The Turks responded by invading Cyprus, and the Greek junta realised the magnitude of the mistake. Samson was removed and the Greek offensive collapsed. The Turkish troops continued to advance until they occupied the northern third of the island, forcing some 180,000 Greek Cypriots to flee their homes for the safety of southern Cyprus. Neither the UK nor the USA intervened.

Cyprus remains a divided island. From time to time violence between the two sides erupts, like that which occurred in August 1996. Unsuccessful peace talks, mostly under the auspices of the UN, have been held sporadically. During recent years Richard Holbrooke, the US diplomat who had done much to end the war in Bosnia, has attempted to effect a reconciliation, but as yet to no avail.

There is some hope of reunification because both sides want to join the EU. Despite pressure from major world powers, talks are still in progress and the tension looks set to continue.

GEOGRAPHY

There are two mountain ranges: the Kyrenia Mountains in Northern Cyprus and the Troödos Massif in the centre of the Republic in the south. Between them is the Mesaoria Plain.

CLIMATE

Cyprus enjoys an intense Mediterranean climate with a typically strongly marked seasonal rhythm. Summers are hot and dry and last from June until September. Winters are changeable, with cold and warmer weather alternating and conditions also vary with the elevation.

ECOLOGY & ENVIRONMENT

Much of southern Cyprus' coastline has been spoilt by tourism, so most of the island's impressive range of flora and fauna is restricted to the well-managed areas of the Troödos Mountains and the Akamas Peninsula.

In the North, where authorities have not yet experienced the advantages and disadvantages of mass tourism, they have had the chance to monitor encroachment more carefully. In some large areas – notably the Karpas Peninsula – large scale development is now banned.

GOVERNMENT & POLITICS

In 1960 Cyprus was declared an independent sovereign republic with a presidential system of government. It is currently ruled by the Democratic Rally Party (DISY) led by Glafkos Clerides.

CYPRUS

In November 1983, Rauf Denktash declared northern Cyprus the independent Turkish Republic of Northern Cyprus, with himself as president. Only Turkey recognises this self-styled nation. Denktash leads a coalition of the National Unity Party and the Communal Liberation Party.

ECONOMY
Partition had a devastating effect on the Cypriot economy. The Republic (southern Cyprus), with its own currency, has made a steady recovery and tourism is now its biggest source of income.

The north uses the Turkish lira, tying the area's economy to Turkey's high inflation; agriculture and a developing tourist industry provide most of the income.

POPULATION & PEOPLE
Since partition, the vast majority of Greek Cypriots live in the Republic, while Turkish Cypriots and colonists live in the north. The total population of Cyprus' is 926,000 with 185,000 living in the north.

ARTS
Reminders of Cyprus' history include ancient Greek temples, Roman mosaics and 15th-century church frescoes. Building on a rich and varied tradition, the visual arts are very much alive today.

Many villages specialise in one or another, whether it be pottery, silver and copperware, basket-weaving, tapestry work, or the famous lace from Lefkara.

SOCIETY & CONDUCT
Since the island's split, Greek Cypriots have become more culturally defined. An example of this is the Republic's decision to change some of its place names, making them more Cypriot than English. In the north, the Turks have succeeded in imbuing the region with an all-pervasive Turkishness. They have changed the Greek place names to Turkish ones and embraced the culture of Turkey.

On both sides of the Green Line, the people are friendly, honest and law-abiding (there is hardly any crime or vandalism anywhere). Family life, marriage and children still play a central role in society, as does religion. Greek and Turkish Cypriots are fiercely patriotic.

RELIGION
Most Greek Cypriots belong to the Greek Orthodox Church and most Turkish Cypriots are Sunni Muslims.

LANGUAGE
Most Cypriots in the Republic speak English and many road signs are in Greek and English. In Northern Cyprus this is not the case outside the touristy areas and you'll have to brush up on your Turkish.

Since mid-1995 the Republic has converted all place names into Latin characters according to the official system of Greek transliteration. As a result, Nicosia has become Lefkosia, and Limassol is now Lemesos. Throughout this chapter the new names are given since the old ones are being phased out on all tourist maps and road signs.

See the Turkish and Greek language guides at the back of the book for pronunciation guidelines and useful words and phrases.

Facts for the Visitor

HIGHLIGHTS
Republic of Cyprus
Nine of the frescoed Byzantine churches in the Troödos Massif are on Unesco's World Heritage List and they really are special. The Tombs of the Kings, dating back to the 3rd century BC, are a lot more fun than the famous Pafos Mosaics, and only half as crowded.

Northern Cyprus
With the castle at one end, Kyrenia's waterfront must be one of the most beautiful in the Mediterranean. Some people are a bit disappointed by the archaeological site at Salamis, but the number of well-preserved upright columns in the gymnasium is incredible.

SUGGESTED ITINERARIES
Republic of Cyprus
Depending on the length of your stay, you might want to see and do the following things:

One week
Allow two days for Lefkosia, two days for Pafos, one day for exploring the ancient coastal sites between Pafos and Lemesos, and the rest in the Troödos Massif.

Two weeks
   As above but make two trips into Northern
   Cyprus, add Polis and the Akamas Peninsula
   (beaches and walks) and have a steam and/or
   massage at the hammam in Lemesos.

Northern Cyprus
One week
   Allow one day for North Nicosia (Lefkoşa), one
   day for Famagusta, half a day for Salamis, and
   spend the rest staying in Kyrenia and visiting
   the castles in the Kyrenia Mountains.
Two weeks
   As above but have a Turkish bath in North
   Nicosia and spend some time exploring the
   near-deserted Karpasia Peninsula and its archaeological sites.

PLANNING
When to Go
Cyprus has a typical Mediterranean climate.
April/May and September/October are the
most pleasant times to visit.

Maps
Most of the tourist offices have free tourist
maps that are adequate for most purposes.

TOURIST OFFICES
Local Tourist Offices
The Cyprus Tourism Organisation (CTO) has
offices in major towns in the Republic. Its
leaflets and maps are excellent.
   In Northern Cyprus there are tourist offices in North Nicosia (Lefkoşa), Famagusta
(Gazimağusa) and Kyrenia (Girne), which
have free country and town maps plus many
comprehensive brochures.

Tourist Offices Abroad
The CTO has branches in most European
countries, the USA, Russia, Israel and Japan.
   Northern Cyprus tourist offices can be
found in the UK, Belgium, the USA, Pakistan
and Turkey; otherwise inquiries are handled
by Turkish tourist offices.

VISAS & DOCUMENTS
In both the Republic and Northern Cyprus,
nationals of the USA, Australia, Canada,
Japan, New Zealand, Singapore and EU
countries can enter and stay for up to three
months without a visa.

If you have a Northern Cyprus stamp in
your passport you can still visit the Republic
(and Greece), but it will be deleted by
customs on entry. Despite this, it is advisable
to get immigration to stamp a separate piece
of paper instead of your passport when entering Northern Cyprus.

EMBASSIES & CONSULATES
Cypriot Embassies & Consulates
The Republic of Cyprus has diplomatic representation in 27 countries, including:

Australia (☎ 02-6281 0832) 30 Beale Crescent,
   Deakin, ACT 2600
Germany (☎ 228-367 980) Kronprinzenstrasse
   58, D-53173 Bonn
Greece (☎ 1-723 2727) Irodotou 16, 10675,
   Athens
Israel (☎ 3-525 0212) 50 Dizengoff St, 14th
   floor, Top Tower, Dizengodd Centre, 64322 Tel
   Aviv
UK & Ireland (☎ 020-7499 8272) 93 Park St,
   London W1Y 4ET
USA (☎ 202-462 5772) 2211 R St North West,
   Washington, DC, 20008

The Northern Cyprus Administration has
offices in:

Canada (☎ 905-731 4000) 328 Highway 7 East,
   Suite 308, Richmond Hill, Ontario L4B 3P7
Germany (☎ 02683 32748) Auf Dem Platz 3,
   53577 Neustadt Wied-Neschen
Japan (☎ 03-203 1313) 4th Floor, 6th Arai Blog-
   1-4, Kabohi-Cho, Shinytku-Ku, Tokyo 160
Turkey (☎ 312-437 6031) Rabat Sokak No 20,
   Gaziosmanpasa 06700, Ankara
UK (☎ 020-7631 1920) 29 Bedford Sq, London
   WC1B 3EG
USA (☎ 212-687 2350) 821 United Nations
   Plaza, 6th floor, New York, NY 10017

Embassies & Consulates in Cyprus
Countries with diplomatic representation in
the Republic of Cyprus include:

Australia (☎ 02-473001) Gonia Leoforos Stass-
   inou 4 & Annis Komninis, 2nd floor, 1060
   Lefkosia
Canada (☎ 02-451630) Office 403, Themistokli
   Dervi 15, Lefkosia
Germany (☎ 02-664362) Nikitara 10, 1080
   Lefkosia
Greece (☎ 02-441880) Leoforos Vyronos 8-10,
   PO Box 21799, 1513 Lefkosia

CYPRUS

Israel (☎ 02-445195) I Grypari 4, PO Box 21049, 1500 Lefkosia
UK (☎ 02-771131) Alexandrou Palli, PO Box 21978, 1587 Lefkosia
USA (☎ 02-776400) Gonia Metochiou & Ploutarchou, 2406 Egkomi, Lefkosia

Countries with diplomatic representation in Northern Cyprus include:

Australia (☎ 227 1115) Saray Hotel, Attatürk Square, North Nicosia
Turkey (☎ 222 72314, fax 222 82209) Bedreddin Demirel Caddesi, North Nicosia, KKTC, Mersin 10, Turkey
UK (☎ 228 7051) Mehmet Akif Sokak 29, North Nicosia
USA (☎ 227 2443) Güner Türkmen Caddesi 20, North Nicosia

CUSTOMS

Items which can be imported duty-free into the Republic are 250g of tobacco or the equivalent in cigarettes, 2L of wine or 1L of spirits, and one bottle of perfume not exceeding 600ml. In Northern Cyprus it is 500g of tobacco or 400 cigarettes, and 1L or spirits or 1L of wine.

MONEY
Currency

The Republic's unit of currency is the Cyprus pound (CY£), divided into 100 cents. There is no limit on the amount of Cyprus pounds you can bring into the country, but foreign currency equivalent to US$1000 or above must be declared. You can leave Cyprus with either CY£500 or the amount with which you entered. The unit of currency in Northern Cyprus is the Turkish lira (TL), and there are no restrictions.

Banks throughout Cyprus will exchange all major currencies in either cash or travellers cheques. Most shops, hotels etc in Northern Cyprus accept CY£ and other hard currencies.

In the Republic you can get a cash advance on Visa, MasterCard, Diners Club, Eurocard and American Express at one or more banks, and there are plenty of ATMs. In Northern Cyprus cash advances are given on Visa cards at the Vakıflar and Kooperatif banks in North Nicosia and Kyrenia; major banks in large towns have ATMs.

Exchange Rates

country	unit		pound
Australia	A$1	=	CY£0.37
Canada	C$1	=	CY£0.43
euro	€1	=	CY£0.58
France	1FF	=	CY£0.09
Germany	DM1	=	CY£0.29
Japan	¥100	=	CY£0.60
New Zealand	NZ$1	=	CY£0.29
UK	£1	=	CY£0.96
USA	US$1	=	CY£0.64

Exchange rates for the Turkish lira have not been given because of the high inflation rate (estimated at 106% in 2000). All prices quoted in the Northern Cyprus section are in UK pounds.

Costs

Cyprus is a cheaper place to visit than most European countries, and in Northern Cyprus costs are slightly lower still. Living frugally, you could just get by on CY£14 a day, or live quite adequately on CY£30. Accommodation costs tend to go up between April and November, peaking during July and August.

If not free, admission costs to all museums and sites are between CY£0.50 to CY£2, and so are not detailed in the text.

Tipping & Bargaining

In both parts of the island a 10% service charge is sometimes added to a restaurant bill, but if not, then a tip of similar percentage is expected. Taxi drivers and hotel porters always appreciate a small tip. It is not normal to bargain for goods in markets.

POST & COMMUNICATIONS
Post

In the Republic, postal rates for cards and letters are between 25 and 41 cents. There are poste restante services in Lefkosia, Larnaka, Pafos and Lemesos.

In Northern Cyprus, rates are between UK£0.39 and UK£0.45. There are poste restante services in North Nicosia, Kyrenia and Famagusta. All mail must be addressed to Mersin 10, Turkey, *not* Northern Cyprus.

Telephone & Fax

In the Republic, you can make overseas calls from all telephone boxes but they only take phonecards available from newsagents, some banks or the Republic's telephone company (CYTA). At peak times, a three minute call to the USA will cost CY£1.83, and CY£1.53 during off-peak (10 pm to 8 am, and Sunday). The Republic's country code is ☎ 357.

In Northern Cyprus most public telephone boxes only take phonecards bought at a Turkish Telecom administration office or shops. A peak three minute call to the USA will set you back UK£1.35 and off-peak UK£0.90. To call Northern Cyprus from abroad dial ☎ 90 (Turkey), the country code ☎ 392, and then the area code and the number. Area codes also must be used when calling locally (codes have been incorporated into all phone numbers in the Northern Cyprus section).

In both regions most people now use mobile phones, but if you have an international one it won't work in Northern Cyprus.

In the south you can send faxes from the post office, in the north from the Turkish Telecom administration offices, or from shops in both regions.

Email & Internet Access
There are Internet cafes in all main towns in southern Cyprus and several in the north. The majority open late, close in the early hours of the morning and have become real social centres. They all charge in the region of CY£2.50 for the first hour and CY£1 for subsequent hours. Despite this, practically no tourist facilities (accommodation, restaurants etc) have email addresses.

INTERNET RESOURCES
The Internet has lots of interesting information on Cyprus, and the most comprehensive site on Northern Cyprus is at www.cypnet .com/cyradise/cyradise.html

BOOKS
Lonely Planet's *Cyprus* by Paul Hellander provides a full and comprehensive guide to the whole island. *Bitter Lemons* by Lawrence Durrell is an interesting read.

NEWSPAPERS & MAGAZINES
The Republic's English-language papers are the *Cyprus Mail* and the *Cyprus Weekly*. The Northern Cyprus publications are the *Turkish Daily News* and *Cyprus Today*.

RADIO & TV
CyBC (Cyprus Broadcasting Corporation) has programs and news bulletins in English on Radio 2 (FM 91 to 1MHz) at 10 am, 2 and 8 pm. BFBS (British Forces Broadcasting Services) broadcasts 24 hours a day in English, and the BBC World Service is easily picked up.

CyBC TV has news in English at 8 pm on Channel 2. Satellite dishes are very common, so many hotels have CNN, BBC, SKY or NBC.

TIME
Cyprus is two hours ahead of GMT/UTC. Clocks go forward one hour on the last weekend in March and back one hour on the last weekend in October.

LAUNDRY
There are plenty of dry-cleaners and laundrettes can be found in all main towns, but they are not common. Most hotels have a laundry service.

TOILETS
There are public toilets in the main towns and at tourist sites. They are invariably clean and Western-style, although in Northern Cyprus you occasionally come across dirtier ones or those of the squat variety.

WOMEN TRAVELLERS
Women travelling alone will receive a lot of attention, especially when exploring the less touristy areas. A firm 'no thankyou' should be enough to deter any unwanted interest.

GAY & LESBIAN TRAVELLERS
Homosexuality is legal in the Republic but still illegal in Northern Cyprus.

DISABLED TRAVELLERS
Any CTO can send you the *What the Disabled Visitor Needs to Know about Cyprus* factsheet, which lists some useful organisations. The Republic's airports have truck-lifts for arriving or departing disabled travellers. Some of the hotels have facilities for the disabled, but there's little help at sites or museums.

In Northern Cyprus there are few facilities for the disabled visitor.

CYPRUS

SENIOR TRAVELLERS
Cyprus is a popular holiday destination with older visitors and they will find travelling around both the Republic and Northern Cyprus fairly easy. In general, no concessions exist for seniors.

BUSINESS HOURS
Opening hours vary according to whether it is winter, spring or summer.

During summer, banks in the Republic are open 8.15 am to 12.30 pm Monday to Friday, and 3.15 to 4.45 pm on Monday; some large banks offer a tourist service on other afternoons. In Northern Cyprus banks are open 8 am to noon and in winter from 2 to 4 pm also.

In summer, shops are open 8 am to 1 pm and 4 to 7.30 pm Monday to Saturday, closing at 2 pm on Wednesday and Saturday. In Northern Cyprus they are open 4 to 7 pm every afternoon Monday to Saturday.

PUBLIC HOLIDAYS & SPECIAL EVENTS
Holidays in the Republic are the same as in Greece, with the addition of Greek Cypriot Day (1 April) and Cyprus Independence Day (1 October). Easter is the most important religious festival and just about everything stops. Fifty days before this is carnival time. A useful publication is the *Diary of Events* available from any CTO.

Northern Cyprus observes Muslim holidays, including the month of Ramadan, which means the north can sometimes shut down for periods of up to a week. It also has Turkish Cypriot Resistance Day (1 August) and the Proclamation of the Turkish Republic of Northern Cyprus (15 November).

ACTIVITIES
Cyprus has a wide range of activities that cater for many different interests. The coastal resorts have beautiful beaches for those travellers wanting to relax in the summer heat, as well as water sports, such as parasailing, for the more adventurous. Travel agencies and tour operators have many day trips and cruises that cater for all ages and interests. For those with a taste for history and archaeology you are spoilt for choice. There are many sites dotted all over the island but make sure to take along a guidebook – information

is not always comprehensive and it is sometimes difficult to know what you are looking at. The inland area around the Troödos Massif is home to a vast variety of flora and fauna. Walking and hiking trails are well marked and graded for all abilities.

WORK
In the Republic, work permits can only be obtained through a prospective employer applying on your behalf. The best place to look for jobs is in the *Cyprus Weekly*. During the tourist season you can sometimes pick up bar or cafe work in return for bed and board (payment is rare if you don't have a permit).

To work in Northern Cyprus, a permit must also be obtained through a prospective employer applying on your behalf. The application is examined by the Department of Labour and granted where the qualifications sought are not locally available.

ACCOMMODATION
Camping
There are seven licensed camping grounds in the Republic, mostly with limited opening times. They are all equipped with hot showers, a minimarket and a snack bar, and charge around CY£1.50 a day for a tent space and CY£1 per person per day. In the North there are four camping grounds.

Hostels
There are four Hostelling International (HI) hostels in the Republic; these are slightly cheaper if you are a member. The Cyprus Youth Hostel Association (☎ 670027) is at PO Box 1328, 1506 Lefkosia. There are no HI hostels in Northern Cyprus.

Hotels
Hotels in the Republic are classified from one to five stars and prices for a double room range from CY£17 to CY£210. Guesthouses cost between CY£10 and CY£32. Prices are negotiable in winter. In Northern Cyprus these prices are slightly lower.

Other Accommodation
In southern Cyprus you can sometimes stay overnight in monasteries, ostensibly for free, but a donation is expected.

FOOD

Cypriot food is a combination of Greek and Turkish cuisine, based primarily on meat, salad and fruit. The local cheese is *halloumi*. The barbecue is a very popular way of cooking meat and fish, and a *meze* is a traditional meal consisting of around 20 different small dishes.

DRINKS

Cypriot wine, made in the villages of the Troödos, is excellent and Greek/Turkish coffee and instant coffee (called Nescafé) are widely available. Raki is widely available in Northern Cyprus, but ouzo is less frequently drunk.

ENTERTAINMENT

Restaurants sometimes have live music and there are cinemas, clubs and Internet cafes open until 2 am or later in most major towns and tourist areas.

SHOPPING

Good buys include local wine and spirits, most leather items and the crafts mentioned in the Arts section.

Getting There & Away

AIR

The Republic's airports are at Larnaka and Pafos. There are scheduled and charter flights from most European cities and the Middle East (around UK£230 return from London, including tax), with discounts for students, but they are heavily booked in the high season. From Cyprus there are daily flights to Greece (CY£87), and frequent services to Israel (CY£79), Egypt (CY£87), Jordan (CY£70), Lebanon (CY£68) and Syria (CY£58) – prices include taxes.

Ercan airport in Northern Cyprus is not recognised by the international airline authorities, so you can't fly there direct. Turkish airlines touch down in Turkey and then continue on to Northern Cyprus (around UK£315 from London, including tax) and other airlines can fly you to Turkey, where you change planes.

SEA

The Republic's passenger ferry port is in Lemesos. In summer there are regular boats to Greece (CY£49) and Israel (CY£44) – prices include taxes but are deck-only. Student reductions are available. In summer there is sometimes a ferry that goes to Rhodes, Crete and Piraeus (Greece). See the Lemesos section for cruise details.

From Northern Cyprus there are two routes to mainland Turkey: Famagusta to Mersin (UK£10) and Kyrenia to Taşucu (from UK£15).

DEPARTURE TAX

In the Republic, departure tax is CY£7 when leaving by air and CY£11 when leaving by sea. In Northern Cyprus it is UK£6 for air departures and UK£6 by sea. At the time of purchase make sure that the taxes are included in your ticket price.

Getting Around

You can make a day trip into Northern Cyprus from the Republic (see the Lefkosia section). It is impossible to travel in the opposite direction.

BUS

Urban and long-distance buses run Monday to Saturday and are operated by a host of private companies. There are few services on Sunday. Buses between major towns are frequent and efficient, charging around CY£1.50 for most journeys.

SERVICE TAXI

Service taxis, which take up to eight people, are run by a central company called Travel Express. Their head office can be contacted on ☎ 077 7474. Each region has its own contact number (see the relevant text). The fixed fares are still competitive with bus travel. For details of departure and arrivals call the relevant number for your area. Northern Cyprus has service taxis between Kyrenia, Famagusta and North Nicosia. There are also normal (more expensive) taxis everywhere.

CAR & MOTORCYCLE

Cars and 4WD vehicles are widely available for hire and cost between CY£12 and CY£50 a day. You can also rent motorbikes (from CY£12) or mopeds (CY£8) in some towns. Driving is on the left and international road signs are used.

In the Republic, children under five must not sit in the front seat and you are advised against travelling due west in the late afternoon because of the sun's glare. The blood alcohol limit is 0.09%. Any car or motorcycle license is valid in the Republic, but you must be over 21 years of age to drive a car. If you're over 18 you can ride a motorcycle of 50cc and above, and 17-year-olds can ride a motorcycle of less than 49cc. In Northern Cyprus you can drive from the age of 18. Officially, you need either a British or an international driving license. Both of these laws also apply to motorcycles.

Parking is cheap. Super and low-lead petrol cost 38 cents for 1L, regular costs 35 cents and diesel just 13 cents.

The Cyprus Automobile Association (☎ 313131) is at Chr Mylona 12, Lefkosia.

BICYCLE
Bicycles can be hired in most areas but particularly in the Troödos. Rates start from around CY£4 to CY£5 a day.

The Republic of Cyprus

In the Republic, which comprises 63% of the island, you'll find a real mix of Greek, eastern and western cultures. The British legacy lives on in the island's two UK military bases – at Akrotiri near Lemesos, and Dhekelia near Larnaka.

LEFKOSIA
☎ 02

Lefkosia (formerly Nicosia and known as Lefkoşa in Turkish), is the capital, bisected by the Green Line separating the Republic from Northern Cyprus. According to the sign at the UN-patrolled barrier at Lidras St, this is 'the last divided capital', and a visit is essential to appreciate the island's plight. Being inland, it attracts far fewer visitors, and so is much more genuinely Cypriot than the coastal towns.

Orientation
The old town is inside the 16th-century Venetian wall and is the most interesting area for visitors; the new town sprawls around it. Reduced in height and dissected by wide thoroughfares, the wall is hardly visible in places. The city centre is Plateia Eleftherias on the south-western edge of the wall. The UN crossover point (Ledra Palace Hotel checkpoint) is at the far west and Famagusta Gate is to the east. At the base of the wall there are car parks and municipal gardens.

Information
Tourist Offices The CTO (☎ 674264) in the old town is in Laïki Yitonia, a fairly touristy, restored area. It is open 8.30 am to 4 pm Monday to Friday and 8.30 am to 2 pm Saturday. The CTO head office (☎ 337715, fax 331644, ⊜ cytourcto.org.cy) is in the new town at Leoforos Lemesou 19.

Money The Hellenic Bank, Leoforos Konstantinou Paleologou 5, near the CTO, is open 8.15 am to 12.30 pm Monday to Friday.

Post & Communications The main post office is on Leoforos Konstantinou Paleologou. Opening hours are 7.30 am to 1.30 pm and 3 to 6 pm (closed Wednesday afternoon), and 8.30 to 10.30 am on Saturday. The telecommunications office (CYTA) is on Leoforos Egyptou and opens from 7.30 am to 1.30 pm daily, but from 3 to 5.30 pm on Tuesday.

Email & Internet Access In the old town, Nicosia Palace Arcade (⊜ n.palace@cytanet .com.cy) on Leoforos Kostaki Pantelidi is open daily. In the new town there is Web.net Cafe (⊜ webnet1@dial.cylink.com.cy), Stasandrou 10C, open from 10.30 am (to around 2 am) Monday to Saturday, and from 5.30 pm on Sunday.

Laundry Express Dry-Cleaners at Ippokratous 49, in the old town, will do a service wash for you.

Medical & Emergency Services The police station (☎ 671434) in the old town is at the top of Lidras, by the barrier. The emergency number for the police is ☎ 199.

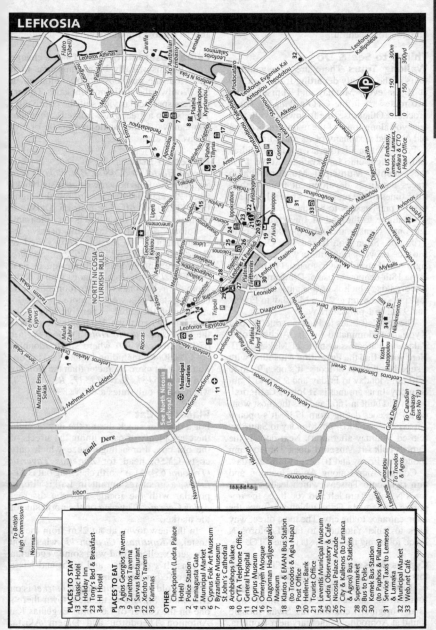

LEFKOSIA

PLACES TO STAY
13 Classic Hotel
14 Holiday Inn
23 Tony's Bed & Breakfast
34 HI Hostel

PLACES TO EAT
3   Agios Georgios Taverna
9   Zanettos Taverna
15 Savvas Restaurant
22 Xefoto's Tavern
35 Kantinas

OTHER
1   Checkpoint (Ledra Palace Hotel)
2   Police Station
4   Famagusta Gate
5   Municipal Market
6   Cyprus Folk Art Museum
7   Byzantine Museum; St John's Cathedral
8   Archbishops Palace
10 CYTA Telephone Office
11 General Hospital
12 Cyprus Museum
16 Omeriyeh Mosque
17 Dragoman Hadjigeorgakis
18 Klarios & EMAN Bus Station (to Troodos & Agia Napa)
19 Post Office
20 Hellenic Bank
21 Tourist Office
24 Leventis Municipal Museum
25 Ledra Observatory & Cafe
26 Nicosia Palace Arcade
27 City & Kallenos (to Larnaca & Agros) Bus Stations
28 Supermarket
29 Bus to Polis
30 Kemek Bus Station (to Paphos & Platres)
31 Service Taxis to Lemesos & Larnaka
32 Municipal Market
33 Web.net Café

Lefkosia's general hospital (☎ 801400) is on Leoforos Nechrou.

Things to See & Do

Walking Tours There are free walking tours of the old city departing from the CTO at 10 am every Monday and Thursday; the two routes are in the CTO's *Walking Tours* brochure. Otherwise, the following walk will take you along some of the main streets of the old city and past many of its museums.

From Plateia Eleftherias go along Lidras and turn right onto Ippokratous. At No 17 is the **Leventis Municipal Museum**, which traces the city's development from prehistoric times to the present. It's open 10.30 am to 4.30 pm Tuesday to Sunday.

Continue to the end of Ippokratous, turn left onto Thrakis and take the dogleg onto Trikoupi. Soon you'll see the Omeriyeh Mosque on your right, after which you turn right onto Patriarhou Grigoriou. On the right is the 18th-century house of **Dragoman Hadjigeorgakis**, which is now a museum. Opening times are 8 am to 2 pm Monday to Friday and 9 am to 1 pm Saturday.

The next left leads to Plateia Arhiepikopou Kyprianou, dominated by the **Archbishop's Palace** and a colossal statue of Makarios III. Here you'll find the **Byzantine Museum**, with a superb collection of icons. It's open 9 am to 4.30 pm Monday to Friday and 9 am to 1 pm Saturday. In its grounds is **St John's Cathedral**, which was built in 1662 and has the most wonderful frescoes dating from 1736. It's open 9 am to noon and 2 to 4 pm Monday to Saturday (closed Saturday afternoon). Next door is the **Cyprus Folk Art Museum**, open 9 am to 4 pm Monday to Friday and 10 am to 1 pm Saturday.

Continue north along Agiou Ioannou and turn right onto Thiseos, which leads to Leoforos N Foka. Turn left and you'll see the imposing **Famagusta Gate**, which was once the main entrance to the city. The most direct way back to Laïki Yitonia is to take Leoforos N Foka, following the signposts to the CTO.

Cyprus Museum Near the CYTA office, this museum has an extraordinary collection of 2000 7th-century BC terracotta figurines found at the sanctuary of Ayia Irini, as well as the original Leda and the Swan mosaic found at Aphrodite's sanctuary near Kouklia.

It's open 9 am to 5 pm Monday to Saturday, and 10 am to 1 pm Sunday.

Ledra Observatory If you fancy a change from the historically based museums then check out the new observatory. Situated in the Woolworths Building (Shokalas Tower) it offers spectacular views of the entire city. There's also a great glass-fronted cafe where you can watch the hustle and bustle of city life as you eat.

Places to Stay

The HI *Hostel* (☎ 674808, Hatzidaki 5) is in a quiet part of the new town about six blocks from Plateia Eleftherias. Follow the signs from Tefkrou, off Themistokli Dervi. It charges CY£4/5 a night and is very pleasant.

Solonos is good for fairly inexpensive accommodation. The best is *Tony's Bed & Breakfast* (☎ 666752, fax 662225, Solonos 13) where singles/doubles/triples/quads cost CY£14/22/34/40, slightly more with a bathroom. Tony also has cheaper rooms for self-catering stays of a week or more.

Most of the more expensive hotels are found in the new town, but inside the walls is the three-star *Classic Hotel* (☎ 664006, fax 670072, Rigenis 90) where singles/doubles are CY£30/40, including breakfast. This option has a lot more character than the *Holiday Inn* (☎ 665131, fax 673337, Rigenis 70) where room-only rates are CY£89/138.

Places to Eat

For a drink or snack during the day or night there are plenty of cafes lining the streets of the old city. For a huge meze which only costs CY£6, head for *Zanettos Taverna* (Trikoupi 65). Also worth checking out is *Xefoto's*, a great restaurant in Laïki Yitonia popular with the locals, and the discreet *Agios Georgios Taverna* on the north side of the market.

In the new town, about 2km from the HI hostel, is *Kantinas* (Chytron 11) where you can get excellent food with some vegetarian options. It's open day and night and has a lively cafe/bar atmosphere.

In the old city, the *municipal market* is on Diogenous St, and in the new town there's one on the corner of Leoforos Evgenias Kai Antoniou Theodotou and Digeni Akrita.

Gardens of the Chateau de Villandry, Loire Valley

Traversing the Alps, Chamonix, France

The Eiffel Tower, Paris' most prominent landmark

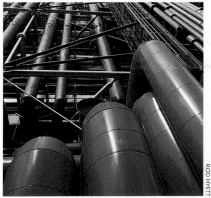

Get to know Paris inside out, Pompidou Centre

The village of Porto in Corsica, dwarfed by huge outcrops of red granite, is renowned for its sunsets.

Monet's garden, Giverny, Normandy, France

They're called bottle cages, after all; Bordeaux region

Ruins of a manor, l'Argentella, Corsica, France

There's a decent *supermarket* on Plateia Solomou.

Getting There & Away

Northern Cyprus Depending on diplomatic relations, you're usually allowed into Northern Cyprus for one day, but check at the CTO first. The border crossing at the Ledra Palace Hotel is open 8 am to 1 pm, returning at 5 pm. You simply walk to the Turkish checkpoint with your passport and request an entry permit. Private cars can be taken over the border, but not hired ones. There is no limit to the number of times you can do this.

However, the Greek Cypriot authorities will not let you across with 'luggage' that exceeds that of a small bag or rucksack. If you continue on to Turkey from Northern Cyprus you will be put on the Greek Cypriot 'black list' and you may never be able to re-enter the South again. Abandoning luggage may seem like a great way to save time and money but remember that it's unlikely that you'll ever be able to collect it!

Air Lefkosia's international airport is in the UN buffer zone and is no longer a passenger airport.

Bus There are lots of private bus companies operating out of Lefkosia.

Intercity, at Omirou 3, off Leonidou, has five buses a day to Lemesos (CY£1.50; fewer on Saturday), one to Pafos (CY£3) and one to Platres (CY£2) at 12.15 pm. Kallenos operates from Plateia Solomou and has five buses a day to Larnaka (CY£1.50). Also from Plateia Solomou is a direct bus to Polis (C£Y4) at noon.

Klarios goes to Troödos (CY£1.50) once a day at 11.30 am and much more frequently to Kakopetria (CY£1.20). EMAN goes to Agia Napa (CY£2) daily at 3 pm, departing from the Constanza car park.

Service Taxi Travel Express (☎ 771444) have service taxis operating to Larnaka (CY£2.10) and Lemesos (CY£3).

Getting Around

The city bus station is at Plateia Solomou; Lefkosia Buses operates numerous routes to and from the city and suburbs.

Also at Plateia Solomou is A Petsas & Sons (☎ 662650) where you can hire cars.

There are no bicycles for rent in or around the old city.

LARNAKA
☎ 04

Larnaka is a coastal resort built over the ancient city of Kition. It has a city beach, a new waterfront promenade, an old Turkish area and a fort. North of the fort, touristy cafes line the seafront, but the other side is less spoilt and much quieter.

The CTO (☎ 654322) is on Plateia Vasileos Pavlou, two blocks west of the Sun Hall Hotel. It's open 8.15 am to 2.30 pm and 3 to 6.30 pm Monday to Friday, but is closed on Wednesday and Saturday afternoons. There is also a CTO at the airport.

There are several Internet cafes in town. The first established was Web Café (@ webcafe@webcafe.com.cy) at Lordou Vyronos 54, a seven-minute walk south-west from the CTO.

Things to See

The site of ancient **Kition** is about 1.5km outside Larnaka. It dates back to the 13th century BC but was completely rebuilt by the Phoenicians in the 9th century BC after an earthquake. The city walls are impressive, otherwise it's not that thrilling.

En route is the **District Archaeological Museum** where artefacts found at Kition are on display. Kition and the museum are open 7am and 9 am respectively to 2.30 pm Monday to Friday. Both are signposted from the town centre.

On Agiou Lazarou, the ornate Byzantine church of **St Lazaros** and its museum are worth a visit, as is the **medieval fort**.

Places to Stay & Eat

The nearest camping ground is *Forest Beach Camping* (☎ 644514), 8km along the beach road towards Agia Napa, but it's a bit run-down. To get there take the tourist bus from the north side of the Sun Hall Hotel.

The HI *Hostel* (☎ 621188, N Rossou 27) is just east of St Lazaros church and charges CY£4/10 for a dorm/double per night; nothing to write home about. In a very quiet part of town, 500m west of the fort, is the friendly

CYPRUS

two-star *Onisillos Hotel* (☎ *651100, fax 654468, Onisillos 17)* where singles/doubles with bathroom cost C£18/25, including breakfast.

North-east from here towards the sea is an area called Laïki Geitonia, where you'll find some lively bars, and a predictable *Hard Rock Cafe*. South, beside the mosque, is *Prasino Amaxoudi* where you'll get good-value, freshly prepared souvlaki, doner kebab or halloumi pitta sandwiches.

South of the fort on the waterfront is *Militzis Restaurant* where all the locals eat. At the other end of town, near the CTO is the *1900 Art Café (Stasinou 6)*. It's an art gallery, a bookshop and also a restaurant with an ever-changing menu of home-cooked Cypriot dishes for CY£4.

The *municipal market* is at the northern end of N Rossou St.

Getting There & Away
Bus The bus stop for Lefkosia (CY£1.50), Lemesos (CY£1.70) and Agia Napa (CY£1) is almost opposite the Dolphin Cafe Restaurant on the waterfront. On Sunday there is only a service to Agia Napa.

Service Taxi Travel Express (☎ 661010) operates service taxis to Lemesos (CY£2.60) and Lefkosia (CY£2.10).

Getting Around
To/From the Airport Bus No 19 from St Lazaros church goes near the airport (6km away) on request. The first bus is at 6.20 am and the last at 7 pm in summer, 5.45 pm in winter. A private taxi costs CY£3.

Bus A Makris buses run every 30 minutes from the north side of the Sun Hall Hotel to the tourist hotel area, 8km along the coast towards Agia Napa (CY£0.80 return).

Car & Motorcycle Thames (☎ 656333), next door to A Makris, rents cars and there are also car-rental booths at the airport. You can hire motorcycles or mopeds from Anemayia (☎ 658333) on the Larnaka to Dhekelia road; ring for free delivery.

Bicycle Bicycles can be hired at Anemayia (see under Car & Motorcycle for details).

AGIA NAPA
☎ 03
On the coast 35km east of Larnaka is Agia Napa. Once a small fishing village with a coastline of beautiful beaches, it is now Cyprus' main package-tourist resort and accommodation is scarce if not booked through a tour operator. Bars, clubs and pubs line the streets and if you're after 24-hour nightlife then Agia Napa is the place to be. See the Larnaka and Lefkosia sections for transport details.

LEMESOS
☎ 05
Lemesos (Limassol) is Cyprus' second-largest city and the main passenger and cargo port. Bland apartments and public gardens line the waterfront; behind these to the west is the more attractive old town with crumbling houses, a mosque, old-fashioned artisans' shops and a castle. Behind the old section sprawls the new town.

The CTO (☎ 362756) is at Spyros Araouzou 15 on the waterfront near the old harbour. It is open 8.15 am to 2.30 pm and 3 to 6 pm Monday to Saturday, closed Wednesday and Saturday afternoons.

Currently, there are about 14 Internet cafes in Lemesos. The most successful is CyberNet (✆ cafeinfo@zenon.logos.cy.net) at Eleftherias 79, a couple of blocks behind the CTO. On weekdays it doesn't open until 1pm.

Things to See
The main attraction is the well-restored **castle** where Richard the Lionheart married Berengaria of Navarre in 1191 and which now houses the **Medieval Museum**. Close by, near the mosque, is a newly restored **hammam** where for CY£5 you can get a steam and sauna or a massage. It is open 2 to 10 pm daily and all sessions are mixed.

Lemesos has a number of other museums but of greater interest are the sites to the west. Fourteen kilometres on the road to Pafos is **Kolossi Castle**, and a further 5km away are the extensive remains of **Kourion** and the nearby **Sanctuary of Apollon Ylatis**. Probably the most visited site in Cyprus, the amphitheatre at Kourion now hosts plays and concerts in summer. For details contact the CTO.

Organised Tours

Two and three-day cruises depart from Lemesos all year. They go to Haifa (Israel), Port Said (Egypt), a selection of Greek islands, and sometimes (in summer) to Lebanon. You can book at any travel agent, but these are not designed for one-way travel.

Places to Stay & Eat

The nearest camping ground is *Governor's Beach Camping* (☎ 632300 or ☎ 632878), 20km east of town.

The cheapest hotels are clustered in the old town, to the east of the castle. A good one with large, clean rooms is the *Luxor Guest House* (☎ 362265, Agiou Andreou 101) which charges CY£5 per person, no breakfast.

Otherwise, the two-star *Continental Hotel* (☎ 362530, fax 373030, Spyrou Araouzou 137) on the waterfront, has very pleasant singles/doubles with bathroom and breakfast for CY£15/25.

A good place to lunch or snack is the unlikely *Richard & Berengaria* cafe, just by the castle. For an evening meal try *Rizitiko's Tavern*. Tucked away down a side street, the friendly atmosphere is only beaten by the delicious traditional food that it serves.

The *municipal market* is at the northern end of Saripolou.

Getting There & Away

Bus Intercity has frequent daily services to Lefkosia (CY£1.50) and Pafos (CY£1.50) from the corner of Enoseos and Eirinis, north of the castle. From here there is also a weekday bus at noon to Agros (CY£1.50) in the Troödos Mountains.

Kallenos goes to Larnaka (CY£1.70) from outside the CTO. From Monday to Saturday, the Kyriakos/Karydas service-taxi company has a minibus which goes to Platres (CY£2) at 11.30 am from its office.

Service Taxi Travel Express (☎ 364114) has service taxis operating to Lefkosia (CY£3), Larnaka (CY£2.60) and Pafos (CY£2.30).

Ferry You can buy ferry tickets from any travel agency or direct from Salamis Tours Ltd (☎ 355555) or Poseidon Lines (☎ 745666). The port is 5km south-west of

town. See the Getting There & Away section at the start of this chapter.

Getting Around

The city bus station is on A Themistokleous, close to the municipal market. Bus No 1 goes towards the port, bus No 16-17 goes to Kolossi and bus No 30 goes north-east along the seafront. Frequent buses also run from the castle to Kourion and its beach. From April to November there's a daily Governor's Beach bus which leaves from the CTO 9.50 am, returning at 4.30 pm.

Lipsos Rent-a-Car (☎ 365295) is at Richard & Berengaria 6 (opposite the castle). The Oceanic Supermarket at 232 Oktovriou 28 rents mopeds and bicycles.

TROÖDOS MASSIF

☎ 05

The mountains of the Troödos region are beautiful with their secluded Byzantine monasteries, 15th-century frescoed churches, small wine-making villages, pine forests and numerous walking trails. In summer the area offers some respite from the heat, and in winter there's enough snow to ski.

The CTO (☎ 421316) in the square at Platres is open 9 am to 3.30 pm Monday to Friday and 9 am to 2.30 pm Saturday. There's enough in this area to keep you busy for at least a week. Check at the CTO for suggested walking trails and information on the flora and fauna you may encounter.

Things to See & Do

The **Kykkos Monastery**, 20km west of Pedhoulas, is the best known but also the most touristy of the monasteries. Although it dates from the 12th century, it has been completely renovated and all the mosaics, frescoes and stonework are new. It also has a museum containing priceless religious icons and relics.

In Pedhoulas is the small, World Heritage-listed **Church of Archangelos**, with frescoes dating from 1474. The key to the church is at a nearby house (signposted). Another fine church is **St Nicholaos of the Roof**, near Kakopetria, open 9 am to 4 pm Tuesday to Saturday, and 11 am to 4 pm Sunday.

Omodos is in the wine-growing region, almost directly south of Pedhoulas, with local wine available for sale and tastings. You can also visit **Socrates' Traditional House**, a 500-year-old house with a wine cellar and period distillery. Also in Omodos is the **Stavros Monastery,** more intimate than the larger, more renowned ones.

Places to Stay & Eat

Even though there are hotels or rooms in almost all the villages, there aren't enough so in July and August you'd be wise to book. Outside these months, you can negotiate on prices.

The only reason to stay in Troödos itself, more a touristy hill station than a village, is the walks. Two kilometres north, in a pine forest, there is a *camping ground* (☎ 420124) which is open May to October. The Troödos HI *Hostel* (☎ 420200) is usually open from May to October (depending on the weather) and charges CY£5 for the first night and CY£4 thereafter. Rather more luxurious is the three-star *Troödos Hotel* (☎ 420135, fax 420160), where singles/doubles cost CY£27/38, including breakfast.

A good regional base is Platres. The cosy *Minerva Hotel* (☎ 421731, fax 421075) is situated on the top road and charges CY£16/30 for singles/doubles with bathroom and breakfast. The Swiss-style *Petit Palais* (☎ 421723, fax 421065) charges CY£20/32 for an en suite room with breakfast. These hotels, and others, are signposted.

The best restaurant in Platres is the good-value *Kalidonia*. Just outside Platres on the road to Troödos is the *Psilo Dendro* lunch restaurant and trout farm, where fresh trout costs CY£5.25.

Getting There & Away

At 7 am there is a daily service taxi from Platres to Lemesos (CY£2). At 7 am there is a daily bus from Agros to Lemesos (CY£1). At 1.30 pm there is a bus from Troödos to Kakopetria (CY£0.60) where you must change to carry on to Lefkosia. There are around 12 buses a day to Lefkosia and the journey costs CY£1.20. At 6 am there is a bus from Pedoulas to Lefkosia (CY£2) but it no longer stops at Platres.

PAFOS
☎ 06

Once the capital of Cyprus, Pafos has always been historically and mythologically important. Today it consists of Kato (lower) Pafos on the coast, where you'll find most of the places of interest, and Pafos, which is 1km inland. Kato Pafos is full of huge hotels and expensive bars and eateries which spoil the old harbour and port area. Pafos itself is much more pleasant, with an authentic life of its own.

The tourist office (☎ 232841) is at Gladstonos 3, just down from Pafos' main square. Its opening hours are the same as the Lemesos CTO, although in July and August it often closes at 3.45 pm. There's another tourist office at the airport.

The most central Internet cafe is Maroushia Fashion Café (@ maroushia@cyling.com.cy) at 6 Kennedy Square, very close to the CTO.

Things to See

There is lots to see in Pafos but most renowned are the **Pafos Mosaics**, well-preserved (if dusty) floors from the villas of 3rd-century AD Roman nobles. They mostly depict mythological themes, emphasising the exploits of Dionysos, the uninhibited God of Wine. The site is open daily, closing at 7.30 pm in summer and 5.45 pm in winter. On the way to the mosaics you pass the remains of a **Byzantine castle** and an **odeon**.

About 2km north of Kato Pafos, on the coastal road to Polis, are the **Tombs of the Kings** which date from the 3rd century BC. These underground tombs are fascinating to explore and the site opens the same hours as the Pafos Mosaics.

Places to Stay & Eat

The nearest camping ground is *Zenon Gardens* (☎ 242277), 5km south of Kato Pafos and behind the summer cinema. It is close to the beach and you camp in the shade of trees.

The HI *Hostel* (☎ 232588, Leoforos Eleftheriou Venizelou 37) is quite a way north of Pafos centre. To get there, walk up Leoforos Evagora Pallikaridi and it is off on the right. The hostel is unkempt and costs CY£5 for the first night and CY£4 thereafter.

Trianon Hotel (☎ 232193, Leoforos Arhiepikopou Makariou III 99) provides singles/doubles for CY£5/12. The rooms are bright and airy but bathroom and kitchen facilities are shared. The friendly two-star *Axiothea Hotel* (☎ 232866, fax 245790, Eves

Malioti 2) charges CY£23/31.50 for singles/ doubles with bathroom and breakfast. On the high ground to the south of the CTO, it has a glass-fronted bar and reception with wonderful views of the sea – perfect for sunset watching.

A highly recommended restaurant in Pafos is *Fettas Corner (Iannis Agrotis 33)*, not far from the Axiothea Hotel. It is where the locals eat and a large meal for two with wine will cost around CY£13. In Kato Pafos try the family-owned *Ifigenia (Agamemnonos 2)* situated opposite the Sofianna Hotel.

The *municipal market* is near the covered bazaar area, not far from the Trianon Hotel.

Getting There & Away
Bus The Amaroza bus company operates to Polis, Lemesos and Lefkosia. Their office is at Leoforos Evagora Pallikaridi 79, north of Pafos' main square; there are around 10 buses a day to Polis (CY£1) and two to Lemesos, which continue to Lefkosia at 8.30 am and 2.30 pm. Alepa Ltd (☎ 234455) also has daily buses to Lemesos (CY£2) and Lefkosia (CY£3). If you book in advance they'll pick you up from your hotel; otherwise they leave from the urban bus station, and outside the municipal market.

Service Taxi Travel Express (☎ 233181) have service taxis operating to Lemesos (CY£2.30).

Getting Around
There are no buses or service taxis to/from the airport; a normal taxi costs CY£7.

The urban bus station is at Karavella Parking, behind the Amaroza bus company office. Bus No 1 goes to Geroskipou Tourist Beach, 9km north of Pafos; bus No 11 goes to Kato Pafos; and bus No 10 goes to Coral Bay. They all stop at the municipal market.

D Antoniades Ltd (☎ 233301), Leoforos Evagora Pallikaridi 111-113, rents mountain bikes, motorcycles and mopeds.

POLIS
☎ 06
In the heart of Chrysochou Bay, near the wild, remote hiking region of the Akamas Peninsula, is the large village of Polis. At present it isn't as spoilt by tourism as Cyprus' other coastal towns. However, an enormous five-star hotel has been built at the gateway to the protected Akamas area, and others look to follow so Polis' charm and serenity is under threat.

The new CTO (☎ 322468) at Agiou Nikolaou 2 is very central and opens from 9 am to 1 pm and 2.30 to 5.45 pm Monday to Saturday, but closes Wednesday and Saturday afternoons. There are plenty of mountain bike, motorcycle and car-rental companies.

Things to See & Do
The **Akamas Peninsula** is a rugged patchwork of barren rock and lush vegetation, with a wide variety of flora and fauna, including some rare species. A network of paths crisscross the peninsula, making it ideal for walkers.

At the start of these trails are the famous and much-visited **Baths of Aphrodite**, 10km west of Polis. According to one legend, the goddess bathed there to restore her virginity after encounters with her many lovers.

In the village, Byzantine frescoes have recently been uncovered in the church of **Agios Andronikos**. The key is held at the **Archaeological Museum**.

Places to Stay & Eat
About 1km north of Polis towards the sea is a *camping ground (☎ 321526)* surrounded by eucalyptus trees; it is signposted from the town centre. Many houses have rooms to rent from CY£7, and there are plenty of apartments for hire. Otherwise, a good hotel is the *Akamas (☎ 321521, fax 321561)*, on the main street, where smallish rooms (mostly with wonderful views) cost CY£6/10 for a single/double. The hotel has a good restaurant too.

There are now lots of cafes and restaurants, but the most popular eatery remains the *Arsinoe Fish Tavern*, on Grigori Digeni on the south side of the pedestrian zone, where you can get a delicious fish meze for CY£6, and other fresh fish dishes.

Getting There & Away
The New Amaroza bus company office is on Kyproleontos, beside the Old Town Restaurant. It runs 10 buses a day to Pafos (CY£1)

and in summer also has services to Latsi (CY£0.35) and the Baths of Aphrodite (CY£0.50). There is a daily bus to Lefkosia at 5 am or 5.30 am, depending on the day, that costs CY£5. Seats must be reserved one day in advance and can be arranged through the CTO.

Northern Cyprus

The Turkish Republic of Northern Cyprus (TRNC) occupies 37% of the island. Almost completely unspoilt by tourism, it has some of the island's best beaches, as well as awe-inspiring monasteries, archaeological sites and castles.

In this section, Greek place names are used with the Turkish in brackets.

NORTH NICOSIA (LEFKOŞA)
North Nicosia, the capital of Northern Cyprus, is a quiet city with some good examples of Gothic and Ottoman architecture. Although it can sometimes seem populated only by soldiers, if you wander the back-streets of the old town you'll find lots of locals toiling away in small workshops, making or mending a whole variety of everyday articles.

Orientation
The city centre is Atatürk Meydanı in the old city. Girne Caddesi is the main thoroughfare which runs north from Atatürk Meydanı to the well-preserved Kyrenia Gate (Girne Kapısı). To the east of the square is the Selimiye quarter, where you'll find most of the interesting places.

Information
Inside Kyrenia Gate there's an excellent tourist office with all the relevant maps and brochures for Northern Cyprus. There's also a tourist office (☎ 22-79112, fax 85625) at the Ministry of Tourism, about 2km north on Bedrettin Demirel Caddesi in the new town. Both are closed on Sunday, but the one at Ledra checkpoint is open.

Post & Communication
The main post office is on Sarayönü Sokak, just west of Atatürk Meydanı. The telecommunications office is on Kizilay Sokak, in the new town, west of the telecom tower; it's open 8 am to midnight daily.

In an emergency ring ☎ 112 for the hospital, ☎ 155 for the police or ☎ 199 for the fire station.

Email & Internet Access
The most conveniently located Internet facility is situated just near the city walls opposite the football grounds (✉ megabir@cypronet.net).

Things to See & Do
The Turkish Museum is at the northern end of Girne Caddesi in a 17th-century Islamic monastery which was used by 19th-century dervishes (Muslim ascetics), and now displays dervish artefacts. Extending from the museum is a long, thin mausoleum containing the tombs of 16 sheikhs. The museum is open 7.30 am to 2 pm Monday to Friday.

The old quarter east of Atatürk Meydanı is dominated by the Selimiye Mosque, which was originally a cathedral built between 1209 and 1326. Next door is the Bedesten, a building comprising two churches, which became an Ottoman bazaar.

A few blocks west of the Bedesten is the Büyük Hammam, a world-famous Turkish bath frequented by locals and tourists of both genders. A steam bath and a massage (male masseurs only) costs UK£10.

Places to Stay & Eat
Most of the budget accommodation is intended for the local workforce and is not recommended for tourists (particularly lone female travellers). Passable is the *Altin Pansiyon* (☎ 22-85049, Girne Caddesi 63) which costs UK£5/6 for singles/doubles without breakfast. The best hotel in the old town is the three-star *Saray* (☎ 22-83115, fax 84808, Atatürk Meydanı) charging UK£26/40 for singles/doubles, with breakfast. It is advisable (safer and cheaper) to move on from the capital and stay in one of the outlying towns.

On Girne Caddesi there are two friendly restaurants, *Saricizmeli* and *Öz Amasyali*, which are open all day. A substantial plate of mixed fare will cost around UK£3 in either. There's also a *restaurant* in the Saray Hotel.

NORTH NICOSIA (LEFKOŞA)

To Main Tourist Office
(Ministry of Tourism)

PLACES TO STAY
8 Altın Pansiyon
13 Saray Hotel

PLACES TO EAT
9 Öz Amasyalı Restaurant
10 Sarıcizmeli Restaurant

OTHER
1 Long-Distance Bus Terminal
2 Telecommunications Office
3 Post Office
4 Minibuses to Famagusta
5 Minibuses to Kyrenia
6 Tourist Office
7 Turkish Museum
11 Checkpoint (Ledra Palace)
12 Main Post Office
14 Büyük Hammam
15 Selimiye Mosque
16 Bedesten
17 Belediyepazari
18 Football Ground

LEFKOSIA (REPUBLIC OF CYPRUS)

See Lefkosia map

In Arasta Sokak, opposite the Bedesten, is a shop which makes delicious halva on the premises. Nearby is the *Belediyepazari*, a large covered market selling fresh produce as well as clothes and knick-knacks.

Getting There & Away
The long-distance bus station is on the corner of Atatürk Caddesi and Kemal Aşık Caddesi in the new town. However, it is much easier to catch the frequent minibuses to Kyrenia (UK£0.60) and Famagusta (UK£0.90) from the bus stop and Itimat bus station just east of Kyrenia Gate.

Local minibuses leave from just west of Kyrenia Gate.

Getting Around
There are no buses to Ercan airport. A taxi will cost UK£8. There are plenty of taxi ranks, and cars can be hired from Memo Rent-a-Car (☎ 22-87700), Cumhuriyet Caddesi 2, to the east of Kyrenia Gate; prices are around UK£25, but you can bargain.

When you cross into Northern Cyprus there are usually a number of taxi drivers waiting to show you all the sights in one day for around UK£55.

FAMAGUSTA (GAZIMAĞUSA)

The old part of Famagusta is enclosed by a very impressive, well-preserved Venetian wall. The tourist office (☎ 36-62864) is on Fevzi Cakmak Caddesi outside the wall, about 300m east of the **Victory Monument** (a monstrosity depicting soldiers in battle) on the right.

Things to See

Famagusta's **St Nicholas Cathedral**, now the Mustafa Pasha Mosque, is the finest example of Cypriot Gothic architecture. Rather incongruously, a small minaret perches on top of one of its ruined towers.

Othello's Castle, part of the city walls and battlements, was built by the Lusignans in the 13th century. According to legend, it was here that Christophore Moro (Venetian governor of Cyprus from 1506 to 1508) killed his wife, Desdemona, in a fit of jealous rage. It is said that Shakespeare, confusing Moro's surname with his race, based his tragedy on this tale. There are good views from the ramparts, and it's open daily.

Places to Stay & Eat

Inside the city walls is the pleasant *Altun Tabaya Hotel* (☎ 36-65363, *Kizilkule Yolu 7*), which charges UK£8/12 for singles/doubles with a private bathroom and breakfast; follow the signs from the gate east of the Victory Monument. In a run-down section of the new town on Ilker Karter Caddesi (not far from the tourist office) is the friendly *Panorama Hotel* (☎ 36-65880, *fax 65990*) where cosy singles/doubles cost UK£7/11 without breakfast. They also offer reduced rates for weekly stays.

In the old town opposite St Nicholas Cathedral is *Viyana Restaurant*, where good food is served in a lovely outside eating area. A meal with meat and dips costs around UK£6. Also on Yiman Yolu Sokak is the wonderful *Petek Confectioner* where you can drink tea and eat cake and Turkish delight. In the new town, *Cyprus House Restaurant* (*Polatpaşa Bulvari Caddesi*) has a beautiful outside dining area. It's about 400m down the first right east of the Victory Monument.

Getting There & Away

Minibuses to North Nicosia (UK£0.90) go frequently from the Itimat bus station on the Victory Monument roundabout and from the small bus terminus on Lefkoşa Yolu, west of the Monument. Also from here minibuses for Kyrenia leave every half hour or so (UK£1).

Ferries to Mersin in Turkey leave on Tuesday, Thursday and Sunday from the port behind Canbulat Yolu. They take eight hours and the trip costs about UK£10 one way. You can buy tickets from Bulent Ecevit Bulvari 3 (☎ 36-65995, fax 36-67840).

SALAMIS

Nine kilometres north of Famagusta is the huge site of Cyprus' most important classical city. Among many other remains, there is a fully restored Roman amphitheatre, a gymnasium still surrounded by the majority of its marble columns with adjacent baths, and some mosaics. The site is open 7 am to 7.30 pm daily in summer. There is a bar/restaurant (with very clean Western-style toilets) in the car park by the ticket office.

Allow at least half a day here as there is also a long sandy beach next to the site, and a camping ground. There are no buses to Salamis and a return taxi will cost UK£6.

KYRENIA (GIRNE)

Kyrenia is a very attractive town built around a horseshoe-shaped harbour dominated on one side by an impressive Byzantine castle. Behind the harbour is Hürriyet Caddesi which runs from the town hall roundabout westward; at the very far end on the left you'll find the tourist office (☎ 81-52145). The waterfront is lined with lovely outdoor cafes and restaurants where it is delightful to sit and watch the boats.

Just down from the roundabout you will find Cafe Net (✉ cafenet–girne@hotmail.com) which is open 9.30 am until midnight daily.

Things to See

The star attraction of the castle is the **Shipwreck Museum**, which houses the world's oldest shipwreck and its cargo. The ship is believed to have sunk in a storm near Kyrenia around 3000 BC. The castle was built by the Byzantines as a defence against marauding Arabs. Both the castle and the museum are open 9 am to 7 pm daily.

Places to Stay & Eat

There's lots of accommodation in Kyrenia, with much of the cheaper options along

Ecevit Caddessi and between Hürriyet Caddesi and the harbour. *Bingöl Guest House* (☎ 81-52749) on the main roundabout is good and central and costs UK£6 per person with bathroom and breakfast; they also have triples and quads. At the *New Bristol Hotel* (☎ 81-56570, fax 57365, Hürriyet Caddesi 42) pleasant singles/doubles go for CY£8/12. If you want a sea view and old-fashioned charm, *Girne Harbour Lodge Motel* (☎ 81-57392, fax 53744) at the west end of the harbour charges UK£10/18 for singles/doubles with bathroom and breakfast.

Little Arif's Restaurant, on the same side of the road as the New Bristol Hotel, is very good value; turn right into a cul-de-sac opposite the European Travel Services office.

You can't really go wrong with any of the restaurants and cafes on the harbour, and they all have such a picturesque view. Try *Set Fish Restaurant* where a fresh seafood dinner costs around UK£6.

Getting There & Away

The long-distance bus station is on Ecevit Caddesi in the south of the new town. Minibuses to Famagusta (UK£0.90) and North Nicosia (UK£0.60), as well as shared taxis to North Nicosia (UK£0.75), all depart from the roundabout in front of the town hall.

There are express boats to Taşucu in Turkey (UK£21 one-way, departs at 9.30 am daily, three hours). There's also a daily ferry which takes about seven hours (UK£15 one-way). Tickets can be bought from the passenger lounge at the port or from Fergün Shipping Co Ltd (☎ 81-52344) in front of the town hall.

France

France's most salient characteristic is its exceptional diversity. The largest country in Western Europe, France stretches from the rolling hills of the north to the seemingly endless beaches of the south; from the wild coastline of Brittany to the icy crags of the Alps, with cliff-lined canyons, dense forest and vineyards in between.

Over the centuries, France has received more immigrants than any other country in Europe. From the ancient Celtic Gauls and Romans to the more recent arrivals from France's former colonies in Indochina and Africa, these peoples have introduced new elements of culture, cuisine and art to France's unique and diverse civilisation.

Once on the western edge of Europe, today's France stands firmly at the crossroads: between England and Italy, Belgium and Spain, North Africa and Scandinavia. Of course, this is exactly how the French have always regarded their country – at the very centre of things.

Facts about France

HISTORY
Prehistory to Medieval
Human presence in France dates from the middle Palaeolithic period, about 90,000 to 40,000 years ago. Around 25,000 BC the Stone Age Cro-Magnon people appeared and left their mark in the form of cave paintings and engravings.

The Celtic Gauls moved into what is now France between 1500 and 500 BC. Julius Caesar's Roman legions took control of the territory around 52 BC, and France remained under Roman rule until the 5th century, when the Franks (thus 'France') and other Germanic groups overran the country.

Two Frankish dynasties, the Merovingians and the Carolingians, ruled from the 5th to the 10th centuries. In 732, Charles Martel defeated the Moors at Poitiers, ensuring that France would not follow Spain and come under Muslim rule. Charles Martel's grandson, Charlemagne, extended the boundaries of the kingdom and was crowned Holy

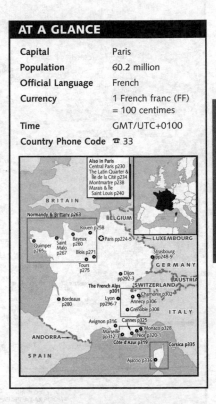

AT A GLANCE

Capital	Paris
Population	60.2 million
Official Language	French
Currency	1 French franc (FF) = 100 centimes
Time	GMT/UTC+0100
Country Phone Code	☎ 33

Also in Paris
Central Paris p230
The Latin Quarter & Île de la Cité p234
Montmartre p238
Marais & Île Saint Louis p240

BRITAIN

Normandy & Brittany p263

Rouen p258

Quimper p265
Saint Malo p267
Bayeux p260
Blois p271
✪ Paris pp224-5

BELGIUM
LUXEMBOURG

Strasbourg pp248-9
GERMANY

Tours p275

Dijon pp292-3
SWITZERLAND
AUSTRIA

The French Alps p301
Chamonix p302-3
Annecy p306
Grenoble p308
ITALY

Bordeaux p280
Lyon pp296-7

Avignon p316   Cannes p325

Marseille pp312-3
Monaco p328
Nice p320-1

ANDORRA
Côte d'Azur p319
Corsica p335

SPAIN

Ajaccio p336

Roman Emperor in 800. During the 9th century, Scandinavian Vikings (the Normans) began raiding France's western coast and eventually founded the Duchy of Normandy.

Under William the Conqueror (the Duke of Normandy), Norman forces occupied England in 1066, making Normandy – and later, Plantagenet-ruled England – a formidable rival of the kingdom of France. A further third of France came under the control of the English Crown in 1154, when Eleanor of Aquitaine married Henry of Anjou (later King Henry II of England).

In 1415, French forces were defeated at Agincourt; in 1420, the English took control of Paris, and two years later King Henry IV

FRANCE

FRANCE

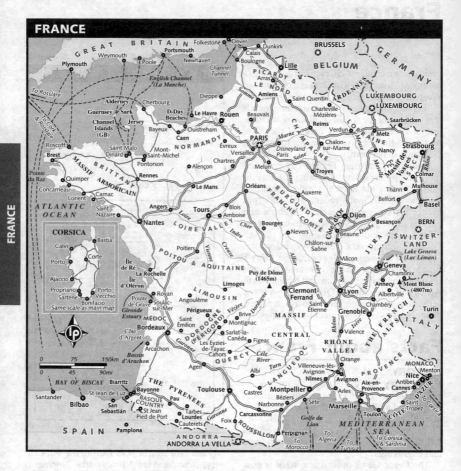

of England became king of France. But a 17-year-old peasant girl known to history as Jeanne d'Arc (Joan of Arc) surfaced in 1429 and rallied the French troops at Orléans. She was captured, convicted of heresy and burned at the stake two years later, but her efforts helped to turn the war in favour of the French.

Renaissance & Reformation

The ideals and aesthetics of the Italian Renaissance were introduced in the 15th century, partly by the French aristocracy returning from military campaigns in Italy. The influence was most evident during the reign of François I, and the chateaux of Fontainebleau, near Paris, and Chenonceau in the Loire are good examples of Renaissance architectural style.

By the 1530s the Protestant Reformation had been strengthened in France by the ideas of the Frenchman John Calvin, an exile in Geneva. The Wars of Religion (1562-98) involved three groups: the Huguenots (French Protestants); the Catholic League, led by the House of Guise; and the Catholic monarchy. The fighting brought the French state close to disintegration. Henry of Navarra, a Huguenot who had embraced Catholicism, eventually became King Henry IV. In 1598, he promulgated the Edict of Nantes, which guaranteed the Huguenots many civil and political rights.

Louis XIV & the Ancien Régime

Louis XIV – also known as Le Roi Soleil (the Sun King) – ascended the throne in 1643 at the age of five and ruled until 1715. Throughout his long reign, he sought to extend the power of the French monarchy. He also involved France in a long series of costly wars and poured huge sums of money into his extravagant palace at Versailles.

His successor, Louis XV (ruled 1715-74), was followed by the incompetent – and later universally despised – Louis XVI. As the 18th century progressed, new economic and social circumstances rendered the old order (ancien régime) dangerously at odds with the needs of the country.

The Seven Years' War (1756-63), fought by France and Austria against Britain and Prussia, was one of a series of ruinous wars pursued by Louis XV, culminating in the loss of France's flourishing colonies in Canada, the West Indies and India to the British.

The French Revolution

By the late 1780s, Louis XVI and his queen, Marie-Antoinette, had managed to alienate virtually every segment of society. When the king tried to neutralise the power of reform-minded delegates at a meeting of the Estates General in 1789, the urban masses took to the streets and, on 14 July, a Parisian mob stormed the Bastille prison.

The Revolution began in the hands of the moderate, republican Girondists (Girondins in French), but they soon lost power to the radical Jacobins, led by Robespierre, Danton and Marat, who established the First Republic in 1792. In January 1793, Louis was guillotined in what is now place de la Concorde in Paris. Two months later the Jacobins set up the notorious Committee of Public Safety, which had near-dictatorial control during the Reign of Terror (September 1793 to July 1794).

In the resulting chaos, a dashing young general by the name of Napoleon Bonaparte chalked up a string of victories in the Italian campaign of the war against Austria, and his success soon turned him into an independent political force.

Napoleon

In 1799, when it appeared that the Jacobins were again on the ascendancy, Napoleon assumed power himself. Five years later he had himself crowned Emperor of the French by Pope Pius VII, and the scope and nature of Napoleon's ambitions became obvious to all.

In 1812, in an attempt to do away with his last major rival on the Continent, Tsar Alexander I, Napoleon invaded Russia. Although his Grande Armée (Grand Army) captured Moscow, it was wiped out shortly thereafter by the brutal Russian winter. Prussia and Napoleon's other enemies quickly recovered from earlier defeats, and less than two years later the Allied armies entered Paris. Napoleon abdicated and was exiled to his tiny Mediterranean island-kingdom of Elba.

At the Congress of Vienna (1814-15), the Allies restored the House of Bourbon to the French throne. But in March 1815, Napoleon escaped from Elba, landed in southern France and gathered a large army as he marched northward towards Paris. His 'Hundred Days' back in power ended when his forces were defeated by the English at Waterloo in Belgium. Napoleon was banished to the remote South Atlantic island of St Helena where he died in 1821.

19th Century

The 19th century was a chaotic one for France. Louis XVIII's reign (1815-24) was dominated by the struggle between extreme monarchists and those who saw the changes wrought by the Revolution as irreversible. Charles X (ruled 1824-30) handled the struggle between reactionaries and liberals with great ineptitude and was overthrown in the July Revolution of 1830. Louis-Philippe (ruled 1830-48), an ostensibly constitutional monarch of upper bourgeois sympathies and tastes, was then chosen by parliament to head what became known as the July Monarchy.

Louis-Philippe was in turn ousted in the February Revolution of 1848, in whose wake the Second Republic was established. In presidential elections held that year, Napoleon's undistinguished nephew Louis-Napoleon Bonaparte was overwhelmingly elected. A

FRANCE

legislative deadlock led Louis-Napoleon to lead a coup d'etat in 1851, after which he was proclaimed Napoleon III, Emperor of the French.

The second empire lasted from 1852 until 1870, when the Prussian prime minister, Bismarck, goaded Napoleon III into declaring war on Prussia. Within months the thoroughly unprepared French army had been defeated and the emperor taken prisoner. When news of the debacle reached the French capital, the Parisian masses took to the streets and demanded that a republic be declared – the Third Republic.

WWI

Central to France's entry into WWI was the desire to regain Alsace and Lorraine, lost to Germany in 1871. This was achieved but at immense human cost: of the eight million French men who were called to arms, 1.3 million were killed and almost one million crippled. The war was officially ended by the Treaty of Versailles in 1919, which laid down severe terms (Germany was to pay US$33 billion in reparations).

WWII

During the 1930s the French, like the British, did their best to appease Hitler, but two days after the 1939 German invasion of Poland, the two countries reluctantly declared war on Germany. By June of the following year, France had capitulated. The British forces sent to help the French barely managed to avoid capture by retreating to Dunkirk and crossing the English Channel in small boats.

The Germans divided France into zones of direct occupation (in the north and along the west coast) and a puppet state based in the spa town of Vichy. Both the collaborationist government and French police forces in the German-occupied areas were very helpful to the Nazis in rounding up French Jews and other targeted groups for deportation to concentration camps.

General Charles de Gaulle, France's undersecretary of war, fled to London and set up a French government-in-exile. He also established the Forces Françaises Libres (Free French Forces), a military force dedicated to continuing the fight against Germany. The liberation of France began with the US, British and Canadian landings in Normandy on D-Day (6 June 1944). Paris was liberated on 25 August.

The Fourth Republic

De Gaulle soon returned to Paris and set up a provisional government, but in January 1946 he resigned as its president, miscalculating that this move would create a popular outcry for his return. A few months later, a new constitution was approved by referendum. The Fourth Republic was a period of unstable coalition cabinets, characterised by slow economic recovery fuelled by massive US aid, an unsuccessful war to reassert French colonial control of Indochina and an uprising by Arab nationalists in Algeria, whose population included over one million French settlers.

The Fifth Republic

The Fourth Republic came to an end in 1958; de Gaulle was brought back to power to prevent a military coup and even civil war. He soon drafted a new constitution that gave considerable powers to the president at the expense of the National Assembly.

In 1969, de Gaulle was succeeded as president by the Gaullist leader Georges Pompidou, who in turn was followed by Valéry Giscard d'Estaing in 1974. François Mitterrand, a Socialist, was elected president in 1981 and re-elected seven years later. The closely contested presidential election of May 1995 resulted in Jacques Chirac winning the mandate with 52% of the vote.

Chirac called a snap election in 1997 and remained president, but his party lost support to a coalition of Socialists, Communists and Greens, led by Lionel Jospin, who became prime minister. The popular Jospin remains the favourite to succeed Chirac in the next presidential ballot, scheduled for 2002.

GEOGRAPHY

France (551,000 sq km) is the largest country in Europe after Russia and Ukraine. It's shaped like a hexagon bordered by either mountains or water except for the relatively flat, north-east frontier that abuts Germany, Luxembourg and Belgium.

ECOLOGY & ENVIRONMENT

France has a rich variety of flora and fauna, including some 113 species of mammals (more than any other country in Europe).

About three-quarters of France's electricity is produced by nuclear power plants. France maintains an independent arsenal of nuclear weapons; in 1992, the government finally agreed to suspend nuclear testing on the Polynesian island of Moruroa and a nearby atoll. However, one last round of tests was concluded in January 1996 before France signed a nuclear test-ban treaty in April 1998.

GOVERNMENT & POLITICS

Despite a long tradition of highly centralised government, the country remains linguistically and culturally heterogeneous. There are even groups in the Basque Country, Brittany and Corsica who still demand complete independence from France.

France has had 11 constitutions since 1789. The present one, instituted by de Gaulle in 1958, established what is known as the Fifth Republic (see the previous History section). It gives considerable power to the president of the republic.

The 577 members of the National Assembly are directly elected in single-member constituencies for five-year terms. The 321 members of the rather powerless Sénat, who serve for nine years, are indirectly elected. The president of France is elected directly for a seven-year term (at the time of writing, a five-year term was under discussion).

Executive power is shared by the president and the Council of Ministers, whose members, including the prime minister, are appointed by the president but are responsible to parliament. The president, who resides in the Palais de l'Élysée in Paris, makes all major policy decisions.

France is one of the five permanent members of the UN Security Council. It withdrew from NATO's joint military command in 1966.

Local Administration

Regional names still exist, but for administrative purposes the country has been divided into units called *départements*, of which there are 96 in metropolitan France and another five abroad. The government in Paris is represented in each department by a *préfet* (prefect).

A department's main town, where the departmental government and the prefect are based, is known as a *préfecture*.

ECONOMY

After sluggish growth through much of the 1990s, the French economy has finally started to hum again. Some think tanks were predicting a rise of 3.5% or more in 2000, and unemployment – which was stuck around 12% in the late 1990s – has dropped to its lowest level in almost a decade and was seen falling below 9% by 2001.

The government has long played a significant interventionist *(dirigiste)* role in the French economy. More than 50% of GDP is still spent by the state, which employs one in every four French workers despite a series of heavyweight privatisations during the 1990s.

France is one of the world's most industrialised countries, with around 40% of the workforce employed in the industrial sector. But it's also the largest agricultural producer and exporter in the EU. Nearly one in 10 workers is engaged in agricultural production, which helps to account for the attention given by the government to French farmers during their periodic protests against cheaper imports.

POPULATION & PEOPLE

France has a population of 60.2 million, more than 20% of whom live in the Paris metropolitan area. During the last 150 years France has received more immigrants than any other European country (4.3 million between 1850 and 1945), including significant numbers of political refugees. In the late 1950s and early 1960s, as the French colonial empire collapsed, more than one million French settlers returned to France from Algeria, Morocco, Tunisia and Indochina. In recent years, there has been a racist backlash against France's non-white immigrant communities, led by the extreme-right Front National (FN) party.

ARTS
Architecture

A religious revival in the 11th century led to the construction of a large number of Romanesque churches, so called because their architects adopted elements from Gallo-Roman

FRANCE

buildings. Romanesque buildings typically have round arches, heavy walls that let in very little light and a lack of ornamentation bordering on the austere.

The Gothic style originated in the mid-12th century in northern France, whose great wealth enabled it to attract the finest architects, engineers and artisans. Gothic structures are characterised by ribbed vaults, pointed arches and stained-glass windows, with the emphasis on space, verticality and light. The invention of the flying buttress meant that greater height and width were now possible. By the 15th century, decorative extravagance led to the Flamboyant Gothic style, so named because its wavy stone carving was said to resemble flames.

Painting

An extraordinary flowering of artistic talent took place in France during the late 19th and early 20th centuries. The impressionists, who endeavoured to capture the ever-changing aspects of reflected light, included Edouard Manet, Claude Monet, Edgar Degas, Camille Pissarro and Pierre-Auguste Renoir. They were followed by the equally creative post-impressionists, among whose ranks were Paul Cézanne, Paul Gauguin and Georges Seurat. A little later, the Fauves (literally, 'wild beasts'), the most famous of whom was Henri Matisse, became known for their radical use of vibrant colour. In the years before WWI Pablo Picasso, who was living in Paris, and Georges Braque pioneered cubism, a school of art which concentrated on the analysis of form through abstract and geometric representation.

Music

When French music comes to mind, most people hear accordions and *chansonniers* (cabaret singers) like Édith Piaf. But at many points in history, France has been at the centre of musical culture in Europe.

France's two greatest classical composers of the 19th century were the Romantic Hector Berlioz, the founder of modern orchestration, and César Franck, who specialised in organ compositions. Their output sparked a musical renaissance that would produce such greats as Gabriel Fauré and the impressionists Claude Debussy and Maurice Ravel.

Jazz hit Paris in the 1920s and has remained popular ever since. Violinist Stéfane Grappelli, pianist Michel Petrucciani and electric violinist Jean-Luc Ponty are among those who have left their mark on the world jazz scene.

Popular music has come a long way since the *yéyé* (imitative rock) of the 1960s sung by Johnny Halliday. Watch out for rappers MC Solaar, Doc Gynéco, Alliance Ethnik, and I Am from Marseille. Evergreen balladeers/folk singers include Francis Cabrel and Julien Clerc. The new age space music of Jean-Michel Jarre splits audiences around the globe.

France's claim to fame in recent years has been *sono mondial* (world music) – Algerian *raï*, Senegalese *mbalax* and West Indian *zouk*. Etienne Daho continues to top the charts with his trance numbers, and a recent development is Astérix rock, a homegrown folk-country sound based on accordions.

Literature

To get a feel for France and its literature of the 19th century, you might pick up a translation of novels by Victor Hugo (*Les Misérables or The Hunchback of Notre Dame*), Stendahl (*The Red and the Black*), Honoré de Balzac (*Old Goriot*), Émile Zola (*Germinal*) or Gustave Flaubert (*A Sentimental Education or Madame Bovary*).

After WWII, existentialism emerged – a significant literary movement based upon the philosophy that people are self-creating beings. Its most prominent figures – Jean-Paul Sartre (*Being and Nothingness*), Simone de Beauvoir, and Albert Camus (*The Plague*) – stressed the importance of the writer's political commitment. De Beauvoir also wrote *The Second Sex*, which has had a profound influence on feminist thinking.

The *roman policier* (detective novel) has always been a great favourite with the French and among its greatest exponents has been the Belgian-born Georges Simenon and his novels featuring Inspector Maigret as well as Frédéric Dard (alias San Antonio), Léo Malet and Daniel Pennac, widely read for his witty crime fiction.

Other contemporary authors who enjoy a wide following include Françoise Sagan, Jean Auel, Emmanuel Carrère, Pascal Quignard and Stéphane Bourguignon.

Cinema

Film has always been taken very seriously as an art form in France. Some of the most innovative and influential filmmakers of the 1920s and 1930s were Jean Vigo, Marcel Pagnol and Jean Renoir.

After WWII, a new generation of directors burst onto the scene. Known as the *nouvelle vague* (new wave), this genre includes directors such as Jean-Luc Godard, François Truffaut, and Claude Chabrol, whose main tenet was that a film should be the conception of the filmmaker – not the product of a studio or a producer.

Despite the onslaught of American films, France is still producing commercially viable (albeit subsidised) films. Contemporary directors of note include Bertrand Blier *(Trop belle pour toi)*, Jean-Jacques Beineix *(Betty Blue)* and Olivier Assayas *(Les Destinées)*. The French film industry's main annual event is the Cannes Film Festival held in May.

SOCIETY & CONDUCT

Some visitors to France conclude that it would be a lovely country if it weren't for the French. The following tips might prove useful: Never address a waiter or bartender as *garçon* (boy); *s'il vous plaît* is the way it's done nowadays. Avoid discussing money, keep off the manicured French lawns and resist handling produce in markets. Always address people as *Monsieur* (Mr/sir), *Madame* (Mrs) and *Mademoiselle* (Miss); when in doubt use 'Madame'.

Finally, when you go out for the evening, it's a good idea to follow the local custom of dressing relatively well, particularly in a restaurant.

RELIGION

Some 80% of French people say they are Catholic, but although most have been baptised very few attend church. Protestants, who were severely persecuted during much of the 16th and 17th centuries, now number about one million.

France now has between four and five million Muslims, making Islam the second-largest religion in the country. The majority are immigrants (or their offspring) who came from North Africa during the 1950s and 1960s.

There has been a Jewish community in France almost continuously since Roman times. About 75,000 French Jews were killed during the Holocaust. The country's Jewish community now numbers some 650,000.

LANGUAGE

Around 122 million people worldwide speak French as their first language, and various forms of creole are used in Haiti, French Guiana and southern Louisiana. Thus the French tend to assume that all human beings should speak French; it was the international language of culture and diplomacy until WWI.

Your best bet is always to approach people politely in French, even if the only words you know are *'Pardon, Monsieur/Madame/Mademoiselle, parlez-vous Anglais?'* ('Excuse me sir/madam/miss, do you speak English?').

See the Language chapter at the back of this book for pronunciation guidelines and useful words and phrases.

Facts for the Visitor

HIGHLIGHTS

Museums

Many of the country's most exceptional museums are in Paris. Besides the rather overwhelming Louvre, Parisian museums not to be missed include the Musée d'Orsay (late-19th and early-20th-century art), the Pompidou Centre (modern and contemporary art), the Musée Rodin, and the Musée National du Moyen Age (Museum of the Middle Ages) at the Hôtel de Cluny. Other cities known for their museums include Nice, Bordeaux, Strasbourg and Lyon.

Palaces & Chateaux

The royal palace at Versailles is the largest and most grandiose of the hundreds of chateaux located all over the country. Many of the most impressive ones, including Chambord, Cheverny, Chenonceau and Azay-le-Rideau, are in the Loire Valley around Blois and Tours. The cathedrals at Chartres, Strasbourg and Rouen are among the most beautiful in France.

FRANCE

FRANCE

Beaches

The Côte d'Azur – the French Riviera – has some of the best known beaches in the world, but you'll also find lovely beaches farther west on the Mediterranean.

SUGGESTED ITINERARIES

Two days
    Paris – the most beautiful city in the world.
One week
    Paris plus a nearby area, such as the Loire Valley, Champagne, Alsace or Normandy.
Two weeks
    As above, plus one area in the west or south, such as Brittany, the Alps or Provence.
One month
    As above, but spending more time in each place and visiting more of the west or south – Brittany, say, or the Côte d'Azur.

PLANNING
When to Go

France is at its best in spring, though wintry relapses aren't uncommon in April and the beach resorts only begin to pick up in mid-May. Autumn is pleasant, too, but by late October it's a bit cool for sunbathing. Winter is great for snow sports in the Alps and Pyrenees, but over Christmas, New Year and the February/March school holidays create surges in tourism. On the other hand, Paris always has all sorts of cultural activities during its rather wet winter.

In summer, the weather is warm and even hot, especially in the south, and the beaches, resorts and camping grounds get packed to the gills. Also, millions of French people take their annual month-long holiday (congé) in August. Resort hotel rooms and camp sites are in extremely short supply, while in the half-deserted cities many shops, restaurants, cinemas, cultural institutions and even hotels simply shut down. Avoid travelling in France during August.

Maps

For driving, the best road map is Michelin's *Motoring Atlas France* (1:200,000), which covers the whole country. Éditions Didier & Richard's series of 1:50,000 trail maps are adequate for most hiking and cycling excursions.

The Institut Géographique National (IGN) publishes maps of France in both 1:50,000 and 1:25,000 scale. Topoguides are little booklets for hikers that include trail maps and information (in French) on trail conditions, flora, fauna, villages en route and more.

TOURIST OFFICES
Local Tourist Offices

Every city, town, village and hamlet seems to have either an *office de tourisme* (a tourist office run by some unit of local government) or a *syndicat d'initiative* (a tourist office run by an organisation of local merchants). Both are an excellent resource and can almost always provide a local map at the very least. Many tourist offices will make local hotel reservations, usually for a small fee.

Details on local tourist offices appear under Information at the beginning of each city, town or area listing.

Tourist Offices Abroad

The French Government Tourist Offices in the following countries can provide brochures and tourist information.

Australia (☎ 02-9231 5244, fax 9221 8682, ◙ frencht@ozemail.com.au) 25 Bligh St, 22nd floor, Sydney, NSW 2000
Canada (☎ 514-288 4264, fax 845 4868, ◙ mfrance@mtl.net) 1981 McGill College Ave, Suite 490, Montreal, Que H3A 2W9
UK (☎ 020-7399 3500, fax 7493 6594, ◙ info@co.uk) 178 Piccadilly, London W1V OAL
USA (☎ 212-838 7800, fax 838 7855, ◙ info@francetourism.com) 444 Madison Ave, New York, NY 10020

VISAS & DOCUMENTS

Citizens of the USA, Canada, Australia and New Zealand, and most European countries can enter France for up to three months without a visa. South Africans, however, must have a visa to visit France (to avoid delays, apply before leaving home).

If you're staying in France for over three months to study or work, apply to the French consulate nearest where you live for a long-stay visa. If you're not an EU citizen, it's extremely difficult to get a work visa; one of the few exceptions allows holders of student visas to work part-time. Begin the paperwork several months before you leave home.

By law, everyone in France, including tourists, must carry identification with them. For visitors, this means a passport. A national identity card is sufficient for EU citizens.

Visa Extensions

Tourist visas *cannot* be extended. If you qualify for an automatic three-month stay upon arrival, you'll get another three months if you exit and then re-enter France. The fewer French entry stamps you have in your passport, the easier this is likely to be.

EMBASSIES & CONSULATES
French Embassies & Consulates

French embassies abroad include:

Australia (☎ 02-6216 0100, fax 6216 0127, ✉ embassy@france.net.au) 6 Perth Ave, Yarralumla, ACT 2600

Canada (☎ 613-789 1795, fax 562 3735, ✉ res@amba-Ottowa.fr) 42 Sussex Drive, Ottawa, Ont K1M 2C9

Germany (☎ 030-206 39000, fax 206 39010) Kochstrasse 6-7, D-10969 Berlin

Italy (☎ 06-686 011, fax 860 1360, ✉ france-italia@france-italia.it) Piazza Farnese 67, 00186 Rome

New Zealand (☎ 04-384 2555, fax 384 2577, ✉ consulfrance@actrix.gen.nz) Rural Bank Building, 34-42 Manners Street, Wellington

Spain (☎ 91-423 8900, fax 423 8901) Calle de Salustiano Olozaga 9, 28001 Madrid.

UK (☎ 020-7201 1000, fax 7201 1004, ✉ press@ambafrance.org) 58 Knightsbridge, London SW1X 7JT. Visa inquiries: ☎ 0891-887733

USA (☎ 202-944 6000, fax 944 6166, ✉ visaswashington@amb-wash.fv) 4101 Reservoir Rd, NW Washington, DC, 20007

Embassies & Consulates in France

Countries with embassies in Paris include:

Australia (☎ 01 40 59 33 00, fax 01 40 59 33 10, ✉ information.paris@dfat.gov.au) 4 rue Jean Rey, 15e (metro Bir Hakeim)

Canada (☎ 01 44 43 29 00, 01 44 43 29 99) 35 ave Montaigne, 8e (metro Franklin D Roosevelt)

New Zealand (☎ 01 45 00 24 11, 01 45 01 43 44) 7ter rue Léonard de Vinci, 16e (metro Victor Hugo)

Spain (☎ 01 44 43 18 00, fax 01 47 23 59 55, ✉ emba.espa@wanadoo.fr) 22 ave Marceau, 8e (metro Alma Marceau)

UK (☎ 01 44 51 31 00, fax 01 44 51 31 27, ✉ ambassade@amb-grandebretagne.fr) 35 rue du Faubourg St Honoré, 8e (metro Concorde)

USA (☎ 01 43 12 22, fax 01 42 66 97 83, ✉ ambassade@amb-usa.fr) 2 ave Gabriel, 1er (metro Concorde)

MONEY
Currency

One French franc (FF) equals 100 centimes. French coins come in denominations of five, 10 and 20 centimes and half, one, two, five, 10 and 20FF (the last two are two-tone). Banknotes are issued in denominations of 20, 50, 100, 200 and 500FF. The higher the denomination, the larger the bill.

Exchange Rates

country	unit		franc
Australia	A$1	=	4.21FF
Canada	C$1	=	4.89FF
euro	€1	=	6.55FF
Germany	DM1	=	3.35FF
Japan	¥100	=	6.68FF
New Zealand	NZ$1	=	3.26FF
Spain	100 ptas	=	3.94FF
UK	UK£1	=	10.9FF
USA	US$1	=	7.26FF

Exchanging Money

Cash & Travellers Cheques Generally you'll get a better exchange rate for travellers cheques than for cash. The most useful ones are issued by American Express in US dollars. Do not bring travellers cheques in Australian dollars as they are hard to change; US$100 bills can also be difficult.

Visa (Carte Bleue in France) is more widely accepted than MasterCard (Eurocard). Visa card-holders with a PIN number can get cash advances from banks and ATMs nationwide. American Express cards aren't very useful, except to get cash at American Express offices in big cities or to pay in upmarket shops and restaurants.

Many post offices make exchange transactions at a very good rate and accept American Express travellers cheques; there's no commission on US dollar travellers cheques (1.2% to 1.5% for ones in French francs).

The Banque de France, France's central bank, offers good rates on travellers cheques and take no commission (except 1% on French franc travellers cheques). Branches are open Monday to Friday but only offer currency services in the morning.

FRANCE

Commercial banks usually charge a stiff 20FF to 35FF per foreign currency transaction. In larger cities, exchange bureaus are faster, easier, open longer hours and often give better rates than the banks.

If your American Express travellers cheques are lost or stolen, call ☎ 0800 90 86 00, a 24-hour toll-free number. For lost or stolen Visa cards, call ☎ 0836 69 08 80 or 0800 90 20 33.

Costs

If you stay in hostels or the cheapest hotels and buy provisions from grocery stores rather than eating at restaurants, it's possible to tour France on as little as US$30 a day (US$35 in Paris). Eating out, lots of travel or treating yourself to France's many little luxuries can increase this figure dramatically.

Discounts Museums, cinemas, the SNCF, ferry companies and other institutions offer price breaks to people under the age of either 25 or 26; students with ISIC cards (age limits may apply); and seniors (people over 60 or, in some cases, 65.) Look for the words *demi-tarif* or *tarif réduit* (half-price tariff or reduced rate) on rate charts.

Tipping & Bargaining

It's not necessary to leave a *pourboire* (tip) in restaurants or hotels; under French law, the bill must already include a 15% service charge. Some people leave a few francs on the table for the waiter, but this isn't expected (especially for drinks). At truly posh restaurants, however, a more generous gratuity is expected. For a taxi ride, the usual tip is 2FF to 5FF no matter what the fare. Bargaining is rarely done in France except at flea markets.

Taxes & Refunds

France's VAT (value-added tax, ie, sales tax) is known in French as TVA *(taxe sur la valeur ajoutée)*. The TVA is 19.6% on the purchase price of most goods (and for noncommercial vehicle rental). Prices that include TVA are often marked TTC *(toutes taxes comprises)*, which means 'all taxes included'.

It's possible (though rather complicated) to get a reimbursement for TVA if you meet several conditions: you are not an EU national and are over 15 years of age; you have

stayed in France less than six months; you are buying more than 1200FF worth of goods (not more than 10 of the same item); and the shop offers duty-free sales *(vente en détaxe)*.

To claim a TVA, you fill out an export sales invoice *(bordereau de vente)* when you make your purchase, and this is stamped at your port of exit. The shop then reimburses you – by mail or bank transfer within 30 days – for the TVA you've paid. Note that duty-free shopping within the EU was abolished in mid-1999.

POST & COMMUNICATIONS
Postal Rates

La Poste, the French postal service, is fast, reliable and expensive. Postcards and letters up to 20g cost 3FF within the EU, 4.40FF to the USA, Canada and the Middle East, and 5.20FF to Australasia. Aerograms cost 5FF to all destinations. Overseas packages are now sent by air only, which is expensive.

Receiving Mail Mail to France *must* include the area's five-digit postcode, which begins with the two-digit number of the department. In Paris, all postcodes begin with 750 and end with the arrondissement number, eg, 75004 for the 4th arrondissement, 75013 for the 13th.

Poste restante mail is held alphabetically by family name, so make sure your last name is written in capital letters. If not addressed to a particular branch, poste restante mail ends up at the town's main post office *(recette principale)*. In Paris, this means the central post office (☎ 01 40 28 20 00) at 52 rue du Louvre (1er; metro Sentier or Les Halles). There's a 3FF charge for every poste restante claimed.

You can also receive mail care of American Express offices, although if you don't have an American Express card or travellers cheques there's a 5FF charge each time you check to see if you have received any mail.

Telephone
Public Telephones Almost all public phones now require *télécartes* (phonecards), which are sold at post offices, *tabacs* (tobacco shops), Paris metro ticket counters and supermarket check-out counters. Cards worth 50/120 units cost 48.60/97.50FF. Each unit is good for one three-minute local call. To make a call with a phonecard, pick up the receiver,

insert the card and dial when the LCD screen reads 'Numérotez'. All telephone cabins can take incoming calls; give the caller the 10-digit number written after the words *'ici le'* on the information sheet next to the phone.

Domestic Dialling France has five telephone zones and all telephone numbers comprise 10 digits. Paris and Île de France numbers begin with 01. The other codes are: ☎ 02 for the north-west; ☎ 03 for the north-east; ☎ 04 for the south-east (including Corsica); and ☎ 05 for the south-west.

Numbers beginning with 0800 are free, but others in the series (eg, 0836) generally cost 2.23FF per minute. For directory assistance, dial ☎ 12.

International Dialling France's international country code is ☎ 33. When dialling from abroad, omit the initial '0' at the beginning of 10-digit phone numbers.

To place a direct call, dial ☎ 00 and then the country code, area code and local number. A three-minute call to the USA costs about 5/3FF peak/off-peak.

To make a reverse-charge call *(en PCV)* or person-to-person *(avec préavis)* from France to other countries, dial ☎ 00 (the international operator), wait for the second tone and then dial ☎ 33 plus the country code of the place you're calling (for the USA and Canada, dial 11 instead of 1).

For directory inquiries outside France, dial ☎ 00, and when the second tone sounds, dial 33, then 12, and finally the country code. For information on home-country direct calls, see the Telephones Appendix in the back of this book.

Telephone Cards You can buy prepaid phone cards in France that make calling abroad cheaper than with a standard télécarte. Carte Intercall Monde, Carte Astuce and Eagle Télécom International are among popular cards that give up to 60% off standard French international call rates. They're available in denominations of 50FF and 100FF from *tabacs*, newsagents, phone shops and other sales points.

Minitel Minitel is a computerised information service peculiar to France. Though useful, it can be expensive to use and the Internet is becoming a popular alternative. Minitel numbers consist of four digits (eg, 3611, 3614, 3615) and a string of letters. Most of the terminals in post offices are free for directory inquiries.

Fax
Virtually all French post offices can send and receive domestic and international faxes *(télécopies* or *téléfaxes)*. It costs around 12/60FF to send a one-page fax within France/to the USA.

Email & Internet Access
Email can be sent and received at cybercafes throughout France. La Poste has set up Internet centres at some 1000 post offices around France; a 50FF Cybercarte gives you an hour's access, and each 30FF 'recharge' is good for another hour. Commercial cybercafes charge about 20FF to 30FF for a half-hour's surfing.

INTERNET RESOURCES
Useful Web sites in English include the Paris Tourist Office (www.paris-touristoffice.com), the French Government Tourist Office (www.francetourism.com) and GuideWeb (www.guideweb.com), which has information about selected regions in France. Many towns have their own Web sites. Gay and lesbian travellers should check the Queer Resources Directory (www.france.qrd.org).

BOOKS
Lonely Planet
Lonely Planet's *France* guide has comprehensive coverage of France and includes chapters on Andorra and Monaco. *Paris Condensed* is a pocket companion with short visits in mind. Regional guides include *Provence & Côte D'Azur*, *The Loire*, *South-Western France* and *Corsica*. The *French phrasebook* is a complete guide to *la langue française*.

Guidebooks
Michelin's hardcover *Guide Rouge* (red guide) lists middle and upper-range hotels and rates France's greatest restaurants with the famous stars. Michelin's *guides verts* (green guides) cover all of France in 24 regional volumes (12 in English).

FRANCE

The best general French-language guides are by *Guide Bleu*. Its blue-jacketed all-France and regional guides provide accurate, balanced information on history, culture and architecture.

Travel

Paul Rambali's *French Blues* is a series of uncompromising yet sympathetic snapshots of modern France. *A Year in Provence* by Peter Mayle is an irresistible account of country life in southern France. *A Moveable Feast* by Ernest Hemingway portrays Bohemian life in 1920s Paris. Henry Miller also wrote some pretty dramatic stuff set in the French capital of the 1930s, including *Tropic of Cancer*. Gertrude Stein's *The Autobiography of Alice B Toklas* is an entertaining account of Paris' literary and artistic circles from WWI to the mid-1930s.

History & Politics

There are many excellent histories of France in English. Among the best is Fernand Braudel's two-volume *The Identity of France*, which recently went out of print. *France Today* by John Ardagh provides excellent insights into the way French society has evolved since WWII.

NEWSPAPERS & MAGAZINES

The excellent *International Herald Tribune* is sold at many news kiosks throughout France for 10FF. Other English-language papers you can find include the *Guardian*, the *Financial Times*, and the colourful *USA Today*. *Newsweek*, *Time* and the *Economist* are also widely available.

RADIO & TV

The BBC World Service can be picked up on 195kHz AM and 6195kHz, 9410kHz, 9760kHz and 12095kHz short wave. In northern France, BBC for Europe is on 648kHz AM. Upmarket hotels often offer cable TV access to CNN, BBC Prime, Sky and other networks. Canal+ (pronounced ka-NAHL pluce), a French subscription TV station available in many mid-range hotels sometimes shows undubbed English movies.

PHOTOGRAPHY & VIDEO

Be prepared to have your camera and film forced through the ostensibly film-safe x-ray machines at airports and when entering sensitive public buildings. Ask to have your film hand-checked, if not your whole camera. Film is widely available, and costs about 35/46FF for a 36-exposure roll of 100ASA print/slide film, excluding processing.

Note that French videotapes cannot be played on British, Australian or American video cassette recorders or TVs unless they are equipped with SECAM.

TIME

France is GMT/UTC plus one hour. Clocks are turned one hour ahead on the last Sunday in March and back again on the last Sunday in September.

LAUNDRY

Self-service laundrettes *(laveries libre service)* generally charge 18FF to 20FF a load and around 2FF for five minutes of drying. Bring lots of coins; few laundrettes have change machines.

TOILETS

Public toilets are scarce, though small towns often have one near the town hall *(mairie)*. In Paris, you're more likely to come upon one of the tan, self-disinfecting toilet pods. Many public toilets cost 2FF or even 2.50FF. Except in the most tourist-filled areas, cafe owners usually allow you to use their toilets provided you ask politely.

WOMEN TRAVELLERS

In general, women need not walk around in fear, although the French seem to have given little thought to sexual harassment – many men tend to stare hard at passing women, for instance. If you're subject to catcalls or hassled on the street, the best strategy is usually to walk on and ignore the comment. Making a cutting retort is ineffective in English and risky in French if your slang isn't proficient.

France's national rape crisis hotline, which is run by a women's organisation called Viols Femmes Informations, can be reached toll-free by dialling ☎ 0800 05 95 95 on weekdays from 10 am to 6 pm.

GAY & LESBIAN TRAVELLERS

Centre Gai et Lesbien (CGL; ☎ 01 43 57 21 47), 3 rue Keller (11e; metro Ledru Rollin),

500m east of place de la Bastille, is headquarters for numerous organisations. Its bar, library and other facilities open 2 to 8 pm Monday to Saturday. Paris' Gay Pride parade is held on the last weekend in June. Gay publications include the monthlies *3 Keller*, *Action* and *Gay*. The monthly *Lesbia* gives a rundown of what's happening around the country.

DISABLED TRAVELLERS

France isn't well-equipped for *handicapés* – kerb ramps are few and far between, older public facilities and budget hotels often lack lifts, and the Paris metro is hopeless. Details of train travel for wheelchair users are available in SNCF's booklet *Guide du Voyageur à Mobilité Réduite*. You can also contact SNCF Accessibilité (the French rail company) toll-free at ☎ 0800 15 47 53.

Hostels in Paris that cater to disabled travellers include the Foyer International d'Accueil de Paris Jean Monnet and the Centre International de Séjour de Paris Kellermann (see Hostels & Foyers in the Paris section).

DANGERS & ANNOYANCES

The biggest crime problem for tourists in France is theft – especially of and from cars. Pickpockets are a problem, and women are a common target because of their handbags. Be especially careful at airports and on crowded public transport in cities.

France's laws regarding even small quantities of drugs are very strict, and the police have the right to search anyone at any time.

The rise in support for the extreme rightwing Front National in recent years reflects the growing racial intolerance in France. Especially in the south, entertainment places such as bars and discos are, for all intents and purposes, segregated.

Emergency national numbers include: ambulance ☎ 15, fire ☎ 18 and police ☎ 17.

BUSINESS HOURS

Most museums are closed on either Monday or Tuesday and on public holidays, though in summer some open daily. Most small businesses open 9 or 10 am to 6.30 or 7 pm daily except Sunday and perhaps Monday, with a break between noon and 2 pm or between 1 and 3 pm. In the south, midday closures are more like siestas and may continue until 3.30 or 4 pm.

Many food shops open daily except Sunday afternoon and Monday. Most restaurants open only for lunch (noon to 2 or 3 pm) and dinner (6.30 to about 10 or 11 pm); outside Paris, very few serve meals throughout the day. In August, lots of establishments simply close down for the annual month-long holiday.

Banque de France branches open Monday to Friday, but will change money and travellers cheques only in the morning (usually 8.45 am to 12.15 pm). Opening hours of other banks vary.

PUBLIC HOLIDAYS & SPECIAL EVENTS

National *jours fériés* (public holidays) in France include New Year's Day, Easter Sunday and Monday, 1 May (May Day), 8 May (1945 Victory Day), Ascension Thursday, Pentecost/Whit Sunday and Whit Monday, 14 July (Bastille Day), 15 August (Assumption Day), 1 November (All Saints' Day), 11 November (1918 Armistice Day) and Christmas Day.

Some of the biggest and best events in France include: the Festival d'Avignon (early July to early August), with some 300 daily music, dance and drama events; Bastille Day celebrations, spread over 13 and 14 July; Francofolies, a six-day dance and music festival held in mid-July in La Rochelle, with performers from all over the French-speaking world; the Festival Interceltique, a 10-day Celtic festival in early August held in the Breton town of Lorient; Lyon's Biennale de la Danse/d'Art Contemporain, a month-long festival (from mid-September) that's held in even-numbered years (in odd-numbered years the city holds a festival of contemporary art); and the Carnaval de Nice, held in Nice every spring around Mardi Gras (Shrove Tuesday).

ACTIVITIES
Skiing

The French Alps have some of the finest (and priciest) skiing in Europe, but there are cheaper, low-altitude ski stations in the Pyrenees; www.skifrance.fr provides information in English about ski resorts, services, conditions and more.

FRANCE

Surfing

The best surfing in France (and some of the best in all of Europe) is on the Atlantic coast around Biarritz.

Hiking

France has thousands of kilometres of hiking trails in every region of the country. These include *sentiers de grande randonnée*, long-distance hiking paths whose alphanumeric names begin with the letters GR and are sometimes hundreds of kilometres long (as in Corsica). These paths are run by an organisation called Fédération Française de Randonnée Pédestre (FFRP; ☎ 01 44 89 93 93, fax 01 40 35 85 67), which also publishes guides to these routes.

Canoeing

The Fédération Française de Canoë-Kayak (☎ 01 45 11 08 50) at 87 quai de la Marne, 94340 Joinville-le-Pont, can supply information on canoeing and kayaking clubs around the country. The sports are very popular in the Dordogne (Périgord) area.

Cycling

The French take their cycling very seriously, and whole parts of the country almost grind to a halt during the annual Tour de France.

A *vélo tout-terrain* (VTT; mountain bike) is a fantastic tool for exploring the countryside. Some GR and GRP hiking trails are open to mountain bikes; a *piste cyclable* is a bicycle path.

Mountain bike enthusiasts who can read French should look for the books of *Les Guides VTT*, a series of cyclists' topoguides published by Didier & Richard. Lonely Planet's *Cycling in France* is an essential resource when touring. *France by Bike: 14 Tours Geared for Discovery* by Karen and Terry Whitehall ($12) is a worthy rival.

Some of the best areas for cycling are around the Alpine resorts of Annecy and Chambery (see the French Alps & Jura section for details). The Loire Valley and coastal regions such as Brittany, Normandy and the Atlantic Coast offer a wealth of easier options.

Details on places that rent bikes appear at the end of individual city or town listings under Getting Around.

COURSES

For details on language and cooking courses, see Courses in the Paris section. Information on studying in France is available from French consulates and French Government Tourist Offices abroad. In Paris, you might also get in touch with the Ministry of Tourism-sponsored International Cultural Organisation (ICO; ☎ 01 42 36 47 18, fax 01 40 26 34 45, metro Châtelet) at 55 rue de Rivoli (1er), BP 2701, 75027 Paris CEDEX.

WORK

Getting a *carte de séjour* (temporary residence permit), which in most cases lets you work in France, is almost automatic for EU citizens; contact the Préfecture de Police in Paris or, in the provinces, the *mairie* (town hall) or nearest prefecture. For anyone else it's almost impossible, though the government tolerates undocumented workers helping out with agricultural work.

Working as an au pair is very common in France, especially in Paris. Single young people – particularly women – receive board, lodging and a bit of money in exchange for taking care of the kids and doing light housework. Knowing some French may be a prerequisite. For information on au pair placement, contact a French consulate or the Paris tourist office.

ACCOMMODATION
Camping

France has thousands of seasonal and year-round camping grounds. Facilities and amenities, reflected in the number of stars the site has been awarded, determine the price. At the less fancy places, two people with a small tent pay 20FF to 55FF a night. Campers without a vehicle can usually get a spot, even late in the day, but not in July and August, when most are packed with families.

Refuges & Gîtes d'Étape

Refuges (mountain huts or shelters) are basic dorms operated by national park authorities, the Club Alpin Français and other private organisations. They are marked on hiking and climbing maps. Some open year-round.

In general, refuges have mattresses and blankets but not sheets. Charges average 50FF to 70FF per night (more in popular areas), and meals are sometimes available. It's a good idea to call ahead and make a reservation.

Gîtes d'étape, which are usually better equipped and more comfortable than refuges, are found in less remote areas, often in villages. They also cost around 50FF to 70FF per person.

Hostels

In the provinces, *Auberges de Jeunesse* (hostels) generally charge 48FF to 73FF for a bunk in a single-sex dorm. In Paris, expect to pay 100FF to 140FF a night, including breakfast. In the cities, especially Paris, you'll find *foyers*, student dorms used by travellers in summer. Most of France's hostels belong to one of three Paris-based organisations:

Fédération Unie des Auberges de Jeunesse (FUAJ; ☎ 01 44 89 87 27, fax 01 44 89 87 10, www.fuaj.org) 27 rue Pajol, 18e, 75018 Paris (metro La Chapelle)

Ligue Française pour les Auberges de la Jeunesse (LFAJ; ☎ 01 44 16 78 78, fax 01 44 16 78 80) 67 rue Vergniaud, 75013 Paris (metro Glacière)

Union des Centres de Rencontres Internationales de France (UCRIF; ☎ 01 40 26 57 64, fax 01 40 26 58 20, ✉ ucrif@aol.com) 27 rue de Turbigo, 2e, 75002 Paris (metro Étienne Marcel)

Only FUAJ is affiliated with the Hostelling International (HI) organisation.

Hotels

For two people sharing a room, budget hotels are often cheaper than hostels. Unless otherwise indicated, prices in this chapter refer to rooms in unrated or one-star hotels equipped with a washbasin. Most doubles, which generally cost the same or only marginally more than singles, have only one bed. Doubles with two beds usually cost a little more. A hall *douche* (shower) can be free or cost between 10FF and 25FF. If you'll be arriving after noon (after 10 am at peak times), it's wise to book ahead, though if you call on the day of your arrival, many will hold a room for you until a set hour. Local tourist offices also make reservations, usually for a small fee.

FOOD

A fully-fledged traditional French dinner – usually begun about 8.30 pm – has quite a few distinct courses: an apéritif or cocktail;

an *entrée* (first course); the *plat principal* (main course); *salade* (salad); *fromage* (cheese); *dessert*; *fruit* (fruit; pronounced fwee); *café* (coffee); and a *digestif* liqueur.

Restaurants usually specialise in a particular cuisine while brasseries – which look very much like cafes – serve quicker meals of more standard fare (eg, steak and chips/French fries or omelettes). Restaurants tend to open only for lunch (noon to 2 or 3 pm) and dinner (6.30 to about 10 or 11 pm); brasseries serve meals throughout the day.

Most restaurants offer at least one fixed-price, multicourse meal known in French as a *menu*. In general, *menus* cost much less than ordering each dish *a la carte* (separately).

Sitting in a cafe to read, write or talk with friends is an integral part of everyday life in France. A cafe located on a grand boulevard will charge considerably more than a place that fronts a side street. Once inside, progressively more expensive tariffs apply at the counter *(comptoir)*, in the cafe itself *(salle)* and outside on the *terrasse*. The price of drinks goes up at night, usually after 8 pm.

DRINKS
Nonalcoholic Drinks

Tap water in France is perfectly safe. Make sure you ask for *une carafe d'eau* (a jug of water) or *de l'eau du robinet* (tap water) or you may get costly *eau de source* (mineral water). A small cup of espresso is called *un café*, *un café noir* or *un express*; you can also ask for a *grand* (large) one. *Un café crème* is espresso with steamed cream. *Un café au lait* is espresso served in a large cup with lots of steamed milk. Decaffeinated coffee is *un café décaféiné* or simply *un déca*.

Other popular hot drinks include: *thé* (tea) – if you want milk you ask for '*un peu de lait frais*'; *tisane* (herbal tea); and *chocolat chaud* (hot chocolate).

Alcoholic Drinks

The French almost always take their meals with wine – *rouge* (red), *blanc* (white) or *rosé*. The least expensive wines cost less per litre than soft drinks. The cheapest wines are known as *vins ordinaires* or *vins de table* (table wines).

Alcoholic drinks other than wine include apéritifs, such as *kir* (dry white wine sweetened with *cassis* – blackcurrant liqueur), *kir royale* (champagne with cassis), and *pastis* (anise-flavoured alcohol drunk with ice and water); and *digestifs* such as brandy or Calvados (apple brandy). A *demi* of beer (about 250ml) is cheaper *à la pression* (on draught) than from a bottle.

Getting There & Away

AIR

Air France and scores of other airlines link Paris with every part of the globe. Other French cities with international air links (mainly to places within Europe) include Bordeaux, Lyon, Marseille, Nice, Strasbourg and Toulouse. For information on Paris' two international airports, Orly and Roissy-Charles de Gaulle, see Getting There & Away in the Paris section.

Flights between London and Paris are sometimes available for as little as UK£50 return; with the larger companies expect to pay at least UK£88. One-way discount fares to Paris start at L229,000 from Rome, 55,000 dr from Athens, I£55 from Dublin, 1200FF from Istanbul, and 16,000 ptas from Madrid. Student travel agencies can supply details.

In France, inexpensive flights offered by charter clearing houses can be booked through many regular travel agents – look in agency windows and pamphlets advertising Go Voyages (☎ 01 53 40 44 29) or Look Voyages (☎ 01 55 49 49 60 or ☎ 0803 313 613). Web sites: www.govoyages.com and www.look-voyages.fr. Reliable travel agency chains include the French student travel company OTU (☎ 01 40 29 12 12) and Nouvelles Frontières (☎ 0803 33 33 33). Web sites: www.otu.fr and www.newfrontiers.com.

LAND
Britain
The highly civilised Eurostar (☎ 0990-186 186 in the UK; ☎ 0836 35 35 39 in France) links London's Waterloo Station with Paris' Gare du Nord via the Channel Tunnel, which passes through a layer of impermeable chalk marl 25m to 45m below the floor of the English Channel. The journey takes about three hours (including 20 minutes in the tunnel), not including the one-hour time change. Tickets for people aged 25 and under cost UK£45/75 one-way/return; return fares booked 14/seven days ahead cost UK£69/80. Student travel agencies often have youth fares not available direct from Eurostar. Web site: www.eurostar.com.

Eurotunnel shuttle trains (☎ 0990-35 35 35 in the UK; ☎ 03 21 00 61 00 in France) whisk buses and cars (and their passengers) from near Folkstone to Coquelles (just west of Calais) in 35 minutes. The regular one-way fare for a car and its passengers ranges from UK£109.50 (February and March) to UK£174.50 (July and August). For promotional fares you must book at least one day ahead. Web site: www.eurotunnel.com.

Elsewhere in Europe
Bus For details on Eurolines coach services (☎ 0836 69 52 52 in France) linking France with other European countries, see Getting There & Away in the Paris section. Web site: www.eurolines.fr.

Train Paris, France's main rail hub, is linked with every part of Europe. Depending on where you're coming from, you sometimes have to change train stations in Paris to reach the provinces. For details on Paris' six train stations, see Getting There & Away in the Paris section.

BIJ (Billets International de Jeunesse, ie, International Youth Tickets) tickets, available to people aged 25 or under, save you at least 20% on international 2nd class rail travel (one way or return); on some routes discounts – not available to Italy – are limited to night trains. BIJ tickets are not sold at train-station ticket windows – you have to go to an office of Voyages Wasteels or one of the student travel agencies. There's almost always at least one BIJ-issuer in the vicinity of major train stations.

On the super-fast *Thalys* trains that link Paris with Brussels, Amsterdam and Cologne, people aged 12 to 25 get significant discounts.

SEA
Ferry tickets are available from almost all travel agents.

Britain & the Channel Islands

Hoverspeed (☎ 0870-524 0 241 in the UK; ☎ 0820 00 35 55 in France) runs giant catamarans (SeaCats) from Folkestone to Boulogne (55 minutes). Foot passengers are charged UK£24 one-way (or return if you come back within five days). Depending on the season, a car with up to nine passengers is charged UK£109 to UK£175 one-way. Web site: www.hoverspeed.co.uk.

The Dover-Calais crossing is also handled by car ferries (one to 1½ hours, 44 a day) run by SeaFrance (☎ 0870-571 1711 in the UK; ☎ 0804 04 40 45 in France) and P&O Stena (☎ 0870-598 0980 in the UK; ☎ 0802 010 020 in France). Pedestrians pay UK£15/24 with SeaFrance/P&O Stena; cars are charged UK£122.50 to UK£170 one-way. Web sites: www.seafrance.com and www.posl.com.

If you're travelling to Normandy, the Newhaven-Dieppe route is handled by Hoverspeed's SeaCats (2¼ hours, one to three a day). Poole is linked to Cherbourg by Brittany Ferries (☎ 0870-536 0360 in the UK; ☎ 02 98 29 28 00 in France), which has one or two 4¼-hour crossings a day; the company also has ferries from Portsmouth to Caen (Ouistreham). On the Portsmouth-Cherbourg route, P&O Portsmouth (☎ 0870-598 0555 in the UK; ☎ 0803 013 013 in France) has three car ferries a day and, from mid-March to mid-October, two faster catamarans a day; the company also links Portsmouth with Le Havre. Web sites: www.brittany-ferries.com and www.poef.com.

If you're going to Brittany, Brittany Ferries links Plymouth with Roscoff (six hours, one to three a day) from mid-March to mid-November; the company also has services from Portsmouth to Saint Malo (8¾ hours). For information on ferries from Saint Malo to Weymouth, Poole, Portsmouth and the Channel Islands, see Getting There & Away in the Saint Malo (Brittany) section.

Ireland

Irish Ferries (☎ 01-638 3333 in Ireland; ☎ 02 33 23 44 44 in Cherbourg) has overnight runs from Rosslare to either Cherbourg (18 hours) or Roscoff (16 hours) every other day (three times a week from mid-September to October, with a possible break in service from November to February). Pedestrians pay I£40 to I£80 (I£32 to I£66 for students and seniors). Eurailpass holders are charged 50% of the adult pedestrian fare. Visit the Web site at www.irish-ferries.com.

Italy

For information on ferry services between Corsica and Italy, see Getting There & Away in the Corsica section.

North Africa

France's SNCM (☎ 0836 67 21 00) and the Compagnie Tunisienne de Navigation (CTN; ☎ 01-341 777 in Tunis) link Marseille with Tunis (about 24 hours; three or four a week). The standard adult fare is 900/1620FF one-way/return. Visit the Web site at www.sncm.fr.

Sète, 29km south-west of Montpellier, is linked with the Moroccan port of Tangier (Tanger; 36 hours, five to seven a month) by the Compagnie Marocaine de Navigation (☎ 04 99 57 21 21 in Sète; ☎ 09-94 23 50 in Tangier). The cheapest one-way berth costs 970FF. Discounts are available if you're under 26 or in a group of four or more.

Getting Around

AIR

France's long-protected domestic airline industry is being opened up to competition, though Air France still handles the majority of domestic flights. Web site: www.airfrance.fr.

Full-fare flying within France is extremely expensive, but very significant discounts are available to people aged 12 to 24, couples, families and seniors. The most heavily discounted flights may be cheaper than long-distance rail travel. Details on the complicated fare structures are available from travel agents.

BUS

Because the French train network is state-owned and the government prefers to operate a monopoly, the country has only very limited intercity bus service. However, buses (some run by the SNCF) are widely used for short distances, especially in rural areas with relatively few train lines (eg, Brittany and Normandy).

FRANCE

TRAIN

Eurail and Inter-Rail passes are valid in France.

France's excellent rail network, operated by the Société Nationale des Chemins de Fer Français (SNCF), reaches almost every part of the country. The most important train lines fan out from Paris like the spokes of a wheel. The SNCF's nationwide telephone number for inquiries and reservations (☎ 0836 35 35 39 in English) costs 2.23FF a minute. Web site: www.sncf.com.

The pride and joy of the SNCF is the high-speed TGV ('teh-zheh-veh'). There are now three TGV lines that go under a variety of names: the TGV Sud-Est and TGV Midi-Mediterranée link Paris' Gare de Lyon with the south-east, including Dijon, Lyon, the Alps, Avignon, Marseille, Nice and Montpellier; the TGV Atlantique Sud-Ouest and TGV Atlantique Ouest link Paris' Gare Montparnasse with western and south-western France, including Brittany, Tours, La Rochelle, Bordeaux, Biarritz and Toulouse; and the TGV Nord links Paris' Gare du Nord with Arras, Lille and Calais.

Reservation fees are optional unless you're travelling by TGV or want a couchette or special reclining seat. On popular trains (eg, on holiday weekends) you may have to reserve ahead to get a seat. Eurail-pass holders must pay all applicable reservation fees.

Before boarding the train, you must validate your ticket (and your reservation card, if it's separate) by time-stamping it in one of the *composteurs*, the bright orange posts that are located somewhere between the ticket windows and the tracks. Eurail and some other rail passes *must* be validated at a train station ticket window to initiate the period of validity.

Discounts
Passes for Nonresidents of Europe
The France Railpass allows unlimited rail travel within France for three to nine days over the course of a month. In 2nd class, the three-day version costs US$180 (US$145 each for two people travelling together); each additional day of travel costs US$30. The France Youthpass, available if you're 25 and under, costs US$164 for four days of travel over two months; additional days (up to a maximum of 10) cost US$20. In North

America, Rail Europe (☎ 800-456 7245) has details. Web site: www.raileurope.com.

Passes for Residents of Europe The Euro Domino France flexipass gives European residents who don't live in France three to eight days of midnight-to-midnight travel over a period of one month. The youth version (for people 25 and under) costs €120 three days and €24 each additional day; the adult version costs €150 three days and €30 each additional day.

Other Discounts Discounts of 25% on one-way or return travel within France are available at all train station ticket windows to: people aged 12 to 25 (the Découverte 12/25 fare); one to four adults travelling with a child aged four to 11 (the Découverte Enfant Plus fare); people over 60 (the Découverte Senior fare); and – for return travel only – any two people who are travelling together (the Découverte À Deux fare).

No matter what age you are, the Découverte Séjour excursion fare gives you a 25% reduction for return travel within France if you meet two conditions: the total length of your trip is at least 200km; and you'll be spending a Saturday night at your destination. The Découverte J30, which must be purchased 30 to 60 days before the date of travel, offers savings of 45% to 55%. The Découverte J8, which you must buy at least eight days ahead, gets you 20% to 30% off.

CAR & MOTORCYCLE
Travelling by car or motorcycle is expensive; petrol is costly and tolls can reach hundreds of francs a day if you're going cross-country in a hurry. Three or four people travelling together, however, may find that renting a car is cheaper than taking the train. In the centres of almost all French cities, parking is metered.

Unless otherwise posted, speed limits are 130km/h (110km/h in the rain) on *autoroutes* (dual carriageways/divided highways whose names begin with A); 110km/h (100km/h in the rain) on *routes nationales* (highways whose names begin with N) that have a divider down the middle; and 90km/h (80km/h if it's raining) on nondivided routes nationales and rural highways. When you pass a sign with a place name, you have entered the boundaries of a town or village; the speed limit automatically drops to 50km/h and stays there until you pass an identical sign with a red bar across it.

The maximum permissible blood-alcohol level in France is 0.05%.

Petrol *sans plomb* (unleaded) costs around 7FF a litre, give or take 10%. *Gasoil* or *gazole* (diesel) is about 5FF to 6FF a litre. Fuel is most expensive at the autoroute rest stops, and tends to be cheapest at the big supermarkets on the outskirts of towns.

If you don't live in the EU and need a car in France (or Europe) for 17 days (or a bit more) to six months, it's *much* cheaper to 'purchase' one from the manufacturer and then 'sell' it back than it is to rent one. The purchase-repurchase *(achat-rachat)* paperwork is not your responsibility. Both Renault's Eurodrive (☎ 1-800 221 1052 in the USA) and Peugeot's Vacation Plan/Sodexa (☎ 1-800-572 9655 or ☎ 1-800-223 1516 in the USA) offer great deals that – incredibly – include insurance with no deductible (excess). Web sites: www.eurodrive.renault.com and www.sodexa.com.

HITCHING

Hitching in France can be difficult, and getting out of big cities like Paris, Lyon and Marseille or travelling around the Côte d'Azur by thumb is well nigh impossible. Remote rural areas are your best bet, but few cars are likely to be going farther than the next large town. Women should not hitch alone.

It's an excellent idea to hold up a sign with your destination followed by the letters *s.v.p.* (for *s'il vous plaît* – 'please'). Some people have reported good luck hitching with truck drivers from truck stops. It's illegal to hitch on autoroutes but you can stand near the entrance ramps.

Organisations around France match people looking for rides with drivers going to the same destination. The best known is Allostop Provoya (☎ 01 53 20 42 42 or, from outside Paris; ☎ 01 53 20 42 43, ☻ allostop@ecritel.fr), based in Paris at 8 rue Rochambeau (9e; metro Cadet). If you're not a member (240FF for up to eight journeys over two years), there's a per-trip fee of between 30FF (for distances under 200km) and 70FF (for distances over 500km). Drivers charge 0.22FF per kilometre for expenses. Web site: www.ecritel.fr/allostop.

Paris

pop 2.2 million, metropolitan area 9.4 million

Paris has almost exhausted the superlatives that can reasonably be applied to a city. Notre Dame and the Eiffel Tower – at sunrise, at sunset, at night – have been described ad nauseam, as have the Seine and the subtle (and not-so-subtle) differences between the Left and Right banks. But what writers have been unable to capture is the grandness and even the magic of strolling along the city's broad, 19th-century avenues leading from impressive public buildings and exceptional museums to parks, gardens and esplanades. Paris is enchanting at any time, in every season.

ORIENTATION

In central Paris (which the French call Intra-Muros – 'within the walls'), the Rive Droite (Right Bank) is north of the Seine, while the Rive Gauche (Left Bank) is south of the river. For administrative purposes, Paris is divided into 20 *arrondissements* (districts) that spiral out from the centre. Paris addresses always include the arrondissement number, listed here after the street address, using the usual French notation, ie, 1er stands for *premier* (1st), 19e for *dix-neuvième* (19th), etc. When an address includes the full five-digit postal code, the last two digits indicate the arrondissement, eg, 75014 for the 14e.

Maps

Lonely Planet's *Paris City Map* includes central Paris, the Paris Métro, Montmartre, a walking tour and an index of all streets and sights.

INFORMATION
Tourist Offices

Paris' main tourist office (☎ 0836 68 31 12, fax 01 49 52 53 00, metro Georges V) at 127 Ave des Champs-Élysées, 8e, opens 9 am to 8 pm every day of the year, except 1 May and 25 December, (11 am to 6 pm on Sunday in winter). This is the best source of information on what's going on in the city. For a small fee and a deposit, the office can find you accommodation in Paris for that night or (up to eight days in advance) in the provinces. The tourist office has branches (☎/fax the same) in the Gare de Lyon open 8 am to 8 pm Monday to Saturday and at the base of the Eiffel Tower open 11 am to 6 pm daily (May to September).

Money

All of Paris' six major train stations have exchange bureaus open seven days a week until at least 7 pm. Avoid the big exchange-bureau chains like Chequepoint and ExactChange. Exchange offices at both airports are open until 11 pm.

Banque de France The best rate in town is offered by Banque de France, whose headquarters (☎ 01 42 92 22 27, metro Palais Royal) is three blocks north of the Louvre at 31 rue Croix des Petits Champs, 1er. The exchange service is open 9.30 am to 12.30 pm weekdays. The branch (☎ 01 44 61 15 30, metro Bastille) at 3 bis place de la Bastille, 4e, opens for exchange 9 am to 12.15 pm weekdays.

American Express Paris' landmark American Express office (☎ 01 47 77 77 75, metro Auber or Opéra) at 11 rue Scribe, 9e, faces the west side of Opéra Garnier. Exchange services are available 9.30 am to 6 pm (7 pm June to September) weekdays, and 10 am to 5 pm on the weekend.

Notre Dame (4e & 5e) Le Change de Paris (☎ 01 43 54 76 55, metro St Michel) at 2 place St Michel, 6e, has good rates. Open 10 am to 7 pm daily. Another exchange bureau (☎ 01 46 34 70 46), one block south of place St Michel at 1 rue Hautefeuille, 6e, is open 9 am to 9 pm daily.

Champs-Élysées (8e) Thanks to fierce competition, the Champs-Élysées is an excellent place to change money. The bureau de change (☎ 01 42 25 38 14, metro Franklin D Roosevelt) at 25 Ave des Champs-Élysées is open 9 am to 8 pm daily.

Montmartre (18e) The bureau de change (☎ 01 42 52 67 19, metro Abbesses) at 6 rue Yvonne Le Tac opens 10 am to 6.30 pm weekdays (10.30 am to 6 pm Saturday and Sunday, June to September).

Post & Communications

Paris' main post office (☎ 01 40 28 20 00, metro Sentier or Les Halles) at 52 rue du Louvre, 1er, is open 24 hours, 365 days. Foreign exchange is available during regular post office hours – 8 am to 7 pm weekdays, til noon on Saturday.

Email & Internet Access

Café Orbital (☎ 01 43 25 76 77, ✉ info@orbital.fr, metro Luxembourg), 13 rue de Médi-

cis, 6e, opens 9 am (noon on Sunday) to 10 pm Monday to Saturday. The Web Bar (☎ 01 42 72 66 55, ✉ webbar@webbar.fr, metro Temple or République) at 32 rue de Picardie, 3e, opens 8.30 am (11 am at the weekend) to 2 am weekdays.

Travel Agencies

Nouvelles Frontières (☎ 0825 00 08 25, metro Luxembourg) has 14 outlets around the city including one at 66 blvd St Michel, 6e, open 9 am to 7 pm Monday to Saturday. Voyageurs du Monde (☎ 01 42 86 16 00, metro Pyramides or Quartre Septembre), 55 rue Ste Anne, 2e, is a huge agency open 9.30 am to 7 pm Monday to Saturday.

Bookshops

The famous Shakespeare & Company (☎ 01 43 26 96 50, metro St Michel) English-language bookshop is at 37 rue de la Bûcherie, 5e, across the Seine from Notre Dame Cathedral.

WH Smith (☎ 01 44 77 88 99, metro Concorde) at 248 rue de Rivoli is the largest English-language bookshop in the city. At 29 rue de la Parcheminerie, 5e, the mellow, Canadian-run Abbey Bookshop (☎ 01 46 33 16 24, metro Cluny-La Sorbonne) has an eclectic selection of new and used fiction titles. Les Mots à la Bouche (☎ 01 42 78 88 30, metro Hôtel de Ville) at 6 rue Ste Croix de la Bretonnerie, 4e, is Paris' premier gay bookshop.

Cultural & Religious Centres

The British Council (☎ 01 49 55 73 00, metro Invalides), 9-11 rue de Constantine, 7e, has libraries and runs language courses. The American Church (☎ 01 47 05 07 99, metro Invalides) at 65 quai d'Orsay, 7e, is a place of worship and something of a community centre for English speakers; its announcement board is an excellent source of information regarding accommodation and employment.

Laundry

The laundrettes (laveries) mentioned here open daily and are near many of the places to stay listed later. Laverie Libre Service (metro Louvre Rivoli), 7 rue Jean-Jacques Rousseau, is near the BVJ hostels, or another branch at 25 rue des Rosiers (metro St Paul), in the Marais. There's a laundrette four blocks south-west of the Panthéon at 216 rue St

FRANCE

Jacques (metro Luxembourg). Lavomatique is at 63 rue Monge (metro Monge). Near Gare de l'Est is the Lav' Club (metro Gare de l'Est) at 55 blvd de Magenta, or try another Laverie Libre Service branch (metro Blanche) at 4 rue Burq, Montmartre.

Lost Property

Paris' Bureau des Objets Trouvés (Lost and Found Office; ☎ 01 55 76 20 20, metro Convention) is at 36 rue des Morillons, 15e. Since telephone inquiries are impossible, the only way to find out if a lost item has been located is to go there and fill in the forms. The office is open 8.30 am to 5 pm Monday, Wednesday and Friday, and to 8 pm Tuesday and Thursday. During July and August it closes at 3.45 pm. For items lost in the metro call ☎ 01 40 30 52 00.

Medical & Emergency Services

An easy *Assistance Publique* (public health service) to find is the Hôtel Dieu hospital (☎ 01 42 34 81 31, metro Cité), on the northern side of place du Parvis Notre Dame, 4e. A 24-hour emergency service (service des urgences) is provided.

Dangers & Annoyances

For its size, Paris is a safe city but you should always use common sense; for instance, avoid the large Bois de Boulogne and Bois de Vincennes parks after nightfall. And some stations are best avoided late at night, especially if you are on your own. These include Châtelet and its seemingly endless tunnels, Château Rouge in Montmartre, Gare du Nord, Strasbourg-St Denis, Montparnasse-Bienvenüe and Réaumur-Sébastopol.

THINGS TO SEE

The Carte Musées et Monuments museum pass gets you into some 75 museums and monuments without having to queue for a ticket. The card costs 80/160/240FF for one/three/five consecutive days and is on sale at the museums and monuments it covers, at some metro ticket windows and at the tourist office.

Left Bank

Île de la Cité (1er & 4e) Paris was founded sometime during the 3rd century BC when members of a tribe known as the Parisii set up a few huts on Île de la Cité. By the Middle Ages the city had grown to encompass both banks of the Seine, though Île de la Cité remained the centre of royal and ecclesiastical power.

Notre Dame (4e) Paris' cathedral (☎ 01 42 34 56 10, metro Cité or St Michel) is one of the most magnificent achievements of Gothic architecture. Begun in 1163 and completed around 1345, features include the three spectacular rose windows. One of the best views of Notre Dame's ornate flying buttresses can be had from the lovely little park behind the cathedral. The haunting **Mémorial des Martyrs de la Déportation**, in memory of the more than 200,000 people deported by the Nazis and French fascists during WWII, is close by.

Notre Dame is open 8 am to 6.45 pm daily. Entry is free, as are **guided tours** in English at noon on Wednesday and Thursday and at 2.30 pm on Saturday (daily in August). Concerts held here don't keep to a schedule but are advertised on posters around town. The **North Tower**, from which you can view many of the cathedral's most fierce-looking gargoyles, can be climbed via long, spiral steps (35/23FF).

Ste Chapelle (1er) The gem-like upper chapel of Ste Chapelle (☎ 01 53 73 78 51, metro Cité), illuminated by a veritable curtain of 13th-century stained glass, is inside the **Palais de Justice** (Law Courts) at 4 blvd du Palais, 1er. Consecrated in 1248, Ste Chapelle was built in three years to house a crown of thorns (supposedly worn by the crucified Christ) and other relics purchased by King Louis IX (later St Louis) earlier in the 13th century. Open daily, admission costs 35FF (23FF for those aged 12 to 25). A ticket valid for both Ste Chapelle and the Conciergerie costs 50/25FF.

Conciergerie (1er) The Conciergerie (☎ 01 53 73 78 50, metro Cité) was a luxurious royal palace when it was built in the 14th century. During the Reign of Terror (1793-94), it was used to incarcerate 'enemies' of the Revolution before they were brought before the tribunal, which met next door in what is now the

FRANCE

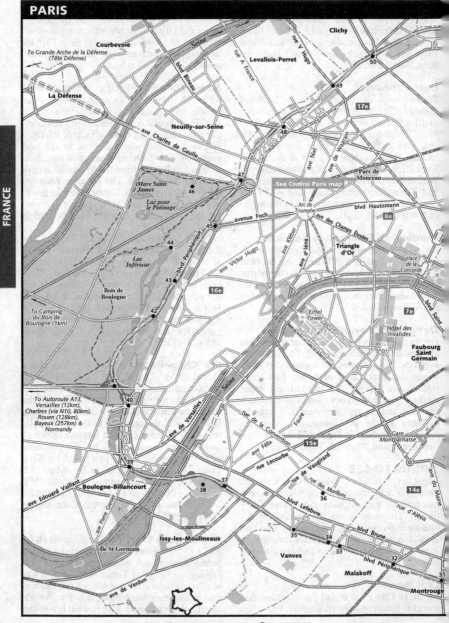

PARIS

To Grande Arche de la Défense
(Tête Défense)

Courbevoie

La Défense

Seine

Clichy

rue V Hugo

50

Levallois-Perret

rue A France

blvd Bineau

49

Neuilly-sur-Seine

ave Charles de Gaulle

48

ave Niel

ave de Wagram

17e

Parc de
Monceau

47

Mare Saint
James

46

Lac pour
le Patinage

45

avenue Foch

See Central Paris map

Arc de
Triomphe

ave des Champs Élysées

blvd Haussmann

8e

44

Lac
Inférieur

blvd Périphérique

ave Victor Hugo

ave Kléber

ave d'Iéna

Triangle
d'Or

place
de la
Concorde

43

Bois de
Boulogne

16e

Eiffel
Tower

7e

blvd Saint

42

To Camping
du Bois de
Boulogne (1km)

Hôtel des
Invalides

Faubourg
Saint
Germain

41

Seine

40

To Autoroute A13,
Versailles (12km),
Chartres (via N10, 80km),
Rouen (128km) &
Bayeux (257km) &
Normandy

ave de Versailles

rue de la Convention

Faure

Gare
Montparnasse

15e

ave Félix

rue Lecorbe

rue de Vaugirard

39

ave Edouard Vaillant

Boulogne-Billancourt

ave Pierre Grenier

37

38

rue des Morillons

36

blvd Lefebvre

rue d'Alésia

14e

ave du Maine

Issy-les-Moulineaux

Île St Germain

35

34

33

blvd Brune

blvd Périphérique

32

31

ave de Verdun

Vanves

Malakoff

Montrouge

euro currency converter €1 = 6.55FF

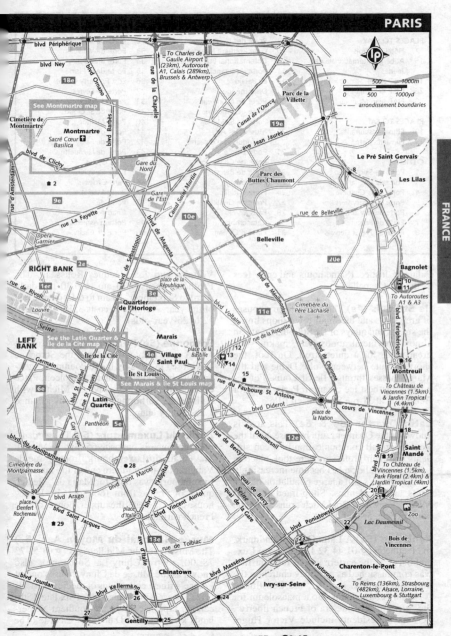

PARIS

	PLACES TO STAY				
2	Hôtel des Trois	9	Porte des Lilas	32	Porte de Châtillon
15	Auberge Internationale des	10	Gare Routière Internationale	33	Porte de Vanves
	Jeunes		(International Bus Terminal)	34	Porte Brancion
19	CISP Ravel	11	Porte de Bagnolet	35	Porte de la Plaine
26	CISP Kellermann	13	Le Balajo	36	Lost Property Office
29	FIAP Jean Monnet		Discothèque	37	Porte de Sèvres
		16	Porte de Montreuil	38	Paris Heliport
	PLACES TO EAT	17	Porte de Vincennes	39	Porte de St Cloud
12	Ethnic Restaurants	18	Porte de St Mandé	40	Porte Molitor
14	Havanita Café	20	Musée des Arts	41	Porte d'Auteuil
			d'Afrique et d'Océanie	42	Porte de Passy
	OTHER	21	Porte Dorée	43	Porte de la Muette
1	Porte de Saint Ouen	22	Porte de Charenton	44	Paris Cycles
3	Porte de Clignancourt	23	Porte de Bercy	45	Porte Dauphine
4	Porte de la Chapelle	24	Porte d'Ivry	46	Paris Cycles
5	Porte d'Aubervilliers	25	Porte d'Italie	47	Porte Maillot
6	Porte de la Villette	27	Porte de Gentilly	48	Porte de
7	Porte de Pantin	28	Paris á Vélo		Champerret
8	Porte du Pré St Gervais	30	Catacombes	49	Porte d'Asnières
		31	Porte d'Orléans	50	Porte de Clichy

Palais de Justice. (Same hours and entry fees as the Ste Chapelle.)

Île St Louis (4e) The 17th-century houses of grey stone and the small-town shops lining the streets and quays of Île St Louis create an almost provincial atmosphere, making it a great place for a quiet stroll. On foot, the shortest route between Notre Dame and the Marais passes through Île St Louis. For reputedly the best ice cream in Paris, head for Berthillon at 31 rue St Louis en l'Île.

Latin Quarter (5e & 6e) This area is known as the Quartier Latin because, until the Revolution, all communication between students and their professors here took place in Latin. Whilst the 5e has become increasingly touristy, there's still a large population of students and academics. Shop-lined **Blvd St Michel**, known as 'Boul Mich', runs along the border of the 5e and the 6e.

Panthéon (5e) A Latin Quarter landmark, the Panthéon (☎ 01 44 32 18 00, metro Luxembourg), at the eastern end of rue Soufflot, was commissioned as an abbey church in the mid-18th century. In 1791, the Constituent Assembly converted it into a mausoleum for the 'great men of the era of French liberty'. Permanent residents include Victor Hugo,

Voltaire and Jean-Jacques Rousseau. The Panthéon opens 9.30 am to 6.30 pm daily April to September, 10 am to 6.15 pm the rest of the year. Admission costs 35FF (23FF for 12 to 25-year-olds).

Sorbonne (5e) Founded in 1253 as a college for 16 poor theology students, the Sorbonne was closed in 1792 by the Revolutionary government but reopened under Napoleon. **Place de la Sorbonne** links blvd St Michel with **Église de la Sorbonne**, the university's domed 17th-century church.

Jardin du Luxembourg (6e) The gardens' main entrance is opposite 65 blvd St Michel. The **Palais du Luxembourg**, fronting rue de Vaugirard at the northern end of the Jardin du Luxembourg, was built for Maria de' Medici, queen of France from 1600 to 1610. It now houses the Sénat, the upper house of the French parliament.

Musée National du Moyen Age (5e) The Museum of the Middle Ages (☎ 01 53 73 78 00, metro Cluny-La Sorbonne), also known as the Musée de Cluny, houses one of France's finest collections of medieval art. Its prized possession is a series of six late-15th-century tapestries from the southern Netherlands known as La Dame à la Licorne (The

Lady and the Unicorn). The museum is open 9.15 am to 5.45 pm daily, except Tuesday. Admission costs 38FF (28FF for those aged 18 to 25, and for everyone on Sunday).

Mosquée de Paris (5e) Paris' ornate central mosque (☎ 01 45 35 97 33, metro Monge) at place du Puits de l'Ermite was built between 1922 and 1926. There are tours 9 am to noon and 2 to 6 pm daily, except Friday. The mosque complex includes a small souk (marketplace), a *salon de thé* (tearoom), an excellent couscous restaurant and a **hammam** (Turkish bath; ☎ 01 43 31 18 14); enter at 39 rue Geoffroy St Hilaire. The hammam (85FF) opens to men from 2 to 9 pm on Tuesday and 10 am to 9 pm on Sunday only; on other days (10 am to 9 pm) it is reserved for women.

The mosque is opposite the **Jardin des Plantes** (Botanical Gardens), which includes a small **zoo** as well as the recently renovated **Musée d'Histoire Naturelle** (Museum of Natural History; ☎ 01 40 79 30 00, metro Monge), open weekdays, except Tuesday, 10 am to 6 pm (until 10 pm on Thursday). Admission 40/30FF.

Catacombes (14e) In 1785, the bones of millions of Parisians were exhumed from overflowing cemeteries and moved to the tunnels of three disused quarries. One such ossuary is the Catacombes (☎ 01 43 22 47 63, metro Denfert Rochereau). During WWII, these tunnels were used by the Résistance as headquarters. The route through the Catacombes begins from the small green building at 1 place Denfert Rochereau. The site is open 2 to 4 pm Tuesday to Friday, and 9 to 11 am and 2 to 4 pm on weekends. Tickets cost 33FF (22FF for students and seniors; 17FF for children). Take a flashlight (torch).

Musée d'Orsay (7e) The Musée d'Orsay (☎ 01 40 49 48 48, metro Musée d'Orsay), 1 rue de Bellechasse, exhibits works of art produced between 1848 and 1914. Spectacularly housed in a 1900 train station, it opens 10 am (9 am on Sunday and throughout summer) to 6 pm (to 9.45 pm on Thursday) Tuesday to Sunday from late Sepetmber to late June. Admission costs 40FF (30FF for those aged 18 to 25 and over 60, and everyone on Sunday; free for under 18s); tickets are valid all day.

Musée Rodin (7e) The Musée Auguste Rodin (☎ 01 44 18 61 10, metro Varenne), 77 rue Varenne, is one of the most pleasant museums in Paris. It is open 9.30 am to 5.45 pm daily from April to September (to 4.45 pm the rest of the year). Entrance costs 28FF (18FF for those aged 18 to 25 and over 60, and everyone on Sunday; free for under 18s). Visiting just the garden (5 pm close) costs 5FF.

Invalides (7e) The Hôtel des Invalides (metro Invalides for the Esplanade, metro Varenne or Latour Maubourg for the main building) was built in the 1670s by Louis XIV to provide housing for 4000 disabled veterans *(invalides)*. It also served as the headquarters of the military governor of Paris, and was used as an armoury. On 14 July 1789 the Paris mob forced its way into the building and took all 28,000 firearms before heading for the Bastille prison.

The **Église du Dôme**, built between 1677 and 1735, is considered one of the finest religious edifices erected under Louis XIV. In 1861 it received the remains of Napoleon, encased in six concentric coffins.

The buildings on either side of the **Cour d'Honneur** (Main Courtyard) house the **Musée de l'Armée** (☎ 01 44 42 37 72), a huge military museum, and the light and airy **Tombeau de Napoléon 1er** (Napoleon's Tomb), both open 10 am to 4.45 pm (5.45 pm in summer) daily. Admission is 38/28FF.

Tour Eiffel (7e) The Tour Eiffel (☎ 01 44 11 23 23, metro Champ de Mars-Tour Eiffel) faced massive opposition from Paris' artistic and literary elite when it was built for the 1889 Exposition Universelle (World's Fair), held to commemorate the Revolution. It was almost torn down in 1909 but was spared for practical reasons – it proved an ideal platform for newfangled transmitting antennae. The Eiffel Tower is 320m high, including the television antenna at the very tip.

Three levels are open to the public. The lift (west and north pillars) costs 22FF for the 1st platform (57m), 47FF for the 2nd (115m) and 62FF for the 3rd (276m). Children four to 12 pay 13/23/32FF respectively; there are no other discounts. The escalator in the south pillar to the 1st and 2nd platforms costs 18FF.

FRANCE

FRANCE

Open 9.30 am to 11 pm (9 am till midnight mid-June to August) daily.

Champ de Mars (7e) The Champ de Mars, a grassy park around the Eiffel Tower, was once a parade ground for the 18th-century **École Militaire** (France's military academy) at the south-eastern end of the lawns.

Right Bank
Jardins du Trocadéro (16e)
The Trocadéro gardens (metro Trocadéro), whose fountain and nearby sculpture park are grandly illuminated at night, are across the Pont d'Iéna from the Eiffel Tower. The colonnaded Palais de Chaillot, built in 1937, houses the anthropological and ethnographic Musée de l'Homme (Museum of Mankind; ☎ 01 44 05 72 72), open 9.45 am to 5.15 pm Wednesday to Monday (30/20FF); and the Musée de la Marine (Maritime Museum; ☎ 01 53 65 69 69), known for its beautiful model ships. The maritime museum opens 10 am to 5.45 pm Wednesday to Monday (38/28FF).

Musée Guimet (16e) The Guimet Museum (☎ 01 47 23 88 11, metro Iéna) at 6 place d'Iéna displays antiquities and art from throughout Asia. It opens 10.15 am to 1 pm and 2.30 to 6 pm Wednesday to Monday. Admission costs 16FF (12FF for 18 to 25-year-olds, students, and everyone on Sunday).

Louvre (1er) The Louvre Museum (☎ 01 40 20 53 17, or ☎ 01 40 20 51 51 for a recorded message, metro Palais Royal-Musée du Louvre), constructed around 1200 as a fortress and rebuilt in the mid-16th century as a royal palace, became a public museum in 1793. The collections on display have been assembled by French governments over the past five centuries and include works of art and artisanship from all over Europe as well as important collections of Assyrian, Egyptian, Etruscan, Greek, Coptic, Roman and Islamic art. The Louvre's most famous work is undoubtedly Leonardo da Vinci's *Mona Lisa*.

The Louvre is open 9 am to 6 pm (9.45 pm Monday and Wednesday) daily, except Tuesday. Ticket sales end 45 minutes before closing time. Admission to the permanent collections costs 45FF (26FF after 3 pm and all day Sunday); the first Sunday of every

month is free. There are no student/senior discounts, but under 18s get in free. Admission to temporary exhibits varies. Tickets are valid for the whole day, so you can leave and re-enter as you please. By advance purchasing your tickets at the *billeteries* (ticket office) at FNAC, or other department stores, for an extra 6FF, you can walk straight in without queuing at all.

For English-language guided tours (38/22FF) and audioguide tours (30FF), go to the mezzanine level beneath the glass pyramid.

Place Vendôme (1er) The 44m-high column in the middle of place Vendôme consists of a stone core wrapped in bronze from 1250 cannons captured by Napoleon at the Battle of Austerlitz (1805). The shops around the square are among Paris' most fashionable and expensive.

Musée de l'Orangerie (1er) This museum (☎ 01 42 97 48 16, metro Concorde), usually home to important impressionist works including a series of Monet's spectacular *Nymphéas* (Water Lilies), is being renovated and is due to reopen at the end of 2001.

Place de la Concorde (8e) This vast, cobbled square between the Jardin des Tuileries and the Champs-Élysées was laid out between 1755 and 1775. Louis XVI was guillotined here in 1793 – as were another 1343 people, including his wife Marie Antoinette, over the next two years. The 3300-year-old Egyptian obelisk in the middle of the square was given to France in 1829 by the ruler of Egypt, Mohammed Ali.

La Madeleine (8e) The church of St Mary Magdalene (metro Madeleine), built in the style of a Greek temple, was consecrated in 1842 after almost a century of design changes and construction delays.

Champs-Élysées (8e) The 2km-long Ave des Champs-Élysées links place de la Concorde with the Arc de Triomphe. Once popular with the aristocracy as a stage on which to parade their wealth, it has, in recent decades, been partly taken over by fast-food restaurants and overpriced cafes. The nicest bit is the park between place de la Concorde and Rond Point des Champs-Élysées.

Musée du Petit Palais (8e) The Petit Palais (☎ 01 42 65 12 73) will close in late 2000 for refurbishment.

West of the Petit Palais, the **Grand Palais** (☎ 01 44 13 17 17), 3 ave du Général du Eisenhower, built for the 1900 World Fair, is now used for temporary exhibitions. It is open 10 am to 8 pm (10 pm Wednesday) daily, except Tuesday. Admission varies.

Arc de Triomphe (8e) Paris' second most famous landmark, the Arc de Triomphe (☎ 01 55 37 73 77, metro Charles de Gaulle-Étoile) is 2.2km north-west of place de la Concorde in the middle of place Charles de Gaulle. Also called place de l'Étoile, this is the world's largest traffic roundabout and the meeting point of 12 avenues. Commissioned in 1806 by Napoleon to commemorate his imperial victories, it remained unfinished until the 1830s. An Unknown Soldier from WWI is buried under the arch, his fate and that of countless others like him commemorated by a memorial flame lit each evening at around 6.30 pm.

The platform atop the arch (lift up, steps down) is open 9.30 am to 11 pm daily from April to September, except on public holidays, and 10 am to 10.30 pm the rest of the year. It costs 40/25FF. The only sane way to get to the arch's base is via the underground passageways.

The **Voie Triomphale** (Triumphal Way) stretches 4.5km from the Arc de Triomphe along Ave de la Grande Armée to the sky-scraper district of **La Défense**, whose best known landmark, the **Grande Arche** (Grand Arch), is a hollow cube (112m to a side).

Centre Georges Pompidou (4e) Thanks in part to its outstanding temporary exhibitions, Centre Pompidou (☎ 01 44 78 12 33, metro Rambuteau or Châtelet-Les Halles) – also known as Centre Beaubourg – is by far the most frequented sight in Paris. **Place Igor Stravinsky**, south of the centre, and the large square to the west attract all kinds of street artists.

The **Musée National d'Art Moderne** (MNAM; National Museum of Modern Art)

on the 4th floor displays France's national collection of 20th-century art. It's open 11 am to 9 pm Wednesday to Monday and costs 30FF (20FF for 18 to 26-year-olds, students and seniors; free for under 18s). The **Bibliothèque Publique d'Information**, a huge, nonlending library, is on the 2nd floor.

Les Halles (1er) Paris' main wholesale food market, Les Halles, occupied this site from the 12th century until 1969, when it was moved out to the suburb of Rungis; a huge underground shopping mall (Forum des Halles) was built in its place. Just north of the grassy area on top of Les Halles is the mostly 16th-century **Église St Eustache**, noted for its wonderful pipe organ.

Hôtel de Ville (4e) Paris' city hall (☎ 01 42 76 40 40, metro Hôtel de Ville) at place de l'Hôtel de Ville was burned down during the Paris Commune of 1871 and rebuilt (1874-82) in the neo-Renaissance style. Enter at 29 rue de Rivoli; open 9.30 am to 6 pm Monday to Saturday.

Marais Area (4e) A marsh *(marais)* converted to agricultural use in the 13th century, this area was, during the 17th century – when the nobility erected luxurious but discreet mansions known as *hôtels particuliers* – the most fashionable part of the city. Eventually the Marais was taken over by ordinary Parisians and by the time renovation began in the 1960s, it had become a poor but lively Jewish neighbourhood. In the 1980s the area underwent serious gentrification and today it is the centre of Paris' gay life.

Place des Vosges (4e) Built in 1605 and originally known as place Royal, place des Vosges (metro Chemin Vert) is a square ensemble of 36 symmetrical houses. Duels were once fought in the elegant park in the middle. Today, the arcades around place des Vosges are occupied by upmarket art galleries, antique shops and salons de thé.

The nearby **Maison de Victor Hugo** is where the author lived from 1832 to 1848 (22/15FF; closed Monday).

Musée Picasso (3e) The Picasso Museum (☎ 01 42 71 25 21, metro St Paul or Chemin

FRANCE

CENTRAL PARIS

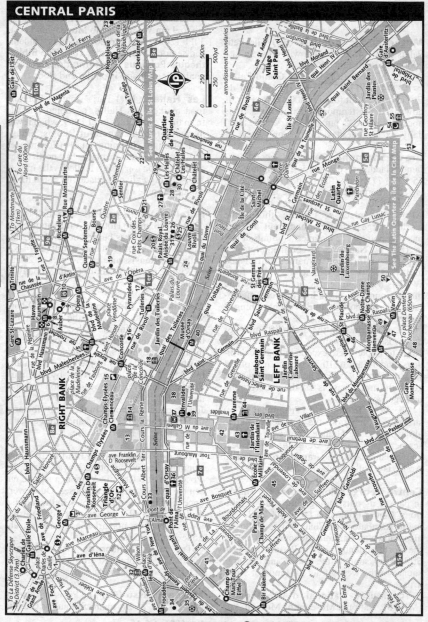

FRANCE

CENTRAL PARIS

PLACES TO STAY		5	La Madeleine Church	30	Roue Libre
23	Auberge de Jeunesse Jules Ferry	6	Au Printemps (Department Store)	32	Musée Guimet
26	Centre International BVJ Paris-Louvre & Laundrette	7	Galeries Lafayette (Department Store)	33	Bateaux Mouches (Boat Tours)
		8	Eurostar & Ferry Offices	34	Palais de Chaillot
PLACES TO EAT		9	American Express	35	Jardins du Trocadéro.
11	Chartier Restaurant	10	Opéra Garnier	36	American Church
17	Food Shops	12	Canadian Embassy	37	Aérogare des Invalides (Buses to Orly)
29	Joe Allen	13	Grand Palais	38	Palais Bourbon (National Assembly Building)
31	Le Petit Mâchon	14	Musée du Petit Palais		
47	Mustang Café	15	US Embassy	39	British Council
49	Le Caméléon Restaurant	16	WH Smith Bookshop	40	Musée d'Orsay
50	CROUS Restaurant Universitaire	18	Musée de l'Orangerie	41	Eiffel Tower
		19	Voyageurs du Monde	42	Hôtel des Invalides
51	CROUS Restaurant Universitaire Bullier	20	Banque de France	43	Église du Dôme
		21	Main Post Office	44	Musée Rodin
53	Founti Agadir	22	Rue Saint Denis Sex District	45	École Militaire
		24	Louvre Museum	46	FNAC Store & Ticket Outlet
OTHER		25	Change du Louvre (Currency Exchange)	48	Cimetière du Montparnasse
1	Arc de Triomphe			52	Institut du Monde Arabe
2	Main Tourist Office	27	Église Saint Eustache	54	Paris Mosque & Hammam
3	Post Office	28	Forum des Halles (Shopping Mall & Park)		
4	Bureau de Change			55	Museum of Natural History

Vert) is just north-east of the Marais at 5 rue de Thorigny. Paintings, sculptures, ceramics, engravings and drawings donated to the French government by the heirs of Pablo Picasso (1881-1973) to avoid huge inheritance taxes are on display, as is Picasso's personal art collection (Braque, Cézanne, Matisse, Rousseau, etc). The museum opens 9.30 am to 6 pm (8 pm on Thursday) Wednesday to Monday; October to March it closes at 5.30 pm. Admission costs 30/20FF (free for under 18s).

Bastille (4e, 11e & 12e) The Bastille is the most famous nonexistent monument in Paris; the notorious prison was demolished shortly after the mob stormed it on 14 July 1789. The site is known as place de la Bastille. The 52m-high **Colonne de Juillet** in the centre was erected in 1830. The new (and rather drab) **Opéra Bastille** (☎ 01 44 73 13 99 or ☎ 0836 69 78 68, metro Bastille) is at 2-6 place de la Bastille.

Opéra Garnier (9e) Paris' renowned opera house (see Opera & Classical Music under Entertainment for contact details) was designed in 1860 by Charles Garnier. The **ceiling** of the auditorium was painted by Marc

Chagall in 1964. The building also houses the **Musée de l'Opéra**, open 10 am to 5 pm daily. Entrance is 30/20FF.

Montmartre (18e) During the 19th century Montmartre was a vibrant centre of artistic and literary creativity. Today it's an area of mimes, buskers, tacky souvenir shops and commercial artists. The **Moulin Rouge** (☎ 01 53 09 82 82, metro Blanche) at 82 blvd de Clichy, founded in 1889, is known for its twice-nightly revues of near-naked girls.

Basilique du Sacré Cœur Sacré Cœur (☎ 01 53 41 89 00, metro Anvers) was built to fulfil a vow taken by Parisian Catholics after the disastrous Franco-Prussian War of 1870-71. It is open 7 am to 11 pm daily (to 6 pm October to March). Admission is 15FF, students 8FF. The funicular up the hill's southern slope costs one metro/bus ticket each way.

Place du Tertre Just west of **Église St Pierre**, place du Tertre is filled with cafes, restaurants, portrait artists and tourists – though the real attractions of the area are the quiet, twisting streets. Look for the **windmills** on rue Lepic and Paris' last **vineyard**,

FRANCE

on the corner of rue des Saules and rue St Vincent.

Pigalle (9e & 18e) Although the area along blvd de Clichy between the Pigalle and Blanche metro stops is lined with sex shops and striptease parlours, there are plenty of legitimate nightspots to choose from (see Entertainment).

Musée de l'Érotisme (Museum of Eroticism; ☎ 01 42 58 28 73, metro Blanche), 72 blvd de Clichy, tries to raise erotic art both antique and modern to a loftier plane – but we know why we visited. Open 10 am to 2 am daily (40FF, students 30FF).

Cimetière du Père Lachaise (20e) Père Lachaise Cemetery (☎ 01 43 70 70 33, metro Père Lachaise), final resting place of such notables as Chopin, Proust, Oscar Wilde and Édith Piaf, may be the most visited cemetery in the world. The best known tomb is that of 1960s rock star Jim Morrison, lead singer for The Doors, who died in 1971. The cemetery is free and open daily to at least 5.30 pm.

Bois de Vincennes (12e) Highlights of this 9.29-sq-km English-style park include the **Parc Floral** (Floral Garden; metro Château de Vincennes); the **Parc Zoologique de Paris** (Paris Zoo; ☎ 01 44 75 20 10, metro Porte Dorée); and the **Jardin Tropical** (Tropical Garden; RER stop Nugent-sur-Marne).

Château de Vincennes (12e) A *bona fide* royal chateau, the Château de Vincennes (☎ 01 48 08 31 20, metro Château de Vincennes) is at the northern edge of the Bois de Vincennes. You can walk around the grounds for free, but to see the Gothic **Chapelle Royale** and the 14th-century **donjon** (keep), you must take a tour (in French, with an information booklet in English). The chateau opens 10 am to 5 pm daily.

Musée des Arts d'Afrique et d'Océanie (12e) Specialising in art from Africa and the South Pacific, this museum (☎ 01 44 74 84 80, metro Porte Dorée) at 293 Ave Daumesnil opens 10 am to noon and 1.30 to 5.30 pm (6 pm on weekends) Wednesday to Monday. The admission fee is 40FF (reduced tariff 30FF, students 10FF).

Bois de Boulogne (16e) The 8.65-sq-km Bois de Boulogne is endowed with meandering trails, forests, cycling paths and *belle époque*-style cafes. Rowing boats can be rented at the **Lac Inférieur** (metro Ave Henri Martin).

Paris Cycles (☎ 01 47 47 76 50 for a recorded message or ☎ 01 47 47 22 37 to book) rents bicycles on ave du Mahatma Gandhi (metro Les Sablons) and at the northern end of the Lac Inférieur (metro Ave Foch). Rental costs 20/30FF for 30 minutes/one hour and 60/80FF for a half-day/day.

LANGUAGE COURSES

Alliance Française (☎ 01 45 44 38 28, metro St Placide) at 101 blvd Raspail, 6e, offers month-long French courses. Accord Language School (☎ 01 42 36 24 95, metro Les Halles) at 52 rue Montmartre, 1er, gets high marks from students.

ORGANISED TOURS

Bus

From April to late September, RATP's Balabus follows a 50-minute return route from Gare de Lyon to the Grande Arche in La Défense. Buses depart about every 20 minutes and cost one metro/bus ticket. L'Open Tour (☎ 01 43 46 52 06, fax 01 43 46 53 06) runs open-deck buses along three circuits year round, allowing you to jump on and off at more than 30 stops. Tickets cost 135/150FF for one/two days (less if you're holding a Carte Orange, Paris Visite or Batobus pass).

Bicycle

Both Roue Libre (☎ 01 53 46 43 77, fax 01 40 28 01 00, metro Les Halles), 95 bis rue Rambuteau, 1er, and Paris à Vélo C'est Sympa! (☎ 01 48 87 60 01, ✉ info@parisvelosympa.com, metro Bastille), 37 blvd Bourdon, 4e, offer bicycle tours on Saturday and Sunday (and during the week depending on demand). Paris à Vélo charges 185FF (160FF for under 26s) while Roue Libre's tours are 135FF and 85FF for children aged four to 12. Both include a guide, the bicycle and insurance. A 1½-hour Sunday morning Paris à Vélo tour costs 100/60FF.

Bullfrog Bike Tours (mobile/cellphone ☎ 06 09 98 08 60, ✉ bullfrogbikes@hotmail.com) head off from the Champ de Mars at 11 am and

3.30 pm from early May to late August (150FF). Night tours (170FF) leave at 8 pm.

Boat

Every 25 minutes, mid-April to early November, the Batobus river shuttle (☎ 01 44 11 33 99) docks at six places including Notre Dame and the Musée d'Orsay. A one/two day pass costs 60/80FF (35/40FF for children under 12). Bateaux Mouches (☎ 01 42 25 96 10 or for an English-language recording ☎ 01 40 76 99 99, metro Alma Marceau) makes a 1½-hour cruise for 40FF (20FF for under 14s) with commentary. Vedettes du Pont Neuf (☎ 01 46 33 98 38, metro Pont Neuf) operates one-hour boat circuits day and night for 50FF (25FF for under 12s).

PLACES TO STAY
Accommodation Services

Accueil des Jeunes en France (AJF; *☎ 01 42 77 87 80, metro Rambuteau*) is at 119 rue St Martin, 4e, just west of the Centre Pompidou (open 10 am to 5.45 pm daily except Sunday). It makes same-day reservations at hostels, hotels and private homes for a 10FF fee; you pay at the office and take a voucher to the establishment. Prices start at 120FF per person (excluding 10FF fee).

The main tourist office (see Information earlier) and its Gare de Lyon annexe can also make same day bookings. It also has information on *pensions de famille*, similar to B&Bs, and homestays.

Camping

At the far western edge of the Bois de Boulogne, *Camping du Bois de Boulogne* (*☎ 01 45 24 30 00, Allée du Bord de l'Eau, 16e*) is Paris' only camping ground. Two people with a tent pay from 67/105FF with/without a vehicle. The Porte Maillot metro stop is linked to the camping ground by RATP bus No 244 (6 am to 8.30 pm) and, April to October, by privately operated shuttle bus (10FF).

Hostels & Foyers

Many hostels allow a three-night maximum stay, especially in summer. Only official *auberges de jeunesse* (youth hostels) require guests to present Hostelling International (HI) cards or equivalent. Curfew – if enforced – tends to be 1 or 2 am. Few hostels accept reservations by telephone.

Louvre Area (1er) *Centre International BVJ Paris-Louvre* (*☎ 01 53 00 90 90, metro Louvre-Rivoli, 20 rue Jean-Jacques Rousseau*) has bunks in single-sex rooms for 130FF, including breakfast.

Marais (4e) The Maison Internationale de la Jeunesse et des Étudiants *(MIJE; ☎ 01 42 74 23 45, fax 01 40 27 81 64)* runs three hostels in attractively renovated 17th and 18th-century Marais residences. Beds start at 145/240FF dorm/single, including breakfast. *MIJE Maubisson (12 rue des Barres, metro Hôtel de Ville)* is in our opinion the best. *MIJE Fourcy (6 rue de Fourcy, metro St Paul)*, the largest hostel, and *MIJE Fauconnier (11 rue du Fauconnier, metro Pont Marie)*, two blocks south of MIJE Fourcy, are the other options.

Panthéon Area (5e) The clean and friendly *Y&H Hostel* (*☎ 01 45 35 09 53, fax 01 47 07 22 24, ✉ smile@youngandhappy.fr, 80 rue Mouffetard, metro Monge*) is popular with a younger crowd. A bed in a three or four-bed room costs 117FF (137FF in a double).

11e Arrondissement *Auberge de Jeunesse Jules Ferry* (*☎ 01 43 57 55 60, 8 blvd Jules Ferry, metro République*) has dorm beds for 115FF (120FF in a double; 19FF extra without an HI card), including breakfast. Internet access costs 5FF.

The clean and friendly *Auberge Internationale des Jeunes* (*☎ 01 47 00 62 00, fax 01 47 00 33 16, ✉ aijaijparis.com, 10 rue Trousseau, metro Ledru Rollin*) attracts a young crowd and gets full in summer. Beds cost 81FF from November to February, 91FF from March to October, including breakfast.

12e Arrondissement *Centre International de Séjour de Paris (CISP) Ravel* (*☎ 01 44 75 60 00, fax 01 43 44 45 30, ✉ 100616 .2215@compuserve.com, 4-6 Ave Maurice Ravel, metro Porte de Vincennes*) charges 126FF for a bed in a two to four-bed room, 156FF in a double and 206FF for a single, including breakfast.

FRANCE

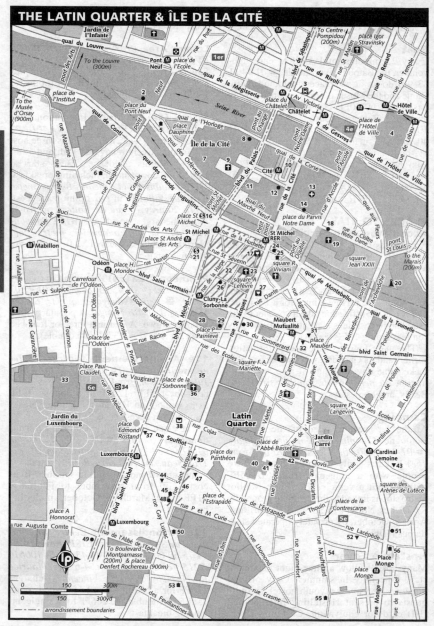

THE LATIN QUARTER & ÎLE DE LA CITÉ

PLACES TO STAY
- 5 Hôtel Henri IV
- 6 Hôtel de Nesle
- 25 Hôtel Esmeralda
- 45 Hôtel de Médicis
- 50 Hôtel Gay Lussac
- 53 Grand Hôtel du Progrès
- 55 Y & H Hostel
- 56 Hôtel Saint Christophe

PLACES TO EAT
- 15 Food Shops
- 22 Restaurants ('Bacteria Alley')
- 31 Food Shops
- 32 Fromagerie (Cheese Shop)
- 37 McDonald's
- 39 Perraudin
- 43 Le Petit Légume
- 44 Douce France Sandwich Bar
- 46 Food Shops
- 47 Tashi Delek
  Tibetan Restaurant
- 52 Ed l'Épicier Supermarket
- 54 Restaurants

OTHER
- 1 Samaritaine
  (Department Store)
- 2 Vedettes du Pont Neuf (Boat
  Tours)
- 3 Noctambus (All-Night Bus)
  Stops
- 4 Hôtel de Ville (City Hall)
- 7 Palais de Justice &
  Conciergerie
- 8 Conciergerie Entrance
- 9 Sainte Chapelle
- 10 Flower Market
- 11 Préfecture de Police
- 12 Préfecture Entrance
- 13 Hôtel Dieu (Hospital)
- 14 Hospital Entrance
- 16 Le Change de Paris
- 17 Caveau de la Huchette
  Jazz Club
- 18 Notre Dame Tower Entrance
- 19 Notre Dame Cathedral
- 20 WWII Deportation Memorial
- 21 Bureau de Change

- 23 Église Saint Séverin
- 24 Shakespeare & Co Bookshop
- 26 Abbey Bookshop
- 27 Le Cloître Pub; Polly
  Maggoo Pub
- 28 Musée du Moyen Age
  (Thermes de Cluny)
- 29 Musée du Moyen Age
  Entrance
- 30 Eurolines Bus Office
- 33 Palais du Luxembourg
  (French Senate Building)
- 34 Café Orbital
- 35 Sorbonne
  (University of Paris)
- 36 Église de la Sorbonne
- 38 Post Office
- 40 Panthéon
- 41 Panthéon Entrance
- 42 Église Saint Étienne du Mont
- 48 Laundrette
- 49 Nouvelles Frontières
  (Travel Agency)
- 51 Laundrette

FRANCE

13e & 14e Arrondissements The *Foyer International d'Accueil de Paris (FIAP) Jean Monnet* (☎ 01 43 13 17 00, fax 01 45 81 63 91, 30 rue Cabanis, metro Glacière) has modern rooms for five to eight/three to four/two people for 139/172/194FF per person, including breakfast. Rooms specially outfitted for disabled people *(handicapés)* are available. Reservations are accepted up to 15 days ahead.

The *Centre International de Séjour de Paris (CISP) Kellermann* (☎ 01 44 16 37 38, 17 blvd Kellermann, 13e, metro Porte d'Italie)* has dorm beds for 113FF and singles for 156FF. Prices include sheets and breakfast. This place also has facilities for disabled people on the 1st floor. Reservations are accepted up to 48 hours in advance.

Hotels
Marais (4e) The friendly *Hôtel Rivoli* (☎ 01 42 72 08 41, 44 rue de Rivoli, metro Hôtel de Ville)* is still a good deal with singles (no shower) starting at 200FF, doubles (with bath and toilet) at 300FF.

Hôtel de Nice (☎ 01 42 78 55 29, fax 01 42 78 36 07, 42 bis rue de Rivoli, metro Hôtel de Ville)* is a family-run place with singles/doubles/triples/quads for 380/450/550/680FF; some rooms have balconies. *Grand Hôtel Malher* (☎ 01 42 72 60 92, fax 01 42 72 25 37, 5 rue Malher, metro St Paul)* has nice singles/doubles starting at 490/590FF (100FF more in the high season).

Notre Dame Area (5e) The *Hôtel Esmeralda* (☎ 01 43 54 19 20, fax 01 40 51 00 68, 4 rue St Julien, metro St Michel)* is everybody's favourite. Its three simple singles (180FF) are booked well in advance. Doubles with bath and toilet start at 450FF.

Panthéon Area (5e) Basic singles at *Hôtel de Médicis* (☎ 01 43 54 14 66, 214 rue St Jacques, metro Luxembourg)* start at 90FF; doubles/triples are 180/250FF.

A better deal is *Grand Hôtel du Progrès* (☎ 01 43 54 53 18, fax 01 56 24 87 80, 50 rue Gay Lussac, metro Luxembourg)*. Singles start at 160FF; larger doubles with a view at 240FF, including breakfast. The nearby, family-run *Hôtel Gay Lussac* (☎ 01 43 54 23 96, fax 01 40 51 79 49, metro Luxembourg)* is a cut above, with small singles averaging 220FF; larger doubles/quads start at 360/450FF.

euro currency converter 1FF = €0.15

Hôtel St Christophe (☎ 01 43 31 81 54, fax 01 43 31 12 54, ✉ hotelstchristophe@compous erve.com, 17 rue Lacépède, metro place Monge) is a classy small hotel with 31 well-equipped rooms at 550/680FF, although discounts are often available.

St Germain des Prés (6e) *Hôtel de Nesle*
(☎ 01 43 54 62 41, 7 rue de Nesle, metro Odéon or Mabillon) is a relaxed, colourfully decorated hotel in a quiet street. Singles/doubles with shower are 275/350FF (450FF for a double with bath and toilet). Reservations not accepted. The well-positioned *Hôtel Henri IV (☎ 01 43 54 44 53, 25 place Dauphine, metro Pont Neuf)* at the western end of Île de la Cité has adequate singles/doubles starting at 125/200FF (hall showers 15FF). Book well ahead.

Montmartre (18e)
Singles/doubles at the attractive *Hôtel des Arts (☎ 01 46 06 30 52, fax 01 46 06 10 83, 5 rue Tholozé, metro Abesss)* start at 360/460FF. *Hôtel de Rohan (☎ 01 42 52 32 57, fax 01 55 79 79 63, 90 rue Myrha, metro Château Rouge)* has basic, tidy singles/doubles for 120/150FF (hall showers 20FF). *Hôtel des Trois Poussins (☎ 01 53 32 81 81, fax 01 53 32 81 82, ✉ h3p@les3po ussins.com, 15 rue Clauzel, metro St Georges)* is a lovely hotel due south of place Pigalle. Singles/doubles start at 680/780FF. Many of the rooms are small studios (from 780/880FF per single/double) with their own cooking facilities.

PLACES TO EAT
Restaurants
Except for those in the very touristy areas, most of the city's thousands of restaurants are pretty good value for money.

Forum des Halles *Le Petit Mâchon (☎ 01 42 60 08 06, 158 rue St Honoré, metro Palais Royal)* bistro has Lyon-inspired specialities, with main courses from 68FF and a 98FF *menu*. American bar/restaurant *Joe Allen (☎ 01 42 36 70 13, 30 rue Pierre Lescot, metro Étienne Marcel)* serves Californian wines and two/three course *menus* for 112/140FF.

Opéra Area (2e & 9e) *Chartier (☎ 01 47 70 86 29, 7 rue du Faubourg Montmartre, metro Grands Boulevards)*, famous for its 330-seat *belle époque* dining room, has mains from 34FF and more elaborate two/three/four course *menus* for 74/110/190FF.

Marais (4e)
Rue des Rosiers (metro St Paul), the heart of the old Jewish neighbourhood, has a few *kascher* (kosher) restaurants. Paris' best known Jewish (but not kosher) restaurant, founded in 1920, is *Restaurant Jo Goldenberg* at No 7, with main dishes for around 80FF. *Minh Chau (10 rue de la Verrerie, metro Hôtel de Ville)* is a tiny but welcoming Vietnamese place with tasty main dishes for about 30FF. For vegetarian fare head to *Aquarius (54 rue Ste Croix de la Bretonnerie, metro Rambuteau)*, where a tasty two-course lunch costs 64/92FF and a three-course dinner is 95FF.

Bastille (4e, 11e & 12e)
While the area around Bastille has many ethnic restaurants, traditional French food is also available. *Havanita Café (☎ 01 43 55 96 42, 11 rue de Lappe, metro Bastille)* serves Cuban-inspired food and drinks. Excellent main courses are 69FF to 94FF. *Bofinger (☎ 01 42 72 87 82, 5-7 rue de la Bastille, metro Bastille)*, with an Art Nouveau interior, has *menus* for 119/178/189FF.

Latin Quarter (4e, 5e & 6e)
This area has plenty of good Greek, North African and Middle Eastern restaurants – but avoid rue de la Huchette (aka 'bacteria alley') and its nearby streets, unless you're after shwarma (20FF), available at several places.

The Moroccan *Founti Agadir (☎ 01 43 37 85 10, 117 rue Monge, metro Censier Daubenton)* has some of the best couscous, grills and tajines on the Left Bank. Lunch *menus* are 75/89FF. Or, if you fancy classics like *bœuf bourguignon* (59FF), try *Perraudin (☎ 01 46 33 15 75, 157 rue St Jacques, metro Luxembourg)*, a reasonably priced traditional French restaurant.

Le Petit Légume (☎ 01 40 46 06 85, 36 rue des Boulangers, metro Cardinal Lemoine), a great choice for home-made vegetarian fare, has *menus* for 50/64/75FF.

Some of the best crepes in Paris are sold from a little stall opposite 68 rue Mouffetard. *Tashi Delek (☎ 01 43 26 55 55, 4 rue St Jacques, metro Luxembourg)* offers good, cheap, Tibetan lunch/dinner *menus* for 65/105FF. *Douce France (7 rue Royer Collard, metro Luxembourg)* is a popular hole-in-the-wall selling great sandwiches.

Montparnasse (6e & 14e)
For innovative food in a traditional setting, you couldn't do better than *Le Caméléon (☎ 01 43 20 63 43, 6 rue de Chevreuse, 6e, metro Vavin)*; the lobster ravioli (92FF) alone is worth a visit.

There are *creperies* at 20 rue d'Odessa and around the corner on rue du Montparnasse. *Mustang Café (☎ 01 43 35 36 12, 84 blvd du Montparnasse, metro Montparnasse-Bienveniie)* serves passable Tex-Mex (platters and chilli from 47FF) until 5 am.

Montmartre (9e & 18e)
Restaurants around place du Tertre tend to be touristy and overpriced – but there are alternatives. An old favourite is *Refuge des Fondus (☎ 01 42 55 22 65, 17 rue des Trois Frères, metro Abbesses)* where 92FF buys an apéritif, wine, and either cheese or meat fondue (meat: minimum of two). *Le Mono (☎ 01 46 06 99 20, 40 rue Véron)* serves West African dishes priced from 25FF to 70FF.

Il Duca (☎ 01 46 06 71 98, 26 rue Yvonne le Tac, metro Abbesses) serves good Italian food in an intimate setting. The lunch *menu* is 89FF and home-made pasta dishes are 55FF to 76FF.

University Restaurants
Paris has 15 *restaurants universitaires* (student cafeterias) run by the Centre Régional des Œuvres Universitaires et Scolaires (CROUS; ☎ 01 40 51 36 00). Students with ID pay 14.50FF, guests about 24FF. Opening times vary, so check the schedule outside any of the following: *Assas (☎ 01 46 33 61 25, 92 rue d'Assas, 6e, metro Port Royal or Notre Dame des Champs)*; *Bullier (☎ 01 43 54 93 38, 39 ave Georges Bernanos, 5e, metro Port Royal)*; *Châtelet (☎ 01 43 31 51 66, 8 rue Jean Calvin, 5e, metro Censier Daubenton)*, just off rue Mouffetard; and *Mabillon (☎ 01 43 25 66 23, 3 rue Mabillon, 6e, metro Mabillon)*.

Self-Catering
Supermarkets are always cheaper than small grocery shops. The *Monoprix Supermarket (21 Avenue de l'Opéra)* opposite metro Pyramides is convenient for the Louvre area, or

try *Ed l'Épicier (37 rue Lacépède, metro Monge)* if you're in the Latin Quarter. For a different shopping experience altogether, head to *Fauchon (☎ 01 47 62 60 11, 26 place de la Madeleine, metro Madeleine)*, Paris' most famous gourmet-food shop.

Food Markets
Paris' *marchés découverts* (open-air markets), open 7 am to 2 pm, pop up in various squares and streets two or three times a week. *Marchés couverts* (covered markets) open 8 am to about 1 pm and 4 to 7 or 7.30 pm Tuesday to Sunday. Ask at your hotel for the location of the nearest market.

Notre Dame Area (4e & 5e)
There are a number of *fromageries* and *groceries* along rue St Louis en l'Île (metro Pont Marie) and place Maubert hosts a food market (Tuesday, Thursday, Saturday) and various other *food shops*.

St Germain des Prés (6e)
Food shops are clustered on rue de Seine and rue de Buci (metro Mabillon) and at rue St Jacques. The covered *Marché St Germain* on rue Lobineau, just north of the eastern end of Église St Germain des Prés, has a huge array of produce and prepared foods.

Marais (4e)
Flo Prestige (10 rue St Antoine, metro Bastille) has picnic supplies and, more importantly, delectable pastries and baked goods.

Montmartre (18e)
Most of the *food shops* in this area are along rue Lepic and rue des Abbesses, about 500m south-west of Sacré Cœur.

ENTERTAINMENT
It's virtually impossible to sample the richness of Paris' entertainment scene without consulting *Pariscope* (3FF; includes an English-language insert) or *L'Officiel des Spectacles* (2FF), both published on Wednesday and available at any newsstand.

Tickets
Tickets can be reserved and bought at the ticket outlets in the FNAC stores at 136 rue de Rennes, 6e (☎ 01 49 54 30 00, metro St Placide) and at the 3rd underground level of

MONTMARTRE

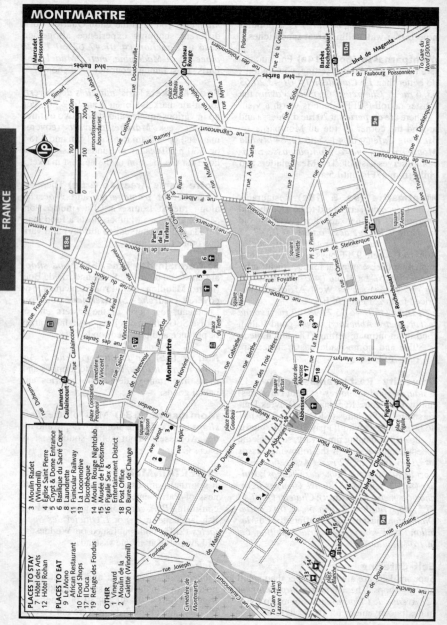

PLACES TO STAY
7 Hôtel des Arts
12 Hôtel Rohan

PLACES TO EAT
9 Le Mono
     African Restaurant
10 Food Shops
17 Il Duca
19 Refuge des Fondus

OTHER
1 Vineyard
2 Moulin de la
     Galette (Windmill)
3 Moulin Radet
     (Windmill)
4 Église Saint Pierre
5 Crypt & Dome Entrance
6 Basilique du Sacré Cœur
8 Laundrette
11 Funicular Railway
13 La Locomotive
     Discothèque
14 Moulin Rouge Nightclub
15 Musée de l'Erotisme
16 Pigalle Sex &
     Entertainment District
18 Post Office
20 Bureau de Change

the Forum des Halles shopping mall (☎ 01 40 41 40 00, metro Châtelet-Les Halles) at 1-7 rue Pierre Lescot, 1er; and in the Virgin Megastores at 52-60 Ave des Champs-Élysées, 8e (☎ 01 49 53 50 00, metro Franklin D Roosevelt) and 99 rue de Rivoli, 1er (☎ 01 49 53 52 09, metro Franklin D Roosevelt).

Pubs

Unpretentious and relaxed, *Le Cloître (☎ 01 43 25 19 92, 19 rue St Jacques, 5e, metro St Michel)* seems to please the young Parisians who congregate there. Informal, friendly *Polly Maggoo (☎ 01 46 33 33 64, 11 rue St Jacques, metro St Michel)* was founded in 1967 and still plays music from that era.

Café Oz (☎ 01 43 54 30 48, 18 rue St Jacques, metro Luxembourg) is a casual, friendly pub with Foster's on tap. Anglophone and always crowded, *Stolly's (☎ 01 42 76 06 76, 16 rue de la Cloche Percée, 4e, metro Hôtel de Vllle)* is on a tiny street just off rue de Rivoli.

Clubs & Dance Venues

The clubs and other dancing venues favoured by the Parisian 'in' crowd change frequently, and many are officially private, which means bouncers can deny entry to whomever they don't like the look of. For example, single men may not be admitted; women, on the other hand, get in free some nights.

Le Balajo (☎ 01 47 00 07 87, 9 rue de Lappe, 11e, metro Bastille), a mainstay of the Parisian dance-hall scene since 1935, is two blocks north-east of place de la Bastille. DJs play old-fashioned *musette* (accordion music) for retro tea dancing 2.30 to 6.30 pm on Thursday and 3 to 7 pm on Sunday (50FF). Night admission (100FF) includes one drink.

La Locomotive (☎ 01 53 41 88 88, 90 blvd de Clichy, 18e, metro Blanche), an enormous, ever popular disco open 11 pm (midnight on Monday) until 6 am, charges 70/100FF (including one drink) on weekdays/weekends. Women get in free before 12.30 am.

Jazz

A favourite for live Jazz, *Caveau de la Huchette (☎ 01 43 26 65 05, 5 rue de la Huchette, 5e, metro St Michel)* opens 9.30 pm to 2 am (later on weekends); entry costs 60FF

(students 55FF) during the week, 70FF (no discounts) at the weekend.

Opera & Classical Music

Paris plays host to dozens of concerts each week. The Opéra National de Paris splits its performances between Opéra Garnier (☎ 01 44 73 13 99), its original home built in 1875, and the modern Opéra Bastille (☎ 01 44 73 13 99), which opened in 1989. Both opera houses also stage ballets and concerts. Opera tickets (September to July only) cost 90FF to 670FF; ballets 70FF to 420FF; and concerts 85FF to 240FF. Check its Web site at www.opera-de-paris.fr. Unsold tickets are offered 15 minutes prior to showtime to students, under 25s or over 65s for about 100FF – ask for the *tarif spécial*.

Cinemas

Going to the movies in Paris is expensive (about 50FF), though most cinemas give discounts on Wednesday (and sometimes Monday). Check *Pariscope* and *L'Officiel des Spectacles* for listings: 'vo' *(version originale)* indicates subtitled movies.

SHOPPING
Fashion

Some of Paris' fanciest shops are along Ave Montaigne and rue du Faubourg St Honoré, 8e; rue St Honoré, 1er and 8e; and place Vendôme, 1er. Rue Bonaparte, 6e, offers a good choice of mid-range boutiques.

Department Stores

Paris' three main department stores, open 9.30 am to 7 pm Monday to Saturday (10 pm on Thursday) are: Au Printemps (☎ 01 42 82 50 00), 64 blvd Haussmann, metro Havre Caumartin; Galeries Lafayette (☎ 01 42 82 36 40), 40 blvd Haussmann, metro Auber or Chaussée; and Samaritaine (☎ 01 40 41 20 20), metro Pont Neuf, which provides an amazing view from the 10th-floor terrace of Building 2 at 19 rue de la Monnaie.

GETTING THERE & AWAY
Air

Paris has two major international airports. Aéroport d'Orly is 14km south of central Paris. For flight and other information call ☎ 01 49 75 15 15 or ☎ 0836 25 05 05. Aéroport Charles

FRANCE

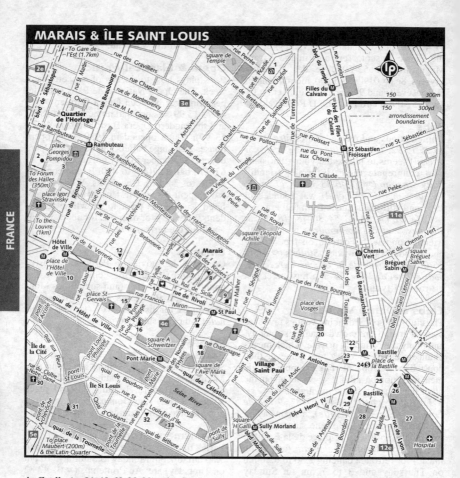

MARAIS & ÎLE SAINT LOUIS

de Gaulle (☎ 01 48 62 22 80), also known as Roissy-Charles de Gaulle in the suburb of Roissy, is 23km north-east of central Paris. For airline information call ☎ 01 48 62 22 80 or ☎ 0836 25 05 05.

Telephone numbers for information at Paris' airline offices are:

Air France	☎ 0802 80 28 02
Air Liberté	☎ 0803 80 58 05
Air New Zealand	☎ 01 40 53 82 23
Air UK	☎ 01 44 56 18 08
American Airlines	☎ 0801 87 28 72
British Airways	☎ 0825 82 54 00
Continental	☎ 01 42 99 09 09
Lufthansa	☎ 0802 02 00 30
Northwest Airlines	☎ 01 42 66 90 00
Qantas	☎ 0803 84 68 46
Singapore Airlines	☎ 01 53 65 79 00
Thai	☎ 01 44 20 70 80
United	☎ 0801 72 72 72

Bus

Eurolines terminal, Gare Routière Internationale (☎ 0836 69 52 52, metro Gallieni), is at Porte de Bagnolet, 20e, on the eastern edge of Paris. Its ticket office in town (☎ 01 43 54 11 99, metro Cluny-La Sorbonne) at 55 rue St Jacques, 5e, opens 9.30 am to 6.30 pm week-

MARAIS & ÎLE SAINT LOUIS

PLACES TO STAY		21	Ethnic Restaurants	14	Stolly's
9	Grand Hôtel Mahler	22	Bofinger	16	Memorial to the Unknown
11	Hôtel Rivoli	23	Flo Prestige		Jewish Martyr
13	Hôtel de Nice	32	Berthillon Ice Cream	20	Maison de Victor Hugo
15	MIJE Maubisson	33	Food Shops	24	Banque de France
17	MIJE Fourcy			25	Colonne de Juillet
18	MIJE Fauconnier	**OTHER**		26	Entrance to Opéra-Bastille
		1	Web Bar	27	Opéra-Bastille
PLACES TO EAT		2	Accueil des Jeunes en France	28	Port de Plaisance de Paris
4	Aquarius Vegetarian Restaurant		(AJF)		Arsenal
7	Restaurants	3	Centre Pompidou	29	Paris à Vélo C'est Sympa!
8	Restaurant Jo Goldenberg	5	Musée Picasso	30	Notre Dame
12	Minh Chau	6	Laundrette	31	Mémorial des Martyrs de la
19	Food Shops	10	Hôtel de Ville (City Hall)		Déportation

days and 10 am to 5 pm on Saturday. There is no domestic, intercity bus service to or from Paris.

Train

Paris has six major train stations (*gares*), each handling traffic to different destinations. For information in English call ☎ 0836 35 35 35, 7 am to 10 pm. The metro station attached to each train station bears the same name as the gare. Paris' major train stations are:

Gare d'Austerlitz (13e) Loire Valley, Spain and Portugal and non-TGV trains to south-western France.

Gare de l'Est (10e) Parts of France east of Paris (Champagne, Alsace and Lorraine), Luxembourg, parts of Switzerland (Basel, Lucerne, Zürich), southern Germany (Frankfurt, Munich) and points farther east.

Gare de Lyon (12e) Regular and TGV Sud-Est trains to places south-east of Paris, including Dijon, Lyon, Provence, the Côte d'Azur, the Alps, parts of Switzerland (Bern, Geneva, Lausanne), Italy and points beyond.

Gare Montparnasse (15e) Brittany and places between (Chartres, Angers, Nantes) and the terminus of the TGV Atlantique serving Tours, Nantes, Bordeaux and other destinations in south-western France.

Gare du Nord (10e) Northern suburbs of Paris, northern France, the UK, Belgium, northern Germany, Scandinavia, Moscow etc; terminus of the TGV Nord (Lille and Calais), and the Eurostar to London.

Gare St Lazare (8e) Normandy, including Dieppe, Le Havre and Cherbourg.

GETTING AROUND

Paris' public transit system, most of which is operated by the RATP (Régie Autonome des Transports Parisians; ☎ 0836 68 77 14), is cheap and efficient. For information in English ring ☎ 0836 68 41 14.

To/From Orly Airport

Orly Rail is the quickest way to reach the Left Bank and the 16e. Take the free shuttle bus to the Pont de Rungis-Aéroport d'Orly RER station, which is on the C2 line, and get on a train heading into the city. Another fast way into town is the Orlyval shuttle train (57FF); it stops near Orly-Sud's Porte F and links Orly with the Antony RER station, which is on line B4. Orlybus (35FF) takes you to the Denfert-Rochereau metro station, 14e. Air France buses (45FF) go to/from Gare Montparnasse, 15e, (every 12 minutes) along Aérogare des Invalides in the 7e. RATP bus No 183 (8FF or one bus/metro ticket) goes to Porte de Choisy, 13e, but is very slow. Jetbus, the cheapest option, links both terminals with the Villejuif-Louis Aragon metro stop (26.50FF; 20 minutes). All services between Orly and Paris run every 15 minutes or so (less frequently late at night) from 5.30 or 6.30 am to 11 or 11.30 pm. A taxi to/from Orly costs from 120FF to 175FF, plus 6FF per piece of luggage over 5kg.

To/From Charles de Gaulle Airport

Roissyrail links the city with both of the airport's train stations (49FF, 35 minutes). To get to the airport, take any line B train whose four letter destination code begins with E (eg, EIRE). Regular metro ticket windows can't

FRANCE

always sell these tickets, so you may have to buy one at the RER station where you board. Trains run every 15 minutes from 5.30 am to around 11 pm.

Air France bus No 2 will take you to Porte Maillot and the corner of Ave Carnot near the Arc de Triomphe for 60FF; bus No 4 to Gare Montparnasse costs 70FF.

RATP bus No 350 (24FF or three bus/metro tickets) links both aérogares with Porte de la Chapelle, 18e, and stops at Gare du Nord and Gare de l'Est, both in the 10e. RATP Bus No 351 goes to ave du Trône, on the eastern side of place de la Nation in the 11e and runs every half-hour or so until 8.20 pm (9.30 pm from the airport to the city). The trip costs 24FF or three bus/metro tickets.

Bus

Short trips cost one bus/metro/RER ticket (see Metro/RER/Bus Tickets below), while longer rides require two. Travellers without tickets can purchase them from the driver. Whatever kind of ticket (*coupon*) you have, you must cancel it in the little machine next to the driver. The fines are hefty if you're caught without a ticket or without a cancelled ticket. If you have a Carte Orange, Formule 1 or Paris Visite pass (see the following Metro & RER section), just flash it at the driver – do not cancel it in the machine.

After the metro shuts down at around 12.45 am, the Noctambus network, whose symbol is a black owl silhouetted against a yellow moon, links the Châtelet-Hôtel de Ville area with most parts of the city. Noctambuses begin their runs from Ave Victoria, 4e, between the Hôtel de Ville and place du Châtelet, every hour on the half-hour from 1.30 to 5.30 am seven days a week. A single ride costs 15FF and allows one immediate transfer onto another Noctambus.

Metro & RER

Paris' underground rail network consists of two separate but linked systems: the Métropolitain, known as the metro, which now has 14 lines and over 300 stations, and the suburban commuter rail network, the RER which, along with certain SNCF lines, is divided into eight concentric zones. The whole system has been designed so that no point in Paris is more than 500m from a metro stop.

How it Works Each metro train is known by the name of its terminus; trains on the same line have different names depending on which direction they are travelling in. On lines that split into several branches and thus have more than one end-of-the-line station, the final destination of each train is indicated on the front, sides and interior of the train cars. In the stations, white-on-blue *sortie* signs indicate exits and black-on-orange *correspondance* signs show how to get to connecting trains. The last metro train sets out on its final run at 12.30 am. Plan ahead so as not to miss your connection. The metro starts up again at 5.30 am.

Metro/RER/Bus Tickets

The same tickets are valid on the metro, the bus and, for travel within the Paris city limits, the RER's 2nd-class carriages. They cost 8FF if bought individually and 55FF (half for children aged four to 11) for a *carnet* of 10. One ticket lets you travel between any two metro stations, including stations outside of the Paris city limits, no matter how many transfers are required. You can also use it on the RER system within zone 1.

For travel on the RER to destinations outside the city, purchase a special ticket *before* you board the train or you won't be able to get out of the station and could be fined. Always keep your ticket until you reach your destination and exit the station.

The cheapest and easiest way to travel the metro is with a Carte Orange, a bus/metro/RER pass whose accompanying magnetic coupon comes in weekly and monthly versions. You can get tickets for travel in up to eight urban and suburban zones; the basic ticket – valid for zones 1 and 2 – is probably sufficient.

The weekly ticket costs 82FF for zones 1 and 2 and is valid Monday to Sunday. Even if you'll be in Paris for only three or four days, it may very well work out cheaper than purchasing a carnet – you'll break even at 16 rides – and it will certainly cost less than buying a daily Mobilis or Paris Visite pass. The monthly Carte Orange ticket (255FF for zones 1 and 2) begins on the first day of each calendar month. Both are on sale in metro and RER stations and at certain bus terminals.

To get a Carte Orange, bring a passport-size photograph of yourself to any metro or

RER ticket counter (four photos for 25FF are available from automatic booths). Request a Carte Orange (which is free) and the kind of coupon you'd like. To prevent tickets being used by more than one person, you must write your surname *(nom)* and given name *(prénom)* on the Carte Orange, and the number of your Carte Orange on each weekly or monthly coupon you buy (next to the words Carte No).

Mobilis and Paris Visite passes, designed for tourists, are on sale in many metro and train stations and international airports. The Mobilis card (and its *coupon*) allows unlimited travel for one day in two to eight zones (32FF to 110FF). Paris Visite passes, providing discounts on entries to certain museums and activities as well as transport, are valid for one/two/three/five consecutive days of travel in either three, five or eight zones. The one to three-zone version costs 55/90/120/175FF for one/two/three/five days. Children aged four to 11 pay half-price. They can be purchased at larger metro and RER stations, at SNCF bureaus in Paris and at the airports.

Taxi

The *prise en* charge (flag fall) is 13FF. Within the city limits, it costs 3.53FF per kilometre for travel 7 am to 7 pm Monday to Saturday (tariff A). At night and on Sunday and holidays (tariff B), it's 5.83FF per kilometre. An extra 8FF is charged for taking a fourth passenger, but most drivers refuse to take more than three people because of insurance constraints. Luggage over 5kg costs 6FF extra and for pick-up from SNCF mainline stations there's a 5FF supplement. The usual tip is 2FF no matter what the fare.

There are 500 taxi stands *(tête de station)* in Paris. Radio-dispatched taxis include Taxis Bleus (☎ 01 49 36 10 10) and G7 Taxis (☎ 01 47 39 47 39). If you order a taxi by phone, the meter is switched on as soon as the driver gets your call.

Car & Motorcycle

Driving in Paris is nerve-wracking but not impossible. The fastest way to get across Paris is usually the Périphérique.

Street parking can cost 15FF an hour; large municipal parking garages usually charge 15/130/200FF per hour/10 hours/24 hours. Fines (75FF or 200FF) are dispensed by parking attendants with great abandon.

Renting a small car (Peugeot 106) for one day without insurance and no kilometres costs about 290FF, but cheaper deals from smaller agencies are available.

Rental agencies in Paris include:

Avis (☎ 0802 05 05 05 or ☎ 01 42 66 67 58)
Budget (☎ 0800 10 00 01)
Europcar (☎ 0803 35 23 52)
Hertz (☎ 01 39 38 38 38)
National/Citer (☎ 01 42 06 06 06)
Thrifty (☎ 0801 45 45 45)

Bicycle

There are 130km of bicycle lanes running throughout Paris. Some of them aren't particularly attractive or safe, but cyclists may be fined about 250FF for failing to use them. The tourist office distributes a free brochure-map called *Paris à Vélo*.

RATP-sponsored Roue Libre (see Bicycle under Organised Tours earlier) is the best place to rent bikes. Hire costs 20/75FF per hour/day or 115/225FF for a weekend/week, insurance included. See Bois de Boulogne (Things to See) for more information.

Around Paris

The region surrounding Paris is known as the Île de France (Island of France) because of its position between the rivers Aube, Marne, Oise and Seine.

DISNEYLAND PARIS

It took US\$4.4 billion to turn beet fields 32km east of Paris into the much heralded Disneyland Parls. Now the most popular tourist attraction in Europe, it opens 365 days a year. From early September to March the hours are 10 am to 6 pm (8 pm on Saturday, some Sundays and perhaps during school holidays); in spring and early summer, the park opens 9 am to 8 pm (to 11 pm at the weekend and from early July to early September). Admission costs 220FF (170FF for those aged three to 11) from April to early November; the rest of the year, except during the Christmas holidays, prices drop to 165/135FF. Multiple-day passes are available.

FRANCE

FRANCE

VERSAILLES
pop 95,000
Versailles served as the country's political capital and the seat of the royal court from 1682 until 1789. After the Franco-Prussian War of 1870-71, the victorious Prussians proclaimed the establishment of the German empire from the chateau's Galerie des Glaces (Hall of Mirrors), and in 1919 the Treaty of Versailles was signed in the same room, officially ending WWI.

The chateau can be jammed with tourists, especially on weekends, in summer and most especially on summer Sundays. Arrive early to avoid the queues.

Information
The tourist office (☎ 01 39 24 88 88, @ touri sme@ot-versailles.fr) is just north of the Versailles-Rive Gauche train station at 2 bis ave de Paris. Open 9 am to 7 pm daily April to October (to 6 pm the rest of the year).

Château de Versailles
The enormous Château de Versailles (☎ 01 30 83 78 00 or ☎ 01 30 83 77 77) was built in the mid-17th century during the reign of Louis XIV (the Sun King). The chateau essentially consists of four parts: the main palace building; the vast 17th-century gardens; the late-17th-century Grand Trianon; and the mid-18th-century Petit Trianon.

Opening Hours & Tickets
The main building opens 9 am to 5.30 pm (6.30 pm May to September) daily, except Monday and public holidays. Admission to the **Grands Appartements** (State Apartments), including the 73m-long **Galerie des Glaces** (Hall of Mirrors) and the **Appartement de la Reine** (Queen's Suite), costs 45FF (after 3.30 pm daily 35FF, free for under 18s on Sunday). Tickets are on sale at Entrée A (Entrance A) off to the right from the equestrian statue of Louis XIV as you approach the building. You won't be able to visit other parts of the main palace unless you take one of the guided tours (see Guided Tours below). Entrée H has facilities for the disabled, including a lift.

The **Grand Trianon** (25FF; 15FF reduced rate) opens noon to 6.30 pm daily April to October; the rest of the year it closes at 5.30 pm. The **Petit Trianon**, open the same days and hours, costs 15/10FF. A combined ticket for both costs 30/20FF.

The gardens are open 7 am (8 am in winter) to nightfall daily (except if it's snowing). Entry is free, except on Saturday, July to September, and on Sunday early April to early October when the baroque fountains 'perform' the **Grandes Eaux**, 3.30 to 5 pm (30FF, students 20FF).

Guided Tours To make a reservation go to entrées C or D. A one-hour tour costs 25FF in addition to the regular entry fee; 80-minute audioguide tours available at entrée A for 35FF.

Getting There & Away
Bus No 171 (8FF or one metro/bus ticket, 35 minutes) links Pont de Sèvres in Paris with the place d'Armes and Versailles but it's faster to go by train. Each of Versailles' three train stations is served by RER and/or SNCF trains coming from a different group of Paris stations.

RER line C4 takes you from Paris' Left Bank RER stations to Versailles-Rive Gauche station (14.50FF). From Paris, catch any train whose four-letter code begins with the letter 'V'. There are up to 70 trains a day (half on Sunday), and the last train back to Paris leaves shortly before midnight.

RER line C5 links Paris' Left Bank with Versailles-Chantiers station (14.50FF). From Paris, take any train whose code begins with 'S'. Versailles-Chantiers is also served by some three dozen SNCF trains a day (20 on Sunday) from Gare Montparnasse (14.50FF, 15 minutes); all trains on this line continue on to Chartres.

From Paris' Gare St Lazare (20FF) and La Défense (12FF), the SNCF has about 70 trains a day to Versailles-Rive Droite, which is 1200m from the chateau. The last train to Paris leaves a bit past midnight.

CHARTRES
pop 40,300
The indescribably beautiful 13th-century cathedral of Chartres rises abruptly from the corn fields 88km south-west of Paris.

Orientation
The medieval sections of Chartres are situated along the Eure River and the hillside to

the west. The cathedral is about 500m east of the train station.

Information

The tourist office (☎ 02 37 18 26 26, ☻ chartres.tourism@wanadoo.fr) is across place de la Cathédrale from the cathedral's main entrance. There's a Banque de France branch at 32 rue du Docteur Maunoury, and the main post office is at place des Épars.

Cathédrale Notre Dame

Chartres' 13th-century cathedral (☎ 02 37 21 75 02), unlike so many of its contemporaries, has not been significantly modified – construction of this early Gothic masterpiece took only 25 years, which is why the cathedral has a high degree of architectural unity.

The cathedral is open 7.30 am (8.30 am on Sunday) to 7.15 pm daily, except during Mass, weddings and funerals. Fascinating tours (35FF, students 25FF) are conducted by Englishman Malcolm Miller from Easter to November; audioguides (15FF to 30FF) are available from the cathedral bookshop. The 112m-high **Clocher Neuf** (new bell tower) is well worth the ticket price (25FF; 15FF for those aged 12 to 25) and the long, spiral climb.

Inside, the cathedral's most exceptional feature is its extraordinary **stained-glass windows**, most of which are 13th-century originals. The **trésor** (treasury) displays a piece of cloth given to the cathedral in 876 said to have been worn by the Virgin Mary.

The early-11th-century Romanesque **crypt**, the largest in France, can be visited by a half-hour guided tour in French (with a written English translation) for 11FF.

Old City

Streets with buildings of interest include **rue de la Tannerie**, which runs along the Eure, and **rue des Écuyers**, midway between the cathedral and the river. **Église St Pierre** at place St Pierre has a massive bell tower dating from around 1000 and some fine (often overlooked) medieval stained-glass windows.

Places to Stay

Camping *Les Bords de l'Eure* (☎ 02 37 28 79 43, 9 rue de Launay), about 2.5km southeast of the train station, is open May to early September. Bus No 8 (direction Hôpital) from the train station goes to the Vignes stop.

Hostel The pleasant and calm *Auberge de Jeunesse* (☎ 02 37 34 27 64, fax 02 37 35 75 85, 23 Ave Neigre) has beds for 68FF, including breakfast. From the train station, take bus No 5 (direction Mare aux Moines) to the Rouliers stop. Reception opens 2 to 10 pm daily.

Hotels Somewhat dingy rooms at *Hôtel de l'Ouest* (☎ 02 37 21 43 27, 3 place Pierre Sémard) start at 120FF. The eight-room *Hôtel Au Départ* (☎ 02 37 36 80 43, 1 rue Nicole) has singles/doubles/triples with washbasin and bidet for 120/190/300FF. Reception is at the Brasserie L'Ouest, 9 place Pierre Sémard (closed Sunday).

Hôtel de la Poste (☎ 02 37 21 04 27, fax 02 37 36 42 17, 3 rue du Général Koening), near place des Épars, has singles/doubles starting at 250/320FF.

Places to Eat

At *Café Serpente* (☎ 02 37 21 68 81, 2 rue du Cloître Notre Dame), across from the south porch of the cathedral, the plat du jour costs 78FF to 98FF. *La Vesuvio* (☎ 02 37 21 56 35, 30 place des Halles) serves pizzas (35FF to 60FF) and light meals; or there's always the *Monoprix* supermarket at 21 rue Noël Ballay, north-east of place des Épars.

Getting There & Around

Train There are three dozen trains a day (20 on Sunday) to/from Paris' Gare Montparnasse (72FF, 55 to 70 minutes) also stopping at Versailles' Chantiers station (61FF, 45 minutes). The last train back to Paris leaves Chartres a bit after 9 pm (7.40 pm on Saturday, after 10 pm on Sunday and holidays).

Alsace & Lorraine

The charming and beautiful region of Alsace, long a meeting place of Europe's Latin and Germanic cultures, is in France's far northeastern corner, nestled between the Vosges Mountains and, about 30km to the east, the Rhine River, marking the Franco-German border. The Alsatian language is a Germanic dialect similar to that spoken in nearby parts of Germany and Switzerland.

Most of Alsace became part of France in 1648 (Strasbourg, the region's largest city, retained its independence until 1681). But more than two centuries of French rule did little to dampen 19th and early-20th-century German enthusiasm for a foothold on the west bank of the southern Rhine, and the region (along with part of Lorraine) was twice annexed by Germany – from the Franco-Prussian War (1871) until the end of WWI, and again between 1939 and 1944.

STRASBOURG
pop 423,000

Strasbourg, just a few kilometres west of the Rhine, is Alsace's great metropolis and its intellectual and cultural capital. Towering above the restaurants and pubs of the lively old city is the marvellous cathedral, near which you'll find one of the finest ensembles of museums in France.

When it was founded in 1949, the Council of Europe decided to base itself in Strasbourg as a symbol of Franco-German (and pan-European) cooperation. The city is also the seat of the European Parliament (the legislative branch of the EU).

Orientation

The train station is 400m west of the Grande Île ('Large Island'), the city centre, which is delimited by the Ill River to the south and the Fossé du Faux Rempart to the north. place Kléber, the main public square on the Grande Île, is 400m north-west of the cathedral.

Information

The main tourist office (☎ 03 88 52 28 28, fax 03 88 52 28 29), 17 place de la Cathédrale, opens 9 am to 7 pm daily. There's a branch office (☎ 03 88 32 51 49) in front of the train station, in the underground complex beneath place de la Gare. Both offices sell the three-day Strasbourg Pass (58FF), which gets you a variety of discounts. Web site: www.strasbourg.com.

Money The Banque de France is at 3 place Broglie (open weekday mornings). The American Express office, 19 rue des Francs Bourgeois, opens weekdays and, from May to September, on Saturday.

Post & Communications The main post office, a neo-Gothic structure at 5 ave de la Marseillaise, is open 8 am to 7 pm weekdays and until noon Saturday. It has exchange services and a Cyberposte.

The Best Coffee Shop, 10 quai des Pêcheurs, offers cheap email access from 10 am (2 pm on weekends) to 11.30 pm.

Laundry On the Grande Île, there are laundrettes at 29 Grand' Rue (open until 8 pm) and 15 rue des Veaux (open until 9 pm).

Things to See

With its bustling public squares, busy pedestrianised areas and upmarket shopping streets, the **Grande Île** is a great place for aimless ambling.

Strasbourg's lacy Gothic cathedral, **Cathédrale Notre Dame**, was begun in 1176. The west facade was completed in 1284, but the spire (its southern companion was never built) wasn't in place until 1439. The interior can be visited daily until 7 pm; the astronomical clock goes through its paces at 12.30 pm (5FF). The 66m-high platform above the facade (from which the tower and its spire soar another 76m) can be visited daily – if you don't mind the 330 steps to the top (20/10FF).

Crisscrossed by narrow lanes, canals and locks, **Petite France**, in the south-west corner of the Grande Île, is the stuff of fairy tales, with half-timbered houses sprouting veritable thickets of geraniums.

The hugely expensive **European Parliament building** (☎ 03 88 17 20 07), inaugurated in 1999, and the Council of Europe's **Palais de l'Europe** (☎ 03 90 21 49 40), opened in 1977 – both about 2km north-east of the cathedral – can be visited on tours. Phone ahead for reservations.

Museums

Except for the Musée de l'Œuvre Notre-Dame and the Musée d'Art Moderne et Contemporain, which close on Monday, all of the city's museums open daily except Tuesday. Opening hours (except for the Musée d'Art Moderne) are 10 am to noon and 1.30 to 6 pm

(10 am to 5 pm on Sunday). Most museums (except the Musée d'Art Moderne, 30FF) charge 20/10FF.

The outstanding **Musée de l'Œuvre Notre Dame** is housed in several 14th and 15th-century buildings at 3 place du Château and displays one of France's finest collections of Romanesque, Gothic and Renaissance sculpture, including many of the cathedral's original statues.

The **Château des Rohan**, 2 place du Château, was built between 1732 and 1742 as a residence for the city's princely bishops. It now houses three museums (combined ticket 40/20FF): the **Musée Archéologique** covers the period from prehistory to 800 AD; the **Musée des Arts Décoratifs** give you a sense of the lifestyle of the rich and powerful during the 18th century; and the **Musée des Beaux-Arts** has paintings from the 14th to 19th centuries.

The new, superb **Musée d'Art Moderne et Contemporain** at place Hans Jean Arp has a diverse collection of works representing every major art movement of the past century or so.

The **Musée Alsacien** at 23 quai St Nicolas, housed in three 16th and 17th-century houses, affords a glimpse into Alsatian life over the centuries.

Organised Tours

Call to reserve a brewery tour at Kronenbourg (☎ 03 88 27 41 59, tram stop Duc d'Alsace), at 68 Route d'Oberhausbergen in the suburb of Cronenbourg, and Heineken (☎ 03 88 19 59 53), at 4 rue St Charles in Schiltigheim. Both are about 2.5km from the city centre. To get to Heineken, take bus No 4 to the Schiltigheim Mairie stop.

Places to Stay

It's *extremely* difficult to find last-minute accommodation from Monday to Thursday when the European Parliament is in plenary session one week each month (except August, and twice in October). Contact the tourist office for dates.

Camping The grassy *Camping de la Montagne Verte* (☎ 03 88 30 25 46, 2 rue Robert Forrer) opens mid-March to October. It's a few hundred metres from the *Auberge de Jeunesse René Cassin* (see Hostels), where you

can pitch a tent for 42FF per person, including breakfast.

Hostels The modern *CIARUS* (☎ 03 88 15 27 88, fax 03 88 15 27 89, 7 rue Finkmatt) a 285-bed Protestant-run hostel about 1km north-east of the train station, has beds from 92FF, including breakfast. By bus, take Nos 4, 10, 20 or 72 to the place de Pierre stop.

The 286-bed *Auberge de Jeunesse René Cassin* (☎ 03 88 30 26 46, fax 03 88 30 35 16, 9 rue de l'Auberge de Jeunesse), 2km south-west of the train station, has beds for 73FF. To get there, take bus No 3 or 23 to the Auberge de Jeunesse stop.

Hotels The 15-room *Hôtel Le Colmar* (☎ 03 88 32 16 89, fax 03 88 21 97 17, 1 rue du Maire Kuss) has clean singles/doubles from 167/218FF. *Hôtel Weber* (☎ 03 88 32 36 47, fax 03 88 32 19 08, ✆ hotelpatricia@hotmail.com, 22 blvd de Nancy) is hardly in the most attractive part of town, but quiet doubles start at 140FF.

The 16-room, family-run *Hôtel Michelet* (☎ 03 88 32 47 38, 48 rue du Vieux Marché aux Poissons) has simple singles/doubles from 145/170FF. The dark, rustic *Hôtel Patricia* (☎ 03 88 32 14 60, fax 03 88 32 19 08, ✆ hotelpatricia@hotmail.com, 1a rue du Puits) has ordinary but spacious doubles with great views from 180FF.

Facing the train station, the 61-room *Hôtel du Rhin* (☎ 03 88 32 35 00, fax 03 88 23 51 92, ✆ hotel-rhin@strasbourg.com, 7-8 place de la Gare) has doubles with washbasin starting at 200FF (360FF with shower and toilet). The 27-room, two-star *Hôtel de l'Ill* (☎ 03 88 36 20 01, fax 03 88 35 30 03, 8 rue des Bateliers) has tasteful doubles for 295FF.

Places to Eat

A *winstub* (pronounced VEEN-shtub) serves both wine and hearty Alsatian fare such as *choucroute* (sauerkraut) and *baeckeoffe* (pork, beef and lamb marinated in wine and cooked with vegetables).

Indulge yourself at *Au Crocodile* (☎ 03 88 32 13 02, 10 rue de l'Outre), with its three Michelin stars. It often plays host to visiting heads of state. The *menus* start at 410FF (including wine) for lunch on weekdays, otherwise 460FF (closed Sunday and Monday).

FRANCE

FRANCE

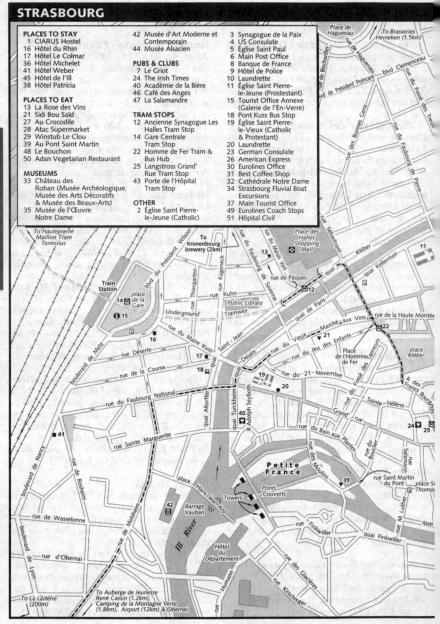

STRASBOURG

PLACES TO STAY
1 CIARUS Hostel
16 Hôtel du Rhin
17 Hôtel Le Colmar
36 Hôtel Michelet
41 Hôtel Weber
45 Hôtel de l'Ill
38 Hôtel Patricia

PLACES TO EAT
13 La Rose des Vins
21 Sidi Bou Saïd
27 Au Crocodile
28 Atac Supermarket
29 Winstub Le Clou
39 Au Pont Saint Martin
48 Le Bouchon
50 Adan Vegetarian Restaurant

MUSEUMS
33 Château des
    Rohan (Musée Archéologique,
    Musée des Arts Décoratifs
    & Musée des Beaux-Arts)
35 Musée de l'Œuvre
    Notre Dame

42 Musée d'Art Moderne et
    Contemporain
44 Musée Alsacien

PUBS & CLUBS
7 Le Griot
24 The Irish Times
40 Académie de la Bière
46 Café des Anges
47 La Salamandre

TRAM STOPS
12 Ancienne Synagogue Les
    Halles Tram Stop
14 Gare Centrale
    Tram Stop
22 Homme de Fer Tram &
    Bus Hub
25 Langstross Grand'
    Rue Tram Stop
43 Porte de l'Hôpital
    Tram Stop

OTHER
2 Église Saint Pierre-
    le-Jeune (Catholic)

3 Synagogue de la Paix
4 US Consulate
5 Église Saint Paul
6 Main Post Office
8 Banque de France
9 Hôtel de Police
10 Laundrette
11 Église Saint Pierre-
    le-Jeune (Prostestant)
15 Tourist Office Annexe
    (Galerie de l'En-Verre)
18 Pont Kuss Bus Stop
19 Église Saint Pierre-
    le-Vieux (Catholic
    & Protestant)
20 Laundrette
23 German Consulate
26 American Express
30 Eurolines Office
31 Best Coffee Shop
32 Cathédrale Notre Dame
34 Strasbourg Fluvial Boat
    Excursions
37 Main Tourist Office
49 Eurolines Coach Stops
51 Hôpital Civil

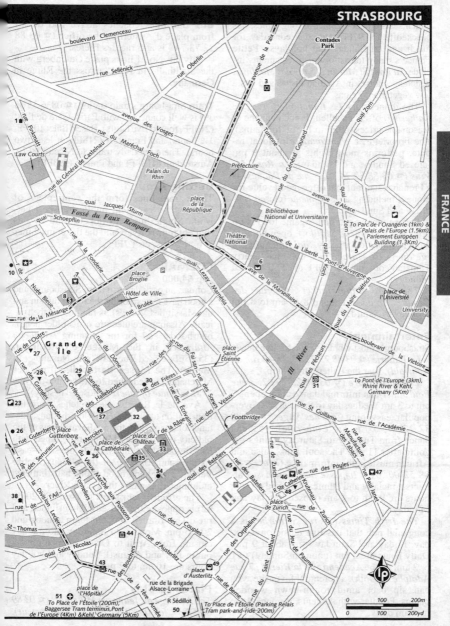

STRASBOURG

Contades Park

boulevard Clemenceau

rue Sellénick

rue Oberlin

avenue de la Paix

1

rue Finkmatt

Law Courts

2

rue du Général de Castelnau

avenue des Vosges

rue du Maréchal Foch

rue Turenne

rue du Général Gouraud

quai Zorn

3

avenue d'Alsace

Préfecture

Palais du Rhin

quai Jacques Sturm

place de la République

Bibliothèque National et Universitaire

4

quai Zorn

To Parc de l'Orangerie (1km) &
Palais de l'Europe (1.5km)
Parlement Européen
Building (1.3Km)

5

quai Schoepflin

Fossé du Faux Rempart

Théâtre National

avenue de la Liberté

6

ave de la Marseillaise

Pont d'Auvergne

rue de la Fonderie

9

10

rue de la Nuée Bleue

7

place Broglie

P

quai Lezay-Marnésia

quai du Maire Dietrich

place de l'Université

University

8

Hôtel de Ville

rue Brûlée

rue de la Mésange

rue de l'Outre

Grande Île

27

28

rue du Dôme

rue des Juifs

rue du Fil

place Saint Étienne

Ill River

boulevard de la Victoire

29

des Orfèvres

rue des Hallebardes

rue du Sanglier

30

rue des Frères

rue des Écrivains

rue des Sœurs

rue des Veaux

quai des Pêcheurs

31

To Pont de l'Europe (3km),
Rhine River & Kehl,
Germany (5Km)

23

37

32

rue Mercière

place Gutenberg

rue du Vieux Marché aux Poissons

place de la Cathédrale

place du Château

33

Footbridge

rue St Guillame

rue de l'Académie

26

36

35

34

quai des Bateliers

45

rue des Bateliers

rue des Frères

rue de Zurich

46

R Ste Catherine

rue Krutenau

rue des Poules

48

rue des Serruriers

de la Division Leclerc

38

rue

St~Thomas

quai Saint Nicolas

44

rue d'Austerlitz

rue des Couples

rue des Orphelins

place de Zurich

rue de Zurich

rue du Jeu de Paume

47

rue Paul Janet

de la Manufacture des Tabacs

43

rue des Bouchers

de la Mésange

49

place d'Austerlitz

rue de la Brigade Alsace-Lorraine

R Sédillot

50

place de l'Hôpital

51

To Place de l'Étoile (200m),
Baggersee Tram terminus, Pont
de l'Europe (4Km) & Kehl, Germany (5Km)

To Place de l'Étoile (Parking Relais
Tram park-and-ride 200m)

rue de Berne

rue du Saint Gothard

0   100   200m
0   100   200yd

euro currency converter 1FF = €0.15

FRANCE

Winstub Le Clou (*3 rue du Chaudron*), which seats diners together at long tables, has baeckeoffe for 97FF (closed Wednesday for lunch and on Sunday and holidays). Petite France's many tourist-oriented restaurants include *Au Pont St Martin* (*15 rue des Moulins*), which specialises in Alsatian dishes and has a few vegetarian options.

The dinner-only *Le Bouchon* (*6 rue Ste Catherine*) offers excellent French cuisine at reasonable prices (69FF to 125FF for mains). The proprietor, a *chansonnière* of local repute, performs most nights at about 9 pm (closed Sunday and Monday). *La Rose des Vins* (☎ 03 88 32 74 40, *5 rue de Pâques*) is a French restaurant that offers good value for money, including a 98FF *menu* (closed Saturday and Sunday).

Self-service vegetarian-organic food is on offer at *Adan* (*6 rue Sédillot*), open noon to 2 pm Monday to Saturday. *Sidi Bou Saïd* (*22 rue du Vieux Marché aux Vins*) has hearty Tunisian couscous for 60FF to 75FF (closed Monday).

The *Atac Supermarket* (*47 rue des Grandes Arcades*) is open 8.30 am to 8 pm Monday to Saturday.

Entertainment

Strasbourg's most vibrant venue for live music is *La Laiterie* (☎ 03 88 23 72 37, *11-13 rue du Hohwald*), near the Laiterie tram stop.

La Salamandre (☎ 03 88 25 79 42, *3 rue Paul Janet*), an informal dance club, opens 9 pm to 3 am Wednesday to Saturday. At ever-popular, easygoing *Café des Anges* (☎ 03 88 37 12 67, *5 rue Ste Catherine*), you can dance from Tuesday to Saturday; things get going after 11 pm. The soul, funk, salsa and African music at the informal *Le Griot* (☎ 03 88 52 00 52, *6 Impasse de l'Écrevisse*) attracts a racially and ethnically mixed crowd; hours are 9 pm to 4 am (closed Sunday and Monday).

The Irish Times (*19 rue St Barbe*) is a congenial pub that has live music on Tuesday, Friday and Saturday from about 9 pm. Daily hours are 2 pm (noon on Sunday) to 1 or 2 am. At the *Académie de la Bière* (*17 rue Adolphe Seyboth*), a perennial favourite, you can sip beer amid rough-hewn wooden beams. Popular with students, it opens 9 am to 4 am daily.

Getting There & Away

Bus Eurolines coaches arrive and depart from place d'Austerlitz; the office (☎ 03 88 22 73 74) is at 5 rue des Frères.

City bus No 21 links place Gutenberg with the Stadthalle in Kehl, across the Rhine in Germany.

Train Strasbourg's train station (☎ 0836 35 35 39) is well connected with Paris' Gare de l'Est (215FF, four to five hours), Basel (Bâle; 103FF, 1½ hours) and Frankfurt (218FF, at least two hours). There are daily trains to Nice (468FF), Amsterdam (413FF) and Prague (593FF).

Getting Around

Three tram lines form the centrepiece of Strasbourg's excellent public transport network. Single bus/tram tickets, sold by bus (but not tram) drivers and the ticket machines at tram stops, cost 7FF.

COLMAR
pop 64,000

Colmar, an easy day trip from Strasbourg (and a good base for exploring the Route du Vin and the Massif des Vosges), is famous for the typically Alsatian architecture of its older neighbourhoods, and for the stunning *Issenheim Altarpiece* in the **Musée d'Unterlinden** (35/25FF; closed Tuesday from November to March). The **Musée Bartholdi**, 30 rue des Marchands, is dedicated to the creator of New York's *Statue of Liberty* (closed Tuesday).

Ave de la République stretches from the train station to the Musée d'Unterlinden, a distance of about 1km; the medieval streets of the old city (eg, **rue des Marchands**), lined with half-timbered buildings, are to the south-east. At the southern edge of the old city, **Petite Venise**, a neighbourhood of old, half-timbered buildings, runs along the Lauch River.

The efficient tourist office (☎ 03 89 20 68 92) is opposite the Musée d'Unterlinden at 4 rue d'Unterlinden. It opens 9 am to noon and 2 to 6 pm, Monday to Saturday (no midday closure from April to October; open until 7 pm in July and August). Sunday and holiday hours are 10 am to 2 pm.

Places to Stay

The *Auberge de Jeunesse Mittelhart* (☎ 03 89 80 57 39, fax 03 89 80 76 16, *2 rue Pasteur*),

2km north-west of the train station, has beds for 69FF, including breakfast. Reception is closed from 10 am to 5 pm. By bus, take No 3 to the Pont Rouge stop.

Near the train station, the cosy, 18-room **Hôtel La Chaumière** (*π 03 89 41 08 99, 74 ave de la République*) has simple and rather small doubles from 180FF (240FF with shower and toilet). The blush-pink (but fading) **Hôtel Primo** (*π 03 89 24 22 24, fax 03 89 24 55 96, ✉ hotel-primo-99@rmcnet.fr, 5 rue des Ancêtres*) has rooms with washbasin for up to three people for 159FF; doubles/quads with shower and toilet are 329/399FF.

Places to Eat
Alsatian specialities including spit-roasted ham (60FF) are served at **La Maison Rouge** (*π 03 89 23 53 22, 9 rue des Écoles*). A four-course Alsatian *menu* costs 84FF (closed on Sunday and Wednesday).

Djerba La Douce (*π 03 89 24 17 12, 10 rue du Mouton*) has Tunisian couscous for 53FF to 95FF (closed on Sunday).

There's a **Monoprix** supermarket across the square from the Musée d'Unterlinden (closed Sunday).

Getting There & Away
Colmar is served by frequent trains from Strasbourg (56FF, at least 30 minutes). Many destinations on the Route du Vin and in the Massif des Vosges are accessible by bus – check timetables at the tourist office and at the bus station next to the train station. Seven buses a day (three or four on weekends) go to the German university city of Freiburg (34FF or 10DM; 65 minutes).

ROUTE DU VIN
Meandering for some 120km along the eastern foothills of the Vosges, the Alsace Wine Route passes through picturesque villages guarded by ruined hill top castles. At places twee and touristy, it stretches from Marlenheim, about 20km west of Strasbourg, southward to Thann, about 35km south-west of Colmar.

Riquewihr, Ribeauvillé and **Kaysersberg** are perhaps the most attractive villages – and the most heavily touristed. Less touristy places include **Mittelbergheim, Eguisheim** and **Turkheim**. If you have your own transport, visit the imposing chateau of **Haut-Koenigsbourg**,

rebuilt early this century by Emperor Wilhelm II. The wine route is a good place to spot some of Alsace's famous storks.

Natzweiler-Struthof (*π 03 88 97 04 49*), the only Nazi concentration camp on French soil, is about 30km west of Obernai (open daily; closed 25 December to February).

The industrial city of **Mulhouse** (pronounced Moo-LOOZE), 43km south of Colmar, has a number of world-class museums dedicated to such subjects as historic motor-cars, railways, firefighting, textile printing and wallpaper.

MASSIF DES VOSGES
The rounded mountaintops, deep forests, glacial lakes, rolling pastureland and tiny villages of the Vosges Mountains are a hiker's paradise, with an astounding 7000km of marked trails. In the winter, the area has 36 modest skiing areas with 170 ski lifts.

The **Route des Crêtes** (Route of the Crests), which begins in Cernay (36km south-west of Colmar), takes you to (or near) the Vosges' highest *ballons* (bald, rounded mountain peaks), as well as to several WWI sites. Mountaintop lookouts afford spectacular views of the Alsace plain, the Schwarzwald (Black Forest) across the Rhine in Germany, the Jura and – on clear days – the Alps. The highest point in the Vosges is the dramatic, windblown summit of the 1424m-high **Grand Ballon**.

NANCY
pop 102,000
Delightful Nancy has an air of refinement found nowhere else in Lorraine, the region that borders Alsace to the west. Thanks to the stunning, gilded **place Stanislas** (the central square), sumptuous cream-coloured buildings, and shop windows filled with fine glassware, the former capital of the dukes of Lorraine seems as opulent today as it did during the 16th to 18th centuries.

The **Musée de l'École de Nancy** houses a superb collection of the sinuous, dream-like works of the Art Nouveau movement, which once flourished here (30/20FF, closed Tuesday). It's about 2km south-west of the centre – by bus, take Nos 5 or 25 to the Nancy Thermal stop.

Other outstanding museums include the newly-reopened **Musée des Beaux-Arts** (Fine

Arts Museum) at place Stanislas (30/15FF), and the **Musée Historique Lorrain** (Lorraine Historical Museum) at 64 and 66 Grande Rue (30FF). Both are closed Tuesday.

Orientation & Information

The heart of Nancy is the beautifully proportioned place Stanislas. The train station, at the bottom of busy rue Stanislas, is 800m southwest of place Stanislas.

The tourist office (☎ 03 83 35 22 41) is inside the Hôtel de Ville on place Stanislas. It opens 9 am to 6 pm, Monday to Saturday (7 pm from April to October), and Sunday and holidays 10 am to 1 pm (5 pm from April to October).

Places to Stay

The 60-bed *Auberge de Jeunesse Remicourt* (☎ 03 83 27 73 67, fax 03 83 41 41 35, 149 rue de Vandœuvre in Villers-lès-Nancy), in an old chateau, is 4km south of the centre. A bed costs 80FF, including breakfast. By bus, take No 26 to the St Fiacre stop.

Two blocks south-west of place Stanislas, the welcoming and slightly off-beat, 29-room *Hôtel de l'Académie* (☎ 03 83 35 52 31, fax 03 83 32 55 78, 7 bis des Michottes) has singles/ doubles with shower from 110/160FF. The friendly, two-star, 20-room *Hôtel des Portes d'Or* (☎ 03 83 35 42 34, fax 03 83 32 51 41, 21 rue Stanislas) has charming and well-kept doubles with upholstered doors from 280FF.

Places to Eat

Restaurant Le Gastrolâtre (☎ 03 83 35 51 94, 1 place Vaudémont) has Lorraine and Provençal *menus* from 95FF to 195FF (closed on Monday at midday and Sunday). Around the corner (and just a block from place Stanislas), rue des Maréchaux is lined with restaurants of all sorts.

The *covered market* (place Henri Mangin) opens 7 am to 6 pm Tuesday to Saturday. Across the square, inside the St Sébastien shopping centre, the *Casino* supermarket opens until 8.30 pm (closed Sunday).

Getting There & Away

From the train station on place Thiers there are direct services to Strasbourg (109FF, 70 to 95 minutes) and Paris' Gare de l'Est (206FF, three hours).

Far Northern France

Le Nord de France is made up of three historical regions: Flanders (Flandre or Flandres), Artois and Picardy (Picardie). Densely populated and laden with rustbelt industry, this is not one of the more fabled corners of France, but if you're up for a short trip from the UK, or inclined to do a little exploring, the region offers lots to do and some excellent dining.

LILLE

pop 1.1 million

Thanks to the Eurostar and other fast rail links, Lille – France's northern-most metropolis – is a popular first stop for visitors coming from across the Channel and Belgium. Long a major industrial centre, today's Lille has two renowned art museums and an attractive old town graced with ornate Flemish-style buildings.

Orientation & Information

Lille is centred around place du Général de Gaulle, place du Théâtre, and place Rihour. Vieux Lille (Old Lille) lies on the north side of the centre. Lille-Flandres train station is about 400m south-east of place du Général de Gaulle; the ultra-modern Lille-Europe train station is 500m farther east.

The tourist office (☎ 03 20 21 94 21, fax 03 20 21 94 20, ✉ ot.lille@wanadoo.fr), place Rihour, occupies a remnant of the 15th-century Palais Rihour. It is open 9.30 am to 6.30 pm Monday to Saturday; and 10 am to noon and 2 to 5 pm Sundays and holidays. Web site: www .cci-lille.fr.

Money The Banque de France at 75 rue Royale exchanges money 8.30 am to 12.15 pm weekdays. There's a Credit du Nord with an ATM on the corner of rue Jean Roisin and place Rihour.

Post & Communications The main post office, 8 place de la République, exchanges currency and has a Cyberposte. Net Arena Games (☎ 03 28 38 09 20), 10 rue des Bouchers, charges 20FF per half-hour of Web surfing.

Laundry The Laverie O'Claire, 57 rue du Molinel, lets you begin your last wash at 8 pm and the last dry cycle at 8.30 pm.

Things to See & Do

On place du Général de Gaulle, the ornate, Flemish Renaissance **Vieille Bourse** (Old Stock Exchange) consists of 24 separate buildings around a courtyard. Nearby, place du Théâtre is dominated by the neoclassical **Opéra** and the tower-topped neo-Flemish **Chambre de Commerce building**. North of place du Général de Gaulle, **Vieux Lille** gleams with nicely-restored 17th and 18th-century houses.

Lille's outstanding **Palais des Beaux-Arts** (Fine Arts Museum, metro République) has a superb collection of 15th to 20th-century paintings and exhibits of archaeology, medieval sculpture and ceramics. It opens noon (2 pm on Monday) to 6 pm (8 pm on Friday); it's closed Tuesday and bank holidays. Tickets cost 30/20FF.

North of Vieux Lille at 9 rue Princesse is the **Musée Charles de Gaulle** (☎ 03 20 31 96 03), where the premier-to-be was born in 1890. It opens 10 am to noon and 2 to 5 pm (closed Monday, Tuesday and holidays). Admission costs 15/5FF.

Special Events

The Braderie, a flea market extraordinaire covering most of the old town, is held on the first weekend of September. The Festival de Lille is a four-week series of concerts and other events held in September and October.

Places to Stay

Camping *Camping L'Image* (☎ 03 20 35 69 42, 140 rue Brune) 10km north-west of Lille in the suburb of Houplines, opens year-round. It charges 11/18FF per adult/tent site. By car, take the A25 towards Dunkerque and get off at exit No 8 (Chapelle d'Armentières).

Hostels The modern, 170-bed *Auberge de Jeunesse* (☎ 03 20 57 08 94, fax 03 20 63 98 93, ✉ lille@fuaj.org, 12 rue Malpart, metro République or Mairie de Lille) is in a former maternity hospital with dorm beds starting at 73FF, including breakfast. Reception opens 8 am to noon and 2 pm to 2 am. It's closed from 20 December to the end of January.

Hotels The place de la Gare has quite a few hotels. *Hôtel des Voyageurs* (☎ 03 20 06 43 14, fax 03 20 74 19 01) at No 10 has simple and clean singles/doubles, reached via a vintage lift, starting at 130/160FF (205/250FF with shower and toilet). A hall shower is 20FF.

The two-star *Hôtel de France* (☎ 03 20 57 14 78, fax 03 20 57 06 01, 10 rue de Béthune) has airy singles/doubles with washbasin for 150/170FF (200/240FF with shower and toilet). Hall showers are free. Drivers unloading luggage should take rue des Fossés.

Hôtel Moulin d'Or (☎ 03 20 06 12 67, fax 03 20 06 33 50, 15 rue du Molinel) has very simple, linoleum-floored doubles from 160FF, 280FF with shower, and 300FF with shower and toilet. There are no hall showers. Curfew is midnight.

Places to Eat

In Vieux Lille, the relaxed *La Pâte Brisée* (☎ 03 20 74 29 00, 63-65 rue de la Monnaie) has savoury and sweet *tartes*, salads, meat dishes and *gratin* in one/two/three-course *menus* for 47/69/84FF, including a drink. Try the great regional *menu* for 89FF at the intimate *La Tarterie de la Voûte* (☎ 03 20 42 12 16, 4 rue des Débris St Étienne), closed Monday night and Sunday.

The elegant *Le Hochepot* (☎ 03 20 54 17 59, 6 rue du Nouveau Siècle) serves Flemish dishes such as *coq à la bière*. The *menus* cost 125FF, including drinks. It's closed Saturday lunch and Sunday.

For a splurge, *À l'Huîtrière* (☎ 03 20 55 43 41, 3 rue des Chats Bossus), decorated with mosaics dating from 1928, has great seafood and traditional French cuisine. The lunch *menu* is 245FF; mains are about 170FF. It opens noon to 2.30 pm and 7 to 9.30 pm (closed Sunday evening and late July to late August). Reserve ahead.

Self-Catering The lively *Wazemmes food market* (*place Nouvelle Aventure, metro Gambetta*), 1.2km south-west of the centre, opens till 7 pm (closed Monday). There's a *Monoprix supermarket* at 31 rue du Molinel (closed Sunday).

Entertainment

Classical Music & Jazz Well-regarded *Orchestre National de Lille* (☎ 03 20 12 82 40)

FRANCE

plays in the Palais de la Musique. *Le 30 (☎ 03 20 30 15 54, 30 rue de Paris)* has live jazz nightly (except Sunday); the audience sits on soft, modular couches in what looks like a 1960s airport VIP lounge.

Pubs & Bars *Café Oz (☎ 03 20 55 15 15, 33 place Louise de Bettignies)*, a branch of Paris' famous Australian bar, has Foster's on tap (18FF for 250mL) and good cocktails (45FF).

In Vieux Lille, the laid-back *Le Balatum (☎ 03 20 57 41 81, 13 rue de la Barre)* has numerous beers from 13FF. *L'Illustration Café (☎ 03 20 12 00 90, 18 rue Royale)* is a mellow Art Nouveau-style bar. Both open until 2 am.

Getting There & Away
Bus The Eurolines office (☎ 03 20 78 18 88), 23 parvis St Maurice, has direct buses to Brussels (50FF, 2½ hours), London (250FF, five hours) and other destinations. It opens 9 am to 6 or 8 pm (two-hour break at noon on Monday to Wednesday, closed Sunday).

Train Lille has frequent rail links to almost everywhere in France. Its two train stations (☎ 0836 35 35 35) are linked by metro line No 2.

Gare Lille-Flandres handles almost all regional services and most TGVs to Paris' Gare du Nord (208FF to 278FF, one hour, one to two per hour). The information office opens 9 am to 7 pm (closed Sunday and holidays).

Gare Lille-Europe is served by Eurostar trains to London (700FF at weekends, 1050FF on weekdays, 2 hours) and TGVs and Eurostars to Brussels (85FF to 98FF, 38 minutes, 15 a day). Other options include Calais (84FF, 1½ hours, eight to 15 a day).

Getting Around
Transpole (☎ 03 20 40 40 40) runs Lille's metro, trams and buses. Tickets (7.50FF) are sold on the bus but must be purchased (and validated in the orange posts) before boarding the metro or tram. A carnet of 10/weekly passes costs 64/71FF.

CALAIS
pop 78,000
Calais, only 34km from the English town of Dover, has long been a popular port for passenger travel between the UK and continental Europe. Its dominance of trans-Channel transport was sealed in 1994 when the Channel Tunnel was opened at Coquelles, 5km south-west of the town centre. Over 20 million people pass through Calais each year.

Orientation & Information
The centre of Calais, whose main square is place d'Armes, is encircled by canals and harbour basins, with Calais-Ville train station 650m to the south. The car ferry terminal is 1.7km north-east of place d'Armes; the hoverport is another 1.5km farther out.

The tourist office (☎ 03 21 96 62 40, fax 03 21 96 01 92, ✉ ot@ot-calais.fr), 12 blvd Georges Clemenceau, opens 9 am to 7 pm Monday to Saturday and Sunday morning. Web site: www.ot-calais.fr.

Money The Banque de France at 77 blvd Jacquard exchanges money 8.30 am to 12.10 pm weekdays. There are commercial banks along rue Royale.

Post & Communications The post office on place de Rheims opens until 6 pm weekdays and until noon on Saturday. It has a currency desk and a Cyberposte terminal.

Laundry The Lavorama on the eastern side of place d'Armes is open 7 am to 9 pm daily.

Things to See
A cast of Auguste Rodin's famous bronze statue of six emaciated but proud figures, known in English as **The Burghers of Calais**, stands in front of the Flemish Renaissance-style Hôtel de Ville, which is topped with an ornate 75m clock tower.

Across the street in Parc St Pierre is the **Musée de la Guerre** (☎ 03 21 34 21 57), an intriguing WWII museum housed in a 94m-long concrete bunker. You can begin your visit from 11 am to 4.15 pm (10 am to 5.15 pm from April to September). Admission costs 25/20FF.

The newly-renovated **Musée des Beaux-Arts et de la Dentelle** (Museum of Fine Arts & Lace; ☎ 03 21 46 48 40), 25 rue Richelieu, has exhibits on mechanised lacemaking (the first machines were smuggled to Calais from England in 1816). It opens 10 am to noon and 2 or 2.30 to 5.30 pm daily (6.30 pm at weekends; closed Tuesday). Admission costs 15FF/10FF (free on Wednesday).

Places to Stay

Camping The grassy but soulless *Camping Municipal* (☎ *03 21 97 89 79, ave Raymond Poincaré*) opens all year. It charges 18.90/13.20FF per adult/tent or caravan site. From the train station, take bus No 3 to the Pluviose stop.

Hostels The modern and nicely furnished *Auberge de Jeunesse* (☎ *03 21 34 70 20, fax 03 21 96 87 80, ave Maréchal De Lattre de Tassigny),* also called the Centre Européen de Séjour, is 200m from the beach. A spot in a two-bed double costs 94FF, and a single costs 136FF, including breakfast. Take bus No 3 to the Pluviose stop.

Hotels At Parc St Pierre near the train station, the nicely-renovated *Hôtel-Pension L'Ovale* (☎/*fax 03 21 97 57 00, 38-40 ave Wilson)* has bright, cheery rooms with high ceilings and sparkling new TVs. Singles or doubles cost 160FF, triples 180FF (all with private shower). The central and friendly *Hôtel Bristol* (☎/*fax 03 21 34 53 24, 15 rue du Duc de Guise)* has cosy singles/doubles from 150/160FF (180/220FF with shower and toilet); hall showers are free. Rooms for four and five people are also available.

The family-run *Hôtel Richelieu* (☎ *03 21 34 61 60, fax 03 21 85 89 28, 17 rue Richelieu)* is a very quiet place. It has singles/doubles/quads with soft beds and a range of amenities for 250/254/314FF, including breakfast.

Places to Eat

Restaurants *Histoire Ancienne* (☎ *03 21 34 11 20, 20 rue Royale)* is a Paris-style bistro specialising in meat dishes grilled over a wood fire. *Menus* go for 98FF to 158FF (closed Monday night and Sunday). Show a ferry or shuttle ticket and get a free bottle of takeaway wine.

The rustic *Au Coq d'Or* (☎ *03 21 34 79 05, 31 place d'Armes)* serves grilled meat dishes and seafood daily. *Menus* run from 64FF to 245FF (closed Wednesday).

For a real treat, try the family-run *La Pléiade* (☎ *03 21 34 03 70, 32 rue Jean Quéhen),* an elegant, mainly seafood restaurant whose

menus cost 85FF to 160FF, plus dessert (closed Saturday midday and Monday).

Self-Catering Place d'Armes hosts a *food market* Wednesday and Saturday mornings. There's a *Match supermarket (place d'Armes)* that also opens Sunday morning in July and August.

Getting There & Away

For details on the Channel Tunnel and ferry fares and schedules, see Britain under Land and Sea in the Getting There & Away section.

Bus Bus Inglard (☎ 03 21 96 49 54) runs buses three times daily (except Sunday) from Calais-Ville train station and place du Théâtre to Boulogne (27FF, 1¼ hours). Cariane Littoral (☎ 03 21 34 74 40), 10 rue d'Amsterdam, has express BCD services to Boulogne (38FF, 35 minutes, six on weekdays and two on Saturday) and Dunkerque (40FF, 30 minutes, 11 weekdays and three on Saturday).

Train Calais has two train stations: Gare Calais-Ville (☎ 0836 35 35 35) and Gare Calais-Fréthun, 10km south-west of town near the Channel Tunnel entrance.

Calais-Ville has direct, non-TGV trains to Paris' Gare du Nord (182FF, 3½ hours, three to six a day), Boulogne (35FF, 35 minutes, hourly), and Lille-Flandres (84FF, 1½ hours, seven to 15 a day).

Calais-Fréthun is well-served by TGVs to Paris' Gare du Nord (215FF, 1½ hours, two a day) as well as the Eurostar to London (700FF to 1050FF, 1¾ hours, three a day). Calais-Fréthun is linked to the Calais-Ville station by Opale Bus No 7 (7.20FF).

Car To reach the Channel Tunnel's vehicle loading area, follow the road signs on the A16 to the 'Tunnel Sous La Manche'.

Boat P&O Stena and SeaFrance Sealink car ferries to/from Dover dock at the busy Terminal Est, just over 1km north-east of place d'Armes.

P&O Stena's office (☎ 0802 01 00 20) is at 41 place d'Armes. Nearby at No 2 is SeaFrance Sealink's office (☎ 0803 04 40 45). Both open weekdays and Saturday morning.

SeaCats to/from Dover, operated by Hoverspeed (☎ 0820 00 35 55 or ☎ 03 21 46 14 00), use the hoverport, 3km north-east of the town centre. Hovercraft no longer run on the Dover-Calais route.

Getting Around

Bus To reach the car ferry terminal, take a free shuttle run by SeaFrance Sealink and P&O Stena – they stop at the Calais-Ville train station and near each company's office at place d'Armes. Hoverspeed's buses to the hoverport (5FF) leave the train station about 45 minutes before each departure.

Opale Bus (☎ 03 21 00 75 75) operates local buses from place du Théâtre, which is 700m south of the train station. Almost all the lines stop at the Calais-Ville train station.

DUNKERQUE
pop 209,000

Dunkerque was flattened shortly before one of the dullest periods in Western architecture – 1950s brick low-rise. Unless you're planning to spend time on the beach or to join in the colourful pre-Lent carnival, there's little reason to spend the night here.

Orientation & Information

The train station is 600m south-west of Dunkerque's main square, place Jean Bart. The beach and its waterfront esplanade, Digue de Mer, are 2km north-east of the centre. The tourist office (☎ 03 28 26 27 28, fax 03 28 63 38 40, ✉ dunkerque@tourism.norsys.fr) is in the medieval belfry on rue de l'Amiral Ronarc.

Things to See & Do

The **Musée Portuaire** (Harbour Museum; ☎ 03 28 63 33 39), 9 quai de la Citadelle, housed in a former tobacco warehouse, has splendid ship models and exhibits on the history of Dunkerque as a port. Admission costs 25/20FF.

One-hour **boat tours** (☎ 03 28 58 85 12 for reservations) depart from place du Minck and afford views of the huge port and some of France's most important steel and petroleum works. Tickets cost 35FF (children 27FF).

Places to Stay & Eat

The *Auberge de Jeunesse* (☎ 03 28 63 36 34, fax 03 28 63 24 54, place Paul Asseman) is on the beach 3km north of the train station. Spots in eight-bed dorm rooms cost 48FF, plus 19FF for breakfast. Take bus No 3 to the 'Piscine' stop, walk past the pool and the hostel's on your right.

Opposite the tourist office, the two-star *Hôtel du Tigre* (☎/fax 03 28 66 75 17, 8 rue Clemenceau) has nice singles/doubles from 90/130FF (190/240FF with shower and toilet).

Kim Thanh Restaurant (☎ 03 28 51 22 98, 14 place Roger Salengro) 100m north-west of the tourist office, does Chinese-Vietnamese lunch *menus* (oodles of chicken) for 55FF (closed Tuesday and Saturday lunch).

Getting There & Away

BCD (☎ 03 21 83 51 51) runs buses to/from Dunkerque train station to Calais (40FF, 45 minutes, 11 on weekdays and three on Saturday). Dunkerque has frequent train links to Lille (73FF, 1¼ hours, 16 a day), Calais (83FF, 1¼ to 1¾ hours, 13 per day) and Paris Gare du Nord by TGV (280FF to 320FF, 1½ hours, hourly).

BATTLE OF THE SOMME MEMORIALS

The First Battle of the Somme, the WWI Allied offensive waged in the villages and woodlands north-east of Amiens, was designed to relieve pressure on the beleaguered French troops at Verdun (for more details see the Alsace & Lorraine chapter). On 1 July 1916, British, Commonwealth and French troops 'went over the top' in a massive assault along a 34km front. But German positions proved virtually unbreachable, and on the first day of the battle an astounding 20,000 British troops were killed and another 40,000 were wounded. Most casualties were infantrymen mowed down by German machine guns.

By the time the offensive was called off in mid-November, some 1.2 million lives had been lost on both sides. The British had advanced 12km, the French only 8km. The Battle of the Somme has become a metaphor for the meaningless slaughter of war, and its killing fields are a site of pilgrimage.

Commonwealth Cemeteries & Memorials

Over 750,000 soldiers from Canada, Australia, New Zealand, South Africa, the Indian subcontinent, the West Indies and other parts of the British Empire died on the Western Front, two-thirds of them in France. By Commonwealth tradition, they were buried where they fell, in over 1000 military cemeteries and 2000 civilian cemeteries. Today, hundreds of neatly-tended Commonwealth plots dot the landscape along a wide line running roughly from Albert and Cambrai north via Arras and Béthune to Armentières and Ypres (Ieper) in Belgium. Some 26 memorials (20 of them in France) bear the names of over 300,000 Commonwealth soldiers whose bodies were never recovered or identified. The French, Americans and Germans reburied their dead in large war cemeteries after the war.

Except where noted, all the monuments listed here are always open. Larger Commonwealth cemeteries usually have a plaque (often inside a little marble pavilion) with historical information in English. Touring the area is only really feasible by car or bicycle.

Maps & Brochures All of the memorials and cemeteries mentioned here (and hundreds of others) are indicated on Michelin's 1:200,000 scale maps. For more information, pick up Michelin's yellow maps Nos 51 and/or 52 overprinted by the Commonwealth War Graves Commission (☎ 03 21 21 77 00 in Beaurains) with all the Commonwealth cemeteries in the region (25FF). The brochure *The Somme – Remembrance Tour of the Great War* (5FF) is on offer at area tourist offices.

Normandy

Normandy (Normandie) derives its name from the Norsemen (Vikings) who took control of the area in the early 10th century. Modern Normandy is the land of the *bocage*, farmland subdivided by hedges and trees.

ROUEN
pop 107,000
The city of Rouen, for centuries the lowest bridging point on the Seine, is known for its many spires, church towers and half-timbered houses, not to mention its Gothic cathedral and excellent museums. Rouen can be visited on a day or overnight trip from Paris.

Orientation & Information
The train station (Gare Rouen-Rive Droite) is at the northern end of rue Jeanne d'Arc, the major thoroughfare running south to the Seine.

The tourist office (☎ 02 32 08 32 40, fax 02 32 08 32 44, @ otrouen@mcom.fr) is at 25 place de la Cathédrale. The office opens 9 am to 7 pm Monday to Saturday, and 9.30 am to 12.30 pm and 2.30 to 6 pm on Sunday, May to September; and 9 am to 6 pm Monday to Saturday, and 10 am to 1 pm on Sunday the rest of the year. Guided city tours (35FF) depart from the office in summer at 10.30 am and 3 pm daily.

Things to See
Rouen's main street, rue du Gros Horloge, runs from the cathedral to **place du Vieux Marché**, where 19-year-old Joan of Arc was burned at the stake for heresy in 1431. You'll learn more about her life from its stained-glass windows at the adjacent Église Jeanne d'Arc than at the tacky **Musée Jeanne d'Arc** across the square at No 33.

Rouen's **Cathédrale Notre Dame**, the subject of a series of paintings by Claude Monet, is a masterpiece of French Gothic architecture. There are several guided visits (15/10FF) a day to the crypt, ambulatory (containing Richard the Lion-Heart's tomb) and Chapel of the Virgin.

The **Musée Le Secq des Tournelles** on rue Jacques Villon (opposite 27 rue Jean Lecanuet) is devoted to the blacksmith's craft and displays some 12,000 locks, keys and tongs made between the 3rd and 19th centuries (15/10FF, closed Tuesday).

The **Musée des Beaux-Arts** facing the square at 26 bis rue Jean Lecanuet features some major paintings from the 16th to 20th centuries, including some of Monet's cathedral series (20/13FF, closed Tuesday).

La Tour Jeanne d'Arc on rue du Donjon, south of the train station, is the tower where Joan of Arc was imprisoned before her execution. There are two exhibition rooms (10FF, closed Tuesday).

Places to Stay
The year-round *Camping Municipal* (☎ 02 35 74 07 59, rue Jules Ferry), in the suburb of Déville-lès-Rouen, is 5km north-west of town. From the Théâtre des Arts or the nearby

FRANCE

FRANCE

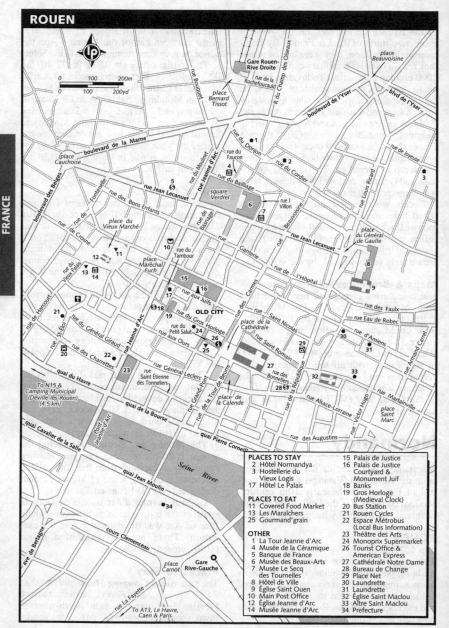

ROUEN

place Beauvoisine

Gare Rouen-Rive Droite

place Bernard Tissot

boulevard de l'Yser

blvd de l'Yser

rue de la Rochefoucauld

R du Champ des Oiseaux

rue Bouquet

place Cauchoise

boulevard de la Marne

place du Général de Gaulle

rue de Joyeuse

rue Louis Ricard

rue du Donjon

rue du Faucon

rue du Cordier

rue du Bailliage

rue Jean Lecanuet

rue Jeanne d'Arc

rue du Moulinet

square Verdrel

rue J Villon

rue de Beauvoisine

boulevard des Belges

boulevard de la Marne

rue de Fontenelle

rue des Bons Enfants

place du Vieux Marché

rue de Crosne

rue de Basnage

rue Ganterie

rue Jean Lecanuet

rue de l'Hôpital

place Maréchal Fuch

place du Tambour

rue du Tambour

rue du Vieux Palais

rue aux Juifs

OLD CITY

rue des Carmes

rue Saint Nicolas

place de la Cathédrale

rue des Faulx

rue Eau de Robec

rue d'Amiens

rue de Harcourt

rue St-Eloi

rue du Général Giraud

rue Jeanne d'Arc

rue du Gros Horloge

rue du Petit Salut

rue aux Ours

rue des Charrettes

rue Saint Romain

rue des Bonnetiers

rue Amand Carrel

quai du Havre

To N15 & Camping Municipal (Déville-lès-Rouen) (4.5 km)

rue Général Leclerc

rue Saint Étienne des Tonneliers

rue Grand-Pont

rue de la Tour de Beurre

place de la Calende

rue de la République

rue Alsace-Lorraine

rue Martainville

place Saint Marc

quai de la Bourse

Pont Jeanne d'Arc

quai Cavalier de la Salle

quai Jean Moulin

Seine River

quai Pierre Corneille

quai des Augustins

rue Victor Hugo

cours Clemenceau

ave de Bretagne

place Carnot

Gare Rive-Gauche

rue La Fayette

To A13, Le Havre, Caen & Paris

PLACES TO STAY
2 Hôtel Normandya
3 Hostellerie du Vieux Logis
17 Hôtel Le Palais

PLACES TO EAT
11 Covered Food Market
13 Les Maraîchers
25 Gourmand'grain

OTHER
1 La Tour Jeanne d'Arc
4 Musée de la Céramique
5 Banque de France
6 Musée des Beaux-Arts
7 Musée Le Secq des Tournelles
8 Hôtel de Ville
9 Église Saint Ouen
10 Main Post Office
12 Église Jeanne d'Arc
14 Musée Jeanne d'Arc

15 Palais de Justice
16 Palais de Justice Courtyard & Monument Juif
18 Banks
19 Gros Horloge (Medieval Clock)
20 Bus Station
21 Rouen Cycles
22 Espace Métrobus (Local Bus Information)
23 Théâtre des Arts
24 Monoprix Supermarket
26 Tourist Office & American Express
27 Cathédrale Notre Dame
28 Bureau de Change
29 Place Net
30 Laundrette
31 Laundrette
32 Église Saint Maclou
33 Aître Saint Maclou
34 Prefecture

euro currency converter €1 = 6.55FF

bus station, take bus No 2 and get off at the *mairie* (town hall) of Déville-lès-Rouen. It's 59FF for two people and a tent.

The spotless and friendly **Hôtel Normandya** (*☎ 02 35 71 46 15, 32 rue du Cordier*) is on a quiet street 300m south-east of the train station. Singles (some with shower) are 110FF to 140FF, doubles 10FF to 20FF more. The very French **Hostellerie du Vieux Logis** (*☎ 02 35 71 55 30, 5 rue de Joyeuse*), 1km east of the train station, has a pleasantly frayed atmosphere and a lovely garden out the back. Singles/doubles start at 100FF. The **Hôtel Le Palais** (*☎ 02 35 71 41 40, 12 rue du Tambour*), between the Palais de Justice and the Gros Horloge, has doubles with shower for 140FF.

Places to Eat
A *covered market* is held daily (except Monday) from 6 am to 1.30 pm at place du Vieux Marché. The bistro-style **Les Maraîchers** at No 37 is the pick of the Vieux Marché's many restaurants, with its terrace and varied *menus* from 69FF (89FF in the evening).

Gourmand'grain (*☎ 02 35 98 15 74, 3 rue du Petit Salut*) behind the tourist office, is a lunchtime vegetarian cafe with *menus* for 45FF and 69FF.

Getting There & Away
Buses to Dieppe (68FF, two hours) and Le Havre (84FF, three hours) are slower and more expensive than the train. The bus station (*☎ 02 35 52 92 00*) is at 25 rue des Charrettes near the Théâtre des Arts.

There are at least 20 trains a day to/from Paris' Gare St Lazare (124FF, 70 minutes). For train information, call ☎ 0836 35 35 39.

Getting Around
TCAR operates the local bus network and metro line. The metro links the train station with the Théâtre des Arts before crossing the Seine into the southern suburbs. Bus tickets cost 8FF, or 63FF for a magnetic card good for 10 rides.

BAYEUX
pop 15,000
Bayeux is celebrated for two trans-Channel invasions: the AD 1066 conquest of England by William the Conqueror (an event chronicled in the Bayeux Tapestry) and the Allied D-Day landings of 6 June 1944; Bayeux was the first town in France to be liberated from the Nazis.

Bayeux is an attractive – though fairly touristy – town with several excellent museums. It's also a good base for the D-Day beaches.

Orientation & Information
The cathedral, Bayeux's central landmark, is 1km north-west of the train station.

The tourist office (*☎ 02 31 51 28 28, fax 02 31 51 28 29*) is at Pont St Jean just off the northern end of rue Larcher. It opens 9 am to noon and 2 to 6 pm Monday to Saturday; and also on Sunday from 9.30 am to noon and 2.30 to 6 pm in July and August. A *billet jumelé* (multipass ticket) valid for most of Bayeux's museums (but not the Musée Mémorial) costs 38/22FF.

Things to See
The world-famous **Bayeux Tapestry** – a 70m-long strip of coarse linen decorated with woollen embroidery – was commissioned by Odo, bishop of Bayeux and half-brother to William the Conqueror, for the consecration of the cathedral in Bayeux in 1077. The tapestry recounts the story of the Norman invasion of 1066 – from the Norman perspective. Halley's Comet, which visited our solar system in 1066, also makes an appearance. The tapestry is housed in the **Musée de la Tapisserie de Bayeux** on rue de Nesmond, open 9 am to 7 pm daily (closed at lunch in off-season). Entry is 38/16FF.

Bayeux's **Cathédrale Notre Dame** is an exceptional example of Norman-Gothic architecture, dating from the 13th century.

The **Musée Mémorial 1944 Bataille de Normandie**, Bayeux's huge war museum on blvd Fabien Ware, displays a haphazard collection of photos, uniforms, weapons and life-like scenes associated with D-Day and the Battle of Normandy. An excellent 30-minute film is screened in English. Admission is 33/16FF.

The **Bayeux War Cemetery**, a British cemetery on blvd Fabien Ware, a few hundred metres west of the museum, is the largest of the 18 Commonwealth military cemeteries in Normandy. Many of the headstones are inscribed with poignant epitaphs.

FRANCE

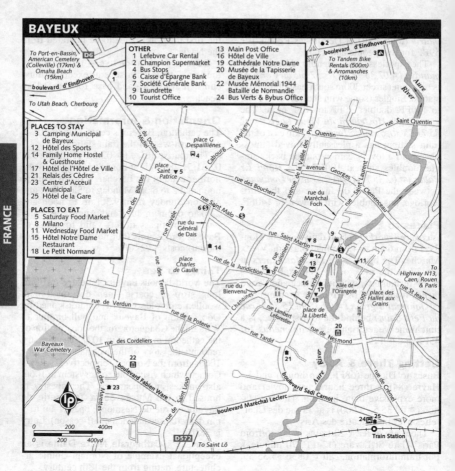

BAYEUX

OTHER
1 Lefebvre Car Rental
2 Champion Supermarket
4 Bus Stops
6 Caisse d'Épargne Bank
7 Société Générale Bank
9 Laundrette
10 Tourist Office
13 Main Post Office
16 Hôtel de Ville
19 Cathédrale Notre Dame
20 Musée de la Tapisserie de Bayeux
22 Musée Mémorial 1944 Bataille de Normandie
24 Bus Verts & Bybus Office

PLACES TO STAY
3 Camping Municipal de Bayeux
12 Hôtel des Sports
14 Family Home Hostel & Guesthouse
17 Hôtel de l'Hôtel de Ville
21 Relais des Cèdres
23 Centre d'Acceuil Municipal
25 Hôtel de la Gare

PLACES TO EAT
5 Saturday Food Market
8 Milano
11 Wednesday Food Market
15 Hôtel Notre Dame Restaurant
18 Le Petit Normand

Places to Stay

Camping *Camping Municipal de Bayeux* (☎ 02 31 92 08 43) is 2km north of town, just south of blvd d'Eindhoven. It's open mid-March to mid-November, and charges 9.20/17.10FF per tent/person. Bus Nos 5 and 6 from the train station stop here.

Hostels The *Family Home* hostel and guesthouse (☎ 02 31 92 15 22, fax 02 31 92 55 72, 39 rue du Général de Dais) in three old buildings, is an excellent place to meet other travellers. Dorm beds are 100FF (95FF with HI card), singles 160FF. There's a kitchen, or you can have a multicourse French dinner (with wine) for 65FF.

The modern, if slightly sterile, *Centre d'Accueil Municipal* (☎ 02 31 92 08 19, 21 rue des Marettes) is 1km south-west of the cathedral. Singles are good value at 90FF.

Hotels The old but well-maintained *Hôtel de la Gare* (☎ 02 31 92 10 70, fax 02 31 51 95 99, 26 place de la Gare), opposite the train station, has singles/doubles from 85/100FF. The central *Hôtel de l'Hôtel de Ville* (☎ 02 31 92 30 08, 31ter rue Larcher) has large and quiet rooms for 140/160FF.

Showers are free. Phone reservations are not accepted. A few hundred metres north, *Hôtel des Sports* (☎ 02 31 92 28 53, 19 rue St Martin) has decent rooms (most with shower) starting at 160/200FF.

Places to Eat
There are *food markets* on rue St Jean (Wednesday morning) and on place St Patrice (Saturday morning).

Le Petit Normand (☎ 02 31 22 88 66, 35 rue Larcher) specialises in traditional Norman food and has simple *menus* starting at 58FF (closed Sunday night and Wednesday, except in July and August). *Hôtel Notre Dame* restaurant (☎ 02 31 92 87 24) offers Norman fare at its best; lunch *menus* cost 60FF, dinner *menus* 95FF (closed Sunday lunch and Monday from November to March). *Milano* (☎ 02 31 92 15 10, 18 rue St Martin) serves good pizza (closed Sunday from September to May).

Getting There & Away
The train station office (☎ 02 31 92 80 50) opens 7 am to 8.45 pm daily. Trains serve Paris' Gare St Lazare (171FF, via Caen), Cherbourg, Rennes and points beyond.

D-DAY BEACHES
The D-Day landings were the largest military operation in history. Early on the morning of 6 June 1944, swarms of landing craft – part of a flotilla of almost 7000 boats – ferried ashore 135,000 Allied troops along 80km of beaches north of Bayeux. The landings on D-Day were followed by the 76-day Battle of Normandy that began the liberation of Europe from Nazi occupation.

Things to See
Arromanches In order to unload the vast quantities of cargo necessary for the invasion, the Allies established two prefabricated ports. The remains of one of them, Port Winston, can be seen at Arromanches, a seaside town 10km north-east of Bayeux.

The **Musée du Débarquement** (Landing Museum; ☎ 02 31 22 34 31) explains the logistics and importance of Port Winston and makes a good first stop before visiting the beaches (35/20FF, closed Monday and in January).

Omaha Beach The most brutal combat of 6 June was fought 20km west of Arromanches at Omaha Beach. Today, little evidence of the war remains except the bunkers and munitions sites of a German fortified point to the west (look for the tall obelisk on the hill).

American Military Cemetery The remains of the Americans who lost their lives during the Battle of Normandy were either sent back to the USA or buried in the American Military Cemetery at Colleville-sur-Mer, containing the graves of 9386 American soldiers and a memorial to 1557 others whose bodies were never found.

Organised Tours
Tours of the D-Day beaches are offered by Bus Fly (☎ 02 31 22 00 08), based at the Family Home hostel in Bayeux (see Places to Stay in Bayeux). An afternoon tour to major D-Day sites costs 160/140FF, including museum entry fees.

Getting There & Away
Bus Bus Verts (☎ 02 31 92 02 92), with an office opposite Bayeaux's train station (closed weekends and in July), sends bus No 70 west to the American cemetery at Colleville-sur-Mer and Omaha Beach. Bus No 74 serves Arromanches, and Gold and Juno beaches. In July and August only, Bus No 75 goes to Caen via Arromanches, Gold, Juno and Sword beaches and the port of Ouistreham. There are timetables posted in the train station and at place G Despallières.

Car For three or more people, renting a car can actually be cheaper than a tour. Lefebvre Car Rental (☎ 02 31 92 05 96) on blvd d'Eindhoven in Bayeux charges 350FF per day with 200km free.

MONT ST MICHEL
pop 42
It is difficult not to be impressed by Mont St Michel with its massive abbey anchored at the summit of a rocky island. Around the base are the ancient ramparts and a jumble of buildings that house the handful of people who still live there.

At low tide, Mont St Michel looks out over bare sand stretching into the distance. At high

FRANCE

tide – about six hours later – this huge expanse of sand is under water, though only the very highest tides cover the 900m causeway that connects the islet to the mainland. The French government is currently spending millions to restore Mont St Michel to its former glory, so parts of it may be scaffolded.

The Mont's major attraction is the **Abbaye du Mont St Michel** (☎ 02 33 89 80 00), at the top of the Grande rue, up the stairway. It opens 9 am to 5.30 pm daily (9.30 am to 5 pm from October to April). It's worth taking the guided tour (in English) included in the ticket price (40/25FF). There are also self-paced evening tours (60/35FF) at 9 or 10 pm (except Sunday) of the illuminated and music-filled rooms.

Pontorson The nearest town, Pontorson is 9km south and the base for most travellers. Route D976 from Mont St Michel runs right into Pontorson's main thoroughfare, rue du Couësnon.

Information
The tourist office (☎ 02 33 60 14 30, fax 02 33 60 06 75, ✉ ot.Mont.Saint.Michel@wanadoo .fr) is up the stairs to the left as you enter Mont St Michel at Porte de l'Avancée. It opens 9 am to noon and 2 to 5.45 pm Monday to Saturday. From Easter to September, it opens 9.30 am to noon and 1 to 6.30 pm daily. In July and August it opens 9 am to 7 pm daily.

There's another tourist office in Pontorson, open daily (closed Sunday in winter).

Places to Stay
Camping *Camping du Mont Saint Michel* (☎ 02 33 60 09 33), open mid-February to mid-November, is on the road to Pontorson (D976), 2km from the Mont. It charges 20/22FF per tent/person. Two-person bungalows with shower and toilet are 220FF.

Hostels Pontorson's *Centre Duguesclin* (☎ 02 33 60 18 65) operates as a 10-room hostel from Easter to mid-September. Beds are 48FF. The hostel is closed from 10 am to 6 pm, but there is no curfew. The hostel is 1km west of the train station on rue du Général Patton, which runs parallel to the Couësnon River north of rue du Couësnon. The hostel is on the left side in a three-storey stone building opposite No 26.

Hotels Mont St Michel has about 15 hotels but most are expensive. *La Mère Poulard* (☎ 02 33 60 14 01, fax 02 33 48 52 31), the first hotel on the left as you walk up the Grande rue, has doubles with shower from 300FF.

In Pontorson, across place de la Gare from the train station, there are a couple of cheap hotels. *Hôtel de l'Arrivée* (☎ 02 33 60 01 57, 14 rue du Docteur Tizon) has doubles for 95FF, or 165FF with shower.

Places to Eat
The tourist restaurants around the base of the Mont have lovely views but tend to be mediocre; *menus* start at about 80FF. A few places along the Grande rue sell sandwiches, quiches and such like. The nearest **supermarket** to the Mont is next to Camping du Mont St Michel on the D976.

In Pontorson, *La Crêperie du Couësnon* (☎ 02 33 60 16 67, 21 rue du Couësnon) has crepes and savoury galettes (10FF to 30FF). *La Tour de Brette* (☎ 02 33 60 10 69, 8 rue du Couësnon) across from the river, has good *menus* from 60FF.

Getting There & Away
STN (☎ 02 33 58 03 07) sends bus No 15 from Pontorson's train station to Mont St Michel daily year-round; most of the buses connect with trains to/from Paris, Rennes and Caen.

There are trains to Pontorson from Caen (via Folligny) and Rennes (via Dol). From Paris, take the train to Caen (from Gare St Lazare), Rennes (from Gare Montparnasse) or direct to Pontorson via Folligny (Gare Montparnasse).

Getting Around
Bikes can be rented at Pontorson's train station (55FF per day plus 1000FF deposit) and from E Videloup (☎ 02 33 60 11 40), 1 bis rue du Couësnon, which charges 50FF/80FF per day for one-speeds/mountain bikes.

Brittany

Brittany (Bretagne in French, Breizh in Breton), the westernmost region of France, is famous for its rugged countryside and wild coastline. Traditional costumes, including extraordinarily tall headdresses worn by the

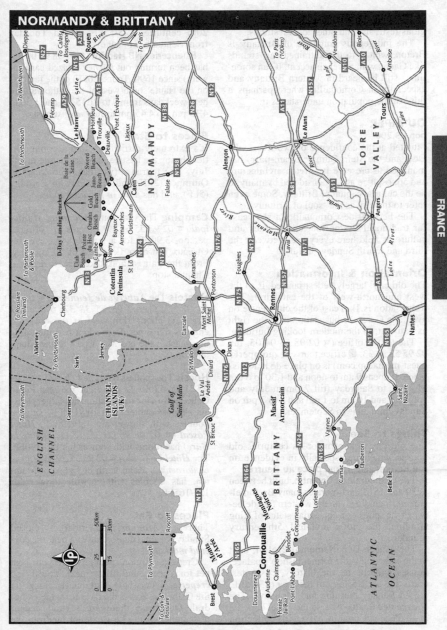

NORMANDY & BRITTANY

FRANCE

euro currency converter 1FF = €0.15

women, can still be seen at *pardons* (religious festivals) and other local festivals.

The indigenous language of Brittany is Breton, which, to the untrained ear, sounds like Gaelic with a French accent. It can sometimes still be heard in western Brittany and especially in Cornouaille, where perhaps a third of the population understands it.

QUIMPER
pop 63,200
Situated at the confluence of two rivers, the Odet and the Steïr, Quimper (cam-**pair**) has managed to preserve its Breton architecture and atmosphere and is considered by many to be the cultural capital of Brittany. Some even refer to the city as the 'soul of Brittany'.

The Festival de Cornouaille, a showcase for traditional Breton music, costumes and culture, is held here every year between the third and fourth Sundays in July.

Orientation & Information
The old city, largely pedestrianised, is to the west and north-west of the cathedral. The train station is 1km east of the city centre on ave de la Gare; the bus station is to the right as you exit, in the modern-looking building.

The tourist office (☎ 02 98 53 04 05, fax 02 98 53 31 33, ✉ office.tourisme.quimper@ ouest-mediacap.com) is on place de la Résistance. It opens 9 am to noon and 1.30 to 6 pm Monday to Saturday (till 7 pm in July and August), and 10 am to 1 pm and 3 to 7 pm on Sunday, mid-June to September.

Things to See
The old city is known for its centuries-old houses, which are especially in evidence on **rue Kéréon** and around **place au Beurre**.

The **Cathédrale St Corentin**, built between 1239 and 1515, incorporates many Breton elements, including – on the western facade between the spires – an equestrian statue of King Gradlon, the city's mythical 5th-century founder.

The **Musée Départemental Breton**, next to the cathedral in the former bishop's palace, houses exhibits on the history, costumes, crafts and archaeology of the area (25/15FF, closed Sunday morning and Monday). The **Musée des Beaux-Arts**, in the Hôtel de Ville at 40 place St Corentin, has a wide collection

of European paintings from the 16th to early 20th centuries (25/15FF, closed Tuesday from September to June).

Faïenceries HB Henriot (☎ 02 98 90 09 36) has been turning out *faïence* (glazed earthenware) since 1690. Tours (20FF) of the factory, on rue Haute south-west of the cathedral, are held weekdays from 9 to 11.15 am and 1.30 to 4.15 pm (to 4.45 pm in July and August).

Places to Stay
It's extremely difficult to find accommodation during the Festival de Cornouaille in late July. The tourist office makes bookings in Quimper (2FF) and elsewhere in Brittany (5FF), and has a list of *private rooms*.

Camping The year-round *Camping Municipal* (☎ 02 98 55 61 09) charges 17.70FF per person, 3.90FF for a tent. It's on ave des Oiseaux just over 1km west of the old city. From the train station, take bus No 1 to the Chaptal stop.

Hostels The *Auberge de Jeunesse* (☎ 02 98 64 97 97, fax 02 98 55 38 37, 6 ave des Oiseaux) about 1km west of the old city, charges 67FF per dorm-room bed including breakfast. Take bus Nos 1 or 8 to the Chaptal stop.

Hotels The spotless *Hôtel de l'Ouest* (☎ 02 98 90 28 35, 63 rue Le Déan), up rue Jean-Pierre Calloch from the train station, has large, pleasant singles/doubles from 100/150FF. Singles/ doubles with shower are 180/190FF. *Hôtel Pascal* (☎ 02 98 90 00 81, 17 bis ave de la Gare) has rooms with shower for 180/190FF. The *Hôtel Le Celtic* (☎ 02 98 55 59 35, 13 rue Douarnenez), 100m north of Église St Mathieu, has doubles without/with shower for 125/165FF.

Places to Eat
There's a *Monoprix* supermarket (closed Sunday) on quai du Port au Vin, near the *covered market*.

Crepes, a Breton speciality, are your best bet for a cheap and filling meal. You'll find *creperies* everywhere, particularly along rue Ste Catherine across the river from the cathedral. Otherwise there are several decent restaurants on rue Le Déan not far from the

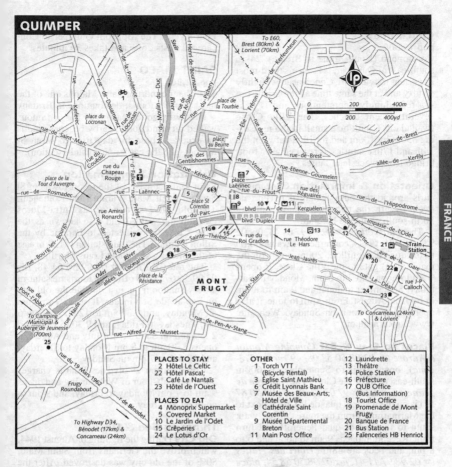

QUIMPER

Map legend:

PLACES TO STAY
2 Hôtel Le Celtic
22 Hôtel Pascal;
   Café Le Nantaïs
23 Hôtel de l'Ouest

PLACES TO EAT
4 Monoprix Supermarket
5 Covered Market
10 Le Jardin de l'Odet
15 Crêperies
24 Le Lotus d'Or

OTHER
1 Torch VTT
   (Bicycle Rental)
3 Église Saint Mathieu
6 Crédit Lyonnais Bank
7 Musée des Beaux-Arts;
   Hôtel de Ville
8 Cathédrale Saint
   Corentin
9 Musée Départemental
   Breton
11 Main Post Office

12 Laundrette
13 Théâtre
14 Police Station
16 Préfecture
17 QUB Office
   (Bus Information)
18 Tourist Office
19 Promenade de Mont
   Frugy
20 Banque de France
21 Bus Station
25 Faïenceries HB Henriot

train station, including Chinese-Vietnamese *Le Lotus d'Or* (☎ 02 98 53 02 54) at No 53 (closed Wednesday).

Le Jardin de l'Odet (☎ 02 98 95 76 76, 39 blvd Amiral de Kerguélen) is a good splurge, with tasty Lyonnais cuisine and *menus* from 80FF (closed Sunday).

Getting There & Away
A half-dozen companies operate out of the bus station (☎ 02 98 90 88 89). Destinations include Brest, Pointe du Raz, Roscoff (for ferries to Plymouth, England), Concarneau and Quimperlé.

Inquire at the train station for SNCF buses to Douarnenez, Camaret-sur-Mer, Concarneau and Quiberon. A one-way ticket on the TGV train to Paris' Gare Montparnasse costs 384FF (4 hours). You can also reach Saint Malo by train via Rennes. For rail information call ☎ 0836 35 35 35.

Getting Around
Bicycle Torch VTT (☎ 02 98 53 84 41) at 58 rue de la Providence rents out mountain bikes for 65/90FF per half-day/day (cheaper in winter). It's closed Sunday, Monday and Thursday morning.

euro currency converter 1FF = €0.15

AROUND QUIMPER
Concarneau
pop 19,500

Concarneau (Konk-Kerne in Breton), 24km south-east of Quimper, is France's third-most important trawler port. Concarneau is slightly scruffy and at the same time a bit touristy, but it's refreshingly unpretentious and is near several decent beaches. The **Ville Close** (walled city), built on a small island measuring 350m by 100m and fortified between the 14th and 17th centuries, is reached via a footbridge from place Jean Jaurès.

Orientation & Information Concarneau curls around the busy fishing port (Port de Pêche), with the two main quays running north-south along the harbour.

The tourist office (☎ 02 98 97 01 44, fax 02 98 50 88 81, ✉ otsi.concarneau@wanadoo.fr) is on quai d'Aiguillon, 200m north of the main (west) gate to the Ville Close. It opens 9 am to noon and 2 to 6 pm, Monday to Saturday, September to June; and 9 am to 8 pm in July and August. From April to June, it also opens 9 am to noon on Sunday. Web site: www.concarneau.org

Places to Stay & Eat *Camping Moulin d'Aurore* (☎ *02 98 50 53 08, 49 rue de Trégunc*), open April to September, is 600m south-east of the Ville Close. The *Auberge de Jeunesse* (☎ *02 98 97 03 47, fax 02 98 50 87 57*) is on the water at quai de la Croix, next to the Marinarium. From the tourist office, walk south to the end of quai Peneroff and turn right. Reception opens 9 am to noon and 6 to 8 pm, and beds are 48FF. *Hôtel des Halles* (☎ *02 98 97 11 41, fax 02 98 50 58 54, place de l'Hôtel de Ville*) charges 220FF for a double with shower and TV.

L'Escale (☎ *02 98 97 03 31, 19 quai Carnot*) is popular with local Concarnois – a hearty lunch or dinner *menu* costs just 51FF (closed Saturday night and Sunday). For excellent home-style crepes, try the unpretentious *Crêperie du Grand Chemin* (*17 ave de la Gare*).

Getting There & Away The bus station is in the parking lot north of the tourist office. Caoudal (☎ 02 98 56 96 72) runs up to four buses a day (three on Sunday) between Quimper and Quimperlé (via Concarneau and Pont Aven). The trip from Quimper to Concarneau costs 26FF and takes 30 minutes.

SAINT MALO
pop 52,300

The Channel port of Saint Malo is one of the most popular tourist destinations in Brittany – and with good reason. It has a famous walled city and good nearby beaches, and is an excellent base for day trips to Mont St Michel (see the earlier Normandy section).

Orientation & Information

Saint Malo consists of the resort towns of St Servan, Saint Malo, Paramé and Rothéneuf. The old city, signposted as Intra-Muros ('within the walls') and also known as the Ville Close, is connected to Paramé by the Sillon Isthmus. The train station is 1.2km east of the old city along ave Louis Martin.

The tourist office (☎ 02 99 56 64 48, fax 02 99 56 67 00, ✉ office.de.tourisme.saint-malo@wanadoo.fr) is just outside the old city on Esplanade St Vincent. It opens 2 to 6 pm on Monday, and 9.30 am to 12.30 and 2 to 6 pm, Tuesday to Friday; and 9.30 am to 1 pm and 2 to 5 pm on Saturday. In July and August, it opens 8.30 am to 8 pm Monday to Saturday, and 10 am to 7 pm on Sunday.

Cop Imprimu, 29 blvd des Talards, charges 30FF per half-hour of Web surfing and opens 9 am to 7 pm Monday to Friday, and 9 am to noon on Saturday.

Things to See & Do

Old City During the fighting of August 1944, which drove the Germans from Saint Malo, 80% of the old city was destroyed. After the war, the main historical monuments were lovingly reconstructed but the rest of the area was rebuilt in the style of the 17th and 18th centuries. The **ramparts**, built over the course of many centuries, are largely original. They afford superb views in all directions.

The **Musée de la Ville**, in the Château de Saint Malo at Porte St Vincent, deals with the history of the city and the Pays Malouin, the area around Saint Malo (27/13.50FF, closed Monday in winter).

The **Aquarium Intra-Muros** with over 100 tanks is built into the walls of the old city next to place Vauban (30/25FF). Europe's

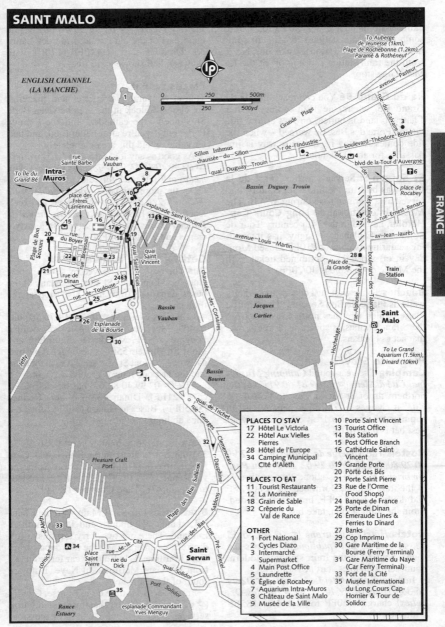

SAINT MALO

ENGLISH CHANNEL
(LA MANCHE)

FRANCE

PLACES TO STAY
17 Hôtel Le Victoria
22 Hôtel Aux Vielles
   Pierres
28 Hôtel de l'Europe
34 Camping Municipal
   Cité d'Aleth

PLACES TO EAT
11 Tourist Restaurants
12 La Morinière
18 Grain de Sable
32 Crêperie du
   Val de Rance

OTHER
1 Fort National
2 Cycles Diazo
3 Intermarché
   Supermarket
4 Main Post Office
5 Laundrette
6 Église de Rocabey
7 Aquarium Intra-Muros
8 Château de Saint Malo
9 Musée de la Ville

10 Porte Saint Vincent
13 Tourist Office
14 Bus Station
15 Post Office Branch
16 Cathédrale Saint
   Vincent
19 Grande Porte
20 Porte des Bés
21 Porte Saint Pierre
23 Rue de l'Orme
   (Food Shops)
24 Banque de France
25 Porte de Dinan
26 Émeraude Lines &
   Ferries to Dinard
27 Banks
29 Cop Imprimu
30 Gare Maritime de la
   Bourse (Ferry Terminal)
31 Gare Maritime du Naye
   (Car Ferry Terminal)
33 Fort de la Cité
35 Musée International
   du Long Cours Cap-
   Hornier & Tour de
   Solidor

euro currency converter   1FF = €0.15

first circular aquarium, **Le Grand Aquarium Saint Malo**, is on ave Général Patton 1.5km south of the train station (56/44FF in summer, 44/30FF off-season). Take bus No 5 from the train station and hop off at the La Madelaine stop.

Île du Grand Bé You can reach the Île du Grand Bé, where the 18th-century writer Chateaubriand is buried, on foot at low tide via the Porte des Bés. Be warned – when the tide comes rushing in, the causeway is impassable for about six hours.

St Servan St Servan's fortress, **Fort de la Cité**, was built in the mid-18th century and served as a German base during WWII. The **Musée International du Long Cours Cap-Hornier**, housed in the 14th-century Tour de Solidor on Esplanade Menguy, has interesting seafaring exhibits (20/10FF, closed Monday in off-season). A combined ticket with the Musée de la Ville is 40/20FF.

Beaches To the west, just outside the old city walls, is **Plage de Bon Secours**. The **Grande Plage**, which stretches north-eastward from the Sillon Isthmus, is spiked with tree trunks that act as breakers.

Places to Stay
Camping The year-round *Camping Municipal Cité d'Aleth* (☎ 02 99 81 60 91) is at the northern tip of St Servan next to Fort de la Cité. It charges 21/28FF per person/tent. In summer take bus No 1; at other times your best bet is bus No 6.

Hostels The *Auberge de Jeunesse* (☎ 02 99 40 29 80, fax 02 99 40 29 02, 37 ave du Père Umbricht, Paramé) is about 2km north-east of the train station. Dorm beds start at 72FF and doubles cost 170FF, breakfast included. From the train station, take bus No 5.

Hotels *Hôtel de l'Europe* (☎ 02 99 56 13 42, 44 blvd de la République) is across the roundabout from the train station. Modern, nondescript doubles start at 180FF.

In the old city, *Hôtel Le Victoria* (☎ 02 99 56 34 01, fax 02 99 40 32 78, 4 rue des Orbettes) charges 150FF for doubles (185FF with shower).

The friendly, family-run *Hôtel Aux Vieilles Pierres* (☎ 02 99 56 46 80) is in a quiet part of the old city at 4 rue des Lauriers. Doubles start at 140FF (170FF with shower); hall showers are free.

Places to Eat
Tourist restaurants, creperies and pizzerias are chock-a-block in the area between Porte St Vincent, the cathedral and the Grande Porte, but if you're after better food, and better value, avoid this area completely.

As good as any for seafood is *La Morinière* (☎ 02 99 40 85 77, 9 rue Jacques Cartier), with *menus* at 70FF and 90FF (closed Wednesday). Or try the more intimate *Grain de Sable* (☎ 02 99 56 68 72) at No 2, which serves an excellent fish soup. In St Servan, *Crêperie du Val de Rance (11 rue Dauphine)* serves Breton-style crepes and galettes (8FF to 42FF).

Getting There & Away
Bus The bus station, served by several operators, is at Esplanade St Vincent. Many of the buses departing from here also stop at the train station.

Courriers Bretons (☎ 02 99 19 70 70) has regular services to Cancale (21.50FF), Fougères (81FF, Monday to Saturday) and Mont St Michel (55FF, one hour). The first daily bus to Mont St Michel leaves at 9.50 am and the last one returns around 4.30 pm.

TIV (☎ 02 99 40 82 67) has buses to Cancale (21FF), Dinan (33FF), and Rennes (56.50FF). Buses to Dinard (20FF) run about once an hour until around 7 pm.

Train From the train station (☎ 0836 35 35 35) there is a direct service to Paris' Gare Montparnasse (315FF, 4¼ hours). Some go via Rennes (70FF). There are local services to Dinan (47FF) and Quimper (221FF).

Boat Ferries link Saint Malo with the Channel Islands, Weymouth and Portsmouth in England. There are two ferry terminals: hydrofoils, catamarans and the like depart from Gare Maritime de la Bourse; car ferries leave from the Gare Maritime du Naye. Both are south of the walled city.

From Gare Maritime de la Bourse, Condor (☎ 02 99 20 03 00) has catamaran and jetfoil services to Jersey (295FF, one-day excursion) and Guernsey (295FF) from mid-March to mid-November. Condor's service to Weymouth (270FF, 4 hours) operates daily from late May to mid-October.

Émeraude Lines (☎ 02 23 18 01 80) has ferries to Jersey, Guernsey and Sark from Gare Maritime du Naye. Service is most regular between late March and mid-November.

Between mid-March and mid-December, Brittany Ferries (☎ 0803 82 88 28) has boats to Portsmouth (passengers 270FF, 850FF to 1620FF with a car) three times a day from the Gare Maritime du Naye. In winter, ferries sail four or five times a week.

The Bus de Mer ferry (run by Émeraude Lines) links Saint Malo with Dinard (20/30FF single/return, 10 minutes) from April to September. In Saint Malo, the dock is just outside the Porte de Dinan; the Dinard quay is at 27 ave George V.

AROUND SAINT MALO
Dinard
pop 10,400
While Saint Malo's old city and beaches are geared towards middle-class families, Dinard attracts a well-heeled clientele – especially from the UK. Indeed, Dinard has the feel of an early-20th-century beach resort, with its candy-cane bathing tents and carnival rides.

Beautiful seaside trails extend along the coast in both directions from Dinard. The famous **Promenade du Clair de Lune** (Moonlight Promenade) runs along the Baie du Prieuré. The town's most attractive walk is the one that links the Promenade du Clair de Lune with Plage de l'Écluse via the rocky coast of **Pointe du Moulinet**. Bikes are not allowed.

The tourist office (☎ 02 99 46 94 12, fax 02 99 88 21 07, ✉ dinard.office.de.tourime@ wanadoo.fr) is in the colonnaded building at 2 blvd Féart. It opens 9 am to noon and 2 to 6 pm Monday to Saturday (9.30 am to 7.30 pm in July and August). Staying in Dinard can strain the budget, so consider making a day trip from Saint Malo (see that town's Getting There & Away section for details).

Loire Valley

From the 15th to 18th centuries, the fabled Loire Valley (Vallée de la Loire) was the playground of kings and nobles who expended vast fortunes and the wealth of the nation to turn it into a vast neighbourhood of lavish chateaux. Today, this region is a favourite destination of tourists seeking architectural glories from the Middle Ages and the Renaissance.

The earliest chateaux were medieval fortresses, thrown up in the 9th century to fend of marauding Vikings. As the threat of invasion diminished by the 15th century, chateaux architecture changed: fortresses gave way to pleasure palaces as the Renaissance ushered in whimsical, decorative features. From the 17th century onwards, grand country houses – built in the neoclassical style amid formal gardens – took centre stage.

BLOIS
pop 49,300
The medieval town of Blois (pronounced blwah) was a hub of court intrigue between the 15th and 17th centuries, and in the 16th century served as a second capital of France. Some dramatic events involving some of France's most important kings and historical figures took place inside the outstanding Château de Blois. The old city, seriously damaged by German attacks in 1940, retains its steep, twisting medieval streets.

Several of the Loire Valley's most rewarding chateaux, including Chambord and Cheverny, are a pleasant 20km-or-so cycle ride from Blois.

Orientation
Almost everything of interest is within walking distance of the train station, which is at the western end of ave Dr Jean Laigret. The old city lies south and east of Château de Blois, which towers over place Victor Hugo.

Information
Tourist Offices The tourist office (☎ 02 54 90 41 41, fax 02 54 90 41 49, ✉ blois.tourism@wanadoo.fr), 3 ave Dr Jean Laigret, opens 9 am (10 am on Sunday) to 7 pm, May to September; and 9 am to 12.30 pm and 2 to 6 pm, Monday to Saturday, and 9.30 am to 12.30 pm on Sunday, the rest of the year.

Money & Post Banque de France, 4 ave Dr Jean Laigret, opens 9 am to 12.15 pm and

1.45 to 3.30 pm on weekdays. Several commercial banks face the river along quai de la Saussaye, near place de la Résistance.

The post office, rue Gallois, opens 8.30 am to 7 pm on weekdays, and 8 am to noon on Saturday.

Email & Internet Access The post office has Cyberposte. L'Étoile Tex (☎ 02 54 78 46 93, ✉ etoiletex.cybercafe@caramail.com), in the hotel of the same name at 7 rue du Bourg Neuf, is a busy bar charging 1FF per minute on its sole Internet terminal.

Things to See
Château de Blois Château de Blois (☎ 02 54 74 16 06) has a compellingly bloody history and an extraordinary mixture of architectural styles. Its four distinct sections are: early Gothic (13th century); Flamboyant Gothic (1498-1503), dating to the reign of Louis XII; early Renaissance (1515-24), from the reign of François I; and Classical (17th century). The chateau also houses an **archaeological museum** and the **Musée des Beaux-Arts** (Musem of Fine Arts), both open 9 am to noon and 2 to 5 pm, mid-October to mid-March; and 9 am to 6.30 pm (8 pm in July and August), the rest of the year (35/25FF). The chateau's evening **sound-and-light show** (60/30FF) runs May to September. For a chateau visit *and* show, buy the combination ticket (75/55FF).

Opposite, the **Maison de la Magie** (House of Magic) has magic shows, interactive exhibits and displays of clocks invented by the Blois-born magician Jean-Eugène Robert-Houdin (1805-71), after whom the great Houdini named himself. It opens 10.30 am to noon and 2 to 6.30 pm, July and August; 10 am to noon and 2 to 6 pm, April to June and in September, October and November; and the same hours Wednesdays and at the weekend, February and March (48/42FF).

Old City Large brown signs in English pinpoint tourist sights around the predominantly-pedestrian, old city. **Cathédrale St-Louis** is named after Louis XIV, who had it rebuilt after a hurricane in 1678. There's a great view of Blois and the River Loire from the lovely **Jardins de l'Évêché** (Gardens of the Bishop's Palace), behind the cathedral.

The 15th-century **Maison des Acrobates** (House of Acrobats), 3 bis rue Pierre de Blois, is one of Blois' few medieval houses to survive the bombings of WWII. It's named after the cheeky characters carved in its timbers.

Places to Stay
Camping Two-star *Camping du Lac de Loire* (☎ 02 54 78 82 05), open April to mid-October, is in Vineuil, 4km south of Blois. It costs 49FF for two people and a tent. There's no bus service from town except in July and August (phone the camp site or the tourist office for details).

Hostels The *Auberge de Jeunesse* (☎/fax 02 54 78 27 21, 18 rue de l'Hôtel Pasquier) in Les Grouëts, is 4.5km south-west of Blois train station. It opens March to mid-November. Call first – it's often full. Dorm beds cost 68FF. The hostel closes 10 am to 6 pm. From place de la République, take bus No 4.

Hotels Near the train station, your best bet is *Hôtel St-Jacques* (☎ 02 54 78 04 15, fax 02 54 78 33 05, 7 rue Ducoux). Basic doubles cost upwards of 130FF. Opposite at No 6, family-run *Hôtel Le Savoie* (☎ 02 54 74 32 21, fax 02 54 74 29 58) has well-kept singles/doubles with shower, toilet and TV starting at 180/200FF.

North of the old city, 12-room *Hôtel du Bellay* (☎ 02 54 78 23 62, fax 02 54 78 52 04, 12 rue des Minimes) touts doubles costing 135FF to 160FF (185FF with bath or shower). *Hôtel L'Étoile Tex* (☎ 02 54 78 46 93, ✉ etoiletex.cybercafe@caramail.com, 7 rue du Bourg Neuf) has nine rooms costing 150FF to 180FF, and has Internet access (1FF per minute).

Places to Eat
In the old city, *Le Rond de Serviette* (☎ 02 54 74 48 04, 18 rue Beauvoir) claims to be Blois' most humorous and cheapest restaurant; its 49FF *menu* is unbeatable. Nearby, tuck into pasta and pizza at *La Scala* (☎ 02 54 74 88 19, 8 rue des Minimes). Its leafy summer terrace gets full fast.

La Mesa (☎ 02 54 78 70 70, 11 rue Vauvert) is a busy Franco-Italian joint, up an alleyway from 44 rue Foulerie. Its lovely courtyard is perfect for dining alfresco.

FRANCE

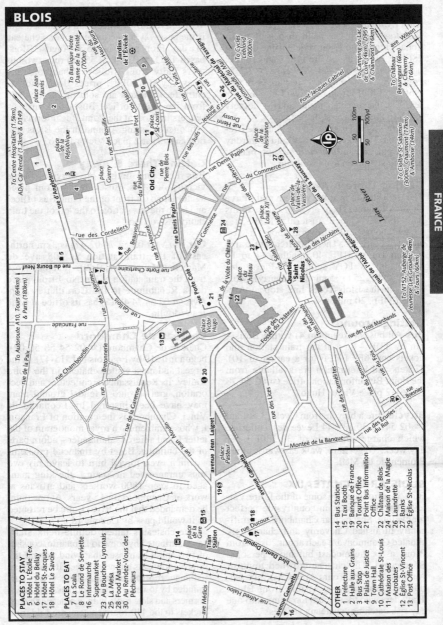

BLOIS

PLACES TO STAY
5 Hôtel L'Étoile Tex
6 Hôtel du Bellay
17 Hôtel St-Jacques
18 Hôtel Le Savoie

PLACES TO EAT
7 La Scala
8 Le Rond de Serviette
16 Intermarché
   Supermarché
23 Au Bouchon Lyonnais
25 La Mesa
28 Food Market
30 Au Rendez-Vous des
   Pêcheurs

OTHER
1 Préfecture
2 Halle aux Grains
3 Bus Stop
9 Palais de Justice
10 Town Hall
11 Maison des
   Acrobates
12 Église St-Vincent
13 Post Office
14 Bus Station
15 Taxi Booth
19 Banque de France
20 Tourist Office
21 Point Bus Information
   Office
22 Château de Blois
24 Maison de la Magie
26 Laundrette
27 Banks
29 Église St-Nicolas

euro currency converter 1FF = €0.15

FRANCE

Those seeking a splurge can try *Au Bouchon Lyonnais* (☎ 02 54 74 12 87, *25 rue des Violettes*) which has main dishes of traditional French and Lyon-style cuisine costing 78FF to 128FF; *menus* are 118FF and 165FF.

Au Rendez-Vous des Pêcheurs (☎ 02 54 74 67 48, *27 rue du Foix*) specialises in fish (96FF to 140FF) from the River Loire and the sea. The handwritten menu adds a homely touch to this cottage-style restaurant.

There's a *food market* on rue Anne de Bretagne on Tuesday, Thursday and Saturday until 1 pm, and an *Intermarché* supermarket near the station on ave Gambetta.

Getting There & Away
The train station is at the western end of ave Dr Jean Laigret. There are four direct trains daily to Paris' Gare d'Austerlitz (123FF, 1½ to two hours), plus several more if you change at Orléans. There are frequent trains to/from Tours (51FF, 40 minutes, 11 to 17 daily) and its TGV station, St-Pierre des Corps (49FF, 25 to 35 minutes, hourly). Most trains on the Blois-Tours line stop at Amboise (34FF, 20 minutes).

Getting Around
Bus All buses (except No 4) within Blois – run by TUB – stop at the train station and tickets cost 6FF (41FF for a carnet of 10). Tickets and information are available from the Point Bus information office (☎ 02 54 78 15 66), 2 place Victor Hugo.

Bicycle Hire a bicycle from Cycles Leblond (☎ 02 54 74 30 13), 44 Levée des Tuileries, which charges upwards of 30/180FF per day/week. To get here, walk eastwards along Promenade du Mail.

BLOIS AREA CHATEAUX
Blois is surrounded by some of the Loire Valley's finest chateaux in countryside perfect for cycling. Spectacular Chambord, magnificently furnished Cheverny and charmingly situated Chaumont are each about 20km from Blois, as is the modest but more personal Beauregard. The chateau-crowned town of Amboise (see the Tours Area Chateaux section) is also easily accessible from Blois. Travellers who try to cram too many into one day risk catching 'chateaux sickness'.

Organised Tours
Without your own wheels, an organised tour is the best way to see more than one chateau in a day. From mid-May to 31 August, Blois-based TLC (☎ 02 54 58 55 55) runs two bus tours daily from Blois to Chambord and Cheverny (65/50FF); prices don't include entry fees. Tickets are sold on the bus and from the tourist office. Buses pick up passengers in Blois at the Point Bus information office (see Getting Around in the Blois section earlier) at 2 place Victor Hugo.

Getting There & Away
Bus TLC runs limited bus services in the vicinity of Blois. Buses depart from place Victor Hugo (in front of the Point Bus office) and from the bus station to the left of the train station as you exit.

Car ADA (☎ 02 54 74 02 47) is 3km north-east of the train station at 108 ave du Maréchal Maunoury (D149). Take bus No 1 from the train station or bus No 4 from place de la République to the Cornillettes stop. Avis (☎ 02 54 74 48 15) has its office at 6 rue Jean Moulin.

Château de Chambord
Château de Chambord (☎ 02 54 50 50 02), begun in 1519 by François I (1515-47), is the largest and most visited chateau in the Loire Valley. Its Renaissance architecture and decoration, grafted onto a feudal ground plan, may have been inspired by Leonardo da Vinci. Chambord is the creation of François I, whose emblems – a royal monogram of the letter F and a fierce salamander – adorn parts of the building. Beset by financial problems – which even forced him to leave his two sons unransomed in Spain – the king managed to keep 1800 workers and artisans at work on Chambord for 15 years. At one point he demanded that the River Loire be rerouted so it would pass by Chambord.

The chateau's famed **double-helix staircase**, attributed by some to Leonardo, consists of two spiral staircases that wind around the same central axis but never meet. It leads to an Italianate **rooftop terrace**, where you're surrounded by towers, cupolas, domes, chimneys, dormers and slate roofs with geometric shapes. Tickets to the 440-room chateau are sold from

9.30 am to 4.45 pm, July and August; 9.30 am to 5.45 pm, April to June and September; and 9.30 am to 4.45 pm, October to March. Visitors already in the chateau can stay 45 minutes after ticket sales end (40/25FF).

From mid-July to mid-October, Chambord hosts a **light show** nightly. Tickets are sold from 10.30 pm until midnight in July, 10 to 11.30 pm in August, and 8.30 to 9.30 or 10 pm September to mid-October (80/50FF). Tickets covering show and chateau are available (100/55F).

Getting There & Away Chambord is 16km east of Blois and 20km north-east of Cheverny. During the school year, TLC bus No 2 average three return trips (two on Saturday, one on Sunday) from Blois to Chambord (18.50FF, 45 minutes). In July and August, your only bus option is TLC's guided tour (see the Blois Area Chateaux introduction).

Getting Around You can rent a bicycle from the Echapée Belle kiosk, next to Pont St-Michel in the castle grounds (25/70FF per hour/day).

Château de Cheverny

Château de Cheverny (☎ 02 54 79 96 29), the most magnificently furnished of the Loire Valley chateaux and still privately owned, was completed in 1634. Visitors wander through sumptuous rooms outfitted with the finest canopied beds, tapestries, paintings, painted ceilings and walls covered with embossed Córdoba leather. Three dozen panels illustrate the story of *Don Quixote* in the upstairs dining room.

The lush grounds shelter an 18th-century **Orangerie** where Leonardo da Vinci's *Mona Lisa* was hidden during WWII. The antlers of almost 2000 stags cover the walls of the **Salle des Trophées**, while the kennels keep a pack of 90 hunting hounds. Near the lake is a **balloon pad** where you can take to the skies in a hot-air balloon, mid-March to mid-October. The 10 to 12-minute ascent costs 47/43FF.

Cheverny (☎ 02 54 79 96 29, 🄴 chateau .cheverny@wanadoo.fr) opens 9.15 or 9.30 am to 6.15 pm (6.30 pm July and August), April to September; and 9.15 or 9.30 am to noon and 2.15 to 5.30 pm (5 pm November to February), the rest of the year (35/24FF).

Getting There & Away Cheverny is 16km south-east of Blois and 20km south-west of Chambord.

The TLC bus from Blois to Villefranche-sur-Cher stops at Cheverny (14.60FF). Buses leave Blois at 6.50 am and 12.25 pm Monday to Saturday. The last bus back to Blois leaves at 6.58 pm. Times vary on Sunday and holidays; check schedules first.

Château de Beauregard

Built in the 16th century as a hunting lodge for François I, Beauregard is most famous for its **Galerie des Portraits**, which displays 327 portraits of notable faces from the 14th to 17th centuries.

Beauregard (☎ 02 54 70 36 74) opens from 9.30 am to noon and 2 to 5 or 6.30 pm, April to September (no break in July and August); and the same hours Thursday to Tuesday, February, March and October to January. Admission costs 40FF (students and children 30FF).

Getting There & Away

Beauregard is 6km south of Blois or a pleasant 15km cycle ride through forests from Chambord. There's road access to the chateau from the Blois-Cheverny D765 and the D956 (turn left at the village of Cellettes).

The TLC bus from Blois to St-Aignan stops at Cellettes (8.80FF), 1km south-west of the chateau, on Wednesday, Friday and Saturday; the first Blois-Cellettes bus leaves at 12.25 pm. There's no afternoon bus back except the Châteauroux-Blois line operated by Transports Boutet (☎ 02 54 34 43 95), which passes through Cellettes around 6.15 pm Monday to Saturday, and – except during August – at about 6 pm on Sunday.

Château de Chaumont

Château de Chaumont (☎ 02 54 51 26 26), set on a bluff overlooking the River Loire, resembles a feudal castle. Built in the late 15th century, it served as a booby prize for Diane de Poitier when her lover, Henry II, died in 1559, and hosted Benjamin Franklin several times when he served as ambassador to France after the American Revolution.

FRANCE

Its luxurious **stables** are the most famous feature, but the **Salle du Conseil** (Council Chamber) on the 1st floor, with its majolica tile floor and tapestries, and **Catherine de' Medici's bedroom** overlooking the chapel, are also remarkable. Tickets are sold from 9.30 am to 6 pm, mid-March to September; 10 am to 4.30 pm, the rest of the year (33FF).

Getting There & Away Château de Chaumont is 17km south-west of Blois and 20km north-east of Amboise in Chaumont-sur-Loire. The path leading up to the chateau begins at the intersection of rue du Village Neuf and rue Maréchal Leclerc (D751). Local trains run from Blois to Onzain (36FF, 10 minutes, eight or more daily), a 2km walk across the river from the chateau.

TOURS
pop 270,000

Lively Tours has the cosmopolitan and bourgeois air of a miniature Paris, with wide 18th-century avenues and cafe-lined boulevards. The city was devastated by German bombardment in June 1940, but much of it has been rebuilt since. The French spoken in Tours is said to be the purest in France.

Orientation
Tours' focal point is place Jean Jaurès, where the city's major thoroughfares – rue Nationale, blvd Heurteloup, ave de Grammont and blvd Béranger – join up. The train station is 300m east along blvd Heurteloup. The old city, centred around place Plumereau, is about 400m west of rue Nationale.

Information
Tourist Offices The tourist office (☎ 02 47 70 37 37, fax 02 47 61 14 22, **ⓔ** info@ligeris.com), 78-82 rue Bernard Palissy, opens 8.30 am to 7 pm Monday to Saturday, 10 am to 12.30 pm and 2.30 to 5 pm on Sunday, May to October; and 9 am to 12.30 pm and 1.30 to 6 pm Monday to Saturday, 10 am to 1 pm on Sunday, the rest of the year.

Money Banque de France, 2 rue Chanoineau, has an exchange service, open 8.45 am to noon on weekdays. Commercial banks overlook place Jean Jaurès.

Post & Communications The post office, 1 blvd Béranger, opens 8 am to 7 pm on weekdays, and 8 am to noon on Saturday. It has a Cyberposte.

Alli@nce Micro (☎ 02 47 05 49 50), 7ter rue de la Monnaie, and Le Cyberspace (☎ 02 47 66 29 96), 13 rue Lavoisier, both charge around 25FF per hour to surf the Web; the latter is housed in a pub, open 2 pm to 5 am.

Things to See
Tours offers lovely quarters for strolling including the **old city** around place Plumereau, which is surrounded by half-timbered houses, as well as **rue du Grand Marché** and **rue Colbert**. The neighbourhood around the **Cathédrale St-Gatien**, built between 1220 and 1547 is renowned for its 13th and 15th-century stained glass. Its Renaissance **cloister** can be visited.

The **Musée de l'Hôtel Goüin** at 25 rue du Commerce is an archaeological museum, housed in a splendid Renaissance mansion built around 1510 (21/16FF). The **Musée du Compagnonnage** (Guild Museum) overlooking the courtyard of **Abbaye St-Julien**, 8 rue Nationale, is a celebration of the skill of the French artisan (25/15FF). The **Musée des Vins de Touraine** (Museum of Touraine Wines) at No 16 is in the 13th-century wine cellars of Abbaye St-Julien (16/10FF).

The **Musée des Beaux-Arts** (Museum of Fine Arts), 18 place François Sicard, has a good collection of works from the 14th to 20th centuries (30/15FF).

Most museums in Tours close Tuesday.

Places to Stay
Camping Three-star *Camping Les Rives du Cher* (☎ 02 47 27 27 60, 63 rue de Rochpinard, St-Avertin), 5km south of Tours, opens April to mid-October. It charges 14/14/8FF per tent/person/car. From place Jean Jaurès, take bus No 5 to the St-Avertin bus terminal, then follow signs.

Hostels *Le Foyer* (☎ 02 47 60 51 51, fax 02 47 20 75 20, **ⓔ** fjt.tours@wanadoo.fr, 16 rue Bernard Palissy), about 500m north of the train station, is a workers' dormitory. When there's space for travellers, singles/doubles cost 100/160FF. Reception closes Sunday.

FRANCE

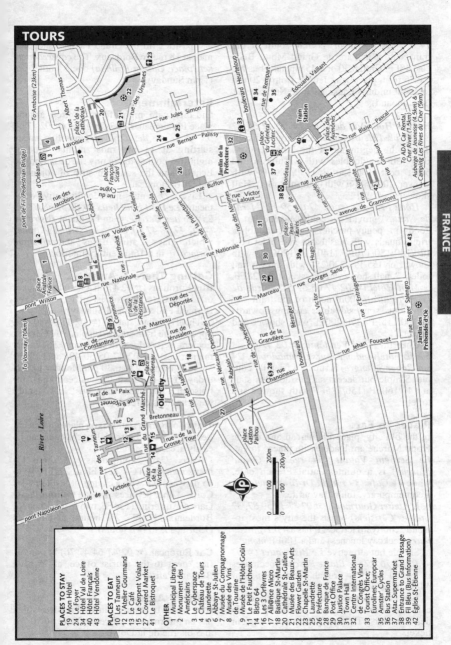

TOURS

PLACES TO STAY
19 Mon Hôtel
24 Le Foyer
34 Hôtel Val de Loire
40 Hôtel Français
43 Hôtel Vendôme

PLACES TO EAT
10 Les Tanneurs
12 L'Atelier Gourmand
13 Le Café
15 Le Serpent Volant
27 Covered Market
41 Le Bistroquet

OTHER
1 Municipal Library
2 Monument des Américains
3 Le Cyberspace
4 Château de Tours
5 Laundrette
6 Abbaye St-Julien
7 Musée du Compagnonnage
8 Musée des Vins de Touraine
9 Musée de l'Hôtel Goüin
11 Le Petit Faucheux
14 Bistro 64
16 Les 3 Orfèvres
17 Alli@nce Micro
18 Basilique St-Martin
20 Cathédrale St-Gatien
21 Musée des Beaux-Arts
22 Flower Garden
23 Chapelle St-Martin
25 Laundrette
26 Préfecture
28 Banque de France
29 Post Office
30 Justice Palace
31 Town Hall
32 Centre International de Congrès Vinci
33 Tourist Office; Eurolines; Europcar
35 Amster' Cycles
36 Bus Station
37 Atac Supermarket
38 Entrance to Grand Passage
39 Fil Bleu (Bus Information)
42 Église St-Étienne

euro currency converter 1FF = €0.15

Tours' *Auberge de Jeunesse* (☎ *02 47 25 14 45, ave d'Atsnval*) is 5km south of the train station in Parc de Grand Mont. Beds cost 48FF. Until 8.30 or 8.45 pm, take bus No 1 or 6 from place Jean Jaurès; from 9.20 pm to about midnight, take Bleu de Nuit bus N1 (southbound).

Hotels *Hôtel Val de Loire* (☎ *02 47 05 37 86, 33 blvd Heurteloup*) looks almost like it did at the beginning of the 20th century. Basic singles/doubles with washbasin and bidet cost 100/150FF (130/180FF with shower, 200/250FF with bath and toilet). Hall showers cost 15FF.

Hôtel Français (☎ *02 47 05 59 12, 11 rue de Nantes*) provides a cold welcome but is good for penny-pinchers: singles/doubles/ triples/quads with washbasin and bidet cost 120/140/150/170FF (140/160/170/180 with shower or 155/190/220/250 with shower and toilet). A hall shower/breakfast costs 10/28FF.

Mon Hôtel (☎ *02 47 05 67 53, 40 rue de la Préfecture*), 500m north of the train station, touts singles/doubles costing upwards of 100/115FF (170/200FF with shower and toilet).

Cheerful *Hôtel Vendôme* (☎ *02 47 64 33 54,* ✉ *hotelvendome.tours@wanadoo.fr, 24 rue Roger Salengro*) is run by a friendly couple. Simple but decent singles/doubles start at 140/160FF (150/185FF with shower and toilet).

Places to Eat
In the old city, place Plumereau and rue du Frand Marché are loaded with places to eat. *Le Serpent Volant* (*54 rue du Grand Marché*) is a quintessential French cafe, while *Le Café* (*39 rue du Dr Bretonneau*) is a contemporary, funky favourite.

L'Atelier Gourmand (☎ *02 47 38 59 87, 37 rue des Cerisiers*) boasts the city's most romantic courtyard terrace. It has a 49FF *plat du jour* (weekday lunches) and a 100FF *menu*.

Simple but attractive *Le Bistroquet* (☎ *02 47 05 12 76, 17 rue Blaise Pascal*) specialises in paella but has French food *menus* for 44FF, 51FF and 62FF.

Les Tanneurs is a university resto-cum-cafe near the main university building on rue des Tanneurs. To dine you need a student ticket.

Sandwich stalls selling well-filled baguettes and pastries fill the Grand Passage shopping mall at 18 rue de Bordeaux. The *covered market* (*place Gaston Pailhou*) opens until 7 pm (1 pm Sunday).

Entertainment
Old-city cafe nightlife is centred around place Plumereau. *Les 3 Orfèvres* (☎ *02 47 64 02 73, 6 rue des Orfèvres*) has live music starting at 11 pm most nights. Student nightlife abounds down tiny rue de la Longue Echelle and the southern strip of adjoining rue Dr Bretonneau.

Live jazz venues include alternative cafe-theatre *Le Petit Faucheux* (☎ *02 47 38 67 62, 23 rue des Cerisiers*) and brilliant *Bistro 64* (☎ *02 47 38 47 40, 64 rue du Grand Marché*) which plays Latin, Blues and *musique Française* in a 16th-century interior.

Getting There & Away
Bus Eurolines (☎ 02 47 66 45 56) has a ticket office next to the tourist office at 76 rue Bernard Palissy (closed Sunday).

The Tours bus station (☎ 02 47 05 30 49), opposite the train station on place du Général Leclerc, serves local destinations. The information desk (☎ 02 47 05 30 49) opens 7.30 am to noon and 2 to 6.30 pm Monday to Saturday. You can visit Chenonceau and Amboise in a day using CAT bus No 10 (study the schedules carefully).

Train Tours train station is on place du Général Leclerc. Several Loire Valley chateaux can be easily accessed by rail.

Paris' Gare Montparnasse is about 1¼ hours away by TGV (211FF to 277FF, 10 to 15 daily), often with a change at St-Pierre des Corps. Other services include to/from Paris' Gare d'Austerlitz (154FF, two to three hours), Bordeaux (224FF, 2¾ hours) and Nantes (135FF, 1½ to two hours).

Car Europcar (☎ 02 47 64 47 76) has an office, next to the tourist office, at 76 blvd Bernard Palissy.

Getting Around
Bus Local buses are run by Fil Bleu which has an information office (☎ 02 47 66 70 70) at 5 bis rue de la Dolve.

Bicycle From May to September, Amster' Cycles (☎ 02 47 61 22 23, fax 02 47 61 28 48), 5 rue du Rempart, rents road and mountain bikes for 80/330FF per day/week.

TOURS AREA CHATEAUX

Several chateaux around Tours can be reached by train, SNCF bus or bicycle. Several companies offer English-language tours of the chateaux – reserve at the Tours tourist office or contact the company directly.

Services Touristiques de Touraine (STT; ☎/fax 02 47 05 46 09, ✉ info@stt-millet.fr) runs half/full-day coach tours, April to mid-October, costing 190/300FF (including admission fees to three to four chateaux). STT's Web site is at www.stt-millet.fr.

Château de Chenonceau

With its stylised moat, drawbridge, towers and turrets straddling the River Cher, 16th-century Chenonceau is everything a fairy-tale castle should be, although its interior is only of moderate interest.

Of the many remarkable women who created Chenonceau, Diane de Poitiers, mistress of King Henri II, planted the garden to the left (east) as you approach the chateau. After Henri's death in 1559, his widow Catherine de Médicis laid out the garden to the right (west) as you approach the castle.

Between 1940 and 1942, the demarcation line between Vichy-ruled France and the German-occupied zone ran down the middle of the Cher: the castle itself was under direct German occupation, but southern entrance to the 60m-long **Galerie** was in the area controlled by Marshal Pétain. For many trying to escape to the Vichy zone, this room served as a crossing point.

Chenonceau (☎ 02 47 23 90 07, ✉ chateau .de.chenonceau@wanadoo.fr) opens 9 am until sometime between 4.30 pm (mid-November to January) and 7 pm (mid-March to mid-September). Admission costs 50/40FF.

Getting There & Away Château de Chenonceau, in the town of Chenonceaux (spelt with an 'x') is 34km east of Tours. Between Tours and Chenonceaux there are two or three trains daily (32FF, 30 minutes); alternatively, trains on the Tours-Vierzon line stop at Chisseaux (33FF, 24 minutes, six

daily), 2km east of Chenonceaux. In summer, take CAT bus No 10 to/from Tours (13FF, one hour, one daily).

Château d'Azay-le-Rideau

Built on an island in the River Indre, Azay-le-Rideau is among the most elegant of Loire chateaux. The seven rooms open to the public are disappointing (apart from a few 16th-century Flemish tapestries), but it's one of the few chateaux which allows picnicking in its beautiful park.

The chateau (☎ 02 47 45 42 04) opens 9.30 am to 6 pm, April to June and September; 9 am to 7 pm, July and August; and 9.30 am to 12.30 pm and to 5.30 pm, October to March (35/23FF).

Getting There & Away Azay-le-Rideau, 26km south-west of Tours, is on SNCF's Tours-Chinon line (four or five daily Monday to Saturday, one on Sunday). From Tours, the 30-minute trip (50 minutes by SNCF bus) costs 27FF; the station is 2.5km from the chateau.

Amboise
pop 11,000

Picturesque Amboise, an easy day trip from Tours, is known for its **Château d'Amboise** (☎ 02 47 57 00 98), perched on a rocky outcrop overlooking the town. The remains of Leonardo da Vinci (1452-1519), who lived in Amboise for the last three years of his life, are supposedly under the chapel's northern transept.

Inside the chateau walls, opposite 42 place Michel Debré, is the innovative **Caveau des Vignerons d'Amboise**, a wine cellar where you can taste (for free) regional Touraine wines, Easter to October. The chateau (☎ 02 47 57 00 98) opens 9 am to noon and 2 to 5 or 5.30 pm; April to October, hours are 9 am to 6.30 pm (8 pm in July and August). Admission costs 40/33FF.

Da Vinci, who came to Amboise at the invitation of François I in 1516, lived and worked in **Le Clos Lucé** (☎ 02 47 57 62 88) at 2 rue du Clos Lucé, a 15th-century brick manor house 500m south-east of the chateau along rue Victor Hugo. The building contains restored rooms and scale models of some 40 of Leonardo's fascinating inventions. Le Clos Lucé opens 9 am to 7 pm (8 pm, July and August), March to

FRANCE

December; and 9 am to 6 pm (10 am to 5 pm in January), the rest of the year (39/32FF).

Information Amboise tourist office (☎ 02 47 57 09 28, fax 02 47 57 14 35, **@** tourisme .amboise@wanadoo.fr) is next to the river, opposite 7 quai du Général de Gaulle (closed Sunday November to Easter).

Getting There & Away Several daily trains run to Amboise from both Tours (28FF, 20 minutes) and Blois (34km, 20 minutes). From Tours, you can also take CAT bus No 10 (19.60FF, 30 to 50 minutes).

South-Western France

The south-western part of France is made up of a number of diverse regions, ranging from the Bordeaux wine-growing area near the beach-lined Atlantic seaboard, to the Basque Country and the Pyrenees mountains in the south. The region is linked to Paris, Spain and the Côte d'Azur by convenient rail links.

LA ROCHELLE
pop 120,000
La Rochelle, a lively port city midway down France's Atlantic coast, is popular with middle-class French families and students on holiday. The ever-expanding Université de La Rochelle, opened in 1993, adds to the city's vibrancy. The nearby Île de Ré is ringed by long, sandy beaches.

Orientation & Information
The old city is north of the Vieux Port (old port), which is linked to the train station – 500m south-east – by ave du Général de Gaulle.

The tourist office (☎ 05 46 41 14 68) is in Le Gabut, the quarter on the south side of the Vieux Port. It opens 10 am to noon and 2 to 6 pm, Monday to Saturday (9 am to 7 pm in June and September, until 8 pm in July and August). Sunday hours are 10 am to noon (11 am to 5 pm in June and September, 9 am to 8 pm in July and August). Visit the Web site at www.ville-larochelle.fr

Things to See
To protect the harbour at night and defend it in times of war, a chain used to be stretched between the two 14th-century stone towers at the harbour entrance, the 36m **Tour St Nicolas** and **Tour de la Chaîne**; the latter houses displays on local history. West along the old city wall is **Tour de la Lanterne**, long used as a prison. All three towers are open daily; admission to each costs 25/15FF (45FF for combined ticket).

The **Musée Maritime Neptunea**, an excellent maritime museum at Bassin des Chalutiers, will soon be the permanent home of Jacques Cousteau's research ship *Calypso*. The entry fee (50/35FF) includes tours of a *chalutier* (fishing trawler). Next door, a vast, new **aquarium** is scheduled to open in early 2001.

Île de Ré
This flat, 30km-long island, fringed by beaches, begins 9km west of La Rochelle. It's connected to the mainland by a 3km toll bridge.

In July and August, and on Wednesdays, weekends and holidays in June, city buses Nos 1 or 50 (known as No 21 between the train station and place de Verdun) go to Sablanceaux (10FF, 25 minutes). Year-round, Rébus (☎ 05 46 09 20 15 in St Martin de Ré) links La Rochelle (the train station and place de Verdon) with St Martin de Ré and other island towns.

Places to Stay
Camping du Soleil (☎ 05 46 44 42 53, ave Marillac), about 1.5km south of the city centre, opens mid-May to mid-September and is often full. It's served by bus No 10.

The *Centre International de Séjour-Auberge de Jeunesse* (☎ 05 46 44 43 11, fax 05 46 45 41 48, ave des Minimes) is 2km south-west of the train station. A dorm bed costs 72FF, including breakfast. To get there, take bus No 10.

The two-star, 63-room *Hôtel Le Commerce* (☎ 05 46 41 08 22, fax 05 46 41 74 85, 6-10 place Verdun) has 11 doubles with washbasin for 135FF (165FF from May to September); doubles with shower and toilet are 235FF (290FF in season). In summer, breakfast (33FF) may be obligatory. In the pedestrianised old city, the friendly, 24-room

Hôtel Henri IV (☎ 05 46 41 25 79, fax 05 46 41 78 64, at place de la Caille) has spacious doubles from 170FF (220FF with shower and toilet).

A few blocks from the train station, the 32-room *Terminus Hôtel* (☎ 05 46 50 69 69, fax 05 46 41 73 12, ✉ terminus@cdl-lr.com, 7 rue de la Fabrique) offers comfortable doubles for 260FF to 300FF, depending on the season. One block north, the 22-room *Hôtel de Bordeaux* (☎ 05 46 41 31 22, fax 05 46 41 24 43, ✉ hbordeaux@free.fr, 43 rue St Nicolas), has quiet, pastel doubles from 175FF (285FF from June to September, including breakfast).

Places to Eat
The rustic *La Galathée* (45 rue St Jean du Perot) serves French *menus* for 65FF (weekday lunch), 85FF and 130FF (closed Tuesday and Wednesday except in July and August). The stylish *Bistrot l'Entracte* (22 rue St Jean du Pérot), specialises in fish and seafood; the four-course *menu* costs 160FF (closed Sunday). There are dozens of other eateries along the northern side of the port and on nearby streets.

An all-you-can-eat Chinese and Vietnamese lunch/dinner buffet costs 69/75FF at *Loan Phuong* (quai du Gabut). Couscous is on offer at *Shéhérazade* (35 rue Gambetta), which is closed Monday at midday.

The lively *covered market* (place du Marché) opens 7 am to 1 pm daily. There's a *Prisunic* supermarket across from 55 rue du Palais (closed Sunday).

Getting There & Away
Eurolines ticketing is handled by Citram Littoral (☎ 05 46 50 53 57) at 30 cours des Dames (closed Saturday afternoon, Monday morning and Sunday).

You can take a TGV from Paris' Gare Montparnasse (320FF to 380FF, three hours) or a non-TGV from Gare d'Austerlitz (264FF). Other destinations include Bordeaux (134FF, two hours) and Tours (160FF).

Getting Around
The innovative local transport system, Autoplus (☎ 05 46 34 02 22), has its main bus hub at place de Verdun. Most lines run until sometime between 7.15 and 8 pm.

Autoplus' *Le Passeur* (4FF) ferry service links Tour de la Chaîne with the Avant Port. It runs whenever there are passengers – just press the red button on the board at the top of the gangplank.

Les Vélos Autoplus, a branch of the public transport company, will furnish you with a bike (lock included) for free for two hours (6FF per hour after that). Bikes are available daily at the Electrique Autoplus office at place de Verdun, open 6.45 am (1 pm on Sunday) to 7 pm. From May to September, they can also be picked up at the Vieux Port (across the street from 11 quai Valin).

The Electric Autoplus office at place de Verdun also rents electric motorcars with a range of 50km for 60/100FF per half-day/day. Electric Barigo scooters cost 40/70FF.

BORDEAUX
pop 650,000
Bordeaux is known for its neoclassical (if somewhat grimy) architecture, wide avenues and well-tended public parks. The city's cultural diversity (including 60,000 students), excellent museums and untouristy atmosphere make it much more than just a convenient stop between Paris and Spain. The marketing and export of Bordeaux wine are the town's most important economic activities.

Orientation
Cours de la Marne stretches for about 2km from the train station north-westward to place de la Victoire, which is linked to the tourist office area (1.5km farther north) by the pedestrians-only rue Ste Catherine. The city centre lies between place Gambetta and the Garonne River.

Information
The main tourist office (☎ 05 56 00 66 00, fax 05 56 00 66 01), 12 cours du 30 Juillet, opens 9 am to 7 pm, Monday to Saturday, and 9.45 am to 4.30 pm on Sunday. From May to September or October, it's open until 8 pm (7 pm on Sunday). Web site: www.bordeaux-tourisme.com

Money Banque de France, 15 rue de l'Esprit des Lois, changes money 9 am to noon on weekdays. There are commercial banks near the tourist office on cours de l'Intendance, rue

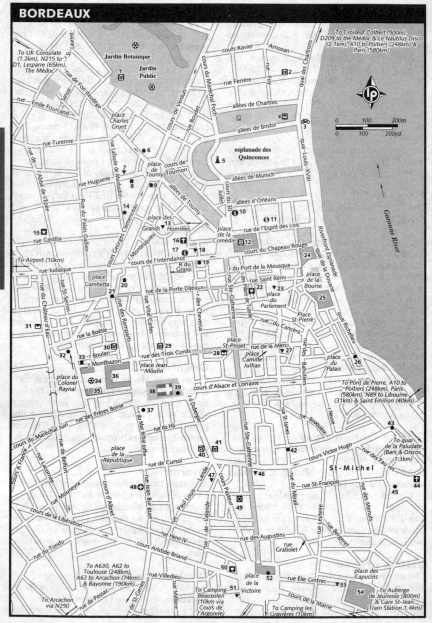

BORDEAUX

To Croiseur Colbert (500m),
D209, to the Médoc & Le Nautilus Disco
(2.1km), A10 to Poitiers (248km) &
Paris (580km)

To UK Consulate
(1.2km), N215 to
D1, Lesparre (65km),
The Médoc

Jardin Botanique

Jardin
Public

cours Xavier   Arnozan

rue Ferrère

quai des Chartrons

place
Charles Gruet

cours de Verdun

allées de Chartres

allées de Bristol

esplanade des
Quinconces

quai Louis-XVIII

To Airport (10km)

rue Emile Fourcand

rue-Turenne

rue Huguerie

allées de Munich

allées d'Orléans

Garonne River

place
de
Tourny

cours de
Tourny/Tournon

allées de Tourny

place de
la Comédie

rue de l'Esprit des Lois

cours du Chapeau Rouge

place des
Grands Hommes

cours de l'Intendance

R du
Grassi

r du Port de la Mousque

rue Saint Rémi

place
de la
Bourse

place
de la
Douane

rue de la Porte Dijeaux

place
Gambetta

rue des Remparts

rue Vital Carles

rue Ste-Catherine

place
du
Parlement

Place
St-Pierre

rue du Cancéra

place
du
Palais

To Arcachon
via N250

To A630, A62 to
Toulouse (248km),
A63 to Arcachon (74km)
& Bayonne (190km)

rue des Trois Conils

place
St-Projet

place
Camille
Jullian

rue de la Merci

place Jean
Moulin

cours d'Alsace et Lorraine

To Pont de Pierre, A10 to
Poitiers (248km), Paris
(580km), N89 to Libourne
(31km) & Saint Émilion (40km)

place
de la
République

cours Victor Hugo

St-Michel

To quai
de la Paludate
(Bars & Discos,
1.3km)

rue de Cursol

place
de la
Victoire

To Camping
Beausoleil
(10km via
Cours de
l'Argonne)

To Camping les
Gravières (10km)

place des
Capucins

To Auberge
de Jeunesse (800m)
& Gare St-Jean
(Train Station, 1.4km)

rue Élie Gintrec

cours Aristide Briand

cours de la Libération

0   100   200m
0   100   200yd

BORDEAUX

PLACES TO STAY		
8	Hôtel Touring & Hôtel Studio	
9	Hôtel de Famille	
20	Hôtel de la Tour Intendance	
33	Hôtel Boulan	

PLACES TO EAT		
7	Restaurant Baud et Millet	
13	Champion Supermarket (Marché des Grands Hommes)	
18	La Chanterelle	
23	Chez Édouard	
27	Claret's	
46	Champion Supermarket	
47	La Fournaise	
51	Cassolette Café	
53	Fruit & Vegetable Stalls	
54	Marche des Capucins	

ENTERTAINMENT		
12	Grand Théâtre	

22	Calle Ocho
50	The Down Under

OTHER	
1	Musée d'Histoire Naturelle
2	Musée d'Art Contemporain
3	Bord'Eaux Velos Loisirs
4	Halte Routière (Bus Station)
5	Girondins Fountain-Monument
6	Laundrette
10	Tourist Office
11	Banque de France
14	Laundrette
15	Hôtel de Police
16	Église Notre Dame
17	Maison du Tourisme de la Gironde
19	American Express
21	Porte Dijeaux
24	Bourse du Commerce
25	Hôtel de la Douane

26	Porte Cailhau
28	Post Office Branch
29	Centre National JeanMoulin
30	Musée des Arts Décoratifs
31	Main Post Office
32	Galerie des Beaux-Arts
34	Jardin de la Mairie
35	Musée des Beaux-Arts
36	Hôtel de Ville
37	Tribunal de Grande Instance (Court; 1998)
38	Cathédrale Saint André
39	Tour Pey-Berland (Belfry)
40	Cyberstation
41	Musée d'Aquitaine
42	Porte de la GrosseCloche
43	Porte des Salinières
44	Église Saint Michel
45	Tour Saint Michel
48	Hôpital Saint André
49	Synagogue
52	Porte d'Aquitaine

FRANCE

Esprit des Lois and cours du Chapeau Rouge. American Express (☎ 05 56 00 63 36) at 14 cours de l'Intendance is open on weekdays and, from June to September, also on Saturday morning.

Post & Communications The main post office, 37 rue du Château d'Eau, opens 8.30 am to 6.30 pm weekdays and until 12.30 pm on Saturday. The branch post office at place St Projet opens until 6.30 pm (noon on Saturday). Currency exchange and Cyberpostes are available at both.

Cyberstation (☎ 05 56 01 15 15), 23 Cour Pasteur, opens 11 am to 2 am (2 pm to midnight on Sunday).

Laundry The laundrettes at 5 rue de Fondaudège and 8 rue Lafaurie de Monbadon open 7 am to 9 pm.

Things to See

The following sights are listed roughly north to south. Admission to each museum costs 25/15FF (free for students and on the first Sunday of the month).

The excellent **Musée d'Art Contemporain** at 7 rue Ferrère hosts exhibits by contemporary artists (closed Monday). The **Jardin Public**, an 18th-century English-style park, is along cours de Verdun and includes Bordeaux's **botanical garden** and **Musée d'Histoire Naturelle** (Natural History Museum); closed Tuesday.

The most prominent feature of **Esplanade des Quinconces**, a vast square laid out in 1820, is a towering fountain-monument to the Girondins, a group of moderate, bourgeois legislative deputies executed during the French Revolution.

The neoclassical **Grand Théâtre** at place de la Comédie was built in the 1770s. **Porte Dijeaux**, which dates from 1748, leads from **place Gambetta**, which has a garden in the middle, to the pedestrianised commercial centre. A few blocks south, the **Musée des Arts Décoratifs** (Museum of Decorative Arts), 39 rue Bouffard, specialises in faïence, porcelain, silverwork, glasswork, furniture and the like; closed Tuesday.

In 1137, the future King Louis VII married Eleanor of Aquitaine in **Cathédrale St André**. Just east of the cathedral, there's the 15th-century, 50m-high belfry, **Tour Pey-Berland**, which can be climbed for 25/15FF (closed Monday). The **Centre National Jean Moulin** (Jean Moulin Documentation Centre), facing the north side of the cathedral, has exhibits on France during WWII; closed Monday.

At 20 cours d'Albert, the **Musée des Beaux-Arts** occupies two wings of the 18th-century Hôtel de Ville and houses a large collection of paintings, including 17th-century Flemish, Dutch and Italian works (closed Tuesday). The outstanding **Musée d'Aquitaine**, 20 cours Pasteur, illustrates the history and ethnography of the Bordeaux area (closed Monday).

The **Synagogue** (1882) on rue du Grand Rabbin Joseph Cohen (just west of rue Ste Catherine) is a mixture of Sephardic and Byzantine styles. During WWII the Nazis turned the complex into a prison. Visits are generally possible Monday to Thursday from 9 am to noon and 2 to 4 pm – ring the bell marked *gardien* at 213 rue Ste Catherine.

Places to Stay

The 150-spot *Camping Les Gravières* (☎ 05 56 87 00 36, *place de Courréjean in Villenave d'Ornon)*, open all year, is 10km south-east of the city centre. By bus, take line B from place de la Victoire towards Corréjean and get off at the terminus.

About 700m west of the train station, the *Auberge de Jeunesse* (☎ 05 56 91 59 51, *22 cours Barbey)* is being completely renovated and is scheduled to reopen in April 2001.

North of the centre near place de Tourny (from the station take bus Nos 7 or 8), *Hôtel Studio* (☎ 05 56 48 00 14, *fax 05 56 81 25 71, 26 rue Huguerie)* and three affiliated hotels offer charmless singles/doubles with shower, toilet and (in most cases) cable TV starting at an absolute minimum of 98/120FF. The hotel's mini-cybercafe charges guests 10FF an hour. Web site: www.hotel-bordeaux.com. *Hôtel de Famille* (☎ 05 56 52 11 28, *fax 05 56 51 94 43, 76 cours Georges Clemenceau)* has rather ordinary but homy doubles from 120FF (185FF with shower and toilet).

A few blocks south-west of place Gambetta, the quiet *Hôtel Boulan* (☎ 05 56 52 23 62, *fax 05 56 44 91 65, 28 rue Boulan)* has decent singles/doubles from 100/110FF (120/140FF with shower).

Just east of place Gambetta, you're assured of a warm welcome at the two-star *Hôtel de la Tour Intendance* (☎ 05 56 81 46 27, *fax 05 56 81 60 90, 16 rue de la Vieille Tour)*, where ordinary doubles/triples cost 250/320FF. Another excellent deal is the two-star

Hôtel Touring (☎ 05 56 81 56 73, *fax 05 56 81 24 55, 16 rue Huguerie)*, which has gigantic and spotless singles/doubles with shower for 180/220FF (220/240FF with toilet, too).

Places to Eat

La Chanterelle (3 rue de Martignac) serves moderately priced traditional French and regional cuisine; *menus* cost 75FF (lunch only) and 98FF (closed on Wednesday night and Sunday). Bistro-style cuisine and south-western French specialities are on offer at *Claret's* (☎ 05 56 01 21 21, *place Camille Julien)*, whose *menus* cost 65FF (lunch only), 98 and 160FF (closed Saturday lunchtime and Sunday). The popular *Chez Édouard* (16 place du Parlement) purveys French bistro-style meat and fish dishes; *menus* cost 59FF (lunch except Sunday), 70FF and 99FF. There are lots of eateries along nearby rue du Parlement Ste Catherine, rue des Piliers de Tutelle and rue St Rémi.

Restaurant Baud et Millet (19 rue Huguerie) serves cheese-based cuisine (most dishes are vegetarian), including all-you-can-eat raclette for 110FF (closed Sunday).

The dinner-only *La Fournaise* (23 rue de Lalande) serves the delicious cuisine of Réunion; *menus* cost 80FF to 140FF (closed Sunday and Monday).

The inexpensive cafes and restaurants around place de la Victoire include the *Cassolette Café* (20 place de la Victoire), which serves family-style French food on small/large *cassolettes* (terracotta plates) that cost 11/33FF (open daily).

There's a *Champion* supermarket at place des Grands Hommes in the basement of the mirror-plated Marché des Grands Hommes (closed Sunday). Near *Marché des Capucins*, a covered food market just east of place de la Victoire (open 6 am to 1 pm, closed Monday), you'll find super-cheap *fruit and vegetable stalls* along rue Élie Gintrec (open until 1 pm, closed Sunday).

Entertainment

Bordeaux has a hopping nightlife scene. *The Down Under* (104 cours Aristide Briand), run by an ex-Aucklander, is a favourite of Anglophones; hours are 7 or 8 pm to 2 am daily. One of the really hot venues is a

Cuban-style bar called *Calle Ocho (24 rue des Piliers de Tutelle)*, open 5 pm to 2 am (closed Sunday).

Among the best of the late-late dancing bars is tropical beach-themed *La Plage (☎ 05 56 49 02 46, 40 quai de la Paludate)* along the river east of the train station, which opens from midnight to 5 am Wednesday to Saturday nights.

Getting There & Away

Buses to places all over the Gironde and nearby departments leave from the Halte Routière (☎ 05 56 43 68 43), in the north-east corner of esplanade des Quinconces; schedules are posted.

Bordeaux's train station, Gare St Jean (☎ 0836 35 35 39), is about 3km south-east of the city centre at the end of cours de la Marne. By TGV it takes only about three hours to/from Paris' Gare Montparnasse (352FF to 399FF). The trip to Bayonne (135FF) takes 1¾ hours.

BORDEAUX VINEYARDS

The Bordeaux wine-producing region, 1000 sq km in extent, is subdivided into 57 production areas called *appellations*, whose climate and soil impart distinctive characteristics to the wines grown there.

Over 5000 chateaux (also known as *domaines*, *crus* and *clos*) produce the region's highly regarded wines, which are mainly reds. Many smaller chateaux accept walk-in visitors (some are closed during the October grape harvest); the larger and better known ones usually require that you phone ahead.

Each vineyard has different rules about tasting – at some it's free, others charge entry fees, and others don't serve wine at all. Look for signs reading *dégustation* (wine tasting), *en vente directe* (direct sales), *vin à emporter* (wine to take away) and *gratuit* (free).

Opposite Bordeaux's main tourist office, the Maison du Vin de Bordeaux (☎/fax 05 56 00 22 66), open weekdays (and, in summer, on Saturday), has details on vineyard visits. It can also supply information on the many local *maisons du vin* (special wine-oriented tourist offices). Web site: www.vins-bordeaux.fr.

On Wednesday and Saturday (daily from May to October), the Bordeaux tourist office runs five-hour bus tours in French and English to local wine chateaux (160/140FF).

St Émilion
pop 400

The medieval village of St Émilion, 39km east of Bordeaux, is surrounded by vineyards renowned for their full-bodied, deeply coloured red wines. The most interesting historical sites – including the **Église Monolithe**, carved out of solid limestone from the 9th to the 12th centuries – can be visited only on the 45-minute guided tours (33/20FF) offered by the tourist office (☎ 05 57 55 28 28), which is at place des Créneaux (open daily). The 50 or so wine shops include the cooperative Maison du Vin (☎ 05 57 55 50 55) at place Pierre Meyrat, around the corner from the tourist office, which is owned by the 250 chateaux whose wines it sells (open daily).

From Bordeaux, St Émilion is accessible by train (44FF, 35 minutes, two or three a day) and bus (at least once a day, except on Sundays and holidays from October to April). The last train back usually departs at 6.27 pm.

THE MÉDOC

North-west of Bordeaux, along the western shore of the Gironde Estuary, lie some of Bordeaux's most celebrated vineyards. To the west, fine sandy beaches bordered by dunes stretch for some 200km from Pointe de Grave south along the **Côte d'Argent** (Silver Coast) to the Bassin d'Arcachon and beyond. The coastal dunes abut a vast pine forest planted in the 19th century to stabilise the drifting sands.

The most beautiful part of this renowned wine-growing area is north of **Pauillac**, along the D2 and the D204 (towards Lesparre). Vineyards around here include the **Château Lafitte Rothschild** (☎ 01 53 89 78 00 in Paris) and the equally illustrious **Château Mouton Rothschild** (☎ 05 56 73 21 29). Both places require advance reservations; the latter charges 30FF.

Seaside resorts include the beach resort of **Soulac-sur-Mer** (population 2800), where the two-star, 13-room *Hôtel La Dame de Cœur (☎ 05 56 09 80 80, fax 05 56 09 97 47, @ la.dame.de.coeur@wanadoo.fr, 103 rue de la Plage)* has doubles from 250FF.

The relaxed naturist village of **Euronat** (☎ 05 56 09 33 33, fax 05 56 09 30 27), about 80km north of Bordeaux, covers 3.3 sq km (including 1.5km of dune-lined beachfront). The cheapest four-person bungalows range from 210FF a night (in winter) to 390FF a night (July and August), minimum three nights. Web site: www.euronat.fr.

Getting There & Away

The northern tip of the Médoc, Pointe de Grave, is linked to Royan by car ferries. Three to five Citram Aquitaine buses a day connect Bordeaux with Lesparre, Soulac-sur-Mer (two hours) and Point de Grave (76FF, 2¼ hours). SNCF bus-train combos linking Bordeaux with Margaux, Pauillac (54FF, one hour), Lesparre, Soulac (83FF, two hours) and Pointe de Grave (or nearby Le Verdon, 89FF) run five times a day (twice on weekends).

ARCACHON
pop 11,800

The beach resort of Arcachon, in the southwest corner of the triangular **Bassin d'Arcachon** (Arcachon Bay), became popular with bourgeois residents of Bordeaux at the end of the 19th century. Its major attractions are the sandy seashore and the extraordinary, 114m-high **Dune de Pyla**, Europe's highest sand dune, which is 8km south of town.

The flat area that abuts the **Plage d'Arcachon** (the town's beach) is known as the **Ville d'Été** (Summer Quarter). The liveliest section is around **Jetée Thiers**, one of the two piers, which is linked to pine-shaded **Cap Ferret** by boat. The **Ville d'Hiver** (Winter Quarter), on the tree-covered hillside south of the centre, was built about a century ago.

A few kilometres east of Arcachon, the oyster port of **Gujan Mestras** sprawls along 9km of coastline. Super-fresh and remarkably cheap oysters can be sampled at **Port de Larros**, one of the town's seven ports.

The tourist office (☎ 05 57 52 97 97, fax 05 57 52 97 77) is a few hundred metres from the train station at place Président Roosevelt (closed on Sunday and holidays except from April to September, when hours are 10 am to 1 pm). Web site: www.arcachon.com.

Places to Stay

The steep, inland side of the Dune de Pyla is gradually burying five large and rather pricey *camping grounds*, open about mid-April to mid-October.

Hotel rooms are nearly impossible to find in July and August. The 15-room *Hôtel Saint*

Christaud (☎/fax 05 56 83 38 53, 8 Allée de la Chapelle) has modern doubles for 99FF to 200FF, depending on the season. The down-to-earth *La Paix* (☎ 05 56 83 05 65, 8 ave de Lamartine), open late May to September, has simple doubles/quads from 171/283FF (25% more from mid-June to early September), including breakfast.

Getting There & Away

Some of the trains from Bordeaux to Arcachon (54FF, 55 minutes, 11 to 18 a day) – which also stop at Gujan Mestras near the Port de Larros – are coordinated with TGVs from Paris' Gare Montparnasse.

BAYONNE
pop 40,000

Bayonne is the most important city in the French part of the Basque Country (Euskadi in Basque, Pays Basque in French), a region straddling the French-Spanish border.

Its most important festival is the annual Fêtes de Bayonne, beginning on the first Wednesday in August. The festival includes a 'running of the bulls' like Pamplona's except that here they have cows rather than bulls.

Orientation & Information

The Adour and Nive Rivers split Bayonne into three: St Esprit, north of the Adour; Grand Bayonne, the oldest part of the city, on the west bank of the Nive; and the very Basque Petit Bayonne to its east.

The tourist office (☎ 05 59 46 01 46, fax 05 59 59 37 55, ❷ bayonne.tourisme@wanadoo.fr) is on place des Basques. It opens 9 am to 6.30 pm weekdays (10 am to 6 pm on Saturday). July and August hours are 9 am to 7 pm daily (10 am to 1 pm Sunday). Its brochure *Fêtes* is useful for cultural and sporting events while *Promenades and Discoveries*, in English, describes a self-guided walk around town.

You can log on at Cyber Net Café (☎ 05 59 55 78 98) on place de la République. Open 7 am to 2 am daily (from midday on Sunday), it charges 1FF per minute or 45FF an hour.

Things to See & Do

Construction of the Gothic **Cathédrale Ste Marie** on place Monseigneur Vansteenberghe began in the 13th century and was completed in 1451. The entrance to the beautiful 13th-century **cloister** is on place Louis Pasteur.

The **Musée Bonnat** (20/10FF; closed Tuesday) at 5 rue Jacques Laffitte in Petit Bayonne, has a diverse collection, including a whole gallery of paintings by Rubens.

Places to Stay

Camping *Camping de Parme* (☎ *05 59 23 03 00, route de l'Aviation)*, 1.25km northeast of the Biarritz-La Négresse train station, charges 79FF for two people and tent. Open all year, it's usually booked during July and August.

Hostels The lively *Auberge de Jeunesse d'Anglet* (☎ *05 59 58 70 00, fax 05 59 58 70 07,* ✪ *biarritz@fuaj.fr, 19 route des Vignes)* at 19 Route des Vignes in Anglet comes complete with a Scottish pub. Popular with surfers, it's open from mid-February to mid-November; reservations are essential in summer. B&B costs 73FF and you can also pitch a tent here for 48FF per person, including breakfast.

From Bayonne, take bus No 7 and get off at Moulin Barbot, a 10-minute walk away. From Biarritz, town or station, take bus No 9.

Hotels You can tumble off the train into hyperfriendly *Hôtel Paris-Madrid* (☎ *05 59 55 13 98, fax 05 59 55 07 22)*, just beside the station. Cheapest singles are 95FF, and pleasant doubles without/with shower start at 130/160FF. Big rooms with bathroom and cable TV which can take up to four cost from 210FF. Nearby at 1 rue Ste Ursule *Hôtel Monte Carlo* (☎ *05 59 55 02 68)* has simple rooms from 90FF and larger ones with bathroom for two to four people at 170FF to 250FF.

In Petit Bayonne, *Hôtel des Basques* (☎ *05 59 59 08 02)* on place Paul Bert has large, pleasant rooms with washbasin and toilet for between 135FF and 180FF and ones with full bathroom from 170FF. Showers cost 10FF.

The mid-range *Hôtel des Basses-Pyrénées* (☎ *05 59 59 00 29, fax 05 59 59 42 02, 12 rue Tour de Sault, closed January)* is built around a 17th-century tower. Doubles/triples/quads with bathroom start at 300/330/350FF. It also has a few rooms with washbasin for 150FF to 170FF and private parking (30FF).

Places to Eat

Nowhere in town is more Basque than *Restaurant Euskalduna Ostatua*, near Hôtel des Basques at 61 rue Pannecau, where main dishes are a bargain 35FF to 50FF. It's open for lunch, weekdays only. Over the Nive River the family-run *Bar-Restaurant du Marché (39 rue des Basques)*, where the cooking's homely and the owner's wife mothers everyone, will fill you to bursting for under 100FF. Open for lunch only.

A couple of blocks west, cheerful *Restaurant Dacquois* (*48 rue d'Espagne)* serves juicy sandwiches from 12FF and has a great value 65FF *menu*.

The central market, *Les Halles*, on the west quay (quai Amiral Jauréguiberry) of the Nive River, is open every morning except Sunday.

Entertainment

The greatest concentration of pubs and bars is in Petit Bayonne, especially along rue Pannecau and quai Galuperie. *La Pompe* (☎ *05 59 25 48 12, 7 rue des Augustins)*, a lively discotheque, throbs from 10 pm to dawn Thursday to Sunday.

Getting There & Away

Bus From place des Basques, ATCRB buses (☎ 05 59 26 06 99) run to St-Jean de Luz (22FF, 40 minutes, 10 daily) with connections for Hendaye (36FF, one hour). Two Transportes Pesa buses run to Irún and San Sebastián in Spain (38FF, 1¾ hours, daily except Sunday).

From the train station car park, RDTL (☎ 05 59 55 17 59) runs services northwards into Les Landes. For beaches north of Bayonne, such as Mimizan Plage and Moliets Plage, get off at Vieux Boucau (39FF, 1¼ hours). TPR (☎ 05 59 27 45 98) has three buses daily to Pau (85FF, 2¼ hours).

Bayonne is one of three hubs in South-West France for Eurolines, whose buses stop in place Charles de Gaulle, opposite the company office (☎ 05 59 59 19 33) at No 3.

Train The train station is just north of Pont St Esprit bridge. TGVs run to/from Paris' Gare Montparnasse (428FF, five hours). Two daily non-TGV trains go overnight to Paris' Gare d'Austerlitz (401FF or 471FF with couchette) in about eight hours.

FRANCE

There's a frequent service to Biarritz (13FF, 10 minutes), St-Jean de Luz (26FF, 25 minutes) and St-Jean Pied de Port (47FF, one hour), plus the Franco-Spanish border towns of Hendaye (37FF, 40 minutes) and Irún (45 minutes).

Some other destinations are Bordeaux (145FF, 2¼ hours, about 12 daily), Lourdes (126FF, 1¾ hours, six daily) and Pau (82FF, 1¼ hours, eight daily).

BIARRITZ
pop 30,000

The classy coastal town of Biarritz, 8km west of Bayonne, has fine beaches and some of Europe's best surfing. Unfortunately, it can be a real budget-buster – consider making it a day trip from Bayonne, as lots of French holidaymakers do. Many surfers camp or stay at one of the two excellent youth hostels – in Biarritz and in Anglet (see the Bayonne section).

Biarritz's Festival International de Folklore is held in early July.

Orientation & Information

Place Clemenceau, at the heart of Biarritz, is just south of Grande Plage, the main beach. The tourist office (☎ 05 59 22 37 10, fax 05 59 24 14 19, ✉ biarritz.tourisme@biarritz.tm.fr), 1 square d'Ixelles, is one block east of the square. It opens 9 am to 6.45 pm daily. In July and August it's open 8 am to 8 pm. It publishes Biarritzcope, a free monthly guide to what's on. In July and August, it has a branch at the train station.

Check your emails at Génius Informatique (1FF per minute, 50FF an hour).

Things to See & Do

The Grande Plage, lined in season with striped bathing tents, stretches from the Casino Bellevue to the stately Hôtel du Palais. North of the hotel is Plage Miramar and the 1834 Phare de Biarritz. Beyond this lighthouse the superb surfing beaches of Anglet extend for 4km (take bus No 9 from place Clemenceau).

The Musée de la Mer, Biarritz' sea museum, is on Pointe Atalaye overlooking Rocher de la Vierge, an islet reached by a short footbridge which offers sweeping coastal views. The museum (45/30FF) has a 24-tank aquarium plus seal and shark pools.

Places to Stay

Camping Biarritz Camping (☎ 05 59 23 00 12, 28 rue d'Harcet), open June to late September, is about 3km south-west of the centre and costs 105FF for two people and tent. Take bus No 9 to the Biarritz Camping stop.

Hostels For Biarritz's Auberge de Jeunesse (05 59 41 76 00, fax 05 59 41 76 07, ✉ auber gejeune.biarritz@wanadoo.fr, 8 rue Chiquito de Cambo), follow the railway westwards from the train station for 800m. B&B is 85FF and half-board, 120FF.

The otherwise expensive Hôtel Barnetche (☎ 05 59 24 22 25, fax 05 59 24 98 71, 5 avenue Charles Floquet) has dorm bunks for 100FF.

Hotels Nowhere is cheap in Biarritz, but prices drop by up to 25% outside summer.

In the Vieux Port area, trim Hôtel Palym (☎ 05 59 24 16 56, 7 rue du Port Vieux) has singles/doubles with toilet for 170/220FF (290FF with bathroom). Hôtel Atlantic (☎ 05 59 24 34 08) at No 10 has singles/doubles with washbasin for 195/215FF and doubles/triples/quads with bathroom for 295/330/350FF.

Attractive Hôtel Etche-Gorria (☎ 05 59 24 00 74, 21 ave du Maréchal Foch) has doubles without/with bathroom for 180/290FF.

Places to Eat

Popular Le Bistroye (☎ 05 59 22 01 02, 6 rue Jean Bart), closed Wednesday evening and all Sunday, has delicious main dishes between 75FF and 95FF. Next door, La Mamounia (☎ 05 59 24 76 08) doles out couscous from 80FF and other Moroccan specialities from 95FF.

There are quite a few decent little restaurants around Les Halles. At Bistrot des Halles (☎ 05 59 24 21 22, 1 rue du Centre), for example, a three-course meal with wine from the chalkboard menu will set you back about 150FF.

The covered market off ave Victor Hugo is open 7 am to 1.30 pm daily.

Entertainment

Popular bar areas include the streets around rue du Port Vieux, the covered market area and around place Clemenceau. Two central discos are Le Caveau, 4 rue Gambetta and Le Flamingo inside the Casino.

Getting There & Away

Most local STAB buses stop beside the town hall, from where Nos 1 and 2 go to Bayonne's town hall and station.

Biarritz-La Négresse train station is 3km south of the centre and served by buses Nos 2 and 9. SNCF has a downtown office (☎ 05 59 24 00 94) at 13 ave du Maréchal Foch.

AROUND BIARRITZ
St-Jean Pied de Port
pop 1500

The walled Pyrenean town of St-Jean Pied de Port, 53km south-east of Bayonne, was once the last stop in France for pilgrims heading for the Spanish pilgrimage city of Santiago de Compostela. Nowadays it's a popular departure point for latter day hikers and bikers but can be hideously crowded in summer. The climb to the 17th-century **Citadelle** merits the effort with fine views.

The tourist office (☎ 05 59 37 03 57) is on place Charles de Gaulle. Riverside *Camping Municipal Plaza Berri* (☎ *05 59 37 11 19, ave du Fronton*), open Easter to September, charges 42FF for two people and tent. Cheerful *Hôtel des Remparts* (☎ *05 59 37 13 79, 16 place Floquet*) has rooms with bathroom from 210FF.

For lunch, *Chez Dédé* (☎ 05 59 37 16 40), just inside the porte de France, has as many as seven good value, tasty *menus*, ranging from the modest *menu du routard* at 50FF to the *suggestion du chef* at 135FF.

Half the reason for coming to St-Jean Pied de Port is the scenic train trip from Bayonne (47FF, one hour, up to four daily).

LOURDES
pop 15,000

In 1858, 14-year-old Bernadette Soubirous saw the Virgin Mary within a small grotto in a series of 18 visions, later confirmed as bona fide apparitions by the Vatican. This simple peasant girl, who lived out her short life as a nun, was canonised as Ste Bernadette in 1933.

Some five million pilgrims annually, including many seeking cures for their illnesses, converge on Lourdes from all over the world.

In counterpoint to the fervent, almost medieval piety of the pilgrims is a tacky display of commercial exuberance.

Orientation & Information

Lourdes' two main east-west streets are rue de la Grotte and, 300m north, blvd de la Grotte. Both lead to the Sanctuaires Notre Dame de Lourdes. The principal north-south thoroughfare connects the train station with place Peyramale and the tourist office (☎ 05 62 42 77 40, fax 05 62 94 60 95, ✉ lourdes@ sudfr.com), which opens 9 am to noon and 2 to 6 pm, Monday to Saturday (to 7 pm between Easter and mid-October, when it's also open 10 am to 6 pm on Sunday). From June to September, there is no midday closure.

The office sells the *Visa Passeport Touristique* (169FF), allowing entry to five museums in Lourdes.

Things to See

The huge religious complex that has grown around the cave where Bernadette saw the Virgin, is just west of the town centre. The main Pont St Michel entrance is open from 5 am to midnight.

Major sites include the **Grotte de Massabielle**, where Bernadette had her visions, its walls today worn smooth by the touch of millions of hands, the nearby **pools** in which 400,000 people immerse themselves each year; and the **Basilique du Rosaire** (Basilica of the Rosary). Dress modestly.

From the Sunday before Easter to mid-October, solemn **torch-lit processions** leave nightly at 8.45 pm from the Grotte de Massabielle while the **Procession Eucaristique** (Blessed Sacrament Procession) takes place daily at 5 pm.

Places to Stay

Camping Tiny *Camping de la Poste* (☎ 05 62 94 40 35, 26 rue de Langelle), a few blocks east of the tourist office, is open Easter to mid-October. Charging 15/21FF per person/tent, it also has a few excellent value rooms with bathroom for 150FF.

Hotels Lourdes has plenty of budget hotels. Near the train station, friendly *Hôtel d'Annecy* (☎ 05 62 94 13 75, 13 ave de la Gare) is open from Easter to October.

FRANCE

Singles/doubles/triples/quads with wash-basin are 95/152/176/198FF (140/195/215/223FF with bathroom). In the town centre, *Hôtel St Sylve* (☎/fax 05 62 94 63 48, 9 rue de la Fontaine) has large singles/doubles for 75/140FF (100/160FF with shower). Open April to October.

The stylish *Hôtel de la Grotte* (☎ 05 62 94 58 87, fax 05 62 94 20 50, 66 rue de la Grotte) has fine balconies and a gorgeous garden. Its singles/doubles with all mod-cons start at 390/420FF. Open April to October.

Places to Eat
Restaurants close early in this pious town; even *McDonald's* (7 place du Marcadal) is slammed shut at 10.30 pm. *Restaurant le Magret* (10 rue des Quatre Frères Soulas), opposite the tourist office, has excellent value *menus* at 80FF and 150FF. Next door, *La Rose des Sables* specialises in couscous (from 78FF). Both close Mondays. The covered *market* is on place du Champ Commun, south of the tourist office.

Getting There & Away
Bus The bus station, down rue Anselme Lacadé east of the covered market, serves regional towns including Pau (32FF, 1¼ hours, four to six daily). SNCF buses to the Pyrenean towns of Cauterets (39FF, one hour, five daily) and Luz-St-Sauveur (40FF, one hour, six daily) leave from the train station's car park.

Train The train station is 1km east of the sanctuaries. Trains connect Lourdes with many cities including Bayonne (106FF, 1¾ hours, three to four daily), Bordeaux (172FF, 2½ hours, six daily), Pau (39FF, 30 minutes, over 10 daily) and Toulouse (125FF, 2¼ hours, seven daily). There are five TGVs daily to Paris' Gare Montparnasse (478FF, 6 hours) and one overnight train to Gare d'Austerlitz (409FF, nine hours).

The Dordogne

The Dordogne (better known as Périgord in France) was one of the cradles of human civilisation, and a number of local caves, including the world-famous Lascaux, are adorned with extraordinary prehistoric paint-ings. The region is also renowned for its cuisine, which makes ample use of those quintessential French delicacies, *truffes du Périgord* (black truffles) and *foie gras*, the fatty liver of force-fed geese.

PÉRIGUEUX
pop 33,000
Founded over 2000 years ago on a curve in the gentle Isle River, Périgueux has one of France's best museums of prehistory, the **Musée du Périgord** at 22 cours Tourny (closed Tuesday and holidays). Admission costs 20/10FF.

The old city, known as **Puy St Front**, lies between blvd Michel Montaigne and the Isle River. The tourist office (☎ 05 53 53 10 63, fax 05 53 09 02 50, ☻ tourisme.perigueux@ perigord.tm.fr) is at 26 place Francheville, next to a fortified, medieval tower called **Tour Mataguerre**. It opens 9 am to 6 pm (closed Sunday). From mid-June to mid-September, daily hours are 9 am to 7 pm (10 am to 6 pm Sunday and holidays).

Places to Stay
The year-round *Barnabé Plage Campground* (☎ 05 53 53 41 45) is about 2.5km east of the train station along the Isle River. By bus, take line No 8 to the rue des Bains stop.

About 600m south of the cathedral, the *Foyer des Jeunes Travailleurs* (☎ 05 53 53 52 05, rue des Thermes Prolongée), just off blvd Lakanal, charges 73FF for a bed, including breakfast.

Near the train station, the cheapest hotel is the family-run, 16-room *Hôtel des Voyageurs* (☎ 05 53 53 17 44, 26 rue Denis Papin), where basic but clean doubles cost only 80FF (100FF with shower). Reception may be closed on weekend afternoons (hours posted).

Getting There & Away
The bus station (☎ 05 53 08 91 06), on place Francheville (just south-west of the tourist office), has buses to Sarlat (50.50FF, 1½ hours, one or two a day) via the Vézère Valley town of Montignac (35FF, 55 minutes).

The train station (☎ 0836 35 35 39), on rue Denis Papin (about 1km north-west of the tourist office), is served by local buses Nos 1, 4 and 5. Destinations include Bordeaux (99FF, 1¼ hours), Les Eyzies de Tayac (41FF,

30 minutes, two to four a day), Paris' Gare d'Austerlitz (268FF, four to five hours) and Sarlat (75FF).

SARLAT-LA-CANÉDA
pop 10,000

This beautiful town, situated between the Dordogne and Vézère Rivers, is graced by numerous Renaissance-style, 16th and 17th-century stone buildings. On Saturday mornings there's a colourful market on place de la Liberté and along rue de la République – edible (though seasonal) offerings include truffles, mushrooms, geese and parts thereof.

The main drag is known as rue de la République where it passes through the heart-shaped old town. The tourist office (☎ 05 53 59 27 67) occupies the 15th and 16th-century Hôtel de Maleville on place de la Liberté.

Places to Stay

The modest but friendly, 15-bed *Auberge de Jeunesse* (☎ 05 53 59 47 59 or ☎ 05 53 30 21 27, *77 ave de Selves*) opens mid-March to mid-November. A bed costs 50FF; small tents can be pitched in the tiny back garden for 30FF a person (5FF more for the first night). Cooking facilities are available. Call ahead to check availability.

Doubles start at 250FF at the two-star places: *Hôtel de la Mairie* (☎ 05 53 59 05 71, *13 place de la Liberté*), near the tourist office (open March to December); and *Hôtel Les Récollets* (☎ 05 53 31 36 00, fax 05 53 30 32 62, 📧 otelrecol@aol.com, *4 rue Jean-Jacques Rousseau*), up an alley just west of rue de la République.

Getting There & Away

There are one or two buses a day (fewer in July and August) from place de la Petite Rigaudie to Périgueux (50.50FF, 1½ hours) via the Vézère Valley town of Montignac (35 minutes).

Sarlat's tiny train station (☎ 0836 35 35 39) is linked to Bordeaux (119FF, 2½ hours), Périgueux (75FF) and Les Eyzies de Tayac (47FF, 50 minutes, two a day).

VÉZÈRE VALLEY

Périgord's most important prehistoric sites are about 45km south-east of Périgueux and 20km north-west of Sarlat in the Vézère Valley, mainly between Les Eyzies de Tayac and Montignac. Worthwhile caves not mentioned below include the **Grotte du Grand Roc** and **La Roque St Christophe**. For details on public transport, see Getting There & Away under Périgueux and Sarlat.

Les Eyzies de Tayac
pop 850

This dull, touristy village offers one of the region's best introductions to prehistory, the **Musée National de Préhistoire** (22/15FF), built into the cliff above the tourist office (closed Tuesday, except in July and August). Also of interest is the **Abri Pataud** (28/14FF), an impressive Cro-Magnon rock shelter in the cliff face (closed Monday, except in July and August).

The **Grotte de Font de Gaume**, a cave with 230 remarkably sophisticated polychrome figures of bison, reindeer and other creatures, and the **Grotte des Combarelles**, decorated with 600 often-superimposed engravings of animals, are 1km and 3km respectively north-east of Les Eyzies de Tayac on the D47. It charges 35/23FF for a tour, which must be reserved in advance on ☎ 05 53 06 86 00 (closed Wednesday).

Les Eyzies' tourist office (☎ 05 53 06 97 05, fax 05 53 06 90 79) is on the town's main street (closed on Sunday from October to February).

Montignac
pop 3100

Montignac, 25km north-east of Les Eyzies, achieved sudden fame thanks to the **Lascaux Cave**, 2km to the south-east, discovered in 1940 by four teenage boys who, it is said, were out searching for their dog. The cave's main room and a number of steep galleries are decorated with 15,000-year-old figures of wild oxen, deer, horses, reindeer and other creatures depicted in vivid reds, blacks, yellows and browns.

Lascaux has long been closed to the public to prevent deterioration, but you can get a good idea of the original at **Lascaux II**, a meticulous replica of the main gallery that opens daily (except on Monday from November to March) from 10 am to 12.30 pm and 1.30 to 6 pm (no midday closure from April to October; until 8 pm in July and August);

FRANCE

closed for three weeks in January. The last tour begins about an hour before closing time. Tickets, which from April to October are sold *only* in Montignac (next to the tourist office), cost 50FF (children 20FF).

SOUTH-WEST OF SARLAT

Along the Dordogne River about 15km south-west of Sarlat you'll find a number of lovely towns and spectacular fortified chateaux.

The trapezoid-shaped, walled village of **Domme**, set on a steep promontory high above the river, is one of the few bastides to have retained most of its 13th-century ramparts. The hamlet of **La Roque Gageac** is built halfway up the cliff face on the right bank of the river.

The 12th to 16th-century **Château de Castelnaud** (30FF) has everything you'd expect from a cliff-top castle. The interior is occupied by a **museum of medieval warfare** (open daily from March to mid-November). Across the river – also perched atop a sheer cliff – is Castelnaud's archrival, the dramatic **Château de Beynac** (40FF, open daily).

Quercy

South-east of the Dordogne department lies the warm, unmistakably southern region of Quercy. The dry limestone plateau in the north-east is covered with oak trees and cut by dramatic canyons created by the serpentine Lot River and its tributaries.

CAHORS
pop 21,432

Cahors, nestled in a bend of the Lot River, is a quiet town with a relaxed Midi atmosphere. The train station lies about 600m west of north-south oriented blvd Léon Gambetta, the main commercial thoroughfare.

A bit south of the train station is **Pont Valentré**, one of France's finest fortified medieval bridges. **Vieux Cahors** is the medieval quarter situated east of blvd Léon Gambetta.

The cavernous nave of the Romanesque-style **Cathédrale St Étienne**, consecrated in 1119, is crowned with two 18m-wide cupolas, the largest in France. The heavily mutilated, Flamboyant Gothic **cloître** (cloister) opens May to September.

The small, free **Musée de la Résistance** (☎ 05 65 22 14 25), on the north side of place Charles de Gaulle, has exhibits on the Resistance, the concentration camps and the liberation of France (open 2 to 6 pm daily).

Information

The tourist office (☎ 05 65 53 20 65, fax 05 65 53 20 74) is on place François Mitterrand. It opens 9 am to 12.30 pm and 1.30 to 6.30 pm, Monday to Saturday (6 pm on Saturday). In July and August, it's also open on Sunday and holidays from 10 am to noon.

About 500m south of the train station at 430 Allée des Soupirs, the municipal centre Les Docks offers Internet access from about 2 to 8 pm (until 6 pm at weekends, until 10 or 11 pm from Wednesday to Friday).

Places to Stay

The three-star *Camping Rivière de Cassebut* (☎ 05 56 30 06 30), on the left bank of the Lot about 1km north of Pont de Cassebut (the bridge just east of Vieux Cahors), is open April to October.

The *Auberge de Jeunesse* (☎ 05 65 35 64 71, fax 05 65 35 95 92, 20 rue Frédéric Suisse) is in the same building as the Foyer des Jeunes Travailleurs. Accommodation in four to 11-bed rooms cost 51FF. Telephone reservations are advisable.

In Vieux Cahors, *Hôtel de la Paix* (☎ 05 65 35 03 40, fax 05 65 35 40 88, place des Halles) has basic but clean doubles from 160FF (210FF with shower and toilet). Reception is closed on Sunday and holidays.

Places to Eat

Inexpensive restaurants around the Marché Couvert include the unpretentious *Restaurant Le Troquet des Halles* (rue St Maurice), where the four-course *menu* costs only 60FF, including wine. Except on Sunday, lunch is noon to 2 pm; dinner is available only from June to September.

Cahors' covered market, the *Marché Couvert* (on place des Halles), opens 7.30 am to 12.30 pm and 3 to 7 pm, Tuesday to Saturday and Sunday mornings.

Getting There & Away

The train station (☎ 0836 35 35 39), on place Jouinot Gambetta (place de la Gare), is on the main SNCF line linking Paris' Gare d'Austerlitz (314FF, 5¼ hours) with Toulouse (87FF, 1¼ hours). To get to Sarlat-la-Canéda, take a train to Souillac and an SNCF bus from there.

AROUND CAHORS

East of Cahors, the limestone hills between Cahors and Figeac are cut by the dramatic, cliff-flanked Lot and Célé Rivers. The **Grotte de Pech Merle** (☎ 05 65 31 27 05), 30km east of Cahors, has thousands of stalactites and dozens of paintings drawn by Cro-Magnon people over 16,000 years ago (open from the week before Easter until October). Arrive early as only 700 people a day are allowed to visit.

The village of **St Cirq Lapopie**, 25km east of Cahors, is perched on a cliff 100m above the Lot River. The harmonious riverside town of **Figeac** is on the Célé about 70km northeast of Cahors. Both are linked to Cahors by four to six SNCF buses a day.

Burgundy & the Rhône

DIJON

pop 230,000

Dijon, the prosperous capital of the dukes of Burgundy for almost 500 years, is one of France's most appealing provincial cities. Graced by elegant medieval and Renaissance residences, it has a distinctly youthful air, in part because of the major university situated there.

Dijon is a good starting point for visits to the vineyards of the Côte d'Or, arguably the greatest wine-growing region in the world (don't mention this when you're in Bordeaux).

Orientation & Information

Dijon's main thoroughfare runs eastward from the train station to Église St Michel: ave Maréchal Foch links the train station with the tourist office; rue de la Liberté continues eastward past the Palais des Ducs.

The tourist office (☎ 03 80 44 11 44, fax 03 80 42 18 83) is 300m east of the train station at place Darcy. It opens 9 am to 8 pm daily; from mid-October to April, hours are 10 am to 5.30 or 6 pm, until 1 pm on Sunday and holi-

days. The annexe, at 34 rue des Forges, faces the north side of the Palais des Ducs (closed Sunday and, from mid-October to April, on Saturday). Web site: www.ot-dijon.fr.

Money & Post The Banque de France, 2 place de la Banque, changes money on weekdays from 8.45 to 11.45 am.

The main post office, at place Grangier, open 8 am to 7 pm weekdays, Saturday to noon. Exchange services and a Cyberposte are available.

Laundry The laundrettes at 41 rue Auguste Comte and Nos 28 and 55 rue Berbisey are open until 8.30 or 9 pm daily.

Things to See

Dijon's major museums open daily except Tuesday, with the exception of the Musée National Magnin, which opens daily except Monday. Except where noted, entry is free for under 18s and students and, on the first Sunday of the month, for everyone. La Clé de la Ville combination ticket (45FF), available at the tourist office, gives access to all of Dijon's museums and to one of the tourist office's tours.

The **Palais des Ducs et des États de Bourgogne** (Palace of the Dukes and States General of Burgundy), remodelled in the neoclassical style in the 17th and 18th centuries, was once the home of the powerful dukes of Burgundy. The east wing houses the outstanding **Musée des Beaux-Arts**, one of the richest and most renowned fine arts museums in France. Hours are 10 am to 6 pm; admission costs 22FF.

Some of the finest of Dijon's many medieval and Renaissance townhouses are just north of the Palais des Ducs along **rue Verrerie** and **rue des Forges**, Dijon's main street until the 18th century. The splendid Flamboyant Gothic **Hôtel Chambellan** (1490) at 34 rue des Forges now houses the tourist office annexe.

Many great figures of Burgundy's history are buried in the Burgundian-Gothic **Cathédrale St Bénigne**, built in the late 13th century. **Église St Michel**, begun in 1499, is a Flamboyant Gothic church with an impressive Renaissance facade. The unusual **Église Notre Dame** was built in the Burgundian-Gothic

FRANCE

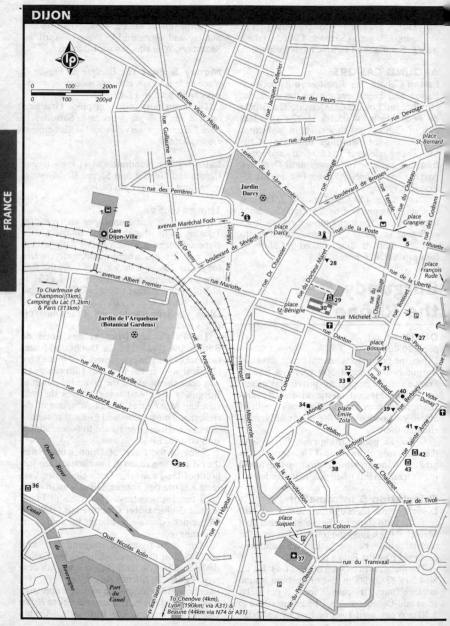

DIJON

0 _____ 100 _____ 200m
0 _____ 100 _____ 200yd

avenue Victor Hugo

rue Jacques Cellerier

rue des Fleurs

rue Devosge

place St-Bernard

rue Audra

avenue de la 1ère Armée

rue Guillaume Tell

rue des Perrières

boulevard de Brosses

rue du Château

place Grangier

Jardin Darcy

rue de la Poste

rue Devosge

rue des Godrans

rue Temple

1

Gare Dijon-Ville

avenue Maréchal Foch

2

place Darcy

3

4

5

r Musette

place François Rude

place de la Liberté

avenue Albert Premier

rue du Dr Remy

boulevard de Sévigné

rue Millotet

rue du Dr Chausser

rue de la Poste

rue du Docteur Maret

28

rue Mariotte

rue du Chapeau Rouge

rue Bossuet

To Chartreuse de Champmoi (1km), Camping du Lac (1.2km) & Paris (313km)

Jardin de l'Arquebuse (Botanical Gardens)

place St-Bénigne

29

30

rue Michelet

rue Danton

place Bossuet

27

rue Pron

rue de l'Arquebuse

rue Jehan de Marville

rue du Faubourg Raines

32

33

31

rue Brulard

40

rue Berbisey

r Victor Dumay

34

rue Monge

place Émile Zola

39

rempart Misericorde

rue Crébillon

rue Berbisey

41

rue Sainte Anne

42

43

35

38

rue de la Manutention

rue de Chaignot

Ouche River

36

Canal

Quai Nicolas Rolin

rue de l'Hôpital

place Suquet

rue Colson

rue de Tivoli

37

rue du Transvaal

Port du Canal

de Bourgogne

av Jean Jaurès

To Chenôve (4km), Lyon (190km; via A31) & Beaune (44km via N74 or A31)

rue du Petit Cîteaux

euro currency converter €1 = 6.55FF

FRANCE

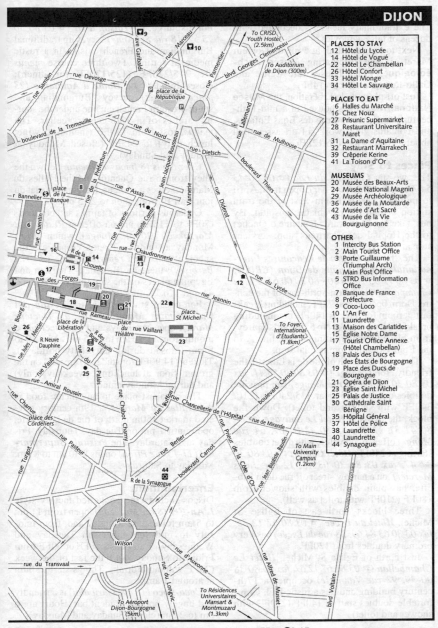

FRANCE

style during the first half of the 13th century. The extraordinary facade is decorated with dozens of false gargoyles.

Next to the cathedral, at 5 rue du Docteur Maret, is the fascinating **Musée Archéologique**, which houses rare Celtic and Gallo-Roman artefacts (14FF).

Just off place de la Libération, the **Musée National Magnin** is housed in a mid-17th-century residence at 4 rue des Bons Enfants, and contains 2000 works of art assembled about a century ago (16/12FF).

Places to Stay

The two-star *Camping du Lac* (☎ *03 80 43 54 72, 3 blvd Chanoine Kir)*, open from April to mid-October, is 1.4km west of the train station behind the psychiatric hospital. By bus, take No 12 (towards Fontaine d'Ouche) to the Hôpital des Chartreux stop; services stop at around 8 pm.

The 260-bed *Centre de Rencontres Internationales et de Séjour de Dijon (CRISD; ☎ 03 80 72 95 20, fax 03 80 70 00 61, 1 blvd Champollion)* is 2.5km north-east of the centre. Dorm beds start at 72FF, including breakfast; a room for three is 140FF, not including breakfast. By bus, take No 5 (towards Épirey) from place Grangier; at night take line A to the Épirey Centre Commercial stop.

Three blocks south of rue de la Liberté, the friendly *Hôtel Monge* (☎ *03 80 30 55 41, fax 03 80 30 30 15, 20 rue Monge)* can provide doubles/quads starting at 135/240FF (210/340FF with shower and toilet). Down the block, the two-star *Hôtel Le Sauvage* (☎ *03 80 41 31 21, fax 03 80 42 06 07, 64 rue Monge)* offers good value, with quiet doubles starting at 240FF. *Hôtel Confort* (☎ *03 80 30 37 47, fax 03 80 30 03 43, 12 rue Jules Mercier)*, on a narrow street off rue de la Liberté, has plain doubles with shower from 180FF (210FF with toilet as well).

Three blocks north-east of Église St Michel, *Hôtel du Lycée* (☎ *03 80 67 12 35, fax 03 80 63 84 69, 28 rue du Lycée)* has very ordinary doubles from 120FF.

Just north of Église St Michel, *Hôtel Le Chambellan* (☎ *03 80 67 12 67, fax 03 80 38 00 39, 92 rue Vannerie)* occupies a 17th-century building and has a rustic feel. Comfortable doubles start at 140FF (220FF with shower and toilet).

Places to Eat

For a splurge, *La Toison d'Or* (☎ *03 80 30 73 52, 18 rue Ste Anne)* serves up traditional Burgundian and French cuisine in a rustic medieval setting. Two/three course *menus* are 215/270FF (125/170FF for lunch); closed Sunday. *La Dame d'Aquitaine (23 place Bossuet)* purveys Burgundian and south-western French cuisine under the soaring arches of a 13th-century cellar. The *menus* cost from 138FF (including wine; lunch only) to 245FF (closed Monday at midday and Sunday).

Chez Nous (8 Impasse Quentin), down the alley from 6 rue Quentin and the Halles du Marché, serves a copious, Burgundian plat du jour (60FF) from noon to 2.15 pm.

Generous portions of tajines and couscous (70FF to 115FF) are on offer at *Restaurant Marrakech (20 rue Monge)*, which closes Monday at midday. Breton crepes are the speciality of the *Crêperie Kerine (36 rue Berbisey)*; there are Brazilian, Tunisian and Egyptian places on the same street at Nos 42, 44 and 116.

For cheap student eats, try *Restaurant Universitaire Maret (3 rue du Docteur Maret)*, open weekdays and one weekend a month from 11.40 am to 1.15 pm and 6.40 to 8 pm (closed during university holidays). Tickets (14.90FF for students) are sold on the ground floor at lunchtime (weekdays only) and during Monday dinner.

The cheapest place to buy picnic food is the *Halles du Marché*, a 19th-century covered market 150m north of rue de la Liberté, open until 1 pm on Tuesday, Thursday, Friday and Saturday. The *Prisunic Supermarket (11-13 rue Piron)* opens 8.30 am to 8 pm, Monday to Saturday.

Entertainment

Discos include the converted-factory-style *L'An-Fer (8 rue Marceau)*, open from 11 pm to 5 am (closed on Monday and, from mid-July to mid-September, on Tuesday and Wednesday). Entry costs 50FF or 60FF from Friday to Sunday, 40FF the rest of the week (25FF without a drink). Things start to hum at around 1 am.

Coco-Loco (18 ave Garibaldi) is a friendly and hugely popular student bar. Hours are 6 pm to 2 am (closed Sunday and Monday).

Getting There & Away

Transco buses link the bus station (attached to the train station; ☎ 03 80 42 11 00) with some of the winemaking towns along the Côte d'Or, including Beaune.

The train station, Gare Dijon-Ville (☎ 0836 35 35 39), has TGV services to/from Paris' Gare de Lyon (227FF to 275FF, 1¾ hours). There are non-TGV trains to Lyon (133FF to 153FF, 1½ to two hours) and Nice (380FF, eight hours).

Getting Around

Dijon's extensive urban bus network is run by STRD (☎ 03 80 30 60 90). Bus lines are known by their number and the name of the terminus station. In the city centre, seven different lines stop along rue de la Liberté, and five more have stops around place Grangier. A Forfait Journée ticket, valid all day, costs 16FF at the STRD office at place Grangier (closed on Sunday).

CÔTE D'OR

Burgundy's finest vintages come from the vine-covered Côte d'Or, the eastern slopes of the limestone escarpment running for about 60km south from Dijon. The northern section, known as the Côte de Nuits, includes Gevrey-Chambertin, Vougeot, Vosne-Romanée and Nuits St Georges, known for their fine reds; the southern section, the Côte de Beaune, includes Pommard, Volnay, Meursault and Puligny-Montrachet. The tourist offices in Dijon and Beaune can provide details on *caves* (wine cellars) that offer tours and *dégustation* (wine tasting).

The Beaune tourist office handles ticketing for year-round, two-hour minibus tours of the Côte (190FF).

Beaune
pop 22,000

Beaune, a famous wine-making centre about 40km south of Dijon, makes an excellent day trip from Dijon. Its most notable historical site is the **Hôtel-Dieu**, France's most opulent medieval charity hospital (32/25FF). The tourist office (☎ 03 80 26 21 30), 1km west of the train station, is opposite the entrance to the Hôtel-Dieu. It opens 9 am (10 am in winter) to sometime between 6 pm (in winter) and 8 pm (from mid-June

to late September, 7 pm on Sunday). Web site: www.ot-beaune.fr.

At the **Marché aux Vins**, on rue Nicolas Rolin 30m south of the tourist office, you can sample 18 wines for 50FF. **Patriarche Père et Fils** at 6 rue du Collège has one of the largest wine cellars in Burgundy; one-hour visits include sampling and begin from 10.30 am (9.30 am in the warm months) to 11 am and 2 to 5 pm.

Places to Stay & Eat The best deal in town is *Hôtel Rousseau (☎ 03 80 22 13 59, 11 place Madeleine)*. Run by a friendly older woman, it has large, old-fashioned singles/doubles from 140/185FF; a room for five is 380FF. The 106-room, two-star *Hôtel Au Grand St Jean (☎ 03 80 24 12 22, fax 03 80 24 15 43, ✉ hotel.saint.jean@netclic.fr, 18 rue du Faubourg Madeleine)* has impersonal doubles/quads from 235/295FF.

Caves Madeleine (8 rue du Faubourg Madeleine) is a cosy wine bar with family-style Burgundian *menus* for 69FF and 115FF (closed on Thursday and Sunday). *Restaurant Maxime (3 place Madeleine)* offers reasonably priced Burgundian cuisine in a rustic but elegant dining room; *menus* range from 76FF to 150FF (closed Sunday night, Monday and, except from June to September, on Thursday night).

The refined *Restaurant Bernard & Martine Morillon (31 rue Maufoux)* has traditional French *menus* for 180FF to 480FF (closed Tuesday midday, Monday and in January).

Getting There & Away Beaune is linked to Dijon by train (38FF, 20 to 25 minutes, 18 to 24 a day) and Transco buses (☎ 03 80 42 11 00; 40FF, one hour, seven to nine a day, two on Sunday and holidays). The latter stop at a number of wine villages, including Vougeot, Nuits St Georges and Aloxe-Corton.

LYON
pop 415,500

The grand city of Lyon is part of a prosperous urban area of almost two million people, France's second-largest conurbation. Founded by the Romans over 2000 years ago, it has spent the last 500 years as a commercial, industrial and banking powerhouse. Lyon sports outstanding museums, a dynamic cultural life,

FRANCE

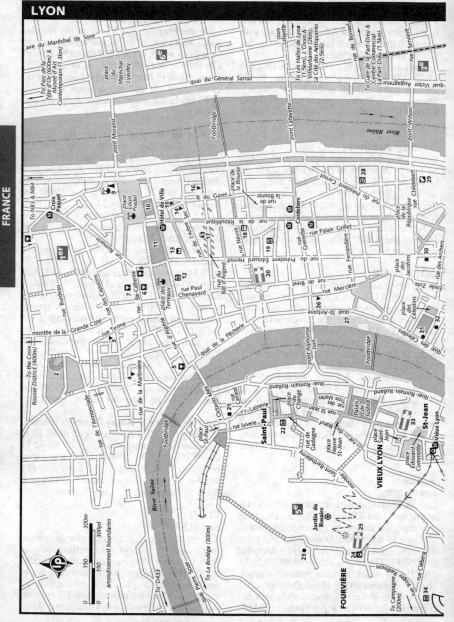

LYON

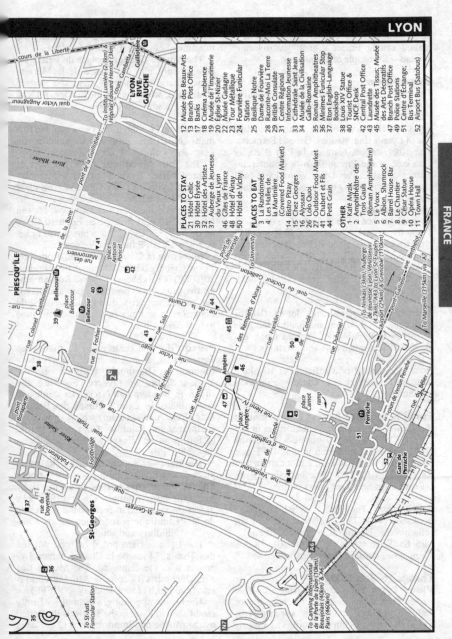

LYON

FRANCE

PLACES TO STAY
21 Hôtel Celtic
30 Hôtel Elysée
32 Hôtel des Artistes
37 Auberge de Jeunesse du Vieux Lyon
46 Gîtes de France
48 Hôtel d'Ainay
50 Hôtel de Vichy

PLACES TO EAT
3 La Randonnée
4 Les Halles de la Martinière (Covered Food Market)
14 Bistro Pizay
15 Chez Georges
16 Alyssaar
26 Lolo Quoi
27 Outdoor Food Market
41 Chabert et Fils
44 Petit Grain

OTHER
1 Káfé Myzik
2 Amphithéâtre des Trois Gauls
5 Le Voxx
6 Albion, Shamrock
7 Barrel House Bar
8 Le Chantier
9 César Statue
10 Opéra House
11 Town Hall
12 Musée des Beaux-Arts
13 Branch Post Office
17 Banks
18 Cinéma Ambience
19 Musée de l'Imprimerie
20 Église St-Nizier
22 Musée Gadagne
23 Tour Métallique
24 Fourvière Funicular Station
25 Basilique Notre Dame de Fourvière
28 Raconte-Moi La Terre
29 British Consulate
31 Centre Regional Information Jeunesse
33 Cathédrale Saint Jean
34 Musée de la Civilisation Gallo-Romaine
35 Roman Amphitheatres
36 Minimes Funicular Stop
37 Eton English-Language Bookshop
38 Tony X Statue
40 Tourist Office & SNCF Desk
42 Central Post Office
43 Laundrette
45 Musée des Tissus; Musée des Arts Décoratifs
47 Branch Post Office
49 Police Stations
51 Centre d'Echange; Bus Terminal
52 Airport Bus (Satobus)

an important university, lively pedestrian malls and such excellent cuisine that it's ranked among France's great gastronomic capitals – for people of all budgets.

Orientation

The city centre is on the Presqu'île, a peninsula bounded by the Rhône and Saône Rivers. Place Bellecour is 1km south of place des Terreaux and 1km north of place Carnot, next to one of Lyon's train stations, Gare de Perrache. The other station, Gare de la Part-Dieu, is 2km east of the Presqu'île in a commercial district called La Part-Dieu. Vieux Lyon (old Lyon) sprawls across the Saône's west bank.

Information

Tourist Offices The tourist office (☎ 04 72 77 69 69, fax 04 78 42 04 32, ✉ lyoncvb@lyon-france.com), place Bellecour, opens 10 am to 6 or 7 pm. Its Web site at www.lyon-france.com is worth a surf. The same building houses an SNCF reservations desk (closed Sunday).

Money Commercial banks dot rue Victor Hugo, rue Bât d'Argent and nearby sections of rue de la République. Thomas Cook exchange offices grace both train stations.

Post The central post office is at 10 place Antonin Poncet (closed Saturday afternoon and Sunday).

Email & Internet Access Check email at the Centre Régional Information Jeunesse (☎ 04 72 77 00 66), 9 quai des Célestins (10FF for initial subscription plus 10FF per 30 minutes). Rates at the Internet cafe inside Raconte-Moi La Terre (see bookshops) are 60/130FF for one/three hours online.

Bookshops The Eton English-language bookshop (☎ 04 78 92 92 36), 1 rue du Plat, sells novels. The travel bookshop, Raconte-Moi La Terre (☎ 04 78 92 60 20), 38 rue Thomassin, stocks a superb map selection.

Things to See & Do

Vieux Lyon The old city, whose cobble streets form a picture-postcard ensemble of restored **medieval and Renaissance houses**, lies at the base of Fourvière hill. The mainly Romanesque **Cathédrale St Jean** has a Flamboyant Gothic facade and a 14th-century astronomical clock in the north transept.

The **Musée Gadagne**, place du Petit Collège, is split into the Musée de la Marionnette, featuring puppets, and the Musée Historique, which paints the history of Lyon (closed Tuesday, 25/13FF).

Fourvière Two thousand years ago, the Romans built the city of Lugdunum on Fourvière's slopes. Today the hill – topped by the **Tour Métallique** (1893), a sort of stunted Eiffel Tower – offers spectacular views of Lyon, its two rivers and – on clear days – Mont Blanc. The easiest way to the top is to ride the funicular railway (between 6 am and 10 pm) from place Édouard Commette in Vieux Lyon. Use a bus/metro ticket or buy a 12.50FF funicular return.

Musée de la Civilisation Gallo-Romaine, 17 rue Cléberg (closed Monday and Tuesday; 20/10FF) is neighboured by two **Roman amphitheatres** which host rock, pop and classical music concerts during Les Nuits de Fourvière, a summer festival held mid-June to mid-September.

Presqu'île The centrepiece of **place des Terreaux** is a monumental 19th-century fountain by Bartholdi, sculptor of New York's *Statue of Liberty*. Fronting the square is the **town hall** (1655). Its south side is dominated by Lyon's **Musée des Beaux-Arts** (Fine Arts Museum) which showcases sculptures and paintings from every period of European art (closed Monday and Tuesday; 25/13FF).

The **statue of a giant on roller skates** on place Louis Pradel, north-east of the **opera house**, was sculpted from scrap metal by Marseille-born sculptor César (1921-98). Skaters buzz around its feet. To the south, **rue de la République** is renowned for its 19th-century buildings and shops.

The Lyonnais are proud of their **Musée des Tissus**, 34 rue de la Charité, where Lyonnais silks are displayed. The **Musée des Arts Décoratifs** (Decorative Arts Museum) is also here (both closed Monday, 30/15FF).

The history of printing, a technology firmly established in Lyon in the 1480s, is illustrated by the **Musée de l'Imprimerie** at 13 rue de la

Poulaillerie (closed Monday and Tuesday; 25/13FF).

Other Attractions The main city park **Parc de la Tête d'Or** sits on the east bank of the Rhône, north of La Part-Dieu. The inspirational **Musée d'Art Contemporain** (Contemporary Art Museum), borders the river at 81 quai Charles de Gaulle and hosts fantastic modern art exhibitions. It also has a multimedia centre devoted to digital art (closed Monday and Tuesday, 25/13FF).

The **Institut Lumière** (☎ 04 78 78 18 95, @ contact@institut-lumiere.org) at 25 rue du Premier-Film brings to life the work of the motion-picture pioneers Auguste and Louis Lumière (closed Monday, 25/20FF). Classic and cult films are screened in its cinema. Program details are posted on its Web site at www.institut-lumiere.org.

Places to Stay

Camping *Camping International de la Porte de Lyon* (☎ 04 78 35 64 55) is some 10km north-west of Lyon in Dardilly. Open year round, it charges 80FF for two people with tent and car. Bus Nos 3 or 19 (towards Ecully-Dardilly) from the Hôtel de Ville metro station stop right out front.

Hostels *Auberge de Jeunesse du Vieux Lyon* (☎ 04 78 15 05 50, fax 04 78 15 05 51, @ lyon@fuaj.org, 40-45 montée du Chemin Neuf) in Vieux Lyon has dorm beds for 71FF including breakfast. Sheets cost 17FF. Non-HI members must buy a welcome stamp (19FF). Reception opens 24 hours.

Auberge de Jeunesse Lyon-Vénissieux (☎ 04 78 76 39 23, fax 04 78 77 51 11, @ lyonvenissieux@fuaj.fr, 51 rue Roger Salengro) is 5.5km south-east of Gare de Perrache in Vénissieux. A dorm bed costs 68FF including breakfast and reception opens 7.30 to 12.30 am. You can take bus No 35 from place Bellecour to the Georges Lévy stop or bus No 53 from Gare de Perrache to the États-Unis-Viviani stop.

Chambres d'Hôtes The *Gîtes de France* (☎ 04 72 77 17 55, fax 04 78 38 21 15, @ gites.rhone.alpes@wanadoo.fr, 1 rue Général Plessier) arranges B&B-type accommodation around Lyon and has lists of

gîtes (self-catering farms and cottages) to rent on a weekly basis.

Hotels At rock-bottom *Hôtel de Vichy* (☎ 04 78 37 42 58, 60 bis rue de la Charité) singles/doubles go for 140/150FF (180/200FF with shower and TV). Heading into town *Hôtel d'Ainay* (☎ 04 78 42 43 42, fax 04 72 77 51 90, 14 rue des Remparts d'Ainay) has basic singles/doubles for 165/175FF (205/215FF with shower and TV).

Old city lovers can try *Hôtel Celtic* (☎ 04 78 28 01 12, fax 04 78 28 01 34, 10 rue François Vernay) in Vieux Lyon. Singles/doubles are 135/160FF (170/200FF with shower).

Two-star spots include the hostelry-style *Hôtel Élysée* (☎ 04 78 42 03 15, fax 04 78 37 76 49, 92 rue du Président Édouard Herriot) which has singles/doubles from 340/360FF; and charming, three-star *Hotel des Artistes* (☎ 04 78 42 04 88, fax 04 78 42 93 76, 8 rue Gaspard André) which touts theatrically furnished, singles/doubles starting at 390/450FF.

Places to Eat

Fresh fruit, olives, cheese and bread are piled high at the *outdoor morning food market* (daily except Monday) on quai St Antoine. *Les Halles de la Martinière* (covered food market) in the northern Presqu'île at 24 rue de la Martinière and *Les Halles de Lyon*, walking distance from Gare de la Part-Dieu at 102 cours Lafayette, offer an equally tasty choice (both closed Sunday afternoon and Monday).

Piggy-part cuisine is the speciality of a traditional Lyonnais *bouchon* – literally 'traffic jam' elsewhere in France but a small, unpretentious bistro-style restaurant in Lyon. Bouchons worth a nibble include *Chez Georges* (☎ 04 78 28 30 46, 8 rue du Garet); *Bistro Pizay* (☎ 04 78 28 37 26, 4 rue Verdi); or *Chabert et Fils* (☎ 04 78 37 01 94, 11 rue des Marronniers). Both have good-value lunch deals (around 50FF).

Favoured for its elephant-sized portions is *La Randonnée* (☎ 04 78 27 86 81, 4 rue Terme) which has vegetarian platters (50FF), lunchtime/evening *formules* (which allows you to pick a set number of courses from 32/38FF) and *menus* (from 49/65FF).

Terraces great for lounging in the sun include *Campagne* (☎ 04 78 36 73 85, 20 rue

FRANCE

Cardinal Gerlier) atop Fourvière hill and any one of the *cafes* on place des Terreaux. On touristy rue Mercière *Lolo Quoi* (☎ 04 72 77 60 90, 40-4 rue Mercière) is a chic spot, dressed in funky furnishings and it's not too wallet-crunching if you stick to a tasty bowl of pasta (50FF).

Syrian *Alyssaar* (☎ 04 78 29 57 66, 29 rue du Bât d'Argent) has spicy *menus* for 78FF, 87FF and 105FF, while Vietnamese *Petit Grain* (☎ 04 72 41 77 85, 19 rue de la Charité) sports salads, meats and vegetarian platters from 43FF. Rue Ste-Marie des Terreaux and rue Ste-Catherine are lined with Chinese, Turkish and other quick-eating joints.

Entertainment
Rue Ste-Catherine is cluttered with bars. At funky *Le Chantier* (☎ 04 78 39 05 56), at No 20, clubbers slide down bum-first – courtesy of a metal slide – to the basement dance floor. On the Saône's left bank *Le Voxx* (☎ 04 78 28 33 87, 1 rue d'Algérie) lures live bands and a boisterous drinking crowd. On the right bank *La Bodéga* (☎ 04 78 29 42 35, 35 quai Pierre Scize) also rocks 'til late.

Bands play at *Kafé Myzik* (☎ 04 72 07 04 26, 20 Montée St-Sébastien), a hole-in-the-wall club; at *Ninkasi* (☎ 04 72 76 89 09, 267 rue Marcel Mérieux), a micro-brewery next to the stadium which serves its own beer and runs a great-value food bar; and at *L'Oxxo* (☎ 04 78 93 62 03, 7 ave Albert Einstein), a student bar in Villeurbanne which sports a decor of recycled aeroplanes and cable cars.

Getting There & Away
Bus Most intercity buses depart from the terminal next to Gare de Perrache. Timetables are available from the TCL information office (☎ 04 78 71 70 00), on the middle level of the Centre d'Échange. Tickets are sold by the driver. Buses for destinations west of Lyon (☎ 04 78 43 40 74) leave from outside the Gorge de Loup metro station.

Train You can travel between Gare de Perrache and Gare de la Part-Dieu by metro (change at Charpennes) or by SNCF train. Lyon has direct rail links to all parts of France and Europe. Trains to/from Paris (318FF to 398FF, two hours) use the capital's Gare de Lyon.

Getting Around
Lyon's metro system has four lines (A to D), which run 5 am to midnight. Tickets (8FF) are valid for one-way travel on buses, trolleybuses, the funicular and the metro for one hour after time-stamping. A carnet of 10 tickets is 68FF. The Ticket Liberté (24FF; allows one day of unlimited travel) and the Ticket Liberté 2h (24FF; two hours of unlimited travel from 9 am to 4 pm) can be bought at metro ticket machines, or at the TCL information office (☎ 04 78 71 70 00) in the Centre d'Échange; at 43 rue de la République; or at the Vieux Lyon metro station.

The French Alps

The French Alps, where craggy, snowbound peaks soar above fertile, green valleys, is one of the most awe-inspiring mountain ranges in the world. In summer, visitors can take advantage of hundreds of kilometres of hiking trails and lots of other sporting activities, while the area's ski resorts attract enthusiasts from around the world in winter.

If you're going to ski or snowboard, expect to pay at least 260FF a day (including equipment hire, lifts and transport) at low-altitude stations, which usually operate from December to March. The larger, high-altitude stations cost 360FF to 460FF a day. The cheapest time to go skiing is in January, between the school holiday periods.

CHAMONIX
pop 9830
The town of Chamonix sits in a valley surrounded by the most spectacular scenery in the French Alps. The area is almost Himalayan in its awesomeness: deeply crevassed glaciers many kilometres long ooze down the valleys between the icy peaks and pinnacles around Mont Blanc, which soars almost four vertical kilometres above the valley floor.

There are some 330km of hiking trails in the Chamonix area. In winter, the valley offers superb skiing, with dozens of ski lifts and over 200km of downhill and cross-country ski runs.

Information
The tourist office (☎ 04 50 53 00 24, fax 04 50 53 58 90, @ info@chamonix.com) at

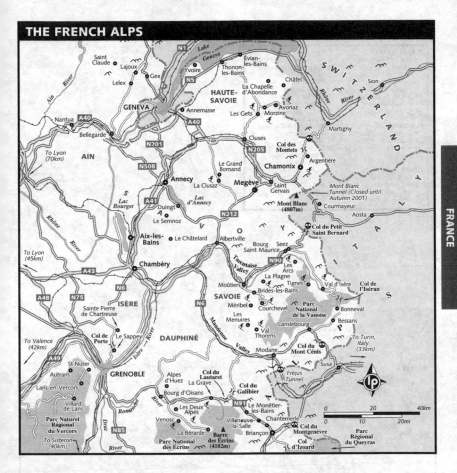

THE FRENCH ALPS

FRANCE

place du Triangle de l'Amitié, opposite place de l'Église, opens 8.30 am to 12.30 pm and 2 to 7 pm daily. Useful brochures on ski-lift hours and costs, refuges, camping grounds and parapente schools are available. In winter it sells a range of ski passes, valid for bus transport and all the ski lifts in the valley.

The Maison de la Montagne, near the tourist office at 109 place de l'Église, houses the Office de Haute Montagne (2nd floor; ☎ 04 50 53 22 08), which has information and maps for walkers and mountaineers (closed Sunday).

You can log onto the Internet at the busy cyBar (☎ 04 50 53 64 80), 81 rue Whymper,

or at the Santa Fe Bar & Restaurant (☎ 04 50 53 99 14), 148 rue du Docteur Paccard. Both charge 1FF per minute.

Climate Weather changes rapidly in Chamonix. Bulletins from *la météo* (the meteorological service) are posted in the window of the tourist office and at the Maison de la Montagne.

Things to See & Do
Aiguille du Midi The Aiguille du Midi (3842m) is a lone spire of rock 8km from the summit of Mont Blanc. The téléphérique

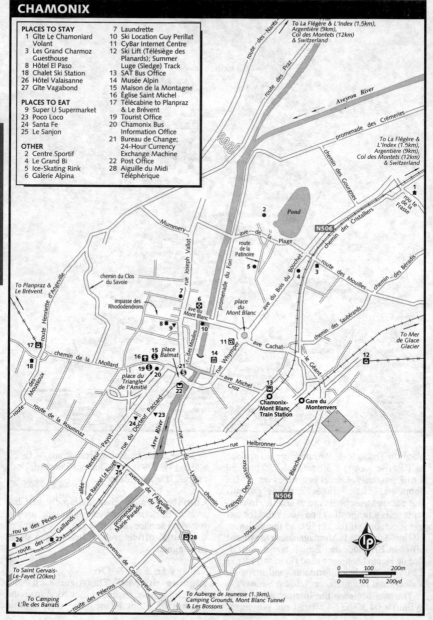

CHAMONIX

PLACES TO STAY
1 Gîte Le Chamoniard
  Volant
3 Les Grand Charmoz
  Guesthouse
8 Hôtel El Paso
18 Chalet Ski Station
26 Hôtel Valaisanne
27 Gîte Vagabond

PLACES TO EAT
9 Super U Supermarket
23 Poco Loco
24 Santa Fe
25 Le Sanjon

OTHER
2 Centre Sportif
4 Le Grand Bi
5 Ice-Skating Rink
6 Galerie Alpina

7 Laundrette
10 Ski Location Guy Perillat
11 CyBar Internet Centre
12 Ski Lift (Télésiège des
  Planards); Summer
  Luge (Sledge) Track
13 SAT Bus Office
14 Musée Alpin
15 Maison de la Montagne
16 Église Saint Michel
17 Télécabine to Planpraz
  & Le Brévent
19 Tourist Office
20 Chamonix Bus
  Information Office
21 Bureau de Change;
  24-Hour Currency
  Exchange Machine
22 Post Office
28 Aiguille du Midi
  Téléphérique

FRANCE

from Chamonix to the Aiguille du Midi (200FF) is the highest and probably scariest cable car in the world – the final leg rises almost vertically up to the Aiguille. In general, visibility is best early in the morning.

The Musée Alpin (☎ 04 50 53 25 93), just off ave Michel Croz in Chamonix, displays artefacts, lithographs and photos illustrating the history of mountain climbing and other Alpine sports. It's open from 2 to 7 pm from June to mid-October; its hours are 3 to 7 pm between Christmas and Easter. It's closed during the rest of the year. Entrance costs 20FF.

Between April and September, you can usually take a second cable car – depending on the winds – from the Aiguille du Midi across the glacier to **Pointe Helbronner** (3466m) and down to the Italian ski resort of **Courmayeur** (an extra 98FF return). A ride from Chamonix to the cable car's halfway point, **Plan de l'Aiguille** (2308m) – an excellent place to start hikes in summer – costs 66/85FF one way/return.

The téléphérique operates 8 am to 3.45 pm all year (6 am to 4.45 pm in July and August). To avoid long queues, arrive before 9.30 am when the buses start to arrive. You can make advance reservations 24 hours a day by calling ☎ 04 50 53 40 00. Pick up your boarding pass and ticket from the ticket office to the right.

Le Brévent Le Brévent (2525m), the highest peak on the west side of the valley, is known for its great views of Mont Blanc. It can be reached from Chamonix by a combination of *télécabine* (gondola) and téléphérique (☎ 04 50 53 13 18) for 57/84FF single/return. Services run from 8 am (9 am in winter) to 5 pm (an hour or so earlier in winter). Numerous hiking trails, including routes back to the valley, can be picked up at Le Brévent or at the cable car's midway station, **Planpraz** (1999m, 48/58FF one way/return).

Mer de Glace The heavily crevassed Mer de Glace (Sea of Ice), the second-largest glacier in the Alps, is 14km long, 1950m across at its widest point and up to 400m deep. It has become a popular tourist destination thanks to a cog-wheel railway, which has an upper terminus at an altitude of 1913m.

The train, which runs year-round (weather permitting), leaves from Gare du Montenvers

(☎ 04 50 53 12 54) in Chamonix. Tickets cost 79/42FF single/return. A combined ticket valid for the train, the gondola to the ice cave (Grotte de la Mer de Glace, 15FF return) and entry to the cave (14FF) costs 116FF. The ride takes 20 minutes each way.

Activities
Hiking In late spring and summer (mid-June to October), the Chamonix area has some of the most spectacular hiking trails anywhere in the Alps. The combined map and guide, *Carte des Sentiers du Mont Blanc* (Mountain Trail Map, 75FF), is ideal for straightforward day hikes. The best map of the area is the 1:25,000 scale IGN map (No 3630OT) entitled *Chamonix-Massif du Mont Blanc* (58FF). Lonely Planet publishes *Walking in France*, a useful guide for walks throughout the whole country.

The fairly level **Grand Balcon Sud** trail, which traverses the Aiguilles Rouges (western) side of the valley at about 2000m, offers great views of Mont Blanc and the glaciers to the east and south. If you'd prefer to avoid 1km of hard uphill walking, take either the Planpraz (46FF one way) or La Flégère lift (43FF one way).

From Plan de l'Aiguille, the midway point on the Aiguille du Midi cable car, the **Grand Balcon Nord** takes you to the Mer de Glace, from where you can hike down to Chamonix. There are a number of other trails from Plan de l'Aiguille.

Skiing & Snowboarding The Chamonix area has 160km of marked ski runs, 42km of cross-country trails and 64 ski lifts of all sorts. Count on paying around 39/220FF a day/week for regular skis or boots. Ski Location Guy Perillat (☎ 04 50 53 54 76) at 138 rue des Moulins is open daily and also rents out snowboards (100/150FF a day without/with boots or 600/700FF a week).

Places to Stay
Camping There are some 13 camp sites in the Chamonix region. In general, camping costs 25FF per person and 12FF to 26FF for a tent site. *L'Île des Barrats* open May to September, is near the base of the Aiguille du Midi cable car. The three-star *Les Deux Glaciers (route des Tissières)* in Les Bossons, 3km south of

FRANCE

Chamonix, is closed mid-November to mid-December. To get there, take the train to Les Bossons or Chamonix Bus to the Tremplin-le-Mont stop.

Refuges Most mountain refuges, which cost 90FF to 100FF a night, are accessible to hikers and are generally open mid-June to mid-September.

The easier-to-reach refuges include one at *Plan de l'Aiguille* (☎ 04 50 53 55 60) at 2308m, the intermediate stop on the Aiguille du Midi cable car, and another at *La Flégère* (☎ 04 50 53 06 13) at 1877m. It's advisable to reserve ahead.

Hostels *Chalet Ski Station* (☎ 04 50 53 20 25, 6 Route des Moussoux)* is a gîte d'étape (next to the Planpraz/Le Brévent télécabine station). Beds cost 60FF a night. It's closed 10 May to 20 June and 20 September to 20 December.

The semi-rustic *Gîte Le Chamoniard Volant* (☎ 04 50 53 14 09, 45 Route de la Frasse)* is on the north-eastern outskirts of town. A bunk in a cramped, functional room costs 66FF. An evening meal is available for 66FF. The nearest bus stop is La Frasse.

The *Auberge de Jeunesse* (☎ 04 50 53 14 52, fax 04 50 55 92 34, ✉ chamonix@fuaj.org, 127 Montée Jacques Balmat)* is a few kilometres south-west of Chamonix in Les Pélerins. By bus, take the Chamonix-Les Houches line and get off at the Pélerins École stop. Beds are 74FF. In winter, only weekly packages are available, including bed, food, ski pass and ski hire for six days from 1450/2990FF in the low/high season.

The *Gîte Vagabond* (☎ 04 50 53 15 43, fax 04 53 68 21, 365 ave Ravanel le Rouge)* is a neat little hostelry with a guest kitchen, bar/restaurant with Internet access, BBQ area, climbing wall and parking. A bed in a four or six person dorm costs 70FF or 149FF for half board.

Hotels At 468 Chemin des Cristalliers next to the railway tracks, *Les Grands Charmoz Guesthouse* (☎ 04 50 53 45 57) has doubles for 184FF. The lively *Hôtel El Paso* (☎ 04 50 53 64 20, fax 04 50 53 64 22, 37 Impasse des Rhododendrons)* is great value. Doubles with shared bath in the low/high season cost

166/224FF, triples are 236/306FF. In summer a dorm bed costs 90FF.

Hôtel Valaisanne (☎ 04 50 53 17 98, 454 ave Ravanel Le Rouge)* is a small, family-owned place 900m south-west of Chamonix town centre. It has doubles for 170/270FF in the low/high season.

Places to Eat
Handy *Poco Loco* (☎ 04 50 53 43 03, 47 rue du Docteur Paccard)* has pizzas from 33FF to 45FF and *menus* from 50FF. It also serves great hot sandwiches (from 23FF), sweet crepes (from 8FF), and burgers to eat in or take away.

Abuzz with hungry diners looking for salads, pizzas, vegetarian platters and Tex Mex specialities is the sometimes crowded *Santa Fe* (☎ 04 50 53 88 14, 148 rue du Docteur Paccard)*, a popular eating as well as meeting place. *Le Sanjon* (☎ 04 50 53 56 44, 5 ave Ravanel le Rouge)* is a picturesque wooden chalet restaurant serving *raclette* (a block of melted cheese, usually eaten with potatoes and cold meats, 99FF) and fondue (69F).

The well-stocked *Super U* supermarket is at 117 rue Joseph Vallot.

Getting There & Away
Bus Chamonix' bus station is next to the train station. SAT Autocar (☎ 04 50 53 01 15) has buses to Annecy (95.30FF), Geneva (170FF, two hours), Grenoble (161FF). There are currently no services to Italy.

Train The narrow-gauge train line from St Gervais-Le Fayet (20km west of Chamonix) to Martigny, Switzerland (42km north of Chamonix), stops at 11 towns in the Chamonix Valley. You have to change trains at the Swiss border. From St Gervais there are trains to destinations all over France.

Chamonix-Mont Blanc train station (☎ 04 50 53 00 44) is on the east side of town. Major destinations include Paris' Gare de Lyon (469FF, six to seven hours), Lyon (186FF, 4½ hours) and Geneva (100FF, 2½ hours via St Gervais).

Getting Around
Bus transport in the valley is handled by Chamonix Bus (☎ 04 50 53 05 55), with an office at place de l'Église opposite the tourist office.

FRANCE

Between April and October, Le Grand Bi (☎ 04 50 53 14 16), 240 ave du Bois du Bouchet, rents three and 10-speed bikes for 65FF a day, mountain bikes for 100FF (closed Sunday).

ANNECY
pop 50,348

Annecy, situated at the northern tip of the incredibly blue Lac d'Annecy, is the perfect place to spend a relaxing holiday. Visitors in a sedentary mood can choose to sit along the lake and feed the swans or mosey around the geranium-lined canals of the old city. Museums and other sights are limited, but the town is an excellent base for water sports, hiking and biking.

Orientation & Information

The train and bus stations are 500m northwest of the old city, which is centred around the canalised Thiou River. The modern town centre is between the main post office and the Centre Bonlieu complex. The lake town of Annecy-le-Vieux is just east of Annecy.

The tourist office (☎ 04 50 45 00 33, fax 04 50 51 87 20, @ ancytour@cybercable.tm.fr) is in the Centre Bonlieu north of place de la Libération. It opens 9 am to 12.30 pm and 1.45 to 6 pm Monday to Saturday, 15 September to 15 May, and 9 am to 6.30 pm, May to September. Sunday openings vary.

The Emailerie (☎ 04 50 10 18 91) on Faubourg de Annonciades, opens 10 am to 10 pm daily (June to October) and 2 to 10 pm (closed Sunday) the rest of the year. Access charges are 25/45FF per 30 minutes/one hour.

Things to See & Do

The Vieille Ville, an area of narrow streets on either side of the Canal du Thiou, retains much of its 17th-century appearance despite recent gentrification. On the island in the middle, the Palais de l'Isle (a former prison) houses the **Musée d'Histoire d'Annecy et de la Haute-Savoie** (20/5FF, closed Tuesday).

The **Musée d'Annecy** (☎ 04 50 33 87 30), housed in the 16th-century **Château d'Annecy** overlooking the town, puts on innovative temporary exhibitions and has a permanent collection of local craftwork (30/10FF, closed Tuesday). The climb up to the chateau is worth it just for the view.

Beaches A kilometre north-east of the Champ de Mars there is a free beach, **Plage d'Annecy-le-Vieux**. Slightly closer to town, next to the casino, is the **Plage de l'Impérial**, which costs 18FF and is equipped with changing rooms. Perhaps Annecy's most pleasant stretch of lawn-lined swimming beach is the free **Plage des Marquisats**, 1km south of the old city along rue des Marquisats. The beaches are officially open from June to September.

Places to Stay

Camping *Camping Municipal Le Belvédère* (☎ 04 50 45 48 30, fax 04 50 45 55 56, Forêt du Crêt du Maure) is 2.5km south of the train station in a shaded forest. From mid-June to early September you can take bus No 91 (Ligne des Vacances) from the train station. It costs about 47/67FF for one/two people to pitch a tent.

Hostels The *Auberge de Jeunesse* (☎ 04 50 45 33 19, fax 04 50 52 77 52, 4 Route du Semnoz) is 1km south of town in the Forêt du Semnoz. From mid-June to early September, bus No 91 goes there. Beds cost 72FF.

Hotels The small *Hôtel Rive du Lac* (☎ 04 50 51 32 85, fax 04 50 45 77 40, 6 rue des Marquisats), superbly located near the Vieille Ville and the lake, has one or two-bed rooms with shower for 146FF.

One of the cheapest places close to the Vieille Ville is the *Central Hôtel* (☎ 04 50 45 05 37, 6 bis rue Royale) in a quiet courtyard. Doubles start at 160FF.

In the heart of the old city, the *Auberge du Lyonnais* (☎ 04 50 51 26 10, fax 04 50 51 05 04, 14 quai de l'Évêché) occupies an idyllic setting next to the canal. Singles/doubles with toilet are 170/240FF.

One of the most oddly-placed hotels in Savoy is the *Hôtel de Savoie* (☎ 04 50 45 15 45, fax 04 50 45 11 99, @ hotel.savoie@mail.dotcom.fr, 1 place de St François), with its entrance on the left side of the Église St François de Sales – spooky. Simple rooms with washbasin cost from 150/220FF.

Places to Eat

In the new town centre, there are good pizzas (from 38FF), large salads (19FF to 43FF) and

FRANCE

FRANCE

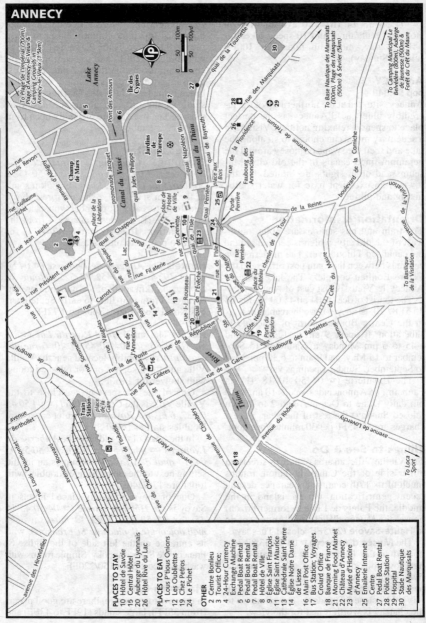

ANNECY

a children's *menu* (42FF) at **Lous P'tious Onions** (☎ 04 50 51 34 41, 36 rue Sommeiller) in the Grand Passage. *Menus* start at 65FF. There are also inexpensive places along rue du Pâquier.

Les Oubliettes (☎ 04 50 45 39 78, 10 quai de l'Isle), right next to the canal in the Old Town, has pizzas from 40FF to 55FF and a wide choice of other main courses such as an expansive *menu Savoyard* for 99FF. Just across the canal, **Le Pichet** (☎ 04 50 45 32 41, 13 rue Perrière), has a big terrace and three-course *menus* for 66FF and 78FF.

Chez Petros (☎ 04 50 45 50 26, 13 Faubourg Ste Claire) is a small but busy Greek restaurant with classic Greek *menus* from 65FF to 115FF, as well as excellent vegetarian dishes such as stuffed aubergines or peppers (40FF), haricot beans (42FF), or okra (54FF).

Getting There & Away

Bus The bus station, Gare Routière Sud, is on rue de l'Industrie next to the train station. Voyages Crolard (☎ 04 50 45 08 12) has regular services to Roc de Chère on the eastern shore of Lac d'Annecy and Bout du Lac at the far southern tip, as well as to Albertville and Chamonix.

Autocars Frossard (☎ 04 50 45 73 90) sells tickets to Geneva, Grenoble, Nice and elsewhere. Autocars Francony (☎ 04 50 45 02 43) has buses to Chamonix.

Train The train station (☎ 0836 35 35 35) is at place de la Gare. There are frequent trains to Paris' Gare de Lyon (451FF, 3¾ hours by TGV), Nice (404FF via Lyon, 352FF via Aix-les-Bains, eight to nine hours), Lyon (115FF, two hours), Chamonix (105FF, three hours) and Aix-les-Bains (39FF, 30 to 45 minutes).

GRENOBLE
pop 153,317

Grenoble is the intellectual and economic capital of the French Alps. Set in a broad valley surrounded by spectacular mountains, this spotlessly clean city has a Swiss feel to it.

Orientation & Information

The old city is centred around place Grenette, with its many cafes, and place Notre Dame.

Both are about 1km east of the train and bus stations.

The Maison du Tourisme at 14 rue de la République houses the tourist office (☎ 04 76 42 41 41, fax 04 76 00 18 98, ✉ office-de-tourism-de-grenoble@wanadoo.fr), an SNCF information counter and an information desk for the local bus network (TAG). The tourist office opens 9 am to 12.30 pm and 1.30 to 6 pm (closed Sunday). From June to mid-September, it opens Sunday from 10 am to noon.

Cybernet (☎ 04 76 51 73 18, ✉ services@neptune.fr), 8 rue Hache, charges 30/47FF for 30/60 minutes online. It opens noon to 2 pm and 10 pm to 1 am.

Things to See

Built in the 16th century to control the approaches to the city (and expanded in the 19th), **Fort de la Bastille** sits on the north side of the Isère River, 263m above the old city. The fort affords superb views of Grenoble and the surrounding mountain ranges. To reach the fort you can take the *téléphérique* (cable car; ☎ 04 76 44 33 65) from quai Stéphane Jay (24/35FF single/return, 19/28FF for students). Several hiking trails lead up the hillside to the fort.

Housed in a 17th-century convent at 30 rue Maurice Gignoux (at the foot of the Fort de la Bastille hill), the **Musée Dauphinois** has displays on the history of the Dauphiné region (20/10FF; closed Tuesday).

Grenoble's fine-arts museum, the **Musée de Grenoble**, 5 place de Lavalette, has a good collection of paintings and sculpture, including works by Matisse, Picasso and Chagall (25/15FF; closed Monday and Tuesday).

The **Musée de la Résistance et de la Déportation de l'Isère**, 14 rue Hébert, examines the region's role in the Resistance, and the deportation of Jews from Grenoble to Nazi concentration camps (20/10FF, closed Tuesday).

The double **Notre Dame** and **St Hugues Cathedral** on place Notre Dame and the adjoining 14th-century **Bishop's Palace** at 3 rue Très Cloîtres have had complete face-lifts and now contain three museums: the **crypte archéologique**, with its Roman-era walls and baptistery dating from the 4th to 10th century; the **Musée d'Art Sacré**, containing liturgical and other religious objects; and the **Centre Jean Achard**, with exhibits

FRANCE

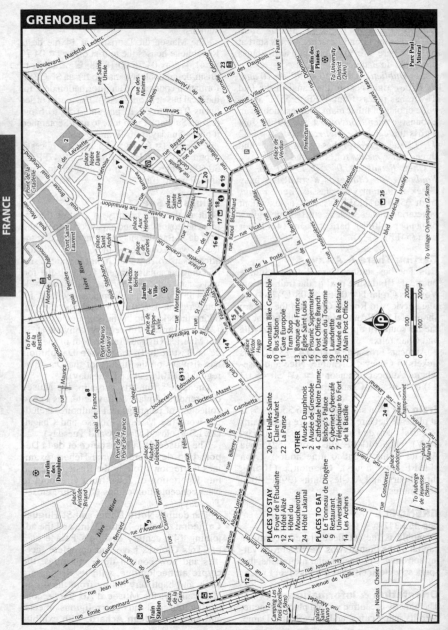

GRENOBLE

PLACES TO STAY
3 Foyer de l'Étudiante
12 Hôtel Alizé
21 Hôtel du
     Moucherotte
24 Hôtel Lakanal

PLACES TO EAT
6 Le Tonneau de Diogène
9 Restaurant
     Universitaire
14 Les Archers

20 Les Halles Sainte
     Claire Market
22 La Panse

OTHER
1 Musée Dauphinois
2 Musée de Grenoble
4 Cathédrale Notre Dame;
     Bishop's Palace
5 Cybernet Cybercafé
7 Téléphérique to Fort
     de la Bastille

8 Mountain Bike Grenoble
10 Bus Station
11 Gare Europole
     Tram Stop
13 Banque de France
15 Église Saint Louis
16 Prisunic Supermarket
17 Post Office Branch
18 Maison du Tourisme
19 Laundrette
23 Musée de la Résistance
25 Main Post Office

of art from the Dauphiné region. Admission is 20FF.

Activities
Skiing & Snowboarding There are a number of inexpensive, low-altitude ski stations near Grenoble, including Col de Porte and Le Sappey (north of the city) and St Nizier du Moucherotte, Lans-en-Vercors, Villard-de-Lans and Méaudre (west of the city). The tourist office has comprehensive information, including accommodation lists.

Hiking The place to go for hiking information is Info-Montagne (☎ 04 76 42 45 90), on the 1st floor of the Maison du Tourisme. It sells hiking maps and has detailed info on gîtes d'étape and refuges (closed Sunday).

Places to Stay
Camping The year-round *Camping Les Trois Pucelles (58 rue des Allobroges)* is one block west of the Drac River in Grenoble's western suburb of Seyssins. From the train station, take the tram towards Fontaine and get off at the Maisonnat stop, then take bus No 51 to Mas des Îles and walk east on rue du Dauphiné.

Hostels The *Auberge de Jeunesse* (☎ 04 76 09 33 52, fax 04 76 09 38 99, **@** grenoble-echirolles@fuaj.org, 10 ave du Grésivaudan) is in Échirolles 5.5km south of the train station. From cours Jean Jaurès, take bus No 8 (direction Pont de Claix) and get off at the Quinzaine stop – look for the Casino supermarket. Reception opens 7.30 am to 11 pm, and beds cost 68FF.

Friendly and central *Foyer de l'Étudiante* (☎ 04 76 42 00 84, 4 rue Ste Ursule) accepts travellers of both sexes from the end of June to the end of September. Singles/doubles cost 90/130FF a day and, for those who want to linger longer, 450/700FF a week. It opens 7 to 12.30 am.

Hotels Near the train station, *Hôtel Alizé* (☎ 04 76 43 12 91, fax 04 76 47 62 79, 1 rue Amiral Courbet) has modern singles/doubles with washbasin for 138/202FF and doubles with shower for 162/212FF.

There are lots of inexpensive hotels in the place Condorcet area, about 800m south-east of the train station. One of the best is *Hôtel*

Lakanal (☎ 04 76 46 03 42, fax 04 76 17 21 24, 26 rue des Bergers). It attracts a young and friendly crowd and has simple singles/doubles with toilet for just 100/120FF. Rooms with shower and toilet cost 140/180FF. Breakfast is 20FF.

In the city centre, *Hôtel du Moucherotte* (☎ 04 76 54 61 40, fax 04 76 44 62 52, 1 rue Auguste Gaché) is a dark and rather old-fashioned place with huge, clean rooms. Its singles/doubles with shower start at 145/178FF. Breakfast is 30FF extra.

Places to Eat
Les Halles Ste Claire food market, near the tourist office, is open daily till 1 pm. The *Restaurant Universitaire (5 rue d'Arsonval)* opens 11.20 am to 1.15 pm and 6.20 to 7.50 pm weekdays between mid-September and mid-June. Tickets (about 15/30FF for students/nonstudents) are sold at lunchtime only.

For good food at reasonable prices, try *Le Tonneau de Diogène* (☎ 04 76 42 38 40, 6 place Notre Dame) which attracts a young, lively crowd. The plat du jour is 55FF, salads cost from 15FF to 38FF. It's open 8.30 am to 1 am.

La Panse (☎ 04 76 54 09 54, 7 rue de la Paix) offers a 50FF and 76FF lunch *menu* and a 100FF day and evening *menu* that are especially good value. It opens noon to 1.30 pm and 7.15 to 10 pm (closed Sunday).

Les Archers (☎ 04 76 46 27 76, 2 rue Docteur Bailly) is a brasserie-style restaurant with great outside seating in summer. The plat du jour is 57FF, *huîtres* (oysters) are 106FF a dozen, and it opens 10 am to 10 pm.

Getting There & Away
Bus The bus station (☎ 04 76 87 90 31) is next to the train station at place de la Gare. VFD (☎ 04 76 47 77 77) has services to Geneva (151FF, 2½ hours), Nice (311FF, five hours), Annecy (99FF, 1¾ hours), Chamonix (161FF, three hours), and to a number of ski resorts. Intercars (☎ 04 76 46 19 77, fax 04 76 47 96 34) handles long-haul destinations such as Budapest (580FF), Madrid (540FF), Lisbon (830FF), London (550FF), Prague (520FF) and Venice (260FF).

Train The train station (☎ 0836 35 35 39) is served by both tram lines (get off at the Gare

FRANCE

Europole stop). There's a regular fast service to Paris' Gare de Lyon (371FF, 3½ hours by TGV). There are three trains a day to Turin (246FF) and Milan (321FF) in Italy, and two trains a day to Geneva (118FF), and regular services to Lyon, Nice and Monaco.

Getting Around
Buses and trams take the same tickets (7.50FF, or 56FF for a carnet of 10), which are sold by bus (but not tram) drivers and by ticket machines at tram stops. They're valid for transfers within an hour of time-stamping, but not for return trips.

Mountain Bike Grenoble (☎ 04 76 47 58 76), 6 quai de France, has mountain bikes for 60/95FF for a half/full day, 170FF for two days, plus a 2000FF deposit (closed Sunday and Monday).

Provence

Provence was settled by the Ligurians, the Celts and the Greeks, but it was after its conquest by Julius Caesar in the mid-1st century BC that the region really began to flourish.

Many well-preserved amphitheatres, aqueducts and other buildings from the Roman period can still be seen in Arles and Nîmes (see the Languedoc-Roussillon section later). During the 14th century, the Catholic Church, then led by a series of French-born popes, moved its headquarters from feud-riven Rome to Avignon, thus beginning the most resplendent period in that city's history.

MARSEILLE
pop 1.23 million
The cosmopolitan and much maligned port of Marseille, France's second-largest city and third-most populous urban area, isn't in the least bit prettified for the benefit of tourists. Its urban geography and atmosphere derive from the diversity of its inhabitants, the majority of whom are immigrants (or their descendants) from the Mediterranean basin, West Africa and Indochina. Although Marseille is notorious for organised crime and racial tensions, the city is worth exploring for a day or two.

Orientation
The city's main street, La Canebière, stretches eastward from the Vieux Port. The train station is north of La Canebière at the top of blvd d'Athènes. The city centre is around rue Paradis, which becomes more fashionable as you move south.

Information
The tourist office (☎ 04 91 13 89 00, fax 04 91 13 89 20, @ accueil@marseille-tourisme .com) is next to the Vieux Port at 4 La Canebière. It opens 9 am to 7 pm (Sunday from 10 am to 5 pm). From mid-June to mid-September, it opens till 7.30 pm daily. Staff can make hotel reservations. The annexe (☎ 04 91 50 59 18) at the train station opens weekdays only (Monday to Saturday in July and August).

The Le Rezo Cybercafé (☎ 04 91 42 70 02, @ lerezo@lerezo.com), 68 cours Julien (6e) charges 30/50FF for 30 minutes/one hour access and opens 9.30 am to 8 pm Monday, 9.30 am to 10 pm Tuesday to Friday, and 10 am to 11 pm Saturday.

Dangers & Annoyances Despite its fearsome reputation, Marseille is probably no more dangerous than other French cities. As elsewhere, beware of bag-snatchers and pickpockets, especially at the train station. At night avoid the Belsunce area – the neighbourhood south-west of the train station and streets bordering La Canebière.

Things to See & Do
Marseille grew up around the **Vieux Port**, where Greeks from Asia Minor established a settlement around 600 BC. The quarter north of quai du Port (around the Hôtel de Ville) was blown up by the Germans in 1943 and rebuilt after the war. The lively **place Thiars** pedestrian zone, with its many late-night restaurants and cafes, is south of the quai de Rive Neuve.

If you like great panoramic views or overwrought mid-19th-century architecture, consider a walk up to the **Basilique Notre Dame de la Garde**, on a hill top 1km south of the Vieux Port – the highest point in the city. Bus No 60 will get you back to the Vieux Port.

Museums All the museums listed here charge 12FF to 18FF for admission; all admit students for half-price. The 'Passeport pour les musées' (50/25FF) is valid for 15 days and allows unlimited entry to all museums.

The **Centre de la Vieille Charité** is home to Marseille's Museum of Mediterranean Archaeology and has superb permanent exhibits on ancient Egypt and Greece (closed weekends). It's in the mostly North African Panier quarter (north of the Vieux Port) at 2 rue de la Charité.

The **Musée Cantini** off rue Paradis, at 19 rue Grignan, has changing exhibitions of modern and contemporary art (closed weekends).

Roman history buffs should visit the **Musée d'Histoire de Marseille** on the ground floor of the Centre Bourse shopping mall, just north of La Canebière (closed Tuesday). Its exhibits include the remains of a merchant ship that plied the waters of the Mediterranean in the late 2nd century AD.

Château d'If Château d'If (☎ 04 91 59 02 30), the 16th-century island fortress-turned-prison made infamous by Alexandre Dumas' *The Count of Monte Cristo*, can be visited daily from 9 am until 7 pm (closed Monday from October to March). Admission costs 22FF. Boats (20 minutes each way; 50FF return) depart from quai des Belges in the Vieux Port and continue to the nearby **Îles du Frioul** (80FF return for chateau and islands).

Places to Stay

Camping & Hostels Tents can usually be pitched (26FF per person) on the grounds of the *Auberge de Jeunesse Château de Bois Luzy* (☎ 04 91 49 06 18, fax 04 91 49 06 18, *Allées des Primevères*), 4.5km east of the city centre in the Montolivet neighbourhood. Otherwise dorm beds (HI card required) are 44FF. Take bus No 6 from near the Canebière-Réformés metro stop or bus No 8 from La Canebière.

The *Auberge de Jeunesse de Bonneveine* (☎ 04 91 73 21 81, fax 04 91 73 97 23, ☻ *mar seille@fuaj.org, Impasse du Docteur Bonfils (8e)*), 4.5km south of the Vieux Port, has beds for 72FF (closed in January). Take bus No 44 from the Rond-Point du Prado metro stop and get off at place Louis Bonnefon.

Hotels – Train Station Area The two-star *Hôtel d'Athènes* (☎ 04 91 90 12 93, fax 04 91 90 72 03, 37-39 blvd d'Athènes, 1er) is at the foot of the grand staircase leading from the train station into town. Average but well-kept singles and doubles with shower and toilet cost 220FF to 300FF. Rooms in its adjoining annexe called the *Hôtel Little Palace* cost between 120FF and 280FF for singles/doubles.

Hotels – Around La Canebière *Hôtel Ozea* (☎ 04 91 47 91 84, 12 rue Barbaroux, 1er) welcomes new guests 24 hours a day (at night just ring the bell to wake up the night clerk). Clean, old-fashioned doubles without/with shower are 120/150FF. There are no hall showers. There are well-kept singles and doubles at *Hôtel Pied-à-Terre* (☎ 04 91 92 00 95, 18 rue Barbaroux, 1er) costing 120/150FF without/with shower.

A little more expensive but definitely worth the money is the homely and very clean *Hôtel Lutetia* (☎ 04 91 50 81 78, fax 04 91 50 23 52, 38 Allées Léon Gambetta) with smallish rooms equipped with TV and phone for 230/260FF for singles/doubles.

Places to Eat

Fresh fruits and vegies are sold at the *Marché des Capucins*, one block south of La Canebière on place des Capucins, and at the *fruit and vegetable market* on cours Pierre Puget. Both are closed Sunday.

Restaurants along and near the pedestrianised cours Julien, a few blocks south of La Canebière, offer an incredible variety of cuisines: Antillean, Pakistani, Thai, Lebanese, Tunisian, Italian and more. An excellent value Caribbean-themed eatery with 'student dishes' for 29FF is the *Mosaic (38 cours Julien)*. Its *plat du jour* is only 19FF. *La Caucase (62 cours Julien)* specialising in Armenian dishes, is open nightly from about 6 pm and has *menus* from 88FF. *Le Resto Provençal (54 cours Julien)* does regional French cuisine and has outdoor tables; mains are around 115FF, the plat du jour is 43FF and the lunch *menu* is 65FF (closed Sunday and Monday). The West Indian *Restaurant Antillais (10 cours Julien)* has starters from 20FF, main dishes from 40FF, and a 100FF *menu* that includes house wine.

Countless cafes and restaurants line the pedestrian streets around place Thiars, which is on the south side of the Vieux Port. Though many offer bouillabaisse, the rich fish stew

FRANCE

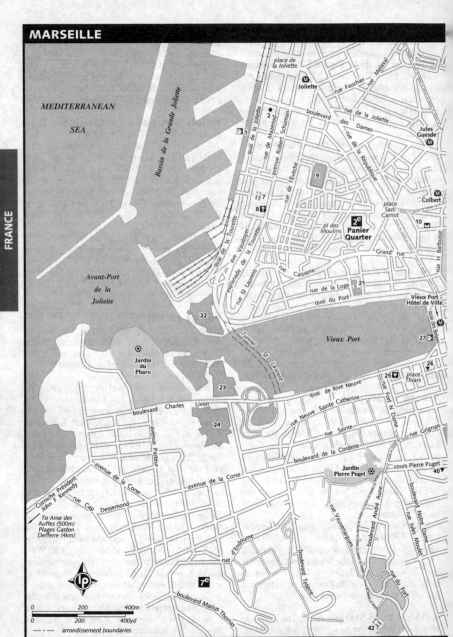

MARSEILLE

MEDITERRANEAN

SEA

Bassin de la Grande Joliette

place de la Joliette

Joliette

rue Malaval

rue Faucher

boulevard des Dames

rue de la Joliette

Jules Guesde

rue de la République

quai de la Joliette

rue de Mazenod

avenue Robert Schuman

rue de l'Évêché

9

place Sadi Carnot

Colbert

Panier Quarter

2e

pl des Moulins

rue H Barbusse

10

Grand' rue

quai de la Tourette

esplanade de la Tourette

ave Vaudoyer

rue St Laurent

rue Caisserie

rue de la Loge

21

quai du Port

Vieux Port - Hôtel de Ville

Avant-Port de la Joliette

22

Tunnel St Laurent

Vieux Port

27

26

Jardin du Pharo

23

25

place Thiars

quai de Rive Neuve

rue Fort N Dame

boulevard Charles Livon

rue Neuve Sainte Catherine

24

avenue Pasteur

rue Sainte

rue Grignan

boulevard de la Corderie

Jardin Pierre Puget

cours Pierre Puget

40

Corniche Président John F Kennedy

avenue de la Corse

rue Cap Dessemond

avenue de la Corse

rue Vauvenargues

boulevard André Aune

boulevard Notre Dame

rue Jules Moulet

To Anse des Auffes (500m) Plages Gaston Defferre (4km)

rue d'Endoume

boulevard Tellène

rue du Fort

7e

0   200   400m
0   200   400yd

boulevard Marius Thomas

42

- - - arrondissement boundaries

FRANCE

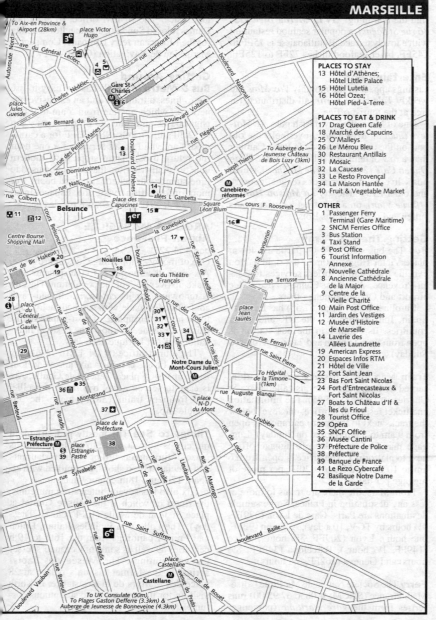

FRANCE

PLACES TO STAY
13 Hôtel d'Athènes;
   Hôtel Little Palace
15 Hôtel Lutetia
16 Hôtel Ozea;
   Hôtel Pied-à-Terre

PLACES TO EAT & DRINK
17 Drag Queen Café
18 Marché des Capucins
25 O'Malleys
26 Le Mérou Bleu
30 Restaurant Antillais
31 Mosaic
32 La Caucase
33 Le Resto Provençal
34 La Maison Hantée
40 Fruit & Vegetable Market

OTHER
1 Passenger Ferry
   Terminal (Gare Maritime)
2 SNCM Ferries Office
3 Bus Station
4 Taxi Stand
5 Post Office
6 Tourist Information
   Annexe
7 Nouvelle Cathédrale
8 Ancienne Cathédrale
   de la Major
9 Centre de la
   Vieille Charité
10 Main Post Office
11 Jardin des Vestiges
12 Musée d'Histoire
   de Marseille
14 Laverie des
   Allées Laundrette
19 American Express
20 Espaces Infos RTM
21 Hôtel de Ville
22 Fort Saint Jean
23 Bas Fort Saint Nicolas
24 Fort d'Entrecasteaux &
   Fort Saint Nicolas
27 Boats to Château d'If &
   Îles du Frioul
28 Tourist Office
29 Opéra
35 SNCF Office
36 Musée Cantini
37 Préfecture de Police
38 Préfecture
39 Banque de France
41 Le Rezo Cybercafé
42 Basilique Notre Dame
   de la Garde

for which Marseille is famous, it's difficult to find the real thing. Try **Le Mérou Bleu** (*32-36 rue St Saëns*), a popular seafood restaurant with a lovely terrace. Bouillabaisse is 75FF to 145FF, other seafood dishes 72FF to 125FF.

Entertainment

Listings appear in the monthly *Vox Mag* and weekly *Taktik* and *Sortir*, all distributed for free at the tourist office.

One of Marseille's two Irish pubs, **O'Malleys** (*quai de Rive Neuve*) overlooks the old port on the corner of rue de la Paix. Camper than a row of tents and full of fun is the **Drag Queen Café** (*2 rue Sénac de Meilhan*), which hosts live bands. For rock, reggae, country and other live music, try **La Maison Hantée** (*10 rue Vian*), on a hip street between cours Julien and rue des Trois Rois.

Getting There & Away

Bus The bus station (☎ 04 91 08 16 40) at place Victor Hugo, 150m to the right as you exit the train station, offers services to Aix-en-Provence, Avignon, Cannes, Nice, Nice airport and Orange, among others.

Eurolines (☎ 04 91 50 57 55) has buses to Spain, Italy, Morocco, the UK and other countries. Its counter in the bus station is open from 8 am to noon and 2 to 6 pm (closed Sunday).

Train Marseille's passenger train station, served by both metro lines, is called Gare St Charles (☎ 0836 35 35 35). The information and ticket reservation office, one level below the tracks next to the metro entrance, is open from 9 am to 8 pm (closed on Sunday). Luggage may be left at the left-luggage office next to platform 1. The office is open from 6 am to 10 pm and it costs 20FF per piece of luggage per day.

From Marseille there are trains to more or less any destination in France. Some sample destinations are Paris' Gare de Lyon (379FF, 4¼ hours by TGV, 10 a day), Avignon (92FF, one hour), Lyon (209FF, 3¼ hours), Nice (149FF, 1½ hours), Barcelona (342FF, 8½ hours) and Geneva (262FF, 6½ hours).

Ferry The Société Nationale Maritime Corse-Méditerranée (SNCM; ☎ 0836 67 95 00) runs ferries from the *gare maritime* (passenger ferry terminal) at the foot of blvd des Dames to Corsica. The SNCM office, 61 blvd des Dames (closed Sunday), also handles ticketing for the Moroccan ferry company, Compagnie Marocaine de Navigation (COMANAV).

Getting Around

Bus & Metro Marseille has two easy-to-use metro lines, a tram line and an extensive bus network, which operate from 5 am to 9 pm. Night buses and tram No 68 run from 9 pm to 12.30 am. Tickets (9FF, 42FF for a carnet of six) are valid on all services for one hour (no return trips). Tram stops have modern blue ticket distributors that should be used to time-stamp your ticket before you board. For more information, visit the Espace Infos RTM (☎ 04 91 91 92 10), 6-8 rue des Fabres.

AROUND MARSEILLE
Aix-en-Provence
pop 134,222

One of the most appealing cities in Provence, Aix owes its atmosphere to the students who make up over 20% of the population. The city is renowned for its *calissons*, almond-paste confectionery made with candied melon, and for being the birthplace of post-impressionist painter Cézanne. Aix hosts the Festival International d'Art Lyrique each July.

The tourist office (☎ 04 42 16 11 61, fax 04 42 16 11 62, @ infos@aixenprovencetour ism.com) is on place Général de Gaulle. Aix is easy to see on a day trip from Marseille, and frequent trains (38FF) make the 35-minute trip.

Things to See The mostly pedestrianised old city is a great place to explore, with its maze of tiny streets full of ethnic restaurants and specialist food shops, intermixed with elegant 17th and 18th-century mansions.

Aix also has several interesting museums, the finest of which is the **Musée Granet** at place St Jean de Malte (10FF, closed Tuesday). The collection includes Italian, Dutch and French paintings from the 16th to 19th centuries as well as some of Cézanne's lesser known paintings. The **Musée des Tapisseries**, in the former bishop's palace at 28 place des Martyrs de la Résistance, is worth visiting for its tapestries and sumptuous costumes (15FF, closed Sunday).

AVIGNON
pop 85,935

Avignon acquired its ramparts and its reputation as a city of art and culture during the 14th century, when Pope Clement V and his court, fleeing political turmoil in Rome, established themselves here. From 1309 to 1377 huge sums of money were invested in building and decorating the popes' palace. Even after the pontifical court returned to Rome amid bitter charges that Avignon had become a den of criminals and brothel-goers, the city remained an important cultural centre.

Today, Avignon maintains its tradition as a patron of the arts, most notably through its annual performing arts festival. The city's other attractions include a bustling walled town and some interesting museums, including several across the Rhône in Villeneuve-lès-Avignon.

The world-famous Festival d'Avignon, held in the last three weeks of July, attracts many hundreds of artists who put on some 300 performances of all sorts each day. Avignon was Europe's first of the twelve Capitals of Culture in 2000.

Orientation
The main avenue in the walled city runs northward from the train station to place de l'Horloge; it's called cours Jean Jaurès south of the tourist office and rue de la République north of it. The island that runs down the middle of the Rhône between Avignon and Villeneuve-lès-Avignon is known as Île de la Barthelasse.

Information
The tourist office (☎ 04 32 74 32 74, fax 04 90 82 95 03, ☻ information@ot-avignon.fr), 41 cours Jean Jaurès, is 300m north of the train station. It opens 9 am to 6 pm (5 pm on Saturday, 10 am to midday on Sunday). During the Avignon Festival it opens 10 am to 8 pm daily (5 pm on Sunday).

The main post office is on cours Président Kennedy, which is through Porte de la République from the train station.

Cyberdrome (☎ 04 90 16 05 15, fax 04 90 16 05 14, ☻ cyberdrome@wanadoo.fr), on rue Guillaume Puy, charges 25FF for 30 minutes online access or 400FF for 10 hours and opens 7 am to 1 am.

Things to See & Do
Palais des Papes & Around Avignon's leading tourist attraction is the fortified Palace of the Popes, built during the 14th century. The seemingly endless halls, chapels, corridors and staircases were once sumptuously decorated, but these days they are nearly empty except for a few damaged frescoes. The palace opens 9 am to 7 pm (9 pm in July and 8 pm in August and September). Admission costs 45/37F.

At the far northern end of place du Palais, the **Musée du Petit Palais** houses an outstanding collection of 13th to 16th-century Italian religious paintings (30/15FF, closed Tuesday). Just up the hill is **Rocher des Doms**, a park with great views of the Rhône, Pont St Bénézet and Villeneuve-lès-Avignon.

Pont St Bénézet Originally built in the 12th century to link Avignon and Villeneuve-lès-Avignon, this is the 'Pont d'Avignon' mentioned in the French nursery rhyme. Once 900m long, the bridge was repaired and rebuilt several times until all but four of its 22 spans were washed away in the 17th century. Entry to the bridge (closed Monday) costs 17/9FF.

Museums Housed in an 18th-century mansion, the **Musée Calvet**, 65 rue Joseph Vernet, has a collection of ancient Egyptian, Greek and Roman artefacts as well as paintings from the 16th to 20th centuries (30/15FF). Its annexe, the **Musée Lapidaire**, 27 rue de la République, houses sculpture and statuary from the Gallo-Roman, Romanesque and Gothic periods (10FF, closed Tuesday).

At 17 rue Victor Hugo, the **Musée Louis Vouland** exhibits a fine collection of ceramics and some superb 18th-century French furniture (20/10FF, closed Sunday and Monday).

Villeneuve-lès-Avignon Avignon's picturesque sister city also has a few interesting sights, all of which are included in a 45FF combined ticket sold at the major sights. From Avignon, Villeneuve can be reached by foot or bus No 10 from the main post office.

The **Chartreuse du Val de Bénédiction**, 60 rue de la République, was once the largest and most important Carthusian monastery in France (32/21FF). The **Musée Pierre de**

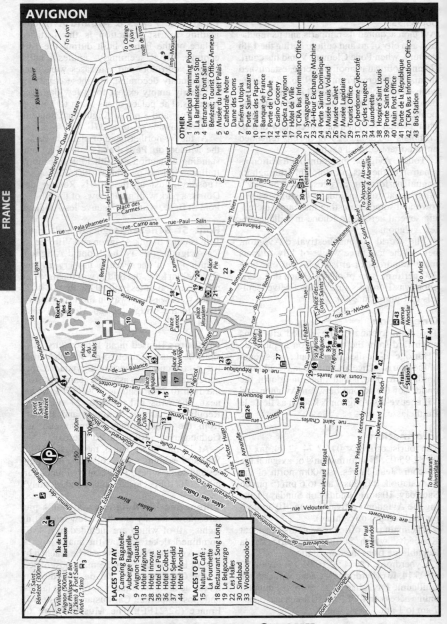

FRANCE

AVIGNON

OTHER
1 Municipal Swimming Pool
3 La Barthelasse Bus Stop
4 Entrance to Pont Saint Bénézet; Tourist Office Annexe
5 Musée du Petit Palais
6 Cathédrale Notre Dame des Doms
7 Cinéma Utopia
8 Porte Saint Lazare
10 Palais des Papes
11 Banque de France
12 Porte de l'Oulle
14 Casino Grocery
16 Opéra d'Avignon
17 Hôtel de Ville
20 TCRA Bus Information Office
21 Synagogue
23 24-Hour Exchange Machine
24 Porte Sainte Dominique
25 Musée Louis Voland
26 Musée Calvet
27 Musée Lapidaire
29 Tourist Office
31 Cyberdrome Cybercafé
32 Cycles Peugeot
34 Laundrette
38 Hospice Saint Louis
39 Porte Saint Roch
40 Main Post Office
41 Porte de la République
42 TCRA Bus Information Office
43 Bus Station

PLACES TO STAY
2 Camping Bagatelle; Auberge Bagatelle;
9 Avignon Squash Club
13 Hôtel Mignon
28 Hôtel Innova
35 Hôtel Le Parc
36 Hôtel Colbert
37 Hôtel Splendid
44 Hôtel Monclar

PLACES TO EAT
15 Natural Café; La Fourchette
18 Restaurant Song Long
19 Le Belgocargo
30 Sindabad
33 Woolloomooloo

euro currency converter €1 = 6.55FF

Luxembourg on rue de la République has a fine collection of religious paintings (20/12FF, closed Mondays and in February).

The **Tour Philippe le Bel**, a defensive tower built in the 14th century at what was then the north-western end of Pont St Bénézet, has great views of Avignon's walled city, the river and the surrounding countryside. Admission costs 10FF. Another Provençal panorama can be enjoyed from the 14th-century **Fort St André** (25/15FF).

Special Events
The world-famous Festival d'Avignon is held every year during the last three weeks of July. Information on the official festival can be obtained by contacting the Bureau du Festival (☎ 04 90 27 66 50, fax 04 90 27 66 83), 8 bis rue de Mons, F-84000 Avignon. Tickets can be reserved from mid-June onwards.

Places to Stay
Camping The three-star *Camping Bagatelle* (*Île de la Barthelasse*) open year-round, is an attractive, shaded camping ground just north of Pont Édouard Daladier, 850m from the walled city. High season charges are 23.80FF per adult and 11FF to pitch a tent. Reception opens 8 am to 9 pm. Take bus No 10 from the main post office to the La Barthelasse stop.

Hostels The 210-bed *Auberge Bagatelle* (☎ 04 90 85 78 45, *Île de la Barthelasse*) is part of a large, park-like area that includes Camping Bagatelle. A bed in a room costs 60FF. See the Camping section for bus directions.

From April to September a bunk in a converted squash court at the *Avignon Squash Club* (☎ 04 90 85 27 78, *32 blvd Limbert*) costs 60FF. Reception opens 9 am to 10 pm (closed on Sunday from September to June; open 8 to 11 am and 5 to 11 pm in July and August). Take bus No 7 from the train station to the Université stop.

Hotels – Within the Walls There are three hotels all close to each other on the same street. *Hôtel Le Parc* (☎ 04 90 82 71 55, *18 rue Agricol Perdiguier*) has singles/doubles without shower for 145/175FF and 195/215FF with shower.

The friendly *Hôtel Splendid* (☎ 04 90 86 14 46, fax 04 90 85 38 55, *17 rue Agricol Perdiguier*) has singles/doubles with shower for 130/200FF and rooms with shower and toilet for 170/280FF.

The third in the trio, the two-star *Hôtel Colbert* (☎ 04 90 86 20 20, fax 04 90 85 97 00, *7 rue Agricol Perdiguier*) has well-priced singles with shower for 160FF and doubles/triples with shower and toilet for 210/260FF.

The always busy *Hôtel Innova* (☎ 04 90 82 54 10, fax 04 90 82 52 39, *100 rue Joseph Vernet*) has bright, comfortable and soundproofed rooms ranging in price from 140FF to 220FF. Breakfast is 25FF.

Hôtel Mignon (☎ 04 90 82 17 30, fax 04 90 85 78 46, *12 rue Joseph Vernet*) has spotless, well-kept and soundproofed singles with shower for 150FF and doubles with shower and toilet for 220FF.

Hotels – Outside the Walls The noisy, family-run *Hôtel Monclar* (☎ 04 90 86 20 14, fax 04 90 85 94 94, ✉ hmonclar84@aol.com, *13 ave Monclar*) is in an 18th-century building just across the tracks from the train station. Comfortable doubles start at 165FF with sink and bidet. The hotel has its own parking lot (20FF) and a pretty, little back garden.

Places to Eat
Les Halles food market on place Pie is open daily (except Monday) from 7 am to 1 pm. *Restaurant Universitaire* (*ave du Blanchissage*), south-west of the train station, opens October to June (closed Saturday dinner and Sunday, and during university holidays) from 11.30 am to 1.30 pm and 6.30 to 7.30 pm. People with student IDs can buy tickets (15FF to 30FF) at the CROUS office at 29 blvd Limbert, just east of the walled city on Monday, Tuesday, Wednesday and Friday from 10.30 am to 12.30 pm.

Restaurant Song Long (*1 rue Carnot*) offers a wide variety of excellent Vietnamese dishes, including 16 *plats végétariens* (vegetarian soups, salads, starters and main dishes from 28FF to 40FF). Lunch/dinner *menus* are 35FF, 40 and 45FF. Song Long opens daily.

Le Belgocargo (*7 rue Armand de Pontmartin*), a Belgian place tucked behind Église St Pierre, serves mussels 16 different ways for 49FF to 68FF and *waterzooi de volaille* (a creamy Belgian stew of chicken, leeks and herbs) for 58FF.

FRANCE

For hearty and healthy fodder in a rustic setting (tree trunks for benches etc) look no farther than the atmospheric *Natural Café* (*17 rue Racine*). It is closed on Sunday and Monday. Adjoining it is the more conventional *La Fourchette* (*17 rue Racine*), a Michelin-recommended place with *menus* for 150FF.

On the other side of town, a good choice is *Woolloomooloo* (*16 bis rue des Teinturiers*), a lively spot with vegetarian and Antillean dishes on offer (*menus* from 67FF to 89FF; closed Sunday and Monday). Nearby, the small bohemian *Sindabad* (*53 rue des Teinturiers*) offers good Tunisian, oriental and Provençal home cooking and has a 50FF *plat du jour* (closed Sunday).

Entertainment
Cinéma Utopia (*4 rue des Escaliers Ste Anne*) is a student entertainment/cultural centre with a jazz club, cafe and four cinemas screening nondubbed films.

From October to June, the *Opéra d'Avignon* (☎ 04 90 82 23 44, *place de l'Horloge*) stages operas, plays and concerts. The box office opens 11 am to 6 pm (closed Sunday).

Getting There & Away
Bus The bus station (☎ 04 90 82 07 35) is down the ramp to the right as you exit the train station. Tickets are sold on the buses, which are run by about 20 different companies. Destinations include Aix-en-Provence (86FF, one hour), Arles (38FF, 1½ hours), Nice (165FF), Nîmes (40FF), and Marseille (89FF, 35 minutes). Sunday services are less frequent.

Train The train station (☎ 0836 35 35 39) is across blvd St Roch from Porte de la République. There are frequent trains to Arles (36FF, 25 minutes), Nice (206FF, four hours), Nîmes (44FF, 30 minutes) and Paris (370FF, 3¼ hours via TGV).

Getting Around
TCRA municipal buses operate 7 am to about 7.40 pm. Tickets cost 6.50FF if bought from the driver; a carnet of five tickets (good for 10 rides) costs 48FF from TCRA offices in the walled city at porte de la République and at place Pie (closed Sunday).

Cycles Peugeot (☎ 04 90 86 32 49), 80 rue Guillaume Puy, has three-speeds and 10-speeds for 60/130/240FF for one/three/seven days (plus 1000FF deposit).

AROUND AVIGNON
Arles
pop 50,513
Arles began its ascent to prosperity in 49 BC when Julius Caesar, to whom the city had given its support, sacked Marseille, which had backed the Roman general Pompey. It soon became a major trading centre and by the late 1st century AD, needed a 20,000-seat amphitheatre and a 12,000-seat theatre. Now known as the **Arènes** and the **Théâtre Antique** respectively, they are still used to stage bullfights and cultural events.

Arles is also known for its **Église St Trophime** and **Cloître St Trophime**. Significant parts of both date from the 12th century and are in the Romanesque style. But the city is probably best known as the place where Van Gogh painted some of his most famous works, including *The Sunflowers*. The tourist office (☎ 04 90 18 41 20) is on esplanade des Lices.

There are regular bus services to Marseille (87FF, 2½ hours), Aix-en-Provence (68FF, 1¾ hours) and Avignon (40FF, 1½ hours).

Côte d'Azur

The Côte d'Azur, which includes the French Riviera, stretches along France's Mediterranean coast from Toulon to the Italian border. Many of the towns here – budget-busting St Tropez, Cannes, Antibes, Nice and Monaco – have become world-famous thanks to the recreational activities of the tanned and idle rich. The reality is rather less glamorous, but the Côte d'Azur still has a great deal to attract visitors: sunshine, 40km of beaches, all sorts of cultural activities and, sometimes, even a bit of glitter.

Unless you're camping or hostelling, your best bet is to stay in Nice, which has a generous supply of cheap hotels, and make day trips to other places. Note that theft from backpacks, pockets, cars and even laundrettes is a serious problem along the Côte d'Azur, especially at train and bus stations.

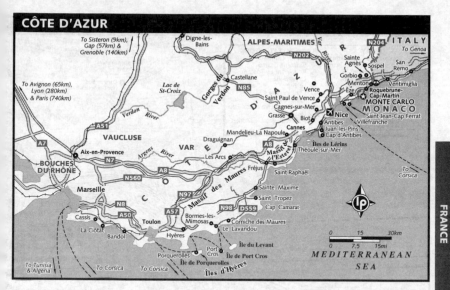

CÔTE D'AZUR

NICE
pop 342,738
Known as the capital of the Riviera, the fashionable yet relaxed city of Nice makes a great base from which to explore the entire Côte d'Azur. The city, which did not become part of France until 1860, has plenty of relatively cheap accommodation and is only a short train or bus ride away from the rest of the Riviera. Nice's beach may be nothing to write home about, but the city is blessed with a fine collection of museums.

Orientation
Ave Jean Médecin runs from near the train station to place Masséna. Vieux Nice is the area delineated by the quai des États-Unis, blvd Jean Jaurès and the 92m hill known as Le Château. The neighbourhood of Cimiez, home to several very good museums, is north of the town centre.

Information
The main tourist office (☎ 04 93 87 07 07, fax 04 93 16 85 16, ℮ otc@nice.coteazur.org) at the train station opens 8 am to 7 pm daily (to 8 pm July to September). The annexe at 5 promenade des Anglais (☎ 04 92 14 48 00) is open Monday to Saturday from 8 am to 6 pm.

The main post office is at 23 ave Thiers, one block from the train station. There are branch post offices at 4 ave Georges Clemenceau, on the corner of rue de Russie, and in the old city at 2 rue Louis Gassin.

Opposite the train station, Le Change (☎ 04 93 88 56 80) at 17 ave Thiers (to the right as you exit the terminal building) offers decent rates and is open from 7 am to midnight. American Express (☎ 04 93 16 53 53) is at 11 Promenade des Anglais (closed Sunday).

The Web Store (☎ 04 93 87 87 99, ℮ info@webstore.fr), 12 rue de Russie, charges 30/50FF for 30/60 minutes of Internet access and is open Monday to Saturday from 10 am to noon and 2 to 7 pm.

Things to See
An excellent-value museum pass (140/70FF), available at tourist offices and participating museums, gives free admission to some 60 Côte d'Azur museums. Unless otherwise noted, the following museums are open Wednesday to Monday from around 10 am to 5 or 6 pm (sometimes with a break for lunch in the off-season), and entry is around 25/15FF.

The **Musée d'Art Moderne et d'Art Contemporain** (Museum of Modern and Contemporary Art), ave St Jean Baptiste, specialises

FRANCE

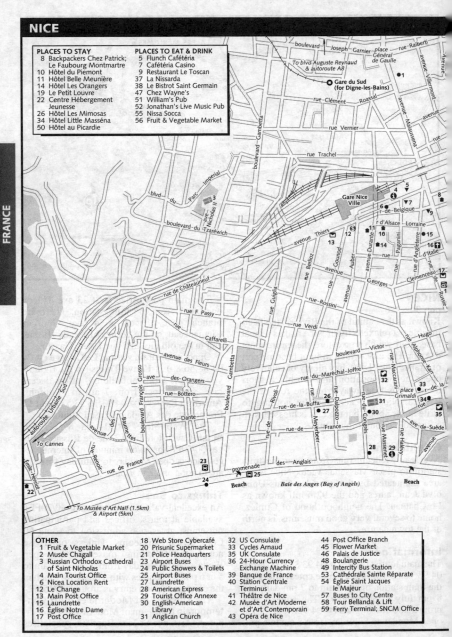

NICE

PLACES TO STAY
- 8 Backpackers Chez Patrick; Le Faubourg Montmartre
- 10 Hôtel du Piemont
- 11 Hôtel Belle Meunière
- 14 Hôtel Les Orangers
- 19 Le Petit Louvre
- 22 Centre Hébergement Jeunesse
- 26 Hôtel Les Mimosas
- 34 Hôtel Little Masséna
- 50 Hôtel au Picardie

PLACES TO EAT & DRINK
- 5 Flunch Cafétéria
- 7 Cafétéria Casino
- 9 Restaurant Le Toscan
- 37 La Nissarda
- 38 Le Bistrot Saint Germain
- 47 Chez Wayne's
- 51 William's Pub
- 52 Jonathan's Live Music Pub
- 55 Nissa Socca
- 56 Fruit & Vegetable Market

OTHER
- 1 Fruit & Vegetable Market
- 2 Musée Chagall
- 3 Russian Orthodox Cathedral of Saint Nicholas
- 4 Main Tourist Office
- 6 Nicea Location Rent
- 12 Le Change
- 13 Main Post Office
- 15 Laundrette
- 16 Église Notre Dame
- 17 Post Office
- 18 Web Store Cybercafé
- 20 Prisunic Supermarket
- 21 Police Headquarters
- 23 Airport Buses
- 24 Public Showers & Toilets
- 25 Airport Buses
- 27 Laundrette
- 28 American Express
- 29 Tourist Office Annexe
- 30 English-American Library
- 31 Anglican Church
- 32 US Consulate
- 33 Cycles Arnaud
- 35 UK Consulate
- 36 24-Hour Currency Exchange Machine
- 39 Banque de France
- 40 Station Centrale Terminus
- 41 Théâtre de Nice
- 42 Musée d'Art Moderne et d'Art Contemporain
- 43 Opéra de Nice
- 44 Post Office Branch
- 45 Flower Market
- 46 Palais de Justice
- 48 Boulangerie
- 49 Intercity Bus Station
- 53 Cathédrale Sainte Réparate
- 54 Église Saint Jacques le Majeur
- 57 Buses to City Centre
- 58 Tour Bellanda & Lift
- 59 Ferry Terminal; SNCM Office

euro currency converter €1 = 6.55FF

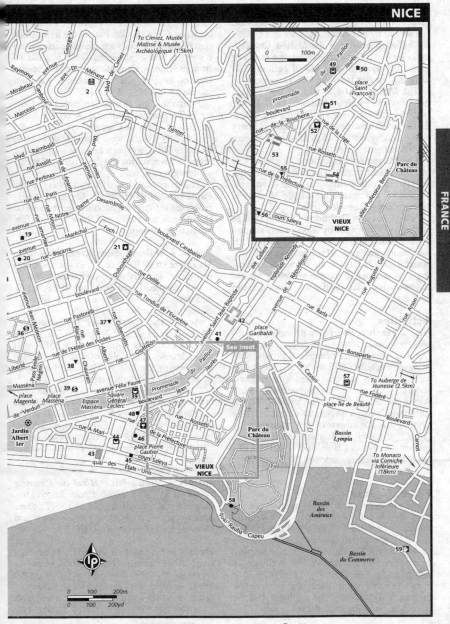

in eye-popping French and American avant-garde works from the 1960s to the present. It's served by bus Nos 3, 5, 7, 16 and 17.

The main exhibit at the **Musée Chagall**, opposite 4 ave Docteur Ménard, is a series of incredibly vivid Marc Chagall paintings illustrating stories from the Old Testament.

The **Musée Matisse**, with its fine collection of works by Henri Matisse (1869-1954), is at 164 ave des Arènes de Cimiez in Cimiez, 2.5km north-east of the train station. Many buses pass by, but No 15 is most convenient; get off at the Arènes stop.

The **Musée Archéologique** (Archaeology Museum) and nearby **Gallo-Roman Ruins** (which include public baths and an amphitheatre) are next to the Musée Matisse at 160 ave des Arènes de Cimiez.

Nice's **Russian Orthodox Cathedral of St Nicholas**, crowned by six onion-shaped domes, was built between 1903 and 1912; step inside and you'll be transported to Imperial Russia (15/10FF; closed Sunday morning). You'll need to dress appropriately: shorts or short skirts and sleeveless shirts are forbidden.

Activities

Nice's **beach** is covered with smooth pebbles, not sand. Between mid-April and mid-October, free public beaches alternate with private beaches (60FF to 70FF a day) that have all sorts of amenities (mattresses, showers, changing rooms, security etc). Along the beach you can hire paddle boats, sailboards and jet skis, and go parasailing (200FF for 15 minutes) and water-skiing (100FF to 130FF for 10 minutes). There are indoor showers (12FF) and toilets (2FF) open to the public opposite 50 Promenade des Anglais.

Places to Stay

There are quite a few cheap hotels near the train station and lots of places in a slightly higher price bracket along rue d'Angleterre, rue d'Alsace-Lorraine, rue de Suisse, rue de Russie and rue Durante, also near the station. In summer the inexpensive places fill up by late morning – book your bed by 10 am.

In summer, lots of backpackers sleep on the beach. Technically this is illegal, but the Nice police usually look the other way.

Hostels The *Auberge de Jeunesse* (☎ 04 93 89 23 64, fax 04 92 04 03 10, Route Forestière de Mont Alban) is 4km east of the train. Beds cost 68.50FF. There's a midnight curfew, and it's often full – call ahead. Take bus No 14 from the Station Centrale terminus on Square Général Leclerc, which is linked to the train station by bus Nos 15 and 17.

From mid-June to mid-September the *Centre Hébergement Jeunesse* (☎ 04 93 86 28 75, 31 rue Louis de Coppet) serves as a hostel. It's half a block north from rue de France. Beds are 50FF, and bags must be stored in the luggage room during the day (10FF). There's a midnight curfew.

The popular 21-bed *Backpackers Chez Patrick* (☎ 04 93 80 30 72, 32 rue Pertinax) is above the Faubourg Montmartre restaurant. Dorm beds are 80FF, and there's no curfew or daytime closure.

Hotels – Train Station Area *Hôtel Belle Meunière* (☎ 04 93 88 66 15, 21 ave Durante) is a clean, friendly place that attracts lots of young people. Dorm beds are 80FF, while doubles/triples with bath are 182/243FF. It's closed in December and January.

Across the street *Hôtel Les Orangers* (☎ 04 93 87 51 41, fax 04 93 82 57 82, 10 bis ave Durante) has dorm beds for 85FF, and great doubles and triples with shower, fridge and balcony for 210FF. The cheerful owner Marc speaks excellent English.

Rue d'Alsace-Lorraine is dotted with two-star hotels. One of the cheapest is the *Hôtel du Piemont* (☎ 04 93 88 25 15, fax 04 93 16 15 18, 19 rue d'Alsace-Lorraine), which has bargain singles/doubles with washbasin from 110/130FF. Singles/doubles with shower start at 140/170FF.

Hotels – Vieux Nice *Hôtel au Picardie* (☎ 04 93 85 75 51, 10 blvd Jean Jaurès) has single/double rooms from 120/150FF; there are also pricier rooms that include toilet and shower. Hall showers are 10FF.

Hotels – Elsewhere in Town The reception of the friendly *Hôtel Little Masséna* (☎ 04 93 87 72 34, 22 rue Masséna), is on the 5th floor (open until 8 pm). Doubles range in price from 140FF to 220FF. Rooms come with a hotplate and fridge. The relaxed, family-style

FRANCE

Hôtel Les Mimosas (☎ 04 93 88 05 59, 26 rue de la Buffa) is two blocks north-east of the (currently closed) Musée Masséna. Utilitarian rooms of a good-size for one/two people cost 120/190FF.

Between the train station and the beach is the colourful *Le Petit Louvre* (☎ 04 93 80 15 54, fax 04 93 62 45 08, 10 rue Emma Tiranty). Singles/doubles with shower, washbasin, fridge and hotplate are 180/205FF.

Places to Eat

In Vieux Nice, there's a *fruit and vegetable market* in front of the préfecture in cours Saleya from 6 am to 5.30 pm (closed Sunday afternoon and Monday). The no-name *boulangerie* at the south end of rue du Marché is the best place for cheap sandwiches, pizza slices and *michettes* (savoury bread stuffed with cheese, olives, anchovies and onions).

Cheap places near the train station include the *Flunch Cafétéria*, to the left as you exit the station building, and the *Cafétéria Casino* (7 ave Thiers) across the street. In the same vicinity, *Restaurant Le Toscan* (1 rue de Belgique), a family-run Italian place, offers large portions of home-made ravioli (closed Sunday).

There are Vietnamese and Chinese restaurants on rue Paganini, rue d'Italie and rue d'Alsace-Lorraine. Nearby, *Le Faubourg Montmartre* (32 rue Pertinax), beneath the Backpackers' Hotel, is always crowded. The house speciality is bouillabaisse (120FF for two), and there's a 68FF *menu*.

La Nissarda (17 rue Gubernatis) has specialities from Nice and Normandy. The *menus* are reasonably priced at 60FF (lunch only) and 78FF, 98FF and 138FF (closed Sunday and in August). Nearby, *Le Bistrot St Germain* (9 rue Chauvain) serves fresh, seasonal food at affordable prices.

In the old city, a perennial favourite with locals is *Nissa Socca* (5 rue Ste Reparate). Its Niçois specialities include *socca* (chickpea rissoles), *farcis* (stuffed vegetables) and ratatouille.

Entertainment

William's Pub (4 rue Centrale) has live music every night (except Sunday) starting at around 9 pm. There's pool, darts and chess in the basement. *Jonathan's Live Music Pub* (1 rue de la Loge) has live music every night in summer. *Chez Wayne's*, (15 rue de la Préfecture) hosts a bilingual quiz on Tuesday, a ladies' night on Wednesday, karaoke on Sunday and live bands on Friday and Saturday. Happy hour is until 9 pm.

Getting There & Away

Bus The intercity bus station, opposite 10 blvd Jean Jaurès, is served by some two dozen bus companies. There are slow but frequent services daily until about 7.30 pm to Cannes (32FF, 1½ hours), Antibes (25.50FF, 1¼ hours), Monaco (20FF return, 45 minutes), and Menton (28.50FF return, 1¼ hours).

Train Nice's main train station, Gare Nice Ville, is 1.2km north of the beach on ave Thiers. There are fast, frequent services (up to 40 daily trains) to points all along the coast, including Monaco (20FF, 20 minutes), Antibes (20FF, 25 minutes) and Cannes (32FF, 40 minutes). The two or three TGVs that link Nice with Paris' Gare de Lyon (455FF, seven hours) are infrequent; it can be more convenient to travel via Marseille.

Trains for Digne-les-Bains make the scenic trip four times daily from Nice's Gare du Sud (☎ 04 93 82 10 17), 4 bis rue Alfred Binet, (109FF, 3¼ hours).

Getting Around

Local buses, run by Sunbus, cost 8/68FF for a single ticket/carnet of 10. Bus information and daily passes are available from the Sunbus information office (☎ 04 93 16 52 10) at the Station Centrale on ave Félix Faure. From the train station to Vieux Nice and the bus station, take bus No 2, 5 or 17. Bus No 12 links the train station with the beach.

Bicycles (80FF a day) can be rented from Nicea Location Rent (☎ 04 93 82 42 71), 9 ave Thiers. Cycles Arnaud (☎ 04 93 87 88 55), 4 place Grimaldi, has mountain bikes for 100/180FF a day/weekend (closed Monday morning and Sunday).

CANNES

pop 67,304

The harbour, the bay, Le Suquet hill, the beachside promenade, and the bronzed sun-worshippers on the beach provide more than enough natural beauty to make Cannes worth at least a day trip. It's also fun watching the

FRANCE

rich drop their money with such fashionable nonchalance.

Cannes is renowned for its many festivals and cultural activities, the most famous being the International Film Festival, which runs for two weeks in mid-May. People come to Cannes all year long, but the main tourist season runs from May to October. During the off season, however, the locals are more inclined to be friendly, prices are lower and there are no crowds to contend with.

Orientation

From the train station, follow rue Jean Jaurès west and turn left onto rue Vénizélos, which runs west into the heart of the Vieux Port. Place Bernard Cornut Gentille (formerly place de l'Hôtel de Ville), where the bus station is located, is on the north-western edge of the Vieux Port. Cannes' most famous promenade, the magnificent blvd de la Croisette, begins at the Palais des Festivals and continues eastward around the Baie de Cannes to Pointe de la Croisette.

Information

The main tourist office (☎ 04 93 39 24 53, fax 04 92 99 84 23, @ semoftou@palais-festivals-cannes.fr) is on the ground floor of the Palais des Festivals (closed Sunday from September to June). It opens 9 am to 7 pm (Monday to Friday) and 10 am to 6 pm on weekends. Daily hours in July and August are 9 am to 8 pm. *There's* an annexe (☎ 04 93 99 19 77) at the train station (closed Sunday); turn left as you exit the station and walk up the stairs next to Frantour Tourisme.

The main post office is at 22 rue Bivouac Napoléon, not far from the Palais des Festivals. Asher Cyber Espace (☎ 04 92 99 03 01, @ asher@riviera.net), 44 blvd Carnot, opens 9.30 am to 7 pm (Friday and Saturday from 9 am to midnight; closed Sunday).

Things to See & Do

Vieux Port Some of the largest yachts you'll ever see are likely to be sitting in the Vieux Port, a fishing port now given over to pleasure craft. The streets around the old port are particularly pleasant on a summer's evening, when the many cafes and restaurants light up the whole area with coloured neon.

The hill just west of the Vieux Port, **Le Suquet**, affords magnificent views of Cannes, especially in the late afternoon and on clear nights. The **Musée de la Castre**, housed in a chateau atop Le Suquet, has Mediterranean and Middle Eastern antiquities as well as objects of ethnographic interest from all over the world (10FF, free for students; closed Tuesday).

Beaches Each of the fancy hotels that line blvd de la Croisette has its own private section of the beach. Unfortunately, this arrangement leaves only a small strip of public sand near the Palais des Festivals. Other free public beaches – the **Plages du Midi** and **Plages de la Bocca** – stretch several kilometres westward from the old port.

Îles de Lérins The eucalyptus and pine-covered **Île Ste Marguerite**, where the Man in the Iron Mask (made famous in the novel by Alexandre Dumas) was held captive during the late 17th century, is just over 1km from the mainland. The island is crisscrossed by many trails and paths. The smaller **Île St Honorat** is home to Cistercian monks who welcome visitors to their monastery and the seven small chapels dotted around the island.

Compagnie Maritime Cannoise (CMC; ☎ 04 93 38 66 33) runs ferries to Île St Honorat (50FF return, 20 minutes) and Île Ste Marguerite (50FF return, 15 minutes). Both islands can be visited for 75FF. The ticket office is at the Vieux Port near the Palais des Festivals.

Places to Stay

Tariffs can be up to 50% higher in July and August – when you'll be lucky to find a room at any price – than in winter. During the film festival, all the hotels are booked up to a year in advance.

Hostels Cannes' *Centre International de Séjour at de la Jeunesse* (☎/fax 04 93 99 26 79, @ centre.sejour.youth.hostel.cannes@wanadoo.fr, 35 ave de Vallauris), in a small villa about 400m north-east of the train station, has dorm beds for 80FF (HI card required; available for 70/100FF for those under/over 26). Reception opens 8 am to 12.30 pm and 2.30 to 10.30 pm (3 to 10 pm on weekends); curfew is

FRANCE

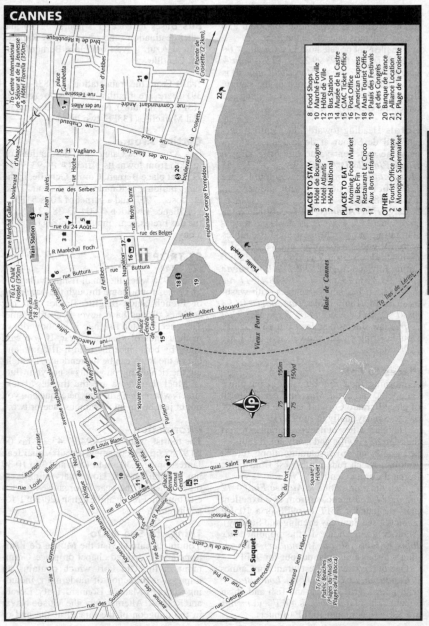

CANNES

euro currency converter 1FF = €0.15

at midnight (2 am on weekends). To get there, follow blvd de la République for 300m and ave de Vallauris runs off to the right.

The pleasant private hostel *Le Chalit* (☎ 06 15 28 07 09, fax 04 93 99 22 11, ✉ le–chalit@ libertysurf.fr, 27 ave du Maréchal Galliéni) is a five-minute walk north-west of the station. Beds are 90FF. Le Chalit opens year-round and there's no curfew.

Hotels Heading towards the Centre International de Séjour at de la Jeunesse, you pass the excellent-value but little known *Hôtel Florella* (☎/fax 04 93 38 48 11, 55 blvd de la République). Singles/doubles are 120/140FF, and doubles with shower and TV are 180FF.

Large *Hôtel Atlantis* (☎ 04 93 39 18 72, fax 04 93 68 37 65, 4 rue du 24 Août) has a two-star rating but its cheapest singles/doubles with TV and minibar cost only 155/195FF during the low season. This rises to 195/220FF during July and August. *Hôtel de Bourgogne* (☎ 04 93 38 36 73, fax 04 92 99 28 41, 11 rue du 24 Août) has singles/doubles with washbasin for 143/186FF. *Hôtel National* (☎ 04 93 39 91 92, fax 04 92 98 44 06, 8 rue Maréchal Joffre) has singles/doubles from 130/220FF. Doubles/triples with shower and toilet are 250/300FF.

Places to Eat
A morning *food market* is held on place Gambetta, and at the *Marché Forville* north of place Bernard Cornut Gentille, both Tuesday to Sunday (daily in summer).

There are a few budget restaurants around the Marché Forville and many small (but not necessarily cheap) restaurants along rue St Antoine, which runs north-west from place Bernard Cornut Gentille.

Near the train station at *Au Bec Fin* (☎ 12 rue du 24 Août), choose from two excellent plats du jour for 55FF to 69FF or a 105FF *menu* (closed Saturday evening and Sunday). Another good choice is the popular *Aux Bons Enfants* (80 rue Meynadier), with regional dishes and a plat du jour for 94FF.

One of the cheapest restaurants in Cannes is *Restaurant Le Croco* (11 rue Louis Blanc), with pizzas, grilled meat and fish and shish kebabs. The *plat du jour* is 49FF and *menus* are 59FF (lunch) and 105FF (dinner).

Getting There & Away
Bus Buses to Nice (1½ hours; 32FF) and other destinations, most operated by Rapides Côte d'Azur, leave from place Bernard Cornut Gentille.

Train From the train station (☎ 0836 35 35 39) there are regular services to Antibes (13FF, 10 minutes), Nice (32FF, 40 minutes) and Marseille (133FF, two hours).

Getting Around
Bus Azur serves Cannes and destinations up to 7km from town. Its office (☎ 04 93 39 18 71) is at place Bernard Cornut Gentille, in the same building as Rapides Côte d'Azur. Tickets cost 7.70FF and a carnet of 10 is 51FF.

Alliance Location (☎ 04 93 38 62 62), 19 rue des Frères, rents mountain bikes for 80FF a day.

ST TROPEZ
pop 5444
Since 1956 when the small fishing village of St Tropez found fame through the patronage of French actor Brigitte Bardot and her acolytes, things have never been the same. The once isolated fishing village now draws in thousands of visitors a year. If you can, come by boat since the road traffic into and out of the town can be horrendous. If watching the rich dining on yachts is not your flute of Moët then there are the timeless backstreets where men still play pétanque and you might just bump into a famous face or two.

Information
The tourist office (☎ 04 94 97 45 21, fax 04 94 97 82 66, ✉ tourisme@nova.fr), quai Jean Jaurès, opens 9.30 am to 1 pm and 3 to 10.30 pm in high season. Hours vary slightly at other times of the year. It organises guided city tours in French and English (20/10FF for adults/children).

Things to See & Do
You might care to visit the **Musée de l'Annonciade**, a disused chapel on place Grammont in the Old Port which contains an impressive collection of modern art, including works by Matisse, Bonnard, Dufy, Derain and Rouault. Alternatively, the **Musée Naval** in the dungeon of the citadel at the end of

FRANCE

Montée de la Citadelle has displays on the town's maritime history and on the Allied landings in 1944.

For a decent beach you need to get 4km out of town to the excellent **Plage de Tahiti**. Naturists will need to get away from St Tropez to the beaches between the town and Le Lavandou to the west.

Places to Stay & Eat

Accommodation isn't cheap and even camping costs more than normal elsewhere. St Tropez's cheapest hotel is the dingy *Hôtel La Méditerranée* (*☎ 04 94 97 00 44, fax 04 94 97 47 83, 21 blvd Louis Blanc*). Doubles start at 200FF. One rung up the price ladder is *Hôtel Les Chimères* (*☎ 04 94 97 02 90, fax 04 94 97 63 57, Port du Pilon*) at the south-western end of ave du Général Leclerc. Singles/doubles with shower and breakfast cost 328/358FF.

Move away from the waterfront to eat. Extremely tasteful and not too expensive is the informal *Café Sud* (*☎ 04 94 97 71 72, 12 rue Étienne Berny*), tucked down a narrow street off Places des Lices. It has a *menu* for 140FF and tables are outside in a star-topped courtyard. Close by, the *Bistrot des Lices* (*☎ 04 94 97 29 00, 3 Places des Lices*) serves traditional Provençal cuisine, including wonderful *ratatouille*, with dishes from 120FF to 190FF.

Getting There & Away

St Tropez bus station, ave Général de Gaulle, is on the south-western edge of town on the one main road out of town. Frequent taxi boats run to Port Grimaud nearby and excursion boats run regularly to and from St Maxime and St Raphaël.

MENTON

pop 28,812

Reputed to be the warmest spot on the Côte d'Azur, Menton is encircled by mountains. The town is renowned for lemons and holds a two-week Fête du Citron (Lemon Festival) each year between mid-February and early March. The helpful tourist office (*☎ 04 93 57 57 00*) is in the Palais de l'Europe at 8 ave Boyer.

It's pleasant to wander around the narrow, winding streets of the Vieille Ville (old city) and up to the cypress-shaded **Cimetière du Vieux Château**, with the graves of English, Irish, North Americans, New Zealanders and others who died here during the 19th century. The view alone is worth the climb.

Église St Michel

The grandest baroque church in this part of France sits perched in the centre of the Vieille Ville. The **beach** along the promenade du Soleil is public and, like Nice's, carpeted with smooth pebbles. Better private beaches lie east of the old city in the port area, the main one being **Plage des Sablettes**.

Camping St Michel (*☎ 04 93 35 81 23, Plateau St Michel*), open from April to mid-October, is 1km north-east of the train station. The adjacent *Auberge de Jeunesse* (*☎ 04 93 35 93 14, fax 04 93 35 93 07, Plateau St Michel*) has beds for 68FF.

The bus station has services to Monaco (12.50FF return, 30 minutes) and Nice (28FF return, 1¼ hours). Take the train to get to Ventimiglia in Italy.

Monaco (Principauté de Monaco)

pop 30,000

The Principality of Monaco, a sovereign state whose territory covers only 1.95 sq km, has been ruled by the Grimaldi family for most of the period since 1297. Prince Rainier III (born in 1923), whose sweeping constitutional powers make him far more than a figurehead, has reigned since 1949. The citizens of Monaco (Monégasques), of whom there are only 5000 out of a total population of 30,000, pay no taxes. The official language is French, although efforts are being made to revive the country's traditional dialect. There are no border formalities and Monaco makes a perfect day trip from Nice.

Orientation

Monaco consists of four principal areas: Monaco Ville, also known as the old city or the Rocher de Monaco, perched atop a 60m-high crag overlooking the Port de Monaco; Monte Carlo, famed for its casino and its Grand Prix motor race, north of the harbour; La Condamine, the flat area surrounding the

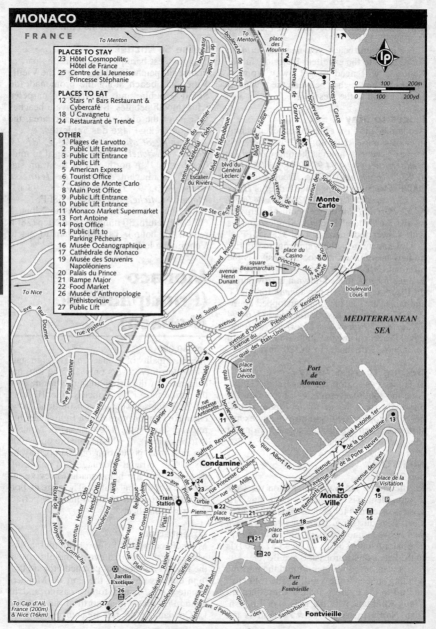

MONACO

FRANCE

PLACES TO STAY
23 Hôtel Cosmopolite;
   Hôtel de France
25 Centre de la Jeunesse
   Princesse Stéphanie

PLACES TO EAT
12 Stars 'n' Bars Restaurant &
   Cybercafé
18 U Cavagnetu
24 Restaurant de Trende

OTHER
1 Plages de Larvotto
2 Public Lift Entrance
3 Public Lift Entrance
4 Public Lift
5 American Express
6 Tourist Office
7 Casino de Monte Carlo
8 Main Post Office
9 Public Lift Entrance
10 Public Lift Entrance
11 Monaco Market Supermarket
13 Fort Antoine
14 Post Office
15 Public Lift to
   Parking Pêcheurs
16 Musée Océanographique
17 Cathédrale de Monaco
19 Musée des Souvenirs
   Napoléoniens
20 Palais du Prince
21 Rampe Major
22 Food Market
26 Musée d'Anthropologie
   Préhistorique
27 Public Lift

euro currency converter €1 = 6.55FF

harbour; and Fontvieille, an industrial area south-west of Monaco Ville and the Port de Fontvieille.

Information

Tourist Offices The Direction du Tourisme et des Congrès de la Principauté de Monaco (☎ 92 16 61 66, fax 92 16 60 00, ✉ dtc@ monaco-congres.com), 2a blvd des Moulins, is across the public gardens from the casino. It opens 9 am to 7 pm (Sunday from 10 am to noon). From mid-June to mid-September, several tourist office kiosks open around the principality.

Money The currency of Monaco is the French franc. Both French and Monégasque coins are in circulation, but the latter are not widely accepted outside the principality.

In Monte Carlo, you'll find lots of banks in the vicinity of the casino. American Express (☎ 93 25 74 45), 35 blvd Princesse Charlotte, is near the main tourist office (closed Saturday and Sunday).

Post & Communications Monégasque stamps are valid only within Monaco, and postal rates are the same as in France. The main post office is at 1 ave Henri Dunant (inside the Palais de la Scala).

Calls between Monaco and the rest of France are treated as international calls. Monaco's country code is ☎ 377. To call France from Monaco, dial ☎ 00 and France's country code (☎ 33). This applies even if you are only making a call from the east side of blvd de France (in Monaco) to its west side (in France)!

Email & Internet Access Stars 'n' Bars (☎ 93 50 95 95, ✉ info@starsnbars.com), a bar and restaurant at 6 quai Antoine 1er, charges 40FF for 30 minutes of Internet access and opens 11 am to midnight (closed Monday).

Things to See & Do

Palais du Prince The changing of the guard takes place outside the Prince's Palace daily at 11.55 am. About 15 state apartments open to the public from 9.30 am to 6.20 pm daily, June to October. Entry is 30/15FF. Guided tours (35 minutes) in English leave every 15 or 20 minutes. A combined ticket

for entry to the **Musée des Souvenirs Napoléoniens** – a display of Napoleon's personal effects in the palace's south wing – is 40/20FF.

Musée Océanographique If you're going to go to one aquarium on your whole trip, the world-famous Oceanographic Museum, with its 90 sea-water tanks, should be it. The museum, which is on ave St Martin in Monaco Ville, opens 9 am to 7 pm daily (to 8 pm in July and August). The entry fee – brace yourself – is 60/30FF.

Cathédrale de Monaco The unspectacular 19th-century cathedral at 4 rue Colonel has one major draw – the grave of Grace Kelly (1929-1982). The Hollywood star married Prince Rainier III in 1956, but was killed in a car crash in 1982. The remains of other members of the royal family, buried in the church crypt since 1885, rest behind Princess Grace's tomb.

Jardin Exotique The steep slopes of the wonderful Jardin Exotique are home to some 7000 varieties of cacti and succulents from all over the world. The spectacular view is worth at least half the admission fee (40/19FF), which also gets you into the **Musée d'Anthropologie Préhistorique** and includes a half-hour guided visit to the **Grottes de l'Observatoire**, a system of caves 279 steps down the hillside. From the tourist office, take bus No 2 to the end of the line.

Places to Stay

Monaco's HI hostel, *Centre de la Jeunesse Princesse Stéphanie* (☎ 93 50 83 20, fax 93 25 29 82, *24 ave Prince Pierre*) is 120m uphill from the train station. You must be aged between 16 and 31 to stay here. Beds (70FF) are given out each morning on a first-come, first-served basis – numbered tickets are distributed around 8 am and registration begins at 11 am.

Hôtel Cosmopolite (☎ 93 30 16 95, fax 93 30 23 05, ✉ hotel-cosmopolite@monte-carlo.mc, 4 rue de la Turbie*) has decent singles/ doubles with shower for 282/314FF, while doubles without shower are 228FF.

The two-star *Hôtel de France* (☎ 93 30 24 64, fax 92 16 13 34, ✉ hotel-france@monte-carlo.mc, 6 rue de la Turbie*) has rooms with shower, toilet and TV starting at 350/390FF, including breakfast.

Places to Eat

There are a few cheap restaurants in La Condamine along rue de la Turbie. Lots of touristy restaurants of more or less the same quality can be found in the streets leading off from place du Palais. The flashy **Stars 'n' Bars** (☎ *93 50 95 95, 6 Quai Antoine 1er*) is a blues bar and restaurant with large portions of great salads (65FF to 75FF). It opens noon to 3 am daily (except Monday); the restaurant closes at midnight.

One of the few affordable restaurants specialising in Monégasque dishes is *U Cavagnetu* (☎ *93 30 35 80, 14 rue Comte Félix-Gastaldi*) where a lunchtime *menu* is 85FF and in the evening jumps to between 115FF and 140FF. Very traditional and cosy is the small **Restaurant de Trende** (☎ *93 30 37 72, 19 rue de la Turbie*). The decor is totally 1930s and the food absolutely Provençal.

Getting There & Away

There is no single bus station in Monaco – intercity buses leave from various points around the city.

The train station, which is part of the French SNCF network (☎ 0836 35 35 39), is on ave Prince Pierre. There are frequent trains to Menton (13FF, 10 minutes), Nice (42FF, 20 minutes) and Ventimiglia in Italy (21FF, 25 minutes).

Languedoc-Roussillon

Languedoc-Roussillon stretches in an arc along the coast from Provence to the Pyrenees. The plains of Bas Languedoc (Lower Languedoc) extend to the coast, where beaches are generally broad and sandy. The wine – Languedoc is France's largest wine-producing area – is red, robust and cheap. Inland are the rugged, sparsely populated mountains of Haut Languedoc (Upper Languedoc), a region of bare limestone plateaus and deep canyons.

Transport is frequent between cities on the plain but buses in the interior are about as rare as camels. For train information throughout the region, ring ☎ 0836 35 35 35.

MONTPELLIER
pop 228,000

Montpellier is one of the nation's fastest-growing cities. It's also one of the youngest, with students making up nearly a quarter of its population.

Montpellier hosts a popular theatre festival in June and a two-week international dance festival in June/July.

Orientation & Information

The Centre Historique has at its heart place de la Comédie, an enormous pedestrianised square. Westward from it sprawls a network of lanes between rue de la Loge and rue Grand Jean Moulin.

Montpellier's main tourist office (☎ 04 67 60 60 60) is at the south end of Esplanade Charles de Gaulle. It's open 9 am to 6.30 pm daily (reduced hours at weekends, later closing in summer).

To snack and surf, visit the Dimension 4 Cybercafé at 11 rue des Balances. It charges a bargain 35FF per hour.

Things to See

Musée Fabre, 39 blvd Bonne Nouvelle, has one of France's richest collections of French, Italian, Flemish and Dutch works from the 16th century onwards. **Musée Languedocien**, 7 rue Jacques Cœur, displays the region's archaeological finds. Both charge 20/10FF.

Beaches The closest beach is at **Palavas-les-Flots**, 12km south of the city. Take bus Nos 17 or 28.

Places to Stay

Camping *L'Oasis Palavasienne* (☎ 04 67 15 11 61, Route de Palavas), 4km south of town, open April to September, charges 106FF for two people and tent. Take bus No 17 to the Oasis stop.

Hostels A bed at the *Auberge de Jeunesse* (☎ 04 67 60 32 22, 2 Impasse de la Petite Corraterie), ideally located in the old city, costs 48FF. Take the tram from the bus or train station.

FRANCE

Hotels At *Hôtel des Touristes* (☎ *04 67 58 42 37, fax 04 67 92 61 37, 10 rue Baudin)*, just off place de la Comédie, there are roomy singles/doubles/triples with shower starting at 150/180/260FF.

Friendly *Hôtel des Étuves* (☎ *04 67 60 78 19, 24 rue des Étuves)* has singles/doubles with bathroom from 130/160FF. Close by, *Hôtel Majestic* (☎ *04 67 66 26 85, 4 rue du Cheval Blanc)* has basic singles/doubles for 110/140FF and doubles/triples/quads with bathroom for 200/300/350FF.

Places to Eat

Eating places abound in Montepellier's old quarter. Vegetarian *Tripti Kulai (20 rue Jacques Cœur)*, has *menus* for 69FF and 85FF. *La Tomate (6 rue Four des Flammes)* does great regional dishes, salads the size of a kitchen garden plus dessert for 50FF and *menus* from 50FF.

Entertainment

For a drink, try the bars flanking rue En-Gondeau, off rue Grand Jean Moulin. *Mash Disco Bar (5 rue de Girone)* is a popular student hangout.

Getting There & Away

Montpellier's bus station (☎ 04 67 92 01 43) is immediately south-west of the train station, itself 500m south of place de la Comédie.

Rail destinations include Paris' Gare de Lyon (379/452FF weekdays/weekends, four to five hours by TGV, about 10 a day), Carcassonne (113FF, 1¾ hours, at least 10 daily) and Nîmes (47FF, 30 minutes, more than 20 daily).

NÎMES

pop 135,000

Nîmes has some of Europe's best-preserved Roman buildings. **Les Arènes**, the amphitheatre (28/22FF), built around AD 100 to seat 24,000 spectators, is used to this day for theatre performances, music concerts and bullfights.

The rectangular **Maison Carrée**, a well-preserved 1st-century Roman temple, survived the centuries as a meeting hall, private residence, stable, church and archive.

Try to coincide with one of Nîmes' three wild *férias* (festivals) – Féria Primavera (Spring Festival) in February, Féria de Pentecôte (Whitsuntide Festival) in June, and the Féria des Vendanges coinciding with the grape harvest in September.

The main tourist office (☎ 04 66 67 29 11) is at 6 rue Auguste.

To check your email, log on at Netgames, right beside the Maison Carrée.

Places to Stay

At year-round *Camping Domaine de la Bastide* (☎ *04 66 38 09 21)*, 4km south of town on the D13, two people with tent pay 55FF. A dorm bed at the *Auberge de Jeunesse* (☎ *04 66 23 25 04)* on Chemin de la Cigale, 3.5km north-west of the train station, costs 52FF.

In the old city, friendly *Hôtel de la Maison Carrée* (☎ *04 66 67 32 89, 14 rue la Maison Carrée)* has singles/doubles/triples/quads with bathroom and TV for 180/220/330/350FF.

Places to Eat

La Truye qui Filhe (9 rue Fresque) blends self-service with a warm, homely atmosphere. Its *menu* is superb value at 52FF; open lunchtime only, closed August. *Le Portofino (3 rue Corneille)* serves great home-made pasta dishes.

Getting There & Away

Bus Nîmes' bus station is beside the train station. Destinations include Pont du Gard (35FF, 45 minutes, five to six daily), Avignon (65FF, 30 minutes, 10 or more daily) and Arles (34FF, 30 to 45 minutes, four to eight daily).

Train The train station is at the south-eastern end of ave Feuchères. Destinations include Paris' Gare de Lyon (366FF to 431FF, four hours by TGV, seven daily), Avignon (65FF, 30 minutes, 10 or more daily), Marseille (76FF, 1¼ hours, 12 daily) and Montpellier (66FF, 30 minutes, 15 or more daily).

AROUND NÎMES
Pont du Gard

The Roman general Agrippa slung the mighty Pont du Gard over the Gard River around 19 BC. You won't be alone; this three-tier aqueduct, 275m long and 49m high, receives over two million visitors a year.

There's a tourist kiosk on each bank and a brand new information centre on the left bank, set back from the river.

FRANCE

Buses from Avignon (26km) and Nîmes (23km) stop 1km north of the bridge.

CARCASSONNE
pop 45,000

From afar, the old walled city of Carcassonne looks like a fairy-tale medieval city. Once inside the fortified walls, however, the magic rubs off. Luring some 200,000 visitors in July and August alone, it can be a tourist hell in high summer. Purists may sniff at Carcassonne's 'medieval' Cité – whose impressive fortifications were extensively renovated and rebuilt in the 19th century – but what the heck; it *is* magic, one of France's greatest skylines.

The Ville Basse (lower town), a more modest stepsister to camp Cinderella up the hill, has cheaper eating places and accommodation and also merits a browse.

Orientation & Information
The Aude River separates the Ville Basse from the Cité on its hillock. The main tourist office (☎ 04 68 10 24 30) is in the Ville Basse opposite Square Gambetta.

Alerte Rouge (Red Alert), 73 rue Verdun, is a cybercafe where you can plug in 10 am to 1 am daily.

Things to See
The 1.7km-long double ramparts of **La Cité** (spectacularly floodlit at night) are spiked with 52 witches' hat towers. Within are narrow, medieval streets and the 12th-century **Château Comtal** (Count's Castle), visited by guided tour only (35/23FF). A 40-minute tour in English departs two or five times a day, according to season.

Places to Stay
Camping *Camping de la Cité* (☎ 04 68 25 11 77), on Route de St Hilaire about 3.5km south of the main tourist office, charges 75FF to 95FF for two people and tent. Take bus No 5 (hourly until 6.40 pm) from Square Gambetta to the route de Cazilhac stop.

Hostels In the heart of the Cité, the large, cheery *Auberge de Jeunesse* (☎ 04 68 25 23 16), on rue Vicomte Trencavel, has dorm beds for 70FF. There's a snack bar offering light meals and a great outside terrace.

The B&B at the *Centre International de Séjour* (☎ 04 68 11 17 00, 91 rue Aimé Ramon) in the Ville Basse, costs 68FF a night.

Hotels Handy for the train station is recommended *Hôtel Astoria* (☎ 04 68 25 31 38, 18 rue Tourtel) where basic singles/doubles cost 110/130FF (from 190FF with bathroom).

Pricing policy at welcoming *Relais du Square* (☎ 04 68 72 31 72, 51 rue du Pont Vieux) couldn't be simpler; large rooms, accommodating one to three people, cost 165FF, whatever their facilities. So in summer get there early if you want your own bathroom.

Places to Eat
In the Ville Basse, *Le Gargantua*, the restaurant of Relais du Square, has a weekday *menu* for 69FF and others from 128FF. *L'Italia* (*32 route Minervoise*), handy for the station, is a pizza-plus joint that also does takeaways. Next door is the more stylish *Restaurant Gil* with Catalan-influenced *menus* from 100FF.

Getting There & Away
The train station is at the northern end of pedestrianised rue Georges Clemenceau. Carcassonne is on the main line linking Toulouse (74FF, 50 minutes, 10 or more daily) with Béziers (70FF, 50 minutes, five daily) and Montpellier (113FF, 1½ hours, 10 or more daily).

TOULOUSE
pop 690,000

Toulouse, France's fourth largest city, is renowned for its high-tech industries, especially aerospace; local factories have built the Caravelle, Concorde and Airbus passenger planes and also the Ariane rocket. Like Montpellier, it's a youthful place with over 110,000 students – more than any other French provincial city.

Most older buildings in the city centre are in rose-red brick, earning the city its nickname *la ville rose* (the pink city).

Orientation
The heart of Toulouse is bounded to the east by blvd de Strasbourg and its continuation, blvd Lazare Carnot and, to the west, by the Garonne River. Its two main squares are place du Capitole and, 300m eastwards, place Wilson.

FRANCE

Information

The busy **tourist office** (☎ 05 61 11 02 22) is in the Donjon du Capitole, a 16th-century tower on Square Charles de Gaulle. It's open 9 am to 6 pm weekdays (shorter hours and a lunch break at weekends), October to April. The rest of the year it opens 9 am to 7 pm, Monday to Saturday, plus 10 am to 1 pm and 2 to 5 pm on Sunday.

The OTU student travel agency (☎ 05 61 12 18 88) at 60 rue du Taur can help with cheap travel options.

Online time at Résomania cybercafe, 85 rue Pargaminières, is 40FF an hour.

Major annual events include Festival Garonne with riverside music, dance and theatre (July), Musique d'Été with music of all definitions around town (July and August) and Jazz sur Son 31, an international jazz festival (October).

Things to See & Do

Cité de l'Espace Space City (☎ 05 62 71 48 71) is a truly mind-boggling interactive space museum and planetarium (69FF). To get there, take bus No 15 from Allées Jean Jaurès to the end of the line, from where it's a 600m walk.

The **Galerie Municipale du Château d'Eau** (15/10FF) is a world-class photographic gallery inside a 19th-century water tower at the western end of Pont Neuf, just across the Garonne River.

Musée des Augustins (12FF, free for students), 21 rue de Metz, has a superb collection of paintings and stone artefacts.

Within the magnificent Gothic **Église des Jacobins**, the remains of St Thomas Aquinas (1225-74), an early head of the Dominican order, are interred on the north side.

The **Basilique St Sernin** is France's largest and most complete Romanesque structure. It's topped by a magnificent eight-sided 13th-century **tower**.

Places to Stay

Camping Year-round, the oft-packed *Camping de Rupé* (☎ 05 61 70 07 35, 21 chemin du Pont de Rupé), 6km north-west of the train station, charges 72FF for two people and tent. Take bus No 59 (last departure at 7.25 pm) from place Jeanne d'Arc to the Rupé stop.

Hotels Avoid the cheap hotels near the train station; most are fairly sordid.

The exceptionally friendly *Hôtel Beauséjour* (☎/fax 05 61 62 77 59, 4 rue Caffarelli), off Allées Jean Jaurès, is great value. Basic rooms start at 110FF and doubles/triples with bathroom are 150/190FF. *Hôtel Splendid* (☎/fax 05 61 62 43 02) at No 13, has simple rooms from 90FF while singles/doubles/triples with bathroom are 130/150/210FF.

Places to Eat

Fill yourself at lunchtime when there are some amazing deals. Look around – many places have lunch *menus* for 50FF to 60FF. Unmissable and an essential Toulouse experience are the small, spartan, lunchtime-only *restaurants* on the 1st floor of Les Halles Victor Hugo covered market (great in itself for atmosphere and fresh produce). They serve up generous quantities of hearty fare for 55FF to 85FF.

Place St Georges is almost entirely taken over by cafe tables. Both blvd de Strasbourg and place du Capitole are lined with restaurants and cafes.

Restaurant Saveur Bio (22 rue Maurice Fonvieille) serves tasty vegetarian food, including a 40FF lunchtime mixed plate, a great value 60FF buffet and three 85FF *menus*.

Entertainment

For what's on where, pick up a copy of *Toulouse Hebdo* (3FF) or Intramuros (free from the tourist office). For life after dark, ask at the tourist office for its free listing *Toulouse By Night*.

Cafes around place St-Pierre beside the Garonne pull in a mainly young crowd. Nearby, the *Why Not Café* (5 rue Pargaminières) has a beautiful terrace while *Café des Artistes* (13 place de la Daurade) is an art-student hangout.

Two hot discos near the centre are *La Strada* (4 rue Gabriel Péri) and *L'Ubu* (16 rue St-Rome).

Getting There & Away

Bus Toulouse's bus station (☎ 05 61 61 67 67), just north of the train station, serves mainly regional destinations including Andorra (75FF, 4 hours, one to two daily). For longer distance travel, both Intercars (☎ 05 61 58 14 53) and

FRANCE

Eurolines (☎ 05 61 26 40 04) have offices in Toulouse.

Train The train station, Gare Matabiau, is on blvd Pierre Sémard, about 1km north-east of the city centre.

Destinations served by multiple daily direct trains include Bayonne (196FF, 3¾ hours), Bordeaux (165FF, 2½ hours) and Carcassonne (74FF, one hour).

The fare to Paris is 356FF by Corail (6½ hours, Gare d'Austerlitz) and 447FF by TGV (5½ hours, Gare Montparnasse via Bordeaux).

SNCF has an information and ticketing office at 5 rue Peyras.

Corsica (Corse)

Corsica, the most mountainous and geographically diverse of all the Mediterranean islands, has spent much of its history under foreign rule. From the 13th century it remained under Genoese control until the Corsicans, led by the extraordinary Pasquale Paoli, declared the island independent in 1755. But France took over in 1769 and has ruled Corsica since – except in 1794-96, when it was under English domination, and during the German and Italian occupation of 1940-43.

The island has 1000km of coastline, soaring granite mountains that stay snowcapped until July, a huge national park, flatland marshes, an uninhabited desert in the northwest and a 'continental divide' running down the middle of the island. It's a popular holiday destination for the French and increasingly for foreigner travellers who come for its exceptional hiking and diving opportunities.

AJACCIO (AIACCIU)
pop 52,880
The port city of Ajaccio, birthplace of Napoleon Bonaparte (1769-1821), is a great place to begin a visit to Corsica and a fine place for strolling. The many museums and statues dedicated to Bonaparte speak volumes – not about Napoleon himself, but about how the people of his native town prefer to think of him.

Orientation
Ajaccio's main street is cours Napoléon, which stretches from place du Général de Gaulle northward to the train station and beyond. The old city is south of place Foch. The ferry port is central to both the old and new town.

Information
Tourist Offices The tourist office (☎ 04 95 51 53 03, fax 04 95 51 53 01, ✉ ajaccio.tourisme@wanadoo.fr), 1 place Foch, is open 8 am to 6 pm daily (8 am to noon and 2 to 5 pm on Saturday). From July to mid-September it opens 8 am to 8.30 pm daily (9 am to 1 pm on Sunday). It closes at 7 pm from April to June and in October. The airport information counter (☎ 04 95 23 56 56) is open 6 am to 10.30 pm.

Money & Post The Banque de France is at 8 rue Sergent Casalonga. The main post office, which has an exchange service, is at 13 cours Napoléon.

Hiking The Maison d'Informations Randonnées (☎ 04 95 51 79 10, fax 04 95 21 88 17), 2 rue Major Lambroschini, provides information on the Parc Naturel Régional de la Corse and its hiking trails. It opens 8.30 am to 12.30 pm and 2 to 6 pm (5 pm on Friday; closed weekends).

Things to See & Do
Museums The house where Napoleon was born and raised, the **Maison Bonaparte** (☎ 04 95 21 43 89) on rue St Charles in the old city, was sacked by Corsican nationalists in 1793 but rebuilt later in the decade. It opens 9 am (10 am from October to April) to 11.45 am and 2 to 5.45 pm (4.45 pm from October to April), closed Sunday afternoon and Monday morning. Admission costs 22/15FF, including a guided tour in French.

The sombre **Salon Napoléonien** (☎ 04 95 21 90 15), on the 1st floor of the Hôtel de Ville at place Foch, exhibits memorabilia of the emperor. It opens 9 am to 11.45 am and 2 to 4.45 pm (closed weekends). Between 15 June and 15 September it opens until 5.45 pm and on Saturday. Entry is 5FF and visitors must be properly dressed.

The **Musée A Bandera** (☎ 04 95 51 07 34), 1 rue Général Lévie, deals with Corsican military history and costs 20/10FF. It's open 9 am to noon and 2 to 6 pm Monday to Saturday.

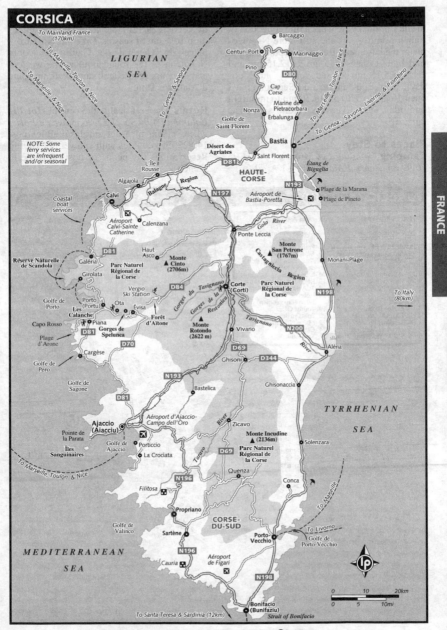

CORSICA

To Mainland France (170km)

To Marseille, Toulon & Nice

To Marseille & Nice

LIGURIAN SEA

To Genoa & Savona

To Marseille, Toulon & Nice

To Genoa, Savona, Livorno & Piombino

Barcaggio

Centuri-Port

Macinaggio

Pino

D80

Cap Corse

Nonza

Marine de Pietracorbara

Golfe de Saint-Florent

Erbalunga

Bastia

NOTE: Some ferry services are infrequent and/or seasonal

Désert des Agriates

D81²

Saint Florent

HAUTE-CORSE

Étang de Biguglia

L'Île Rousse

N193

Algajola

Balagne Region

N197

Aéroport de Bastia-Poretta

Plage de la Marana

Plage de Pineto

Coastal boat services

Calvi

Aéroport Calvi-Sainte Catherine

Calenzana

Golo River

Ponte Leccia

Monte San Petrone (1767m)

Castagniccia Region

Moriani-Plage

Réserve Naturelle de Scandola

D81

Galéria

Haut Asco

Monte Cinto (2706m)

Parc Naturel Régional de la Corse

Girolata

Vergio Ski Station

D84

Gorges du Tavignano

Corte (Corti)

Parc Naturel Régional de la Corse

N198

To Italy (80km)

Golfe de Porto

Porto (Portu)

Ota

Évisa

Forêt d'Aïtone

Gorges de la Restonica

Les Calanche

Piana

Monte Rotondo (2622 m)

Tavignano River

Vivario

N200

Capo Rosso

D81

Gorges de Spelunca

D70

Ghisoni

D69

D344

Aléria

Plage d'Arone

Cargèse

Golfe de Pero

N193

Bastelica

Ghisonaccia

TYRRHENIAN SEA

Golfe de Sagone

D81

Aéroport d'Ajaccio-Campo dell'Oro

River

Ajaccio (Aiacciu)

Zicavo

Monte Incudine (2136m)

Solenzara

Pointe de la Parata

Porticcio

Parc Naturel Régional de la Corse

Îles Sanguinaires

Golfe de Ajaccio

La Crociata

D69

Quenza

Conca

To Marseille, Toulon & Nice

Taravo River

N196

Filitosa

To Marseille

Propriano

CORSE-DU-SUD

MEDITERRANEAN SEA

Golfe de Valinco

Sartène

Porto-Vecchio

To Livorno

Golfe de Porto-Vecchio

N196

Cauria

Aéroport de Figari

N198

0   10   20km

0   5   10mi

Bonifacio (Bunifaziu)

To Santa Teresa & Sardinia (12km)

Strait of Bonifacio

Musée Fesch (☎ 04 95 21 48 17), 50-52 rue du Cardinal Fesch, has a fine collection of Italian primitive art and still more Napoleonia in the basement. Between September and mid-June it opens 9.15 am to 12.15 pm and 2.15 to 5.15 pm (closed Sunday and Monday); from mid-June to mid-September it's open 10 am to 5.30 pm (9.30 pm to midnight on Friday, closed Tuesday). Admission costs 25/15FF.

Places to Stay

Camping *Camping Les Mimosas* (☎ 04 95 20 99 85, Route d'Alata), open 1 April to 15 October, is about 3km north of the town centre. It costs 29/12FF per adult/tent site. Prices drop 10% out of season. Take bus No 4 from place du Général de Gaulle or cours Napoléon to the roundabout at the western end of cours Jean Nicoli, and walk up route d'Alata for 1km.

Hotels The best deal is the central *Hôtel le Colomba* (☎ 04 95 21 12 66, 8 ave de Paris) where clean, pleasant singles/doubles cost 140/200FF; doubles with shower are 180FF. Reservations (by phone or post) must be in French.

AJACCIO (AIACCIU)

PLACES TO STAY
1 Hôtel Kallisté
16 Hôtel Colomba

PLACES TO EAT
2 Monoprix Supermarket
7 Marché Municipal
21 La Pizza
23 U Scampi; Le Bosco
26 Café de Paris; Dolce Piacere

OTHER
3 Musée Fesch; Chapelle Impériale
4 Terminal Routier
5 Terminal Maritime
6 SNCM Ticketing Office
8 Main Post Office
9 Banque de France
10 Maison d'Information Randonnées
11 Préfecture
12 Musée A Bandera
13 Assemblée Régionale de la Corse
14 Laundrette
15 Relais des Gîtes Ruraux
17 TCA Boutique
18 Hôtel de Ville; Salon Napoléonien
19 Tourist Office
20 Boats to Îles Sanguinaires
22 Maison Bonaparte
24 Cathédrale
25 Taxi Rank

The friendly and efficiently run *Hôtel Kallisté* (☎ 04 95 51 34 45, fax 04 95 21 79 00, ✉ hotelkalliste@cyrnos.com, 51 cours Napoléon) has classy singles/doubles with shower and toilet for 240/280FF in low season; 320/360FF in June, July and September; and 380/430FF in August. Most rooms have both air-conditioning and mini-bar. Breakfast (38FF) is served in your room and there are English-speaking staff.

Places to Eat

Ajaccio's restaurants are mostly seasonal and mediocre. Cafes can be found along blvd du Roi Jérôme, quai Napoléon and the north side of place de Gaulle. *Café de Paris* and the neighbouring *Dolce Piacere*, on the west side of place du Général de Gaulle, both have giant terraces with good views of the sea and the square.

The best pizza (45FF to 59FF) is served at *La Pizza* (☎ 04 95 21 30 71, 2 rue des Anciens Fosées). Try the *quatre saisons* pizza, liberally sprinkled with chilli-laced olive oil.

The popular *U Scampi* (☎ 04 95 21 38 09, 11 rue Conventionnel Chiappe) serves fish and Corsican specialities – including octopus stew – on a flower-filled terrace. Lunch and dinner *menus* start at 85FF. It opens year-round (closed Friday night and Saturday lunchtime). *Le Bosco* (☎ 04 95 21 25 06) next door shares the same terrace as the Scampi and offers the same sort of *menus*, including a 195FF shellfish platter.

On Square Campinchi, the *Marché Municipal* open-air food market operates until 1 pm (closed Monday). There's a *Monoprix* supermarket opposite 40 cours Napoléon (closed Sunday).

Getting There & Away

Bus The Terminal Maritime et Routier on Quai l'Herminier houses Ajaccio's bus station. A dozen-odd companies have services, daily except Sunday and holidays, to Bastia (110FF, two a day), Bonifacio (110FF, two or three a day), Calvi (120FF, with a change at Ponte Leccia), Corte (60FF, two a day), Porto and Ota (70FF, 2½ hours, two a day), Sartène (70FF, two or three a day) and many small villages.

The bus station's information counter (☎ 04 95 51 55 45), which can provide schedules,

opens 7 am to 7 or 8 pm daily. Eurocorse (☎ 04 95 21 06 30 or 04 95 51 05 08), responsible for most of the long-distance lines, opens 8.30 am to 4 pm (closed Sunday).

Train The train station (☎ 04 95 23 11 03), blvd Sampiero (place de la Gare), is staffed 6.15 or 7.30 am to 6.30 pm daily (8 pm from late May to late September).

Ferry The Terminal Maritime is on quai l'Herminier next to the bus station. SNCM's ticketing office (☎ 04 95 29 66 99), across the street at 3 quai l'Herminier, opens 8 to 11.45 am and 2 to 6 pm (closed Saturday afternoon and Sunday). Ajaccio is connected to the mainland (Marseille, Toulon or Nice) by at least one daily ferry; the SNCM bureau in the ferry terminal opens two or three hours before the scheduled departure time.

Getting Around

Bus Local bus maps and timetables can be picked up at the TCA Boutique (☎ 04 95 51 43 23), 2 ave de Paris, open 8 am to noon and 2.30 to 6 pm (closed Sunday). Single tickets/carnet of 10 cost 7.50/58FF.

Taxi There's a taxi rank on place du Général de Gaulle, or call Radio Taxis Ajacciens (☎ 04 95 25 09 13).

Scooter The Hôtel Kallisté (see Places to Stay) rents scooters for 195/986FF per day/week. Prices drop between October and April.

BASTIA
pop 37,884

Bustling Bastia, Corsica's most important business and commercial centre, has rather an Italian feel to it. It was the seat of the Genoese governors of Corsica from the 15th century, when the *bastiglia* (fortress) from which the city derives its name was built. There's not all that much to see or do, but this pleasant place makes a good base for exploring **Cap Corse**, the wild, 40km-long peninsula to the north.

Orientation

The focal point of the town centre is 300m-long place St Nicolas. Bastia's main thoroughfares are the east-west ave Maréchal

FRANCE

Sébastiani, which links the ferry terminal with the train station, and the north-south blvd Paoli, a fashionable shopping street one block west of place St Nicolas.

Information
The tourist office (☎ 04 95 55 96 85, fax 04 95 55 96 00), place St Nicolas, opens 8 am to noon and 2 to 6 pm daily (closed on Sunday afternoon). In July and August it opens 8 am to 8 pm daily.

The Banque de France is at 2 bis cours Henri Pierangeli, half a block south of place St Nicolas. The main post office (with exchange services) is on the even-numbered side of ave Maréchal Sébastiani, a block west of place St Nicolas.

Things to See & Do
Bastia's **place St Nicolas**, a palm and plane tree-lined esplanade, was laid out in the late 19th century. The narrow streets and alleyways of **Terra Vecchia**, which is centred around place de l'Hôtel de Ville, lie just south. The 16th-century **Oratoire de l'Immaculée Conception** is opposite 3 rue Napoléon and was decorated in rich baroque style in the early 18th century.

The picturesque, horseshoe-shaped **Vieux Port** is between Terra Vecchia and the **Citadelle** and is probably the most colourful part of Bastia with its crumbling buildings and lively restaurants.

Places to Stay
Camping Small *Camping Les Orangers* (☎ *04 95 33 24 09*), open from April to mid-October, is about 4km north of Bastia in Miomo. Fees are 13/10/25FF for a tent site/ parking/per adult. Take the bus to Sisco from opposite the tourist office.

Hotels *Hôtel Le Riviera* (☎ *04 95 31 07 16, fax 04 95 34 17 39, 1 bis rue du Nouveau Port*) has doubles with shower and toilet for 200/250FF in the low/high season. Reception is on the 1st floor. The family-run *Hôtel Central* (☎ *04 95 31 71 12, fax 04 95 31 82 40, 3 rue Miot*) has basic singles/doubles with shower and toilet from 180/200FF and better-equipped rooms with TV from 230/250FF.

If your budget can handle it, the central, upmarket *Hôtel Napoléon* (☎ *04 95 31 60 30,*

fax 04 95 31 77 83, 43 blvd Paoli) has small but comfortable doubles equipped with all the amenities for around 290FF to 590FF. Prices rise early July to early September.

Places to Eat
Cafes and brasseries line the western side of place St Nicolas. More restaurants are on the north side of the Vieux Port, on quai des Martyrs de la Libération and on place de l'Hôtel de Ville in Terra Vecchia, where the *Café Pannini* sells great jumbo sandwiches.

Le Colomba (☎ *04 95 32 79 14, Vieux Port)* is a large place serving 32 varieties of pizza (39FF to 57FF). The Brazilian pizza is the house speciality.

A bustling *food market* is held at place de l'Hôtel de Ville in Terra Vecchio every morning except Monday, and there's a *Spar supermarket* on the corner of rue César Campinchi and rue Capanelle.

Getting There & Away
Air France's fifth-busiest airport, Aéroport de Bastia-Poretta (☎ 04 95 54 54 54) is 20km south of the town. Municipal buses to the airport (50FF) depart from the roundabout opposite the train station about an hour before each flight's departure (eight or nine times a day). The tourist office has timetables.

Bus Rapides Bleus (☎ 04 95 31 03 79), 1 ave Maréchal Sebastiani, has buses to Porto-Vecchio and Bonifacio (via Porto-Vecchio) and handles tickets for Eurocorse buses to Corte and Ajaccio. The afternoon bus to Calvi run by Les Beaux Voyages (☎ 04 95 65 02 10) leaves from outside the train station.

Train The train station (☎ 04 95 32 60 06) is at the northern end of ave Maréchal Sébastiani. See Getting Around at the start of the Corsica section for more information.

Ferry Bastia is linked by ferry to both France and Italy. The ferry terminal is at the eastern end of ave Pietri. SNCM's office (☎ 04 95 54 66 81) across the roundabout handles ferries to mainland France, and opens 8 to 11.45 am and 2 to 5.45 pm daily (closed Sunday, and Saturday afternoon). The SNCM counter in the ferry terminal opens two hours before each sailing.

For Italy, Mobylines' office (☎ 04 95 34 84 94, fax 04 95 32 17 94), 4 rue du Commandant Luce de Casabianca, is 200m north of place St Nicolas. It opens 8 am to noon and 2 to 6 pm (until noon Saturday; closed Sunday). Corsica Ferries (☎ 04 95 32 95 95, fax 04 95 32 14 71), 15 bis rue Chanoine Leschi, opens 8.30 am to noon and 2 to 6.30 pm (closed on Sunday).

The cheapest low season fare to/from the mainland is around 184FF for passengers under 25 years of age.

CALVI
pop 5177

Calvi, where Admiral Horatio Nelson lost his eye, serves both as a military town and a rather upmarket holiday resort. The Citadelle, garrisoned by a crack regiment of the French Foreign Legion, sits atop a promontory at the western end of a beautiful half-moon shaped bay.

Orientation

The Citadelle – also known as the Haute Ville (upper town) – is north-east of the port. blvd Wilson, the main thoroughfare in the Basse Ville (lower town), is up the hill from quai Landry and the marina.

Information

The tourist office (☎ 04 95 65 16 67, fax 04 95 65 14 09) near the marina opens 9 am to 1.30 pm and 2 to 7 pm (closed Saturday afternoon and Sunday).

The Crédit Lyonnais, blvd Wilson, opens until 4.30 pm (closed on weekends) and sports a handy ATM. The main post office is about 100m to the south on the same street.

Things to See & Do

The Citadelle, set atop an 80m-high granite promontory and enclosed by massive Genoese ramparts, affords great views of the surrounding area. The 13th-century Église St Jean Baptiste was rebuilt in 1570; inside is a miraculous ebony icon of Christ. West of the church, a marble plaque marks the site of the house where, according to local tradition, Christopher Columbus was born. The imposing 13th-century Palais des Gouverneurs (Governors' Palace) is above the entrance to the citadel. Now known as Caserne Sampiero, it serves as a barracks and mess hall for officers of the French Foreign Legion.

Beaches Calvi's 4km-long beach begins just south of the marina and stretches around the Golfe de Calvi. Other nice beaches, including one at **Algajola**, are west of town. The port and resort town of L'Île Rousse (Isula Rossa) east of Calvi is also endowed with a long, sandy beach with incredibly clean water.

Places to Stay

Camping & Studios Three-star *Camping Les Castors* (☎ 04 95 65 13 30, route de Pietra Maggiore), open from April to mid-October, is 800m south-east of the centre of town. Charges are 30/12FF per adult/tent site. Prices rise in July and August.

Farther south, the two-star *Camping La Clé des Champs* (☎ 04 95 65 00 86, route de Pietra Maggiore), open April to October, charges 25/10/12FF per adult/tent site/car.

Hostels The 130-bed *Auberge de Jeunesse BVJ Corsotel* (☎ 04 95 65 14 15, fax 04 95 65 33 72, ave de la République) opens from late March to October. Beds in two to eight-person rooms cost 120FF per person, including a filling breakfast.

Hotels *Hôtel du Centre* (☎ 04 95 65 02 01, 14 rue Alsace-Lorraine) is the cheapest place after the youth hostel. Open 1 June to 13 September, rooms with showers cost between 180FF and 250FF, depending on season.

Places to Eat

Calvi's attractive marina is lined with fairly pricey restaurants and cafes, but there are several budget places on rue Clemenceau, which runs parallel to blvd Wilson. *Best Of*, at the south end of the street, sells good sandwiches (around 25FF) including some with Corsican fillings.

Quai Landry's line-up of waterfront cafes and restaurants includes *Île de Beauté* (☎ 04 95 65 00 46), which specialises in fish and Corsican cuisine and has *menus* for 100FF and 150FF. *Callelu Restaurant* (☎ 04 95 65 22 18, quai Landry) does great fish dishes (110FF to 120FF).

The tiny *Marché Couvert* near Église Ste Marie Majeure opens 8 am to noon (closed

FRANCE

Sunday). The *Super U* supermarket is south of the town centre on ave Christophe Colomb.

Getting There & Away
Bus Buses to Bastia and Calenzana are run by Les Beaux Voyages (☎ 04 95 65 15 02), place de la Porteuse d'Eau. From mid-May to mid-October, an Autocars SAIB (☎ 04 95 26 13 70) bus serves the island's spectacular north-west coast from Calvi's Monument aux Morts (war memorial) to Galéria (1¼ hours) and Porto (three hours).

Train Calvi's train station (☎ 04 95 65 00 61), just off ave de la République, opens until 7.30 pm. From mid-April to mid-October, one-car shuttle trains *(navettes)* run by Tramways de la Balagne make 19 stops between Calvi and L'Île Rousse. The line is divided into three sectors and each costs one ticket (10FF).

Ferry SNCM ferries (☎ 04 95 65 01 38) sail to Calvi from Nice, Marseille and Toulon, but during winter they can be very infrequent. Between mid-May and mid-September, Corsica Ferries links Calvi with Genoa. You can also travel by the fast NGV *(Navire à Grande Vitesse)* boat back to the mainland.

PORTO (PORTU)
pop 460
The pleasant seaside town of Porto, nestled among huge outcrops of red granite and renowned for its sunsets, is an excellent base for exploring some of Corsica's natural wonders. **Les Calanche**, a spectacular mountain landscape of red and orange granite outcrops, towers above the azure waters of the Mediterranean slightly south of Porto along route D81. The **Gorges de Spelunca**, Corsica's most famous river gorge, stretches almost from the town of Ota, 5km east of Porto, to the town of Evisa, 22km away.

Orientation & Information
The marina is about 1.5km downhill from Porto's pharmacy – the local landmark – on the D81. The area, known as Vaïta, is spread out along the road linking the D81 to the marina. The Porto River just south of the marina is linked by an arched pedestrian bridge to a fragrant eucalyptus grove and a small, pebble beach.

The tourist office (☎ 04 95 26 10 55, fax 04 95 26 14 25) near the marina opens 9.30 am to noon and 2.30 to 6.30 pm Monday to Friday (9 am to 8 pm Monday to Saturday in July and August). Just around the corner is a Parc Naturel Régional de Corse office, open in summer. The only ATM between Ajaccio and Calvi is here at Porto.

Things to See & Do
A short trail leads to the 16th-century **Genoese tower** on the outcrop above the town. It's open 10 am and 6 pm, April to October (10FF).

From April to mid-October, the Compagnie des Promenades en Mer (☎ 04 95 26 15 16) runs **boat excursions** (170FF) to the fishing village of Girolata (passing by the Scandola Nature Reserve), and occasionally to Les Calanche in the evenings (80FF).

Places to Stay
Camping The friendly *Funtana al' Ora* (☎ 04 95 26 11 65), 2km east of Porto on the road to Évisa, charges 28FF per person and 11FF for a tent. It's open May to November.

Hostels In the nearby village of Ota, *Gîte d'Étape Chez Félix* (☎ 04 95 26 12 92) and *Gîte d'Étape Chez Marie* (☎ 04 95 26 11 37) both open year-round and charge 60FF for a dorm bed.

Hotels There are plenty of hotels in Vaïta and at the marina. One of the best deals is the *Hôtel du Golfe* (☎ 04 95 26 13 33) which charges 180FF for shower-equipped doubles with toilet (add 20FF per person in summer). *Hôtel Monte Rosso* (☎ 04 95 26 11 50, fax 04 95 26 12 30) nearby has doubles with shower and toilet for 240FF (300FF in July and August).

Getting There & Away
Autocars SAIB (☎ 04 95 22 41 99) has two buses a day linking Porto and nearby Ota with Ajaccio (2½ hours). From mid-May to mid-October a bus also goes from Porto to Calvi (three hours).

CORTE (CORTI)
pop 6329
When Pasquale Paoli led Corsica to independence in 1755, he made Corte, a fortified town at the geographical centre of the island,

the country's capital. To this day, the town remains a potent symbol of Corsican independence. In 1765, Paoli founded a national university there, but it was closed when his short-lived republic was taken over by France in 1769. The Università di Corsica Pasquale Paoli was reopened in 1981 and now has about 3000 students, making Corte the island's liveliest and least touristy town.

Ringed with mountains, snowcapped until as late as June, Corte is an excellent base for hiking; some of the island's highest peaks rise west of the town.

Information
The tourist office (☎ 04 95 46 26 70, fax 04 95 46 34 05, ✆ Corte.Tourisme@wanadoo.fr), La Citadelle, opens 9 am to noon and 2 to 5 pm (closed on weekends). In July and August it opens 9 am to 8 pm.

There are several banks with ATMs along the northern part of cours Paoli. The post office also has an ATM.

Things to See & Do
The **Citadelle**, built in the early 15th century and largely reconstructed during the 18th and 19th centuries, is perched on top of a hill, with the steep and twisted alleyways and streets of the **Ville Haute** and the Tavignanu and Restonica river valleys below.

The **Château** – the highest part, also known as the Nid d'Aigle (Eagle's Nest) – was built in 1419 by a Corsican nobleman and expanded by the French.

The impressive **Museu di a Corsica** (Musée de la Corse; ☎ 04 95 45 25 45) houses an outstanding exhibition on Corsican folk traditions, crafts, agriculture, economy and anthropology. It also has a small cinema and hosts temporary art and music exhibitions on the ground floor. Hours are 10 am to 8 pm in July and August; admission costs 35/20FF.

The **Gorges de la Restonica**, a deep valley cut through the mountains by the Restonica River, is a favourite with hikers. The river passes Corte, but some of the choicer trails begin about 16km south-west of town at the Bergeries Grotelle sheepfolds.

Places to Stay
Camping *Camping Alivetu* (☎ 04 95 46 11 09, *Faubourg de St Antoine*), open 1 April to

15 October, is just south of Pont Restonica. It charges 32/15FF per adult/tent site.

Hostels The quiet and very rural *Gîte d'Étape U Tavignanu* (☎ 04 95 46 16 85, fax 04 95 61 14 01, *chemin de Baliri*) opens all year and charges 80FF per person, including breakfast. From Pont Tavignanu (the first bridge on Allée du Neuf Septembre), walk westward along chemin de Baliri and follow the signs (almost 1km).

Hotels The 135-room *Hôtel HR* (☎ 04 95 45 11 11, fax 04 95 61 02 85, 6 allée du 9 Septembre) has clean, utilitarian rooms for one/two people for 135/250FF in low season and 135/400FF in high season.

Hôtel de la Poste (☎ 04 95 46 01 37, 2 place Padoue) has spacious, simple rooms with shower for between 140FF and 170FF (with toilet). The family-run *Hôtel du Nord et de L'Europe* (☎ 04 95 46 00 68, fax 04 95 47 40 72, 22 cours Paoli) accommodates students in winter but accepts travellers from April to October. Rooms with shower cost 180FF to 270FF.

Places to Eat
The *Restaurant Universitaire* on the main campus of the Università di Corsica on ave Jean Nicoli, in Résidence Pasquale Paoli, opens 11.30 am to 1.30 pm and 6.30 to 9 pm, October to June (closed at weekends). Meal tickets are sold 11 am to 1 pm.

Restaurant Le Bip's (☎ 04 95 46 06 26, 14 cours Paoli) is a nice cellar restaurant at the bottom of the flight of stairs 20m down the hill from *Brasserie Le Bip's* (☎ 04 95 46 04 48). The 80FF *menu* changes daily.

Corte's best restaurant is *U Museu* (☎ 04 95 61 08 36, Rampe Ribanella) which has an excellent range of tasty local fare. Unusual dishes include *civet de sanglier aux myrtes sauvages* (wild boar in myrtle).

There's a *Eurospar Supermarket* (7 ave Xavier Luciani) and a *Casino Supermarket* (allée du 9 Septembre).

Getting There & Away
Corte is on Eurocorse's Bastia-Ajaccio route, served by two buses a day in each direction (no Sunday service). The stop is at 3 ave Xavier Luciani where a schedule is posted.

FRANCE

The train station (☎ 04 95 46 00 97) is staffed 8 am to noon and 2 to 6.30 pm (closed on Sunday after 11 am, early September to late June).

BONIFACIO (BUNIFAZIU)
pop 2658

The famed **Citadelle** of Bonifacio sits 70m above the translucent waters of the Mediterranean, atop a long, narrow and easily defensible promontory – 'Corsica's Gibraltar'. On all sides, limestone cliffs sculpted by the wind and the waves drop almost vertically to the sea; the north side looks out on 1.6km-long Bonifacio Sound, at the eastern end of which is the **marina**. The southern ramparts afford views of the coast of Sardinia, 12km away.

Bonifacio was long associated with the Republic of Genoa. The local dialect – unintelligible to other Corsicans – is Genoese and many local traditions (including cooking methods) are Genoa-based.

Information

In the Citadelle, the tourist office (☎ 04 95 73 11 88, fax 04 95 73 14 97), 2 rue Fred Scamaroni, opens 9 am to 8 pm daily in summer and 9 am to noon and 2 to 6 pm Monday to Friday the rest of the year.

The Société Générale, outside the Citadelle at 38 rue St Érasme, has poor rates, charges 25FF commission (closed at weekends), and sports the only ATM in town. In summer, there are exchange bureaus along the marina.

Things to See & Do

Looking down the dramatic cliffs to the sea is a delight; the best views are to be had from **place du Marché** and from the walk west towards and around the cemetery. Don't miss **Porte de Gênes**, which is reached by a tiny 16th-century drawbridge, or the Romanesque **Église Ste Marie Majeure**, the oldest building in Bonifacio. **Rue des Deux Empereurs** (Street of the Two Emperors) is so-called because both Charles V and Napoleon slept there; look for the plaques at Nos 4 and 7. The **Foreign Legion Monument** east of the tourist office was brought back from Algeria in 1963 when that country won its independence.

Places to Stay

The olive-shaded **Camping Araguina** (☎ 04 95 73 02 96, ave Sylvère Bohn), open mid-March to October, is 400m north of the marina. It charges 31/34FF per person in the low/high season and 11FF for a tent.

The 32-room **Hôtel des Étrangers** (☎ 04 95 73 01 09, fax 04 95 73 16 97, ave Sylvère Bohn), 500m north of the marina, opens early April to October. Doubles with shower and toilet cost 220FF (280FF to 390FF from July to September).

In the Citadelle, the two-star **Hôtel Le Royal** (☎ 04 95 73 00 51, fax 04 95 73 04 68, rue Fred Scamaroni) has rooms for 225FF, 250FF and 290FF, October to April; prices double in July and August.

Places to Eat

In the Citadelle, **Pizzeria-Grill de la Poste** (☎ 04 95 73 13 31, 5 rue Fred Scamaroni) has Corsican dishes, pizza and pasta (45FF to 69FF). **Cantina Doria** (☎ 04 95 73 50 49, 27 rue Doria) is a neat, rustic hole-in-the-wall where you dine on wooden benches among old farming utensils. Their enormous soupe Corse (40FF) is enough for two people.

At the marina, **Super Marché Simoni** (93 quai Jérôme Comparetti) opens 8 am to 12.30 pm and 3.30 to 7.30 pm (closed Sunday afternoon). The **Coccinelle** supermarket next door has a fresh bakery counter.

Getting There & Away

Bus Eurocorse (☎ 04 95 70 13 83 in Porto-Vecchio) has buses to Ajaccio via Sartène. To Bastia, change buses at Porto-Vecchio, which is served by two buses daily (four in summer). All buses leave from the parking lot next to the Eurocorse kiosk at the east end of the marina.

Ferry Saremar (☎ 04 95 73 00 96) and Moby Lines (☎ 04 95 73 00) both offer a daily car and passenger ferry service year-round from Bonifacio's ferry port to Santa Teresa (50 minutes, two to seven per day).

Saremar charges 45/65FF for a one-way passenger fare in low/high season while Moby Lines charges 50/65FF. There's an additional 18.50FF port tax.

Greece

The first travel guide to Greece was written 1800 years ago by the Greek geographer and historian Pausanias, so the tourism industry isn't exactly in its infancy.

The country's enduring attraction is its archaeological sites; those who travel through Greece journey not only through the landscape but also through time, witnessing the legacy of Europe's greatest ages – the Mycenaean, Minoan, classical, Hellenistic and Byzantine.

You cannot wander far in Greece without stumbling across a broken column, a crumbling bastion or a tiny Byzantine church, each perhaps neglected and forgotten but still retaining an aura of former glory.

Its culture is a unique blend of East and West, inherited from the long period of Ottoman rule and apparent in its food, music and traditions. The mountainous countryside is a walker's paradise crisscrossed by age-old donkey tracks leading to stunning vistas.

The magnetism of Greece is also due to less tangible attributes – the dazzling clarity of the light, the floral aromas that permeate the air, the spirit of places – for there is hardly a grove, mountain or stream which is not sacred to a deity, and the ghosts of the past still linger.

Then again, many visitors come to Greece simply to get away from it all and relax in one of Europe's friendliest and safest countries.

Facts about Greece

HISTORY

Greece's strategic position at the crossroads of Europe and Asia has resulted in a long and turbulent history.

During the Bronze Age, which lasted from 3000 to 1200 BC in Greece, the advanced Cycladic, Minoan and Mycenaean civilisations flourished. The Mycenaeans were eventually swept aside by the Dorians in the 12th century BC. The next 400 years are often referred to as the 'age of darkness' (1200-800 BC), which sounds a bit unfair for

AT A GLANCE

Capital	Athens
Population	10.6 million
Official Language	Greek
Currency	1 drachma = 100 lepta
Time	GMT/UTC+0200
Country Phone Code ☏ 30	

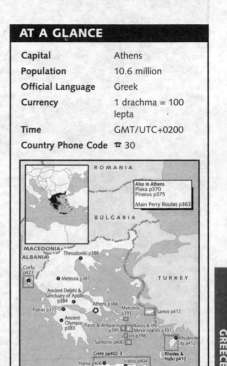

a period that saw the arrival of the Iron Age and emergence of geometric pottery. Homer's *Odyssey* and *Iliad* were composed at this time.

By 800 BC, when Homer's works were first written down, Greece was undergoing a cultural and military revival with the evolution of the city-states, the most powerful of which were Athens and Sparta. Greater Greece – Magna Graecia – was created, with southern Italy as an important component. The unified Greeks repelled the Persians twice, at Marathon (490 BC) and Salamis (480 BC). The period which followed was an unparalleled time of growth and prosperity, resulting in what is called the classical (or golden) age.

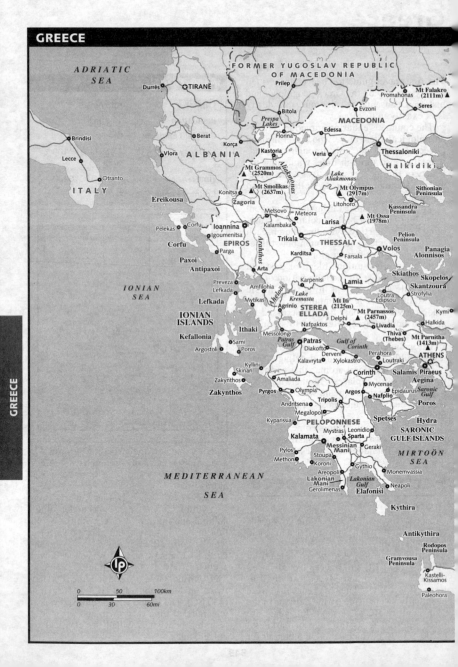

GREECE

BULGARIA

Smolyan

Edirne

TURKEY

BLACK SEA

İstanbul

İzmit

Drama Xanthi Komotini

THRACE

Didymotiho

Evros

Kavala

SEA OF MARMARA

Alexandroupolis

THRACIAN SEA

Bandırma

Bursa

Thasos

Gallipoli

Samothraki

Gökçeada

Çanakkale

Balıkesir

Karyes
Mt Athos
(2033m)
Athos
Peninsula

Myrina

Limnos

Kyra

NORTH-EASTERN
AEGEAN ISLANDS

SPORADES

Gioura
Piperi

Agios
Efstratios

Lesvos

Ayvalık

Mytilini

Uşak

Skyros

Psara

Inousses

Manisa

EVIA

AEGEAN
SEA

Chios

Çeşme

İzmir

TURKEY

Nea Styra

Chios

Karystos

Andros

Kuşadası

Aydın

Denizli

Gavrio

Samos

Kea

Gyaros

Tinos

Ikaria

Syros

Mykonos

Fourni
Islands

Agathonisi

Arki

Kythnos

Renia Delos

Patmos

Lipsi

Farmako

Milas

Naxos

Donousa

Leros

Paros

Naxos

Bodrum

Serifos
Sifnos
Kimolos

Antiparos

Amorgos

Kalymnos

Kos

Marmaris

Iraklia

Kos

Datça

Sikinos

Ios

Astypalea

Milos

Folegandros

Anafi

Sirna

Nisyros

Tilos

Symi

Rhodes

Thirasia

Halki

Alimia

Rhodes

CYCLADES

Santorini
(Thira)

DODECANESE
ISLANDS

Kattavia

Lindos

Kastellorizo

Saria

SEA OF CRETE

Karpathos

Pigadia

Hania

CRETE

Rethymno

Iraklio

Kassos

Hora
Sfakion

Mt Ida (2456m)

Agios
Nikolaos

Sitia

Matala

Ierapetra

Gavdos

The Golden Age

This is the period when the Parthenon was commissioned by Pericles, Sophocles wrote *Oedipus the King*, and Socrates taught young Athenians to think. At the same time, the Spartans were creating a military state. The golden age ended with the Peloponnesian War (431-404 BC) in which the militaristic Spartans defeated the Athenians. So embroiled were they in this war that they failed to notice the expansion of Macedonia under King Philip II, who easily conquered the war-weary city-states.

Philip's ambitions were surpassed by those of his son Alexander the Great, who marched triumphantly into Asia Minor, Egypt, Persia and what are now parts of Afghanistan and India. In 323 BC he met an untimely death at the age of 33, and his generals divided his empire between themselves.

Roman Rule & the Byzantine Empire

Roman incursions into Greece began in 205 BC, and by 146 BC Greece and Macedonia had become Roman provinces. After the subdivision of the Roman Empire into eastern and western empires in AD 395, Greece became part of the eastern (Byzantine) Empire, based at Constantinople.

In the centuries that followed, Venetians, Franks, Normans, Slavs, Persians, Arabs and, finally, Turks took their turns to chip away at the Byzantine Empire.

The Ottoman Empire & Independence

The end came in 1453, when Constantinople fell to the Turks. Most of Greece soon became part of the Ottoman Empire. Crete was not captured until 1670, leaving Corfu the only island never occupied by the Turks. By the 19th century the Ottoman Empire had become the 'sick man of Europe'. The Greeks, seeing nationalism sweep Europe, fought the War of Independence (1821-32). The great powers – Britain, France and Russia – intervened in 1827, and Ioannis Kapodistrias was elected the first Greek president.

Kapodistrias was assassinated in 1831 and the European powers stepped in again, declaring that Greece should become a monarchy. In January 1833 Otho of Bavaria was installed as king. His ambition, called the

Great Idea, was to unite all the lands of the Greek people to the Greek motherland. In 1862 he was peacefully ousted and the Greeks chose George I, a Danish prince, as king.

In WWI, Prime Minister Venizelos allied Greece with France and Britain. King Constantine (George's son), who was married to the Kaiser's sister Sophia, disputed this and left the country.

Smyrna & WWII

After the war, Venizelos resurrected the Great Idea. Underestimating the new-found power of Turkey under the leadership of Atatürk, he sent forces to occupy Smyrna (the present-day Turkish port of İzmir) which had a large Greek population. The army was repulsed and many Greeks were slaughtered. This led to a brutal population exchange between the two countries in 1923.

In 1930 George II, Constantine's son, was reinstated as king and he appointed the dictator General Metaxas as prime minister. Metaxas' grandiose ambition was to take the best from Greece's ancient and Byzantine past to create a Third Greek Civilisation. What he actually created was more a Greek version of the Third Reich. His chief claim to fame is his celebrated *okhi* (no) to Mussolini's request to allow Italian troops into Greece in 1940.

Despite Allied help, Greece fell to Germany in 1941. Resistance movements polarised into royalist and communist factions, leading to a bloody civil war which lasted until 1949. The country was left in chaos. More people were killed in the civil war than in WWII, and 250,000 people were homeless. The sense of despair became the trigger for a mass exodus. Almost a million Greeks headed off in search of a better life elsewhere, primarily to Australia, Canada and the USA. Villages – whole islands even – were abandoned as people gambled on a new start in cities such as Melbourne, Toronto, Chicago and New York. While some have drifted back, the majority have stayed away.

The Colonels

Continuing political instability led to the colonels' coup d'etat in 1967. King Constantine (son of King Paul, who succeeded George II) staged an unsuccessful counter coup, then fled the country. The colonels' junta then distinguished itself by inflicting appalling brutality, repression and political incompetence upon the people. In 1974 they attempted to assassinate Cyprus' leader, Archbishop Makarios. When Makarios escaped, the junta replaced him with the extremist Nikos Samson, prompting Turkey to occupy Northern Cyprus. The continued occupation remains one of the most contentious issues in Greek politics. The junta, now discredited, had little choice but to hand back power to civilians. In November 1974 a plebiscite voted against restoration of the monarchy, and Greece became a republic. An election brought the right-wing New Democracy (ND) party into power.

The Socialist 1980s

In 1981 Greece entered the then EC (European Community, now the EU). Andreas Papandreou's Panhellenic Socialist Movement (PASOK) won the next election, giving Greece its first socialist government. PASOK promised removal of US air bases and withdrawal from NATO, which Greece had joined in 1951. Instead Papandreou presided over seven years of rising unemployment and spiralling debt.

He was forced to step aside in 1989 while an unprecedented conservative and communist coalition took over to investigate a scandal involving the Bank of Crete. Papandreou and four ministers were ordered to stand trial, and the coalition ordered fresh elections for October 1990.

The 1990s

The elections brought New Democracy back to power with a majority of two. Tough economic reforms introduced by Prime Minister Konstantinos Mitsotakis soon made his government deeply unpopular. By late 1992, allegations began to emerge about the same sort of corruption and dirty tricks that had brought Papandreou unstuck. Mitsotakis himself was accused of having a secret horde of Minoan art, and he was forced to call an election in October 1993.

Greeks again turned to PASOK and the ailing Papandreou, who eventually had been cleared of all charges. He had little option but to continue with the austerity program begun by Mitsotakis, quickly making his government equally unpopular.

Papandreou was forced to step down in January 1996 after a lengthy spell in hospital. His departure produced a dramatic change of direction for PASOK, with the party abandoning its leftist policies and electing experienced economist and lawyer Costas Simitis as its new leader. Cashing in on his reputation as the Mr Clean of Greek politics, Simitis romped to a comfortable majority at a snap poll called in October 1996.

His government has focussed almost exclusively on the push for further integration with Europe, which has meant more tax reform and more austerity measures. While unpopular at the time, Simitis appears to have accomplished his objectives. At the time of writing, Greece was expecting to be admitted to the single European currency in mid-2001.

The electorate showed its appreciation of his achievements by handing Simitis a mandate for another four years at elections held in April 2000.

Foreign Policy

Greece's foreign policy is dominated by its extremely sensitive relationship with Turkey, its giant Muslim neighbour to the east.

At the time of writing, these two uneasy NATO partners appeared to be trying hard to be friends. It's a dramatic turnaround after years of mutual antagonism, when even the smallest incident brought talk of all-out war. The trigger was the massive earthquake that struck western Turkey in August 1999. Television images of the devastation prompted Greece to join the rescue effort. Its rescue teams were greeted like heroes, and grateful Turks were quick to return the favour following the earthquake that struck northern Athens a month later. The two have kept talking ever since.

The break-up of former Yugoslavia and the end of the Stalinist era in Albania have given Greece two new issues to worry about.

GEOGRAPHY

Greece consists of the southern tip of the Balkan peninsula and about 2000 islands, only 166 of which are inhabited. The land mass is 131,900 sq km and Greek territorial waters cover a further 400,000 sq km.

Most of the country is mountainous. The Pindos Mountains in Epiros are the southern extension of the Dinaric Alps, which run the length of former Yugoslavia. The range continues down through Central Greece and the Peloponnese, and re-emerges in the mountains of Crete. Less than a quarter of the country is suitable for agriculture.

CLIMATE

The climate is typically Mediterranean with mild, wet winters followed by very hot, dry summers.

There are regional variations. The mountains of Northern Greece have a climate similar to the Balkans, with freezing winters and very hot, humid summers, while the west coast and the Ionian Islands have the highest rainfall.

Mid-October is when the rains start in most areas, and the weather stays cold and wet until February – although there are also occasional winter days with clear blue skies and sunshine. Crete stays warm the longest – you can swim off its southern coast from mid-April to November.

ECOLOGY & ENVIRONMENT

Looking at the harsh, rocky landscapes today, it's hard to believe that in ancient times Greece was a fertile land with extensive forests. The change represents an ecological disaster on a massive scale. The main culprit has been the olive tree. In ancient times, native forest was cleared on a massive scale to make way for a tree whose fruit produced an oil that could be used for everything from lighting to lubrication. Much of the land cleared was hill country that proved unsuitable for olives. Without the surface roots of the native trees to bind it, the topsoil quickly disappeared. The ubiquitous goat has been another major contributor to ecological devastation.

The news from the Aegean Sea is both good and bad. According to EU findings, it is Europe's least polluted sea – apart from areas immediately surrounding major cities. Like the rest of the Mediterranean, it has been overfished.

FLORA & FAUNA
Flora

The variety of flora is unrivalled in Europe. The wild flowers are spectacular. They continue to thrive because much of the land is too poor for agriculture and has escaped the ravages of modern fertilisers. The best places to see the amazing variety are the mountains of Crete and the southern Peloponnese.

Fauna

You won't encounter many animals in the wild, mainly due to the macho habit of blasting to bits anything that moves. Wild boar are still found in reasonable numbers in the north and are a favourite target for hunters. Squirrels, rabbits, hares, foxes and weasels are all fairly common on the mainland; less common is the cute European suslik – a small ground squirrel. Reptiles are well represented. The snakes include several viper species, which are poisonous.

Bird-watchers have more chance of coming across something unusual than animal spotters. Lake Mikri Prespa in Macedonia has the richest colony of fish-eating birds in Europe, while the Dadia Forest Reserve in Thrace numbers such majestic birds as the golden eagle and the giant black vulture among its residents.

Endangered Species

The brown bear, Europe's largest land mammal, still survives in very small numbers in the mountains of Northern Greece, as does the grey wolf.

Europe's rarest mammal, the monk seal, was once very common in the Mediterranean, but is now on the brink of extinction in Europe. There are about 400 left in Europe, half of which live in Greece. There are about 40 in the Ionian Sea and the rest are found in the Aegean.

The waters around Zakynthos are home to the last large sea turtle colony in Europe, that of the loggerhead turtle (*Careta careta*). The Sea Turtle Protection Society of Greece (☎/fax 01-523 1342, ✉ stps@compulink .gr), Solomou 57, Athens 104 32, runs monitoring programs and is always looking for volunteers.

National Parks

Visitors who expect Greek national parks to provide facilities on a par with those in countries like Australia and the USA will be very disappointed. Although they all have refuges and some have marked hiking trails, Greek national parks have little else by way of facilities.

The most visited parks are Mt Parnitha, just north of Athens, and the Samaria Gorge on Crete. The others are Vikos-Aoös and Prespa national parks in Epiros; Mt Olympus on the border of Thessaly and Macedonia; and Parnassos and Iti national parks in Central Greece.

If you want to see wildlife, the place to go is the Dadia Forest Reserve in eastern Thrace.

There is also a National Marine Park off the coast of Alonnisos, and another around the Bay of Laganas area off Zakynthos.

GOVERNMENT & POLITICS

Since 1975, democratic Greece has been a parliamentary republic with a president as head of state. The president and parliament, which has 300 deputies, have joint legislative power. Prime Minister Simitis heads a 43-member cabinet.

ECONOMY

Traditionally, Greece has been an agricultural country, but the importance of agriculture in the economy is declining. Tourism is by far the biggest industry; shipping comes next.

POPULATION & PEOPLE

The population of Greece is 10.6 million. Women outnumber men by more than 200,000. Greece is now a largely urban society, with 68% of people living in cities. By far the largest is Athens, with more than 3.7 million in the greater Athens area – which includes Piraeus (171,000). Other major cities are Thessaloniki (750,000), Patras (153,300), Iraklio (127,600), Larisa (113,400) and Volos (110,000). Less than 15% of the population live on the islands. The most populous are Crete (537,000), Evia (209,100) and Corfu (107,592).

Contemporary Greeks are a mixture of all of the invaders who have occupied the country since ancient times. There are a number of distinct ethnic minorities – about 300,000 ethnic Turks in Thrace; about 100,000 Britons; about 5000 Jews; Vlach and Sarakatsani shepherds in Epiros; Roma (Gypsies); and lately, a growing number of Albanians.

ARTS

The arts have been integral to Greek life since ancient times. In summer, Greek dramas are staged in the ancient theatres where they were originally performed.

The visual arts follow the mainstream of modern European art, and traditional folk arts such as embroidery, weaving and tapestry continue.

The *bouzouki* is the most popular musical instrument, but each region has its own speciality of instruments and sounds. *Rembetika* music, with its themes of poverty and suffering, was banned by the junta, but is now enjoying a revival. Rembetika is the music of the working classes and has its roots in the sufferings of the refugees from Asia Minor in the 1920s. Songs are accompanied by bouzouki, guitar, violin and accordion.

The blind bard Homer composed the narrative poems *Odyssey* and *Iliad*. These are tales of the Trojan war and the return to Greece of Odysseus, King of Ithaki, linking together the legends sung by bards during the dark age. Plato was the most devoted pupil of Socrates, writing down every dialogue he could recall between Socrates, other philosophers and the youth of Athens. His most widely read work is the *Republic*, which argues that the perfect state could only be created with philosopher-rulers at the helm.

Nikos Kazantzakis, author of *Zorba the Greek* and numerous other novels, plays and poems, is the most famous of 20th-century Greek novelists. The Alexandrian, Constantine Cavafy (1863-1933), revolutionised Greek poetry by introducing a personal, conversational style. He is considered the TS Eliot of Greek literary verse. Poet George Seferis (1900-71) won the Nobel Prize for literature in 1963, and Olysseus Elytis (1911-96) won the same prize in 1979.

Theophilos (1866-1934) is famous for his primitive style of painting. The country's most famous painter was a young Cretan painter called Domenikos Theotokopoulos, who moved to Spain in 1577 and became known as the great El Greco.

SOCIETY & CONDUCT

Greece is steeped in traditional customs. Name days (celebrated instead of birthdays),

GREECE

weddings and funerals all have great significance. On someone's name day there is an open house and refreshments are served to well-wishers who stop by with gifts. Weddings are highly festive, with dancing, feasting and drinking sometimes continuing for days.

If you want to bare all, other than on a designated nude beach, remember that Greece is a conservative country, so take care not to offend the locals.

MYTHOLOGY

The myths are accounts of the gods whom the Greeks worshipped in ancient times. The main characters are the 12 principle deities, who lived on Mt Olympus – which the Greeks thought to be at the exact centre of the world.

The supreme deity was **Zeus**, who was also god of the heavens. He was the possessor of an astonishing libido and mythology is littered with his offspring. Zeus was married to his sister, **Hera**, who was the protector of women and the family. She was able to renew her virginity each year by bathing in a spring. She was the mother of **Ares**, the god of war, and **Hephaestus**, god of the forge.

Demeter was the goddess of earth and fertility, while the goddess of love (and lust) was the beautiful **Aphrodite**. The powerful goddess of wisdom and guardian of Athens was **Athena**, who is said to have been born (complete with helmet, armour and spear) from Zeus' head.

Poseidon, the brother of Zeus, was god of the sea and preferred his sumptuous palace in the depths of the Aegean to Mt Olympus. **Apollo**, god of the sun, was also worshipped as the god of music and song. His twin sister, **Artemis**, was the goddess of childbirth and the protector of suckling animals.

Hermes, messenger of the gods, completes the first XI – the gods whose position in the pantheon is agreed by everyone. The final berth is normally reserved for **Hestia**, goddess of the hearth. She was too virtuous for some, who promoted the fun-loving **Dionysos**, god of wine, in her place.

Other gods included **Hades**, god of the underworld; **Pan**, god of the shepherds; **Asclepius**, the god of healing; and **Eros**, the god of love.

Heroes such as **Heracles** and **Theseus** were elevated almost to the ranks of the gods. **Xena**, sadly, does not feature anywhere. The strapping warrior princess of TV fame is a script writer's invention – not a myth!

RELIGION

About 97% of Greeks nominally belong to the Greek Orthodox Church. The rest of the population is split between the Roman Catholic, Protestant, Evangelist, Jewish and Muslim faiths. While older Greeks and those in rural areas tend to be deeply religious, most young people are decidedly more interested in the secular.

LANGUAGE

Greeks are naturally delighted if you can speak a little of their language, but you don't need to be able to speak Greek to get around. English is almost a second language, especially with younger people. You'll also find many Greeks have lived abroad, usually in Australia or the USA, so even in remote villages there are invariably one or two people who can speak English.

See the Language chapter at the back of this book for pronunciation guidelines and useful Greek words and phrases.

Transliteration

Travellers in Greece will frequently encounter confusing and seemingly illogical English transliterations of Greek words. Transliteration is a knotty problem – there are six ways of rendering the vowel sound 'ee' in Greek, and two ways of rendering the 'o' sound and the 'e' sound.

This guidebook has merely attempted to be consistent within itself, not to solve this long-standing difficulty.

As a general rule, the Greek letter gamma (γ) appears as a 'g' rather than a 'y'; therefore it's *agios*, not *ayios*. The letter delta (δ) appears as 'd' rather than 'dh', so it's *domatia*, not *dhomatia*. The letter phi (φ) can be either 'f' or 'ph'. Here, we have used the general rule that classical names are spelt with a 'ph' and modern names with an 'f' – so it's Phaestos (not Festos), but Folegandros, not Pholegandros. Please bear with us if signs in Greek don't agree with our spelling. It's that sort of language.

Facts for the Visitor

HIGHLIGHTS
Islands
Many islands are overrun with visitors in summer. For tranquillity, try lesser-known islands such as Kassos, Sikinos and Kastellorizo. If you enjoy mountain walks, Naxos, Crete, Samothraki and Samos are all very rewarding. If you prefer the beach, try Paros.

Museums & Archaeological Sites
Greece has more ancient sites than any other country in Europe. It's worth seeking out some of the lesser lights where you won't have to contend with the crowds that pour through famous sites like the Acropolis, Delphi, Knossos and Olympia.

The leading museum is the National Archaeological Museum in Athens, which houses Heinrich Schliemann's finds from Mycenae and Minoan frescoes from Akrotiri on Santorini (Thira). The Thessaloniki Museum contains treasures from the graves of the Macedonian royal family, and the Iraklio Museum houses a vast collection from the Minoan sites of Crete.

Museums and sites are free for card carrying students and teachers from EU countries. An International Student Identification Card (ISIC) gets non-EU students a 50% discount.

Historic Towns
Two of Greece's most spectacular medieval cities are in the Peloponnese. The ghostly Byzantine city of Mystras, west of Sparta, clambers up the slopes of Mt Taygetos, its winding paths and stairways leading to deserted palaces and churches. In contrast, Byzantine Monemvasia is still inhabited, but equally dramatic and full of atmosphere.

There are some stunning towns on the islands. Rhodes is the finest surviving example of a fortified medieval town, while Naxos' *hora* (main village) is a maze of narrow, stepped alleyways of whitewashed Venetian houses, their tiny gardens ablaze with flowers.

SUGGESTED ITINERARIES
Depending on the length of your stay, you might want to see and do the following:

One day
  Spend the day in Athens seeing its museums and ancient sites.
One week
  Spend one day in Athens, two days in the Peloponnese visiting Nafplio/Mycenae and Olympia, and four days in the Cyclades.
Two weeks
  Spend two days in Athens, two days in the Peloponnese, and two days in Central Greece visiting Delphi and Meteora. Follow up with a week of island-hopping through the Cyclades.
One month
  Spend two days in Athens, two days in the Peloponnese; catch an overnight ferry from Patras to Corfu for two days; head to Ioannina and spend two days exploring the Zagorohoria villages of northern Epiros; spend three days travelling back to Athens vía Meteora and Delphi. Take a ferry from Piraeus to Chios and spend two weeks island-hopping back through the North-Eastern Aegean Islands, the Dodecanese and the Cyclades.

PLANNING
When to Go
Spring and autumn are the best times to visit. Winter is pretty much a dead loss, unless you're going to take advantage of the cheap skiing. The islands go into hibernation between late November and early April. Hotels and restaurants close up, and buses and ferries operate on drastically reduced schedules.

The cobwebs are dusted off in time for Easter, and conditions are perfect until the end of June. Everything is open, public transport operates normally, but the crowds have yet to arrive. From July until mid-September, it's on for young and old as northern Europe heads for the Mediterranean en masse. If you want to party, this is the time to go. The flip side is that everywhere is packed out, and rooms can be hard to find.

The pace slows down again by about mid-September, and conditions are ideal once more until the end of October.

Maps
Unless you are going to trek or drive, the free maps given out by tourist offices will probably suffice. The best motoring maps are

GREECE

produced by local company Road Editions, which also produces a good trekking series.

What to Bring

In summer, bring light cotton clothing, a sun hat and sunglasses; bring sunscreen too – it's expensive in Greece. In spring and autumn, you will need light jumpers (sweaters) and thicker ones for the evenings.

In winter, thick jumpers and a raincoat are essential. You will need to wear sturdy walking shoes for trekking in the country, and comfortable shoes are a better idea than sandals for walking around ancient sites. An alarm clock for catching early-morning ferries, a torch (flashlight) and a small daypack will also be useful.

TOURIST OFFICES

The Greek National Tourist Organisation (GNTO) is known as EOT in Greece. There is either an EOT office or a local tourist office in almost every town of consequence and on many islands. Most do no more than give out brochures and maps. Popular destinations have tourist police, who can often help in finding accommodation.

Local Tourist Offices

The EOT head office (☎ 01-321 0561/62, fax 325 2895, ☻ gnto@eexi.gr) is at Amerikis 2, Athens 105 64. Other tourist offices are listed through the book.

Tourist Offices Abroad

Australia (☎ 02-9241 1663) 51 Pitt St, Sydney, NSW 2000

Canada (☎ 416-968 2220) 1300 Bay St, Toronto, Ont M5R 3K8
(☎ 514-871 1535) 1233 Rue de la Montagne, Suite 101, Montreal, Que H3G 1Z2

France (☎ 01 42 60 65 75) 3 Ave de l'Opéra, Paris 75001

Germany (☎ 069-237 735) Neue Mainzer-strasse 22, 60311 Frankfurt
(☎ 089-222 035) Pacellistrasse 2, W 80333 Munich 2
(☎ 040-454 498) Abteistrasse 33, 20149 Hamburg 13
(☎ 030-217 6262) Wittenplatz 3A, 10789 Berlin 30

Italy (☎ 06-474 4249) Via L Bissolati 78-80, Rome 00187
(☎ 02-860 470) Piazza Diaz 1, 20123 Milan

Japan (☎ 03-3505 5911) Fukuda Bldg West, 5th Floor 2-11-3 Akasaka, Minato-ku, Tokyo 107

UK (☎ 020-7499 4976) 4 Conduit St, London W1R ODJ

USA (☎ 212-421 5777) Olympic Tower, 645 5th Ave, New York, NY 10022
(☎ 312-782 1084) Suite 160, 168 North Michigan Ave, Chicago, Illinois 60601
(☎ 213-626 6696) Suite 2198, 611 West 6th St, Los Angeles, California 92668

VISAS & DOCUMENTS

Nationals of Australia, Canada, EU countries, Israel, New Zealand and the USA are allowed to stay in Greece for up to three months without a visa. For longer stays, apply at a consulate abroad or at least 20 days in advance to the Aliens Bureau (☎ 01-770 5711), Leoforos Alexandros 173, Athens. Elsewhere in Greece, apply to the local police authority. Singapore nationals can stay in Greece for 14 days without a visa.

In the past, Greece has refused entry to those whose passport indicates that they have visited Turkish-occupied North Cyprus, though there are reports that this is less of a problem now. To be on the safe side, however, ask the North Cyprus immigration officials to stamp a piece of paper rather than your passport. If you enter North Cyprus from the Greek Republic of Cyprus, no exit stamp is put in your passport.

Driving Licence & Permits

Greece recognises all national driving licences, provided the licence has been held for at least one year. It also recognises an International Driving Permit, which should be obtained before you leave home.

Hostel Card

A Hostelling International (HI) card is of limited use in Greece. The only place you will be able to use it is at the Athens International Youth Hostel.

Student & Youth Cards

The most widely recognised (and thus the most useful) form of student ID is the International Student Identity Card (ISIC). Holders qualify for half-price admission to museums and ancient sites and for discounts at some budget hotels and hostels.

Seniors Cards
See the Senior Travellers section later in this chapter.

EMBASSIES & CONSULATES
Greek Embassies Abroad
Greece has diplomatic representation in the following countries:

Australia (☎ 02-6273 3011) 9 Turrana St, Yarralumla, Canberra, ACT 2600
Canada (☎ 613-238 6271) 76-80 Maclaren St, Ottawa, Ont K2P 0K6
France (☎ 01 47 23 72 28) 17 Rue Auguste Vaquerie, 75116 Paris
Germany (☎ 0228-83010) Koblenzer St 103, 5300 Bonn 2
Italy (☎ 06-854 9630) Via S Mercadante 36, Rome 00198
Japan (☎ 03-340 0871/72) 16-30 Nishi Azabu, 3-chome, Minato-ku, Tokyo 106
New Zealand (☎ 04-473 7775) 5-7 Willeston St, Wellington
South Africa (☎ 021-24 8161) Reserve Bank Bldg, St George's Rd, Cape Town
Turkey (☎ 312-446 5496) Ziya-ul-Rahman Caddesi 9-11, Gazi Osman Pasa 06700, Ankara
UK (☎ 020-7229 3850) 1A Holland Park, London W11 3TP
USA (☎ 202-667 3169) 2221 Massachusetts Ave NW, Washington, DC, 20008

Foreign Embassies in Greece
The following countries have diplomatic representation in Greece:

Australia (☎ 01-644 7303) Dimitriou Soutsou 37, Athens 115 21
Canada (☎ 01-725 4011) Genadiou 4, Athens 115 21
France (☎ 01-339 1000) Leoforos Vasilissis Sofias 7, Athens 106 71
Germany (☎ 01-728 5111) Dimitriou 3 & Karaoli, Kolonaki 106 75
Italy (☎ 01-361 7260) Sekeri 2, Athens 106 74
Japan (☎ 01-775 8101) Athens Tower, Leoforos Messogion 2-4, Athens 115 27
New Zealand (honorary consulate; ☎ 01-771 0112) Semitelou 9, Athens 115 28
South Africa (☎ 01-680 6645) Kifissias 60, Maroussi, Athens 151 25
Turkey (☎ 01-724 5915) Vasilissis Georgiou B 8, Athens 106 74
UK (☎ 01-723 6211) Ploutarhou 1, Athens 106 75
USA (☎ 01-721 2951) Leoforos Vasilissis Sofias 91, Athens 115 21

CUSTOMS
Duty-free allowances in Greece are the same as for other EU countries. Import regulations for medicines are strict; if you are taking medication, make sure you get a statement from your doctor before you leave home. It is illegal, for example, to take codeine into Greece. The export of antiques is prohibited. You can bring as much foreign currency as you like, but if you want to leave with more than US$1000 in foreign banknotes the money must be declared on entry. It is illegal to bring in more than 100,000 dr, and to leave with more than 20,000 dr.

MONEY
Banks will exchange all major currencies, in either cash or travellers cheques and also Eurocheques. Post offices charge less commission than banks, but won't cash travellers cheques.

All major credit cards are accepted, but only in larger establishments. You'll find ATMs everywhere, particularly in tourist areas.

Currency
The Greek unit of currency is the drachma (dr). Coins come in denominations of five, 10, 20, 50 and 100 dr, while banknotes come in 50, 100, 500, 1000, 5000 and 10,000 dr denominations.

Exchange Rates
country	unit		drachma
Australia	A$1	=	216.27 dr
Canada	C$1	=	251.62 dr
euro	€1	=	337.20 dr
France	1FF	=	51.41 dr
Germany	DM1	=	172.41 dr
Japan	¥100	=	343.81 dr
New Zealand	NZ$1	=	167.89 dr
UK	UK£1	=	560.86 dr
USA	US$1	=	373.22 dr

Costs
Greece is still a cheap country by European standards. A rock-bottom daily budget would be about 7000 dr, which would mean staying in hostels, self-catering and seldom taking buses or ferries. Allow at least 12,000 dr per day if you want your own room and plan to eat out regularly, as well as travelling and

GREECE

seeing the sites. If you want a real holiday – comfortable rooms and restaurants all the way – reckon on 20,000 dr per day.

Tipping & Bargaining

In restaurants the service charge is included on the bill, but it is the custom to leave a small tip – just round off the bill. Accommodation is nearly always negotiable outside peak season, especially if you are staying more than one night. Souvenir shops are another place where substantial savings can be made. Prices in other shops are normally clearly marked and non-negotiable.

Taxes & Refunds

Value-added tax (VAT) varies from 15% to 18%. A tax-rebate scheme applies at a restricted number of shops and stores; look for a Tax Free sign in the window. You must fill in a form at the shop and present it with the receipt at the airport on departure. A cheque will (hopefully) be sent to your home address.

POST & COMMUNICATIONS
Post

Postal rates for cards and small airmail letters (up to 20g) are 140 dr to EU destinations, and 170 dr elsewhere. The service is slow but reliable – five to eight days within Europe and about 10 days to the USA, Australia and New Zealand.

Post offices are usually open 7.30 am to 2 pm. In major cities they stay open until 8 pm and also open 7.30 am to 2 pm on Saturday. Do not wrap up a parcel until it has been inspected at the post office.

Mail can be sent poste restante to any main post office and is held for up to one month. Your surname should be underlined and you will need to show your passport when you collect your mail. Parcels are not delivered in Greece – they must be collected from a post office.

Telephone

The phone system is modern and efficient. All public phone boxes use phonecards, sold at OTE offices and *periptera* (kiosks). Four cards are available: 100 units (1000 dr), 200 units (1800 dr), 500 units (4200 dr) and 1000 units (8200 dr). The 'i' at the top left hand of the dialling panel on public phones brings up the operating instructions in English.

Direct-dial long-distance and international calls can also be made from public phones. Many countries participate in the Home Country Direct scheme, which allows you to access an operator in your home country for reverse-charge calls. A three-minute call to the USA costs 708 dr.

If you're calling Greece from abroad, the country code is ☎ 30. If you're making an international call from Greece, the international access code is ☎ 00.

Fax

Main city post offices have fax facilities.

Email & Internet Access

Greece was slow to embrace the wonders of the Internet, but is now striving to make up for lost time. Internet cafes are springing up everywhere, and are listed under the Information section for cities and islands where available.

There has also been a huge increase in the number of hotels and businesses using email, and addresses also have been listed where available.

INTERNET RESOURCES

There has also been a huge increase in the number of Web sites providing information about Greece.

A good place to start is the 500 Links to Greece listed at www.viking1.com/corfu/link.htm. It has links to a huge range of sites covering everything from accommodation to Zeus. One site that it doesn't provide a link to is www.greektravel.com, front door for an assortment of interesting sites by Matt Barrett.

The Greek Ministry of Culture has put together an excellent site at www.culture.gr with loads of information about museums and ancient sites.

BOOKS
Lonely Planet

Lonely Planet's *Greece* contains more comprehensive information on all the areas covered by this chapter as well as coverage of less-visited areas, particularly in Central and Northern Greece. *Greek Islands* is especially tailored for island-hoppers; if you want to concentrate on specific regions, pick up Lonely Planet's *Corfu & the Ionians* or *Crete* guides. In mid-2001, guides to *Athens* and *Rhodes & the Dodecanese* will be published.

Travel
The ancient Greek traveller Pausanias is acclaimed as the world's first travel writer. His *Guide to Greece* was written in the 2nd century AD and still makes fascinating reading.

History
A Traveller's History of Greece by Timothy Boatswain & Colin Nicholson is probably the best choice for the layperson who wants a good general reference.

General
There are numerous books to choose from if you want to get a feel for the country. *Zorba the Greek* by Nikos Kazantzakis may seem an obvious choice, but read it and you'll understand why it's the most popular of all Greek novels translated into English.

English writer Louis de Bernières has become almost a cult figure following the success of *Captain Corelli's Mandolin*, which tells the emotional story of a young Italian army officer sent to the island of Kefallonia during WWII.

Other modern authors to look out for include Anne Michaels *(Fugitive Pieces)* and Gillian Bouras *(A Foreign Wife* and *Aphrodite and the Others)*.

NEWSPAPERS & MAGAZINES
The main English-language newspaper is the daily *Athens News* (300 dr). The Athens edition of the *International Herald Tribune* (400 dr) carries an eight-page English translation of the popular Greek daily *Kathimerini*.

Foreign newspapers are widely available, although only between April and October in smaller resort areas.

RADIO & TV
There are plenty of radio stations to choose from, especially in Athens, but not many broadcast in English. If you have a short-wave radio, the best frequencies for the World Service are 618, 941 and 1507MHz.

The nine TV channels offer nine times as much rubbish as one channel. You'll find the occasional American action drama in English (with Greek subtitles). News junkies can get their fix with CNN and Euronews.

PHOTOGRAPHY
Major brands of film are widely available, but quite expensive outside major towns and on the islands.

Never photograph military installations or anything else with a sign forbidding pictures.

TIME
Greece is two hours ahead of GMT/UTC, and three hours ahead on daylight-saving time, which begins at 12.01 am on the last Sunday in March, when clocks are put forward one hour. Clocks are put back an hour at 12.01 am on the last Sunday in September.

Out of daylight-saving time, at noon in Greece it is also noon in Istanbul, 10 am in London, 2 am in San Francisco, 5 am in New York and Toronto, 8 pm in Sydney and 10 pm in Auckland. These times do not make allowance for daylight saving in the other countries.

LAUNDRY
Large towns and some islands have laundrettes. Most charge about 2000 dr to wash and dry a load, whether you do it yourself or leave it to them.

TOILETS
You'll find public toilets at all major bus and train stations, but they are seldom very pleasant. You will need to supply your own paper. In town, a cafe is the best bet, but the owner won't be impressed if you don't buy something.

Warning
Greek plumbing cannot handle toilet paper; always put it in the bin provided.

WOMEN TRAVELLERS
Many foreign women travel alone in Greece. Hassles occur, but they tend to be a nuisance rather than threatening. Violent offences are very rare. Women travelling alone in rural areas are usually treated with respect. In rural areas it's sensible to dress conservatively; it's perfectly OK to wear shorts, short skirts etc in touristy places.

GREECE

GAY & LESBIAN TRAVELLERS

In a country where the church still plays a major role in shaping society's views on issues such as sexuality, it should come as no surprise that homosexuality is generally frowned upon. Although there is no legislation against homosexual activity, it is wise to be discreet and to avoid open displays of togetherness.

This has not prevented Greece from becoming a popular destination for gay travellers. Athens has a busy gay scene, but most people head for the islands – Mykonos and Lesvos in particular. Paros, Rhodes, Santorini and Skiathos also have their share of gay hang-outs.

DISABLED TRAVELLERS

If mobility is a problem, the hard fact is that most hotels, museums and ancient sites are not wheelchair accessible. Lavinia Tours (☎ 031-23 2828), Egnatia 101 (PO Box 11106), Thessaloniki 541 10, has information for disabled people coming to Greece.

SENIOR TRAVELLERS

Elderly people are shown great respect in Greece. There are some good deals available for EU nationals. For starters, those over 60 qualify for a 50% discount on train travel plus five free journeys per year. Take your ID card or passport to a Greek Railways (OSE) office and you will be given a Senior Card. Pensioners also get a discount at museums and ancient sites.

DANGERS & ANNOYANCES

Greece has the lowest crime rate in Europe. Athens is developing a bad reputation for petty theft and scams, but elsewhere crimes are most likely to be committed by other travellers. Drug laws are very strict.

BUSINESS HOURS

Banks are open 8.30 am to 2.30 pm Monday to Thursday, to 2 pm Friday. Some city banks also open 3.30 to 6.30 pm and on Saturday morning. Shops are open 8 am to 1.30 pm and 5.30 to 8.30 pm on Tuesday, Thursday and Friday, and 8 am to 2.30 pm on Monday, Wednesday and Saturday, but these times are not always strictly adhered to. Periptera (kiosks) are open from early morning to midnight. All banks and shops, and most museums and archaeological sites, close during holidays.

PUBLIC HOLIDAYS & SPECIAL EVENTS

Public holidays are as follows:

New Year's Day 1 January
Epiphany 6 January
First Sunday in Lent February
Greek Independence Day 25 March
Good Friday/Easter Sunday March/April
Spring Festival/Labour Day 1 May
Feast of the Assumption 15 August
Okhi Day 28 October
Christmas Day 25 December
St Stephen's Day 26 December

Easter is Greece's most important festival, with candle-lit processions, feasting and firework displays. The Orthodox Easter is 50 days after the first Sunday in Lent.

A number of cultural festivals are also held during the summer months. The most important is the Athens Festival, when plays, operas, ballet and classical music concerts are staged at the Theatre of Herodes Atticus. The festival is held in conjunction with the Epidaurus Festival, which features ancient Greek dramas at the theatre at Epidaurus.

ACTIVITIES
Windsurfing

Sailboards are widely available for hire, priced from 2000 dr an hour. The top spots for windsurfing are Hrysi Akti on Paros, and Vasiliki on Lefkada – reputedly one of the best places in the world to learn.

Skiing

Greece offers some of the cheapest skiing in Europe. There are 16 resorts dotted around the mainland, most of them in the north. They have all the basic facilities and are a pleasant alternative to the glitzy resorts of northern Europe. What's more, there are no package tours. More information is available from the Hellenic Ski Federation (☎ 01-524 0057, fax 524 8821), PO Box 8037, Omonia, Athens 100 10, or from the EOT.

Hiking

The mountainous terrain is perfect for trekkers who want to get away from the crowds.

The popular routes are well marked and well maintained, including the E4 and E6 trans-European treks, which both end in Greece.

If you want someone to do the organising for you, Trekking Hellas (☎ 01-323 4548, fax 325 1474, ✉ trekking@compulink.gr), Filelli-non 7, Athens 105 57 offers a range of treks and other adventure activities throughout the country.

LANGUAGE COURSES

If you are serious about learning Greek, an intensive course at the start of your stay is a good way to go about it. Most of the courses are in Athens and are covered in the Athens section later in this chapter. More information about courses is available from EOT offices and Greek embassies.

WORK

Your best chance of finding work is to do the rounds of the tourist hotels and bars at the beginning of the season. The few jobs available are hotly contested, despite the menial work and dreadful pay. EU nationals don't need a work permit, but everyone else does.

ACCOMMODATION

There is a range of accommodation in Greece to suit every taste and pocket. All places to stay are subject to strict price controls set by the tourist police. By law, a notice must be displayed in every room, which states the category of the room and the price for each season. If you think you've been ripped off, contact the tourist police. Prices quoted in this book are for the high season, unless otherwise stated. Prices are about 40% cheaper between October and May.

Camping

Greece has almost 350 camping grounds. Prices vary according to facilities, but reckon on about 1500 dr per person and about 1200 dr for a small tent. Many sites close in winter. Freelance camping is officially forbidden, but often tolerated in remoter areas.

Refuges

Greece has 55 mountain refuges, which are listed in the booklet *Greece Mountain Refuges & Ski Centres*, available free of charge at EOT and EOS (Ellinikos Orivatikos Syndesmos, the Greek Alpine Club) offices.

Hostels

You'll find youth hostels in most major towns and on half a dozen islands. The only place affiliated to Hostelling International (HI) is the excellent Athens International Youth Hostel (☎ 01-523 4170).

Most other youth hostels in Greece are run by the Greek Youth Hostel Organisation (☎ 01-751 9530, fax 751 0616, ✉ y-hostels@ otenet.gr), Damareos 75, Athens 116 33. There are affiliated hostels in Athens, Olympia, Patras and Thessaloniki on the mainland, and on the islands of Crete and Santorini. Rates vary from 1600 dr to 2000 dr and you don't have to be a member *to* stay in any of them.

There is a XEN (YWCA) hostel for women in Athens.

Domatia

Domatia are the Greek equivalent of the British bed and breakfast, minus the breakfast. Once upon a time, domatia consisted of little more than spare rooms that families would rent out in summer to supplement their income. Nowadays many domatia are purpose-built appendages to the family house. Rates start at about 6000/9000 dr for singles/doubles.

Hotels

Hotels are classified as deluxe, A, B, C, D or E class. The ratings seldom seem to have much bearing on the price, but expect to pay 6000/9000 dr for singles/doubles in D and E class, and from 10,000/15,000 dr in a decent C-class place with private bathroom.

Some places are classified as pensions and rated differently. Both are allowed to levy a 10% surcharge for stays of less than three nights, but they seldom do. It normally works the other way – you can bargain if you're staying more than one night.

Apartments

Self-contained family apartments are available in some hotels and domatia, particularly on the islands.

Traditional Settlements

Traditional settlements are old buildings of architectural merit that have been converted

GREECE

into tourist accommodation. They are terrific places to stay if you can afford 10,000 dr to 15,000 dr for a double.

Houses & Flats

For long-term rental accommodation in Athens, check the advertisements in the English-language newspapers. In rural areas, ask around in *tavernas*.

FOOD

If Greek food conjures up an uninspiring vision of lukewarm *moussaka* collapsing into a plate of olive oil, take heart – there's a lot more on offer.

Snacks

Greece has a great range of fast-food options for the inveterate snacker. Foremost among them are the *gyros* and the *souvlaki*. The gyros is a giant skewer laden with seasoned meat that grills slowly as it rotates, the meat being steadily trimmed from the outside. Souvlaki are small, individual kebabs. Both are served wrapped in pitta bread with salad and lashings of *tzatziki* (a yogurt, cucumber and garlic dip). Other snacks are pretzel rings, *spanakopitta* (spinach and cheese pie) and *tyropitta* (cheese pie). Dried fruits and nuts are also very popular.

Starters

Greece is famous for its appetisers, known as *mezedes* (literally, 'tastes'). Standards include tzatziki, *melitzanosalata* (aubergine dip), *taramasalata* (fish-roe dip), *dolmades* (stuffed vine leaves), *fasolia* (beans) and *oktapodi* (octopus). A selection of three or four represents a good meal and can be a good option for vegetarians. Most dishes cost between 600 dr and 1000 dr.

Main Dishes

You'll find moussaka (layers of aubergine and mince, topped with bechamel sauce and baked) on every menu, alongside a number of other taverna staples. They include *moschari* (oven-baked veal and potatoes), *keftedes* (meatballs), *stifado* (meat stew), *pastitsio* (macaroni with mince meat and bechamel sauce, baked) and *yemista* (either tomatoes or green peppers stuffed with mince meat and

rice). Most main courses cost between 1000 dr and 1600 dr.

The most popular fish are *barbouni* (red mullet) and *ksifias* (swordfish), but they don't come cheap. Prices start at about 3000 dr for a serve. *Kalamaria* (fried squid) is readily available and cheap at about 1400 dr.

Fortunately for vegetarians, salad is a mainstay of the Greek diet. The most popular is *horiatiki salata*, normally listed on English menus as Greek or country salad. It's a mixed salad of cucumbers, peppers, onions, olives, tomatoes and feta (sheep or goat's-milk white cheese).

Desserts

Turkish in origin, most desserts are variations on pastry soaked in honey. Popular ones include *baklava* (thin layers of pastry filled with honey and nuts) and *kadaifi* (shredded wheat soaked in honey).

Restaurants

There are several varieties of restaurants. An *estiatoria* is a straightforward restaurant with a printed menu. A taverna is often cheaper and more typically Greek, and you'll probably be invited to peer into the pots. A *psistaria* specialises in charcoal-grilled dishes. *Ouzeria* (ouzo bars) often have such a good range of mezedes that they can be regarded as eating places.

Kafeneia

Kafeneia are the smoke-filled cafes where men gather to drink coffee, play backgammon and cards and engage in heated political discussion. They are a bastion of male chauvinism. Female tourists tend to avoid them, but those who venture in invariably find they are treated courteously.

Self-Catering

Buying and preparing your own food is easy in Greece. Every town of consequence has a supermarket, as well as fruit and vegetable shops.

DRINKS
Nonalcoholic Drinks

Bottled mineral water is cheap and available everywhere, as are soft drinks and packaged juices.

Alcohol

Greece is traditionally a wine-drinking society. If you're spending a bit of time in the country, it's worth acquiring a taste for retsina (resinated wine). The best (and worst) flows straight from the barrel in the main production areas of Attica and Central Greece. Tavernas charge from 800 dr to 1500 dr for 1L. Retsina is available by the bottle everywhere. Greece also produces a large range of regular wines from traditional grape varieties.

Mythos and Alpha are two Greek beers to look out for. Amstel is the most popular of several northern European beers produced locally under licence. Expect to pay about 200 dr in a supermarket, or 500 dr in a restaurant. The most popular aperitif is the aniseed-flavoured ouzo.

ENTERTAINMENT

The busy nightlife is a major attraction for many travellers. Nowhere is the pace more frenetic than on the islands in high season; Ios and Paros are famous for their raging discos and bars. Discos abound in all resort areas. If you enjoy theatre and classical music, Athens and Thessaloniki are the places to be.

Greeks are great film-goers. Cinemas show films in the original language (usually English) with Greek subtitles.

SPECTATOR SPORTS

Greek men are sports mad. Basketball has almost overtaken soccer as the main attraction. If you happen to be eating in a taverna on a night when a big match is being televised, expect indifferent service.

SHOPPING

Greece produces a vast array of handicrafts, including woollen rugs, ceramics, leather work, hand-woven woollen shoulder bags, embroidery, copperware and carved-wood products.

Getting There & Away

AIR

There are no less than 16 international airports, but most of them handle only summer charter flights to the islands. Athens handles the vast majority of international flights, including all intercontinental flights. Athens has regular scheduled flights to all the European capitals, and Thessaloniki is also well served.

Most flights are with the national carrier, Olympic Airways, or the flag carrier of the country concerned.

Europe

Flying is the fastest, easiest and cheapest way of getting to Greece from northern Europe. What's more, scheduled flights are so competitively priced that it's hardly worth hunting around for charter cheapies.

Olympic Airways, British Airways and Virgin Atlantic all offer 30-day return tickets from London for about UK£240 (midweek departures) in high season, and Olympic and British Airways offer returns to Thessaloniki for about UK£225.

At the time of writing, the cheapest fares were being offered by EasyJet (☎ 0870 600 0000), which was offering London (Luton) to Athens from UK£69 one way.

Charter flights from London to Athens are readily available for UK£99/189 one way/return in high season, dropping to UK£79/129 in low season. Fares are about UK£109/209 to most island destinations in high season. Similar deals are available from charter operators throughout Europe.

Athens is a good place to buy cheap air tickets. Examples of one-way fares include London (25,000 dr), Madrid (73,000 dr), Paris (55,000 dr) and Rome (42,000 dr). Remember to add the international departure tax of 6800 dr.

The USA & Canada

Olympic Airways has daily flights to Athens from New York and up to three a week from Boston. Delta also has daily flights from New York. Apex fares range from US$960 to US$1550. It's worth shopping around for cheaper deals from the major European airlines.

You should be able to get to Athens from Toronto and Montreal for about C$1150 or from Vancouver for C$1500. Olympic has up to five flights a week to Athens from Toronto via Montreal.

Australia

Olympic flies to Athens twice a week from Sydney via Melbourne. Fares range from A$1595 to A$2400.

LAND
Northern Europe

Overland travel between northern Europe and Greece is virtually a thing of the past. Buses and trains can't compete with cheap air fares, and the turmoil in the former Yugoslavia has cut the shortest overland route. All bus and train services now go via Italy and take the ferries over to Greece.

Train Unless you have a Eurail pass, travelling to Greece by train is prohibitively expensive. Greece is part of the Eurail network, and passes are valid on ferries operated by Adriatica di Navigazione and Hellenic Mediterranean Lines from Brindisi to Corfu, Igoumenitsa and Patras.

Neighbouring Countries

Bus The Hellenic Railways Organisation (OSE) has buses from Athens to Istanbul (23,000 dr, 22 hours) at 11 pm every day, and to Tirana (12,600 dr, 21 hours) at 8.30 am every day except Sunday.

Train There are daily trains between Athens and Istanbul for 20,000 dr, leaving Athens at 11.15 pm. The trip takes 23 hours.

Car & Motorcycle The crossing points into Turkey are at Kipi and Kastanies, the crossings into the Former Yugoslav Republic of Macedonia (FYROM) are at Evzoni and Niki, and the Bulgarian crossing is at Promahonas. All are open 24 hours a day. The crossing points to Albania are at Kakavia and Krystallopigi.

Hitching If you want to hitchhike to Turkey, look for a through-ride from Alexandroupolis because you cannot hitchhike across the border.

SEA
Italy

The most popular crossing is from Brindisi to Patras (18 hours), via Corfu (nine hours) and Igoumenitsa (10 hours). There are numerous services. Deck-class fares start at about 7500

dr one way in low season, 12,000 dr in high season. Eurail pass-holders can travel free with both Adriatica di Navigazione and Hellenic Mediterranean. You still need to make a reservation and pay port taxes – L8000 in Italy and 1800 dr in Greece.

There are also ferries to Patras from Ancona, Bari, Trieste and Venice, stopping at either Corfu or Igoumenitsa on the way. In summer there are also ferries from Bari and Brindisi to Kefallonia.

Turkey

There are five regular ferry services between the Greek islands and Turkey: Lesvos-Ayvalık, Chios-Çeşme, Samos-Kuşadası, Kos-Bodrum and Rhodes-Marmaris. All are daily services in summer, dropping to weekly in winter. Tickets must be bought a day in advance and you will be asked to hand over your passport. It will be returned on the boat.

Cyprus & Israel

Salamis Lines and Poseidon Lines operate services from Piraeus to the Israeli port of Haifa, via Rhodes and Lemessos (formerly Limassol) on Cyprus. Deck-class fares from Piraeus are 19,000 dr to Lemessos and 28,000 dr to Haifa. Given the amount of time you'll be spending on board, it's worth getting a cabin – 34,000 dr to Lemessos and 47,000 dr to Haifa. Port tax costs an additional 3000 dr.

Students and travellers aged under 30 qualify for a 20% discount on these fares.

LEAVING GREECE

An airport tax of 6800 dr for international flights is included in air fares. Port taxes are 1800 dr to Italy and 3000 dr to Turkey, Cyprus and Israel.

Getting Around

AIR

Most domestic flights are operated by Olympic Airways and its offshoot, Olympic Aviation. They offer a busy schedule in summer with flights from Athens to 25 islands and a range of mainland cities. Sample fares include Athens-Iraklio for 21,400 dr, Athens-Rhodes for 23,400 dr and Athens-Santorini for 22,200 dr. There are also flights from Thessaloniki to the islands. It is advisable to book at least two weeks in advance, especially in summer. Services to the islands are fairly skeletal in winter. Aegean Air, Air Greece and Cronus Airlines provide competition on a few major routes. Air Manos specialises in package deals to the islands.

These fares include the 3400 dr tax on domestic flights, paid when you buy your ticket.

BUS

Buses are the most popular form of public transport. They are comfortable, they run on time and there are frequent services on all the major routes. Almost every town on the mainland (except in Thrace) has at least one bus a day to Athens. Local companies can get you to all but the remotest villages. Reckon on paying about 1200 dr per hour of journey time. Sample fares from Athens include 8700 dr to Thessaloniki (7½ hours) and 3650 dr to Patras (three hours). Tickets should be bought at least an hour in advance to ensure a seat.

Major islands also have comprehensive local bus networks. In fact, every island with a road has a service of some sort, but they tend to operate at the whim of the driver.

TRAIN

Trains are generally looked on as a poor alternative to bus travel. The main problem is that there are only two main lines: to Thessaloniki and Alexandroupolis in the north and to the Peloponnese. In addition there are a number of branch lines, such as Pyrgos-Olympia and the spectacular Diakofto-Kalavryta mountain railway.

If there are trains going in your direction, they are a good way to travel. Be aware that there are two distinct levels of service: the painfully slow, dilapidated trains that stop at all stations and the faster, modern intercity trains.

The slow trains represent the cheapest form of transport. It may take five hours to crawl from Athens to Patras, but the 2nd-class fare is only 1580 dr. Intercity trains do the trip in just over three hours for 2980 dr – still cheaper than the bus.

Inter-Rail and Eurail passes are valid in Greece, but you still need to make a reservation. In summer, make reservations at least two days in advance.

CAR & MOTORCYCLE

Car is a great way to explore areas that are off the beaten track. Bear in mind that roads in remote regions are often poorly maintained. You'll need a good road map.

You can bring a vehicle into Greece for four months without a carnet – only a Green Card (international third-party insurance) is required.

Average prices for fuel are 255 dr per litre for super, 240 dr for unleaded and 170 dr for diesel.

Most islands are served by car ferries, but they are expensive. Sample fares for small cars from Piraeus include 19,600 dr to Crete and 24,000 dr to Rhodes.

Road Rules

Greek motorists are famous for ignoring the road rules, which is probably why the country has one of the highest road fatality rates in Europe. No casual observer would ever guess that it is compulsory to wear seat belts in the front seats of vehicles, nor that it is compulsory to wear a crash helmet on motorcycles of more than 50cc – always insist on a helmet when renting a motorcycle.

The speed limit for cars is 120km/h on toll roads, 90km/h outside built-up areas and 50km/h in built-up areas. For motorcycles, the speed limit outside built-up areas is 70km/h. Speeding fines start at 30,000 dr.

Drink-driving laws are strict – a blood alcohol content of 0.05% incurs a penalty and over 0.08% is a criminal offence.

Rental

Car hire is expensive, especially from the multinational hire companies. High-season weekly rates with unlimited mileage start at about 110,000 dr for the smallest models, dropping to 90,000 dr in winter – and that's without tax and extras.

You can generally do much better with local companies. Their advertised rates are 25% lower and they're often willing to bargain.

Mopeds, however, are cheap and available everywhere. Most places charge about 3000 dr per day.

Warning If you plan to hire a motorcycle or moped, check that your travel insurance covers you for injury resulting from motorbike accidents. Many policies don't.

Lonely Planet receives a lot of letters complaining about companies hiring out poorly maintained machines. Most insurance policies won't pay out for injuries caused by defective machines.

Automobile Association

The Greek automobile club, ELPA, offers reciprocal services to members of other national motoring associations. If your vehicle breaks down, dial ☎ 104.

BICYCLE

People do cycle in Greece, but you'll need strong leg muscles to tackle the mountainous terrain. You can hire bicycles, but they are not nearly as widely available as cars and motorcycles. Prices range from about 1000 dr to 3000 dr. Bicycles are carried free on most ferries.

HITCHING

The further you are from a city, the easier hitching becomes. Getting out of major cities can be hard work, and Athens is notoriously difficult. In remote areas, people may stop to offer a lift even if you aren't hitching.

BOAT
Ferry

Every island has a ferry service of some sort. They come in all shapes and sizes, from the state-of-the-art 'superferries' that run on the major routes to the ageing open ferries that operate local services to outlying islands.

The hub of the vast ferry network is Piraeus, the main port of Athens. It has ferries to the Cyclades, Crete, the Dodecanese, the Saronic Gulf Islands and the North-Eastern Aegean Islands. Patras is the main port for ferries to the Ionian Islands, while Volos and Agios Konstantinos are the ports for the Sporades.

Some of the smaller islands are virtually inaccessible in winter, when schedules are cut back to a minimum. Services start to pick up in April and are running at full steam from June to September.

Fares are fixed by the government. The small differences in price you may find between ticket agencies are the result of some agencies sacrificing part of their designated commission to qualify as a 'discount service'. The discount seldom amounts to more than 50 dr. Tickets can be bought at the last minute from quayside tables set up next to the boats. Prices are the same, contrary to what you will be told by agencies.

Unless you specify otherwise, you will automatically be sold deck class, which is the cheapest fare. Sample fares from Piraeus include 4800 dr to Mykonos and 5900 dr to Santorini (Thira).

Hydrofoil

Hydrofoils offer a faster alternative to ferries on some routes, particularly to islands close to the mainland. They take half the time, but cost twice as much. Most routes operate only during high season.

Catamaran

High-speed catamarans have rapidly become an important part of the island travel scene. They are just as fast as the hydrofoils – if not faster, and much more comfortable. They are also much less prone to cancellation in rough weather.

Yacht

It's hardly a budget option, but *the* way to see the islands is by yacht. There are numerous places to hire boats, both with and without crew. If you want to go it alone, two crew members must have sailing certificates. Prices start at about US$1300 per week for a four-person boat. A skipper will cost an extra US$800 per week.

LOCAL TRANSPORT

You'll find taxis almost everywhere. Flag fall is 200 dr, followed by 66 dr per kilometre in towns and 120 dr per kilometre outside towns. The rate doubles from midnight to 5 am. There's a surcharge of 300 dr from airports and 160 dr from ports, bus stations and train stations. Luggage is charged at 55 dr per item over 10kg. Taxis in Athens and Thessaloniki often pick up extra passengers along the way (yell out your destination as they cruise by; when you get out, pay what's on the meter, minus what it read when you got in, plus 200 dr).

In rural areas taxis don't have meters, so make sure you agree on a price with the driver before you get in.

GREECE - MAIN FERRY ROUTES

ORGANISED TOURS

Greece has many companies which operate guided tours, predominantly on the mainland, but also on larger islands. The major operators include CHAT, Key Tours and GO Tours, all based in Athens. It is cheaper to travel independently – tours are only worthwhile if you have extremely limited time.

STREET NAMES

Odos means street, *plateia* means square and *leoforos* means avenue. These words are often omitted on maps and other references,

so we have done the same throughout this chapter, except when to do so would cause confusion.

Athens Αθήνα

☎ 01 • pop 3.7 million

Ancient Athens ranks alongside Rome and Jerusalem for its glorious past and its influence on Western civilisation, but the modern city is a place few people fall in love with.

However inspiring the Acropolis might be, most visitors have trouble coming to

GREECE

terms with the surrounding urban sprawl, the appalling traffic congestion and the pollution.

However, the city is not without its redeeming features. The Acropolis is but one of many important ancient sites, and the National Archaeological Museum has the world's finest collection of Greek antiquities.

Culturally, Athens is a fascinating blend of East and West. King Otho and the middle class that emerged after independence may have been intent on making Athens a European city, but the influence of Asia Minor is everywhere – the coffee, the kebabs, the raucous street vendors and the colourful markets.

ORIENTATION

Although Athens is a huge, sprawling city, nearly everything of interest to travellers is located within a small area bounded by Omonia Square (Plateia Omonias) to the north, Monastiraki Square (Plateia Monastirakiou) to the west, Syntagma Square (Plateia Syntagmatos) to the east and the Plaka district to the south. The city's two major landmarks, the Acropolis and Lykavittos Hill, can be seen from just about everywhere in this area.

Syntagma is the heart of modern Athens. Flanked by luxury hotels, banks and fast-food restaurants, the square is dominated by the old royal palace – home of the Greek parliament since 1935.

Omonia is slowly being cleaned up following the completion of metro construction, but is still better known for its prostitutes and pickpockets than its neoclassical architecture. The major streets of central Athens all meet here. Panepistimiou (El Venizelou) and Stadiou run parallel south-east to Syntagma, while Athinas leads south to the market district of Monastiraki. Monastiraki is in turn linked to Syntagma by Ermou – home to some of the city's smartest shops – and Mitropoleos.

Mitropoleos skirts the northern edge of Plaka, the delightful old Turkish quarter which was virtually all that existed when Athens was declared the capital of independent Greece. Its labyrinthine streets are nestled on the north-eastern slope of the Acropolis, and most of the city's ancient

sites are close by. It may be touristy, but it's the most attractive and interesting part of Athens and the majority of visitors make it their base.

Streets are clearly signposted in Greek and English. If you do get lost, it's very easy to find help. A glance at a map is often enough to draw an offer of assistance. Anyone you ask will be able to direct you to Syntagma (say SYN-tag-ma).

INFORMATION
Tourist Offices

The main EOT tourist office (☎ 331 0561/62, fax 325 2895, ✉ gnto@eexi.gr) is close to Syntagma at Amerikis 2. It has a useful free map of Athens as well as information about public transport in Athens, including ferry departures from Piraeus. The office is open 9 am to 7 pm Monday to Friday and 9.30 am to 2 pm Saturday.

The EOT office (☎ 969 4500) at the East airport terminal is open 9 am to 7 pm Monday to Friday and 11 am to 5 pm Saturday.

The tourist police (☎ 924 2700) are open 24 hours a day at Dimitrakopoulou 77, Koukaki. Take trolleybus No 1, 5 or 9 from Syntagma. They also have a 24-hour information service (☎ 171).

Money

Most of the major banks have branches around Syntagma, open 8 am to 2 pm Monday to Thursday and 8 am to 1.30 pm Friday. The National Bank of Greece has an automatic exchange machine.

American Express (☎ 324 4975) is at Ermou 2, and Eurochange (☎ 322 0155) has an office nearby at Karageorgi Servias 4. It changes Thomas Cook travellers cheques without commission.

In Plaka, Acropole Foreign Exchange, Kydathineon 23, is open 9 am to midnight daily. The banks at the East and West airport terminals are open 7 am to 9 pm.

Post & Communications

The main post office is at Eolou 100, Omonia (postcode 102 00), which is where mail addressed to poste restante will be sent unless specified otherwise. If you're staying in Plaka, it's best to get mail sent to the Syntagma post office (postcode 103 00). Both are open 7.30 am to 8 pm Monday to Friday, to 2 pm Saturday, and 9 am to 1.30 pm Sunday. Parcels over 2kg going abroad must be posted from the parcels office at Stadiou 4 (in the arcade). They should not be wrapped until they've been inspected.

The OTE telephone office at 28 Oktovriou-Patission 85 is open 24 hours a day. There are also offices at Stadiou 15, Syntagma, and at Athinas 50, south of Omonia. They are open 7 am to 11.30 pm daily.

Email & Internet Access
Internet cafes are popping up like mushrooms all over Athens. Most charge from 1000 dr to 1500 dr per hour of computer time, whether you log on or not. They include:

Skynet Internet Centre
  At the corner of Voulis and Apollonos, Plaka, open 9.30 am to 8.30 pm Monday to Friday and 10 am to 8.30 pm Saturday
Sofokleus.com Internet Café
  Stadiou 5, Syntagma, open 10 am to 10 pm Monday to Saturday and 1 to 11 pm Sunday
Museum Internet Café
  Oktovriou-Patission 46, open 9 am to 2.30 am daily

Travel Agencies
The bulk of the city's travel agencies are around Syntagma square, particularly in the area just south of the square on Filellinon, Nikis and Voulis.

Reputable agencies include STA Travel (☎ 321 1188, fax 321 1194, 🄯 robissa@spark.net.gr), Voulis 43, and Etos Travel (☎ 324 1884, fax 322 8447, 🄯 usit@usitetos.gr), Filellinon 1. Both these places also issue International Student Identity Cards.

Bookshops
Athens has three good English-language bookshops. The biggest is Eleftheroudakis, which has branches at Panepistimiou 17 and Nikis 4. The others are Pantelides Books, Amerikis 11, and Compendium Books, Nikis 28. Compendium also has a second-hand books section.

Cultural Centres
The British Council (☎ 363 3215), Plateia Kolonaki 17, and the Hellenic American Union (☎ 362 9886), Massalias 22, hold frequent concerts, film shows, exhibitions etc. Both also have libraries.

Laundry
Plaka has a convenient laundry at Angelou Geronta 10, just off Kydathineon near the outdoor restaurants.

Medical & Emergency Services
For emergency medical treatment, ring the tourist police (☎ 171) and they'll tell you where the nearest hospital is. Don't wait for an ambulance – get a taxi. Hospitals give free emergency treatment to tourists. For hospitals with outpatient departments on duty, ring ☎ 106. For first-aid advice, ring ☎ 166. You can get free dental treatment at the Evangelismos Hospital, Ipsilandou 45.

Dangers & Annoyances
Athens has its share of petty crime.

Pickpockets Pickpockets have become a major problem. Their favourite hunting grounds are the metro system and the crowded streets around Omonia, particularly Athinas. The Sunday market on Ermou is another place where it pays to take extra care of your valuables.

Taxi Touts Taxi drivers working in league with some overpriced C-class hotels around Omonia are a problem. The scam involves taxi drivers picking up late-night arrivals, particularly at the airport and Bus Terminal A, and persuading them that the hotel they want to go to is full. The taxi driver will pretend to phone the hotel of choice, announce that it's full and suggest an alternative. You can ask to speak to your chosen hotel yourself, or insist on going where you want.

Bar Scams Lonely Planet receives a steady flow of letters warning about bar scams, particularly around Syntagma. The most popular version runs something like this: friendly Greek approaches solo male traveller and discovers that the traveller knows little about Athens; friendly Greek then reveals that he, too, is from out of town. Why don't they go to this great little bar that he's just discovered and have a beer? They order a drink, and the equally friendly owner then offers another

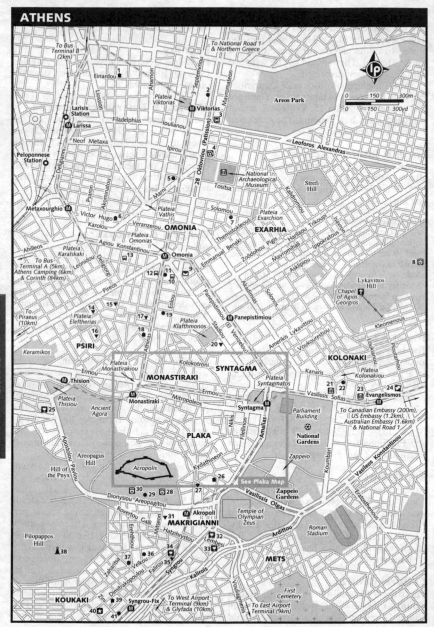

ATHENS

drink. Women appear, more drinks are provided and the visitor relaxes as he realises that the women are not prostitutes, just friendly Greeks. The crunch comes at the end of the evening when the traveller is presented with an exorbitant bill and the smiles disappear. The con men who cruise the streets playing the role of the friendly Greek can be very convincing – some people have been taken in more than once.

ACROPOLIS

Most of the buildings now gracing the Acropolis were commissioned by Pericles during the golden age of Athens in the 5th century BC. The site had been cleared for him by the Persians, who destroyed an earlier temple complex on the eve of the Battle of Salamis.

The entrance to the Acropolis is through the **Beule Gate**, a Roman arch that was added in the 3rd century AD. Beyond this is the **Propylaia**, the monumental gate that was the entrance in ancient times. It was damaged by Venetian bombing in the 17th century, but it has since been restored. To the south of the Propylaia is the small, graceful **Temple of Athena Nike**, which is not accessible to visitors.

Standing supreme over the Acropolis is the monument which more than any other epitomises the glory of ancient Greece – the **Parthenon**. Completed in 438 BC, this building is unsurpassed in grace and harmony. To achieve perfect form, its lines were ingeniously curved to counteract unharmonious optical illusions. The base curves upwards slightly towards the ends, and the columns become slightly narrower towards the top, with the overall effect of making them both look straight.

Above the columns are the remains of a Doric frieze, which was partly destroyed by Venetian shelling in 1687. The best surviving pieces are the controversial Elgin Marbles, carted off to Britain by Lord Elgin in 1801. The Parthenon, dedicated to Athena, contained an 11m-tall gold-and-ivory statue of the goddess completed in 438 BC by Phidias of Athens (only the statue's foundations exist today).

To the north is the **Erechtheion** and its much-photographed Caryatids, the six maidens who support its southern portico. These are plaster casts – the originals (except for the one taken by Lord Elgin) are in the site's museum.

The site and museum are open 8 am to 8 pm daily. The combined admission fee is 2000 dr.

SOUTH OF THE ACROPOLIS

The importance of theatre in the life of the Athenian city-state can be gauged from the dimensions of the enormous **Theatre of Dionysos**, just south of the Acropolis. Built between 342 and 326 BC on the site of an earlier theatre, it could hold 17,000 people spread over 64 tiers of seats, of which about 20 survive. The entrance is on Dionysiou Areopagitou. It's open 8.30 am to 2.30 pm daily; admission is 500 dr.

GREECE

The **Stoa of Eumenes**, built as a shelter and promenade for theatre audiences, runs west from the Theatre of Dionysos to the **Theatre of Herodes Atticus**, built in Roman times. It is used for performances during the Athens Festival, but is closed at other times.

TEMPLE OF OLYMPIAN ZEUS

Begun in the 6th century BC, this massive temple took more than 700 years to complete. The Emperor Hadrian eventually finished the job in AD 131. It was the largest temple in Greece, impressive for the sheer size of its 104 Corinthian columns (17m high with a base diameter of 1.7m). The site is just southeast of Plaka, and the 15 remaining columns are a useful landmark for travellers arriving in the city by bus or taxi from the airport. The site is open 8.30 am to 2.30 pm Tuesday to Sunday; admission is 500 dr.

ROMAN STADIUM

The stadium, just east of the temple, hosted the first Olympic Games of modern times in 1896. It was originally built in the 4th century BC as a venue for the Panathenaic athletic contests. The seats were rebuilt in Pentelic marble by Herodes Atticus in the 2nd century AD, and faithfully restored in 1895.

ANCIENT AGORA

The Agora was the marketplace of ancient Athens and the focal point of civic and social life. Socrates spent much time here expounding his philosophy. The main monuments are the well-preserved **Temple of Hephaestus**, the 11th-century **Church of the Holy Apostles** and the reconstructed **Stoa of Attalos**, which houses the site's museum.

The site is open 8 am to 8 pm Tuesday to Sunday (to 5 pm in winter); admission is 1200 dr.

ROMAN AGORA

The Romans built their agora just west of its ancient counterpart. Its principle monument is the wonderful **Tower of the Winds**, built in the 1st century BC by a Syrian astronomer named Andronicus. Each side represents a point of the compass, and has a relief carving depicting the associated wind. The site is open 8.30 am to 2.30 pm Tuesday to Sunday; admission is 500 dr.

MUSEUMS

Athens has no less than 28 museums, displaying everything from ancient treasures to old theatre props. You'll find a complete list at the tourist office. These are the highlights:

National Archaeological Museum

This is the undoubted star of the show – the most important museum in the country, with finds from all the major sites. The crowd-pullers are the magnificent, exquisitely detailed gold artefacts from Mycenae and the spectacular **Minoan frescoes** from Santorini (Thira), which are here until a suitable museum is built on the island. The museum is at 28 Oktovriou-Patission 44, open 8.30 am to 8 pm Tuesday to Sunday and noon to 8 pm on Monday; admission is 2000 dr.

Benaki Museum

This museum, on the corner of Vasilissis Sofias and Koumbari, houses the collection of Antoine Benaki, the son of an Alexandrian cotton magnate named Emmanual Benaki. The collection includes ancient sculpture, Persian, Byzantine and Coptic objects, Chinese ceramics, icons, two El Greco paintings and a superb collection of traditional costumes.

Goulandris Museum of Cycladic & Ancient Greek Art

This private museum was custom-built to display a fabulous collection of Cycladic art, with an emphasis on the early Bronze Age. Particularly impressive are the beautiful marble figurines. These simple, elegant forms, mostly of naked women with arms folded under their breasts, inspired 20th-century artists such as Brancusi, Epstein, Modigliani and Picasso.

It's at Neofytou Douka 4 and is open 10 am to 4 pm daily, except Tuesday and Sunday; admission is 1000 dr.

LYKAVITTOS HILL

Pine-covered Lykavittos is the highest of the eight hills dotted around Athens. From the summit there are all-embracing views of the city, the Attic basin and the islands of Salamis and Aegina – pollution permitting.

The southern side of the hill is occupied by the posh residential suburb of Kolonaki. The main path to the summit starts at the top of

Loukianou, or you can take the funicular railway from the top of Ploutarhou (500 dr).

WHAT'S FREE
Changing of the Guard
Every Sunday at 11 am a platoon of traditionally costumed *evzones* (guards) marches down Vasilissis Sofias, accompanied by a band, to the Tomb of the Unknown Soldier in front of the parliament building on Syntagma.

LANGUAGE COURSES
Try the Athens Centre (☎ 701 2268, fax 701 8603, ℮ athenscr@compulink.gr), Arhimidous 48, Mets, or the Hellenic American Union (☎ 362 9886, fax 363 3174, ℮ dto lias@hau.gr), Massalias 22, Pefkakia.

ORGANISED TOURS
Key Tours (☎ 923 3166), Kallirois 4; CHAT Tours (☎ 322 3137), Stadiou 4; and GO Tours (☎ 322 5951), Voulis 31-33, are the main operators. You'll see their brochures everywhere, offering identical tours and prices. They include a half-day bus tour (10,000 dr), which does no more than point out major sights.

SPECIAL EVENTS
The Athens Festival is the city's most important cultural event, running from mid-June to the end of August. It features plays, ballet and classical-music concerts at venues like the Theatre of Herodes Atticus and the Lykavittos Theatre. Information and tickets are available from the Festival Box Office, Stadiou 4.

PLACES TO STAY
Camping
The closest camping ground is *Athens Camping (☎ 581 4114, 581 1562/63)*, 7km west of the city centre at Athinon 198 – on the road to Corinth. There are several camping grounds south-east of Athens on the coast road to Cape Sounion.

Hostels
There are a few places around town making a pitch for the hostelling market by tagging 'youth hostel' onto their name. There are some dreadful dumps among them.

There are only a couple of youth hostels worth knowing about. They include the excellent HI-affiliated *Athens International Youth Hostel (☎ 523 4170, fax 523 4015, Victor Hugo 16)*. Location is the only drawback, otherwise the place is almost too good to be true. The spotless rooms, each with bathroom, sleep two to four people. Rates are 1720 dr per person for HI members. If you're not a member, you can either pay 4200 dr to join or 700 dr for a daily stamp.

XEN (YWCA; ☎ 362 4291, Amerikis 11) is an option for women only. Singles/doubles with bathroom are 10,000/12,000 dr. Annual membership costs 1000 dr.

Hotels
Athens is a noisy city and Athenians keep late hours, so an effort has been made to select hotels in quiet areas. Plaka is the most popular place to stay, and it has a good choice of accommodation right across the price spectrum. Rooms fill up quickly in July and August, so it's wise to make a reservation.

Plaka Student & Travellers' Inn (☎ 324 4808, fax 321 0065, ℮ students-inn@ath.forthnet.gr) right in the heart of Plaka at Kydathineon 16 is a well-run place with spotless rooms. It has beds in large dorms for 4000 dr, four-person dorms for 4500 dr and three-person dorms for 5000 dr. There are also singles/doubles for 8000/11,000 dr. All rooms share communal bathrooms. The place stays open all year, and rooms are heated in winter.

Festos Youth & Student Guest House (☎ 323 2455, ℮ consolas@hol.gr, Filellinon 18), Filellinon 18, has dorm beds priced from 3000 dr to 3500 dr. The owners have better rooms nearby at *Hotel Dioskouros (☎ 324 8165, Pittakou 6)*, where doubles with shared bathroom are 9000 dr.

Plaka also has some good mid-range accommodation. *Acropolis House Pension (☎ 322 2344, fax 322 6241, Kodrou 6-8)* is a beautifully preserved 19th-century house. Singles/doubles with private bathroom are 15,000/18,000 dr. *Hotel Adonis (☎ 324 9737, fax 323 1602, Kodrou 3)*, opposite, is a comfortable modern hotel with air-con singles/doubles from 12,000/17,000 dr. It has good views of the Acropolis from the 4th-floor rooms, and from the rooftop bar.

GREECE

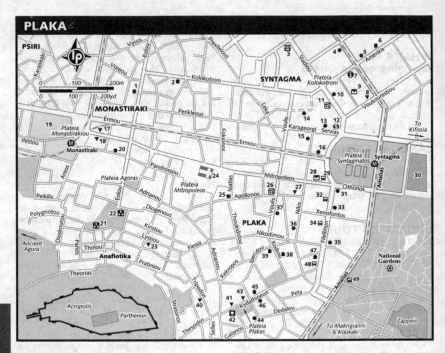

Monastiraki The friendly, family-run *Hotel Tempi (☎ 321 3175, fax 325 4179, ☺ tempiho tel@travelling.gr, Eolou 29)* is a quiet place on the pedestrian precinct part of Eolou. Rooms at the front overlook a small square with a church and a flower market. It's 6000/10,000 dr for singles/doubles with shared bathroom, or 11,500 dr for doubles with private bathroom. It has a small communal kitchen where the guests can prepare breakfast.

The nearby *Hotel Carolina (☎ 324 3551/52, fax 324 3550, Kolokotroni 55)* has singles/doubles with outside bathroom for 7000/11,000 dr, or 8000/12,000 dr with inside bathroom. All the rooms have air-con available.

Hotel Cecil (☎ 321 8005, fax 321 9606, Athinas 39) occupies a fine old classical building with beautiful high, moulded ceilings. It looks immaculate after a complete refit, and singles/doubles with private bathroom are good value at 10,000/15,000 dr, including breakfast.

Koukaki *Marble House Pension (☎ 923 4058, fax 922 6461, Zini 35A)* is a quiet place tucked away on a small cul-de-sac. Rates are 5500/9500 dr for singles/doubles with shared bathroom, or 6500/11,000 dr with private bathroom. All rooms come equipped with bar fridge, ceiling fans and safety boxes for valuables.

Art Gallery Hotel (☎ 923 8376, fax 923 3025, ☺ ecotec@otenet.gr, Erehthiou 5) is a friendly place that's always brimming with fresh flowers. It offers comfortable singles/doubles/triples for 14,000/16,500/19,800 dr with balcony and private bathroom.

Both these places are just a short ride from Syntagma on trolleybus No 1, 5, 9 or 18.

Omonia & Surrounds There are dozens of hotels around Omonia, but most of them are either bordellos masquerading as cheap hotels or uninspiring, overpriced C-class hotels.

Hostel Aphrodite (☎ 881 0589, fax 881 6574, ☺ hostel-aphrodite@ath.forthnet.gr, Einardou 12) is a fair way north of Omonia,

PLAKA

PLACES TO STAY			
1	Hotel Tempi	41	Plaka Psistaria
2	Hotel Carolina	43	Byzantino
6	XEN (YWCA) Hostel		
38	Hotel Adonis	**OTHER**	
39	Acropolis House Pension	3	OTE
45	Student & Travellers' Inn	4	Eleftheroudakis Books
47	Festos Youth & Student	5	Pantilides Books
	Guest House	7	Tourist Office (EOT)
		9	Parcel Post Office
PLACES TO EAT		10	Athens Festival Box Office
8	Brazil Coffee Shop	11	Sofokleos.com Internet Café
17	Savas	12	National Bank of Greece
18	Thanasis	13	Eurochange
23	Eden Vegetarian	14	Pan Express Travel
	Restaurant	15	Eleftheroudakis Books
27	Furin Kazan Japanese	16	American Express
	Restaurant	19	Flea Market
40	Ouzeri Kouklis	20	Centre of Hellenic Tradition
		21	Roman Agora

22	Tower of the Winds
24	Athens Cathedral
25	National Welfare Organisation
26	Skynet Internet Centre
28	Syntagma Post Office
29	Buses to Airport
30	Parliament
31	ETOS Travel
32	Bus 040 to Piraeus
33	Olympic Airways
34	Buses to Cape Sounion
35	OSE Office (Train Tickets)
36	Compendium Books
37	STA Travel
42	Brettos (bar)
44	Laundrette
46	Acropole Foreign Exchange
48	Trolley Stop for Plaka
49	Bus 024 to Bus Terminal B

but it's only 10 minutes from the train stations. It's a long-standing favourite with travellers, with Internet access and a bar. Dorm beds are priced from 3500 dr. There are also singles/doubles with shared bathroom for 6000/10,000 dr, and doubles with private bathroom for 11,000 dr.

PLACES TO EAT
Plaka
For most people, Plaka is the place to be. It's hard to beat the atmosphere of dining out beneath the floodlit Acropolis.

You do, however, pay for the privilege – particularly at the outdoor restaurants around the square on Kydathineon. The best of this bunch is *Byzantino (Kydathineon 20)*, which prices its menu more reasonably and is popular with Greek family groups. The nearby *Plaka Psistaria (Kydathineon 28)* has a range of gyros and souvlakia to eat there or take away.

Ouzeri Kouklis (Tripodon 14) is an old-style ouzeri with an oak-beamed ceiling, marble tables and wicker chairs. It serves only mezedes, which are brought round on a large tray for you to take your pick. They include flaming sausages – ignited at your table – and cuttlefish for 1200 dr, as well as the usual dips for 600 dr. The whole selection, enough for four hungry people, costs 9800 dr.

Vegetarian restaurants are thin on the ground in Athens. *Eden Vegetarian Restaurant (Lyssiou 12)* is one of only three. The Eden has been around for years, substituting soya products for meat in tasty vegetarian versions of moussaka and other Greek favourites. Reckon on 8000 dr for two people.

For a real treat, head to *Daphne Restaurant (☎ 322 7971, Lysikratous 4)*. It's an exquisitely restored 1830s neoclassical mansion decorated with frescoes from Greek mythology. The menu includes regional specialities like rabbit cooked in mavrodaphne wine. Reckon on about 10,000 dr per person. It's open every night from 7 pm.

Syntagma
Fast food is the order of the day around busy Syntagma with an assortment of Greek and international offerings.

Anyone suffering from a surfeit of Greek salad and souvlaki should head for *Furin Kazan Japanese Fast-Food Restaurant (Apollonos 2, Syntagma)*. It has noodle dishes from 1800 dr and rice dishes from 1600 dr. It's open 11.30 am to 5.30 pm Monday to Saturday.

Follow your nose to the *Brazil Coffee Shop* on Voukourestiou for the best coffee in town.

South of the Acropolis
To 24 Hours (Syngrou 44) is a great favourite with Athenian night owls. As the name suggests, it's open 24 hours. It calls itself a *patsadakia*, which means that it specialises in

GREECE

patsas (tripe soup), but it always has a wide selection of taverna dishes.

Socrates Prison *(Mitseon 20)* is not named after the philosopher, but after the owner – who reckons the restaurant is his prison. It's a stylish place with an imaginative range of mezedes from 850 dr and main dishes from 1500 dr.

Monastiraki

There are some excellent cheap places to eat around Monastiraki, particularly for gyros and souvlaki fans. **Thanasis** and **Savas**, opposite each other at the bottom end of Mitropoleos, are the places to go.

Psiri

There are loads of possibilities in Psiri, just north-west of Monastiraki. Once rated as 'Athens at its most clapped out', the district has undergone an amazing transformation in the past two years. The narrow streets are now dotted with numerous trendy ouzeris, tavernas and music bars, particularly the central area between Plateia Agion Anargyron and Plateia Iroön.

If none of the places grabs your attention as you wander around, try **Embros** *(Plateia Agion Anargyron 4)*. It's a popular spot with seating in the square, and a choice of about 20 mezedes. They include delicious cheese croquettes (1150 dr) and chicken livers wrapped in bacon (1600 dr).

The streets north of Psiri, around Plateia Eletherias, have been adopted by the city's Bangladeshi community and it's the place to head for a good curry and a cold beer. Try **Bengal Garden** *(Korinis 12)* or the smarter **Pak Bangla Indian Restaurant** *(Menandrou 13)*.

Self-Catering

Supermarkets are few and far between in central Athens. Those that do exist are marked on the main Athens map. **Vasilopoulou** *(Stadiou 19)* is an excellent delicatessen with a good selection of cold meats and cheeses. For the best range of fresh fruit and vegetables, head for the **markets** on Athinas.

ENTERTAINMENT

Friday's edition of the *Athens News* carries a 16-page weekly entertainment guide, while the *Kathimerini* supplement that accompanies the *International Herald Tribune* has daily listings.

Discos & Bars

Discos operate in central Athens only between October and April. In summer, the action moves to the coastal suburbs of Glyfada and Ellinikon.

Most bars around Plaka and Syntagma are places to avoid, especially if there are guys outside touting for customers. One place that's recommended is **Brettos** *(Kydathineon 41)*, a delightful old family-run place right in the heart of Plaka. Huge old barrels line one wall, and the shelves are stocked with an eye-catching collection of coloured bottles.

Most bars in Athens have music as a main feature. Thisio is a good place to look, particularly on Iraklidon. **Stavlos** *(Iraklidon 10)* occupies an amazing old rabbit warren of a building.

Gay Bars

The greatest concentration of gay bars is to be found on the streets off Syngrou, south of the Temple of Olympian Zeus. Popular spots include the long-running **Granazi Bar** *(Lembesi 20)* and the more risque **Lamda Club** *(Lembesi 15)*. Lesbians should check the nearby **Porta Bar** *(Falirou 10)*.

Rock & Jazz Concerts

The **Rodon Club** *(Marni 24)*, north of Omonia, hosts touring international rock bands, while local bands play at the *AN Club (Solomou 20, Exarhia)*.

Rembetika Clubs

Rembetika Stoa Athanaton *(☎ 321 4362, Sofokleous 19)* above the meat market is a good place to check, although it's closed from mid-May to the end of September. For the rest of the year, it's open 3 to 7.30 pm daily, except Sunday, and from midnight to 6 am.

Folk Dancing

The **Dora Stratou Dance Company** performs at its theatre on Filopappos Hill at 10.15 pm every night from mid-May to October, with additional performances at 8.15 pm on Wednesday. Tickets are 1500 dr. Filopappos

Hill is west of the Acropolis, off Dionysiou Areopagitou. Bus No 230 from Syntagma will get you there.

Sound-and-Light Show

Athens' endeavour at this spectacle is not one of the world's best. There are shows in English every night at 9 pm from April to October at the theatre on the *Hill of the Pnyx* (☎ 322 1459). Tickets are 1500 dr. The Hill of the Pnyx is opposite Filopappos Hill, and the show is timed so that you can cross straight to the folk dancing.

SPECTATOR SPORTS

Almost half of the 18 soccer teams in the Greek first division are based in Athens or Piraeus. The most popular are Olympiakos (Piraeus), Panathinaikos (Athens), which plays at the Olympic Stadium on alternate Sundays, AEK (Athens), and PAOK (Thessaloniki). Fixtures and results are listed in the *Athens News*.

SHOPPING

The National Welfare Organisation shop, on the corner of Apollonos and Ipatias, Plaka, is a good place to go shopping for handicrafts. It has top-quality goods and the money goes to a good cause – the organisation was formed to preserve and promote traditional Greek handicrafts.

The Centre of Hellenic Tradition, Pandrossou 36, Plaka, has a display of traditional and modern handicrafts from each region of Greece. Most of the items are for sale.

GETTING THERE & AWAY
Air

Athens' dilapidated airport, Ellinikon, is 9km south of the city. There are two main terminals: West for all Olympic Airways flights, and East for all other flights. The airport's old military terminal is dusted off for charter flights in peak season.

Facilities are equally primitive at all the terminals. Nothing is likely to change, however, until the new international airport at Spata (21km east of Athens) opens in 2002.

The Olympic Airways head office (☎ 926 7251/54) is at Syngrou 96. Much more convenient is the office at Filellinon 13, near Syntagma.

Bus

Athens has two main intercity bus stations. The EOT gives out schedules for both with departure times, journey times and fares.

Terminal A, north-west of Omonia at Kifissou 100, has departures to the Peloponnese, the Ionian Islands and western Greece. To get there, take bus No 051 from the junction of Zinonos and Menandrou, near Omonia. Buses run every 15 minutes from 5 am to midnight.

Terminal B is north of Omonia off Liossion and has departures to Central and Northern Greece as well as to Evia. To get there, take bus No 024 from outside the main gate of the National Gardens on Amalias. EOT misleadingly gives the terminal's address as Liossion 260, which turns out to be a small workshop. Liossion 260 is where you should get off the bus. Turn right onto Gousiou and you'll see the terminal at the end of the road.

Buses for Attica leave from the Mavromateon terminal at the junction of Alexandras and 28 Oktovriou-Patission.

Train

Athens has two train stations, about 200m apart on Deligianni, about 1km north-west of Omonia. Trains to the Peloponnese leave from the Peloponnese station, while trains to the north leave from Larisis station – as do all international services.

Services to the Peloponnese include eight trains to Patras, four of which are intercity express (2980 dr, 3½ hours), while services north include 10 trains a day to Thessaloniki, five of which are intercity express (8250 dr, six hours). The 7 am service from Athens is express right through to Alexandroupolis, arriving at 7 pm. There are also trains to Volos and Halkida on Evia.

The easlest way to get to the stations is on Metro Line 2 to Larissa, outside Larisis station. The Peloponnese station is across the footbridge at the southern end of Larisis station. Tickets can be bought at the stations or at the OSE offices at Filellinon 17, Sina 6 and Karolou 1.

Car & Motorcycle

National Rd 1 is the main route north from Athens. It starts at Nea Kifissia. To get there from central Athens, take Vasilissis Sofias from Syntagma and follow the signs. National

GREECE

Rd 8, which begins beyond Dafni, is the road to the Peloponnese. Take Agiou Konstantinou from Omonia.

The northern reaches of Syngrou, just south of the Temple of Olympian Zeus, are packed solid with car-rental firms.

Hitching

Athens is the most difficult place in Greece to hitchhike from. Your best bet is to ask the truck drivers at the Piraeus cargo wharves. Otherwise, for the Peloponnese, take a bus from Panepistimiou to Dafni, where National Rd 8 begins. For Northern Greece, take the metro to Kifissia, then a bus to Nea Kifissia and walk to National Rd 1.

Ferry

See the Piraeus section later in this chapter for information on ferries to/from the islands.

GETTING AROUND
To/From the Airport

There is a 24-hour express-bus service between central Athens and both the East and West terminals, also calling at the special charter terminal when in use.

Service No E91 leaves Stadiou, near Omonia, every 20 minutes from 6 am to 9 pm, every 40 minutes from 9 pm until 12.20 am, and then hourly through the night. It stops at Syntagma (outside the post office) five minutes later. The trip takes from 30 minutes to an hour, depending on traffic. The return service is No E92. The fare is 250 dr (500 dr from midnight to 6 am), and you pay the driver. There are also express buses between the airport and Plateia Karaïskaki in Piraeus.

A taxi from the airport to Syntagma should cost from 1500 dr to 2500 dr, depending on the time of day.

Bus & Trolleybus

Blue-and-white suburban buses operate from 5 am to midnight and charge a flat rate of 120 dr. Route numbers and destinations, but not the actual routes, are listed on the free EOT map.

The map does, however, mark the routes of the yellow trolleybuses, making them easy to use. They also run from 5 am to midnight and cost 120 dr.

There are special buses that operate 24 hours a day to Piraeus. Bus No 040 leaves from the corner of Syntagma and Filellinon, and No 049 leaves from the Omonia end of Athinas. They run every 20 minutes from 6 am to midnight, and then hourly.

Tickets can be bought from ticket kiosks and regular periptera. Once on a bus, you must validate your ticket by putting it into a machine; the penalty for failing to do so is 4800 dr.

Metro

Although sections of the long-awaited new metro system finally came on line in late 1999, much work remains to be done before the system becomes fully operational – supposedly before the Olympics in 2004.

Line 1 runs from Piraeus (Great Harbour) to the northern suburb of Kifissia, with useful stops at Monastiraki, Omonia (city centre) and Plateia Viktorias (National Archaeological Museum).

Line 2 has useful stops at Larissa (for the train stations), Omonia, Panepistimiou and Syntagma (city centre). Line 3 will eventually run north-east from Monastiraki to Stavros, where it will connect with trains to the international airport at Spata.

Ticket prices are 150 dr for most journeys, including Monastiraki-Piraeus. There are ticket machines and ticket booths at all stations, and validating machines at platform entrances. The penalty for travelling without a validated ticket is 4800 dr.

Trains operate between 5 am and midnight.

Taxi

Athenian taxis are yellow. The flag fall is 200 dr, with a 160 dr surcharge from ports and train and bus stations, and a 300 dr surcharge from the airport. After that, the day rate (tariff 1 on the meter) is 66 dr per kilometre. The rate doubles between midnight and 5 am (tariff 2 on the meter). Baggage is charged at the rate of 55 dr per item over 10kg. The minimum fare is 500 dr, which covers most journeys in central Athens.

Around Athens

PIRAEUS Πειραιάς
☎ 01 • pop 171,000

Piraeus has been the port of Athens since classical times. These days it's little more

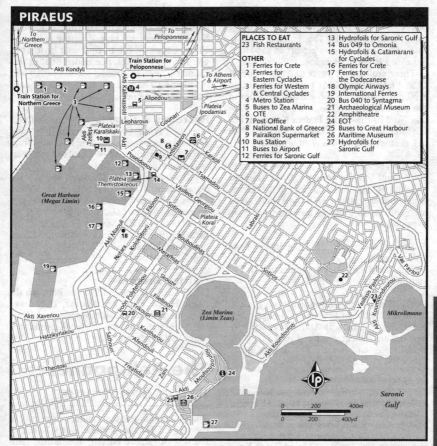

PIRAEUS

PLACES TO EAT	13 Hydrofoils for Saronic Gulf
23 Fish Restaurants	14 Bus 049 to Omonia
	15 Hydrofoils & Catamarans
OTHER	for Cyclades
1 Ferries for Crete	16 Ferries for Crete
2 Ferries for	17 Ferries for
Eastern Cyclades	the Dodecanese
3 Ferries for Western	18 Olympic Airways
& Central Cyclades	19 International Ferries
4 Metro Station	20 Bus 040 to Syntagma
5 Buses to Zea Marina	21 Archaeological Museum
6 OTE	22 Amphitheatre
7 Post Office	24 EOT
8 National Bank of Greece	25 Buses to Great Harbour
9 Pairaikon Supermarket	26 Maritime Museum
10 Bus Station	27 Hydrofoils for
11 Buses to Airport	Saronic Gulf
12 Ferries for Saronic Gulf	

GREECE

than an outer suburb of the space-hungry capital, linked by a mish-mash of factories, warehouses and apartment blocks. The streets are every bit as traffic-clogged as Athens, and behind the veneer of banks and shipping offices most of Piraeus is pretty seedy. The only reason to come here is to catch a ferry or hydrofoil.

Orientation & Information

Piraeus consists of a peninsula surrounded by harbours. The most important of them is the Great Harbour. All ferries leave from here, as well as hydrofoil and catamaran services to

Aegina and the Cyclades. There are dozens of shipping agents around the harbour, as well as banks and a post office.

Zea Marina, on the other side of the peninsula, is the main port for hydrofoils to the Saronic Gulf Islands (except Aegina). North-east of here is the picturesque Mikrolimano (small harbour), lined with countless fish restaurants. There's a tourist office (☎ 452 2586) at Zea Marina.

Getting There & Away

Bus There are two 24-hour bus services between central Athens and Piraeus. No 049

runs from Omonia to the Great Harbour, and bus No 040 runs from Syntagma to the tip of the Piraeus peninsula. This is the service to catch for Zea Marina – get off at the Hotel Savoy on Iroön Politehniou.

There are express buses to Athens airport from Plateia Karaïskaki between 5 am and 8.20 pm, and between 6 am and 9.25 pm in the other direction. The fare is 250 dr. Blue bus No 110 runs from Plateia Karaïskaki to Glyfada and Voula every 15 minutes (120 dr). It stops outside the West terminal.

Metro The metro offers the fastest and most convenient link between the Great Harbour and Athens. The station is close to the ferries, at the northern end of Akti Kalimassioti. There are metro trains every 10 minutes from 5 am to midnight.

Train All services to the Peloponnese from Athens start and terminate at Piraeus, although some schedules don't mention it. The station is next to the metro.

Ferry The following information is a guide to departures between June and mid-September. Schedules are similar in April, May and October, but are radically reduced in winter – especially to small islands. The Athens tourist office has a reliable schedule, updated weekly.

Cyclades
　There are daily ferries to Amorgos, Folegandros, Ios, Kimolos, Kythnos, Milos, Mykonos, Naxos, Paros, Santorini, Serifos, Sifnos, Sikinos, Syros and Tinos; two or three ferries a week to Iraklia, Shinoussa, Koufonisi, Donoussa, and Anafi; none to Andros or Kea.
Dodacanese
　There are daily ferries to Kalymnos, Kos, Leros, Patmos and Rhodes; three a week to Karpathos and Kassos; and weekly services to the other islands.
North-Eastern Aegean
　There are daily ferries to Chios, Lesvos (Mytilini), Ikaria and Samos; and two a week to Limnos.
Saronic Gulf Islands
　There are daily ferries to Aegina, Poros, Hydra and Spetses all year.
Crete
　There are two boats a day to Iraklio; daily services to Hania and Rethymno; and three a week to Agios Nikolaos and Sitia.

The departure points for the various ferry destinations are shown on the map of Piraeus. Note that there are two departure points for Crete. Check where to find your boat when you buy your ticket. See under Boat in this chapter's Getting Around section earlier and the Getting There & Away sections for each island for more information.

Hydrofoil & Catamaran Minoan Lines operate Flying Dolphins (hydrofoils) and high-speed catamarans to the Cyclades from early April to the end of October, and year-round services to the Saronic Gulf.

All services to the Cyclades and Aegina leave from Great Harbour, near Plateia Themistokleous. Some services to Poros, Hydra and Spetses also leave from here, but most leave from Zea Marina. For the latest departure information, pick up a timetable from the Flying Dolphin office at Filellinon 3 (Syntagma) in Athens.

Getting Around
Local bus Nos 904 and 905 run between the Great Harbour and Zea Marina. They leave from the bus stop beside the metro at Great Harbour, and drop you by the maritime museum at Zea Marina.

The Peloponnese
Η Πελοπόννησος

The Peloponnese is the southern extremity of the rugged Balkan peninsula. It's linked to the rest of Greece only by the narrow Isthmus of Corinth, and this has long prompted people to declare the Peloponnese to be more an island than part of the mainland. It technically became an island after the completion of the Corinth Canal across the isthmus in 1893, and it is now linked to the mainland only by road and rail bridges.

The Peloponnese is an area rich in history. The principal site is Olympia, which is the birthplace of the Olympic Games, but there are many other sites which are worth seeking out. Epidaurus, Corinth and Mycenae in the north-east are all within easy striking distance of the pretty Venetian town of Nafplio.

In the south are the magical old Byzantine towns of Monemvasia and Mystras. The rugged Mani Peninsula is famous for its spectacular wild flowers in spring, as well as for the bizarre tower settlements sprinkled across its landscape.

The beaches south of Kalamata are some of the best in Greece.

PATRAS Πάτρα
☎ 061 • pop 153,300

Patras is Greece's third-largest city and the principal port for ferries to Italy and the Ionian Islands. It's not particularly exciting and most travellers hang around only long enough for transport connections.

Orientation & Information

The city is easy to negotiate and is laid out on a grid stretching uphill from the port to the old *kastro* (castle). Most services of importance to travellers are to be found along the waterfront, known as Othonos Amalias, in the middle of town and Iroön Politehniou to the north. All the various shipping offices are to be found along here. The train station is right in the middle of town on Othonos Amalias, and the bus station is close by.

PATRAS

PLACES TO STAY
20 Hotel Rannia
23 Pension Nicos

PLACES TO EAT
7 Europa Centre

OTHER
1 Customs
2 Tourist Police
3 EOT
4 OTE
5 Minoan Lines
6 Kronos Supermarket
8 Adriatica
9 Boats to Ionian Islands
10 Superfast Ferries
11 Strintzis
12 Med Link Lines
13 First-Aid Centre
14 Main Bus Station
15 ANEK
16 Olympic Airways
17 Archaeological Museum
18 Post Office
19 Laundrette
21 National Bank of Greece
22 Buses to Zakynthos
24 Kronos Supermarket
25 Rocky Racoon Music Bar
26 Kastro

GREECE

The tourist office (☎ 620 353) is inside the port fence off Iroön Politehniou, and the tourist police (☎ 451 833) are upstairs in the embarkation hall.

Money The National Bank of Greece on Plateia Trion Symahon has a 24-hour automatic exchange machine.

Post & Communications The post office is on the corner of Zaïmi and Mezonos. There's a telephone office opposite the tourist office at the port. For Internet access, head inland to the Rocky Racoon Music Bar, Gerokostopoulou 56. It's open 9 am to 3 am daily.

Things to See & Do
There are great views of Zakynthos and Kefallonia from the Venetian **kastro**, which is reached by the steps at the top of Agiou Nikolaou.

Places to Stay & Eat
Most travellers go to *Pension Nicos* (☎ 623 757), up from the waterfront on the corner of Patreos and Agiou Andreou 121. Its doubles with shared facilities are 6500 dr, and singles/doubles with bathroom are 4000/7000 dr.

C-class *Hotel Rannia* (☎ 220 114, fax 220 537, Riga Fereou 53) facing Plateia Olgas has comfortable air-con singles/doubles with TV for 10,000/15,000 dr – 8000/12,000 dr outside peak season.

The *Europa Centre* (Othonos Amalias 10) is a convenient cafeteria-style place close to the international ferry dock. It has a range of taverna dishes as well as spaghetti (from 900 dr) and a choice of vegetarian meals (900 dr).

Getting There & Away
For transport from Athens, see that city's Getting There & Away section earlier in this chapter.

The best way to travel to Athens is by train. The buses may be faster, but they drop you a long way from the city centre at Terminal A on Kifissou. This can be a real hassle if you're arriving in Athens after midnight – when there are no connecting buses to the city centre, leaving newcomers at the mercy of the notorious Terminal A taxi drivers.

The trains take you close to the city centre, five minutes from Syntagma on the new metro system.

Bus Buses to Athens (3650 dr, three hours) run every 30 minutes, with the last at 9.45 pm. There are also 10 buses a day to Pyrgos (for Olympia) and two to Kalamata.

Train There are nine trains a day to Athens. Four are slow trains (1580 dr, five hours) and five are intercity express (2580 dr, 3½ hours). The last intercity train leaves at 6 pm. Trains also run south to Pyrgos and Kalamata.

Ferry There are daily ferries to Kefallonia (3450 dr, four hours), Ithaki (3500 dr, six hours) and Corfu (6000 dr, 10 hours). Services to Italy are covered in the Getting There & Away section at the start of this chapter. Ticket agents line the waterfront.

DIAKOFTO-KALAVRYTA RAILWAY
This spectacular rack-and-pinion line climbs up the deep gorge of the Vouraikos River from the small coastal town of Diakofto to the mountain resort of **Kalavryta**, 22km away. It is a thrilling journey, with dramatic scenery all the way. There are four trains a day in each direction.

Diakofto is one hour east of Patras on the main train line to Athens.

CORINTH
☎ 0741 • pop 27,400
Modern Corinth is an uninspiring town which gives the impression that it has never quite recovered from the devastating earthquake of 1928. It is, however, a convenient base from which to visit nearby ancient Corinth.

Places to Stay & Eat
Corinth Beach Camping (☎ 27 967) is about 3km west of town. Buses to ancient Corinth can drop you there.

Corinth's budget hotels are a grim bunch. The least awful of them is *Hotel Apollon* (☎ 22 587, Pirinis 18) near the train station, even though it doubles as a brothel. From the outside the place looks to be on the verge of collapse, but the rooms have been redecorated and are reasonable value at 5000/7000 dr for singles/doubles with bathroom.

If you can afford it, head for the friendly family-run *Hotel Ephira (☎ 24 021, fax 24 514, Ethnikis Antistaseos 52)*. It costs 9000/ 14,500 dr for clean air-con singles/doubles with bathroom.

Taverna O Theodorakis near the port on the side street next to the Hotel Corinthos is a lively place specialising in fish.

Getting There & Away

Bus Corinth has two main bus stations. There are buses to Athens (1500 dr, 1½ hours) every 30 minutes from the bus station on the corner of Ermou and Koliatsou, on the south-eastern side of the park in the city centre. Buses to Nafplio leave from the junction of Ethnikis Antistaseos and Aratou, while buses to other parts of the Peloponnese leave from a new bus station on the southern side of town. Hourly buses to ancient Corinth (240 dr, 20 minutes) leave from Koliatsou, north-west of the central park.

Train There are 14 trains a day to Athens, five of them intercity services. There are also trains to Kalamata, Nafplio and Patras.

ANCIENT CORINTH & ACROCORINTH

The sprawling ruins of ancient Corinth lie 7km south-west of the modern city. Corinth (Κόρινθος) was one of ancient Greece's wealthiest and most wanton cities. When Corinthians weren't clinching business deals, they were paying homage to Aphrodite in a temple dedicated to her, which meant they were frolicking with the temple's sacred prostitutes. The only ancient Greek monument remaining here is the imposing **Temple of Apollo**; the others are Roman. Towering over the site is Acrocorinth, the ruins of an ancient citadel built on a massive outcrop of limestone.

Both sites are open 8 am to 6 pm daily. Admission is 1200 dr for ancient Corinth and free for Acrocorinth.

NAFPLIO Ναύπλιο
☎ 0752 • pop 11,900
Nafplio ranks as one of Greece's prettiest towns. The narrow streets of the old quarter are filled with elegant Venetian houses and neoclassical mansions.

There's a small municipal tourist office (☎ 24 444) on 25 Martiou in the modern part

of town. It's open 9 am to 1.30 pm and 4.30 to 9 pm daily. The bus station is on Syngrou, the street which separates the old town from the new.

Palamidi Fortress

There are terrific views of the old town and the surrounding coast from this ruined hilltop fortress. The climb is strenuous – there are almost 1000 steps – so start early and take water with you. The fortress is open 8 am to 4.30 pm Monday to Friday, and 8 am to 2.30 pm weekends; admission is 800 dr.

Places to Stay & Eat

The cheapest rooms are in the new part of town along Argous, the road to Argos.

Hotel Economou (☎ 23 955, Argonafton 22) is run by the manager of the former youth hostel, now closed. Two rooms have been set up as dorms, with beds for 2500 dr. Argonafton runs off Argous.

Most people prefer to stay in the old part of town, where there are numerous signs for domatia. Singles/doubles cost from 5000/8000 dr. Stylish *Hotel Byron (☎ 22 351, fax 26 338, ✉ byronhotel@otenet.gr, Platanos 2)* has beautifully furnished singles for 13,000 dr, and doubles range from 16,000 dr to 22,000 dr.

The old town has dozens of restaurants. Most close in winter, when the choice shrinks to a few long-standing favourites like *Taverna Paleo Arhontiko (☎ 22 449)* on the corner of Ypsilandou and Sofroni. Reservations are essential on Friday and Saturday nights. Reckon on 6000 dr for two, plus wine.

Another popular spot is the *Mezedopoleio O Noulis*. It serves a fabulous range of mezes (snacks) which can easily be combined into a meal. Check the *saganaki flambé*, ignited with Metaxa (brandy) as it reaches your table.

Getting There & Away

There are hourly buses to Athens (2650 dr, 2½ hours) via Corinth, as well as services to Argos (for Peloponnese connections), Mycenae and Epidaurus.

EPIDAURUS Επίδαυρος

The crowd-puller at this site is the huge and well-preserved **Theatre of Epidaurus**, but don't miss the more peaceful **Sanctuary of Asclepius** nearby. Epidaurus was regarded as

GREECE

the birthplace of Asclepius, the god of healing, and the sanctuary was once a flourishing spa and healing centre. The setting alone would have been enough to cure many ailments.

The site is open 8 am to 5 pm daily, to 7 pm in summer; admission is 1500 dr.

You can enjoy the theatre's astounding acoustics first-hand during the Epidaurus Festival from mid-June to mid-August.

Getting There & Away

There are two buses a day from Athens (2250 dr, 2½ hours), as well as three a day from Nafplio (600 dr, 40 minutes). During the festival, there are excursion buses from Nafplio and Athens.

MYCENAE Μυκήνες

Mycenae was the most powerful influence in Greece for three centuries until about 1200 BC. The rise and fall of Mycenae is shrouded in myth, but the site was settled as early as the sixth millennium BC. Historians are divided as to whether the city's eventual destruction was wrought by invaders or internal conflict between the Mycenaean kingdoms. Described by Homer as 'rich in gold', Mycenae's entrance, the **Lion Gate**, is Europe's oldest monumental sculpture.

Excavations have uncovered the palace complex and a number of tombs. The so-called **Mask of Agamemnon**, discovered by Heinrich Schliemann in 1873, now holds pride of place at the National Archaeological Museum in Athens along with other finds from the site.

The site is open 8 am to 7 pm daily; admission is 1500 dr.

Places to Stay

Most people visit on day trips from Nafplio, but there are several hotels in the modern village below the site. The *Belle Helene Hotel* (☎ 76 255, fax 76 179) has singles/doubles for 5000/7500 dr.

Getting There & Away

There are buses from Argos and Nafplio.

SPARTA Σπάρτη

☎ 0731 • pop 14,100

The bellicose Spartans sacrificed all the finer things in life to military expertise and left no

monuments of any consequence. Ancient Sparta's forlorn ruins lie amid olive groves at the northern end of town. Modern Sparta is a neat, unspectacular town, but it's a convenient base from which to visit Mystras.

Orientation & Information

Sparta is laid out on a grid system. The main streets are Paleologou, which runs north-south through the town, and Lykourgou, which runs east-west. The tourist office (☎ 24 852) is in the town hall on the main square, Plateia Kentriki. It's open 8 am to 2.30 pm Monday to Friday.

Places to Stay & Eat

Camping Paleologou Mystras (☎ 22 724), 2km west of Sparta on the road to Mystras, is a friendly, well-organised site with good facilities – including a swimming pool. It's open all year. Buses to Mystras can drop you off there.

There's a good choice of hotels back in town. The popular family-run *Hotel Cecil* (☎ 24 980, fax 81 318, Palaeologou 125) has singles/doubles with bathroom and TV for 8000/10,000 dr.

The *Restaurant Elysse (Palaeologou 113)* offers Lakonian specialities like *chicken bardouniotiko* (1300 dr), which is chicken cooked with onions and feta cheese.

Getting There & Away

The bus terminal is at the eastern end of Lykourgou. There are 10 buses a day to Athens (3900 dr, four hours), three to Monemvasia and two to Kalamata. There are also frequent buses to Mystras (250 dr, 30 minutes).

MYSTRAS Μυστράς

Mystras, 7km from Sparta, was once the shining light of the Byzantine world. Its ruins spill from a spur of Mt Taygetos, crowned by a mighty fortress built by the Franks in 1249. The streets of Mystras are lined with palaces, monasteries and churches, most of them dating from the period between 1271 and 1460, when the town was the effective capital of the Byzantine Empire.

The site is open 8 am to 7 pm daily. Admission is 1200 dr, which includes entrance to the museum (closed Monday). You'll need to take an entire day to do this vast

GREECE

place justice. Take a taxi or hitch a ride to the upper Fortress Gate and work your way down. Take some water.

MONEMVASIA Μονεμβασία
☎ 0732

Monemvasia is no longer an undiscovered paradise, but mass tourism hasn't lessened the impact of one's first encounter with this extraordinary old town – nor the thrill of exploring it.

Things to See

Monemvasia occupies a great outcrop of rock that rises dramatically from the sea opposite the village of Gefyra. It was separated from the mainland by an earthquake in AD 375 and access is by a causeway from Gefyra. From the causeway, a road curves around the base of the rock for about 1km until it comes to a narrow L-shaped tunnel in the massive fortifying wall. You emerge, blinking, in the **Byzantine town**, hitherto hidden from view.

The cobbled main street is flanked by stairways leading to a complex network of stone houses with tiny walled gardens and courtyards. Steps (signposted) lead to the ruins of the **fortress** built by the Venetians in the 16th century. The views are great, and there is the added bonus of being able to explore the Byzantine **Church of Agia Sophia**, perched precariously on the edge of the cliff.

Places to Stay & Eat

There is no budget accommodation in Monemvasia, but there are domatia in Gefyra as well as cheap hotels.

Basic *Hotel Akrogiali* (**☎** *61 360*), opposite the National Bank of Greece, has singles/ doubles with shower for 6000/9000 dr.

If your budget permits, treat yourself to a night in one of the beautifully restored traditional settlements in Monemvasia. The pick of them is *Malvasia Guest Houses* (**☎** *61 113, fax 61 722*), with singles for 9000 dr, and doubles from 12,000 dr to 15,000 dr. Prices include a generous breakfast.

The *Taverna O Botsalo* is the place to go for a hearty meal in Gefyra, while *To Kanoni*, on the right of the main street in Monemvasia, has an imaginative menu.

Getting There & Away

Bus There are four buses a day to Athens (5800 dr, six hours), travelling via Sparta, Tripolis and Corinth.

Ferry In July and August, there are at least two hydrofoils a day to Piraeus via the Saronic Gulf Islands.

GYTHIO Γύθειο
☎ 0731 • pop 4900

Gythio, once the port of ancient Sparta, is an attractive fishing town at the head of the Lakonian Gulf. It is the gateway to the rugged Mani Peninsula to the south.

The main attraction is the picturesque islet of **Marathonisi**, linked to the mainland by a causeway. According to mythology it is ancient Cranae, where Paris (a prince of Troy) and Helen (the wife of Menelaus of Sparta) consummated the love affair that sparked the Trojan War. An 18th-century tower on the islet has been turned into a **museum** of Mani history.

Places to Stay & Eat

Meltemi Camping (**☎** *22 833*) is the pick of the sites along the coast south of town. Buses to Areopoli can drop you there.

You'll find plenty of domatia signs around town. They include *Xenia Rooms to Rent* (**☎** *22 719*), opposite the causeway to Marathonisi. It has singles/doubles with bathroom for 4000/6000 dr. The nearby *Saga Pension* (**☎** *23 220, fax 24 370*) charges 7000/10,000 dr for singles/doubles with TV and breakfast.

The waterfront is lined with countless fish tavernas with very similar menus. For something completely different, head inland to the tiny *General Store & Wine Bar* (**☎** *24 113, Vasileos Georgiou 67*). You'll find an unusually varied and imaginative menu featuring dishes like orange and pumpkin soup (600 dr) and fillet of pork with black pepper and ouzo (2800 dr).

Getting There & Away

Bus There are five buses a day to Athens (4700 dr, 4¼ hours) via Sparta (750 dr, one hour), five to Areopoli (500 dr, 30 minutes), two to Gerolimenas (1150 dr, two hours), and one to the Diros Caves (700 dr, one hour).

GREECE

Ferry There are daily ferries to Kythira (1600 dr, two hours) in summer, continuing twice a week to Kastelli-Kissamos on Crete (5100 dr, seven hours). Tickets are sold at Golden Ferries (☎ 22 996, fax 22 410) opposite the tourist office on Vasileos Pavlou.

THE MANI

The Mani is divided into two regions, the Lakonian (inner) Mani in the south and Messinian (outer) Mani in the north-west below Kalamata.

Lakonian Mani
☎ 0733

The Lakonian Mani is wild and remote, its landscape dotted with the dramatic stone tower houses that are a trademark of the region. They were built as refuges from the clan wars of the 19th century. The best time to visit is in spring, when the barren countryside briefly bursts into life with a spectacular display of wild flowers.

The region's principal village is **Areopoli**, about 30km south-west of Gythio. There are a number of fine towers on the narrow, cobbled streets of the old town at the lower end of the main street, Kapetan Matapan.

Just south of here are the magnificent **Diros Caves**, where a subterranean river flows. The caves are open 8 am to 5.30 pm from June to September, closing at 2.30 pm from October to May. Admission is 3500 dr.

Gerolimenas, 20km farther south, is a tiny fishing village built around a sheltered bay. **Vathia**, a village of towers built on a rocky peak, is 11km south-east of Gerolimenas. Beyond Vathia, the coastline is a series of rocky outcrops sheltering pebbled beaches.

Places to Stay & Eat There are no camping grounds in the Lakonian Mani.

In Areopoli, there are basic singles/doubles for 4000/6000 dr at **Perros Bathrellos Rooms** (☎ 51 205) on Kapetan Matapan. It's above the popular **Taverna Barbar Petros**. The **Hotel Kouris** (☎ 51 340) on the main square charges 7500/9500 dr with bathroom.

In Gerolimenas, comfortable singles/doubles with bathroom at **Hotel Akrogiali** (☎ 54 204) go for 8000/12,000 dr. It also has a good restaurant.

Getting There & Around There are five buses a day from Areopoli to Sparta via Gythio.

Areopoli is the focal point of the local bus network. There are three buses a day to Itilo, two a day to the Diros Caves and Gerolimenas, and occasional buses to Vathia.

Crossing to the Messinian Mani involves changing buses at Itilo.

Messinian Mani
☎ 0721

The Messinian Mani runs north along the coast from Itilo to Kalamata. The beaches here are some of the best in Greece, set against the dramatic backdrop of the Taygetos mountains.

Itilo, the medieval capital of all the Mani, is split by a ravine that is the traditional dividing line between inner and outer Mani.

The picturesque coastal village of **Kardamyli**, 37km south of Kalamata, is the starting point for walks up the **Taygetos Gorge**. It takes about 2½ hours to walk to the deserted **Monastery of the Saviour**. Strong footwear is essential and take plenty of water.

Stoupa, 10km south of Kardamyli, has a great beach and is a popular package destination in summer.

Places to Stay & Eat There are several camping grounds along the coast, including two at Stoupa.

There are numerous domatia around Kardamyli with singles/doubles for 5000/8000 dr. **Stavros Bravacos** (☎ 73 326) has doubles with kitchen facilities for 9000 dr. The popular **Taverna Perivolis** is one of nine tavernas around the village.

Accommodation in Stoupa is monopolised by package operators in summer. **Hotel Stoupa** (☎ 54 308) on the road into town has doubles with bathroom for 11,000 dr. **Taverna Akrogiali** has a great setting overlooking the main beach.

Getting There & Away There are two buses a day from Kalamata to Itilo, stopping at Kardamyli and Stoupa.

OLYMPIA Ολυμπία
☎ 0624

The site of ancient Olympia lies 500m beyond the modern town, surrounded by the green foothills of Mt Kronion. There is a well-

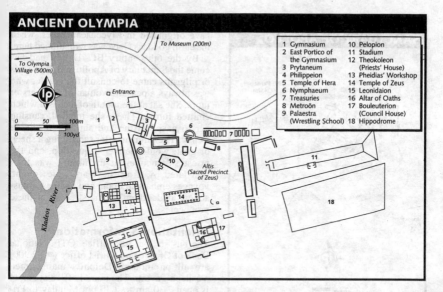

ANCIENT OLYMPIA

To Museum (200m)

To Olympia Village (500m)

Entrance

1 Gymnasium	10 Pelopion
2 East Portico of	11 Stadium
the Gymnasium	12 Theokoleon
3 Prytaneum	(Priests' House)
4 Philippeion	13 Pheidias' Workshop
5 Temple of Hera	14 Temple of Zeus
6 Nymphaeum	15 Leonidaion
7 Treasuries	16 Altar of Oaths
8 Metroön	17 Bouleuterion
9 Palaestra	(Council House)
(Wrestling School)	18 Hippodrome

Altis
(Sacred Precinct of Zeus)

Kladeos River

organised municipal tourist office on the main street, open 9 am to 9 pm daily between June and September, and 8 am to 2.45 pm Monday to Saturday the rest of the year. It also changes money.

Things to See

In ancient times, Olympia was a sacred place of temples, priests' dwellings and public buildings, as well as being the venue for the quadrennial Olympic Games. The first Olympics were staged in 776 BC, reaching the peak of their prestige in the 6th century BC. The city-states were bound by a sacred truce to stop fighting for three months and compete.

The site is dominated by the immense, ruined **Temple of Zeus**, to whom the games were dedicated. The site is open 8 am to 7 pm Monday to Friday, and 8.30 am to 3 pm weekends. Admission is 1200 dr. There's also a **museum** north of the archaeological site. It keeps similar hours and admission is also 1200 dr. Allow a whole day to see both.

Places to Stay & Eat

There are three good camping grounds to choose from. The most convenient is *Camping Diana* (☎ 22 314), 250m west of town. It has excellent facilities and a pool.

The *youth hostel* (☎ 22 580, Praxitelous Kondyli 18) has dorm beds for 1700 dr, including hot showers.

Pension Achilleys (☎ 22 562, Stefano-poulou 4) has singles/doubles with shared bathroom for 3000/6000 dr.

Fast Food Vassilakis at the corner of Spiliopoulou and Karamanli is better value than most places in town with pasta from 1000 dr and grilled meats from 1500 dr.

Getting There & Away

There are four buses a day to Olympia from Athens (5900 dr, 5½ hours). There are also regular buses and trains to Olympia from Pyrgos, 24km away on the coast.

Central Greece

Central Greece has little going for it in terms of attractions – with the notable exceptions of Delphi and surroundings.

DELPHI Δελφοί
☎ 0265 • pop 2400

Like so many of Greece's ancient sites, the setting at Delphi – overlooking the Gulf of Corinth from the slopes of Mt Parnassos – is

GREECE

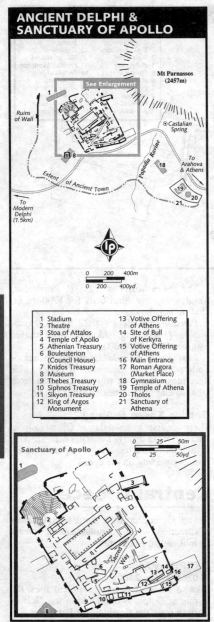

ANCIENT DELPHI & SANCTUARY OF APOLLO

Mt Parnassos
(2457m)

See Enlargement

Ruins
of Wall

Castalian
Spring

To
Arahova
& Athens

Extent of Ancient Town

To
Modern
Delphi
(1.5km)

Papadia Ravine

0   200   400m
0   200   400yd

1	Stadium	13	Votive Offering
2	Theatre		of Athens
3	Stoa of Attalos	14	Site of Bull
4	Temple of Apollo		of Kerkyra
5	Athenian Treasury	15	Votive Offering
6	Bouleuterion		of Athens
	(Council House)	16	Main Entrance
7	Knidos Treasury	17	Roman Agora
8	Museum		(Market Place)
9	Thebes Treasury	18	Gymnasium
10	Siphnos Treasury	19	Temple of Athena
11	Sikyon Treasury	20	Tholos
12	King of Argos	21	Sanctuary of
	Monument		Athena

Sanctuary of Apollo

0   25   50m
0   25   50yd

Sacred Way

stunning. The Delphic oracle is thought to have originated in Mycenaean times, when the earth goddess Gaea was worshipped here.

By the 6th century BC, Delphi had become the Sanctuary of Apollo and thousands of pilgrims came to consult the oracle, who was always a peasant woman of 50 years or more. She sat at the mouth of a chasm which emitted fumes. These she inhaled, causing her to gasp, writhe and shudder in divine frenzy. The pilgrim, after sacrificing a sheep or goat, would deliver a question, and the priestess' incoherent mumbling was then translated by a priest. Wars were fought, voyages embarked upon, and business transactions undertaken on the strength of these prophecies.

Orientation & Information

The bus station, post office, OTE, National Bank of Greece and tourist office (☎ 82 900) are all on modern Delphi's main street, Vasileon Pavlou. The tourist office at No 44 is open 7.30 am to 2.30 pm Monday to Friday. The ancient site is 1.5km east of modern Delphi.

Sanctuary of Apollo

The **Sacred Way** leads up from the entrance of the site to the **Temple of Apollo**. It was here that the oracle supposedly sat, although no chasm, let alone vapour, has been detected. The path continues to the theatre and stadium. Opposite this sanctuary is the **Sanctuary of Athena** (free admission) and the much-photographed **tholos**, a 4th-century BC columned rotunda of Pentelic marble.

The site is open 7.30 am to 7.15 pm Monday to Friday, and 8.30 am to 2.45 pm weekends and public holidays. The museum is open similar hours. Entry to each is 1200 dr.

Places to Stay & Eat

There are lots of hotels in town, starting with *Hotel Tholos* (*☎/fax 82 268, Apollonos 31*). It has singles/doubles with bathroom for 5000/9000 dr. It's open from March to November and on Friday and Saturday in winter. *Hotel Parnassos* (*☎ 82 321, Vasileon Pavlou and Frederikis 32*) charges 8000/10,000 dr with breakfast.

The food is good value at *Taverna Vakhos* next to the Hotel Tholos.

GREECE

Getting There & Away

There are five buses a day to Delphi from Athens (2900 dr, three hours).

Northern Greece

Northern Greece covers the regions of Epiros, Thessaly, Macedonia and Thrace. It includes some areas of outstanding natural beauty, such as the Zagoria region of north-western Epiros.

IGOUMENITSA Ηγουμενίτσα
☎ 0665 • pop 6800

Igoumenitsa, opposite the island of Corfu, is the main port of north-western Greece. Few people stay any longer than it takes to buy a ticket out. The bus station is on Kyprou. To get there from the ferries, follow the waterfront (Ethnikis Antistasis) north for 500m and turn up El Venizelou. Kyprou is two blocks inland and the bus station is on the left.

Places to Stay & Eat

If you get stuck for the night, you'll find signs for *domatia* around the port. The D-class *Egnatia* (☎ 23 648, Eleftherias 2) has comfortable rooms for 8500/11,500 dr with private bathroom.

Bilis (☎ 26 214, Agion Apostolon 15) opposite the Corfu ferry quay is handy for a quick meal.

Getting There & Away

Bus Services include nine buses a day to Ioannina (1900 dr, two hours), and four a day to Athens (8850 dr, 8½ hours).

Ferry There are international services to the Italian ports of Ancona, Bari, Brindisi, Trieste and Venice. Ticket agents are opposite the port.

Ferries to Corfu (1400 dr, 1½ hours) operate every hour between 5 am and 10 pm.

IOANNINA Ιωάννινα
☎ 0651 • pop 90,000

Ioannina is the largest town in Epiros, sitting on the western shore of Lake Pamvotis. In Ottoman times, it was one of the most important towns in the country.

Orientation & Information

The town centre is around Plateia Dimokratias where the main streets of the new town meet. All facilities of importance to travellers are nearby.

The helpful EOT office (☎ 25 086) is set back on a small square at Napoleon Zerva 2, 100m to the south-west along Dodonis. It's open 7.30 am to 2.30 pm and 5.30 to 8.30 pm Monday to Friday, and 9 am to 1 pm Saturday. Robinson Travel (☎ 29 402), 8th Merarhias Gramou 10, specialises in treks in the Zagoria region.

For Internet access, try the Giannena Club, 100m from the tourist office at Stoa Saka 30-32.

Things to See

The **old town** juts out into the lake on a small peninsula. Inside the impressive fortifications lies a maze of winding streets flanked by traditional Turkish houses.

The **Nisi** (island) is a serene spot in the middle of the lake, with four monasteries set among the trees. Ferries to the island leave from just north of the old town. They run half-hourly in summer and hourly in winter. The fare is 200 dr.

Places to Stay & Eat

Camping Limnopoula (☎ 25 265) is on the lakeside 2km north of town.

The cheapest hotel is *Agapi Inn* (☎ 20 541, Tsirigoti 6) near the bus station. Basic singles/doubles cost 5000/7000 dr. Next door is the co-owned *Hotel Paris*, which has more comfortable singles/doubles for 6000/9000 dr. There are *domatia* on the island.

There are several restaurants outside the entrance to the old town. *To Manteio Psistaria* is recommended.

Getting There & Away

Ioannina has two flights a day to Athens (18,400 dr) and one servicing Thessaloniki (12,100 dr).

The main bus terminal is 300m north of Plateia Dimokratias on Zossimadon, the northern extension of Markou Botsari. Services include 12 buses a day to Athens (7700 dr, seven hours), nine to Igoumenitsa, five to Thessaloniki and three to Trikala via Kalambaka.

GREECE

ZAGORIA & VIKOS GORGE
☎ 0653

The Zagoria (Zagória) region covers a large expanse of the Pindos Mountains north of Ioannina. It's a wilderness of raging rivers, crashing waterfalls and deep gorges. Snowcapped mountains rise out of dense forests. The remote villages that dot the hillsides are famous for their impressive grey-slate architecture.

The fairytale village of **Monodendri** is the starting point for treks through the dramatic **Vikos Gorge**, with its awesome sheer limestone walls. It's a strenuous 7½-hour walk from Monodendri to the twin villages of **Megalo Papingo** and **Mikro Papingo**. The trek is very popular and the path is clearly marked. Ioannina's EOT office has information.

Other walks start from **Tsepelovo**, near Monodendri.

Places to Stay & Eat
There are some wonderful places to stay, but none of them come cheap. The options in Monodendri include the traditional **Monodendri Pension & Restaurant** (☎ 71 300). Doubles are 9000 dr. **Pension Gouris** (☎ 094-789 909) in Tsepelovohas is a delightful place with doubles for 12,000 dr. The owner, Alexis, also runs a shop and restaurant and can advise on treks.

Xenonas tou Kouli (☎ 41 138) is one of several options in Megalo Papingo. Rates start at 12,000 dr for doubles. The owners are official EOS guides. The only rooms in Mikro Papingo are at **Xenonas Dias** (☎ 41 257), a beautifully restored mansion with doubles for 11,000 dr. It has a restaurant specialising in charcoal grills.

Getting There & Away
Buses to the Zagoria leave from the main bus station in Ioannina. There are buses to Monodendri on weekdays at 6 am and 4.15 pm; to Tsepelovo on Monday, Wednesday and Friday at 6 am and 3 pm; and to the Papingo villages on Monday, Wednesday and Friday at 6 am and 2.30 pm.

TRIKALA Τρίκαλα
Trikala is a major transport hub, but otherwise has little of interest. Eight buses a day run between Trikala and Athens (5400 dr, 5½ hours).

There are also six buses a day to Thessaloniki, two to Ioannina and hourly buses to Kalambaka (for Meteora).

METEORA Μετέωρα
☎ 0432

Meteora is an extraordinary place. The massive, sheer columns of rock that dot the landscape were created by wave action millions of years ago. Perched precariously atop these seemingly inaccessible outcrops are monasteries that date back to the late 14th century.

Meteora is just north of the town of Kalambaka, on the Ioannina-Trikala road. The rocks behind the town are spectacularly floodlit at night. **Kastraki**, 2km from Kalambaka, is a charming village of red-tiled houses just west of the monasteries.

Things to See
There were once monasteries on each of the 24 pinnacles, but only five are still occupied. They are Megalou Meteorou (Metamorphosis, open 9 am to 1 pm and 3 to 6 pm, closed Tuesday), Varlaam (open 9 am to 1 pm and 3.30 to 6 pm, closed Friday), Agiou Stefanou (open 9 am to 1 pm and 3 to 5 pm daily), Agias Triados (open 9 am to 5 pm, closed Thursday), Agiou Nikolaou (open 9 am to 5 pm daily) and Agias Varvaras Rousanou (open 9 am to 6 pm, closed Wednesday). Admission is 500 dr for each monastery; free for Greeks.

Meteora is best explored on foot, following the old paths where they exist. Allow a whole day to visit all of the monasteries and take food and water. Women must wear skirts that reach below their knees, men must wear long trousers, and arms must be covered.

Places to Stay & Eat
Kastraki is the best base for visiting Meteora. **Vrachos Camping** (☎ 22 293), on the edge of the village, is an excellent site.

There are dozens of **domatia** in town, charging from 4000/6000 dr for singles/doubles. **Hotel Sydney** (☎/fax 23 079) on the road into town from Kalambaka has comfortable doubles with bathroom for 9000 dr.

In Kalambaka, **Koka Roka Rooms** (☎ 24 554) at the beginning of the path to Agia Triada is a popular travellers place. Doubles

METEORA

Ypapanti
(closed to the public)

Megalou Meteorou
(Grand Meteora)

Varlaam

Agiou Nikolaou Anapafsa

Agias Varvaras
Rousanou

Psaropetra

Boufidis
Camping

Agiou Antoniou
(closed to
the public)

Kastraki

Panagia

Bantowas

Agias Triados
(Holy Trinity)

Agiou Stefanou

Vrachos
Camping

Kalambaka

To
Ioannina

To
Trikala

with bath are 8000 dr; the taverna downstairs is good value. Telephone for a lift from the bus or train station.

Getting There & Away

Kalambaka is the hub of the transport network. There are frequent buses to Trikala and two a day to Ioannina. Local buses shuttle constantly between Kalambaka and Kastraki; five a day continue to Metamorphosis.

Trains between Kalambaka and Volos weren't operating at the time of research. The line was being upgraded and services were scheduled to resume in 2001. These trains connect with trains from Athens and Thessaloniki at Paleofarsalos.

THESSALONIKI Θεσσαλονίκη
☎ 031 • pop 750,000

Thessaloniki, also known as Salonica, is Greece's second-largest city. It's a bustling, sophisticated place with good restaurants and a busy nightlife. It was once the second city of Byzantium, and there are some magnificent Byzantine churches, as well as a scattering of Roman ruins.

Orientation

Thessaloniki is laid out on a grid system. The main thoroughfares – Tsimiski, Egnatia and Agiou Dimitriou – run parallel to Nikis, on the waterfront. Plateias Eleftherias and Aristotelous, both on Nikis, are the main squares. The city's most famous landmark is the White Tower (no longer white) at the eastern end of Nikis.

The train station is on Monastiriou, the westerly continuation of Egnatia beyond Plateia Dimokratias, and the airport is 16km to the south-east. The old Turkish quarter is north of Athinas.

Information

Tourist Offices The EOT office (☎ 271 888), Plateia Aristotelous 8, is open 8.30 am to 8 pm Monday to Friday, and 8.30 am to 2 pm Saturday. The tourist police (☎ 554 871) are at Dodekanisou 4, 5th floor, open 7.30 am to 11 pm daily.

Money The National Bank and the Commercial Bank have branches on Plateia Dimokratias. The branch of the National Bank of Greece at Tsimiski 11 is open at weekends for currency exchange. American Express (☎ 269 521) is at Tsimiski 19.

Post & Communications The main post office is at Aristotelous 26 and the OTE telephone office is at Karolou Dil 27.

Email & Internet Access Globus Internet Café (☎ 232 901) is a long-established place near the Roman Agora at Amynta 12.

Laundry Bianca Laundrette, just north of the Arch of Galerius on Antoniadou, charges 1400 dr to wash and dry a load.

Medical Services There is a first-aid centre (☎ 530 530) at Navarhou Koundourioti 6.

Things to See

The **archaeological museum**, at the eastern end of Tsimiski, houses a superb collection of treasures from the royal tombs of Philip II. It is open 8 am to 7 pm Tuesday to Friday

GREECE

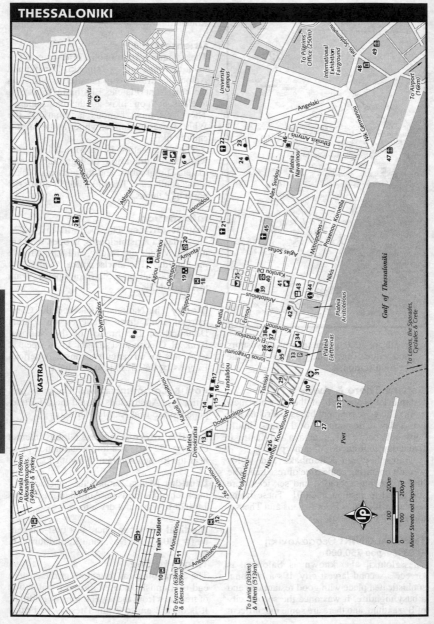

THESSALONIKI

GREECE

KASTRA

Hospital

University Campus

Angelaki

Ethnikis Amynis

Plateia Navarinou

Nik Germanou

To Pilgrims' Office (250m)
International Exhibition Fairground

To Airport (16km)

Avgoustou

Athinas

Iasonidou

Alex Svolou

Agias Sofias

Gulf of Thessaloniki

Agiou Dimitriou

Amynta

Olympou

Filippou

Egnatia

Ermou

Aristotelous

Karolou Dil

Mitropoleos

Proxenou Koromila

Nikis

Plateia Aristotelous

To Lesvos, the Sporades, Cyclades & Crete

Olympiados

Ionos Dragoumi

Tantalidou

Tsimiski

L Venizelou

Komninon

Plateia Eleftherias

Kalapothaki

Karaoli & Dimitriou

Dodekanisou

Navarinou Koundourioti

Port

To Kavala (169km), Alexandroupolis (349km) & Turkey

Langada

Polytehniou

26 Oktovriou

Plateia Dimokratias

Monastiriou

Anegenisgos

To Evzoni (63km) & Edessa (89km)

To Larisa (303km) & Athens (513km)

Train Station

0   100   200m
0   100   200yd

Minor Streets not Depicted

THESSALONIKI

PLACES TO STAY
14 Hotel Acropol
16 Hotel Averof
17 Hotel Atlas
46 Youth Hostel

PLACES TO EAT
15 Ta Nea Ilysia
38 O Loutros Fish Taverna

OTHER
1 Kavala Bus Station
2 Church of Osios David
3 Monastery of Vlatadon
4 Atatürk's House
5 Turkish Consulate
6 Show Avantaz
7 Church of Agios Dimitrios
8 Ministry of Macedonia & Thrace
9 Alexandroupolis Bus Station
10 Airport Bus Terminal
11 Athens & Trikala Bus Station
12 Katerini Bus Station
13 Tourist Police
18 Local Bus Station
19 Roman Agora
20 Globus Internet Café
21 Church of Panagia Ahiropiitos
22 Rotonda
23 Bianca Laundrette
24 Arch of Galerius
25 Main Post Office
26 Olympic Airways Office
27 Hydrofoil Departure Point
28 Olympic Airways
29 Ta Ladadika (area)
30 Karaharsis Travel & Shipping Agency
31 First-Aid Centre
32 Ferry Departure Point
33 Car Parking
34 UK Consulate
35 Molho Bookshop
36 National Bank of Greece
37 American Express
39 Train Tickets Office (OSE)
40 OTE
41 US Consulate
42 Foreign Newspapers Kiosk
43 Olympian Cinema
44 EOT
45 Church of Agia Sofia
47 White Tower
48 Archaeological Museum
49 Museum of Byzantine Culture

and 12.30 to 7 pm Monday; admission is 1500 dr.

The **White Tower** is the city's most prominent landmark. It houses a **Byzantine Museum**, with splendid frescoes and icons. It's open 8 am to 2.30 pm Tuesday to Sunday; admission is free.

Places to Stay & Eat
The *youth hostel* (☎ 225 946, Alex Svolou 44) has dorm beds for 2000 dr. To get there, take bus No 10 from outside the train station to the Kamara stop.

The best budget hotel in town is *Hotel Acropol* (☎ 536 170) on Tandalidou, a quiet side street off Egnatia. Clean singles/doubles with shared bath are listed at 6000/9000 dr, but most of the time it charges a bargain 5000 dr per room. You'll find similar prices at the quiet *Hotel Averof* (☎ 538 498, Leontos Sofou 24).

Hotel Atlas (☎ 537 046, Egnatia 40) has singles/doubles with shared bathroom for 6000/9000 dr and doubles with bath for 12,000 dr. The rooms at the front get a lot of traffic noise.

Ta Nea Ilysia opposite the Hotel Averof on Leontos Sofou is a popular place, with main dishes priced from 1300 dr.

O Loutros Fish Taverna, which occupies an old Turkish hammam near the flower market on Komninon, is a lively place full of local colour. Most dishes cost from 2000 dr to 3000 dr.

Entertainment
You will find live bouzouki and folk music every night at *Show Avantaz*, opposite the Turkish consulate at Agiou Dimitriou 156. It opens at 11 pm.

A good area to check is *Ta Ladadika*, near the ferry quay, where former shipping warehouses have been converted into numerous trendy cafes, bars and restaurants.

Getting There & Away
Air There are up to 20 flights a day to Athens, priced from 19,400 dr with Air Greece to 23,400 dr with Olympic. Olympic has daily flights to Ioannina, Lesvos and Limnos, and occasional flights to Chios, Mykonos and Rhodes. Aegean Airlines has two flights a day to Iraklio. Olympic Airways (☎ 230 240) is at Nav Koundourioti 3.

Bus There are several bus terminals, most of them near the train station. Buses to Athens, Igoumenitsa and Trikala leave from Monastiriou 65 and 67; buses to Alexandroupolis leave from Koloniari 17; and buses to Litihoro (for Mt Olympus) leave from Promitheos 10. Buses to the Halkidiki Peninsula leave from

GREECE

Karakasi 68 (in the eastern part of town; it's marked on the free EOT map). To get there, take local bus No 10 from Egnatia to the Botsari stop.

The OSE has two buses a day to Athens from the train station, as well as international services to Istanbul and Tirana (Albania).

Train There are nine trains a day to Athens, five of them intercity express services (8250 dr, six hours). There are also five trains to Alexandroupolis, two of which are express services (4990 dr, 5½ hours). All the international trains from Athens stop at Thessaloniki. You can get more information from the OSE office at Aristotelous 18, or from the train station.

Ferry & Hydrofoil There's a Sunday ferry to Lesvos, Limnos and Chios throughout the year. In summer there are at least three ferries a week to Iraklio (Crete), stopping in the Sporades and the Cyclades on the way. In summer there are daily hydrofoils to Skiathos, Skopelos and Alonnisos. Karaharisis Travel & Shipping Agency (π 524 544, fax 532 289), Koundourioti 8, handles tickets for both ferries and hydrofoils.

Getting Around

There is no bus service from the Olympic Airways office to the airport. Take bus No 78 from the train station (150 dr). A taxi from the airport costs about 2000 dr.

There is a flat fare of 100 dr on bus services within the city.

HALKIDIKI Χαλκιδική

Halkidiki is the three-pronged peninsula south-east of Thessaloniki. It's the main resort area of Northern Greece, with superb sandy beaches right around its 500km of coastline. **Kassandra**, the south-western prong of the peninsula, has surrendered irrevocably to mass tourism. **Sithonia**, the middle prong, is not as over-the-top and has some spectacular scenery.

Mt Athos

Halkidiki's third prong is occupied by the all-male Monastic Republic of Mt Athos (also called the Holy Mountain), where monasteries full of priceless treasures stand amid an impressive landscape of gorges, wooded mountains and precipitous rocks.

Obtaining a four-day visitors permit involves a bit of work. Start early, because only 10 foreign adult males may enter Mt Athos per day and there are long waiting lists in summer. You can start the process from outside Thessaloniki, but you will have to pass through Thessaloniki anyway to pick up your reservation.

You must first book a date for your visit with the Mount Athos Pilgrims' Office (π 031-861 611, fax 861 811), Leoforos Karamanli 14, just east of the Exhibition Site (off map) in Thessaloniki. This office is open 8.30 am to 1.30 pm and 6 to 8 pm weekdays (except Wednesday). Call first and make a telephone booking.

Letters of recommendation are no longer required, but you must declare your intention to be a pilgrim. You need to supply a photocopy of your passport details and, if you are Orthodox, a photocopied certificate showing your religion.

You must then call at the Pilgrims' Office in person to collect the forms confirming your reservation. You can then proceed from Thessaloniki to the port of Ouranoupolis, departure point for boats to Mt Athos, where you will be given your actual permit.

Armed at last with your permit, you can explore, on foot, the 20 monasteries and dependent religious communities of Mt Athos. You can stay only one night at each monastery.

MT OLYMPUS Ολυμπος Ορος
π 0352

Mt Olympus is Greece's highest and mightiest mountain. The ancients chose it as the abode of their gods and assumed it to be the exact centre of the Earth. Olympus has eight peaks, the highest of which is Mytikas (2917m). The area is popular with trekkers, most of whom use the village of **Litohoro** as a base. Litohoro is 5km inland from the Athens-Thessaloniki highway.

The EOS office (π 81 944) on Plateia Kentriki has information on the various treks and conditions. The office is open 9 am to 1 pm and 6 to 8.30 pm Monday to Friday, and 9 am to 1 pm Saturday.

The main route to the top takes two days, overnighting at one of the refuges on the mountain. Good protective clothing is essential, even in summer.

Places to Stay & Eat
The cheapest rooms are at *Hotel Markesia* (☎ 81 831) near Plateia Kentriki. It has clean singles/doubles with bathroom for 6500/7500 dr. It's open from June to October. At other times, try the cheery *Hotel Enipeas* (☎/fax 81 328) on Plateia Kentriki, where you'll find singles/doubles for 9000/12,000 dr. *Olympus Taverna* on Agiou Nikolaou serves standard fare at reasonable prices.

There are four *refuges* on the mountain at altitudes ranging from 940m to 2720m. They are open from May to September.

Getting There & Away
There are eight buses a day to Litohoro from Thessaloniki and three from Athens (7500 dr, six hours).

ALEXANDROUPOLIS
Αλεξανδρούπολη
☎ 0551 • pop 37,000
Dusty Alexandroupolis doesn't have much going for it, but if you're going to Turkey or Samothraki, you may end up staying overnight here. There's a tourist office (☎ 24 998) in the town hall on Dimokratias.

Places to Stay & Eat
Hotel Lido (☎ 28 808, Paleologou 15), one block north of the bus station, is a great budget option. It has singles/doubles with shared bathroom for 4000/5000 dr, and doubles with private bathroom for 6500 dr.

Neraida Restaurant on Kyprou has a good range of local specialities priced from 1600 dr. Kyprou starts opposite the pier where ferries leave for Samothraki.

Getting There & Away
There are five flights a day to Athens (19,700 dr) from the airport 7km west of town. There are five trains and five buses (5400 dr) a day to Thessaloniki. There's also a daily train and a daily OSE bus to Istanbul.

In summer there are at least two boats a day to Samothraki (2300 dr, two hours), dropping to one in winter. There are also hydrofoils to Samothraki and Limnos.

Saronic Gulf Islands
Νησιά του Σαρωνικού

The Saronic Gulf Islands are the closest island group to Athens. Not surprisingly, they are a very popular escape for residents of the congested capital. Accommodation can be hard to find between mid-June and September, and on weekends year-round.

Getting There & Away
Ferries to all four islands, and hydrofoils to Aegina, leave from the Great Harbour in Piraeus. Hydrofoils to the other islands run from Zea Marina in Piraeus.

AEGINA Αίγινα
☎ 0297 • pop 11,000
Aegina is the closest island to Athens and a popular destination for day-trippers. Many make for the lovely **Temple of Aphaia**, a well-preserved Doric temple 12km east of Aegina town. It is open 8.15 am to 7 pm weekdays (to 5 pm in winter) and 8.30 am to 3 pm weekends. Admission is 800 dr. Buses from Aegina town to the small resort of **Agia Marina** can drop you at the site. Agia Marina has the best beach on the island, which isn't saying much.

Most travellers prefer to stay in Aegina town, where the *Hotel Plaza* (☎ 25 600) has singles/doubles overlooking the sea for 4500/7500 dr.

POROS Πόρος
pop 4000
Poros is a big hit with the Brits, but it's hard to work out why. The beaches are nothing to write home about and there are no sites of significance. The main attraction is pretty Poros town, draped over the Sferia Peninsula. Sferia is linked to the rest of the island, known as Kalavria, by a narrow isthmus. Most of the package hotels are here. There are a few *domatia* in Poros town, signposted off the road to Kalavria.

The island lies little more than a stone's throw from the mainland, opposite the Peloponnesian village of Galatas.

GREECE

HYDRA Ύδρα
☎ 0298 • pop 3000

Hydra is the island with the most style and is famous as the haunt of artists and jet-setters. Its gracious stone mansions are stacked up the rocky hillsides that surround the fine natural harbour. The main attraction is peace and quiet. There are no motorised vehicles on the island – apart from a garbage truck and a few construction vehicles.

Accommodation is expensive, but of a high standard. *Hotel Dina* (☎ 52 248) has singles/doubles overlooking the harbour for 10,000/12,000 dr, less on weekdays.

SPETSES Σπέτσες
☎ 0298 • pop 3700

Pine-covered Spetses is perhaps the most beautiful island in the group. It also has the best beaches, so it's packed with package tourists in summer. The **old harbour** in Spetses town is a delightful place to explore.

Orloff Apartments (☎ 72 246) has well-equipped studios behind the harbour for 6000/10,000 dr.

Cyclades Κυκλάδες

The Cyclades, named after the rough circle they form around Delos, are quintessential Greek islands with brilliant white architecture, dazzling light and golden beaches.

Delos, historically the most important island of the group, is uninhabited. The inhabited islands of the archipelago are Mykonos, Syros, Tinos, Andros, Paros, Naxos, Ios, Santorini (Thira), Anafi, Amorgos, Sikinos, Folegandros and the tiny islands of Koufonisi, Shinousa, Iraklia and Donousa, lying east of Naxos. A further six – Kea, Kythnos, Serifos, Sifnos, Kimolos and Milos (all with small permanent populations) – are referred to as the Western Cyclades.

Some of the Cyclades, like Mykonos, Ios and Santorini, have embraced tourism, filling their coastlines with bars and their beaches with sun lounges. Others, like Anafi, Sikinos and the tiny islands east of Naxos, are little more than clumps of rock, each with a village, secluded coves and few tourists.

To give even the briefest rundown on every island is impossible in a single chapter.

For more detailed information, see Lonely Planet's *Greek Islands*.

History
The Cyclades enjoyed a flourishing Bronze Age civilisation (3000 to 1100 BC), more or less concurrent with the Minoan civilisation.

By the 5th century BC, the island of Delos had been taken over by Athens, which kept its treasury there.

Between the 4th and 7th centuries AD, the islands, like the rest of Greece, suffered a series of invasions and occupations. During the Middle Ages they were raided by pirates – hence the labyrinthine character of their towns, which was meant to confuse attackers. On some islands the whole population would move into the mountainous interior to escape the pirates, while on others they would brave it out on the coast. Hence on some islands the hora (main town) is on the coast and on others it is inland.

The Cyclades became part of independent Greece in 1827.

Getting There & Away
Air Mykonos and Santorini have international airports that receive charter flights from northern Europe. There are daily flights from Athens to Milos, Syros, Naxos, Paros, Mykonos and Santorini. In addition there are direct flights between Santorini and Mykonos. Both islands have direct connections with Rhodes and Thessaloniki, and there are two flights a week from Santorini to Iraklio (Crete).

Ferry There are daily boats from Piraeus to most islands, but in winter, services are severely curtailed. A daily ferry travels between Mykonos, Paros, Naxos, Ios and Santorini. In summer, hydrofoils and catamarans link Paros, Naxos, Syros, Tinos, Ios and Santorini. In July, August and September, the Cyclades are prone to the *meltemi*, a ferocious north-easterly wind which can disrupt ferry schedules.

MYKONOS Μύκονος
☎ 0289 • pop 6170

Mykonos is perhaps the most visited – and most expensive – of all Greek islands. It has the most sophisticated nightlife and is a mecca for gay travellers.

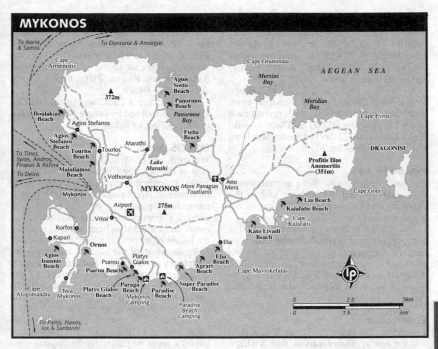

MYKONOS

Orientation & Information

There is no tourist office. The tourist police (☎ 22 482) are at the port, in the same building as the hotel reservation office (☎ 24 540), the association of rooms and apartments office (☎ 26 860), and the camping information office (☎ 22 852). The post office is not far from the south bus station, and the OTE is near the north bus station. There's slow and expensive Internet access at Porto Market, opposite the port. A useful Web site is www.mykonosgreece.com.

Things to See

The island's capital and port is warren-like Mykonos town, with chic boutiques, houses with brightly painted wooden balconies, and flowering plants cascading down dazzling white walls.

The **archaeological museum** and **maritime museum** are OK. The **folklore museum**, near the Delos quay, is well stocked with local memorabilia. It's open 5.30 to 8.30 pm daily; admission is free.

The most popular beaches are **Platys Gialos**, with wall-to-wall sun lounges, the mainly nude **Paradise** and mainly gay **Super Paradise**, **Agrari** and **Elia**. The less crowded ones are **Panormos**, **Kato Livadi** and **Kalafatis**.

Places to Stay

Paradise Beach Camping (☎ 22 852, fax 24 350, ℮ paradise@paradise.myk.forthnet.gr) charges 1500 dr per person and 1100 dr per tent. Two-person beach cabins with shared facilities are 10,000 dr; cabins for four with private bath cost 22,000 dr. *Mykonos Camping* (☎ 24 578) near Platys Gialos beach charges 2000/1100 dr per person/tent. Minibuses for these sites usually meet the ferries and there are regular buses into town.

Rooms fill up quickly in summer, so it's prudent to succumb to the first domatia owner who accosts you. Outside of the high season (July and August), you can get some excellent bargains.

Kalogera is a good street to seek out lodgings – there are a number of mid-range hotels here, including **Hotel Philippi** (☎ 22 294, fax 24 680), offering simple doubles/triples with bath for 17,000/22,000 dr. Nearby, **Rooms Chez Maria** (☎ 22 480) has attractive rooms for 15,000/20,000 dr. There's a good (pricey) restaurant here as well.

Hotel Delos (☎ 22 517, fax 22 312, ✉ ero stravel@myk.forthnet.gr) on the small town beach has spotless doubles with private bath and water views for 20,000 dr. The old-world **Hotel Apollon** (☎ 22 223) on the harbourfront also offers doubles for 20,000 dr.

Places to Eat

For food with a view, there are numerous restaurants around the harbour and in the charming area known as Little Venice, on the western waterfront.

Busy **Niko's Taverna**, near the Delos quay, serves good seafood. **Sesame Kitchen**, next to the maritime museum on Matogianni, offers a variety of vegetarian dishes. **Antonini's Taverna**, on Taxi Square, is popular with locals for its good-value traditional fare.

Entertainment

Troubador (formerly the Down Under Bar) and the nearby **Skandinavian Bar & Disco** are very popular. **Rhapsody** in Little Venice plays jazz and blues. Next door, **Montparnasse Piano Bar** plays classical music at sunset.

Cavo Paradiso, 300m above Paradise Beach, has all-night raves starting at 3 am. Entry is 5000 dr.

Porta, **Kastro Bar**, **Icaros** and **Manto** are among the many popular gay haunts. **Pierro's** is the place for late-night dancing.

Getting There & Away

Daily flights from Mykonos to Athens cost 19,100 dr and to Santorini 15,400 dr. In summer there are also flights to/from Rhodes and Thessaloniki. The Olympic Airways office (☎ 22 490) is on Plateia Louka, by the south bus station.

There are ferries daily to Mykonos from Piraeus (4800 dr). From Mykonos there are daily ferries and hydrofoils to most Cycladic islands, and weekly services to Crete, the North-Eastern Aegean and the Dodecanese. For the port police, call ☎ 22 218.

Getting Around

The north bus station is near the port, behind the OTE office. It serves Agios Stefanos, Elia, Kalafatis and Ano Mera. The south bus station, south-east of the windmills, serves Agios Yiannis, Psarou, Platys Gialos, Ornos and Paradise Beach.

Paradise, Super Paradise, Agrari and Elia Beaches are served by caïque from Mykonos town and Platys Gialos.

DELOS Δήλος

Just south-east of Mykonos, the uninhabited island of Delos is the Cyclades' archaeological jewel. According to mythology, Delos was the birthplace of Apollo – the god of light, poetry, music, healing and prophecy. The island flourished as an important religious and commercial centre from the 3rd millennium BC, reaching the height of its power in the 5th century BC.

To the north of the island's harbour is the **Sanctuary of Apollo**, containing temples dedicated to him, and the **Terrace of the Lions**. These proud beasts were carved in the 7th century BC from marble from Naxos, and their function was to guard the sacred area. (At the time of research the marble lions had been moved to the island's museum and copies were to be placed on the original site.) The **Sacred Lake** (dry since 1926) is where Leto supposedly gave birth to Apollo. The **museum**, with impressive but poorly labelled artefacts, is east of this section.

South of the harbour is the **Theatre Quarter**, where private houses were built around the **Theatre of Delos**. East of here are the **Sanctuaries of the Foreign Gods**. Climb **Mt Kynthos** (113m) for a spectacular view of Delos and the surrounding islands.

Excursion boats leave Mykonos for Delos (30 minutes) between 9 and 10.15 am daily except Monday, when the site is closed. The round trip is 1900 dr; entrance to the site is 1200 dr. The boat schedule allows you only about three hours on the island – for full appreciation of the site, it's worth investing in a guidebook or, better still, a guided tour. There is a cafeteria on the island.

PAROS Πάρος
☎ 0284 • pop 9591

Paros is an attractive island, although less dramatically so than Naxos, 16km to the east. Its

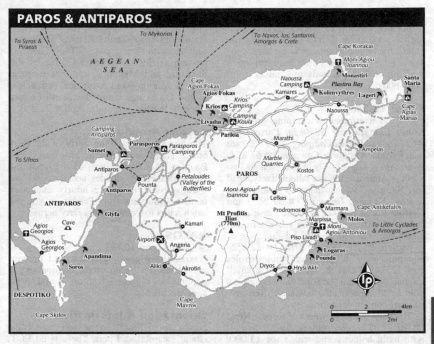

PAROS & ANTIPAROS

softly contoured and terraced hills culminate in one central mountain, Profitis Ilias. It has some of the finest beaches in the Cyclades, and is famous for its pure white marble – no less than the *Venus de Milo* herself was created from it.

Orientation & Information

Paros' main town and port is Parikia, on the west coast. Agora, also known as Market St, is Parikia's main commercial thoroughfare running south-west from the main square, Plateia Mavrogenous (opposite the ferry terminal). There is no tourist office but countless agencies can help with information. The OTE is on the south-west waterfront; turn right from the ferry pier. The post office is also on the waterfront, but to the north of the pier.

Wired Cafe is on Market St, while just north of the quay is Memphis.net, a bar-cum-cybercafe. A good Web site is at parosweb.com.

Things to See & Do

One of the most notable churches in Greece is Parikia's **Panagia Ekatontapyliani** (Our Lady of the Hundred Gates), which features a beautiful, highly ornate interior. Visitors must be 'modestly attired' (ie, no shorts).

Petaloudes, 8km from Parikia, is better known as the Valley of the Butterflies. In summer, huge swarms of the creatures almost conceal the copious foliage.

The charming village of **Naoussa**, filled with white houses and labyrinthine alleyways, is still a working fishing village, despite an enormous growth in tourism over the last few years. Naoussa has good beaches served by caïque, including popular **Kolimvythres**, with bizarre rock formations; **Monastiri**, a mainly nude beach; and **Santa Maria**, which is good for windsurfing. Paros' longest beach, **Hrysi Akti** (Golden Beach) on the south coast, is also popular with windsurfers.

The picturesque inland villages of **Lefkes**, **Marmara** and **Marpissa** are all worth a visit and offer good walking opportunities. The Moni Agiou Antoniou (Monastery of St Anthony), on a hill above Marpissa, offers breathtaking views.

Antiparos This small island, less than 2km from Paros, has superb beaches but is becoming too popular for its own good. One of the chief attractions in Antiparos is the **cave**, considered one of Europe's most beautiful (open 9.45 am to 4.45 pm daily in summer only; entry 600 dr).

Places to Stay
Paros has a number of camping grounds. *Koula Camping* (☎ 22 081), *Parasporas* (☎ 22 268) and *Krios Camping* (☎ 21 705) are near Parikia. *Antiparos Camping* (☎ 61 221) is on Agios Giannis Theologos Beach, just north of Antiparos village. Alternatively, head for Naoussa, which has two camp sites nearby: *Naoussa Camping* (☎ 51 595) and *Surfing Beach* (☎ 51 013). There's also an information office at Naoussa's bus terminal which can help with accommodation.

Back in Parikia, *Rooms Mike* (☎ 22 856) is popular with backpackers. Doubles/triples cost 12,000/15,000 dr, with use of a small kitchen. Walk 50m left from the pier and it's next to Memphis.net cybercafe. Mike also has self-contained studios.

The very friendly owners of *Rooms Rena* (☎/fax 21 427) offer spotless doubles/triples with bath, balcony and fridge for 13,000/16,000 dr; turn left from the pier then right at the ancient cemetery.

Hotel Argonauta (☎ 21 440, fax 23 442) on the main square offers comfortable rooms for 18,000/21,000 dr.

Places to Eat
There are countless tavernas and cafes lining the waterfront and surrounding the main square. If you're after a cheap, quick fix, *Zorba's* on the main square does a mean gyros. Just off Market St is the oddly named *Happy Green Cow*, dishing up good vegetarian fare. For something more upmarket, try *I Trata* or *Porphyra*, on opposite sides of the ancient cemetery, north of the pier. Both offer excellent seafood at reasonable prices.

Entertainment
There are a few good bars tucked away in the old town, including the mellow *Pirate* jazz and blues bar. The far southern end of Parikia's waterfront has *Slammers*, *Comma Club* and *The Dubliner Irish Bar* to keep you going.

Getting There & Away
Flights to/from Athens cost 18,900 dr. Paros is a major transport hub for ferries. Daily connections with Piraeus cost 4900 dr. There are frequent ferries and hydrofoils to Naxos, Ios, Santorini and Mykonos, and less frequent ones to Amorgos and Astypalea, then across to the Dodecanese and the North-Eastern Aegean. For the port police, call ☎ 21 240.

Getting Around
The bus station is 100m north of the ferry quay. There are frequent buses to Aliki, Pounta, Naoussa, Lefkes, Piso Livadi and Hrysi Akti. For Petaloudes, take the Aliki bus.

In summer there are hourly excursion boats to Antiparos from Parikia, or you can catch a bus to Pounta and a ferry across.

NAXOS Νάξος
☎ 0285 • pop 16,703
Naxos, the biggest, greenest and perhaps most beautiful island of the archipelago, is popular but big enough to allow you to escape the hordes.

Orientation & Information
Naxos town (Chora), on the west coast, is the island's capital and port. There is no EOT, but the privately owned Naxos Tourist Information Centre (NTIC; ☎ 25 201, fax 25 200) opposite the quay makes up for this, thanks to the inimitable Despina. The office is open 8 am to midnight daily and offers many services, including luggage storage and laundry.

To find the OTE, turn right from the quay and it's on the waterfront, 150m past the National Bank of Greece. The post office is three blocks farther on. Internet access is available at Rental Centre on Plateia Protodikiou, also known as Central Square.

Things to See & Do
The winding alleyways of **Naxos town**, lined with immaculate whitewashed houses, clamber up to the crumbling 13th-century kastro walls. The well-stocked archaeological museum is here, housed in a former school where Nikos Kazantzakis was briefly a pupil. It's open 8 am to 2.30 pm Tuesday to Sunday; admission is 600 dr.

After the town beach of Agios Georgios, south beyond the harbourfront, sandy **beaches**

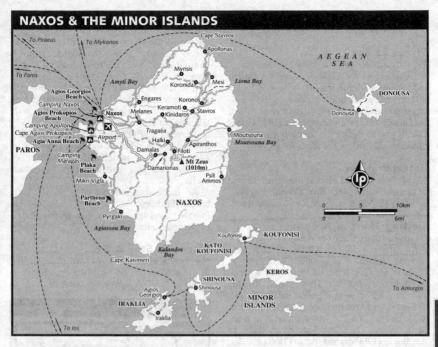

NAXOS & THE MINOR ISLANDS

– which become progressively less crowded – continue southwards as far as Pyrgaki Beach.

On the north coast, **Apollonas** has a rocky beach and a pleasant sheltered bay. If you're curious about the *kouros* statues, you can see the largest one, 10.5m long and dating from the 7th century BC, just outside of Apollonas, lying abandoned and unfinished in an ancient marble quarry.

The gorgeous **Tragaea region** is a vast Arcadian olive grove with Byzantine churches and tranquil villages. **Filoti**, the largest settlement, perches on the slopes of **Mt Zeus** (1004m). It takes three hours to climb the trail to the summit. The village of **Apiranthos** is a gem, with many old houses of uncharacteristically bare stone.

Minor Islands This string of tiny islands is off the east coast of Naxos. Of the seven, only Koufonisi, Donousa, Shinousa and Iraklia are inhabited. They see few tourists and have few amenities, but each has some domatia. They are served by two or three ferries

a week from Piraeus via Naxos, some of which continue to Amorgos.

Places to Stay

Naxos' three camping grounds are *Camping Naxos* (☎ 23 500), 1km south of Agios Georgios Beach; *Camping Maragas* (☎ 24 552), Agia Anna Beach; and *Camping Apollon* (☎ 24 117), 700m from Agios Prokopios Beach.

Dionyssos Youth Hostel (☎ 22 331) is the best budget choice, with dorm beds for 2000 dr, doubles/triples with private bath for 4000/5000 dr and cooking facilities for guests. It's signposted from Agiou Nikodemou, also known as Market St. Book through the NTIC.

Pension Irene (☎ 23 169), south-east of the town centre, has doubles for around 14,000 dr. Near the kastro, *Hotel Panorama* (☎ 24 404) has lovely quiet doubles/triples for 15,000/18,000 dr.

There are also some good accommodation options by Agios Giorgios Beach, including

GREECE

Hotel St George (☎ 23 162), with very pleasant doubles/triples for 18,000/20,000 dr.

Places to Eat
Popi's Grill on the waterfront serves good-value souvlaki for 1700 dr. *Taverna Galini* out by Pension Irene is a favourite with locals and serves up delicious seafood. In the winding streets and alleys around the kastro, you'll find *Manolis Garden* serving excellent Greek fare. If you're hankering for curry in this part of the world, follow the signs for *Dolfini*.

Entertainment
Nightlife is centred around the southern end of the waterfront; *Med Bar*, *Cream*, *Veggera* and *Day & Night* will keep you entertained.

Getting There & Around
Naxos has daily flights to Athens (20,100 dr), daily ferries to Piraeus (4900 dr) and good ferry and hydrofoil connections with most islands in the Cyclades. At least once a week there are boats to Crete, Thessaloniki, Rhodes and Samos. For the port police, call ☎ 22 300.

Buses run to most villages and the beaches as far as Pyrgaki. The bus terminal is in front of the quay. There are four buses daily to Apollonas (1200 dr) and five to Filoti (450 dr).

IOS Ιος
☎ 0286 • pop 2000
Ios epitomises the Greece of sun, sand and sex; in high season it's the *enfant terrible* of the islands. Come here if you want to bake on a beach all day and drink all night. Yet it's not only young hedonists who holiday on Ios – the island is also popular with the older set (anyone over 25) – but the two groups tend to be polarised. The young stay in the 'village' and others at the Ormos port. Nonravers should avoid the village from June to September.

Ios has a tenuous claim to being Homer's burial place. His tomb is supposedly in the island's north, although no one seems to know exactly where.

Gialos Beach, at the port, is OK. **Koumbara Beach**, a 20-minute walk west of Gialos, is less crowded and mainly nudist. **Milopotas**, 1km east, is a superb long beach. Vying with Milopotas for best beach is **Manganari**, on the south coast, reached by bus or, in summer, by excursion boats from the port.

Orientation & Information
The capital, Ios town ('the village', also known as the Hora), is 2km inland from the port of Ormos. The bus terminal in Ormos is straight ahead from the ferry quay on Plateia Emirou. To walk from Ormos to Ios town, turn left from Plateia Emirou, then immediately right and you'll see the stepped path leading up to the right after 100m. The walk takes about 20 minutes.

There is no EOT tourist office, but information is available at the port from travel agents, most of which offer free luggage storage and free use of safes to reduce thefts.

An increasing number of venues – from hotels (Francesco's, Far Out) and bars (Fun Pub) to travel agents – are now offering Internet access to their patrons.

Places to Stay & Eat
Far Out Camping (☎ 91 468, fax 92 303, ✉ farout@otenet.gr) on Milopotas Beach is a seriously slick operation, attracting up to

2000 people a night in summer. Open from May to October, camping costs 1600 dr per person; tents can be hired for 400 dr. Bungalows cost from 2500 dr to 4000 dr per person. There are loads of features – pools, bar, restaurants, minimarket, travel agency, safe boxes, sports facilities. Next door is *Far Out Village Hotel* (☎ 92 305), with lovely double rooms and access to all the Far Out facilities for 20,000 dr.

If you prefer a quieter camp site, try *Camping Stars* (☎ 91 302), also in Milopotas, or *Camping Ios* (☎ 91 050) in Ormos.

There is a wonderful view of the bay from *Francesco's* (☎/fax 91 223, ✉ fragesco@otenet.gr) in the village. Dorm beds cost 2500 dr; doubles/triples with private bath are 10,000/12,000 dr. It's a lively meeting place with a bar and terrace.

In the port, head right from the ferry quay to *Hotel Poseidon* (☎ 91 091) for lovely rooms (18,000 dr for a double) with great views across the harbour.

In the village, *Taverna Lord Byron*, *Pithari Taverna* and *Fun Pub* are the most popular eateries. For a seafood treat, head to *Filippos* on the road between the port and Koumbara Beach. At the port, try *The Octopus Tree*, a quaint, authentic eatery by the fishing boats (so you know the fish is fresh!).

Entertainment

The party crowd reckons the port is dull, while the older set thinks the village is crazy, so take your pick. At night the tiny central square has so many party-goers that it can take 30 minutes to get from one side to the other. Surprisingly, bars in the square charge competitive prices.

Scorpions, *Dubliners* and *Sweet Irish Dreams* are perennial favourites in the village; *Blue Note* and *Red Bull* are also very popular.

Getting There & Around

Ios has daily connections with Piraeus (5300 dr), and there are frequent hydrofoils and ferries to the major Cycladic islands. For up-to-date schedules contact the port police (☎ 91 264).

There are regular buses between the port, the village and Milopotas Beach.

SANTORINI (THIRA)

Σαντορίνη (Θήρα)
☎ 0286 • pop 9360

Around 1450 BC, the volcanic heart of Santorini exploded and sank, leaving an extraordinary landscape. Today the startling sight of the malevolently steaming core almost encircled by sheer cliffs remains – this is certainly the most dramatic of all Greek islands. It's possible that the catastrophe destroyed the Minoan civilisation, but neither this theory nor the claim that the island was part of the lost continent of Atlantis has been proven.

Orientation & Information

The capital, Fira, perches on top of the caldera (submerged crater) on the west coast. The port of Athinios is 12km away. There is no EOT or tourist police, but the helpful Dakoutros Travel Agency (☎ 22 958 or 24 286, fax 22 686) makes up for this. It's in the southern part of the main square (Plateia Theotokopoulou) opposite the taxi station and is open 8 am to 9 or 10 pm daily. The post office is a block south of the taxi station, the OTE is 200m north of the main square, and the Lava Internet Cafe is just north of the main square.

Things to See & Do

Fira The commercialism of Fira has not quite reduced its all-pervasive dramatic aura. The best of the town's museums is the exceptional new **Museum of Prehistoric Thera**, with wonderful displays of well-preserved, well-labelled artefacts predominantly from ancient Akrotiri. The large-scale wall paintings from the 17th century BC are a highlight. The museum is open 8.30 am to 3 pm Tuesday to Sunday; at the time of writing the admission price had not been determined – expect to pay around 1200 dr. To get there, walk south from the main square, past the bus station and take the next street on the right.

The **Megaron Gyzi Museum**, behind the Catholic monastery, houses local memorabilia, including fascinating photographs of Fira before and immediately after the 1956 earthquake. Opening hours are erratic; check the notice on the door.

Around the Island Excavations in 1967 uncovered the remarkably well-preserved Minoan settlement of **Akrotiri**. There are remains

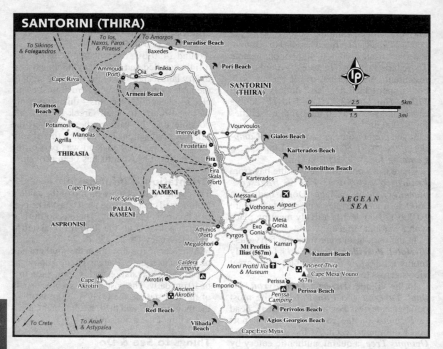

SANTORINI (THIRA)

To Sikinos & Folegandros

To Ios, Naxos, Paros & Piraeus

To Amorgos

Paradise Beach

Baxedes

Pori Beach

Ammoudi (Port)

Finikia

Oia

Cape Riva

SANTORINI (THIRA)

Armeni Beach

Potamos Beach

Potamos

Manolas

Agrilla

Imerovigli

Vourvoulos

Gialos Beach

THIRASIA

Firostefani

Karterados Beach

Fira

Monolithos Beach

Fira Skala (Port)

Karterados

Cape Trypiti

NEA KAMENI

Messaria

Hot Springs

Vothonas

Airport

AEGEAN SEA

PALIA KAMENI

ASPRONISI

Athinios (Port)

Megalohori

Exo Gonia

Pyrgos

Mesa Gonia

Kamari

Caldera Camping

Mt Profitis Ilias (567m)

Kamari Beach

Moni Profiti Ilia & Museum

Ancient Thira

Cape Mesa Vouno

Cape Akrotiri

Akrotiri

Emporio

Perissa

567m

Perissa Beach

Ancient Akrotiri

Perissa Camping

Red Beach

Perivolos Beach

To Crete

To Anafi & Astypalea

Vlihada Beach

Agios Georgios Beach

Cape Evo Mytis

0   2.5   5km
0   1.5   3mi

---

of two and three-storey buildings, and evidence of a sophisticated drainage system. The site is open 8.30 am to 3 pm Tuesday to Sunday; admission is 1200 dr.

Less impressive than Akrotiri, the site of **Ancient Thira** is still worth a visit for the stunning views. **Moni Profiti Ilia**, a monastery built on the island's highest point, can be reached along a path from Ancient Thira; the walk takes about one hour.

Santorini's **beaches** are of black volcanic sand that becomes very hot, making a beach mat essential. Kamari and Perissa get crowded – those near Oia and Monolithos are quieter. Red Beach, a 10-minute walk from Akrotiri, is popular.

From Imerovigli, just north of Fira, a 12km coastal path leads to the picturesque village of **Oia** (pronounced **ee**-ah), famed for postcard-perfect sunsets. On a clear day there are breathtaking views of neighbouring islands.

Of the surrounding islets, only **Thirasia** is inhabited. At Palia Kameni you can bathe in

hot springs, and on Nea Kameni you can clamber around on volcanic lava. A six-hour tour to these three islands by either caïque or glass-bottom boat costs 5500 dr. Tickets are available from most agencies in town.

Places to Stay

Beware of the aggressive accommodation owners who meet boats and buses and claim that their rooms are in Fira when in fact they're in Karterados. Ask to see a map to check their location.

Camping Santorini (☎ 22 944), 1km east of the main square, has many facilities including a restaurant and swimming pool. The cost is 1000 dr per person and 1000 dr per tent.

Thira Hostel (☎ 23 864), 200m north of the square, is a good place to meet people and sleeps as many as 145. It has dorms with up to 10 beds for 3000 dr per person, roof beds for 2000 dr, plus doubles/triples with private bath for 10,000/12,000 dr. It also has a very cheap restaurant.

GREECE

There are plenty of rooms to rent near the main square and on the road running east towards Camping Santorini, including *Pension Petros* (☎ *22 573*), offering basic but pleasant doubles for 17,000 dr. The location can be a bit noisy, however.

A short walk north-east of the centre of town will take you to a quiet rural area with plenty of domatia. *Pension Stella* has doubles/triples for 16,000/19,000 dr, *Pension Horizon* charges 17,000/20,000 dr and *Villa Gianna* – which has a pool – charges 21,000/25,000 dr. All have private bath, some have balcony. To book any of these, ring Dakoutros Travel (see Orientation & Information earlier in this section). The same agent has properties in Oia on its books; most are in traditional houses with fine views. Double studios cost from 25,000 dr; a house for four starts at 35,000 dr.

Places to Eat
Toast Club, on the square, is a fast-food operation (pizza and pasta) and a favourite with budget travellers. *Restaurant Stamna*, just east of the square, has good-value daily specials. *Naoussa*, not far from the cable-car station, is excellent. The food served by other restaurants in this area does not always represent good value for money, but you may not mind given the million-dollar view. For something special, visit upmarket *Kukumavlos*, by the Orthodox cathedral, where you can enjoy fine dining while admiring the sunset.

Entertainment
Bars and clubs are clustered along one street, Erythrou Stavrou. From the main square, facing north, turn left at George's Snack Corner then take the first right. *Koo Club*, *Enigma* and *Murphy's* are all popular, and *Kira Thira Jazz Bar* is an old favourite.

Getting There & Away
Flights cost 22,200 dr to Athens, 22,900 dr to Rhodes, 15,400 dr to Mykonos and to Iraklio (Crete). The Olympic Airways office (☎ 22 493) is 200m south of the hospital.

Daily ferries to Piraeus cost 5900 dr. There are frequent connections with Crete, Ios, Paros and Naxos. Ferries travel less frequently to/from Anafi, Sikinos, Folegandros, Sifnos, Serifos, Kimolos, Milos, Karpathos and Rhodes. For the port police call ☎ 22 239.

Getting Around
There are daily boats from Athinios and Fira Skala to Thirasia and Oia. The islets surrounding Santorini can only be visited on excursions from Fira.

Large ferries use Athinios port, where they are met by buses. Small boats use Fira Skala, which is served by donkey or cable car (1000 dr each); otherwise it's a clamber up 600 steps. The cable car runs every 20 minutes from 6.40 am to 9 pm.

The bus station is just south of Fira's main square. Buses go to Oia, Kamari, Perissa, Akrotiri and Monolithos frequently. Port buses usually leave Fira, Kamari and Perissa 90 minutes to an hour before ferry departures.

Crete Κρήτη

Crete, Greece's largest island, is divided into four prefectures: Hania, Rethymno, Iraklio and Lassithi. All of Crete's large towns are on the north coast, and it's here that the package tourist industry thrives – Crete has the dubious distinction of playing host to a quarter of all visitors to Greece. You can escape the hordes by visiting the undeveloped west coast, heading into the rugged mountainous interior, or staying in one of the villages of the Lassithi Plateau which, when the tour buses depart, return to rural tranquillity.

Crete has many opportunities for superb trekking and climbing. It's also the best place in Greece for buying high-quality, inexpensive leather goods.

For more detailed information, see Lonely Planet's *Crete*.

History
Crete was the birthplace of Minoan culture, Europe's first advanced civilisation, which flourished from 2800 to 1450 BC. Very little is known of Minoan civilisation, which came to an abrupt end, possibly destroyed by Santorini's volcanic eruption.

Later, Crete passed from the warlike Dorians to the Romans, and then to the Genoese,

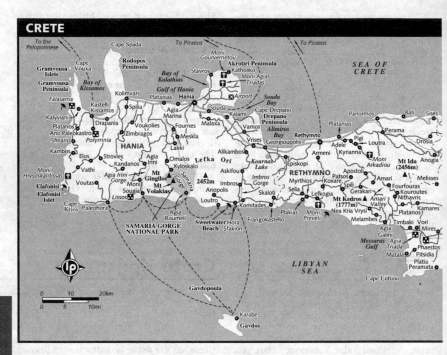

CRETE

who in turn sold it to the Venetians. Under the Venetians, Crete became a refuge for artists, writers and philosophers who fled Constantinople after it fell to the Turks. Their influence inspired the young Cretan painter Domenikos Theotokopoulos, who moved to Spain and there won immortality as the great El Greco.

The Turks finally conquered Crete in 1670. It became a British protectorate in 1898 after a series of insurrections and was united with independent Greece in 1913. There was fierce fighting during WWII when a German airborne invasion defeated Allied forces in the 10-day Battle of Crete. An active resistance movement drew heavy reprisals from the German occupiers.

Getting There & Away
Air The international airport is at Iraklio, Crete's capital. Hania and Sitia have domestic airports. There are several flights a day from Athens to Iraklio and Hania, and weekly flights to Sitia. In summer there are three flights a week to Rhodes from Iraklio and two to Santorini.

Ferry Kastelli-Kissamos, Rethymno, Hania, Iraklio, Agios Nikolaos and Sitia have ferry ports. Ferries travel most days to Piraeus from Hania (5900 dr), Rethymno and Iraklio (7000 dr); less frequently from Agios Nikolaos and Sitia (7600 dr). There are at least two boats a week from Iraklio to Santorini and on to other Cycladic islands.

In summer there's at least one ferry a week from Iraklio to Rhodes (6200 dr) via Kassos and Karpathos and at least three a week from Agios Nikolaos to Rhodes via Sitia, Kassos and Karpathos. In summer, a twice-weekly boat sails from Iraklio to Cyprus via Rhodes and then on to Israel.

Getting Around
Frequent buses run between towns on the north coast, and less frequently to the south

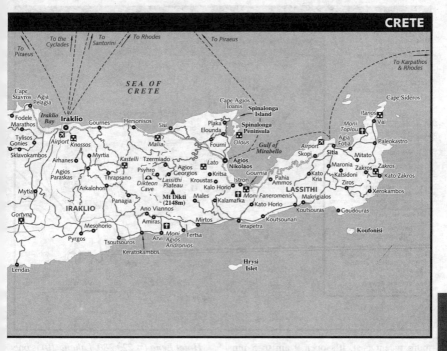

CRETE

coast and mountain villages. For more information, visit the long-distance bus Web site at www.ktel.org .

Parts of the south coast are without roads, so boats are used to connect villages.

IRAKLIO Ηράκλειο
☎ 081 • pop 127,600

Iraklio, Crete's capital, lacks the charm of Rethymno or Hania, its old buildings swamped by modern apartment blocks. Its neon-lit streets do exude a certain dynamism, but apart from its archaeological museum and proximity to Knossos, there's little point in lingering here.

Orientation & Information

Iraklio's two main squares are Plateia Venizelou and Plateia Eleftherias. Dikeosynis and Dedalou run between them, and 25 Avgoustou is the main thoroughfare leading from the waterfront to Plateia Venizelou. The EOT (☎ 228 225), open 8 am to 2.30 pm

weekdays, and Olympic Airways (☎ 229 191) are on Plateia Eleftherias. The tourist police (☎ 283 190) are at Dikeosynis 10.

Most of the city's banks are on 25 Avgoustou. The American Express representative, Adamis, is at 25 Avgoustou 23.

The central post office is on Plateia Daskalogiani, and there is a temporary post office by El Greco Park in summer. The OTE is just north of El Greco Park. You can access the Internet at Netcafe, on 1878, or Istos Cyber Cafe, Malikouti 2.

There is a laundrette and left-luggage storage area at Washsalon, Handakos 18.

Things to See

Don't leave Iraklio without seeing the magnificent collection at the **archaeological museum**. Opening times are 8 am to 7 pm Tuesday to Sunday, 12.30 to 7 pm Monday. Admission is 1500 dr.

Close to the waterfront is the **Historical Museum of Crete**, covering the island's

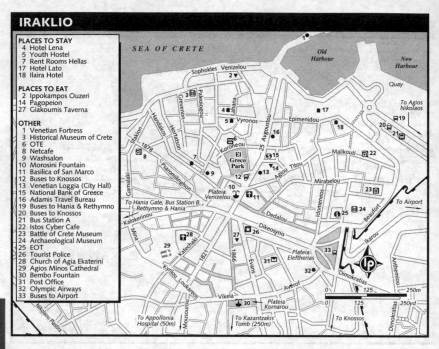

IRAKLIO

PLACES TO STAY
- 4   Hotel Lena
- 5   Youth Hostel
- 7   Rent Rooms Hellas
- 17 Hotel Lato
- 18 Ilaira Hotel

PLACES TO EAT
- 2   Ippokampos Ouzeri
- 14 Pagopeion
- 27 Giakoumis Taverna

OTHER
- 1   Venetian Fortress
- 3   Historical Museum of Crete
- 6   OTE
- 8   Netcafe
- 9   Washsalon
- 10 Morosini Fountain
- 11 Basilica of San Marco
- 12 Buses to Knossos
- 13 Venetian Loggia (City Hall)
- 15 National Bank of Greece
- 16 Adamis Travel Bureau
- 19 Buses to Hania & Rethymno
- 20 Buses to Knossos
- 21 Bus Station A
- 22 Istos Cyber Cafe
- 23 Battle of Crete Museum
- 24 Archaeological Museum
- 25 EOT
- 26 Tourist Police
- 28 Church of Agia Ekaterini
- 29 Agios Minos Cathedral
- 30 Bembo Fountain
- 31 Post Office
- 32 Olympic Airways
- 33 Buses to Airport

more recent past. It's open 9 am to 5 pm weekdays, to 2 pm Saturday. Admission is 1000 dr.

You can pay homage to the great writer Nikos Kazantzakis by visiting his grave. To get there, walk south on Evans and turn right onto Plastira.

Places to Stay

Beware of taxi drivers who tell you that the pension of your choice is dirty, closed or has a bad reputation. They're paid commissions by the big hotels.

There's few domatia in Iraklio and not much budget accommodation. *Rent Rooms Hellas* (☎ 288 851, *Handakos 24*) is a hostel popular with backpackers despite the number of draconian rules posted in the rooftop reception and bar. Singles/doubles/triples are 4500/6000/7500 dr; dorm beds are 2000 dr. As a last resort there's also the *youth hostel* (☎ 286 281, *Vyronos 5*) off 25 Avgoustou, where beds in small, crowded dorms cost 1800 dr.

Hotel Lena (☎ 223 280, *Lahana 10*) is one of the nicer budget hotels. Singles/doubles with shared facilities cost 6500/9000 dr; with private bath 8500/11,000 dr.

Ilaira Hotel (☎ 227 103, *Epimenidou 1*) near the old harbour and bus stations is situated among a cluster of decent mid-range hotels. It has hints of the 1970s (lots of brown and orange), but it offers clean, comfortable singles/doubles for 10,000/14,000 dr, plus it has a rooftop terrace. Across the road is the very upmarket *Hotel Lato* (☎ 228 103, *Epimenidou 15*) with rooms for 25,000/31,000 dr.

Places to Eat

Plateia Venizelou has countless fast-food outlets and cafe-bars, while Theosadaki, the little street between 1866 and Evans, is lined with traditional tavernas. One of the best is *Giakoumis Taverna* (*Theosadaki 5*).

Ippokampos Ouzeri, on the waterfront just west of 25 Avgoustou, offers a huge range of good-value mezedes and is always packed. Go early to get a table.

Pagopeion, by Agios Titos church, has good food with imaginative titles, and the toilets alone are worth a visit.

There's a bustling, colourful *market* all the way along 1866.

Getting There & Away

For air and ferry information, see Getting There & Away at the start of the Crete section. For the port police, call ☎ 244 912.

Iraklio has two bus stations. Bus station A, just inland from the new harbour, serves eastern Crete (Agios Nikolaos, Ierapetra, Sitia, Malia and the Lassithi Plateau). Bus station B, 50m beyond the Hania Gate, serves the south (Phaestos, Matala, Anogia). The Hania/Rethymno terminal is opposite bus station A.

Getting Around

Bus No 1 goes to/from the airport (180 dr) every 15 minutes between 6 am and 1 am; it stops at Plateia Eleftherias adjacent to the archaeological museum. Local bus No 2 goes to Knossos (260 dr) every 10 minutes from bus station A and also stops on 25 Avgoustou.

Car and motorcycle-rental firms are mostly along 25 Avgoustou.

KNOSSOS Κνωσσός

Knossos, 8km south-east of Iraklio, is the most famous of Crete's Minoan sites and is the inspiration for the myth of the Minotaur. According to legend, King Minos of Knossos was given a bull to sacrifice to the god Poseidon, but instead decided to keep it. This enraged Poseidon, who punished the king by causing his wife Pasiphae to fall in love with the animal. The result of this bizarre union was the Minotaur – half-man and half-bull – who lived in a labyrinth beneath the king's palace, feeding on youths and maidens.

In 1900 the ruins of Knossos were uncovered by Arthur Evans. Although archaeologists tend to disparage Evans' reconstruction, the buildings – an immense palace, courtyards, private apartments, baths and more – give a good idea of what a Minoan palace may have looked like. The delightful frescoes depict plants and animals, as well as people participating in sports, ceremonies and festivals, and generally enjoying life, in contrast to the battle scenes found in the art of classical Greece.

A whole day is needed to see the site, and a guidebook is immensely useful. The site is open 8 am to 7 pm daily from April to October; entry is 1500 dr. Arrive early to avoid the crowds. See Getting Around under Iraklio, earlier, for transport details.

PHAESTOS & OTHER MINOAN SITES

Phaestos (Φαιστός), Crete's second-most important Minoan site, is not as impressive as Knossos but worth a visit for its stunning views of the plain of Mesara. The palace was laid out on the same plan as Knossos, but excavations have not yielded many frescoes. The site is open 8 am to 7 pm daily; entry is 1200 dr.

Crete's other important Minoan sites are **Malia**, 34km east of Iraklio, where there is a palace complex and adjoining town, and **Zakros**, 40km from Sitia. This was the smallest of the island's palatial complexes. The site is rather remote and overgrown, but the ruins are on a more human scale than at Knossos, Phaestos or Malia.

HANIA Χανιά
☎ 0821 • pop 65,000

Lovely Hania, the old capital of Crete, has a harbour with crumbling, softly hued Venetian buildings. It oozes charm; it also oozes package tourists.

Orientation & Information

Hania's bus station is on Kydonias, a block south-west of Plateia 1866, the town's main square. Halidon runs from here to the old harbour. The fortress separates the old harbour from the new. Hania's port is at Souda, 10km from town.

The EOT office (☎ 92 943) is at Kriari 40, 20m from Plateia 1866. It's open 7.30 am to 2 pm weekdays. The central post office is at Tzanakaki 3 and the OTE is next door. Internet access is available at Vranas Studios on Agion Deka, or from e-Kafe.com, Theotokopoulou 53.

Things to See

The **archaeological museum** at Halidon 30 is housed in the former Venetian Church of San Francesco; the Turks converted it into a mosque. It's open 8 am to 7 pm Tuesday to

HANIA

*SEA OF
CRETE*

Lighthouse

To
Camping
Hania

*Venetian
Port*

Ritsou

Angelou

Theofanous

Akti-Kountourioti

Apostolidou

Patriarhou Ioanikeiou

NEA HORA

Patriarhou Gerasimou

Skoufon

Kondylaki

Portou

Pireos

Douka

Zambeliou

K Melaxaki

Piga

**Promahonas
Hill**

Dounopapa

Kirilou

Selnou

Kissamou

To Kastelli-
Kissamos

Skalidi

P Kaladi

Kydonias

Akti-Tombazi

*Plateia
Katehaki*

Ag. Markou

Lithinon

Kanevaro

Karre

Sifaka

*Plateia
Venizelou*

Karaoli Dimitriou

Isodion

Potie

Betola

Halidon

Skridlof

*Plateia
Afinagora*

Gianari

Kriari

**Plateia
1866**

Koraka

Karaiskaki

Mihali Dalani

*Plateia
Hortatson*

*Plateia
Tsouderon*

Mousouron

Ag. Markou

Anfroleon

Sifaka

Kalistou

Akti Enosis

Kalergon

SPLANTZIA

Epimenidou

*Plateia
1821*

Vourdouba

Dastalogianni

Minos

Sarpaki

Nikiforou Episkopou

*Plateia
Markopoulou*

Nikiforou Foka

Food
Market

El Venizelou

Akti-Miaouli

To Akrotiri
Peninsula &
Airport (14km)

Kipnou

Trikoupi

Dimokratias

Plastira

Tzanakaki

Bonali

Sfakion

Kornarou

Apokoronou

Solomou

To Souda, Rethymno
& Iraklio

To Souda, Rethymno
& Iraklio

Korai

Stadium

**Public
Garden
& Zoo**

Melidoni

Plateia
Markopoulou

PLACES TO STAY	12 Tholos Restaurant	16 Buses to Souda
3 Hotel Meltemi		17 EOT
7 Rooms for Rent George	**OTHER**	18 Buses to Western Beaches
13 Vranas Studios	1 e-Kafe.com	19 Main Bus Station
14 Pension Fidias	2 Naval Museum	20 National Bank of Greece
	4 Mosque of the Janissaries	21 Post Office
PLACES TO EAT	5 Archaeological Site	22 OTE
8 Tsikoydadiko	6 Cafe Crete	23 Olympic Airways
9 Tamam	11 Archaeological Museum	24 EOS
10 Suki Yaki	15 Orthodox Cathedral	25 War Museum

Sunday. Admission is 500 dr. There's also the **naval museum**, by the fortress, and the **war museum** at Tzanakaki 23.

Places to Stay

The nearest camping ground is *Camping Hania (☎ 31 138)*, 3km west of town, on the beach. Take a Kalamaka bus from Plateia 1866.

The budget choice is *Pension Fidias (☎ 52 494, Sarpaki 6)*, behind the Orthodox cathedral, which offers beds in three-bed dorms for 2500 dr. Doubles, some with bath, cost from 5500 dr.

The most interesting rooms are in the ancient Venetian buildings around the old harbour. *Hotel Meltemi (☎ 92 802, Agelou 2)* next to the fortress is quite run-down but has character and a great location. Doubles cost from 7000 dr. *Rooms for Rent George (☎ 88 715, Zambeliou 30)*, one block from the waterfront, has singles/doubles/triples for 4000/7000/9000 dr.

Vranas Studios (☎/fax 58 618, ✉ vranas@yahoo.com, Agion Deka 10) by the cathedral has lovely, spacious studios sleeping up to three and costing 17,000 dr in August but considerably less (11,000 dr) at other times.

Places to Eat

The lively central *food market* houses a few inexpensive tavernas.

For alfresco dining, try *Tsikoydadiko (Zambeliou 31)*, or the lovingly preserved ruins at the classy *Tholos Restaurant (Agion Deka 36)*. Both serve good Greek cuisine at reasonable prices. Another good choice is the excellent *Tamam (Zambeliou 51)*, while atmospheric *Suki Yaki (Halidon 26)*, under the archway, serves up authentic – albeit pricey – Chinese and Thai meals.

Entertainment

The authentic *Cafe Crete (Kalergon 22)* has live Cretan music every evening.

There are numerous cafes and bars around the harbour, particularly near the fortress.

Getting There & Away

For air and ferry information, see Getting There & Away at the start of the Crete section. Olympic Airways (☎ 40 268) is at Tzanakaki 88. For the port police at Souda, call ☎ 89 240.

There are frequent buses to Iraklio, Rethymno and Kastelli-Kissamos, and less frequent ones to Paleohora, Omalos, Hora Sfakion, Lakki and Elafonisi from the bus station on Kydonias. Buses for Souda (the port) leave frequently from outside the food market, and for beaches just west of Hania from the south-eastern corner of Plateia 1866.

THE WEST COAST

This is Crete's least developed coastline. At Falasarna, 16km west of Kastelli-Kissamos, there's a magnificent sandy beach and a few tavernas and domatia. There are buses in summer from Kastelli-Kissamos and Hania. South of Falasarna there are good sandy beaches near the villages of Sfinario and Kambos.

Farther south you can wade out to more beaches on beautiful Elafonisi islet. Travel agents in Hania and Paleohora run excursions to the area.

SAMARIA GORGE

Φαράγγι της Σαμαριάς

It's a wonder the rocks underfoot haven't worn away completely as so many people trample through the Samaria Gorge. But it is one of Europe's most spectacular gorges, and

worth seeing. You can do it independently by taking a bus from Hania to the head of the gorge at Omalos and walking the length of the gorge (16km) to Agia Roumeli, from where you take a boat to Hora Sfakion and then a bus back to Hania. Or you can join one of the daily excursions from Hania (many companies also offer an 'easy' option, which starts from Agia Roumeli and goes about 4km into the gorge).

The first public bus leaves Hania at 6.15 am and excursion buses also leave early so that people get to the top of the gorge before the heat of the day. The walk takes about five or six hours, and you need good walking shoes and a hat, as well as water and food. The gorge is open early May to mid-October; admission is 1200 dr.

LEFKA ORI Λευκά Ορι

Crete's rugged White Mountains are south of Hania. For information on climbing and trekking, contact the EOS (☎ 24 647), Tzanakaki 90, Hania. Alpine Travel (☎ 53 909, ✉ info@alpine.gr), in Hania, offers many trekking programs; check its comprehensive Web site at www.alpine.gr. Also based in Hania is Trekking Plan (☎ 60 861), which rents mountain bikes and organises bike tours into the mountains. Its Web site is at www.cycling.gr.

PALEOHORA & THE SOUTH-WEST COAST
☎ 0823

Paleohora (Παλαιοχώρα) was discovered by hippies back in the 1960s and from then on its days as a tranquil fishing village were numbered. It remains a relaxing, if overrated, resort favoured by backpackers. There's a helpful tourist office three blocks south of the bus stop.

Farther east, along Crete's south-west coast, are the resorts of Sougia, Agia Roumeli, Loutro and Hora Sfakion; of these, Loutro is the most appealing and is the least developed.

Places to Stay & Eat

Camping Paleohora (☎ 41 120) is 1.5km north-east of the town, near the pebble beach. There's also a restaurant and nightclub here.

In Paleohora, **Homestay Anonymous** (☎ *41 509*) is a great place for backpackers. It has clean rooms set around a small courtyard; singles/doubles are 4000/5500 dr and there is a communal kitchen. **Oriental Bay Rooms** (☎ *41 076*) at the northern end of the pebble beach (on the road to the camping ground), has comfortable doubles/triples with bath for 7000/8000 dr.

There are numerous domatia and taverna along the harbourfront. There's a good vegetarian restaurant, **The Third Eye**, close to the sandy beach.

Getting There & Away

There are at least three buses a day between Hania and Paleohora (1600 dr).

There's no road linking the coastal resorts, but they are connected by boats from Paleohora in summer. Twice weekly the boat goes to Gavdos Island (Europe's southernmost point).

Coastal paths lead from Paleohora to Sougia and from Agia Roumeli to Loutro. Both walks take five to six hours.

RETHYMNO Ρέθυμνο
☎ 0831 • pop 24,000

Although similar to Hania, with its Venetian and Turkish buildings (not to mention its package tourists), Rethymno is smaller and has a distinct character.

The EOT (☎ 29 148) is on the beach side of El Venizelou and is open 8 am to 2 pm weekdays. The tourist police (☎ 28 156) occupy the same building.

The post office is at Moatsou 21 and the OTE is at Kountouriotou 28. There's Internet access upstairs at Galero cafe, beside the Rimondi fountain.

Things to See & Do

The imposing **Venetian fortress** is open 8 am to 8 pm daily except Monday; entry is 900 dr. The **archaeological museum** opposite the fortress entrance is open 8.30 am to 3 pm Tuesday to Sunday; entry is 500 dr. The **historical and folk art museum** on Vernardou has a well-presented display of Cretan crafts. Its opening hours are 9.30 am to 1.30 pm Monday to Saturday; entry is 600 dr.

The Happy Walker (☎ 52 920), Tombazi 56, has a program of daily walks in the countryside costing from 7000 dr per person.

Places to Stay

The nearest camping ground is **Elisabeth Camping** (☎ *28 694*) on Myssiria beach, 3km east of town.

The **youth hostel** (☎ *22 848, Tombazi 45*) is a friendly place; beds are 1800 dr in dorms or on the roof. **Olga's Pension** (☎ *53 206, Souliou 57*) in the heart of town is colourful and eclectically decorated, with rooms spread off a network of terraces bursting with greenery. Doubles/triples with private bath are 9000/12,000 dr. The tranquil **Rent Rooms Garden** (☎ *28 586, Nikiforou Foka 82*) is an old Venetian house with a delightful garden; rooms are 10,000/15,000 dr.

Places to Eat

Stella's Kitchen, beneath Olga's Pension, offers hearty breakfasts and cheap snacks. **Taverna Kyria Maria** (*Diog Mesologiou 20*), tucked behind the Rimondi fountain, is a cosy family-run taverna.

Gounakis Restaurant & Bar (*Koroneou 6*) has live Cretan music every evening and reasonably priced food.

The area east of Rimondi fountain is a good place to investigate. Arabatzoglou and Radamanthios have a number of upmarket places, including **Avli** and **Taverna Larenzo**. The **Punch Bowl** Irish bar is also here.

Getting There & Away

For ferries, see Getting There & Away at the start of the Crete section. For the port police, call ☎ 22 276.

There are frequent buses to Iraklio (1800 dr) and Hania (1600 dr), and less frequent ones to Agia Galini, Arkadi Monastery and Plakias.

LASSITHI PLATEAU Οροπέδιο Λασιθίου

The first view of this mountain-fringed plateau, laid out like an immense patchwork quilt, is breathtaking. The plateau, 900m above sea level, is a vast expanse of orchards and fields, dotted by some 7000 metal windmills with white canvas sails.

Lassithi's major sight, the **Dikteon Cave**, on the side of Mt Dikti, is where, according to mythology, the Titan Rhea hid the newborn Zeus from Cronos, his offspring-gobbling father. It's open 8 am to 4 pm daily and entry is 800 dr.

Places to Stay & Eat

Psyhro is the best place to stay; it's near the cave and has the best views. *Zeus Hotel* (☎ *0844-31 284*) has singles/doubles with private bath for 5000/8000 dr. On the main street, *Stavros* and *Platanos* tavernas serve decent food at similar prices.

Getting There & Away

There are daily buses to the area from Iraklio and three a week from Agios Nikolaos.

SITIA Σητεία
☎ 0843 • pop 8000

Back on the north coast, the manifestations of package tourism gather momentum as they advance eastwards, reaching a crescendo in Agios Nikolaos. The tourist overkill dies down considerably by the time you reach Sitia, an attractive town with a hotel-lined bay and long sandy beach.

The municipal tourist office is on the waterfront just before the town beach. The post office is on Dimokratou, off El Venizelou, and the OTE is on Kapetan Sifis, which runs inland from Plateia El Venizelou, the main square. The ferry port is a bit of a hike; it's signposted from the main square.

Places to Stay & Eat

There are no camping grounds near Sitia, but it's possible to camp in the grounds of the *youth hostel* (☎ *22 693, Therissou 4*) on the road to Iraklio for 1200 dr. Dorm beds cost 1500 dr; doubles/triples with shared facilities are 3500/5000 dr.

There is no shortage of domatia behind the waterfront. The immaculate *Hotel Arhontiko* (☎ *28 172, Kondylaki 16*) has doubles/triples for 5000/6500 dr. To find it, walk towards the ferry dock along El Venizelou, turn left up Filellinon and then right onto Kondylaki.

The waterfront is buzzing with tavernas and bars; inland you'll find *Kali Kardia Taverna* (*Foundalidhou 20*) and *O Mixos* (*Kournarou 15*). Both are excellent value and popular with locals.

Getting There & Away

For air and ferry information, see Getting There & Away at the start of the Crete section. To contact the port police, call ☎ 22 310.

There are at least three buses daily to Ierapetra and five to Iraklio via Agios Nikolaos. In summer there are two or three buses daily to Vaï and Zakros.

AROUND SITIA

The reconstructed **Toplou Monastery**, 15km from Sitia, houses some beautifully intricate icons and other relics. To get there, take a Vaï bus from Sitia, get off at the fork for the monastery and walk the last 3km.

Superb **Vaï Beach**, famous for its palm trees, gets crowded, but it's well worth a visit.

Dodecanese
Δωδεκάνησα

The Dodecanese are more verdant and mountainous than the Cyclades and have comparable beaches. And here, more than other islands, you get a sense of Greece's proximity to Asia. Ancient temples, massive crusader fortifications, mosques and imposing Italian-built neoclassical buildings stand juxtaposed, vestiges of a turbulent past.

There are 16 inhabited islands in the group; the most visited are Rhodes, Kos, Patmos and Symi.

RHODES Ρόδος

According to mythology, the sun god Helios chose Rhodes as his bride and bestowed light, warmth and vegetation upon her. The blessing seems to have paid off, for Rhodes produces flowers in profusion and enjoys more sunny days than most Greek islands.

The ancient sites of Lindos and Kamiros are legacies of Rhodes' importance in antiquity. In 1291 the Knights of St John, having fled Jerusalem under siege, came to Rhodes and established themselves as masters. In 1522 Süleyman I, sultan of the Ottoman Empire, staged a massive attack on the island and took Rhodes City. The island, along with the other Dodecanese, then became part of the Ottoman Empire.

In 1912 it was the Italians' turn and in 1944 the Germans took over. The following year Rhodes was liberated by British and Greek commandos. In 1948 the Dodecanese became part of Greece.

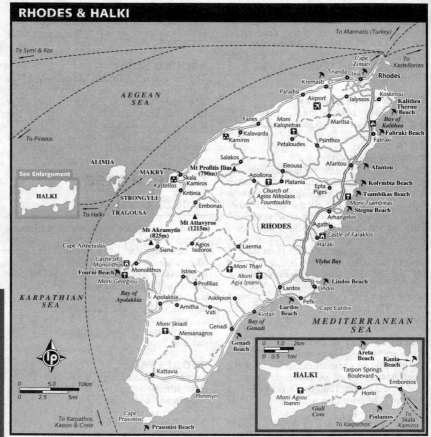

RHODES & HALKI

Rhodes City

☎ 0241 • pop 43,500

Rhodes' capital and port is Rhodes City, on the northern tip of the island. Almost everything of interest here lies in the old town. The main thoroughfares are Sokratous, Pythagora, Agiou Fanouriou and Ipodamou, with mazes of narrow streets between them. The new town to the north is a monument to package tourism.

The main port is east of the old town, and north of here is Mandraki Harbour, supposed site of the Colossus of Rhodes, a giant bronze statue of Apollo (built in 292-280 BC) – one of the Seven Wonders of the World. The statue stood for a mere 65 years before being toppled by an earthquake.

Information The EOT office (☎ 23 255, ✉ eot-rodos@otenet.gr) is on the corner of Makariou and Papagou. It's open 7.30 am to 3 pm weekdays. The tourist police (☎ 27 423) are next door. In summer there is also a municipal tourist office on Plateia Rimini, open longer hours than the EOT.

The main post office is on Mandraki and the OTE is at Amerikis 91. There is a cyber-cafe, Rock Style, at Dimokratias 7, just south of the old town, and Minoan Internet Cafe is at Iroön Politehniou 13 (new town).

Things to See & Do In the old town, the 15th-century Knights' Hospital is a splendid building. It was restored by the Italians and is now the **archaeological museum**, housing an impressive collection, including the exquisite statue of *Aphrodite of Rhodes*. Opening times are 8.30 am to 3 pm Tuesday to Sunday. Admission is 800 dr.

Odos Ippoton – the Avenue of the Knights – is lined with magnificent medieval buildings, the most imposing of which is the **Palace of the Grand Masters**, restored, but never used, as a holiday home for Mussolini. It's open 8.30 am to 3 pm daily except Monday. Admission is 1200 dr.

The old town is reputedly the world's finest surviving example of medieval fortification. The 12m-thick walls are closed to the public, but you can take a **guided walk** along them on Tuesday and Saturday, starting at 2.45 pm in the courtyard at the Palace of the Grand Masters (1200 dr).

The 18th-century **Turkish bath** on Plateia Arionos (signposted from Ipodamou) offers a rare opportunity to bathe Turkish-style in Greece. It's open 1 to 6 pm Tuesday, 11 am to 6 pm Wednesday, Thursday and Friday, and 8 am to 6 pm Saturday. Entry is 500 dr (300 dr on Wednesday and Saturday).

Places to Stay *Faliraki Camping* (☎ 85 358) about 15km south of Rhodes City near Faliraki Beach, has good facilities including a pool and charges 1500/800 dr per person/tent. Take a bus from the east-side bus station.

The old town is well supplied with accommodation. The unofficial *Rodos Youth Hostel* (☎ 30 491, Ergiou 12) off Agiou Fanouriou is popular and has a lovely garden. Dorm beds cost 1500 dr, doubles with shared facilities are 3500 dr; with bath 6000 dr. There is a kitchen available for self-caterers and during the summer there are roof beds (1000 dr) and barbecue facilities.

Sunlight Hotel (☎ 21 435, Ipadomou 32) above Stavros Bar has doubles/triples with private bath and fridge for 10,000/12,000 dr. The friendly *Pension Andreas* (☎ 34 156, fax 74 285, Omirou 28D) has a terrace bar with terrific views, and email facilities for guests.

Clean, pleasant doubles with shared bathroom cost 10,000 dr, doubles/triples/quads with private bath are 12,500/15,500/18,000 dr.

Other good choices include the *Pink Elephant* (☎ 22 469, Irodotou 42) and *Hotel Spot* (☎ 34 737, Perikleous 21). Both have clean, bright doubles with private bath for 12,000 dr.

Sara from Kafe Besara (see Places to Eat) has well located, self-contained *apartments* set around a lovely courtyard. Apartments sleeping two/four cost 20,000/30,000 dr a night. Visit the cafe (✆ cafe_besara@yahoo.com) or call ☎ 30 363.

Most of Rhodes' other villages have hotels or a few domatia.

Places to Eat Away from the venues with tacky photo menus, you'll find some good eateries.

For the best Greek coffee in town and a game of backgammon or chess, try *Kafekopteion* (Sokratous 76). Head to *Kringlan Swedish Bakery* (I Dragoumi 14) in the new town for exceptional sandwiches and delicious pastries.

One of the best-value places to eat in the old town is the *Fisherman's Ouzeria* on Sofokleous. *Taverna Kostas* (Pythagora 62) and *Yiannis Taverna* on Platanos are highly popular and also good value.

If you're tired of Greek food, however, there are some excellent options. *Le Bistrot de L'Auberge* (Praxitelous 21) in a beautifully restored medieval house serves terrific French dishes. Indian food fans should visit *India Restaurant* (Konstantopedos 16) opposite the Swedish bakery. *Kasbah* (Platonos 4) serves huge Moroccan-influenced meals; the delicious couscous mains (3800 dr) are enough to satisfy two hungry people. For a seafood treat, head to the upmarket *Alexis* (Sokratous 18).

The funky *Kafe Besara* (Sofokleous 11), run by Australian expat Sara, and *Marco Polo Cafe* (Agiou Fanouriou 40) are both popular for daytime coffees and evening drinks.

Entertainment There is a distinctly average *sound-and-light show* at the Palace of the Knights, depicting the Turkish siege. A noticeboard outside gives the times for performances

GREECE

RHODES CITY

MEDITERRANEAN SEA

PLACES TO STAY
31 Sunlight Hotel
33 Rodos Youth Hostel
36 Pink Elephant
37 Pension Andreas
47 Hotel Spot

PLACES TO EAT
4 Kringlan Swedish Bakery
5 India Restaurant
28 Kafekopteion
35 Marco Polo Cafe
38 Alexis
40 Yiannis Taverna
41 Kasbah
42 Fisherman's Ouzeria
43 Kafe Besara
44 Taverna Kostas
45 Le Bistrot de L'Auberge

OTHER
1 Aquarium
2 Bars
3 Hospital
6 Minoan Internet Cafe
7 Mosque of Murad Reis
8 National Theatre
9 Olympic Airways
10 OTE
11 Post Office
12 Port Police
13 Departure Points for Hydrofoils, Diving & Excursion Boats
14 Triton Holidays
15 EOT
16 Tourist Police
17 Bus Station (West Side)
18 Bus Station (East Side)
19 Taxi Rank
20 Dodecanese Hydrofoil Company
21 Municipal Tourist Office
22 Entrance to Sound & Light Show
23 Temple of Aphrodite
24 Byzantine Museum
25 Museum of Decorative Arts
26 Palace of the Grand Masters
27 Archaeological Museum
29 Mosque of Süleyman
30 Turkish Library
32 Turkish Bath
34 Greek Folk Dance Theatre
39 Castellania Fountain
46 Synagogue
48 Departure Point for Boats to Turkey
49 Customs Office
50 Port Police
51 Rock Style Internet Cafe

GREECE

in different languages, or you can check the schedule with the EOT. Admission is 1200 dr.

The **Greek Folk Dance Theatre** (☎ 29 085) on Andronikou gives first-rate performances, beginning at 9.20 pm. Admission is 3500 dr.

The old town has some great bars, but a popular place for big-time bar-hopping is Orfanidou in the city's north-west, lined with bars representing almost every nationality.

Around the Island
The imposing **Acropolis of Lindos**, Rhodes' most important ancient city, shares a rocky outcrop with a **crusader castle**. The site is open 8 am to 7 pm Tuesday to Friday, and 8.30 am to 3 pm weekends. Admission is 1200 dr. Below the site is Lindos town, with labyrinths of winding streets full of whitewashed, elaborately decorated houses. It's undeniably beautiful but very touristy. The bus to Lindos from Rhodes City's east-side station costs 1000 dr.

The extensive ruins of **Kamiros**, an ancient Doric city on the west coast, are well preserved, with the remains of houses, baths, a cemetery and a temple, but the site should be visited as much for its lovely setting on a gentle hillside overlooking the sea.

Between Rhodes City and Lindos the **beaches** are crowded. If you prefer isolation, venture south to the bay of Lardos. Even farther south, between Genadi and Plimmyri, you'll find good stretches of deserted sandy beach. On the west coast, beaches tend to be pebbly and the sea is often choppy.

Getting There & Away
Air There are daily flights from Rhodes to Athens (23,400 dr) and Karpathos (12,800 dr). In summer there are regular services to Iraklio, Mykonos, Santorini, Kassos and Kastellorizo. The Olympic Airways office (☎ 24 571) is at Ierou Lohou 9.

For information and efficient service, Triton Holidays (☎ 21 690, fax 31 625, ✉ info@tritondmc.gr) near the New Market at Plastira 9 is hard to beat.

Ferry There are daily ferries from Rhodes to Piraeus (9000 dr). Most sail via the Dodecanese north of Rhodes, but at least three times a week there is a service via Karpathos, Kassos, Crete and the Cyclades. The EOT gives out a schedule.

There are daily excursion boats to Symi (5000 dr return), as well as a hydrofoil (3000 dr one way) and regular ferry service (1600 dr). Similar services also run to Kos, Kalymnos, Nysiros, Tilos, Patmos and Leros.

Between April and October there are regular boats from Rhodes to Marmaris (Turkey); one-way tickets cost 11,000 dr (13,500 dr return). There is an additional US$10 Turkish port tax each way.

From March to August there are regular ferries to Israel (from 28,000 dr) via Cyprus (17,000 dr). Prices do not include foreign port tax.

For the port police, call ☎ 27 695.

Getting Around
To/From the Airport There are frequent buses between the airport and Rhodes City's west-side bus station (450 dr). A taxi to the airport costs about 3500 dr.

Bus Rhodes City has two bus stations. The west-side bus station, next to the New Market, serves the airport, the west coast, Embona and Koskinou; the east-side station, nearby on Plateia Rimini, serves the east coast and inland southern villages. The EOT has a schedule.

Car & Motorcycle You'll be tripping over independent car and motorcycle-rental outlets in Rhodes City's new town, particularly on and around 28 Oktovriou. Try to bargain – competition is fierce.

Many parts of the old town are prohibited to cars, but there are car parks around the periphery.

SYMI Σύμη
☎ 0241 • pop 2332
Symi town is outstandingly attractive, with pastel-coloured neoclassical mansions surrounding the harbour and covering the surrounding hills. The island is easily accessible by boat from Rhodes, but you'll have more fun if you stay over when the day-trippers have gone.

There is no tourist office or tourist police. Perhaps the best source of information is the English-language *Symi Visitor* newspaper, widely available and free of charge. It includes useful maps of the town, which is divided into

GREECE

two parts: Gialos, the harbour, and Horio, above it, crowned by the kastro.

There is little by way of budget accommodation on the island; double rooms average about 14,000 dr. *Catherinettes Rooms to Let* (☎ 72 698), *Hotel Glafkos* (☎ 71 358) and *Rooms to Let Helena* (☎ 71 931), all scattered around the harbour, are some good options. The bulk of the restaurants are at the end of the harbour. *O Meraklis* and *Taverna Neraida* are cheap and cheerful eateries; at night, the *Sunflower* sandwich and salad bar turns into an excellent vegetarian restaurant. *Hellenikon* has a cellar of 140 different Greek wines, while *Tholos*, a five-minute walk from the harbour towards the tiny town beach, offers well-prepared, imaginative fare.

Aside from the excursion boats, a number of ferries and hydrofoils between Rhodes and Kos also call at Symi. The port police are on ☎ 71 205.

KARPATHOS Κάρπαθος
☎ 0245 • pop 5323

The picturesque, elongated island of Karpathos lies midway between Crete and Rhodes. It's a relaxed place, with little of the hype that surrounds more touristed islands.

Orientation & Information

The main port and capital is Pigadia, and there's a smaller port at Diafani. There's no EOT or tourist police; your best bet is to see one of the travel agencies. Karpathos Travel (☎ 22 148) is on Dimokratias. There is Internet access at Caffe Galileo, two doors from the Olympic Airways office on Apodimon Karpathou, the main thoroughfare running parallel to the waterfront.

Things to See & Do

Karpathos has glorious **beaches**, particularly at Apella, Kira Panagia and Lefkos.

The northern village of **Olymbos** is like a living museum and is endlessly fascinating to ethnologists. Women wear brightly coloured and embroidered skirts, waistcoats and headscarves and goatskin boots. Interiors of houses are decorated with embroidered cloth and their facades with brightly painted moulded-plaster reliefs, and the inhabitants speak a dialect which retains some

Doric words. A two-hour uphill walking trail leads from Diafani to Olymbos, and there are infrequent local buses between these two towns. There are excursions to Olymbos from Pigadia, but these leave you with an excessive 4½ hours in the small town.

Places to Stay & Eat

There's plenty of accommodation and owners usually meet the boats. *Harry's Rooms* (☎ 22 188), just off 28 Oktovriou, has spotless singles/doubles with shared bathroom for 4500/5500 dr. *Hotel Avra* (☎ 22 388, 28 Oktovriou) has comfortable doubles with/without private bath for 8000/6000 dr. Basic accommodation is also available at Diafani, Olymbos and several other villages.

To sample traditional local dishes, head for busy *Taverna Karpathos*, near the quay. On Apodimon Karpathou there is a wonderful *taverna* that serves great mezedes and often has locals playing music. The place has no sign – it's a white and blue building just up from the National Bank of Greece.

Getting There & Away

Karpathos has an international airport that receives charter flights from northern Europe. There are daily flights to Rhodes (12,700 dr) and three a week to Kassos (6800 dr) and Athens (25,900 dr).

There are three ferries a week to Rhodes (4400 dr) and to Piraeus (7900 dr) via the Cyclades and Crete. In bad weather, ferries do not stop at Diafani. There is also a weekly high-speed catamaran on the Kassos-Karpathos-Halki-Rhodes route. For the port police, call ☎ 22 227.

KOS Κως
☎ 0242 • pop 26,379

Kos is renowned as the birthplace of Hippocrates, father of medicine. Kos town manifests the more ghastly aspects of mass tourism, and the beaches are pretty horrendous, with wall-to-wall sun lounges and beach umbrellas. The island is crowded but there are a few areas where you can try to escape the masses.

Orientation & Information

Kos town, on the north-east coast, is the main town and port. The municipal tourist office

(☎ 24 460, ✉ dotkos@hol.gr), Vasileos Georgiou 1, is near the hydrofoil pier. The post office is on Vasileos Pavlou; the OTE is on the corner of Vironos and Xanthou. Internet access is available at Cafe Del Mare, Megalou Alexandrou 4.

Things to See
Before you beat a hasty retreat from Kos town, check the 13th-century **fortress** and the **archaeological museum**, open 8 am to 3 pm Tuesday to Sunday. Entry is 800 dr. The **ancient agora** and the **odeion** are also worth seeing.

On a pine-clad hill, 4km from Kos town, stand the extensive ruins of the renowned healing centre of **Asclepion**, where Hippocrates practised medicine. The site is open 8 am to 3 pm Tuesday to Sunday; admission is 800 dr.

The villages in the **Asfendion** region of the Dikeos Mountains are reasonably tranquil. There is a long stretch of beach along Kefalos Bay. **Paradise** is the most appealing of these beaches, but don't expect to have it to yourself.

Places to Stay & Eat
Kos Camping (☎ 23 910) is 3km along the eastern waterfront. There are frequent buses from the harbourfront in town; take any heading to Agios Fokas.

Otherwise, head for the convivial *Pension Alexis* (☎ 28 798, 25 594, Irodotou 9) close to the harbour (the entrance is on Omirou). Singles/doubles/triples with shared bath cost 5000/7500/9000 dr. The friendly English-speaking Alexis is a font of information. He is also the owner of *Hotel Afendoulis* (☎ 25 321, Evripilou 1), where comfortable, well-kept singles/doubles/triples with private bath cost 7500/11,000/13,0000 dr.

Olympiada behind the Olympic Airways office, and *Filoxenia Taverna* on the corner of Pindou and Alikarnassou, are popular with locals. *Creta Corner* on the corner of Artemisias and Korai serves excellent, well-priced food, and there's often live Greek music.

Entertainment
Kos town is well known for its nightlife. The streets of Diakon and Nafklirou are lined with bars that are jam-packed in high season.

Getting There & Away
Apart from European charter flights, there are daily flights from Kos to Athens (21,400 dr). The Olympic Airways office (☎ 28 331) is at the southern end of Vasileos Pavlou.

There are frequent ferries from Rhodes that continue on to Piraeus (7700 dr) via Kalymnos, Leros and Patmos. There are less frequent connections to Nisyros, Tilos, Symi, Samos and Crete. Daily excursion boats also go to Nisyros, Kalymnos and Rhodes. Ferries travel daily in summer to Bodrum in Turkey costing 9000 dr one way (10,000 dr return). A particularly helpful agency is Pulia Tours (☎ 26 388), Vasileos Pavlou 3.

For the port police, call ☎ 26 594.

Getting Around
Buses for Asclepion, Agios Fokas (for the camping ground) and Lampi leave from opposite the town hall on the harbourfront; all other buses leave from the station behind the Olympic Airways office.

PATMOS Πάτμος
☎ 0247 • pop 2663
Starkly scenic Patmos gets crowded in summer, but manages to remain remarkably tranquil. Orthodox and Western Christians have long made pilgrimages to this holy island.

Orientation & Information
The tourist office (☎ 31 666), post office and police station are all in the white Italianate building at the island's port and capital of Skala. There is an Internet cafe, Millennium, a few blocks inland from the port, just up from the OTE.

Things to See
The **Monastery of the Apocalypse**, on the site where St John wrote the book of Revelations, is between the port and the hora. The attraction here is the cave where the saint lived and dictated his revelations. Opening times are 8 am to 1 pm daily and 4 to 6 pm on Tuesday, Wednesday and Sunday.

The hora's whitewashed houses huddle around the fortified **Monastery of St John the Theologian**, which houses a vast collection of monastic treasures, including embroidered robes, Byzantine jewellery and early manuscripts and icons. It's open the same hours as

GREECE

the Monastery of the Apocalypse. Admission to the monastery is free, but it costs 1200 dr to see the treasury.

Appropriate dress (ie, no shorts) is requested for visitors to the holy sites.

Patmos' indented coastline provides numerous secluded coves, mostly with pebble beaches. The best is Psili Ammos in the south, reached by excursion boat.

Places to Stay & Eat
Stefanos Camping (☎ 31 821) is on Meloi Beach, 2km north-east of Skala. Someone usually meets the ferries, but call ahead to make sure.

There are a few budget pensions along the hora road, including *Pension Maria Paskeledi* (☎ 32 152), where singles/doubles/triples with shared bathroom cost 4000/7000/9000 dr.

There is a cluster of mid-range hotels about 500m to the right of the port as you disembark. *Hotel Australis* (☎ 31 576) and *Villa Knossos* (☎ 32 189), next to each other, offer pleasant singles/doubles for 10,000/15,000 dr, and both have wonderful gardens. Hotel Australis also has pricier studio apartments.

O Pantelis Taverna, one block back from the waterfront, and *Grigoris Taverna*, opposite the passenger-transit port building, are popular eateries. *Restaurant Pisofani* serves up good fresh fish.

Cafe Aman, a five-minute walk from the port (turn left facing inland), offers excellent salads and pastas in a lovely setting. Aman and its neighbouring bars are popular for late-night drinks.

Getting There & Around
Frequent ferries travel between Patmos and Piraeus (7200 dr), and to Rhodes (4400 dr) via Leros, Kalymnos and Kos. There are also frequent boats to Samos. For the port police, call ☎ 34 131. Skala, Hora, Grikos and Kambos are connected by buses which depart from the port. In summer there are frequent excursion boats to the various beaches and to the islets of Arki and Marathi.

KASTELLORIZO Καστελλόριζο (MEGISTI)
☎ 0241 • pop 275
Tiny Kastellorizo lies 116km east of Rhodes, its nearest Greek neighbour, and only 2.5km

from the southern coast of Turkey. Its **Blue Grotto** is spectacular and comparable to its namesake in Capri. The name derives from the blue appearance of the water in the grotto, caused by refracted sunlight. Excursion boats will take you to the cave, and also to some of the surrounding islets, all of which are uninhabited. The island's remoteness is drawing a steady trickle of visitors, but as yet it remains pristine. There are plenty of rooms for rent – owners usually meet the boats. Three flights (10,900 dr) and two ferries (3700 dr) a week operate between Rhodes and Kastellorizo.

North-Eastern Aegean Islands

These islands are less visited than the Cyclades and the Dodecanese. There are seven major islands in this group: Chios, Ikaria, Lesvos, Limnos, Samos, Samothraki and Thasos.

SAMOS Σάμος
☎ 0273 • pop 32,000
Samos was an important centre of Hellenic culture and is reputedly the birthplace of the philosopher and mathematician Pythagoras. Lush and humid, its mountains are skirted by pine, sycamore and oak-forested hills.

Orientation & Information
Samos has three ports: Vathy (Samos town) and Karlovasi on the north coast, and Pythagorio on the south-east coast.

Vathy's unhelpful EOT office (☎ 28 530) is in a side street one block north of Plateia Pythagora. A better bet is ITSA Travel (☎ 23 605/06, 📧 itsa@otenet.gr), directly opposite the port. Friendly staff here can help with ferries, excursions and accommodation, plus there's free luggage storage.

The post office is on Smyrnis, four blocks from the waterfront. The OTE is on Plateia Iroön, behind the municipal gardens. There is a cybercafe on the waterfront, 250m from Plateia Pythagora and next to the police station.

Things to See & Do
Very little is left of the **ancient city** of Samos, on which the town of Pythagorio now stands. The Sacred Way, once flanked by

DIANA MAYFIELD

Sunrise over Vieux Bassin, Honfleur, Normandy, France

ROD HYETT

Street art in Paris

FRANCES LINZEE GORDON

The ever-popular beignet (doughnut), France

DIANA MAYFIELD

The stunning 13th-century stained glass (the oldest and finest in Paris) of the Sainte Chappelle

Decorative wedding bread

Golden sand and crystalline waters of Smugglers Cove, Zakynthos

Traditionally black, Crete

Bell tower near Loutro, Crete.

Soaking up the sun, sand and sea in Hania, Crete, Greece.

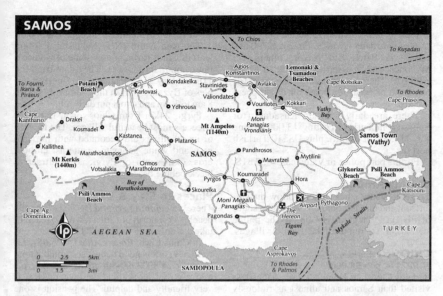

SAMOS

2000 statues, has now metamorphosed into the airport's runway.

The extraordinary **Evpalinos Tunnel**, built in the 6th century BC, is the site's most impressive surviving relic. The 1km tunnel was dug by political prisoners and used as an aqueduct to bring water from the springs of Mt Ampelos. Part of it can still be explored. It's 2km north of Pythagorio and is open 8.30 am to 3 pm daily, except Monday. Entry is 800 dr.

Vathy's **archaeological museum**, by the municipal gardens, is outstanding, the highlight being a 4.5m kouros statue. It's open 8.30 am to 3 pm daily, except Monday. Admission is 800 dr.

The villages of **Manolates** and **Vourliotes** on the slopes of Mt Ampelos are excellent walking territory, as there are many marked pathways. There's also good walking in the area north-east of Vathy. Quiet beaches can be found on the south-west coast in the Marathokampos area.

Places to Stay & Eat
Pythagorio, where you'll disembark if you've come from Patmos, is touristy and expensive. Vathy, 20 minutes away by bus, is cheaper. **Pythagoras Hotel** (☎ 28 422, fax 28 893, ☺ smicha@otenet.gr) is a good budget option.

Doubles/triples in high season go for 9000/11,000 dr, but considerably less at other times. There's also a good-value restaurant here. The hotel is 800m to the left of the quay. Call ahead to be met at the port.

The friendly **Pension Vasso** (☎ 23 258) is open year-round and has singles/doubles/triples for 5000/9000/12,000 dr with balcony and bath. To get there from the quay, turn right onto the waterfront, left onto Stamatiadou and walk up the steps. Nearby, **Hotel Ionia** (☎ 28 782) is cheap. Singles/doubles with shared bathroom are 4000/6000 dr.

Hotel Samos (☎ 28 377, fax 23 771, ☺ hot samos@otenet.gr) on the waterfront just near the port is a decent choice, offering singles/doubles/triples for 9900/12,600/17,450 dr. The hotel has lots of facilities, including rooftop pool, bar and restaurant.

The popular **Taverna Gregoris**, near the post office, serves good food at reasonable prices. **O Kipos** (The Garden), one block back from the waterfront on Kalomiri, offers good traditional food in a lovely outdoor setting.

Getting There & Away
Samos has an international airport receiving European charter flights. There are also daily

flights to Athens (17,400 dr) and two flights a week to Thessaloniki (25,400 dr).

There are daily ferries to Piraeus (6700 dr), some via Paros and Naxos, others via Mykonos, and two ferries a week to Chios (3000 dr). There are ferries to Patmos (3100 dr one way) or excursion boats for day-trippers (8000 dr return).

There are daily boats to Kuşadası (for Ephesus) in Turkey, costing 13,000 dr one way (14,000 dr return), plus US$10 Turkish port tax.

For the port police in Vathy call ☎ 27 318.

Getting Around
To get to Vathy's bus station, follow the waterfront and turn left onto Lekadi, 250m south of Plateia Pythagora (just before the police station). Buses run to all the island's villages.

CHIOS Χίος
☎ 0271 • pop 54,000
'Craggy Chios', as Homer described it, is less visited than Samos and almost as riotously fertile. It is famous for its mastic trees, which produce a resin still used in chewing gum.

In 1822 an estimated 25,000 inhabitants of the island were massacred by the Turks after an uprising against Turkish rule.

Orientation & Information
The main town and port is Chios town, which is unattractive and noisy; only the old Turkish quarter has any charm. It is, however, a good base from which to explore the island.

The municipal tourist office (☎ 44 389) is at Kanari 18, the main street running from the waterfront to Plateia Vounakiou in the town centre. Manos Center (☎ 20 002), right by the ferry dock, can help with accommodation and transport arrangements and is open to meet the 4 am ferry from Piraeus.

The OTE is 100m beyond the tourist office, and the post office is on Rodokanaki, a block back from the waterfront. On the southern waterfront at Egeou 98 is Enter Internet Café (the cafe is upstairs; enter from the side street).

Things to See
The **Philip Argenti Museum**, in the same building as the Korais library near the cathedral in Chios town, contains exquisite embroideries and traditional costumes. It's open 8 am to 2

pm weekdays (also 5 to 7.30 pm Friday) and 8 am to 12.30 pm Saturday. Admission is 300 dr.

The **Nea Moni** (New Monastery), 14km west of Chios town, houses some of Greece's most important mosaics. They date from the 11th century and are among the finest examples of Byzantine art in the country. It's open 8 am to 1 pm and 4 to 8 pm daily; entry is free.

Pyrgi, 24km from Chios town, is one of Greece's most beautiful villages. The facades of its dwellings are decorated with intricate grey and white geometric patterns. **Emboreios**, 6km south of Pyrgi, is an attractive black-pebble beach.

Places to Stay & Eat
There's a *camping ground* (☎ 74 111) on the beach 14km north of Chios town. To reach it, take a Kardamyla or Langada bus.

In Chios town, *Rooms Alex* (☎ 26 054, Livanou 29) offers good budget accommodation. Rooms cost 8000 dr with private bath, there's a lovely roof terrace and the owner, Alex, is very friendly and helpful. The pension is one block back from the waterfront, about 500m south of the quay. *Chios Rooms* (☎ 20 196) at the opposite end of the harbour to the ferry dock, has clean, simple rooms in a lovely old building. Singles/doubles with shared bath are 5000/9000 dr, with private bathroom 7000/11,000 dr.

By the police station, 50m to the right of the ferry disembarkation point, is *Ouzeri Theodosiou*, a popular establishment serving delectable mezedes. Opposite Rooms Alex is *Ta Duo Aderfi* (The Two Brothers), with a pleasant garden and good food.

There's an astonishing number of bars lining the waterfront, catering largely to the 2000 students from the island's university.

Getting There & Away
There are daily flights from Chios to Athens (15,800 dr) and twice-weekly flights to Thessaloniki (22,400 dr) and Lesvos (10,900 dr).

Ferries sail at least twice a week to Samos (3000 dr) and Piraeus (5800 dr) via Lesvos, and once a week to Thessaloniki (8400 dr) via Lesvos and Limnos. There are a few boats to the small islands of Psara, west of Chios, and Inousses, to the east. In summer daily boats travel to Çeşme in Turkey; tickets cost 15,000 dr one way (20,000 dr return), plus

US$10 Turkish port tax. For the port police call ☎ 44 433.

Getting Around

There are two bus stations. Blue buses go to local villages (Vrontados, Karyes, Karfas) and leave from the right side (coming from the waterfront) of Plateia Vounakiou, by the garden. Green, long-distance buses (to Pyrgi and Mesta) leave from the station one block to the left of Plateia Vounakiou.

LESVOS (MYTILINI) Λέσβος

(Μυτιλήνη)

Lesvos is the third largest Greek island. It has always been a centre of artistic and philosophical achievement and creativity, and it remains a spawning ground for innovative ideas in the arts and politics.

A useful source of information on the island is the Web site www.greeknet.com.

Mytilini

☎ 0251 • pop 23,970

Mytilini, the capital and port of Lesvos, is a large working town built around two harbours. All passenger ferries dock at the southern harbour. The tourist police (☎ 22 776) are at the entrance to the quay; the EOT (☎ 42 511) is 50m up the road at Aristarhou 6. The post office is on Vournazon, west of the southern harbour, and the OTE is on the same street. Internet access is available at Net Club, 200m south of the southern harbour on Eliti; it's open from 4 pm weekdays, from 10 am Saturday and Sunday.

Things to See Mytilini's imposing **castle**, built in early Byzantine times and renovated in the 14th century, opens 8.30 am to 3 pm daily, except Monday. The new **archaeological museum**, signposted north of the quay, is open 8.30 am to 3 pm Tuesday to Sunday. Don't miss the **Theophilos Museum**, which houses the works of the prolific primitive painter Theophilos. It's 4km from Mytilini in the village of Varia (take a local bus) and is open 9 am to 2.30 pm and 6 to 8 pm Tuesday to Sunday. Entry to each of these attractions costs 500 dr.

Places to Stay & Eat Domatia owners belong to a cooperative called Sappho Room Finding Service; most of these domatia are in little side streets off Ermou, near the northern harbour. *Salina's Garden Rooms* (☎ 42 073, *Fokeas 7*) has doubles from 6500 dr with shared facilities; nearby, *Thalia Rooms* (☎ 24 640, *Kinikiou 1*) has doubles from 7500 dr with private bath. Nearest to the quay is *Iren* (☎ 22 787, *Komninaki 41*), where clean but simple doubles/triples cost 9000/11,000 dr.

The ramshackle but atmospheric *Ermis Ouzeri* has yet to be discovered by the tourist crowd. It's at the northern end of Ermou on the corner with Kornarou. There are popular tavernas spilling over the pavement south of the harbour; *Stratos Psarotaverna* offers good fish dishes.

The Lazy Fish (*Imvrou 5*) is an atmospheric place for a drink.

Around the Island

Northern Lesvos is best known for its exquisitely preserved traditional town of **Mithymna** (also known as Molyvos), which is a good place to spend a few days. The neighbouring beach resort of **Petra**, 6km south, is affected by low-key package tourism, while the villages surrounding **Mt Lepetymnos** are authentic, picturesque and worth a day or two of exploration.

Western Lesvos is a popular destination for lesbians who come on a kind of pilgrimage in honour of Sappho, one of the greatest poets of ancient Greece. The beach resort of **Skala Eresou** is built over ancient Eresos, where she was born in 628 BC.

Southern Lesvos is dominated by **Mt Olympus** (968m), with pine forests decorating its flanks. **Plomari**, a large traditional coastal village, is popular with visitors, and the picturesque village of **Agiasos** is a favourite day-trip destination.

Getting There & Away

There are daily flights from Lesvos to Athens (19,900 dr), and less frequent services to Thessaloniki (20,900 dr), Limnos (13,400 dr) and Chios (10,900 dr). The Olympic Airways office (☎ 28 659) is at Kavetsou 44.

In summer there are daily boats to Piraeus (7200 dr), some via Chios. There are three a week to Kavala (6500 dr) via Limnos and two a week to Thessaloniki (8400 dr). Ferries to Ayvalik, Turkey cost 16,000 dr one

way (21,000 dr return). The port police
(☎ 28 827) are 75m from the port on Pavlou
Kountouriotou.

Getting Around

There are two bus stations in Mytilini. The
one for long-distance buses is just beyond the
south-western end of Pavlou Kountouriotou.
For local buses go to the harbour's northern-
most section.

SAMOTHRAKI Σαμοθράκη
☎ 0551 • pop 2800

This wild, alluring island has only recently
been discovered by holiday-makers and is deservedly popular with walkers. Experienced
trekkers can climb **Mt Fengari** (1611m), the
highest mountain in the Aegean.

Samothraki's big attraction is the **Sanctuary
of the Great Gods**, an ancient site at Paleopo-
lis shrouded in mystery. No one knows quite
what went on here, only that it was a place of
initiation into the cult of the Kabeiroi, the gods
of fertility. They were believed to help sea-
farers, and to be initiated into their mysteries
was seen as a safeguard against shipwreck and
other misfortune. The site's winding pathways
lead through lush shrubbery to extensive ruins.
The site's most celebrated relic, the *Winged
Victory of Samothrace*, which now has pride of
place in Paris' Louvre, was discovered here in
1863. Both the site and its small museum are
open 8.30 am to 3 pm Tuesday to Sunday. Admission to each is 500 dr.

Samothraki's port is Kamariotissa on the
north-west coast. The island's capital, the
hora (also called Samothraki), is 5km inland.
Most people stick to the resorts of Kamariotissa, Loutra (Therma) and Pahia Ammos,
leaving the rest of the island untouched.

There are two camping grounds at Loutra
and a number of domatia in the port and hora.
Ferries link Samothraki with Limnos, and
with Kavala and Alexandroupolis on the
mainland.

Sporades Σποράδες

The Sporades group comprises the lush, pine-
forested islands of Skiathos, Skopelos and
Alonnisos, south of the Halkidiki Peninsula,
and far-flung Skyros, off Evia.

Getting There & Away

Air Skiathos receives many charter flights
from northern Europe. In summer there are
daily flights from Athens to Skiathos (16,700
dr) and two a week between Athens and Skyros (14,200 dr).

Ferry Skiathos, Skopelos and Alonnisos
have frequent ferry services to the mainland
ports of Volos and Agios Konstantinos, as
well as one or two a week to Kymi (Evia), via
Skyros. In high season there are also connections to Thessaloniki.

There is an extensive hydrofoil service
from these mainland ports and between the
islands. The hydrofoils are more frequent,
faster and more convenient, but fares are double those for the ferries.

In summer, three hydrofoils a week connect
Skyros with other islands in the Sporades.

SKIATHOS Σκίαθος
☎ 0427 • pop 4100

Skiathos is tagged the Mykonos of the Sporades, which means it's crowded and expensive, but it does have good beaches,
particularly on the south coast. However, the
island lacks the charm of Skopelos and
Alonissos.

Orientation & Information

There is a tourist information booth and helpful touch-screen computer to the left as you
disembark from the boats. Skiathos town's
main thoroughfare is Papadiamanti, running
inland from opposite the port. Here you'll
find the post office, the OTE and the tourist
police (☎ 23 172). Around the corner from
the post office, on Evangelistrias, is Internet
Zone Cafe. A good source of information is
the Web site at www.n-skiathos.gr.

Places to Stay & Eat

There is a Rooms to Let kiosk on the waterfront, to the right as you disembark, or you
can wander Papadiamanti and its side streets
looking for hotels or domatia. Be warned that
accommodation is hard to come by in July and
August.

There is a *camping ground* (☎ 49 250) at
Koukounaries Beach on the south coast. In
town, the best value is at *Hotel Karafelas*
(☎ 21 235) at the end of Papadiamanti. Quite

comfortable single/doubles are available for 10,000/14,000 dr.

Numerous fast-food outlets, cafes and bars line Papadiamanti. *Niko's Cafe Bar* offers an extensive menu at reasonable prices. The waterfront restaurants are much of a muchness, catering to the tourist trade. A notable exception is popular *Ta Psaradiki Ouzeri* at the far end of the old harbour by the fish market.

Getting There & Around

See earlier for information about flights to/from Skiathos.

There are frequent ferries to Volos (2700 dr) and Agios Konstantinos (3300 dr) and regular connections to Skopelos, Alonissos and Skyros. The port police are on ☎ 22 017.

Crowded buses ply the south-coast road between Skiathos town and Koukounaries Beach every 20 to 30 minutes, stopping at the beaches along the way.

SKOPELOS Σκόπελος
☎ 0424 • pop 5000
Skopelos is less commercialised than Skiathos, but following hot on its trail.

Information

There is no tourist office or tourist police in Skopelos town. The post office is well hidden in the labyrinth of alleyways behind the waterfront. To find it, walk up the road opposite the bus station, take the first left, the first right, the first left again, and it's on the right. The OTE is signposted from the middle of the waterfront, and there's a cybercafe, Click & Surf, one block back from the waterfront on Nirvana.

Things to See

Attractive **Skopelos town**, with white houses built on a hillside, hides mazes of narrow streets and stairways leading up to the kastro. **Glossa**, the island's other town, lying inland in the north, is similarly appealing with fewer concessions to tourism.

Staphylos, 4km from Skopelos town, is a decent beach that gets very crowded; over a headland is **Velanio**, the island's designated nudist beach. The 2km stretch of tiny pebbles at **Milia**, 10km farther on, is considered the island's best beach.

Places to Stay & Eat

The Rooms & Apartments Association of Skopelos (☎ 24 567), in a small office on the waterfront, can help you find accommodation.

Pension Sotos (☎ 22 549) in a charming old building in the middle of the waterfront has charming doubles/triples with private bath for 10,000/15,000 dr. There's also a communal kitchen and courtyard garden.

A 10-minute walk from the port is *Pension Soula (☎ 22 930)* with rooms for 12,000/15,000 dr, a communal kitchen and garden. To find it, walk right from the port and turn left at Hotel Amalia. Follow the road, bearing right after about 200m, and the pension is on the right.

Zio Peppe on the waterfront has excellent pizza from 700 dr. For a cheap, basic and popular restaurant, try *O Platanos*, just in from the bus station. *Restaurant Alexander*, beyond the OTE (follow the signs), is more upmarket but offers good, reasonably priced fare in a lovely garden setting.

Getting There & Around

There are frequent ferries to Volos (3400 dr) and Agios Konstantinos (4100 dr). These boats also call at Alonnisos and Skiathos. Large ferries dock behind the bus station; other boats at the quay to the harbour's north. Many hydrofoil services to Skopelos also call at Loutraki, the port for Glossa. You can contact the port police on ☎ 22 180.

The bus station is on the waterfront. There are frequent buses from Skopelos town to Glossa, stopping at the beaches on the way.

ALONNISOS Αλόννησος
☎ 0424 • pop 3000
Alonnisos is the least visited of these islands and is green and serene. The water surrounding the island has been declared a marine park and is the cleanest in the Aegean.

The harbour town is Patitiri; the hora is a few kilometres inland. A winding path starting from just beyond Pension Galini in Patitiri leads within 40 minutes to the hora. Alonnisos is an ideal island for walking and there is a network of well-signposted trails, as well as guided walks offered by many of the travel agencies.

Kokkinokastro and **Hrysia Milia** are among the good beaches lining the coast.

GREECE

Places to Stay & Eat

There are two camping grounds: large, shady *Camping Rocks* (☎ 65 410) in Patitiri and smaller *Ikaros Camping* (☎ 65 258) on the east coast at Steni Vala beach. There is a Rooms to Let service (☎ 65 577) opposite the quay.

Pension Galini (☎ 65 573, fax 65 094) is a good choice: doubles/triples cost 15,000/17,000 dr with private bath. Spacious, well-equipped apartments for four/six people are also available for 20,000/25,000 dr. The pension is 400m up Pelasgon, on the left beside the lobster restaurant (there's no sign).

For imaginatively prepared local cuisine, try *To Kamaki Ouzeri*, on Ikion Dolopon.

Getting There & Away

There are frequent ferries to Volos (3800 dr) and Agios Konstantinos (4400 dr) via Skiathos and Skopelos. The port police can be reached at ☎ 65 595.

Ionian Islands
Τα Επτάνησα

The Ionian Islands stretch down the west coast of Greece from Corfu in the north to remote Kythira, situated off the southern tip of the Peloponnese.

Getting There & Away

Air There are lots of charter flights to Corfu from northern Europe in summer, as well as a few flights to Kefallonia and Zakynthos. Olympic has daily flights from Athens to Corfu, Zakynthos, Kefallonia and Kythira.

Ferry Most ferries between Italy and Patras call at Corfu. In summer, there are also services from Brindisi to Kefallonia, Zakynthos and Paxi.

CORFU Κέρκυρα

Corfu is the most important island in the group, with a population of 107,592.

Corfu Town
☎ 0661 • pop 36,000

The old town of Corfu, wedged between two fortresses, occupies a peninsula on the island's east coast. The narrow alleyways of high shuttered tenements in mellow ochres and pinks are an immediate reminder of the town's long association with Venice.

Orientation & Information The town's old fortress (Palaio Frourio) stands on an eastern promontory, separated from the town by an area of parks and gardens known as the Spianada. The new fortress (Neo Frourio) lies to the north-west. Ferries dock at the new port, just west of the new fortress. The long-distance bus station is on Avrami, just inland from the port.

The EOT office (☎ 37 520) is on Rizospaston Voulefton, between the OTE and the post office, and the tourist police (☎ 30 265) are at Samartzi 4. All the major Greek banks are in town, including the National Bank on the corner of Voulgareos and Theotoki. American Express is represented by Greek Skies Tours (☎ 30 883), Kapodistriou 20A.

Things to See The **archaeological museum**, Vraili 5, houses a collection of finds from Mycenaean to classical times. The star attraction is the pediment from the Temple of Artemis, decorated with gorgons. Opening times are 8.45 am to 3 pm Tuesday to Saturday and 9.30 am to 2.30 pm Sunday; admission is 800 dr.

The **Church of Agios Spiridon**, Corfu's most famous church, has an elaborately decorated interior. Pride of place is given to the remains of St Spiridon, displayed in a silver casket; four times a year they are paraded around the town.

Places to Stay & Eat There are no decent budget places in town. A lot of people wind up at the *Hotel Evropi* (☎ 39 304), but only because it's close to the port – it's signposted off Xenofondos Stratigou. It charges 5500/6000 dr for singles/doubles.

The cheapest reasonable rooms are at the *Hotel Ionian* (☎ 30 628), also near the port at Xenofondos Stratigou 46. It charges 8500/11,000 dr for singles/doubles with bathroom. The C-class *Hotel Konstantinopolis* (☎ 48 716, fax 48 718, Zavitsianou 3) is a splendid Art Nouveau hotel. Singles/doubles are 12,500/18,600 dr.

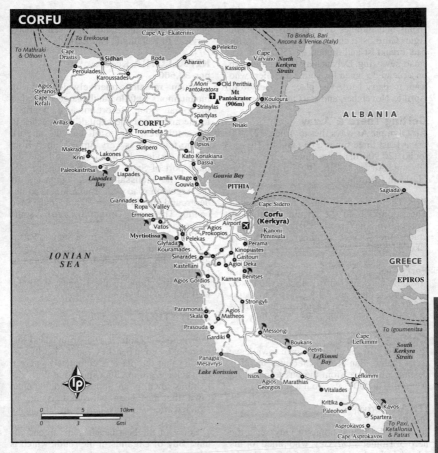

CORFU

There are several cheap restaurants near the new port. The tiny *O Thessalonikios* on Xenofondos Stratigou does succulent spit-roast chicken (1200 dr). In town, try *Hryso-malis (Nik Theotaki 6)* near the Spianada.

Around the Island
There's hardly anywhere in Corfu that hasn't made its play for the tourist dollar, but the north is totally over the top. The only real attraction there is the view from the summit of **Mt Pantokrator** (906m), Corfu's highest mountain. There's a road to the top from the village of **Strinila**.

The main resort on the west coast is **Paleo-kastritsa**, which is built round a series of pretty bays. Farther south, there are good beaches around the small village of **Agios Gordios**. Between Paleokastritsa and Agios Gordios is the hill-top village of **Pelekas**, supposedly the best place on Corfu to watch the sunset.

Places to Stay
Accommodation on Corfu is dominated by package groups. Most backpackers head straight for the **Pink Palace** (☎ *53 103/04, fax 53 025, ✆ pink-palace@ker.forthnet.gr)*, a

huge complex of restaurants, bars and budget rooms that tumbles down a hillside outside Agios Gordios. It charges 6500 dr per day for bed, breakfast and dinner, or 7500 dr in the smart new wing. Debauchery is the main item on a menu designed for young travellers who want to party hard. The place is open from April to November, and staff meet the boats.

Getting There & Away
Air Olympic Airways flies to Athens (23,400 dr) at least three times a day and to Thessaloniki (20,900 dr) three times a week. The Olympic Airways office (☎ 38 694) is at Polila 11 in Corfu town.

Bus There are daily buses to Athens and Thessaloniki from the Avrami terminal in Corfu town. The fare of 8650 dr to Athens includes the ferry to Igoumenitsa. The trip takes 11 hours.

Ferry There are hourly ferries to Igoumenitsa (1400 dr, 1½ hours) and a daily ferry to Paxoi. In summer, there are daily services to Patras (5800 dr, 10 hours) on the international ferries that call at Corfu on their way from Italy.

Getting Around
Buses for villages close to Corfu town leave from Plateia San Rocco. Services to other destinations leave from the bus terminal on Avrami. The EOT gives out a schedule.

ITHAKI Ιθάκη
pop 3100
Ithaki is the fabled home of Odysseus, the hero of Homer's *Odyssey*, who pined for his island during his journeys to far-flung lands. It's a quiet place with some isolated coves. From the main town of Vathy you can walk to the **Fountain of Arethousa**, the fabled site of Odysseus' meeting with the swineherd Eumaeus on his return to Ithaki. Take water with you, as the fountain dries up in summer.

Ithaki has daily ferries to the mainland ports of Patras and Astakos, as well as daily services to Kefallonia and Lefkada.

KEFALLONIA Κεφαλλονιά
pop 32,500
Tourism remains relatively low-key on mountainous Kefallonia, the largest island of the Ionian group. Resort hotels are confined to the areas near the capital, the beaches in the south-west, Argostoli and the airport. Public transport is very limited, apart from regular services between Argostoli and the main port of Sami, 25km away on the east coast. The **Melissani Cave**, signposted off the Argostoli road 4km from Sami, is an underground lake lit by a small hole in the cave ceiling. The nearby **Drogarati Cave** has some impressive stalactites.

There are daily ferries from Sami to Patras (3450 dr, four hours), as well as from Argostoli and the south-eastern port of Poros to Kyllini in the Peloponnese. There are also ferry connections to the islands of Ithaki, Lefkada and Zakynthos.

ZAKYNTHOS Ζάκυνθος
pop 32,560
Zakynthos, or Zante, is a beautiful island surrounded by great beaches – so it's hardly surprising that the place is completely overrun by package groups. Its capital and port, Zakynthos town, is an imposing old Venetian town that has been painstakingly reconstructed after being levelled by an earthquake in 1953.

Some of the best beaches are around the huge **Bay of Laganas** in the south, which is where endangered loggerhead turtles come ashore to lay their eggs in August – at the peak of the tourist invasion. Conservation groups are urging people to stay away and the Greek government has declared this area a National Marine Park.

There are regular ferries between Zakynthos and Kyllini in the Peloponnese.

Italy

During a visit to Italy, an 18th-century English traveller wrote: 'Of all the countries in the world, Italy is the most adorned by the arts. Of all the countries in the world, she has the least need of them.' As inspiring today as it was then, Italy is a magnificently complex – if unevenly woven – tapestry of natural splendour and human achievement.

Centuries ago, well-to-do northern Europeans were drawn to the Mediterranean light, and so the Grand Tour (of Europe) was born. What they found in Italy was an extraordinary cocktail: next to the awe-inspiring artistic wealth of Rome, Venice and Florence they often encountered squalid decadence, poverty and spivs on the make.

The economic miracles of the past decades have transformed the country, but beneath all the style, fine food and delicious wine, there remains, happily, a certain chaotic air. Not everything is wonderful – expanding industry, poor urban planning, unchecked resort construction and what at times seems like an almost wilful indifference to the nation's art treasures have too often blighted the cities and countryside.

You could not hope to experience all the wonders of the country in even a year's non-stop travel. From the grandeur of the Dolomites to the rainbow-coloured sea of Sardinia, there is much more to the country than St Peter's and the Uffizi.

AT A GLANCE

Capital	Rome
Population	57.8 million
Official Language	Italian
Currency	1 Italian lira (L) = 100 centesimi
Time	GMT/UTC+0100
Country Phone Code	☎ 39

Facts about Italy

HISTORY

The traditional date for the founding of Rome by Romulus is 753 BC, but the country had already been inhabited for thousands of years. Palaeolithic Neanderthals lived in Italy during the last Ice Age more than 20,000 years ago, and by the start of the Bronze Age, around 2000 BC, the peninsula had been settled by several Italic tribes.

From about 900 BC the Etruscan civilisation developed until these mysterious people, whose origins are still controversial, dominated the area between the Arno and Tiber Valleys. After the foundation of Rome, Etruscan civilisation continued to flourish until the end of the 3rd century BC, when the Romans overwhelmed the last Etruscan city.

The Roman Republic

The new Roman republic, after recovering from the invasion of the Gauls in 390 BC, began its expansion into southern Italy. Rome claimed Sicily following the First Punic War against Hannibal in 241 BC, after his legendary crossing of the Alps. Rome defeated Carthage in 202 BC and within a few years claimed Spain and Greece as colonies.

ITALY (ITALIA)

Expansion & Empire

In the 1st century BC, under Julius Caesar, Rome conquered Gaul and moved into Egypt. After Caesar's assassination by his nephew, Brutus, on the Ides of March in 44 BC, a power struggle began between Mark Antony and Octavius, leading to the deaths of Antony and Cleopatra in Egypt in 31 BC and the establishment of the Roman Empire in 27 BC. Octavius, who had been adopted by Julius Caesar as his son and heir, took the title of Augustus Caesar and became the first emperor. Augustus ruled for 45 years, a period of great advancement in engineering, architecture, administration and literature.

The Eastern & Western Empires

By the end of the 3rd century, the empire had grown to such an extent that Emperor Diocletian divided it between east and west for administrative purposes. His successor, Constantine, declared religious freedom for Christians and moved the seat of power to the eastern capital, Byzantium, which he renamed Constantinople. During the 4th century, Christianity was declared the official state religion and grew in power and influence.

By the early 5th century, German tribes had entered Rome, and in 476 the Western Roman Empire ended when the German warrior, Odoacer, deposed the emperor and declared himself ruler of Italy. The south and Sicily were dominated by Muslim Arabs until the Normans invaded in 1036.

The City-States & the Renaissance

The Middle Ages in Italy were marked by the development of powerful city-states in the north. This was the time of Dante, Petrarch and Boccaccio, Giotto, Cimabue and Pisano.

In the 15th century the Renaissance, which began in Florence, spread throughout the country, fostering genius of the likes of Brunelleschi, Donatello, Bramante, Botticelli, da Vinci, Masaccio, Lippi, Raphael and, of course, Michelangelo.

By the early 16th century much of the country was under Spanish rule. This lasted until 1713 when, following the War of Spanish Succession, control of Italy passed to the Austrians. It was not until after the invasion by Napoleon in 1796 that a degree of unity was introduced into Italy, for the first time since the fall of the Roman Empire.

The Risorgimento

In the 1860s Italy's unification movement, known as the Risorgimento, gained momentum, and in 1861 the Kingdom of Italy was declared under the rule of King Vittorio Emanuele. Venice was wrested from Austria in 1866 and Rome from the papacy in 1870.

Mussolini & WWII

In the years after WWI, Italy was in turmoil. In 1921 the Fascist Party, formed by Benito Mussolini in 1919, won 35 of the 135 seats in parliament. In October 1921, after a period of considerable unrest and strikes, the king asked Mussolini to form a government, whereupon he became prime minister with only 7% representation in parliament.

Mussolini formed the Rome-Berlin axis with Hitler in 1936 and Italy entered WWII as an ally of Germany in June 1941. After a series of military disasters and an invasion by the Allies in 1943, the king led a coup against Mussolini and had him arrested. After being rescued by the Germans, Mussolini tried to govern in the north, but was fiercely opposed by Italian partisans, who finally shot him in April 1945.

The Italian Republic

In 1946, following a referendum, the constitutional monarchy was abolished and the republic established. Italy was a founding member of the European Economic Community in 1957 and was seriously disrupted by terrorism in the 1970s following the appearance of the Red Brigades, who kidnapped and assassinated the Christian Democrat prime minister, Aldo Moro, in 1978.

In the decades that followed WWII, Italy's national government was dominated by the centre-right Christian Democrats, usually in coalition with other parties (excluding the Communists). Italy enjoyed significant economic growth in the 1980s, but the 1990s heralded a new period of crisis for the country, both economically and politically.

The 1990s

Against the backdrop of a severe economic crisis, the very foundations of Italian politics

ITALY

were shaken by a national bribery scandal known as *tangentopoli* (bribesville). Investigations eventually implicated thousands of politicians, public officials and businesspeople, and left the main parties in tatters, effectively demolishing the centre of the Italian political spectrum.

After a period of right-wing government, new elections in 1996 brought a centre-left coalition known as the Olive Tree to power. Led by economist Romano Prodi, it included the communists for the first time in Italian history. A program of fiscal austerity was ushered in to guarantee Italy's entry into Europe's economic and monetary union (EMU), which occurred in 1998. Although the prime minister has been replaced three times (the government is currently led by socialist Giuliano Amato, who inherited the poisoned chalice from Prodi's successor Massimo d'Alema in March 2000) the Olive Tree coalition is holding on. If it survives until the planned elections of 2001 it will be the first government to serve out a full five-year term.

The Mafia

The 1990s have also seen Italy moving more decisively against the Sicilian Mafia, prompted by the 1992 assassinations of two prominent anti-Mafia judges. A major offensive in Sicily, plus the testimonies of several *pentiti* (informers or supergrasses), led to several important arrests – most notably of the Sicilian godfather, Salvatore 'Toto' Riina, who is now serving a life sentence. The man believed to have taken power after Riina's arrest, Giovanni Brusca, was arrested in May 1996 and implicated in the murders of anti-Mafia judges, Giovanni Falcone and Paolo Borsellino. A number of subsequent high profile arrests have undoubtedly dented the Mafia's confidence, but the battle is far from won.

GEOGRAPHY

Italy's boot shape makes it one of the most recognisable countries in the world. The country, incorporating the islands of Sicily and Sardinia, is bound by the Adriatic, Ligurian, Tyrrhenian and Ionian seas, which all form part of the Mediterranean Sea. About 75% of the Italian peninsula is mountainous, with the Alps dividing the country from France, Switzerland and Austria, and the

Apennines forming a backbone which extends from the Alps into Sicily. There are four active volcanoes: Stromboli and Vulcano (in the Aeolian Islands), Vesuvius (near Naples) and Etna (Sicily).

CLIMATE

Italy lies in a temperate zone, but the climates of the north and south vary. Summers are uniformly hot, but are often extremely hot and dry in the south. Winters can be severely cold in the north – particularly in the Alps, but also in the Po Valley – whereas they are generally mild in the south and in Sicily and Sardinia.

ECOLOGY & ENVIRONMENT

The countryside can be dramatically beautiful, but the long presence of humans on the peninsula has had a significant impact on the environment. Aesthetically the result is not always displeasing – much of the beauty of Tuscany, for instance, lies in the interaction of olive groves with vineyards, fallow fields and stands of cypress and pine. Centuries of tree clearing, combined with illegal building have also led to extensive land degradation and erosion. The alteration of the environment, combined with the Italians' passion for hunting *(la caccia)*, has led to many native animals and birds becoming extinct, rare or endangered. Under laws progressively introduced this century, many animals and birds are now protected.

There are numerous national parks in Italy. Among the most important are the Parco Nazionale del Gran Paradiso and the Parco Nazionale dello Stelvio, both in the Alps, and the Parco Nazionale d'Abruzzo.

Central and southern Italy are sometimes subject to massive earthquakes. A series of quakes devastated parts of the Appenine areas of Umbria and the Marche in September 1997. There was an earthquake after four days of tremors in central Italy in April 1998.

GOVERNMENT & POLITICS

For administrative purposes Italy is divided into 20 regions, each of which have some degree of autonomy. The regions are then subdivided into provinces and municipalities.

The country is a parliamentary republic, headed by a president who appoints the prime minister. The parliament consists of a senate and chamber of deputies, both of which have equal legislative power. The seat of national government is in Rome. Until reforms were introduced in 1994, members of parliament were elected by what was probably the purest system of proportional representation in the world. Two-thirds of both houses are now elected on the basis of who receives the most votes in their district, basically the same as the first-past-the-post system in the UK. The old system generally produced unstable coalition governments – Italy had 53 governments in the 48 years between the declaration of the republic and the introduction of electoral reforms.

ECONOMY

Italy has the fifth-largest economy in the world, thanks to some spectacular growth in the 1980s. However, the severe economic crisis of 1992-93 prompted a succession of governments to pull the economy into line with draconian measures such as the partial privatisation of the country's huge public sector. The Olive Tree coalition worked hard to meet the Maastricht criteria for entry into the European Monetary Union (EMU), cutting the budget deficit and lowering inflation in time to be included in the first intake of countries in May 1998.

Despite years of effort and the expenditure of trillions of lire, a significant economic gap still exists between Italy's northern and southern regions. The fact remains that Italy's richest regions (Piedmont, Lombardy, Veneto and Emilia-Romagna) are all northern, and its poorest (Calabria, Campania and Sicily) are all southern.

POPULATION & PEOPLE

The population of Italy is 57.8 million. The country has the lowest birthrate in Europe – a surprising fact considering the Italians' preoccupation with children and family. Foreigners may like to think of Italy as a land of passionate, animated people who gesticulate wildly when speaking, love to eat, drive like maniacs and don't like to work. However, it will take more than a holiday in Italy to understand its vigorous and remarkably diverse inhabitants. Overall the people remain fiercely protective of their regional customs, including their dialects and cuisine.

ARTS
Architecture, Painting & Sculpture

Italy has often been called a living art museum and certainly it is not always necessary to enter a gallery to appreciate the country's artistic wealth – it is all around you as you walk through Florence or Venice, or a medieval hill-top village in Umbria. In the south of Italy and in Sicily, where Greek colonisation preceded Roman domination, there are important Greek archaeological sites such as the temples at Paestum, south of Salerno, and at Agrigento in Sicily. Pompeii and Herculaneum give an idea of how ancient Romans actually lived.

Byzantine mosaics adorn churches throughout Italy, most notably at Ravenna, in the Basilica of San Marco in Venice, and in Monreale cathedral near Palermo. There are also some interesting mosaics in churches in Rome. In Apulia, you can tour the magnificent Romanesque churches, a legacy of the Normans (the region's medieval rulers) and their successors, the Swabians.

The 15th and early 16th centuries in Italy saw one of the most remarkable explosions of artistic and literary achievement in recorded history – the Renaissance. Patronised mainly by the Medici family in Florence and the popes in Rome, painters, sculptors, architects and writers flourished and many artists of genius emerged. The High Renaissance (about 1490-1520) was dominated by three men – Leonardo da Vinci (1452-1519), Michelangelo Buonarrotti (1475-1564) and Raphael (1483-1520).

The baroque period (17th century) was characterised by sumptuous, often fantastic architecture and richly decorative painting and sculpture. In Rome there are innumerable works by the great baroque sculptor and architect Gianlorenzo Bernini (1598-1680).

Neoclassicism in Italy produced the sculptor, Canova (1757-1822). Of Italy's modern artists, Amedeo Modigliani (1884-1920) is perhaps the most famous. The early 20th century also produced an artistic movement known as the Futurists, who rejected the sentimental art of the past and were infatuated by new technology, including modern warfare. Fascism produced its own style of architecture in Italy, characterised by the EUR satellite city and the work of Marcello Piacentini

ITALY

(1881-1960), which includes the *Stadio dei Marmi* at Rome's Olympic Stadium complex.

Music

Few modern Italian singers or musicians have made any impact outside Italy – one exception is Zucchero (Adelmo Fornaciari), who has become well known in the USA and UK as Sugar. Instead, it is in the realms of opera and instrumental music where Italian artists have triumphed. Antonio Vivaldi (1675-1741) created the concerto in its present form. Verdi, Puccini, Bellini, Donizetti and Rossini, composers from the 19th and early 20th centuries, are all stars of the modern operatic era. Tenor Luciano Pavarotti (1935-) is today's (fading) luminary of Italian opera. Not so with Andrea Bocelli (1958-) who soared to international stardom in the 1990s.

Literature

Before Dante wrote his *Divina Commedia* (Divine Comedy) and confirmed vernacular Italian as a serious medium for poetic expression, Latin was the language of writers. Among the greatest writers of ancient Rome were Cicero, Virgil, Ovid and Petronius.

A contemporary of Dante was Petrarch (1304-74). Giovanni Boccaccio (1313-75), author of the *Decameron*, is considered the first Italian novelist.

Machiavelli's *The Prince*, although a purely political work, has proved the most lasting of the Renaissance works.

Italy's richest contribution to modern literature has been in the novel and short story. Cesare Pavese and Carlo Levi both endured internal exile in southern Italy during Fascism. Levi based *Christ Stopped at Eboli* on his experiences in exile in Basilicata. Umberto Eco shot to fame with his first and best-known work, *The Name of the Rose*.

Theatre

At a time when French playwrights ruled the stage, the Venetian Carlo Goldoni (1707-93) attempted to bring Italian theatre back into the limelight with the *commedia dell'arte*, the tradition of improvisational theatre. Luigi Pirandello (1867-1936), author of *Six Characters in Search of an Author*, won the Nobel Prize in 1934. Modern Italian theatre's most enduring representative is actor/director Dario Fo, who won the Nobel Prize in 1998.

Cinema

From 1945 to 1947, Roberto Rossellini produced three neorealist masterpieces, including *Rome Open City* starring Anna Magnani. Vittorio de Sica produced another classic in 1948, *Bicycle Thieves*. Schooled with the masters of neorealism, Federico Fellini in many senses took the creative baton from them and carried it into the following decades, with films such as *La Dolce Vita*. The career of Michelangelo Antonioni reached a climax with *Blow-up* in 1967. Bernardo Bertolucci had his first international hit with *Last Tango in Paris*. He made the blockbuster *The Last Emperor* in 1987, *The Sheltering Sky* (1990), *Stealing Beauty* (1995) and *Beseiged* (1998). Franco Zeffirelli's most recent film was *Tea with Mussolini*. Other notable directors include the Taviani brothers, Giuseppe Tornatore, Nanni Moretti and Roberto Benigni, director of the Oscar-winning *Life is Beautiful* (1998).

SOCIETY & CONDUCT

It is difficult to make blanket assertions about Italian culture, if only because Italians have lived together as a nation for little over 100 years. Prior to unification, the peninsula was long subject to a varied mix of masters and cultures. This lack of unity contributed to the survival of local dialects and customs. Even today many Italians tend to identify more strongly with their region or home town than with the nation. An Italian is first and foremost a Tuscan or Sicilian, or even a Roman or Neapolitan.

In some parts of Italy, especially in the south, women might be harassed if they wear skimpy or see-through clothing. Modest dress is expected in all churches. Those that are major tourist attractions, such as St Peter's in Rome, strictly enforce dress codes (no shorts, bare arms or shoulders).

RELIGION

Around 85% of Italians profess to be Catholic. The remaining 15% includes about 700,000 Muslims, 500,000 evangelical Protestants, 140,000 Jehovah's Witnesses and smaller communities of Jews, Waldenses and Buddhists.

ITALY

LANGUAGE

English is most widely understood in the north, particularly in major centres such as Milan, Florence and Venice. Staff at most hotels and restaurants usually speak a little English, but you will be better received if you attempt to communicate in Italian.

Italian, a Romance language, is related to French, Spanish, Portuguese and Romanian. Modern literary Italian developed in the 13th and 14th centuries, predominantly through the works of Dante, Petrarch and Boccaccio, who wrote chiefly in the Florentine dialect. Although many dialects are spoken in everyday conversation, so-called standard Italian is the national language of schools, media and literature, and is understood throughout the country.

Many older Italians still expect to be addressed by the third person formal, ie, *Lei* instead of *Tu*. It is not polite to use the greeting *ciao* when addressing strangers, unless they use it first; use *buongiorno* and *arrivederci*.

See the Language chapter at the back of this book for pronunciation guidelines and useful words and phrases.

Facts for the Visitor

HIGHLIGHTS

Coming up with a Top 10 list for Italy is a little like trying to find the 10 shiniest gold ingots in Fort Knox. Bearing that in mind, you could try the following:

1. Florence
2. Aeolian Islands
3. Amalfi Coast
4. Siena
5. Italian food
6. The Cinque Terre
7. Ancient ruins of Rome, Pompeii & Paestum
8. Venice
9. Parco Naturale di Fanes-Sennes-Braies (in the Dolomites)
10. Carnevale in Ivrea (Piemonte)

SUGGESTED ITINERARIES

Depending on the length of your stay, you might want to see and do the following things:

Two days
Visit Rome to see the Forum, the Colosseum, St Peter's Basilica and the Vatican museums.

One week
Visit Rome and Florence, with detours in Tuscany to Siena and San Gimignano. Or visit Rome and Naples, with detours to Pompeii, Vesuvius and the Amalfi Coast.

Two weeks
As above, plus Bologna, Verona, Ravenna and at least three days in Venice.

PLANNING
When to Go

The best time to visit Italy is in the off season, particularly April-June and September-October, when the weather is good, prices are lower and there are fewer tourists. During July and August (the high season) it is very hot, prices are inflated, the country swarms with tourists and hotels by the sea and in the mountains are usually booked out. Note that many hotels and restaurants in seaside areas close down for the winter months.

Maps

Michelin map No 988 (1:1,000,000) covers the entire country. There is also a series of area maps at 1:400,000 – Nos 428 to 431 cover the mainland, No 432 covers Sicily and No 433 Sardinia.

If you're driving, the AA's *Big Road Atlas – Italy* (UK£9.99) is scaled at 1:250,000 and includes 39 town maps.

What to Bring

A backpack is a definite advantage in Italy, but if you plan to use a suitcase and portable trolley, be warned about the endless flights of stairs at train stations and in many of the smaller medieval towns, as well as the petty thieves who prey on tourists who have no hands free because they are carrying too much luggage. A small pack (with a lock) for use on day trips or for sightseeing is preferable to a handbag or shoulder bag, particularly in the southern cities where motorcycle bandits are very active. A money belt is absolutely essential in Italy, particularly in the south and in Sicily, but also in the major cities, where groups of dishevelled-looking women and children prey on tourists with bulging pockets.

In the more mountainous areas the weather can change suddenly, even in high summer, so remember to bring at least one item of warm clothing. Most importantly, bring a pair of hardy, comfortable, worn-in walking shoes.

ITALY

In many cities, pavements are uneven and often made of cobblestones.

TOURIST OFFICES
Local Tourist Offices

There are three main categories of tourist office in Italy: regional, provincial and local. Their names vary throughout the country. Provincial offices are sometimes known as the Ente Provinciale per il Turismo (EPT) or, more commonly, the Azienda di Promozione Turistica (APT). The Azienda Autonoma di Soggiorno e Turismo (AAST) and Informazioni e Assistenza ai Turisti (IAT) offices usually have information only on the town itself. In some of the very small towns and villages the local tourist office is called a Pro Loco, and is often little more than a room with a desk. At most offices you should be able to get an *elenco degli alberghi* (a list of hotels), a *pianta della cittá* (map of the town) and information on the major sights. Staff speak English in larger towns, but in the more out-of-the-way places you may have to rely on sign language. Tourist offices are generally open 8.30 am to 12.30 or 1 pm and 3 to 7 pm Monday to Friday and on Saturday morning. Hours are usually extended in summer.

The Centro Turistico Studentesco e Giovanile (CTS) has offices all over Italy and specialises in discounts for students and young people, but is also useful for travellers of any age looking for cheap flights and sightseeing discounts. It is linked with the International Student Travel Confederation. You can get a student card here if you have documents proving that you are a student.

Tourist Offices Abroad

Information about Italy can be obtained at Italian State Tourist Offices (Web site www.enit .it) throughout the world, including:

Australia (☎ 02-9262 1666, fax 9262 5745) c/o Italian Chamber of Commerce, Level 26, 44 Market St, Sydney, NSW 2000

Canada (☎ 514-866 7668, ✉ initaly@ican.net) Suite 1914, 1 Place Ville Marie, Montreal, Quebec H3B 2C3

UK (☎ 020-7408 1254, ✉ enitlond@globalnet.co.uk) 1 Princes St, London W1R 8AY

USA (☎ 212-245 4822, ✉ enitny@bway.net) Suite 1565, 630 Fifth Ave, New York, NY 10111; (☎ 310-820 1819) Suite 550, 12400 Wilshire Blvd, Los Angeles, CA 90025; (☎ 312-644 0996, ✉ enitch@italiantouism.com) 500 North Michigan Ave, Chicago, IL 60611

Sestante CIT (Compagnia Italiana di Turismo), Italy's national travel agency, also has offices throughout the world (known as CIT outside Italy). It can provide extensive information on Italy, as well as book tours and accommodation. It can also make train bookings. Offices include:

Australia (☎ 03-9650 5510) Level 4, 227 Collins St, Melbourne, Vic 3000; (☎ 02-9267 1255), 263 Clarence St, Sydney, NSW 2000

Canada (☎ 514-845 4310, 800 361 7799) Suite 750, 1450 City Councillors St, Montreal, Quebec H3A 2E6 (☎ 905-415 1060, 800 387 0711) Suite 401, 80 Tiverton Court, Markham, Toronto, Ontario L3R 0G4

UK (☎ 020-8686 0677, 8686 5533, ✉ ciao@citalia.co.uk) Marco Polo House, 3/5 Lansdown Rd, Croydon CR9 1LL

USA (☎ 212-730 2121, ✉ citnewyork@msn.com) 10th floor, 15 West 44th Street, New York, NY 10036 (☎ 310-338 8615, ✉ citlax@email.msm.com) 6033 West Century Blvd, suite 980, Los Angeles, CA 90045

VISAS & DOCUMENTS

EU citizens require only a national identity card or a passport to stay in Italy for as long as they like and since Italy is now a member of the Schengen Area, EU citizens can enter the country without passport controls.

Citizens of many other countries including the USA, Australia, Canada and New Zealand do not need to apply for visas before arriving in Italy if they are entering the country as tourists only. If you are entering the country for any reason other than tourism, you should insist on having your passport stamped. Visitors are technically obliged to report to a *questura* (police station) if they plan to stay at the same address for more than one week, to receive a *permesso di soggiorno* – in effect, permission to remain in the country for a nominated period up to the three-month limit. Tourists who are staying in hotels or youth hostels are not required to do this since proprietors need to register their guests with the police. A permesso di soggiorno only becomes

ITALY

a necessity (for non-EU citizens) if you plan to study, work (legally) or live in Italy.

EMBASSIES & CONSULATES
Italian Embassies & Consulates
Italian diplomatic missions abroad include:

Australia
Embassy: (☎ 02-6273 3333, fax 6273 4223, ✉ ambital2@dynamite.com.au) 12 Grey St, Deakin, Canberra, ACT 2600
Consulate: (☎ 03-9867 5744, fax 9866 3932, ✉ itconmel@netlink.com.au) 509 St Kilda Rd, Melbourne, Vic 3004
Consulate: (☎ 02-9392 7900, fax 9252 4830, ✉ itconsyd@armadillo.com.au) Level 43, The Gateway, 1 Macquarie Place, Sydney, NSW 2000

Canada
Embassy: (☎ 613-232 2401, fax 233 1484, ✉ italcomm@trytel.com) 21st floor, 275 Slater St, Ottawa, Ontario K1P 5H9
Consulate: (☎ 514-849 8351, fax 499 9471, ✉ consitmtl@cyberglobe.net) 3489 Drummond St, Montreal, Quebec H3G 1X6
Consulate: (☎ 416-977 1566, ✉ consolato.it@toronto.italconsulate.org) 136 Beverley St, Toronto, Ontario M5T 1Y5

France
Embassy: (☎ 01 49 54 03 00, fax 01 45 49 35 81, ✉ stampa@dial.oleane.com) 7 rue de Varenne, Paris 75007
Consulate: (☎ 01 44 30 47 00, fax 01 45 66 41 78) 5 blvd Augier, Paris 75116

New Zealand
Embassy: (☎ 04-473 53 39, fax 472 72 55, ✉ ambwell@xtra.co.nz) 34 Grant Rd, Thorndon, Wellington

UK
Embassy: (☎ 020-7312 2209, fax 7312 2230, ✉ emblondon@embitaly.org.uk) 14 Three Kings Yard, London W1Y 2EH
Consulate: (☎ 020-7235 9371, fax 7823 1609) 38 Eaton Place, London SW1X 8AN

USA
Embassy: (☎ 202-328 5500, fax 328 5593, ✉ itapress@ix.netcom.com) 1601 Fuller St, NW Washington, DC 20009
Consulate: (☎ 213-820 0622, fax 820 0727, ✉ cglos@aol.com) Suite 300, 12400 Wilshire Blvd, West Los Angeles, CA 90025
Consulate: (☎ 212-737 9100, fax 249 4945, ✉ italconsny@aol.com) 690 Park Ave, New York, NY 10021-5044
Consulate: (☎ 415-931 4924, fax 931 7205) 2590 Webster St, San Francisco, CA 94115

Embassies & Consulates in Italy
The headquarters of most foreign embassies are in Rome, although there are generally British and US consulates in other major cities. The following addresses and phone numbers are for Rome:

Australia (☎ 06 85 27 21) Via Alessandria 215
Austria (☎ 06 844 01 41) Via Pergolesi 3
Consulate: (☎ 06 855 29 66) Viale Liegi 32
Canada (☎ 06 44 59 81) Via G B de Rossi 27
Consulate: (☎ 06 44 59 81) Via Zara 30
France (☎ 06 68 60 11) Piazza Farnese 67
Consulate: (☎ 06 68 80 21 52) Via Giulia 251
Germany (☎ 06 88 47 41) Via Po 25c
Consulate: (☎ 06 88 47 41) Via Francesco Siacci 2c
New Zealand (☎ 06 440 29 28) Via Zara 28
Spain (☎ 06 687 81 72) Largo Fontanella Borghese 19
Consulate: (☎ 06 687 14 01) Via Campo Marzio 34
Switzerland (☎ 06 808 36 41) Via Barnarba Oriani 61
Consulate: (☎ 06 808 83 61) Largo Elvezia 15
UK (☎ 06 482 54 41) Via XX Settembre 80a
USA (☎ 06 467 41) Via Vittorio Veneto 119a-121

For a complete list of all foreign embassies in Rome and other major cities throughout Italy, look in the local telephone book under *ambasciate* or *consolati*, or ask for a list at the tourist office.

CUSTOMS
As of 1 July 1999, duty-free sales within the EU were abolished. Under the rules of the single market, goods bought in and exported within the EU incur no additional taxes, provided duty has been paid somewhere within the EU and the goods are for personal consumption.

Travellers coming from outside the EU, on the other hand, can import, duty free: 200 cigarettes, 1L of spirits, 2L of wine, 60mls of perfume, 250mls of *eau de toilet*, and other goods up to a total value of L340,000 (€175); anything over this limit must be declared on arrival and the appropriate duty paid (it is advisable to carry all receipts).

MONEY
A combination of travellers cheques and credit cards is the best way to take your

ITALY

money. If you buy travellers cheques in lire there should be no commission charged for cashing them. There are exchange offices at all major airports and train stations, but it is advisable to obtain a small amount of lire before arriving to avoid problems and queues at the airport and train stations.

Major credit cards, including Visa, Master-Card and American Express, are widely accepted in Italy and can be used for purchases for payment in hotels and restaurants (although smaller places might not accept them). They can also be used to get money from ATMs (*bancomats*) or, if you don't have a PIN, over the counter in major banks, including the Banca Commerciale Italiana, Cassa di Risparmio and Credito Italiano. If your credit card is lost, stolen or swallowed by an ATM, you can telephone toll-free (☎ 167-82 20 56) to have it cancelled. To cancel a MasterCard the number in Italy is ☎ 167-86 80 86, or you can make a reverse-charge call to St Louis in the USA (☎ 314-275 66 90). To cancel a Visa card in Italy, phone ☎ 167-82 10 01. The toll-free emergency number to report a lost or stolen American Express card varies according to where the card was issued. Check with American Express in your country or contact American Express in Rome (☎ 06 722 82) which has a 24-hour card-holders' service.

The fastest way to receive money is through Western Union (☎ 167-01 38 39 toll-free). This service functions in Italy through the Mail Boxes Etc chain of stores, which you will find in the bigger cities. The sender and receiver have to turn up at a Western Union outlet with passport or other form of ID and the fees charged for the virtually immediate transfer depend on the amount sent.

Currency

Until the euro notes and coins are in circulation, Italy's currency will remain the lira (plural: lire). Notes come in denominations of L1000, L2000, L5000, L10,000, L50,000, L100,000 and L500,000. Coin denominations are L50, L100 (two types of silver coin), L200, L500 and L1000.

Remember that, like other continental Europeans, Italians indicate decimals with commas and thousands with points.

Exchange Rates

country	unit		lire
Australia	A$1	=	L1241.85
Canada	C$1	=	L1444.84
euro	€1	=	L1936.27
France	1FF	=	L295.182
Germany	DM1	=	L989.999
Ireland	£IR1	=	L2458.56
Japan	¥100	=	L1972.57
New Zealand	NZ$1	=	L964.079
UK	UK£1	=	L3222.28
USA	US$1	=	L2143.12

Costs

A *very* prudent traveller could get by on L80,000 per day, but only by staying in youth hostels, eating one meal a day (at the hostel), buying a sandwich or pizza by the slice for lunch and minimising the number of galleries and museums visited, since the entrance fee to most major museums is cripplingly expensive at around L12,000. You save on transport costs by buying tourist or day tickets for city bus and underground services. When travelling by train, you can save money by avoiding the fast Eurostars which charge a *supplemento rapido*. Italy's railways also offer a few cut-price options for students, young people and tourists for travel within a nominated period (see the Getting Around section in this chapter for more information).

Museums and galleries usually give discounts to students, but you will need a valid student card which you can obtain from CTS offices if you have documents proving you are a student.

A basic breakdown of costs during an average day could be: accommodation L25,000 (youth hostel) to L60,000; breakfast (coffee and croissant) L3000; lunch (sandwich and mineral water) L6000; public transport (bus or underground railway in a major town) L6000; entry fee for one museum L12,000; a sit-down dinner L14,000 to L30,000.

Tipping & Bargaining

You are not expected to tip on top of restaurant service charges, but it is common practice among Italians to leave a small amount, say around 10%. In bars they will leave any small change as a tip, often only L100 or L200. You can tip taxi drivers if you wish but it's not obligatory.

Bargaining is common throughout Italy in the various flea markets, but not normally in shops. You can try bargaining for the price of a room in a *pensione*, particularly if you plan to stay for more than a few days or out of season.

POST & COMMUNICATIONS
Post
Stamps (*francobolli*) are available at post offices and authorised tobacconists (look for the official *tabacchi* sign: a big 'T', often white on black). Since letters often need to be weighed, what you get at the tobacconist's for international air mail will occasionally be an approximation of the proper rate. Main post offices in the bigger cities are generally open from around 8 am to 6 pm. Many open on Saturday morning too.

Postcards and letters up to 20g sent air mail cost L1400 to Australia and New Zealand, L1300 to the USA and L800 to EU countries (L900 to the rest of Europe). Aerograms are a cheap alternative, costing only L900 to send anywhere. They can be purchased at post offices only.

A new service, *posta prioritaria* (priority post – a little like the UK's 1st class post), began in 1999. For L1200, postcards and letters up to 20g posted to destinations within Italy, the EU, Switzerland and Norway are supposed to arrive the following day.

Sending letters express (*espresso*) costs a standard extra L3600, but may help speed a letter on its way.

Telephone & Fax
Italy's country code is ☎ 39. Area codes are an integral part of the telephone number, even if you're dialling a local number. Not content to make the area code part of the phone number, it is planned to convert the initial 0 into a 4 by the end of 2000. Thus any number in Rome will begin with 46.

Local and long distance calls can be made from any public phone, or from a Telecom office in larger towns. Italy's rates, particularly for long-distance calls, are among the highest in Europe. Local calls cost a minimum of L200. Most public phones accept only phonecards, sold in denominations of L5000, L10,000 and L15,000 phonecards at tobacconists and newsstands, or from vending machines at Telecom offices.

To make a reverse-charge (collect) call from a public telephone, dial ☎ 170. All operators speak English. Numbers for this Home Country Direct service are displayed in the first pages of Italian phone books and include: Australia (☎ 172 10 61, Telstra), Canada (☎ 172 10 01, Teleglobe), New Zealand (☎ 172 10 64), UK (☎ 172 01 44, BT Automatic) and USA (☎ 172 10 11, AT&T). For international directory inquiries call ☎ 176.

International faxes can cost L8000 for the first page and L5000 per page thereafter. You can transmit faxes from specialist fax/photocopy shops, post offices and from some tabacchi. Some Telecom public phones can also send faxes.

Email & Internet Access
Italy has a growing number of Internet cafes, where you can send and receive email or surf the Net for around L10,000 to L15,000 an hour.

INTERNET RESOURCES
There is an Italy page at Lonely Planet's Web site at www.lonelyplanet.com. The following are just a few of the huge number of useful Web sites for travellers to Italy.

Alfanet at www.alfanet.it has a Welcome Italy page, with a link to information about a number of cities; CTS at www.cts.it has useful information (but in Italian only) from Italy's leading student travel organisation; Rome at www.informaroma.it has information on the city's monuments and museums, virtual tours and links to other pertinent sites.

Travel Italy at www.travel.it provides useful tourist information; and Il Vaticano at www.christusrex.org has detailed information about the Vatican City, including virtual tours of the main monuments and the Musei Vaticani.

BOOKS
For a more comprehensive guide to Italy, pick up a copy of Lonely Planet's *Italy*. If you want to concentrate on specific regions, pick up Lonely Planet's new *Rome*, *Venice*, *Tuscany & Umbria* and *Sicily* guides. Also useful are the *Italian phrasebook*, *World Food Italy* and *Rome City Map*. If you're a

ITALY

hiking enthusiast, a good companion is Lonely Planet's *Walking in Italy*.

For a potted history of the country, try the *Concise History of Italy* by Vincent Cronin. A *History of Contemporary Italy – Society and Politics 1943-1988* by Paul Ginsborg is well written and absorbing. Luigi Barzini's classic *The Italians* is a great introduction to Italian people and culture, while *Excellent Cadavers: The Mafia and the Death of the First Italian Republic* by Alexander Stille is a shocking and fascinating account of the Mafia in Sicily.

Interesting introductions to travelling in Italy include *A Traveller in Italy* by HV Morton, who also wrote similar guides to Rome and southern Italy.

NEWSPAPERS & MAGAZINES

Major English-language newspapers available in Italy are the *Herald Tribune,* the English *Guardian*, the *Times* and the *Telegraph*. *Time* magazine, *Newsweek* and the *Economist* are available weekly.

TIME

Italy is one hour ahead of GMT/UTC, and two hours ahead during summer. Daylight-saving time starts on the last Sunday in March, when clocks are put forward an hour. Clocks are put back an hour on the last Sunday in September. Remember to make allowances for daylight-saving time in your own country. Note that Italy operates on a 24-hour clock.

LAUNDRY

Coin laundrettes, where you can do your own washing, are catching on in Italy. You'll find them in most of the main cities and towns. A load will cost around L8000. Many camping grounds have laundry facilities.

WOMEN TRAVELLERS

Italy is not a dangerous country for women, but women travelling alone will often find themselves plagued by unwanted attention from men. Most of the attention falls into the nuisance/harassment category and it is best simply to ignore the catcalls, hisses and whistles. However, women touring alone should use common sense. Avoid walking alone in dark and deserted streets and look for centrally located hotels that are within easy walking distance of places where you can eat at night. In the south, including Sicily and Sardinia, the unwelcome attention paid to women travelling alone can border on the highly intrusive, particularly in the bigger cities. Women should also avoid hitchhiking alone.

GAY & LESBIAN TRAVELLERS

Homosexuality is legal in Italy and generally well tolerated in major cities, though overt displays of affection might get a negative response in smaller towns and villages, particularly in the south.

The national organisation for gays (men and women) is AGAL (☎ 051 644 70 54, fax 051 644 67 22) in Bologna.

DISABLED TRAVELLERS

The Italian travel agency CIT can advise on hotels which have special facilities. The UK-based Royal Association for Disability and Rehabilitation, or RADAR (☎ 020-7250 3222), publishes a useful guide called *Holidays & Travel Abroad; A Guide for Disabled People*.

DANGERS & ANNOYANCES

Theft is the main problem for travellers in Italy, mostly in the form of petty thievery and pickpocketing, especially in the bigger cities. Although not something you should be particularly worried about, a few precautions are necessary to avoid being robbed. Always carry your cash in a money belt and avoid flashing your dough in public. Pickpockets operate in crowded areas, such as markets and on buses.

Watch out for groups of dishevelled-looking kids, who can be lightening fast as they empty your pockets. Motorcycle bandits are a minor problem in Rome, Naples, Palermo and Syracuse. If you are using a shoulder bag, make sure that you wear the strap across your body and have the bag on the side away from the road.

Never leave valuables in a parked car – in fact, try not to leave anything in the car if you can help it.

It is a good idea to park your car in a supervised car park if you are leaving it for any amount of time. Car theft is a major problem in Rome and Naples. Throughout Italy you can call the police (☎ 113) or *carabinieri* (☎ 112) in an emergency.

BUSINESS HOURS

Business hours can vary from city to city, but generally shops and businesses are open 8.30 am to 1 pm and 5 to 7.30 pm Monday to Saturday, and some are also open on Sunday mornings. Banks are generally open 8.30 am to 1.30 pm and from 2.30 to 4.30 pm Monday to Friday, but hours vary between banks and cities. Large post offices are open 8 am to 6 or 7 pm Monday to Saturday. Most museums close on Monday, and restaurants and bars are required to close for one day each week.

All of this has become more flexible since opening times were liberalised under new trading hours laws that went into effect in April 1999. At the time of writing it was difficult to determine what effect this would have on day to day practicalities, as Italians tend to value their time off and are not necessarily rushing to keep their shops open throughout the week.

PUBLIC HOLIDAYS & SPECIAL EVENTS

National public holidays include: 6 January (Epiphany); Easter Monday; 25 April (Liberation Day); 1 May (Labour Day); 15 August (*Ferragosto* or Feast of the Assumption); 1 November (All Saints' Day); 8 December (Feast of the Immaculate Conception); 25 December (Christmas Day); and 26 December (Feast of St Stephen).

Individual towns also have public holidays to celebrate the feasts of their patron saints. Some of these are the Feast of St Mark in Venice on 25 April; the Feast of St John the Baptist on 24 June in Florence, Genoa and Turin; the Feast of St Peter and St Paul in Rome on 29 June; the Feast of St Januarius in Naples on 19 September; and the Feast of St Ambrose in Milan on 7 December.

Annual events in Italy worth keeping in mind include:

Carnevale During the 10 days before Ash Wednesday, many towns stage carnivals. The one held in Venice is the best known, but there are also others, including at Viareggio in Liguria and Ivrea near Turin.

Holy Week There are important festivals during this week everywhere in Italy, in particular the colourful and sombre traditional festivals of Sicily. In Assisi the rituals of Holy Week attract thousands of pilgrims.

Scoppio del Carro Literally 'Explosion of the Cart', this colourful event held in Florence in Piazza del Duomo on Easter Sunday features the explosion of a cart full of fireworks and dates back to the Crusades. If all goes well, it is seen as a good omen for the city.

Corso dei Ceri One of the strangest festivals in Italy, this is held in Gubbio (Umbria) on 15 May, and features a race run by men carrying enormous wooden constructions called *ceri*, in honour of the town's patron saint, Sant'Ubaldo.

Il Palio On 2 July and 16 August, Siena stages this extraordinary horse race in the town's main piazza.

ACTIVITIES
Hiking

It is possible to go on organised treks in Italy, but if you want to go it alone you will find that trails are well marked and there are plenty of refuges in the Alps, in the Alpi Apuane in Tuscany and in the northern parts of the Appennines. The Dolomites in particular provide spectacular walking and trekking opportunities. In Sardinia head for the eastern mountain ranges between Oliena and Urzulei and along the coastal gorges between Dorgali and Baunei (see the Sardinia section for details). If you plan on hiking, a good companion guide is Lonely Planet's *Walking in Italy*.

Skiing

The numerous excellent ski resorts in the Alps and the Apennines usually offer good skiing conditions from December to April.

Cycling

This is a good option if you can't afford a car but want to see the more isolated parts of the country. Classic cycling areas include Tuscany and Umbria.

ACCOMMODATION

The prices mentioned here are intended as a guide only. There is generally a fair degree of fluctuation throughout the country, depending on the season. Prices usually rise by 5% to 10% each year, although sometimes they remain fixed for years, or even drop.

ITALY

Camping

Facilities throughout Italy are usually reasonable and vary from major complexes with swimming pools, tennis courts and restaurants, to simple camping grounds. Average prices are around L8000 per person and L11,000 or more for a site. Lists of camping grounds in and near major cities are usually available at tourist information offices.

The Touring Club Italiano (TIC) publishes an annual book on all camping sites in Italy, *Campeggi e Villaggi Turistici in Italia* (L32,000). Free camping is forbidden in many of the more beautiful parts of Italy, although the authorities seem to pay less attention in the off season.

Hostels

Hostels in Italy are called *ostelli per la gioventú* and are run by the Associazione Italiana Alberghi per la Gioventú (AIG), which is affiliated with Hostelling International (HI). Prices, including breakfast, range from L16,000 to L24,000. Closing times vary, but are usually from 9 am to 3 or 5 pm and curfews are around midnight. Men and women are often segregated, although some hostels have family accommodation.

An HI membership card is not always required, but it is recommended that you have one. Membership cards can be purchased at major hostels, from student and youth travel centre (CTS) offices and from AIG offices throughout Italy. Pick up a list of all hostels in Italy, with details of prices, locations etc from the AIG office (☎ 06 487 11 52) in Rome, Via Cavour 44.

Pensioni & Hotels

Establishments are required to notify local tourist boards of prices for the coming year and by law must then adhere to those prices (although they do have two legal opportunities each year to increase charges). If tourists believe they are being overcharged, they can make a complaint to the local tourist office. The best advice is to confirm hotel charges before you put your bags down, since many proprietors employ various methods of bill padding. These include charges for showers (usually around L2000), a compulsory breakfast (up to L14,000 in the high season) and compulsory half or full board, although this can often be a good deal in some towns.

The cheapest way to stay in a hotel or pensione is to share a room with two or more people: the cost is usually no more than 15% of the cost of a double room for each additional person. Single rooms are uniformly expensive in Italy (from around L45,000) and quite a number of establishments do not even bother to cater for the single traveller.

There is often no difference between an establishment that calls itself a pensione and one that calls itself an *albergo* (hotel); in fact, some use both titles. *Locande* (similar to pensioni) and *alloggi*, sometimes also known as *affitta-camere*, are generally cheaper, but not always.

Rental Accommodation

Finding rental accommodation in the major cities can be difficult and time-consuming and you will often find the cost prohibitive, especially in Rome, Florence, Milan and Venice. In major resort areas, such as the Aeolian Islands and other parts of Sicily, and in the Alps, rental accommodation is reasonably priced and readily available and many tourist offices will provide information by mail or fax.

One organisation which publishes booklets on villas and houses in Tuscany, Umbria, Veneto, Sicily and Rome is Cuendet. Write to Cuendet & Cie spa, Strada di Strove 17, 53035 Monteriggioni, Siena (☎ 0577 57 63 10, fax 0577 30 11 49, ✉ cuende@mbox .vol.it) and ask for a catalogue (US$17). Prices, however, are expensive. CIT offices throughout the world also have lists of villas and apartments for rent in Italy.

Agriturismo

This is basically a farm holiday and is becoming increasingly popular in Italy. Traditionally, the idea was that families rented out rooms in their farmhouses. For detailed information on all facilities in Italy contact Agriturist (☎ 06 68 52 33 37), Corso Vittorio Emanuele 89, 00186 Rome; Web site: www.agriturist.it. It publishes a book (L40,000) listing establishments throughout Italy which is available at its office and in selected bookshops.

Refuges

Before you go hiking in any part of Italy, obtain information about refuges *(rifugi)* from the local tourist offices. Some refuges have private rooms, but many offer dorm-style accommodation, particularly those which are more isolated. Average prices are from L18,000 to L40,000 per person for B&B. A meal costs around the same as at a trattoria. The locations of refuges are marked on good hiking maps and most open only from late June to September. The alpine refuges of CAI (Italian Alpine Club) offer discounts to members of associated foreign alpine clubs.

FOOD & DRINK

Eating is one of life's great pleasures for Italians. Cooking styles vary notably from region to region and significantly between the north and south. In the north the food is rich and often creamy; in central Italy the locals use a lot of olive oil and herbs and regional specialities are noted for their simplicity, fine flavour and the use of fresh produce. As you go further south the food becomes hotter and spicier and the *dolci* (cakes and pastries) sweeter and richer.

Vegetarians will have no problems eating in Italy. Most eating establishments serve a selection of *contorni* (vegetables prepared in a variety of ways).

If you have access to cooking facilities, buy fruit and vegetables at open-air markets and salami, cheese and wine at *alimentari* or *salumerie* (a cross between a grocery store and a delicatessen). Fresh bread is available at a *forno* or *panetteria*.

Restaurants are divided into several categories. A *tavola calda* (literally 'hot table') usually offers inexpensive, pre-prepared meat, pasta and vegetable dishes in a self-service style. A *rosticceria* usually offers cooked meats, but also often has a larger selection of takeaway food. A *pizzeria* will of course serve pizza, but usually also a full menu. An *osteria* is likely to be either a wine bar offering a small selection of dishes, or a small *trattoria*. Many of the establishments that are in fact restaurants (*ristoranti*) call themselves trattoria and vice versa for reasons best known to themselves.

Most eating establishments charge a *coperto* (cover charge) of around L2000 to L3000, and a *servizio* (service charge) of 10% to 15%. Restaurants are usually open for lunch from 12.30 to 3 pm, but will rarely take orders after 2 pm. In the evening, opening hours vary from north to south. In the north they eat dinner earlier, usually from 7.30 pm, but in Sicily you will be hard-pressed to find a restaurant open before 8.30 pm. Very few restaurants stay open after 11.30 pm.

A full meal will consist of an antipasto, which can vary from *bruschetta*, a type of garlic bread with various toppings, to fried vegetables, or *prosciutto e melone* (ham wrapped around melon). Next comes the *primo piatto*, a pasta dish or risotto, followed by the *secondo piatto* of meat or fish. Italians often then eat an *insalata* (salad) or contorni and round off the meal with dolci and *caffé*, often at a bar on the way home or back to work.

Italian wine is justifiably world-famous. Fortunately, wine is reasonably priced, so you will rarely pay more than L12,000 for a bottle of drinkable wine and as little as L6000 will still buy something of reasonable quality. Try the famous chianti and *brunello* in Tuscany, but also the *vernaccia* of San Gimignano, the *barolo* in Piedmont, the *lacrima christi* or *falanghina* in Naples and the *cannonau* in Sardinia. Beer is known as *birra* and the cheapest local variety is Peroni.

ENTERTAINMENT

Whatever your tastes, there should be some form of entertainment in Italy to keep you amused, including opera, theatre, classical music concerts, rock concerts and traditional festivals. Major entertainment festivals are also held, such as the Festival of Two Worlds in June/July at Spoleto, Umbria Jazz in Perugia in July, Rome's Estate Romana in July, and the Venice Biennale every odd-numbered year. Operas are performed in Verona and Rome throughout summer (for details see the Entertainment sections under both cities) and at various times of the year throughout the country, notably at the opera houses in Milan and Rome.

SPECTATOR SPORTS

Soccer (*calcio*) is the national passion and there are stadiums in all the major towns. If you'd rather watch a game than visit a Roman ruin, check newspapers for details of who's playing where, although tickets for the bigger matches can be hard to find. The Italian Formula One Grand Prix races are held at Monza,

ITALY

just north of Milan in September. The San Marino Grand Prix is held at Imola in May. Good luck finding a ticket, though.

SHOPPING

Italy is synonymous with elegant, fashionable and high-quality clothing, leather goods, glass and ceramics. The problem is that most are very expensive. However, if you happen to be in the country during the summer sales in July and August and the winter sales in January and February, you can pick up incredible bargains.

Getting There & Away

AIR

Although paying full fare to travel by plane in Europe is expensive, there are various discount options, including cut-price fares for students and people aged under 25 or 26 (depending on the airline). There are also standby fares which are usually around 60% of the full fare. Several airlines offer cut-rate fares on legs of international flights between European cities. These are usually the cheapest fares available, but the catch is that they are often during the night or very early in the morning, and the days on which you can fly are severely restricted. Some examples of cheap one-way fares at the time of writing are: Rome-Paris L220,000 (L360,000 return); Rome-London L210,000 (L258,000 return); and Rome-Amsterdam L329,000 return.

Another option is to travel on charter flights. There are several companies throughout Europe which operate these, and fares are usually cheaper than for normal scheduled flights. Italy Sky Shuttle (☎ 020-8748 1333), part of the Air Travel Group, 227 Shepherd's Bush Rd, London W6 7AS, specialises in charter flights, but also offers scheduled flights.

Look in the classified pages of the London Sunday newspapers for information on other cheap flights. Campus Travel (☎ 020-7730 3402), 52 Grosvenor Gardens, SW1W OAG, and STA Travel (☎ 020-7361 6161), 86 Old Brompton Rd, London SW7 3LH, both offer reasonably cheap fares. Within Italy, information on discount fares is available from

CTS and Sestante CIT offices (see the earlier Tourist Offices section).

LAND

If you are travelling by bus, train or car to Italy it will be necessary to cross various borders, so remember to check whether you require visas for those countries before leaving home.

Bus

Eurolines is the main international carrier in Europe, with representatives in Italy and throughout the continent. Its head office (☎ 020-7730 8235) is at 52 Grosvenor Gardens, Victoria, London SW1. In Italy the main bus company operating this service is Lazzi, with offices in Florence (☎ 055 35 71 10) at Piazza Adua and in Rome (☎ 06 884 08 40) at Via Tagliamento 27b. Buses leave from Rome, Florence, Milan, Turin, Venice and Naples, as well as numerous other Italian towns, for major cities throughout Europe including London, Paris, Barcelona, Madrid, Amsterdam, Budapest, Prague, Athens and Istanbul. Some ticket prices are Rome-Paris L187,000 (L297,000 return), Rome-London L260,000 (L398,000 return) and Rome-Barcelona L211,000 (L376,000 return).

Train

Eurostar (ES) and Eurocity (EC) trains run from major destinations throughout Europe direct to major Italian cities. On overnight hauls you can book a *cuccetta* (known outside Italy as a couchette or sleeping berth).

Travellers aged under 26 can take advantage of Billet International de Jeunesse tickets (BIJ, also known in Italy as BIGE), which can cut fares by around 50%. They are sold at Transalpino offices at most train stations and at CTS and Sestante CIT offices in Italy, Europe and overseas. Examples of one-way 2nd-class fares are: Rome-Amsterdam L218,900, Rome-Paris L170,000 and Rome-London L284,300. Throughout Europe and in Italy it is worth paying extra for a couchette on night trains. A couchette from Rome to Paris is an extra L48,000.

You can book tickets at train stations or at CTS, Sestante CIT and most travel agencies. Eurostar and Eurocity trains carry a supplement (determined by the distance you are travelling and the type of train).

Car & Motorcycle

Travelling with your own vehicle certainly gives you more flexibility. The drawbacks in Italy are that cars can be inconvenient in larger cities where you'll have to deal with heavy traffic, parking problems, the risk of car theft, the exorbitant price of petrol and toll charges on the autostrade.

If you want to rent a car or motorcycle, you will need a valid EU driving licence, an International Driving Permit, or your driving permit from your own country. If you're driving your own car, you'll need an international insurance certificate, known as a Carta Verde (Green Card), which can be obtained from your insurer.

Hitching

Hitching is never safe in any country and we don't recommend it. Your best bet is to inquire at hostels throughout Europe, where you can often arrange a lift. The International Lift Centre in Florence (☎ 055 28 06 26) and Enjoy Rome (☎ 06 445 18 43) might be able to help organise lifts. It is illegal to hitch on the autostrade.

SEA

Ferries connect Italy to Spain, Croatia, Greece, Turkey, Tunisia and Malta. There are also services to Corsica (from Livorno) and Albania (from Bari and Ancona). See Getting There & Away under Brindisi (for ferries to/from Greece), Ancona (to/from Greece, Albania and Turkey), Venice (to/from Croatia) and Sicily (to/from Malta and Tunisia).

Getting Around

AIR

Travelling by plane is expensive within Italy and it makes much better sense to use the efficient and considerably cheaper rail and bus services. The domestic airlines are Alitalia, Meridiana and Air One. The main airports are in Rome, Pisa, Milan, Bologna, Genova, Torino, Naples, Catania, Palermo and Cagliari, but there are other, smaller airports throughout Italy. Domestic flights can be booked directly with the airlines or through Sestante CIT, CTS and other travel agencies.

Alitalia offers a range of discounts for students, young people and families, and for weekend travel.

BUS

Numerous bus companies operate within Italy. It is usually necessary to make reservations only for long trips, such as Rome-Palermo or Rome-Brindisi. Otherwise, just arrive early enough to claim a seat.

Buses can be a cheaper and faster way to get around if your destination is not on major rail lines, for instance from Umbria to Rome or Florence, and in the interior areas of Sicily and Sardinia.

TRAIN

Travelling by train in Italy is simple, relatively cheap and generally efficient. The Ferrovie dello Stato (FS) is the partially privatised state train system and there are several private railway services throughout the country.

There are several types of trains: Regionale (R), which usually stop at all stations and can be very slow; interRegionale (iR), which run between the regions; Intercity (IC) or Eurocity (EC), which service only the major cities; and Eurostar Italia (ES), which serves major Italian and European cities.

To go on the Intercity, Eurocity and Eurostar Italia trains, you have to pay a *supplemento*, an additional charge determined by the distance you are travelling and the type of train.

All tickets must be validated in the yellow machines at the entrance to all train platforms.

It is not worth buying a Eurail or Inter-Rail pass if you are going to travel only in Italy. The FS offers its own discount passes for travel within the country. These include the Cartaverde for those aged 26 years and under. It costs L40,000, is valid for one year, and entitles you to a 20% discount on all train travel. You can also buy a *biglietto chilometrico* (kilometric ticket), which is valid for two months and allows you to cover 3000km, with a maximum of 20 trips. It costs L214,000 (2nd class) and you must pay the supplement if you catch an Intercity or Eurostar train. Its main attraction is that it can be used by up to five people, either singly or together.

Some examples of 2nd-class fares (plus IC supplement) are Rome-Florence L26,600

(IC L13,100) and Rome-Naples L18,600 (IC L13,200).

CAR & MOTORCYCLE

Roads are generally good throughout the country and there is an excellent system of autostrade (freeways). The main north-south link is the Autostrada del Sole, which extends from Milan to Reggio di Calabria (called the A1 from Milan to Naples and the A3 from Naples to Reggio).

In Italy people drive on the right-hand side of the road and pass on the left. Unless otherwise indicated, you must give way to cars coming from the right. It is compulsory to wear seat belts if they are fitted to the car (front seat belts on all cars and back seat belts on cars produced after 26 April 1990). If you are caught not wearing your seat belt, you will be required to pay a L62,500 on-the-spot fine.

Helmets are now compulsory for every motorcycle and moped rider and passenger.

Some of the Italian cities, including Rome, Bologna, Florence, Milan and Turin have introduced restricted access to both private and rental cars in their historical centres. The restrictions, however, do not apply to vehicles with foreign registrations. *Motorini* (mopeds) and scooters (such as Vespas) are able to enter the zones without any problems.

Speed limits, unless otherwise indicated by local signs, are: on autostrade 130km/h for cars of 1100cc or more, 110km/h for smaller cars and motorcycles under 350cc; on all main, nonurban highways 100km/h; on secondary nonurban highways 90km/h; and in built-up areas 50km/h.

Petrol prices are high in Italy – around L1950 per litre. Petrol is called *benzina*, unleaded petrol is *benzina senza piombo* and diesel is *gasolio*.

The blood-alcohol limit is 0.08% and random breath tests have now been introduced.

Call the Automobile Club d'Italia (ACI) on ☎ 116 for roadside assistance.

BOAT

Navi (large ferries) service the islands of Sicily and Sardinia, and *traghetti* (smaller ferries) and *aliscafi* (hydrofoils) service areas such as Elba, the Aeolian Islands, Capri and Ischia. The main embarkation points for Sicily and Sardinia are Genoa, La Spezia, Livorno, Civitavecchia, Fiumicino and Naples.

Tirrenia Navigazione is the major company servicing the Mediterranean and it has offices throughout Italy. Most long-distance services travel overnight and all ferries carry vehicles (you can usually take a bicycle free of charge).

BICYCLE

Bikes are available for rent in most Italian towns – the cost can be up to L25,000 a day and up to L110,000 a week (see the Getting Around section in each city). However, if you are planning to do a lot of cycling, consider buying a bike in Italy; you can buy a decent second-hand bicycle for L200,000. Bikes can travel in the baggage compartment of some Italian trains (not on the Eurostars or Intercity trains).

Rome

pop 2.6 million

A phenomenal concentration of history, legend and monuments coexist in chaotic harmony in Rome (Roma), as well as an equally phenomenal concentration of people busily going about their everyday lives. It is easy to pick the tourists because they are the only ones to turn their heads as the bus passes the Colosseum.

Rome's origins date to a group of Etruscan, Latin and Sabine settlements on the Palatine, Esquiline, Quirinal and surrounding hills, but it is the legend of Romulus and Remus – the twins raised by a she-wolf – which has captured the popular imagination. The myth says Romulus killed his brother during a battle over who should govern, and then established the city on the Palatine (Palatino), one of the famous Seven Hills of Rome. From the legend grew an empire that eventually controlled almost the entire world known to Europeans at the time.

In Rome there is visible evidence of the two great empires of the western world: the Roman Empire and the Christian Church. On the one hand is the Forum and Colosseum, and on the other St Peter's and the Vatican. In between, in almost every piazza, lies history on so many levels that what you see is only the tip of the iceberg – this is exemplified by

St Peter's Basilica, which stands on the site of an earlier basilica built by the Emperor Constantine over the necropolis where St Peter was buried.

ORIENTATION

Rome is a vast city, but the historical centre is relatively small. Most of the major sights are west – and within walking distance – of the central train station, Stazione Termini. Invest L6000 in the street map and bus guide *Roma*, with a red-and-blue cover; it's available at any newsstand in Stazione Termini.

Plan an itinerary if your time is limited. Many of the major museums and galleries open all day until 5 or 7 pm, and some remain open until 10 pm. Many museums are closed on Monday, but it is a good idea to check.

The main bus terminus is in Piazza del Cinquecento, directly in front of the train station. Many intercity buses arrive and depart from the Piazzale Tiburtina, in front of the Stazione Tiburtina, accessible from Termini on the Metropolitana Linea B.

INFORMATION
Tourist Offices

There is an APT tourist information office (☎ 06 487 12 70) at Stazione Termini, open 8.15 am to 7.15 pm daily. It's in the central courseway.

The main APT office (☎ 06 48 89 92 53/55) is at Via Parigi 5 and opens 8.15 am to 7.15 pm Monday to Friday and until 1.45 pm on Saturday. Walk north-west from Stazione Termini, through Piazza della Repubblica. Via Parigi runs to the right from the top of the piazza, about a five-minute walk from the station. The office has information on hotels and museum opening hours and entrance fees. Staff can also provide information about provincial and Intercity bus services, but you need to be specific about where and when you want to go (see the Getting Around section for further information).

It's likely that you'll get all the information and assistance you need at Enjoy Rome (☎ 06 445 18 43, fax 06 445 07 34) Via Varese 39 (five minutes north-east of the station). Check out the Web site at www.enjoyrome.com. This is a privately run tourist office that offers a free hotel-reservation service. The English-speaking staff can also organise alternative accommodation such as apartments. They have extensive up-to-date information about Rome and good information about accommodation in other cities. The office is open 8.30 am to 1 pm and 3.30 to 6 pm Monday to Friday and 8.30 am to 1 pm on Saturday.

Money

Banks are open 8.30 am to 1.30 pm and usually from 2.45 to 3.45 pm Monday to Friday. You will find a bank and exchange offices at Stazione Termini. There is also an exchange office (Banco di Santo Spirito) at Fiumicino airport, to your right as you exit from the customs area.

Numerous other exchange offices are scattered throughout the city, including American Express (☎ 06 676 41), at Piazza di Spagna 38, and Thomas Cook (☎ 06 4 82 81 82), at Piazza Barberini 21.

Otherwise, go to any bank in the city centre. The Banca Commerciale Italiana, Piazza Venezia, is reliable for receiving money transfers and will give cash advances on both Visa and MasterCard. Credit cards can also be used in automatic teller machines (ATMs), known as bancomats, to obtain cash 24 hours a day. You'll need to get a PIN from your bank.

Post & Communications

The main post office is at Piazza San Silvestro 19, just off Via del Tritone, and is open 9 am to 6 pm Monday to Sunday (Saturday to 2 pm). *Fermo posta* (poste restante) is available here. You can send telegrams from the office next door (open 24 hours).

The Vatican post office (☎ 06 69 88 34 06) in Piazza di San Pietro (St Peter's Square) is open 8 am to 7 pm Monday to Saturday (8.30 am to 2.15 pm Monday to Saturday, July and August). The service is faster and more reliable, but there's no fermo posta. The postcode for central Rome is 00100, although for fermo posta at the main post office it is 00186.

There is a Telecom office at Stazione Termini, from where you can make international calls direct or through an operator. Another office is near the station, on Via San Martino della Battaglia opposite the Pensione Lachea. International calls can easily be made with a phonecard from any public telephone. Phonecards can be purchased at tobacconists and newspaper stands.

ITALY

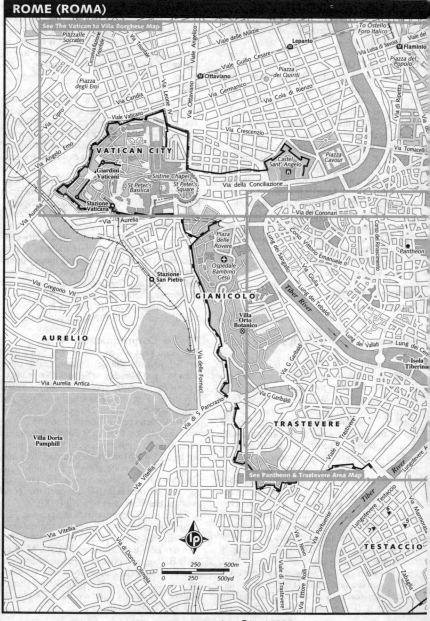

ROME (ROMA)

See The Vatican to Villa Borghese Map

Piazzalle Socrates

Via Triofiale

Via delle Milizie

Viale Angelico

To Ostello Foro Italico

Lepanto

Via Luisa di Savoia

Viale del

Flaminio

Piazza del Popolo

Via di Ripetta

Circonvallazione Trionfale

Viale Guilio Cesare

Piazza degli Eroi

M Ottaviano

Piazza dei Quiriti

Via Candia

Via Germanico

Via Cola di Rienzo

Via Tomacelli

Via Cipro

Viale Vaticano

Via Leone IV

Via Ottaviano

Via Crescenzio

VATICAN CITY

Piazza Cavour

Via Angelo Emo

Giardini Vaticani

Castel Sant'Angelo

Sistine Chapel

St Peter's Basilica

St Peter's Square

Via della Conciliazione

Stazione Vaticana

Via Aurelia

Via dei Coronari

Via — Aurelia

Plaza delle Rovere

Corso del Rinascimento

Pantheon

Ospedale Bambino Gesù

Corso Vittorio Emanuele II

Lung del Sangallo

Lung dei Tebaldi

Via Giulia

Stazione San Pietro

GIANICOLO

Tiber River

Via Gregorio VII

Villa Orto Botanico

Lung dei Vallati

Lung dei Cen

AURELIO

Isola Tiberina

Via delle Fornaci

Via G. Garibaldi

Via Aurelia Antica

Via G Garibaldi

TRASTEVERE

Via di S Pancrazio

Villa Doria Pamphill

Viale di Trastevere

River

Lungotevere A

Via Vitellia

See Pantheon & Trastevere Area Map

Tiber

Lungotevere Testaccio

Via Marmorata

Via Vitellia

6

Via di Donna Olimpia

5

TESTACCIO

Via Portuense

Via Nino Bixio

Via Ettore Rolli

Viale di Trastevere

Zabaglia

0   250   500m
0   250   500yd

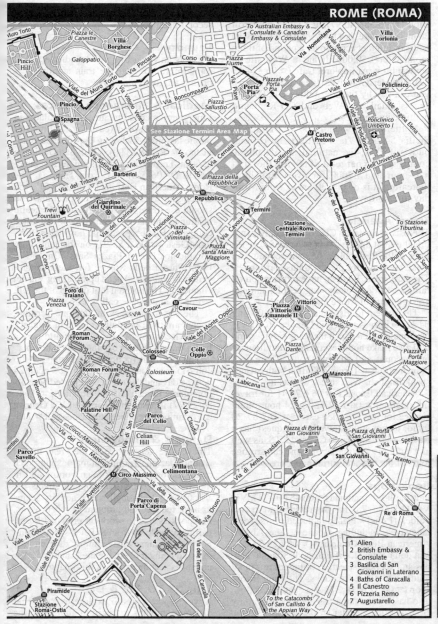

ROME (ROMA)

To Australian Embassy &
Consulate & Canadian
Embassy & Consulate

Piazza le
di Canestre

Villa
Borghese

Villa
Torlonia

Galoppatio

Via Nomentana

Via Regina
Margherita

Pincio
Hill

Viale del Muro Torto

Corso d'Italia

Piazza
Fiume

Viale del Policlinico

Policlinico

Muro Torto

Via Pinciana

Via Vittorio Veneto

Piazzale
Porta
Pia

Via Regina Elena

Pincio

Via Boncompagni

Porta
Pia

2

Policlinico
Umberto I

Spagna

Via Sistina

Via Barberini

Piazza
Sallustio

Via Piave

Piazza
della
Repubblica

Castro
Pretorio

Viale del Policlinico

Viale dell'Università

To Stazione
Tiburtina

Trevi
Fountain

Via del Tritone

Barberini

See Stazione Termini Area Map

Via Orlando

Via Cernaia

Via Solferino

Giardino
del Quirinale

Repubblica

Via Nazionale

Piazza
del
Viminale

Termini

Stazione
Centrale-Roma
Termini

Via del Corso

Via del Quirinale

Via Cavour

Via Carlo Alberto

Via Cavour

Piazza
Santa Maria
Maggiore

Via di Castro Pretorio

Via Tiburtina

Via dei Sardi

Foro di
Traiano

Via dei Fori Imperiali

Piazza
Venezia

Via Cavour

Cavour

Viale del Monte Oppio

Via Merulana

Piazza
Vittorio
Emanuele II

Vittorio

Via Principe
Eugenio

Via di Porta
Maggiore

Piazza di
Porta
Maggiore

Roman
Forum

Colosseo

Colle
Oppio

Piazza
Dante

Via L. Petroselli

Roman Forum

Colosseum

Via Labicana

Viale Manzoni

Manzoni

Via Merulana

Via Emanuele Filiberto

Palatine Hill

Via di San Gregorio VII

Parco
del Celio

Via Claudia

Via del Circo Massimo

Celian
Hill

Piazza di Porta
San Giovanni

Piazza di Porta
San Giovanni

Via La Spezia

Parco
Savello

Villa
Celimontana

3

San Giovanni

Via Taranto

Via Appia Nuova

Circo Massimo

Via di Amba Aradam

Via Druso

Via della Terme di Caracalla

Re di Roma

Viale Aventino

Parco di
Porta Capena

4

Via delle Terme di Caracalla

Via Gallia

Viale M. Gelsomini

Viale di Piramide Cestia

Piramide

Stazione
Roma-Ostia

To the Catacombs
of San Callisto &
the Appian Way

1 Alien
2 British Embassy &
   Consulate
3 Basilica di San
   Giovanni in Laterano
4 Baths of Caracalla
5 Il Canestro
6 Pizzeria Remo
7 Augustarello

ITALY

euro currency converter L1000 = €0.52

Email & Internet Access

Bibli (☎ 06 588 40 97), at Via dei Fienaroli 28 in Trastevere, is a bookshop that offers 10 hours of Internet access over a period of three months for L50,000. It has a Web site at www.bibli.it. At Explorer Café (☎ 06 324 17 57), Via dei Gracci 85 (near the Vatican), you can pay by the hour (about L12,000) to access email, the Web and CD-Rom and multimedia libraries.

Nolitel Italia (☎ 06 42 00 70 01) at Via Sicilia 54 near Via Veneto, is an official outlet of TIM, the national mobile phone company. It charges L8000 for the first half-hour and L7000 for every half-hour thereafter. It is open 9.30 am to 7 pm Monday to Saturday.

Travel Agencies

There is a Sestante CIT office (Italy's national tourist agency; ☎ 06 474 65 55) at Piazza della Repubblica 65, where you can make bookings for planes, trains and ferries. The staff speak English, have information on fares for students and young people, and can arrange tours of Rome and surrounds.

The student tourist centre, CTS (☎ 06 462 04 31, ✉ info@cts.it), Via Genova 16 off Via Nazionale, offers much the same services and will also make hotel reservations, but focuses on discount and student travel. There is a branch office at Termini. Staff at both offices speak English. Web site: www.cts.it.

American Express (☎ 06 6 76 41 for travel information; ☎ 06 7 22 82 for 24-hour client service for lost or stolen cards; ☎ 167 87 20 00 for lost or stolen travellers cheques) has a travel service similar to CIT and CTS, as well as a hotel-reservation service, and can arrange tours of the city and surrounding areas.

Bookshops

Feltrinelli International (☎ 06 487 01 71), Via VE Orlando 78, has literature and travel guides (Lonely Planet included) in several languages, including Japanese. The Anglo-American Book Company (☎ 06 679 52 22), Via della Vite 27, off Piazza di Spagna, also has an excellent selection of literature, travel guides and reference books. The Lion Bookshop (☎ 06 32 65 04 37), Via dei Greci 33-36, also has a good range, as does the Economy Book & Video Center (☎ 06 474 68 77), Via

Torino 136, off Via Nazionale, which also has second-hand books.

Laundry

There is an Onda Blu coin laundrette at Via Lamarmora 10, near the train station. It is open 8 am to 10 pm daily.

Medical & Emergency Services

Emergency medical treatment is available in the *pronto soccorso* (casualty sections) at public hospitals, including Ospedale San Gallicano (☎ 06 588 23 90), Via di San Gallicano 25/a in Trastevere; and Ospedale Fatebenefratelli (☎ 06 5 87 31), Isola Tiberina. The Rome American Hospital (☎ 06 2 25 51), Via E Longoni 81, is a private hospital and you should use its services only if you have health insurance and have consulted your insurance company. Rome's paediatric hospital is Bambino Gesú (☎ 06 6 85 91) on the Janiculum (Gianicolo) Hill at Piazza Sant' Onofrio 4. From Piazza della Rovere (on the Lungotevere near St Peter's) head uphill along Via del Gianicolo. The hospital is at the top of the hill.

For an ambulance call ☎ 118.

There is a pharmacy in Stazione Termini, open 7 am to 11 pm daily (closed in August). Otherwise, closed pharmacies should post a list in their windows of others open nearby.

The *questura* (police headquarters; ☎ 06 468 61) is at Via San Vitale 15. It's open 24 hours a day and thefts can be reported here. Its Foreigners Bureau (Ufficio Stranieri; ☎ 06 46 86 29 77) is around the corner at Via Genova 2. For immediate police attendance call ☎ 113.

Dangers & Annoyances

Thieves are very active in the areas in and around Stazione Termini, at major sights such as the Colosseum and Roman Forum, and in the city's most expensive shopping streets, eg, Via Condotti, although police activity seems to have reduced the problem in recent years. Pickpockets like to work on crowded buses, particularly No 40 from St Peter's to Termini. For more comprehensive information on how to avoid being robbed, see the Dangers & Annoyances section earlier in this chapter.

THINGS TO SEE & DO

It would take years to explore every corner of Rome, months to begin to appreciate the incredible number of monuments and weeks for a thorough tour of the city. You can, however, cover most of the important monuments in five days, or three at a minimum.

Piazza del Campidoglio

Designed by Michelangelo in 1538, the piazza is on the Capitolino (Capitoline Hill), the most important of Rome's seven hills. Formerly the seat of the ancient Roman government, it is now the seat of Rome's municipal government. Michelangelo also designed the facades of the three palaces that border the piazza. A modern copy of the bronze equestrian statue of Emperor Marcus Aurelius stands at its centre: the original is now on display in the ground-floor portico of the Palazzo Nuovo (also called Palazzo del Museo Capitolino). This and the other two palaces flanking the piazza (Palazzo del Museo Capitolino and Palazzo dei Conservatori) make up the **Musei Capitolini**, well worth visiting for their collections of ancient Roman sculpture, including the famous *Capitoline Wolf*, an Etruscan statue dating from the 6th century BC. They are open 10 am to 9 pm Tuesday to Sunday. Admission is L12,000.

Walk to the right of the Palazzo del Senato to see a panorama of the Roman Forum. Walk to the left of the same building to reach the ancient Roman **Carcere Mamertino**, where St Peter was believed to have been imprisoned.

The **Chiesa di Santa Maria d'Aracoeli** is between the Campidoglio and the Monumento Vittorio Emanuele II at the highest point of the Capitoline Hill. It is built on the site where legend says the Tiburtine Sybil told the Emperor Augustus of the coming birth of Christ.

Piazza Venezia

This piazza is overshadowed by a neoclassical monument dedicated to Vittorio Emanuele II, often referred to by Italians as the *macchina da scrivere* (typewriter) because it resembles one. Built to commemorate Italian unification, the piazza incorporates the **Altare della Patria** and the tomb of the unknown soldier, as well as the **Museo del Risorgimento**. Also in the piazza is the 15th-century **Palazzo Venezia**, which was Mussolini's official residence and now houses a museum.

Roman Forum & Palatine Hill

The commercial, political and religious centre of ancient Rome, the Forum stands in a valley between the Capitoline and Palatine (Palatino) hills. Originally marshland, the area was drained during the early republican era and became a centre for political rallies, public ceremonies and senate meetings. Its importance declined along with the empire after the 4th century, and the temples, monuments and buildings constructed by successive emperors, consuls and senators over a period of 900 years fell into ruin, eventually to be used as pasture.

The area was systematically excavated in the 18th and 19th centuries, and excavations are continuing. You can enter the Forum from Via dei Fori Imperiali, which leads from Piazza Venezia to the Colosseum. Entrance to the Forum is free, but it costs L12,000 to head up to the Palatine. The Forum and Palatine Hill are open 9 am to 7 pm Monday to Saturday in summer (to 4 pm in winter), and 9 am to 1 pm on Sunday year-round.

As you enter the Forum, to your left is the **Tempio di Antonino e Faustina**, erected by the senate in 141 AD and transformed into a church in the 8th century. To your right are the remains of the **Basilica Aemilia**, built in 179 BC and demolished during the Renaissance, when it was plundered for its precious marble. The Via Sacra, which traverses the Forum from north-west to south-east, runs in front of the basilica. Towards the Campidoglio is the **Curia**, once the meeting place of the Roman senate and converted into a Christian church in the Middle Ages. The church was dismantled and the Curia restored in the 1930s. In front of the Curia is the **Lapis Niger**, a large piece of black marble which legend says covered the grave of Romulus. Under the Lapis Niger is the oldest known Latin inscription, dating from the 6th century BC.

The **Arco di Settimo Severo** was erected in 203 AD in honour of this emperor and his sons, and is considered one of Italy's major triumphal arches. A circular base stone beside the arch marks the *umbilicus urbis*, the symbolic centre of ancient Rome. To the south is the **Rostrum**, used in ancient times by public speakers and once decorated by the rams of captured ships.

South along the Via Sacra is the **Tempio di Saturno**, one of the most important temples in

ITALY

ancient Rome. Eight granite columns remain. The **Basilica Julia**, in front of the temple, was the seat of justice, and nearby is the **Tempio di Giulio Cesare** (Temple of Julius Caesar), which was erected by Augustus in 29 BC on the site where Caesar's body was burned and Mark Antony read his famous speech. Back towards the Palatine Hill is the **Tempio dei Castori**, built in 489 BC in honour of the Heavenly Twins, or Dioscuri. It is easily recognisable by its three remaining columns.

In the area south-east of the temple is the **Chiesa di Santa Maria Antiqua**, the oldest Christian church in the Forum. It is closed to the public. Back on the Via Sacra is the **Case delle Vestali**, home of the virgins who tended the sacred flame in the adjoining **Tempio di Vesta**. If the flame went out, it was seen as a bad omen. The next major monument is the vast **Basilica di Costantino**. Its impressive design inspired Renaissance architects. The **Arco di Tito**, at the Colosseum end of the Forum, was built in 81 AD in honour of the victories of the emperors Titus and Vespasian against Jerusalem.

From here climb the Palatino, where wealthy Romans built their homes and where legend says that Romulus founded the city. Archaeological evidence shows that the earliest settlements in the area were on the Palatine. Like the Forum, the buildings of the Palatine fell into ruin and in the Middle Ages the hill became the site of convents and churches. During the Renaissance, wealthy families established their gardens here. The Farnese gardens were built over the ruins of the Domus Tiberiana, which is now under excavation.

Worth a look is the impressive **Domus Augustana**, which was the private residence of the emperors; the **Domus Flavia**, the residence of Domitian; the **Tempio della Magna Mater**, built in 204 BC to house a black stone connected with the Asiatic goddess Cybele; and the **Casa di Livia**, thought to have been the house of the wife of Emperor Augustus, and decorated with frescoes.

Colosseum
Originally known as the Flavian Amphitheatre, Rome's most famous monument was begun by Emperor Vespasian in 72 AD in the grounds of Nero's Golden House, and completed by his son Titus. The massive structure could seat 80,000 and featured bloody gladiatorial combat and wild beast shows that resulted in thousands of human and animal deaths.

In the Middle Ages the Colosseum became a fortress and was later used as a quarry for travertine and marble for the Palazzo Venezia and other buildings. Restoration works have been underway since 1992. Opening hours are 9 am to 7 pm daily in summer (to one hour before sunset in winter). Entry is L10,000.

Arch of Constantine
On the west side of the Colosseum is the triumphal arch built to honour Constantine following his victory over his rival Maxentius at the battle of Milvian Bridge (near the present-day Zona Olimpica, north-west of the Villa Borghese) in 312 AD. Its decorative reliefs were taken from earlier structures.

Circus Maximus
There is not much to see here apart from the few ruins that remain of what was once a chariot racetrack big enough to hold 300,000 spectators.

Baths of Caracalla
The huge Terme di Caracalla complex, covering 10 hectares, could hold 1600 people and included shops, gardens, libraries and entertainment. Begun by Antonius Caracalla and inaugurated in 217 AD, the baths were used until the 6th century. From the 1930s to 1993 they were an atmospheric venue for opera performances in summer. These performances have now been banned to prevent further damage to the ruins. The baths are open 9 am to 7 pm Monday to Saturday and to 2 pm on Sunday in summer; in winter until 3 pm daily. Entry is L8000.

Some Significant Churches
Down Via Cavour from Stazione Termini is **Santa Maria Maggiore**, built in the 5th century. Its main baroque facade was added in the 18th century, preserving the 13th-century mosaics of the earlier facade. Its bell tower is Romanesque and the interior is baroque. There are 5th-century mosaics decorating the triumphal arch and nave.

Follow Via Merulana to reach **Basilica di San Giovanni in Laterano**, Rome's cathedral.

ITALY

Fira, perched on the lip of the caldera, Santorini

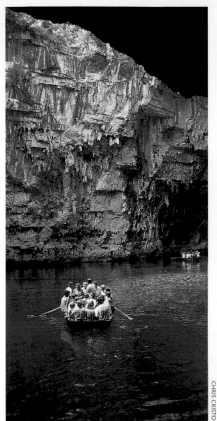

The Mellisani Cave near Sami, Kefallonia, Greece

Detail of Pisa's Leaning Tower, Italy

The gilded mosaics of Cattedrale Monreale, Sicily

Your gondola awaits you on the Bacino Canal, San Marco, Venice, Italy

Self-catering at the markets in Italy

Venetian facades at Carnival (Carnevale), Venice

Windmill on the salt pans in Mothia, Sicily, Italy

The original church was built in the 4th century, the first Christian basilica in Rome. Largely destroyed over a long period of time, it was rebuilt in the 17th century.

Basilica di San Pietro in Vincoli, just off Via Cavour, is worth a visit because it houses Michelangelo's *Moses* and his unfinished statues of Leah and Rachel, as well as the chains worn by St Peter during his imprisonment before being crucified.

Chiesa di San Clemente, Via San Giovanni in Laterano, near the Colosseum, defines how history in Rome exists on many levels. The 12th-century church at street level was built over a 4th-century church which was, in turn, built over a 1st-century Roman house containing a temple dedicated to the pagan god Mithras.

Santa Maria in Cosmedin, north-west of Circus Maximus, is regarded as one of the finest medieval churches in Rome. It has a seven-storey bell tower and its interior is heavily decorated with Cosmatesque inlaid marble, including the beautiful floor. The main attraction for the tourist hordes is, however, the **Bocca della Verità** (Mouth of Truth). Legend has it that if you put your right hand into the mouth and tell a lie, it will snap shut.

Baths of Diocletian

Started by Emperor Diocletian, these baths were completed in the 4th century. The complex of baths, libraries, concert halls and gardens covered about 13 hectares and could house up to 3000 people. After the aqueduct that fed the baths was destroyed by invaders in 536 AD, the complex fell into decay. Parts of the ruins are now incorporated into the Basilica di Santa Maria degli Angeli.

Basilica di Santa Maria degli Angeli

Designed by Michelangelo, this church incorporates what was the great central hall and *tepidarium* (lukewarm room) of the original baths. During the following centuries his work was drastically changed and little evidence of his design, apart from the great vaulted ceiling of the church, remains. An interesting feature of the church is a double meridian in the transept, one tracing the polar star and the other telling the precise time of the sun's zenith. The church is open from 7.30 am to 12.30 pm and from 4 to 6.30 pm. Through the sacristy is an entrance to a stairway leading to the upper terraces of the ruins.

Museo Nazionale Romano

This museum, located in three separate buildings, houses an important collection of ancient art, including Greek and Roman sculpture. The museum is largely housed in the restored Palazzo Altemps, Piazza Sant'Apollinare 44, near Piazza Navona. It contains numerous important pieces from the Ludovisi collection, including the *Ludovisi Throne*. Entry is L10,000. Another part of the same museum is in the Palazzo Massimo alle Terme, in Piazza dei Cinquecento. It contains a collection of frescoes and mosaics from the Villa of Livia, excavated at Prima Porta. Entry is L12,000. Both sections open 9 am to 6.45 pm Tuesday to Saturday (to 7.45 pm on Sunday).

Via Vittorio Veneto

This was Rome's hot spot in the 1960s, where film stars could be spotted at the expensive outdoor cafes. These days you will find only tourists, and the atmosphere of Fellini's *La Dolce Vita* is long dead.

Piazza di Spagna & Spanish Steps

This piazza, church and famous staircase (Scalinata della Trinitá dei Monti) have long provided a major gathering place for foreigners. Built with a legacy from the French in 1725, but named after the Spanish Embassy to the Holy See, the steps lead to the church of Trinitá dei Monti, which was built by the French.

In the 18th century the most beautiful men and women of Italy gathered there, waiting to be chosen as artists' models. To the right as you face the steps is the house where Keats spent the last three months of his life, and where he died in 1821. In the piazza is the boat-shaped fountain of the **Barcaccia**, believed to be by Pietro Bernini, father of the famous Gian Lorenzo. One of Rome's most elegant shopping streets, **Via Condotti**, runs off the piazza towards Via del Corso.

Piazza del Popolo

This vast piazza was laid out in the 16th century and redesigned in the early 19th century by Giuseppe Valadier. It is at the foot of the

ITALY

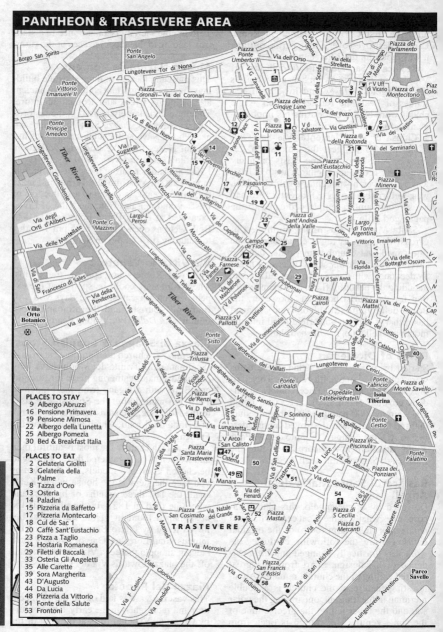

PANTHEON & TRASTEVERE AREA

PLACES TO STAY
9   Albergo Abruzzi
16 Pensione Primavera
19 Pensione Mimosa
22 Albergo della Lunetta
25 Albergo Pomezia
30 Bed & Breakfast Italia

PLACES TO EAT
2   Gelateria Giolitti
3   Gelateria della
    Palme
8   Tazza d'Oro
13 Osteria
14 Paladini
15 Pizzeria da Baffetto
17 Pizzeria Montecarlo
18 Cul de Sac 1
20 Caffè Sant'Eustachio
24 Hostaria Romanesca
33 Osteria Gli Angeletti
43 Alle Carette
39 Sora Margherita
43 D'Augusto
44 Da Lucia
48 Pizzeria da Vittorio
51 Fonte della Salute
53 Frontoni

ITALY

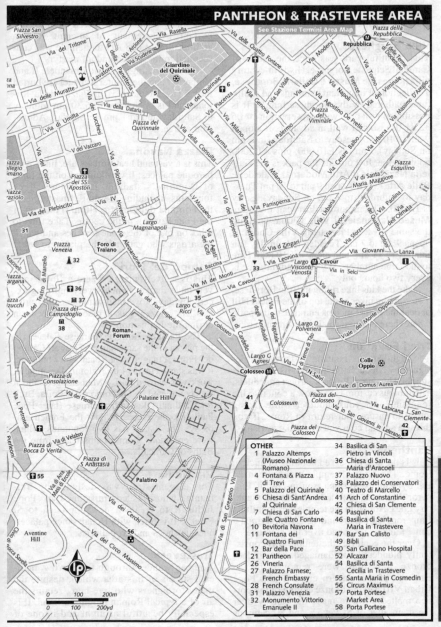

PANTHEON & TRASTEVERE AREA

See Stazione Termini Area Map

OTHER
1 Palazzo Altemps (Museo Nazionale Romano)
4 Fontana & Piazza di Trevi
5 Palazzo del Quirinale
6 Chiesa di Sant'Andrea al Quirinale
7 Chiesa di San Carlo alle Quattro Fontane
10 Bevitoria Navona
11 Fontana dei Quattro Fiumi
12 Bar della Pace
21 Pantheon
26 Vineria
27 Palazzo Farnese; French Embassy
28 French Consulate
31 Palazzo Venezia
32 Monumento Vittorio Emanuele II
34 Basilica di San Pietro in Vincoli
36 Chiesa di Santa Maria d'Aracoeli
37 Palazzo Nuovo
38 Palazzo dei Conservatori
40 Teatro di Marcello
41 Arch of Constantine
42 Chiesa di San Clemente
45 Pasquino
46 Basilica di Santa Maria in Trastevere
47 Bar San Calisto
49 Bibli
50 San Gallicano Hospital
52 Alcazar
54 Basilica di Santa Cecilia in Trastevere
55 Santa Maria in Cosmedin
56 Circus Maximus
57 Porta Portese Market Area
58 Porta Portese

ITALY

Pincio Hill, from where there is a panoramic view of the city.

Villa Borghese

This beautiful park was once the estate of Cardinal Scipione Borghese. His 17th-century villa houses the **Museo e Galleria Borghese**, a collection of important paintings and sculptures gathered by the Borghese family. It is possible to visit only with a reservation (☎ 06 32 81 01), so call well in advance. It's open 9 am to 10 pm Tuesday to Saturday (to 8 pm on Sunday). Entry is L10,000, plus a L2000 booking fee. Just outside the park is the **Galleria Nazionale d'Arte Moderna**, Viale delle Belle Arti 131. It's open 9 am to 10 pm Tuesday to Saturday (to 8 pm on Sunday). Entry is L8000. The important Etruscan museum, **Museo Nazionale di Villa Giulia**, is along the same street in Piazzale di Villa Giulia. It opens 9 am to 7 pm Tuesday to Saturday (on Sunday to 11 am) and entry is L10,000. Due to the large numbers of visitors admittance is every two hours only.

Take the kids bike riding in Villa Borghese. You can hire bikes at the top of the Pincio Hill or near the Porta Pinciana entrance to the park, where there is also a small amusement park.

Trevi Fountain

The high-baroque Fontana di Trevi was designed by Nicola Salvi in 1732. Its water was supplied by one of Rome's earliest aqueducts. The famous custom is to throw a coin into the fountain (over your shoulder while facing away) to ensure your return to Rome. If you throw a second coin you can make a wish.

Pantheon

This is the best preserved building of ancient Rome. The original temple was built in 27 BC by Marcus Agrippa, son-in-law of Emperor Augustus, and dedicated to the planetary gods. Although the temple was rebuilt by Emperor Hadrian around 120 AD, Agrippa's name remains inscribed over the entrance.

Over the centuries the temple was consistently plundered and damaged. The gilded-bronze roof tiles were removed by an emperor of the eastern empire, and Pope Urban VIII had the bronze ceiling of the portico melted down to make the canopy over the main altar of St Peter's and 80 cannons

for Castel Sant'Angelo. The Pantheon's extraordinary dome is considered the most important achievement of ancient Roman architecture. In 608 AD the temple was consecrated to the Virgin and all martyrs.

The Italian kings Vittorio Emanuele II and Umberto I and the painter Raphael are buried there. The Pantheon is in Piazza della Rotonda and is open 9 am to 6.30 pm Monday to Saturday and to 1 pm on Sunday. Admission is free.

Piazza Navona

This is a vast and beautiful square, lined with baroque palaces. It was laid out on the ruins of Domitian's stadium and features three fountains, including Bernini's masterpiece, the **Fontana dei Quattro Fiumi** (Fountain of the Four Rivers), in the centre. Take time to relax on one of the stone benches and watch the artists who gather in the piazza to work.

Campo de' Fiori

This is a lively piazza where a flower and vegetable market is held every morning except Sunday. Now lined with bars and trattorias, the piazza was a place of execution during the Inquisition.

The **Palazzo Farnese** (Farnese Palace), in the piazza of the same name, is just off Campo de' Fiori. A magnificent Renaissance building, it was started in 1514 by Antonio da Sangallo, work was carried on by Michelangelo and it was completed by Giacomo della Porta. Built for Cardinal Alessandro Farnese (later Pope Paul III), the palace is now the French embassy. The piazza has two fountains, which were enormous granite baths taken from the Baths of Caracalla.

Via Giulia

This elegant street was designed by Bramante, who was commissioned by Pope Julius II to create a new approach to St Peter's. It is lined with Renaissance palaces, antique shops and art galleries.

Trastevere

You can wander through the narrow medieval streets of this area which, despite the many foreigners who live here, retains the air of a typical Roman neighbourhood. It is especially beautiful at night and is one of

ITALY

the more interesting areas for bar-hopping or a meal.

Of particular note here is the **Basilica di Santa Maria in Trastevere**, in the lovely piazza of the same name. It is believed to be the oldest church dedicated to the Virgin in Rome. Although the first church was built on the site in the 4th century, the present structure was built in the 12th century and features a Romanesque bell tower and facade, with a mosaic of the Virgin. Its interior was redecorated during the baroque period, but the vibrant mosaics in the apse and on the triumphal arch date from the 12th century. Also take a look at the **Basilica di Santa Cecilia** in Trastevere.

Gianicolo

Go to the top of the Gianicolo (Janiculum), the hill between St Peter's and Trastevere, for a panoramic view of Rome.

Catacombs

There are several catacombs in Rome, consisting of miles of tunnels carved out of volcanic rock, which were the meeting and burial places of early Christians in Rome. The largest are along the Via Appia Antica, just outside the city and accessible on bus No 660 (from Piazza dei Cinquecento). The **Catacombs of San Callisto** and **Catacombs of San Sebastiano** are almost next to each other on the Via Appia Antica. San Callisto is open 8.30 am to noon and 2.30 to 5.30 pm (closed Wednesday and all of February). San Sebastiano is open 8.30 am to noon and 2.30 to 5 pm (closed Sunday and all of November). Admission to each costs L8000 and is with a guide only.

Vatican City

After the unification of Italy, the papal states of central Italy became part of the new kingdom of Italy, causing a considerable rift between church and state. In 1929, Mussolini, under the Lateran Treaty, gave the pope full sovereignty over what is now the Vatican City.

The tourist office (☎ 06 69 88 44 66), in Piazza San Pietro to the left of the basilica, is open 8.30 am to 7 pm Monday to Saturday. Guided tours of the Vatican City gardens (L18,000) can be organised here. A few doors up is the Vatican post office (☎ 06 69 88 34 06), said to offer a much more reliable service

than the normal Italian postal system. It is open 8 am to 7 pm Monday to Saturday (8.15am to 2.15 pm Monday to Saturday, July and August).

The city has its own postal service, currency, newspaper, radio station, train station and army of Swiss Guards.

St Peter's Basilica & Square The largest and most famous church in the Christian world, **San Pietro** (St Peter's) stands on the site where St Peter was buried. The first church on the site was built during Constantine's reign in the 4th century, and in 1506 work started on a new basilica, designed by Bramante.

Although several architects were involved in its construction, it is generally held that St Peter's owes more to Michelangelo, who took over the project in 1547 at the age of 72 and was particularly responsible for the design of the dome. He died before the church was completed. The cavernous interior contains numerous treasures, including Michelangelo's superb *Pietá*, sculpted when he was only 24 years old and the only work to carry his signature (on the sash across the breast of the Madonna). It has been protected by bulletproof glass since an attack in 1972 by a hammer-wielding vandal.

Bernini's huge, baroque *Baldacchino* (a heavily sculpted bronze canopy over the papal altar) stands 29m high and is an extraordinary work of art. Another point of note is the red porphyry disc near the central door, which marks the spot where Charlemagne and later emperors were crowned by the pope.

Entrance to Michelangelo's soaring dome is to the right as you climb the stairs to the atrium of the basilica. Make the entire climb on foot for L7000, or pay L8000 and take the elevator for part of the way (recommended).

The basilica is open 7 am to 7 pm daily (6 pm in winter) and dress rules are stringently enforced – no shorts, miniskirts or sleeveless tops. Prams and strollers must be left in a designated area outside the basilica.

Bernini's **Piazza San Pietro** (St Peter's Square) is considered a masterpiece. Laid out in the 17th century as a place for Christians of the world to gather, the immense piazza is bound by two semicircular colonnades, each of which is made up of four rows of Doric

ITALY

columns. In the centre of the piazza is an obelisk that was brought to Rome by Caligula from Heliopolis (in ancient Egypt). When you stand on the dark paving stones between the obelisk and either of the fountains, the colonnades appear to have only one row of columns.

The Pope usually gives a public audience at 10 or 11 am every Wednesday in the Papal Audience Hall. You must make a booking, either in person or by fax to the Prefettura della Casa Pontifica (☎ 06 69 88 30 17, fax 06 69 88 58 63), on the Monday or Thursday before the audience between 9 am and 1 pm. Go

through the bronze doors under the colonnade to the right as you face the basilica.

Vatican Museums From St Peter's follow the wall of the Vatican City (to the right as you face the basilica) to the museums, or catch the regular shuttle bus (L2500) from the piazza in front of the tourist office. The museums are open 8.45 am to 3.45 pm Monday to Friday (to 12.45 on Saturday). Admission is L15,000. The museums are closed on Sunday and public holidays, but open on the last Sunday of every month from 9 am to 1 pm (free admission, but queues are always very

STAZIONE TERMINI AREA

PLACES TO STAY & EAT			
1 Pensione Katty	31 Pensione Everest	15 Telecom Office	26 Museo Nazionale Romano
3 Pensione Lachea;	33 Hotel Kennedy	16 Urban Bus Station	27 Teatro dell'Opera
Hotel Pensione Dolomiti	35 Hotel Sandy	17 Baths of Diocletian	28 Questura (Police Station)
5 Pensione Ester		18 APT Tourist Office	29 Foreigners' Bureau
6 Pensione Restivo	**OTHER**	19 Feltrinelli International	30 CTS
7 Hotel Positano	2 Telecom Office	21 Sestante CIT Office	32 Italian Youth Hostels
8 Papa Germano	4 Hospital (Policlinico Umberto I)	22 Basilica di Santa	Association Office
10 Trattoria Da Bruno	9 ENIT Tourist Office	Maria degli Angeli	34 Basilica di Santa
12 Fawlty Towers	11 Enjoy Rome	23 Eurojet	Maggiore Maria
20 Hotel Oceania	13 CTS	24 SAIS & Segesta Bus Office	36 The Druid's Den
	14 APT Branch Tourist Office	25 Economy Book & Video Center	37 Circolo degli Artisti

long). Guided visits to the Vatican gardens cost L18,000 and can be booked by calling ☎ 06 69 88 44 66.

The Vatican museums contain an incredible collection of art and treasures collected by the popes, and you will need several hours to see the most important areas and museums. The Sistine Chapel comes towards the end of a full visit; otherwise, you can walk straight there and then work your way back through the museums.

The **Museo Pio-Clementino**, containing Greek and Roman antiquities, is on the ground floor near the entrance. Through the tapestry and map galleries are the **Stanze di Rafaello**, once the private apartments of Pope Julius II, decorated with frescoes by Raphael. Of particular interest is the magnificent **Stanza della Segnatura**, which features **Raphael's masterpieces** *The School of Athens* and *Disputation on the Sacrament*.

From Raphael's rooms, go down the stairs to the sumptuous **Appartamento Borgia**, decorated with frescoes by Pinturicchio, then go down another flight of stairs to the **Sistine Chapel**, the private papal chapel built in 1473 for Pope Sixtus IV. Michelangelo's wonderful frescoes of the *Creation* on the barrel-vaulted ceiling and *Last Judgment* on the end wall have both been restored to their original brilliance. It took Michelangelo four years, at the height of the Renaissance, to paint the ceiling; 24 years later he painted the extraordinary *Last Judgment*. The other walls of the chapel were painted by artists including Botticelli, Ghirlandaio, Pinturicchio and Signorelli. To best enjoy the ceiling frescoes, a pocket mirror is recommended so that you don't have to strain your neck.

ORGANISED TOURS

Enjoy Rome (☎ 06 445 18 43, 167-27 48 19 toll-free), Via Varese 39, offers walking or bike tours of Rome's main sights for L35,000 per person and a shuttle service for Pompeii. ATAC bus No 110 leaves daily at 3.30 pm (2.30 pm in winter) from Piazza dei Cinquecento, in front of Stazione Termini, for a three-hour tour of the city. The cost is L15,000. Vastours (☎ 06 481 43 09), Via Piemonte 34, operates half-day coach tours of Rome from L48,000 and full-day coach tours

of the city from L130,000, as well as tours to Tivoli, the Castelli Romani and other Italian cities. American Express (☎ 06 676 41) in Piazza di Spagna 38 and the CIT office in Piazza della Repubblica also offer guided tours of the city.

SPECIAL EVENTS

Although Romans desert their city in summer, particularly in August when the weather is relentlessly hot and humid, cultural and musical events liven up the place. The Comune di Roma coordinates a diverse series of concerts, performances and events throughout summer under the general title Estate Romana (Roman Summer). The series usually features major international performers. Information is published in Rome's daily newspapers.

A jazz festival is held in July and August in the Villa Celimontana, a park on top of the Celian Hill (access from Piazza della Navicella).

The Festa de' Noantri is held in Trastevere in the last two weeks of July in honour of Our Lady of Mt Carmel. Street stalls line Viale di Trastevere, but head for the backstreets for live music and street theatre.

At Christmas the focus is on the many churches of Rome, each setting up its own nativity scene. Among the most renowned is the 13th-century crib at Santa Maria Maggiore. During Holy Week, at Easter, the focus is again religious and events include the famous procession of the cross between the Colosseum and the Palatino on Good Friday, and the Pope's blessing of the city and the world in St Peter's Square on Easter Sunday.

The Spanish Steps become a sea of pink azaleas during the Spring Festival in April.

PLACES TO STAY
Camping

About 15 minutes from the centre by public transport is *Village Camping Flaminio* (☎ 06 333 26 04, Via Flaminia Nuova 821). It costs L16,000 per person and L22,000 for a site. Tents and bungalows are available for rent. From Stazione Termini catch bus No 910 to Piazza Mancini, then bus No 200 to the camping ground. At night, catch bus No 24n from Piazzale Flaminio (just north of Piazza del Popolo).

ITALY

THE VATICAN TO VILLA BORGHESE

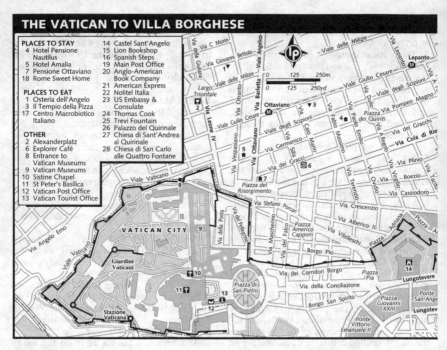

PLACES TO STAY
- 4 Hotel Pensione Nautilus
- 5 Hotel Amalia
- 7 Pensione Ottaviano
- 18 Rome Sweet Home

PLACES TO EAT
- 1 Osteria dell'Angelo
- 3 Il Tempio della Pizza
- 17 Centro Macrobiotico Italiano

OTHER
- 2 Alexanderplatz
- 6 Explorer Café
- 8 Entrance to Vatican Museums
- 9 Vatican Museums
- 10 Sistine Chapel
- 11 St Peter's Basilica
- 12 Vatican Post Office
- 13 Vatican Tourist Office
- 14 Castel Sant'Angelo
- 15 Lion Bookshop
- 16 Spanish Steps
- 19 Main Post Office
- 20 Anglo-American Book Company
- 21 American Express
- 22 Nolitel Italia
- 23 US Embassy & Consulate
- 24 Thomas Cook
- 25 Trevi Fountain
- 26 Palazzo del Quirinale
- 27 Chiesa di Sant'Andrea al Quirinale
- 28 Chiesa di San Carlo alle Quattro Fontane

Hostels

The HI *Ostello del Foro Italico* (☎ *06 323 62 67, Viale delle Olimpiadi 61*) costs L25,000 a night, breakfast and showers included. Take Metro Linea A to Ottaviano, then bus No 32 to Foro Italico. The head office of the Italian Youth Hostels Association (☎ 06 487 11 52) is at Via Cavour 44, 00184 Rome. It will provide information about all the hostels in Italy. You can also join HI here.

B&Bs

This type of accommodation in private houses is a recent addition to Rome's accommodation options for budget travellers. *Bed & Breakfast Italia* (☎ *06 687 86 18, fax 06 687 86 19, ❸ md4095@mclink.it, Corso Vittorio Emanuele II 282*) is one of several B&B networks. Central singles/doubles with shared bathroom cost L50,000/95,000, or L70,000/130,000 with private bath. Also well worth checking is *Rome Sweet Home* (☎/fax 06 69 92 48 33, ❸ romesweethome@tisc alinet.it, Via della Vite 32). Prices are more expensive (L70,000/

100,000) but the B&Bs are stunning. It has a Web site at www.romesweethome.it.

Hotels & Pensioni

North of Stazione Termini To reach the pensioni in this area, head to the right as you leave the train platforms onto Via Castro Pretorio. The excellent *Fawlty Towers* (☎ *06 445 48 02, Via Magenta 39*) offers hostel-style accommodation at L40,000 per person, or L45,000 with a shower. Run by the people at Enjoy Rome, it offers lots of information about Rome and added bonuses are the sunny terrace and satellite TV.

Nearby in Via Palestro are several reasonably priced pensioni. *Pensione Restivo* (☎ *06 446 21 72, ❸ info@enjoyrome.com, Via Palestro 55*) has reasonable singles/doubles at L70,000/110,000, including the cost of showers. There's a midnight curfew. *Pensione Katty* (☎ *06 444 12 16, Via Palestro 35*) has basic rooms from L55,000/90,000. Around the corner is *Pensione Ester* (☎ *06 495 71 23, Viale Castro Pretorio 25*) with comfortable

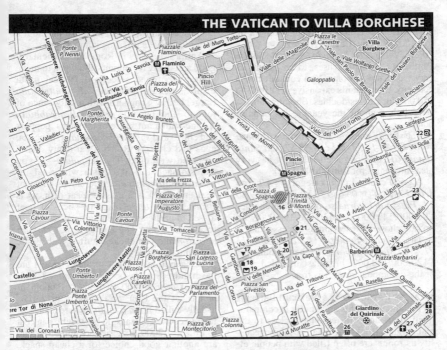

THE VATICAN TO VILLA BORGHESE

doubles/triples for L70,000/100,000. **Hotel Positano** (☎ 06 49 03 60, Via Palestro 49) is a more expensive option. Very pleasant rooms with bathroom, TV and other comforts cost L120,000/160,000.

Two good pensioni are in the same building. **Pensione Lachea** (☎ 06 495 72 56, Via San Martino della Battaglia 11) has large rooms for L70,000/90,000. **Hotel Pensione Dolomiti** (☎ 06 49 10 58) has singles/doubles for L65,000/95,000.

Papa Germano (☎ 06 48 69 19; **e** info@hotelpapagermano.it, Via Calatafimi 14a) is one of the more popular budget places in the area. It has singles/doubles for L55,000/80,000, or a double with private bathroom for L100,000.

Across Via XX Settembre, about 1km from the station, **Pensione Ercoli** (☎ 06 474 54 54, Via Collina 48) has rooms for L90,000/140,000.

South of Stazione Termini This area is seedier, but prices remain the same. As you exit to the left of the station, follow Via Gioberti to Via G Amendola, which becomes Via F Turati. This street, and the parallel Via Principe Amedeo, harbours a concentration of budget pensioni, so you should easily find a room. The area improves as you get closer to the Colosseum and Roman Forum.

On Via Cavour, the main street running south-west from the piazza in front of Termini, is **Everest Pensione** (☎ 06 488 16 29, Via Cavour 47), with clean and simple singles/doubles for L60,000/90,000. **Hotel Sandy** (☎ 06 445 26 12, Via Cavour 136) has dormitory beds for L35,000 a night.

Better quality hotels in the area include **Hotel Oceania** (☎ 06 482 46 96, Via Firenze 50), which can take up to five people in a room; it has doubles for up to L260,000. **Hotel Kennedy 2** (☎ 06 446 53 73, Via F Turati 62) has good quality singles/doubles with bath for up to L149,000/249,000.

City Centre At **Pensione Primavera** (☎ 06 68 80 31 09, Piazza San Pantaleo 3) on a

ITALY

square just off Via Vittorio Emanuele II, there are immaculate doubles with bathroom for up to L180,000. The *Albergo Abruzzi* (☎ 06 679 20 21, Piazza della Rotonda 69) overlooks the Pantheon – which excuses, to an extent, its very basic, noisy rooms. You couldn't find a better location, but it's expensive at L105,000/150,000 for singles/doubles. Bookings are essential throughout the year at this popular hotel.

The strictly nonsmoking *Pensione Mimosa* (☎ 06 68 80 17 53, fax 683 35 57, Via Santa Chiara 61), off Piazza della Minerva, has very pleasant rooms for L90,000/110,000.

A good choice in this category is *Albergo della Lunetta* (☎ 06 686 10 80, fax 06 689 20 28, Piazza del Paradiso 68), which charges L90,000/140,000, or L110,000/190,000 with private shower. Reservations are essential.

The *Albergo Pomezia* (☎/fax 06 686 13 71, Via dei Chiavari 12) has rooms for L120,000/170,000, breakfast included. Use of the communal shower is free.

Near St Peter's & the Vatican Bargains do not abound in this area, but it is comparatively quiet and still reasonably close to the main sights. Bookings are an absolute necessity as rooms are often filled with people attending conferences and so on at the Vatican. The simplest way to reach the area is on the Metropolitana Linea A to Ottaviano. Bus No 64 from Termini stops at St Peter's.

The best bargain in the area is *Pensione Ottaviano* (☎ 06 39 73 72 53, ✉ gi.costantini@agora.stm.it, Via Ottaviano 6), near Piazza Risorgimento. It has beds in dormitories for L35,000 per person. *Hotel Pensione Nautilus* (☎ 06 324 21 18, Via Germanico 198) offers basic singles/doubles for L90,000/110,000; or L130,000/160,000 with private bathroom. *Hotel Amalia* (☎ 06 39 72 33 56, fax 39 72 33 65, ✉ hotelamalia@iol.it, Via Germanico 66) has a beautiful courtyard entrance and clean, sunny rooms. Rooms are L105,000/140,000 and include breakfast and use of the communal shower. Triples are L182,000.

PLACES TO EAT

Rome bursts at the seams with trattorias, pizzerias and restaurants – and not all of them overrun by tourists. Eating times are generally

from 12.30 to 3 pm and 8 to 11 pm. Most Romans head out for dinner around 9 pm, so it's better to arrive earlier to claim a table.

Antipasto dishes in Rome are particularly good and many restaurants allow you to make your own mixed selection. Typical pasta dishes include *bucatini all'Amatriciana* (large, hollow spaghetti with a salty sauce of tomato and bacon), *penne all'arrabbiata* (penne with a hot sauce of tomatoes, peppers and chilli) and *spaghetti carbonara* (pancetta, eggs and cheese). Romans eat many dishes prepared with offal. Try the *paiata* – if you can stomach it – it's pasta with veal intestines. *Saltimbocca alla Romana* (slices of veal and ham) is a classic meat dish, as is *straccetti con la rucola*, fine slices of beef tossed in garlic and oil and topped with fresh rocket. In winter you can't go past *carciofi alla Romana* (artichokes stuffed with garlic and mint or parsley).

Good options for cheap, quick meals are the hundreds of bars, where *panini* (sandwiches) cost L2500 to L5000 if taken *al banco* (at the bar), or takeaway pizzerias, usually called *pizza a taglio*, where a slice of freshly cooked pizza, sold by weight, can cost as little as L2000. Bakeries are numerous and are another good choice for a cheap snack. Try a huge piece of *pizza bianca*, a flat bread resembling focaccia, costing from around L2000 a slice (sold by weight).

Try *Paladini* (Via del Governo Vecchio 29) for sandwiches, and *Pizza a Taglio* on Via Baullari for takeaway pizza.

There are numerous outdoor *markets*, notably the lively daily market in Campo de' Fiori. Other, cheaper food markets are held in Piazza Vittorio Emanuele, near the station, and in Via Andrea Doria, near Largo Trionfale, north of the Vatican.

Restaurants, Trattorias & Pizzerias

The restaurants near Stazione Termini are generally to be avoided if you want to pay reasonable prices for good food. The side streets around Piazza Navona and Campo de' Fiori harbour many budget trattorias and pizzerias, and the areas of San Lorenzo (to the east of Termini, near the university) and Testaccio (across the Tiber near Piramide) are popular local eating districts. Trastevere offers an excellent selection of rustic eating

ITALY

places hidden in tiny piazzas, and pizzerias where it doesn't cost the earth to sit at a table on the street.

City Centre The *Pizzeria Montecarlo (Vicolo Savelli 12)* is a very traditional pizzeria, with paper sheets for tablecloths. A pizza with wine or beer will cost as little as L17,000. The *Pizzeria da Baffetto (Via del Governo Vecchio 11)* is a Roman institution. The pizzas are huge and delicious. Expect to join a queue if you arrive after 9 pm and don't be surprised if you end up sharing a table. Pizzas cost around L10,000 to L15,000, a litre of wine costs L9000 and the cover charge (coperto) is only L2000. Farther along the street at No 18 is a tiny, nameless *osteria* where you can eat an excellent, simple meal for around L25,000. There's no written menu, but don't be nervous – the owner/waiter will explain slowly (in Italian). Back along the street towards Piazza Navona is *Cul de Sac 1 (Piazza Pasquino 73)*, a wine bar which also has light meals at reasonable prices.

Centro Macrobiotico Italiano (Via della Vite 14), is a vegetarian restaurant which also serves fresh fish in the evenings. It charges an annual membership fee (which reduces as the year goes by), but tourists can usually eat there and pay only a small surcharge.

There are several small restaurants in Campo de' Fiori. *Hostaria Romanesca* is tiny, so arrive early in winter. In summer there are numerous tables outside. A dish of pasta will cost around L12,000, a full meal around L40,000.

Just off Campo de' Fiori is *Filetti di Baccalá* in the Largo dei Librari, which serves only deep-fried cod fillets for L6500 and wine for L9000 a litre. Across Via Arenula in the Jewish quarter is *Sora Margherita (Piazza delle Cinque Scole 30)*. Open only at lunchtime, it serves traditional Roman and Jewish food and a full meal will cost around L38,000.

West of the Tiber On the west bank of the Fiume Tevere (Tiber River), good-value restaurants are concentrated in Trastevere and the Testaccio district, past Piramide. Many of the establishments around St Peter's and the Vatican are geared for tourists and can be very expensive. There are, however, some good options. Try *Il Tempio della*

Pizza (Viale Giulio Cesare 91) or the highly recommended *Osteria dell'Angelo (Via G Bettolo 24)*, along Via Leone IV from the Vatican City, although this place can be difficult to get into if you get there after 8 pm.

In Trastevere, try *Frontoni*, on Viale di Trastevere opposite Piazza Mastai, for fantastic panini made with pizza bianca. *D'Augusto*, in Piazza dei Renzi just around the corner from the Basilica di Santa Maria in Trastevere (turn right as you face the church and walk to Via della Pelliccia), is a very popular cheap eating spot. The food might be average, but the atmosphere, especially in summer with tables outside in the piazza, is as traditionally Roman as you can get. A meal with wine will cost around L29,000. *Da Lucia (Vicolo del Mattinato 2)* is more expensive at around L50,000 a full meal, but the food is good and the owners are delightful. In summer you'll sit beneath the neighbours' washing.

For a Neapolitan-style pizza, try *Pizzeria da Vittorio (Via San Cosimato 14)*. You'll have to wait for an outside table if you arrive after 8.30 pm, but the atmosphere is great. A bruschetta, pizza and wine will cost around L30,000.

You won't find a cheaper, noisier, more chaotic pizzeria in Rome than *Pizzeria Remo (Piazza Santa Maria Liberatrice 44)* in Testaccio. Nearby is *Il Canestro* on Via Maestro Giorgio, which specialises in vegetarian food and is relatively expensive; you won't get much change out L60,000. *Augustarello (Via G Branca 98)*, off the piazza, specialises in the very traditional Roman fare of offal dishes. The food is reasonable and a meal will cost around L25,000.

Between Termini & the Forum If you have no option but to eat near Stazione Termini, try to avoid the tourist traps offering overpriced full menus. *Trattoria da Bruno (Via Varese 29)* has good food at reasonable prices – around L8500 for pasta and up to L17,000 for a second course. Home-made gnocchi are served on Thursday. A decent pizzeria is *Alle Carrette (Vicolo delle Carrette 14)*, off Via Cavour near the Roman Forum. A pizza and wine will cost around L16,000. Just off Via Cavour is *Osteria Gli Angeletti (Via dell'Angeletto)*, an excellent little restaurant with prices at the higher end of the budget range. You'll pay L10,000 to

ITALY

L14,000 for a pasta and around L16,000 for a second course.

Cafes

Remember that prices skyrocket in bars as soon as you sit down, particularly near the Spanish Steps, in the Piazza della Rotonda and in Piazza Navona, where a *cappuccino a tavola* (at a table) can cost L5000 or more. The same cappuccino taken at the bar will cost around L1800 – but passing an hour or so watching the world go by over a cappuccino, beer or wine in any of the above locations can be hard to beat!

For the best coffee in Rome head for *Tazza d'Oro*, on Via degli Orfani just off Piazza della Rotonda; and *Caffé Sant'Eustachio* (*Piazza Sant'Eustachio 82*). Try the *granita di caffé* at either one.

Gelati

Both *Gelateria Giolitti* (*Via degli Uffici del Vicario 40*) near the Pantheon and *Gelateria della Palme* (*Via della Maddalena 20*) just around the corner have a huge selection of flavours. In Trastevere, *Fonte della Salute* (*Via Cardinale Marmaggi 2-6*) also has excellent gelati.

ENTERTAINMENT

Rome's best entertainment guide is the weekly *romac'é* (L2000), available at all newsstands. It has an English-language section. Another good entertainment guide is *Trovaroma*, a weekly supplement in the Thursday edition of the newspaper *La Repubblica*. It provides a comprehensive listing of what's happening in the city, but in Italian only. The newspaper also publishes a daily listing of cinema, theatre and concerts.

Metropolitan is a fortnightly magazine for Rome's English-speaking community (L1500). It has good entertainment listings and is available at outlets including the Economy Book & Video Center, Via Torino 136, and at newsstands in the city centre, including Largo Argentina.

Cinema

There are a handful of cinemas in Trastevere that show English-language movies. There are daily shows at *Pasquino* (☎ *06 580 36 22, Vicolo del Piede 19*), just off Piazza Santa

Maria. *Alcazar* (☎ *06 588 00 99, Via Merry del Val 14*) shows an English-language film every Monday. *Nuovo Saucer* (☎ *06 581 81 16, Largo Ascianghi*) shows films in their original language on Monday and Tuesday.

Nightclubs

Among the more interesting and popular Roman live music clubs is *Radio Londra* (*Via di Monte Testaccio 67*), on the Testaccio area. On the same street are the more sedate music clubs *Caruso Caffé* at No 36 and *Caffé Latino* at No 96, both generally offering jazz or blues. More jazz and blues can be heard at *Alexanderplatz* (*Via Ostia 9*) and *Big Mama* (*Via San Francesco a Ripa 18*) in Trastevere. *Circolo degli Artisti* (*Via Lamarmora 28*), near Piazza Vittorio Emanuele, is a lively club, popular among Rome's hip set.

Roman discos are outrageously expensive. Expect to pay up to L30,000 to get in, which may or may not include one drink. Perennials include *Alien* (*Via Velletri 13*), *Piper '90* (*Via Tagliamento 9*) and *Gilda-Swing* (*Via Mario de' Fiori 97*). The best gay disco is *L'Alibi* (*Via di Monte Testaccio 44*).

Exhibitions & Concerts

From November to May, opera is performed at the *Teatro dell'Opera* (☎ *06 481 70 03, Piazza Beniamino Gigli*). A season of concerts is held in October and November at the *Accademia di Santa Cecilia* (*Via della Conciliazione 4*) and the *Accademia Filarmonica* (*Via Flaminia 118*). A series of concerts is held from July to the end of September at the *Teatro di Marcello* (*Via Teatro di Marcello 44*) near Piazza Venezia. For information call ☎ 06 482 74 03.

Rock concerts are held throughout the year. For information and bookings, contact the ORBIS agency (☎ *06 482 74 03*) in Piazza Esquilino near Stazione Termini.

Bars

Vineria in Campo de' Fiori, also known as Giorgio's, has a wide selection of wine and beers. In summer it has tables outside, but prices are steep – better to stand at the bar. *Bar della Pace* (*Via della Pace 3-7*) is big with the trendy crew, but being hip has a price. *Bevitoria Navona* (*Piazza Navona 72*) has wine by the glass. In Trastevere, the slacker-alternative set seems to prefer *Bar San Calisto (Piazza San Calisto)*, probably because you don't have to pay extra to sit at the outside tables. Near Piazza Santa Maria Maggiore, *The Druid's Den (Via San Martino ai Monti 28)* is a popular Irish pub, which means you can get Guinness and Kilkenny on tap.

SHOPPING

It is probably advisable to stick to window-shopping in the expensive Ludovisi district, the area around Via Veneto. The major fashion shops are in Via Sistina and Via Gregoriana, heading towards the Spanish Steps. Via Condotti and the parallel streets heading from Piazza di Spagna to Via del Corso are lined with moderately expensive clothing and footwear boutiques, as well as shops selling accessories.

It is cheaper, but not as interesting, to shop along Via del Tritone and Via Nazionale. There are some interesting second-hand clothes shops along Via del Governo Vecchio.

If clothes don't appeal, wander through the streets around Via Margutta, Via Ripetta, Piazza del Popolo and Via Frattina to look at the art galleries, artists' studios and antiquarian shops. Antique shops line Via Coronari, between Piazza Navona and Lungotevere di Tor di Nona.

Everyone flocks to the famous Porta Portese market every Sunday morning. Hundreds of stalls selling anything you can imagine line the streets of the Porta Portese area parallel to Viale di Trastevere, near Trastevere. Take time to rummage through the piles of clothing and bric-a-brac and you will find some incredible bargains. Catch tram No 8 from Largo Argentina and ask the driver where to get off (it's a 10-minute ride).

The market on Via Sannio, near Porta San Giovanni, sells new and second-hand clothes and shoes at bargain prices.

GETTING THERE & AWAY
Air

The main airline offices are in the area around Via Veneto and Via Barberini, north of Stazione Termini. Qantas, British Airways, Alitalia, Air New Zealand, Lufthansa and Singapore Airlines are all on Via Bissolati. The main airport is Leonardo da Vinci, at Fiumicino (see the Getting Around section).

Bus

The main terminal for intercity buses is in Piazzale Tiburtina, in front of the Stazione Tiburtina. Catch the Metropolitana Linea B from Termini to Tiburtina. Buses connect with cities throughout Italy. Numerous companies, some of which are listed here, operate these services. For information about which companies operate services to which destinations and from where, go to the APT office, or Enjoy Rome (see Tourist Offices). At Eurojet (☎ 06 481 74 55, fax 06 474 45 21, @ eurojet@adv.it), Piazza della Repubblica 54, you can buy tickets for and get information about several bus services. Otherwise, there are ticket offices for all of the companies inside the Tiburtina station. COTRAL buses, which service Lazio, depart from numerous points throughout the city, depending on their destinations.

Some useful bus lines are:

COTRAL (☎ 167-43 17 84) Via Ostiense 131 – services throughout Lazio
Lazzi (☎ 06 884 08 40) Via Tagliamento 27b – services to other European cities (Eurolines) and the Alps
Marozzi (information at Eurojet) – services to Bari and Brindisi, as well as to Pompeii, Sorrento and the Amalfi Coast and Matera in Basilicata
SAIS & Segesta (☎ 06 481 96 76) Piazza della Repubblica 42 – services to Sicily
SENA (information at Eurojet) – service to Siena
SULGA (information at Eurojet) – services to Perugia and Assisi

Train

Almost all trains arrive at and depart from Stazione Termini. There are regular connections to all major cities in Italy and throughout Europe. For train timetable information phone ☎ 147 88 80 88 (from 7 am to 9 pm), or go to the information office at the station (English is spoken). Timetables can be bought at most newsstands in and around Termini and are particularly useful if you are travelling mostly by train. Services at Termini include telephones, money exchange (see the earlier Information section) and luggage storage (☎ 147 30 62 75; L5000 per piece every six hours, beside track 22). Some trains depart from the stations Ostiense and at Tiburtina.

ITALY

Car & Motorcycle

The main road connecting Rome to the north and south is the Autostrada del Sole A1, which extends from Milan to Reggio di Calabria. On the outskirts of the city it connects with the Grande Raccordo Anulare (GRA), the ring road encircling Rome. If you are entering or leaving Rome, use the Grande Raccordo and the major feeder roads which connect it to the city; it might be longer, but it is simpler and faster. From the Grande Raccordo there are 33 exits into Rome. If you're approaching from the north, take the Via Salaria, Via Nomentana or Via Flaminia exits. From the south, Via Appia Nuova, Via Cristoforo Colombo and Via del Mare (which connects Rome to the Lido di Ostia) all provide reasonably direct routes into the city. The A12 connects the city to Civitavecchia and to Fiumicino airport.

Car rental offices at Stazione Termini in Rome include Avis (☎ 06 419 99/98), Hertz (☎ 06 321 68 31) and Maggiore (☎ 147 86 70 67). All have offices at both airports. Happy Rent (☎ 06 481 81 85), Via Farini 3, rents scooters and bicycles (with baby seats available), as well as some cars and video cameras. It also offers a free baggage deposit and a free email service to its customers. It has a Web site at www.happyrent.com. Another option for scooters and bicycles is I Bike Rome (☎ 06 322 52 40), Via Veneto 156.

Boat

Tirrenia and the Ferrovie dello Stato (FS) ferries leave for various points in Sardinia (see Sardinia's Getting There & Away section) from Civitavecchia. A Tirrenia fast ferry leaves from Fiumicino, near Rome, and Civitavecchia. Bookings can be made at Sestante CIT, or any travel agency displaying the Tirrenia or FS sign. You can also book directly with Tirrenia (☎ 06 474 20 41), Via Bissolati 41, Rome; or at the Stazione Marittima (ferry terminal) at the ports. Bookings can be made at Stazione Termini for FS ferries.

GETTING AROUND
To/From the Airport

The main airport is Leonardo da Vinci (☎ 06 65 95 36 40 for flights only) at Fiumicino. Access to the city is via the airport-Stazione Termini direct train (follow the signs to the station from the airport arrivals hall), which costs L16,000. The train arrives at and leaves from platform No 22 at Termini and there is a ticket office on the platform. The trip takes 35 minutes. The first train leaves the airport for Termini at 7.37 am and the last at 10.07 pm. Another train makes stops along the way, including at Trastevere and Ostiense, and terminates at Stazione Tiburtina (L8000). The trip takes about 50 minutes. A night bus runs from Stazione Tirburtina to the airport from 12.30 to 3.45 am, stopping at Termini at the corner of Via Giolitti about 10 minutes later. The airport is connected to Rome by an autostrada, accessible from the Grande Raccordo Anulare (ring road).

Taxis are prohibitively expensive from the airport – don't even bother.

The other airport is Ciampino, which is used for most domestic and international charter. Blue COTRAL buses (running from 6.50 am to 11.40 pm) connect with the Metropolitana (Linea A at Anagnina), where you can catch the subway to Termini or the Vatican. But if you arrive very late at night, you could end up being forced to catch a taxi. A metropolitan train line, the FM4, connects Termini with the Ciampino airport and Albano Laziale. The airport is connected to Rome by Via Appia Nuova.

Bus

The city bus company is ATAC (☎ 167 43 17 84 for information in English). Details on which buses head where are available at the ATAC information booth in the centre of Piazza dei Cinquecento. Another central point for main bus routes in the centre is Largo Argentina, on Corso Vittorio Emanuele south of the Pantheon. Buses run from 5.30 am to midnight, with limited services throughout the night on some routes. A fast tram service, the No 8, connects Largo Argentina with Trastevere, Porta Portese and the suburb of Monte Verde.

Rome has an integrated public transport system, so you can use the same ticket for the bus, subway and suburban railway. Tickets cost L1500 and are valid for 75 minutes. They must be purchased *before* you get on the bus and validated in the orange machine as you enter. The fine for travelling without a ticket is L100,000, to be paid on the spot, and there is no sympathy for 'dumb tourists'.

Tickets can be purchased at any tobacconist, newsstand, or at the main bus terminals. Daily tickets cost L6000 and weekly tickets cost L24,000.

Metropolitana

The Metropolitana (Metro) has two lines, A and B. Both pass through Stazione Termini. Take Linea A for Piazza di Spagna, the Vatican (Ottaviano) and Villa Borghese (Flaminio), and Linea B for the Colosseum, Circus Maximus and Piramide (for Testaccio and Stazione Ostiense). Tickets are the same as for city buses (see under Bus in this section). Trains run approximately every five minutes between 5.30 am and 11.30 pm (12.30 am on Saturday).

Taxi

Taxis are on radio call 24 hours a day in Rome. Cooperativa Radio Taxi Romana (☎ 06 35 70) and La Capitale (☎ 06 49 94) are two of the many operators. Major taxi ranks are at the airports, Stazione Termini and Largo Argentina in the historical centre. There are surcharges for luggage (L2000 per item), night service (L5000), Sunday and public holidays (L2000) and travel to/from Fiumicino airport (L14,000/11,500). The flag fall is L4500 (for the first 3km), then L1200 for every kilometre. There is a L5000 supplement from 10 pm to 7 am and L2000 from 7 am to 10 pm on Sunday and public holidays.

Car & Motorcycle

Negotiating Roman traffic by car is difficult enough, but you are taking your life in your hands if you ride a motorcycle in the city. The rule in Rome is to watch the vehicles in front and never take for granted that the vehicles behind are watching you. Pedestrians should watch out for motorcycles, which never seem to stop at red lights.

If your car goes missing after being parked illegally, check with the traffic police (☎ 06 676 91). It will cost about L180,000 to get it back plus L15,600 for each day it has been in the police yard.

A major parking area close to the centre is at the Villa Borghese. Entrance is from Piazzale Brasile at the top of Via Veneto. There is a supervised car park at Stazione Termini. There are large car parks at Stazione Tiburtina and Piazza dei Partigiani at Stazione Ostiense

(both accessible to the centre of Rome by the Metro). See the preceding Getting There & Away section for information about car, scooter and bike rental.

Around Rome

OSTIA ANTICA

The Romans founded this port city at the mouth of the Tiber in the 4th century BC and it became a strategically important centre of defence and trade. It was populated by merchants, sailors and slaves, and the ruins of the city provide a fascinating contrast to a place such as Pompeii. It was abandoned after barbarian invasions and the appearance of malaria, but Pope Gregory IV re-established the city in the 9th century.

The Rome EPT office or Enjoy Rome can provide information about the ancient city, or call the ticket office on ☎ 06 56 35 80 99.

Things to See

Of particular note in the excavated city are the mosaics of the **Terme di Nettuno** (Baths of Neptune); a **Roman theatre** built by Augustus; the **forum** and **temple**, dedicated to Jupiter, Juno and Minerva; and the **Piazzale delle Corporazioni**, where you can see the offices of Roman merchants, distinguished by mosaics depicting their trades. The site is open 9 am to 7 pm (last admission 6 pm) Tuesday to Sunday and entry is L8000.

Getting There & Away

To get to Ostia Antica take the Metropolitana Linea B to Magliana and then the Ostia Lido train (getting off at Ostia Antica). By car, take the SS8bis (aka Via del Mare) or Via Ostiense.

TIVOLI
pop 52,372

Set on a hill by the Anio River, Tivoli was a resort town of the ancient Romans and became popular as a summer playground for the rich during the Renaissance. It is famous today for the terraced gardens and fountains of the Villa d'Este and the ruins of the spectacular Villa Adriana, built by the Roman emperor Hadrian.

The local tourist office (☎ 0774 33 45 22) is in Largo Garibaldi near the COTRAL bus stop.

ITALY

Things to See

Hadrian built his summer villa, **Villa Adriana**, in the 2nd century AD. Its construction was influenced by the architecture of the famous classical buildings of the day. It was successively plundered by barbarians and Romans for building materials and many of its original decorations were used to embellish the Villa d'Este. However, enough remains to give an idea of the incredible size and magnificence of the villa. You will need about four hours to wander through the vast ruins.

Highlights include La Villa dell'Isola (the Villa of the Island) where Hadrian spent his pensive moments, the Imperial Palace and its Piazza d'Oro (Golden Square), and the floor mosaics of the Hospitalia. The villa is open 9 am to about one hour before sunset daily (around 7.30 pm; last entry at 6.30 pm) between April and September. Entry is L8000.

The Renaissance **Villa d'Este** was built in the 16th century for Cardinal Ippolito d'Este on the site of a Franciscan monastery. The villa's beautiful gardens are decorated with numerous fountains, which are its main attraction. Opening hours are the same as for Villa Adriana and entry is L8000. Both villas are closed on Monday.

Getting There & Away

Tivoli is about 40km east of Rome and accessible by COTRAL bus. Take Metro Linea B from Stazione Termini to Ponte Mammolo; the bus leaves from outside the station every 20 minutes. The bus also stops near the Villa Adriana, about 1km from Tivoli. Otherwise, catch local bus No 4 from Tivoli's Piazza Garibaldi to Villa Adriana.

TARQUINIA

pop 14, 020

Believed to have been founded in the 12th century BC and to have been the home of the Tarquin kings who ruled Rome before the creation of the republic, Tarquinia was an important economic and political centre of the Etruscan League. The major attractions here are the painted tombs of its *necropoli* (burial grounds). The IAT tourist information office (☎ 0766 85 63 84) is at Piazza Cavour 1.

Things to See

The 15th-century Palazzo Vitelleschi houses the **Museo Nazionale Tarquiniense** and an excellent collection of Etruscan treasures, including frescoes removed from the tombs. There are also numerous sarcophagi that were found in the tombs. The museum is open 9 am to 7 pm Tuesday to Sunday. Entry is L8000 and the same ticket covers entry to the **necropolis**, a 15 to 20-minute walk away (or catch one of four daily buses). The necropolis has the same opening hours as the museum. Ask at the tourist office for directions. The tombs are richly decorated with frescoes, though many are seriously deteriorated.

Places to Stay & Eat

Tarquinia has limited (and overpriced) accommodation, so it is best visited as a day trip from Rome. If you must stay, remember to book well in advance. The nearest camp site is *Tusca Tirrenica* (☎ 0766 86 42 94), Viale Nereidi, 5km from the town. *Hotel Miramare* (☎ 0766 86 40 20, Viale dei Tirreni 36) is in the newer part of town, about a 10-minute walk downhill from the medieval centre. Singles/doubles with private bath cost L90,000/140,000.

For a good, cheap meal, try *Cucina Casareccia (Via G Mazzini 5)*, off Piazza Cavour, or the *Trattoria Arcadia* opposite at No 6.

Getting There & Away

Buses leave approximately every hour for Tarquinia from Via Lepanto in Rome, near the Metropolitana Linea A Lepanto stop, arriving at Tarquinia a few steps away from the tourist office. You can also catch a train from Ostiense, but Tarquinia's station is at Tarquinia Lido (beach), approximately 3km from the centre. You will then need to catch one of the regular local buses.

CERVETERI

Ancient Caere was founded by the Etruscans in the 8th century BC and enjoyed a period of great prosperity as a maritime centre from the 7th to 5th centuries BC. The main attractions here are the tombs known as *tumoli*, great mounds with carved stone bases. Treasures taken from the tombs can be seen in the Vatican Museums, the Villa Giulia Museum

ITALY

and the Louvre. The Pro Loco tourist office is at Piazza Risorgimento 19.

The main necropolis area, **Banditaccia**, is open 9 am to 6 pm daily, while in winter it closes one hour before sunset. Entry is L8000. You can wander freely once inside the area, though it is best to follow the recommended routes in order to see the best preserved tombs. Banditaccia is accessible by local bus in summer only from the main piazza in Cerveteri, but it is also a pleasant 3km walk west from the town.

Cerveteri is accessible from Rome by COTRAL bus from Via Lepanto, outside the Lepanto stop on Metropolitana Linea A.

Northern Italy

Italy's affluent north is capped by the Alps and bound by the beaches of Liguria and lagoons of Venice, with the gently undulating Po River plain at its heart. Venice and Milan are the big drawcards, but leave room for the historic cities and towns of Piedmont, Lombardy, Emilia-Romagna and the Veneto.

GENOA
pop 950,849
Travellers who write off Genoa (Genova) as simply another seedy port town, bypassing the city for the coastal resorts, do the town a disservice. This once-powerful maritime republic, birthplace of Christopher Columbus (1451-1506) and now capital of the region of Liguria, can still carry the title La Superba. It is a city of contrasts, where humble backstreets lead onto grand thoroughfares and piazzas lined with marble and stucco palaces.

Orientation
Most trains stop at Genoa's two main stations, Principe and Brignole. The area around Brignole is closer to the city centre and a better bet for accommodation than Principe, which is close to the port. Women travelling alone should avoid the port area at night.

From Brignole walk straight ahead along Via Fiume to get to Via XX Settembre and the historical centre. Walking around Genoa is easier than using the local ATM bus service, but most useful buses stop outside both stations.

Information
Tourist Offices The main IAT tourist information office (☎ 010 24 87 11, fax 010 246 76 58, @ aptgenova@apt.genova.it) is on the waterfront at Via del Porto Antico, in the Palazzina Santa Maria building. It's open 9 am to 6.30 pm daily. There are branches at Stazione Principe and the airport (open 8 am to 8 pm Monday to Saturday; the Stazione Principe office also opens 9 am to noon on Sunday).

Post & Communications The main post office is in Via Dante, just off Piazza de Ferrari. You'll also find public phones here. There is a Telecom office to the left of Stazione Brignole on Piazza Verdi, open from 8 am to 9 pm daily. Genoa's postcode is 16100.

Medical & Emergency Services The Ospedale San Martino (☎ 010 55 51) is in Via Benedetto XV. In an emergency, call ☎ 118 for an ambulance and ☎ 113 for the police.

Things to See & Do
Start by wandering around the labyrinthine old port area, searching out the 12th-century, black-and-white marble **Cattedrale di San Lorenzo** and the **Palazzo Ducale** in Piazza Matteotti. The palaces of the Doria family, one of the city's most important families in the 14th and 15th centuries, can be found in **Piazza San Matteo**. To see some of the city's other palaces, take a walk along **Via Garibaldi**, which is lined with grand buildings. Several are open to the public and contain art galleries, including the 16th-century **Palazzo Bianco** and 17th-century **Palazzo Rosso**. Italian and Flemish Renaissance works are displayed in the **Galleria Nazionale di Palazzo Spinola**, Piazza Superiore di Pellicceria 1. The gallery is open 9 am to 7 pm Tuesday to Saturday (from 2 pm on Sunday); entry is L8000.

Genoa's **aquarium** is Europe's biggest, and well worth a visit. It's on the waterfront at Ponte Spinola and opens 9.30 am to 7 pm Monday to Friday and until 8 pm on weekends (11 pm on Thursday in summer and closed on Monday in winter). Admission is L19,000.

Places to Stay
The HI *Ostello Genova* (☎ *010 242 24 57,* @ *hostelge@iol.it*) is at Via Costanzi 120 in Righi, just outside Genoa. B&B costs L23,000

ITALY

and an evening meal of pasta is L5000. Catch bus No 40 from Stazione Brignole.

On the 3rd floor of a gracious old palazzo near Stazione Brignole, **Carola** (*☎ 010 839 13 40, Via Gropallo 4*) has a family atmosphere and pleasant singles/doubles/triples with shower for L45,000/75,000/100,000. To get there, turn right as you leave the station, walk up Via de Amicis to Piazza Brignole and turn right onto Via Gropallo. **Albergo Rita** (*☎/fax 010 87 02 07*), a few doors up at No 8, has singles for L50,000/75,000 and doubles for L75,000/90,000 without/with bathroom.

Splash out a little at **Hotel Bel Soggiorno** (*☎ 010 54 28 80, fax 010 58 14 18, Via XX Settembre 19*), where chintzy rooms with bathroom, TV and minibar start at L85,000/110,000. One of the city's grandest establishments is the **Bristol Palace** (*☎ 010 59 25 41, fax 010 56 17 56, Via XX Settembre 35*), where rooms with all the trimmings are L185,000/330,000.

Places to Eat

Don't leave town without trying *pesto genovese*, *pansoti* (ravioli in walnut sauce), *farinata* (a Tuscan torte made with chickpea flour) and, of course, *focaccia*. Plenty of shops sell sandwiches and pizza by the slice in the Brignole and port areas. For seafood, head to the **Via Sottoripo arcades** on the waterfront; at No 113 the takeaway fried calamari, sardines and zucchini cost around L4000.

The basic but authentic **Trattoria Da Maria** (*Vico Testa d'Oro 14*), off Via XXV Aprile, offers a full meal including wine for L13,000. Hidden away at Vico degli Orefici 5, **La Santa** has a reputation for good regional cooking; the tourist menu is L20,000 (not including drinks) and pasta starts at L8000.

Entertainment

The Genoa Theatre Company performs at the **Politeama Genovese** (*☎ 010 839 35 89*) and the **Teatro della Corte** (*☎ 010 534 22 00*). **Teatro della Tosse in Sant'Agostino** (*☎ 010 247 07 93, Piazza R Negri 4*) has a season of diverse shows from October to May.

Getting There & Away

Air Cristoforo Colombo airport at Sestri Ponente, 6km west of the city, has regular domestic and international connections. The Volabus (*☎ 010 558 24 14*) airport bus service leaves from Piazza Verdi, just outside Stazione Brignole, and also stops at Stazione Principe. Service is half-hourly from 5.30 am to 11 pm.

Bus Buses for Rome, Florence, Milan and Perugia leave from Piazza della Vittoria, south of Stazione Brignole. Eurolines buses leave from the same piazza for Barcelona, Madrid and Paris. Book at Geotravels (*☎ 010 58 71 81*) in the piazza.

Train Genoa is connected by train to major cities. For train information call *☎ 147 88 80 88*.

Boat The city's busy port is a major embarkation point for ferries to Sicily, Sardinia and Corsica. Major companies are Corsica Ferries (*☎ 019 21 55 11 in Savona*); Moby Lines (*☎ 010 25 27 55*) at Ponte Asserato (for Corsica); Tirrenia (*☎ 010 254 30 58*) at the Stazione Marittima, Ponte Colombo (for Sicily and Sardinia); and Grandi Navi Veloci and Grandi Traghetti (*☎ 010 58 93 31*) at Via Fieschi 17 (for Sardinia, Sicily, Malta and Tunisia). For more information, see the Getting There & Away sections under Sicily and Sardinia, and under Corsica in the France chapter.

RIVIERA DI LEVANTE

The Ligurian coastal region from Genoa to La Spezia (on the border with Tuscany) rivals the Amalfi Coast in its spectacular beauty. Several of the resorts have managed to remain relatively unspoiled, despite attracting thousands of summer tourists. There's a chance of suitable beach weather in both spring and autumn.

There are IAT tourist offices in most of the towns, including Santa Margherita Ligure (*☎ 0185 28 74 86, fax 0185 29 02 22*), Via XXV Aprile 4 in the town centre, and in La Spezia (*☎ 0187 77 09 00, fax 0187 77 09 08*), near the waterfront at Via Mazzini 45. They can advise on accommodation, which is often hard to find.

Things to See & Do

Pretty Santa Margherita Ligure is a good base from which to explore the nearby resorts of **Portofino**, a haunt of the rich and famous,

ITALY

and **Camogli**, a fishing village turned resort town, just a short bus ride away. The medieval Benedictine monastery of **San Fruttuoso** is a 2½-hour hilly walk from Camogli or Portofino, with sensational views along the way; you may want to catch the ferry back.

The five tiny coastal villages of the **Cinque Terre** – Riomaggiore, Manorola, Corniglia, Vernazza and Monterosso – are easily reached by train from La Spezia. Linked by unforgettably scenic walking and hiking tracks, these once-secluded mountainside fishing and wine-growing villages are attracting increasing numbers of visitors.

Places to Stay & Eat

Santa Margherita's *Nuova Riviera* (☎/fax 0185 28 74 03, ☻ gisabin@tin.it, Via Belvedere 10) is an immaculate, nonsmoking, family-run hotel 15 minutes or so from the station (follow Via Roma to Piazza Mazzini). Singles/doubles/triples are around L110,000/125,000/155,000 (negotiable) with shower and breakfast; B&B accommodation is also offered. Nearby, *Albergo Annabella* (☎ 0185 28 65 31, Via Costasecca 10) has large rooms for L60,000/80,000. Right by the station, *Albergo Azalea* (☎ 0185 28 81 60, Via Roma 60) has rooms from L65,000/95,000 with bathroom.

The orderly and well-run *Ostello 5 Terre* (☎ 0187 92 02 15, ☻ ostello@cdh.it, Via B Riccobaldi 21) in Manorola has B&B from L25,000, and an evening meal for around L12,000; book well ahead.

In La Spezia, *Albergo Parma* (☎ 0187 74 30 10, fax 0187 74 32 40, Via Fiume 143) is opposite the station, with rooms from L75,000/90,000 with shower, TV and phone.

In Santa Margherita, *Trattoria San Siro* (Corso Matteotti 137) is about 15 minutes from the beach; a full meal costs around L35,000. La Spezia's many good trattorias include *La Tavernetta* (Via Fiume 57), with pizza or pasta for L9000, and *Dino* (Via Da Passano 17), for reasonably priced seafood near the seafront.

Getting There & Away

The entire coast is served by train and all points are accessible from Genoa. Buses leave from Santa Margherita's Piazza Martiri della Libertà for Portofino.

Boats leave from near the bus stop in Santa Margherita for Portofino (L10,000 return),

San Fruttuoso (L20,000) and the Cinque Terre (L35,000); from La Spezia to the Cinque Terre by boat it's L33,000.

TURIN
pop 962,507

Turin (Torino) is the capital of the Piedmont region. The House of Savoy, which ruled this region for hundreds of years (and Italy until 1945), built a gracious baroque city of boulevards, porticoes and arcades. Italy's industrial expansion began here with companies such as Fiat and Olivetti.

Orientation & Information

The Porta Nuova train station is the point of arrival for most travellers. To reach the city centre, cross Corso Vittorio Emanuele II and walk straight ahead through the grand Carlo Felice and San Carlo piazzas until you come to Piazza Castello. The tourist office is at Piazza Castello 161 (☎ 011 53 51 81, fax 011 53 00 70), open 9.30 am to 7 pm Monday to Saturday, and Sunday to 3 pm. There's also a branch at the Porta Nuova train station (☎ 011 53 13 27, fax 011 561 70 95).

Things to See

Piazza San Carlo, known as Turin's drawing room, is capped by the baroque churches of **San Carlo** and **Santa Cristina**. The centre of historical Turin is **Piazza Castello**, which features the sumptuous **Palazzo Madama**, home to the **Museo Civico d'Arte Antica**. The gardens of the adjacent 17th-century **Palazzo Reale** (Royal Palace) were designed in 1697 by Louis le Nôtre, whose other works include the gardens at Versailles.

The **Cattedrale di San Giovanni Battista**, west of the Palazzo Reale and off Via XX Settembre, houses the **Shroud of Turin**, the linen cloth believed to have been used to wrap the crucified Christ. Scientists have established that the shroud dates from the 12th century. The shroud is displayed for only a few days each year; for further details call ☎ 800 329 329. A reasonable copy is displayed in the cathedral, and a museum devoted to the legend of the shroud is at Via San Domenico 28, open 9 am to noon and 3 to 7 pm daily (L9000).

Turin's **Museo Egizio** (☎ 011 561 77 76), Via Accademia delle Scienze 6, is considered

ITALY

one of the best museums of ancient Egyptian art after those in London and Cairo. It opens 9 am to 7 pm Tuesday to Saturday (to 2 pm on Sunday); admission is L12,000.

Places to Stay & Eat

Turin has plenty of cheap, if a little run-down, accommodation.

Campeggio Villa Rey (☎ 011 819 01 17, *Strada Superiore Val San Martino 27)* opens March to October. *Ostello Torino* (☎ 011 660 29 39, Via Alby 1), on the corner of Via Gatti, is in the hills east of the Po River. Catch bus No 52 from the Porta Nuova station (No 64 on Sunday). B&B is L22,000 and a meal is L14,000.

The one-star *Canelli* (☎ 011 54 60 78, Via San Dalmazzo 5b), off Via Garibaldi, has bare singles/doubles/triples with shower for L40,000/55,000/66,000. The two-star *Albergo Magenta* (☎ 011 54 26 49, fax 011 54 47 55, Corso Vittorio Emanuele II 67) is near Porta Nuova station, and has singles/doubles for L50,000/75,000 or L90,000/120,000 with bathroom. In a great location, *San Carlo* (☎ 011 562 78 46, fax 011 53 86 53, Piazza San Carlo 197) has rooms with bathroom, TV and old-world style for L85,000/120,000. Not far away near Piazza Castello, *Hotel Venezia* (☎ 011 562 30 12, fax 011 562 37 26, Via XX Settembre 70) offers three-star luxury for L180,000/230,000.

One of Turin's better self-service restaurants is *La Grangia* (Via Garibaldi 21), where a full meal costs around L15,000.

At *Pizzeria alla Baita dei 7 Nani* (Via A Doria 5) you can grab a pizza and a beer for around L12,000. For gelati, head for *Caffè Fiorio* (Via Po 8); try the gooey *gianduia* (chocolate; L2500).

Getting There & Away

Turin is serviced by Caselle international airport (☎ 011 567 63 61), with flights to European and national destinations. Sadem (☎ 011 311 16 16) buses run to the airport every 45 minutes from the corner between Via Sacchi and Corso Vittorio Emanuele II, on the western side of the Porta Nuova train station. Sadem's intercity buses terminate at the main bus station at Corso Inghilterra 1, near Porta Susa train station. Buses serve the Valle d'Aosta, most of the towns and ski resorts in Piedmont and major Italian cities. Regular trains connect with Milan, Aosta, Venice, Genoa and Rome.

Getting Around

The city is well serviced by a network of buses and trams. A map of public-transport routes is available at the station information office.

MILAN

pop 1,308,000

The economic and fashion capital of Italy, Milan (Milano) has long been an elegant and cultural city. Its origins are believed to be Celtic, but it was conquered by the Romans in 222 BC and became a major trading and transport centre. From the 13th century the city flourished under the rule of two powerful families: the Visconti, followed by the Sforza.

Milan closes down almost completely in August, when most of the city's inhabitants take their annual holidays.

Orientation

From Milan's central train station (Stazione Centrale), it's easy to reach the centre of town on the efficient underground railway (known as the Metropolitana Milanese, or MM). The city of Milan is huge, but most sights are in the centre. Use the Duomo and the Castello Sforzesco as your points of reference; the main shopping areas and sights are around and between the two.

Information

Tourist Offices The main branch of the APT tourist office (☎ 02 72 52 43 01/02/03, fax 02 72 52 43 50) is at Via Marconi 1, in Piazza del Duomo, where you can pick up the useful city guides *Milan is Milano* (with a good map), *Hello Milan* and *Milano Mese*. The office is open 8.30 am to 7 pm Monday to Friday, 9 am to 1 pm and 2 to 6 pm on Saturday, and to 5 pm on Sunday. The branch office at Stazione Centrale (☎ 02 72 52 43 60), near the Telecom office, has useful listings in English posted outside.

Milan City Council operates an information office in Galleria Vittorio Emanuele II, open 8.30 am to 5 pm Monday to Friday, to 2.30 pm on Saturday.

Foreign Consulates Foreign consulates include Australia (☎ 02 777 04 21) at Via Borgogna 2, Canada (☎ 02 675 81) at Via Vittorio Pisani 19, France (☎ 02 655 91 41) at Via Mangili 1, the UK (☎ 02 72 30 01) at Via San Paolo 7 and the USA (☎ 02 29 03 51) at Via P Amedeo 2/10.

Money Banks in Milan open 8.30 am to 1.30 pm and 2.45 to 3.45 pm Monday to Friday. Exchange offices on Piazza Duomo include Banca Ponti at No 19, and there are offices open daily at Stazione Centrale. The American Express office (☎ 02 87 66 74) is at Via Brera 3 and opens 9 am to 5 pm Monday to Friday.

Post & Communications The main post office is at Via Cordusio 4, off Via Dante, near Piazza del Duomo, and is open 8 am to 7 pm Monday to Friday and 9.30 am to 1 pm on Saturday. Fermo posta is open from 8.15 am to 12.30 pm. There are also post offices at the station and at Linate airport.

There is a Telecom Italia telephone office in the upper level of Stazione Centrale, open 8 am to 8 pm daily; it has international telephone directories. The Telecom office in the Galleria has Internet access (L200 per minute), a fax machine and phonecards; it closes at 9.30 pm. Milan's postcode is 20100.

The Hard Disk Cafe at Corso Sempione 44 (www.hdc.it) was Milan's first cybercafe and it's still the best in town, with snacks, cocktails and 60 screens. For basic Internet access closer to the station, Boomerang on the corner of Via Gasparotto and F Filzi charges L3000 for 10 minutes, L8000 per half-hour.

Bookshops The American Bookstore, Via Campiero 16, provides a good selection of English-language books.

Laundry The Lavanderia Self-Service on Via Tadino charges L5000 or L10,000 for a megaload. It's open 7.30 am to 9.30 pm daily.

Medical & Emergency Services For an ambulance call ☎ 118. The public hospital, Ospedale Maggiore Policlinico (☎ 02 550 31), is at Via Francesco Sforza 35, close to the centre. There is an all-night pharmacy (☎ 02 669 09 35) in Stazione Centrale. In an emergency call the police on ☎ 113. The questura (police headquarters) for foreigners is at Via Montebello (☎ 02 62 26 34 00); English is spoken. For lost property call the Milan City Council (☎ 02 546 52 99) at Via Friuli 30.

Dangers & Annoyances Milan's main shopping areas are popular haunts for groups of thieves, who are as numerous here as in Rome and just as lightning-fast. They use the same technique of waving cardboard or newspaper in your face to distract you while they head for your pockets or purse. Be particularly careful in the piazza in front of the Stazione Centrale. Don't hesitate to make a racket if you are hassled.

Things to See & Do

Start with the extraordinary **Duomo**, begun in 1386 to an unusual French Gothic design. With its spiky marble facade shaped into pinnacles, statues and pillars, this tumultuous structure is certainly memorable – as is the view from the roof (stairs L6000, lift L9000).

Join the throngs and take a *passeggiata* through the magnificent **Galleria Vittorio Emanuele II** to **La Scala**, Milan's famed opera house. The theatre's **museum** is open 9 am to noon and 2 to 5.30 pm daily (closed on Sunday from November to April). Admission is L6000.

At the end of Via Dante is the immense **Castello Sforzesco**, originally a Visconti fortress and entirely rebuilt by Francesco Sforza in the 15th century. Its museum collections include furniture, artefacts and sculpture, notably Michelangelo's unfinished *Pietà Rondanini*. The castle is open 9.30 am to 5.30 pm Tuesday to Sunday. Admission is free.

Nearby on Via Brera is the 17th-century Palazzo di Brera, home to the **Pinacoteca di Brera**. This gallery's vast collection includes Mantegna's masterpiece, the *Dead Christ*, and is open 9 am to 5.45 pm Tuesday to Saturday, and on Sunday to 8 pm. Admission is L12,000.

Leonardo da Vinci's *Last Supper* can be viewed by prior appointment in the Cenacolo Vinciano, Piazza Santa Maria delle Grazie 2; phone ☎ 199 199 100 to make a booking. After centuries of damage from floods, heavy-handed restorations, bombing and decay, the recently restored fresco was unveiled in 1999

ITALY

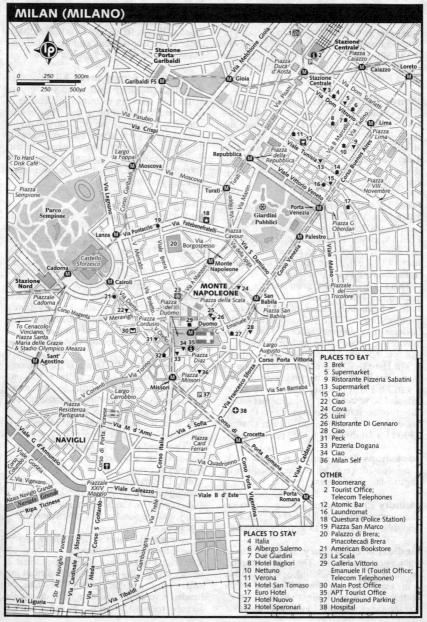

MILAN (MILANO)

PLACES TO EAT
3 Brek
5 Supermarket
9 Ristorante Pizzeria Sabatini
13 Supermarket
15 Ciao
22 Ciao
24 Cova
25 Luini
26 Ristorante Di Gennaro
28 Ciao
31 Peck
33 Pizzeria Dogana
34 Ciao
36 Milan Self

OTHER
1 Boomerang
2 Tourist Office;
   Telecom Telephones
12 Atomic Bar
16 Laundromat
18 Questura (Police Station)
19 Piazza San Marco
20 Palazzo di Brera;
   Pinacotecadi Brera
21 American Bookstore
23 La Scala
29 Galleria Vittorio
   Emanuele II (Tourist Office;
   Telecom Telephones)
30 Main Post Office
35 APT Tourist Office
37 Underground Parking
38 Hospital

PLACES TO STAY
4 Italia
6 Albergo Salerno
7 Due Giardini
8 Hotel Bagliori
10 Nettuno
11 Verona
14 Hotel San Tomaso
17 Euro Hotel
27 Hotel Nuovo
32 Hotel Speronari

ITALY

euro currency converter €1 = L1936

to a mixed reception: judge for yourself. The building is open Tuesday to Saturday from 9 am to 7 pm, Sunday to 8 pm. Admission is L12,000.

Special Events
St Ambrose's Day (7 December) is Milan's major festival, with celebrations at the Fiera di Milano (MM1: Amendola Fiera).

Places to Stay
Hostels The HI *Ostello Piero Rotta* (☎/*fax 02 39 26 70 95, Viale Salmoiraghi 1)* is north-west of the city centre; B&B is L26,000. Take the MM1 to the QT8 stop. The hostel is closed between 9 am and 3.30 pm, and lights out is 12.30 am. *Protezione della Giovane* (☎ *02 29 00 01 64, Corso Garibaldi 123)* is run by nuns for single women aged 16 to 25 years. Beds cost from L37,000 a night. Pre-booking is required.

Hotels Milan's hotels are among the most expensive and heavily booked in Italy, particularly due to trade fairs held in the city, so it's strongly recommended to book in advance. There are numerous budget hotels around Stazione Centrale, but the quality varies. The tourist office will make bookings, held by hotels for one hour.

Stazione Centrale & Corso Buenos Aires
One of Milan's nicest one-star hotels is *Due Giardini* (☎ *02 29 52 10 93, fax 02 29 51 69 33, Via B Marcello 47)*, with rooms overlooking a tranquil back garden; comfortable doubles are L150,000 with bathroom and TV. To get there turn right off Via D Scarlatti, which is to the left as you leave the station.

Budget options nearby on busy Via Dom Vitruvio, off Piazza Duca d'Aosta, include *Albergo Salerno* (☎ *02 204 68 70)* at No 18, with clean singles/doubles for L65,000/ 90,000 (add L30,000 for a bathroom). *Italia* (☎ *02 669 38 26)* at No 44 has less attractive rooms for L55,000/85,000; L90,000/130,000 with bathroom.

The no-frills *Nettuno* (☎ *02 29 40 44 81, Via Tadino 27)* has rooms with bathroom for L75,000/115,000. Near Piazza della Repubblica, *Verona* (☎ *02 66 98 30 91, Via Carlo Tenca 12)* has rooms for L80,000/150,000 with shower, satellite TV and telephone.

Just off Corso Buenos Aires, the friendly *Hotel San Tomaso* (☎ *02 29 51 47 47,* @ *hotelsantomaso@tin.it, Viale Tunisia 6)* on the 3rd floor has singles/doubles/triples for L60,000/100,000/135,000, all with shower and TV.

Closer to the centre, off Piazza G Oberdan, *Euro Hotel* (☎ *02 20 40 40 10,* @ *eurohotel.viasirtori@tin.it, Via Sirtori 26)* is a good bet, with modern rooms with shower, satellite TV and breakfast for L110,000/140,000/ 180,000.

For some three-star comfort, try the *Hotel Baglioni* (☎ *02 29 52 68 84, fax 02 29 52 68 42, Via Boscovich 43)*. Singles range seasonally from L140,000 to L220,000, doubles from L220,000 to L320,000.

The Centre In a great location near Piazza del Duomo, *Hotel Speronari* (☎ *02 86 46 11 25, fax 02 72 00 31 78, Via Speronari 4)* has comfortable singles/doubles for L75,000/110,000; L95,000/160,000 with bathroom. *Hotel Nuovo* (☎ *02 86 46 05 42, Piazza Beccaria 6)* is also in the thick of things, just off Corso Vittorio Emanuele II and the Duomo. Basic rooms cost L60,000/80,000, and a double with bathroom is L120,000.

Places to Eat
There are plenty of fast-food outlets and sandwich bars in the station and Duomo areas, extremely popular during the lunch-time rush.

For something less hectic, try one of the many trattorias or fill up on the snacks served in bars from around 5 pm.

Restaurants If you're looking for a traditional trattoria, try the side streets south of the station and along Corso Buenos Aires.

Around Stazione Centrale The *Ciao* outlet *(Corso Buenos Aires 7)* is part of a self-service chain (there are a multitude of others, including those surrounding the Duomo, on Corso Europa and at Via Dante 5), but the food is pretty good and relatively cheap. Pizza and pasta dishes cost from L5000 and salads start at around L4500. The *Brek* chain is a similar but superior alternative.

Ristorante Pizzeria Sabatini (Via Boscovich 54), around the corner from Corso Buenos

ITALY

Aires, serves imaginative pasta dishes such as gorgonzola with nuts (L13,000), as well as traditionally prepared meat and fish dishes; pizza is a speciality (from L9000).

City Centre The *Ristorante Di Gennaro* *(Via Santa Radegonda 14)* is reputed to be one of the city's first pizzerias, and the pizzas and focaccias are still excellent. *Pizzeria Dogana*, on the corner of Via Capellari and Via Dogana near the Duomo, has outside tables and pasta and pizza for around L10,000.

For a more authentic self-service experience, join the city workers at *Milan Self (Via Baracchini 9)*, with pasta for L6000 and salad at L4500. It's open for lunch Monday to Friday.

Cafes & Sandwich Bars The popular *Luini (Via Santa Radegonda 16)*, just off Piazza del Duomo, is one of Milan's oldest fast-food outlets and a favourite haunt of teenagers and students.

For a classy cuppa in elegant surroundings, head to *Cova (Via Monte Napoleone 8)*, established in 1817.

The best gourmet takeaway is *Peck*. Its rosticceria is at Via Cesare Cantù 3, where you can buy cooked meats and vegetables, and there's another outlet near the Duomo at Via Spadari 7-9.

Self-Catering There's a reasonable *supermarket* inside the station, as well as those close by at Via D Vitruvio 32 and on the corner of Via Lecco and F Casati.

Entertainment
Music, theatre and cinema dominate Milan's entertainment calendar. The opera season at *La Scala* opens on 7 December. For tickets go to the box office (☎ 02 72 00 37 44) in the portico in Via Filodrammatici, open noon to 6 pm daily, but don't expect a good seat unless you book well in advance.

Milan has a reasonable selection of bars, from the disco-pubs and wine bars surrounding Piazza San Marco to pricey bars such as *Atomic (Via Casati 24)*.

For football fans a visit to *Stadio Olympico Meazza* (in San Siro) is a must, with AC Milan and Inter Milan drawing crowds of up to 85,000. Ticket prices start at

around L25,000, and can be bought at branches of Cariplo (AC Milan) and Banca Popolare di Milano (Inter) banks.

Shopping
Looking good is more than just a Milanese pastime, but designer threads don't come cheap. Hit the main streets behind the Duomo around Corso Vittorio Emanuele II for clothing, footwear and accessories, or dream on and window-shop for couturier fashions in Via Monte Napoleone, Via Borgospesso and Via della Spiga.

The areas around Via Torino, Corso Buenos Aires and Corso XXII Marzo are less expensive. Markets are held around the canals (south-west of the centre), notably on Viale Papiniano on Tuesday and Saturday morning. A flea market is held in Viale Gabriele d'Annunzio each Saturday, and there's an antique market in Brera at Via Fiori Chiari every third Saturday of the month.

Getting There & Away
Air Most international flights use Malpensa airport, about 50km north-west of Milan. Domestic and European flights use Linate airport, about 7km east of the city. For flight information for the two airports call ☎ 02 74 85 22 00.

Bus Bus stations are scattered throughout the city, although some major companies use Piazza Castello as a terminal. Check with the APT.

Train Regular trains go from Stazione Centrale to Venice, Florence, Bologna, Genoa, Turin and Rome, as well as major cities throughout Europe. For timetable information call ☎ 147 88 80 88 or go to the busy office in Stazione Centrale (English is spoken), open from 7 am to 11 pm. Regional trains stop at Stazione Porta Garibaldi and Stazione Nord in Piazzale Cadorna on the MM2 line.

Car & Motorcycle Milan is the major junction of Italy's motorways, including the Autostrada del Sole (A1) to Rome, the Milano-Torino (A4), the Milano-Genova (A7) and the Serenissima (A4) for Verona and Venice, and the A8 and A9 north to the lakes and the Swiss border.

ITALY

All these roads meet with the Milan ring road, known as the Tangenziale Est and Tangenziale Ovest (the east and west bypasses). From here follow the signs which lead into the centre. The A4 in particular is an extremely busy road, where an accident can hold up traffic for hours. In winter all roads in the area become extremely hazardous because of rain, snow and fog.

Getting Around

To/From the Airport STAM airport shuttle buses leave for Linate airport from Piazza Luigi di Savoia, on the east side of Stazione Centrale, every 30 minutes from 5.40 am to 9 pm (25 minutes, L5000). Airpullman Service runs shuttle buses from the same piazza to Malpensa airport every 20 minutes from 5.20 am to 10 pm (50 minutes, L13,000). Buses link the airports hourly from 4 am to 11.30 pm.

The Malpensa Express train links Malpensa airport with Cadorna underground station in the centre of Milan. Trains leave Cadorna from 5 am to 11.10 pm, and Malpensa from 6 am to 1.30 am. The journey takes 40 minutes and tickets cost L15,000.

Bus & Metro Milan's public transport system is extremely efficient, with underground (MM), tram and bus services. Tickets are L1500, valid for one underground ride and/or 75 minutes on buses and trams.

You can buy tickets in the MM stations, as well as at authorised tobacconists and newsstands.

Taxi Taxis won't stop if you hail them in the street – head for the taxi ranks, all of which have telephones. A few of the radio taxi companies serving the city are Radiotaxidata (☎ 02 53 53), Prontotaxi (☎ 02 52 51), Autoradiotaxi (☎ 02 85 85) and Arco (☎ 02 67 67).

Car & Motorcycle Entering central Milano by car is a hassle. The city is dotted with expensive car parks (look for the blue sign with a white 'P'). A cheaper alternative is to use one of the supervised car parks at the last stop on each MM line. In the centre there are private garages that charge around L4000 per hour (L6000 first hour). Hertz, Avis, Maggiore and Europcar all have offices at Stazione Centrale.

MANTUA
pop 53,065
Mantua (Mantova) is closely associated with the Gonzaga family, who ruled from the 14th to 18th centuries. The powerful family embellished the city with sumptuous palaces, built to impress and amuse, making Mantua a byword for courtly excess. As a result, the city is also known for its master works by painter Andrea Mantegna and architect Giulio Romano, who were summoned to work for the Gonzaga. You can easily visit the city on a day trip from Milan, Verona or Bologna.

Information
The APT tourist office (☎ 0376 32 82 53), Piazza Andrea Mantegna 6, is a 10-minute walk from the station along Corso Vittorio Emanuele, which becomes Corso Umberto 1. The office is open 8.30 am to 12.30 pm and 3 to 6 pm Monday to Saturday and 9.30 am to 12.30 pm on Sunday.

Things to See
Mantua's **Piazza Sordello** is surrounded by impressive buildings, including the eclectic **cattedrale**, which combines a Romanesque tower, baroque facade and Renaissance interior. The piazza is dominated by the massive **Palazzo Ducale**, former seat of the Gonzaga family. The palace has more than 500 rooms and courtyards, but its showpieces are the Gonzaga apartments and art collection, and the **Camera degli Sposi** (Bridal Chamber), with frescoes by Mantegna. The palace is open 9 am to 6 pm Tuesday to Sunday. Admission is L12,000.

Don't miss the Gonzaga's lavishly decorated summer palace, **Palazzo del Tè**, completed in 1534 by the master of Mannerism, Giulio Romano. It's open 9 am to 5.30 pm Tuesday to Sunday. Admission is L12,000.

Places to Stay & Eat
There are camping sites 2km from Mantua at *Corte Chiara* (☎ 0376 39 08 04) and 7km from town at *Sacchini* (☎ 0376 44 87 63), priced at around L20,000 per person. In Mantua, *Albergo ABC* (☎ 0376 32 33 47, *Piazza Don Leoni 25*) has singles/doubles with bathroom and breakfast for L100,000/140,000.

For cheap but good pizza or pasta head to *Pizzeria Capri* (*Via Bettinelli 8*), opposite the

ITALY

station, or **La Masseria** *(Piazza Broletto 7)*. For finer dining, **Ristorante Pavesi** *(Piazza delle Erbe 13)* serves full meals for around L40,000.

Getting There & Away
Mantua is accessible by train and bus from Verona (about 40 minutes), and by train from Milan and Bologna with a change at Modena.

VERONA
pop 255,824
Forever associated with Romeo and Juliet, Verona has much more to offer than the fabricated relics of a tragic love story. Once an important Roman city, Verona reached its peak under the rule of the della Scala (also known as the Scaligeri) family in the 13th and 14th centuries, a period noted for the savage family feuding on which Shakespeare based his play.

Orientation & Information
Buses leave for the historical centre from outside the train station; otherwise, it's a 20-minute walk, heading right to leave the bus station, crossing the river and walking along Corso Porta Nuova to Piazza Brà. From there take Via Mazzini and turn left at Via Cappello to reach Piazza delle Erbe.

The main APT tourist office (☎ 045 806 86 80, ✆ veronapt@tin.it) is at Via degli Alpina 9, facing Piazza Brà. It's open 9 am to 6 pm Monday to Saturday (to 8 pm and on Sunday to 2.30 pm from July to September). The branch at the train station (☎ 045 800 08 61) is open from 7 am to 9 pm.

The main post office is on Piazza Viviani. The Ospedale Civile Maggiore (☎ 045 807 11 11) is at Piazza A Stefani.

Things to See & Do
Piazza Brà's Roman amphitheatre, known as the **Arena**, was built in the 1st century and is now Verona's opera house.

Walk along Via Mazzini to Via Cappello and **Juliet's House** (Casa di Giulietta), its entrance smothered with lovers' graffiti. Further along the street to the right is **Porta Leoni**, one of the gates to the old Roman Verona; **Porta Borsari**, the other gate to the city, is north of the Arena at Corso Porta Borsari.

Piazza delle Erbe, the former site of the Roman forum, is lined with Verona's characteristic pink marble palaces and filled with market stalls. The piazza remains the lively heart of the city. Just off the square is the elegant **Piazza dei Signori**, flanked by the medieval town hall, the Renaissance **Loggia del Consiglio** and the della Scala (Scaligeri) residence, partly decorated by Giotto and nowadays known as the **Governor's Palace**. Take a look at the **Duomo**, on Via Duomo, for its Romanesque main doors and Titian's glorious *Assumption*.

Places to Stay & Eat
The lovingly restored HI **Ostello Villa Francescatti** (☎ 045 59 03 60, fax 800 91 27, Salita Fontana del Ferro 15) has B&B for L22,000 (including sheets) and dinner for L14,000. An HI or student card is necessary. The **camping ground** (L10,000 per person with your own tent) next door is run by the hostel management. To get there catch bus No 73 from the station to Piazza Isolo and follow the signs.

Albergo Castello (☎/fax 045 800 44 03, Corso Cavour 43) has singles/doubles with shower for L90,000/140,000; the entrance is around the corner. **Albergo Ciopeta** (☎ 045 800 68 43, ✆ ciopeta@iol.it, Vicolo Teatro Filarmonico 2), just off Piazza Brà, has quaint rooms for L80,000/130,000. For some three-star luxury, **Antica Porta Leona** (☎ 045 59 54 99, fax 045 59 52 14, Corticella Leoni 3) has well-appointed rooms for around L140,000/200,000.

Boiled meats are a Veronese speciality, as is the crisp Soave white wine. Both the Castello and Ciopeta hotels have well-priced restaurants. **Pizzeria Liston** *(Via dietro Liston 19)* has good pizzas from L11,000 and a full meal for around L35,000. **Brek** in Piazza Brà has a view of the Arena and the usual cheap dishes from L8000.

Entertainment
Verona hosts musical and cultural events throughout the year, culminating in a season of opera and drama from July to September at the *Arena* (tickets from around L40,000). There is a lyric-symphonic season in winter at the 18th-century **Teatro Filarmonico** (☎ 045 800 28 80, Via dei Mutilati 4), just off

ITALY

Piazza Brà. Information is available from the Fondazione Arena di Verona (☎ 045 805 18 11), Piazza Brà 28. The box office (☎ 045 800 51 51) is at Via dietro Anfiteatro 6b, or book on the Web at www.arena.it.

Getting There & Away
The Verona-Villafranca airport (☎ 045 809 56 66) is just outside town and accessible by bus and train.

The main APT bus station is in the piazza in front of the train station, known as Porta Nuova. Buses leave for surrounding areas, including Mantua, Ferrara and Brescia.

Verona is on the Brenner Pass railway line to Austria and Germany, and is directly linked by train to Milan, Venice, Florence and Rome.

The city sits at the intersection of the Serenissima A4 (Milan-Venice) and the Brennero A22 autostrade.

Getting Around
The APT airport bus leaves from Porta Nuova and from Piazza Cittadella, off Corso Porta Nuova near Piazza Brà. Bus Nos 11, 12 and 13 connect the station with Piazza Brà, and Nos 72 and 73 go to Piazza delle Erbe.

If you arrive by car, you should have no trouble reaching the centre – simply follow the 'centro' signs. There are also signs marking the directions to most hotels. There's a free car park in Via Città di Nimes (near the train station) – a good bet, as parking in the centre is limited.

PADUA
pop 215,137
Although famous as the city of St Anthony and for its university, which is one of the oldest in Europe, Padua (Padova) is often merely seen as a convenient and cheap place to stay while visiting Venice. In fact the city offers a rich collection of art treasures, and its many piazzas and porticoed streets are a stress-free pleasure to explore.

Orientation & Information
It's a 15-minute walk from the train station to the centre of town, or you can take bus No 3 or 8 along Corso del Popolo (which becomes Corso Garibaldi).

The IAT tourist office (☎ 049 875 20 77, fax 049 875 50 08) at the station opens

9.15 am to 6.30 pm Monday to Saturday and 9 am to noon on Sunday.

The post office is at Corso Garibaldi 33 and there's a telephone office nearby (open 8 am to 9.30 pm). Padua's postcode is 35100.

Things to See
Thousands of pilgrims arrive in Padua every year to visit the **Basilica del Santo** in the hope that St Anthony, patron saint of Padua and of lost things, will help them find whatever it is they are looking for. The saint's tomb is in the basilica, along with artworks including the 14th-century frescoes and bronze sculptures by Donatello which adorn the high altar. Donatello's bronze equestrian statue, known as the *Gattamelata* (Honeyed Cat), is outside the basilica.

The **Musei Civici agli Eremitani** and **Cappella degli Scrovegni** are at Piazza Eremitani 8. The chapel's emotionally charged frescoes depicting the life of Christ were painted by Giotto between 1303 and 1305. The transcendent 38 panels are considered one of the world's greatest works of figurative art. The museum and chapel are open 9 am to 7 pm (to 6 pm in winter) Tuesday to Sunday; it's advisable to book in summer, and a combined ticket to both costs L10,000.

A combined L15,000 ticket (L10,000 for students) allows entry to the city's monuments and can be bought at any of the main sights.

Places to Stay & Eat
Padua has no shortage of budget hotels, but they fill up quickly in summer. The non-HI *Ostello della Città di Padova* (☎ 049 875 22 19, fax 049 65 42 10, Via A Aleardi 30) has B&B for L23,000. Take bus No 3, 8 or 12 from the station to Prato della Valle (a piazza about five minutes away) and then ask for directions.

Verdi (☎ 049 875 57 44, Via Dondi dell' Orologio 7) has clean singles/doubles for L40,000/64,000 and is in the university district off Via Dante. The two-star *Sant'Antonio* (☎ 049 875 13 93, fax 049 875 25 08, Via Santo Fermo 118), near the river and the northern end of Via Dante, has comfortable rooms with TV and phone for L95,000/120,000. In the heart of the old city, the *Leon Bianco* (☎ 049 875 08 14, fax 049 875 61 84, Piazzetta Pedrocchi 12) has three-star rooms for L115,000/170,000.

ITALY

Grab a snack at **Dalla Zita** (*Via Gorizia 16*), off Piazza Pedrocchi, where you'll be spoilt for choice with more than 100 sandwich fillings on offer. **Birroteca da Mario** (*Via Breda 3*), off Piazza della Frutta, is a good choice for panini and pizza. **Trattoria al Pero** (*Via Santa Lucia 72*), near Piazza dei Signori, serves delectable regional dishes for around L15,000. Daily food **markets** are held in Piazza delle Erbe and Piazza della Frutta.

Getting There & Away
Padua is directly linked by train to Milan, Venice and Bologna, and is easily accessible from most other major cities. Regular buses serve Venice, Milan, Trieste and surrounding towns. The bus terminal is in Piazzale Boschetti, off Via Trieste, near the train station. There is a large public car park in Prato della Valle, a massive piazza near the Basilica del Santo.

VENICE
pop 309,422
La Serenissima, the Most Serene Republic, perhaps no other city in the world has inspired the superlatives heaped upon Venice (Venezia) by great writers and travellers through the centuries. Byron's 'fairy city of the heart, rising like water-columns from the sea' was, and forever will be, an inspired phenomenon.

The secret to discovering its romance and beauty is to *walk*. Parts of Dorsoduro and Castello see few tourists even in the high season (July to September), and it's here that you'll appreciate just how seductive Venice can be. It's easy to happily lose yourself for hours in the narrow winding streets between the Accademia and the train station, where the signs pointing to San Marco and the Rialto never seem to make any sense – but what a way to pass the time!

The islands of the lagoon were first settled during the barbarian invasions of the 5th and 6th centuries AD, when the people of the Veneto sought refuge in the marshy region, gradually building the unique city on a raft of wooden posts driven into the subsoil. The waters that today threaten the city's existence once protected it from its enemies. Following centuries of Byzantine rule, Venice evolved into a republic ruled by a succession of doges (chief magistrates) and enjoyed a period of

independence that lasted 1000 years. It was the point where east met west, and the city eventually grew in power to dominate half the Mediterranean, the Adriatic and the trade routes to the Levant. It was from Venice that Marco Polo set out on his voyage to China.

Today, Venice is increasingly being left to the tourists – the regular floods (caused by high tides) and soaring property values make it impractical as a place of residence. Most of the 'locals' live in industrial Mestre, which is linked to the city by the 4km-long bridge across the lagoon.

Orientation
Venice is built on 117 small islands and has some 150 canals and 400 bridges. Only three bridges cross the Grand Canal (Canal Grande): the Rialto, the Accademia and, at the train station, the Scalzi. The city is divided into six *sestieri* (quarters): Cannaregio, Castello, San Marco, Dorsoduro, San Polo and Santa Croce. A street can be called a *calle*, *ruga* or *salizzada*; a street beside a canal is a *fondamenta*; a canal is a *rio*; and a quay is a *riva*. The only square in Venice called a *piazza* is San Marco – all the others are called *campo*.

If all that isn't confusing enough, Venice also has its own style of street numbering. Instead of a system based on individual streets, each sestiere has a long series of numbers. There are no cars in the city and all public transport is via the canals, on *vaporetti* (water buses). To cross the Grand Canal between the bridges, use a *traghetto* (basically a public gondola, but much cheaper). Signs will direct you to the various traghetto points. Of course the other mode of transportation is *a piedi* (on foot).

To walk from the *ferrovia* (train station) to San Marco along the main thoroughfare, Lista di Spagna (whose name changes several times), will take a good half-hour – follow the signs to San Marco. From San Marco the routes to other main areas, such as the Rialto, the Accademia and the ferrovia, are well signposted but can be confusing, particularly in the Dorsoduro and San Polo areas.

It's worth buying the street-referenced *Venezia* map published by FMB, as the free tourist office map provides only a vague guide to the complicated network of streets.

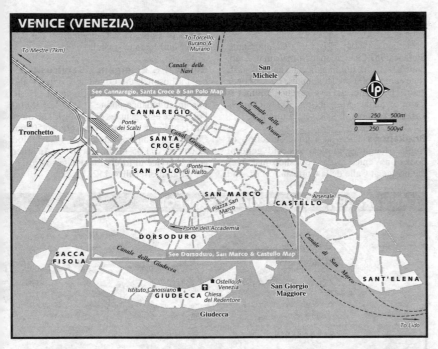

VENICE (VENEZIA)

Information

Tourist Offices Venice has three APT tourist office branches: at the train station (☎ 041 529 87 27), open 8 am to 7 pm daily; at Piazza San Marco 71f (☎ 041 520 89 64), open from 9.30 am to 3.30 pm daily and the Venice Pavilion (☎ 041 522 63 56), on the waterfront next to the Giardini Ex Reali (turn right from San Marco), open 10 am to 6 pm daily. Hours can vary a little seasonally.

Visitors aged between 14 and 29 can buy a Rolling Venice card (L5000), which offers significant discounts on food, accommodation, shopping, transport and entry to museums. It is available from tourist offices July to September, and from a number of private offices at other times; check at the tourist offices for details.

Foreign Consulates The British consulate (☎ 041 522 72 07) is in the Palazzo Querini near the Accademia, Dorsoduro 1051.

Money Most of the main banks have branches in the area around the Rialto and San Marco.

The American Express office at Salizzada San Moisè (exit from the western end of Piazza San Marco onto Calle Seconda dell'Ascensione) will exchange money without charging commission. Its opening hours are 9 am to 5.30 pm Monday to Friday and to 12.30 pm at weekends. There's an ATM for card-holders.

Thomas Cook, Piazza San Marco 141, is open 9.10 am to 7.45 pm Monday to Saturday and 9.30 am to 5 pm on Sunday. There is also a bank at the train station, or you can change money at the train ticket office between 7 am and 9.30 pm daily.

Post & Communications The main post office is on Salizzada del Fontego dei Tedeschi, just near the Ponte di Rialto (Rialto Bridge) on the main thoroughfare to the station. Stamps are sold at window Nos 9 and 10 in the central courtyard. There's a branch post office just off the western end of Piazza San Marco, and at the train station.

There are several Telecom offices in the city, including those at the post office, near

ITALY

the Rialto and on Strada Nova. Venice's postcode is 30100.

Nethouse (☎ 041 277 11 90), Campo Santo Stefano 2967-2958, is open from 9 am to 2 am, with 60 screens, printing, fax and helpful staff. Rates are L4500 for 15 minutes, L18,000 per hour. The smaller and less frenetic Puntonet at Campo Santa Margherita 3002 charges L10,000 per hour, L3000 for 15 minutes.

Bookshops There is a good selection of English-language guidebooks and general books on Venice in the bookshop just over the bridge at Calle de la Cortesia 3717d, and at Studium, behind St Mark's Basilica on the corner of Calle de la Canonica, on the way from San Marco to Castello.

Medical & Emergency Services If you need a hospital, the Ospedale Civile (☎ 041 529 45 17) is on Campo SS Giovanni e Paolo. For an ambulance phone ☎ 041 523 00 00. For police emergencies call ☎ 113. The questura is at Fondamenta di San Lorenzo 5056 in Castello, and on the mainland at Via Nicolodi 22 (☎ 041 271 55 11) in Marghera. An emergency service in foreign languages is run by the carabinieri; call ☎ 112.

CANNAREGIO, SANTA CROCE & SAN POLO

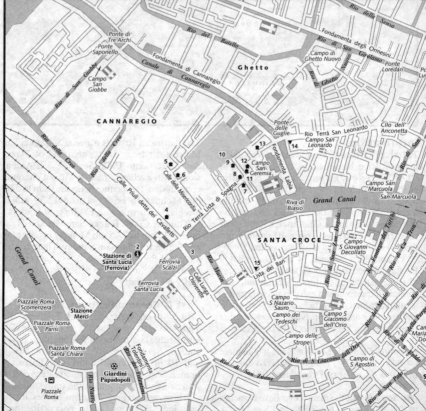

Things to See & Do

Before you visit Venice's principal monuments, churches and museums, you should catch the No 1 vaporetto along the Grand Canal, lined with Gothic, Moorish, Renaissance and rococo palaces. Then you can stretch your legs by taking a long walk: start at **San Marco** and either delve into the tiny lanes of tranquil **Castello** or head for the **Accademia Bridge** (Ponte dell'Accademia) to reach the narrow streets and squares of **Dorsoduro** and **San Polo**.

Remember that most museums are closed on Monday.

Piazza & Basilica di San Marco San Marco's dreamlike, 'can this be real' quality has you pinching yourself no matter how many times you visit. Napoleon felt so at home he called it the finest drawing room in Europe. The piazza is enclosed by the basilica and the elegant arcades of the Procuratie Vecchie, Procuratie Nuove and Libreria Sansoviniana. San Marco hosts flocks of pigeons and tourists, and both compete for space in the high season. While you're standing gob-smacked you might be lucky enough to see the bronze *mori* (Moors) strike the bell of the 15th-century Torre dell'Orologio (clock tower).

CANNAREGIO, SANTA CROCE & SAN POLO

PLACES TO STAY
4 Edelweiss Stella Alpina
5 Hotel Villa Rosa
6 Hotel Santa Lucia
7 Albergo Adua
8 Hotel Minerva
9 Hotel Rossi
11 Hotel Guerrini
12 Casa Gerotto; Alloggi Calderan
13 Al Gobbo
16 Ostello Santa Fosca
22 Giorgione

PLACES TO EAT
14 Trattoria alla Palazzina
15 Pizzeria all'Anfora
19 Standa
20 Cantina do Mori
21 Osteria del Bomba
23 Rosa Salva

OTHER
1 Intercity Bus Station
2 Tourist Office
3 Ponte dei Scalzi
10 Park & Playground
17 Paradiso Perduto
18 Iguana
24 SS Giovanni e Paolo
25 Ospedale Civile

ITALY

With its spangled spires, Byzantine domes and seething facade of mosaics and marble, the Basilica di San Marco is the western counterpart of Constantinople's Santa Sophia. The elaborately decorated basilica was built to house the body of St Mark, stolen from its burial place in Egypt by two Venetian merchants and carried to Venice in a barrel of pork. The saint has been reburied several times in the basilica (at least twice the burial place was forgotten) and his body now lies under the high altar. The present basilica was built in the 11th century and richly decorated with mosaics, marbles, sculpture and a jumble of other looted embellishments over the ensuing five centuries. The bronze horses prancing above the entrance are replicas of the famous statues liberated in the Sack of Constantinople in 1204. The originals can be seen in the basilica's **museum** (entry is L3000).

Don't miss the **Pala d'Oro** (L3000), a stunning gold altarpiece decorated with silver, enamels and precious jewels. It is behind the basilica's altar.

The basilica's 99m freestanding **bell tower** dates from the 10th century, although it suddenly collapsed on 14 July 1902 and had to be rebuilt. It costs L8000 to get to the top.

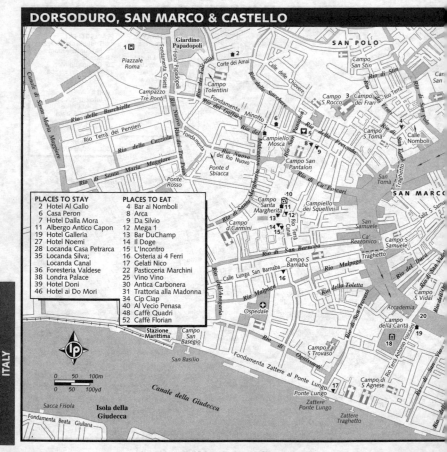

DORSODURO, SAN MARCO & CASTELLO

PLACES TO STAY
2 Hotel Al Gallo
6 Casa Peron
7 Hotel Dalla Mora
11 Albergo Antico Capon
19 Hotel Galleria
27 Hotel Noemi
28 Locanda Casa Petrarca
35 Locanda Silva;
    Locanda Canal
36 Foresteria Valdese
38 Londra Palace
39 Hotel Doni
46 Hotel ai Do Mori

PLACES TO EAT
4 Bar ai Nomboli
8 Arca
9 Da Silvio
12 Mega 1
13 Bar DuChamp
14 Il Doge
15 L'Incontro
16 Osteria ai 4 Ferri
17 Gelati Nico
22 Pasticceria Marchini
25 Vino Vino
30 Antica Carbonera
31 Trattoria alla Madonna
34 Cip Ciap
40 Al Vecio Penasa
48 Caffè Quadri
52 Caffè Florian

Palazzo Ducale The official residence of the doges and the seat of the republic's government, this palace also housed many government officials and the prisons. The original palace was built in the 9th century and later expanded, remodelled and given a Gothic tracery facade. Visit the **Sala del Maggior Consiglio** to see the paintings by Tintoretto and Veronese. The palace is open 9 am to 7 pm daily (to 5 pm November to March) and the ticket office closes 1½ hours beforehand. Admission is L18,000 and the same ticket covers entry to the nearby Museo Correr, Biblioteca Marciana and Museo Archeologico, as well as the Palazzo Mocenigo (San Stae area), and Burano and Murano museums.

The **Bridge of Sighs** (Ponte dei Sospiri) connects the palace to the old prisons. The bridge evokes romantic images, probably because of its association with Casanova, a native of Venice who spent some time in the prisons. In fact it was the thoroughfare for prisoners being led to the dungeons.

Galleria dell'Accademia The Academy of Fine Arts' collection traces the development of Venetian art, and includes masterpieces by Bellini, Carpaccio, Tintoretto,

OTHER
1 Intercity Bus Station
3 Frari
5 Cafe Blue
10 Puntonet
18 Galleria dell'Accademia
20 Ponte dell'Accademia
21 Nethouse
23 Collezione Peggy Guggenheim
24 Chiesa di Santa Maria della Salute
26 American Express
29 Bookshop
32 Ponte di Rialto
33 Main Post Office; Telecom Telephones
37 Questura (Police Station)
41 Bridge of Sighs
42 Palazzo Ducale
43 Basilica di San Marco
44 Studium Bookshop
45 Torre dell'Orologio (Clock Tower)
47 Thomas Cook
49 Procuratie Vecchie
50 Tourist Office
51 Procuratie Nuove
53 Bell Tower
54 Libreria Sansoviniana
55 Tourist Office; Venice Pavilion

Titian, Giorgione and Veronese. The gallery is open 9 am to 7 pm Tuesday to Saturday, to 8 pm on Sunday and to 2 pm on Monday. Admission is L12,000.

For a change of pace, visit the nearby **Collezione Peggy Guggenheim**, displayed in the former home of the American heiress. The collection runs the gamut of modern art from Bacon to Pollock, and the palazzo is set in a sculpture garden where Miss Guggenheim and her many pet dogs are buried. It is open 10 am to 6 pm Wednesday to Monday (to 10 pm on Saturday). Admission is L12,000.

Churches Venice has many gorgeous churches, and most of them boast an art treasure or two. The **Chiesa del Redentore** (Church of the Redeemer) on Giudecca Island was built by Palladio to commemorate the end of the great plague of 1576, and is the scene of the annual Festa del Redentore (see the Special Events section). Longhena's **Chiesa di Santa Maria della Salute** guards the entrance to the Grand Canal and contains works by Tintoretto and Titian. Be sure to visit the great Gothic churches **SS Giovanni e Paolo**, with glorious stained-glass, and the **Frari**, home to Titian's tomb and his uplifting *Assumption*. Entry to each is L3000, or you can buy the Chorus Pass (L15,000) which gets you into 13 of the city's most famous churches.

The Lido This thin strip of land, east of the centre, separates Venice from the Adriatic and is easily accessible by vaporetto Nos 1, 6, 14 and 61. Once *the* most fashionable beach resort – and still very popular – it's almost impossible to find a space on its long beach in summer.

Islands The island of **Murano** is the home of Venetian glass. Tour a factory for a behind-the-scenes look at its production, or visit the Glassworks Museum to see some exquisite historical pieces. Despite the constant influx of tourists, **Burano** is still a relatively sleepy fishing village, renowned for its lace-making. **Torcello**, the republic's original island settlement, was abandoned due to malaria. Just about all that remains on the hauntingly deserted island is the Byzantine cathedral, its exquisite mosaics intact. Excursion boats travel to the three islands from San Marco (L30,000 return). Vaporetto

No 12 goes to all three from Fondamenta Nuove (L6000 one way).

Gondolas These might represent the quintessential romantic Venice, but at around L120,000 (L150,000 after 8 pm) for a 50-minute ride, they are very expensive. It is possible to squeeze up to six people into one gondola and still pay the same price. Prices are set for gondolas, so check with the tourist office if you have problems.

Organised Tours

The Associazione Guide Turistiche (☎ 041 520 90 38), Castello 5327, arranges group tours in various languages for a hefty L200,000. Shop around the various travel agencies for the best deals on guided walks and collective gondola rides with serenade (around L50,000 per person).

Special Events

The major event of the year is Venice's famed Carnevale, held during the 10 days before Ash Wednesday, when Venetians don spectacular masks and costumes for what is literally a 10-day street party. At its decadent height in the 18th century, the Carnevale lasted for six months!

The Venice Biennale, a major exhibition of international visual arts, is held every odd-numbered year, and the Venice International Film Festival is held every September at the Palazzo del Cinema, on the Lido.

The most important celebration on the Venetian calendar is the Festa del Redentore (Festival of the Redeemer), held on the third weekend in July and featuring a spectacular fireworks display. The Regata Storica, a gondola race on the Grand Canal, is held on the first Sunday in September.

Places to Stay

Simply put, Venice is expensive. The average cost of a basic single/double without bath in a one-star hotel is around L90,000/120,000; prices quoted in this section are high season. Some hotels include breakfast, which allows their proprietors to charge a little more. Prices skyrocket in peak periods (Christmas, Carnevale, Easter etc), but can drop dramatically at other times of the year. It is advisable to make a booking

ITALY

before you arrive. As Venice does not have a traditional street numbering system, the best idea is to ring your hotel when you arrive and ask for specific directions.

Camping Litorale del Cavallino, north-east of the city along the Adriatic coast has numerous camping grounds, many with bungalows. The tourist office has a full list, but you could try *Marina di Venezia* (☎ *041 530 09 55,* **e** *camping@marinave.it, Via Montello 6, Punta Sabbioni),* which is open from mid-April to the end of August.

Hostels The HI *Ostello di Venezia* (☎ *041 523 82 11, fax 041 523 56 89, Fondamenta delle Zitelle 86)* is on the island of Giudecca. It is open to members only, though you can buy a card there. B&B is L27,000 and full meals are available for L14,000. Take vaporetto No 82 from the station (L6000 one way) and get off at Zitelle; curfew is 11.30 pm. *Istituto Canossiano* (☎/fax *041 522 21 57, Ponte Piccolo 428)* is nearby on Giudecca, with dorm beds for women only at L23,000 per night. Take vaporetto No 82 and get off at Palanca.

Foresteria Valdese (☎/fax *041 528 67 97, Castello 5170)* has dorm beds for L30,000 and doubles from L85,000 per night. Follow Calle Lunga from Campo Santa Maria Formosa. Students will feel at home at *Ostello Santa Fosca* (☎ *041 71 57 75,* **e** *cpu@ iuav.unive.it, Cannaregio 2372),* less than 15 minutes from the station through Campo Santa Fosca. Dorm beds are L30,000 and check-in is 4 to 7 pm.

Hotels Not surprisingly, bargain hotels are few and far between in Venice.

Cannaregio The two-star *Edelweiss Stella Alpina* (☎ *041 71 51 79,* **e** *stelalpina@tin.it, Calle Priuli detta dei Cavalletti 99d),* near the station on the first street on the left after the Scalzi church, has decent singles/doubles for L110,000/160,000; with bathroom they're L150,000/235,000. The next street on the left is Calle della Misericordia, with two recommended hotels. *Hotel Santa Lucia* (☎/fax *041 71 51 80),* at No 358, is a newish building (ie, 20th century) with a strip of terrace garden. Doubles with shower and breakfast go for L170,000 (L140,000 without shower),

and singles without shower or breakfast are L80,000. At No 389, the friendly *Hotel Villa Rosa* (☎/fax *041 71 89 76)* has pleasant, well-furnished singles/doubles/triples/quads with bathroom, breakfast and satellite TV for L130,000/190,000/240,000/280,000.

On Lista di Spagna, the main drag, *Albergo Adua* (☎ *041 71 61 84, fax 041 244 01 62)* at No 233a has clean singles/doubles with shower for L130,000/200,000. Across the road at No 230, *Hotel Minerva* (☎ *041 71 59 68,* **e** *lchecchi@tin.it)* has modest rooms for L70,000/95,000.

Hotel Rossi (☎ *041 71 51 64, fax 041 71 77 84)* is just off Lista di Spagna (via a Gothic archway) at the end of tiny Calle de le Procuratie. Singles/doubles/triples/quads with bathroom and bare essentials are L100,000/ 160,000/195,000/230,000. On the same street, the two-star *Hotel Guerrini* (☎ *041 71 53 33, fax 041 71 51 14)* has comfortable singles without/with bathroom for L80,000/120,000, and doubles for L160,000/230,000. Around the corner, *Casa Gerotto* (☎/fax *041 71 53 61, Campo San Geremia 283)* and the neighbouring *Alloggi Calderan* together offer singles/ doubles in a hostel atmosphere for around L110,000/140,000. *Al Gobbo* (☎ *041 71 50 01),* at No 312 in the same campo, provides sparkling-clean rooms with bathroom and breakfast for L120,000/150,000.

For a multistar splurge in this less touristy area, the 15th-century *Giorgione* (☎ *041 522 58 10, fax 041 523 90 92, Calle Larga dei Proverbi 4587),* just off Campo dei SS Apostoli, has tranquil doubles with the lot starting at around L235,000.

San Marco Although this is the most touristy area of Venice, it has some surprisingly good-quality (relatively) budget pensioni. *Hotel Noemi* (☎ *041 523 81 44,* **e** *hotelnoemi@tin.it, Calle dei Fabbri 909)* is only a few steps from Piazza San Marco and has simple singles/doubles for L90,000/ 130,000.

Locanda Casa Petrarca (☎ *041 520 04 30, Calle delle Schiavine 4386)* is one of the area's nicest cheaper hotels, with singles for L75,000 and doubles without/with shower for L140,000/170,000. To get there, find Campo San Luca, go along Calle dei Fusari, then take the second street on the left and turn

ITALY

right onto Calle delle Schiavine; the hotel is at the end of Schiavine, overlooking a canal.

Just off Piazza San Marco, *Hotel ai Do Mori* (☎ 041 520 48 17, fax 041 520 53 28, Calle Larga San Marco 658) has pleasant singles/doubles, some with views of St Mark's basilica, for L120,000/150,000.

Castello This area is to the east of Piazza San Marco. Although close to the piazza it's less touristy, and eerily reminiscent of the atmospheric movie *Don't Look Now*. *Locanda Silva* (☎ 041 522 76 43, fax 041 528 68 17, Fondamenta del Rimedio 4423) has rather basic singles/doubles for L70,000/110,000, and *Locanda Canal* (☎ 041 523 45 38, fax 041 241 91 38), next door at No 4422c, has better doubles with bathroom for L160,000. To get there, head off from Campo Santa Maria Formosa towards San Marco.

Hotel Doni (☎/fax 041 522 42 67, Fondamenta del Vin 4656) is a little establishment off Salizzada San Provolo. It has clean, quiet rooms without bathroom for L75,000/95,000; a double with bathroom is L140,000.

On the waterfront, live like a doge at the *Londra Palace* (☎ 041 520 05 33, fax 041 522 50 32, Riva degli Schiavoni 4171), where views and pampering up the rates to L375,000 (and upwards) a double.

Dorsoduro, San Polo & Santa Croce This is the most authentic area of Venice, in which you can still find the atmosphere of a living city. *Hotel Al Gallo* (☎ 041 523 67 61, fax 041 522 81 88, Corte dei Amai 197g), off Fondamenta Tolentini heading down from the station, has excellent doubles with shower for L115,000. *Casa Peron* (☎ 041 71 00 21, fax 041 71 10 38, Salizzada San Pantalon 84) has clean singles/doubles with shower for L100,000/150,000 including breakfast. To get to the Casa Peron from the station, cross Ponte dei Scalzi and follow the signs to San Marco and Rialto till you reach Rio delle Muneghette, then cross the wooden bridge. Nearby, *Hotel Dalla Mora* (☎ 041 71 07 03, fax 041 72 30 06, Santa Croce 42a) is on a lovely small canal just off Salizzada San Pantalon. It has airy rooms, some with canal views and a common open terrace. Singles/doubles/triples/quads with bathroom are L95,000/150,000/190,000/230,000. Bookings are a must.

In one of the nicest squares in Venice, *Albergo Antico Capon* (☎/fax 041 528 52 92, Campo Santa Margherita 3004b) provides singles/doubles with bathroom for L120,000/150,000.

Hotel Galleria (☎ 041 523 24 89, ✆ galleria@tin.it, Dorsoduro 878a) has elegant rooms in a 17th-century palace facing the Grand Canal at Ponte dell'Accademia. But don't panic: this must be the last remaining affordable hotel on the Grand Canal. A double with bathroom costs L180,000, and singles/doubles without facilities are L100,000/150,000.

Mestre Mestre makes an economical if somewhat drab alternative to staying in Venice. There are a number of good hotels as well as plenty of cafes and places to eat around the main square. If you're travelling by car, the savings on car-parking charges are considerable. The two-star *Albergo Roberta* (☎ 041 92 93 55, fax 041 93 09 83, Via Sernaglia 21) has good-sized, clean singles/doubles with bathroom for L90,000/130,000. The one-star *Albergo Giovannina* (☎ 041 92 63 96, fax 041 538 84 42, Via Dante 113) has decent singles for L50,000 and doubles with bathroom for L90,000.

Places to Eat
Unless you choose carefully, eating in Venice can be an expensive business.

Bars serve a wide range of tasty panini, *tramezzini* (sandwiches) and rolls with every imaginable filling. They cost around L2500 to L5000 if you eat them while standing at the bar. Head for one of the many *bacari* (traditional wine bars) for wine by the glass *(ombra)* and interesting bite-sized snacks *(cichetti)*. The staples of the Veneto region's cucina are rice and beans. Try the *risi e bisi* (risotto with peas), followed by a glass of *fragolino*, the Veneto's fragrant strawberry wine.

Restaurants Avoid the tourist traps around San Marco and near the train station, where prices are high and the quality is poor.

Cannaregio Heading from the station, *Trattoria alla Palazzina* (Cannaregio 1509) is just over the first bridge after Campo San Geremia. It has a garden at the rear and serves good if pricey pizzas for L13,000 to L20,000. A full meal will cost around L50,000. The authentic *Osteria del Bomba (Calle de l'Oca 4297)*, parallel to Strada Nova near Campo dei SS Apostoli, has pasta from L8000 and a mouthwatering array of cichetti.

Around San Marco & Castello The popular bar/osteria *Vino Vino (San Marco 2007)* is at Ponte Veste near Teatro La Fenice. The good-quality menu changes daily, with pasta or risotto for L10,000 and a main dish for around L15,000. Wine is sold by the glass. *Antica Carbonera*, on Calle Bembo (a continuation of Calle dei Fabbri), is an atmospheric old trattoria with pasta from L13,000 and a full meal for around L60,000. Just off Campo Santa Maria Formosa and over Ponte del Mondo Novo, *Cip Ciap* serves filling pizza by the slice for L3000 to L5000.

Dorsoduro, San Polo & Santa Croce This is the best area for small, authentic trattorias and pizzerias. The pizzas are particularly good at *Pizzeria all'Anfora*, across the Ponte dei Scalzi from the station at Lista dei Bari 1223, with a garden at the rear. Pizzas cost L7500 to L14,000.

L'Incontro (Rio Terrà Canal 3062a), between Campo San Barnaba and Campo Santa Margherita, serves excellent food, with a full meal around L45,000.

Cantina do Mori, on Sottoportego dei do Mori, off Ruga Rialto, is a small, very popular wine bar which also serves sandwiches. *Trattoria alla Madonna*, Calle della Madonna, two streets west of the Rialto, specialises in seafood – a full meal costs up to L70,000, but it's worth the extra lire.

The stylish *Arca (Calle San Pantalon 3757)*, past Campo San Pantalon, has pasta and pizza for L9000 to L16,000.

Around the corner is *Da Silvio (Crosera San Pantalon 3817)*, which is a good-value pizzeria/trattoria with outside tables in a garden setting.

Cafes & Bars If you can cope with the idea of paying L15,000 for a cappuccino, spend an hour or so sitting at an outdoor table in Piazza San Marco, listening to the orchestra at either *Caffè Florian* or *Caffè Quadri*. For a cheaper alternative, try Campo Santa Margherita's

Bar DuChamp, a student favourite where panini cost around L6000 and you can sit outside at no extra charge.

Bar ai Nomboli, between Campo San Polo and the Frari on the corner of Calle dei Nomboli and Rio Terrà dei Nomboli, has a huge selection of gourmet sandwiches and tramezzini. In the Castello area you can choose from an extensive range of cheap panini at the bar *Al Vecio Penasa (Calle delle Rasse 4585)*.

If you're looking for a typical osteria serving Venetian cichetti, try *Osteria ai 4 Ferri* on Calle Lunga San Barnaba, off Campo San Barnaba in Dorsoduro.

Gelati & Pastries Some of the best gelati in Venice is served at *Gelati Nico (Fondamenta Zattere ai Gesuati 922)*. You can join the locals taking their evening stroll along the fondamenta or take a seat at an outside table. *Il Doge*, Campo Santa Margherita, also has excellent gelati. A popular place for cakes and pastries is *Pasticceria Marchini (Calle del Spezier 2769)*, just off Campo Santo Stefano. *Rosa Salva*, on Campo SS Giovanni e Paolo, is frequented by locals for its gelati and extra special pastries. Try the hot chocolate.

Self-Catering For fruit and vegetables, as well as delicatessens, head for the *market* in the streets on the San Polo side of the Rialto Bridge. There's a *Standa* supermarket on Strada Nova and a *Mega 1* supermarket just off Campo Santa Margherita.

Entertainment
The free weekly booklet *Un Ospite di Venezia*, available at hotels and tourist offices, has entertainment listings, or buy a copy of the monthly *Venezia News* from newsagents for L4000. The tourist office also has brochures listing events and performances for the entire year.

Venice lost its opera house, the magnificent Teatro La Fenice, to a fire in January 1996. Reconstruction is slowly under way, and in the interim performances are held at *PalaFelice (☎ 041 521 01 61)*, a tentlike structure on the car-park island of Tronchetto.

Major art exhibitions are held at *Palazzo Grassi* (San Samuele vaporetto stop), and smaller exhibitions are held at various venues in the city throughout the year.

ITALY

In Cannaregio, *Paradiso Perduto (Fondamenta della Misericordia 2539)* has live music and outdoor tables; the food's good too. A few doors up at No 2515, *Iguana* pumps out live and loud Latino music, with burritos on the side. In Dorsoduro, there's *Café Blue (Salizzada San Pantalon 3778)*, a pub-like drinking den near trendy Campo Santa Margherita.

Shopping

For many visitors, Venice is synonymous with its elaborate glassware. There are several workshops and showrooms in Venice, particularly in the area between San Marco and Castello and on the island of Murano, designed mainly for tourist groups. If you're interested in buying some Venetian glass, shop around carefully because quality and prices can vary dramatically.

Venice is a trinket box of jewellery, crystals, grotesque Carnevale masks and bronze lions. You'll find them in shops throughout the city. Lace is another characteristic product of the Venetian lagoon, produced mainly on the island of Burano and available in Venice at Annelie Pizzi e Ricami, at Calle Lunga San Barnaba 2748. Marbled paper and luscious velvet fabrics are other Venetian specialities. Window-shop at Venice's oldest traditional papermaking establishment, Legatoria Piazzesi, Campiello della Feltrina 2551c, San Marco.

The main shopping area for designer-label clothing, shoes, accessories and jewellery is in the narrow streets between San Marco and the Rialto, particularly the Merceria and the area around Campo San Luca. Luxury items can be found in the area near La Fenice.

Getting There & Away

Air Marco Polo airport (☎ 041 260 92 60) is just east of Mestre and services domestic and European flights. It is accessible by regular *motoscafo* (motorboat) from San Marco and the Lido (L17,000). From Piazzale Roma there are also ATVO buses (☎ 041 520 55 30) for L5000 or the ACTV city bus No 5 for L1500. A water taxi from San Marco will cost around L110,000.

Bus ACTV buses (☎ 041 528 78 86) leave from Piazzale Roma for surrounding areas including Mestre and Chioggia, a fishing port at the southernmost point of the lagoon. Buses also go to Padua and Treviso. Tickets and information are available at the office in Piazzale Roma.

Train The train station, Stazione Santa Lucia (☎ 147 88 80 88), is directly linked to Padua, Verona, Trieste, Milan and Bologna, and so is easily accessible for Florence and Rome. You can also head to major points in Germany, Austria and the former Yugoslavia. The Venice Simplon *Orient Express* runs between Venice and London, via Innsbruck, Zürich and Paris, twice weekly. Ask at any travel agent or phone ☎ 041 528 58 11.

Boat Minoan Lines (☎ 041 271 23 45), Porto Venezia, Zona Santa Marta, runs ferries to Greece four times a week in winter and daily in summer. Deck class costs L126,000 one way in the high season.

Getting Around

Once you cross the bridge from Mestre, cars must be left at the car park on the island of Tronchetto or at Piazzale Roma (cars are allowed on the Lido – take car ferry No 17 from Tronchetto). The car parks are not cheap at around L25,000 a day. A cheaper alternative is to leave the car at Fusina, near Mestre, and catch the vaporetto to Zattere and then the No 82 either to Piazza San Marco or the train station. Ask for information at the tourist information office just before the bridge to Venice.

As there are no cars in Venice, vaporetti are the city's mode of public transport. From Piazzale Roma, vaporetto No 1 zigzags its way along the Grand Canal to San Marco and then to the Lido. There is the faster No 82 if you are in a hurry to get to San Marco. The No 12 vaporetto leaves from Fondamenta Nuove for the islands of Murano, Burano and Torcello. A full timetable is available at vaporetto ticket offices. A single vaporetto ticket costs L6000 (plus L6000 for luggage), even if you only ride to the next station; a return is L10,000. A 24-hour ticket costs L18,000 for unlimited travel, a 72-hour ticket is L35,000 (worthwhile) and a one-week ticket costs L60,000.

Water taxis are exorbitant, with a set charge of L27,000 for a maximum of seven

ITALY

minutes, then L500 every 15 seconds. It's an extra L8000 if you phone for a taxi, and various other surcharges add up to make a gondola ride seem cheap.

FERRARA
pop 138,015

The seat of the Este dukes from the 13th century to the end of the 16th century, Ferrara retains much of the austere splendour of its heyday. Graceful palaces line the city's streets, which radiate from the imposing Castello Estense and are largely traffic-free.

Information

The tourist information office (☎ 0532 20 93 70, ◪ infotur.comfe@fe.nettuno.it) is inside the Castello Estense. It opens 9 am to 1 pm and 2 to 6 pm daily.

Things to See

The small historical centre encompasses medieval Ferrara, to the south of the **Castello Estense** and the area to the north. The castle – complete with moat and drawbridges – was begun by Nicolò II d'Este in 1385. It now houses government offices, and the areas open to the public have a suitably chilling atmosphere.

The pink-and-white striped **Duomo** dates from the 12th century, with Gothic and Renaissance additions and an unusual triple facade. Its museum has a superb collection of Renaissance art. The Renaissance Palazzo dei Diamanti, along Corso Ercole I d'Este, contains the **Pinacoteca Nazionale** and exhibitions of modern art. The gallery is open 9 am to 2 pm Tuesday to Saturday (Sunday to 1 pm). Entry is L8000.

The **Palazzo Schifanoia**, Via Scandiana 23, is one of the city's earliest major Renaissance buildings and another of the Este palaces. It features the 'Room of the Months', decorated with Ferrara's finest Renaissance frescoes, portraying courtly life. The palace, whose name means 'chase your cares away', is open 9 am to 7 pm daily; entry is L8000.

Places to Stay & Eat

Ferrara is a cheap alternative to Bologna, and can be used as a base for visiting Venice. *Albergo Centro Storico (☎ 0532 20 33 74, Via Vegri 15)* is central but basic, with singles/

doubles for L40,000/60,000. South of the cathedral, *Pensione Artisti (☎ 0532 76 10 38, Via Vittoria 66)* has singles for L30,000 and doubles without/with bathroom for L60,000/85,000. Better rooms are available at the two-star *Albergo Nazionale (☎ 0532 20 96 04, Corso Porta Reno 32)* for L80,000/120,000 with bathroom. Opposite the cathedral, the four-star *Annunziata (☎ 0532 20 11 11, fax 0532 20 32 33, Piazza Repubblica 5)* combines period features with modern themes. Comfortable rooms cost L220,000/320,000.

Pizzeria il Ciclone (Via Vignatagliata 11) has pizzas for around L10,000. Closer to the cathedral at Via Adelardi 11, **Al Brindisi** serves up traditional dishes like salami cooked in red wine for L15,000. Next door, *Pappagallo* is a simple but satisfying self-service where a meal including wine costs L12,000. In the medieval quarter, *Angeli (Via delle Volte 4)* is a rustic but stylish osteria, with roast beef for L19,000 and tortellini for L12,000.

Getting There & Away

Ferrara is on the Bologna-Venice train line, with regular trains to both cities. It is 40 minutes from Bologna and 1½ hours from Venice. Regular trains also run directly to Ravenna. Buses run from the train station to Modena (also in the Emilia-Romagna region).

BOLOGNA
pop 404,378

Bologna is not only an elegant, wealthy and intellectual centre, it's also one of Italy's more attractive larger cities. The regional capital of Emilia-Romagna, it is famous for its porticoed streets, harmonious rusty-hued architecture, university (the oldest in Europe) and, above all, its gastronomic tradition. The Bolognese have given the world tortellini, lasagne, mortadella and the inescapable spaghetti bolognese – known in Bologna as *spaghetti al ragù* – hence one of the city's nicknames, Bologna la Grassa (Bologna the Fat).

Information

The IAT tourist office (☎ 051 23 96 60, fax 051 23 14 54), at Piazza Maggiore 6, under the portico of the town hall, is open 9 am to 7 pm Monday to Saturday, to 2 pm on Sunday. There are branch offices at the train station

ITALY

and airport. Pick up a map and the useful booklet *Welcome to Bologna*.

The main post office is in Piazza Minghetti. Telecom telephones are at Piazza VIII Agosto 24, and at the train station. In a medical emergency call ☎ 118, or Ospedale Maggiore on ☎ 051 647 81 11. For the police call ☎ 113.

Things to See & Do

Perfect for a stroll, Bologna's traffic-free centre is formed by **Piazza Maggiore**, the adjoining **Piazza del Nettuno** and **Fontana di Nettuno** (Neptune's Fountain), sculpted in bronze by the French artist who became known as Giambologna, and **Piazza di Porta Ravegnana**, with its two leaning towers to rival Pisa's (originally there were 42).

The **Basilica di San Petronio** in Piazza Maggiore is dedicated to the city's patron saint, Petronius. It was here that Charles V was crowned emperor by the pope in 1530. The incomplete red-and-white marble facade displays the colours of Bologna, and the chapels inside contain notable works of art. The adjacent **Palazzo Comunale** (town hall) is a huge building combining several architectural styles in remarkable harmony. It features a bronze statue of Pope Gregory XIII (a native of Bologna, and the creator of the Gregorian calendar), an impressive staircase attributed to Bramante and Bologna's collection of art treasures.

The **Basilica di Santo Stefano** is a group of four churches (originally there were seven) and includes the 11th-century Chiesa del Crocefisso, which houses the bones of San Petronio.

The **Basilica di San Domenico**, erected in the early 16th century, houses the elaborate sarcophagus of St Dominic, the founder of the Dominican order. The chapel was designed by Nicoló Pisano and its shrine features figures carved by a young Michelangelo.

The **Museo Civico Archeologico**, **Pinacoteca Nazionale**, French Gothic **Basilica di San Francesco** and Romanesque **Basilica di Santo Stefano** are also well worth a visit.

Places to Stay

Budget hotels in Bologna are virtually nonexistent and it is almost impossible to find a single room. The city's busy trade-fair calendar means that hotels are often heavily booked, so always book in advance.

The best options are the two HI hostels: ***Ostello San Sisto*** (☎ *051 51 92 02, Via Viadagola 14*) charges L18,000 with breakfast and ***Ostello Due Torri*** (☎/*fax 051 50 18 10*), on the same street at No 5, charges L21,000. Take bus Nos 93 or 20b from Via Irnerio (off Via dell'Indipendenza south of the station), ask the bus driver where to alight, then follow the signs to the hostel.

Right in the historic centre, ***Albergo Garisenda*** (☎ *051 22 43 69, fax 051 22 10 07, Galleria del Leone 1*) looks onto the two towers and Via Rizzoli, and provides decent singles/doubles without shower for L70,000/100,000. ***Apollo*** (☎ *051 22 39 55, fax 051 23 87 60, Via Drapperie 5*) nearby has singles/doubles for L60,000/95,000, and doubles/triples with bathroom for L130,000/165,000. Away from the centre, ***Albergo Marconi*** (☎ *051 26 28 32, Via G Marconi 22*) provides rather anonymous single/double rooms for L55,000/70,000, with shower for L88,000/110,000.

Bologna has plenty of two and three-star hotels, although standards are disappointing. ***Accademia*** (☎ *051 23 23 18, fax 051 26 35 90, Via delle Belle Arti 6*) is a good two-star midway between the train station and old centre, with rooms for L130,000/190,000. Closer to the station, the three-star ***Donatello*** (☎/*fax 051 24 81 74, Via dell'Indipendenza 65*) offers cut-price rates if there are no trade fairs happening, with roomy doubles for L160,000.

Places to Eat

Pizzeria Bella Napoli (*Via San Felice 40*) serves some of Bologna's best pizzas at reasonable prices. *Pizzeria Altero* (*Via Ugo Bassi 10*) has good pizza by the slice for only L1500. Grab a coffee and cake at *Zanarini* (*Via Luigi Carlo Farini 2*), the city's grandest tearoom. The self-service *Due Torri* (*Via dei Giudei 4*) is excellent value for lunch, with mains from L13,000 and pasta or salad for L4000 to L9000. For something fancier, try the elegant and airy *Diana* (*Via dell'Indipendenza 24a*) or the traditional, wood-lined *Cesari* (*Via Carbonesi 8*), where a sampling of the local cuisine will set you back around L70,000.

Shop at *Mercato Ugo Bassi* (*Via Ugo Bassi 27*), a covered market offering all the

BOLOGNA

PLACES TO STAY
3 Donatello
5 Accademia
7 Albergo Marconi
16 Apollo
17 Albergo Garisenda

PLACES TO EAT
6 Diana
8 Pizzeria Bella Napoli
9 Mercato Ugo Bassi
11 Pizzeria Altero
18 Due Torre
24 Zanarini
25 Cesari

OTHER
1 Tourist Office
2 Intercity Bus Terminal
4 Pinacoteca Nazionale
10 Basilica di San Francesco
12 Questura (Police Station)
13 Palazzo Comunale
14 IAT Tourist Office
15 Fontana di Nettuno
19 Le Due Torri
   (Leaning Towers)
20 Basilica di Santo Stefano
21 Main Post Office
22 Museo Civico Archeologico
23 Basilica di San Petronio
26 Basilica di San Domenico

local fare. There's also a *market* in the streets
south-east of Piazza Maggiore.

Getting There & Away

Bologna is a major transport junction for
northern Italy and trains from virtually all
major cities stop here. Buses to major cities
depart from the terminal in Piazza XX Settembre, around the corner from the train station in Piazza delle Medaglie d'Oro.

The city is linked to Milan, Florence and
Rome by the A1 (Autostrada del Sole). The
A13 heads directly for Venice and Padua, and
the A14 goes to Rimini and Ravenna.

Getting Around

Traffic is restricted in the city centre, so it's
best to park at one of the many public car
parks outside the city walls. Bus No 25 will
take you from the train station to the historical centre.

RAVENNA
pop 135,844

Ravenna is best known for its exquisite mosaics, relics of the time it was capital of the
Western Roman Empire, stronghold of
Theodoric the Great (king of the Ostrogoths)
and western seat of the Byzantines, notably

ITALY

under Justinian and Theodora. The town is easily accessible from Bologna and is worth a day trip, at the very least.

Information
The IAT tourist office (☎ 0544 354 04, fax 0544 48 26 70) is at Via Salara 8 and is open 8.30 am to 6 pm Monday to Saturday and 10 am to 4 pm on Sunday. The Ospedale Santa Maria delle Croci (☎ 0544 40 91 11) is at Via Missiroli 10. In a police emergency call ☎ 113.

Things to See
The pick of Ravenna's mosaics are found in the **Basilica di Sant'Apollinare Nuovo**, the **Basilica di San Vitale**, the **Mausoleo di Galla Placidia** (these are the oldest) and the **Battistero Neoniano**. These buildings are all in the town centre and an admission ticket to the four, as well as to the **Museo Arcivescovile**, costs L10,000. The mosaics in the **Basilica di Sant'Apollinare in Classe**, 5km away, are also notable.

Special Events
Ravenna hosts a music festival from late June to early August, featuring international artists. An annual theatre and literature festival is held in September in honour of Dante, who spent his last 10 years in the city and is buried here. In winter, opera and dance are staged at the *Teatro Alighieri* (☎ *0544 325 77, Piazza Garibaldi 5*).

Places to Stay & Eat
The HI *Ostello Dante* (☎ *0544 42 11 64, Via Aurelio Nicolodi 12*) opens March to November. Take bus No 1 from Viale Pallavacini, to the left of the train station. B&B are L23,000 and family rooms are available for L25,000 per person. An evening meal is L14,000. *Al Giaciglio* (☎/fax *0544 394 03, Via Rocca Brancaleone 42*) is Ravenna's sole one-star establishment, with singles/doubles and shower for L55,000/ 80,000. To find it, go straight ahead from the station along Viale Farini and turn right onto Via Rocca Brancaleone. Two-star *Ravenna* (☎ *0544 21 22 04, fax 0544 21 20 77, Via Maroncelli 12*), just outside the train station, has rooms for around L80,000/100,000. In the heart of the city's historic centre, the three-star *Hotel Centrale Byron* (☎ *0544 334

79, fax 0544 341 14, Via IV Novembre 14*) has classy rooms from L90,000/126,000, including breakfast.

For a quick meal, you can try the *Bizantino* self-service restaurant in the city's fresh-produce market in Piazza Andrea Costa. *Cá de Vén (Via Corrado Ricci 24)* is a popular place for a regional dish or glass of wine in medieval surroundings.

Getting There & Away
Ravenna is accessible by train from Bologna, sometimes with a change at Castel Bolognese. The trip takes around 1½ hours.

Getting Around
Cycling is a popular way to get around the sights. Rental is L15,000 per day or L2000 per hour from COOP San Vitale, Piazza Farini, to the left as you leave the station.

SAN MARINO
The world's oldest surviving republic, San Marino was founded in 300 AD by a stonemason said to have been escaping religious persecution. The tiny state (only 61 sq km) strikes its own coins, has its own postage stamps and army – and is an unashamed tourist trap. The main attraction is the splendid view of the mountains and coast. You can also wander along the city walls and visit the two fortresses.

The tourist office (☎ 0549 88 29 98) is in the Palazzo del Turismo at Contrada Omagnano 20. San Marino is accessible from Rimini by bus.

The Dolomites

The limestone Dolomites (Dolomiti) stretch across Trentino-Alto Adige and into the Veneto. This spectacular Alpine region is the Italians' favoured area for skiing and there are excellent hiking trails.

Information
Information about Trentino-Alto Adige can be obtained in Trent at the APT del Trentino (☎ 0461 83 90 00, @ apt@provincia.tn.it), Via Romagnosi 3; in Rome (☎ 06 36 09 58 42, fax 06 320 24 13), Via del Babuino 20; and in Milan (☎ 02 86 46 12 51, fax 02 72 00

21 88), Piazza Diaz 5. Bolzano's tourist office (☎ 0471 30 70 00, ✉ bolzano@ sudtirol.com), Piazza Walther 8, also has information on the region, and there's a telephone information service on ☎ 0471 41 38 08.

The APT Dolomiti at Cortina (☎ 0436 27 11) can provide information on trekking and skiing in the Veneto.

Skiing

The Dolomites' numerous ski resorts range from expensive and fashionable Cortina d'Ampezzo in the Veneto to family-oriented resorts such as those in the Val Gardena in Trentino-Alto Adige. All the resorts have helpful tourist offices with loads of information on facilities, accommodation and transport.

The high season is generally from Christmas to early January and from early February to April, when prices increase considerably. A good way to save money is to buy a *settimana bianca* (literally, 'white week'), a package-deal ski holiday available through travel agencies throughout Italy. This covers accommodation, food and ski passes for seven days.

If you want to go it alone, but plan to do a lot of skiing, invest in a ski pass. Most resort areas offer their own passes for unlimited use of lifts at several resorts for a nominated period. The cost in the 2000-01 high season for a six-day pass was around L270,000. The Superski Dolomiti pass (☎ 0471 79 53 97), which allows access to 460 lifts and 1200km of ski runs in 12 valleys, costs L300,000. The average cost of ski and boot hire in the Alps is around L25,000 a day for downhill and L20,000 for cross-country.

Trekking

Without doubt, the Dolomites provide the most breathtaking opportunities for walking in the Italian Alps – from a half-day stroll with the kids to demanding treks that combine walking with mountaineering skills. The walking season is roughly from July to late September. Alpine refuges (*rifugi*) usually close around 20 September.

Buy a map of the hiking trails which also shows the locations of Alpine refuges. The best maps are the Tabacco 1:25,000 series, which can be bought in newsagents and bookshops in the area where you plan to hike, and often in major bookshops in larger cities. Lonely Planet's *Walking in Italy* outlines several treks in detail and the *Italy* guide also details some suggested treks.

Hiking trails are generally well marked with numbers on red-and-white painted bands (which you will find on trees and rocks along the trails), or by numbers inside different coloured triangles for the Alte Vie (the four High Routes through the Dolomites which link a chain of rifugi and can take up to two weeks to walk – the APT in Trent has a booklet).

Recommended hiking areas include:

Alpe di Siusi
  A vast plateau above the Val Gardena, at the foot of the spectacular Sciliar.
Cortina area
  Featuring the magnificent Parco Naturale di Fraies-Sennes-Braies.
Pale di San Martino
  Accessible from San Martino di Castrozza.

Warning Remember that even in summer the weather is extremely changeable in the Alps: although it might be sweltering when you set off, you should be prepared for very cold and wet weather on even the shortest of walks. Essentials include a pair of good-quality, worn-in walking boots, an anorak or pile/wind jacket, a lightweight backpack, a warm hat and gloves, a waterproof poncho, light food and plenty of water.

Getting There & Away

The region has an excellent public transport network – the two principal bus companies are SAD in Alto Adige and the Veneto, and Atesina in Trentino. There's a network of long-distance buses operated by a number companies (eg, Lazzi, SITA, Sena, STAT and ATVO) connecting the main towns and many of the ski resorts with major cities such as Rome, Florence, Venice, Bologna, Milan and Genoa. Information is available from tourist offices and *autostazioni* (bus stations) in the region. For long-distance travel information, Lazzi Express (☎ 06 884 08 40, fax 06 841 23 96) is at Via Tagliamento 27b in Rome, and in Florence (☎ 055 28 71 18, fax 055 21 43 28) at Piazza Stazione 47r. SITA (☎ 055 21 47 21, fax 055 48 36 51) is at Via Santa Caterina da Siena 17 in Florence.

Getting Around

If you are planning to hike in the Alps during the warmer months, you'll find that hitchhiking is no problem, especially near the resort towns. The areas around the major resorts are well serviced by local buses, and tourist offices will be able to provide information on local bus services. During winter, most resorts have 'ski bus' shuttle services from the towns to the main ski facilities.

CORTINA D'AMPEZZO
pop 1200

Italy's most fashionable and expensive ski resort, Cortina is also one of the best equipped and certainly the most picturesque. The area is very popular for trekking and climbing, with well-marked trails and numerous rifugi.

The main APT tourist office (☎ 0436 27 11) has information on Cortina's (expensive!) accommodation. *International Camping Olympia (☎ 0436 50 57)* is north of Cortina at Fiames and is open year-round. *Casa Tua (☎ 0436 22 78, ✉ casatua@tin.it, Zuel 100)* in Cortina charges L50,000 to L90,000 per person, depending on the season. SAD buses connect Cortina with Bolzano, via Dobbiaco, and long-distance services are operated by ATVO, Zani, Lazzi and SITA.

CANAZEI
pop 1730

Set in the Fassa Dolomites, the resort of Canazei has more than 100km of trails and is linked to the challenging network of runs known as the **Sella Ronda**. Canazei also offers cross-country skiing and summer skiing on Marmolada, which at 3342m is the highest peak in the Dolomites.

The Marmolada *camping ground (☎ 0462 60 16 60)* is open all year, and there is also a choice of hotels, furnished rooms and apartments. Contact the AAST tourist office (☎ 0462 60 11 13, fax 0462 60 25 02) for full details. The resort is accessible by Atesina bus from Trent and SAD bus from Bolzano.

VAL GARDENA

This is one of the most popular skiing areas in the Alps, due to its reasonable prices and first-class facilities for downhill, cross-country and Alpine skiing. There are superb walking trails in the Sella Group and the Alpe di Siusi. The Vallunga, behind Selva, is great for family walks and cross-country skiing.

The valley's main towns are Ortisei, Santa Cristina and Selva, all offering plenty of accommodation and easy access to runs. The tourist offices at Santa Cristina (☎ 0471 79 30 46, fax 0471 79 31 98) and Selva (☎ 0471 79 51 22, fax 0471 79 42 45) have extensive information on accommodation and facilities. Staff speak English and will send details on request. The Val Gardena is accessible from Bolzano by SAD bus, and is connected to major Italian cities by coach services (Lazzi, SITA and STAT).

SAN MARTINO DI CASTROZZA

Located in a sheltered position beneath the Pale di San Martino, this resort is popular among Italians and offers good facilities and ski runs, as well as cross-country skiing and a toboggan run. The APT office (☎ 0439 76 88 67, fax 0439 76 88 14) will provide a full list of accommodation, or try *Garni Suisse (☎ 0439 680 87, Via Dolomiti 1)*, where singles/doubles with breakfast cost L43,000/86,000. Buses travel regularly from Trent, Milan, Venice, Padua and Bologna.

Central Italy

Miraculously, the rolling hills and soft golden light of Tuscany, and rugged hill towns of Umbria and the Marches – so familiar to us through the works of the Renaissance artists – seem virtually unchanged today. The locals remain close to the land, but in each of the regions there is a strong artistic and cultural tradition – even the smallest medieval hill town can harbour extraordinary works of art.

FLORENCE
pop 403,294

Cradle of the Renaissance, home of Dante, Machiavelli, Michelangelo and the Medici. Florence's (Firenze) dazzling wealth of art, culture and history overwhelms most visitors, making it one of the most enticing cities in Italy – as the throngs of visitors attest.

Florence was founded as a colony of the Etruscan city of Fiesole in about 200 BC and later became the strategic Roman garrison settlement of Florentia. In the Middle Ages the city developed a flourishing economy based on banking and commerce, which sparked a period of building and growth previously unequalled in Italy. It was a major focal point for the Guelph and Ghibelline struggle of the 13th century, which saw Dante banished from the city. But Florence truly flourished in the 15th century under the Medici, reaching the height of its cultural, artistic and political development as it gave birth to the Renaissance.

The Grand Duchy of the Medici was succeeded in the 18th century by the House of Lorraine (related to the Austrian Habsburgs). Following the Risorgimento unification, Florence was the capital of the new kingdom of Italy from 1865 to 1871. During WWII parts of the city were destroyed by bombing, including all of the bridges except the Ponte Vecchio, and in 1966 a devastating flood destroyed or severely damaged many important works of art.

Orientation

Whether you arrive by train, bus or car, the main train station, Santa Maria Novella, is a good reference point. Budget hotels and pensioni are concentrated around Via Nazionale to the east of the station, and Piazza Santa Maria Novella to the south. The main thoroughfare to the centre is Via de' Panzani and then Via de' Cerretani, about a 10-minute walk. You'll know you've arrived when you first glimpse the Duomo.

Once at Piazza del Duomo you will find Florence easy to negotiate, with most of the major sights within easy walking distance. Most museums stay open until 10 pm (virtually all are closed on Monday), but Florence is a living art museum and you won't waste your time by just strolling through its streets. Take the city ATAF buses for longer distances such as to Piazzale Michelangelo or the nearby suburb of Fiesole, both of which offer panoramic views of the city.

Information

Tourist Offices The Florence City Council (Comune di Firenze) operates a tourist information office (☎ 055 21 22 45, fax 055 238 12 26) opposite the main train station at Piazza della Stazione 4, next to the Chiesa di Santa Maria Novella; there's another office at

Borgo Santa Croce 29r (☎ 055 234 04 44). Opening hours are 8.30 am to 5.30 pm Monday to Saturday (to 1.30 pm on Sunday). The main APT office (☎ 055 29 08 32/33, fax 055 276 03 83) is just north of the Duomo at Via Cavour 1r, open 8.15 am to 7.15 pm Monday to Saturday and Sunday to 1.30 pm. At all offices you can pick up a map of the city, a list of hotels and other useful information.

The Consorzio ITA, inside the station on the main concourse, has a computerised system for checking the availability of hotel rooms and can book you a night for a small fee; there are no phone bookings. A good map of the city, on sale at newsstands, is the one with the white, red and black cover called *Firenze: Pianta della Città*.

Foreign Consulates The US consulate (☎ 055 239 82 76) is at Lungarno Vespucci 38, the UK's (☎ 055 28 41 33) is at Lungarno Corsini 2 and the French consulate (☎ 055 230 25 56) is at Piazza Ognissanti 2.

Money The main banks are concentrated around Piazza della Repubblica. You can also use the service at the information office in the station, but it has poor exchange rates.

Post & Communications The main post office is on Via Pellicceria, off Piazza della Repubblica, and is open 8.15 am to 7 pm Monday to Saturday. Poste restante mail can be addressed to 50100 Firenze. There is a Telecom office at Via Cavour 21r, open 7 am to 11 pm daily, and another at the station.

Internet Train has 10 branches in Florence, including offices not far from the station at Via Guelfa 24r (☎ 055 21 47 94) and in Santa Croce at Via dei Benci 36 (☎ 055 263 85 55). It charges L6000/12,000 per half-hour/hour and also offers postal and money-transfer services. The lively Caffè Mambo at Via G Verdi 49 has a separate Internet area and charges L2500 for 15 minutes.

Bookshops The Paperback Exchange, Via Fiesolana 31r (closed Sunday), offers a vast selection of new and second-hand English-language books. Internazionale Seeber, Via de' Tornabuoni 70r; and Feltrinelli International, Via Cavour 12 20r, also have good selections.

ITALY

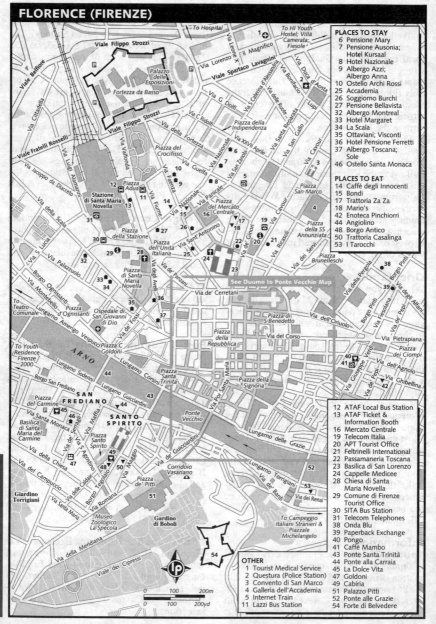

FLORENCE (FIRENZE)

PLACES TO STAY
6 Pensione Mary
7 Pensione Ausonia;
   Hotel Kursaal
8 Hotel Nazionale
9 Albergo Azzi;
   Albergo Anna
10 Ostello Archi Rossi
25 Accademia
26 Soggiorno Burchi
27 Pensione Bellavista
32 Albergo Montreal
33 Hotel Margaret
34 La Scala
35 Ottaviani; Visconti
36 Hotel Pensione Ferretti
37 Albergo Toscana;
   Sole
46 Ostello Santa Monaca

PLACES TO EAT
14 Caffè degli Innocenti
15 Bondi
17 Trattoria Za Za
18 Mario's
42 Enoteca Pinchiorri
44 Angiolino
48 Borgo Antico
50 Trattoria Casalinga
53 I Tarocchi

OTHER
1 Tourist Medical Service
2 Questura (Police Station)
3 Convento di San Marco
4 Galleria dell'Accademia
5 Internet Train
11 Lazzi Bus Station
12 ATAF Local Bus Station
13 ATAF Ticket &
   Information Booth
16 Mercato Centrale
19 Telecom Italia
20 APT Tourist Office
21 Feltrinelli International
22 Passamaneria Toscana
23 Basilica di San Lorenzo
24 Cappelle Medicee
28 Chiesa di Santa
   Maria Novella
29 Comune di Firenze
   Tourist Office
30 SITA Bus Station
31 Telecom Telephones
38 Onda Blu
39 Paperback Exchange
40 Pongo
41 Caffè Mambo
43 Ponte Santa Trinità
44 Ponte alla Carraia
45 La Dolce Vita
47 Goldoni
49 Cabiria
51 Palazzo Pitti
52 Ponte alle Grazie
54 Forte di Belvedere

See Duomo to Ponte Vecchio Map

0   100   200m
0   100   200yd

euro currency converter €1 = L1936

Laundry Onda Blu, east of the Duomo at Via degli Alfani 24bR and at Via Guelfa 22a rosso, is self-service and charges L5500 to wash and L5500 to dry.

Medical & Emergency Services For an ambulance call ☎ 118. The main public hospital is Ospedale Careggi (☎ 055 427 71 11), Viale Morgagni 85, north of the city centre. Tourist Medical Service (☎ 055 47 54 11), Via Lorenzo il Magnifico 59, can be phoned 24 hours and the doctors speak English, French and German. An organisation of volunteer interpreters (English, French and German) called the Associazione Volontari Ospedalieri (☎ 055 234 45 67, ☎ 055 40 31 26) will translate free of charge once you've found a doctor. Hospitals have a list of volunteers. All-night pharmacies include the Farmacia Comunale (☎ 055 28 94 35), inside the station; and Molteni (☎ 055 28 94 90) in the city centre at Vìa dei Calzaiuoli 7r.

Call ☎ 113 for the police. The questura (☎ 055 497 71) is at Via Zara 2. There is an office for foreigners where you can report thefts etc. For information about lost property call ☎ 055 328 39 42. Towed-away cars (☎ 055 30 82 49) can be collected from Via dell'Arcovata 6 (south-west of the centre).

Dangers & Annoyances Crowds, heavy traffic, noisy Vespas and summer heat can combine to make Florence unpleasant. Air pollution can be a problem for small children, people with respiratory problems and the elderly. Pickpockets are active in crowds and on buses: beware of the groups of dishevelled women and children carrying newspapers and cardboard, whose trick is to distract you while others rifle through your bag and pockets.

Things to See & Do

Duomo With its nougat facade and sykline-dominating dome, the Duomo is one of Italy's most famous monuments, and the world's fourth-largest cathedral. Named the Cattedrale di Santa Maria del Fiore, the breathtaking structure was begun in 1294 by the Sienese architect Arnolfo di Cambio but took almost 150 years to complete.

The Renaissance architect Brunelleschi won a public competition in 1420 to design the enormous dome, the first of its kind since antiquity. The octagonal dome is decorated with frescoes by Vasari and Zuccari, and stained-glass windows by Donatello, Paolo Uccello and Lorenzo Ghiberti. For a bird's-eye view of Florence, climb to the top of the cupola (open 8.30 am to 7.30 pm Monday to Friday and to 5 pm on Saturday; entry L10,000). The Duomo's marble facade is a 19th-century replacement of the unfinished original, which was pulled down in the 16th century.

Giotto designed and began building the graceful **bell tower** next to the cathedral in 1334, but died before it was completed. The campanile is 82m high and you can climb its stairs daily between 9 am and 7.30 pm; entry is L10,000.

The Romanesque **baptistry**, believed to have been built between the 5th and 11th centuries on the site of a Roman temple, is the oldest building in Florence. Dante was baptised here, and it is particularly famous for its gilded-bronze doors. The celebrated *Gates of Paradise* by Lorenzo Ghiberti face the Duomo to the east; Ghiberti also designed the north door. The south door, by Andrea Pisano, dates from 1336 and is the oldest. Most of the doors are copies – the original panels are being removed for restoration and placement in the Museo dell'Opera del Duomo. The baptistry is open noon to 6.30 pm Monday to Saturday and 8.30 am to 1.30 pm on Sunday; entry costs L5000.

Uffizi Gallery The Palazzo degli Uffizi, built by Vasari in the 16th century, contains some of the world's best-loved Renaissance paintings. The collection is Italy's most important, and represents the huge legacy of the Medici family. Be prepared to swoon – and to join a lengthy queue.

The gallery's inordinate number of masterpieces include 14th-century gems by Giotto and Cimabue; Botticelli's *Birth of Venus* and *Allegory of Spring* from the 15th century; and works by Filippo Lippi, Fra Angelico and Paolo Uccello. *The Annunciation* by Leonardo da Vinci is also here, along with Michelangelo's *Holy Family*, Titian's *Venus of Urbino* and renowned works by Raphael, Andrea del Sarto, Tintoretto, Caravaggio and Tiepolo. The gallery is open 8.30 am to 10 pm daily except Monday (Sunday to 8 pm). Entry is L12,000.

ITALY

Piazza della Signoria & Palazzo Vecchio Designed by Arnolfo di Cambio and built between 1298 and 1340, the Palazzo Vecchio is the traditional seat of the Florentine government. In the 16th century it became the ducal palace of the Medici (before they moved to the Palazzo Pitti), and was given an interior facelift by Vasari. Visit the Michelozzo courtyard just inside the entrance and the lavishly decorated apartments upstairs. The palazzo is open 9 am to 7 pm (Thursday and Sunday to 2 pm) daily. Admission is L11,000.

The palace's turrets, battlements and bell tower form an imposing backdrop to Piazza della Signoria, scene of many pivotal political events in the history of Florence, including the execution of the religious and political reformer Savonarola; a bronze plaque marks the spot where he was burned at the stake in 1498. The **Loggia della Signoria**, at right angles to the Palazzo Vecchio, displays sculptures such as Giambologna's *Rape of the Sabine Women*, but Cellini's famous *Perseus* has been relocated to the Uffizi. The statue of *David* is a fine copy of Michelangelo's masterpiece; the original was installed on the site in 1504, and is now safely indoors in the Galleria dell'Accademia.

Ponte Vecchio This famous 14th-century bridge, lined with gold and silversmiths' shops, was the only one to survive Nazi bombing in WWII. Originally, the shops housed butchers, but when a corridor along the 1st floor was built by the Medici to link the Palazzo Pitti and Palazzo Vecchio, it was ordered that goldsmiths rather than noisome butchers should trade on the bridge.

Palazzo Pitti This immense and imposing palazzo was built for the Pitti family, great rivals of the Medici, who moved in a century later. The **Galleria Palatina** has works by Raphael, Filippo Lippi, Titian and Rubens, hung in lavishly decorated rooms. The gallery and gloriously over-the-top **royal apartments** are open 8.30 am to 10 pm Tuesday to Saturday and to 8 pm on Sunday; entry L12,000. The palace also houses the **Museo degli Argenti** (Silver Museum) and **Galleria d'Arte Moderna**, open 8.30 am to 2 pm Tuesday to Sunday.

Don't leave without visiting the Renaissance **Giardino di Boboli** (Boboli Gardens), with grottoes, fountains, leafy walkways and panoramic city views. Entry is L4000.

Museo del Bargello Also known as the Palazzo del Podestà, the medieval Palazzo del Bargello has a grim history as the seat of the local ruler and, later, of the chief of police. The palace now houses Florence's rich collection of sculpture, notably Michelangelo's *Bacchus*, Donatello's bronze *David*, Giambologna's *Mercury* and works by Benvenuto Cellini and the della Robbias. The Bargello is at Via del Proconsolo 4, and is open 8.30 am to 2 pm Tuesday to Sunday; entry is L8000.

Galleria dell'Accademia Michelangelo's *David* is housed in this gallery, as are four of the artist's unfinished *Slaves*. Early Florentine works are on show in the gallery upstairs. The Accademia is at Via Ricasoli 60, and opens 8.30 am to 10 pm Tuesday to Saturday and Sunday to 8 pm. Entry is L12,000.

Convento di San Marco The Monastery of St Mark pays homage to the work of Fra Angelico, who decorated many of the monks' cells with sublime frescoes and lived here from 1438 to 1455. Don't miss the peaceful cloisters (depicted in his *Annunciation*). The monastery also contains works by Fra Bartolomeo and Ghirlandaio, as well as the cell of the monk Savonarola. It's open 8.30 am to 2 pm Tuesday to Sunday, and entry is L8000.

Basilica di San Lorenzo & Cappelle Medicee The basilica was built by Brunelleschi in the early 15th century for the Medici and includes his mathematically precise **Sagrestia Vecchia** (Old Sacristy), with sculptural decoration by Donatello. The cloister leads to the **Biblioteca Laurenziana**, the huge library built to house the Medici collection of some 10,000 manuscripts and entered via Michelangelo's flowing Mannerist stairway.

The Cappelle Medicee (Medici Chapels) are around the corner in Piazza Madonna degli Aldobrandini. The **Cappella dei Principi**, sumptuously decorated with marble and semiprecious stones, was the principal burial

ITALY

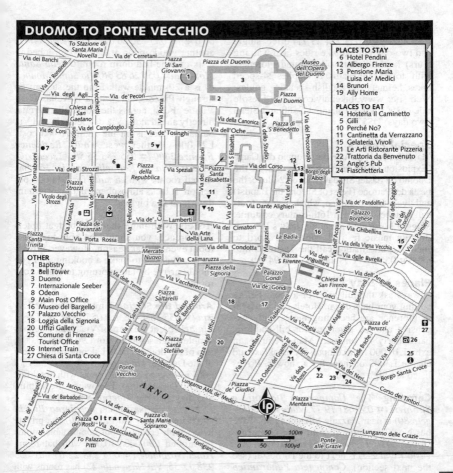

DUOMO TO PONTE VECCHIO

PLACES TO STAY
6 Hotel Pendini
12 Albergo Firenze
13 Pensione Maria
   Luisa de' Medici
14 Brunori
19 Aily Home

PLACES TO EAT
4 Hosteria Il Caminetto
5 Gilli
10 Perché No?
11 Cantinetta da Verrazzano
15 Gelateria Vivoli
21 Le Arti Ristorante Pizzeria
22 Trattoria da Benvenuto
23 Angie's Pub
24 Fiaschetteria

OTHER
1 Baptistry
2 Bell Tower
3 Duomo
7 Internazionale Seeber
8 Odeon
9 Main Post Office
16 Museo del Bargello
17 Palazzo Vecchio
18 Loggia della Signoria
20 Uffizi Gallery
25 Comune di Firenze
   Tourist Office
26 Internet Train
27 Chiesa di Santa Croce

place of the Medici grand dukes. The incomplete **Sagrestia Nuova** was Michelangelo's first architectural effort, and contains his *Medici Madonna*, *Night & Day* and *Dawn & Dusk* sculptures, which adorn the Medici tombs. The chapels are open 8.30 am to 5 pm Tuesday to Sunday, and admission is L11,000.

Other Attractions The Tuscan Gothic **Chiesa di Santa Maria Novella** was constructed for the Dominican Order during the 13th and 14th centuries; its white-and-green marble facade was designed by Alberti in the 15th century. The church features Masaccio's *Trinity*, a masterpiece of perspective, and is decorated with frescoes by Ghirlandaio (who was perhaps assisted by a very young Michelangelo). **Cappella di Filippo Strozzi** has frescoes by Filippino Lippi, and those in the cloisters are by Paolo Uccello.

Head up to **Piazzale Michelangelo** for unparalleled views of Florence. To reach the piazzale from the city centre, cross the Ponte Vecchio, turn left and walk along the river, then turn right at Piazza Giuseppe Poggi; if you're footsore, take bus No 13 from the station.

ITALY

Cycling

I Bike Italy (☎ 055 234 23 71) offers single and two-day guided bike rides (and walking tours) in the countryside around Florence, with stops at vineyards. It supplies 24-speed bikes, helmets and English-speaking guides; Web site: www.ibikeitaly.com. The Fiesole ride costs US$65, Chianti US$80 and Siena (two days) US$235.

Special Events

Major festivals include the Scoppio del Carro (Explosion of the Cart), held in front of the Duomo on Easter Sunday; and, on 24 June, the Festa del Patrono (Feast of St John the Baptist) and lively Calcio Storico, which features football matches played in 16th-century costume. Maggio Musicale Fiorentino, Italy's longest-running music festival, runs from April to June. For information call the Teatro Comunale (☎ 055 21 11 58, fax 055 277 94 10).

Places to Stay

Always ask the full price of a room before putting your bags down. Hotels and pensioni in Florence are becoming increasingly expensive and are notorious for bill-padding, particularly in summer. Many require an extra L10,000 for a compulsory breakfast and charge L3000 or more for a shower. Prices listed are high season.

Camping The *Campeggio Italiani e Stranieri* (☎ 055 681 19 77, *Viale Michelangelo 80*) is near Piazzale Michelangelo. Take bus No 13 from the station. *Villa Camerata* (☎ 055 60 03 15, fax 055 61 03 00, *Viale Augusto Righi 2-4*) is next to the HI hostel (see the next section). *Campeggio Panoramico* (☎ 055 59 90 69, fax 055 591 86, *Via Peramonda 1*), in Fiesole, also has bungalows. Take bus No 7 from the station.

Hostels The HI *Ostello Villa Camerata* (☎ 055 60 14 51, fax 055 61 03 00, *Viale Augusto Righi 2-4*) charges L26,000 for B&B and L14,000 for dinner; there is also a bar. Take bus No 17, which leaves from the right of the station as you leave the platforms and takes 20 minutes. Daytime closing is 9 am to 2 pm. It is open to HI members only and reservations can be made by mail (essential in summer).

The private *Ostello Archi Rossi* (☎ 055 29 08 04, fax 055 230 26 01, *Via Faenza 94r*) is another good option at L30,000 for a bed in a six or nine-bed dorm room. *Ostello Santa Monaca* (☎ 055 26 83 38, *Via Santa Monaca 6*) is a 20-minute walk from the station: go through Piazza Santa Maria Novella, along Via de' Fossi, across the Ponte alla Carraia, directly ahead along Via de' Serragli, and Via Santa Monaca is on the right. A bed costs L25,000. Further west, *Youth Residence Firenze 2000* (☎ 055 233 55 58, ✉ scatizzi@ dada.it, *Via le Raffaello Sanzio 16*) has shared rooms with *en suite* for L55,000 per person. It lacks atmosphere, but the warm indoor pool is a big plus.

Hotels With more than 150 budget hotels in Florence, you should be able to find a room even in peak season. However, it is always advisable to make a booking, and you should arrive by late morning to claim your room.

Around the Station Tiny *Pensione Bellavista* (☎ 055 28 45 28, fax 055 28 48 74, *Largo Alinari 15*), at the start of Via Nazionale, has simple singles/doubles for L90,000/130,000; two of the doubles have balconies and a view of the Duomo. *Albergo Azzi* (☎/fax 055 21 38 06, *Via Faenza 56*) has rooms with breakfast for L70,000/110,000. The owners are helpful, and they also run *Albergo Anna* upstairs.

Across Via Nazionale, *Soggiorno Burchi* (☎ 055 41 44 54, *Via Faenza 20*) is a private house with eccentric but comfortable rooms for around L90,000/110,000 with bathroom. *Hotel Nazionale* (☎ 055 238 22 03, fax 055 238 17 35, *Via Nazionale 22*) has rooms with shower for L100,000/150,000, breakfast included. A few doors up at No 24, the recently renovated *Pensione Ausonia* (☎ 055 49 65 47, fax 055 462 66 15) has something for everyone. Run by a young couple who go out of their way to help travellers, the accommodation ranges from standard singles/doubles/triples with breakfast for L90,000/145,000/190,000 to rooms with bathroom for L115,000/165,000/ 220,000; downstairs in their two-star *Hotel Kursaal* (☎ 055 49 63 24), superior doubles/ triples with balcony, air-con and satellite TV are L210,000/255,000. *Pensione Mary* (☎/fax 055 49 63 10, *Piazza dell'Indipendenza 5*) has

ITALY

singles/doubles with bathroom and breakfast for L120,000/160,000.

Closer to the station, the two-star *Accademia* (☎ 055 29 34 51, fax 055 21 97 71, *Via Faenza 7*) is housed in an 18th-century palace, replete with magnificent stained-glass doors and carved wooden ceilings. Singles are L140,000 and doubles with bathroom go for L230,000, including breakfast and satellite TV.

Around Piazza Santa Maria Novella Via della Scala, which runs north-west off the piazza, is lined with pensioni. *La Scala* (☎ 055 21 26 29) at No 21 has small doubles/triples for L85,000/150,000. *Hotel Margaret* (☎ 055 21 01 38), at No 25, has pleasantly furnished singles/doubles with bathroom for L95,000/120,000. At No 43, the no-frills *Albergo Montreal* (☎ 055 238 23 31, fax 055 28 74 91) has clean singles for L85,000 and doubles/triples/quads with bathroom for L110,000/150,000/185,000.

Sole (☎/fax 055 239 60 94, *Via del Sole 8*) charges L70,000/100,000 for basic singles/doubles; a double with bathroom costs L120,000. Ask for a quiet room, as the street can be noisy. *Albergo Toscana* (☎/fax 055 21 31 56), in the same building, has pretty rooms with bathroom for L90,000/150,000. Slightly north, the family-run *Hotel Pensione Ferretti* (☎ 055 238 13 28, fax 055 21 92 88, *Via delle Belle Donne 17*) has comfortable singles for L70,000; rooms with bathroom are L90,000/140,000, including breakfast.

Ottaviani (☎ 055 239 62 23, fax 055 29 33 55, *Piazza Ottaviani 1*), just off Piazza Santa Maria Novella, has singles/doubles for a reasonable L70,000/90,000, breakfast included. *Visconti* (☎/fax 055 21 38 77), in the same building, has statues galore and a pleasant breakfast terrace. Singles are L65,000 and doubles are L90,000/140,000 without/with bathroom.

The Duomo to Ponte Vecchio This area is a 15-minute walk from the station and is right in the heart of old Florence. One of the best deals is the small *Aily Home* (☎ 055 239 65 05, *Piazza Santo Stefano 1*), overlooking the Ponte Vecchio. Its singles are L40,000 and doubles (three of which overlook the bridge) go for L70,000 a night. *Albergo Firenze*

(☎ 055 21 42 03, fax 055 21 23 70, *Piazza dei Donati 4*), just south of the Duomo, offers singles/doubles with bathroom and breakfast for L100,000/140,000. *Brunori* (☎ 055 28 96 48, *Via del Proconsolo 5*) has doubles for L96,000, with bathroom for L124,000. *Pensione Maria Luisa de' Medici* (☎/fax 055 28 00 48, *Via del Corso 1*) is in a 17th-century palace. It has no singles, but its large rooms cater for up to five people. A double starts at L80,000.

Up several notches, the three-star *Hotel Pendini* (☎ 055 21 11 70, fax 055 28 18 07, *Via degli Strozzi 2*) is just around the corner from Piazza della Repubblica. Light and airy rooms on the 4th floor are L180,000/260,000. A family suite for six is L570,000.

Villa Experience life in an old villa at *Bencistà* (☎/fax 055 591 63, ✉ bencista@uol.it, *Via Benedetto da Maiano 4*), about 1km from Fiesole in the hills overlooking Florence. Compulsory half-board is a budget-breaking L270,000/300,000 without/with bathroom.

Places to Eat
Tuscany is known for its simple but fine cuisine. At its most basic, how can you beat a thick slice of crusty bread drizzled with olive oil and downed with a glass of ripe Chianti? Try the *ribollita*, a very filling soup of vegetables and white beans, reboiled with chunks of bread and garnished with olive oil. Another traditional dish is *bistecca alla Fiorentina* (steak Florentine), big enough for two.

The *covered market* in San Lorenzo, open 7 am to 2 pm Monday to Friday, offers fresh produce, cheeses and meat at reasonable prices.

Restaurants – City Centre At the *Trattoria da Benvenuto* (*Via Mosca 16r*), on the corner of Via dei Neri, a full repast will cost around L45,000 and a quick meal of pasta, bread and wine L16,000. For more atmospheric surroundings, there's the attractively timbered *Le Arti Ristorante Pizzeria* (*Via dei Neri 57*). The menu is more varied than most, with good pizza for around L10,000 and pasta for L13,000. At No 35r on the same street, *Angie's Pub* has focaccia for around L6000, as well as hamburgers and hot dogs, swilled down with beer on tap; there's no extra charge to sit. *Fiaschetteria* (*Via dei Neri 17r*) has a

ITALY

good range of panini from L2500 and value-for-money pastas for around L8000.

At *Hosteria Il Caminetto* (*Via dello Studio 34*), just south of Piazza del Duomo, pasta for L14,000 or a full meal for around L45,000 can be enjoyed on its small vine-covered terrace. *Enoteca Pinchiorri* (☎ 24 27 77, *Via Ghibellina 87*), just north of Chiesa di Santa Croce, is arguably the city's finest restaurant. The cuisine is Italian-style nouvelle, the surroundings are palatial and, at more than L150,000 per head, the prices are prohibitive.

Restaurants – Around San Lorenzo
Tiny but popular *Mario's* (*Via Rosina 2r*), near the Mercato Centrale, is open at lunchtime only, and serves delicious pasta for around L7000. Around the corner at Piazza del Mercato Centrale 24, *Trattoria Za Za* is another local favourite, with outdoor seating and reasonable prices. *Bondi* (*Via dell'Ariento 85*) specialises in focaccia and pizza from L3000.

Restaurants – In the Oltrarno *Trattoria Casalinga* (*Via dei Michelozzi 9r*) is a bustling place popular with the locals. The food is great and a filling meal of pasta, meat or contorni, and wine will cost around L15,000 to L20,000. *I Tarocchi* (*Via de' Renai 16*) serves superior pizza from L7500 to L10,000, as well as regional dishes including a good range of pasta from L9000 to L11,000 and plenty of salads for around L8000. *Angiolino* (*Via Santo Spirito 36r*) is an excellent trattoria where a full meal will cost around L40,000. In trendy Piazza Santo Spirito, *Borgo Antico* is a great summer retreat for alfresco dining, but at L25,000 for spaghetti vongole it's not cheap.

Cafes & Snack Bars
Perhaps the city's finest cafe is the wonderfully intact *belle époque Gilli*, on Piazza della Repubblica. If you can't resist the bountiful display of mouthwatering sweet and savoury delights, you'll save lire if not calories by eating and drinking at the bar.

Caffè degli Innocenti (*Via Nazionale 57*), near the Mercato Centrale, has a selection of pre-prepared panini and good cakes for around L2500 to L4500. The streets between the Duomo and the Arno harbour many pizzerias where you can buy takeaway pizza by the slice for around L2000 to L4000, depending on the weight.

Cantinetta da Verrazzano (*Via dei Tavolini 18r*) wine bar/cafe is a tight fit and deservedly popular. Grab a snack from the takeaway bakery, have a meal or quaff some memorable Chianti.

Gelati Two of the city's best outlets for gelati are *Gelateria Vivoli* in Via dell'Isola delle Stinche, south of Via Ghibellina, and *Perché No?* (*Via dei Tavolini 19r*), off Via dei Calzaiuoli. Tiny tubs cost L3000, but at Vivoli it's well worth it for the comfy seats and welcome bathroom.

Entertainment
Hotels and tourist offices should have copies of the various free publications listing the theatrical and musical events and festivals held in the city and surrounding areas. Look out for the bimonthly *Florence Today* and the monthly *Florence Concierge Information*. The monthly *Firenze Spettacolo* entertainment guide is available from newsstands, where you can also pick up English-language publication *Vista*.

Concerts, opera and dance are performed year-round at the *Teatro Comunale* (*Corso Italia 16*), with the main seasons running from September to December and January to April. Contact the theatre's box office (☎ 055 277 92 36).

English films are screened at a number of cinemas: the *Astro* in Piazza San Simone, near Santa Croce (every night except Monday); the *Odeon* in Piazza Strozzi (Monday and Wednesday); and the *Goldoni*, Via de' Serragli (Wednesday).

Nightclubs include *La Dolce Vita*, spilling onto Piazza del Carmine, south of the Arno, and *Pongo* (*Via Giuseppe Verdi 59r*), with an assortment of live music. The tiny but noisy *Cabiria* bar in Piazza Santo Spirito is popular, especially in summer.

A more sedate pastime is the nightly *passeggiata* (stroll) in Piazzale Michelangelo, overlooking the city (take bus No 13 from the station or the Duomo).

Shopping
The main shopping area is between the Duomo and the Arno, with boutiques concentrated

along Via Roma, Via dei Calzaiuoli and Via Por Santa Maria, leading to the goldsmiths lining the Ponte Vecchio. Window-shop along Via de' Tornabuoni, where top designers such as Gucci, Prada and Ferragamo hawk their wares.

The open-air market (open Monday to Saturday) held in the streets surrounding San Lorenzo near the Mercato Centrale offers leather goods, clothing and jewellery at low prices but often dodgy quality. Check carefully before you buy. You can bargain, but not if you use a credit card. The flea market at Piazza dei Ciompi, off Borgo Allegri and north of Santa Croce, is not as extensive but there are often some great bargains. It opens from around 9 am to 6 pm Monday to Saturday and on the last Sunday of the month.

Florence is renowned for its beautifully patterned paper, which is stocked in the many *cartolerie* (stationer's shops) throughout the city and at the markets. Lovers of Florentine velvet cushions, tapestries and decorative tassels should head for Passamaneria Toscana, Piazza San Lorenzo 12r.

Getting There & Away

Air Florence is served by two airports, Amerigo Vespucci and Galileo Galilei. Amerigo Vespucci (☎ 055 37 34 98, flight info ☎ 055 306 17 00/02), a few kilometres north-west of the city centre, serves domestic and European flights. Galileo Galilei (☎ 055 21 60 73, Firenze Air Terminal at Santa Maria Novella station), just under an hour away from Florence near Pisa, is one of northern Italy's main international and domestic airports.

Bus The SITA bus station (☎ 055 21 47 21, fax 055 48 36 51), Via Santa Caterina da Siena 17, is just west of the train station. Buses leave for Siena, San Gimignano and Volterra. Lazzi (☎ 055 28 71 18, fax 055 21 43 28) is at Piazza Stazione 47r.

Train Florence is on the main Rome-Milan line. Most of the trains are the fast Eurostars, for which you have to book and to pay a *rapido* supplement. Regular trains also go to/from Venice (three hours) and Trieste. For train information ring ☎ 147 88 80 88.

Car & Motorcycle Florence is connected by the Autostrada del Sole (A1) to Bologna and Milan in the north and Rome and Naples to the south. The Firenze-Mare motorway links Florence with Prato, Pistoia, Lucca, Pisa and the Versilia coast, and a *superstrada* (dual carriageway) joins the city to Siena. Exits from the autostrade into Florence are well signposted, and either one of the exits marked 'Firenze nord' or 'Firenze sud' will take you to the centre of town. There are tourist information offices on the A1 both to the north and south of the city.

Getting Around

To/From the Airport Regular trains to Pisa airport leave from platform No 5 at Florence's Santa Maria Novella station daily from 6.46 am to 5 pm. Check your bags in at the air terminal (☎ 055 21 60 73) near platform 5, at least 15 minutes before train departure time.

You can get to Amerigo Vespucci airport by ATAF bus No 62 from the train station (every 20 minutes from 6.30 am to 10.20 pm) or, more directly, by SITA coach from the depot in Via Santa Caterina da Siena (every hour or so from 8.15 am to 7.30 pm).

Bus ATAF buses service the city centre and Fiesole. The terminal for the most useful buses is in a small piazza to the left as you go out of the station onto Via Valfonda. Bus No 7 leaves from here for Fiesole and also stops at the Duomo. Tickets must be bought before you get on the bus and are sold at most tobacconists and newsstands or from automatic vending machines at major bus stops (L1500 for one hour, L2500 for three hours, L6000 for 24 hours).

Car & Motorcycle If you're spending the day in Florence, use the underground parking areas at the train station or in Piazza del Mercato Centrale (L4000 an hour). Less expensive parking is available from November to February at the Fortezza da Basso (L3000 an hour).

To rent a car, try Hertz (☎ 055 28 22 60), Via M Finiguerra 33r, or Avis (☎ 055 21 36 29), Borgo Ognissanti 128r. For motorcycles and bicycles try Alinari (☎ 055 28 05 00), Via Guelfa 85r. Ask at the station for information about the city council's free bicycles for use between 8 am and 7.30 pm.

ITALY

Taxi You can find taxis outside the station, or call ☎ 055 4798 or ☎ 055 4390 to book one.

PISA
pop 98,928

Once a maritime power to rival Genoa and Venice, Pisa now makes the most of its one remaining claim to fame: its leaning tower. The busy port city was also the site of an important university and the home of Galileo Galilei (1564-1642). Pisa was devastated by the Genoese in the 13th century, and its history eventually merged with that of Florence. Like that city, Pisa straddles the Arno River; unlike Florence, however, the city has a pleasing intimacy and charm so far intact despite the many day-trippers.

Orientation & Information

The focus for visitors is the Campo dei Miracoli, a 1.5km walk from the train station across the Arno. Bus No 4 will save you the walk. The medieval town centre around Borgo Stretto is a kilometre or so from the station.

There are APT tourist information offices at the station (☎ 050 422 91), the airport and at Via Carlo Cammeo 2, west of Campo dei Miracoli. The offices open 9 am to 7 pm Monday to Saturday, and 9.30 am to 1.30 pm Sunday. Pisa's postcode is 56100.

Things to See & Do

The Pisans can justly claim that their **Campo dei Miracoli** (Field of Miracles) is one of the most beautiful squares in the world, whether by day or by night. A welcome expanse of well-kept lawns provides the perfect setting for the dazzling white marble cathedral, baptistry and bell tower – all of which lean to varying degrees.

The striped Pisan-Romanesque **cathedral**, begun in 1063, has a graceful facade of tiered arches and a cavernous column-lined interior. The transept's bronze doors, facing the leaning tower, are by Bonanno Pisano, while the 16th-century bronze doors of the main entrance are by Giambologna. The cathedral's cupcake-like **baptistry**, which was started in 1153 and took two centuries to complete, contains a pulpit sculpted by Nicola Pisano.

The famous leaning **bell tower** found itself in trouble from the start, because of the marshy nature of the land on which it was built. Its architect, Bonanno Pisano, managed to complete only three of the tower's eventual seven tiers before it started to lean. It has continued to lean by an average 1mm a year, and today it is almost 5m off the perpendicular. The tower has been closed for over a decade, and is braced by strengthening cables, weighted with more than 1000 tons of lead and undergoing a ground-levelling process – all in all, it resembles a construction site. It's hoped that the weights and steel cables will be removed in 2001, leaving the tower still leaning but without the risk of collapse, and open to a limited number of visitors.

The pricing structure for the Campo is staggered; in essence, it costs L3000 to see the cathedral, and from L18,000 to L10,000 for all or just a few of the sights.

After taking in the Campo dei Miracoli, wander down Via Santa Maria, along the Arno and into the Borgo Stretto to explore the old city.

Places to Stay & Eat

Pisa has a range of reasonably priced hotels. Many of the budget places double as residences for students during the school year, so it can sometimes be difficult to find a cheap room.

The non-HI *Ostello per la Gioventù* (☎/fax 050 89 06 22, *Via Pietrasantina 15*) has dorm beds for L24,000, and is closed between 9 am and 6 pm. Take bus No 3 from the station. Right by the Campo dei Miracoli, *Albergo Gronchi* (☎ 050 56 18 23, *Piazza Arcivescovado 1*) has modern singles/doubles for L35,000/58,000. The two-star *Hotel di Stefano* (☎ 050 55 35 59, fax 050 55 60 38, *Via Sant'Apollonia 35*) is not far away and offers good-quality rooms with shower for L100,000/125,000. *Albergo Milano* (☎ 050 231 62, fax 050 442 37, *Via Mascagni 14*) is just outside the station, with pleasant rooms and a friendly owner. Basic rooms go for L60,000/80,000; rooms with shower cost L85,000/115,000.

Splash out with a view of the Arno at the grand *Royal Victoria* (☎ 050 94 01 11, fax 050 94 01 80, *Lungarno Pacinotti 12*), which dates from 1839 and offers lovely rooms for L145,000/175,000.

Being a university town, Pisa has a number of cheap eating places. Head for Borgo

ITALY

Stretto and the university area. *Trattoria da Matteo (Via l'Arancio 46)* is a good choice for cheap pizza and pasta. *Antica Trattoria il Campano*, in an old tower near the market at Vicolo Santa Margherita, is full of medieval atmosphere; a meal costs around L35,000. *Spaghetteria alle Bandierine (Via Mercanti 4)* has a rustic farmhouse feel and serves a multitude of delicious spaghetti dishes, particularly seafood. Leave room for the *panna cotta* with strawberries (L5000). Head to *La Bottega del Gelato* in Piazza Garibaldi for gelati, or grab a cocktail and bar snack at *Krott (Lungarno Pacinotti 2)*. There's an open-air food *market* in Piazza delle Vettovaglie, off Borgo Stretto.

Getting There & Away

The airport, with domestic and European flights, is only a few minutes away by train, or by bus No 3 from the station. Lazzi (☎ 050 462 88) buses run to Florence via Lucca; somewhat surprisingly, there's an original Keith Haring mural opposite its office in Piazza Vittorio Emanuele. CPT (☎ 050 50 55 11) operates buses to Livorno via Tirrenia. Pisa is linked by direct train to Florence, Rome and Genoa. Local trains head for Lucca and Livorno.

SIENA

pop 56,956

Italy's best preserved medieval town, Siena, is built on three hills and surrounded by its historic ramparts. The maze-like historic centre is jam-packed with majestic Gothic buildings in various shades of the colour known as burnt sienna; it's also usually crammed to bursting with visitors.

According to legend, Siena was founded by the sons of Remus (one of the founders of Rome). In the Middle Ages the city became a free republic, but its success and power led to serious rivalry with Florence, both politically and culturally. Painters of the Sienese School produced significant works of art, and the city was home to St Catherine and St Benedict.

Siena is divided into 17 *contrade* (districts) and each year 10 are chosen to compete in the Palio, a tumultuous horse race and pageant held in the shell-shaped Piazza del Campo on 2 July and 16 August.

Orientation

Leaving the train station, cross the concourse to the bus stop opposite and catch bus No 9 or 10 to Piazza Gramsci, then walk into the centre along Via dei Termini (it takes about five minutes to reach Piazza del Campo). From the intercity bus station in Piazza San Domenico, it's a five-minute walk along Via della Sapienza and then turn right onto Via delle Terme. Visitors' cars are not allowed into the medieval centre.

Information

Tourist Office The APT office (☎ 0577 28 05 51, fax 0577 27 06 76) is at Piazza del Campo 56. It opens 8.30 am to 7.30 pm Monday to Saturday (8.30 am to 1 pm and 3 to 7 pm Monday to Friday and to 1 pm on Saturday from 11 November to 21 March).

Post & Communications The main post office is at Piazza Matteotti 1. Telecom is at Via dei Termini 40.

There is a branch of the Internet Train at di Città 121, with 20 screens.

Laundry Onda Blu, at Via Casato di Sotto 17, charges L10,000 to wash and dry.

Medical & Emergency Services For an ambulance, call ☎ 118. The public hospital (☎ 0577 58 51 11) is on Viale Bracci, just north of Siena at Le Scotte.

For police attendance call ☎ 113. The questura is at Via del Castoro 23 and its Foreigners' Bureau is in Piazza Jacopo della Quercia (facing the Duomo).

Things to See

Siena's uniquely shell-shaped **Piazza del Campo** (known simply as Il Campo) has been the city's focus since the 14th century. The piazza's sloping base is formed by the nobly proportioned **Palazzo Pubblico** (town hall), considered one of Italy's most graceful Gothic buildings. Its Sienese art treasures include Simone Martini's *Maestà* and Ambrogio Lorenzetti's *Allegories of Good & Bad Government*. The town hall is open 10 am to 7 pm daily (to 11 pm in July and August), and entry is L10,000 (L5000 for students).

The spectacular **Duomo** is another Gothic masterpiece, and one of the most enchanting

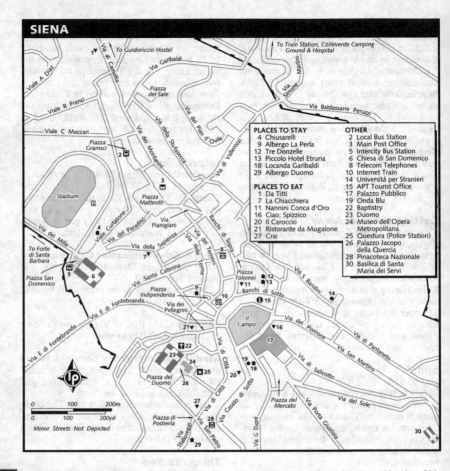

SIENA

PLACES TO STAY
4 Chiusarelli
9 Albergo La Perla
12 Tre Donzelle
13 Piccolo Hotel Etruria
18 Locanda Garibaldi
29 Albergo Duomo

PLACES TO EAT
1 Da Titti
7 La Chiacchiera
11 Nannini Conca d'Oro
16 Ciao; Spizzico
20 Il Caroccio
21 Ristorante da Mugalone
27 Crai

OTHER
2 Local Bus Station
3 Main Post Office
5 Intercity Bus Station
6 Chiesa di San Domenico
8 Telecom Telephones
10 Internet Train
14 Universitá per Stranieri
15 APT Tourist Office
17 Palazzo Pubblico
19 Onda Blu
22 Baptistry
23 Duomo
24 Museo dell'Opera
   Metropolitana
25 Questura (Police Station)
26 Palazzo Jacopo
   della Quercia
28 Pinacoteca Nazionale
30 Basilica di Santa
   Maria dei Servi

cathedrals in Italy; plans to enlarge it were stymied by the arrival of the Black Death in 1348. Its black-and-white striped marble facade has a Romanesque lower section, with carvings by Giovanni Pisano, and the inlaid-marble floor (largely covered) features various works depicting biblical stories. The marble and porphyry **pulpit** was carved by Nicola Pisano, father of Giovanni; other artworks include a bronze statue of St John the Baptist by Donatello, and statues of St Jerome and Mary Magdalene by Bernini.

A door in the north aisle leads to the **Libreria Piccolomini**, built by Pope Pius III to house the magnificent illustrated books of his uncle, Pope Pius II. It features frescoes by Pinturicchio and a Roman statue of the Three Graces. Entry is L2000.

The **Museo dell'Opera Metropolitana** (Duomo Museum) is in Piazza del Duomo. Its many works of art formerly adorned the cathedral, including the *Maestà* by Duccio di Buoninsegna and the 12 marble statues by Giovanni Pisano, which once graced the Duomo's facade; other works include those by Ambrogio Lorenzetti, Simone Martini and Taddeo di Bartolo. From mid-March to the end of September the museum is open 9 am to 7.30 pm daily. In October it closes at 6 pm and during the rest of the year at 1.30 pm. Entry is L6000.

The **baptistry**, behind the cathedral, has a Gothic facade and is decorated with 15th-century frescoes. The highlight is the font by Jacopo della Quercia, with sculptures by Donatello and Ghiberti. It opens 9 am to 7.30 pm daily (in October it closes at 6 pm and during the rest of the year its hours are 10 am to 1 pm and 2.30 to 5 pm); entry is L3000.

The 15th-century Palazzo Buonsignori houses the **Pinacoteca Nazionale** (National Picture Gallery), whose Sienese masterpieces include Duccio di Buoninsegna's *Madonna dei Francescani, Madonna col Bambino* by Simone Martini and a series of Madonnas by Ambrogio Lorenzetti. The gallery is open 9 am to 7 pm Tuesday to Saturday, Monday to 1.30 pm and 8 am to 1 pm on Sunday. Admission is L8000.

Places to Stay

It is always advisable to book a hotel in Siena, particularly in August and during the Palio, when accommodation is impossible to find for miles around.

Colleverde camping ground (☎ *0577 28 00 44, fax 0577 33 32 98*) is outside the historical centre at Strada di Scacciapensieri 47 (take bus No 3 from Piazza Gramsci). It opens 21 March to 10 November and costs L15,000 for adults, L8000 for children and L15,000 for a site.

Guidoriccio (☎ *0577 522 12, Via Fiorentina*) hostel is about 3km out of the centre in Stellino. B&B is L29,000 and an evening meal is L16,000. Take bus No 3 from Piazza Gramsci.

In the heart of the old town, *Tre Donzelle* (☎ *0577 28 03 58, fax 0577 22 39 33, Via delle Donzelle 5*) offers serviceable singles/doubles for L50,000/80,000 and doubles with shower for L100,000. Nearby, the two-star *Piccolo Hotel Etruria* (☎ *0577 28 80 88, fax 0577 28 84 61, Via delle Donzelle 1*) has renovated rooms for L75,000/120,000 with bathroom. *Albergo La Perla* (☎ *0577 471 44, Via delle Terme 25*) has small but clean rooms with shower for L80,000/110,000. Behind the town hall, *Locanda Garibaldi* (☎ *0577 28 42 04, Via Giovanni Dupré 18*) has rooms for

L45,000/85,000. Its small trattoria is reasonably priced.

The three-star *Duomo* (☎ *0577 28 90 88, fax 0577 430 43, Via Stalloreggi 38*) has rooms with views for L150,000/220,000. *Chiusarelli* (☎ *0577 28 05 62, fax 0577 27 11 77, Viale Curtatone 15*) is well placed for drivers near the Stadio Comunale car park; pleasant singles are L95,000, while singles/doubles with bathroom are L125,000/185,000.

Agriturismo is well organised around Siena. The tourist office can provide a list of establishments.

Places to Eat

The ubiquitous self-service *Ciao* and ready-to-go *Spizzico* are right on the Campo at No 77. For a traditional hostaria, try *Il Caroccio*, off the Campo at Via Casato di Sotto 32, where a meal costs around L35,000 and bistecca alla Fiorentina is L40,000 a kilogram. *Ristorante da Mugalone* (*Via dei Pelligrini 8*) is another good place for local specialities. Pasta is around L12,000, second courses L16,000 and bistecca is L6000 per 100gms.

Tiny *La Chiacchiera* (*Costa di Sant'Antonio 4*), off Via Santa Caterina, serves local specialities. Pasta dishes cost from L7000 and a bottle of house wine is L5000. A full meal will cost L30,000. There are several trattorias further north of here, in a less frenetic neighbourhood. *Da Titti* (*Via di Camollia 193*) is a no-frills establishment with big wooden bench tables where a full meal with wine costs around L28,000.

Supermarkets in the town centre include *Crai* (*Via di Città 152-156*) and *Consorzio Agrario*, Via Piani Giani. *Nannini Conca d'Oro* (*Banchi di Sopra 22*) is one of the city's finest cafes and a good place to stock up on panforte.

Getting There & Away

Regular Tra-In buses run from Florence to Siena, arriving at Piazza San Domenico. Buses also go to San Gimignano, Volterra and other points in Tuscany, and there's a daily bus to Rome. For timetable information about buses to Perugia, ask at the Balzana travel agency (☎ 0577 28 50 13); these buses leave from the train station.

Siena is not on a main train line, so from Rome it is necessary to change at Chiusi and from Florence at Empoli, making buses a better alternative.

SAN GIMIGNANO
pop 6956
Few places in Italy rival the beauty of San Gimignano, a town which has barely changed since medieval times. Set on a hill overlooking the misty pink, green and gold Tuscan landscape, the town is best known for its huge pockmarked towers (13 of the original 72 remain), the 11th-century fortified homes of its leading feuding families.

The tiny town is packed with tourists on weekends, so try to visit during the week. The Pro Loco tourist information office (☎ 0577 94 00 08, 🖂 prolocosg@tin.it) is at Piazza del Duomo 1 in the town centre.

Things to See & Do
Climb San Gimignano's tallest tower, **Torre Grossa** (also known as the town hall tower), off Piazza del Duomo, for a memorable view of the Tuscan hills. The tower is reached from within the **Palazzo del Popolo**, which houses the **Museo Civico**, whose star attraction is Lippo Memmi's 14th-century *Maestà*. The **Duomo** has a Romanesque interior, frescoes by Ghirlandaio in the **Cappella di Santa Fina** and a particularly gruesome *Last Judgment* by Taddeo di Bartolo. The city's most impressive piazza is **Piazza della Cisterna**, named for the 13th-century well at its centre.

Places to Stay & Eat
San Gimignano offers few options for budget travellers. The nearest camping ground is *Il Boschetto di Piemma* (☎ 0577 94 03 52, fax 0577 94 19 82), about 3km from San Gimignano at Santa Lucia. It costs L9000 a night for adults, L7000 for children and L12,000 for a tent site. It is open from April to mid-October and there is a bus service to the site. The non-HI *hostel* (☎ 0577 94 19 91, Via delle Fonti 1) opens 1 March to 31 October and charges L29,000 for B&B, L16,000 for a meal.

Hotels in town are expensive but there are numerous rooms for rent in private homes, and agriturismo is well organised in this area. For information, contact the tourist office. If you can afford a treat, soak up the medieval ambience at *Hotel La Cisterna* (☎ 0577 94 03 28,

fax 0577 94 20 80, Piazza dell Cisterna 24), where singles/doubles are L120,000/200,000.

Friendly *Trattoria Chiribiri* (*Piazzetta della Madonna 1*), off Via San Giovanni, has hearty minestrone for L8000 and ravioli for L10,000. A fresh-produce *market* is held on Thursday morning in Piazza del Duomo.

Getting There & Away
Regular buses connect San Gimignano with Florence and Siena. Buses arrive at Porta San Giovanni and timetables are posted outside the tourist office. Enter through the Porta and continue straight ahead to reach Piazza del Duomo.

CERTALDO
pop 15,942
Located in the Val d'Elsa between Florence and Siena, this small medieval town is definitely worth a visit. Giovanni Boccaccio, one of the fathers of the Italian language, was born here in 1313.

Fattoria Bassetto (☎ 0571 66 83 42, 🖂 bassetto@dedalo.com), 2km east of the town on the road to Siena, is a former 14th-century Benedictine convent, surrounded by a garden with swimming pool. Dorm-style accommodation is L35,000 and a private room is L65,000.

Umbria

Mountainous Umbria is characterised by its many medieval hill towns, and noted for its Romanesque and Gothic architecture. Towns such as Assisi, Gubbio, Spello, Spoleto, Todi and Orvieto are accessible by bus or train from Perugia, the region's capital.

PERUGIA
pop 144,732
Perugia is one of Italy's best-preserved medieval hill towns, with panoramic views at every turn. The city has a lively and bloody past, due to the internal feuding of the Baglioni and Oddi families, and the violent wars waged against its neighbours during the Middle Ages. Perugia also has a strong artistic and cultural tradition: it was the home of the painter Perugino, and Raphael, his student, also worked here. Its University for Foreigners, established

in 1925, attracts thousands of students from all over the world, and the Umbria Jazz festival is held here in July.

Orientation & Information

Perugia's hub is the old town's central main drag, Corso Vannucci, running north-south from Piazza Italia, through Piazza Repubblica and ending at Piazza IV Novembre and the Duomo.

The IAT tourist office (☎ 075 572 33 27, fax 075 573 93 86) is opposite the Duomo at Piazza IV Novembre 3, and is open 8.30 am to 1.30 pm and 3.30 to 6.30 pm Monday to Saturday (9 am to 1 pm on Sunday). The main post office is in Piazza Matteotti. The monthly magazine *Viva Perugia: What, Where, When* (L1000 at newsstands) has events listings and other useful information.

Things to See

Perugia's austere **Duomo** has an unfinished facade in the characteristic Perugian red-and-white marble. Inside are frescoes and decorations by artists from the 15th to 18th centuries. The **Palazzo dei Priori**, just down from the Duomo on Corso Vannucci, is a rambling 13th-century palace which houses

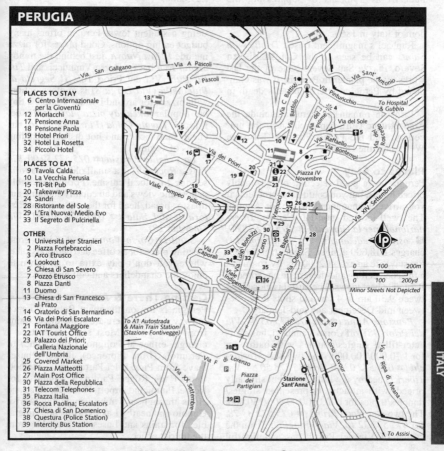

PERUGIA

PLACES TO STAY
6 Centro Internazionale per la Gioventù
12 Morlacchi
17 Pensione Anna
18 Pensione Paola
19 Hotel Priori
32 Hotel La Rosetta
34 Piccolo Hotel

PLACES TO EAT
9 Tavola Calda
10 La Vecchia Perusia
15 Tit-Bit Pub
20 Takeaway Pizza
24 Sandri
28 Ristorante del Sole
29 L'Era Nuova; Medio Evo
33 Il Segreto di Pulcinella

OTHER
1 Università per Stranieri
2 Piazza Fortebraccio
3 Arco Etrusco
4 Lookout
5 Chiesa di San Severo
7 Pozzo Etrusco
8 Piazza Danti
11 Duomo
13 Chiesa di San Francesco al Prato
14 Oratorio di San Bernardino
16 Via dei Priori Escalator
21 Fontana Maggiore
22 IAT Tourist Office
23 Palazzo dei Priori; Galleria Nazionale dell'Umbria
25 Covered Market
26 Piazza Matteotti
27 Main Post Office
30 Piazza della Repubblica
31 Telecom Telephones
35 Piazza Italia
36 Rocca Paolina; Escalators
37 Chiesa di San Domenico
38 Questura (Police Station)
39 Intercity Bus Station

To Hospital & Gubbio

Minor Streets Not Depicted

To A1 Autostrada & Main Train Station (Stazione Fontivegge)

To Assisi

ITALY

the impressively frescoed **Sala dei Notari** and the **Galleria Nazionale dell'Umbria**, with works by Perugino and Fra Angelico. Between the two buildings, in Piazza IV Novembre, is the 13th-century **Fontana Maggiore**, designed by Fra Bevignate in 1278 and carved by Nicola and Giovanni Pisano.

At the other end of Corso Vannucci is the **Rocca Paolina** (Paolina Fortress), the ruins of a massive 16th-century fortress built upon the foundations of the palaces and homes of powerful families of the day, notably the Baglioni. The homes were destroyed and the materials used to build the fortress under orders of Pope Paul III as a means of suppressing the Baglioni. The fortress itself was destroyed by the Perugians after the declaration of the kingdom of Italy in 1860.

Raphael's magnificent fresco *Trinity with Saints* can be seen in the **Chiesa di San Severo**, Piazza San Severo. One of the last works by the painter in Perugia, it was completed by Perugino after Raphael's death in 1520.

Etruscan remains in Perugia include the **Arco Etrusco** (Etruscan Arch), near the university, and the **Pozzo Etrusco** (Etruscan Well), near the Duomo.

Places to Stay

Perugia has a good selection of reasonably priced hotels, but you could have problems if you arrive unannounced in July or August. The well-located non-HI **Centro Internazionale per la Gioventù** (☎ 075 572 28 80, ✉ ostello@edisons.it, Via Bontempi 13) charges L18,000 a night. Sheets (for the entire stay) are an extra L2000. Its TV room has a frescoed ceiling and the terrace has some of Perugia's best views. The hostel is closed between 9.30 am to 4 pm and shuts down between mid-December and mid-January.

Pensione Anna (☎/fax 075 573 63 04, Via dei Priori 48), off Corso Vannucci, has character-filled singles/doubles with bathroom for L70,000/100,000. The two-star **Morlacchi** (☎ 075 572 03 19, fax 075 573 50 84, Via Tiberi 2) nearby is a little better but similarly priced, with attractively presented singles/doubles/triples for L70,000/100,000/130,000. The two-star **Hotel Priori** (☎ 075 572 33 78, fax 075 572 32 13, Via Vermiglioli 3), on the corner of Via dei Priori, has a delightful breakfast terrace and small but serviceable singles/doubles for L90,000/140,000, including breakfast.

Pensione Paola (☎ 075 572 38 16, Via della Canapina 5) is down the escalator from Via dei Priori, with pleasant rooms without bathroom for L43,000/65,000. Off the Piazza Italia end of Corso Vannucci, **Piccolo Hotel** (☎ 075 572 29 87, Via Luigi Bonazzi 25) has small doubles without/with bathroom for L60,000/75,000.

If you're feeling flush, the four-star **La Rosetta** (☎/fax 075 572 08 41, Piazza Italia 19) has palatial period-detailed rooms from L215,000.

Places to Eat

Being a student town, Perugia offers many budget eating options. Good places for pizza include *L'Era Nuova*, just behind the trendy **Medio Evo** bar on Corso Vannucci, and **Tit-Bit Pub**, Via dei Priori 105. **Il Segreto di Pulcinella** (Via Larga 8) is another option, with pizzas for around L9000. There's a tiny but popular *takeaway pizza place* at Via dei Priori 3. **Tavola Calda** (Piazza Danti 16) has cheap sandwiches and hot dishes, including heaps of vegies.

La Vecchia Perusia (☎ 075 572 59 00, Via Ulisse Rocchi 9) is a small old-style trattoria serving fine local cuisine. For unforgettable panoramic views and an equally stunning antipasto spread, head for the ever-popular **Ristorante del Sole** (☎ 075 573 50 31, Via Oberdan 28).

Sandri (Corso Vannucci 32) is a great meeting place for a coffee and delicious cake, where you don't pay extra to sit down to enjoy the chandeliers and ceiling frescoes.

Getting There & Away

Perugia is not on the main Rome-Florence railway line, but there are some direct trains from both cities. Most services require a change, either at Foligno (from Rome) or Terontola (from Florence). Intercity buses leave from Piazza dei Partigiani (at the bottom of the Rocca Paolina escalators) for Rome, Fiumicino airport, Florence, Siena and cities throughout Umbria including Assisi, Gubbio and nearby Lake Trasimeno. Timetables for trains and buses are available from the tourist office.

ITALY

Getting Around

The main train station is a few kilometres downhill from the historical centre. Catch any bus heading for Piazza Italia. Tickets cost L1200 and must be bought before you get onboard.

Most of the historical centre is closed to normal traffic, but tourists are allowed to drive to their hotels. It is probably wiser not to do this, as driving in central Perugia is a nightmare because of the extremely narrow, winding streets, most of which are one way. The solution is to park at one of the large car parks downhill, and take the pedestrian elevator up to the old centre. There is a supervised car park (L13,000 for the first two days, then L8500 per day) at Piazza dei Partigiani, from where you can catch the Rocca Paolina escalator leading to Piazza Italia. There are two major car parks at the foot of the Via dei Priori escalator.

ASSISI

pop 24,626

Home of St Francis, Assisi retains a modicum of spirituality despite attracting millions of visitors each year. Away from the hullabaloo, tranquillity can still be found in the medieval laneways. Assisi's inhabitants have been aware of the visual impact of their city since Roman times, perched halfway up Mt Subasio. From the valley its pink-and-white marble buildings shimmer in the sunlight. In September 1997, a strong earthquake rocked the town, causing part of the vault of the upper church of the Basilica di San Francesco to collapse. While the upper basilica has since reopened, the painstaking task of restoration continues.

The APT tourist office (☎ 075 81 25 34, @ aptas@krenet.it), Piazza del Comune, has all the information you need on hotels, sights and events in Assisi. It's open 8 am to 2 pm and 3.30 to 6.30 pm Monday to Friday, 9 am to 1 pm and 3.30 to 6.30 pm on Saturday and 9 am to 1 pm Sunday.

Things to See

Most people come to Assisi to visit its religious monuments. Dress rules are applied rigidly – absolutely no shorts, miniskirts or low-cut dresses/tops are allowed.

St Francis' Basilica is composed of two churches, one built on top of the other. The lower church is decorated with frescoes by Simone Martini, Cimabue and a pupil of Giotto, and contains the crypt where St Francis is buried. The Italian Gothic upper church has a stone-vaulted roof, and was decorated by the great painters of the 13th and 14th centuries, in particular Giotto and Cimabue. The frescoes in the apse and entrance received the most damage in the 1997 earthquake.

The impressively frescoed 13th-century **Basilica di Santa Chiara** contains the remains of St Clare, friend of St Francis and founder of the Order of Poor Clares.

For spectacular views of the valley below, head to the massive 14th-century **Rocca Maggiore** fortress. You'll easily be able to spot the huge **Basilica di Santa Maria degli Angeli**, built around the first Franciscan monastery. St Francis died in its **Cappella del Transito** in 1226.

Places to Stay & Eat

Assisi is well geared for tourists and there are numerous budget hotels and *affittacamere* (rooms for rent). Peak periods, when you will need to book well in advance, are Easter, August and September, and the Feast of St Francis on 3 and 4 October. The tourist office has a full list of affittacamere and religious institutions.

The small HI *Ostello della Pace* (☎/fax 075 81 67 67, Via Valecchi 177) is open all year; B&B is L25,000. The hostel is on the bus line between Santa Maria degli Angeli and Assisi. The non-HI hostel *Fontemaggio* and camping ground (☎ 075 81 36 36, fax 075 81 37 49) has B&B for L25,000 and singles/doubles for L50,000/100,000. From Piazza Matteotti, at the far end of town from the basilica, it's a 30-minute uphill walk along Via Eremo delle Carceri to No 8.

Albergo Italia (☎ 075 81 26 25, fax 075 804 37 49, Vicolo della Fortezza), just off Pizza del Comune, has rooms with shower for L45,000/69,000. Nearby, the three-star *Dei Priori* (☎ 075 81 22 37, fax 075 81 68 04, Corso Mazzini 15) has comfortable rooms for L75,000/100,000.

For a snack of pizza by the slice for around L2000, head for *Pizza Vincenzo*, just off Piazza del Comune at Via San Rufina 1a. A good self-service in the same area is *Il Foro Romano (Via Portico 23)*. *Il Pozzo Romano (Via*

ITALY

Santa Agnese 10), off Piazza Santa Chiara, has pizzas for around L9000 and a tourist menu for L22,000. Dine under ancient architraves at *Dal Carro (Vicolo dei Nepis 2)*, off Corso Mazzini, with superior pasta dishes from L7000. If you want to splash some cash, try the stylish *Medio Evo (Via Arco dei Priori 4)*.

Getting There & Away

Buses connect Assisi with Perugia, Foligno and other local towns, leaving from Piazza Matteotti. Buses for Rome and Florence leave from Piazzale dell'Unità d'Italia. Assisi's train station is in the valley, in the suburb of Santa Maria degli Angeli. It's on the same line as Perugia and a shuttle bus runs between the town and the station.

ANCONA
pop 101,285

The main reason to visit Ancona, a largely unattractive and industrial port city in the Marches, is to catch a ferry to Croatia, Greece or Turkey.

The easiest way to get from the train station to the port is by bus No 1. There are tourist information offices at the train station and the stazione marittima (seasonal). The main APT office (☎ 071 35 89 91, ✆ aptanc ona@tin.it) is out of the way at Via Thaon de Revel 4. It has a good Web site at www.com une.ancona.it. The main post office is at Piazza XXIV Maggio, open 8.15 am to 7 pm Monday to Saturday.

If you're stuck here waiting for a ferry, there are a couple of options for dining and accommodations. Many backpackers choose to bunk down at the ferry terminal, although the city has many cheap hotels. The relatively new *Ostello della Gioventú (☎/fax 071 4 22 57, Via Lamaticci)* has B&B for L24,000.

In the old town, *Trattoria da Dina (☎ 523 39, Vicolo ad Alto 3)* has full meals for L19,000.

Getting There & Away

Buses depart from Piazza Cavour for towns throughout the Marches region. Rome is served by Marozzi (☎ 0734 85 91 18). Ancona is on the Bologna-Lecce train line and thus easily accessible from major towns throughout Italy. It is also directly linked to Rome via Foligno.

All ferry operators have information booths at the ferry terminal, off Piazza Kennedy. Most lines offer discounts on return fares. Prices listed are for one-way deck class in the 2000 high season.

Companies include Superfast (☎ 071 207 02 40) to Patras in Greece (L136,000), Minoan Lines (☎ 071 20 17 08) to Igoumenitsa and Patras (L124,000) and Adriatica (☎ 071 20 49 15) to Durrës in Albania (L155,000) and to Split in Croatia (L80,000).

URBINO
pop 15,114

This town in the Marches can be difficult to reach, but it is worth the effort to see the birthplace of Raphael and Bramante – little changed since the Middle Ages and still a centre of art, culture and learning.

The IAT tourist information office (☎ 0722 27 88, ✆ iat@comune.urbino.ps.it) is at Piazza Duca Federico 35 and is open 9 am to 1 pm Monday to Saturday. The Banca Nazionale del Lavoro on Via Vittorio Emanuele has an ATM, as do most banks spread about the town centre. The main post office is at Via Bramante 18. There are Telecom offices at Via Puccinotti 4 and at Piazza San Francesco 1.

Things to See

Urbino's main sight is the huge **Palazzo Ducale**, designed by Laurana and completed in 1482. The best view is from Corso Garibaldi to the west, from where you can appreciate the size of the building and see its towers and loggias. Enter the palace from Piazza Duca Federico and visit the **Galleria Nazionale delle Marches**, featuring works by Raphael, Paolo Uccello and Verrocchio. The palace is open 9 am to 7 pm Tuesday to Saturday, to 9 pm on Sunday and to 2 pm Monday. Between February and May visits must be arranged in advance by calling ☎ 0722 32 90 57. Entry is L8000. Also visit the **Casa di Rafaello**, Via Raffaello 57, where the artist Raphael was born, and the **Oratorio di San Giovanni Battista**, with 15th-century frescoes by the Salimbeni brothers.

Places to Stay & Eat

Urbino is a major university town and most cheap beds are taken by students during the school year. The tourist office has a full list of affittacamere. The **Pensione Fosca** (☎ 0722 32 96 22, Via Raffaello 61) has singles/doubles for L42,000/60,000.

There are numerous bars around Piazza della Repubblica in the town centre and near the Palazzo Ducale which sell good panini. Try **Pizzeria Galli**, Via Vittorio Veneto 19, for takeaway pizza by the slice. **Ristorante Da Franco**, just off Piazza del Rinascimento, next to the university, has a self-service section where you can eat a full meal for around L22,000.

Getting There & Away
There is no train service to Urbino, but it is connected by SAPUM and Bucci buses on weekdays to cities including Ancona, Pesaro and Arezzo. There is a bus link to the train station at the town of Fossato di Vico, on the Rome-Ancona line. There are also buses to Rome twice a day. All buses arrive at Borgo Mercatale, down Via Mazzini from Piazza della Repubblica. The tourist office has timetables for all bus services.

Southern Italy

Although much poorer than the north, the land of the *mezzogiorno* (midday sun) is rich in history and cultural traditions. The attractions here are simpler and more stark, the people more vibrant and excitable, and myths and legends are inseparable from official history. Campania, Apulia and Basilicata cry out to be explored and absolutely nothing can prepare you for Naples.

NAPLES
pop 1,067,365

Crazy and confusing, but also seductive and fascinating, Naples (Napoli), capital of the Campania region, has an energy that is palpable. Beautifully positioned on the Bay of Naples and overshadowed by Mt Vesuvius, it is one of the most densely populated cities in Europe. The city's homegrown mafia, the Camorra, is not as internationally infamous as its Sicilian counterpart, but in Naples it is just as pervasive.

While in the city, look out for its famous *presepi* (nativity cribs).

Orientation
Both the Stazione Centrale (central train station) and the main bus terminal are just off the vast Piazza Garibaldi. Naples is divided into *quartieri* (districts). The main shopping thoroughfare into the historical centre, Spaccanapoli, is Corso Umberto I, which heads south-west from Piazza Garibaldi to Piazza Bovio. West on the bay are Santa Lucia and Mergellina, both fashionable and picturesque and a far cry from the chaotic, noisy historical centre. South-west of Mergellina is Posillipo, where the ultra-wealthy live, and in the hills overlooking the bay is the residential Vomero district, a natural balcony across the city and bay to Vesuvius.

Information
Tourist Offices The EPT office at the station (☎ 081 26 87 79) will make hotel bookings, but make sure you give specific details on where you want to stay and how much you want to pay. Some staff speak English. Ask for *Qui Napoli* (Here Naples), published monthly in English and Italian, which lists events in the city, as well as information about transport and other services. The office is open 8.30 am to 8 pm Monday to Saturday and 9 am to 2 pm on Sunday.

There's an AAST office in Piazza del Gesú Nuovo (☎ 081 552 33 28), near Piazza Dante, open 8.30 am to 7.30 pm Monday to Saturday and until 3.30 pm on Sunday. The student travel centre, CTS (☎ 081 552 79 60), is at Via Mezzocannone 25.

Money There is a branch of the Banca Nazionale del Lavoro at Via Firenze 39; otherwise, there are plenty of exchange booths throughout the city which often offer lower rates than the banks.

Post & Communications The main post office is in Piazza G Matteotti, off Via Armando Diaz. It's open 8.15 am to 7.30 pm Monday to Friday and to 1 pm on Saturday. There is a Telecom office at Via A Depretis 40, open 9 am to 10 pm daily. Internetbar, Piazza Bellini 74, provides Internet access. The postcode for central Naples is 80100.

Medical & Emergency Services For an ambulance call ☎ 081 752 06 96. Each city

ITALY

NAPLES (NAPOLI)

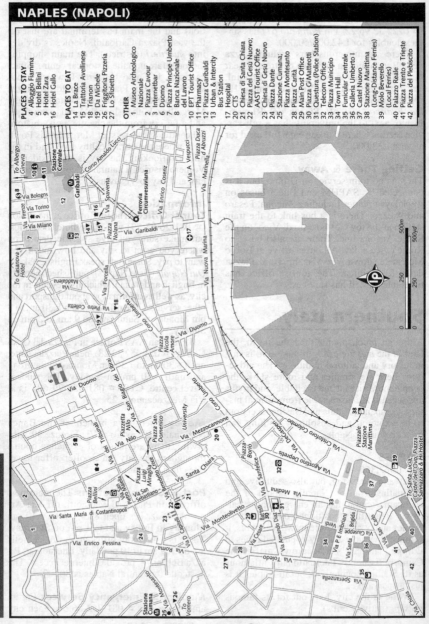

PLACES TO STAY
4 Alloggio Fiamma
5 Hotel Bellini
9 Hotel Zara
16 Hotel Gallo

PLACES TO EAT
14 La Brace
15 Trattoria Avellinese
18 Trianon
19 Da Michele
26 Friggitoria Pizzeria
27 Lo Sfizietto

OTHER
1 Museo Archeologico Nazionale
2 Piazza Cavour
3 Internetbar
6 Duomo
7 Piazza Principe Umberto
8 Banca Nazionale del Lavoro
10 EPT Tourist Office
11 Pharmacy
12 Piazza Garibaldi
13 Urban & Intercity Bus Station
17 Hospital
20 CTS
21 Chiesa di Santa Chiara
22 Piazza del Gesù Nuovo; AAST Tourist Office
23 Chiesa di Gesù Nuovo
24 Piazza Dante
25 Stazione Cumana; Piazza Montesanto
28 Piazza Carità
29 Main Post Office
30 Piazza G Matteotti
31 Questura (Police Station)
32 Telecom Office
33 Piazza Municipio
34 Town Hall
35 Funicular Centrale
36 Galleria Umberto I
37 Castel Nuovo
38 Stazione Marittima (Long-Distance Ferries)
39 Molo Beverello (Local Ferries)
40 Palazzo Reale
41 Piazza Trento e Trieste
42 Piazza del Plebiscito

district has a Guardia Medica (after hours medical service); check in *Qui Napoli* for details. The Ospedale Loreto-Mare (☎ 081 20 10 33) is near the station on Via A Vespucci. The pharmacy in the central station is open 8 am to 8 pm daily.

The questura (☎ 081 794 11 11) is at Via Medina 75, just off Via A Diaz, and has an office for foreigners where you can report thefts and so on. To report a stolen car call ☎ 081 794 14 35.

Dangers & Annoyances The petty crime rate in Naples is extremely high, particularly of the bag-snatching kind. Car theft is also a major problem, so think twice before bringing a vehicle to the city. Women should be careful at night near the station and around Piazza Dante. The area west of Via Toledo and as far north as Piazza Caritá can be particularly threatening.

Naples' legendary traffic is less chaotic these days, but you will still need to take care when crossing roads.

Things to See & Do

Start by walking around Spaccanapoli, the historic centre of Naples. From the station and Corso Umberto I turn right onto Via Mezzocannone, which will take you to Via Benedetto Croce, the main street of the quarter. To the left is Piazza del Gesú Nuovo, with the Neapolitan baroque **Chiesa di Gesú Nuovo** and the 14th-century **Chiesa di Santa Chiara**, restored to its original Gothic-Provençal style after it was severely damaged by bombing during WWII. The beautiful **Chiostro delle Clarisse** (Nuns' Cloisters) should not be missed.

The **Duomo** has a 19th-century facade but was built by the Angevin kings at the end of the 13th century, on the site of an earlier basilica. Inside is the **Cappella di San Gennaro**, which contains the head of St Januarius (the city's patron saint) and two vials of his congealed blood. The saint is said to have saved the city from plague, volcanic eruptions and other disasters. Every year the faithful gather to pray for a miracle, namely that the blood will liquefy and save the city from further disaster (see under Special Events).

Turn off Via Duomo onto **Via Tribunali**, one of the more characteristic streets of the area, and head for Piazza Dante, through the 17th-century **Port'Alba**, one of the gates to the city. Via Roma, the most fashionable street in old Naples, heads to the left (becoming Via Toledo) and ends at Piazza Trento e Trieste and the **Piazza del Plebiscito**.

In the piazza is the **Palazzo Reale**, the former official residence of the Bourbon and Savoy kings, now a museum. It is open 9 am to 1.30 pm Tuesday to Sunday and also from 4 to 7.30 pm on weekends. Admission is L8000. Just off the piazza is the **Teatro San Carlo**, one of the most famous opera houses in the world thanks to its perfect acoustics and beautiful interior.

The 13th-century **Castel Nuovo** overlooks Naples' ferry port. The early-Renaissance triumphal arch commemorates the entry of Alfonso I of Aragon into Naples in 1443. It is possible to visit the **Museo Civico** in the castle. Situated south-west along the waterfront at Santa Lucia is the **Castel dell'Ovo**, originally a Norman castle, which is surrounded by a tiny fishing village, the **Borgo Marinaro**.

The **Museo Archeologico Nazionale** is in Piazza Museo, north of Piazza Dante. It contains one of the most important collections of Graeco-Roman artefacts in the world, mainly the rich collection of the Farnese family, and the art treasures that were discovered at Pompeii and Herculaneum. The museum opens 9 am to 10 pm Tuesday to Saturday (Sunday to 8 pm). Admission is L12,000.

To escape the noisy city centre, catch the Funicolare Centrale (funicular), on Via Toledo, to the suburb of **Vomero** and visit the Certosa di San Martino, a 14th-century Carthusian monastery, rebuilt in the 17th century in Neapolitan-baroque style. It houses the **Museo Nazionale di San Martino**. The monastery's church is well worth a visit, as are its terraced gardens, which afford spectacular views of Naples and the bay. The monastery is open 9 am to 2 pm Tuesday to Sunday. Entry is L8000.

Special Events

Religious festivals are lively occasions in Naples, especially the celebration of St Januarius, the patron saint of the city, held three times a year (the first Sunday in May, 19 September and 16 December) in the Duomo.

ITALY

Places to Stay

Hostel The HI *Ostello Mergellina Napoli* (☎ 081 761 23 46, *Salita della Grotta 23*), in Mergellina, is modern and safe. B&B is L26,000. It's open all year and imposes a maximum three-night stay in summer. Take the Metropolitana to Mergellina, and signs will direct you to the hostel from the waterfront.

Hotels Most of the cheap hotels are near the station and Piazza Garibaldi in a rather unsavoury area, and some of the cheaper hotels double as brothels. It is best to ask the tourist office at the station to recommend or book a room.

Station Area The following hotels are safe and offer a reasonable standard of accommodation. The *Hotel Zara* (☎ 081 28 71 25, ✉ hotelzar@tin.it, *Via Firenze 81*) is clean, with singles/doubles for L35,000/60,000. Via Firenze is off Corso Novara, to the right as you leave the train station. *Albergo Ginevra* (☎ 081 28 32 10, *Via Genova 116*), about 300m from the station, is another reliable and well-kept place with rooms for L42,000/67,000. The *Casanova Hotel* (☎ 081 26 82 87, *Corso Garibaldi 333*) is quiet and safe. Rooms are L35,000/70,000; triples with shower are L95,000. *Hotel Gallo* (☎ 081 20 05 12, fax 081 28 18 49, *Via Spaventa 11*), to the left out of the train station, has rooms of different standards (ask to see them first) for L110,000/160,000.

Around Spaccanapoli The best option in this area is the popular *Hotel Bellini* (☎ 081 45 69 96, *Via San Paolo 44*), which offers singles/doubles for L70,000/120,000. *Alloggio Fiamma* (☎ 081 45 91 87, *Via Francesco del Giudice 13*) has pretty basic doubles/triples for L80,000/110,000.

Out of the Centre In Santa Lucia, *Pensione Astoria* (☎ 081 764 99 03, *Via Santa Lucia 90*) has basic singles/doubles for L45,000/70,000. In the same building is *Albergo Teresita* (☎ 081 764 01 05), with rooms for L45,000/70,000. At Vomero, just near the funicular station, *Pensione Margherita* (☎ 081 556 70 44, *Via D Cimarosa 29*) charges L60,000/110,000; ask for a room with a bay view. Have a L50 coin on hand for the lift.

Places to Eat

Naples is the home of pasta and pizza. In fact, once you have eaten a good Neapolitan pizza, topped with fresh tomatoes, oregano, basil and garlic, no other pizza will taste the same. Try a *calzone*, a filled version of a pizza, or *mozzarella in carozza* (mozzarella deep-fried in bread) which is sold at tiny street stalls. Also sold at street stalls is the *misto di frittura* (deep-fried vegetables). Don't leave town without trying the *sfogliatelle* (light, flaky pastry filled with ricotta).

Restaurants There are several inexpensive places to eat in and around Naples' centre.

City Centre According to the locals the best pizza in Naples (and Italy) is served at *Da Michele* (*Via Cesare Sersale 1*). The place is always crowded and you'll need to queue with a numbered ticket. Another excellent option is the nearby *Trianon* (*Via Pietro Colletta 46*) near Via Tribunali, where there's a wide selection from L5000. *La Brace* (*Via Spaventa 14*) is also recommended. You can eat well for around L25,000. Down the same street at Nos 31-35 is *Trattoria Avellinese*, Via Silvio Spaventa 31-35, just off Piazza Garibaldi, which specialises in cheap seafood.

Mergellina & Vomero For a good meal, Neapolitans head for the area around Piazza Sannazzaro, south-west of the centre, which is also handy to the HI hostel. *Pizzeria da Pasqualino* (*Piazza Sannazzaro 79*) has outdoor tables and serves good pizzas and seafood. A meal will cost around L20,000 with wine. *Daniele* (*Via A Scarlatti 104*) is a bar with a restaurant upstairs. *Cibo Cibo* (*Via Cimarosa 150*) is another good budget spot. In Vomero, *Trattoria da Sica* (*Via Bernini 17*) has excellent local dishes – try the spaghetti *alle vongole e pomodorini* (clams and cherry tomatoes).

Food Stalls On the corner of Vico Basilico Puoti and Via Pignasecca is *Lo Sfizietto*. *Friggitoria Pizzeria* is at Piazza Montesanto. Both offer lots of cheap goodies.

Entertainment

The monthly *Qui Napoli* and the local newspapers are the only real guides to what's on.

ITALY

In July there is a series of free concerts called Luglio Musicale a Capodimonte held outside the archaeological museum. The *Teatro San Carlo* (☎ *081 797 21 11*) has year-round performances of opera, ballet and concerts. Tickets start at L20,000.

Getting There & Away

Air Capodichino airport (☎ 081 789 62 68), Viale Umberto Maddalena, is 5km north-east of the city centre. There are connections to most Italian and several European cities. Bus No 14 or 14R leaves from Piazza Garibaldi every 30 minutes for the airport (20 minutes).

Bus Buses leave from Piazza Garibaldi, just outside the train station, for destinations including Salerno, Benevento, Caserta (every 20 minutes) and Bari, Lecce and Brindisi in Apulia.

Train Naples is a major rail-transport centre for the south, and regular trains for most major Italian cities arrive and depart from the Stazione Centrale. There are up to 30 trains a day for Rome.

Car & Motorcycle Driving in Naples is not recommended. The traffic is chaotic, and car and motorcycle theft is rife. However, the city is easily accessible from Rome on the A1. The Naples-Pompeii-Salerno road connects with the coastal road to Sorrento and the Amalfi Coast.

Boat *Traghetti* (small ferries), *aliscafi* (hydrofoils) and *navi veloce* (fast ships) leave for Capri, Sorrento, Ischia and Procida from the Molo Beverello, in front of the Castel Nuovo. Some hydrofoils leave for the bay islands from Mergellina, and ferries for Ischia and Procida also leave from Pozzuoli. All operators have offices at the various ports from which they leave.

Tickets for the hydrofoils cost around double those for ferries, but the trip takes half the time.

Ferries to Palermo and Cagliari (Tirrenia ☎ 147 89 90 00) and to the Aeolian Islands (Siremar ☎ 091 761 36 88) leave from the Stazione Marittima on Molo Angioino, next to Molo Beverello (see the Getting There & Away sections under Sicily and Sardinia).

SNAV (☎ 081 761 23 48) runs regular ferries and, in summer, hydrofoils to the Aeolian Islands.

Getting Around

You can make your way around Naples by bus, tram, Metropolitana (underground) and funicular. City buses leave from Piazza Garibaldi in front of the central station bound for the centre of Naples, as well as Mergellina. Tickets cost L1500 for 90 minutes and are valid for buses, trams, the Metropolitana and funicular services. Day tickets cost L4500. Useful buses include No 14 or 14Rto the airport; Nos R2 and R1 to Piazza Dante; and No 110 from Piazza Garibaldi to Piazza Cavour and the archaeological museum. Tram No 1 leaves from east of Stazione Centrale for the city centre. To get to Molo Beverello and the ferry terminal from the train station, take bus No R2 or 152, a bus called 'La Sepsa', or the M1.

The Metropolitana station is downstairs at the train station. Trains head west to Mergellina, stopping at Piazza Cavour, Piazza Amedeo and the funicular to Vomero, and then head on to the Campi Flegrei and Pozzuoli. Another line, now under construction, will eventually connect Piazza Garibaldi and Piazza Medaglie d'Oro, with stops including the Museo Archeologico Nazionale.

The main funicular connecting the city centre with Vomero is the Funicolare Centrale in Piazza Duca d'Aosta, next to Galleria Umberto I, on Via Toledo.

The Ferrovia Circumvesuviana operates trains for Herculaneum, Pompeii and Sorrento. The station is about 400m south-west of Stazione Centrale, in Corso Garibaldi (take the underpass from Stazione Centrale). The Ferrovia Cumana and the Circumflegrei, based at Stazione Cumana in Piazza Montesanto, operate services to Pozzuoli, Baia and Cumae every 20 minutes.

AROUND NAPLES

From Naples it's only a short distance to the **Campi Flegrei** (Phlegraean Fields) of volcanic lakes and mud baths, which inspired both Homer and Virgil in their writings. Today part of suburban Naples, the area is dirty and overdeveloped, but still worth a day trip. The Greek colony of **Cumae** is certainly

ITALY

worth visiting, particularly to see the Cave of the Cumaean Sybil, home of one of the ancient world's greatest oracles. Also in the area is **Lake Avernus**, the mythical entrance to the underworld, and **Baia** with its submerged Roman ruins visible from a glass-bottomed boat.

Reached by CPTC bus from Naples' Piazza Garibaldi or by train from the Stazione Centrale is the **Palazzo Reale** at Caserta (☎ 0823 32 11 37), usually called the Reggia di Caserta. Built by the Bourbon king Charles III, this massive 1200-room palace is set in gardens modelled on Versailles.

Pompeii & Herculaneum

Buried under a layer of lapilli (burning fragments of pumice stone) during the devastating eruption of Mt Vesuvius in 79 AD, **Pompeii** provides a fascinating insight into how the ancient Romans lived. It was a resort town for wealthy Romans, and among the vast ruins are impressive temples, a forum, one of the largest known Roman amphitheatres, and streets lined with shops and luxurious houses. Many of the site's mosaics and frescoes have been moved to Naples' Museo Archeologico Nazionale. The exception is the Villa dei Misteri, where the frescoes remain *in situ*. Many houses and shops are closed, but efforts are under way to open more of Pompeii to the public.

There are tourist offices (AACST) at Via Sacra 1 (☎ 081 850 72 55) in the new town, and just outside the excavations at Piazza Porta Marina Inferiore 12 (☎ 167 01 33 50 toll-free). Both offer information for visitors, notes on guided tours and a simple map of the ancient city. The ruins are open from 9 am to one hour before sunset; entry is L12,000.

Catch the Ferrovia Circumvesuviana train from Naples and get off at the Pompeii-Villa dei Misteri stop; the Porta Marina entrance is close by.

Herculaneum (Ercolano) is closer to Naples and is also a good point from which to visit Mt Vesuvius. Legend says the city was founded by Hercules. First Greek, then Roman, it was also destroyed by the 79 AD eruption, buried under mud and lava. Most inhabitants of Herculaneum had enough warning and managed to escape. The ruins here are smaller and the buildings, particularly the private houses, are

remarkably well preserved. Here you can see better examples of the frescoes, mosaics and furniture that used to decorate Roman houses.

Herculaneum is also accessible on the Circumvesuviana train from Naples. The ruins are open daily from 9 am to one hour before sunset. Entry is L12,000.

If you want to have a look into the huge crater of Mt Vesuvius, catch the Trasporti Vesuviani bus (☎ 081 739 28 33) from the piazza in front of the Ercolano train station or from Pompeii's Piazza Anfiteatro. The return ticket costs L7000 from Ercolano and L12,000 from Pompeii. The first bus leaves Pompeii at 8.30 am and takes 30 minutes to reach Herculaneum. You'll then need to walk about 1.5km to the summit, where you must pay L9000 to be accompanied by a guide to the crater. See Lonely Planet's *Walking in Italy* guide for detailed information on walking circuits on Vesuvius. The last bus returns to Pompeii from Herculaneum's Quota 1000 car park at 5.45 pm in summer and at 5 pm in winter.

SORRENTO
pop 16,459

This major resort town is in a particularly beautiful area, but is heavily overcrowded in summer with package tourists and traffic. However, it is handy to the Amalfi Coast and Capri.

Information

The centre of town is Piazza Tasso, a short walk from the train station along Corso Italia. The AAST tourist office (☎ 081 807 40 33), Via Luigi de Maio 35, is located inside the Circolo dei Forestieri complex. It is open 8.45 am to 2.30 pm and 4 to 6.45 pm Monday to Saturday.

The post office is at Corso Italia 210 and the Telecom telephone office is at Piazza Tasso 37. The Deutsche Bank on Piazza Angelina Laura has an ATM. Sorrento's postcode is 80067.

For medical assistance contact the Ospedale Civile (☎ 081 533 11 11).

Places to Stay & Eat

There are several camping grounds, including *Nube d'Argento (☎ 081 878 13 44, Via del Capo 21)*, which costs L12,000 per person and up to L15,000 for a tent site.

The HI *Ostello La Caffeteria* (☎ *081 807 29 25, Via degli Aranci 160)*, near the train station, offers B&B for L26,000.

Hotel City (☎ *081 877 22 10, Corso Italia 221)* has singles/doubles with bathroom for L75,000/105,000. *Pensione Linda* (☎ *081 878 29 16, Via degli Aranci 125)* has very pleasant rooms with bathroom for L60,000/100,000.

You can get a cheap meal at *Self-Service Angelina Lauro* in Piazza Angelino Lauro. *Giardinello (Via dell'Accademia 7)* has pizzas from about L6500. On Via San Cesareo, off Piazza Tasso are several *alimentari* (grocery shops) where you can buy food for picnics.

Getting There & Away

Sorrento is easily accessible from Naples on the Circumvesuviana train line. SITA buses leave from outside the train station for the Amalfi Coast. Hydrofoils and ferries leave from the port, along Via de Maio and down the steps from the tourist office, for Capri and Napoli year-round and Ischia in summer only.

In summer, traffic is heavy along the coastal roads to Sorrento.

CAPRI
pop 7075

This beautiful island, an hour by ferry from Naples, retains the mythical appeal that attracted Roman emperors, including Augustus and Tiberius, who built 12 villas here, although the steady flow of summer tourists have somewhat spoilt its tranquil exclusivity. A short bus ride will take you to Anacapri, the town uphill from Capri – a good alternative if rooms are full in Capri. The island is famous for its grottoes, but is also a good place for walking. There are tourist offices at Marina Grande (☎ 081 837 06 34), where all the ferries arrive; in Piazza Umberto I (☎ 081 837 06 86, fax 081 837 09 18, ✉ touristoffice@capri.it) in the centre of town; and at Piazza Vittoria 4 in Anacapri (☎ 081 837 15 24). Online information can be found at www.capri.it.

Things to See & Do

There are expensive boat tours of the grottoes, including the famous **Grotta Azzurra** (Blue Grotto). Boats leave from the Marina Grande and a return trip will cost L26,500 (which includes the cost of a motorboat to the grotto, rowing boat into the grotto and entrance fee). It is cheaper to catch a bus from Anacapri (although the rowboat and entrance fee still total around L16,000). It is possible to swim into the grotto before 9 am and after 5 pm, but do so only in company and when the sea is very calm. You can walk to most of the interesting points on the island. Sights include the **Giardini d'Augusto**, in the town of Capri, and **Villa Jovis**, the ruins of one of Tiberius' villas, along the Via Longano and Via Tiberio. The latter is a one-hour walk uphill from Capri. Also visit Axel Munthe's wonderful **Villa San Michele** at Anacapri, home of the Swedish writer at the end of the 19th century.

Places to Stay & Eat

The *Stella Maris* (☎ 081 837 04 52, Via Roma 27), just off Piazza Umberto I, is right in the noisy heart of town. Doubles range from L100,000 to L160,000, depending on the season. *Villa Luisa* (☎ *081 837 01 28, Via D Birago 1)* is a private house with a couple of doubles for rent at L95,000; the views are terrific.

In Anacapri near the town centre, the *Loreley* (☎ *081 837 14 40*, ✉ *loreley@caprinet.it, Via G Orlandi 16)* has singles/doubles with bathroom starting at L80,000/135,000. *Caesar Augustus* (☎ *837 14 21, Via G Orlandi 4)* is a beautiful hotel that becomes a knockout bargain in the off season and when there are empty rooms – in season, rooms start at L150,000/200,000. It opens from 1 May to the end of October.

In Capri, try *La Cisterna (Via M Serafina 5)* for a pizza. In Anacapri try the *Trattoria il Solitario (Via G Orlandi 54)*, in a garden setting. Another good place is *Il Saraceno*, Via Trieste e Trento 18, where a full meal could cost up to L30,000. Try the lemon liqueur.

Getting There & Away

Getting to Capri is no problem, as there are hydrofoils and ferries virtually every hour from Naples' Molo Beverello and Mergellina, at least in summer. The Naples daily *Il Mattino* has all sailing times.

Several companies make the trip, including Caremar (☎ 081 551 3882), which runs ferries for L12,000 one way; and Linee Marittime Veloci (☎ 081 552 7209 in Beverello and

☎ 081 761 2348 in Mergellina), which runs hydrofoils for L20,000 one way.

Getting Around

From Marina Grande, the funicular directly in front of the port takes you to the town of Capri (L1700), which is at the top of a steep hill some 3km from the port up a winding road. Small local buses connect the port with Capri, Anacapri and other points around the island (L1700 for one trip).

AMALFI COAST

The 50km-stretch of the Amalfi Coast swarms with rich tourists in summer and prices are correspondingly high. However, it remains a place of rare and spectacular beauty and if you can manage to get there in spring or autumn, you will be surprised by the reasonably priced accommodation and peaceful atmosphere.

There are tourist information offices in the individual towns, including in Positano (☎ 089 87 50 67) at Via Saracino 2, and Amalfi (☎ 089 87 11 07), on the waterfront at Corso Roma 19.

Positano

pop 3638

This is the most beautiful town on the coast, but for exactly this reason it has also become the most fashionable. It is, however, still possible to stay here cheaply.

Villa Maria Luisa (☎ *089 87 50 23, Via Fornillo 40*) is the pick of the budget options, with double rooms with terraces for L100,000 in the low season and L130,000, breakfast included, in August. The *Villa delle Palme* (☎ 089 87 51 62), around the corner in Via Pasitea, is run by the same management and charges L125,000 for a double in the low season, L140,000 at the height of summer. Next door is the pizzeria *Il Saraceno d'Oro*.

Around Positano

The hills behind Positano offer some great walks if you tire of lazing on the beach. The tourist office at Positano has a brochure listing four routes, ranging in length from two to four hours. Visit **Nocelle**, a tiny, isolated village above Positano, accessible by walking track from the end of the road from Positano. Have lunch at *Trattoria Santa Croce* (☎ 089

81 12 60), which has a terrace with panoramic views. It is open for both lunch and dinner in summer, but at other times of the year it is best to telephone and check in advance. From Nocelle, a walking track leads directly up into the hills overlooking the Amalfi Coast. Nocelle is accessible by local bus from Positano, via Montepertuso.

On the way from Positano to Amalfi is the town of **Praiano**, which is not as scenic but has more budget options, including the only camping ground on the Amalfi Coast. *La Tranquillitá* (☎ *089 87 40 84,* @ *contraq@ contraqpraiano.com*) has a pensione, bungalows and a small camping ground. It costs L25,000 per head to camp there if you have your own tent. For a double room or bungalow it is L100,000 (with breakfast) and in summer there is compulsory half-pension at L105,000 per head including room, private bathroom, breakfast and dinner. The SITA bus stops outside the pensione. The entire establishment closes down in winter, reopening at Easter.

Amalfi

pop 5589

One of the four powerful maritime republics of medieval Italy, Amalfi today is a popular tourist resort. It has an impressive **Duomo**, and nearby is the **Grotta dello Smeraldo**, which rivals Capri's Grotta Azzurra.

In the hills behind Amalfi is **Ravello**, accessible by bus and worth a visit if only to see the magnificent 11th-century **Villa Rufolo**, once the home of popes and later of the German composer Wagner. The 20th-century **Villa Cimbrone** is set in beautiful gardens, which end at a terrace offering a spectacular view of the Gulf of Salerno. There are numerous walking paths in the hills between Amalfi and Ravello. Pick up *Walks from Amalfi – The Guide to a Web of Ancient Italian Pathways* (L12,000) in Amalfi.

Places to Stay & Eat The HI *Ostello Beato Solitudo* (☎ *081 802 50 48, Piazza G Avitabile*) is in Agerola San Lazzaro, a village just 16km west of Amalfi. It charges L17,500 for bed only. A bus leaves every 45 minutes from Amalfi, the last at 8.50 pm.

For a room in Amalfi, *Albergo Proto* (☎ *089 87 10 03, Salita dei Curiali 4*) has

ITALY

doubles/triples from L125,000/175,000, breakfast included. *Hotel Lidomare* (☎ 87 13 32, *Via Piccolomini 9*) provides homy singles/doubles for L80,000/135,000 – just follow the signs from Piazza del Duomo and go left up a flight of stairs.

Ristorante al Teatro (*Via E Marini 19*) offers good food in very pleasant surroundings; you should get a main for around L8500. To get there, follow the signs to the left from Via Pietro Capuana, the main shopping street off Piazza del Duomo. *Pizzeria da Maria* (*Via Lorenzo d'Amalfi 14*) has pizzas for around L6000 and a good set menu for L28,000.

Getting There & Away

Bus The coast is accessible by regular SITA buses, which run between Salerno (a 40-minute train trip from Naples) and Sorrento (accessible from Naples on the Circumvesuviana train line). Buses stop in Amalfi at Piazza Flavio Gioia, from where you can catch a bus to Ravello.

Car & Motorcycle The coastal road is narrow and in summer it is clogged with traffic, so be prepared for long delays. At other times of the year you should have no problems. Hire a motorcycle in Sorrento, Salerno or Maiori.

Boat Hydrofoils and ferries also service the coast, leaving from Salerno and stopping at Amalfi and Positano. From Positano in summer you can catch a boat to Capri.

PAESTUM

The evocative image of three Greek temples standing in fields of poppies is not easily forgotten and makes the trek to this archaeological site well worth the effort. The three temples, just south of Salerno, are among the world's best preserved monuments of the ancient Greek world. There is a tourist office (☎ 0828 81 10 16) open 9 am to 2 pm daily and an interesting museum (L8000) at the site, open 9 am to 7 pm (to 10 pm in summer) daily (except the first and third Monday of the month). The ruins are open daily from 9 am to two hours before sunset and entry is L8000.

Paestum is accessible from Salerno by ATACS bus or by train.

MATERA
pop 20,000

This ancient city in the region of Basilicata evokes powerful images of a peasant culture which existed until just over 30 years ago. Its famous *sassi* (the stone houses built in the two ravines that slice through the city) were home to more than half of Matera's population until the 1950s, when the local government built a new residential area just out of Matera and relocated the entire population. The wards are now a major tourist attraction, and have been designated a World Heritage Site by Unesco – a far cry from the days when Matera struggled against poverty, deprivation and malaria. Francesco Rosi's excellent film *Cristo si é fermato a Eboli* (Christ stopped at Eboli) is a poignant illustration of what life was like in Basilicata.

There is a tourist office (☎ 0835 33 19 83) at Via de Viti De Marco 9, off the main Via Roma. Itinera (☎ 0835 26 32 59, ✉ arttur@tin.it) organises guided tours in English of the sassi wards for around L50,000 an hour (maximum five people). There is online information about Matera at www.materanet.com.

Things to See

The two main sassi wards, known as **Barisano** and **Caveoso**, had no electricity, running water or sewerage until well into last century. The oldest sassi are at the top of the ravines, and the dwellings which appear to be the oldest were established in the 20th century. As space ran out in the 1920s, the population started moving into hand-hewn or natural caves, an extraordinary example of civilisation in reverse. The sassi zones are accessible from Piazza Vittorio Veneto and Piazza del Duomo in the centre of Matera. Be sure to see the rock churches, **Santa Maria d'Idris** and **Santa Lucia alla Malve**, both with amazingly well-preserved Byzantine frescoes. The 13th-century Apulian-Romanesque **cathedral**, overlooking Sasso Barisano, is also worth a visit. In Sasso Caveoso you could be approached by young children wanting to act as tour guides.

Some parts of the wards are now being restored and some people have begun to move back into the area. Excavations in Piazza Vittorio Veneto have revealed the ruins of parts of **Byzantine Matera**, including a castle and a rock church decorated with frescoes. The excavations are ongoing but the site is now open to the public.

Places to Stay & Eat
There are few options for budget accommodation here and it is best to book in advance. The fairly bare *Albergo Roma* (☎ *0835 33 39 12, Via Roma 62)* offers singles/doubles for L45,000/65,000.

The local fare is simple and the focus is on vegetables. *Da Aulo (Via Padre Minozzo 21)* is economical and serves typical dishes of Basilicata. There is a fruit and vegetable *market* near Piazza V Veneto, between Via Lucana and Via A Persio.

Getting There & Away
SITA buses connect Matera with Potenza, Taranto and Metaponto. The town is on the private Ferrovie Apulo-Lucane train line, which connects with Bari, Altamura and Potenza. There are also three Marozzi buses a day from Rome to Matera. Buses arrive in Piazza Matteotti, a short walk down Via Roma to the town centre.

APULIA
The province of Apulia, the thin heel of the Italian peninsula, has long been isolated from the rest of the country and dismissed as a rural backwater with endemic poverty and not much else. Yet for centuries the 400-km strip of territory that makes up the province has been fought over by virtually every major colonial power, from the Greeks to the Spanish, who were intent on establishing a strategic foothold right on the Mediterranean. Each culture left its distinctive architectural mark, still in evidence today, albeit crumbling, untended and often ruined.

Brindisi
pop 95,383
As the major embarkation point for ferries to Greece, the city swarms with travellers in transit. There is not much to do here, other than wait, so most backpackers gather at the train station or at the port in the Stazione Marittima. The two are connected by Corso Umberto I – which becomes Corso Garibaldi – and are a 10-minute walk from each other; otherwise, you can take bus No 3 or 9.

The EPT tourist information office (☎ 0831 56 21 26) is at Lungomare Regina Margherita 12. Another information office is inside the ferry terminal. Be careful of bag snatchers and pickpockets in the area around the train station and the port.

If you need to bunk down for the night while awaiting a ferry, the non-HI *Ostello per la Gioventú* (☎ *0831 56 80 24, Via N Brandi 4, Casale)* is about 2km out of town. B&B costs L20,000. Take bus No 3 from Via Cristoforo Colombo near the train station. *Hotel Venezia* (☎ *0831 52 75 11, Via Pisanelli 4)* has singles/doubles for L27,000/50,000. Turn left off Corso Umberto I onto Via S Lorenzo da Brindisi to get there.

There are numerous takeaway outlets along the main route between the train and boat stations, but if you want a meal, head for the side streets. The *Vecchio Vicolo (Vicolo D'Orimini 13)* between the station and the port has good-value meals for around L20,000.

Getting There & Away Marozzi runs several buses a day to/from Rome (Stazione Tiburtina), leaving from Viale Regina Margherita in Brindisi. Appia Travel (☎ 0831 52 16 84), Viale Regina Margherita 8-9, sells tickets (L65,000; nine hours). There are rail connections to the major cities of northern Italy, as well as Rome, Ancona and Naples.

Boat Ferries leave Brindisi for Greek destinations including Corfu, Igoumenitsa, Patras and Cefalonia. Adriatica (☎ 0831 52 38 25), Corso Garibaldi 85-87, is open from 9 am to 1 pm and 4 to 7 pm; you must check in here until 7 pm (after 8 pm check-in is in front of the ship). Other major ferry companies are Hellenic Mediterranean Lines (☎ 0831 52 85 31), Corso Garibaldi 8; and Italian Ferries (☎ 0831 59 03 21), Corso Garibaldi 96-98.

Adriatica and Hellenic are the most expensive, but also the most reliable. They are also the only lines which can officially accept Eurail and Inter-Rail passes, which means you pay only L20,500 to travel deck class. For a *poltrona* (airline-type chair) you'll pay L32,000, and L48,000 for a 2nd-class cabin. If you want to use your Eurail or Inter-Rail pass, it is important to reserve some weeks in advance in summer. Even with a booking in summer, you must still go to the Adriatic or

Hellenic embarkation office in the Stazione Marittima to have your ticket checked.

Discounts are available for travellers under 26 years of age and holders of some Italian rail passes. Note that fares increase by 40% in July and August. Ferry services are also increased during this period. Average prices in the 2000 high season for deck class were: Adriatica and Hellenic to Corfu, Igoumenitsa, Cefalonia or Patras cost L120,000 (L100,000 return); Med Link to Patras cost L70,000 on deck. Prices go up by an average L25,000 for a poltrona, and for the cheapest cabin accommodation prices jump by L40,000 to L65,000. Bicycles can be taken aboard free, but the average high-season fare for a motorcycle is L60,000 and for a car around L130,000.

The port tax is L12,000, payable when you buy your ticket. It is essential to check in at least two hours prior to departure.

Lecce
pop 100,884

Baroque can be grotesque, but never in Lecce. The style here is so refined and particular to the city that the Italians call it Barocco Leccese (Lecce baroque). Lecce's numerous bars and restaurants are a pleasant surprise in such a small city.

There is an APT information office (☎ 0832 24 80 92) at Via Vittorio Emanuele 24 near Piazza Duomo. Take bus No 2 from the station to the town centre.

Things to See & Do The most famous example of Lecce baroque is the **Basilica di Santa Croce**. Artists worked for 150 years to decorate the building, creating an extraordinarily ornate facade. In the **Piazza del Duomo** are the 12th-century **cathedral** (which was completely restored in the baroque style by the architect Giuseppe Zimbalo of Lecce) and its 70m-high **bell tower**; the **Palazzo del Vescovo** (Bishop's Palace); and the **Seminario**, with its elegant facade and baroque well in the courtyard. In Piazza Sant'Oronzo are the remains of a **Roman amphitheatre**.

Places to Stay & Eat Cheap accommodation is not abundant in Lecce, but camping facilities abound in the province of Salento. *Torre Rinalda (☎ 0832 38 21 62)*, near the sea at Torre Rinalda is accessible by STP bus

from the terminal in Lecce's Via Adua. It costs L12,000/16,000 per person/site.

In Lecce try *Hotel Cappello (☎ 0832 30 88 81, Via Montegrappa 4)* near the station. Singles/doubles are L57,000/90,000 with bathroom.

A good snack bar is *Da Guido e Figli (Via Trinchese 10)*. A more traditional eating place is *Angiolino (Via Principi di Savoia)* near Porta Napoli. A full meal could cost L20,000.

Getting There & Away STP buses connect Lecce with towns throughout the Salentine peninsula, leaving from Via Adua. Lecce is directly linked by train to Brindisi, Bari, Rome, Naples and Bologna. The Ferrovie del Sud Est runs trains to all major points in Apulia.

Sicily

Sicily, the largest island in the Mediterranean, is a land of Greek temples, Norman churches and castles, Arab and Byzantine domes and splendid baroque churches and palaces. Its landscape, dominated by the volcano Mt Etna (3323m) on the east coast, ranges from fertile coast to mountains in the north to a vast, dry plateau at its centre.

Sicily, with a population of about five million, has a mild climate in winter. Summer can be relentlessly hot, when the beaches swarm with holidaying Italians and other Europeans. The best times to visit are in spring and autumn, when it is hot enough for the beach, but not too hot for sightseeing.

Most ferries from Italy arrive at Sicily's capital, Palermo, which is a convenient jumping-off point. If you're short on time, spend a day in Palermo and then perhaps head for Taormina and Agrigento. Syracuse is another highlight.

The Mafia remains a powerful force in Sicily, despite taking a hammering from the authorities throughout the 1990s. But the 'men of honour' are little interested in the affairs of tourists, so there is no need to fear you will be the target in a gang war while in Sicily.

Getting There & Away
Air There are flights from major cities in Italy and throughout Europe to Palermo and

ITALY

Catania. The easiest way to get information is from any Sestante CIT or Alitalia office.

Bus & Train Bus services from Rome to Sicily are operated by Segesta (in Rome ☎ 06 481 96 76), which has two departures daily from Rome's Piazza Tiburtina. The buses service Messina (L55,000; 9 hours), Palermo (L66,000; 12 hours) and Syracuse (L66,000; 12 hours). SAIS Trasporti (in Palermo ☎ 091 617 11 41) also has a daily service to Catania and Palermo (L75,000).

One of the cheapest ways to reach Sicily is to catch a train to Messina. The cost of the ticket covers the 3km-ferry crossing from Villa San Giovanni (Calabria) to Messina.

Boat Sicily is accessible by ferry from Genova, Livorno, Naples, Reggio di Calabria and Cagliari, and also from Malta and Tunisia. The main companies servicing the Mediterranean are Tirrenia (in Palermo ☎ 091 33 33 00; in Rome ☎ 06 474 20 41); and Grimaldi (in Palermo ☎ 091 58 74 04; in Rome ☎ 06 42 81 83 88), which runs Grandi Traghetti and Grandi Navi Veloci. Prices are determined by the season and jump considerably in the summer period (July to September). Timetables can change each year and it's best to check at a travel agency that takes ferry bookings. Be sure to book well in advance during summer, particularly if you have a car.

At the time of writing, high-season fares for a poltrona were Genoa-Palermo with Grimaldi Grandi Navi Veloci (L150,000; 20 hours); Naples-Palermo with Tirrenia (L88,000; 10 hours); and Cagliari-Palermo with Tirrenia, (L70,000; 10 hours). A bed in a shared cabin with four beds costs an additional L25,000 to L35,000. Cars cost upwards of L130,000.

Other ferry lines servicing the island are Grandi Traghetti for Livorno-Palermo and Gozo Channel for Sicily-Malta. For information on ferries going from the mainland directly to Lipari, see the Getting There & Away section under Aeolian Islands.

Getting Around
Bus is the most common mode of public transport in Sicily. Numerous companies run services between Syracuse, Catania and Palermo as well as to Agrigento and towns in the interior. The coastal train service between Messina and Palermo and Messina to Syracuse is efficient and reliable.

PALERMO
pop 730,000
An Arab emirate and later the seat of a Norman kingdom, Palermo was once regarded as the grandest and most beautiful city in Europe. Today it is in a remarkable state of decay, due to neglect and heavy bombing during WWII, yet enough evidence remains of its golden days to make Palermo one of the most fascinating cities in Italy.

Orientation
Palermo is a large but easily manageable city. The main streets of the historical centre are Via Roma and Via Maqueda, which extend from the central station to Piazza Castelnuovo, a vast square in the modern part of town.

Information
Tourist Offices The main APT tourist office (☎ 091 58 61 22) is at Piazza Castelnuovo 35. It's open 8.30 am to 2 pm and 2.30 to 6 pm Monday to Friday (to 2 pm on Saturday). There are branch offices at the Stazione Centrale (☎ 091 616 59 14) and airport (☎ 091 59 16 98) with the same opening hours as the main office.

Money The exchange office at the Stazione Centrale is open 8 am to 8 pm daily. American Express is represented by Ruggieri & Figli (☎ 091 58 71 44), Via Emerico Amari 40, near the Stazione Marittima.

Post & Communications The main post office is at Via Roma 322 and the main Telecom telephone office is opposite the station in Piazza G Cesare, open 8.30 am to 9.30 pm daily. The postcode for Palermo is 90100.

Medical & Emergency Services For an ambulance call ☎ 091 30 66 44. The public hospital, Ospedale Civico (☎ 091 666 22 07), is at Via Carmelo Lazzaro. The all-night pharmacy, Lo Cascio (☎ 091 616 21 17), is near the train station at Via Roma 1. The questura (☎ 091 21 01 11) is at Piazza della Vittoria and is open 24 hours a day.

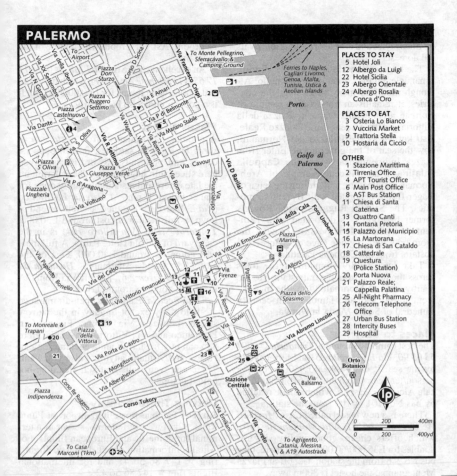

PALERMO

PLACES TO STAY
1 Hotel Joli
12 Albergo da Luigi
22 Hotel Sicilia
23 Albergo Orientale
24 Albergo Rosalia
   Conca d'Oro

PLACES TO EAT
3 Osteria Lo Bianco
7 Vucciria Market
9 Trattoria Stella
10 Hostaria da Ciccio

OTHER
1 Stazione Marittima
2 Tirrenia Office
4 APT Tourist Office
6 Main Post Office
8 AST Bus Station
11 Chiesa di Santa
   Caterina
13 Quattro Canti
14 Fontana Pretoria
15 Palazzo del Municipio
16 La Martorana
17 Chiesa di San Cataldo
18 Cattedrale
19 Questura
   (Police Station)
20 Porta Nuova
21 Palazzo Reale;
   Cappella Palatina
25 All-Night Pharmacy
26 Telecom Telephone
   Office
27 Urban Bus Station
28 Intercity Buses
29 Hospital

Dangers & Annoyances Contrary to popular opinion, Palermo is not a hotbed of thievery, but you will have to watch your valuables, which may attract pickpockets and bag snatchers. The historical centre can be a little dodgy at night, especially for women walking alone. Travellers should also avoid walking alone in the area north-east of the station, between Via Roma and the port (though there is safety in numbers).

Things to See

The intersection of Via Vittorio Emanuele and Via Maqueda marks the **Quattro Canti** (four corners of historical Palermo). The four 17th-century Spanish baroque facades are each decorated with a statue. Nearby is **Piazza Pretoria**, with a beautiful fountain, **Fontana Pretoria**, created by Florentine sculptors in the 16th century. Locals used to call it the Fountain of Shame because of its nude figures. Also in the piazza are the baroque **Chiesa di Santa Caterina** and the **Palazzo del Municipio** (town hall). Just off the piazza is Piazza Bellini and Palermo's most famous church, **La Martorana**, with a beautiful Arab-Norman bell tower and an interior decorated with Byzantine mosaics. Next to it is the Norman **Chiesa** di San Cataldo, which also mixes Arab and Norman styles and is easily recognisable by its red domes.

The huge **cattedrale** is along Via Vittorio Emanuele, on the corner of Via Bonello. Although modified many times over the centuries, it remains an impressive example of Norman architecture. Opposite Piazza della Vittoria and the gardens is the **Palazzo Reale**, also known as the Palazzo dei Normanni, now the seat of the government. Enter from Piazza Indipendenza to see the **Cappella Palatina**, a magnificent example of Arab-Norman architecture, built during the reign of Roger II and decorated with Byzantine mosaics. The **Sala di Ruggero** (King Roger's former bedroom), is decorated with 12th-century mosaics. It is possible to visit the room only with a guide (free of charge). Go upstairs from the Cappella Palatina.

Take bus No 8/9 from under the trees across the piazza from the train station to the nearby town of **Monreale** to see the magnificent mosaics in the famous 12th-century cathedral of **Santa Maria la Nuova**.

Places to Stay

The best camping ground is *Trinacria* (☎ 091 53 05 90, Via Barcarello 25), at Sferracavallo by the sea. It costs L9000/L9500/L500 per person/tent/car. Catch bus No 616 from Piazzale Alcide de Gasperi, which can be reached by bus Nos 101 or 107 from the station.

There is a new hostel called *Casa Marconi* (☎ 091 657 06 11, Via Monfenera 140), which offers cheap, good quality singles/doubles for L35,000/60,000. To get there, take bus No 246 from the station. Get off at Piazza Montegrappa; the hostel is 300m away.

Near the train station try *Albergo Orientale* (☎ 091 616 57 27, Via Maqueda 26), in an old and somewhat decayed palace; rooms are L35,000/55,000. Around the corner is *Albergo Rosalia Conca d'Oro* (☎ 091 616 45 43, Via Santa Rosalia 7), with rather basic singles/doubles/triples from L40,000/60,000/90,000 without bath.

The *Hotel Sicilia* (☎ 091 616 84 60, Via Divisi 99), on the corner of Via Maqueda, has singles/doubles of a higher standard at L50,000/75,000 with bath. *Albergo da Luigi* (☎ 091 58 50 85, Via Vittorio Emanuele 284), next to the Quattro Canti, has rooms from

L30,000/50,000, or L40,000/60,000 with bathroom. Ask for a room with a view of the fountain.

An excellent choice is *Hotel Joli* (☎ 091 611 17 65, Via Michele Amari 11), which has clean and comfortable rooms for L60,000/90,000. It is a popular choice so book early.

Places to Eat

A popular Palermitan dish is *pasta con le sarde* (pasta with sardines, fennel, peppers, capers and pine nuts). Swordfish is served here sliced into huge steaks. The Palermitani are late eaters and restaurants rarely open for dinner before 8 pm. At *Osteria Lo Bianco* (Via E Amari 104), at the Castelnuovo end of town, a full meal will cost around L30,000. *Trattoria Stella* (Via Alloro 104) is in the courtyard of the old Hotel Patria. A full meal will come to around L40,000. One of the city's best-loved restaurants is *Hostaria da Ciccio* (Via Firenze 6), just off Via Roma. A meal will come to around L30,000.

The *Vucciria*, Palermo's open-air markets, are held daily except Sunday in the narrow streets between Via Roma, Piazza San Domenico and Via Vittorio Emanuele. Here you can buy fresh fruit and vegetables, meat, cheese and virtually anything else you want. There are even stalls that sell steaming-hot boiled octopus.

Getting There & Away

Air The Falcone-Borsellino airport at Punta Raisi, 32km west of Palermo, serves as a terminal for domestic and European flights. For Alitalia information about domestic flights, ring ☎ 147 86 56 41 and for international flights ring ☎ 147 86 56 42.

Bus The main (Intercity) terminal for destinations throughout Sicily and the mainland is in the area around Via Paolo Balsamo, to the right (east) as you leave the station. Offices for the various companies are all in this area, including SAIS Traporti (☎ 091 616 60 28), Via Balsamo 16; and Segesta (☎ 091 616 79 19), Via Balsamo 26.

Train Regular trains leave from the Stazione Centrale for Milazzo, Messina, Catania and Syracuse, as well as for nearby towns such as Cefalú. Direct trains go to Reggio di Calabria,

Naples and Rome. For a one-way ticket to Rome you pay L73,200 in 2nd class plus a L26,000 Intercity supplement.

Boat Boats leave from the port (Molo Vittorio Veneto) for Sardinia and the mainland (see the earlier Sicily Getting There & Away section). The Tirrenia office (☎ 091 33 33 00) is at the port.

Getting Around
Taxis to/from the airport cost upwards of L70,000. The cheaper option is to catch one of the regular blue buses which leave from outside the station roughly every 45 minutes from 5 am to 9.45 pm. The trip takes one hour and costs L6500. Palermo's buses are efficient and most stop outside the train station. Bus No 7 runs along Via Roma from the train station to near Piazza Castelnuovo and No 39 goes from the station to the port. You must buy tickets before you get on the bus; they cost L1500 and are valid for one hour.

AEOLIAN ISLANDS
Also known as the Lipari Islands, the seven islands of this archipelago just north of Milazzo are volcanic in origin. They range from the well-developed tourist resort of Lipari and the understated jet-set haunt of Panarea, to the rugged Vulcano, the spectacular scenery of Stromboli (and its fiercely active volcano), the fertile vineyards of Salina, and the solitude of Alicudi and Filicudi, which remain relatively undeveloped. The islands have been inhabited since the Neolithic era, when migrants sought the valuable volcanic glass, obsidian. The Isole Eolie (Aeolian Islands) are so named because the ancient Greeks believed they were the home of Aeolus, the god of wind. Homer wrote of them in the *Odyssey*.

Information
The main AAST tourist information office (☎ 090 988 00 95) for the islands is on Lipari at Corso Vittorio Emanuele 202. Other offices are open on Vulcano, Salina and Stromboli during summer.

Things to See & Do
On **Lipari** visit the citadel (castello), with its archaeological park and museum. You can also go on excellent walks on the island.

Catch a local bus from the town of Lipari to the hill-top village of Quattrocchi for a great view of Vulcano. Boat trips will take you around the island – contact the tourist office for information.

Vulcano, with its ever-present, rotten-egg smell of sulphur (you'll get used to it), is a short boat trip from Lipari's port. The main volcano, Vulcano Fossa, is still active, though the last recorded period of eruption was 1888-90. You can make the one-hour hike to the crater, or take a bath in the therapeutic hot muds.

Stromboli is the most spectacular of the islands. Climb the cone (924m) at night to see the Sciara del Fuoco (Trail of Fire), lava streaming down the side of the volcano, and the volcanic explosions from the crater. Many people make the trip (four to five hours) without a guide during the day, but at night you should go with a guided group. The AGAI and GAE official guides (☎/fax 090 98 62 54, ✉ stromboli@iol.it) organise guided tours which depart at around 5 pm and return at 11.30 pm. It's best to contact them in advance to make a booking, since they only depart if groups are large enough. Remember to take warm clothes, wear heavy shoes and carry a torch and plenty of water.

Places to Stay & Eat
Camping facilities are available on Salina and Vulcano. Most accommodation in summer is booked out well in advance on the smaller islands, particularly on Stromboli, and most hotels close during winter.

Lipari Lipari provides the best options for a comfortable stay. It has numerous budget hotels, affittacamere and apartments, and the other islands are easily accessible by regular hydrofoil. When you arrive on Lipari you will be approached by someone offering accommodation. This is worth checking because the offers are usually genuine. The island's camping ground, *Baia Unci* (☎ 090 981 19 09), is at Canneto, about 3km out of Lipari town. It costs L18,000 a night per person. The HI *Ostello per la Gioventú Lipari* (☎ 090 981 15 40, Via Castello 17) is inside the walls of the citadel. A bed costs L14,500 a night, plus L1000 for a hot shower and L3000 for breakfast. A meal costs L15,000,

ITALY

but you can cook your own. It's open March to October.

Lo Nardo Maria (☎ *090 988 0431, fax 090 981 31 63, Vicolo Ulisse*) is a private home with four comfortable double rooms costing L50,000 between October and April but double that amount during the summer. from L25,000 to L40,000 per person, depending on the season.

You can eat surprisingly cheaply on Lipari. *Da Bartolo* (*Via Garibaldi 53*) is a good choice for seafood; a full meal costs around L35,000. At *Nenzyna* (*Via Roma 2*) you can eat well for L25,000.

Stromboli On Stromboli the popular *Casa del Sole* (☎ *090 98 60 17, Via Soldato Cincotta*), on the road to the volcano, has singles/doubles for L35,000/40,000. If you want to splurge, try the hotel *La Sirena* (☎ *090 988 99 97, Via Pecorini Mare*), which charges L70,000/120,000 for rooms with bath.

Vulcano On Vulcano, try *Pensione Agostino* (☎ *090 985 23 42, Via Favaloro 1*), close to the mud bath, which has doubles with bathroom from L50,000 to L100,000 depending on the season. *Hotel Arcipelago* (☎ *090 985 20 02*) is beautifully positioned on Vulcano's northern coast and costs L185,000 for half-board.

Alicudi & Filicudi If you want seclusion, head for Filicudi or Alicudi. However, the hotels aren't exactly cheap. Alicudi's *Ericusa* (☎ *090 988 99 02*) costs L105,000 for half-board in summer and Filicudi's *La Canna* (☎ *090 988 99 56, Via Rosa 53*) charges L115,000 for half-board.

Getting There & Away
Ferries and hydrofoils leave for the islands from Milazzo (which is easy to reach by train from Palermo and Messina) and all ticket offices are along Via Rizzo at the port. SNAV runs hydrofoils (L19,500 one way). Siremar also runs hydrofoils, but its ferries are half the price. If arriving at Milazzo by train, you will need to catch a bus to the port. If arriving by bus, simply make the five-minute walk back along Via Crispi to the port area. SNAV also runs hydrofoils from Palermo twice a day in summer and three times a week in the off season.

You can travel directly to the islands from the mainland. Siremar runs regular ferries from Naples and SNAV runs hydrofoils from Naples (see the Naples Getting There & Away section), Messina and Reggio di Calabria. Note that occasionally the sea around the islands can be very rough and sailings are cancelled, especially out of season to the outer islands.

Getting Around
Regular hydrofoil and ferry services operate between the islands. Both Siremar and Aliscafi SNAV have offices at the port on Lipari, where you can get full timetable information.

TAORMINA
pop 10,500
Spectacularly located on a hill overlooking the sea and Mt Etna, Taormina was long ago discovered by the European jet set, which has made it one of the more expensive and touristy towns in Sicily. But its magnificent setting, its Greek theatre and the nearby beaches remain as seductive now as they were for the likes of Goethe and DH Lawrence. The AAST tourist office (☎ 0942 2 32 43) in Palazzo Corvaja, just off Corso Umberto near Largo Santa Caterina, has extensive information on the town.

Things to See & Do
The **Greek theatre** (entry L4000) was built in the 3rd century BC and later greatly expanded and remodelled by the Romans. Concerts and theatre are staged here in summer and it affords a wonderful view of Mt Etna. From the beautiful **Trevelyan Gardens** there is a panoramic view of the sea. Along Corso Umberto is the **Duomo**, with a Gothic facade. The local beach is **Isola Bella**, a short bus ride from Via Pirandello or by the *funivia* (cable car), which costs L5000 return.

Trips to Mt Etna can be organised through CST (☎ 0942 2 33 01), Corso Umberto 101. In nearby Catania, Natura e Turismo (NeT; ☎ 095 33 35 43, fax 095 53 79 10, ✉ natetur@tin.it, Via Quartararo 11) organises guided walks and excursions on Mt Etna and in surrounding areas.

Places to Stay & Eat
You can camp near the beach at *Campeggio San Leo* (☎ *0942 2 46 58, Via Nazionale*) at

Capo Taormina. The cost is L10,000 per person per night, and L14,000 for a tent site.

There are numerous *affittacamere* (room rentals) in Taormina and the tourist office has a full list. *Il Leone* (☎ 0942 2 38 78, *Via Bagnoli Croce 127)*, near the Trevelyan Gardens, charges L45,000 per person with breakfast. *Pensione Svizzera* (☎ 0942 237 90, ✆ *sviz zera@tau.it, Via Pirandello 26)*, on the way from the bus stop to the town centre, has very pleasant singles/doubles for L80,000/120,000 with private bathroom.

Ristorante La Piazzetta (Via Paladini 5) has excellent full meals for around L30,000. *Da Rita (Via Calapitrulli 3)* serves pizza, bruschetta and lots of big salads. To drink a good Sicilian wine or sangria, go to *Arco Rosso (Via Naumachie 7)*. Eat a typical Sicilian summer breakfast at *Bam Bar (Via Di Giovanni 45);* order a granita of crushed ice with fresh fruit or almonds.

Getting There & Away

Bus is the easiest way to get to Taormina. SAIS buses leave from Messina, Catania and also from the airport at Catania. Taormina is on the main train line between Messina and Catania, but the station is on the coast and regular buses will take you to Via Pirandello, near the centre; bus services are heavily reduced on Sunday.

ETNA

Dominating the landscape in eastern Sicily between Taormina and Catania, Mt Etna (3323m) is Europe's largest live volcano. It has four live craters at its summit and its slopes are littered with crevices and extinct cones. Eruptions of slow lava flows can occur, but are not really dangerous. Etna's most recent eruption was in 1999. You can climb to the summit (it's a seven-hour hike), but the handiest way is to take the cable car (SITAS ☎ 095 91 41 41) from the **Rifugio Sapienza** on the Nicolosi side of the mountain. The all-in price for the cable car, a 4WD vehicle to near the tip of the crater and a guide is L65,000. From the north side, there is a 4WD minibus (Le Betulle/STAR, ☎ 095 64 34 30) from Piano Provenzana. A three-hour guided tour costs L60,000.

Mt Etna is best approached from Catania by AST bus (☎ 095 53 17 56), which departs Via L Sturzo (in front of the train station) at 8.15 am, returning from Rifugio Sapienza at 4.30 pm (L7000 return). A private Circumetnea train line (☎ 095 37 48 42) circles Mt Etna from Giarre-Riposto to Catania. It starts from Catania at Stazione Borgo, Corso delle Province 13 (take bus Nos 29 or 36 from Catania's main train station). From Taormina, you can take an FS train to Giarre, where you can catch the Circumetnea.

SYRACUSE
pop 125,900

Once a powerful Greek city to rival Athens, Syracuse (Siracusa) is one of the highlights of a visit to Sicily. Founded in 743 BC by colonists from Corinth, it became a dominant sea power in the Mediterranean, prompting Athens to attack the city in 413 BC. Syracuse was the birthplace of the Greek mathematician and physicist Archimedes, and Plato attended the court of the tyrant Dionysius, who ruled from 405 to 367 BC.

Orientation & Information

The main sights of Syracuse are in two areas: on the island of Ortygia and at the archaeological park 2km across town. There are two tourist information offices. The AAT (☎ 0931 46 42 55), Via Maestranza 33 on Ortygia, opens 9 am to 1 pm and 4.30 to 8.30 pm weekdays (morning only on Saturday). The APT (☎ 0931 6 77 10), Via San Sebastiano 45, opens 8.30 am to 1.30 pm Monday to Saturday. There is a branch office of the APT, with the same opening hours, at the archaeological park.

Things to See

Ortygia On the island of Ortygia the buildings are predominantly medieval, with some baroque palaces and churches. The **Duomo** was built in the 7th-century on top of the Temple of Athena, incorporating most of the original columns in its three-aisled structure. The splendid **Piazza del Duomo** is lined with baroque palaces. Walk down Via Picherali to the waterfront and the **Fonte Aretusa** (Fountain of Arethusa), a natural freshwater spring. According to Greek legend, the nymph Arethusa, pursued by the river-god Alpheus, was turned into a fountain by the goddess Diana. Undeterred, Alpheus turned himself into the river which feeds the spring.

ITALY

Neapolis-Parco Archeologico To get to this archaeological zone, catch bus No 1 from Riva della Posta on Ortygia. The main attraction here is the 5th-century BC **Greek theatre**, its seating area carved out of solid rock. Nearby is the **Orecchio di Dionisio**, an artificial grotto in the shape of an ear which the tyrant of Syracuse, Dionysius, used as a prison. The 2nd-century **Roman amphitheatre** is impressively well preserved. The park opens daily from 9 am to one hour before sunset. Admission is L4000.

The **Museo Archeologico Paolo Orsi** (☎ 0931 46 40 22), about 500m east of the archaeological zone, off Viale Teocrito, contains Sicily's best-organised and most interesting archaeological collection. The museum is open 9 am to 1 pm and 3.30 to 6.30 pm Tuesday to Sunday. Admission is L8000.

Places to Stay
Camping facilities are at *Agriturist Rinaura* (☎ *0931 72 12 24)*, about 4km from the city near the sea. Camping costs L8000 per person and L19,000 for a site. Catch bus Nos 21, 22 or 24 from Corso Umberto. The non-HI *Ostello della Gioventú (☎ 0931 71 11 18, Viale Pepoli 45)* is 8km west of town on SS115; catch bus Nos 11 or 25 from Piazzale Marconi. Beds cost L25,000; full board is L42,000.

Hotel Gran Bretagna (☎ 0931 6 87 65, Via Savoia 21), just off Largo XXV Luglio on Ortygia, has very pleasant singles/doubles for L63,000/99,000 with bath or L53,000/87,000 without. *Hotel Aretusa (☎ 0931 2 42 11, Via Francesco Crispi 75)* is close to the train station; comfortable and clean rooms cost L45,000/70,000.

Places to Eat
On Ortygia, *Ristorante Osteria da Mariano (Vicolo Zuccalá 9)* serves typical Sicilian food. *Pizzeria Trattoria Zsa Zsa (Via Roma 73)* serves 65 different kinds of pizza, antipasti and pasta. At both places a full meal will cost less than L25,000. A good pizzeria is *Il Cenacolo (Via del Consiglio Reginale 10)*.

At *Pasticceria Cassarino (Corso Umberto 86)* you can try scrumptious Sicilian sweets including *cannoli di ricotta* and *arancini*.

There is an open-air, fresh produce *market* in the streets behind the Temple of Apollo, open daily (except Sunday) until 1 pm. You will find several *alimentari* and *supermarkets* along Corso Gelone.

Getting There & Away
SAIS buses leave from Riva della Posta on Ortygia for Catania, Palermo, Enna and surrounding small towns. The SAIS service for Rome also leaves from the piazza, connecting with the Rome bus at Catania. AST buses also service Palermo from Piazza della Posta. Syracuse is easy to reach by train from Messina and Catania. Boat services from Syracuse to Malta remain in a state of flux and it is best to check with the tourist offices.

AGRIGENTO
pop 55,200
Founded in approximately 582 BC as the Greek Akragas, Agrigento is today a pleasant medieval town, but the Greek temples in the valley below are the real reason to visit. The Italian novelist and dramatist Luigi Pirandello (1867-1936) was born here, as was the Greek philosopher and scientist Empedocles (circa 490-430 BC).

The AAST tourist office (☎ 0922 2 04 54), Via Cesare Battisti 15, opens 8.30 am to 1.30 pm and 4.30 to 7 pm Monday to Friday (to 1 pm on Saturday).

Things to See & Do
Agrigento's **Valley of the Temples** is one of the major Greek archaeological sights in the world. Its five main Doric temples were constructed in the 5th century BC and are in various states of ruin because of earthquakes and vandalism by early Christians. The only temple to survive relatively intact is the **Tempio della Concordia**, which was transformed into a Christian church. The **Tempio di Giunone**, a five-minute walk uphill to the east, has an impressive sacrificial altar. The **Tempio di Ercole** is the oldest of the structures. Across the main road which divides the valley is the massive **Tempio di Giove**, one of the most imposing buildings of ancient Greece. Although now completely in ruins, it used to cover an area measuring 112m by 56m, with columns 18m high. **Telamoni**, colossal statues of men, were also used in the structure. The remains of one of them are in the **Museo Archeologico**, just north of the temples on Via dei Templi (a copy lies at the archaeological site).

Close by is the **Tempio di Castore e Polluce**, which was partly reconstructed in the 19th century. The temples are lit up at night and are open until one hour before sunset. To get to the temples from the town, catch bus No 1, 2 or 3 from the train station.

Places to Stay & Eat
The *Bella Napoli* (☎ 0922 2 04 35, Piazza Lena 6), off Via Bac Bac at the end of Via Atenea, has clean and comfortable singles/doubles for L25,000/55,000 (L44,000/75,000 with private bathroom). For a decent, cheap meal try the excellent *La Forchetta* (Piazza San Francesco 9); the spaghetti *al pesce di spada* (swordfish) is delicious at L8000.

Getting There & Away
Intercity buses leave from Piazza Rosselli, just off Piazza Vittorio Emanuele, for Palermo, Catania and surrounding small towns.

Sardinia

The second-largest island in the Mediterranean, Sardinia (Sardegna) was colonised by the Phoenicians and Romans, followed by the Pisans, Genoese and finally the Spaniards. But it is often said that the Sardinians, known on the island as Sardi, were never really conquered – they simply retreated into the hills.

The landscape of the island ranges from the 'savage, dark-bushed, sky-exposed land' described by DH Lawrence, to the beautiful gorges and valleys near Dorgali and the unspoiled coastline between Bosa and Alghero. Try to avoid the island in August, when the weather is hot and the beaches are overcrowded.

Getting There & Away
Air Airports at Cagliari, Olbia and Alghero link Sardinia with major Italian and European cities. For information contact Alitalia or the Sestante CIT or CTS offices in all major towns.

Boat The island is accessible by ferry from Genoa, Livorno, Fiumicino (the port of Rome), Civitavecchia, Naples, Palermo, Trapani, Bonifacio (Corsica) and Tunis. The departure points in Sardinia are Olbia, Golfo

Aranci and Porto Torres in the north, Arbatax on the east coast and Cagliari in the south.

The main company, Tirrenia, runs a service between Civitavecchia and Olbia, Arbatax or Cagliari, and between Genoa and Porto Torres, Olbia, Arbatax or Cagliari. There are fast ships between Fiumicino and Golfo Aranci/Arbatax, La Spezia and Golfo Aranci, and Civitavecchia and Olbia. The national railway, Ferrovie dello Stato (FS), runs a slightly cheaper service between Civitavecchia and Golfo Aranci. Moby Lines (which also runs Navarma Lines and Sardegna Lines) and Sardinia Ferries (also known as Elba and Corsica Ferries) both operate services from the mainland to Sardinia, as well as to Corsica and Elba. They depart from Livorno, Civitavecchia and arrive at either Olbia or Golfo Aranci. Grandi Navi Veloci runs a service between Genova and Olbia or Porto Torres from late June to late September. Most travel agencies in Italy have brochures on the various companies' services.

Timetables change and prices fluctuate with the season. Prices for a poltrona on Tirrenia ferries in the 2000 high season were: Genoa to Cagliari (L102,000; 20 hours); Genoa to Porto Torres or Olbia (L83,000; 13 hours); Naples to Cagliari (L78,000; 16 hours); and Palermo to Cagliari (L73,000; 14 hours); Civitavecchia to Olbia, (L40,400; seven hours); Civitavecchia to Cagliari (L77,000; 13½ hours). The cost of taking a small car ranged from L134,100 to L180,000, and for a motorcycle from L40,100 to L53,900.

For online information including departures, timetables and fares, check Tirrenia's Web site at www.tirrenia.com. Moby Lines has a Web site at www.mobylines.it (Italian only).

Getting Around
Bus The two main bus companies are the state-run ARST, which operates extensive services throughout the island, and the privately owned PANI, which links main towns.

Train The main FS train lines link Cagliari with Oristano, Sassari and Olbia. The private railways that link smaller towns throughout the island can be very slow. However, the *trenino* (little train), which runs from Cagliari to Arbatax through the Barbagia, is a very relaxing way to see part of the interior (see the Cagliari Getting There & Away section).

Car & Motorcycle The only way to explore Sardinia properly is by road. Rental agencies are listed under Cagliari and some other towns around the island.

Hitching You might find hitchhiking laborious once you get away from the main towns because of the light traffic. Women should not hitchhike in Sardinia under any circumstances.

CAGLIARI
pop 204,237

This attractive city offers an interesting medieval section, the beautiful beach of Poetto, and salt lakes with a population of pink flamingoes.

Orientation

If you arrive by bus, train or boat, you will find yourself at the port area of Cagliari. The main street along the harbour is Via Roma, and the old city stretches up the hill behind it to the castle. Most of the budget hotels and restaurants are in the area near the port.

Information

Tourist Offices The AAST information booth (☎ 070 66 92 55), Piazza Matteotti 9, is open 8 am to 8 pm daily in July and August and 8 am to 2 pm in other months. There are also information offices at the airport and in the Stazione Marittima.

The Ente Sardo Industrie Turistiche office (ESIT; ☎ 167 01 31 53 or 070 6 02 31, fax 070 66 46 36), Via Goffredo Mameli 97, is open 8 am to 8 pm daily during the summer (reduced hours the rest of the year). It has information on the whole island.

Post & Communications The main post office (☎ 070 6 03 11) is on Piazza del Carmine, up Via La Maddalena from Via Roma. The Telecom office is at Via G M Angioj, north of Piazza Matteotti. The postcode for Cagliari is 09100.

Medical & Emergency Services For an ambulance ring ☎ 070 28 62 00, and for medical attention go to the Ospedale Civile (☎ 070 609 22 67), Via Ospedale. Contact the police on ☎ 113, or go to the questura (☎ 070 6 02 71), Via Amat 9.

Things to See

The **Museo Archeologico Nazionale**, Piazza Arsenale, in the Citadella dei Musei, has a fascinating collection of Nuraghic bronzes. It's open 9 am to 2 pm and 3 to 8 pm daily, April to September (9 am to 7 pm Tuesday to Sunday the rest of the year). Admission is L4000.

It's enjoyable enough to wander through the medieval quarter. The Pisan-Romanesque **Duomo** was built in the 13th century, but later remodelled. It has an interesting Romanesque pulpit.

From the **Bastione di San Remy**, which is in the centre of town in Piazza Costituzione and once formed part of the fortifications of the old city, there is a good view of Cagliari and the sea.

The Pisan **Torre di San Pancrazio**, in Piazza Indipendenza, is also worth a look. The **Roman amphitheatre**, on Viale Buon Cammino, is considered the most important Roman monument in Sardinia. During summer opera is performed here.

Spend a day on the **Spiaggia di Poetto**, east of the centre, and wander across to the salt lakes to see the flamingoes.

Special Events

The Festival of Sant'Efisio, a colourful festival mixing the secular and the religious, is held annually for four days from 1 May.

Places to Stay & Eat

There are numerous budget pensioni near the station. Try the *Locanda Firenze* (☎ 070 66 85 05, Corso Vittorio Emanuele 149), which has comfortable singles/doubles for L43,000/58,000. *Locanda Miramare* (☎ 070 66 40 21, Via Roma 59) has rooms for L56,000/75,000. Nearby is *Albergo La Perla* (☎ 66 94 46, Via Sardegna 18), with rooms for L46,000/58,000.

Several reasonably priced trattorias can be found in the area behind Via Roma, particularly around Via Sardegna and Via Cavour. *Trattoria da Serafino* (Via Lepanto 6), on the corner of Via Sardegna, has excellent food at reasonable prices. *Trattoria Gennargentu* (Via Sardegna 60) has good pasta and seafood and a full meal costs around L33,000. *Trattoria Ci Pensa Cannas*, down the street at No

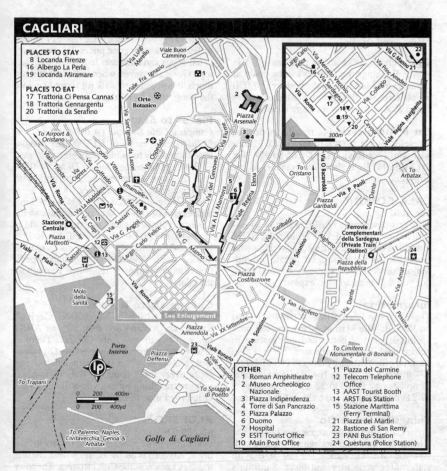

CAGLIARI

PLACES TO STAY
8 Locanda Firenze
16 Albergo La Perla
19 Locanda Miramare

PLACES TO EAT
17 Trattoria Ci Pensa Cannas
18 Trattoria Gennargentu
20 Trattoria da Serafino

OTHER

1	Roman Amphitheatre	11	Piazza del Carmine
2	Museo Archeologico Nazionale	12	Telecom Telephone Office
3	Piazza Indipendenza	13	AAST Tourist Booth
4	Torre di San Pancrazio	14	ARST Bus Station
5	Piazza Palazzo	15	Stazione Marittima (Ferry Terminal)
6	Duomo	21	Piazza dei Martiri
7	Hospital	22	Bastione di San Remy
9	ESIT Tourist Office	23	PANI Bus Station
10	Main Post Office	24	Questura (Police Station)

37, is another good choice, with meals for around L26,000. On Via Sardegna there are also grocery shops and bakeries.

Getting There & Away

Air Cagliari's airport (☎ 070 24 02 00) is to the north-west of the city at Elmas. ARST buses leave regularly from Piazza Matteotti to coincide with flight arrivals and departures. The Alitalia office (☎ 070 24 00 79 or 147 86 56 43) is at the airport.

Bus & Train ARST buses (☎ 070 409 83 24; or in Sardinia ☎ 800 86 50 42) leave from Piazza Matteotti for nearby towns, the Costa del Sud and the Costa Rei. PANI buses (☎ 070 65 23 26) leave from further along Via Roma at Piazza Darsena for towns such as Sassari, Oristano and Nuoro. The main train station is also in Piazza Matteotti. Regular trains leave for Oristano, Sassari, Porto Torres and Olbia. The private Ferrovie della Sardegna (FdS) train station is in Piazza della Repubblica. For information about the *Trenino Verde* which runs along a scenic route between Cagliari and Arbatax, contact ESIT (see Information), or the FdS directly (☎ 070 58 02 46). The most interesting and

ITALY

picturesque section of the route is between Mandas and Arbatax.

Boat Ferries arrive at the port just off Via Roma. Bookings for Tirrenia can be made at the Stazione Marittima in the port area (☎ 070 66 60 65). See the earlier Sardinia Getting There & Away section for more details.

Car & Motorcycle For rental cars or motorcycles try Hertz (☎ 070 66 81 05), Piazza Matteotti 1; or Ruvioli (☎ 070 65 89 55), Via dei Mille 11. Both also have branches at the airport.

CALA GONONE
pop 1002
This fast-developing seaside resort is an excellent base from which to explore the coves along the eastern coastline, as well as the Nuraghic sites and rugged terrain inland. Major points are accessible by bus and boat, but you will need a car to explore.

Information
There is a Pro Loco office (☎ 0784 9 36 96) on Viale del Blu Marino, where you can pick up maps, a list of hotels and information to help you while visiting the area. There is also a tourist office in nearby Dorgali (☎ 0784 9 62 43), at Via Lamarmora 108. At Cala Gonone, Coop Ghivine (☎ 0336 32 69 57, fax 0784 9 67 21) organises guided treks in the region.

Things to See & Do
From Cala Gonone's port, catch a boat to the **Grotta del Bue Marino**, where a guide will take you on a 1km walk to see vast caves with stalagmites, stalactites and lakes. Sardinia's last colony of monk seals once lived here, but have not been sighted in several years. Boats also leave for **Cala Luna**, an isolated beach where you can spend the day by the sea or take a walk along the fabulous gorge called **Codula di Luna**. However, the beach is packed with day-tripping tourists in summer. The boat trip to visit the grotto and beach costs L35,000.

A **walking track** along the coast links Cala Fuili, south of Cala Gonone, and Cala Luna (about three hours one way).

If you want to descend the impressive **Gorropu Gorge**, ask for information from the team of young expert guides based in Urzulei

– Societá Gorropu (☎ 0782 64 92 82, 0347 775 27 06). They also offer a wide range of guided walks in the area at good prices. It is necessary to use ropes and harnesses to traverse the Gorropu Gorge; however, when it doesn't rain too much, it is possible to walk for about 1km into the gorge from its northern entrance.

Places to Stay
Camping Gala Gonone (☎ 0784 931 65, Via Collodi) charges up to L27,000 per person. Free camping is forbidden throughout the area.

Hotels include the *Piccolo Hotel* (☎ 0784 932 32, Via C Colombo) near the port, with singles/doubles for L60,000/99,000.

Su Gologone (☎ 28 75 12) is a few kilometres east of Oliena, near the entrance to the Lanaittu valley. It's on the expensive side at around L155,000 for half-board, but is in a lovely setting and the owners also organise guided tours, treks and horse-riding expeditions. Its restaurant is renowned throughout the island.

Getting There & Away
Catch a PANI bus to Nuoro from Cagliari, Sassari or Oristano and then take an ARST bus to Dorgali and Cala Gonone. There is also a bus from Olbia's port to Oliena or Dorgali, from where you can catch a bus (only every three hours) to Cala Gonone. If you are travelling by car, you will need a detailed road map of the area.

ALGHERO
pop 39,026
One of the most popular tourist resorts in Sardinia, Alghero is on the island's west coast in the area known as the Coral Riviera. The town is a good base from which to explore the magnificent coastline linking it to Bosa in the south, and the famous Grotte di Nettuno (Neptune's Caves) on the Capocaccia to the north.

Information
The train station is on Via Don Minzoni, some distance from the centre, and is connected by a regular bus service to the centre of town.

The AAST tourist office (☎ 079 97 90 54) is at Piazza Porta Terra 9, near the port and just across the gardens from the bus station. The old city and most hotels and restaurants are in the area west of the tourist office.

The main post office is at Via XX Settembre 108. There is a bank of public telephones on Via Vittorio Emanuele at the opposite end of the gardens from the tourist office. The postcode for Alghero is 07041.

In an emergency ring the police on ☎ 113; for medical attention ring ☎ 079 93 05 33, or go to the Ospedale Civile (☎ 079 99 62 33) on Via Don Minzoni.

Things to See & Do

It's worth wandering through the narrow streets of the old city and around the port. The most interesting church is the **Chiesa di San Francesco**, Via Carlo Alberto. The city's **cathedral** has been ruined by constant remodelling, but its bell tower remains a fine example of Gothic-Catalan architecture.

Near Alghero at the beautiful **Capocaccia** are the **Grotte di Nettuno**, accessible by hourly boats from the port (L18,000), or three time a day by the FS bus from Via Catalogna (L4500 one way, 50 minutes).

If you have your own transport, don't miss the **Nuraghe di Palmavera**, about 10km out of Alghero on the road to Porto Conte.

The coastline between Alghero and Bosa is stunning. Rugged cliffs fall down to isolated beaches, and near **Bosa** is one of the last habitats of the griffon vulture. It's quite an experience if you are lucky enough to spot one of these huge birds. The best way to see the coast is by car or motorcycle. If you want to rent a bicycle or motorcycle to explore the coast, try Cicloexpress (☎ 079 98 69 50), Via Garibaldi, at the port.

Special Events

In summer Alghero stages the Estate Musicale Algherese (Alghero's Summer Music Festival) in the cloisters of the church of San Francesco, Via Carlo Alberto. A festival, complete with fireworks display, is held on 15 August for the Feast of the Assumption.

Places to Stay & Eat

It is virtually impossible to find a room in August unless you book months in advance. At other times of the year you should have little trouble. Camping facilities include *Calik* (☎ *079 93 01 11*) in Fertilia, about 6km out of town (L24,000 per person). The HI *Ostello dei Giuliani* (☎ *079 93 03 53, Via Zara 1*) is also in Fertilia. Take the hourly bus 'AF' from Via Catalogna to Fertilia. B&B costs L15,000, a shower is L1000 and a meal costs L15,000. The hostel is open all year.

In the old town is the *Hotel San Francesco* (☎ *079 97 92 58, Via Ambrogio Machin 2*) with singles/doubles for L55,000/90,000.

A pleasant place to eat is *Trattoria Il Vecchio Mulino* (*Via Don Deroma 7*). A full meal will cost around L45,000.

Getting There & Away

Alghero is accessible from Sassari by train. The main bus station is on Via Catalogna, next to the public park. ARST (☎ 079 95 01 79) buses leave for Sassari and Porto Torres. FS buses (☎ 95 04 58) also service Sassari, Macomer and Bosa.

ITALY

Macedonia (Македонија)

The Former Yugoslav Republic of Macedonia (FYROM) is at the south end of what was once the Yugoslav Federation. Its position in the mountainous centre of the Balkan Peninsula between Albania, Bulgaria, Serbia and Greece has often made it a political powder keg. The mix of Islamic and Orthodox influences tell of a long struggle that ended in 1913 when the Treaty of Bucharest divided Macedonia among three of its neighbours. Serbia got the northern part while the southern half went to Greece. Bulgaria received a much smaller slice. Only in 1992 did ex-Yugoslav Macedonia become fully independent, and the country has emerged without being drawn into the wars that have plagued other former Yugoslav republics.

In this book, Lonely Planet uses the name Macedonia rather than the Former Yugoslav Republic of Macedonia. This is to reflect what the inhabitants prefer to call their country and is not intended to prejudice any political claims.

For travellers Macedonia is a land of contrasts, ranging from Skopje with its timeworn Turkish bazaar and lively cafes, to the many medieval monasteries around Ohrid. With its fascinating blend of Orthodox mystery and the exotic Orient, together with Lake Ohrid's world-class beauty, Macedonia offers an unexpected variety of opportunities for relaxation and exploration.

AT A GLANCE

Capital	Skopje
Population	2 million
Official Language	Macedonian
Currency	1 Macedonian denar (MKD) = 100 deni
Time	GMT/UTC+0100
Country phone code ☎ 389	

Facts about Macedonia

HISTORY

Historical Macedonia (from where Alexander the Great set out to conquer the ancient world in the 4th century BC) is today contained mostly in present-day Greece, a point Greeks are always quick to make when discussing contemporary Macedonia's use of that name. The Romans subjugated the Greeks of ancient Macedonia and the territory to the north in the mid-2nd century BC, and when the empire was divided in the 4th century AD, this region became part of the Eastern Roman Empire ruled from Constantinople. Slav tribes settled here in the 7th century, changing the ethnic character of the area.

In the 9th century the region was conquered by the Bulgarian tsar Simeon (r. 893-927) and later, under Tsar Samuel (r. 980-1014), Macedonia was the centre of a powerful Bulgarian state. Samuel's defeat by Byzantium in 1014 ushered in a long period when Macedonia passed back and forth between Byzantium, Bulgaria and Serbia. After the crushing defeat of Serbia by the Turks in 1389, the Balkans became a part of the Ottoman Empire and the region's cultural character again changed.

In 1878 Russia defeated Turkey, and Macedonia was ceded to Bulgaria by the Treaty of San Stefano. The western powers, fearing the creation of a powerful Russian satellite in the heart of the Balkans, forced Bulgaria to give Macedonia back to Turkey.

In 1893 Macedonian nationalists formed the Internal Macedonian Revolutionary Organisation (IMRO) to fight for independence from Turkey, culminating in the Ilinden uprising of August 1903, which was brutally suppressed by October. Although the nationalist leader Goce Delčev died before the revolt he has become the symbol of Macedonian nationalism.

The First Balkan War in 1912 brought Greece, Serbia, Bulgaria and Montenegro together against Turkey. In the Second Balkan War in 1913 Greece and Serbia ousted the Bulgarians and split Macedonia between themselves. Frustrated by this, IMRO continued the struggle against royalist Serbia; the interwar government in Belgrade responded by banning the Macedonian language and

even the name Macedonia. Though some IMRO elements supported the Bulgarian occupation of Macedonia during WWII, many more joined Tito's partisans, and in 1943 it was agreed that post-war Macedonia would have full republic status in future Yugoslavia.

The end of WWII brought Macedonians hopes of unifying their peoples; this was encouraged by the Greek communist party and Bulgaria's recognition of its Macedonian minorities. However, the Stalin-Tito split of 1948 and the end of the Greek civil war in 1949 put an end to such hopes. Nonetheless, the first Macedonian grammar was published in 1952 and an independent Macedonian Orthodox Church was allowed to form.

On 8 September 1991 a referendum on independence was held in Macedonia and 74% voted in favour. In January 1992 the country declared its full independence from former Yugoslavia. Belgrade cooperated by ordering all federal troops present to withdraw and, because the split was peaceful, road and rail links were never broken.

Greece delayed diplomatic recognition of Macedonia by demanding that the country find another name, alleging that the term Macedonia implied territorial claims on northern Greece. Greece is concerned that if the Macedonians use the term Macedonia they may aspire to greater de facto legitimacy to the ambit of ancient Macedonia, which included (and still includes) a large part of Greece. At Greece's insistence, Macedonia was forced to use the absurd 'temporary' title FYROM (Former Yugoslav Republic of Macedonia) for the purpose of being admitted to the UN in April 1993. When the USA (following six EU countries' lead) recognised FYROM in February 1994, Greece declared an economic embargo against Macedonia and closed the port of Thessaloniki to the country's trade. The embargo was lifted in November 1995 after Macedonia changed its flag and agreed to discuss its name with Greece. To date, there has been no resolution of this thorny issue, though relations with Greece on the trade front are looking healthy.

GEOGRAPHY
Much of 25,333-sq-km Macedonia is a plateau between 600 and 900m high. The Vardar River cuts across the middle of the country, passing the capital, Skopje, on its way to the Aegean Sea near Thessaloniki. Ohrid and Prespa Lakes in the south-west drain into the Adriatic via Albania; at 294m, Lake Ohrid is the deepest lake on the Balkan Peninsula. In the north-west the Šar Planina marks Macedonia's border with Kosovo; Titov Vrv (2748m) in this range is Macedonia's highest peak. The country's three national parks are Pelister (west of Bitola), Galičica (between Lakes Ohrid and Prespa) and Mavrovo (between Ohrid and Tetovo). A fourth national park will be established in the Šara Mountain region west of Tetovo, encompassing the ski resort Popova Šapka.

CLIMATE
Macedonia's summers are hot and dry. In winter, warm Aegean winds blowing up the Vardar Valley moderate the continental conditions prevailing farther north. However, Macedonia receives a lot of snowfall, even if temperatures are warmer than those farther north.

GOVERNMENT & POLITICS
The current government is headed by president Boris Trajkovski of the Macedonian Internal Revolutionary Organisation party (VMRO). The main opposition party is the Social Democratic Union of Macedonia (SDSM). Among Albanians, the main party is the Democratic Party of Albanians (DPA).

ECONOMY
Macedonia is a rich agricultural area which feeds itself and exports tomatoes and cucumbers to Western Europe. Cereals, rice, cotton and tobacco are also grown and Macedonian mines yield chromium, manganese, tungsten, lead and zinc. The main north-south trade route from Western Europe to Greece via the valleys of the Danube, Morava and Vardar Rivers passes through the country. Tourism is concentrated around Lake Ohrid.

The collapse of trade with Serbia in the wake of the Kosovo war has undercut Macedonia's main export market, helping to generate 35% unemployment.

POPULATION & PEOPLE
Of the republic's two million-plus population, 66% are Macedonian Slavs who bear no relation whatsoever to the Greek-speaking Macedonians of antiquity. The Macedonian language is much closer to Bulgarian than to Serbian, and many ethnographers in the early part of last century may have considered the Macedonians to be ethnic Bulgarians. However, over the past 50 years, a generation of people have emerged who consider themselves to be Macedonians, not Bulgarians.

The largest minority groups are ethnic Albanians (23%), Turks (4%), Roma (3%), Serbs (2%) and others (2%). Tensions between ethnic Albanians and Macedonians derive partly from the high birth rate of the former (three times the national average), which makes many ethnic Macedonians nervous about losing their majority. Albanians are in a majority in the rural region between Tetovo and Debar in the north-west of the republic. An Albanian-language university in Tetovo, which has 4000 students but is not recognised by the Macedonian government, has deepened tensions, as did the Kosovo war of early 1999, when 250,000 refugees flooded into the country (almost all of these have now returned).

ARTS

Music

The oldest form of Macedonian folk music involves the *gajda* (bagpipes). This is played solo or is accompanied by the *tapan* (two-sided drum), each side of which is played with a different stick to obtain a different tone. These are often augmented by *kaval* (flute) and/or *tambura* (small lute with two pairs of strings). Macedonia has also inherited (from a long period of Turkish influence) the *zurla* (double-reed horn), also accompanied by the *tapan*, and the *Čalgija* music form involving clarinet, violin, *darabuk* (hour-glass shaped drum) and *džumbuš* (banjo-like instrument).

Bands playing these instruments may be heard and enjoyed at festivals such as the folklore festival in Ohrid in mid-July or the Ilinden festival in Bitola in early August. Nearly all Macedonian traditional music is accompanied by dancing.

The Macedonian rock band Leb i Sol is well known.

Folk Dancing

The most famous Macedonian folk dance is probably *Teškoto* (The Difficult One). Music for this male dance is provided by the *tapan* and *zurla*. This beautiful dance, performed in traditional Macedonian costume, is often included in festivals or concerts.

Other dances include *Komitsko,* symbolising the struggle of Macedonian freedom fighters against the Turks, and *Tresenica,* a women's dance from the Mariovo region.

Cinema

Before the Rain, Milcho Manchevski's visually stunning vision of how inter-ethnic war in Macedonia might begin, was filmed mainly in Ohrid in the north-west. *The Peacemaker* was shot in Bitola, to simulate prewar Sarajevo.

SOCIETY & CONDUCT

Macedonians are a proud and hospitable people and welcome visitors. Show respect to your hosts by learning a few words of Macedonian. Be aware that churches and mosques are not built for tourists, but are working places of worship. Dress and behave accordingly.

RELIGION

Most of the Albanians and Turks are Muslim, while most Slavs are Orthodox.

LANGUAGE

Macedonian is a South Slavic language divided into two large groups, the western and eastern Macedonian dialects. The Macedonian literary language is based on the central dialects of Veles, Prilep and Bitola. Macedonian shares all the characteristics that separate Bulgarian from the other Slavic languages, evidence that it's closely related to Bulgarian.

The Cyrillic alphabet is based on the one developed by two Thessaloniki brothers, St Cyril and St Methodius, in the 9th century. It was taught by their disciples at a monastery in Ohrid, from where it spread across the eastern Slavic world.

The Cyrillic alphabet is used predominantly in Macedonia. Street names are printed in Cyrillic script only, so it's a good idea to learn the Cyrillic alphabet before you travel to the country. Road signs use both Cyrillic and Latin scripts.

For a quick introduction to useful Macedonian words and phrases, see the Language chapter at the end of this book.

Facts for the Visitor

HIGHLIGHTS

The Byzantine monasteries of Ohrid, particularly Sveti Sofija and Sveti Kliment, are worth a visit. Lake Ohrid itself is simply beautiful. The Čaršija (old Turkish bazaar) in Skopje is very colourful.

SUGGESTED ITINERARIES

Depending on the length of your stay, you might want to see and do the following things in Macedonia:

Two days
  Visit Ohrid (if your entry point is Skopje, take a bus)
One week
  Visit Ohrid and Skopje
Two weeks
  As above, plus a quick visit to the Heraclea ruins in Bitola and some skiing or hiking in the national parks

PLANNING
Maps
The tourist office has a road and tourist map of the Republic of Macedonia.

What to Bring
You can find most things in Macedonia, but bring along a converter and adaptor if you plan to use electrical appliances.

TOURIST OFFICES
Only Skopje has an official tourist office (see Skopje later in this chapter for details).

VISAS & DOCUMENTS
Citizens of EU countries and New Zealanders do not need visas to enter Macedonia, but visas are required of citizens of most countries. For Americans and Australians the visa is issued free of charge at your port of entry. Canadians and South Africans must buy visas for £7; these are obtainable either before you go or at the border.

EMBASSIES & CONSULATES
Macedonian Embassies & Consulates
Macedonian embassies are found in the following countries. There are no embassies as yet in Australia or New Zealand.

Albania (☎ 042-330 36, fax 325 14) Rruga Lek Dukagjini, Vila 2, Tirana
Canada (☎ 613-234 3882, fax 233 1852) 130 Albert St, Suite 1006, Ottawa ON, K1P 5G4
Turkey (☎ 012-446 9204, fax 446 9206) Filistin sokak 30-2/3, Gaziosman Pasha, Ankara
UK (☎ 020-7499 5152, fax 499 2864) 19a Cavendish Square, London, W1M 9AD
USA (☎ 202-337 3063, fax 337 3093) 3050 K Street NW, Washington DC, 20007
Yugoslavia (☎ 011-633 348, fax 182 287) Gospodar Jevremova 34, 11000 Belgrade

Embassies & Consulates in Macedonia
The following embassies are in Skopje (area code ☎ 091):

Albania (☎ 614 636, fax 614 200) ul H T Karpoš 94a
Bulgaria (☎ 116 320, fax 116 139) ul Zlatko Šnajder 3
Canada (☎ 125 228, fax 122 681) ul Mitropolit Teodosie Gologanov 104

Greece (☎ 130 198, fax 115 718) ul Borka Talevski 6
Turkey (☎ 113 270, fax 117 024) ul Slavej Planina bb
UK (☎ 116 772, fax 117 005) ul Veljko Vlahović 26
USA (☎ 116 180, fax 117 103) Bulevar Ilindenska
Yugoslavia (☎ 129 298, fax 129 427) Pitu Guli 8

CUSTOMS
Customs checks are generally cursory.

MONEY
Currency
Colourful Macedonian denar (MKD) banknotes come in denominations of 10, 50, 100, 500, 1000 and 5000 and there are coins of one, two and five denari. Though it is stable, the denar is useless outside Macedonia. Restaurants, hotels and some shops will accept payment in Deutschmarks (usually) and US dollars (sometimes); prices are often quoted in these currencies. Some prices in this chapter have been converted to denars from Deutschmarks or US dollars, so the listed price may not be exact.

Exchange Rates
Conversion rates for major currencies in mid-2000 are listed below:

country	unit		denar
Australia	A$1	=	35.58 MKD
Canada	C$1	=	40.56 MKD
euro	€1	=	54.32 MKD
France	10FF	=	82.81 MKD
Germany	DM1	=	27.77 MKD
Japan	¥100	=	55.20 MKD
NZ	NZ$1	=	27.15 MKD
UK	UK£1	=	89.72 MKD
USA	US$1	=	59.85 MKD

For the most recent currency rates, point your Web browser at www.xe.net/ucc/full.shtml.

Exchanging Money
Small private exchange offices throughout central Skopje and Ohrid exchange money (cash only) for a rate only slightly better than the banks, but the banks change travellers cheques as well. A handful of ATMs can be found in central Skopje; these offer the best exchange rates.

Costs

Except for accommodation in Skopje, Macedonia is not an expensive country. If you stay in a private room in Skopje, you might keep costs to 1800 MKD to 2100 MKD a day; outside Skopje, frugal travellers may spend 1200 MKD to 1500 MKD per day.

Tipping

It is common practice in Macedonia to round up restaurant bills and taxi fares to the nearest convenient figure.

POST & COMMUNICATIONS
Post

Mail addressed c/o Poste Restante, 1000 Skopje 2, Macedonia, can be claimed at the post office next to Skopje train station. Mail addressed c/o Poste Restante, 1101 Skopje 1, Macedonia, can be picked up at the main post office by the river; go to window No 2. Letters to the USA cost 38 MKD, to Australia 40 MKD and to Europe 35 MKD.

Mail addressed c/o Poste Restante, 6000 Ohrid, Macedonia, can be picked up at Ohrid's main post office near the bus station.

Telephone & Fax

Macedonia's country code is ☎ 389. Long-distance phone calls cost less at main post offices than in hotels. Drop the initial zero in the city codes when calling Macedonia from abroad. For outgoing calls the international access code in Macedonia is ☎ 99. You can purchase phonecards in 100 (155 MKD), 200, 500, or 1000-unit denominations from post offices. Some of the larger kiosks sell the 100-unit cards.

Macedonia has a digital mobile/cellphone network (MOBIMAK); your provider is likely to have a roaming agreement with Macedonia's domestic network.

Fax services are available at the main post offices in Skopje and Ohrid.

Email & Internet Access

Skopje and Ohrid both have numerous Internet cafes to feed Macedonia's Internet craze.

INTERNET RESOURCES

The Virtual Macedonia site (www.vmacedonia.com/index2.html) has useful background and practical information.

BOOKS

Good background books include *Who Are the Macedonians?* by Hugh Poulton, a political and cultural history, Rebecca West's *Black Lamb & Grey Falcon*, a between-the-wars Balkan travelogue, and Robert Kaplan's *Balkan Ghosts*. Lonely Planet's *Mediterranean Europe phrasebook* will help with the language. Zoë Brân's *After Yugoslavia*, part of the Lonely Planet Journeys series, retraces the author's 1978 trip through the now much-changed former Yugoslavia. Brân visits Slovenia, Croatia, Bosnia-Hercegovina and Yugoslavia in an attempt to make sense of what has happened in the intervening years.

NEWSPAPERS & MAGAZINES

Svet World Press, on the corner of ul Dame Gruev and Bul Partizanski Odredi in Skopje, has a wide selection of foreign publications.

RADIO & TV

You have a choice of three state TV stations (one of which plays mostly live CNN) and any number of private and satellite channels, including CBC, Eurosport and Euronews. The BBC World Service is found on 104.4 FM, and the Voice of America on 107.5 FM.

TIME

Macedonia goes on daylight-saving time at the end of March when clocks are turned forward one hour. On the last Sunday of September they're turned back an hour.

LAUNDRY

Macedonia currently has no self-wash laundry services, but your hotel might do a load for a fee. Dry cleaning (*chemisko chistenye*) is available – in Skopje, there's one in the basement of the Trgovski Centar.

TOILETS

Public toilets are invariably of the grotty 'squattie' type. Take toilet paper with you if you must use them, but make use of hotel and restaurant toilets whenever you can.

HEALTH

State health centres should be able to provide basic services for a small fee to travellers. Health insurance to cover private services and evacuation is recommended.

WOMEN TRAVELLERS
Women travellers should feel no particular concern about travel in Macedonia. Other than possible cursory interest from men, travel is hassle-free and easy.

GAY & LESBIAN TRAVELLERS
Homosexuality in Macedonia is technically legal. Given its tenuous social acceptability, however, it's probably best for visitors to maintain a low profile.

DISABLED TRAVELLERS
Few public buildings or streets have facilities for wheelchairs, but some newer buildings provide wheelchair ramps.

DANGERS & ANNOYANCES
Macedonia is a safe country in general. However, travellers should be on the look-out for pickpockets in bus and train stations and exercise common sense in looking after their belongings.

BUSINESS HOURS
Businesses tend to stay open late in Macedonia. Travellers will generally find that businesses will be open from 8 am to 8 pm weekdays and 8 am to 2 pm on Saturday.

PUBLIC HOLIDAYS & SPECIAL EVENTS
Public holidays in Macedonia are New Year (1 and 2 January), Orthodox Christmas (7 January), Easter Monday and Tuesday (March/April), Labour Day (1-2 May), Ilinden or Day of the 1903 Rebellion (2 August), Republic Day (8 September) and 1941 Partisan Day (11 October).

ACTIVITIES
Macedonia's top ski resort is Popova šapka (1845m) on the southern slopes of Šar Planina west of Tetovo near the border with Kosovo. Mavrovo in western Macedonia comes a close second. Hiking in any of the three national parks (Galičica and Pelister in the south, and Mavrovo) is a good way to get to know the countryside. Pelister has a nice lodge from which you can base hiking activities. Spelunking is also a popular sport; a good place to try it is Lake Matka, near Skopje.

COURSES
Via Media (☎ 114 669) at ul Dame Gruev 1/14 has 1½-hour language courses for a cost of 640 MKD.

ACCOMMODATION
Skopje's hotels are very expensive but there are also camping grounds and private-room agencies in Ohrid and Skopje. Skopje's convenient HI hostel is open throughout the year, and the Ohrid hostel opens in summer. Beds are available at student dormitories in Skopje in summer. Prices in more expensive hotels are usually quoted in US dollars (US$).

FOOD
Turkish-style grilled mincemeat is available almost everywhere and there are self-service cafeterias in most towns for the less adventurous. Balkan *burek* (cheese or meat pie) and yoghurt makes for a cheap breakfast. Look out for a sign sporting *burekdžilnica*. Watch for Macedonian *tavče gravče* (beans in a skillet) and Ohrid trout, which is priced according to weight.

Other dishes to try are *teleška čorba* (veal soup), *riblja čorba* (fish soup), *čevapčinja* (kebabs), *mešena salata* (mixed salad) and the *šopska salata* (mixed salad with grated white cheese).

DRINKS
Skopsko Pivo is the local beer. It's strong and reasonably cheap. Brand name European beers are also available. There are a good number of commercially produced wines of average to better quality and the national firewater is *rakija*, a strong distilled spirit made from grapes. *Mastika,* an ouzo-like spirit, is also popular.

ENTERTAINMENT
Entertainment for Macedonia's hip generation consists of hanging out in smart cafes and bars. Live traditional Macedonian music can often be heard in restaurants and Skopje has some jazz bars.

SHOPPING
Macedonian mementoes include rugs and small textiles, paintings, traditional costumes, antique coins, handmade dolls and, from Ohrid, wood carvings.

Getting There & Away

AIR

A host of airlines service Skopje. JAT Yugoslav Airlines, Macedonian Airlines (MAT), Adria Airways, Croatia Airlines, Avioimpex, Olympic Airways, Malev Hungarian Airlines, Turkish Airlines and British Airways offer flights from Skopje to a number of European destinations. Sample one-way prices (not including airport taxes) are: Amsterdam (US$235); Athens (US$195); Belgrade (US$100); London (US$395); Rome (US$183); Zagreb (US$200); and Zürich (300 Sfr). Return prices are usually a much better deal.

It may be cheaper to fly into Thessaloniki in northern Greece. Bear in mind, however, that Greece's transport links with Macedonia are poor, consisting of just one train a day from Thessaloniki. Kompas Holidays (see the Travel Agencies section in Skopje) can arrange shuttles from Thessaloniki for DM60 per person one-way (with a minimum of four people).

Some airline phone numbers in Skopje are:

Adria Airways	(☎ 117 009)
Alitalia	(☎ 118 602)
Avioimpex	(☎ 112 412)
British Airways	(☎ 214 250)
Croatian Airlines	(☎ 115 858)
JAT Yugoslav Airlines	(☎ 116 532)
Macedonian Airlines (MAT)	(☎ 116 333)
Malev Hungarian Airlines	(☎ 111 214)
Olympic Airlines	(☎ 127 127)
Turkish Airlines	(☎ 117 214)

Any of the innumerable travel agents in Skopje or Ohrid can book these flights.

LAND

Avoid transit through Yugoslavia, as visas are very difficult to obtain. The Yugoslav embassy in Skopje says to allow at least 30 days for processing. Prepare to pay a 1220 MKD postage fee (to send the visa application to Belgrade) plus the cost of the visa. Even then, there is no guarantee that a visa will be granted.

Visas are not necessary for travel to Kosovo, and it is actually quite easy to get there; the border crossing is just a 20-minute trip north from Skopje. Unfortunately, the Macedonian border facilities are ill-equipped to handle the heavy traffic, and waits at the border have been reported from one to 10 hours. Even so, this seems mostly to apply to private vehicles. The border guards wave through the buses from Skopje, and if you come by taxi you can just walk across the border (to catch a taxi on the other side) with little or no wait (see Kosovo in the Yugoslavia chapter).

Bus

The international bus station in Skopje is next to the City Museum. Buses go to Sofia (620 MKD, six hours, three times daily), İstanbul (1280 MKD, 14 hours, three to four daily), Belgrade (850 MKD, six hours, three times daily), Munich (4800 MKD, 24 hours, twice a week) and Zagreb (2560 MKD, 15 hours, four a week). Buses also go to Budapest, Vienna, and Sarajevo. Except for Sofia and İstanbul you'll need a transit visa through Yugoslavia.

Buses between Skopje and Prishtina, the capital of Kosovo, are fairly frequent. To/from Albania you can travel between Tetovo and Tirana by bus (five to six hours, two per day), or walk across the border at Sveti Naum (see the Ohrid section).

Train

Trains run between Skopje and Belgrade via Niš (1200 MKD, eight to nine hours, twice daily). Sleepers are available. One train runs daily between Skopje and Thessaloniki (700 MKD, six hours). Note that Thessaloniki in Macedonian is 'Solun'.

All the timetables and arrivals/departures boards at Skopje train station are in Cyrillic script only. Staff at the helpful information desk (☎ 234 255) speak English; it's open daily from 6 am to 10 pm. Feroturist Travel Agency (☎ 163 248) in the train station is open 7 am to 8 pm Monday to Friday, 7 am to 2 pm Saturday, and 7 am to 9 pm on Sunday. It sells international train tickets and books sleepers to Belgrade, Zagreb and Ljubljana (add 700 MKD and 750 MKD extra for Zagreb and Ljubljana).

Car & Motorcycle

There are several main highway border crossings into Macedonia from neighbouring countries. You will probably be charged 160 MKD to bring your car into Macedonia.

Yugoslavia/Kosovo You can cross at Blace (between Skopje and Uroševac) and Tabanovce (10km north of Kumanovo).

Bulgaria The main crossings are just east of Kriva Palanka (between Sofia and Skopje), and east of Delčevo (26km west of Blagoevgrad) and Novo Selo (between Kulata and Strumica).

Greece There are crossings at Gevgelija (between Skopje and Thessaloniki), Dojran (just east of Gevgelija) and Medžitlija (16km south of Bitola).

Albania The crossings are Sveti Naum (29km south of Ohrid), Kafa San (12km south-west of Struga) and Blato (5km northwest of Debar).

DEPARTURE TAX

The airport departure tax at Skopje and Ohrid is about 510 MKD; this may be included in your ticket.

Getting Around

BUS

Bus travel is well developed in Macedonia with fairly frequent services from Skopje to Ohrid and Bitola.

TRAIN

You won't find Macedonia's trains of much use. The local train from Skopje to Bitola takes four hours to cover 229km.

CAR & MOTORCYCLE

Skopje is awash with rental car agencies, from the large ones (Hertz and Avis) to smaller local companies. The tourist office in Skopje has a complete listing. Petrol is widely available.

Speed limits for cars and motorcycles are 120km/h on motorways, 80km/h on open roads and 50 to 60km/h in towns. Speeding

fines typically start from around 1500 MKD. Wearing a seatbelt is compulsory, though you'll probably find that nobody does.

The Macedonia-wide number for emergency highway assistance is ☎ 987.

LOCAL TRANSPORT

A quick way of getting around the country if the buses are not convenient is by taxi, especially if there are two or more of you to share the cost. A half-hour trip, from Skopje to Lake Matka for example, should cost around 350 MKD. Taxis are a convenient way to get to Kosovo: 640 MKD will get you to the Macedonia-Kosovo border, where taxis are waiting on the other side to whisk you to Prishtina. Note that these taxis are more expensive and will probably cost DM35 and up, depending on your negotiating skills.

Skopje (Скопје)

☎ 091 • pop 600,000

Macedonia's capital Skopje is strategically set on the Vardar River at a crossroads of Balkan routes almost exactly midway between Tirana and Sofia, the capitals of neighbouring Albania and Bulgaria. Thessaloniki, Greece, is 260km south-east, near the point where the Vardar flows into the Aegean. The Romans recognised the location's importance long ago when they made Scupi the centre of Dardania Province. Later on conquerors included the Slavs, Byzantines, Bulgarians, Normans and Serbs, until the Turks arrived in 1392 and managed to hold onto Uskub (Skopje) until 1912.

After a devastating earthquake in July 1963 killed 1066 people and virtually demolished the town, aid poured in from all over the world to create the modern urban landscape of today. It's evident that the planners got carried away by the money being thrown their way, erecting oversized, irrelevant structures which are now crumbling due to lack of maintenance. The post office building and telecommunications complex next to it are particularly hideous examples of this architectural overkill. Fortunately, much of the old town survived, along with the fortress atop the hill, preserving Skopje's historic beauty.

MACEDONIA

Orientation

Most of central Skopje is a pedestrian zone, with the 15th-century Turkish stone bridge (Kamen Most) over the Vardar River linking the old and new towns. South of the bridge is Ploštad Makedonija (the former Ploštad Maršal Tito), which gives into ul Makedonija leading south. The train station is a 15-minute walk south-east of the stone bridge. The domestic bus station is just over the stone bridge. Farther north is Čaršija, the old Turkish bazaar.

Detailed maps of Skopje are sold at the tourist information office and at some of the larger kiosks for 250 MKD.

Information

Tourist Office The tourist information office (☎ 116 854) has helpful staff who speak English; it's opposite the Daud Pasha Baths on the viaduct between the Turkish bridge and Čaršija. Opening hours are 9 am to 7 pm Monday to Saturday, and from 9 am to 4 pm Saturday. The tourist office is closed Sunday, and usually closes one hour earlier in winter.

Money There are many private exchange offices scattered throughout the old and new towns where you can change your cash at a good rate. The rate at the banks tends to be only slightly lower.

Skopje has a number of ATMs, though they are not always easy to find. There are two in the Bunjakoveć Shopping Centre, one in Trgovski Centar off Ploštad Makedonija, and another at the Skopje airport.

Post & Communications The telephone centre in the main post office is 75m north of Ploštad Makedonija, along the river. It's open 24 hours and the post office is open from 7 am to 7.30 pm Monday to Saturday and to 2.30 pm on Sunday.

Email & Internet Access The Café Astoria in the Bunjakoveć Shopping Centre at Partizanska 27a charges 100 MKD per hour for online time. Scanning, faxing and printing services are also available. There's also Café Cyberia, on Bulevar Makedonija near its intersection with Sveti Kliment Ohridski, which charges 70 MKD per hour.

Travel Agencies Skopje abounds with travel agencies. A good bet is Kompas Holidays (☎/fax 222 441 or ☎/fax 110 089, @ komphol@mt.net.mk), just inside the Trgovski Centar.

Left Luggage The left-luggage office at the train station is open 24 hours. The domestic bus station also has a left luggage area.

Medical & Emergency Services The city hospital (☎ 130 111) is on the corner of ul 11 Oktomvri and Moše Pijade. The Neuromedica private clinic (☎ 222 170) is at ul Partizanski 3-1-4. The emergency number for ambulance is ☎ 94, and police is ☎ 92.

Things to See

Walking north from the Turkish bridge you'll see the **Daud Pasha Baths** (1466) on the right, once the largest Turkish baths in the Balkans. The **City Art Gallery** (closed on Monday) now occupies its six domed rooms. Almost opposite this building is a functioning Orthodox church **Sveta Dimitrija**.

North again is **Čaršija**, the old market area, which is well worth exploring. Steps up on the left lead to the tiny **Church of Sveti Spas** with a finely carved iconostasis created in 1824. It's half buried because when it was constructed in the 17th century no church was allowed to be higher than a mosque. In the courtyard at Sveti Spas is the tomb of Goce Delčev, a moustached IMRO freedom fighter killed by the Turks in 1903.

Beyond the church is the **Mustafa Pasha Mosque** (1492), with an earthquake-cracked dome. The 100 MKD ticket allows you to ascend the 124 steps of the minaret. In the park across the street are the ruins of **Fort Kale**, with an 11th-century Cyclopean wall and good views of Skopje. Higher up on the same hill is the **Museum of Contemporary Art** (closed Monday), with temporary exhibits.

The lane on the north side of Mustafa Pasha Mosque leads back down to Čaršija and the **Museum of Macedonia**. Its large collection covers the history of the region fairly well, but explanations are in Cyrillic. The museum is housed in the modern white building behind the **Kuršumli Han** (1550), a caravanserai or inn used by traders during the Turkish period. Skopje's old Oriental bazaar

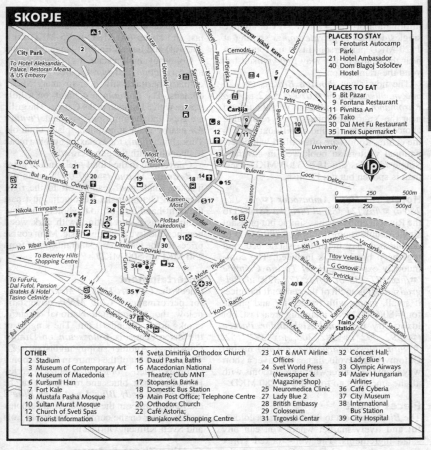

SKOPJE

PLACES TO STAY
1 Feroturist Autocamp Park
21 Hotel Ambasador
40 Dom Blagoj Šošolčev Hostel

PLACES TO EAT
5 Bit Pazar
9 Fontana Restaurant
11 Pivnitsa An
26 Tako
30 Dal Met Fu Restaurant
35 Tinex Supermarket

OTHER
2 Stadium
3 Museum of Contemporary Art
4 Museum of Macedonia
6 Kuršumli Han
7 Fort Kale
8 Mustafa Pasha Mosque
10 Sultan Murat Mosque
12 Church of Sveti Spas
13 Tourist Information
14 Sveta Dimitrija Orthodox Church
15 Daud Pasha Baths
16 Macedonian National Theatre; Club MNT
17 Stopanska Banka
18 Domestic Bus Station
19 Main Post Office; Telephone Centre
20 Orthodox Church
22 Café Astoria; Bunjakoveč Shopping Centre
23 JAT & MAT Airline Offices
24 Svet World Press (Newspaper & Magazine Shop)
25 Neuromedica Clinic
27 Lady Blue 2
28 British Embassy
29 Colosseum
31 Trgovski Centar
32 Concert Hall; Lady Blue 1
33 Olympic Airways
34 Malev Hungarian Airlines
36 Café Cyberia
37 City Museum
38 International Bus Station
39 City Hospital

district is among the largest and most colourful of its kind left in Europe.

Places to Stay

Skopje's prices for accommodation have jumped in response to the influx of Kosovo-bound foreigners.

Camping From April to mid-October you can pitch a tent at the *Feroturist Autocamp Park* (☎ 228 246, fax 162 677) for around 192 MKD per person and tent. The camping ground is located between the river and the stadium, just a 15-minute walk upstream

from the Turkish stone bridge along the right (south) bank.

Hostels The HI *Dom Blagoj Šošolčev Hostel* (☎ 114 849, fax 235 029), at Prolet 25 near the train station, has good, clean rooms and is open 24 hours a day all year round. Single rooms go for 1520/1210 MKD for members/nonmembers, and beds in a double for 1210/865 MKD – though in the off-season you may be able to get a bed alone in a double. A few apartments and three-bed dorms are also available. Breakfast is an additional 60 MKD.

Private Rooms & Pansions The tourist information office (☎ 116 854) can arrange singles/doubles in *private homes* starting at 1120 MKD per person. Insist on something near the centre or you may find yourself beyond the train station.

The tidy, clean *Pansion Brateks* (☎ 176 606, mobile/cellphone ☎ 070 24 3232, ul Atso Karomanov 3), in a pleasant neighbourhood near the Yugoslav embassy, is a reasonable choice if you don't mind a half-hour walk to the centre. Rooms are often filled with international visitors so book well in advance. Singles/doubles are 1920/3200 MKD. German is spoken but not English.

Hotels The *Hotel Ambasador* (☎/fax 121 286 or ☎/fax 121 383, ul Pirinska 38) next to the Russian embassy, has simple but pleasant single/double rooms for 3600/4800 MKD (a double bed may mean two single beds put together); breakfast is included. The continuously expanding *Hotel Tasino Češmiče* (☎/fax 177 333 or ☎/fax 178 329, ul Belgradska 28) is south of the centre. It has nice, if small, rooms with fridge, TV and phone for 4480/6400 MKD including breakfast. For luxury try the *Hotel Aleksandar Palace* (☎ 392 392 or 392 200, fax 392 152, ℮ info@aleksandarpalace.com.mk) on bul Oktomvriska Revolucija near the river a short way from the centre, where great rooms with all the amenities go for 9480/14,280 MKD.

Places to Eat

The *Bit Pazar* next to the Čaršija is a colourful and lively market where you can buy salad ingredients. The well-stocked *Tinex Supermarket* on ul Dame Gruev, near the intersection with ul Makedonija, is well stocked with a variety of necessities. There is a cheap *restaurant* in the basement of the youth hostel (see Places to Stay).

From the bridge, *Dal Met Fu Restaurant* is fairly obvious across Ploštad Makedonija, on the left at the beginning of ul Makedonija. This place is good for pizza and pasta. With the same owner but a bit farther out, along bul Vodnjanska and convenient to Pansion Brateks, are *Dal Fufol* and its fast-food neighbour, *Fufufu* (or just *3Fs*). These offer similar dishes to Dal Met Fu. *Tako* (☎ 114 808), on Sveti Kliment Ohridski, is a small

smoke-free spot for burritos, fajitas and other Mexican delicacies. It's popular with expats, fast and cheap (40 MKD to 75 MKD for a plateful) and has an English-language menu.

Colourful small restaurants in Čaršija serving *čevapčinja* and *burek* reflect a Turkish culinary heritage still dear to many Macedonians. Try *Fontana* restaurant, on a little square with a fountain in the Čaršija. The grills are good and the atmosphere is great. *Pivnitsa An* nearby is an atmospheric place in an old Turkish inn (*hani*) for a relaxing evening meal; it's popular with the expat crowd.

Convenient to the Hotel Aleksander Palace is *Restoran Meana* (☎ 397 070), on an unmarked small road leading off to the right from bul Oktomvriska Revolucija, just past the right-hand turn-off to the hotel. The trout is divine, as is the setting, with dark wood benches and live evening music. Main course prices for the last three restaurants range from 250 MKD to 500 MKD.

Entertainment

Check the *Concert Hall* (ul Makedonija 12) for performances. *Club MNT*, downstairs below the Macedonian National Theatre, cranks up at around 10 pm. The kingpin of the disco scene is *Colosseum* on Dimitri Čupkovski. Another snappy nightspot is *ZZ Top*, south-west of the centre in the shopping complex called – brace yourself – Beverley Hills. Live jazz, blues and rock music can be heard at the *Lady Blue 1* and *Lady Blue 2* clubs, the former in the Concert Hall complex and the latter on the corner of Ivo Ribar Lola and Sveti Kliment Ohridski.

Getting There & Away

Bus There are buses to Ohrid, Bitola, Prishtina and Belgrade.

There are two bus routes from Skopje to Lake Ohrid: the one through Tetovo (167km) is much faster and more direct than the bus that goes via Veles and Bitola (261km). Book a seat to Ohrid the day before if you're travelling in high season (May to August).

Buses to Prishtina leave from the domestic bus station.

Train See the Getting There & Away section earlier in this chapter for details on train travel to/from Skopje.

Getting Around
To/From the Airport There are no buses to the airport so unless you arrange transport in advance, you'll be at the mercy of the airport 'taxi mafia', which charges 1280 MKD to 2240 MKD for a ride into town. Do not get into a taxi that has no official taxi sign. It's better to request the place you're staying to help arrange pick-up in advance. Taxis to the airport from the centre cost about 640 MKD.

Bus Inner-suburban city buses in Skopje cost 15 MKD to 30 MKD per trip, depending on what kind of bus and whether you buy your ticket on the bus or in advance.

Taxi Skopje's taxi system is excellent, once you get beyond the unofficial taxis at the airport. All taxis have meters and they always turn them on without prompting. The first few kilometres is a flat 50 MKD, and then it's 15 MKD per kilometre.

AROUND SKOPJE
Lake Matka
A half-hour's drive south-west of Skopje is Lake Matka, set in a beautiful valley. Macedonia's finest spelunking can be enjoyed in the caves in the hills above the lake. Non-spelunkers can choose from a variety of hikes. Take bus No 60 (30 MKD) to the last stop, Matka (40 minutes) and walk about 300m on the path above the dam. The path will take you to *Pioneerski Dom* (☎ 352 655), right on the lake and next to a monastery, where the spelologists bunk; accommodation is basic and costs 320 MKD a night. Food and heat is available, but the lodge is closed in January and February and when it snows.

Southern Macedonia

OHRID (ОХРИД)
☎ 096
Lake Ohrid, a natural tectonic lake in the south-west corner of Macedonia, is the deepest lake in the Balkans (294m) and one of the world's oldest. One third of its 450-sq-km surface area belongs to Albania. Nestled amid mountains at an altitude of 695m, the Macedonian section of the lake is the more beautiful, with striking vistas of the water from the beach and hills.

The town of Ohrid is *the* Macedonian tourist mecca and is popular with visitors from Macedonia and neighbouring countries. Some 30 'cultural monuments' in the area keep visitors busy. Predictably, the oldest ruins readily seen today are Roman. Part of a Roman amphitheatre has been uncovered in the old town of Lihnidos (Ohrid) on the Via Egnatia, which connected the Adriatic to the Aegean.

Under Byzantium, Ohrid became the episcopal centre of Macedonia. The first Slavic university was founded here in 893 by Bishop (Saint) Kliment of Ohrid, a disciple of St Cyril and St Methodius, and from the 10th century until 1767 the patriarchate of Ohrid held sway. The revival of the archbishopric of Ohrid in 1958 and its independence from the Serbian Orthodox Church in 1967 were important steps on the road to modern nationhood.

Small Orthodox churches housing intact medieval frescoes help make Ohrid enchanting for a long, relaxing stay.

Orientation
Ohrid bus station is next to the post office in the centre of town. To the west is the old town and to the south is the lake.

Information
Tourist Offices The tourist office (☎ 266 494) at ul Partizanska 3 in front of the bus station arranges bus tickets and private rooms. Those needing a guide might try Sonja Jankovska (☎ 266 315), who speaks good English and knows Ohrid thoroughly.

Money The Ohridska Banka, on the Sveti Kliment Ohridski mall, changes travellers cheques and cash and offers Visa advances without commission. Exchange bureaus for cash have proliferated.

Post & Communications The telephone centre in the modern post office near the bus station is open 7 am to 8 pm Monday to Saturday, and 9 am to noon and 6 to 8 pm on Sunday. Phonecard phones are located outside the post office. The post office is in the same building but around the corner, next to the philatelic bureau.

MACEDONIA

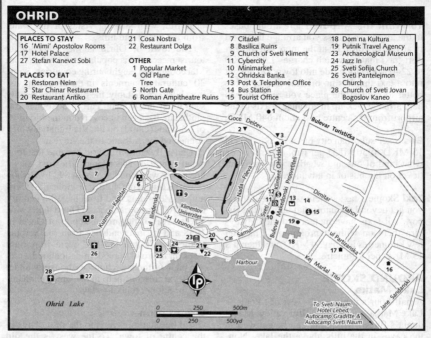

OHRID

PLACES TO STAY	21 Cosa Nostra	7 Citadel	18 Dom na Kultura
16 'Mimi' Apostolov Rooms	22 Restaurant Dolga	8 Basilica Ruins	19 Putnik Travel Agency
17 Hotel Palace		9 Church of Sveti Kliment	23 Archaeological Museum
27 Stefan Kanevči Sobi	**OTHER**	11 Cybercity	24 Jazz In
	1 Popular Market	10 Minimarket	25 Sveti Sofija Church
PLACES TO EAT	4 Old Plane	12 Ohridska Banka	26 Sveti Pantelejmon
2 Restoran Neim	Tree	13 Post & Telephone Office	Church
3 Star Chinar Restaurant	5 North Gate	14 Bus Station	28 Church of Sveti Jovan
20 Restaurant Antiko	6 Roman Ampitheatre Ruins	15 Tourist Office	Bogoslov Kaneo

Email & Internet Access It's hard to miss the sign for the 24-hour, ultra-modern Cybercity, on the 3rd storey of the Ohrid mall across from the post office. Slow Internet access costs 60 MKD per hour. Other Internet cafes have bounced up; ask around town.

Travel Agencies The Putnik Travel Agency, which is opposite the bus station, sells train and plane tickets.

Left Luggage The left-luggage office at the bus station charges 20 MKD per piece per day.

Things to See
The picturesque old town of Ohrid rises from Sveti Kliment Ohridski, the main pedestrian mall, up towards the Church of Sveti Kliment and the citadel. A medieval town wall still isolates this hill from the surrounding valley. Head into the old town on Car Samuil as far as the **Archaeological Museum** in the four-storey dwelling of the Robevi family (1827)

at No 62. The admission price is 100/50 MKD for adults/students. Farther along Car Samuil is the 11th-century **Sveti Sofija**, also worth the 100/30 MKD adult/student price. Aside from the frescoes there's an unusual Turkish *mimbar* (pulpit) remaining from the days when this was a mosque, and an upstairs portico with a photo display of the extensive restoration work. An English-speaking guide is on hand.

Near here ul Ilindenska climbs to the North Gate; to the right is the 13th-century **Church of Sveti Kliment** (100 MKD admission), almost covered inside with vividly restored frescoes of biblical scenes. Opposite this church is an icon gallery with a fine view from the terrace. The walls of the 10th-century **citadel** to the west offer more splendid views.

In the park below the citadel are the ruins of an early Christian **basilica** with 5th-century mosaics covered by protective sand. Nearby is the shell of **Sveti Pantelejmon**, Ohrid's oldest church, which is being refurbished and may reclaim the remains of St

Kliment himself, once held there but later moved to Sveti Sofija.

The tiny 13th-century **Church of Sveti Jovan Bogoslov Kaneo**, on a point overlooking the lake, occupies a very pleasant site. There's a rocky beach at the foot of the cliffs and in summer young men perform death-defying leaps into the water from the clifftop above the lake. Most churches and museums at Ohrid are open 9 am to 3 pm daily, except Monday; some have a morning break from 10.30 to 11 am.

There's a frequent bus service from Ohrid to **Struga**, at the northern end of Lake Ohrid. Each year at the end of August, poets converge on Struga for an international festival of poetry.

Special Events

The five-day Balkan Festival of Folk Dances & Songs, held at Ohrid in early July, draws folkloric groups from around the Balkan region. The Ohrid Summer Festival, held from mid-July to mid-August, features classical concerts in the Church of Sveti Sofija as well as open-air theatre performances and many other events.

Ohrid hosts a swimming marathon each August, when swimmers race the 30km from Sveti Naum to Ohrid.

Places to Stay

Camping The *Autocamp Gradište* (☎ 22 578), open from May to mid-September, is halfway to Sveti Naum. Popular with young people, the place is by some accounts a 24-hour disco. Those opting for peace and quiet might prefer the family-oriented *Autocamp Sveti Naum* (☎ 58 811), 2km north of the monastery of the same name. Both camp sites are accessible on the Sveti Naum bus; ask the driver to let you off at your site.

Private Rooms Private rooms are your best bet at Ohrid as the camping grounds and hostel are far from town and the hotels can be pricey. *Private rooms* organised through the tourist office (☎ 266 494) near the bus station, ul Partizanska 3, cost from 320 MKD to 800 MKD per person per night, plus 20 MKD tax per person per night.

Popular with the diplomatic community, *'Mimi' Apostolov Rooms* (☎/fax 31 549, ul

Strašo Pinđura 2) has eight comfortable, heated rooms with phone and satellite TV for 800 MKD including breakfast. For real rustic flavour right on the lake, it's hard to beat the *sobi* (rooms) of Stefan Kanevče (☎ 34 813) in Kaneo (the small lakeside settlement you'll see below you on the way to the Church of Sveti Jovan Boroslov Kaneo). A room goes for 320 MKD plus an extra 160 MKD for a hearty breakfast, if you want it. Stefan might take you fishing if you're keen.

There are other private rooms available from other travel agencies, or look for signs along the waterfront promenade.

Hostels & Hotels The *Mladost Hostel* (☎ 21 626) is located on the lakeside a little over 2km to the west of Ohrid, towards Struga and is open in summer only. A bed costs 210 MKD per night. Get there on the Struga bus (15 MKD) and ask for Mladost.

Expect to pay around 1568/1920 MKD per night, including breakfast, for a decent single/double room at the fairly central *Hotel Palace* (☎ 260 440, fax 35 460) on ul Partizanska, close to the bus station.

For comfort and some luxury, the *Hotel Lebed* (☎ 36 742, ☎/fax 263 607, e tani@mt.net.mk), about 1km east of town along the water, is an excellent choice. The secluded hotel has eight comfortable rooms with pleasant wood decor. All rooms have phone, satellite TV, and central heating and air-conditioning. Singles/doubles cost 2560/3840 MKD including breakfast. Reserve early (three weeks ahead in summer, three days ahead in the off-season). Visa and MasterCard are accepted.

Places to Eat

Picnic-minded travellers can stock up on fresh vegetables at the busy *Popular Market* just north of the old plane tree. There is a *minimarket* for meat and dairy produce on Sveti Kliment Ohridski.

Any number of fast-food and pizza joints speckle the old town area. Try *Cosa Nostra*, not far from the Archaeological Museum, which serves up tasty pizzas and is quite popular. Across the way, *Restaurant Dolga*, popular with international travellers, has a glorious seaview from its outdoor patio and offers good trout (approximately 500 MKD for a good-sized portion of two trout). One of Ohrid's most atmospheric eating places is the *Restaurant Antiko (Car Samuil 30)*, in an old house in the old town.

The *Star Chinar (Old Plane Tree)* is a neat, modern restaurant near the old plane tree and offers some tasty local specialities. Try *chulban* – lamb, beef and rice patties in sauce. About 100m west of the old plane tree is the Turkish-style *Restoran Neim* on the south side of Goce Delčev which serves some good *musaka* or *polneti piperki* (stuffed peppers).

Entertainment
The mellow *Jazz In*, just towards the water from Sveti Sofija, dominates the after-hours scene. Ohrid's movie theatre is *Dom Na Kultura* at Grigor Prličev, facing the lakeside park. Cultural events are also held here.

Getting There & Away
Air Avioimpex flies once a week from Ohrid to Zürich (250 Sfr plus a 20 Sfr airport tax); MAT flies regularly from Skopje and once a week from Dusseldorf (US$180 plus airport tax). Adria Airlines flies three times a week from Ljubljana (US$120).

Bus No less than 10 buses a day run between Ohrid and Skopje (280 MKD, three hours, 167km), via Kičevo. Another three go via Bitola and another two via Mavrovo. The first route is shorter, faster, more scenic and cheaper, so try to take it. During the summer rush, it pays to book a seat the day before.

There are six buses a day that travel to Bitola (140 MKD, 1¼ hours). Buses to Struga (7km) leave about every 15 minutes (5 am to 9 pm) from stand No 1 at the bus station. Enter through the back doors and pay the conductor (35 MKD).

Yugoslavia An overnight bus from Ohrid to Belgrade (1530 MKD, 694km), via Kičevo, leaves Ohrid at 5.45 pm, reaching Belgrade 14 hours later. Another two buses go to Belgrade via Bitola, leaving at 5 am and 3.30 pm.

Albania To go to Albania catch a bus or boat to Sveti Naum monastery, which is very near the border crossing. In summer there are six buses a day from Ohrid to Sveti Naum (80 MKD, 29km), in winter three daily. The

bus continues on to the border post. From Albanian customs it's 6km to Pogradec; taxis are waiting and should charge only US$6 to US$10 for the ride.

Greece Ohrid has no direct transport links to Greece. See the Getting There & Away section earlier in this chapter.

AROUND OHRID
Sveti Naum
The better part of a second day at Ohrid could be spent on a pilgrimage to Sveti Naum, on the Albanian border 28km south of Ohrid by bus. There you will see the impressive 17th-century **Church of Sveti Naum** rising on a hill above the lake, surrounded by a monastery. The original church was built here in 900, and St Naum was buried here in 910. The gorgeous frescoes inside the church are mostly 19th century, though fragments of 16th and 17th century work remain. You can probably find an English speaker on hand to act as a guide. The monastery offers a view of the Albanian town of Pogradec across the lake.

Places to Stay & Eat The monastery has a new 28-room hotel *Sveti Naum* (☎/fax 096-283 244 or ☎/fax 283 245, ⓔ markoni@ mt.net.mk, ⓔ viomark@mt.net.mk), which has excellent rooms with satellite TV, phone, and central heating and air-conditioning, and (almost uniquely in Macedonia) a tub. Visa and MasterCard are accepted. The hotel is open year-round; book well in advance in summer. High-season rooms (July to August) cost 5440/8640 MKD for a double/suite (5120/8000 MKD in low season). Breakfast is included, and the restaurant serves other meals as well. Fast-food stands line the road to the monastery in summer.

Getting There & Away Six buses a day run from Ohrid to Sveti Naum; it's 70 MKD one-way, payable on the bus. Buses return generally 40 minutes after they set out. The bus makes a stop going both ways at the Albanian border.

In summer you can also come by boat but it only leaves when a group is present; ask about times at the wharf or at the travel agencies in town. The fare should be about 250 MKD each way.

BITOLA (БИТОЛА)
☎ 097

Bitola, the southernmost city of the former Yugoslavia and second largest in Macedonia, sits on a 660m-high plateau between mountains 16km north of the Greek border. The colourful old bazaar area (Stara Čaršija) serves as a reminder that during part of the later Ottoman period, the town housed foreign consulates.

The bus and train station are adjacent to each other, about 1km south of the town centre. The central attraction of Bitola is the magnificent **Heraclea ruins** beyond the old cemetery, 1km south of the bus/train stations, (admission 50 MKD, photos 500 MKD). Founded in the 4th century BC by Philip II of Macedonia, Heraclea was conquered by the Romans two centuries later and became an important stage on the Via Egnatia. From the 4th to 6th centuries AD it was an episcopal seat. Excavations continue but the Roman baths, portico and theatre can now be seen. More interesting are the two early Christian basilicas and the episcopal palace, complete with splendid mosaics.

It's probably best to treat Bitola as a day trip or a stopover between Skopje and Ohrid, as facilities are poor. There are no private rooms, the hotel is dark and overpriced, and no left-luggage office is available. To get to the border, you must take a taxi (320 MKD to 400 MKD) and then get a Greek taxi on the other side to the nearest town, Florina.

PELISTER NATIONAL PARK

Rather than staying in Bitola, consider a trip up to Pelister National Park, capped by the magnificent Mt Pelister (2601m). Up the road to the park, which branches off from the Bitola-Prilep road not far out of Bitola, you will find the secluded and comfortable *Hotel Molika* (*☎ 097-229 406, fax 229 048)*, 140m above sea level and 15km from Bitola, with 46 clean rooms with central heating, TV, in-room phones and minibars. Singles/doubles start from 1500/2300 MKD (breakfast included). High season is July to August and January to February, so book early.

If you're there to ski, a lift ticket will cost about 320 MKD, and the hotel can help arrange ski rentals. At the top of the nearby lift, the mountaineers' club Kopanki offers a simple resthouse with a kitchen and cheap beds (inquire at Hotel Molika).

If you contact the hotel, they will be able to help you find a reasonably priced taxi (250 MKD to 300 MKD) from Bitola.

Malta

Malta, Gozo and Comino don't take up much space on the map, but their strategic position in the eastern Mediterranean between Sicily and Tunisia has for centuries made them irresistible to both navigators and invaders. The British were merely the last of a long series of colonisers to leave, but as a result most Maltese, and most of the tourists who visit the country, speak English. Due to the islands' varied colonial history, the Maltese have developed and retained a unique language and culture in which it is possible to detect Italian, Arabic, English, Jewish, French and Spanish influences.

Malta has long been regarded as an economical and cheerful destination for a beach holiday. The weather is excellent, food and accommodation are good value and the water is clean. However, the coastline is mainly rocky and the few sandy beaches are often crowded. The real highlights are the magnificent 16th-century fortified city of Valletta with its glorious harbour; the bustling Mediterranean life of the city with its lively cafes and bars; the stone villages with their precious baroque churches and exuberant *festas*; the astonishing prehistoric temples and archaeological finds; the beautiful, medieval fortress town of Mdina; and, if you want to get away from it all, the quiet island of Gozo.

AT A GLANCE

Capital	Valletta
Population	378,000
Official Language	Malti, English
Currency	1 Maltese lira (Lm) = 100 cents
Time	GMT/UTC+0100
Country Phone Code	☎ 356

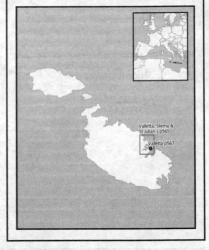

Valletta, Sliema & St Julian's p565
Valletta p567

Facts about Malta

HISTORY

Malta has a fascinating history, and the island is crowded with physical and cultural reminders of the past. The islands' oldest monuments are the beautifully preserved megalithic temples built between 3800 and 2500 BC, which are the oldest surviving free-standing structures in the world.

From around 800 to 218 BC, Malta was colonised by the Phoenicians and, for the last 250 years of this period, by Phoenicia's principal North African colony, Carthage. The Maltese language (Malti) is Semitic in origin and is believed to be based on Phoenician. With watchful eyes painted on the prow, the colourful Maltese fishing boats – *luzzu* and *kajjik* – are scarcely changed from the Phoenician trading vessels that once plied the Mediterranean.

After the Punic Wars between Rome and Carthage and the defeat of the Carthaginian general Hannibal in 208 BC, Malta became part of the Roman Empire. In AD 60, St Paul – a prisoner en route to Rome – was shipwrecked on the island. According to tradition, he converted the islanders to Christianity.

Arabs from North Africa arrived in 870, but tolerated the local Christian population. They introduced citrus fruits and cotton, and

had a notable impact on Maltese customs and language. The Arabs were expelled in 1090 by the Norman King Roger of Sicily. For the next 400 years Malta's history was linked to Sicily, and its rulers were a succession of Normans, Angevins (French), Aragonese and Castilians (Spanish). The relatively small population of downtrodden islanders paid their taxes by trading, slaving and piracy, and were repaid in kind by marauding North Africans (Berbers and Arabs) and Turks.

In 1530, the islands were given to the Knights of the Order of St John of Jerusalem by Charles V, Emperor of Spain; their rent

was two Maltese falcons a year, one to be sent to the emperor and the other to the Viceroy of Sicily. The 12,000 or so local inhabitants were given no say in the matter.

The Order of St John was founded during the crusades to protect Christian pilgrims travelling to and from the Holy Land, and to care for the sick. The knights were drawn from the younger male members of Europe's aristocratic families; in other words, those who were not the principal heirs. The order comprised eight nationalities or *langues* (languages). In order to preserve their identity, the langues built magnificent palaces, called *auberges.* The eight langues – Italy, Germany, France, Provence, Castile, Aragón, Auvergne and England – correspond to the eight points of the Maltese Cross. It was a religious order, with the knights taking vows of celibacy, poverty and obedience, and handing over their patrimony. The Order of St John became extremely prestigious, wealthy and powerful as a military and maritime force, and as a charitable organisation which founded and operated several hospitals.

As soon as they arrived in Malta, the knights began to fortify the harbour and to skirmish with infidels. In May 1565, an enormous Ottoman fleet carrying more than 30,000 men laid siege to the island. The 700 knights and 8000 Maltese and mercenary troops were commanded by a 70-year-old grand master, Jean de la Vallette. The Great Siege lasted for more than three months, with continuous and unbelievably ferocious fighting; after enormous bloodshed on both sides, help finally arrived from Sicily and the Turks withdrew.

The knights were hailed as the saviours of Europe. Money and honours were heaped on them by grateful monarchs, and the construction of the new city of Valletta – named after the hero of the siege – and its enormous fortifications began. Malta was never again seriously threatened by the Turks.

Although the order continued to embellish Valletta, the knights sank into corrupt and ostentatious ways, largely supported by piracy. In 1798 Napoleon arrived, seeking to counter the British influence in the Mediterranean, and the knights, who were mostly French, surrendered to him without a fight.

The Maltese defeated the French in 1800 with the assistance of the British, and in 1814 Malta officially became part of the British Empire. The British decided to develop Malta into a major naval base. In WWII, Malta once again found itself under siege. Considered a linchpin in the battle for the Mediterranean, Malta was subjected to a blockade and, in 1942, to five months of day-and-night bombing raids, which left 40,000 homes destroyed and the population on the brink of starvation.

In 1947 the devastated island was given a measure of self-government. Malta's best known leaders in the postwar period have been the leader of the Nationalist Party and prime minister, Dr George Borg Olivier, who led the country to independence in 1964, and Dominic Mintoff who, as prime minister and leader of the Maltese Labour Party, established the republic in 1974. In 1979 links with Britain were reduced further when Mintoff expelled the British armed services and signed agreements with Libya, the Soviet Union and North Korea. Domestic policy focused on state enterprises.

In 1987 the Nationalist Party assumed power under the prime ministership of Dr Eddie Fenech Adami, and it was returned by a landslide victory in 1992, when one of the party's main platforms was Malta's application to join the EU. However, the 1996 general election saw the Labour Party, led by Dr Alfred Sant, narrowly regain power. One of its main policies was to remove the country's application for full EU membership. In 1998, with the application suspended, Eddie Fenech Adami's Nationalist Party was returned to power.

In recent decades, the Maltese have achieved considerable prosperity, thanks largely to tourism, but increasingly because of shipping, trade and light industries.

GEOGRAPHY

The Maltese archipelago consists of three inhabited islands: Malta (246 sq km), Gozo (67 sq km) and Comino (2.7 sq km). They lie in the middle of the Mediterranean, 93km south of Sicily, 288km east of Tunisia and 350km north of Libya.

The densely populated islands are formed of a soft limestone, which is the golden building material used in all constructions. There are some low ridges and outcrops, but no major hills. The Victoria Lines escarpment traverses the island of Malta from the coast near Baħar ic-Cagħaq almost to the bay of Fomm ir-Riħ. The soil is generally thin and rocky, although in some valleys it is terraced and farmed intensively. There are few trees and, for most of the year, little greenery to soften the stony, sun-bleached landscape. The only notable exception is Buskett Gardens, a lush valley of trees and orange groves protected by the imposing southern Dingli Cliffs. There is virtually no surface water and there are no permanent creeks or rivers. The water table is the main source of fresh water, but it is supplemented by several large desalination plants.

CLIMATE
Malta has an excellent climate, although it can get very warm (around 30°C) in midsummer and occasionally in spring and autumn when the hot sirocco winds blow from Africa. The rainfall is low, at around 580mm a year, and it falls mainly between November and February. However, there's still plenty of sun in winter, when temperatures average around 14°C.

ECOLOGY & ENVIRONMENT
The combined pressures of population, land use and development, as well as pollution and the lack of protection of natural areas, have had a significant environmental impact on the islands. In 1990 the Maltese government drew up a plan which designated development zones and identified areas of ecological importance. Hunting, especially of birds, has always been a way of life in Malta but it is now restricted, as the islands lie on three migratory paths between Europe and Africa – migrating birds being protected species.

GOVERNMENT
Malta is an independent, neutral, democratic republic. The president has a ceremonial role and is elected by parliament. Executive power lies with the prime minister and the cabinet, the latter chosen from the majority party in the 65-member parliament.

There are two major parties: the Partit Tal-Haddiema, or Labour Party, and the Partit Nazzjonalista, or Nationalist Party.

ECONOMY
The Maltese enjoy a good standard of living, low inflation and low unemployment. The government's economic strategy is to concentrate on the development of the tourism industry, manufacturing, and financial services. Tourism in particular is rapidly growing in importance.

POPULATION & PEOPLE
Given its history, it's not surprising that Malta has been a melting pot of Mediterranean peoples. Malta's population is around 378,000, with most people living in Valletta

and its satellite towns; Gozo has 29,000 inhabitants; while Comino has a mere handful of farmers – six or seven in winter.

ARTS
Malta is noted for its fine crafts – particularly its handmade lace, hand-woven fabrics and silver filigree. Lace-making probably arrived with the knights in the 16th century. It was traditionally the role of village women – particularly on the island of Gozo – and, although the craft has developed into a healthy industry, it is still possible to find women sitting on their doorsteps making lace tablecloths.

The art of producing silver filigree was probably introduced to the island in the 17th century via Sicily, which was then under strong Spanish influence. Malta's silversmiths still produce beautiful filigree by traditional methods, but in large quantities to meet tourist demand.

Other handicrafts include weaving, knitting and glass-blowing; the latter is an especially healthy small industry which produces glassware exported throughout the world.

CULTURE & RELIGION
In Malta, the Mediterranean culture is dominant, but there are quite a few signs of British influence. The Catholic Church is the custodian of national traditions and its enormous churches dominate the villages. Although its influence is waning, Catholicism is a real force in most people's daily lives. Divorce and abortion are illegal; however, the possibility of divorce being legalised is a widely discussed issue.

LANGUAGE
Some linguists attribute the origins of Malti to the Phoenician occupation of Malta, but most consider it to be related to the Arabic dialects of Algeria and Tunisia. The language has an Arabic grammar and construction, but is laced with Sicilian, Italian, Spanish, French and English loan-words. Malti is the only Semitic language to be written in a Roman alphabet.

Nearly all Maltese in built-up areas speak English, and an increasing number speak Italian, helped by the fact that Malta receives Italian TV. French and German are also spoken.

See the Language Guide at the back of the book for pronunciation guidelines and useful words and phrases.

Facts for the Visitor

HIGHLIGHTS

The evocative Ħaġar Qim prehistoric temples are without doubt the highlight of a visit to Malta. The hill-top medieval town of Mdina is another must. On Gozo, visit the imposing megalithic temples of Ġgantija and the fascinating Azure Window and nearby Inland Sea at Qawra.

PLANNING
When to Go

The pleasant climate means you can visit Malta at any time. Outside the high season, which is between mid-June and late September, accommodation prices drop by up to 40%. The season of festas (or more correctly *festi*) begins in earnest at the beginning of June and lasts until the end of September.

Maps

A useful map is the *Insight Map Malta Flexi-Map*, which has street names in both English and Malti. Street signs in Valletta and some tourist areas are bilingual, but in many parts of the island they are in Malti only. The Maltese themselves rarely know the English names of streets other than the main thoroughfares. *Triq* means street in Maltese, and *misrah* and *pjazza* mean square.

There are several good bookshops which stock guidebooks, maps and general books. Sapienzas Bookshop (☎ 233621), 26 Republic St, Valletta, is recommended.

What to Bring

Summers can get very hot in Malta, so bring light, cool clothing and a hat (one which will not be blown off by the constant wind). Also bring along sunscreen (it's always more expensive in tourist areas) and comfortable shoes if you plan to do some exploring on foot.

TOURIST OFFICES
Local Tourist Offices

The Malta Tourist Authority (MTA) information offices can provide a range of useful brochures, hotel listings and maps. There are MTA offices at Malta international airport (☎ 249600), open 24 hours a day; in Valletta (☎ 237747) at 1 City Arcade; and on Gozo at Mġarr Harbour (☎ 553343) and Victoria (☎ 558106) on Independence Square.

Tourist Offices Abroad

The MTA has its main office in London at Malta House (☎ 020-7292 4900, fax 020-7734 1880, @ maltauk@aol.com) 36-38 Piccadilly, London, W1V 0PP. There are also offices in Paris, Frankfurt, Milan, Amsterdam and New York, and representative offices in 16 other cities. Embassies and offices of Air Malta can provide information in other countries (see the following Embassies & Consulates section).

VISAS

Entry visas are not required for holiday visits of up to three months by nationals of Australia, New Zealand, Canada, the USA or the UK.

EMBASSIES & CONSULATES
Maltese Embassies & Consulates

Malta has diplomatic missions in the following countries:

Australia (☎ 02-6295 1586) 261 La Perouse St, Red Hill, Canberra, ACT 2603
Canada (☎ 709-722 2744) Suite 1, Puglisevich Building, 611 Torbay Road, St John's, Newfoundland, A1A 5J1
Italy (☎ 06-687 99 47) 12 Lungotevere Marzio, 00186 Rome
UK (☎ 020-7292 4800) 36-38 Piccadilly, London W1V 0PQ
USA (☎ 202-462 3611) 2017 Connecticut Ave, NW Washington, DC 20008

Embassies & Consulates in Malta

The following countries have embassies in Malta:

Australia (☎ 338201) Ta'Xbiex Terrace, Ta'Xbiex MSD 11
Canada (☎ 233122) 103 Archbishop St, Valletta
Germany (☎ 336531) Il-Piazzetta, Entrance B, 1st floor, Tower Rd, Sliema
Italy (☎ 233157/59) 5 Vilhena St, Floriana
Tunisia (☎ 435175) Dar Carthage, Qormi Rd, Attard BZN 02
UK (☎ 233134/37) 7 St Anne St, Floriana

MALTA

USA (☎ 235960/65) Development House, 3rd floor, St Anne St, Floriana

CUSTOMS
Items for personal use are not subject to duty. One litre of spirits, 1L of wine and 200 cigarettes can be imported duty-free. Duty is charged on any gifts over Lm50 intended for local residents.

MONEY
Currency
The Maltese lira (Lm; a £ symbol is also sometimes used) is divided into 100 cents. There are one, two, five, 10, 25, 50 cent and Lm1 coins; and Lm2, Lm5, Lm10 and Lm20 notes. The currency is often referred to as the pound.

Exchange Rates
Banks almost always offer better rates than hotels or restaurants. There is a 24-hour bureau at the airport available to passengers only. Travellers arriving by ferry should note that there are no exchange facilities at the port. Automatic change machines and ATMs can be found in most towns and tourist areas.

country	unit		Maltese lira
Australia	A$1	=	Lm0.26
Belgium	f10	=	Lm0.01
Canada	C$1	=	Lm0.30
euro	€1	=	Lm0.40
France	1FF	=	Lm0.06
Germany	DM1	=	Lm0.21
Japan	¥100	=	Lm0.44
New Zealand	NZ$1	=	Lm0.20
UK	UK£1	=	Lm0.66
USA	US$1	=	Lm0.45

Costs
By European standards, Malta is good value, although prices are increasing slowly. If you can budget on around Lm10 per day, you'll get pleasant hostel accommodation, a simple restaurant meal, a decent street-side snack and enough cold drinks to keep you going. If you cook your own meals your costs will be even lower.

Tipping & Bargaining
Restaurants and taxis expect a 10% tip. Bargaining for handicrafts at stalls or markets is essential, but most shops have fixed prices. Hotels and car hire agencies will often be prepared to bargain in the off season between October and mid-June. You won't get far bargaining for taxis, but make sure you establish the fare in advance.

POST & COMMUNICATIONS
Post
Post office branches are found in most towns and villages. There is a poste restante service at the main post office in Castile Square, Valletta; it's open from 8 am to 6 pm.

Local postage costs six cents; postcards or letters sent air mail to Europe cost 16c, to the USA 22c and to Australia 27c.

Telephone & Fax
Public telephones are widely available and take coins or phonecards, which you can buy at Maltacom offices, post offices and stationery shops for Lm2, Lm3 or Lm5. There are rows of phones at the offices of Maltacom (the country's phone company). The main office is at Mercury House, St George's Rd, Paceville (open 24 hours). Other offices are at South St, Valletta (open from 7 am to 6 pm), and Bisazza St, Sliema (open 8 am to 11 pm).

For local telephone enquiries phone ☎ 190; for overseas enquiries phone ☎ 194. Local calls cost ten cents. The international direct dialling code is ☎ 00. International calls are discounted by around 20% between 6 pm and midnight and all day Saturday and Sunday (off-peak rate), and by up to 36% between midnight and 8 am (night rate). A three-minute call to the USA costs Lm1.50 (standard rate), Lm1.20 (off-peak) and 96c (night).

To call Malta from abroad, dial the international access code, ☎ 356 (the country code for Malta) and the number. There are no area codes in Malta.

Fax and telex services are available at Maltacom offices.

INTERNET RESOURCES
There's a wealth of useful information on the MTA's official Web site at www.tourism.org.mt and on the SearchMalta Web site at www.searchmalta.com (the latter site provides details on services from hotel

accommodation to leisure activities and childcare facilities).

Email & Internet Access
There are Internet cafes in Valletta, Sliema, St Julian's, Mosta and Victoria (Gozo). See the Valletta, Sliema & St Julian's section for details.

BOOKS
For more detailed information on the Maltese Islands check out Lonely Planet's *Malta*.

For a fascinating account of the Turkish siege of Malta in 1565, read *The Great Siege* by Ernle Bradford. Bradford's *Siege: Malta 1940-1943* covers the island's second major crisis. *The Kappillan of Malta* by Nicholas Monsarrat tells the story of a priest's experiences during WWII, interwoven with a potted history of Malta. Monsarrat lived on Gozo for many years. Malta has many fiction writers; those writing in English include Francis Ebejer and Joseph Attard.

NEWSPAPERS & MAGAZINES
The local English-language newspapers are the *Times*, the *Sunday Times*, the *Independent* and *Independent on Sunday*. British, French, German and Italian newspapers are available on the evening of publication.

RADIO & TV
Two local TV stations broadcast in Malti, and all of the main Italian TV stations are received in Malta. Satellite and cable TV are widely available. BBC World Service can be picked up on short-wave radio, and some Maltese radio stations broadcast in English.

TIME
Malta is two hours ahead of GMT/UTC during summer (from the last Sunday in March to the last Sunday in October), and one hour ahead during winter.

TOILETS
Small blocks of clean, sit-down public toilets are located throughout Malta.

WOMEN TRAVELLERS
Malta remains a conservative society by western standards, and women are still expected to be wives and mothers; however, an increasing number of women are now joining the workforce. Young males have adopted the Mediterranean macho style, but they are not usually aggressive. Normal caution should be observed, but problems are unlikely. If you are alone, Paċeville – the nightclub zone at St Julian's – is hectic but not particularly unsafe. Walking alone at night in Gzira is not recommended because this is the centre for prostitution.

Dress conservatively, particularly if you intend to visit churches (shorts are out for both sexes in churches, and shoulders should be covered). Topless bathing is illegal.

DISABLED TRAVELLERS
The Association for the Physically Handicapped (☎ 693863) is a good contact for disabled people wanting to travel to Malta. It is at the Rehabilitation Fund Rehabilitation Centre, Corradino Hill, Paola PLA 07. The MTA can provide details about hotels which have facilities for the disabled.

GAY & LESBIAN TRAVEL
Homosexual sex was legalised in Malta in 1973. Attitudes towards homosexuality in Malta are much the same as in most of southern Europe. Although Malta is not a very 'out' destination, there are several openly gay and lesbian bars, including the Lady Godiva Bar in Triq Wilga, Paċeville (male/female) and the Tom Bar, at the top of Telgħa Tal-Kurċifiss in Floriana. Malta held its first Gay Pride festival in 1996, organised by the Pride of Malta Organisation (☎ 250780).

TRAVEL WITH CHILDREN
Pharmacies are well stocked with baby needs such as formula, bottles, pacifiers and nappies (diapers). Kids might enjoy the Malta Experience (see Things to See in the Valletta section), or a harbour tour (see Organised Tours in the Valletta section). In summer, you can hire snorkelling gear, boats etc at the NSTS Aquacentre Beach Club (see Activities in the Valletta section). There is a Splash & Fun Park (☎ 342724), with water slides and a playground, at Bahar ic-Cagħaq. Another option for older kids (who are not easily frightened) is a visit to the Mdina Dungeons, which are fitted out with spooky sound effects and gory torture scenes (see the Mdina section).

MALTA

DANGERS & ANNOYANCES

Taxi drivers often try to rip off travellers – always agree on a fare before getting into a taxi. On arrival at the airport, ignore any taxi drivers who tell you that the bus stop is a 20-minute walk away, or that the bus won't be along for another hour – they're just touting for business.

If you go walking in the countryside, beware of the national obsession with shooting and trapping birds – the little stone shacks that pepper the cliff-tops are shooters' hides. The close season for shooting is 22 May to 31 August.

BUSINESS HOURS

Shops are open between 9 am and 1 pm, and 3.30 or 4 and 7 pm. Between 1 October and 14 June, banks are open from 8.30 am to 12.30 or 12.45 pm Monday to Friday; some banks also open in the afternoon. On Saturday they're open from 8.30 am to noon. The summer hours are the same (although few banks are open in the afternoon) except for Saturday, when they close at 11.30 am.

Between 1 October and 30 June, offices are open from 8 am to 1 pm and 2.30 or 3 to 5.30 pm Monday to Friday, and from 8.30 am to 1 pm on Saturday; from July to September they open 7.30 am to 1.30 pm Monday to Saturday.

PUBLIC HOLIDAYS & SPECIAL EVENTS

Fourteen national public holidays are observed in Malta: New Year's Day (1 January); St Paul's Shipwreck (10 February); St Joseph's Day (19 March); Good Friday; Freedom Day (31 March); Labour Day (1 May); commemoration of 1919 independence riots (7 June); Feast of Sts Peter and Paul, and Harvest Festival (29 June); Feast of the Assumption (15 August); Feast of Our Lady of Victories (8 September); Independence Day (21 September); Feast of the Immaculate Conception (8 December); Republic Day (13 December); and Christmas (25 December).

Festi are important events in Maltese family and village life. During the past 200 years they have developed from simple village feast days into extravagant spectacles. Every village has a festa, usually to celebrate the feast day of its patron saint. Most of them are in summer, and for days in advance the island reverberates to the sound of explosions announcing the forthcoming celebration.

The main fireworks display is usually on Saturday night, and is accompanied by one or more local brass bands. On Sunday evening the statue of the patron saint is paraded through the streets accompanied by brass bands, fireworks, petards and church bells. Afterwards, people repair to the bars to drink and chat, or sample savoury snacks or sweets such as *qubbajt* (nougat).

If a festa is held while you are visiting, you should definitely go along. Tourist offices can provide details.

ACTIVITIES

Diving

Malta offers excellent conditions for diving and competitive rates on courses. Underwater visibility often exceeds 30m, and there's dramatic scenery with caves and enormous dropoffs sometimes only metres from the shore. The water temperature drops to around 14°C in winter and reaches 25°C in summer. It is nearly always possible to find a protected site with easy access, so conditions are ideal for beginners.

Diving is strictly monitored by the Maltese government, and all divers must provide a medical certificate from either their own doctor or a local doctor (Lm3, available through dive centres). The minimum age for diving is 14 years. People wanting to dive unaccompanied will also need a local diving permit (Malta C-Card; Lm2), which is granted on presentation of a medical certificate, proof of qualification (minimum CMAS two-star) and two passport-sized photos. A PADI openwater dive course will cost from Lm110. One escorted shore dive with equipment hire will cost about Lm12. There are around 30 licensed diving schools. Maltaqua (☎ 571873), St Paul's Bay, and Divecare, (☎ 319994), St Julian's, in Malta, and Calypso Diving (☎ 562000), Marina St, Marsalforn, Gozo, have been recommended. The MTA has a list of all diving centres and also produces a useful brochure on diving.

Horse Riding

There are several registered riding schools – the MTA can provide a list. Try Darmanin's

Riding School (☎ 235649), Stables Lane, Marsa.

Walking
Distances on Malta are relatively small, so you can cover a lot of the islands on foot. Unfortunately, the Maltese show little interest in their countryside, so a lot of it is unkempt and littered with rubbish.

Sports Clubs
Sports clubs abound, and most of their facilities are available to visitors through temporary membership. One of the best is the Marsa Sports Club (☎ 233851), 4km south of Valletta, which offers golf, tennis, squash, cricket and swimming.

Beaches
The best sandy beaches on Malta are Ġnejna Bay; Għajn Tuffieħa and Golden Bay (bus Nos 47, 51 and 652); Paradise Bay (bus Nos 45, 48 and 645); Ramla Bay; Armier Bay (bus No 50); Mellieħa Bay (bus Nos 44, 45 and 48); and St George's Bay (bus Nos 64 and 67).

The best sandy beaches on Gozo are Ramla Bay (bus No 42) and Xlendi Bay (bus No 87). On Comino, the best beaches are Santa Maria Bay and San Niklaw Bay (private). Where bus numbers are not shown, private transport is necessary.

WORK
It is difficult for foreigners to work legally in Malta. Casual (illegal) work waitering or washing dishes in bars and discos can sometimes be found.

ACCOMMODATION
The MTA produces a list of accommodation on Malta, Gozo and Comino. There's a full range of options, from five-star hotels to small guesthouses.

As there are no longer set rates according to class of accommodation, it's best to ring around to get an idea. Prices can be considerably lower in the off season, and two and three-star hotels often work out cheaper than guesthouses. There are hostels on Malta and Gozo (see the Valletta, Sliema and St Julian's section). Camping is not permitted, and apart from hostels the cheapest option is boarding

with families for around Lm3 a night. Try the National Student Travel Service (NSTS); see Air in the Getting There & Away section for contact details.

FOOD
Malta is not known as a destination for gourmets, but the food is both good and cheap. The most obvious influence is Sicilian, and most of the cheaper restaurants serve pasta and pizza. English standards (eg, grilled chops, sausages and mash, roast with three veg) are also commonly available, particularly in the most touristed areas. Vegetarians are well catered for, with many restaurants offering vegetarian dishes as main courses.

It is definitely worth trying some of the Maltese specialities: *pastizzi* (savoury pasties filled with cheese or mushy peas), which are available from small bakeries and bars; *timpana* (a rich macaroni, cheese and egg pie); and *bragioli* (spicy beef rolls). Two favourite, but relatively expensive, dishes are *fenech* (rabbit), which is fried or cooked in a casserole or pie, and *lampuka*, a fish (dorado), which is caught between September and November and usually served grilled, fried or made into a pie.

DRINKS
Local beers are good, with a range of lagers, stouts and pale ales: Hop Leaf (40c for a small bottle) is recommended. The local wine industry is continually improving and most table wines are very drinkable. You get what you pay for (from 45c to Lm4 a bottle). Imported wines and beers are available at reasonable prices.

ENTERTAINMENT
Paċeville is the centre of Malta's nightlife, with lots of bars, clubs and discos.

SHOPPING
Hand-knitted clothing is produced in the villages and can be cheap. Traditional handicrafts include lace, silver filigree, blown glass and pottery. Shop around, though, before you make a purchase; the Malta Crafts Centre, St John's Square, Valletta, is a good place to start. The best bargains are found on Gozo.

MALTA

Getting There & Away

AIR

Malta is well connected to Europe and North Africa. Scheduled prices aren't particularly cheap, but there are some excellent packages. Some bargains are available through NSTS, the representative in Malta for most student travel organisations (including STA Travel, Campus Holidays, CTS etc) and an associate member of Hostelling International (HI). NSTS has offices in Valletta (☎ 244983, fax 230330, ✉ nsts@nsts.org) at 220 St Paul St and on Gozo (☎ 553977) at 45 St Francis Square, Victoria.

Air Malta (☎ 662211) has scheduled flights to/from Amsterdam, Athens, Berlin, Brussels, Cairo, Casablanca, Catania (Sicily), Damascus, Dubai, Dublin, Frankfurt, Hamburg, Istanbul, London (Heathrow and Gatwick), Manchester, Munich, Palermo, Paris, Rome, Tripoli, Tunis, Vienna, Zürich and other destinations.

Air Malta has a series of agents worldwide. They include:

Australia (☎ 02-9244 2111) World Aviation Systems, 403 George St, Sydney, NSW 2000
Canada (☎ 416-604 4112) Trans-Med Aviation Inc., 3323 Dundas Street West, Toronto M6P 2A6
Egypt (☎ 02-578 2692) Air Malta Office, Nile Hilton Commercial Centre, 34 Tahir Square, Cairo
UK (☎ 020-8785 3199) Air Malta House, 314-316 Upper Richmond Rd, Putney, London SW15 6TU
USA (☎ 212-983 8504) World Aviation Systems, 205 East 42nd Street, Suite 1908, New York NY10017

Other airlines servicing the country include Alitalia, KLM, Lufthansa, Swissair and Tunisavia. Avoid buying tickets in Malta if you can, because prices are higher.

Charter flights, usually for trips of one or two weeks from England or Scotland, offer outstanding value, particularly in winter. Contact a travel agent specialising in budget flights and packages.

SEA

Malta has regular sea links in summer with both Sicily (Palermo, Pozzallo, Syracuse and Catania) and northern Italy (Genoa and Livorno). Cars can be brought by ferry from Sicily and may be imported for up to three months. A Green Card (internationally recognised proof of insurance) for Malta is required.

The Italy-Malta ferry services change schedules frequently so it is best to confirm the information given here with a travel agent. SMS Agency (☎ 232211), 311 Republic St, Valletta, has information about all of the services on offer.

Virtù Ferries runs fast catamaran services to Sicily (Catania, Pozzallo and Licata) daily in summer, thrice weekly in winter. The journey to Catania takes three hours and costs Lm34 for an open return, and as little as Lm14/21 for a same-day return in winter/summer. Virtù Ferries has offices in Ta'Xbiex, near Valletta (☎ 3188543, Princess Elizabeth Terrace), and Catania (☎ 095-316711, Piazza Europa 1).

Other companies operate regular car-ferry services to Italian ports and to Tunisia. The journey to Catania takes around 12 hours and a deck passenger is charged Lm20. Cars cost around Lm35 to transport. Ferry companies include Meridiano Lines (☎ 239776) and MA.RE.SI Shipping (☎ 320620), both of which have services to Pozzallo and Reggio Calabria, and Grimaldi Group Grandi Traghetti (☎ 244373), with services to Genoa and Tunis.

It is important to note that ferries do not have exchange facilities and there are none available at Malta's port. Nor is there public transport from the port up to the city of Valletta – you either catch a taxi or make the steep 15-minute walk.

DEPARTURE TAX

All passengers departing by sea are required to pay a Lm4 departure tax which should be added by the travel agent when you buy your ticket.

Getting Around

BUS

Malta and Gozo are served by a network of buses run by the Malta Public Transport Authority (ATP), many of them beautiful and uncomfortable relics of the 1950s. On Malta, fares range from 15c to 50c, depending on the number of fare stages you pass through and whether it's an express or night service. Buses run until about 10 or 11 pm, depending on the route. Route numbers change occasionally, so check them locally. Most buses on Malta originate from the main City Gate bus terminus, which is in a plaza area just outside Valletta's city gates (☎ 250007/08/09 for information). A free bus map is available from ATP kiosks and tourist information offices.

Bus Nos 45, 452 and 453 run regularly from Valletta to Ċirkewwa to connect with the ferry to Gozo. Bus Nos 60 and 63 run from Valletta to Sliema, and bus Nos 62, 67 and 68 go on to St Julian's and Paċeville.

On Gozo, the bus terminus is in the main town of Victoria, on Main Gate St just south of Republic St. A flat fare of 10c will take you anywhere on the island. Note that few buses run after noon (for information phone ☎ 556011). Bus No 25 runs from the ferry port of Mġarr to Victoria, and bus No 21 goes from Victoria to Marsalforn. In the villages, the bus stop is always in or near the church square.

TAXI
Taxis are expensive and should only be used as a last resort or with a group of people. A fare from the airport to Sliema is around Lm8; from Valletta to St Julian's it's around Lm5. Make sure you establish a price in advance. Wembley Motors (☎ 374141) in St Andrews offers a 24-hour service.

CAR & MOTORCYCLE
Like the British, the Maltese drive on the left side of the road. Hiring a car in Malta is a good idea, partly because taxis are so expensive. One late-night fare between Paċeville and Buġibba could easily cost Lm7, which is nearly the cost of a hire car for a day. All the car-hire companies have representatives at the airport but rates vary, so shop around. In 2000 Hertz was offering a weekly summer rate of Lm75 for a small car (Lm53 a week in the low season). Its head office (☎ 314636) is at 66 Gzira Road, Gzira. Local garages such as Ada (☎ 691007) charge slightly less. La

Ronde (☎ 322962), Belvedere Street, Gzira, hires out motorcycles from Lm3 per day (insurance and delivery included). Call ☎ 242222 for 24-hour breakdown assistance and towing.

Road rules
You can't drive fast in Malta. If the speed limits (70km/h on highways and 35km/h in urban areas) don't slow you down, the many potholes in the roads definitely will. At intersections where there are no roundabouts, the first to arrive has right of way. Breathalyser tests were only introduced in Malta in 1998. It is illegal to drive with *any* alcohol in your blood.

BICYCLE
A bike can be a good way to get around Gozo because of the small distances, but hills, heat and erratic driving make cycling on Malta less pleasant. The Cycle Store (☎ 432890), 135 Eucharistic Congress St in Mosta, about 30 minutes by bus from Valletta, has bikes for Lm1.50 a day. The Marsalforn Hotel (☎ 556147) in Gozo has bikes for Lm2 a day, or less if rented for several days.

HITCHING
Hitchhiking is very unusual in Malta and is frowned upon.

BOAT
Regular ferries link Malta and Gozo, and buses connect with all ferry services (see the Bus information earlier in this section). Ferries depart from Ċirkewwa on Malta and from Mġarr on Gozo. Services are more or less hourly from 6 am to 11 pm. The crossing takes 30 minutes and costs Lm1.75 return for passengers, and Lm4 return for cars. Even if you board at Ċirkewwa, you still pay for your ticket at Gozo on the return leg; this means that car drivers arriving at Ċirkewwa should head straight for the queue.

Be warned that Maltese families flock to Gozo on Sunday, particularly in summer, which can cause long delays at ferry terminals. Traffic from Ċirkewwa to the main towns is also very heavy on Sunday evening. All ferries are operated by the Gozo Channel Co (☎ 243964).

There is also a ferry service (☎ 335689) between Valletta and Sliema (at the end of the Strand) approximately every half-hour from 8 am to 6 pm.

HELICOPTER

There is a regular helicopter service between Malta international airport and Gozo. Tickets cost Lm17 one way and Lm25 return. There are also helicopter tours of the islands. Contact any travel agency for information and bookings.

ORGANISED TOURS

A number of companies operate bus tours and they are highly competitive, so shop around the travel agencies. The tours will restrict you to the well-trampled tourist traps, but they can give you a good introduction to the islands nonetheless.

A typical full-day tour of Malta costs Lm3 to Lm6. Tours without lunch are generally cheaper. There are also day tours to Gozo and Comino, and trips to see late-night festa fireworks. Tour guides expect tips.

Day tours to Sicily (up to Lm30) are available through the travel agencies. The journey takes 90 minutes by catamaran and the tour includes a visit to Mt Etna and Taormina. Captain Morgan Cruises (☎ 343373) at The Strand, Sliema, has a great range of cruises, sailing adventures and jeep safaris. See the Valletta section for information on harbour tours.

Valletta, Sliema & St Julian's

Valletta, the city of the Knights of the Order of St John, is architecturally superb and seemingly unchanged since the 16th century. The city is the seat of Malta's government, and overlooks the magnificent Grand Harbour to the south-east and Marsamxett Harbour to the north-west.

On the south-eastern side of the Grand Harbour lie the fortified peninsulas of Vittoriosa and Senglea and the town of Cospicua (known collectively as the Three Cities, or the Cotonera). These are older and in some ways more interesting than Valletta itself. They are dominated by their docks, which date from the time of the Phoenicians and were the principal reason for their existence. They are definitely worth exploring.

On the northern side of Marsamxett Harbour lies Sliema, the most fashionable residential area. Restaurants and high-rise hotels line the shores. Farther north-west are the tourist haunts of St Julian's and Paċeville (**patch**-ey-vill).

Orientation

The Maltese think of the suburbs that surround Valletta – Cospicua, Paola, Hamrun, Qormi, Birkirkara, Gzira, Sliema and St Julian's – as separate towns. This may well have been accurate in the relatively recent past, but they now run into one another and effectively create one large city with a population of around 250,000. The entire eastern half of the island is intensively developed, with large suburbs and towns, the airport and numerous industrial sites.

The ferries from Italy dock in the Grand Harbour below Valletta, and it's a steep 15-minute climb up the hill to the main City Gate bus terminus, outside the southern walls.

Information

Tourist Offices The local tourist office (☎ 237747) is at 1 City Arcade, Valletta.

Money There are several banks in Valletta's main street, Republic St, including branches of the HSBC Bank at Nos 15 and 233. You can also change money at the Thomas Cook office in Valletta (☎ 235948) at 20 Republic St and in Sliema (☎ 322747) at il-Piazzetta, Triq it-Torri.

Email & Internet Access Email checking can be done at the YMCA (☎ 240680), 178 Merchants St, Valletta, where Internet access costs 75c per half-hour. The YMCA is open 10 am to 10 pm Monday to Saturday. At the Għall Kafé (☎ 319686) at 118 St George's Road in Paċeville you'll pay Lm1 for 40 minutes, or Lm2 for 100 minutes.

Laundry The Square Deal laundrette on the Strand, Sliema (opposite the Captain Morgan boats), is one of the few laundries outside the hotels, but it's expensive at Lm2.50 for one load.

MALTA

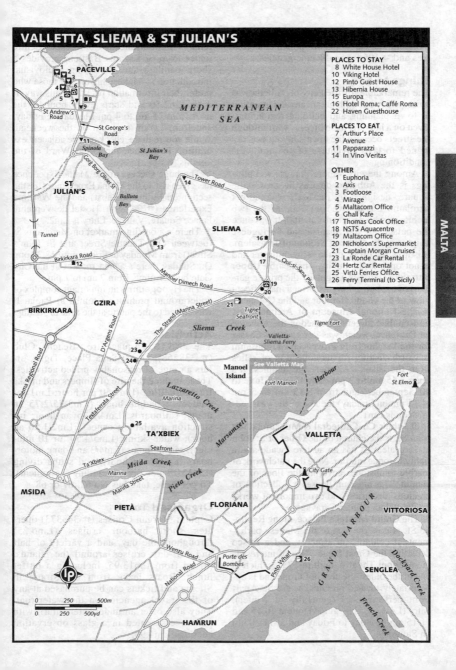

VALLETTA, SLIEMA & ST JULIAN'S

PLACES TO STAY
8 White House Hotel
10 Viking Hotel
12 Pinto Guest House
13 Hibernia House
15 Europa
16 Hotel Roma; Caffé Roma
22 Haven Guesthouse

PLACES TO EAT
7 Arthur's Place
9 Avenue
11 Papparazzi
14 In Vino Veritas

OTHER
1 Euphoria
2 Axis
3 Footloose
4 Mirage
5 Maltacom Office
6 Ghall Kafe
17 Thomas Cook Office
18 NSTS Aquacentre
19 Maltacom Office
20 Nicholson's Supermarket
21 Captain Morgan Cruises
23 La Ronde Car Rental
24 Hertz Car Rental
25 Virtù Ferries Office
26 Ferry Terminal (to Sicily)

MALTA

0   250   500m
0   250   500yd

Medical & Emergency Services Useful numbers include ☎ 191 for police emergencies and ☎ 196 for health emergencies.

Things to See

The remarkable fortified city of Valletta was built swiftly but with great care and attention to town planning and building regulations. Even on a hot day, fresh breezes waft through the streets because the town's layout was designed to take advantage of 'natural' airconditioning.

Among the city's more impressive buildings is the **Auberge de Castile** on Castile Square, designed by the Maltese architect Girolamo Cassar (who was one of the two architects who designed Valletta). It was once the palace for the Spanish and Portuguese knights of the Order of St John of Jerusalem. It is now the office of the prime minister and is not open to the public. The nearby **Upper Barrakka Gardens**, originally the private gardens of the Italian knights, offer a magnificent view of the Grand Harbour and the Cotonera.

The **National Museum of Archaeology**, on Republic Street, is housed in the Auberge de Provence, which was designed by Cassar for the knights from Provence. The museum is worth visiting for its collection of relics from the island's Copper Age temples. It's open 7.45 am to 2 pm daily from 16 June to 30 September, and from 8.15 am to 5 pm (4.15 pm on Sunday) the rest of the year; admission is Lm1.

St John's Co-Cathedral & Museum, on St John St, is the church of the Order of St John of Jerusalem. It has an austere facade and a richly baroque interior. Note the patchwork of marble tombstones covering the floor of the church. The museum houses a collection of precious tapestries, and two important works by the Italian painter Caravaggio.

The **Grand Master's Palace**, along Republic St, is now the seat of the Maltese parliament. It contains an armoury and a fresco depicting the Great Siege. Also of interest is the **Manoel Theatre**, built in 1731, which is one of the oldest theatres in Europe and is appropriately located on Old Theatre St. Apart from performances (generally in winter), entry (Lm1.65) is by guided tour at 10.45 and 11.15 am Monday to Friday and at 11.30 am on Saturday.

The **Malta Experience** (☎ 243776) at Valletta's Mediterranean Conference Centre (enter from St Lazarus Bastion) provides a short, painless and interesting audiovisual introduction to Maltese history for those who prefer their information packaged this way. It costs Lm2.50 and starts every hour on the hour from 11 am to 4 pm Monday to Friday, and from 11 am to 1 pm on the weekend. While you're there, check out the adjacent exhibition hall, once the Great Ward of the knights' hospital.

The huge success of the Malta Experience has given rise to the Mdina Experience (see the section on Mdina & Rabat) and the **Wartime Experience** (☎ 247891), Hostel de Verdelin, Palace Square, Valletta. Entry is Lm2.

There's a bustling **market** on Merchants St (between Old Theatre Street and St John's Street) from Monday to Friday until 12.30 pm. On Sunday there's a **flea market** at the City Gate bus terminus from 7 am to 1 pm.

The **Hypogeum** is an important complex of underground prehistoric tombs at Paola. It was closed to the public at the time of writing.

Activities

The NSTS Aquacentre Beach Club (☎ 338568), Qui-si-Sana Place, Tigne, offers a range of reasonably priced activities. These include the hire of flippers and masks for snorkelling (Lm1.50 per hour; Lm1 for students); paddle boats (Lm3.75/2.75 an hour); sailboards (Lm4/2.75 an hour; instruction available); canoes (Lm2/1.50 an hour); water-skiing (Lm5/4.50 for 10 minutes); sailing boats (Lm4/3 an hour); motorboats (Lm8/6 an hour); and scuba diving (Lm15/13 per dive, including equipment). To get there, take bus No 62, 67 or 68.

Organised Tours

Captain Morgan Cruises (☎ 343373) operates short harbour cruises (Lm6.25) throughout the day, and a variety of half and full-day cruises around the islands, priced from Lm13.95, including a buffet lunch. Boats leave from the Strand in Sliema and tickets can be purchased at any of the travel agencies on the waterfront. They also offer an underwater safari, with passengers seated in a glass observation keel, for Lm4.95.

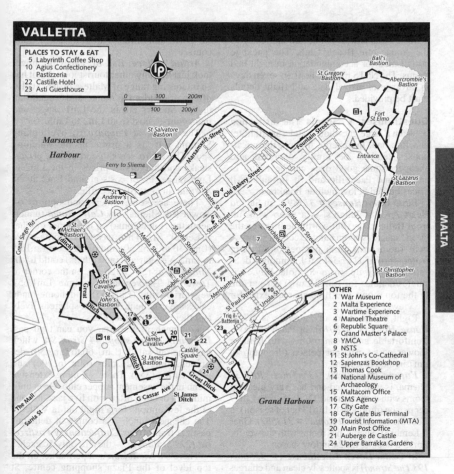

VALLETTA

PLACES TO STAY & EAT
- 5 Labyrinth Coffee Shop
- 10 Agius Confectionery
   Pastizzeria
- 22 Castille Hotel
- 23 Asti Guesthouse

OTHER
- 1 War Museum
- 2 Malta Experience
- 3 Wartime Experience
- 4 Manoel Theatre
- 6 Republic Square
- 7 Grand Master's Palace
- 8 YMCA
- 9 NSTS
- 11 St John's Co-Cathedral
- 12 Sapienzas Bookshop
- 13 Thomas Cook
- 14 National Museum of
   Archaeology
- 15 Maltacom Office
- 16 SMS Agency
- 17 City Gate
- 18 City Gate Bus Terminal
- 19 Tourist Information (MTA)
- 20 Main Post Office
- 21 Auberge de Castile
- 24 Upper Barrakka Gardens

MALTA

Places to Stay

Hostels The NSTS is an associate member of Hostelling International (HI). It runs several hostels in Malta and also has agreements with certain guesthouses to provide cheap accommodation to hostellers. An HI membership card is required in order to stay at any of the hostels in Malta. Cards can be obtained from the NSTS or from the main hostel, *Hibernia House* (☎ 333859, fax 230330) in Depiro St, Sliema, where a bed costs Lm2.85. To get there, take bus No 62 or 67 to Balluta Bay, walk up the hill along Manoel Dimech Rd, then turn left into

Depiro St – the hostel is about 100m along on the right.

There are other hostels, or places which have hostel-price agreements with the NSTS. The University Residence in *Lija* (☎ 436168, fax 434963), on Triq R.M.Bonnici, charges Lm4.75 per night. Take bus No 40 from Valletta. Or you can stay in *Buġibba* (☎ 573022, fax 571975, 100 Triq Iċ-Ċentujun) for Lm4.25; take bus 49 from Valletta or No 70 from Sliema.

The NSTS offers a special hostelling package which includes airport welcome and transfers, seven overnight stays (with breakfast)

including at least one night at Hibernia House, a week's bus pass, a phonecard and entry to the Aquacentre Beach Club. The package costs Lm62 for accommodation in eight-bed dorms. The NSTS must be notified seven days in advance of arrival date and flight details must be provided.

Guesthouses & Hotels The distinction between a large guesthouse and a small hotel is a fine one. In general, though, the guesthouses tend to be family operated and cheaper. Some good ones can be found in and around Paċeville and St Julian's. All prices quoted below include breakfast.

Pinto Guest House (☎ 313897), in Sacred Heart Ave, St Julian's, is a steep walk up from Balluta Bay, but worth the hike for the clean, spacious rooms and excellent view. A twin room costs Lm6 per person. *Viking Hotel* (☎ 316702 or 340930), Spinola Rd, St Julian's, just up from Spinola Bay, has singles/doubles for Lm12/Lm10 per person. In the top rooms you'll be charged extra for the view.

Right in the centre of Paċeville is *White House Hotel* (☎ 378016), in Paċeville Ave. Comfortable and clean rooms with bath or shower cost Lm10 per person (dropping to Lm7 in the off season).

Europa (☎ 330080, 138 Tower Rd), in Sliema, is well located and has very pleasant rooms with bathroom and TV. It charges Lm17 per person (dropping to Lm13 out of season) in a double room. *Hotel Roma* (☎ 318587), Ghar Il-Lembi St, Sliema, has rooms with shower for Lm35 a double, Lm24 in low season.

In Gzira, *Haven Guesthouse* (☎ 335862, 193 The Strand) is spotlessly clean and charges Lm7.70 per person.

In Valletta, there's *Asti Guesthouse* (☎ 239506), 18 St Ursula St, in a former convent. Rooms are very basic and bathrooms are shared, but prices are good at Lm5.50 per person. The charming three-star *Castille Hotel* (☎ 243677), Castile Square, near the Upper Barrakka Gardens, charges Lm25 per person for a room with shower, Lm16 in low season.

Places to Eat
There are cheap restaurants, bars and cafes on The Strand in Sliema, in Paċeville and around St Julian's Bay. Prices tend to be fairly

standard – around Lm2 for a pizza, Lm2.50 for pasta and Lm2.50 to Lm4 for a main course.

Arthur's Place, Ball St, Paċeville, might look just like any other tourist joint, but it has an interesting range of Maltese dishes. It also offers a children's menu and vegetarian dishes. Starters are in the Lm1 range, and main courses cost from Lm2 to Lm3.50.

The terrace at *Papparazzi,* overlooking Spinola Bay, is a prime people-watching spot. The bistro serves good pastas, pizzas, steaks and burgers at prices in the Lm2 to Lm5 range. Pizza costs around Lm2 at the *Avenue*, in Gort St, Paċeville.

There are some other good options on Tower Rd, Sliema. Try *Caffé Roma* (underneath the Hotel Roma) on the corner of Ghar Il-Lembi St. The pasta is home-made (Lm1.30 to Lm2.50) and pizzas cost Lm1.65 to Lm2. Vegetarians (and others) could try *In Vino Veritas* (59 Dingli St), on the corner of Tower Rd. The vegetarian lasagne (Lm1.65), vegetarian rice (Lm1.65) and home-made cakes are excellent. The atmosphere is lively and there are many regulars.

For lunch in Valletta, you can't go past *Labyrinth coffee shop* (44 Strait St), which has generous salads (Lm1.60 to Lm2.50), delicious home-made pies (60c to 70c) and great coffee (35c). There's a more extensive menu in the basement supper club. Open until midnight or later, often with live jazz, it's one of the few options for a night out in Valletta. The cheapest lunch is a couple of delicious pastizzi from *Agius Confectionery Pastizzeria* (273 St Paul St) – they're only 5c each.

There's a *Nicholson's* supermarket on the top level of the Plaza shopping centre, St Anna Square, Sliema.

Entertainment
Paċeville is Malta's nightlife centre. It's quiet from Monday to Thursday but on Friday, Saturday and Sunday the place is jumping. Crowds spill out of the bars onto the street, policemen lounge around, elderly British tourists look bemused and cars crawl around trying to avoid pedestrians' toes. Wander until you find the bar of your choice.

Mirage, a disco club for the young crowd, is opposite *Footloose*, a (loud) rock music pub in St George's Rd. *Euphoria* and *Axis*, also in St George's Rd, are other places in Paceville to dance and party till late. Discos cost around Lm2.50 to enter (some are free) and drinks are expensive. Since bus services stop at around 10 pm, most Maltese group together and catch taxis or walk home.

Getting Around

To/From the Airport Bus No 8 leaves from outside the departures hall at Malta international airport terminal about every half-hour and goes to Valletta City Gate bus terminus. The journey costs 15c (you pay the driver). Most arrivals are transferred by courtesy car or coach to their hotels. Taxis operate on official rates; to Sliema or St Julian's it's Lm8.

Local Transport See the Getting Around section earlier in this chapter for more information on transport.

Around Malta

NORTH COAST

Although the north coast is fairly exposed, it's a good place for walking as it's relatively uninhabited. The sandy beach at Mellieha, west of St Paul's Bay, is the best on Malta, although it does get crowded. Catch bus No 44 or 45 from Valletta.

St Paul's Bay & Bugibba

Bugibba, the traditional name for the town on St Paul's Bay, is the main tourist centre – and it's ghastly. There is no reason to stay here unless you're on a very cheap package. However, the nightlife hots up in summer, and there are numerous cheap hotels and restaurants open throughout the year. Catch bus No 43, 44, 45, 49 or 58 from Valletta.

Cirkewwa

This is the port where the Gozo ferry docks. Paradise Bay, one of Malta's better sandy beaches, is a short walk to the south of the town. See the Getting Around section at the beginning of this chapter for information on the ferry to Gozo.

WEST COAST

The west coast is a great place to get away from the crowds. The best access is by private boat. If you're looking for solitude, keep away from the big tourist development and crowded, sandy beach at Golden Bay.

MOSTA

Mosta is famous for its church which has one of the largest unsupported domes in the world, with a diameter of 39.6m. The church was designed by Maltese architect Giorgio Grognet de Vassé whose plan was closely based on the Pantheon in Rome. The foundation stone was laid in 1833 and the church took 27 years to complete. Take bus No 49, 57 or 58 from Valletta.

MDINA & RABAT

Until the knights arrived and settled around the Grand Harbour, the political centre of Malta was Mdina. Set inland on an easily defendable rocky outcrop, it has been a fortified city for more than 3000 years. You could spend hours wandering through Mdina's narrow, quiet streets.

The city is still home to the Maltese aristocracy and is sometimes called the Noble City or the Silent City. Much of it was rebuilt after an earthquake in 1693, but you can still see some original sections which survived the disaster.

Things to See & Do

The best preserved medieval building is the **Palazzo Falzon**, built in 1495, which has Norman architectural features. Mdina has a beautiful main piazza, dominated by the cathedral. The **Cathedral Museum** is open 9 am to 4.30 pm Monday to Saturday.

The **Mdina Dungeons**, below the Vilhena Palace, St Publius Square, are medieval dungeons that have been restored to all their dubious glory and have tableaux depicting their victims. The dungeons are unlocked daily between 9.30 am and 5 pm, and entry is Lm1.40.

The **Mdina Experience** (☎ 454322), at 7 Mesquita Square, is the local version of Valletta's Malta Experience. It is shown from 10.30 am to 4 pm Monday to Friday, and 10.30 am to 2 pm on Saturday. Entry is Lm1.40.

The adjacent township of Rabat is typically Maltese. **St Paul's Church** and **St Paul's Grotto** lie in the centre of town, both of them classic examples of Maltese baroque. The grotto is believed to be the spot where St Paul lived. The nearby **catacombs** are also worth a look.

Places to Eat

A great place for lunch or a snack is the *Fontanella Tea Garden (1 Bastion St)*, which is built into the fortifications. If you feel like a splurge, dine at *Medina (7 Holy Cross St)*. It's one of Malta's best restaurants, and is just off Mdina's main piazza. An excellent meal with wine will come to around Lm12.

There are plenty of bars and a number of restaurants in Rabat. Visit *Baron* snack bar, 3 Republic St, not so much for the food as for the authentic local atmosphere.

Getting There & Away

Catch bus No 80 or 81 from Valletta to reach Mdina and Rabat.

SOUTH COAST

You can enjoy spectacular views from the 200m-high **Dingli Cliffs**. The most interesting and evocative prehistoric temples on Malta are **Ħaġar Qim** and **Mnajdra**, built between 3600 and 3000 BC near the village of Qrendi. The temples are open from 7.45 am to 2 pm in summer and 8.15 am to 5 pm (4.15 pm on Sunday) in winter; entry costs Lm1. These Copper Age megalithic temples are reminiscent of Stonehenge, and a visit is an absolute must.

EAST COAST
Marsaxlokk

This attractive fishing village has a couple of good fish restaurants and a touristy, harbourside market. Unfortunately, it is now overshadowed by an enormous power station. There are some pleasant swimming spots around **Delimara Point**, south-east of the village.

Gozo

Gozo is considerably smaller than the island of Malta and has a distinctive character of its own; the countryside is more attractive, the pace is slower and there are far fewer tourists.

It seems to have escaped the worst of the 20th century, so don't come for nightlife and bright lights. The capital is Victoria (also known as Rabat), but most tourists stay at the small resort town of Marsalforn. You can cram the sights into one day, but the real charm of Gozo is best appreciated at a slower pace.

VICTORIA (RABAT)

Victoria is an interesting, bustling town and the commercial centre of Gozo. There are no hotels in Victoria, but it has a decent range of shops and banks.

There's a wonderful view over the island from the **citadel**, which was constructed by the knights in the 17th century. The archaeological and folklore **museums** are worth a visit, as is the flat-topped **cathedral**. Money ran out when it came to building the cathedral's dome; its absence is noticeable from the outside but not from within, where there's a magnificent trompe l'oeil painting instead.

The tourist office (☎ 558106), in Independence Square, has a useful brochure and map. It can also supply information about car and bicycle rental on Gozo.

MARSALFORN

Marsalforn is the main resort town on the island and can become crowded on weekends. There are two large hotels, a scattering of smaller places to stay and a dozen restaurants, all built around an attractive bay. Follow the coast road west from the harbour for a fabulous walk past salt pans and weirdly eroded cliffs.

You can change money at the HSBC Bank on the harbour front, which is open 8 am to 12.45 pm (11.30 am on Saturday) from 15 June to 31 October. The diving on Gozo is particularly good (see Activities in the Facts for the Visitor section for further information).

Places to Stay

Outside the high season, the family-run *Atlantis Hotel* (☎ 554685) in Qolla St offers a poolside room and breakfast for Lm6 to Lm8 per person in winter; this jumps to Lm14 to Lm16.50 per person in summer. Lower daily rates can be negotiated for stays of a week or more, and cars and bicycles can be hired.

Calypso Hotel (☎ 562000), on the harbour, also has good off-season deals. Sea-view rooms cost Lm14.50 per person in summer, dropping to Lm6.50 in winter.

Marsalforn Hotel (☎ 556147), Rabat Rd, is a rather garish green and white guesthouse in the middle of town. B&B is Lm6 per person. Self-catering flats for four people are Lm10 to Lm12 per day. The hotel hires out bicycles.

Hostel accommodation can be arranged at *St Joseph Hostel (☎ 556439)* in Għanjsielem, a 15-minute walk uphill from Mġarr Harbour, in summer only – book in advance through NSTS (see Valletta section).

Places to Eat

The restaurants are clustered around the harbour, and there's not really a great deal to distinguish between them. *Smiley's* is the cheapest, but it's pretty basic: burgers cost 60c, fish and chips Lm1.30.

Il-Kartell, on the west side of the bay, is a step up and has good fish, pasta and pizzas; spaghetti is Lm1.20 and main courses and fresh fish are from Lm3 to Lm5. *Arzella Bar Restaurant Pizzeria*, on a terrace suspended over the east side of the bay, is similarly priced but also offers Maltese specialities such as timpana (Lm1.50) and bragioli (Lm3.20).

Getting There & Away

Marsalforn is a 4km walk from Victoria, or you can catch bus No 21 from the terminus in Main Gate St.

AROUND GOZO

Gozo measures only 14km from east to west and 6km from north to south, so a lot of the island can be covered on foot. The Ġgantija temple complex near Xagħra village is the most spectacular in Malta – its walls are 6m high.

There's a dramatic stretch of coastline around **Dwejra Point**, including the imposing **Azure Window**, a gigantic rock arch in the cliff, only a few hundred metres from the Inland Sea. This is the best area in Malta for walking along the scenic rocky coastline.

Xlendi

Xlendi is a small fishing village on the tip of a deep, rocky inlet on the south-west coast. It's a pretty spot but fast becoming over-developed. Some well-marked coastal footpaths start at Xlendi.

Serena ApartHotel (☎ 553719), Upper St, is perched over the town and has great views. A superior suite with a sea view, plus breakfast, costs Lm12 per person. The elegant *St Patrick's Hotel (☎ 562951)* is right on the sea and has rooms from Lm10 per person in the low season, rising to Lm17 in summer (rooms with sea views cost a bit more). There are several restaurants in Xlendi. At the St Patrick's Hotel waterfront restaurant, a salad with Gozo cheese (like a peppery feta) costs Lm1.65.

Catch bus No 87 to get to Xlendi from Victoria.

MALTA

Morocco

Known to the Arabs as *al-Maghreb al-Aqsa*, the 'farthest land of the setting sun', Morocco stands at the western extremity of the Arab and Muslim world. A land saturated with colour and rich in history, it has long held a romantic allure for westerners. For many, its greatest charm lies in the labyrinths of the imperial cities Fès, Meknès, Marrakesh and Rabat.

The countryside, too, exerts its own fascination. The snowcapped High Atlas Mountains, the great river valleys of the south with their magnificent red-earth kasbahs, the vast expanse of the desert all – offer the visitor a taste of the exotic.

Facts about Morocco

HISTORY

Morocco is largely populated by descendants of the Berber settlers who came to the area thousands of years ago. Their independent spirit has outlived conquerors over the centuries and resulted in one of Africa's most colourful cultures.

The first records of the Berbers recount their control of trans-Saharan trade. Later the Romans gained a tenuous hold in this part of North Africa, only to fade slowly away before the arrival of Islam in the 7th century as Arab armies asserted control over the whole North African coast and much of Spain.

Basic tribal divisions soon reasserted themselves, however, and the Berbers, having adopted Islam, developed their own brand of Shi'ism, known as Kharijism. By 829 the Kharijites had established a stable Idrissid state, with its capital at Fès, which dominated all of Morocco.

This unity was short lived. By the 11th century the region had fragmented. Out of the chaos emerged the Almoravids, who overran Morocco and Muslim Spain (Al-Andalus) and founded Marrakesh. They were supplanted by the Almohads, who raised Fès, Marrakesh and Rabat to heights of splendour, before crumbling as Christian armies regained Spain. The

AT A GLANCE

Capital	Rabat
Population	30 million (approx)
Official Language	Arabic
Currency	1 dirham (Dr) = 100 centimes
Time	GMT/UTC+0000
Country Phone Code	☎ 212

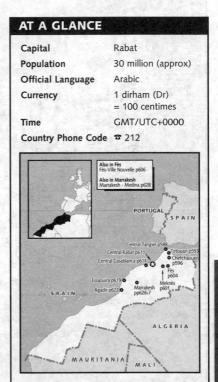

Also in Fès
Fès-Ville Nouvelle p606

Also in Marrakesh
Marrakesh - Medina p628

PORTUGAL
SPAIN

Central Tangier p588
Central Rabat p611
Central Casablanca p614
Tetouan p593
Chefchaouen p596
Fès p604
Essaouira p619
Meknès p601
Agadir p622
Marrakesh pp626-7

S P A I N

ALGERIA

MAURITANIA
MALI

MOROCCO

Merenid dynasty revitalised the Moroccan heartland and established Fès el-Jdid (New Fès), but it too collapsed after Granada fell to the Christians in 1492 and Muslim refugees poured into Morocco.

Morocco managed to retain its independence as colonialism swept the rest of Africa until, by the 1912 Treaty of Fès, France took over much of the country, handing Spain a zone in the north. Rabat was made the capital and Casablanca developed as a major port.

By 1934 the last opposition from Berber mountain tribes had been crushed, but Moroccan resistance moved into political channels in the Istiqlal (independence) party.

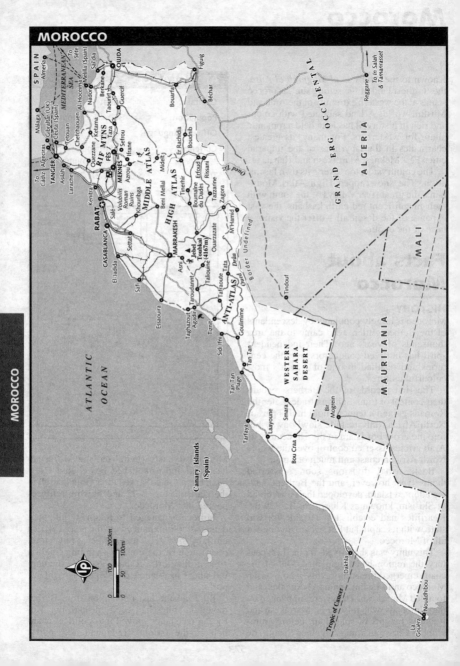

After WWII, opposition again took a more violent turn and in 1953 the French exiled Sultan Mohammed V. This only succeeded in further stoking Moroccan discontent and he was allowed to return in 1955. Independence was granted the following year.

The Spanish withdrew from much of the country around the same time but retained the coastal enclaves of Ceuta and Melilla. Sultan Mohammed V became a king, followed by his son King Hassan II who despite moves towards democracy and several coup attempts, retained all effective power until his death in July 1999. His son, Mohammed VI has already adopted a more populist, reforming agenda vowing to tackle the huge developmental problems in Morocco – specifically high unemployment, poverty and illiteracy.

It was also hoped that with the new king the disputed territory of the Western Sahara would be resolved. The current situation dates back to 1975 and the 'Green March', when 350,000 unarmed Moroccans marched into the Spanish colony as the Spanish were first talking of withdrawal, which took place shortly afterwards. The Polisario Front, which had been struggling for years against Spanish rule, turned to fight its new overlords. In 1991, the United Nations brokered a cease-fire on the understanding that a referendum on the territory's future would be held in 1992. The vote still has not been held, largely due to a dispute over who should be eligible to vote. Publicly all parties still support a vote, but it's unlikely to take place until 2002.

GEOGRAPHY

One of Africa's most geographically diverse areas, Morocco is spectacularly beautiful. It is traversed by four mountain ranges. From north to south, they are the Rif, the Middle Atlas, the High Atlas and the Anti-Atlas. Certain peaks of the High Atlas remain snow-capped all year and are among the highest in Africa.

Between the mountain ranges themselves, and between these ranges and the Atlantic Ocean, are plateaus and plains. Fed by melting snow, they are fertile and well watered, though on many of the plains farther south, agriculture is tenuous, except along certain river courses. In the extreme south the country is characterised by vast, eroded gorges which, like the rivers that flow at their bases, gradually peter out in the endless sand and stone wastes of the Sahara Desert.

CLIMATE

The geological variety is mirrored by wide ranging climatic conditions.

Weather in the coastal regions is generally mild, but can become cool and wet, particularly in the north. Average temperatures in Tangier and Casablanca range from about 12°C (54°F) in winter up to 25°C (77°F) and above in summer. Rainfall is highest in the Rif and northern Middle Atlas, where only the summer months are almost dry. The Atlantic coast remains agreeable year round, cooled by sea breezes. The southern Atlantic coast is more arid.

Marrakesh and the interior of Morocco can become stiflingly hot in summer, easily exceeding 40°C, particularly when the desert winds from the Sahara (known as the *sirocco* or *chergui*, from the Arabic *ash-sharqi*, meaning 'the easterly') are blowing. The chergui can occur at any time of the year, but is most common in spring. Even in winter, these lowlands can be quite hot during the day, with the mercury hitting 30°C, but temperatures drop quickly in the evening. In the desert, the dry atmosphere means that temperatures can swing wildly from baking days to freezing (quite literally) nights.

The rainy season is from November to January, but can go on as late as April. This cooler spell is the best time to visit desert and oases. However, recent years have been typified by drought. Drought years seem to now rotate on a two-year cycle, with devastating effects on agriculture.

In winter the mountains, can get as cold as -20°C (without taking the wind-chill factor into account), with snow often blocking mountain passes so take enough warm clothing to cope with an unwelcome night stuck in an unheated bus.

ECOLOGY & ENVIRONMENT

Deforestation and soil erosion are major problems in some areas. Nevertheless, springtime can see blazes of colourful wildflowers and there are still pine and cedar forests in the north and rolling wooded parkland towards

MOROCCO

the south. The fringes of the desert are graced with verdant *palmeraies* (palm groves).

Many larger 'African' mammals (eg, Barbary lion) have become extinct though wild boar, large wild sheep *(mouflon)* and macaque monkeys can be seen in the Atlas. The more arid regions are home to gazelles and fennec foxes, but they're quite rare.

Thanks to its diverse climate and habitat, and importance as a stopover for migratory birds, Morocco has much to offer the bird-watcher. More than 300 species have been recorded, including huge concentrations of migrating storks, hawks and eagles in spring and autumn; colourful bee-eaters and rollers; and the majestic bustards and graceful cranes.

GOVERNMENT & POLITICS

The kingdom of Morocco is ruled by King Mohammed VI who came to the throne in July 1999. During his father's reign, King Hassan II, the country's constitution had been considerably modernised with the introduction of an elected lowered chamber and a system of multiparty politics. The government is now a coalition, with the socialist Abderrahmane Youssoufi as prime minister.

Mohammed VI intends to build on these developments and has been quick to accelerate the release of political prisoners (a process which began in the early 90s) and has apologised for past political disappearances. While Moroccans now live in a more politically tolerant state, and the climate of fear that many maintain existed under Hassan II has largely disappeared, a few political detentions continue (especially related to the Western Sahara) and insulting the king remains a widely interpreted criminal offence. However, the government continues a dialogue with pressure groups such as Amnesty International.

Despite these democratic moves, Morocco remains essentially an absolute monarchy. The king retains the right to appoint his prime minister and all ministers subsequently chosen by the prime minister must be approved by the king. The major ministries of justice, foreign affairs and internal affairs remain very firmly in the hands of the king. The 275-seat upper house consists of deputies indirectly elected from local and regional government, professional bodies and trade unions.

ECONOMY

The mainstays of Morocco's economy are agriculture, mining, tourism, manufacturing, and remittances from Moroccans abroad.

Morocco is the world's third-largest exporter of phosphates and tourism is now a major foreign exchange earner. However, the country is still largely dependent on agriculture and a series of drought years has greatly restricted Morocco's promising economic growth.

Years of IMF-imposed austerity measures, followed by continued public spending cuts and massive privatisation, have made the economy leaner and fitter – but not without serious social costs, such as rising unemployment.

The economic hope for Morocco is a free trade agreement signed with the European Union (EU) and that came into force in March 2000. By 2012 all trade barriers between Morocco and the EU will have been removed. The payoff for Europe should be a tighter clamp on the flow of drugs (a multi-billion dollar trade) and access to new markets. Huge EU investment in Morocco's infrastructure and development are planned, but for Morocco to benefit from free trade much economic modernisation is needed.

POPULATION & PEOPLE

The population is estimated to be 30 million and growing at around 1.8%. The largest city is Casablanca, with a population of around five million.

The bulk of the population is made up of Arab and Berber peoples who have inter-married over the centuries. Morocco once hosted a large population of Jews, but the vast majority left after the foundation of Israel in 1948. Trade with trans-Saharan Africa brought a population of black Africans into Morocco many of whom originally came as slaves.

ARTS

Two things that immediately strike the visitor to Morocco are the music and the architecture. The former is drawn from many traditions, from classics of the Arab-Andalucían heritage through to the more genuinely African rhythms of Berber music. Raï, a fusion of traditional, tribal and modern Western popular forms and instruments, began in Algeria and has become very popular in Morocco. Cheap cassettes are easily obtained throughout the country.

With the exception of what the Arabs left behind in Spain, nothing in Europe can prepare you for the visual feast of the great mosques and *medersas* (Koranic schools) that bejewel the major Moroccan cities. Lacking the extravagance of the Gothic or rococo, Moroccan monuments are virtuoso pieces of geometric design and harmony.

SOCIETY & CONDUCT

It is easy to be beguiled by appearances in Morocco. Despite the impact of the West, Morocco remains a largely conservative Muslim society. As a rule, a high degree of modesty is demanded of both sexes in dress as well as behaviour. Women, in particular, are well advised to keep their shoulders and upper arms covered and to opt for long skirts or trousers (beach resorts such as Agadir are an exception).

You should always ask permission before taking photographs – urban Moroccans usually have no problem with this. As a rule, women especially do *not* want to be photographed. Respect their right to privacy and don't take photos.

If invited into a Moroccan home, it is customary to remove your shoes before stepping onto the carpet. Food is served in common dishes and eaten with the right hand. In Muslim countries the left hand is used for personal hygiene after visiting the toilet and should not be used to eat with or to touch any common source of food or water, or to hand over money or presents.

All mosques and religious buildings in active use are off limits to non-Muslims. Cemeteries are pretty much no-go areas too – don't take shortcuts through them.

RELIGION

All but a tiny minority of the population is Sunni Muslim, but in Morocco, Islam is far from strictly orthodox. The main difference lies in the worship of local saints and holy people *(marabouts)* a sort of resurgence of pre-Islamic traditions. The whitewashed *koubba* (tomb) of the marabout is a common sight all over the Maghreb (north-west Africa).

Where these local saints have accumulated many followers, prosperous individuals have endowed the koubba with educational institutions known as *zawiyyas*, which offer an alternative to the orthodox medersas attached to mosques.

LANGUAGE

Arabic is the official language, but Berber and French are widely spoken. Spanish is spoken in former Spanish-held territory (particularly the north) and some English in the main tourist centres. Arabic and French are taught in schools and French is important in university education and commerce.

Although many Moroccans speak many different languages passably, don't expect much beyond Moroccan Arabic and French outside the main cities and popular tourist spots.

Spoken Moroccan Arabic *(darija)* is considerably different from what you hear in the Middle East. Pick up a copy of Lonely Planet's *Moroccan Arabic phrasebook* for more detailed coverage. Various Berber dialects are spoken in the countryside and particularly in the mountains.

See the Language Guide at the back of this book for pronunciation guidelines and useful words and phrases.

Facts for the Visitor

HIGHLIGHTS

The four great cities of Morocco's imperial past are Fès, Marrakesh, Meknès and Rabat. Here you will discover Morocco's greatest monuments, mosques and medersas surrounded by the colour of the medina and *souqs* (markets).

In just a few days you can sample the breathtaking heights of the Atlas Mountains, sprinkled with Berber villages, and then head south for the oases and *kasbahs* of the Drâa Valley and the Dadès and Todra Gorges.

The Atlantic coast is dotted with tranquil towns bearing the marks of European occupation. Among the more interesting are the former Portuguese settlements of Asilah and El-Jadida, as well as Essaouira. There are plenty of decent beaches along the Atlantic and Mediterranean coasts.

MOROCCO

SUGGESTED ITINERARIES

Depending on how much time you have, you might want to do the following:

One to two weeks
   Visit the imperial cities (Fès, Meknès, Marrakesh and Rabat).
Two to three weeks
   Visit Marrakesh, the High Atlas, the southern oases and gorges, and finish on the coast at Essaouira.
One month
   At a pinch you could take in the imperial cities, some trekking, the southern oases and gorges, Essaouira and perhaps the Rif Mountains around Chefchaouen.

PLANNING
When to Go

The most pleasant times to explore Morocco are during spring (April to May) and autumn (September to October). Midsummer can be very enjoyable on the coast but viciously hot in the interior. Likewise, winter can be idyllic in Marrakesh and farther south during the day, but you can be chilled to the bone at night.

Snow blocks the passes in the High Atlas during winter when trekkers need to be equipped for sub-zero conditions. During winter it also gets surprisingly cold across the north-western part of the country.

Maps

The best map is the Michelin No 959 *Morocco* (scale 1:1,000,000). In Rabat, the Cartography Division of the Conservation & Topography Department (☎ 295034, fax 295549) is on Ave Hassan II, near the Centre de Transfusion Sanguine, 4km from the city centre. It stocks a range of maps, including topographical sheets (useful for hiking). Unfortunately, you must make an official request for any maps you want, a process that can take days.

What to Bring

Bring any special medication you need. It's a good idea to use sun protection (eg, a hat, sunglasses and sunscreen) year round. A sleeping bag can be useful in winter. Also bring your own contraceptives – you can get hold of condoms and even the pill, but quality is dubious and availability uncertain.

TOURIST OFFICES
Local Tourist Offices

The national tourist body, ONMT, has offices (usually called Délégation Régionale du Tourisme) in the main cities. The head office (☎ 730562) is in Rabat on Rue al-Abtal, Abtal district. A few cities also have local offices known as *syndicats d'initiative*. Some are much better than others, though all have brochures and simple maps to dispense.

Tourist Offices Abroad

The ONMT maintains offices in Australia (Sydney), Belgium (Brussels), Canada (Montreal), France (Paris), Germany (Düsseldorf), Italy (Milan), Japan (Tokyo), Portugal (Lisbon), Spain (Madrid), Sweden (Stockholm), Switzerland (Zürich), the UK (London) and the USA (New York and Orlando).

VISAS

Most visitors to Morocco need no visa and on entry are granted leave to remain in the country for 90 days. Exceptions include nationals of Israel, South Africa and Zimbabwe. Visa requirements can change, so check with the Moroccan embassy in your country or a reputable travel agent before travelling.

Entry requirements for Ceuta and Melilla are the same as for Spain (see that chapter).

Visa Extensions

If the 90 days you are entitled to are insufficient, the simplest thing to do is leave (eg, to the Spanish enclaves) and come back a few days later. Your chances improve if you re-enter by a different route.

People on visas may, however, prefer to try for an extension (this may take up to two weeks). Go to the nearest police headquarters (or *Préfecture*) with your passport, four photos proof of sufficient funds and, preferably, a letter from your embassy requesting a visa extension on your behalf.

EMBASSIES & CONSULATES
Moroccan Embassies & Consulates

Australia (☎ 02-9922 4999) Suite 2, 11 West St, North Sydney, NSW 2060
Canada (☎ 416-236 7391) 38 Range Rd, Ottawa KIN 8J4

France (☎ 01-45 20 69 35) 5 Rue Le Tasse, Paris 75016
Germany (☎ 228 35 50 44) Gotenstrasse, 7-9-5300, Bonn 2
Japan (☎ 03-478 3271) Silva Kingdom 3, 16-3, Sendagaya, Shibuya-ku, Tokyo 151
Netherlands (☎ 70-346 9617) Oranjestraat 9, 2514 JB, The Hague
Spain (☎ 91-563 1090) Calle Serrano 179, 28002 Madrid
Tunisia (☎ 01-782 775) 39 Avenue du 1er Juin, Mutuelleville, Tunis
UK (☎ 0171-581 5001) 49 Queen's Gate Gardens, London SW7 5NE
USA (☎ 202-462 7979) 1601 21st St NW, Washington DC 20009

Embassies & Consulates in Morocco

Most embassies are in Rabat but there are also consulates in Tangier, Marrakesh and Casablanca. Embassies in Rabat (telephone code ☎ 07) include:

Algeria (☎ 765474) 46-8 Ave Tariq ibn Zayid
 Consulate (☎ 710452) 11 Blvd Bir Anzarane, Oujda
Canada (☎ 672880) 13 Rue Jaafar as-Sadiq, Agdal
France (☎ 777822) 3 Rue Sahnoun, Agdal
 Service de Visas (☎ 702404) Rue Ibn al-Khatib
Germany (☎ 709662) 7 Zankat Madnine
Japan (☎ 631782) 39 Ave Ahmed Balafrej Souissi
Netherlands (☎ 733512) 40 Rue de Tunis
Spain (☎ 768989) 3-5 Zankat Madnine
 Consulate (☎ 704147) 57 Rue du Chellah
Tunisia (☎ 730636) 6 Ave de Fès
UK (☎ 729696) 17 Blvd de la Tour Hassan
USA (☎ 762265) 2 Ave de Marrakesh

CUSTOMS

You can import up to 200 cigarettes and 1L of spirits duty-free.

MONEY

The unit of currency is the dirham (Dr), which is equal to 100 centimes. The importation or exportation of local currency is prohibited and there's not much of a black market and little reason to use it.

In the Spanish enclaves of Ceuta and Melilla the currency is the Spanish peseta (pta).

Exchanging Money

Banking services are generally quick and efficient. Branches of BMCE (Banque Marocaine du Commerce Extérieur) are the most convenient and often have separate *bureau de change* sections. Almost all banks charge commission on travellers cheques (around Dr10 per cheque).

Australian, Canadian and New Zealand dollars are not quoted in banks and are generally not accepted.

country	unit		dirham
Australia	A$1	=	Dr6.14
Canada	C$1	=	Dr7.47
euro	€ 1	=	Dr9.57
France	1FF	=	Dr1.46
Germany	DM1	=	Dr4.89
Japan	¥100	=	Dr10.41
New Zealand	NZ$1	=	Dr4.62
UK	UK£1	=	Dr15.61
USA	US$1	=	Dr11.03

Credit and Debit Cards Major credit cards are widely accepted in the main tourist centres although their use often attracts a surcharge. American Express is represented by the travel agency Voyages Schwartz, which can be found in Rabat, Casablanca, Marrakesh and Tangier.

Automatic teller machines *(guichets automatiques)* are now a common site and many accept Visa, MasterCard, Electron, Cirrus, Maestro and InterBank. BMCE and Crédit du Maroc ATMs are a good bet.

Costs

Moroccan prices are refreshingly reasonable. With a few small tips here and there plus entry charges to museums and the like, you can get by on US$20 to US$25 a day per person as long as you stay in cheap hotels, eat at cheap restaurants and are not in a hurry. If you'd prefer some of life's basic luxuries, such as hot showers, the occasional splurge at a good restaurant and the odd taxi, plan on US$30 to US$35 a day.

If you're under 26, an international student card can get you big reductions on internal flights (and some international flights) and international rail fares departing from Morocco.

MOROCCO

Tipping & Bargaining

Tipping and bargaining are integral parts of Moroccan life. Practically any service can warrant a tip, but don't be railroaded. The judicious distribution of a few dirham for a service willingly rendered can, however, make your life a lot easier. Between 5% and 10% of a restaurant bill is about right.

When souvenir-hunting, decide beforehand how much you are prepared to spend on an item (to get an idea of prices, visit the Ensemble Artisanals in the major cities), but be aware that carpet vendors often start with hugely inflated prices. If this is so wait until the price has reduced considerably before making your first (low) offer, then approach your limit slowly.

POST & COMMUNICATIONS
Post

The Moroccan post is fairly reliable, including poste restante. Take your passport to claim mail. There's a small charge for collecting letters.

Outgoing parcels have to be inspected by customs (at the post office) so don't turn up with a sealed parcel. Nifty flat-pack boxes are available.

Telephone & Fax

The telephone system in Morocco is good. Private sector *téléboutiques* are widespread and much quicker (though fractionally more expensive) than the official phone offices, which are being phased out. Attendants sell phonecards (*télécartes*) and provide change. Téléboutiques are marked on maps throughout this chapter. Phone cards for public phones are still available from some post offices

Calls are expensive: a three-minute call to the USA will cost about US$3 and a three-minute call to Europe at least US$2. For international calls, there is a 20% reduction between 8 pm and 8 am weekdays and throughout the weekend.

Reverse charge (collect) calls to most countries are possible. A list of toll-free numbers connecting you to an operator in the country you wish to call can be found in the Moroccan phone book (*Annuaire des Abonnés au Téléphone*).

When calling overseas from Morocco, dial ☎ 00, your country code and then the city code and number. Morocco's country code is 212.

Many téléboutiques have fax machines. Prices per page vary but you can expect to pay about Dr50 to Europe and Dr70 to North America and Australia.

Email & Internet Access

Internet cafes have sprung up all over Morocco. See Information under each town for addresses.

One hour on the Internet costs between Dr10 and Dr25. The machines are new and access fairly reliable, though the Net is quicker in the morning.

INTERNET RESOURCES

There are numerous Internet sites about Morocco – www.maghreb.net, www.mincom.gov.ma, www.morocco.com and www.i-cias.com/mor.htm will get you started.

BOOKS

See Lonely Planet's *Morocco* for more detailed information on the country.

The Moors: Islam in the West by Michael Brett & Werner Forman details Moorish civilisation at its height, with superb colour photographs. *Histoire du Maroc* by Bernard Lugan is a potted history of the country. *The Conquest of Morocco* by Douglas Porch examines the takeover of Morocco by Paris.

Doing Daily Battle by Fatima Mernissi, translated by Mary Jo Lakeland, is a collection of interviews with 11 Moroccan women giving a valuable insight into their lives and aspirations. A number of Western writers have connections with Morocco, including long-term Tangier resident, Paul Bowles.

For High Atlas trekking information beyond the two-day trek, consult the *Great Atlas Traverse Morocco* by Michael Peyron. Volume I (Moussa Gorges to Aït ben Wgemmez) covers the Toubkal area. Another excellent guide (in French) is *Le Haut Atlas Central* by André Fougerolles. Detailed maps are available in Rabat (see Maps in the Facts for the Visitor section).

NEWSPAPERS & MAGAZINES

Foreign press is available at central newsstands in the major centres. News magazines such as *Newsweek* and *Time* are usually fairly easy to find, along with the *International Herald Tribune* and some UK papers, including the *International Guardian*, and their

Continental European equivalents. The French press is the most up-to-date and by far the cheapest.

RADIO & TV
Local radio is in Arabic and French, and you can pick up Spanish broadcasts in most parts of the country. Midi 1 (97.5 FM) is a good French language station covering northern Morocco. The BBC broadcasts into the area on short-wave frequencies 15,070 MHz and 12,095MHz, from about 8 am to 11 pm.

Satellite television provides several foreign channels, including CNN, NBC and Canalǵ. The two government-owned stations, TVM and 2M, broadcast in Arabic and French.

TIME
Moroccan time is GMT/UTC all year, so when it's summer in Europe, Morocco will be two hours behind Spanish time and one hour behind UK time.

LAUNDRY
You're better off doing it yourself. Most cheap hotels will do it for you, but it takes time. Establishments called *Pressings* are really dry-cleaners, and a full load will be very expensive.

TOILETS
Public toilets are few and far between so you're better off using toilets in cafes and hotels – you'll need your own paper, a tip for the attendant, stout-soled shoes and a nose clip. They are mostly of the 'squatter' variety.

WOMEN TRAVELLERS
Although a certain level of sexual harassment is almost the norm, in some ways Morocco can be less problematic than more overtly macho countries such as Italy and Spain. Harassment is generally of the leering, verbal variety. In the bigger cities especially, female travellers will receive hopeful greetings from every male over the age of 13! Ignore them entirely. Women will save themselves a great deal of grief by dressing modestly that means keeping shoulders and upper arms covered, opting for long skirts and trousers and avoiding anything skintight. It's wise not to walk around alone at night as after dark all 'good' Moroccan women are at home.

GAY & LESBIAN TRAVELLERS
Homosexual acts are officially illegal in Morocco – in theory you can go to jail and/or get fined. However, although not openly admitted or shown, male homosexuality remains relatively common. Male homosexuals are advised to be discreet; aggression towards gay male travellers is not unheard of.

Gay women shouldn't encounter any particular problems, though it's commonly believed by Moroccans that there are no lesbians in their country.

DANGERS & ANNOYANCES
Morocco's era as a hippy paradise, riding the Marrakesh Express and all that, is long past. Plenty of fine dope may be grown in the Rif Mountains, but drug busts are common and Morocco is not a good place to investigate local prison conditions. The vast majority of shake-down stories and rip-offs in Morocco are drug related. A common ploy is to get you stoned, force you to buy a piece the size of a house brick and then turn you over to the police (or threaten to).

Those disembarking (and embarking) the ferry in Tangier should expect at least some hassle from touts and hustlers trying to pull you one way or the other (usually to a hotel/ferry ticket office where they can expect a commission). Ceuta and Melilla are far more pleasant ports of entry.

On some of the more popular tourist routes, in particular the road between Marrakesh and Ouarzazate, you may come across professional hitchhikers and people pretending that their cars have broken down. Once you stop to assist them various scams unfold.

Morocco has its share of pickpockets and thieves but they're not a major problem.

The police can be reached on ☎ 19 and the highway emergency service on ☎ 177.

Guides
A few years ago *Brigade Touristique* (special tourist police) were set up in the principal tourist centres to clamp down on Morocco's notorious *faux guides* (false guides) and hustlers. Any person suspected of trying to operate as an unofficial guide could face jail and/or a huge fine.

This has reduced, but not eliminated, the problem of the faux guides. You'll still find plenty hanging around the entrances to the big city medinas and outside bus and train stations. They can be persistent and sometimes unpleasant. If you don't want their services, ignore their offers and try not to get your feathers ruffled – and note they smell fear.

If you end up with one of these people remember their main interest is the commission gained from certain hotels or on articles sold to you in the souqs.

Official guides can be engaged through tourist offices and most hotels at the fixed price of Dr120 per half day (plus tip). It's well worth taking a guide when exploring the intricate and confusing medinas of Fès and Marrakesh. Their local knowledge is extensive and they'll save you from being hassled by other would-be guides. If you don't want a shopping expedition included in your tour, make this clear beforehand.

BUSINESS HOURS

Banking hours are weekdays 8.30 to 11.30 am and 2.30 to 4.30 pm with Friday lunch lasting from 11.15 am to 3 pm. During Ramadan hours are 9 am to 3 pm. These times can vary a little. In some of the main tourist cities currency exchange offices keep longer hours and open over the weekend. Post offices generally keep similar hours, but don't close until around 6 pm. *Téléboutiques* and Internet cafes are open until around 10 pm. Many museums and some monuments are closed on Tuesday.

PUBLIC HOLIDAYS & SPECIAL EVENTS

All banks, post offices and most shops are shut on the main public holidays. The 10 national secular holidays are:

New Year's Day 1 January
Independence Manifesto 11 January
Feast of the Throne 13 July
Labour Day 1 May
National Day 23 May
Young People's Day 9 July
Allegiance of Wadi-Eddahab 14 August
Anniversary of the King's and People's Revolution 20 August
Anniversary of the Green March 6 November
Independence Day 18 November

In addition to secular holidays there are many Islamic holidays and festivals, all tied to the lunar calendar. Some are celebrated all over the country but others are local events.

Probably the most important is the Aïd al-Fitr, held at the end of the month-long Ramadan fast, which is fairly strictly observed by most Muslims. The festivities generally last four or five days, during which just about everything grinds to a halt.

Another important Muslim festival is Aïd al-Adha, which marks the end of the Islamic year. It commemorates Abraham's submission to God through the offer of his son Isaac for sacrifice. Again, most things shut down for four or five days. The third main religious festival, known as Mawlid an-Nabi (or simply Mouloud), celebrates the Prophet Mohammed's birthday.

Local festivals, mostly in honour of marabouts (saints) and known as *moussems* or *amouggars*, are common among the Berbers and usually held in the summer months.

ACTIVITIES
Camel Treks

For many travellers, a camel expedition into the desert is a real highlight of a trip to the south. Though fairly expensive (from Dr300 per person) and hard on the bottom, it's a great way to experience the silence and beauty of the landscape.

Surfing & Windsurfing

With thousands of kilometres of Atlantic coastline, Morocco has some great surfing spots – the surf club in Rabat is a good place for information. Places worth investigating include the beaches around Kenitra; Media Beach, a few kilometres north of Rabat; and Anchor Point in Agadir. For windsurfing, Essaouira is the place to head for.

Trekking

The mountains of Morocco are varied and not to be underestimated – ascending Jebel Toubkal (4167m), the highest peak, may take just two days but the altitude takes its toll. However, by hiring guides and mules (from Dr200 per day) most mountainous areas can be explored for weeks at a time. Early spring is the best time to go (for more details see the High Atlas Trekking section).

ACCOMMODATION
Camping
You can camp anywhere in Morocco if you have permission from the site's owner. There are also many official sites, where you'll pay around Dr10 per person plus Dr10 to pitch a tent. There are extra charges for vehicles, electricity and hot water.

Hostels
There are hostels *(auberges de jeunesse)* at Asni, Azrou, Casablanca, Chefchaouen, Fès, Marrakesh, Meknès, Rabat and Tangier. If you're travelling alone, they are among the cheapest places to stay (between Dr20 to Dr30 a night).

Hotels
You'll find cheap, unclassified hotels clustered in certain parts of the medinas of the bigger cities. Singles/doubles cost from Dr30/50; showers are often cold, but there are always *hammams* (bath houses) nearby. Some of these places are bright and spotless, others haven't seen a mop for years.

For a little more, you can often find better, unclassified or one-star hotels outside the medinas. In one-star hotels, singles/doubles with shower start at around Dr60/120; rooms in two-star hotels start at around Dr150/200. Prices can include breakfast, which is hardly ever a good deal – coffee and a croissant is Dr7 to Dr10 in a cafe.

The additional star in the three-star category (from Dr200/250) gets you a TV and a telephone. Hotels in the five-star category (from Dr1000 for a double) range from rather sterile modern places to former palaces.

FOOD
For those prepared to seek out the best, Moroccan food is superb. Influenced by Berber, Arabic and Mediterranean (particularly Spanish and French) traditions, the cuisine features a sublime use of spices and the freshest of local produce.

Restaurant food, particularly in the touristy zones, can be variable. Head for the places full of locals and you won't go far wrong. Typical dishes include *tajine*, a meat and vegetable stew cooked slowly in an earthenware dish and *couscous*, fluffy steamed semolina served with tender meat and vegetables and sometimes a spicy sauce. The preparation of couscous is laborious and most cheap restaurants only serve it on Fridays, the day it's traditionally eaten.

Harira, a thick soup made from lamb stock, lentils, chickpeas, onions, tomatoes, fresh herbs and spices, is usually eaten as a first course in the evening, but is substantial enough to make a meal on its own. In a cheap restaurant a bowl costs Dr4 or Dr5.

Salads are served everywhere, the nicest being the traditional *salade marocaine* made from finely diced green peppers, tomatoes and red onion. *Brochettes* (skewered meat barbecued over hot coals) or roast chicken served with crispy *frites* (french fries) are other staples.

Pastilla, a speciality of Fès, is a very rich and delicious dish made from pigeon meat and lemon-flavoured eggs, plus almonds, cinnamon, saffron and sugar, encased in layer upon layer of very fine *ouarka* pastry.

Vegetarians shouldn't have any major problems – fresh fruit and vegetables as well as a range of pulses, such as lentils and chickpeas, are widely available. When ordering couscous or tajine, simply ask for your dish to be served *sans viande* (without meat).

Coffee and croissant (around Dr8) is a good, cheap breakfast. Even cheaper and really delicious is a breakfast of *bessara* (pea soup with spices and olive oil), fresh bread and sweet mint tea. You'll find bessara stalls near the central markets.

Morocco is full of patisseries which produce excellent French and Moroccan pastries. This is where the locals head in the early evening.

If you're on a very tight budget, you can eat for as little as Dr50 per day. A three-course meal in a medium-priced restaurant will cost around Dr80 (without beer or wine). If you want to treat yourself to a meal in a traditional Moroccan palace restaurant or a smart French place, expect to pay upwards of Dr150 per person.

DRINKS
Morocco is bursting at the seams with cafes where sipping mint tea or coffee is a serious occupation. More often than not, the cafe is an all-male preserve and female travellers may prefer to head for the patisseries.

MOROCCO

Mint tea is made with Chinese gunpowder tea, fresh mint and vast quantities of sugar. It's usually served in elegant Moroccan teapots and poured into small glasses. In restaurants it may be just served by the glass. English tea is usually served black and is invariably known as *thé Lipton*. Coffee is served in the French style: short black or large milky white. *Qahwa ness-ness* is half coffee, half milk served in a glass.

It's not advisable to drink the tap water in Morocco, though in the major cities you should be all right. Local bottled water is available everywhere and costs Dr5 for a big bottle (more in restaurants). Water taken from streams in the mountains should be treated with purification tablets.

Beer is reasonably easy to find in the villes nouvelles. A bottle of local Stork or Flag beer typically costs from Dr12 to Dr15 in bars (more than double that in fancy hotels). Imported beer is very expensive. Morocco produces some quite palatable wines (the whites and rosés are better than the reds) for as little as Dr35 in liquor stores.

ENTERTAINMENT

Morocco isn't exactly the last word in nightlife. The major cities do have some good cinemas (movies dubbed into French) and there are bars, discos and nightclubs to be found. The latter three tend to be dubious or rather exclusive or both. Plenty of hotels and restaurants provide traditional music to accompany dinner. The best opportunities to hear music, however, will be at the annual festivals and moussems.

SHOPPING

Moroccan crafts are world-famous for their variety and quality. Items to look for include traditional carpets (Rabat) and flatweave rugs, ceramics (Fès and Safi), chased brass and copperware (Marrakesh, Fès and Tetouan), painted woodwork (Fès), thuya woodcarvings (Essaouira), leather work and silver jewellery (Tiznit and Taroudannt).

Look around before buying anything. All the major cities have a government-run Ensemble Artisanal where you can look at good-quality items in peace and quiet and check the upper-range prices. See the Tipping & Bargaining section earlier.

Morocco has a tradition of perfume making and in the bigger cities you'll find large perfumeries where you can buy excellent copies (Dr49 for 20ml) of all the famous names.

Getting There & Away

AIR

Morocco is well served by air travel options from Europe, the Middle East and West Africa. The main entry point is the Mohammed V airport 30km south-east of Casablanca. International flights also land at other cities including Tangier, Agadir, Marrakesh, Fès and Ouarzazate. Air France and Royal Air Maroc (RAM) are the major carriers, but other airlines operating to Morocco include Alitalia, British Airways, Iberia, KLM, Lufthansa, Swissair and Gulf Air.

Europe & the UK

It is possible to find charter flights to Morocco from some Northern European cities such as Paris, Amsterdam, Brussels and Düsseldorf for the equivalent of around UK£200 or less. Charter tickets are generally return tickets and are usually not valid for more than one month.

In the high season, scheduled flights (valid for one month) between London and Casablanca are as much as UK£350. It is much cheaper to fly to Málaga (from as little as UK£69 one way) in southern Spain and then catch a ferry.

There are no cheap one-way flights out of Morocco. Expect to pay around Dr4500 for a standard fare to Northern Europe.

North America & Australasia

Royal Air Maroc and TWA have direct flights from New York to Casablanca (around US$1000), though fares from other Canadian and US cities (via Europe) will cost at least an extra US$200. It may be more economical to fly to Paris, Amsterdam or London and continue from there. There are no direct flights between Australia or New Zealand and Morocco. Head to a destination in Europe first.

LAND
Europe
Bus Eurolines and the Moroccan national bus line, CTM (Compagnie des Transports Marocains), operate buses between Morocco and many European cities. A one-way/return ticket valid for six months from London to Marrakesh costs UK£116/192. CTM buses to Paris, other European cities run regularly from the major Moroccan cities. One-way tickets start at Dr615 (Málaga) rising to Dr1200 (Paris).

The land border between Morocco and Algeria was closed in 1994 and at the time of writing looked set to remain so.

Train Trains give you the option of couchettes and breaking your trip along the way, though for the price of a rail ticket to Paris you can fly to Málaga in Southern Spain. A one-way/return ticket to Algeciras, via the Eurostar, valid for two months costs UK£153/272 – those over 26 pay 30% extra. Heading the other way, a one-way fare from Casablanca to London is Dr2220, less with a student card.

The Moroccan rail system is part of the Inter-Rail network. A two-zone ticket for unlimited 2nd-class train-travel for one month, and covering France, Belgium, the Netherlands, Spain and Morocco, costs UK£235 (or UK£169 if under 26). However, you need to have lived in Europe for six months. A single zone pass covering Spain and Morocco costs UK£179/129 and is valid for 22 days.

For non-EU residents Eurail Passes cover 17 European countries and will get you as far as Algeciras, but do not cover Morocco. Tickets start at US$470 for 15 days unlimited travel, but should be purchased outside the EU. They are also available from Rail Europe (☎ 0990 848848, French Railway House, 179 Piccadilly, W1V OBA) in London. Check out its Web site at www.raileurope.com.

BOAT
Spain
Car ferries are operated by Trasmediterranea, Islena de Navigación SA, Comarit, Limadet, Buquebus and Euroferrys. The most popular route is Algeciras-Tangier; others are Algeciras-Ceuta (Spanish Morocco), Ceuta-Málaga, Almeria-Melilla (Spanish Morocco), Málaga-Melilla, Gibraltar-Tangier and Cadiz-Tangier. Between Spanish Morocco and Spain hydrofoils are commonly used; the Tangier runs use drive-on and drive-off ferries.

Algeciras-Tangier There's a ferry roughly every hour, or 1½ hours, between 7 am to 9.30 pm (more in the high season). Adult one-way fares are 3200 ptas (Dr210). Children under 12 travel at half-price. A car up to 6m long costs 9900 ptas (Dr648). The crossing takes 2½ hours.

Cadiz-Tangier IMTC run this twice daily, three-hour, service. Fares are 3900 ptas (Dr250) one-way; cars 9900 ptas (Dr125).

Algeciras & Málaga-Ceuta There are up to 22 hydrofoil (35 minutes) and six ferry crossings (90 minutes) per day between Algeciras and Ceuta. The one-way fares are 2945ptas and 1800 ptas respectively. Cars cost from 8223 ptas on either service.

Buquebus run the twice daily Ceuta-Málaga hydrofoil (4995 ptas; cars 14900 ptas; 90 minutes).

Almeria & Málaga-Melilla Trasmediterranea has six overnight services a week from Almeria to Melilla, and Málaga to Melilla and vice versa. The crossing takes 6½ to eight hours and 7½ to 10 hours respectively. The cheapest one-way fare is 4020 ptas on either service. Cars cost 10,500 ptas and cabin space is available from 6710 ptas per person.

Gibraltar-Tangier
Bland Shipping run this thrice-weekly, passenger-only, service. The voyage (two hours) costs Dr260/Dr510 (UK£18/35) one way/ return.

France
The Sète-Tangier and Nador ferry service is operated by the Compagnie Marocaine de Navigation and the crossing is usually made every four to five days, takes 38 hours and costs roughly between 1500FF and 3630FF (children half-price) depending on class, season and number of people sharing. Cars cost between 1780FF and 2515FF. Departures, journey time and fares to Nador (summer only) are similar.

MOROCCO

Getting Around

AIR
Royal Air Maroc (RAM) have a good internal network and if you're under 22 or a student under 31, you are entitled to at least 25% (and often up to 60%) off all fares. The standard/student one-way fare between Casablanca and Tangier is Dr688/263 (about US$70/28); between Casablanca and Agadir it's Dr908/323 (about US$90/32).

BUS
There is a good network of bus routes all over the country; departures are frequent and tickets are cheap.

CTM (Compagnie des Transports Marocains) is really the only national company, though other companies (with smaller networks), such as SATAS, are just as good. On major inter-city routes it runs 1st- and 2nd-class services. There are more of the former than the latter, so you'll often be paying the higher fare (about 25% more) unless you're very flexible about departure times. Advance booking is advisable especially in smaller towns with few services. In many places, CTM has its own terminal.

Some examples of 1st-class CTM fares are:

from	to	fare (Dr)
Casablanca	Agadir	140
	Fès	80
	Marrakesh	65
	Tangier	110
Tangier	Fès	85
	Tiznit	260
Marrakesh	Fès	128
	Ouarzazate	52
Agadir	Laayoune	200
	Tangier	237

There is an official baggage charge on CTM buses (Dr5 per pack). On other lines baggage handlers may demand a little cash – Dr3 is OK.

TRAIN
Morocco has one of the most modern rail systems in Africa. Travel by train when you can. You have a choice of 1st and 2nd class in *ordinaire* and *rapide* trains. The latter are in fact no faster, but have air-con and are more comfortable. The former are cheaper, but usually restricted to evening services. The shuttle trains (TNR) between Rabat, Casablanca and Mohammed V international airport are in a class of their own. They are fast (Rabat to Casablanca in 55 minutes) and comfortable. The fares quoted are for 2nd-class travel, roughly comparable with bus fares. There's no need to go 1st class.

Couchettes are available on long-distance night trains between Marrakesh and Tangier. There are refreshment trolleys and sometimes buffet cars on the longer journeys too.

Timetables are prominently displayed in train stations, and a free book of timetables, *Indicateur Horaires,* is sometimes available at stations.

Supratours runs luxury buses in conjunction with trains to some destinations not on the rail network. Useful ones include Tetouan, Agadir and Essaouira. You can buy a bus-rail ticket to any place on the combined network.

CAR & MOTORCYCLE
You drive on the right in Morocco. An International Driving Permit is officially required, but most national licences are sufficient. Main roads are in decent condition, but many secondary roads are not so hot. Some mountain roads can be blocked by snow in winter, and desert roads are sometimes awash with sand drifts.

The traffic accident rate in Morocco is high; night driving can be particularly hazardous since cars, bicycles and donkeys may travel without lights.

The expanding motorway network now stretches from Casablanca to just short of Tangier and from Rabat to Fès. Tolls are payable and the speed limit on the motorway is 120km/h – elsewhere it's 100km/h (40 to 60km/h in built-up areas).

You should give way to traffic entering a roundabout from the right when you're already on one. It's compulsory for drivers and passengers to wear seatbelts.

There are frequent police and customs roadblocks, some set up with tyre-shredding traps. Always stop; often you'll be waved through, but have your licence and passport handy.

Most towns have paid-parking areas. They give some peace of mind and cost a few dirham for a few hours or Dr10 overnight.

Leaded, unleaded and diesel are the most widely available types of fuel. Fuel is much cheaper in the Spanish enclaves and the Western Sahara.

Rental

A hire car is ideal for exploring the southern oases and kasbah routes.

You'll find all the major companies in Moroccan cities, plus plenty of local companies. Renault 4 and Fiat Uno are cheapest (around Dr1400, plus 20% tax, for three days with unlimited kilometres; insurance is extra). You may be asked to leave a deposit of at least Dr3000 if not paying by credit card, and need to be at least 21 years old. Shop around and always haggle for discounts.

BICYCLE

Distances are great and you'll need to carry all supplies with you (including any spare parts you may need, food and plenty of drinking water), but the rewards are also great. Many roads are narrow and dusty. You can transport bikes on trains (the minimum charge is Dr20) and buses, but pack them well.

HITCHING

Hitching in Morocco is possible, but demands a thick skin and considerable diplomatic expertise in the north because of aggressive hustlers. Women should never hitch alone.

LOCAL TRANSPORT

The big cities have reasonable and useful local bus networks. A ride costs about Dr2.50.

Petits taxis (city taxis) are equally useful and cheap, provided the driver uses the meter and you have some idea of the fare. Fares around town shouldn't be more than Dr10. Multiple hire is common, and fares rise by about 50% after 8 pm.

Grands taxis work a little like buses. Usually ageing Mercedes, they take six passengers to a fixed destination for a standard fare and leave when full. They often leave more frequently than buses, are quicker and up to 50% more expensive.

The Mediterranean Coast & the Rif

TANGIER
☎ 09

Tangier is a major port of entry for tourists and was once home to hordes of the world's best hustlers. The Brigade Touristique (see Dangers & Annoyances earlier) has cracked down but Tangier is certainly not hassle free. However, give the place a couple of days, get a handle on the hassle and you'll find it a unique, likeable city buzzing with energy.

Tangier has been coveted for millennia as a strategic site commanding the Strait of Gibraltar. Settled as a trading port by the ancient Greeks and Phoenicians, Tangier has been occupied by the Romans, Vandals, Byzantines, Arabs, Berbers, Fatimids, Almoravids, Almohads, Merenids, Portuguese, Spanish, British and French. All the peoples who have settled here have left their mark.

In the late 19th and early 20th centuries, Tangier (Tanja to the locals) became the object of intense rivalry between the European powers. A solution was finally reached in 1923, when the city and surrounding countryside were declared an 'international zone' controlled by the resident diplomatic agents of France, Spain, Britain, Portugal, Sweden, Holland, Belgium, Italy and the USA. Even the Moroccan sultan was represented by an agent, appointed by the French resident-general.

During the 'Inter Zone' years, which ended with independence in 1956, Tangier became a fashionable Mediterranean resort renowned for its high-profile gay scene, and popular with freebooters, artists, writers, exiles and bankers. It was also an infamous haven for paedophiles.

Orientation

Like many larger Moroccan towns, Tangier is divided between the convoluted streets of the old medina and the wide, ordered boulevards of the ville nouvelle. The modern shops and offices and most of the restaurants and better hotels are in the latter area. The medina has markets, craft shops, cheaper hotels and smaller restaurants. The square known as the Petit Socco is the heart of the medina. The larger Grand Socco lies between the medina and the ville nouvelle.

MOROCCO

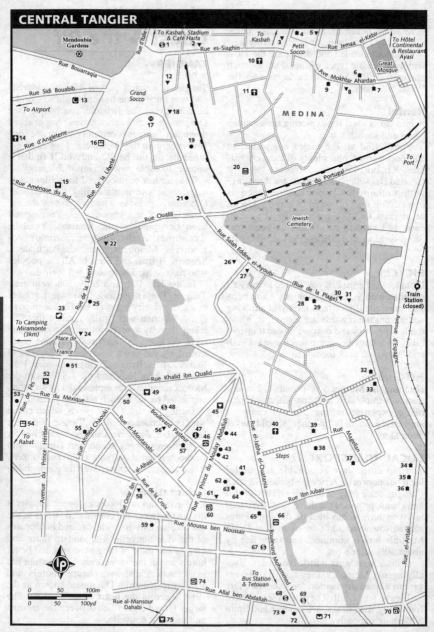

CENTRAL TANGIER

Mendoubia Gardens

Rue d'Italie

To Kasbah, Stadium & Café Haifa

To Kasbah

Rue Jemaa el-Kebir

To Hôtel Continental & Restaurant Ayasi

Great Mosque

Rue Bouarraqia

Rue es-Siaghin

Petit Socco

Ave Mokhtar Ahardan

Rue Sidi Bouabib

To Airport

Grand Socco

MEDINA

Rue d'Angleterre

Rue de la Liberté

Rue Amérique du Sud

To Port

Rue Oualili

Rue du Portugal

Jewish Cemetery

Rue Salah Eddine el-Ayoubi

Rue de la Liberté

(Rue de la Plage)

Train Station (closed)

To Camping Miramonte (3km)

Place de France

Avenue d'Espagne

Rue Khalid ibn Qualid

Rue de Fès

Rue du Méxique

Boulevard Pasteur

Rue Magellan

To Rabat

Rue Ahmed Chaouki

Rue el-Moutanabi

Rue du Prince Moulay Abdallah

Rue el-Jabha el-Ouatania

Rue

Steps

Avenue du Prince Héritier

Rue Omar ibn al-Ahass

Rue de la Croix

Rue ibn Jubair

Rue Moussa ben Noussair

Boulevard Mohammed V

To Bus Station & Tetouan

Rue Allal ben Abdallah

Rue al-Mansour Dahabi

Rue el-Antaki

0   50   100m
0   50   100yd

CENTRAL TANGIER

PLACES TO STAY
4 Pensión Mauritania
6 Hôtel Mamora
7 Hôtel Olid
9 Pension Palace
28 Pensión Miami
29 Pension Le Détroit
32 Pensión Majestic
33 Hôtel l'Marsa
34 Marco Polo & Bar
35 Hôtel El Djenina
36 Youth Hostel
37 Hôtel Magellan
38 Hôtel Ibn Batouta
39 Hôtel El Muniria & Tanger Inn
55 Hôtel Astoria
57 Hôtel de Paris
65 Hôtel Tanjah-Flandria; Le Palace Disco

PLACES TO EAT
2 Restaurant Mamounia Palace
3 Café Tingis
5 Restaurant Andalus
8 Restaurant Ahlan
12 Pâtisserie Charaf
18 Restaurant Economique

22 Restaurant Populaire
24 Café de Paris
26 Sandwich Genève
27 Sandwich Cervantes
30 Hassi Baida Restaurant
31 Restaurant Africa
50 Excel Food
56 Pâtisserie Le Petit Prince
58 Pizzeria Piazza Capri
61 Casa Pepé (Liquor Store)

OTHER
1 BMCE Bank (ATMs)
10 Church of the Immaculate Conception
11 Spanish Church
13 Mosque
14 St Andrew's Church
15 Dean's Bar
16 Cinéma Rif
17 Hammam
19 Covered Market
20 American Legation Museum
21 Covered Market
23 French Consulate
25 British Airways office
40 Church
41 Iberia Airlines
42 Transmediterranea Office

43 Limadet Boat Ticket Office
44 Budget
45 Les Ambassadeurs Bar
46 Telephone & Fax Office; Cyber Espace Pasteur
47 Tourist Office
48 BMCE (Late Bank & ATMs)
49 Paname Bar
51 Royal Air Maroc (RAM)
52 Hole-in-the-Wall Bar
53 Depôt de Nuit (Night Pharmacy)
54 Cinéma Le Paris
59 Paris Pressing (Laundry)
60 Cyber Café Adam
62 Librairie des Colonnes
63 Avis
64 Voyages Schwartz (American Express)
66 Téléboutique
67 Crédit du Maroc
68 Banque Populaire
69 Wafabank
70 Maghrib Net
71 Post Office
72 Hertz
73 Cady Loc (Car Rental)
74 Cyber Café Mam Net
75 London Pub

Information

Tourist Offices The Délégation Régionale du Tourisme (☎ 948050, 29 Blvd Pasteur) can arrange official guides and offers a limited range of brochures.

Money There are several banks along Blvd Pasteur and Blvd Mohammed V. The BMCE on Blvd Pasteur has ATMs and an exchange booth which is open from 8.30 am to 8 pm daily. Crédit du Maroc is further south on Blvd Mohammed V.

Post & Communications The main post office for *poste restante* (c/o Tangier Principle 90000) is on Blvd Mohammed V. The parcel counter is around the back of the building.

Internet services are available at Cyber Café Mam Net (53 Rue du Prince du Moulay Abdallah), and Maghrib Net on Rue al-Antaki. Both charge around Dr10 per hour.

Bookshops The Librairie des Colonnes (☎ 936955, 54 Blvd Pasteur) has a good selection of Francophone literature and some English novels. Librairie Dar Baroud at the Hotel Continental stocks a good range of English books on Morocco and translations of Moroccan authors.

Things to See

In the heart of the medina the **Petit Socco**, with its cafes and restaurants, is the focus of activity. In the days of the international zone this was the sin and sleaze centre and it retains something of its seedy air.

Heading north from the Petit Socco, Rue des Almohades takes you to the **kasbah**. Built on the highest point of the city, you enter from Bab el-Assa at the end of Rue Ben Raissouli in the medina. The gate opens onto a large courtyard leading to the 17th-century **Dar el-Makhzen**, the former sultan's palace. It's now a museum housing beautiful craftwork. It's open from 9 am to 12.30 pm and 3 to 5.30 pm daily, except Tuesday, and from 9 to 11.30 am Friday. Entry is Dr10.

MOROCCO

The **American Legation Museum** is a fascinating reminder that Morocco was the first country in the world to recognise US independence. This fine old building houses a fascinating collection of 17th to 20th-century paintings and prints. Knock on the door, it's open 10 am to 1 pm and 3 to 5 pm weekdays. Entrance is free but donations are greatly appreciated.

Places to Stay

Camping *Camping Miramonte* (☎ 947504) is about 3km west of the centre overlooking Jew's Bay and was undergoing some promising renovation work at the time of writing. It costs Dr15 per adult, plus Dr10 to pitch a tent and Dr10 for a car. Turn left off Ave Hassan II on to Rue des USA then first right down a narrow street to the grey gates (it's a Dr10 petits taxi ride).

Hostel Beds cost Dr27 at the *Youth Hostel* (☎ 946127, 8 Rue al-Antaki). Another Dr5 will get you a hot shower.

Hotels There are numerous small hotels in the medina around the Petit Socco and along Ave Mokhtar Ahardan, which connects the Petit Socco and the port area.

The European-style hotels in the ville nouvelle have the edge on comfort.

Medina Area There are plenty of cheap pensions, though many are now filled with economic refugees from West Africa. Most are basic, some have hot showers and singles/doubles cost around Dr40/80.

Two of the best are *Pension Palace* (☎ 936128) and *Hôtel Olid* (☎ 931310). Basic rooms cost Dr40/80 (Dr10 for a hot shower). The Palace's rooms are small but clean, and some surround a quiet courtyard. The Olid has seen better days, but the rooms come with private cold shower.

The best place on the Petit Socco is *Pensión Mauritania* (☎ 934677). Clean rooms with washbasin cost Dr35-45 per person.

Hôtel Mamora (☎ 934105, 19 Ave Mokhtar Ahardan) offers clean single/double rooms with shower for Dr197/230. Some rooms have beautiful views over the Great Mosque to the sea.

The pick of the crop is *Hôtel Continental* (☎ 931024, fax 931143, 36 Dar Baroud) perched above the port. It was used for some scenes in the film version of Paul Bowles' *The Sheltering Sky* and is full of character. Rooms go for Dr186/240 including breakfast.

There are several hammams around the Petit Socco and one at 80 Rue des Almohades.

Ville Nouvelle The unclassified hotels and pensions along Rue Salah Eddine el-Ayoubi are no better than the cheapies in the medina and similarly priced. Good value, and straight down the line, is *Pension Le Détroit* (☎ 934838), whilst *Pensión Miami* (☎ 932900) remains popular.

Hôtel L'Marsa (☎ 932339, 92 Ave d'Espagne) offers good value (Dr50/100) although the cafe next door can be noisy. Next door is the basic, but adequate, *Pensión Majestic* (☎ 937246). Singles/doubles cost Dr50/100 in summer. Hot showers cost Dr5.

There's a better selection of hotels on the steep and winding Rue Magellan, which starts beside Hotel Biarritz. *Hôtel Magellan* (☎ 372319) has good value rooms (some with views) for Dr40/80. Farther up are hotels *El Muniria* (☎ 935337) and *Ibn Batouta* (☎ 939311) – the latter has recently been renovated and has immaculate en suite rooms (Dr120/200) and a roof cafe. William Burroughs wrote *The Naked Lunch* while staying at the Muniria, which has characterful rooms with shower for Dr110/130.

A good choice of mid-range hotels can be found in the streets off Blvd Pasteur. *Hôtel de Paris* (☎ 931877, 42 Blvd Pasteur) has clean, comfortable rooms with shower for Dr220/270. The straight-forward *Hôtel Astoria* (☎ 937201, 10 Rue Ahmed Chaouki) offers pleasant rooms with showers for Dr136/180.

The German-run *Hôtel Marco Polo* (☎ 941124), on Rue el-Antaki, has impeccable rooms as well as a restaurant and lively bar. Singles/doubles cost Dr189/217. Next door, the recently refurbished *Hôtel El Djenina* (☎ 942244) has similarly priced rooms and a bar/restaurant.

The only top-end hotel in Tangier worth it's salt is the *El Minzah* (☎ 935885, ✉ elminzah@tangeroise.net.ma, 85 Rue de la Liberté). A wonderful reminder of the 1930s, rooms cost Dr1365/1630.

Places to Eat

Medina Area For really cheap food and self-catering head to the covered market and food stalls close to the Grand Socco. Numerous small cafes and restaurants here, and around the Petit Socco, offer cheap traditional fare. Just down the hill from Hôtel Continental, *Restaurant Ayasi (7 Rue Dar el-Baroud; unsigned)* serves excellent bessara in the morning; a filling bowl served with fresh French bread costs Dr5. Fish, chicken and tajines (Dr20) are served after 11 am.

On the east side of the Grand Socco, the tiny stall-like *Restaurant Economique* offers harira, bessara and brochettes all day long. *Restaurant Ahlan*, on Ave Mokhtar Ahardan is popular for lunch.

Just north of the Petit Socco, *Restaurant Andalus (7 Rue Commerce)* is a pleasant hole-in-the-wall serving great cheap meals including liver (Dr35) and sword fish (Dr45). Farther north, not far from the Agadir Bazaar, *Restaurant Sose (15 Mostafa Doukkali; unsigned)* serves a range of Moroccan staples and on Thursday specialises in couscous (Dr20). Closed Friday.

Restaurant Mamounia Palace (☎ 935099) on Rue es-Siaghin, offers full 'Moroccan feasts' tour-group style (Dr100 a throw).

To watch the world go by over coffee or mint tea, try the pleasantly faded *Café Tingis* on the Petit Socco. The *Pâtisserie Charaf*, just off the Grand Socco, serves an excellent selection of pastries.

Ville Nouvelle *Sandwich Cervantes* and *Sandwich Genève,* opposite each other on Rue Salah eddine el-Ayoubi, offer rolls filled with meat or fish and salad for Dr10.

Farther down towards Ave d'Espagne, *Restaurant Africa* at No 83 and, next door, *Hassi Baida* have set meals for around Dr50 or main courses from Dr30. The Africa is licensed and both places are open until 11 pm daily.

Restaurant Populaire, down the steps from Rue de la Liberté, is a local favourite serving excellent Moroccan food (especially fish dishes) at reasonable prices (Dr40). Don't miss it.

If you're desperate for Western-style fast food, *Excel Food* on Blvd Pasteur isn't bad. *Pizzeria Piazza Capri (☎ 937221, 2 Rue de la Croix)* makes a decent pizza for around Dr30.

More expensive meals can be had in the restaurants and cafes near Place de France (a coffee at the ageing *Café de Paris* is a must) and down Rue du Prince du Moulay Abdallah.

For wonderful cakes and savoury pastries try *Pâtisserie Le Petit Prince (34 Blvd Pasteur)*.

Hidden away in a tiny street behind the stadium is *Café Hafa,* set in shaded, terraced gardens overlooking the Straits of Gibraltar. A delightful place to while away the hot afternoon.

The liquor store *Casa Pepé (9 Rue Ibn Rochd)* stocks a decent selection of delicatessen foods such as French and Spanish salami, pâté and cheese.

Entertainment

Bars South of the Grand Socco on Rue Amérique du Sud is the famous *Dean's Bar* – hardly a Westerner of any repute did not prop up this bar at one time or another. Satisfyingly seedy and intimate, beer and tapas costs from Dr13.

Some particularly lively and colourful local bars include the *Hole in the Wall* on Ave du Prince Héritier, the *Paname* at 15 Blvd Pasteur, *Les Ambassadeurs* on Rue du Prince du Moulay Abdallah and the *Marco Polo* on Rue el-Antaki.

London Pub, Rue al-Mansour Dahabi, has live music every night and is a very civilised place. A remnant of Tangier's yesteryear, though a little quite these days, is the tiny *Tanger Inn*, next to the Hôtel El Muniria on Rue Magellan. It's open from 9 pm until late.

The much-reduced European gay population still frequents some of the beach bars south of town. Popular places include the *Macumba*, *Miami Beach* and *Coco Beach*.

Negrescu on the corner of Avenue Mexique and Avenue Prince Héritier, is a clean and calm bar with an adjacent restaurant.

Chico's Pub (10 rue de Soroya) has the feel of a piano bar, though it is very subdued. There's an extensive and expensive selection of liquors.

The Pilo on Avenue de Fes, just past Ave. Mexique intersection is a relaxed place, with high ceilings and '50s decor. There's plently of excellent tapas and the two large windows upstairs overlook Avenue Mexique and all the people cruising in the twilight hours.

MOROCCO

Nightclubs The three most popular night-clubs in town are: *Pasarela*, down by the beach on Ave des FAR; the *Olivia Valere* in the Ahlan Hôtel, about 5km along the road to Rabat; and *Le Palace* disco in Hôtel Tanjah-Flandria. Entry to all the clubs is around Dr100; drinks start at Dr40.

Morocco Palace on Prince Moulay Abdellah is decorated with excellent artisanal work throughout and popular live music (mostly contemporary Arabic music covers). It's a bit sleazy and there's supposedly a belly dancer late Friday and Saturday nights.

Pasarela, in the southern part of the ville nouvelle on Ave des FAR, is a large complex with several bars, an attractive garden and outdoor swimming pool. The music is a Western mix. It's open from 11.30 pm to 3 am.

Another popular place is the *Olivia Valere* nightclub in the Ahlan Hôtel, about 5km outside the city on the road to Rabat. *Le Palace* disco (Dr50) in the Hôtel Tanjah-Flandria. It's open from 9 pm to 3 am. The entrance is next to Cyber Café Adam.

Getting There and Away

Air Royal Air Maroc (☎ 979501, fax 932681) have daily flights to Casablanca (Dr688 one way), plus direct flights to Amsterdam, Brussels, London, Madrid and Paris. Regional Airlines fly to Málaga, Iberia fly to Madrid and British Airways to London.

Bus Most CTM buses leave from an office near the port entrance. Others (and some second class services) leave from the bus station on Place Jamia el-Arabia (an Dr8 Petit Taxi ride away). Most non-CTM buses leave from here to hundreds of destinations.

Regular CTM departures include Casablanca (Dr110), Rabat (Dr83), Tetouan (Dr13.50) and Fès (Dr85).

Train The only train station operating in Tangier, Tangier Morora, is about 5km south-east of town. Trains south from Tangier split at Sidi Kacem to Rabat (five hours), Casablanca (six hours) and Marrakesh (10½ hours), or to Meknès (five hours), Fès (six hours) and Oujda (12 hours). The only cheap *Ordinaire* service south (Marrakesh Dr143, Fès Dr74) leaves at 10.30 pm. There are three other *Rapide* departures. Take a petit taxi from town (about Dr13).

Taxi Grands taxis leave from the bus station; there are frequent departures to Tetouan (Dr20), Asilah (Dr20) and Fnideq (Dr25).

Car The following are among the car-rental agencies in Tangier:

Avis (☎ 933031) 54 Blvd Pasteur
Budget (☎ 948060) 7 Ave Prince Moulay Abdallah
Cady Loc (☎ 322207) 3 Allal Ben Abdellah
Europcar (☎ 941938) 87 Blvd Mohammed V
Hertz (☎ 332210) 36 Blvd Mohammed V

Boat If you're heading to Spain or Gibraltar by boat, you can buy tickets from virtually any travel agency or at the port itself. However, the port and entrance to the port can be a real hassle – be firm or you'll have someone following you around pointing out the bleeding obvious. Both the Limadet and Trasmediterranea offices are on Rue du Prince du Moulay Abdallah.

Getting Around

Local bus services in Tangier are not what they once were and few are of use to the traveller. Local departures leave from outside Mohammed V Mosque on Rue de Belgique.

Petit taxis are metered and cost under Dr10 around town.

TETOUAN
☎ 09

Tetouan's flavour is unmistakably Spanish-Moroccan, as a result of its settlement by Arab-Berber and Jewish refugees from Muslim Andalucía in the 16th century and subsequent occupation by the Spanish during the protectorate years. The whitewashed and tiled houses of the medina are dramatically set against the brooding Rif Mountains.

Although the hassle has calmed down in recent years, be prepared to meet some serious touts and hustlers. That said, it's well worth spending time here.

Information

The tourist office (☎ 961916) is at 30 Blvd Mohammed V. The staff are helpful and speak English.

There are plenty of banks along Blvd Mohammed V. The BMCE, on Place Moulay

TETOUAN

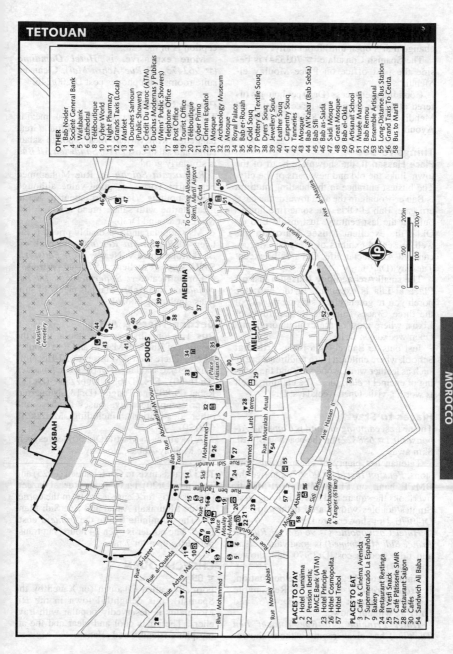

OTHER
1 Bab Noider
4 Société General Bank
5 Wafabank
6 Cathedral
8 Téléboutique
10 Cyber World
11 Night Pharmacy
12 Grands Taxis (Local)
13 Market
14 Douches Sarhoun (Public Showers)
15 Crédit Du Maroc (ATM)
16 Duchas Modernas y Publicas (Mens' Public Showers)
17 Telephone Office
18 Post Office
19 Tourist Office
20 Téléboutique
21 Cyber Primo
29 Cinéma Español
31 Mosque
32 Archaeology Museum
33 Mosque
34 Royal Palace
35 Bab er-Rouah
36 Gold Souq
37 Pottery & Textile Souq
38 Dyers' Souq
39 Jewellery Souk
40 Leather Souq
41 Carpentry Souq
42 Tanneries
43 Mosque
44 Bab M'Kabar (Bab Sebta)
45 Bab Sfli
46 Bab as-Saida
47 Saidi Mosque
48 Great Mosque
49 Bab el-Okla
50 Artisanat School
51 Musée Marocain
52 Bab Remou
53 Ensemble Artisanal
55 Long-Distance Bus Station
56 Grand Taxis To Ceuta
58 Bus to Martil

PLACES TO STAY
2 Hotel Oumaima
22 Pension Iberia; BMCE Bank (ATM)
23 Hotel Principe
26 Hôtel Cosmopolita
57 Hôtel Trébol

PLACES TO EAT
3 Café & Cinema Avenida
9 Bakery
24 Restaurant Restinga
25 El Yesfi Snack
27 Café Pâtisserie SMIR
28 Restaurant Saigon
30 Cafés
54 Sandwich Ali Baba

MOROCCO

el-Mehdi has an ATM and a bureau de change that's open until 8 pm daily.

The Spanish Consulate (☎ 703534) is beside the post office on Place Moulay el-Mehdi.

Good Internet access (Dr10 per hour) is offered at Cyber Primo, on Place Moulay el-Mehdi, and Cyber World (8 Salah Eddine Al Ayoubi).

Things to See
Place Hassan II, the showpiece heart of the town, links the old and new parts of the city. The busiest entrance to the bustling **medina** is Bab er-Rouah. In the area towards the eastern gate, Bab el-Okla, are some fine houses built in the last century. Just inside Bab el-Okla, the excellent **Musée Marocain** has well-presented exhibits of everyday Moroccan and Andalucían life. Open daily except Tuesday (Dr10).

The small **Archaeology Museum** just off Place al-Jala is excellent. In the entrance porch you're greeted by a striking mosaic of the three Graces from the Roman ruins of Lixus, where most of the exhibits originate. Open weekdays; Dr10.

Just outside Bab el-Okla is the **Artisanat School**, where children learn traditional crafts such as leather work, woodwork and the making of enamel (zellij) tiles. The building itself is worth a visit. Open weekdays; Dr10.

Places to Stay
The nearest **camping ground** is **Camping Alboustane** (☎ 688822) on the beach at Martil, 8km away.

Tetouan has plenty of cheap, basic pensions. **Pension Iberia** (☎ 963679), above the BMCE bank on Place Moulay el-Mehdi, overlooks the square and is worth trying first. Singles/doubles with shared bathroom cost Dr40/70. Hot showers are Dr5.

Hôtel Cosmopolita (☎ 964821, 3 Rue du Prince Sidi Mohammed) is good value, clean and tidy. Rooms cost Dr35/70 (hot shower costs Dr7).

Another good bet, close to the bus station, is **Hôtel Trebol** (☎ 962018). Reasonable rooms with shower (cold) cost Dr41/62 and Dr31/52 without shower.

Hotel Príncipe (20 Rue Youssef ben Tachfine) has clean rooms without shower

for Dr60/74, with shower Dr70/100. The reception is in the cafe.

More expensive, is **Hotel Oumaima** (☎ 963473, 10 Rue Achra Mai). Clean en suite rooms with phones cost Dr200/246.

Places to Eat
The best place for a cheap, nutritious meal is **El Yesfi Snack** on Rue ben Tachfine. Great baguettes with various meats, potato salad, chips and salad cost Dr16. **Sandwich Ali Bab** is similarly good.

Restaurant Saigon on Rue Mohammed ben Larbi Torres, is good-value although there's nothing Vietnamese about it. A full meal (tajine with salad, bread and a drink) will cost around Dr30.

Also popular and reasonably priced is the licensed **Restaurant Restinga**, set back off Blvd Mohammed V. Nearby, **Café Pâtisserie SMIR** serves excellent coffee and pastries.

For self-caterers **Supermercado La Española** on Rue Achra Mai has plenty of supplies (including booze).

Getting There & Away
Bus The long-distance bus station is at the junction of Rue Sidi Mandri and Rue Moulay Abbas. There are CTM buses to Al-Hoceima (Dr62.50), Casablanca (Dr105), Chefchaouen (Dr16.50), Fès (Dr68), Ouezzane (Dr33), Rabat (Dr80) and Tangier (Dr13). Numerous other companies have buses to these and other destinations, including Marrakesh (Dr130).

A local bus to Martil (Dr2.50) leaves from Rue Moulay Abbas, close by.

Taxi Grands taxis to Chefchaouen (Dr25) and Tangier (Dr20) leave from Rue al-Jazeer. Grands taxis for Ceuta leave from the corner of Rue Mourakah Anual and Rue Sidi Mandri. The 20-minute trip to the frontera costs Dr15. The border is open 24 hours, but transport dries up after 7 pm.

CHEFCHAOUEN
☎ 09
Formally called Chaouen (or Xauen by the Spanish), this delightful town in the Rif Mountains is deservedly popular with travellers. The air is cool and clear and the atmosphere friendly and relaxed.

The town was founded by Moulay Ali ben Rachid in 1471 after the huge influx of Muslim and Jewish refugees from Andalucía. These refugees gave the town its unique Hispanic look of whitewashed houses, though the blue that the town is so famous for only dates back to the 1930s – before then doors and window frames were a traditional Muslim green.

The town remained isolated until occupied by Spanish troops in 1920, and until then the inhabitants spoke a variant of medieval Castilian.

Information

The post office and two banks (no ATMs) are on the main street, Ave Hassan II.

Groupe Chaouni Info offer Internet access for D10 to Dr20 per hour. Internet Cafe Sefiani Network is opposite the Mobil station which is on Ave Tarik Tetouan (Dr30 per hour).

Things to See & Do

The old **medina** is easy to find your way around – all painted streets are dead-ends. Many of the weaving looms, once so common, are now gone, although you may see a few crammed into tiny ground-floor rooms at the north end of town.

Numerous cafes surround the shady and cobbled **Plaza Uta el-Hammam** which is dominated by the 15th century **kasbah** (entry to the museum and gardens is Dr10) and **Great Mosque**.

The lively **market** in the new town is held on Monday and Thursday.

The mountains around the town provide some excellent **trekking**. Contact the President of the Association Randonnée et Culture at Casa Hassan (☎ 988196).

Places to Stay

The very pleasant Azilan **camping ground,** and the poor **youth hostel,** are situated on the side of the hill north of the Hôtel Asma. It's a steep 30-minute walk (follow the signs to the hotel) from town. Call (☎ 986979) for both. Sleeping out under the stars in the camp site costs Dr10.

The cheapest hotels are in the medina. The best of the bunch is probably **Pensión La Castellana** (☎ 986295, 4 Sidi Ahmed el-Bouhali), just off the western end of Plaza Uta el-Hammam. Singles/doubles cost Dr30/60, including hot showers and use of the kitchen, or you can crash on the wonderful roof terrace for Dr15.

Also popular are **Pension Mauritania** (☎ 986184), with rooms for Dr20/30, and **Pension Znika** (☎ 986624), which is spotlessly clean, light and airy and costs Dr30 per person. Hot showers are included at both places.

The very pleasant **Hostel Gernika** (☎ 987434), north-east of Plaza de Makhzen, is run by two Spanish women. It has nine beautifully furnished rooms, all doubles with own shower, for Dr120.

Outside the medina is the friendly **Hotel Marrakesh** (☎ 987113), offering basic, modern, clean and comfortable singles/doubles for Dr50/80 and rooms with shower and toilet for Dr80/120. Nearby, the newish **Hôtel Madrid** (☎ 987496, fax 987498) is popular with tour groups. Clean rooms with showers, phones and heaters cost Dr180/261.

Casa Hassan (☎ 986153, fax 988196) up from Plaza Uta al-Hammam is the discerning choice in town. Simple, nice doubles are Dr250, with the classy suites Dr550. Rates are half-board.

Places to Eat

Down near the market are some cheap brochette munching places (Dr15), but the most popular places to eat in Chefchaouen are the small restaurants and cafes on Plaza Uta el-Hammam – **Café Snack Mounir** is a good bet for breakfast and lunch. A full meal will cost around Dr20 to Dr30.

Farther north, near Pension Valencia, the **Restaurant Granada** and **Restaurant Chez Fouad** present a variety of dishes at reasonable cost.

Up a small flight of steps on the north side of Plaza de Makhzen you'll find a hole-in-the-wall place which offers excellent bessara for Dr5. There are often stalls selling soup (Dr3) or snails (Dr2 for a bowl of the slippery suckers) in Plaza Uta el-Hammam or just outside Bab al-'Ain.

Restaurant Assada, just inside Bab al-'Ain to the north, is another tiny local spot offering good-value standards (about Dr18). Outside the medina, up the hill from the Bab al-'Ain, the popular **Restaurant Moulay Ali ben**

CHEFCHAOUEN

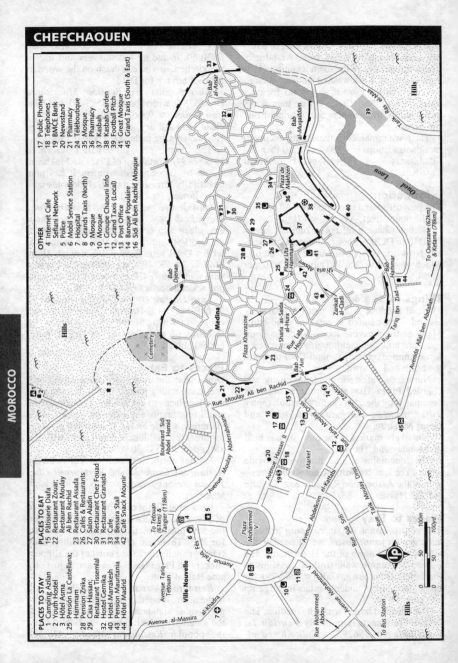

PLACES TO STAY
1 Camping Azilan
3 Youth Hostel
4 Hôtel Asma
25 Pensión La Castellana;
   Hammam
28 Pensión Znika
29 Casa Hassan;
   Restaurant Tissemlal
32 Hostel Gernika
40 Hotel Marrakesh
43 Pension Mauritania
44 Hôtel Madrid

PLACES TO EAT
15 Pâtisserie Diafa
22 Restaurant Zouar;
   Restaurant Moulay
   Ali ben Rachid
23 Restaurant Assada
26 Cafés & Restaurants
27 Salon Aladin
30 Restaurant Chez Fouad
31 Restaurant Granada
33 Cafe
34 Bessara Stall
42 Café Snack Mounir

OTHER
4 Internet Cafe
5 Sefiani Network
5 Police
6 Mobil Service Station
7 Hospital
8 Grands Taxis (North)
9 Mosque
10 Mosque
11 Groupe Chaouni Info
12 Grand Taxis (Local)
13 Post Office
14 Banque Populaire
16 Sidi Ali ben Rachid Mosque
17 Public Phones
18 Telephones
19 BMCE Bank
20 Newsstand
21 Pharmacy
24 Téléboutique
35 Mosque
36 Pharmacy
37 Kasbah
39 Kasbah Garden
39 Football Pitch
41 Great Mosque
45 Grand Taxis (South & East)

Rachid and *Restaurant Zouar* are similarly priced – fish at the Zouar is a good option.

For a splurge (only Dr50 for three courses!), try *Salon Aladin* or *Restaurant Tissemlal*. Both are up a side street just off Plaza Uta el-Hammam. The pastilla at Aladin and the lemon chicken at the Tissemlal are excellent.

Pâtisserie Daifa, on Ave Hassan II just outside the medina close to Bab al-'Ain, has good pastries and fresh bread. Excellent goat's cheese, is available in some shops up from Bab al-'Ain.

Getting There & Away

Bus The bus station is a 20-minute walk south-west of the old town centre. Many of the CTM and other buses (especially to Fès) are through services that often arrive already full. Give yourself a fighting chance and book a seat in advance.

If you're not having any luck getting a bus to Fès (Dr52, 4½ hours), try for Meknès (Dr45, four hours) or Ouezzane (Dr15, 11 hours). There are loads of buses and grands taxis between both places and Fès.

In addition to the numerous buses to Tetouan there are departures to Fnideq (3km short of the Ceuta border), Oued Laou (for the Mediterranean coast), Tangier, Rabat, Casablanca and Nador.

Taxi Grands taxis going north-west to Tetouan (Dr25) and Tangier (Dr50; difficult to get) leave from just off Plaza Mohammed V. Taxis heading to Ouezzane (Dr25) and other points south and east leave from Ave Abdallah.

Eastern Morocco

TAZA

☎ 05

Overlooking the Taza Gap – the only feasible pass from the east between the Rif Mountains and the Middle Atlas – Taza has been important throughout Morocco's history as a base from which to exert control over the country's eastern extremities.

If you have your own transport, the drive around **Mt Tazzeka**, with a visit to the incredible caverns of the **Gouffre du Friouato**, is superb. Said to be the deepest in North Africa, the caverns have only been partially explored.

In the town itself, the old medina is relaxed and worth a wander, particularly around the ramparts to **Bab er-Rih** (Gate of the Wind), from where there are excellent views over the surrounding countryside.

Places to Stay & Eat

In the medina, the basic but cheerful *Hôtel de l'Étoile* (☎ 270179), on Moulay el-Hassan, has rooms with fireplaces and brass beds for Dr35. There is no shower but you'll find a hammam nearby.

In the centre of the new town (about 3km from the medina), *Hôtel Guillaume Tell* (☎ 672347) offers big rooms with double beds for Dr40/60. Showers are cold. The nearby *Hôtel de la Poste* (☎ 672589) has small but comfortable rooms for Dr48/64 but no shower.

Hôtel du Dauphiné (☎ 673567), Place de l'Indépendance, is an attractive colonial-style place with its own restaurant and lively bar. Rooms with shower and toilet cost Dr130/165.

The best of the few eateries in town is *Restaurant Majestic* on Ave Mohammed V, near the hotels. You can eat well for around Dr30.

Getting There & Away

Buses and grands taxis leave for Fès, Tangier, Al-Hoceima, Nador and Oujda several times a day from a lot on the Fès-Oujda road near the train station. The CTM terminal is on Place de l'Indépendance.

There are daily trains to Casablanca via Fès, Meknès and Rabat as well as regular services to Marrakesh, Tangier and Oujda.

OUJDA

Oujda is a sprawling modern city with little obvious attractions to detain travellers. However, it's a pleasant, relaxed place with a bustling medina. It's the last stop before the Algerian border (closed at the time of writing) and something of a crossroads – to the south lies the Sahara and to the north the resort town of Saidia on the Mediterranean Coast.

Information

The OMNT (☎ 685631) is on Place du 16 Août 1953. Close by, opposite the CTM station, is

MOROCCO

the all-night pharmacy. The banks and main post office are on Blvd Mohammed V. Internet access is available at Alf@Net on Blvd Mohammed V and Acrosys Marocon on Rue Tarik Ibn Ziad (Dr10 per hour).

Things to See
About 6km south of Oujda medina is the oasis of Sidi Yahia and a shrine to the man Christians know as John the Baptist, but whom both Muslims and Jews revere as a prophet. The inside of the shrine is off limits to non-Muslims but you are free to wander around the exterior, which is decorated with carved Arabic script and beautiful tile work.

There's a huge and vibrant annual moussem in September, which is well worth attending.

Catch one of Frequent No 1 buses (Dr2) to Sidi Yahia from the square outside Bab el-Ouahab or charter a petit taxi (about Dr12).

Places to Stay & Eat
There are cheap hotels along Rue Marrakesh in the medina. However, *Hôtel Al-Hanna* (☎ 686003, 132 Rue de Marrakesh) is all you need. Spotless singles/doubles with basin go for Dr40/60 (hot showers included).

Hôtel D'Isly (☎ 683928, 26 Rue Ramdane el-Gadhi*) has clean, bright rooms for Dr30/60 (cold showers only).

The cheapest snack food and fruit stalls are just inside **Bab el-Ouahab**, the eastern gate of the medina.

Close to Place du 16 Août 1953, *Restaurant Baraka* serves tasty roast chicken. *Restaurant Nacional* on Blvd Zerktouni is similar and excellent.

Sophisticated cafes line Mohammed V; try *Café Le Trésor*, *Pâtisserie Colombo* and *Café la Defense*.

Getting There & Away
Bus CTM has an office behind the town hall servicing one express bus to Casablanca (10½ hours) via Taza (four hours), Fès (six hours), Meknès (seven hours) and Rabat (9½ hours). SATA and Trans Ghazala, who have offices close by, also go to Casablanca.

All other buses, including CTM's other services, leave from the Gare Routière across Oued Nachef, a 15 minute walk south from

the train station or a petit taxi ride (around Dr6). There are daily CTM departures to Casablanca, Tangier, Nador and Chefchaouen. Non-CTM buses leave for Figuig, Bouarfa, Er Rachidia, Berkane and Saidia (on the coast).

Train Oujda station is close to the centre of town, at the western end of Blvd Zerktouni.

There are daily departures for Casablanca (9¾ hours), Fès (five hours), Rabat (8¾ hours), Tangier (11 hours), Taza (3½ hours), Marrakesh (14 hours), and Meknès (6¼ hours).

Taxi Grands taxis to Taza (Dr50) and Fès (Dr90) leave from outside the main bus station.

Grands taxis to Nador (Dr35), Saidia (Dr20), Ahfrir (Dr10) and Berkane (Dr15) leave from Rue Derfoufi, just north of the Post Office.

Spanish Morocco

Ceuta and Melilla are Spanish enclaves on the northern Moroccan coast. They came under Spanish control in the 15th and 16th centuries respectively and, although administered as city provinces of Spain, are waiting to be granted full autonomous status on an equal footing with the other provinces.

About 70% of the inhabitants are Spanish. The main function of these cities is to supply Spanish troops stationed there, and sell duty-free goods (many of which find their way to destinations all over north-western Africa). Morocco occasionally campaigns half-heartedly for their return, but Rabat is not keen to rock the boat as Spain is an increasingly important trading partner. However, Morocco's Free Trade Agreement with the EU may well remove the need to smuggle goods out of the tiny Spanish enclaves and adversely effect their economies.

Travellers pass through these towns mainly for ferry services to and from Spain but they are also tranquil places for the travel weary. Note that Ceuta and Melilla keep Spanish, not Moroccan, time and have cheap, tax-free petrol.

CEUTA
☎ 956

Known as Sebta in Morocco, Ceuta offers a couple of days' distraction but it's not cheap. If you're heading for Morocco, you could catch an early fast-ferry from Algeciras and continue through to Tetouan or Chefchaouen.

Information

The tourist office (☎ 956 501 401) near the end of Avenida Muelle Cañonero Dato, beside the dock, has an accommodation list. Closed Sunday.

Plenty of banks line the main street, Paseo de Revellín, and its continuation, Calle Camoens. Outside business hours you can change money at Hôtel La Muralla, on Plaza de Africa. There's no need to buy dirham here, as you can do so at the border as long as you have cash.

The main post office *(correos y telégrafos)* is on Plaza de España.

Internet access at the Indy Net costs 700 ptas per hour (it's much cheaper in Tetouan).

There are plenty of Telefonica's blue and green public phones around. They accept coins, phonecards (from Tabacs) and credit cards. Direct overseas dialling is possible and cheaper than in Morocco.

Things to See

The Museo de la Legión, on Paseo de Colón, is dedicated to and run by the Spanish Legion and holds a staggering array of military paraphernalia. Entry is free and includes a guided tour.

Opened in May 1995, the Maritime Park (Parque Marítimo del Mediterráneo) is a huge complex on the seafront, complete with manufactured beach, pools, restaurants, bars and casino. Entry costs 800 ptas per adult and 350 ptas per child.

Places to Stay & Eat

Finding somewhere to stay in Ceuta can be a nightmare, so try and book a room in advance. Not everywhere is signed; look out for the blue-and-white F (for *fondas* or inn) or CH (for *casas de huéspedes* or boarding house) signs close to the entrances.

In mid March, when the annual carnival is held, a decent room can be impossible to find.

The following prices are subject to 3% tax.

Probably the best value in town is the small *Pensión Charito (☎ 956 513 982, 5 Calle Arrabal)* about 15 minutes walk along the waterfront from the ferry terminal. Basic singles/doubles cost 1500 ptas and 2000 ptas. Cold showers only.

Centrally located, *Pensión Revellín (☎ 956 516 762, 2nd floor/2 Paseo de Revellín)* has rooms for 1200/2200 ptas, with hot showers (300 ptas), but it's not amazingly friendly.

If you can afford a little extra, *Pensión La Bohemia (☎ 956 510 615, 16 Paseo de Revellín)* is a pleasant place. Fresh and clean singles/doubles, with piping-hot showers (free) in a shared bathroom, cost 2000/4000 ptas.

Two-star *Hostal Central (☎ 956 516 716, 15 Paseo del Revellín)* has nice, small en suite rooms with TVs for 3600/6000 ptas.

There are plenty of cafes and bars serving snacks and simple meals. Things get cheaper as you head east from the town centre along Calle Real. *Cafetería La Campana (15 Calle Camoens)* is great for breakfast (around 350 ptas) and does a good *menú de la diá for* 975 ptas.

The restaurant *Club Nautico (☎ 956 514 440)*, on Calle Edrisis, has good fish dishes for about 1300 ptas, and a couple of vegetarian options.

Getting There & Away

Morocco The No 7 bus runs every ten minutes or so between Plaza de la Constitución and the *frontera* (75 ptas, 20 minutes). If you arrive by ferry and want to head for the border, there's a No 7 stop just up from the tourist office on Calle Edrisis, opposite the ramparts.

Once through the border, there are plenty of grands taxis to Tetouan (Dr15 a seat). The trip from Ceuta to Tetouan should take no more than two hours.

Mainland Spain The ferry terminal is 800m west of the town centre. There are frequent fast-ferry (hydrofoil), and regular (and cheaper) ferry departures to Algeciras. Two hydrofoil services per day head to Malaga.

There are regular helicopter flights between Malaga airport and Ceuta.

MOROCCO

MELILLA
☎ 952

Smaller but more run-down and more typically 'Moroccan' than Ceuta, Melilla retains a lingering fascination because of its medieval fortress (impressive renovations were taking place at the time of writing). Until the end of the 19th century, almost all of Melilla was contained within these massive walls. This old part of town has a distinctly Castilian flavour with narrow, twisting streets, squares, gates and drawbridges.

Information

There's a well-stocked tourist desk (☎ 952 675 444) in the Palicio de Congresos y Exposiciones on Calle Fortuny. Most of the banks are in Avenida de Juan Carlos I Rey, and you can buy and sell dirham.

There's a Banque Populaire on the Moroccan side of the border – cash exchanges only.

Melilla's band of moneychangers don't offer great rates.

Things to See

The fortress of Melilla la Vieja, also known as the Medina Sidonia, is very impressive and offers great views. Inside the walls are the Iglesia de la Concepción with its gilded *reredos* and shrine to Nuestra Señora la Virgen de la Victoria (the patron of the city), the Museo Municipal and the Museo Militar.

The main entrance to the fortress is through the massive Puerta de la Marina.

Places to Stay & Eat

Be warned – accommodation in Melilla is expensive.

Cheapest, if a little rough and ready, is *Pensión del Puerto* off Avenida General Macías. A bed should cost 1500 ptas.

Expensive, but still among the cheapest places, is the *Hostal Residencia Rioja* (☎ 952 682 709, 10 Calle Ejército Español). Its bright, basic singles/doubles cost 3500/4500 ptas, with communal hot showers.

Hostal R Parque (☎ 952 682 143) fronts Parque Hern-ández, but slightly dingy rooms cost 3000/5500 ptas.

The best area to search for good, cheap *bocadillos* (large sandwich) and the like is along Calle Castelar (not far from the Mercado Municipal). The popular *Antony Pizza*

Factory (☎ 952 684 320, 1 Calle Cándido) serves good pizza (from 575 ptas) and pasta (675 ptas).

Cafe Rossy on Calle General Prim is a good place for breakfast. In the evening head to *La Onubense* and *Cervecería*, two excellent tapas bars on Calle General O'Donnell.

Getting There & Away

Morocco No 2 bus runs from Plaza de España to the border (75 ptas) every 30 minutes from 7.30 am to 10 pm. On the Moroccan side there are frequent buses (Dr2.20) and grands taxis (Dr4) to Nador until about 8pm.

Mainland Spain Trasmediterranea runs daily ferries to Málaga and Almería. Buy your tickets at its office on Plaza de España or in the ferry terminal. Spanish rail and coach tickets can be booked at travel agents in town. It's also worth checking out flights to Málaga.

The Middle Atlas

MEKNÈS
☎ 05

Although a town of considerable size even in the 13th century, Meknès didn't reach its peak until Moulay Ismail, the second Alawite sultan, made it his capital in 1672 and spent the next 55 years building an enormous palace complex. Under Sultan Sidi Mohammed III, however, Morocco's capital was moved back to Marrakesh. In 1755 a large earthquake severely damaged Meknès. No restoration was done and the city was allowed to decay – until recently, when its tourism potential was recognised and major restoration began.

Oued Boufekrane divides the new town from the old.

Information

The tourist office (☎ 524426) is near the main post office facing Place de France.

Banks with ATMs are concentrated in the ville nouvelle. BMCE operates a bureau de change on Ave des FAR (opposite the Hôtel Volubilis), from 10 am to 2 pm and 4 to 8 pm daily.

MOROCCO

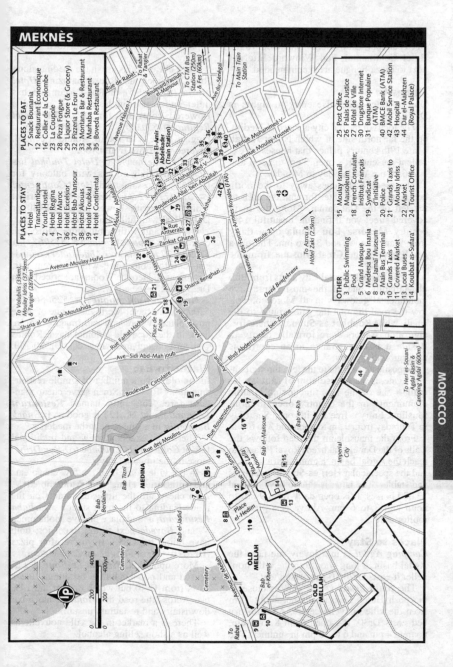

MEKNÈS

PLACES TO STAY
1 Hotel Transatlantique
2 Youth Hostel
4 Hotel Regina
17 Hotel Maroc
36 Hotel Excelsior
37 Hôtel Bab Mansour
38 Hotel Akouas
39 Hotel Toubkal
41 Hotel Continental

PLACES TO EAT
5 Snack Bounania
12 Restaurant Economique
16 Collier de la Colombe
23 La Coupole
28 Pizza Fongue
29 Liquor Store (& Grocery)
32 Pizzeria Le Four
33 Montana Bar & Restaurant
34 Marhaba Restaurant
35 Boveda Restaurant

OTHER
3 Public Swimming Pool
5 Grand Mosque
6 Medersa Bou Inania
8 Dar Jamaï Museum
9 Main Bus Terminal
10 Grands Taxis
11 Covered Market
13 Local Buses
14 Koubbat as-Sufara'
15 Moulay Ismail Mausoleum
18 French Consulate; Institut Français
19 Syndicat d'Initiative
20 Police
21 Grands Taxis to Moulay Idriss
22 Market
24 Tourist Office
25 Post Office
26 Palais de Justice
27 Hôtel de Ville
30 Drugstore Internet
31 Banque Populaire (ATM)
40 BMCE Bank (ATM)
42 Mobil Service Station
43 Hospital
44 Dar el-Makhzen (Royal Palace)

MOROCCO

Internet cafes in the ville nouveau charge Dr10 per hour. Club Internet, next door to the Hotel Continental, and Winword Internet next to Pizza Fongue are recommended.

Things to See

Unless stated otherwise entry to sights is Dr10.

The focus of the old city is Place el-Hedim, on the far north side of which is **Dar Jamai**, a late 19th century palace that houses an excellent museum. It's open 9 am to noon and 3 to 6.30 pm Wednesday to Monday.

The **medina** stretches away to the north behind the square; enter through the arch to the left of the Dar Jamai. Along the main covered street you'll find the beautiful 14th century **Medersa Bou Inania** open daily from 9 am to noon and 3 to 6 pm. There's a good view of the **Great Mosque** from the roof.

A visit to the **Imperial City** starts from **Bab el-Mansour**, one of the most impressive monumental gateways in all Morocco. Follow the road through the gate around to the small, white **Koubbat as-Sufara'**, where foreign ambassadors were formally received. Beside it is the entrance to an enormous underground granary.

Opposite and a little to the left, through another gate, is the **Mausoleum of Moulay Ismail** – one of the few functioning Islamic monuments in the country open to non-Muslims. Entry is free and it's open Saturday to Thursday from 9 am to noon and 3 to 6 pm.

From the mausoleum the road follows the walls of the Dar el-Makhzen (Royal Palace) to reach the **Agdal basin**, a grand artificial lake, and the spectacular **Heri es-Souani** granaries and stables. The latter is said to have housed 12,000 horses. It is open daily from 9 am to noon and 3 to 6 pm. Above is a pleasant rooftop cafe.

Places to Stay

Camping Agdal is in a lovely site near the Agdal basin, a long way from the ville nouvelle. It costs Dr20/10 per person/tent.

The *youth hostel* (☎ 524698) is close to the posh Hotel Transatlantique, about 1km from the ville nouvelle centre. A dormitory bed costs Dr30. It's open from 8 to 9 am, noon to 4 pm and 6 to 10 pm in summer. The

rest of the year, it's open 8 to 10 am, noon to 3 pm and 6 to 10 pm; 10 am to 6 pm on Sunday.

Most cheap hotels are in the medina along Rue Dar Smen and Rue Rouamzine. *Hotel Maroc* (☎ 530075), on Rue Rouamzine, has quiet and clean singles/doubles around a flowered courtyard for Dr60/120. *Hotel Regina* (☎ 530280), on Rue Dar Smen, is a biggish place with rooms around a central, covered courtyard from Dr60.

In the ville nouvelle, *Hotel Toubkal* has clean and bright rooms with balcony for Dr50/90. Across the road, *Hotel Continental* (☎ 525471, 92 Ave des FAR) has bright rooms, some with shower, for Dr110/140; or Dr140/160 with full bathroom.

Quieter and with a bit more Moroccan character is *Hotel Akouas* (☎ 515967, fax 515994, 27 Rue El-Amir Abdelkader), a modern, comfortable place with a decent bar, restaurant and terrace. Rooms are priced from Dr280, ask to see a few.

Hotel Transatlantique (☎ 525050, fax 520057), on Rue el-Merinyne, is one of those posh places where you can imagine you're back in the good old colonial days. Rooms with air-con and great views cost Dr590/750.

Places to Eat

In the old town a number of simple restaurants along Rue Dar Smen serve cheap standard fare. The aptly named *Restaurant Économique* at No 123 is good as is *Snack Bounania* in a square near the medersa.

There's an excellent view and traditional fare at *Collier de la Colombe* (67 Rue Driba) close to the imperial city.

In the ville nouvelle are a few cheap eats and rotisseries along Ave Mohammed V. Also cheap are the little restaurants on the roads leading to the train station. *Marhaba Restaurant*, a tiled place on Ave Mohammed V, and *Boveda* next to the Excelsior; both have tajine for US$3. If you're after pizza (Dr20) try *Pizza Fongue* on Zankat Accra.

More upmarket, *Pizzeria Le Four* is a licensed and popular Italian restaurant. Pizza costs from Dr40 but watch out for the 14% tax. Across the road the *Montana* has a bar downstairs and restaurant upstairs.

There is a market in the ville nouvelle as well as a shop selling alcohol.

Entertainment

There are many bars grouped around Blvd Allal ben Abdallah, mostly attached to hotels and restaurants. Those at *La Coupole* and *Pizzeria Le Four* are two of the better places.

One of the best discos is in *Hôtel Bab Mansour*.

Getting There & Away

Bus The CTM bus station is on Ave des Forces Armées Royales (FAR). The main bus station (where CTM buses also stop) is just outside Bab el-Khemis. CTM destinations include Casablanca (four hours), Chefchaouen (five hours), Fès (one hour), Marrakesh (seven hours), Rabat (2½ hours), Tangier (six hours) and Tetouan (six hours).

Local buses and grands taxis to the same destinations also leave from here.

Train The main train station is on Ave du Sénégal. More convenient is El-Amir Abdelkader station, parallel to Ave Mohammed V. All trains to Fès (one hour), Oujda (6½ hours), Casablanca (4½ hours), Rabat (2¼ hours) and Marrakesh (seven hours) stop here.

AROUND MEKNÈS

About 33km from Meknès are the best-preserved Roman ruins in Morocco. **Volubilis** (Oualili in Arabic) dates largely from the 2nd and 3rd centuries AD, although the site was originally settled by Carthaginian traders in the 3rd century BC. It is noted for its mosaic floors, many of which have been left *in situ*.

The site is open daily from sunrise to sunset and entry is Dr20. To get there, take a grands taxi (Dr7 per person) or bus (Dr6) from Place de la Foire in Meknès and hop out at the turn-off to Moulay Idriss. From there it's a pleasant half-hour walk. Going back, you can hitch or walk to Moulay Idriss and wait for a bus or taxi. If you have a group, you could negotiate to hire a grands taxi for a half-day trip (don't pay more than Dr300).

FÈS

☎ 05

Fès is the oldest of Morocco's imperial cities, founded shortly after the Arabs swept across North Africa following the death of the Prophet Mohammed. It has often been the capital. The city's magnificent buildings reflect the brilliance of Arab-Berber imagination and artistry. Fassis, the people of Fès, justifiably still look on their city as the cultural and spiritual capital of Morocco.

The medina of Fès el-Bali (Old Fès) is one of the largest medieval cities in the modern world. Its narrow, winding alleys and covered bazaars are crammed with craft workshops, restaurants, mosques, medersas, markets and dye pits and tanneries. The exotic smells, the hammering of metal workers, the call of the muezzin and the jostling crowds are an unforgettable experience.

History

Fès was founded in 789 AD by Idriss I on the right bank of the Oued Fès in what is now the Andalus Quarter. His son, Idriss II, extended the city onto the left bank in 809; these two parts of the city constitute Fès el-Bali.

The earliest settlers were mainly refugees from Córdoba (Spain) and Kairouan (Tunisia). Both groups were from well-established Islamic centres of brilliance and their skills laid the groundwork for one of the most important centres of Islamic intellectual and architectural development.

The city reached its height under the Merenids, who took it from the Almohads in 1250 and erected a new quarter, Fès el-Jdid. Fès remained the capital throughout their rule. With the rise of the Saadians in the 16th century, Marrakesh once again gained the ascendancy and Fès slipped into relative obscurity, only to be revived under the Alawite ruler Moulay Abdallah in the 19th century. In 1916, the French began building the ville nouvelle on the plateau to the south-west of the two ancient cities.

Orientation

Fès consists of three distinct parts. The original walled city of Fès el-Bali is east. Southwest is the French-built ville nouvelle with most of the restaurants and hotels. Between them is the Merenid walled city of Fès el-Jdid.

Information

The ONMT office (☎ 623460) is on Place de la Résistance in the ville nouvelle.

Official guides (including nine female guides), at Dr120/150 for a half/full day, are available from the ONMT office or through

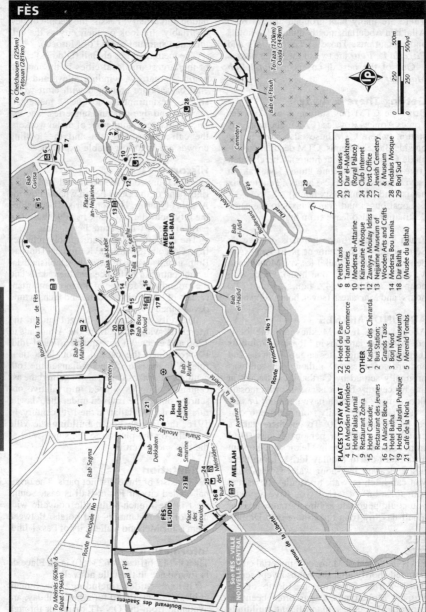

FÈS

PLACES TO STAY & EAT
4 Le Meridien Mérinides
7 Hotel Palais Jamaï
9 Restaurant Zohra
15 Hotel Cascade;
   Restaurant des Jeunes
16 La Maison Bleue
17 Hotel Batha
19 Hotel du Jardin Publique
21 Café de la Noria
22 Hotel du Parc
26 Hotel du Commerce

OTHER
1 Kasbah des Cherarda
2 Bus Station;
   Grands Taxis
3 Borj Nord
   (Arms Museum)
5 Merenid Tombs
6 Petits Taxis
8 Tanneries
10 Medersa el-Attarine
11 Kairaouine Mosque
12 Zawiyya Moulay Idriss II
13 Nejjarine Museum of
   Wooden Arts and Crafts
14 Medersa Bou Inania
18 Dar Batha
   (Musée du Batha)
20 Local Buses
23 Dar el-Makhzen
   (Royal Palace)
24 Club Internet
25 Post Office
27 Jewish Cemetery
   & Museum
28 Andalus Mosque
29 Borj Sud

hotels. Plenty of unofficial guides hang around and will guide you for a lot less. A guide can be useful especially in stopping other would-be guides pestering you.

The main post office is in the ville nouvelle, as are most banks with ATMs. Société General does cash credit card advances and exchanges travellers cheques.

There are dozens of Internet cafes all over town charging Dr10 per hour. Try Club Internet on Rue des Mérinides.

Things to See

Fès el-Bali The old walled medina is the area of most interest. It's an incredible maze of twisting alleys, arches, mosques, medersas, shrines, fountains, workshops and markets. The most convenient entry point is **Bab Bou Jeloud**. Unfortunately, many of the religious sites and monuments are closed to non-Muslims. Entry to the others costs Dr10.

Just in from Bab Bou Jeloud is the **Medersa Bou Inania**, built by the Merenid sultan Bou Inan between 1350 and 1357. It is one of the few functioning religious buildings non-Muslims may enter. The carved woodwork is magnificent. It's open 8 am to 5 pm daily except at prayer times.

In the guts of the city is the **Kairaouine Mosque**, one of the largest mosques in Morocco. Founded between 859 and 862 for refugees from Tunisia, it has one of the finest libraries in the Muslim world. Unfortunately, it's closed to non-Muslims.

Nearby, the **Medersa el-Attarine**, built by Abu Said in 1325, displays some particularly beautiful Merenid craftsmanship. It's open 9 am to noon and 2 to 6 pm daily.

On the boundary between Fès el-Bali and Fès el-Jdid, is the interesting **Dar Batha** (Musée du Batha) on Place de l'Istiqlal. Built as a palace over 100 years ago, it houses historical and artistic artefacts from ruined or decaying medersas, as well as Fassi embroidery, tribal carpets and ceramics. It's open 8.30 am to noon and 2.30 to 6.30 pm Wednesday to Monday.

Fès el-Jdid The other walled city, built by the Merenids in the 13th century, has the old Jewish quarter (mellah) and a couple of mosques and synagogues (one housing a **museum**), but is less interesting than Fès el-Bali.

The grounds of the **Dar el-Makhzen** (Royal Palace) comprise 80 hectares of pavilions, medersas, mosques and pleasure gardens closed to the public.

At the northern end of the main street, Sharia Moulay Suleiman, is the enormous **Bab Dekkaken**, formerly the main entrance to the royal palace. Between it and Bab Bou Jeloud are the **Bou Jeloud Gardens**, through which flows Oued Fès, the city's main water source.

Borj Nord & Merenid Tombs For a spectacular view of Fès, walk or take a taxi up to the Borj Nord fortress and Merenid Tombs. The whole of Fès lies at your feet. The 16th century borj, built by the Saadian sultan Ahmed al-Mansour, houses the **Arms Museum**. Opening hours are as for the Musée du Batha. The tombs, mostly ruins, are dramatic against the city backdrop. Don't come here alone too early or late.

Places to Stay

Camping & Hostels The shady *Camping Diamant Vert* (☎ 608369) at 'Ain Chkef 6km south, off the Ifrane road, sits at the bottom of a valley with a clean stream. Camping costs Dr20/15 per person/tent. Take bus No 17 (to 'Ain Chkef) from Place de Florence or Place Atlas.

More luxurious, *Camping International* (☎ 731439, fax 731554) is about 3km out on the Sefrou road. It's in large gardens with a pool (May to October), tennis courts, restaurants, bar and shops. It costs Dr40/30 per adult/tent. Take bus No 38 from Place Atlas.

The *youth hostel* (☎ 624085, 18 Rue Abdeslam Serghini) in the ville nouvelle is small and clean with a tiled courtyard, TV and hot showers. Members pay Dr45/55 in dormitory/two-bed accommodation with breakfast (non-members Dr50/60). It's open from 8 to 10 am, noon to 3 pm and 6 to 10 pm daily.

Hotels – Medina The most colourful hotels are around Bab Bou Jeloud. They are basic and not all have showers, but there are hammams all over.

Hotel du Jardin Publique (☎ 633086) outside the gate, has clean, large rooms for Dr40/60. Inside the gate, *Hotel Cascade* (☎ 638442) has simple rooms for Dr40/60 and two roof terraces.

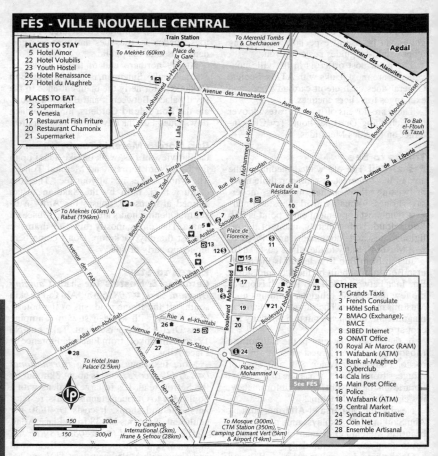

FÈS - VILLE NOUVELLE CENTRAL

PLACES TO STAY
5 Hotel Amor
22 Hotel Volubilis
23 Youth Hostel
26 Hotel Renaissance
27 Hotel du Maghreb

PLACES TO EAT
2 Supermarket
6 Venesia
17 Restaurant Fish Friture
20 Restaurant Chamonix
21 Supermarket

OTHER
1 Grands Taxis
3 French Consulate
4 Hôtel Sofia
7 BMAO (Exchange);
   BMCE
8 SIBED Internet
9 ONMT Office
10 Royal Air Maroc (RAM)
11 Wafabank (ATM)
12 Bank al-Maghreb
13 Cyberclub
14 Cala Iris
15 Main Post Office
16 Police
18 Wafabank (ATM)
19 Central Market
24 Syndicat d'Initiative
25 Coin Net
28 Ensemble Artisanal

Staying in Fès el-Jdid doesn't offer the full-on medina buzz, but it is central. Closest to Bab Bou Jeloud is *Hotel du Parc* with rooms at Dr30/50. The best place is *Hotel du Commerce (Place des Alaouites)* with simple rooms, some with balconies, for Dr40/60.

The only medina mid-range choice is the good *Hotel Batha* (☎ 741077, fax 741078, *Place Batha*) overlooking the Batha museum. It has rooms with bathroom for Dr190/240 and a bar, restaurant and pool.

If you have the money, then the swankiest choice in town is *Hotel Palais Jamaï* (☎ 634331, fax 635096, ✉ resa@palais .jamai.co.ma). Once the pleasure dome of a late-19th-century grand vizier to the sultan, it's set in a lush Andalusían garden. Rooms start at Dr1800 for a double reaching Dr18,000 for the Royal Suite.

For the same kind of money you can forfeit facilities such as the swimming pool for personalised service in a beautifully restored riad. *La Maison Bleue* (☎ 636052, fax 740686, ✉ maisonbleue@fesnet.net.ma, 2 *Place de Batha*) has suites from Dr1500/1700 to Dr3000. Dinner in the restaurant costs residents/non-residents another Dr450/500 (including drinks).

MOROCCO

Hotels – Ville Nouvelle The central *Hotel Renaissance* (☎ 622193, 29 Rue Abdel el-Khattabi) is an old, dark, cavernous place but remains popular. The clean rooms, some with balcony, start at Dr50 and there's a terrace.

Brighter and cleaner, *Hotel du Maghreb* (☎ 621567, 25 Ave Mohammed es-Saloui) has rooms with brass bed and balcony from Dr50 (hot showers cost Dr10).

Closer to the student area, *Hotel Volubilis* has brightly decorated rooms from Dr30 per person.

The pleasant three-star *Hotel Amor* (☎ 623304, 31 Rue Arabie Saoudite) has bright, clean rooms with bathroom for Dr160/190, as well as a restaurant and bar.

Near the Merenid tombs (see the Fès el-Bali map) is *Le Meridien Mérinides* (☎ 645226, fax 645 225) with its sweeping panorama of the old medina. The swimming pool and two restaurants make good spots for a sunset drink. Air-con rooms start at Dr1100/1300.

Places to Eat
There are plenty of snack stands in the popular Bab Bou Jeloud area, where you can get a filling roll for about Dr10. The *Restaurant des Jeunes* has simple meals for around Dr50.

In the ville nouvelle there are a few cheap eats around Blvd Mohammed V and the central market. On Ave de France, the popular *Venisia* is one of the best snack bars in town.

For something more substantial, *Restaurant Chamonix*, a block south of the market, offers the usual (set menu Dr50) plus pizzas. Nearby, on Blvd Mohammed V, the pleasant *Restaurant Fish Friture* serves cheap and good seafood and pizzas from Dr40.

For a splurge (Dr390 per head), try the restaurant *Al Fassia* in the Hôtel Palais Jamaï. A little cheaper are the several traditional restaurants set in centuries-old buildings in the medina. The cheapest, with few crowds, *Restaurant Zohra* (☎ 637699, 3 Derb Ain Nass Blida) has tasty menus from Dr70.

For a peaceful cuppa, the *Café de la Noria* in the Bou Jeloud Gardens is unbeatable. In the ville nouvelle, there's a multitude of cafes and patisseries – take your pick.

There are *supermarkets* near the train station and opposite the central market.

Entertainment
Quite a few bars are scattered around the ville nouvelle. The European-looking *Cala Iris* on Ave Hassan II is a good place to start, as are the hotel bars. Some of the bigger hotels have nightclubs, try the discos in the *Volubilis* and *Mérinides* hotels.

Getting There & Away
Air Fès airport (☎ 674712) is at Saiss, 15km to the south. RAM (☎ 625516) has an office at 54 Ave Hassan II and daily/twice-weekly flights to Casablanca/Paris.

Bus CTM buses (☎ 732384) originate at the bus station at Place Baghdadi, near Bab Bou Jeloud, and call in at the ville nouvelle terminus half an hour later.

There are daily departures to Casablanca (five hours) via Rabat (3½ hours) and Meknès (one hour); Erfoud (eight hours); Marrakesh (nine hours); Oujda (six hours); Rissani (nine hours); Tangier (six hours); and Tetouan (five hours).

Other buses run more regularly and reservations can be made.

Train The train station is in the ville nouvelle, 10 minutes' walk from the town centre.

There are daily departures to Casablanca (5½ hours) via Rabat (3½ hours) and Meknès (one hour); Oujda (six hours); Marrakesh (eight hours); and Tangier (five hours).

Taxi Grands taxis to Casablanca (Dr100), Meknès (Dr15) and Rabat (Dr60) leave from the bus station.

Car The following are among the car-rental agencies located in Fès:

Avis (☎ 626746) 50 Blvd Abdallah Chefchaouni
Budget (☎ 620919) Corner of Ave Hassan II and Rue Bahrein
Europcar (☎ 626545) 45 Ave Hassan II
Hertz (☎ 622812) Ave de France

Getting Around
Bus Fès has good local bus services (around Dr2) although they are like sardine cans at times. Useful routes include:

No 9 Place de l'Atlas-Ave Hassan II-Dar Batha
No 12 Bab Bou Jeloud-Bab Guissa-Bab el-Ftouh

MOROCCO

No **16** train station-airport
No **47** train station-Bab Bou Jeloud

Taxi The drivers of the red petits taxis generally use the meters without any fuss. Expect to pay about Dr10 from the train station to Bab Bou Jeloud. Only grands taxis go out to the airport (Dr80).

AROUND FÈS

Set against jagged mountain bluffs and rich farmland, the picturesque Berber town of **Sefrou** makes a fine contrast to the intensity of Fès, just 28km away. The town boasts a small walled **medina** and **mellah**. The best points of entry/exit are the Bab Taksebt, Bab Zemghila and the Bab Merba. There's a **waterfall** about 1.5km west of town.

Accommodation options are limited. There's a *camping ground* on the hill overlooking the town; the basic *Hôtel Frenaie* (☎ 660030) on the road to Fès (Dr70/100 for singles/doubles); and south of the medina, the two-star *Hôtel Sidi Lahcen el-Youssi* (☎ 683428), on Rue Sidi Ali Bouserghine, which has rooms with hot shower and balcony for Dr165/200.

Regular buses (Dr5) and taxis (Dr8) between Fès and Sefrou drop you off at Place Moulay Hassan in front of the Bab M'Kam and Bab Taksebt.

North Atlantic Coast

ASILAH
☎ 09

The small port of Asilah has enjoyed a tumultuous history disproportionate to its size. Settled first by the Carthaginians and then the Romans, it came under Portuguese and Spanish control in the 15th and 16th centuries respectively. Early this century, Asilah became the residence of Er-Raissouli who, in spite of attempts by the sultan and various European powers to control him, was master of north-eastern Morocco until he was imprisoned in 1925 by a Rif rival, Abd el-Krim.

Things to See
The 15th-century Portuguese **ramparts** are intact, but access is limited to the south-western corner beside the mausoleum of Sidi Ahmed El Mansour. The views are excellent.

The **Palais de Raissouli**, **Hassan II International Center** and **El Kamra** tower are the focus of the annual **Cultural Moussem** held in early August. The latter venues house art exhibitions throughout the year.

Several decent **beaches** stretch north of the town, whilst **Paradise Beach**, a local favourite, is 3km south.

Places to Stay
Camping *Camping As-Saada* and *Camping Echrigui* are a few hundred metres north of town. The latter is the better and has a cafe and shop. Both are secure, have decent facilities and fill up in summer.

Hotels *Hôtel Marhaba* (☎ 417144), which overlooks Place Zelaka in front of Bab Kasaba, is simple and just the job. Rooms cost Dr50 per person, plus Dr5 for hot showers. *Hôtel Asilah* (☎ 417286), on Ave Hassan II, has singles/doubles without shower for Dr35/70 and rooms with for Dr100/120. It may close in winter.

Hôtel Mansour (☎ 417390, fax 417533, 49 Ave Mohammed V) is a friendly place with spotless en suite rooms from Dr112/225.

If you have a little spare cash stay at the intimate and stylish, Spanish-run *Hotel Patio de la Luna* (☎ 416074, 12 Plaza Zelaya), next door to Hôtel Marhaba. Rooms cost Dr150/300.

Places to Eat
There's a string of restaurants and cafes on and around Ave Hassan II. A main course will cost around Dr30. Slightly more expensive restaurants lie across from Bab Kasaba and opposite the new harbour. For Spanish-style fish dishes around Dr50, *Casa García* (☎ 417465) is currently top dog, but *Restaurante Oceano Casa Pepe* (☎ 417395) is close behind.

Getting There & Away
The best way to reach Asilah is by bus (Dr10) or grands taxi (Dr12) from Tangier, or bus from Larache (Dr10). Regular buses leave for Rabat, Casablanca, Fès and Meknès. There are trains, but the station is 1.5km north of town.

CHRISTOPHER GROENHOUT

Wrestling with local Roman wildlife, Piazza Navona

BETHUNE CARMICHAEL

Poppies on the path to ruin, Sicily, Italy

JON DAVISON

Milan's cathedral has a forest of spires and statuary, but no bell tower.

Orthodox fresco, in a church in Ohrid, Macedonia

Church of Kaneo above Lake Ohrid, Macedonia

The Mosta Dome is a prominant landmark, visible from most parts of Malta.

LARACHE
☎ 09

Larache is a tranquil town despite being bigger and scruffier than Asilah. At one time Larache was completely walled, but the kasbah and ramparts are now mostly in ruin. What remains intact is the old tumble-down medina, a fortress known as **Casbah de la Cigogne** and a pocket-sized, Spanish-built citadel that houses the archaeological museum (open every day except Tuesday; Dr10).

The new sections of town are of classic Spanish colonial architecture, though most of Larache is whitewashed with blue painted doors and window frames.

Most people come to Larache to visit the Roman ruins of Lixus, 3 to 4km north of town. The site sits upon a hillock overlooking the Loukkos estuary and the Tangier-Larache highway. The remains of the amphitheatre, temples, mosaics and public baths are impressive; entry is free.

There are also a number of reasonable beaches north of town.

Information
The post office and many of the banks (with ATMs) are on Blvd Mohammed V.

Places to Stay
The best place to stay in the medina is *Pensión Atlas* (☎ 912014, 154 Rue 2 Mars), which charges Dr20/50 for small, moderately clean rooms.

Next to the bus station, *Pension de la Gare* (☎ 913030) has basic clean rooms with a sink for Dr35/70, but no hot water. Much better is *Pension Amal* (☎ 912788, 10 Ave Abdallah ben Yassine), which has smallish, but very clean, rooms for Dr40/65. Hot showers cost Dr6.

Pension Es-Saada (☎ 913641, 16 Ave Mohammed ben Abdallah), close to Place de la Libération has pleasant, clean rooms, some with balconies, for Dr30 per person. The rooms on the ground floor can be a bit noisy.

Once *the* place to stay during Spanish colonial times, the two-star *Hôtel España* (☎ 913195, fax 915628) fronts onto Place de la Libération. It still manages to exude an air of grandeur. Clean, well maintained rooms

without a bathroom cost Dr100/150, en suite singles/doubles are Dr165/195.

All prices tend to rise by 10% in summer.

Places to Eat
The cheapest eateries are the little places around Place de la Libération and the Zoco (inside the medina) which serve very edible Spanish-style fare.

One of the best of them is *Restaurant Commercial*, on the right just before you enter the Zoco through Bab al-Khemis. It serves a plate of seafood for Dr25, and a decent salad for Dr4.

Restaurant Larache, next door to the Pension Es-Saada, is also reasonable.

Still popular since the days of the Spanish are *churros*, a kind of doughnut traditionally eaten for breakfast. A stall three doors down from Bab al-Khemis sells them in the late afternoon (around 5 pm).

Two good places for breakfast are *Salon de thé Lacoste* on Ave Mohammed ben Abdallah and *Le Sourie Salon de thé, Pâtisserie, Glaciér* next to Hôtel España on Ave Hassan. *Café Central* on Place de la Libération is a great place for coffee.

Getting There & Away
Larache is most easily reached by bus. CTM and several private lines run buses through here. Booking is not always possible, so turn up in the morning and get the first service you can.

There are buses to Fès via Meknes (Dr61), Tangier (Dr29), Casablanca (Dr82) via Kenitra (Dr43) and Rabat (Dr56). There are also non-CTM buses to Tetouan (Dr20), Ceuta (Dr25), Kenitra (Dr30), Asilah (Dr10) and Ouezzane (Dr20).

Grands taxis to Asilah (Dr10) leave from outside the bus station.

Getting Around
For the beach or the Lixus ruins catch bus No 4 or 5 opposite the Casbah de la Cicogne, or take a petits taxi (around Dr15, but haggle).

RABAT
☎ 07

Rabat's history goes back 2500 years to Phoenician exploration. Little remains of their influence or that of the Romans, who came

MOROCCO

after and built a settlement known as Sala. The Almohad Sultan Yacoub al-Mansour ushered in a brief period of glory for Rabat in the 12th century. He used the kasbah as a base for campaigns in Spain, and built the magnificent Almohad Bab Oudaia and the unfinished Tour Hassan. However, the city rapidly declined after his death in 1199.

Muslims expelled from Spain resettled the city and neighbouring Salé in the early 17th century and the stage was set for the colourful era of the Sallee Rovers. These corsairs plundered thousands of merchant vessels returning to Europe from Asia, West Africa and the Americas.

Rabat's role as Morocco's capital began during the French protectorate. Few of its people are involved in the tourist trade, many are civil servants, and there's a definite air of French sophistication. It's a relaxed place, even in the souks, and it's worth staying a few days.

Information

Tourist Office The ONMT office (☎ 730562) is inconveniently located on Rue al-Abtal in Agdal, west of the city (take bus No3 from Blvd Hassan II).

Money The banks are concentrated along Ave Mohammed V and Ave Allal ben Abdalla. The Wafa, BMCE, BMCI and Crédit du Maroc banks have bureau de change booths. The one at the BMCE on Ave Mohammed V is open from 8.30 am to 8 pm daily. There's a useful BMCE bureau at Rabat Ville train station.

Plenty of banks in the ville nouvelle have ATMs.

Post & Communications The post office, on the corner of Rue Soekarno and Ave Mohammed V. The parcel ('Colis postaux') and EMS ('Poste Rapide') offices are to the right of the main entrance.

Téléboutiques are found all over town. Wave Cyber Cafe (53 Allal Ben Abdellah) and INT Plus is on Ave Mohammed V, both charge around Dr10 per hour.

Bookshops Reasonable English books are available at the English Bookshop (☎ 706593, 7 Zankat Alyamama) and American Bookstore (☎ 767103, 4 Rue Tanger).

Librairie Livre Service, on Ave Allal ben Abdallah, stocks French books.

Travel Agencies CAP Tours (☎ 733571, fax 731878, ✉ Captours@sis.net.ma), at 7 Rue Damas, Agdal, are a polished operation. Also good are Voyages Schwartz (☎ 681569), on the corner of Av Omar Ben Khattab and Rue Daraa in Agdal.

Things to See

The walled **medina** only dates from the 17th century, but is worth exploring. There are some excellent carpet shops and jewellery stores. Follow Rue Souika, then head north up Rue des Consuls (where there's an informal morning carpet souk on Tuesday and Thursday) to get to the **Kasbah des Oudaias**, built on the bluff overlooking the Atlantic Ocean. The main entry is via the impressive **Almohad Bab Oudaia**, built in 1195.

The kasbah houses a palace built by Moulay Ismail that now contains the **Museum of Moroccan Arts**. The museum is open daily; entry is Dr10.

South-east of the medina within, walking distance of the centre of town, is the Rabat's most famous landmark, the **Tour Hassan**, the incomplete minaret of the great mosque begun by Yacoub al-Mansour. The 1755 earthquake finished off the half-built mosque. On the same site is the **Mausoleum of Mohammed V**, the present king's grandfather.

Bab ar-Rouah, the Gate of the Winds, close to the Royal Palace is very impressive. Beyond the city walls, at the end of Ave Yacoub el-Mansour, are the remains of the ancient Roman city of Sala. It subsequently became the independent Berber city of **Chellah** and then later still the Merenids' royal burial ground. It's open daily, entry is Dr10.

Rabat's **Archaeology Museum** is interesting, but the marvellous Roman bronzes are sometimes away on loan. It's on Rue al-Brihi, almost opposite the Hôtel Chellah, and is open daily (except Tuesday), entry is Dr10.

If you're after something completely different, learn to **surf** at Oudayas Surf Club (☎ 260683). The stylish club-house is perched above the Atlantic Ocean west of the kasbah.

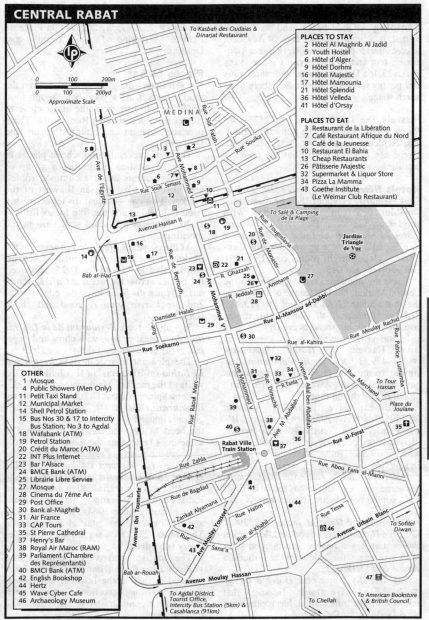

CENTRAL RABAT

To Kasbah des Oudaias &
Dinarjat Restaurant

MEDINA

To Salé & Camping
de la Plage

Jardins
Triangle
de Vuę

Bab al-Had

To Salé & Camping
de la Plage

PLACES TO STAY
2 Hôtel Al Maghrib Al Jadid
5 Youth Hostel
6 Hôtel d'Alger
9 Hôtel Dorhmi
16 Hôtel Majestic
17 Hôtel Mamounia
21 Hôtel Splendid
36 Hôtel Velleda
41 Hôtel d'Orsay

PLACES TO EAT
3 Restaurant de la Libération
7 Café Restaurant Afrique du Nord
8 Café de la Jeunesse
10 Restaurant El Bahia
13 Cheap Restaurants
26 Pâtisserie Majestic
32 Supermarket & Liquor Store
34 Pizza La Mamma
43 Goethe Institute
   (Le Weimar Club Restaurant)

To Tour
Hassan

Place du
Joulane

Rabat Ville
Train Station

To Sofitel
Diwan

To Chellah

To American Bookstore
& British Council

To Agdal District,
Tourist Office,
Intercity Bus Station (5km) &
Casablanca (91km)

Bab ar-Rouah

OTHER
1 Mosque
4 Public Showers (Men Only)
11 Petit Taxi Stand
12 Municipal Market
14 Shell Petrol Station
15 Bus Nos 30 & 17 to Intercity
   Bus Station; No 3 to Agdal
18 Wafabank (ATM)
19 Petrol Station
20 Crédit du Maroc (ATM)
22 INT Plus Internet
23 Bar l'Alsace
24 BMCE Bank (ATM)
25 Librairie Libre Service
27 Mosque
28 Cinema du 7éme Art
29 Post Office
30 Bank al-Maghrib
31 Air France
33 CAP Tours
35 St Pierre Cathedral
37 Henry's Bar
38 Royal Air Maroc (RAM)
39 Parliament (Chambre
   des Représentants)
40 BMCI Bank (ATM)
42 English Bookshop
44 Hertz
45 Wave Cyber Cafe
46 Archaeology Museum

MOROCCO

Places to Stay

Camping At Salé beach, and well signposted, is *Camping de la Plage (☎ 844566)*. It costs Dr15 per person, Dr18 for a two-person tent and Dr12 per car. Camper vans are Dr25. It's Dr10 for power and water, plus Dr7 per hot shower. Unfortunately there's not much shade.

Hostels The *Youth Hostel (☎ 725769, 43 Rue Marassa)*, opposite the walls of the medina, is pleasant and costs Dr32 per night. There are cold showers, but no cooking facilities.

Hotels *Hôtel d'Alger (☎ 724829, 34 Rue Souk Semara)* is about the cheapest, reasonable deal in the medina with singles/doubles for Dr35/70. However, *Hôtel Al Maghrib Al Jadid (☎ 732207, 2 Rue Sebbahi)* is more geared towards travellers – clean, bright rooms cost Dr50/80. Hot showers are Dr5.

There are numerous other cheapies in the Central Market, but in a league of its own, is the immaculate *Hôtel Dorhmi (☎ 723898, 313 Ave Mohammed V)*. Comfortable rooms cost Dr80/100; hot showers are Dr7.

In the ville nouvelle, a block south of Blvd Hassan II, *Hôtel Mamounia (☎ 724479, 10 Rue de la Mamounia)* has simple rooms for Dr50/90. Some rooms have balconies; hot showers cost Dr5. Don't be put off by the entrance.

More expensive is *Hôtel Velleda (☎ 769531, 106 Ave Allal ben Abdallah)*. It's a tidy, bright place on the 4th floor (with a lift) and has good views. Spacious rooms with showers (some have toilets) cost Dr120/165.

Hôtel Splendid (☎ 723283, 8 Rue Ghazza) has some great en suite rooms for Dr150/175 and some poor-value basic rooms for Dr97/118.

The renovated *Hotel Majestic (☎ 722997, 121 Blvd Hassan II)* is a good middle-bracket choice. Large, reasonably furnished en suite rooms (some with balconies and medina views) cost Dr189/223.

The friendly, three-star *Hôtel d'Orsay (☎ 202277, 11 Ave Moulay Youssef)*, just across from the train station, has rooms with good facilities for Dr211/264.

New, swish and modern is *Hôtel Sofitel Diwan (☎ 262727, fax 262424)* on Place de l'Unité Africaine. Double rooms cost Dr1800.

Places to Eat

For self-caters the grocery stalls around the indoor market are a good bet, though food stuffs are cheaper from the stalls close to Bab el Bouiba and along Rue Souika. There is a supermarket and liquor store on Rue Dimachk.

There are several good, cheap places to eat in the medina, including a group of small restaurants under a common roofed area just off Blvd Hassan II, west of the market. You can get meat dishes or freshly fried fish, salad and the like for as little as Dr20. There is a bessara stall here in the mornings.

At the popular *Café de la Jeunesse*, in the medina, you can get a full meal of kebabs, chips, salad and bread for Dr25. However, the tajines across the street at *Café Restaurant Afrique du Nord* have the edge (Dr25) and the *harira* soup is good and cheap (Dr3.50).

Just up the road, *Restaurant de la Libération* does meat or fish, with chips and vegetables (or couscous on Fridays) for Dr29.

The pleasant Moroccan-style *Restaurant El Bahia* on Blvd Hassan II is built into the walls of the medina. Meals cost around Dr35.

For a splurge (about Dr200 per person) try *Restaurant Dinarjat (☎ 704239, 6 Rue Belgnaoui)* housed in a 17th-century mansion in the heart of the medina. The experience is sometimes better than the food.

There are plenty of restaurants in the ville nouvelle. *La Mamma (☎ 707329, 6 Rue Zankat Tanta)*, near the Hôtel Central, is the best (licensed) pizzeria/Italian restaurant in Rabat I and has been run by the same Italian-French family since 1964. Pizzas cost Dr50 and fresh pasta dishes start at around Dr45. The steaks and ice cream are also good; delivery is available.

The stylish, and very European, *Le Weimar Club Restaurant (☎ 732650, 7 Rue Sana'a)* in the Geothe Institute, serves reasonable pizza and excellent German/French cuisine for around Dr50. It has a pleasant and relaxed bar.

There are numerous cafes along Ave Mohammed V, some of which double as bars. *Henry's*, on Avenue Allel ben Abdallah, is OK. *Pâtisserie Majestic* has excellent bread, cakes and coffee. In the south-east corner of the Kasbah des Oudaias, the quiet and shady *Café Maure* overlooks the estuary to Salé.

Getting There & Away

Bus The bus station is inconveniently situated 5km from the centre of town. Take local bus No 30 or a petit taxis (Dr15) to the centre.

CTM offers a comprehensive service, though cheaper non-CTM buses leave for most destinations including Casablanca, Tangier, Fès, Tetouan, Chefchaouen, Tiznit and Marrakesh.

Train *Rabat Ville* train station is centrally located on Ave Mohammed V. Don't get off at Rabat Agdal station. There are 23 trains to Casablanca (Dr27 one-way, 50 minutes). About half are *Trains Navettes Rapides* (TNR) shuttle services which link Rabat with Casablanca's Mohammed V airport (Dr55; 2nd class), via Casa-Port.

There are also daily departures to Tangier (5½ hours), Meknès and Fès (four hours) and Marrakesh (4½ hours). Cheaper, late-night *Ordinaire* services are available.

Taxi Grands taxis for Casablanca (Dr27) leave from outside the main bus station. Taxis for Fès (Dr55), Meknès (Dr40) and Salé (Dr3) leave from near the Hôtel Bou Regreg on Blvd Hassan II.

Car The following are among the car-rental agencies in Rabat:

Avis (☎ 769759) 7 Rue Abou Faris al-Marini
Budget (☎ 705789) train station, Ave Mohammed V
Europcar (☎ 722328) 25 Rue Patrice Lumumba
Hertz (☎ 709227) 46 Ave Mohammed V

Getting Around

Local Transport The main local city bus station is on Blvd Hassan II. From here, the No 16 bus goes to Salé and No 3 to Agdal. Bus Nos 30 and 17 run past Rabat's intercity bus station; they leave from a stop just inside Bab al-Had.

AROUND RABAT

The town of **Salé** is worlds away from Rabat. Largely left to itself since the demise of the corsairs, you can experience the sights, smells and sounds of the Morocco of yesteryear here without the tourist hordes.

In the 13th century the Merenid sultan built the walls and gates that stand today and a canal between the Oued Bou Regreg and the Bab Mrisa to allow safe access for shipping. Salé became the principal seaport through which the sultanate at Fès traded with the outside world until the end of the 16th century.

The main sight inside the walls is the classic Merenid **medersa** built in 1333 next to the grand mosque. Entry costs Dr10.

Grands taxis to Rabat (Dr3) leave from Bab Mrisa. Bus No 16 also links the two. You can catch the small boats across the river below Bab Bou Haja.

CASABLANCA
☎ 02

With a population of at least five million, Casablanca is Morocco's largest city and industrial centre. Although it has a history going back many centuries and was colonised by the Portuguese in the 16th century (who stayed until 1755), it had declined into insignificance by the mid-1880s.

Its renaissance came when the resident-general of the French protectorate, Lyautey, decided to develop Casablanca as a commercial centre. It was largely his ideas that gave Casablanca its wide boulevards, public parks and fountains, and imposing Mauresque civic buildings (a blend of French colonial and traditional Moroccan styles).

Look for the white, medium high-rise 1930s architecture, the many Art Deco touches and the pedestrian precincts thronged with speedy, fashion-conscious young people. Casablanca is cosmopolitan Morocco and an excellent barometer of liberal Islam.

Information

Tourist Offices The helpful ONMT (☎ 271177, 55 Rue Omar Slaoui) is open weekdays. The Syndicat d'Initiative, at 98 Blvd Mohammed V, is open daily.

Money There are BMCE branches with ATMs on Ave Lalla Yacout and Ave des

CENTRAL CASABLANCA

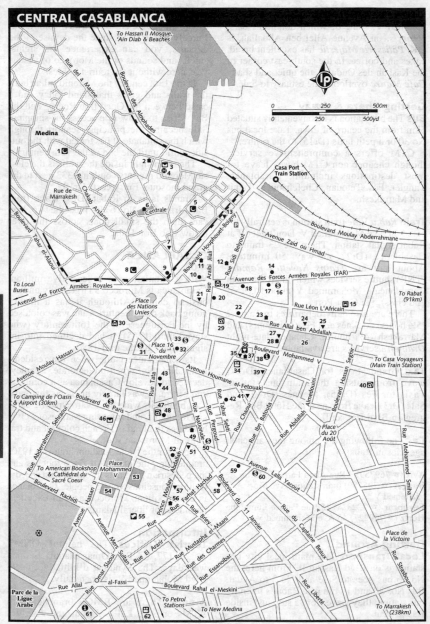

CENTRAL CASABLANCA

PLACES TO STAY		
2	Youth Hostel	
6	Cheap Hotels	
11	Hôtel Plaza	
12	Hôtel du Centre	
23	Hôtel Touring	
28	Hôtel Colbert	
37	Hôtel Rialto	
49	Hôtel de Paris; Swiss Ice Cream Factory	
56	Hôtel du Palais	

PLACES TO EAT		
7	Restaurant Widad	
13	Taverne du Dauphin	
21	Papa Geno	
24	Restaurant de l'Étoile Marocaine	
25	La Bodéga	
27	Rôtisseries; Restaurant Amine	
35	Sphinx Brasserie	
39	Snack Saigon	
41	Grocery Store	
44	Restaurant Snack Bar California	

51	Cafe National	
57	Restaurant Al-Mounia	
58	Pâtisserie de l'Opera	

OTHER		
1	Al-Djemma Mosque	
3	Post Office	
4	Hammam	
5	Great Mosque	
8	Mosque	
9	Clock Tower	
10	Air France	
14	Avis	
15	CTM Bus Terminal	
16	BMCE Bank (ATM)	
17	Europcar	
18	Royal Air Maroc (RAM)	
19	Petit Taxi Stand	
20	Hertz	
22	British Airways Office	
26	Central Market	
29	First Cyber	
30	Grand Taxis for Rabat	
31	Wafabank	
32	Trasmediterranea	

33	Crédit du Maroc (ATM)	
34	Cinéma Rialto	
36	Au Petit Poucet	
38	Syndicat d'Initiative; Post Office	
40	Haloui Cyber Club	
42	Imaphotos	
43	Libraire Liver Service	
45	Citibank	
46	Main Post Office	
47	Euro Net	
48	English Forum Bookshop	
50	BMCE Bank (ATM)	
52	Voyages Schwartz	
53	Palais de Justice	
54	Hôtel de Ville	
55	French Consulate	
59	Le Comptoire Marocaine de Distribution de Disques	
60	BMCI Bank	
61	Tourist Office	
62	Cinéma Lynx	

FAR. The Crédit du Maroc bank on Blvd Mohammed V will change travellers cheques and is open Saturday mornings. There are banks with ATMs at Mohammed V international airport.

American Express is represented by Voyages Schwartz (☎ 222947, 112 Rue Prince Moulay Abdallah).

Post & Communications The main post office (which services poste restante) is on Place Mohammed V. The parcel office is left of the main entrance.

Email & Internet Access Several email places dotted around town charge about Dr20 per hour. Try First Cyber at 62 Rue Allah Ben Abdellah, Euro Net at 51 Rue Tata, and Haloui Cyber Club at 206 Blvd Mohammed V.

Things to See
Don't miss the beautiful **Hassan II Mosque**, which overlooks the ocean just beyond the northern tip of the medina. Finished in 1993, it is the third biggest religious monument in the world. It's also open to non-Muslims. There are guided tours, in various languages,

every day except Friday (Dr100 per person; Dr50 for students).

The central **ville nouvelle** around Place Mohammed V has some of the best examples of Mauresque architecture. They include the *hôtel de ville* (town hall), the *palais de justice* (law courts), the post office, and the extraordinary but shamefully neglected Cathédrale du Sacré Cœur. Casablanca has some wonderful architecture, so look upwards occasionally!

Casablanca's **beaches** are to the west of town along the Blvd de la Corniche and beyond in the suburb of 'Ain Diab. It's a trendy area and very crowded in summer. The beaches are nothing special. Bus No 9 goes to 'Ain Diab from Place Oued al-Makhazine, just to the west of Place des Nations Unies.

Places to Stay
Camping About 5km south-west of town, on the main road to El-Jadida, is *Camping de l'Oasis* (☎ 234257), which charges Dr10 per person, tent and car. Bus No 31 runs past it.

Hostel There's a *Youth Hostel* (☎ 220551, fax 227677, 6 Place de l'Amiral Philibert) in

MOROCCO

the medina, just off Blvd des Almohades. It's large, comfortable and clean, and costs Dr45 per person, including breakfast. Double/triple rooms cost Dr120/180.

Hotels The hotels in the medina are unclassified, without hot showers (use the local hammam), seedy and cost around Dr40 per person. There are a number around Rue Centrale, north-west of the clock tower, but you can do much better outside the medina for a little more.

Outside the medina *Hôtel du Palais* (☎ 276121, 68 Rue Farhat Hachad), near the French consulate, is a good, clean (and cheap) deal. Spacious singles/doubles go for Dr62/Dr76. Showers are cold.

Near the central market and around Rue Allal ben Abdallah, is a cluster of cheapies. *Hôtel Touring* (☎ 310216, 87 Rue Allal ben Abdallah) has big old rooms for Dr62/78 (Dr7 for a hot shower).

A good choice is the friendly *Hôtel Colbert* (☎ 314241, 38 Rue Chaoui), opposite the market. Simple rooms with washbasin go for Dr68/83 (hot showers costs Dr10). En suite rooms cost Dr84/100.

Hôtel Rialto (☎ 27 51 22, 9 Rue Salah Ben Bouchaib) is a welcoming place offering spotless singles/doubles with shower for Dr84/120.

Hôtel du Centre (☎ 446180, fax 446178), just off Ave des FAR, on Rue Sidi Balyout has reasonable modern rooms, with bathroom and phone, for Dr158/195.

Built in 1936, the characterful *Hôtel Plaza* (☎ 297698, 18 Blvd Houphouet-Boigney) has large en suite rooms (some have balconies and sea views) for Dr224/263 and rooms without bathrooms for Dr130/169. It also has a bar.

The three-star *Hôtel de Paris* (☎ 274275, fax 298069, 2 Rue Ech-Cherie Amziane), in the pedestrian zone off Rue Prince Moulay Abdallah, has comfortable, rooms with heating, phone and TV for Dr293/347.

The five-star *Hôtel Royal Mansour* (☎ 313011, fax 312583, ✉ rmansourcom @marocnet.ma, 27 Ave des FAR) is the pick of the crop. Rooms start at Dr2800.

Places to Eat

There are a few cheap restaurants around the clock tower entrance to the medina. A popular one is *Restaurant Widad*, which serves decent Moroccan dishes.

Outside the medina, the best place for good, cheap food is along Rue Chaoui. There are several rotisseries offering roast chicken (Dr15 to Dr25) and the excellent *Restaurant Amine*, which serves large portions of freshly cooked seafood from Dr25.

In the market, opposite, are a number of vegetable and fruit stalls (though expensive) and a good delicatessen (parma ham and pâté). Fresh food is cheaper in the medina.

The friendly *Restaurant de l'Étoile Marocaine* (☎ 314100, 107 Rue Allal Ben Abdallah) serves decent Moroccan dishes in pleasant surroundings. Main courses cost around Dr50.

For excellent Moroccan food in traditional surroundings, check out *Restaurant Al-Mounia* (☎ 222669, 95 Rue du Prince Moulay Abdallah). Main courses start at Dr85 and vegetarian dishes are available.

Papa Geno on Rue el-Amraoui Brahim, is a clean and bright fast food joint, the chef is a complete professional. Dr24 for *kefta*, chips and salad.

The food at *Restaurant Snack Bar California*, 19 Rue Tata remains good, just as well as they are trading on LPs recommendation. Mains, including tajine, couscous and brochettes and some vegetarian dishes, cost Dr30. It's a peaceful and relaxing place for women travellers.

A real locals place is the tiny *Snack Saigon* on Rue Salah Ben Bouchaib. Prices seem to fluctuate with the mood of the waiter but on a good day you'll pay about Dr25 for a world class tajine cooked over a charcoal burner.

For seafood head to the popular *Taverne du Dauphin* (☎ 221200, 115 Blvd Houphouet-Boigny). A fish fillet will cost around Dr65 and calamares Dr45, 20% tax is added. If you don't fancy a full meal, pop in for a snack at the bar, which is a great place for a relaxed drink.

The city centre is filled with French-style cafes. *Cafe National* is a beautiful example of Art Deco style.

Pâtisserie de l'Opéra, 50 Blvd 11 Janvier is a civilised, tranquil place, great for a quiet coffee or tea.

For delicious home-made ice cream visit the *Swiss Ice Cream Factory*. It's a woman friendly place deservedly popular with the young and trendy.

There's a grocery store on Ave Houmane el-Fetouaki.

Entertainment

Bars & Nightclubs Central Casablanca has a large red-light district and plenty of seedy bars and cabaret places. Women should be particularly mindful of this after dark.

A good low key bar is *Au Petit Poucet*, a die-hard relic of 1920s France. Saint-Exupéry, the French author and aviator used to spend time here between mail-flights south across the Sahara on the Toulouse to Chile service.

Just round the corner, the *Sphinx Brasserie* is a spacious, friendly place, but again a bit of a male preserve.

La Bodéga (☎ 541842, 129 Rue Allal Ben Abdallah) is a Spanish-style tapas bar and restaurant. It's expensive but good fun with live music, and it's very woman friendly.

The trendiest clubs and bars are to be found in the wealthy beachside suburb of 'Ain Diab to the west of town.

Cinema *Cinéma Lynx* (☎ 220229), 50 Ave Mers Sultan, is considered to be the best in town. Tickets cost from Dr20. The more central *Cinéma Rialto*, on Rue Salah Ben Bouchaib, is a classic Art Deco building.

Getting There & Away

Air From Casablanca's Mohammed V airport (30km south-east of the city), there are regular connections to Western Europe, the rest of Africa and the Middle East.

Internally, you can get to any destination directly from Casablanca with Royal Air Maroc. There are five daily flights to Agadir (Dr929, one hour), five weekly flights to Fès (Dr578, 50 minutes), at least two daily flights to Marrakesh (Dr451, 50 minutes) and at least one flight a day to Tangier (Dr571, one hour).

Bus The flash CTM bus station (☎ 449224) is on Rue Léon L'Africain. There are daily departures to Agadir (eight-nine hours) Essaouira (seven hours), Fès (five hours) and Meknès (four hours) Marrakesh (four hours) Oujda, Rabat (one hour), Safi (four hours), Tangier (six hours), Taza and Tetouan (four-five hours).

CTM also operates international buses (☎ 458000) to Belgium, France, Germany, Italy and Spain from Casablanca.

Aulad Ziane is the new bus station for almost all non-CTM services. It's bright and almost serene! The only draw-back is its distance from the city centre, which is about a Dr10 taxi ride away or catch bus No 10 from Blvd Mohammed V.

Train Most long distance departures to destinations across the country leave from Casa-Voyageurs station, 4km east of the city. Local bus No 30 runs to Casa-Voyageurs along Ave des FAR and Blvd Mohammed V; a petit taxi costs Dr10.

Rapide shuttle trains to Mohammed V Airport (38 minutes; Dr30) and north to Rabat (50 minutes; Dr27) leave from the central Casa-Port station, via Casa-Voyageurs.

Taxi Grands taxis to Rabat (Dr27) leave from Blvd Hassan Seghir, near the CTM bus station.

Car The following are among the car-rental agencies in Casablanca:

Avis (☎ 312424) 19 Ave des FAR; (☎ 339072) Mohammed V airport
Budget (☎ 313737) Mohammed V airport; (☎ 313124) Tour des Habous, Ave des FAR
Europcar (☎ 313737) Complexe des Habous, Ave des FAR; (☎ 339161) Mohammed V airport
Hertz 25 Rue Aribi Jilali (☎ 484710); Mohammed V airport (☎ 339181)

Getting Around

To/From the Airport Shuttle trains (TNR) run from Mohammed V airport to the Casa-Voyageurs and Casa-Port train stations (24 minutes, Dr25). A grands taxi to Mohammed V airport will cost you Dr150 (Dr200 after 8pm).

Bus Useful local bus routes include:

No 4 Along Rue Strasbourg and down Ave Lalla Yacout to Blvd de Paris
No 5 From the terminal to Place de la Victoire
No 9 From the terminal to 'Ain Diab and the beaches

No 10 From Place de la Concorde (and along
   Blvd Mohammed V) to Ouled Ziane bus station
No 15 From the terminal to the Hassan II
   Mosque
No 30 From the Blvd Ziraoui to Casa-
   Voyageurs train station via Ave des FAR and
   Blvd Mohammed V

Taxi There's no shortage of petits taxis in
Casablanca, but just make sure the meter is
on. Expect to pay Dr10 for a ride in or around
the city centre.

SAFI
☎ 04
Safi (Asfi) is a modern Atlantic fishing port
and industrial centre in a steep crevasse
formed by the Oued Chabah. It has a lively
walled medina and souq, with battlements
dating from the brief Portuguese era, and is
well known for its pottery.

Things to See
In the walled city, which the Portuguese built
and to which the Moroccans later added, the
Qasr al-Bahr (Castle on the Sea) is usually
the first port of call. There are good views
from the ramparts, and a number of 17th-
century Spanish and Dutch cannons. It's open
from 8.30 am to noon and 2.30 to 6 pm daily;
entry costs Dr10.

Across the street lies the **medina**, which is
dominated by the **Kechla**, a massive defensive structure with fine views out to the Qasr
al-Bahr. Inside is the **National Ceramics
Museum** which features both ancient and
contemporary pottery. It's open from 8.30 am
to noon and 2 to 6 pm daily. Entry costs
Dr10.

Safi's famous **potteries**, where traditional
wood-fired kilns are still used, are on the hill
opposite Bab Chabah, to the north-west of the
Kechla. You can purchase pottery here for
very reasonable prices.

Places to Stay
About 2km north of town, just off the coast
road to El-Jadida, is **Camping International**.
It's a shady site with a small swimming pool
and costs Dr12 per person, Dr9 per car, Dr9
per tent and Dr10 for a hot shower.

There are some basic cheapies (from Dr30
per person) clustered around the port end of
Rue du Souq and along Rue de R'bat.

Hôtel Majestic (☎ 464011), next to the
medina wall at the junction of Ave Moulay
Youssef and Place de l'Indépendance, is the
best value. Well-maintained, pleasant
singles/doubles with washbasin and bidet
cost from Dr40. A hot shower is Dr5.

The two-star **Hôtel Anis** (☎ 463078), just
off Rue de R'bat to the south of the medina,
has comfortable rooms with shower and toilet for Dr135/159. **Hôtel Assif** (☎ 622311),
on Ave de la Liberté near Place Mohammed
V, has rooms with shower for Dr200/250.
The hotel has a restaurant.

Places to Eat
The hole-in-the-wall seafood restaurants in
the alleys off Rue du Souq in the medina offer
cheap, excellent food for about Dr20 a head.
Restaurant de Safi, on Rue de la Marine, offers reasonably priced brochettes and other
Moroccan dishes. Almost next door, **Restaurant Gegene** serves fish and Italian dishes.

The more expensive **Restaurant Le
Refuge** (☎ 464354), a few kilometres north
of Safi on the coast road to Sidi Bouzid, has
a good reputation for seafood.

Getting There & Away
CTM and other companies share a terminal
south-east of the town centre. There are regular departures to Casablanca and several to
Marrakesh, Essaouira and Agadir. A couple of
buses head north to El-Jadida. Some are
through services from elsewhere, but you
shouldn't have too much trouble on main runs.

ESSAOUIRA
☎ 04
Essaouira (pronounced Esa-**weera**) is one of
the most popular coastal towns for independent
travellers. Not only does it have a long curve
of magnificent beach (much appreciated by
windsurfers), it also has a pleasantly laid-back
atmosphere. It's a favourite with painters, and
in summer months the cool sea breezes provide
welcome relief from the heat of the interior.

Originally a small Phoenician settlement
called Mogodor, it was occupied by the Portuguese in the 16th century. The present
town, however, dates largely from 1765,
when Sultan Sidi Mohammed bin Abdallah
hired a French architect to redesign the town
for use as a trade centre with Europe.

MOROCCO

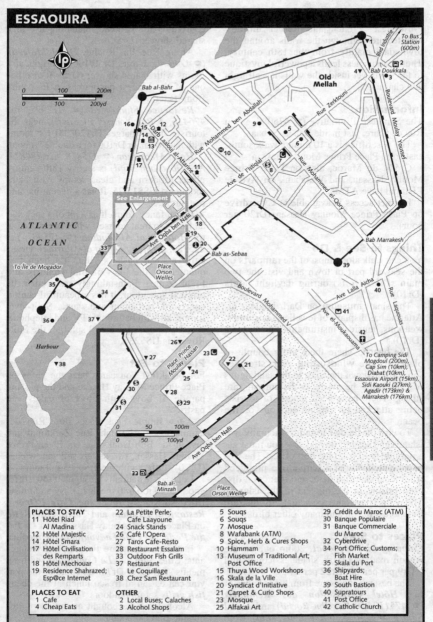

ESSAOUIRA

ATLANTIC OCEAN

To Île de Mogador

Harbour

Old Mellah

To Bus Station (600m)

Bab al-Bahr

Bab Doukkala

Boulevard Moulay Youssef

Rue Zerktouni

Rue Mohammed ben Abdallah

Ave de l'Istiqlal

Rue Mohammed el-Qory

Darb Laalouj al-Attarine

See Enlargement

Ave Oqba ben Nafi

Place Orson Welles

Bab as-Sebaa

Bab Marrakesh

Boulevard Mohammed V

Ave Lalla Aicha

Rue Laayoual

Ave el-Moukaouama

To Camping Sidi Mogdoul (200m), Cap Sim (10km), Diabat (10km), Essaouira Airport (15km), Sidi Kaouki (27km), Agadir (173km) & Marrakesh (176km)

South Bastion

MOROCCO

Place Prince Moulay Hassan

Bab al-Minzah

Place Orson Welles

Ave Oqba ben Nafi

PLACES TO STAY	22 La Petite Perle;	5 Souqs	29 Crédit du Maroc (ATM)
11 Hôtel Riad	Cafe Laayoune	6 Souqs	30 Banque Populaire
Al Madina	24 Snack Stands	7 Mosque	31 Banque Commerciale
12 Hôtel Majestic	26 Café l'Opera	8 Wafabank (ATM)	du Maroc
14 Hôtel Smara	27 Taros Cafe-Resto	9 Spice, Herb & Cures Shops	32 Cyberdrive
17 Hôtel Civilisation	28 Restaurant Essalam	10 Hammam	34 Port Office; Customs;
des Remparts	37 Restaurant	13 Museum of Traditional Art;	Fish Market
18 Hôtel Mechouar	Le Coquillage	Post Office	35 Skala du Port
19 Residence Shahrazed;	38 Chez Sam Restaurant	15 Thuya Wood Workshops	36 Shipyards;
Esp@ce Internet		16 Skala de la Ville	Boat Hire
	OTHER	20 Syndicat d'Initiative	39 South Bastion
PLACES TO EAT	2 Local Buses; Calaches	21 Carpet & Curio Shops	40 Supratours
1 Cafe	3 Alcohol Shops	23 Mosque	41 Post Office
4 Cheap Eats		25 Alfakai Art	42 Catholic Church

The fortifications are an interesting mix of Portuguese, French and Berber military architecture, although the walls around the town date mainly from the 18th century. Their massiveness lends a powerful mystique to the town, yet inside the walls it's all light and charm.

Information

The Syndicat d'Initiative (☎ 475080) is on Rue de Caire, just inside Bab as-Sebaa.

The post office is a 10 minute walk southeast from Place Prince Moulay Hassan.

Crédit du Maroc, also on Place Prince Moulay Hassan, and Wafabank on Ave de l'Istiqlal have ATMs.

Internet access is available at Cyberdrive on Place Prince Moulay Hassan (Dr20 per hour).

Things to See & Do

You can walk along most of the **ramparts** on the seaward part of town and visit the two main *skalas* (forts) during daylight hours (Dr10).

The small **museum** on Darb Laalouj al-Attarine has displays of jewellery, costumes, weapons, musical instruments and carpets (Dr10).

The **beach**, where there are a couple of places to hire **windsurfing** gear, stretches some 10km down the coast to the sand dunes of Cap Sim – be aware as the currents are strong. There have been reports of tourists being attacked on remote sections of the beach.

To visit the Île de Mogador – actually two islands and several tiny islets – you must get a permit (free) from the port office. The Romans manufactured a purple dye produced from local shellfish here; and there is a disused prison on the biggest of the islands. Today the islands are a sanctuary for the rare Eleonora's falcon and many other birds.

Places to Stay

Camping Sidi Mogdoul, 200m out on the Agadir road, is a stark, shadeless compound – Dr9 per person, Dr22 per tent.

The best sea views are from the terraces of the *Hôtel Civilisation des Remparts* (☎ 475110, 18 Rue Ibn Rochd) and *Hôtel Smara* (☎ 475655, 26 Rue de la Skala). Both

have basic singles/doubles around covered courtyards for Dr60/80, including use of a shared shower (Dr5).

Along Rue Ibn Rochd, *Hotel Majestic* (☎ 474909) charges Dr50/100 for bright, airy rooms with shared shower (Dr5). It also has one of the highest panoramas in Essaouira from its terrace.

Residence Shahrazed (☎ 472977, fax 476436, 1 Rue Youssef El Fassi), near the tourist office, charges Dr120/200 for rooms with bathroom, or Dr100 for a double without.

Hotel Mechouar (☎ 475828, fax 784827, Ave Oqba ben Nafii) is a cosy 18th-century place. Modern and clean rooms with bathroom cost US$15/25. It has a decent bar and restaurant.

If you fancy yourself as a bit of a rock star and want to treat yourself while in Essaouira, try *Hotel Riad Al Madina* (☎ 475907, fax 475727, 9 Darb Laalouj al-Attarine). Originally a local pasha's villa, it's been frequented by the likes of Jimi Hendrix and Frank Zappa. Painstakingly restored to its original splendour, it has a beautiful central courtyard, restaurant and sauna. Split-level rooms, all with bathroom, TV and telephone, cost US$44/67; for a real splurge, the Suite Royale is US$236.

Places to Eat

For breakfast you can't beat the cafes on Place Prince Moulay Hassan and the passing parade of boys with trays of cakes and pastries.

A few simple snack places along Rue Mohammed ben Abdallah, Rue Zerktouni and just inside Bab Doukkala. On Place Prince Moulay Hassan, two stands sell sandwiches (Dr20) stuffed with meat, salad and more.

Loads of restaurants throughout town offer good, Dr40 to Dr80 meals in cosy and music filled surrounds, including *Cafe l'Opéra*, *Restaurant Essalam* and *Taros Café-Resto* on Place Prince Moulay Hassan, and *La Petite Perle* and *Cafe Laayoune* in the medina.

In the port area are two seafood restaurants, *Chez Sam* and *Le Coquillage*, with set menus starting at Dr70. En route to the port you can eat an al fresco lunch at the cheap *fish grills* set up outdoors.

Alcohol can be bought at the shops just outside Bab Doukkala.

MOROCCO

Getting There & Away
Air There are regular flights from Essaouira's airport (☎ 476709), 15km north of town, to Casablanca.

Bus The bus terminal is 1km north-east of the town centre. CTM has regular buses to Agadir (three hours), Casablanca (6½ hours) and Marrakesh (2½ hours). Grands taxis to Agadir leave from a nearby lot.

Supratours (☎ 472317) runs buses from near Bab Marrakesh to Marrakesh train station and Agadir.

AGADIR
☎ 08

Most of the original town of Agadir was devastated by an earthquake in 1960; a double tragedy that it should occur in a decade responsible for so much of today's ugly architecture. Sitting by a vast sweep of protected beach, the town has been specifically developed as a resort for short-stay package tourists from Europe. For the independent traveller, although expensive, it's well placed for trips east and south and offers an escape from the restraints of everyday Moroccan life.

If it all gets too much, you can always head for the less-crowded beaches of **Taghazout** and **Cap Rhir**, a local bus ride to the north.

Information
The ONMT tourist office (☎ 846377) is in the market just off Ave Prince Sidi Mohammed. There's also a Syndicat d'Initiative (☎ 840307) on Blvd Mohammed V.

The main post and phone office is on Ave du Prince Moulay Abdallah, and there's another in Talborjt. Internet cafes, including AgadirNet, on Ave Hassan II, charge Dr10 to Dr15 per hour.

Places to Stay
Camping Campervans predominate at Agadir's *camp site* (☎ 846683) on the port side of town. It charges Dr10/15 per adult/tent.

Hotels Most budget hotels are concentrated in the slightly sleazy, but pretty compact area of Rue Yacoub El Mansour in Talborjt.

Hotel Tamri (☎ 821880, 1 Ave du Président Kennedy) has a bright, plant-filled courtyard with rooms with bathroom for Dr80/100.

Hotel Petite Suède (☎ 840779, fax 840057), just off Ave du Général Kettani, is close-ish to the beach. For Dr140/195, rooms with bathroom and balcony are good value.

Central on Ave Hassan II, *Hotel Kamal* (☎ 842817, fax 843940) is a package place so has pool, bar etc and rooms for Dr290/360.

There's no shortage of expensive hotels in Agadir, especially along the beachfront. Dominated by block-booked charter groups, they tend to get more expensive the further south you go. The *Sheraton* (☎ 843232, Blvd Mohammed V) has rooms for Dr1500/1700.

Places to Eat
There are snack stands on Rue Yacoub el-Mansour. *Restaurants,* on the roads leading up here, offer good three-course menus for around Dr35.

If you fancy fresh fish, head to the port entrance where there are dozens of cheap *seafood stalls*. The restaurants lining the *promenade* are great for a sunset dinner. Farther back you'll find the large hotels with Moroccan and international fare, plus a smorgasbord of other restaurants and cafes.

Uniprix is a good place to pick up munchies and alcohol. For healthier food head to the souq.

Entertainment
There are countless bars to choose from in the bigger hotels, often with 'entertainers' or karaoke. *The Pub* in *Hotel Anezi* has magnificent panoramic views. The *Irish bar* in the Tafoukt complex on Blvd du 20 Août, has tempting rows of taps but only serves the usual Moroccan draughts. Otherwise you can down a beer at a beachfront restaurant or cafe.

Two popular nightclubs are *Flamingo* at Hôtel Beach Club and *El Paradiso* at Hôtel Argana.

Getting There & Around
Air Royal Air Maroc (☎ 840793) has an office on Ave du Général Kettani. From Al-Massira airport (☎ 839003), 22km south of Agadir (Dr150 grands taxi ride), it has direct flights to Casablanca (50 minutes; daily) and Marrakesh (30 minutes). International flights go to Paris (3½ hours; four weekly), Las Palmas (1¼ hours; three weekly) in the Canary Islands and Zurich (3½ hours; one weekly).

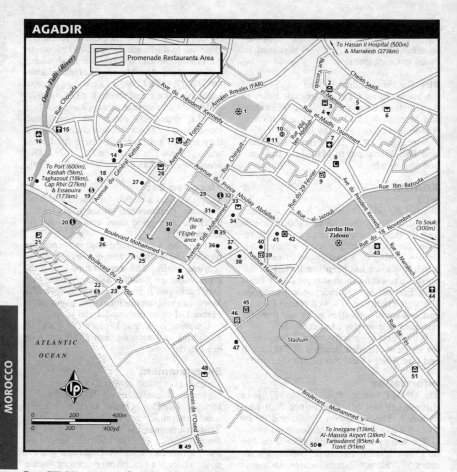

AGADIR

Promenade Restaurants Area

Ouest Tildi (River)

To Hassan II Hospital (500m)
& Marrakesh (273km)

Rue Chouada

Ave du Président Kennedy

Armées Royales (FAR)

Cheikh Saadi

Rue Yacoub el-Mansour

Avenue des Forces

Avenue du Général Kettani

Rue el-Madhi Toummert

Rue Allal ben Abdallah

Rue Chinguit

To Port (600m),
Kasbah (5km),
Taghazout (18km),
Cap Rhir (27km)
& Essaouira
(173km)

Avenue du Prince Moulay Abdallah

Rue du 29 Février

Ave du Président Kennedy

Rue Ibn Batouta

Rue – al-Jazouli

To Souk
(300m)

Boulevard Mohammed V

Place
de
l'Espér-
ance

Avenue Sidi Mohammed

Jardin Ibn
Zidoun

Rue du 18 Novembre

Boulevard du 20 Août

Avenue Hassan II

Rue de Marrakech

Rue de Fès

ATLANTIC
OCEAN

Stadium

Chemin de l'Oued Souss

Boulevard Mohammed V

To Inezgane (13km),
Al-Massira Airport (28km)
Taroudannt (85km) &
Tiznit (91km)

0   200   400m
0   200   400yd

MOROCCO

Bus CTM buses leave from Rue Yacoub el-Mansour daily for Casablanca (10 hours), Essaouira (three hours), Marrakesh (four hours), Rabat (12 hours), Tafraoute (five hours) and Tangier (14 hours).

The main bus terminal is actually in Inezgane, 13km south of Agadir. If you arrive here jump in a grands taxi (Dr3) or local bus No 5 or 6 to Agadir.

TAROUDANNT
☎ 08

Taroudannt, with its magnificent, extremely well-preserved, red-mud walls, has been an important player in Morocco's history. It briefly became the capital in the 16th century under the Saadians, who built the old part of town and the kasbah.

The city narrowly escaped destruction in 1687 at the hands of Moulay Ismail, after it became the centre of a rebellion opposing his rule. Instead, Moulay Ismail contented himself with massacring its inhabitants. Today, it's a pleasant place, with some nice accommodation options, to while away a few days.

Information
Taroudannt has banks with ATMs, a post

AGADIR

PLACES TO STAY & EAT					
4	Talborjt Restaurants	9	Cybernet; Wafabank (ATM)	32	ONMT Tourist Office
11	Hôtel Tamri	10	Hammam	33	Main Post & Phone Offices
14	Hôtel Petite Suède	12	Mosque	34	Town Hall; Pharmacy (All-
16	Camping ground	13	Royal Air Maroc (RAM)		Night Pharmacy)
24	Hotel Anezi	15	Protestant Church	36	Air France
26	Sheraton Hôtel	17	Car Rental Agencies	37	Car Rental Agencies (Local)
35	Hôtel Kamal	18	BCMI (ATM)	38	Travel Agencies
47	Hôtel Argana	19	BCME (ATM)	39	AgadirNet
49	Hôtel Beach Club	20	Syndicat d'Initiative	40	Saawa Supermarket
		21	Municipal Swimming Pool	41	New Labcolor (Kodak)
OTHER		22	Banque Populaire	42	Synagogue
1	Jardin de Olhâ & museum	23	Tourist Train	43	Police
2	Grands Taxis	25	Complexe Tafoukt	44	St Anne's Catholic Church
3	CTM buses	27	Tour Agents	45	Museum of Folk Arts
5	Complexe Artisanal	28	Supratours	46	Municipal Theatre
6	Talborjt Post Office	29	Central Market	48	Post Office
7	Police	30	Valle des Oiseaux	50	Royal Palace
8	Mohammed V Mosque	31	Uniprix (Supermarket);	51	Place Taxies et Bus
			Wafabank Bureau de Change		

office, and Infonet, north of Place Talmoklate, charges Dr10 per hour.

Things to See
You can explore the **ramparts** of Taroudannt by foot, bicycle (Dr5 per hour) or horse-drawn carriage (Dr35).

High-quality items abound in the Berber and Arab **souqs**, especially traditional jewellery, and there are large **markets** held outside the ramparts on Thursday and Sunday. Some modest **tanneries** lie just beyond Bab Taghount, north-west of the centre at Place Assarag.

Places to Stay
There are plenty of cheapie options, around or close to Place Assarag. On the square, *Hotel Roudani* has rooms on a terrace for Dr40 and free hot showers.

Closer to Place Talmoklate Is *Hotel des Oliviers* (☎ 852021). It has clean singles/doubles for Dr30/60 but showers are cold. *Hotel Mantaga* (☎ 852763) has a good terrace overlooking Place la Victoire, cold showers and rooms for Dr30/50/70.

The best deal by far is *Hotel Taroudannt* (☎ 852416). The rooms are gathered around a tranquil, leafy courtyard full of character and cost Dr70/90 without bathroom or Dr100/120 with bath and toilet.

Hotel Palais Salam (☎ 852501), a 19th-century palace within the kasbah, is excellent.

With cool gardens, fountains, salons, pool, bar and restaurants it's a top place for a splurge. Rooms cost Dr500/600; if you can stretch your budget a bit further go for the suites in the riad from Dr780/900.

Places to Eat
Small *restaurants* and *snack stands* line the street between Place Assarag and Place Talmoklate and serve the usual Moroccan fare plus seafood at rock-bottom prices. *Barcelone,* on Place Assarag, is a good one.

The restaurants at *Hotel Taroudannt* and *Hotel Palais Salam* have tasty French and Moroccan fare.

Getting There & Away
SATAS and CTM have offices on Place Assarag; other companies and grands taxis are based just outside Bab Zorgan, the southern gate. CTM has a morning bus to Casablanca via Agadir (1½ hours) and an evening bus to Ouarzazate (5½ hours). SATAS buses run to Tata (five hours) and Ouarzazate. Local buses leave for Marrakesh via the spectacular Tizi n'Test pass.

TIZNIT
☎ 08
In an arid corner of the Souss Valley at the end of the Anti-Atlas range, is Tiznit. With its 6km of encircling red-mud walls, it looks old

MOROCCO

but is actually a recent creation. It makes a pleasant short stop and the silver jewellery is reputed to be some of the best in the south.

There are a couple of banks with ATMs and Internet cafes that charge Dr12.

Places to Stay

There's a fairly bare *camp site* between Bab Oulad Jarrar and the main roundabout. The budget hotels are mostly on or near Place al-Machouar, the main square within the city walls, and are all pretty similar.

Hôtel Belle-Vue (☎ 862109), off the square on Rue du Bain, has large, sunny singles/doubles for Dr40/70. A hot shower costs Dr5. On Place al-Machouar, the *Hôtel/Café Atlas* has rooms (some overlooking the square) for around Dr40 per person.

The two-star *Hôtel de Paris* (☎ 862865), on Ave Hassan II by the roundabout, has clean and comfortable rooms with bathroom for Dr108/135. The hotel also has a restaurant.

Hôtel de Tiznit (☎ 862411), on Rue Bir In-zaran, is a three-star place with a secluded courtyard with pool, bar and restaurant. Rooms cost Dr253/319 and there's parking.

Places to Eat

Several of the hotels on Place al-Machouar have restaurants, and there are a few cafes scattered around inside and outside the walls. The market across Blvd Mohammed V from the main city gates is good for fresh food.

Café/Restaurant du Carrefour, opposite the Hôtel de Paris, offers a particularly good breakfast featuring fresh almond and spicy agane oil and it has a drinking fountain.

Getting There & Away

Buses (including CTM and SATAS) leave from Place al-Machouar to Agadir (two hours), Essaouira (six hours), Casablanca (13 hours), Marrakesh (5¾ hours), Tafraoute (four hours) and Sidi Ifni 1½ hours). Grands taxis to Agadir (Dr20) and Sidi Ifni (Dr20) leave from the main lot opposite the post office.

TAFRAOUTE

Some 107km east of Tiznit is the pretty Berber town of Tafraoute. The reason for visiting is the surrounding countryside. The nearby **Ameln Valley**, with its fields dotted with mud-brick villages, provides days of hiking possibilities. The journey up from Tiznit (or Agadir) into the heart of the Anti-Atlas to Tafraoute is well worth the effort.

There are a couple of banks (no ATMs), a post office and a souq on Monday and Wednesday.

Places to Stay & Eat

Just off the Tiznit road, *Camping Les Trois Palmiers* charges US$1 per person/tent.

The cheapest hotels are the *Hôtel Tanger* (☎ 800033), which offers basic rooms for Dr25 per person, and the *Hôtel Reddouane* (☎ 800066), where singles/doubles cost Dr35/50.

In the centre, *Hotel Tafraout* (☎ 800060, Place Al-Missira Moulay Rachid) has huge, modern and clean rooms for Dr40/80; hot showers are free.

Hotel Les Amandiers (☎ 800088, fax 800343) sits on the crest of the hill overlooking the town and has some pretty impressive views. Rooms with TV and phone cost Dr310/520. Aimed at package tourists, it has a swimming pool (non-residents pay Dr35), bar, restaurant and shaded parking.

You can eat fairly well for about Dr25 in either of the two cheap hotels. The pleasant *Restaurant l'Étoile du Sud*, opposite the post office, has a good set menu for Dr70.

Getting There & Away

CTM and other companies have evening services to Casablanca (11½ hours), Agadir (five hours) and Marrakesh (10 hours); all go via Tiznit (2½ hours). There are also local buses to Tiznit in the morning.

The High Atlas

MARRAKESH
☎ 04

One of Morocco's most important artistic and cultural centres, Marrakesh was founded in 1062 AD by the Almoravid sultan Youssef bin Tachfin, but experienced its heyday under his son, Ali, who built the extensive *khettara* (underground irrigation canals) that still supply the city's gardens with water.

The city was largely razed by the Almohads in 1147, but they soon rebuilt what would remain the capital of the Almohad empire until its collapse in 1269. For the following 300 years the focus of Moroccan brilliance passed to Fès, but the Saadians made Marrakesh the capital again in the 16th century. The Saadians also built the mellah, Mouassine mosque and the mosque of Ali ben Youssef. In the 17th century, Moulay Ismail moved the capital to Meknès, and although Marrakesh remained an important base of power, it only really came into its own again when the French built the ville nouvelle and revitalised the old town. Tourism has ensured its relative prosperity since then.

Orientation & Information

As in other major Moroccan towns, the ville nouvelle and the medina are separate entities. Place Djemaa el-Fna, Marrakesh's atmospheric main square, is the heart of the medina.

The tourist office (☎ 448889) is in the ville nouvelle on Place Abdel Moumen ben Ali. Other offices can be found at 170 Ave Mohammed V and near La Mamounia.

There are plenty of ATMs and money-exchanges, some (ie, Bank Populaire near Djemaa el-Fna) open on Saturday mornings.

The main post office is on Place du 16 Novembre, in the ville nouvelle. There is a branch office (and a phone centre) on the Djemaa el-Fna. Internet places charge between Dr15 and Dr20 an hour.

Things to See

The focal point of Marrakesh is the **Djemaa el-Fna**, a huge square in the medina. Although lively at any time of day, it comes into its own in the late afternoon and evening, when rows of open-air food stalls are set up and mouth-watering aromas fill the air. Musicians, snake charmers, magicians, acrobats and benign lunatics take over the rest of the space, along with hustlers, ageing water sellers and bewildered tourists. It's brilliant for people-watching but if you stand still for too long someone will try to sell you something, dance for you, sing for you, or simply drape a large live serpent around your neck.

The **souqs** of Marrakesh are some of the best in Morocco, producing a wide variety of high-quality crafts, and a fair amount of

rubbish. High-pressure sales tactics are common and you should be very sceptical of what you are told about the quality of most goods – the gold and silver are always plated, and the amber is plastic (put a lighted match to it and smell it).

The **Koutoubia Mosque** is the most famous Marrakesh landmark. Built by the Almohads in the late 12th century, it is the oldest and best preserved of the Almohads' three famous minarets, the other two being the Tour Hassan in Rabat and the Giralda in Seville (Spain).

The **Ali ben Youssef Medersa**, next to the mosque of the same name, was built by the Saadians in 1565 and contains some beautiful examples of stucco decoration. The largest theological college in the Maghreb, it once housed up to 900 students and teachers (Dr10).

The **Palais de la Bahia** was built in the late 19th century as the residence of Bou Ahmed, the grand vizier of Sultan Moulay al-Hassan I. It's a rambling structure with fountains, gardens and shady courtyards. The palace is open daily and entry is free, but you must take (and pay) a guide.

Built about the same time and definitely worth a visit is the nearby Dar Si Said, now the **Museum of Moroccan Arts**. It served as a palace for Bou Ahmed's brother, Sidi Said, and houses Berber jewellery, carpets, Safi pottery and leather work (closed Tuesday, Dr10).

Next to the Kasbah Mosque are the **Saadian Tombs**. Sixty-six of the Saadians, including Al-Mansour, his successors and their closest family members, lie buried under the two main structures. The tombs are open daily (Dr10).

Special Events

The Festival of Folklore, held each June (the dates vary), attracts some of the best troupes in Morocco. In July, the famous Fantasia features charging Berber horsemen outside the ramparts.

Places to Stay

Hostel The *Youth Hostel* (☎ 447713), not far from the train station is a bit far from the action. It costs Dr14 (membership compulsory) and is open from 8 to 9 am and noon to 11 pm.

MOROCCO

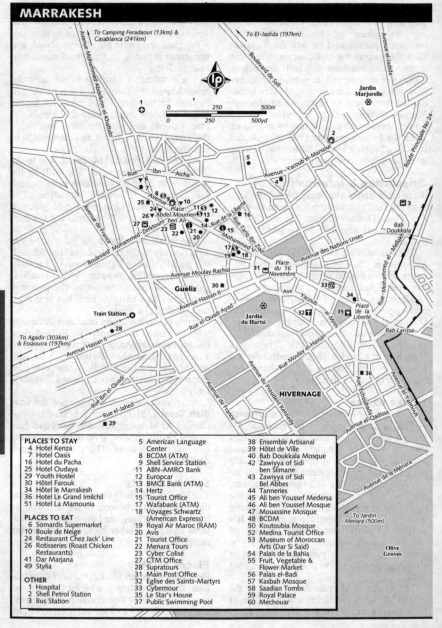

MARRAKESH

To Camping Feradaous (13km) &
Casablanca (241km)

To El-Jadida (197km)

Jardin
Marjorelle

Route Principale No 24-

0   250   500m
0   250   500yd

Avenue Mohammed Abdelkrim el-Khattabi

Boulevard de Safi

Avenue el-Jadida

Avenue Yacoub-el-Mansour

Rue   Ibn   Aicha

Boulevard Mohammed-Zerktouni

Avenue de France

Place
Abdel Moumen
ben Ali

Rue de la Liberté

Rue Tariq Ibn Ziad

Mohammed V

Bab
Doukkala

Avenue des Nations Unies

Avenue Mohammed-el-Mellakah

Avenue Moulay Rachid

Place
du 16
Novembre

Guéliz

Avenue Hassan II.

Avenue el-Quadi Ayad

Ave   Yacoub

Place
de la
Liberté

Bab Larissa

Train Station

Rue el-Quadi

Rue el-Mmm

Jardin
du Hartsi

Bab Larissa

To Agadir (303km)
& Essaouira (197km)

Avenue Hassan II

Rue du Président Kennedy

Rue Moulay el-Hassan

Rue Echouhada

Avenue el-Yarmouk

HIVERNAGE

Avenue el-Qadissa

Rue Ibn el-Quadi

Rue-el-Jahed

Avenue de France

Avenue de la Ménara

To Jardin
Menara (500m)

Olive
Groves

PLACES TO STAY	5 American Language	38 Ensemble Artisanal
4 Hotel Kenza	Center	39 Hôtel de Ville
7 Hotel Oasis	8 BCDM (ATM)	40 Bab Doukkala Mosque
16 Hotel du Pacha	9 Shell Service Station	42 Zawiyya of Sidi
25 Hotel Oudaya	11 ABN-AMRO Bank	ben Slimane
29 Youth Hostel	12 Europcar	43 Zawiyya of Sidi
30 Hôtel Farouk	13 BMCE Bank (ATM)	Bel Abbes
34 Hôtel le Marrakesh	14 Hertz	44 Tanneries
36 Hotel Le Grand Imilchil	15 Tourist Office	45 Ali ben Youssef Medersa
51 Hotel La Mamounia	17 Wafabank (ATM)	46 Ali ben Youssef Mosque
	18 Voyages Schwartz	47 Mouassine Mosque
PLACES TO EAT	(American Express)	48 BCDM
6 Somardis Supermarket	19 Royal Air Maroc (RAM)	52 Medina Tourist Office
10 Boule de Neige	20 Avis	54 Palais de la Bahia
24 Restaurant Chez Jack' Line	21 Tourist Office	55 Fruit, Vegetable &
26 Rotisseries (Roast Chicken	22 Menara Tours	Flower Market
Restaurants)	23 Cyber Colisé	56 Palais el-Badi
41 Dar Marjana	27 CTM Office	57 Kasbah Mosque
49 Stylia	28 Supratours	58 Saadian Tombs
	31 Main Post Office	59 Royal Palace
OTHER	32 Eglise des Saints-Martyrs	60 Mechouar
1 Hospital	33 Cybernour	
2 Shell Petrol Station	35 Le Star's House	
3 Bus Station	37 Public Swimming Pool	

48 Koutoubia Mosque
50 Museum of Moroccan
Arts (Dar Si Said)

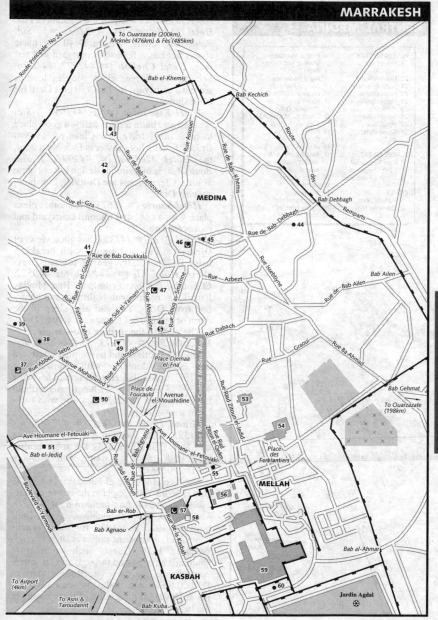

To Ouarzazate (200km),
Meknès (476km) & Fès (485km)

Bab el-Khemis

Bab Kechich

43

42

Rue el-Gza

MEDINA

Bab Debbagh

Rue de-Bab-Debbagh

44

45

46

Rue de Bab Doukkala

41

40

47

Bab Ailen

48

39

38

49

Place Djemaa
el-Fna

Rue Dabach

Rue Graoui

Rue Ba-Ahmad

37

Avenue Mohammed v

Place de
Foucauld

Avenue
el-Mouahidine

Bab Gehmat

50

53

To Ouarzazate
(198km)

Ave Houmane el-Fetouaki

Ave Houmane el-Fetouaki

54

52

51
Bab el-Jedid

Place
des
Ferblantiers

55

MELLAH

56

Bab er-Rob

57

58

Bab Agnaou

Bab al-Ahmar

To Airport
(4km)

KASBAH

59

60

Jardin Agdal

To Asni &
Taroudannt

Bab Ksiba

See Marrakesh–Central Medina Map

MOROCCO

MOROCCO

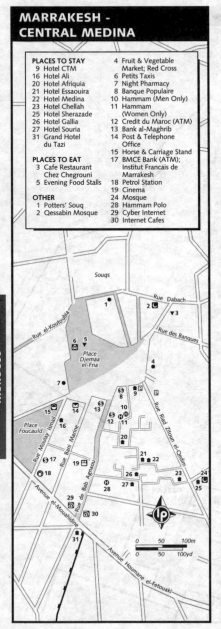

MARRAKESH - CENTRAL MEDINA

PLACES TO STAY
9 Hotel CTM
16 Hotel Ali
20 Hotel Afriquia
21 Hotel Essaouira
22 Hotel Medina
23 Hotel Chellah
25 Hotel Sherazade
26 Hotel Gallia
27 Hotel Souria
31 Grand Hotel
du Tazi

PLACES TO EAT
3 Cafe Restaurant
Chez Chegrouni
5 Evening Food Stalls

OTHER
1 Potters' Souq
2 Qessabin Mosque

4 Fruit & Vegetable
Market; Red Cross
6 Petits Taxis
7 Night Pharmacy
8 Banque Populaire
10 Hammam (Men Only)
11 Hammam
(Women Only)
12 Credit du Maroc (ATM)
13 Bank al-Maghrib
14 Post & Telephone
Office
15 Horse & Carriage Stand
17 BMCE Bank (ATM);
Institut Francais de
Marrakesh
18 Petrol Station
19 Cinema
24 Mosque
28 Hammam Polo
29 Cyber Internet
30 Internet Cafes

Hotels – Medina There are plenty of small hotels in the area south of the Djemaa el-Fna. *Hotel Afriquia* (☎ 442403, 45 Sidi Bouloukat) charges from Dr40 for basic rooms but has a fantastic courtyard and terrace. *Hotel Chellah* (☎ 442977, 14 Derb Sekaya) has large, clean singles/doubles around a courtyard for Dr40/80 plus Dr10 for a hot shower.

Hôtel Essaouira (☎/fax 443805, 3 Sidi Bouloukate) has a terrace cafe – a good place to meet other travellers. Clean rooms cost Dr35/70, and a hot shower is Dr5. Next door, the *Hôtel Medina* (☎ 442997, 1 Sidi Bouloukat) is of a similar design but not quite as nice. Clean rooms are Dr40/80; hot showers cost Dr5.

Hôtel Souria (☎ 426757) is another clean place with a cool and tranquil courtyard and rooms for Dr80/100.

Hôtel CTM (☎ 442325) has good views of Djemaa el-Fna and rooms with breakfast from Dr70. Totally geared towards travellers, *Hôtel Ali* (☎ 444979, fax 440522, ✉ hotelali@hotmail.com), on Rue Moulay Ismail, has rooms with bathroom and breakfast from Dr85. You can also sleep in the dorm or on the roof terrace for around Dr40.

The pick of the medina two-star places is *Hôtel Gallia* (☎ 445913, 30 Rue de la Recette). It's spotless and has a quiet courtyard and singles/doubles with shower for Dr210/270. Similar, *Hotel Sherazade* (☎/fax 429305, 3 Derb Djama) has rooms without bathroom from Dr125/175; those with bathroom start at Dr160/190.

Grand Hotel du Tazi (☎ 442787, fax 442152), on the corner of Ave El-Mouahidine and Rue Bab Agnaou, is the most central place with a pool, has rooms with bathroom for Dr250/290.

On Ave Houmane el-Fetouaki, just inside Bab el-Jedid, is the jewel in the crown of Marrakesh's hotels – *La Mamounia* (☎ 444409, fax 444660, ✉ resa@mamounia.com). Built between 1925 and 1929 for the (French-controlled) Moroccan railways, it was renovated in 1986. Guests such as Winston Churchill have passed through and jet-setters continue to patronise it. Rooms start at Dr2000 for a single in the low season and finish at Dr30,000 for a suite of three rooms in the high season.

Hotels – Ville Nouvelle In the ville nouvelle and handy for the train station, *Hôtel Farouk* (☎ 431989, 66 Ave Hassan II) has rooms with showers from Dr70. There's also a restaurant and excursions are organised.

Another good choice is *Hotel Toulousain* (☎ 430033, 44 Rue Tariq Ibn Ziad), a calm and cool place with courtyard and parking. Rooms without shower are Dr80/100; Dr105/135 with.

Hotel du Pacha (☎ 431327, fax 431326, 33 Rue de la Liberté) is an older style place with a cool central courtyard. Air-con rooms with balcony are priced from Dr200.

Heading back down towards the medina, the three-star *Hotel Le Grand Imilchil* (☎ 447653, fax 446165, Rue Echouhada) charges Dr315/400 for rooms with balcony. There's a pool, gardens, bar and restaurant.

Hotel Oudaya (☎ 448751, fax 435400, ✉ oudaya@iam.net.ma, 147 Rue Mohammed el-Beqal) has a terrace overlooking a small tiled courtyard with pool. Rooms with air-con are Dr320/390.

There are many four- and five-star hotels aimed at tour groups and delegates. Lots of them are on Ave de France (near the Palais du Congress) and further out of town on the road to Casablanca.

The four-star *Hotel Kenza* (☎ 448330, fax 435386), on Ave Yacoub el-Mansour, is pretty good value with comfortable rooms for Dr440/560. There's a pool, bars, restaurants, fitness club and nightclub.

Places to Eat

Medina In the evening, the Djemaa el-Fna fills with all sorts of *food stalls*. You can eat snacks for a few dirham, while a full meal won't cost more than Dr30. At other times you can sit on one of the many terraces (including the ground level *Café Restaurant Chez Chegrouni*) enjoying the spectacle and a meal, coffee or ice cream (consumption is obligatory). Otherwise there are several small *restaurants* along Rue Bani Marine and Rue de Bab Agnaou.

Many of the hotels in the medina have restaurants – *Hôtel Ali* has a good-value buffet nightly from 6.30 to 10.30 pm for Dr60 (Dr50 for hotel guests).

For a splurge (at least Dr300 per head) in a palace restaurant, one of the best for sheer atmosphere is *Dar Marjana* (☎ 445773) near Bab Doukkala. Just eclipsing it for quality of food is *Stylia* (☎ 443587, 34 Rue Ksour). Both restaurants are lost in the winding alleys of the medina. When you make a reservation (obligatory), arrange for a guide to meet you.

Ville Nouvelle A good collection of ville nouvelle restaurants, offering French, Moroccan and Italian cuisine for around Dr60 can be found around Ave Mohammed V and Blvd Mohammed Zerktouni. *Restaurant Chez Jack' Line* (☎ 447547) is a quirky French-style restaurant presided over by Madame Jack' Line and her 23-year-old parrot.

A great place to start the day is *Boule de Neige (30 Place Abdel Moumen ben Ali)* which has fried or scrambled egg breakfasts (Dr50) and cornflakes (Dr15). *Hôtel Farouk* has good value menu for Dr60 (plus 10% service; beer is Dr13), as does *Hotel Oasis* Dr55, on Ave Mohammed.

Somardis supermarket on Rue Ibn Aicha is a reasonable place for supplies and alcohol.

Entertainment

The only bar in the medina is at the *Grand Hotel du Tazi* (see Places to Stay) which remains popular with tourists. Many ville-nouvelle hotels have bars and nightclubs. The better nightclubs include *Diamant Noir* in Hôtel le Marrakesh, *Le Star's House*, opposite Le Marrakesh, and *Shehrazade* at Hotel Kenza on Ave Yacoub el-Mansour.

Getting There & Away

Air Ménara airport (☎ 447865) is 6km southwest of town. RAM (☎ 446444), at 197 Ave Mohammed V, has daily flights to Casablanca (40 minutes) and Agadir (35 minutes). International flights go to Geneva (three hours, weekly), London (3½ hours; weekly) and Paris (2¼ hours, twice weekly).

Bus The bus station is outside the city walls by Bab Doukkala, a 20-minute walk or Dr12 taxi ride from the Djemaa el-Fna. CTM operates from here and its office on Blvd Mohammed Zerktouni in Gueliz. It has daily buses to Fès (eight hours), Agadir (four hours), Casablanca (3½ hours) and M'Hamid (via Zagora). Other buses serve the same destinations plus Rabat, Essaouira (four hours) and Taroudannt (six hours).

MOROCCO

Train The train station is on Ave Hassan II, a taxi or bus No 8 ride from Djemaa el-Fna. There are regular trains to Casablanca (three hours), Fès (eight hours), Meknès (seven hours) and Rabat (four hours).

AROUND MARRAKESH

The road between Marrakesh and Taroudannt goes over the spectacular 2092m **Tizi n'Test pass**, one of the highest passes in Morocco. It's a good, if sometimes hairy, road and the views are magnificent. On the way, a worthwhile stop is the partly restored **Tin Mal Mosque**, the launch pad for the Almohad campaign of conquest in the 12th century.

HIGH ATLAS TREKKING

If you have good shoes or boots, plenty of warm clothes and a sleeping bag, the ascent of Jebel Toubkal (4167m), Morocco's highest mountain, is worth making. It's a beautiful area and on clear days there are incredible views.

You don't need mountaineering skills, as long as you go outside the winter months and take the normal route from Imlil and stay at the Toubkal hut for the night. You can do this trek in two days up to the Toubkal hut the first day, and up to the summit and back down again the second.

The usual starting point for the trek is the village of Imlil, 17km south of Asni on the Tizi n'Test road from Marrakesh to Agadir. Other possible starting points are the villages of Setti Fatma and Oukaïmeden in the Ourika Valley, but these involve longer treks.

For information beyond the normal two-day trek, see Books under Facts for the Visitor in this chapter.

Guides

You don't need a guide for the normal two-day trek, but longer treks will almost certainly require a guide and mule. You can arrange this in Imlil at the CAF Refuge or Bureau des Guides. In Marrakesh, the Hôtel Ali (☎ 444979; fax 440522, ✉ kotelali@hotmail.com) and the Hôtel de Foucauld (☎ 445499; fax 441344), near the Djemaa el-Fna, is a good places to track down experienced mountain guides.

Official guides carry ID cards and the official prices for guides, mules and muleteers are published annually in *The Great Trek through the Moroccan Atlas*, a very useful tourist office booklet generally available only in Marrakesh (and in French). At the time of writing guides charged Dr250 and mules were Dr85 per day.

Imlil

Most trekkers stay in Imlil for the first night. Stock up here for the trek, as there's nothing available farther up the mountain. The Imlil shops have a wide range of food including bread, canned and packaged goods, mineral water, soft drinks and cigarettes, but no beer.

Places to Stay & Eat The cheapest place to stay in Imlil is the *Club Alpin Français (CAF) Refuge* in the village square. It offers dormitory-style accommodation for Dr24 (CAF members), Dr39 (HI members) and Dr52 (nonmembers), plus there's a common room with an open fireplace, cooking facilities (Dr5 for use of gas), cutlery and crockery. You can camp here for Dr12 per tent, Dr6 per person. Bookings for *refuges* (huts) farther up cannot be made from here.

Good deals in Imlil include the *Hôtel L'Aine* (☎ 485625), which charges Dr40 per person in comfortable and bright rooms, and the *Café Soleil* (☎ 485622) which charges Dr40 per person for very basic rooms hot showers included.

Chez Jean Pierre (☎/fax 485609), just out of Imlil on the road to Ouanesskra, has four simple, spotlessly clean rooms and a recommended restaurant. Demi-pension costs Dr135 per person.

Discovery Ltd, a UK company which specialises in small group trips to the High Atlas, has restored the *Kasbah du Toubkal* (☎ 485611, fax 485636, ✉ kasbah@discover.ltd.uk) on the hill above Imlil. Beds are available in three large rooms which have dorm space above mezzanine floors above comfortable Moroccan-style salons (Dr300 per person, full-board. Luxurious double rooms are Dr600 per person.). Meals are excellent.

All the hotels have restaurants offering standard Moroccan meals from around Dr30. *Café Imouzar*, just off the square has cheaper, but excellent eats.

The Two-Day Trek

The first day takes you from Imlil to the Toubkal hut (3207m) via the villages of Aroumd and Sidi Chamharouch. This takes about five hours. Bottled drinks are usually available at both these villages. The Toubkal Refuge (3207m) was totally rebuilt in 1999 and now has dorm beds for over 70 people, hot showers (Dr10), a kitchen (Dr7 per hour for gas) and a generator. Bring your own bedding. Officially, bookings must be made through Caf in Casablanca (☎ 02-270090, fax 297292, BP 6178), Web site: www .clubalpin .com; or in Marrakesh (BP 888). However, you can usually find out if space is available down in Imlil (it's often rammed in July and August) and the warden now has two rather unreliable, mobile phones (☎ 01-655133, 624981). Beds cost Dr64 per person for non-CAF members and Dr48 for HI members.

The ascent from the hut to the summit should take you about four hours and the descent about two. Carry water with you. Any water from the streams on the mountainside should be boiled or treated or there's a fair chance you'll pick up giardia. It can be bitterly cold at the top even in summer.

Other Treks

The five-hour trek north-east from Imlil over the Tizi n'Tamatert pass (2279m) to Tacheddirt is an enjoyable walk. In the village there's a small *CAF refuge* (priced the same as the one in Imlil). It's a great launching point for many of the other treks, including a one or two-day walk to the village of Setti Fatma at the head of the Ourika Valley and the climb up to Oukaïmeden. There are cheap hotels here and transport to Marrakesh from both villages.

The possibilities for even longer treks in the Toubkal area are almost unlimited. A popular seven to 10-day circuit takes in Toubkal, Lake Sidi Ifni, Tacheddirt, Oukaïmeden and Tizi Oussem.

Getting There & Away

There are frequent buses (Dr10) and grands taxis (Dr13) to Asni from Bab er-Rob in Marrakesh. From Asni, trucks operate fairly frequently to Imlil and will take passengers for around Dr15. Grands taxis cost DR15.

Southern Morocco

OUARZAZATE
☎ 04

Ouarzazate (pronounced War-**zazat**) was created by the French as a garrison and regional administrative centre in 1928 and now has about 30,000 inhabitants.

The best thing about Ouarzazate is the journey there from Marrakesh over the Tizi n'Tichka pass which offers superb views over the mountains and into the valleys. Ouarzazate's other draw card is the spectacular **Kasbah of Aït Benhaddou**, 32km north of town off the Marrakesh road.

Information

The tourist office (☎ 882485) is in the centre of town, opposite the post office. The Banque Populaire behind the water tower is open for exchange on weekends. Internet cafes charge Dr15 per hour.

Places to Stay

There's a *camp site* (signposted) off the road towards Tinerhir, about 3km from the bus station. Charges are Dr10 per person and tent.

One of the best is *Hôtel Royal* (☎ 882258, 24 Ave Mohammed V) with singles starting at Dr30. The linen is clean and the showers are hot. Across the road, *Hôtel Es-Salam* (☎ 882512) has large and bright rooms without shower from Dr40. There are cosy lounges and a terrace.

There are also a few places to stay in Aït Benhaddou, which is 32km north-west off the road to Marrakesh and has a fantastic kasbah. In the centre, *Auberge La Baraka* (☎ 890305, fax 886273) has clean doubles for Dr60 with shower. Further along the road, *Auberge Étoile Filante D'or* (☎ 890322, fax 886113) has sparkly bedsheets and a terrace where you can sleep for Dr20. Both have restaurants.

Hôtel Kenzi Azghor (☎ 886501, fax 886353), on Ave Prince Moulay Rachid, has a great terrace overlooking town, loads of sports, kid-friendly facilities and a good bar. Rooms start at Dr359/468 plus taxes.

Places to Eat

Cheap and cheerful eateries surround the bus station and market, and there's more at the Kasbah.

MOROCCO

Restaurant Essalam, off Ave Mohammed V, has all the old favourites and a terrace. Just as good are *Café la Renaissance,* Ave Mohammed V, and the restaurant at the *Hôtel Atlas*. You can eat well for around Dr30.

Restaurant Dimitri (☎ 887346, 22 Ave Mohammed V) has a good range of Moroccan, French and Italian dishes. A full meal (with wine) will set you back about Dr170.

Getting There & Away
Air The airport (☎ 882348) is 1km north of town. Royal Air Maroc (☎ 885102) at 1 Ave Mohammed V has direct flights to Casablanca (Dr557, one hour, at least daily) and to Paris (Dr3402, 3½ hours, twice weekly).

Bus & Taxi CTM has a bus station on Blvd Mohammed V. Buses go to M'Hamid (Dr52.50, seven hours), Zagora (Dr35, four hours), Marrakesh (four hours), Agadir (Dr86, seven hours), Taroudannt, Casablanca, Boumalne du Dadès (Dr24.50) and Tinerhir.

Other buses and grands taxis depart from the bus station 1km north-west of town.

Local buses travel to Aït Benhaddou from Ouarzazate, but it's a lot easier to get there by taxi (Dr7).

Car Since the Drâa Valley makes such a spectacular journey, you might consider renting a car in Ouarzazate, although you'll save cash by doing it in Marrakesh. There are international and local car hire offices along and off the main road through town.

DRÂA VALLEY
For the 100km before Zagora, the Drâa flows through a sea of palmeraies and imposing craggy desert cliffs and past dozens of imposing, earth-red kasbahs. It's a magical drive, especially in the soft mauve light of the early evening.

Largely a creation of the French, **Zagora's** attractions are limited to a sign saying 'Tombouctou 52 jours' (by camel) and its large Wednesday and Sunday **markets**. It's the last stop for banks, supermarkets (no alcohol) and Internet access (Dr25 per hour).

About 18km south of Zagora is the small town of **Tamegroute** which has a *zawiyya* (religious foundation) containing an old Koranic library with texts dating back to the

13th century. There's also a small pottery factory in the town and a Saturday souq.

About 23km south of Zagora, you get your first glimpse of the Sahara at **Tinfou Dunes**. (If you have the time you would be better off going to Merzouga; see the Merzouga & To The Dunes entry later in this chapter.) Continuing on you hit the end of the road at **M'Hamid**, about 40km north of the Algerian border. **Jew's Dunes** to the north of the village is where any overnight camel ride will lead you.

Places to Stay & Eat
Zagora *Camping Sindbad* is the only camp site in Zagora, *Camping d'Amezrou* and *Camping de la Montagne* are off the M'Hamid road. They all charge around Dr10 per person/tent.

Hôtel Vallée du Drâa (☎ 847210) is clean and friendly with rooms for Dr45/70. Next door, *Hôtel des Amis* (☎ 847924) offers basic rooms with shower for Dr35/60/75.

One of Zagora's most relaxing places is *Hôtel La Fibule* (☎ 847318) on the south side of the Oued Drâa. Doubles without/with shower cost Dr180/360, including breakfast and there's an excellent restaurant, bar and swimming pool.

There are plenty of cheap restaurants over and above those at the hotels, all of which produce tasty Moroccan dishes. The popular *Restaurant Timbouctou,* on Blvd Mohammed V, offers meals for around Dr40.

Tinfou *Hotel Repos du Sables* (☎/fax 848566) is a kasbah with simple but comfortable rooms for Dr50 per person. The camels parked outside can take you to the dunes, only a short walk away, for Dr150.

M'Hamid Just before M'Hamid is *Carrefour des Caravanes* (☎ 848665) nestled in dunes and charging Dr10 per person/tent. There are basic rooms for Dr50, or Berber tents for Dr20 per person.

Across the road, without the dunes, is *Bivouac Mille et Une Nuits* (☎ 847061, fax 847922) which has a tiled hammam, small pool and tented accommodation for Dr70 per person; Dr120 half board.

In the village, *Hôtel Restaurant Sahara* (☎ 848009) has grubby facilities for Dr25 per person and shared cold showers. The hotel cafe is pleasant and serves decent meals.

Getting There & Away

A CTM bus leaves M'Hamid at 5 am, reaching Zagora (Dr20) at 7 am before continuing to Ouarzazate (Dr40, seven hours) and Marrakesh (12 hours).

The return bus from Zagora leaves at 4 pm. Other daily buses leave Zagora for Casablanca, Erfoud, Marrakesh, Meknès, Ouarzazate, Rabat and Rissani.

From Zagora, grands taxis to Ouarzazate cost Dr50 per person. On market days you may be able to get to Rissani.

BOUMALNE DU DADÈS & THE DADÈS GORGE
☎ 04

The towering ochre-coloured cliffs and fabulous rock formations of the Dadès Gorge, just over 100km east of Ouarzazate along the road to Er-Rachidia, are one of Morocco's most magnificent natural sights. Along the road are magnificent *ksour* (fortified strongholds), both ruined and lived-in.

From Boumalne du Dadès, a good bitumen road wiggles past 63km of palmeraies, Berber villages and some beautiful ruined kasbahs to Msemrir, before continuing as *piste* (dirt track) to Imilchil, in the heart of the High Atlas.

There's a Banque Populaire and post office in Boumalne, and Wednesday is market day.

Places to Stay & Eat

In the Gorge There are half a dozen simple hotels lining the road – all have restaurants and will let you sleep on their terrace or salon/camp by the river from around Dr10/5 per person.

Close to the narrowest part of the gorge, and right on the river, is *Hotel Atlas Berbere* (☎ 831742). Built in earthen kasbah style, it has rooms for Dr50/80.

Back towards Boumalne, *Chez Pierre* (☎ 830267) is a tasteful auberge with a sumptuous menu and half-board for Dr360 per person.

Boumalne du Dadès *Hotel Bougafer*, across from the bus station, has simple rooms for Dr50/70. Up on the hill, *Kasbah Tizzarouine* (☎/fax 830256) has comfortable cave rooms with bathroom for Dr250 per person half-board.

Getting There & Away

The CTM office is in the centre of town. It has daily buses to Marrakesh and Tinerhir. Other buses leave for Agadir, Casablanca, Erfoud, Fés, Marrakesh, Rabat and Zagora.

Getting Around

Occasional grands taxis – and Berber camionettes on market days – run to Aït Oudinar (Dr10) in the gorge.

TINERHIR & THE TODRA GORGE
☎ 04

The spectacular pink canyons of the Todra Gorge, 15km from Tinerhir, rise up at the end of a lush valley of mud-brick villages and palmeraies. It's best visited in the morning, when the sun penetrates to the bottom, turning the rock from rose pink to a deep ochre. The area is becoming increasingly popular with rock climbers and in the high season can get very busy with large tour groups.

Apart from exploring the gorge itself, you can potter about in the Tinerhir palmeraies or head further north into the wilds of the High Atlas. There are banks, a post office and Internet access in Tinerhir, which has an enormous souq on Sunday and Monday.

Places to Stay & Eat

In the Gorge There are three good camp sites along the road to the gorge, about 9km from Tinerhir. You'll pay about Dr10 per person and up to Dr15 to pitch a tent. There's a small grocery shop near the first place.

Just before the gorge, *Hôtel le Mansour* (☎ 834213) has a Berber tented cafe and basic rooms for Dr50. Next door, *Hôtel Étoile des Gorges* (☎ 835158) has basic rooms for Dr60 and a cheap tented restaurant.

Inside the gorge, *Hôtel Restaurant Les Roches* (☎ 834814, fax 833611) offers doubles without/with shower for Dr100/150. Next door, *Hôtel Restaurant Yasmina* (☎ 834207) has rooms for Dr110/200, and in summer you can sleep on the roof for Dr20.

You can get pretty good food in all places, but you'll have to battle with tour groups at lunch time.

Tinerhir There's a handful of budget hotels virtually in a row on Ave Hassan II. *Hôtel Salam* (☎ 835020), next to the CTM office,

MOROCCO

has basic rooms for Dr30/60. Back behind Ave Hassan II, near the central market, is *Hôtel de l'Avenir* (☎/fax 834599) with pleasant rooms priced from Dr60 including breakfast. Trekking can be organised here and the restaurant does paella.

Hôtel Tomboctou (☎ 834604, fax 833505), on Ave Bir Anzarane, is a beautiful old kasbah; rooms with bathroom cost from Dr250; from Dr90 without. There's a pool and restaurant with international dishes. The hotel also has good local information and mountain trekking and bike trips.

Getting There & Away
CTM has a bus to Marrakesh. Otherwise, several private buses also run to Agadir, Casablanca, Fés, Meknés, Tangier and Zagora.

Some grands taxis head up to the Todra Gorge (Dr7) and, on market days, you can find camionettes heading to more remote High Atlas villages.

MERZOUGA & THE DUNES
About 50km south of Erfoud are the tiny villages of Hassi Labied and Merzouga and the famous **Erg Chebbi**, Morocco's only genuine Saharan dune.

It's a magical landscape with the dunes changing colour from pink to gold to red at different times of the day. Sometimes in spring, shallow lakes appear attracting flocks of pink flamingo and other water birds.

Merzouga itself is tiny but it does have téléboutiques, general stores, a mechanic and, of course, a couple of carpet shops.

Places to Stay & Eat
Simple kasbah-style auberges flank the western side of Erg Chebbi to the north and south of the villages. Basic but comfortable rooms

cost about Dr30/60 and you can usually sleep on the roof, or in the salon or Berber tent for about Dr25. All have views of the dunes and offer food (including the local *kalia*), Berber music, sand toys (snowboard, skis etc) and camel treks (around Dr100 for a couple of hours to Dr200 to Dr300 per night with meals).

South of Merzouga, *Auberge la Palmeraie* is a super chilled-out place with pink rooms, not facing the dunes, from Dr50.

Nearby, *Kasbah Le Touareg* (☎/fax 577215) is slightly more upmarket with colourful rooms for Dr100. The more basic rooftop turret rooms have excellent views for Dr60.

Ksar Sania (☎ 577414, fax 577230) offers the area's most comfortable doubles from Dr70 to Dr180 and its restaurant has a French menu for Dr90.

In Hassi Labied, *Ocean des Dunes* is a very clean but basic place with nice salon type seating outside its Dr50 rooms.

Between the two villages is *Kasbah Hotel Aiour* (☎ 715602), close to the dunes it has rooms with bathroom for Dr90/150.

Getting There & Away
A camionette to Merzouga leaves Rissani and returns daily (1½ hours; there are also 4WD taxis between the two on Sunday, Tuesday and Thursday. If you're driving you may want to engage a local guide (Dr100).

Another daily bus runs between Erfoud and Merzouga (one hour). Apart from the 'sunrise tours', the only other option is to charter a 4WD taxi (about Dr300), or hitch a ride with tourists.

There are daily buses to and from Fés (eight hours) and Meknés (eight hours) from Rissani and Erfoud.

Portugal

Spirited yet unassuming, Portugal has a dusty patina of faded grandeur; the quiet remains of a far-flung colonialist realm. Even as it flows towards the economic mainstream of the European Union (EU) it still seems to gaze nostalgically over its shoulder and out to sea.

For visitors, this far side of Europe offers more than beaches and port wine. Beyond the crowded Algarve, one finds wide appeal: a simple, hearty cuisine based on seafood and lingering conversation, an enticing architectural blend wandering from the Moorish to Manueline to surrealist styles, and a changing landscape that occasionally lapses into impressionism. Like the *emigrantes* (economically inspired Portuguese who eventually find their way back to their roots), *estrangeiros* (foreigners) who have tasted the real Portugal can only be expected to return.

Facts about Portugal

HISTORY

The early history of Portugal goes back to the Celts who settled the Iberian Peninsula around 700 BC. A subsequent pattern of invasion and reinvasion was established by the Phoenicians, Greeks, Romans and Visigoths.

In the 8th century the Moors crossed the Strait of Gibraltar and commenced a long occupation which introduced Islamic culture, architecture and agricultural techniques to Portugal. The Moors were ejected in the 12th century by powerful Christian forces in the north of the country who mobilised attacks against them with the help of European Crusaders.

In the 15th century Portugal entered a phase of conquest and discovery inspired by Prince Henry the Navigator. Explorers such as Vasco da Gama, Ferdinand Magellan and Bartolomeu Diaz discovered new trade routes and helped create an empire that, at its peak, extended to Africa, Brazil, India and the Far East. This period of immense power and wealth ended in 1580 when Spain occupied

the Portuguese throne. The Portuguese regained it within 90 years, but their imperial momentum had been lost.

At the close of the 18th century Napoleon mounted several invasions of Portugal, but was eventually trounced by the troops of the Anglo-Portuguese alliance.

A period of civil war and political mayhem in the 19th century culminated in the abolition of the monarchy in 1910 and the founding of a democratic republic.

A military coup in 1926 set the stage for the dictatorship of António de Oliveira Salazar, who clung to power until his death in 1968. General dissatisfaction with his regime and a ruinous colonial war in Africa led to the

PORTUGAL

euro currency converter €1 = 200 escudo

so-called Revolution of the Carnations, a peaceful military coup on 25 April 1974.

The granting of independence to Portugal's African colonies in 1974-75 produced a flood of nearly a million refugees into the country. The 1970s and early 1980s saw extreme swings between political right and left, and strikes over state versus private ownership.

Portugal's entry into the EU in 1986 and its acceptance as a member of the European Monetary System in 1992 secured a measure of stability, although the 1990s were troubled by recession, rising unemployment and continuing backwardness in agriculture and education.

Expo '98, which attracted eight million visitors, triggered some vast infrastructure projects and launched Portugal into a new era of economic success. Ensuring further attention (and development) are Porto's status as a European Capital of Culture in 2001, and Portugal's role as host of the European football championships in 2004.

GEOGRAPHY & ECOLOGY
Portugal is about twice the size of Switzerland, just 560km from north to south and 220km from east to west.

The northern and central coastal regions are densely populated. The northern interior is characterised by lush vegetation and mountains; the highest range, the Serra da Estrela, peaks at Torre (1993m). The south is less populated and, apart from the mountainous backdrop of the Algarve, flatter and drier.

CLIMATE
Midsummer heat is searing in the Algarve and Alentejo, and in the upper Douro Valley, but tolerable elsewhere. The north is rainy and chilly in winter. Snowfall is common in the Serra da Estrela.

ECOLOGY & ENVIRONMENT
Portugal has one international-standard national park (70,290-hectare Peneda-Gerês), 11 *parques naturais* (natural parks, of which the biggest and best known is 101,060-hectare Serra da Estrela), eight nature reserves and several other protected areas. The government's Instituto da Conservação da Natureza (ICN; Information Division ☎ 213 523 317), Rua Ferreira Lapa 29-A, Lisbon,

manages them all, though information is best obtained from each park's headquarters.

GOVERNMENT & POLITICS
Portugal has a Western-style democracy based on the Assembleiada República, a single-chamber parliament with 230 members and an elected president. The two main parties are the Socialist Party (Partido Socialista or PS) and the right-of-centre Social Democratic Party (Partido Social Democrata or PSD). Other parties include the Communist Party (PCP) and the new Left Bloc (BE). In October 1999 the Socialist Party under the popular António Guterres was re-elected for a second four-year term.

ECONOMY
After severe economic problems in the 1980s, Portugal has tamed inflation to around 2% and enjoys an annual growth rate of around 3.5%, thanks largely to infrastructure investment and privatisation. Agriculture plays a decreasing role compared with industry and services (eg, telecommunications, banking and tourism). Portugal benefits from low labour costs, a young population and massive EU funding which has helped improve its infrastructure dramatically. In 1999 the country made the grade for European monetary union and smoothly joined the euro currency zone.

POPULATION & PEOPLE
Portugal's population of 10 million does not include the estimated three million Portuguese living abroad as migrant workers.

ARTS
Music
The best-known form of Portuguese music is the melancholy, nostalgic songs called *fado,* popularly considered to have originated with the yearnings of 16th-century sailors. Much on offer to tourists in Lisbon is overpriced and far from authentic. The late Amália Rodrigues was the star of Portuguese fado; her recordings are sold in most record shops in Portugal.

Literature
In the 16th century, Gil Vicente, master of farce and religious drama, set the stage for Portugal's dramatic tradition. Later in that century Luís de Camões wrote *Os Lusíadas,* an

PORTUGAL

epic poem celebrating the age of discovery (available in translation as *The Lusiads*). Camões is considered Portugal's national poet.

Two of Portugal's finest 20th-century writers are poet-dramatist Fernando Pessoa (1888-1935), author of the 1934 *Message*; and the 1998 Nobel Prizewinning novelist José Saramago, whose novels (notably *Baltasar and Blimunda* and *The Year of the Death of Ricardo Reis*) weave together the real and imaginary. Others to try are Eça de Queiroz *(The Maias)* and Fernando Namora *(Mountain Doctor)*. A contemporary Portuguese 'whodunnit', close to the political bone, is *The Ballad of Dog's Beach* by José Cardoso Pires.

Architecture

Unique to Portugal is Manueline architecture, named after its patron King Manuel I (1495-1521). It symbolises the zest for discovery of that era and is characterised by boisterous spiralling columns and nautical themes.

Crafts

The most striking Portuguese craft is the decorative tiles called *azulejos,* based on Moorish techniques of the 15th century. Superb examples are to be seen all over the country. Lisbon has its own azulejos museum.

SOCIETY & CONDUCT

Despite prosperity and foreign influence, the Portuguese have kept a firm grip on their culture. Folk dancing remains the pride of villages everywhere, and local festivals are celebrated with gusto. TV soccer matches, a modern element of male Portuguese life, ensure the continuation of the traditional long lunch break.

The Portuguese tend to be very friendly but socially conservative: win their hearts by dressing modestly outside of the beach resorts, and by greeting and thanking them in Portuguese. Shorts and hats are considered offensive inside churches.

RELIGION

Portugal is 99% Roman Catholic, with fewer than 120,000 Protestants and about 5000 Jews.

LANGUAGE

Like French, Italian, Spanish and Romanian, Portuguese is a Romance language, derived from Latin. It's spoken by over 10 million people in Portugal and 130 million in Brazil, and is the official language of five African nations. Nearly all turismo staff speak English. In Lisbon, Porto and the Algarve it's easy to find English-speakers, but they are rare in the countryside, and among older folk. In the north, you'll find returned emigrant workers who speak French or German.

See the Language Guide at the back of the book for pronunciation guidelines and useful words and phrases. For more, pick up Lonely Planet's *Portuguese phrasebook*.

Facts for the Visitor

HIGHLIGHTS

Tops for scenery are the mountain landscapes of the Serra da Estrela and Peneda-Gerês National Park. Architecture buffs should visit the monasteries at Belém and Batalha, and the palaces of Pena (Sintra) and Buçaco. Combining the best of both worlds are Portugal's old walled towns such as Évora and Marvão. In Lisbon don't miss the Gulbenkian museum, and Europe's largest Oceanarium.

SUGGESTED ITINERARIES

Depending on the length of your stay, you might want to see and do the following:

Two days
  Lisbon
One week
  Devote four or five days to Lisbon and Sintra and the rest to Óbidos and Nazaré.
Two weeks
  As for one week, plus two days in Évora and the rest in the Algarve (including one or two days each in Tavira, Lagos and Sagres).
One month
  As above, plus a day each in Castelo de Vide and Marvão, two in Coimbra, five in the Douro Valley (Porto plus a Douro River cruise) and the remainder in either the Serra da Estrela or the Peneda-Gerês National Park.

PLANNING
When to Go

Peak tourist season is June to early September. Going earlier (late March or April) or later (late September to early October) gives you fewer crowds, milder temperatures, spectacular foliage, and seasonal discounts including up to 50% for accommodation (prices in this chapter are for peak season). The Algarve tourist season lasts from late February to November.

Maps

Michelin's No 940 *Portugal; Madeira* map is accurate and useful even if you're not driving. Maps by the Automóvel Club de Portugal (ACP) are marginally less detailed but more current. For maps and information on the national/natural parks it's best to visit the information offices at or near each park, though even here trekkers will find little of use.

Topographic maps are published (and sold) by two mapping agencies in Lisbon: the civilian Instituto Português de Cartográfia e Cadastro (☎ 213 819 600, fax 213 819 697, ✉ ipcc@ipcc.pt), at Rua Artilharia Um 107, and the military Instituto Geográfico do Exército (☎ 218 520 063, fax 218 532 119, ✉ igeoe@igeoe.pt), on Avenida Dr Alfredo Bensaúde. Porto Editora, Praça Dona Filipa de Lencastre 42, in Porto, stocks the (better) military versions.

TOURIST OFFICES
Local Tourist Offices

Called *postos de turismo* or just *turismos*, local tourist offices are found throughout Portugal and offer information, maps and varying degrees of assistance.

Tourist Offices Abroad

Portuguese tourist offices operating abroad under the administrative umbrella of ICEP (Investimentos, Comércio e Turismo de Portugal) include:

Canada Portuguese Trade & Tourism Commission (☎ 416-921-7376, fax 921-1353, ✉ iceptor@idirect.com) 60 Bloor St West, Suite 1005, Toronto, Ontario M4W 3B8
Spain Oficina de Turismo de Portugal (☎ 91-522 4408, fax 522 2382, ✉ acarrilho@mail2.icep.pt) Gran Via 27, 1st floor, 28013 Madrid
UK Portuguese Trade & Tourism Office (☎ 020-7494 1441, fax 7494 1868, ✉ iceplondt@aol.com) 22-25a Sackville St, London W1X 1DE
USA Portuguese National Tourist Office (☎ 212-354 4403, fax 764 6137, ✉ tourism@portugal.org) 590 Fifth Ave, 4th floor, New York, NY 10036-4785

VISAS & DOCUMENTS
Visas

No visa is required for any length of stay by nationals of EU countries. Those from Canada, Israel, New Zealand and the USA can stay up to 60 days in any half-year without a visa. Others, including nationals of Australia and South Africa, need visas (and should try to get them in advance) unless they're spouses or children of EU citizens.

Portugal is a signatory of the Schengen Convention on the abolition of mutual border controls (see Visas in the introductory Facts for the Visitor chapter), but unless you're a citizen of the UK, Ireland or a Schengen country, you should check visa regulations with the consulate of each Schengen country you plan to visit. You must apply in your country of residence.

Outside Portugal, visa information is supplied by Portuguese consulates. In Portugal, contact the Foreigners Registration Service (Serviço de Estrangeiros e Fronteiras; ☎ 213 585 545), Rua São Sebastião da Pedreira 15, Lisbon, for information. It's open 9 am to noon and 2 to 4 pm weekdays.

EMBASSIES & CONSULATES
Portuguese Embassies & Consulates

Portuguese embassies abroad include:

Australia (☎ 02-6290 1733) 23 Culgoa Circuit, O'Malley, ACT 2606
Canada (☎ 613-729-0883) 645 Island Park Drive, Ottawa, Ont K1Y 0B8
France (☎ 01 47 27 35 29) 3 Rue de Noisiel, 75116 Paris
Ireland (☎ 01-289 4416) Knock Sinna House, Knock Sinna, Fox Rock, Dublin 18
Spain (☎ 91-561 78 00) Calle Castello 128, 28006 Madrid
UK (☎ 020-7235 5331) 11 Belgrave Square, London SW1X 8PP
USA (☎ 202-328 8610) 2125 Kalorama Rd NW, Washington, DC 20008

Embassies & Consulates in Portugal

Foreign embassies in Portugal include:

Canada (☎ 213 164 600) Avenida da Liberdade 196, Lisbon
Consulate: (☎ 289 803 757) Rua Frei Lourenço de Santa Maria 1, Faro

PORTUGAL

France (☎ 213 939 100) Calçada Marquês de Abrantes 123, Lisbon
(☎ 226 094 805) Rua Eugénio de Castro 352, Porto
Ireland (☎ 213 929 440) Rua da Imprensa à Estrela 1, Lisbon
Spain (☎ 213 472 381) Rua do Salitre 1, Lisbon
(☎ 225 101 685) Rua de Dom João IV 341, Porto
Consulates: (☎ 251 822 122) Avenida de Espanha, Valença do Minho
(☎ 281 544 888) Avenida Ministro Duarte Pacheco, Vila Real de Santo António
UK (☎ 213 924 000) Rua de São Bernardo 33, Lisbon
(☎ 226 184 789) Avenida da Boavista 3072, Porto
Consulate: (☎ 282 417 800) Largo Francisco A Maurício 7, Portimão
USA (☎ 217 273 300) Avenida das Forças Armadas, Lisbon
(☎ 222 080 061) Rua da Reboleira 7, Porto

There are no embassies for Australia or New Zealand. New Zealand has an honorary consul in Lisbon (☎ 213 509 690; from 9 am to 1 pm weekdays); the nearest embassy is in Rome (☎ 39-6-440 29 28). Australian citizens can call the Australian Policy Liaison Office at the Canadian Embassy (or the Australian Embassy in Paris, ☎ 33-1 40 59 33 00).

MONEY
Currency
The unit of Portuguese currency is the escudo, further divided into 100 centavos. Prices are written with a $ sign between escudos and centavos; eg, 25 escudos 50 centavos is 25$50. There are 200$00, 100$00, 50$00, 20$00, 10$00, 5$00, 2$50 and 1$00 coins. Notes currently in circulation are 10,000$00, 5000$00, 2000$00, 1000$00 and 500$00.

There is no limit on the importation of currency. If you leave Portugal with more than 100,000$00 in escudos or 500,000$00 in foreign currency you must prove that you brought in at least this much.

From 1 January 1999, when Portugal joined the European Monetary Union, goods and services were priced in both escudos and euros. The escudo will be withdrawn on 1 July 2002.

Exchange Rates

country	unit		escudos
Australia	A$1	=	128$58
Canada	C$1	=	149$60
euro	€1	=	200$48
France	1FF	=	30$56
Germany	DM1	=	102$51
Japan	¥100	=	204$24
New Zealand	NZ$1	=	99$82
Spain	100 ptas	=	120$49
UK	UK£1	=	333$64
USA	US$1	=	221$90

Exchanging Money
Portuguese banks can change most foreign cash and travellers cheques but charge a commission of around 2500$00. Better deals for travellers cheques are at private exchange bureaus in Lisbon, Porto and tourist resorts.

Better value (and handier) are the 24-hour Multibanco ATMs at most banks. Exchange rates are reasonable and normally the only charge is a handling fee of about 1.5% to your home bank. Few tourist centres have automatic cash-exchange machines.

Major credit cards – especially Visa and MasterCard – are widely accepted by shops, hotels and a growing number of guesthouses and restaurants.

Costs
Portugal remains one of the cheapest places to travel in Europe. On a rock-bottom budget – using hostels or camping grounds, and mostly self-catering – you can squeeze by on US$20 to US$25 a day. With bottom-end accommodation and cheap restaurant meals, figure around US$30. Travelling with a companion and taking advantage of the off-season discounts (see When to Go earlier in this section), two can eat and sleep well for US$60 to US$70 per day. Outside major tourist areas, and in low season, prices dip appreciably.

Concessions are often available on admission fees etc if you're over 65, under 26 or hold a student card.

Tipping & Bargaining
A reasonable restaurant tip is 10%. For a snack, a bit of loose change is sufficient. Taxi drivers appreciate 10% of the fare, and petrol station attendants 50$00 to 100$00.

The sands of the Sahara Desert

Entrance to the Moulay Ismail Mausoleum, Meknès, Morocco

Hassan II mosque, Casablanca

Berber silver jewellery, Taroudannt, Morocco

Kasbah, near Ouarzazate

Folk dancing, Ponte de Lima, Minho, Portugal

Mosteiro dos Jerónimos, Lisbon, Portugal

Decorated pots from the Alto Alentejo, Portugal

The wild, craggy coastline of The Algarve, Portugal

Good-humoured bargaining is acceptable in markets but you'll find the Portuguese tough opponents! Off season, you can sometimes bargain down the price of accommodation.

Taxes & Refunds

IVA is a sales tax levied on a wide range of goods and services; in most types of shops it's 17%. Tourists from non-EU countries can claim an IVA refund on goods from shops belonging to Europe Tax-Free Shopping Portugal. The minimum purchase for a refund is 11,700$00 in any one shop. The shop assistant fills in a cheque for the refund (minus an administration fee). When you leave Portugal you present goods, cheque and your passport at customs for a cash, postal-note or credit-card refund.

This service is available at Lisbon, Porto and Faro airports (postal refund only at Faro). If you're leaving overland, contact customs at your final EU border point, or call Europe Tax-Free Shopping Portugal (Lisbon ☎ 218 408 813).

POST & COMMUNICATIONS
Post

Postcards and letters up to 20g cost 52$00 within Portugal, 90$00 to Spain, 100$00 to European destinations and 140$00 to destinations outside Europe. For delivery to North America or Australasia allow eight to 10 days; delivery within Europe averages four to six days.

For parcels, 'economy air' (or surface airlift, SAL) costs about a third less than airmail and usually arrives a week or so later. Printed matter is cheapest to send in batches of under 2kg. The post office at Praça dos Restauradores in Lisbon and Porto's main post office are open into the evening and at weekends. Most major towns have a post office with *posta restante* service, though it's not always the main branch. In Lisbon and Porto a charge of 65$00 is levied for each item claimed.

Addresses in Portugal are written with the street name first, followed by the building address and often a floor number with a ° symbol, eg, 15-3°. An alphabetical tag on the address, eg, 2-A, indicates an adjoining entrance or building. R/C (*rés do chão*) means ground floor.

Telephone

In 1999 Portugal completely revised its telephone numbering system. Aside from a few assistance numbers, all domestic numbers now have nine digits. All digits must be dialled from any location, effectively rendering area codes obsolete.

Local calls from public coin telephones start at 30$00, but as the largest acceptable coin is 50$00, these are impractical for long-distance and international calls. Handier and cheaper are 'Credifones', which accept cards sold at newsagents, tobacconists and telephone offices. The cards come in 650$00, 1300$00 or 1900$00 denominations; a youth/student card should get you a 10% discount.

Domestic charges drop by 50% from 9 pm to 9 am on weekdays, and all day Saturday and Sunday. International charges drop by around 10% to 25% from 9 pm to 9 am, and 20% to 50% during the weekend. Hotels typically charge over *three times* the economy/Credifone rate!

A three-minute direct-dial (IDD) evening/weekend call from Portugal using a Credifone costs about 180/90$00 within the EU, 200/90$00 to the USA or Canada, and 360/360$00 to Australia or New Zealand.

To call Portugal from abroad, dial the international access code, then ☎ 351 (the country code for Portugal) and the number. From Portugal, the international access code is ☎ 00. For operator help or to make a reverse-charge (collect) call from Portugal, dial ☎ 172. For domestic inquiries, dial ☎ 118; for numbers abroad, dial ☎ 177. Multilingual operators are available.

For more information on telephoning in Europe, see the Telephones Appendix at the back of this book.

Fax

Post offices operate a domestic and international service called Corfax, costing 820$00 for the first page to Europe and 1250$00 to North America or Australia. Some private shops offer much cheaper services.

Email & Internet Access

Many towns have a branch of the Instituto Português da Juventude or IPJ, a state-funded youth-centre network. Most of these offer free Internet access during certain hours.

PORTUGAL

Some municipal libraries also have free access. Some newer youth hostels have access for around 500$00 per hour. Internet cafes in bigger towns charge 100$00 to 600$00 (or more) per hour.

INTERNET RESOURCES

Three useful Web sites on Portugal are: A Collection of Home Pages about Portugal (www.well.com/user/ideamen/portugal.html; Portugal Info (www.portugal-info.net); and Excite City.Net (www.city.net/countries/portugal).

BOOKS

Rose Macaulay's *They Went to Portugal* and *They Went to Portugal Too* follow a wide variety of visitors from medieval times to the 19th century. Marion Kaplan's *The Portuguese: The Land and Its People* offers a fine overview of Portugal and its place in the modern world.

Walkers and car tourers should pack the *Landscapes of Portugal* series by Brian & Aileen Anderson, including books on the Algarve, Sintra/Estoril and the Costa Verde. More detailed is *Walking in Portugal* by Bethan Davies and Ben Cole.

NEWSPAPERS & MAGAZINES

Portuguese-language newspapers include the dailies *Diário de Notícias, Público* and *Jornal de Notícias,* and weeklies *O Independente* and *Expresso.* For entertainment listings, check local dailies or seasonal cultural-events calendars from tourist offices.

English-language newspapers published in Portugal include *The News,* with regional editions featuring local news and classified pages, and *Anglo-Portuguese News.* Newspapers and magazines from abroad are widely available in major cities and tourist resorts.

RADIO & TV

Portuguese radio is represented by the state-owned stations *Antena 1, 2* and *3,* by *Rádio Renascença* and by a clutch of local stations. BBC World Service is at 12.095MHz or 15.485MHz short-wave, but reception is poor.

Portuguese TV includes state-run channels RTP-1 (or Canal 1) and RTP-2 (or TV2) and two private channels, SIC and TVI. Soaps *(telenovelas)* take up the lion's share of broadcasting time.

LAUNDRY

There are *lavandarias* everywhere, most specialising in dry-cleaning *(limpeza à seco).* They'll often do wash-and-dry *(lavar e secar)* too, though it may take a day or two. Figure 1500$00 to 2500$00 for a 5kg load.

TOILETS

The rare public toilets are of the sit-down variety, generally clean and usually free. Coin-operated toilet booths are increasingly common in bigger cities. Most people, however, go to the nearest cafe for a drink or pastry and use the facilities there.

WOMEN TRAVELLERS

Outside Lisbon and Porto, an unaccompanied foreign woman is an oddity, and older people may fuss over you as if you were in need of protection. Women travelling on their own or in small groups report few hassles. In Lisbon and Porto, women should be cautious about where they go alone after dark. Hitching is not recommended for solo women anywhere in Portugal.

GAY & LESBIAN TRAVELLERS

In this predominantly Catholic country, there is little understanding or acceptance of homosexuality. But Lisbon has a flourishing gay scene, with an annual Gay Pride Festival (around June 28) and a Gay & Lesbian Community Center (Centro Comunitário Gay e Lésbico de Lisboa; ☎ 218 873 918), Rua de São Lazaro 88, open 4 to 9 pm daily. For information on gay-friendly bars, restaurants and clubs in Lisbon and Porto, check the Web sites www.ilga-portugal.org and www.portugalgay.pt.

DISABLED TRAVELLERS

The Secretariado Nacional de Rehabilitação (☎ 217 936 517, fax 217 965 182), Avenida Conde de Valbom 63, Lisbon, publishes the Portuguese-language *Guia de Turismo* with sections on barrier-free accommodation, transport, shops, restaurants and sights in Portugal. It's only available at its offices.

Turintegra, part of the Cooperativa Nacional Apoio Deficientes (CNAD; ☎/fax 218 595 332), Praça Dr Fernando Amado, Lote

PORTUGAL

566-E, 1900 Lisbon, keeps a keener eye on developments and arranges holidays and transport for disabled travellers.

DANGERS & ANNOYANCES

The most widespread crime against foreigners is theft from rental cars, followed by pickpocketing, and pilfering from camping grounds. On the increase are armed robberies, mostly in the Algarve, Estoril Coast, parts of Lisbon and a few other cities. But with the usual precautions (use a money belt or something similar, bag your camera when not in use and don't leave valuables in cars or tents) there's little cause for worry. For peace of mind take out travel insurance.

Avoid swimming on beaches which are not marked as safe: Atlantic currents are notoriously dangerous (and badly polluted near major cities).

The national emergency number is ☎ 112 for police, fire and other emergencies anywhere in Portugal.

BUSINESS HOURS

Most banks are open 8.30 am to 3 pm weekdays. Most museums and other tourist attractions are open 10 am to 5 pm weekdays but are often closed at lunchtime and all day Monday. Shopping hours generally extend from 9 am to 7 pm on weekdays, and 9 am to 1 pm on Saturday. Lunch is given serious and lingering attention between noon and 3 pm.

PUBLIC HOLIDAYS & SPECIAL EVENTS

Public holidays in Portugal include New Year's Day, Carnival (Shrove Tuesday; February/March), Good Friday and the following Saturday, Liberty Day (25 April), May Day, Corpus Christi (May/June), National Day (10 June), Feast of the Assumption (15 August), Republic Day (5 October), All Saints' Day (1 November), Independence Day (1 December), Feast of the Immaculate Conception (8 December) and Christmas Day.

Portugal's most interesting cultural events include:

Holy Week Festival Easter week in Braga features colourful processions including Ecce Homo, with barefoot penitents carrying torches.

Festas das Cruzes Held in Barcelos in May, the Festival of the Crosses is known for processions, folk music and dance, and regional handicrafts.

Feira Nacional da Agricultura In June, Santarém hosts the National Agricultural Fair, with bullfighting, folk singing and dancing.

Festa do Santo António The Festival of Saint Anthony fills the streets of Lisbon on 13 June.

Festas de São João Porto's big street bash is the St John's Festival, from 16 to 24 June.

Festas da Nossa Senhora da Agonia Viana do Castelo's Our Lady of Suffering Festival, for three days nearest to 20 August, is famed for folk arts, parades and fireworks.

ACTIVITIES

Off-road cycling (BTT or *bicyclete tudo terrano*, all-terrain bicycle) is booming in Portugal, with bike trips on offer at many tourist destinations (see Tavira, Setúbal, Évora and Peneda-Gerês National Park).

Despite some fine rambling country, walking is not a Portuguese passion. Some parks are establishing trails, though, and some adventure travel agencies offer walking tours (see Lisbon, Serra da Estrela, Porto and Peneda-Gerês National Park).

Popular water sports include surfing, windsurfing, canoeing, white-water rafting and water-skiing. For information on local specialists see Lagos, Sagres and Peneda-Gerês National Park.

Alpine skiing is possible at Torre in the Serra da Estrela from January through March.

The Instituto Português da Juventude (see Lisbon for more on the IPJ) offers holiday programs for 16 to 30-year-olds (visitors too), including BTT, canoeing and rock climbing. Private organisations with activities including these plus trekking, horse riding, caving and hydrospeed (running white-water without a boat) are listed under Lisbon, Porto and Peneda-Gerês National Park.

COURSES

Interlingua in Portimão (☎/fax 282 416 030, ✉ interlingua@mail.telepac.pt) runs a two-hour fun course in Portuguese language basics for 4000$00. Longer courses are offered by Centro de Línguas in Lagos (☎/fax 282 761 070, ✉ cll@mail.telepac.pt); Cambridge School in Lisbon (☎ 213 124 600, fax 213 534 729, ✉ cambridge@mail.telepac.pt),

PORTUGAL

with Porto and Coimbra branches too; Lisbon-based IPFEL (☎ 213 154 116, fax 213 154 119, @ instituto@ipfel.pt), with a Porto branch; and CIAL-Centro de Linguas in Lisbon (☎ 217 940 448, fax 217 960 783, @ por tuguese@cial.pt), Porto (☎ 223 320 269) and Faro (☎ 289 807 611).

ACCOMMODATION

Most tourist offices have lists of accommodation to suit a range of budgets, and can help you find and book it. Although the government uses stars to grade some types of accommodation, criteria seem erratic.

Camping

Camping is popular, and easily the cheapest option. The multilingual, annually updated *Roteiro Campista* (900$00), sold in larger bookshops, contains details of nearly all Portugal's camping grounds. Depending on facilities and season, most prices per night run to about 300$00 to 600$00 per adult, 300$00 to 500$00 for a small tent and 300$00 to 500$00 per car. Many camping grounds close in the low season.

Hostels

Portugal has 38 *pousadas da juventude* (youth hostels), all part of the Hostelling International (HI) system. Low rates are offset by segregated dorms, midnight curfews and partial daytime exclusion at most (but not all) of them.

In high season, dorm beds cost 1700$00 to 2900$00, and most hostels also offer basic doubles for 3800$00 to 4600$00 (without bath) or 4100$00 to 6500$00 (with). Bed linen and breakfast are included. Many hostels have kitchens where you can do your own cooking, plus TV rooms and social areas.

Advance reservations are essential in summer. Most hostels will call ahead to your next stop at no charge, or you can pay 300$00 per set of bookings (with three days' notice) through the country's central HI reservations office, Movijovem (☎ 213 524 072, fax 213 528 621, @ movijovem@mail.telepac.pt), Avenida Duque d'Ávila 137, Lisbon.

If you don't already have a card from your national hostel association, you can join HI by paying an extra 400$00 (and having a

'guest card' stamped) at each of the first six hostels where you stay.

Private Rooms

Another option is a private room (*quarto particular*), usually in a private house, with shared facilities. Home-owners may approach you at the bus or train station; otherwise watch for 'quartos' signs or ask at tourist offices. Rooms are usually clean, cheap (4500$00 to 6000$00 for a double in summer) and free from hostel-style restrictions. A variant is a rooming house (*dormida*), where doubles are about 4500$00. You may be able to bargain in the low season.

Guesthouses

The most common types of guesthouse, the Portuguese equivalent of B&Bs, are the *residencial* and the *pensão* (plural *pensões*). Both are graded from one to three stars, and the best are often cheaper and better-run than some hotels. High-season pensão rates for a double start around 5000$00; a residencial, where breakfast is normally included, is a bit more. Many have cheaper rooms with shared bathrooms.

Hotels

The government grades hotels with one to five stars. For a high-season double figure on 15,000$00 to as much as 50,000$00. *Estalagem* and *albergaria* refer to upmarket inns. Prices drop spectacularly in low season. Breakfast is usually included.

Other Accommodation

Pousadas de Portugal are government-run former castles, monasteries or palaces, often in spectacular locations. For details contact tourist offices, or Pousadas de Portugal (☎ 218 481 221, fax 218 405 846), Avenida Santa Joana Princesa 10, 1749 Lisbon.

Private counterparts are operated under a scheme called Turismo de Habitação and a number of smaller schemes (often collectively called 'Turihab'), which allow you to stay in anything from a farmhouse to a manor house; some also have self-catering cottages. Tourist offices can tell you about local Turihab properties.

A double in high season costs a minimum of 16,300$00 in a Pousada de Portugal but just 10,000$00 in a Turihab farmhouse.

PORTUGAL

FOOD

Eating and drinking get serious attention in Portugal. The fast-food era has been ignored in favour of leisurely dining and devotion to wholesome ingredients.

The line between snacks and meals is blurred. Bars and cafes offer snacks or even a small menu. For full meals try a *casa do pasto* (a simple, cheap eatery), *restaurante*, *cervejaria* (bar-restaurant) or *marisqueira* (seafood restaurant). Lunchtime typically lasts from noon to 3 pm, evening meals from 7 to 10.30 pm.

The *prato do dia* (dish of the day) is often a bargain at around 800$00; the *ementa turística* (tourist menu) rarely is. A full portion or *dose* is ample for two decent appetites; a *meia dose* (half-portion) is a quarter to a third cheaper. The *couvert* – the bread, cheese, butter, olives and other titbits at the start of a meal – cost extra.

Common snacks are *pastéis de bacalhau* (codfish cakes), *prego em pão* (meat and egg in a roll) and *tosta mista* (toasted cheese and ham sandwich). Prices start around 300$00.

Seafood offers exceptional value, especially *linguado grelhado* (grilled sole), *bife de atum* (tuna steak) and the omnipresent *bacalhau* (dried cod) cooked in dozens of ways. Meat is hit-or-miss, but worth sampling are local *presunto* (ham), *borrego* (roast lamb) and *cabrito* (kid). Main-dish prices start around 900$00.

Cafes and *pastelarias* (pastry shops) offer splendid desserts and cakes. Cheeses from Serra da Estrela, Serpa and the Azores are good but pricey.

Local markets offer fresh seafood, vegetables and fruit. Big cities have grocery shops *(minimercadoes)* and many now have vast *hipermercados*.

DRINKS

Coffee is a hallowed institution with its own nomenclature. A small black espresso is a *bica*. Half-and-half coffee and milk is *café com leite*. For coffee with lots of milk at breakfast, ask for a *galão*. Tea *(chá)* comes with lemon *(com limão)* or with milk *(com leite)*. Fresh orange juice is common. Mineral water *(água mineral)* is carbonated *(com gás)* or still *(sem gás)*.

Local beers *(cerveja)* include Sagres in the south and Super Bock in the north. A 20cL draught is called *um imperial*; *uma garrafa* is a bottle.

Portuguese wine *(vinho)* offers great value in all varieties: red *(tinto)*, white *(branco)* and semi-sparkling young *(vinho verde)*, which is usually white but occasionally red. Restaurants often have *vinho da casa* (house wine) for as little as 350$00 per 350ml jug. You can please the most discerning taste buds for under 800$00 a bottle. Port, synonymous with Portugal, is produced in the Douro Valley east of Porto and drunk in three forms: ruby, tawny and white.

ENTERTAINMENT

Portugal has many local festivals and fairs, often centred on saints' days and featuring music, dance, fireworks, parades, handicraft fairs or animal markets. See the earlier Public Holidays & Special Events section.

Fado, the melancholy Portuguese equivalent of the blues (see Music under Facts about Portugal), is offered in *casas de fado* in Lisbon, Coimbra and Porto. More conventional bars, pubs and clubs abound in Lisbon, Porto and the Algarve.

Some bigger towns sponsor summer cultural programs, especially music (rock, jazz and classical) and dance. Ask at tourist offices for free what's-on publications, or see the local newspaper for listings.

Cinemas cost around 800$00 a ticket, with prices often reduced once weekly to lure audiences from their homes. Foreign films are usually subtitled.

SPECTATOR SPORTS

Football (soccer) dominates the sporting scene. The season lasts from August to May and most villages and towns have a team. The three best are Lisbon's Benfica and Sporting, and Porto's FC Porto. Ask the tourist office about forthcoming matches. The fever will peak in 2004 when Portugal hosts the European football championships.

Bullfighting remains popular despite pressure from international animal-rights activists. The season runs from March to October. Portuguese rules prohibit a public kill, though bulls are often dispatched in private afterwards. In Lisbon, bullfights are held at Campo Pequeno on Thursday. Less touristy versions can be seen at the June

PORTUGAL

agricultural fair in Vila Franca de Xira and Santarém.

SHOPPING

Leather goods, especially shoes and bags, are good value, as are textiles such as lace and embroidered linen. Handicrafts range from inexpensive pottery and basketwork to substantial purchases like Arraiolos rugs, filigree jewellery and made-to-order azulejos.

Getting There & Away

AIR

British Airways (BA), TAP Air Portugal and the no-frills carrier Go have daily direct flights from London to Lisbon; BA and TAP also go to Porto and Faro. On most days there are direct links to Lisbon and Porto from Paris, Frankfurt, Amsterdam, Brussels and Madrid.

From the UK, high-season London-Lisbon return fares start about UK£160 with Go (☎ 0845-605 4321). London-Porto via a third-country carrier can be as low as UK£150, and charter fares to Lisbon or Faro start about UK£170. TAP (☎ 0845-601 0932) and BA (☎ 0845-722 2111) both offer youth/student fares, but the best such deals are with agencies such as Trailfinders (☎ 020-7937 1234), usit CAMPUS (☎ 0870-240 1010) and STA (☎ 020-7361 6161).

France has frequent Portugal connections at reasonable prices. TAP (☎ 08 02 31 93 20) and Air France (☎ 08 02 80 28 02) have youth/student fares but you're better off with agencies like AJF (☎ 01 42 77 87 80), usit CONNECT (☎ 01 43 29 69 50) or Wasteels (☎ 08 03 88 70 00).

For prices from Portugal, ask youth travel agencies usit TAGUS (Lisbon ☎ 213 525 986, Porto ☎ 226 094 146) or Wasteels (Lisbon ☎ 218 869 793, Porto ☎ 225 370 539). TAP (☎ 808 205 700) and BA (☎ 808 212 125) can be contacted at local rates from anywhere in Portugal.

LAND
Bus

Portugal's main Eurolines agents are Internorte (Porto ☎ 226 052 420), Intercentro (Lisbon ☎ 213 571 745) and Intersul (Faro ☎ 289 899 770), serving north, central and southern Portugal, respectively.

UK-based Busabout (☎ 020-7950 1661) is a Europe-wide hop-on-hop-off coach network with stops near hostels and camping grounds, and passes that let you travel as much as you want within a set period. Its Portugal stops are in Porto, Lisbon and Lagos.

Spain Spanish connections of Eurolines (Madrid ☎ 91 327 1381) include Madrid-Lisbon (5700 ptas/6860$00), Madrid-Porto (4560 ptas/5490$00) and Seville-Lisbon (4870 ptas/5870$00), all at least three times weekly; and Seville-Lagos (2630 ptas/3170$00) four to six times weekly.

Spanish operators with Portugal links include AutoRes (☎ 902-19 29 39) and ALSA (Madrid ☎ 91 754 6502), each with twice-daily Madrid-Lisbon services; and Damas (Huelva ☎ 959 25 69 00), running twice daily from Seville to Faro, jointly with the Algarve line EVA. Three times weekly, Transportes Agobe (☎ 902-15 45 68) runs from Granada via Seville and the Algarve to Lisbon, continuing on Saturday to Coimbra and Porto.

The UK & France Eurolines (UK ☎ 08705-143219) runs a variety of services from London (Victoria coach station) via the Channel ferry, with a 7½ hour stopover and change of coach in Paris. These include at least four weekly to Porto (UK£105/770FF one way from London/Paris, 40 hours); five to Lisbon (UK£108/735FF, 42 hours); and two to Faro/Lagos (UK£113/785FF, 45 hours).

The independent line IASA (Paris ☎ 01 43 53 90 82, Porto ☎ 222 084 338, Lisbon ☎ 213 143 979) runs five coaches weekly on four routes: Paris-Viana do Castelo; Paris-Braga; Paris-Porto; and Paris-Coimbra-Lisbon. Its one-way/return fares range from 640/990FF to 695/995FF.

Train

Spain The main rail route is Madrid-Lisbon on the *Talgo Lusitânia* via Valência de Alcántara. The nightly express takes 10½ hours, and a 2nd-class reserved seat costs 6700 ptas/8000$00, a sleeper berth 9300 ptas/11,200$00.

A popular northern route is Vigo-Porto (three expresses daily). Badajoz-Elvas-Lisbon is tedious (two regional services daily, with a change at Entroncamento) but the scenery is grand. There are no direct southern trains: from Seville you can ride to Huelva, change for Ayamonte, bus across the border to Vila Real de Santo António, and catch frequent trains to Faro and Lagos.

The daily Paris-Lisbon train (see the following UK & France section) goes via Salamanca, Valladolid, Burgos, Vitória and San Sebastian.

The UK & France In general, it's only worth taking the train if you can use under-26 rail passes such as Inter-Rail (see the Getting Around chapter at the beginning of this book).

All services from London to Portugal go via Paris, where you change trains (and stations) for the *TGV Atlantique* to Irún in Spain (change trains again). From Irún there are two standard routes: the *Sud-Expresso* across Spain to Coimbra in Portugal, where you can continue to Lisbon or change for Porto; and an express service to Madrid, changing there to the *Lusitânia* to Lisbon. Change at Lisbon for the south of Portugal.

Buying a one-way, 2nd-class, adult/youth London-Lisbon ticket (seat only) for the cheapest route, via the channel ferry, costs UK£166/88; allow at least 30 hours. Tickets for this route are available from bigger train stations or from Connex South Eastern (☎ 0870-001 0174). The Eurostar service to Paris via the Channel Tunnel cuts several hours off the trip but bumps up the cost.

Car & Motorcycle

The quickest routes from the UK are by ferry via northern Spain: from Portsmouth to Bilbao with P&O Stena Line (☎ 08706-003300) and from Plymouth to Santander with Brittany Ferries (☎ 08705-360360). In winter, Brittany sails from Poole or Portsmouth.

Alternatively, motor through France via Bordeaux, and through Spain via Burgos and Salamanca.

DEPARTURE TAX

Airport taxes for return flights between Portugal and other European countries range from about 3000 ptas/3600$00 for Spain to

UK£25/9200$00 for the UK. Taxes are included in the ticket price with a scheduled carrier, but payable at check-in with charter flights.

Getting Around

AIR

Flights within Portugal are poor value unless you have a youth/student card. Both PGA Portugália Airlines (Lisbon ☎ 218 425 559) and TAP (☎ 808 205 700) have multiple daily Lisbon-Porto and Lisbon-Faro links, for about 17,100$00 and 16,300$00 respectively; Portugália offers a 50% youth discount. TAP has a daily Lisbon-Faro service connecting with its international arrivals and departures at Lisbon.

BUS

A welter of regional bus companies together operate a network of comfortable, direct intercity *expressos,* fast regional *rápidas,* and *carreiras* which stop at every crossroad. Local weekend services can thin out to nothing, especially up north and when school is out.

A Lisbon-Porto express (3½ hours) costs 2300$00 and Lisbon-Faro (about five hours) costs 2500$00. A youth card should get you discounts of about 20%.

TRAIN

Caminhos de Ferro Portugueses (CP), the state railway company, operates three main services: *rápido* or *intercidade* (IC on timetables), *interregional* (IR) and *regional* (R). Intercidade and interregional tickets cost at least twice the price of regional services, with reservations either mandatory or recommended. A special fast IC service called Alfa links Lisbon, Coimbra and Porto. If you can match your itinerary and pace to a regional service, rail travel is cheaper, if slower, than by bus.

Sample 2nd-class IC/IR fares include 2650/2080$00 for Lisbon-Porto and 2100/1930$00 for Lisbon-Faro.

Children aged four to 12 and adults over 65 travel at half-price. Youth-card holders get 30% off R and IR services (except at weekends). There are also family discounts. One/two/three-week tourist tickets (*bilhetes*

PORTUGAL

turísticos) at 18,500/31,000/43,300$00 are good for 1st-class travel, but worthwhile only if you're practically living on Portuguese trains.

Frequent train travellers may want to buy the *Guia Horário Oficial* (350$00), with all domestic and international timetables, from ticket windows at most stations.

CAR & MOTORCYCLE

ACP (Automóvel Clube de Portugal), Portugal's representative for various foreign car and touring clubs, provides medical, legal and breakdown assistance for members. But anyone can get road information and maps from its head office (☎ 213 180 100, fax 213 180 227), Rua Rosa Araújo 24, Lisbon. ACP emergency help numbers are ☎ 219 429 103 for southern Portugal and ☎ 228 340 001 for northern Portugal.

Petrol is pricey – eg, 185$00 and up for 1L of 95-octane unleaded fuel *(sem chumbo)*, which is readily available.

Road Rules

There are indeed rules, though Portuguese drivers are among Europe's most accident-prone. Although city driving (and parking) is hectic, rural roads have surprisingly little traffic. EU subsidies have paid for major upgrades of the road system, and there are now long stretches of motorway, some of them toll roads.

Driving is on the right. Speed limits for cars and motorcycles are 50km/h in cities and public centres, 90km/h on normal roads and 120km/h on motorways (but 50, 70 and 100km/h for motorcycles with sidecars). Drivers and front passengers in cars must wear seat belts. Motorcyclists and passengers must wear helmets, and motorcycles must have headlights on day and night.

Drink-driving laws are strict, with a maximum legal blood-alcohol level of 0.05%.

Car Rental

Portugal has dozens of local car-rental firms, many offering lower daily rates than international firms. To rent a small car for a week in high season, figure on about UK£200 from the UK or at least 45,000$00 from Portugal (with tax, insurance and unlimited mileage). However, fly-drive packages from international firms or TAP Air Portugal can be good value. You must be at least 25 and have held your licence for over a year (some companies allow younger drivers at higher rates).

BICYCLE

A growing number of towns have bike rental outfits (1500$00 to 3500$00 a day). If you're bringing your own machine, pack plenty of spares. Bikes can no longer be taken with you on trains, though most bus lines will accept them as accompanied baggage, subject to space and sometimes for an extra fee.

LOCAL TRANSPORT

Except in Lisbon or Porto there's little reason to take a municipal bus. Lisbon's underground system is handy for getting around the city centre and out to Parque das Nações, the former Expo site (see the Lisbon section for details). Porto is building its own underground system.

Taxis offer good value over short distances, especially for two or more people, and are plentiful in towns. Fares go up at night and at weekends, and if your trip leaves the city limits.

Enthusiasts for stately progress shouldn't miss the trams in Lisbon and Porto, an endangered species, and the *elevadores* (funiculars and elevators) of Lisbon, Bom Jesus (Braga) and Nazaré. Commuter ferries cross the Rio Tejo all day to/from Lisbon.

ORGANISED TOURS

Gray Lines (☎ 213 522 594, fax 213 560 668), Avenida Praia da Vitória 12-B, Lisbon, organises multiday coach tours throughout Portugal, through local agents or upper-end tourist hotels. The AVIC coach company (☎ 258 806 180), Avenida dos Combatentes 206, Viana do Castelo, offers short tours of the Douro and Lima Valleys. Miltours (☎ 289 890 600), Veríssimo de Almeida 14, Faro, has day trips in the Algarve and elsewhere.

Among unusual offerings by UK agencies are art, music and history tours by Martin Randall Travel (☎ 020-8742 3355) and wine tours by Arblaster & Clarke (☎ 01730-893344). Two of the UK agencies with Portugal hiking holidays are Explore Worldwide (☎ 01252-760000) and Ramblers Holidays (☎ 01707-331133). For references to the

PORTUGAL

adventure-travel specialists within Portugal, see Activities under Facts for the Visitor in this chapter.

Lisbon

pop 663,000
Although it has the crowds, noise and traffic of a capital city, Lisbon's low skyline and breezy position beside the Rio Tejo (River Tagus) lend it a small, manageable feel. Its unpretentious atmosphere, pleasant blend of architectural styles and diverse attractions appeal to a wide range of visitors. Furthermore, Lisbon (Lisboa to the Portuguese) is one of Europe's most economical destinations.

Orientation
Activity centres on the Baixa district, focused at Praça Dom Pedro IV, known by all as the Rossio. Just north of the Rossio is Praça dos Restauradores, at the bottom of Avenida da Liberdade, Lisbon's park-like 'main street'. West of the Rossio it's a steep climb to the Bairro Alto district, traditional centre of Lisbon's nightlife. East of the Rossio, it's another climb to the Castelo de São Jorge and the adjacent Alfama district, a maze of ancient lanes. Several kilometres west is Belém with its cluster of attractions. Parque das Nações, the former Expo '98 site with its grand Oceanarium, lies on the revamped north-eastern waterfront.

Information
Tourist Offices Turismo de Lisboa (☎ 213 433 672, fax 213 610 359) has a new information centre, CRIA (Centro de Representação, Informação e Animação), in Praça do Comércio, dealing specifically with Lisbon inquiries.

A tourist office (☎ 213 463 314, fax 213 468 772) run by ICEP, the national tourist organisation, in the Palácio Foz on Praça dos Restauradores, deals only with national inquiries. Both offices are open 9 am to 8 pm daily.

Other Turismo de Lisboa kiosks are at Rua Augusta, on Largo Martim Moniz and at Belém. A branch (☎ 218 450 660) at the airport is open 6 am to midnight daily. All have free maps and the bimonthly *Follow me Lisboa,* listing sights and current events. All sell the Lisboa Card, good for unlimited travel on nearly all city transport and free or discounted admission to many museums and monuments; a 24/48/72-hour card costs 2100/3500/4500$00.

Money Banks with 24-hour cash-exchange machines are at the airport, Santa Apolónia train station and Rua Augusta 24. A better deal is the exchange bureau Cota Câmbios, Rossio 41, open 9 am to 9 pm daily. Nearly every bank has an ATM machine.

· Top Tours (☎ 213 155 885, fax 213 155 873), Avenida Duque de Loulé 108, offers American Express card or travellers-cheque holders commission-free currency exchange, help with lost cards or cheques and holding/forwarding of mail and faxes. It's closed at weekends.

Post & Communications The central post office is on Praça do Comércio. Mail addressed to Posta Restante, Central Correios, Terreira do Paço, 1100 Lisboa, comes here. A telephone office at Rossio 68 is open until 11 pm daily. A more convenient post and telephone office on Praça dos Restauradores is open until 10 pm on weekdays and to 6 pm at weekends. Planet Megastore (see Email & Internet Access) has a cheap fax service.

Email & Internet Access Portugal Telecom's Net Center (☎ 213 522 292), Avenida Fontes Pereira de Melo 38, offers Internet access at 200$00 per half-hour, 9 am to 5 pm weekdays. Access costs 100$00 per quarter-hour at Espaço Ágora (☎ 213 940 170), Rua Cintura, Armazém 1 (behind Santos train station), open 2 pm to 1 am daily; and 175$00 per quarter-hour at a bar called the Web Café (☎ 213 421 181), Rua do Diário de Notícias 126, 4 pm to 2 am daily. Planet Megastore (☎ 217 928 100), Avenida da República 41-B, open 8 am to midnight daily, charges 200$00 per quarter-hour.

Travel Agencies Trusty youth-travel agencies are usit TAGUS (☎ 213 525 986, fax 213 532 715), Rua Camilo Castelo Branco 20; and Wasteels (☎ 218 869 793, fax 218 869 797), Rua dos Caminhos do Ferro 90, by Santa Apolónia train station.

PORTUGAL

LISBON

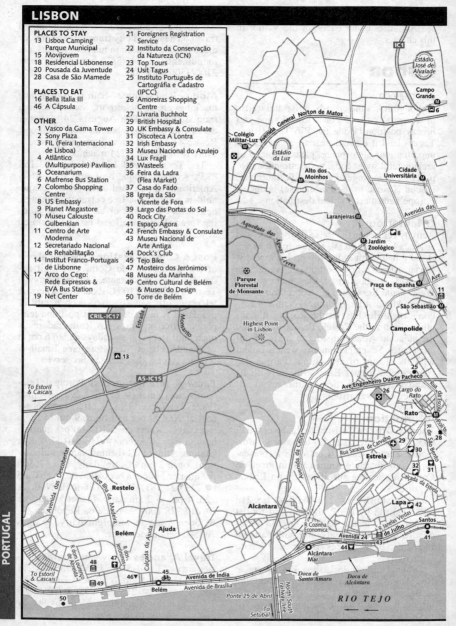

PLACES TO STAY
13 Lisboa Camping Parque Municipal
15 Movijovem
18 Residencial Lisbonense
20 Pousada da Juventude
28 Casa de São Mamede

PLACES TO EAT
16 Bella Italia III
46 A Cápsula

OTHER
1 Vasco da Gama Tower
2 Sony Plaza
3 FIL (Feira Internacional de Lisboa)
4 Atlântico (Multipurpose) Pavilion
5 Oceanarium
6 Mafrense Bus Station
7 Colombo Shopping Centre
8 US Embassy
9 Planet Megastore
10 Museu Calouste Gulbenkian
11 Centro de Arte Moderna
12 Secretariado Nacional de Rehabilitação
14 Institut Franco-Português de Lisbonne
17 Arco do Cego: Rede Expressos & EVA Bus Station
19 Net Center

21 Foreigners Registration Service
22 Instituto da Conservação da Natureza (ICN)
23 Top Tours
24 Usit Tagus
25 Instituto Português de Cartográfia e Cadastro (IPCC)
26 Amoreiras Shopping Centre
27 Livraria Buchholz
29 British Hospital
30 UK Embassy & Consulate
31 Discoteca A Lontra
32 Irish Embassy
33 Museu Nacional do Azulejo
34 Lux Fragil
35 Wasteels
36 Feira da Ladra (Flea Market)
37 Casa do Fado
38 Igreja da São Vicente de Fora
39 Largo das Portas do Sol
40 Rock City
41 Espaço Ágora
42 French Embassy & Consulate
43 Museu Nacional de Arte Antiga
44 Dock's Club
45 Tejo Bike
47 Mosteiro dos Jerónimos
48 Museu da Marinha
49 Centro Cultural de Belém & Museu do Design
50 Torre de Belém

PORTUGAL

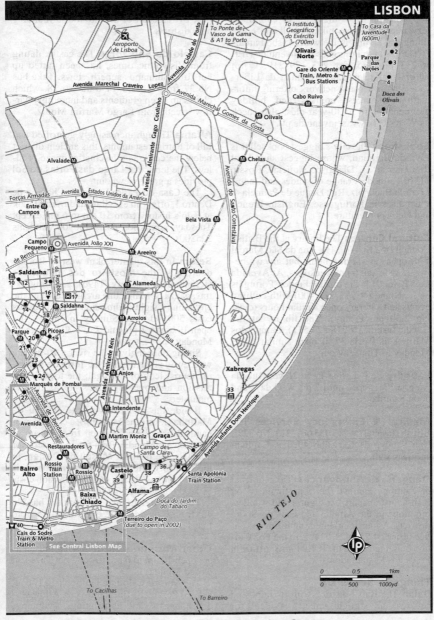

LISBON

To Ponte de Vasco da Gama & A1 to Porto

To Instituto Geográfico do Exército (700m)

To Casa da Juventude (600m)

Aeroporto de Lisboa

Olivais Norte

Gare do Oriente Train, Metro & Bus Stations

Parque das Nações

Avenida Cidade do Porto

Avenida Marechal Craveiro Lopez

Avenida Marechal Gomes da Costa

Cabo Ruivo

Doca dos Olivais

Olivais

Avenida Almirante Gago Coutinho

Chelas

Alvalade

Forças Armadas

Avenida Estados Unidos da América

Entre Campos

Roma

Avenida do Santo Contestável

Bela Vista

Campo Pequeno

Avenida João XXI

Ave. da República

Areeiro

de Berna

Saldanha

Olaias

Alameda

Ave. da República

Saldahna

Arroios

Rua Morais Soares

Parque

Picoas

Xabregas

Anjos

Avenida Almirante Reis

Marquês de Pombal

Avenida de Liberdade

Intendente

Avenida Infante Dom Henrique

Avenida

Martim Moniz

Graça

Campo de Santa Clara

Restauradores

Rossio Train Station

Rossio

Castelo

Santa Apolónia Train Station

Bairro Alto

Baixa Chiado

Alfama

Doca do Jardim do Tabaco

Terreiro do Paço (due to open in 2002)

RIO TEJO

Cais do Sodré Train & Metro Station

See Central Lisbon Map

To Cacilhas

To Barreiro

0   0.5   1km
0   500   1000yd

PORTUGAL

euro currency converter 1 escudo = €0.004

Cabra Montêz (mobile/cellphone ☎ 917 446 668, fax 214 382 285, ☻ cabramon tez@ip.pt) organises biking, walking, horse riding and karting in the wider Lisbon area.

The Instituto Português da Juventude (IPJ; ☎ 213 179 235, fax 213 179 219, ☻ ipj .infor@mail.telepac.pt), Avenida da Liberdade 194, is a youth network offering information resources, courses and holiday programs for 16 to 30-year-olds; also check its Web site (www.sejuventude.pt).

Bookshops The city's biggest bookseller is Livraria Bertrand, whose biggest shop is at Rua Garrett 73. Diário de Notícias, Rossio 11, has a modest range of guides and maps. Livraria Buchholz, Rua Duque de Palmela 4, specialises in Portuguese, English, French and German literature.

Cultural Centres The library at the British Council (☎ 213 476 141), Rua de São Marçal 174, opens at varying hours but always between noon and 6 pm weekdays. At Avenida Luis Bivar 91 is the Institut Franco-Portugais de Lisbonne (☎ 213 111 400) with cultural events and a library open similar hours (closing 2.30 pm Friday). The library at the Goethe Institut (☎ 218 824 511), Campo dos Mártires da Pátria 37, is open similar hours Monday to Thursday only.

Laundry Self-service Lave Neve, Rua da Alegria 37, is open until 7 pm weekdays and noon Saturday.

Medical & Emergency Services The British Hospital (☎ 213 955 067, 213 976 329), Rua Saraiva de Carvalho 49, has English-speaking staff.

Dangers & Annoyances Take normal precautions against theft, particularly on rush-hour transport. At night avoid wandering alone in the Alfama and Cais do Sodré districts. A tourist-oriented, multilingual police office (☎ 213 421 634) is in the Foz Cultura building beside the ICEP tourist office in Praça dos Restauradores.

Things to See & Do

Baixa The Baixa district, with its imposing squares and straight streets, is ideal for strolling. From the Rossio, ascend at a stately pace by funicular or lift into the surrounding hilly districts.

Castelo de São Jorge The castle, dating from Visigothic times, has been tarted up but still commands superb views. Take bus No 37 from Rossio, or tram No 28, which clanks up steep gradients and incredibly narrow streets from Largo Martim Moniz.

Alfama Though increasingly gentrified and full of tourist restaurants, this ancient district below the castle is a fascinating maze of alleys. The terrace at **Largo das Portas do Sol** provides a great viewpoint.

The **Casa do Fado**, Largo do Chafariz de Dentro 1, offers an excellent audiovisual look at fado's history from 10 am to 6 pm except Tuesday; admission costs 450$00 (students 225$00).

Belém In this quarter 6km west of Rossio, don't miss the **Mosteiro dos Jerónimos** (Jerónimos Monastery, 1496), a soaring extravaganza of Manueline architecture and the city's finest sight. Admission to the cloisters costs 500$00 (free Sunday morning). It's open 10 am to 1 pm and 2 to 5.30 pm except Monday.

Sitting obligingly in the river a 10-minute walk away is the Manueline **Torre de Belém**, *the* tourist icon of Portugal; the tower's admission and opening times are as for the monastery.

Beside the monastery is the **Museu da Marinha** (Maritime Museum), a collection of nautical paraphernalia open from 10 am to 6 pm except Monday (to 5 pm in winter), for 500$00. The brilliant **Museu do Design**, in the Centro Cultural de Belém opposite, is open 11 am to 7.15 pm daily; admission costs 500$00 (students 250$00).

To reach Belém take the train (or bus No 43) from Cais do Sodré or tram No 15 from Praça da Figueira.

Other Museums The following museums are open 10 am to 6 pm (from 2 pm Tuesday; closed Monday).

The **Museu Calouste Gulbenkian** is considered Portugal's finest museum. Allow several hours to view its paintings, sculptures,

PORTUGAL

jewellery and more. The adjacent **Centro de Arte Moderna** exhibits a cross section of modern Portuguese art. Entry to each costs 500$00 (free to students, children and seniors, and to all on Sunday). The handiest metro station is São Sebastião.

One of Lisbon's most attractive museums is the **Museu Nacional do Azulejo** (National Azulejos Museum) in the former convent of Nossa Senhora da Madre de Deus. Entry costs 400$00. Take bus No 104 from Praça do Comércio (weekdays) or No 59 from Rossio (weekends).

The **Museu Nacional de Arte Antiga** (Antique Art Museum), Rua das Janelas Verdes, houses the national collection of works by Portuguese painters. Admission costs 500$00 (students 250$00; free to all on Sunday morning). From Praça da Figueira take bus No 40 or 60 or tram No 15.

Parque das Nações The former Expo '98 site, a revitalised 2km-long waterfront area in the north-east, has a range of attractions, notably a magnificent **Oceanarium**, Europe's largest. It's open 10 am to 6 pm daily; entry costs 1500$00 (800$00 seniors and those under 16). Take the metro to Oriente station, an equally impressive Expo project.

Organised Tours

Carris (☎ 213 613 000) offers tours by open-top bus (2000$00) and tram (2800$00). Transtejo (☎ 218 820 348) runs cruises on the Tejo for 3000$00 from the Terreiro do Paço ferry terminal.

Places to Stay

Camping *Lisboa Camping – Parque Municipal* (☎ 217 623 100, *Parque Florestal de Monsanto)* is 6km north-west of Rossio. Take bus No 43 from Cais do Sodré.

Hostels The central *pousada da juventude* (☎ 213 532 696, *Rua Andrade Corvo 46)* is open 24 hours a day.

The closest metro station is Picoas, or take bus No 46 from Santa Apolónia station or Rossio.

The newer *casa da juventude* (☎ 218 920 890, *Via de Moscavide)* is 1km north of Gare do Oriente. Take bus No 44 from Praça dos Restauradores or Oriente to the Avenida da Boa Esperança roundabout; the hostel is 250m down the road.

Reservations are essential at both hostels.

Hotels & Guesthouses In high season – and for central hotels at any time – advance bookings are imperative.

Baixa & Restauradores Adequate doubles with shared bath start around 4000$00 at homely *Pensão Santo Tirso* (☎ 213 470 428, *Praça Dom Pedro IV 18, 3rd floor)* and 5000$00 at *Pensão Prata* (☎ 213 468 908, *Rua da Prata 71, 4th floor)* and *Pensão Arco da Bandeira* (☎ 213 423 478, *Rua dos Sapateiros 226, 3rd floor)*.

Slightly pricier are Pensão Duque (☎ 213 463 444, Calçada do Duque 53) and Pensão Norte (☎ 218 878 941, Rua dos Douradores 159, 2nd floor).

More salubrious, with doubles around 7000$00, are *Pensão Imperial* (☎ 213 420 166, *Praça dos Restauradores 78, 4th floor)* and friendly *Hospedaria Bons Dias* (☎ 213 471 918, *Calçada do Carmo 25, 5th floor)*. Old-fashioned *Pensão Residencial Alcobia* (☎ 218 865 171, fax 218 865 174, *Poço do Borratém 15)* has doubles for 8000$00 with breakfast. Brighter, security-conscious *Pensão Residencial Gerês* (☎ 218 810 497, fax 218 882 006, *Calçada do Garcia 6)* charges 9000$00 (without breakfast).

Bairro Alto & Rato Near the Elevador da Glória, pleasant *Pensão Globo* (☎ 213 462 279, *Rua do Teixeira 37)* has doubles without bath from 4500$00. *Pensão Londres* (☎ 213 462 203, fax 213 465 682, *Rua Dom Pedro V 53)* has spacious rooms, the upper ones with great views; doubles start at 7200$00. *Casa de São Mamede* (☎ 213 963 166, fax 213 951 896, *Rua Escola Politécnica 159)* has doubles in an elegant old house for 15,000$00.

Marquês de Pombal & Saldahna The *Residencial Lisbonense* (☎ 213 544 628, *Rua Pinheiro Chagas 1)* has bright doubles from 8000$00.

A three-star hotel with the facilities of a four-star is *Hotel Presidente* (☎ 213 539 501, fax 213 520 272, *Rua Alexandre Herculano 13)* with doubles for 16,000$00.

PORTUGAL

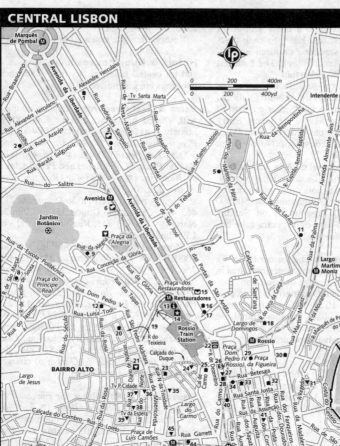

CENTRAL LISBON

CENTRAL LISBON

PLACES TO STAY			
1	Hotel Presidente	39	Adega do Ribatejo
12	Pensão Londres		(Casa de Fado)
16	Pensão Imperial	41	Adega Regional da Beira
18	Pensão Residencial Gerês	45	Café A Brasileira
20	Pensão Globo	50	Martinho da Arcada
23	Pensão Duque	51	Hua Ta Li
25	Hospedaria Bons Dias	53	Solar do Vez
28	Pensão Santo Tirso		
30	Pensão Residencial Alcobia	OTHER	
32	Pensão Norte	2	Automóvel Clube de Portugal
33	Pensão Arco da Bandeira		(ACP)
43	Pensão Prata	3	Canadian Embassy
52	Pensão São João da Praça &	4	Instituto Português da
	Sé Guest House		Juventude (IPJ)
		5	Goethe Institut
PLACES TO EAT		6	Spanish Embassy
24	Restaurante O Sol	7	Hot Clube de Portugal
27	Nicola	8	British Council
31	São Cristóvão	9	Lave Neve
35	Cervejaria da Trindade	10	Elevador de Lavra
36	Sinal Vermelho	11	Gay & Lesbian Community
37	Adega Machado (Casa de		Centre
	Fado)	13	ICEP National Tourist Office
38	A Primavera		& Turismo de Lisboa
		14	Tourist Police Post

15	Post & Telephone Office		
17	ABEP Ticket Kiosk		
19	Elevador da Glória		
21	Web Café		
22	Telephone Office		
26	Cota Câmbios		
29	Carris Kiosk		
34	Diário de Notícias		
40	Elevador de Santa Justa		
42	Santos Ofícios		
44	Livraria Bertrand		
46	Elevador da Bica		
47	Fabrica Sant'Ana		
48	Police Sation		
49	24-Hour Cash Exchange		
	Machine		
54	Terreiro do Paço Ferry Terminal		
55	Cais de Alfândega Ferry		
	Terminal		
56	Turismo de Lisboa (CRIA)		
57	Central Post Office		
58	Ó Gilins Irish Pub		
59	Mercado da Ribeira		
60	Cais do Sodré Car Ferry		
	Terminal		

Alfama Behind the cathedral, at Rua São João da Praça 97, popular *Pensão São João da Praça* (*☎/fax 218 862 591*) on the 2nd floor and genteel *Sé Guest House* (*☎ 218 864 400*) on the 1st floor have doubles from 6000$00 to 12,000$00 (with breakfast).

Places to Eat
There are dozens of restaurants and cafes in the Baixa (best for lunchtime bargains) and Bairro Alto (pricier evening venues). A trendier restaurant and bar zone is riverside Doca de Santo Amaro, near Alcântara-Mar station. The main market, Mercado da Ribeira, is near Cais do Sodré station.

Baixa & Alfama *Adega Regional da Beira* (*☎ 213 467 014, Rua dos Correeiros 132*) is one of many reasonably priced places along this street. Vegetarian *Restaurante O Sol* (*☎ 213 471 944, Calçada do Duque 25*) offers set meals for under 1000$00. A bargain Chinese restaurant is *Hua Ta Li* (*☎ 218 887 91 70, Rua dos Bacalhoeiros 109*).

Among several restaurants with outdoor seating in lower Alfama, *Solar do Vez* (*☎ 218 870 794, Campo das Cebolas 48*) has an ap-

pealing simplicity. *São Cristóvão* (*☎ 218 885 578, Rua de São Cristóvão 30*) is famous for its Cape Verdean dishes.

For a coffee or a meal, two late 19th/early 20th century cafes are *Nicola* (*☎ 213 460 579, Rossio 24*) and *Martinho da Arcada* (*☎ 218 879 259, Praça do Comércio 3*). The literary pedigree of *Café A Brasileira* (*☎ 213 469 547, Rua Garrett 120*) is symbolised by the bronze figure of Fernando Pessoa outside.

Bairro Alto & Saldanha Tiny *Restaurante A Primavera* (*☎ 213 420 477, Travessa da Espera 34*) has a family ambience complemented by honest cooking. Smarter and pricier (with great desserts) is *Restaurante Sinal Vermelho* (*☎ 213 461 252, Rua das Gáveas 89*).

Cervejaria da Trindade (*☎ 213 423 506, Rua Nova da Trindade 20-C*) is a converted convent decorated with azulejos. Main dishes start at around 1400$00.

Bright and cheerful *Bella Italia III* (*☎ 213 528 636, Avenida Duque d'Ávila 40-C*) is a pastelaria-cum-restaurant, with pizzas and half-portions of Portuguese fare for under 1000$00.

PORTUGAL

Belém A row of attractive restaurants in Belém with outdoor seating includes *A Cápsula* (☎ 213 648 768, Rua Vieira Portuense 72).

Entertainment

For current listings, pick up the free bi-monthly *Follow me Lisboa* or monthly *Agenda Cultural* from the tourist office, or *Público* from a newsstand.

Music Many Lisbon *casas de fado* (which are also restaurants) produce pale tourist imitations of fado at high prices. All have a minimum charge of 2000$00 to 4500$00. In the Bairro Alto, try *Adega Machado* (☎ 213 224 640, Rua do Norte 91) or the simpler *Adega do Ribatejo* (☎ 213 468 343, Rua Diário de Notícias 23). The tourist offices can suggest others.

Hot Clube de Portugal (☎ 213 467 369, Praça da Alegria 39) is at the centre of a thriving jazz scene, with live music three or four nights weekly. It's open 10 pm to 2 am (closed Sunday and Monday).

Ó Gilíns Irish Pub (☎ 213 421 899, Rua dos Remolares 8-10) is open 11 am to 2 am daily, with live Irish tunes most Saturday nights and jazz with Sunday brunch.

Disco clubs come and go. Try *Luanda* (☎ 213 633 959, Travessa de Teixeira Júnior 6) or the good *Lux Fragil* (☎ 218 820 890, Avenida Infante Dom Henrique, Cais da Pedra à Santa Apolónia), both raving from midnight until 5 am. Other bar-discos are by the river: *Rock City* (☎ 213 428 640, Rua Cintura do Porto de Lisboa, Armazém 225) has live rock nightly except Monday; *Dock's Club* (☎ 213 950 856, Rua da Cintura do Porto de Lisboa 226) carries on until 4 am nightly except Sunday.

The African music scene (predominantly Cape Verdean) thrives in bars around Rua de São Bento; one of the best known is *Discoteca A Lontra* (☎ 213 956 968, Rua de São Bento 155), open until 4 am nightly except Monday.

Cinemas Lisbon has dozens of cinemas, including multiscreen ones at *Amoreiras* (☎ 213 878 752) and *Colombo* (☎ 217 113 222) shopping complexes. Tickets cost 800$00 (550$00 Monday).

Spectator Sports Lisbon's football teams are Benfica and 2000 national champions Sporting. The tourist offices can advise on match dates and tickets. Bullfights are staged at Campo Pequeno between April and October. Tickets are available at ABEP ticket agency on Praça dos Restauradores.

Shopping

For azulejos, try Fabrica Sant'Ana at Rua do Alecrim 95. The Museu Nacional do Azulejo also has a small shop. Santos Ofícios at Rua da Madalena 87 has an eclectic range of Portuguese folk art. On Tuesday and Saturday, visit the Feira da Ladra, a huge open-air market at Campo de Santa Clara in the Alfama.

Getting There & Away

Air Lisbon is connected by daily flights to Porto, Faro and many European centres (see the introductory Getting There & Away and Getting Around sections of this chapter). For arrival and departure information call ☎ 218 413 700.

Bus A dozen different companies, including Renex (☎ 218 874 871), operate from Gare do Oriente. The Arco do Cego terminal (☎ 213 545 439), Avenida João Crisóstomo, is the base for Rede Expressos (☎ 213 103 111) and EVA (☎ 213 147 710), whose networks cover the whole country.

Train Santa Apolónia station (☎ 218 884 025/027) is the terminus for northern and central Portugal, and for all international services (trains also stop en route at the better-connected Gare do Oriente). Cais do Sodré station is for Belém, Cascais and Estoril. Rossio station serves Sintra.

Barreiro station, across the river, is the terminus for southern Portugal; connecting ferries leave frequently from the pier at Terréiro do Paço.

The North-South railway line, over the Ponte de 25 Abril, goes to suburban areas and will eventually carry farther to southern Portugal.

Ferry Cais da Alfândega is the terminal for several ferries including to Cacilhas (110$00), a transfer point for some buses to Setúbal. A car ferry (for bikes too) runs from Cais do Sodré terminal.

PORTUGAL

Getting Around

To/From the Airport The AeroBus runs every 20 minutes from 7 am to 9 pm, taking 30 to 45 minutes between the airport and Cais do Sodré, including a stop by the ICEP tourist office. A 460/1075$00 ticket is good for one/three days on all buses, trams and funiculars. Local bus Nos 8, 44, 45 and 83 also run near the ICEP tourist office; No 44 links the airport with Gare do Oriente too. A taxi into town is about 1500$00, plus 300$00 if your luggage needs to go in the boot.

Bus & Tram Individual bus and tram tickets are 80$00 from Carris kiosks, most conveniently at Praça da Figueira and the Santa Justa elevador; tickets bought on board cost 160$00. A four/seven-day Passe Turístico, valid for all trams and buses and the metro, costs 1720/2430$00.

Buses and trams run from 6 am to 1 am, with some night services. Pick up a transport map, *Planta dos Transportes Públicas da Carris*, from tourist offices or Carris kiosks.

Wheelchair users can call the Cooperativa Nacional Apoio Deficientes (☎ 218 595 332) for assistance to hire adapted transport. The clattering, antediluvian trams *(eléctricos)* are an endearing component of Lisbon; try No 28 to Alfama from Largo Martim Moniz.

Metro The metro is useful for hops across town and to the Parque das Nações. Individual tickets cost 100$00; a *caderneta* of 10 tickets is 850$00. A day ticket *(bilhete diário)* is 270$00. The metro operates from 6.30 am to 1 am. Beware of pickpockets during rush hour.

Taxi Lisbon's taxis are plentiful. Flagging them down can be tricky: they're best hired from taxi ranks. Some at the airport are less than scrupulous.

Car & Bicycle Car rental companies in Lisbon include Avis (☎ 800 201 002) and Europcar (☎ 219 407 790). Rupauto (☎ 217 933 258, fax 217 931 768) has cheap rates. Tejo Bike (☎ 218 871 976), 300m east of Belém, rents bikes for 750$00 an hour to ride along the waterfront.

Around Lisbon

SINTRA
pop 20,000

If you take only one trip from Lisbon, make it Sintra. Beloved by Portuguese royalty and English nobility, its thick forests and startling architecture provide a complete change from Lisbon. The tourist office (☎ 219 231 157, fax 219 235 176), at Praça da República 23 in the historic centre, has a good map and accommodation information.

At weekends and during the annual July music festival, expect droves of visitors. In high season it's wise to book accommodation ahead.

Things to See

The **Palácio Nacional de Sintra**, Manueline and Gothic, with Moorish origins, dominates the town with its twin chimneys. It's open 10 am to 5.30 pm except Wednesday; admission costs 600$00 (students 300$00).

One of Sintra's best museums is the **Museu do Brinquedo** on Rua Visconde de Monserrate, with 20,000 toys from around the world. It's open 10 am to 6 pm except Monday, and costs 500/300$00.

An easy 3km climb from the centre leads to the ruined **Castelo dos Mouros** with a fine view over the town and surroundings. It's open 9 am to 7 pm daily. Twenty minutes on is the exuberantly Romantic **Palácio da Pena**, built in 1839. It's open 10 am to 6.30 pm (5 pm in winter) except Monday, for 600/300$00. Cars are prohibited; Stagecoach bus No 434 (600$00) runs regularly from the station via the tourist office.

Rambling, romantic **Monserrate Gardens**, 4km from town, are open 10 am to 5 pm daily (admission free). En route is an extraordinary, mystical mansion, **Quinta da Regaleira**, open 10 am to 6 pm (4 pm in winter) daily, for 2000/1000$00.

Places to Stay

The nearest decent camping ground is *Camping Praia Grande* (☎ 219 290 581), on the coast 11km from Sintra and linked by a frequent bus service. A *pousada da juventude* (☎ 219 241 210) is at Santa Eufémia, 4km from the centre; reservations are essential.

PORTUGAL

Casa de Hóspedes Adelaide (☎ 219 230 873, Rua Guilherme Gomes Fernandes 11), a 10-minute walk from the station, has reasonable doubles without bath from 4000$00. Better-value private rooms are around 4500$00 (the tourist office has a list). Across the tracks, friendly **Piela's** (☎ 219 241 691, Rua João de Deus 70 – due to move in 2001 to Avenida Desiderio Cambournac 1-3) has doubles without bath from around 6000$00.

Places to Eat

Close to the tourist office is the recommended **Tulhas** (☎ 219 232 378, Rua Gil Vicente 4-6). Simple **A Tasca do Manel** (☎ 219 230 215, Largo Dr Vergilio Horta 5) serves up standards for around 900$00 a dish. Behind the station, **Restaurante Parririnha** (☎ 219 231 207, Rua João de Deus 41) serves great grilled fish. Cavernous **Bistrobar Ópera Prima** (☎ 219 244 518, Rua Consiglieri Pedroso 2-A) has live jazz, soul and blues several nights weekly.

Getting There & Away

The Lisbon-Sintra railway terminates in the district of Estefânia, 1.5km north-east of the historic centre. Sintra's bus station, and another train station, are a further 1km east in the new-town district of Portela de Sintra. Frequent shuttle buses run to the historic centre from the bus terminal.

Trains run every 15 minutes all day from Lisbon's Rossio station. Buses run regularly from Sintra to Estoril and Cascais.

Getting Around

A taxi to Pena or Monserrate costs around 2000$00 return. Horse-drawn carriages are a romantic alternative: figure on 10,000$00 to Monserrate and back. Old trams run from Ribeira de Sintra (1.5km from the centre) to Praia das Maças, 12km to the west.

CASCAIS

pop 30,000

Cascais, the 'in' beach resort on the coast west of Lisbon, is packed with tourists in summer. The tourist office (☎ 214 868 204, fax 214 672 280), Rua Visconde de Luz 14, has accommodation lists and bus timetables; there's also a police post (☎ 214 863 929) here.

Smartprint (☎ 214 866 776), at Rua Frederico de Arouca 45, has Internet access for 155$00 per five minutes.

Things to See & Do

Two kilometres east of Cascais, **Estoril** is an old-fashioned resort with Europe's biggest casino, open 3 pm to 3 am daily. Estoril's Praia Tamariz beach (beside the train station) has an ocean swimming pool.

The sea roars into the coast at **Boca do Inferno** (Hell's Mouth), 2km west of Cascais. Spectacular, windy **Cabo da Roca**, Europe's westernmost point, is 16km from Cascais and Sintra (served by buses from both towns). Long, wild **Guincho** beach, 3km from Cascais, is a popular surfing venue.

Transrent (☎ 214 864 566) at Centro Commercial Cisne, Avenida Marginal (near the post office), rents bicycles and motorcycles.

Places to Stay & Eat

Camping Orbitur do Guincho (☎ 214 871 014, fax 214 872 167) is 7km from Cascais near Guincho beach. **Residencial Avenida** (☎ 214 864 417, Rua da Palmeira 14) has doubles without bath for 6000$00. The tourist office can recommend private rooms from around 5000$00. **Casa da Pergola** (☎ 214 840 040, fax 214 834 791, Avenida Valbom 13) has fancy doubles from 17,000$00.

A Económica (☎ 214 833 524, Rua Sebastião J C Melo 11) serves standard fare at low prices. Try delicious fish kebabs at **A Tasca** (Rua Afonso Sanches 61).

Getting There & Away

Trains run frequently all day to Estoril and Cascais from Cais do Sodré station in Lisbon.

SETÚBAL

pop 80,000

This refreshingly untouristy city, an easy 50km south of Lisbon, has fine beaches and seafood restaurants, and is a good base for exploring nearby Parque Natural da Arrábida and Reserva Natural do Estuário do Sado.

The tourist office (☎/fax 265 534 402), Praça do Quebedo, is a five-minute walk east from the bus terminal at Avenida 5 de Outubro. A regional tourist office (☎ 265 539 120, fax 265 539 127) is at Travessa Frei Gaspar 10.

The Instituto Português da Juventude (IPJ; ☎ 265 532 707) at Largo José Afonso has free Internet access for limited periods on weekdays. Ciber Centro (☎ 265 234 800), Avenida Bento Gonçalves 21-A, charges 250$00 for 15 minutes. It's open 9 am to 11 pm weekdays.

Things to See

The town's main cultural attraction is the 15th-century **Igreja de Jesus** in Praça Miguel Bombarda, with early Manueline decoration inside. The **Galeria da Pintura Quinhentista** around the corner displays a renowned collection of 16th-century paintings; it's open 9 am to noon and 2 to 5 pm except Sunday and Monday (admission free).

Good **beaches** west of town include Praia da Figuerinha (accessible by bus in summer). Across the estuary at Tróia is a more developed beach, plus the ruins of a Roman settlement. On the ferry trip across you may see some of the estuary's 30 or so bottle-nosed dolphins.

Activities

The Sistemas de Ar Livre (☎ 265 227 685, mobile/cellphone 919 361 725) organises Sunday walks for 1000$00 per person; ask at the tourist office. For jeep safaris, hiking and biking in the Serra da Arrábida, or canoe trips through the Reserva Natural do Estuário do Sado, contact Planeta Terra (☎ 265 532 140), Praça General Luís Domingues 9. Vertigem Azul (☎ 265 238 000), Avenida Luísa Todi 375, offers dolphin-spotting and canoeing trips.

Places to Stay & Eat

A municipal *camping ground* (☎ 265 522 475) is 1.5km west of town. The *pousada da juventude* (☎ 265 534 431, Largo José Afonso) has doubles with bath as well as dorm beds.

Residencial Todi (☎ 265 220 592, Avenida Luísa Todi 244) has doubles without/with bath from 3000/4000$00. *Casa de Hóspedes Bom Amigo* (☎ 265 526 290), in Praça de Bocage, has well-adorned doubles without bath for around 5000$00. Smarter *Residencial Bocage* (☎ 265 543 080, fax 265 543 089, Rua São Cristovão 14) has doubles for 7500$00.

Cheap restaurants east of the regional tourist office include *Triângulo* (☎ 265 233 927, Rua Arronches Junqueiro 76). Seafood restaurants line the western end of Avenida Luísa Todi; friendly *Casa do Chico* (☎ 265 239 502) at No 490 is less touristy than most. Popular *Restaurante Antóniu's* (☎ 265 523 706, Rua Trabalhadores do Mar 31) is also recommended.

Getting There & Away

Buses leave frequently from Lisbon's Gare do Oriente and from Cacilhas, a short ferry ride from Lisbon's Cais de Alfândega. Ferries shuttle across the estuary to Tróia regularly; the tourist office has the latest timetable.

The Algarve

Boisterous and full of foreigners, the Algarve is about as far from traditional Portugal as one can get. The focus is on Albufeira and Lagos, with sun, sand and golf (and surfing along the west coast) the draw cards, but there are other attractions: the forested slopes of Monchique, the fortified village of Silves and windswept, historic Sagres. The district capital and largest town is Faro.

Information

The expat-oriented, English-language newspapers with information on entertainment and coming events include the *Algarve News, APN* and *Algarve Resident.*

Dangers & Annoyances Theft is a significant problem in the Algarve. Don't leave anything valuable unattended in your vehicle, tent or on the beach.

Swimmers should beware of dangerous currents, especially on the west coast. Beaches are marked by coloured flags: red means no bathing, yellow means yes to wading but no to swimming, green means anything goes.

Shopping

Few souvenirs are actually made in the Algarve, but woollens (cardigans and fishing pullovers) and Moorish-influenced ceramics are good value. Algarviana is a local *amaretto* (bitter almond liqueur), and the salubrious bottled waters of Monchique are sold everywhere.

PORTUGAL

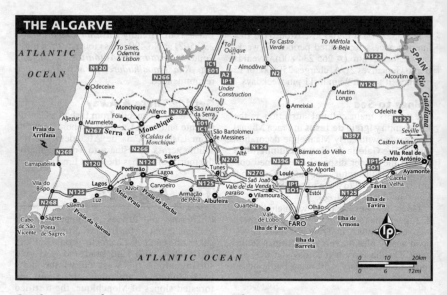

THE ALGARVE

Getting Around

Rede Expressos and EVA together run an efficient network of bus services throughout the Algarve. The IP1/EO1 superhighway, to run the length of the coast, is nearly complete. Bicycles, scooters and motorcycles can be rented everywhere; see town listings.

FARO
pop 40,000

Pleasantly low-key Faro is the main transport hub and commercial centre. The tourist office (☎ 289 803 604, fax 289 800 453) on Rua da Misericórdia has leaflets on just about every Algarve community.

Things to See & Do

The **waterfront** around Praça de Dom Francisco Gomes has pleasant gardens and cafes. Faro's beach, **Praia de Faro**, is 6km southwest of the city on Ilha de Faro; take bus No 16 from opposite the bus station or, from May to September, a ferry from Arco da Porta Nova, close to Faro's port.

At Estói, 12km north of Faro, the romantically ruined **Estói Palace** has a surreal garden of statues, balustrades and azulejos; take the Faro to São Brás de Alportel bus which goes via Estói.

Places to Stay & Eat

A big, cheap *municipal camping ground* (☎ 289 817 876) is on Praia de Faro. The *pousada da juventude (☎ 289 826 521, Rua da Polícia de Segurança Pública 1)* provides double rooms (4200/4600$00 without/with bath) as well as 1900$00 dorm beds. It's open 6 pm to midnight.

Residencial Adelaide (☎ 289 802 383, fax 289 826 870, Rua Cruz dos Mestres 7) is a friendly budget pensão with doubles without/with bath for 5000/6000$00. Close to the bus and train stations is *Pensão Residencial Filipe (☎/fax 289 824 182, Rua Infante Dom Henrique 55)*, which has doubles without/with bath for around 6000/7500$00.

Lively *Sol e Jardim (☎ 289 820 030, Praça Ferreira de Almeida 22)* serves good seafood. *A Garrafeira do Vilaça (☎ 289 802 150, Rua São Pedro 33)* is popular for budget meals.

Getting There & Away

Faro airport has both domestic and international flights (see the introductory Getting There & Away section of this chapter).

From the bus station, just west of the centre, there are at least a dozen daily express coaches to Lisbon (about four hours) and frequent buses to other coastal towns.

The train station is a few minutes' walk west of the bus station. Two IR and three IC trains run daily to Lisbon (Barreiro), and about half a dozen each to Albufeira and Portimão.

Getting Around
The airport is 6km from the centre. The Aero-Bus runs into town in summer only (free to those with airline tickets). Bus Nos 14 and 16 run into town until 9 pm (but infrequently in winter). A taxi costs about 1300$00.

TAVIRA
pop 12,000

Tavira is one of the Algarve's oldest and handsomest towns. The tourist office (☎ 281 322 511) is at Rua da Galeria 9. Bicycles and scooters can be rented from Loris Rent next door (☎ 281 325 203). For walking or bike tours call Exploratio (☎/fax 281 321 973, mobile/cellphone 919 338 226). PostNet (☎ 281 320 910), Rua Dr Silvestre Falcão, Lote 6, has Internet access for 200$00 per 15 minutes.

Things to See & Do
In the old town the **Igreja da Misericórdia** has a striking Renaissance doorway and interior azulejos. From there, it's a short climb to the **castle** dominating the town.

Ilha da Tavira, 2km from Tavira, is an island beach connected to the mainland by ferry. Walk 2km beside the river to the ferry terminal at Quatro Águas or take the (summer only) bus from the bus station.

For a look at the old Algarve, take a bus to near **Cacela Velha**, an unspoilt hamlet 8km from Tavira. Another worthwhile day trip is to the fishing centre of **Olhão**, 22km west of Tavira.

Places to Stay & Eat
Ilha da Tavira has a *camping ground*, but the ferry stops running at 11 pm (usually 1 am from July to September). Popular *Pensão Residencial Lagoas* (☎ 281 322 252, Rua Almirante Cândido dos Reis 24) has doubles without bath from 5000$00. Central *Residencial Imperial* (☎ 289 322 234, Rua José Pires Padinha 24) has doubles with bath and breakfast for 8000$00. Riverside *Pensão Residencial Princesa do Gilão*

(☎ 289 325 171, Rua Borda d'Agua de Aguiar 10) charges 8000$00.

Good budget restaurants on riverside Rua Dr José Pires Padinha include *Restaurante Regional Carmina* (☎ 281 322 236) at No 96 and *Casa de Pasto A Barquinha* (☎ 281 322 843) at No 142. *Cantinho do Emigrante* (☎ 281 323 696, Praça Dr Padinha 27) also has bargain fare.

At Olhão, enjoy a delicious seafood lunch at *Restaurante Isidro* (☎ 289 714 124, Rua 5 de Outubro 68), opposite the market; it's closed Wednesday.

Getting There & Away
Some 15 trains and at least four express buses run daily between Faro and Tavira (30 to 50 minutes).

LAGOS
pop 20,000

This tourist resort has some of the Algarve's finest beaches. The tourist office (☎ 289 763 031) is 1km north-east of the centre, at the Situo São João roundabout; it's closed at weekends during winter. The pousada da juventude (see Places to Stay) has Internet access at 300$00 per half-hour.

Things to See & Do
In the old town, the **municipal museum** houses an assortment of archaeological finds, ecclesiastical treasures, handicrafts and animal foetuses. The adjacent **Igreja de Santo António** has some intricate baroque woodwork.

The beach scene includes **Meia Praia**, a vast strip to the east; and to the west **Praia da Luz** and the more secluded **Praia do Pinhão**.

Espadarte do Sul (☎ 289 761 820) operates **boat trips** from Docapesca harbour, including snorkelling and game fishing. On the seaside promenade, local fishermen offer motorboat jaunts to the nearby **grottoes**.

Places to Stay
Two nearby camping grounds are *Trindade* (☎ 289 763 893), 200m south of the town walls, and *Imulagos* (☎ 289 760 031), with a shuttle bus from the waterfront road. The *pousada da juventude* (☎ 289 761 970) is at Rua Lançarote de Freitas 50.

Residencial Marazul (☎ 289 769 749, Rua 25 de Abril 13) has smart doubles from

PORTUGAL

around 11,000$00. *Private rooms* are plentiful, for around 5500$00.

Places to Eat

For good Algarve specialities, try *O Cantinho Algarvio* (☎ 289 761 289, *Rua Afonso d'Almeida 17*). A local favourite is *Restaurante Bar Barros* (☎ 282 762 276, *Rua Portas de Portugal 83*). *Mullens (Rua Cândido dos Reis 86)* is a wood-panelled pub with good food.

Getting There & Away

Bus and train services depart frequently for other Algarve towns and around a dozen times daily to Lisbon; by train, change at Tunes for Lisbon.

Getting Around

You can rent bicycles, mopeds and motorcycles from Motoride (☎ 289 761 720), Rua José Afonso 23, or agents in town. Figure about 1000$00 a day for a mountain bike or 7000$00 for a motorbike.

MONCHIQUE
pop 4000

This quiet highland town in the forested Serra de Monchique offers a quiet alternative to the discos and beach life on the coast.

Things to See & Do

Monchique's **Igreja Matriz** has an amazing Manueline portal, its stone seemingly tied in knots! Follow the brown pedestrian signs up from the bus station, around the old town's narrow streets.

Caldas de Monchique, 6km south, is a revamped but still charming hot-spring hamlet. Some 8km west is the Algarve's 'rooftop', the 902m **Fóia** peak atop the Serra de Monchique, with terrific views through a forest of radio masts.

Monchique's tourist office (☎ 289 911 189) has details of walking, horseback and mountain-bike trips in the hills.

Places to Stay & Eat

Central *Residencial Estrela de Monchique* (☎ 289 913 111, *Rua do Porto Fundo 46*) has doubles with bath for 5000$00. *Restaurante A Charrete* (☎ 289 912 142, *Rua Dr Samora Gil 30*) is the best in town.

Getting There & Away

Over a dozen buses run daily from Lagos to Portimão, from where five to nine services run daily to Monchique.

SILVES
pop 10,500

Silves was the capital of Moorish Algarve, rivalling Lisbon for influence. Times are quieter now, but the huge castle is well worth a visit.

The tourist office (☎ 289 442 255), Rua 25 de Abril, is open weekdays and Saturday morning.

Places to Stay & Eat

Residencial Sousa (☎ 289 442 502, *Rua Samoura Barros 17*) has doubles without bath for around 5000$00. *Residencial Ponte Romana* (☎ 289 443 275) beside the old bridge has doubles with bath from 6000$00.

Restaurante Rui (☎ 289 442 682, *Rua C Vilarinho 27*), Silves' best fish restaurant, serves a memorable *arroz de marisco* (shellfish rice). For cheaper meals, try the riverfront restaurants opposite the old bridge.

Getting There & Away

Silves train station is 2km from town; trains from Lagos (35 minutes) stop six times daily (from Faro, change at Tunes), to be met by local buses. Six buses run daily to Silves from Albufeira (40 minutes).

SAGRES
pop 2500

Sagres is a small fishing port perched on dramatic cliffs in Portugal's south-western corner. The tourist office (☎ 289 624 873), just beyond the central Praça da República on Rua Comandante Matoso, is open weekdays and Saturday morning. Turinfo (☎ 289 620 003), open daily on Praça da República, rents cars and bikes, books hotels and arranges jeep and fishing trips.

Things to See & Do

In the **fort**, on a wide windy promontory, Henry the Navigator established his school of navigation and primed the explorers who later founded the Portuguese empire.

Among several beaches close to Sagres, a good choice is at the small village of **Salema**, 17km east.

PORTUGAL

No Sagres visit would be complete without a trip to **Cabo de São Vicente** (Cape St Vincent), 6km to the west. A solitary lighthouse stands on this barren cape, Europe's south-westernmost point.

Places to Stay & Eat
Parque de Campismo Sagres (☎ 289 624 351) is 2km from town, off the Vila do Bispo road. Many Sagres folk rent rooms for around 5000$00 a double. Cheap, filling meals can be had at *Restaurante A Sagres* at the roundabout as you enter the village, and at cafes in Praça da República.

Getting There & Away
About 15 buses run daily to Sagres from Lagos (45 to 65 minutes), fewer on Sunday. Three continue out to Cabo de São Vicente on weekdays.

Central Portugal

Central Portugal, good for weeks of desultory rambling, deserves more attention than it receives. From the beaches of the Costa de Prata to the lofty Serra da Estrela and the sprawling Alentejo plains, it is a landscape of extremes.

Some of Portugal's finest wines come from the Dão region, while farther south, the hills and plains are studded with equally famous cork oaks. The mountainous centre is graced with scores of fortresses and walled cities with cobbled streets, clean air and grand panoramas.

ÉVORA
pop 54,000

One of Portugal's architectural gems and a Unesco World Heritage Site, the walled town of Évora is the capital of Alentejo province, a vast landscape of olive groves, vineyards and wheat fields. The town's charm lies in the narrow streets of the well-preserved inner town.

Orientation & Information
The focal point is Praça do Giraldo, from where you can wander through backstreets until you meet the city walls. An annotated map is available from the tourist office (☎ 266 702 671) at Praça do Giraldo 73. For other guides and maps go to Nazareth bookshop, Praça do Giraldo 46.

Outside the tourist office is an automatic cash-exchange machine. Oficin@ bar (☎ 266 707 312) at Rua da Moeda 27 has Internet access for 100$00 per 10 minutes.

Things to See & Do
On Largo do Marquês de Marialva is the **Sé**, Évora's cathedral, with cloisters and a museum of ecclesiastical treasures, both closed Monday. Admission costs 450$00.

The **Museu de Évora** features fantastic 16th-century Portuguese and Flemish painting. Admission costs 350$00. Opposite is the Roman-era **Temple of Diana**, subject of Évora's top-selling postcard.

The **Igreja de São Francisco**, south of Praça do Giraldo, includes the ghoulish Capela dos Ossos (Chapel of Bones), constructed with the bones and skulls of several thousand people. Admission costs 100$00.

Évora's big bash, and one of Alentejo's biggest country fairs, is the Feira de São João, held from approximately 22 June to 2 July.

Places to Stay
Accommodation gets tight in Évora in summer; booking ahead is essential.

An *Orbitur camping ground (☎ 266 705 190)* is about 2km south of town (buses to Alcaçovas stop there). Évora's *pousada da juventude (☎ 266 744 848)* is at Rua Miguel Bombarda 40.

Recommended *private rooms* are those at Rua Romão Ramalho 27 (☎ 266 702 453) with doubles costing 5000$00. *Residencial O Alentejo (☎ 266 702 903, Rua Serpa Pinto 74)* has doubles with bath for 6000$00. Rooms at handsome *Pensão Policarpo (☎/fax 266 702 424, Rua da Freiria de Baixo 16)* start at 9500$00. *Residencial Solar Monfalim (☎ 266 750 000, Largo da Misericórdia 1)* is a mini-palace with doubles from 14,500$00.

Places to Eat
O Portão (☎ 266 703 325, Rua do Cano 27), by the aqueduct, is a popular budget choice with dishes from 700$00. *Café Restaurant O Cruz (☎ 266 744 779, Praça 1 de Maio 20)* offers traditional fare at reasonable prices.

Jovial *Taberna Tipica Quarta-Feira (☎ 266 707 530, Rua do Inverno 16)* packs

PORTUGAL

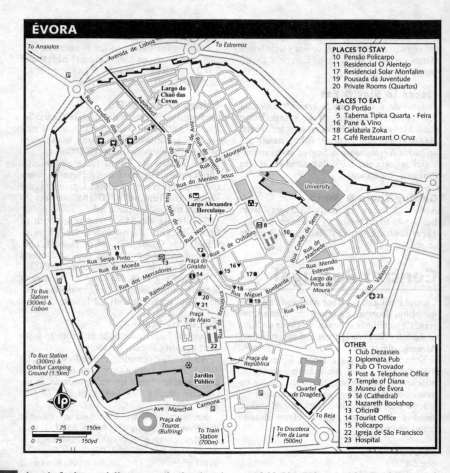

ÉVORA

PLACES TO STAY
10 Pensão Policarpo
11 Residencial O Alentejo
17 Residencial Solar Monfalim
19 Pousada da Juventude
20 Private Rooms (Quartos)

PLACES TO EAT
4 O Portão
5 Taberna Tipica Quarta - Feira
16 Pane & Vino
18 Gelataria Zoka
21 Café Restaurant O Cruz

OTHER
1 Club Dezasseis
2 Diplomata Pub
3 Pub O Trovador
6 Post & Telephone Office
7 Temple of Diana
8 Museu de Évora
9 Sé (Cathedral)
12 Nazareth Bookshop
13 Oficin@
14 Tourist Office
15 Policarpo
22 Igreja de São Francisco
23 Hospital

them in for its speciality creamed spinach and pork dishes. *Pane & Vino* (☎ *266 746 960, Páteo do Salema 22)* has great pasta and pizzas. Ice-cream fans will appreciate *Gelataria Zoka (Largo de São Vicente 14)*.

Entertainment
Student hang-outs include several bars north-west of the centre: *Club Dezasseis* (☎ *266 706 559, Rua do Escrivão da Cámara 16)*; *Diplomata Pub* (☎ *266 705 675, Rua do Apóstolo 4)*, with frequent live music; and *Pub O Trovador* (☎ *266 707 370, Rua da Mostardeira 4)*. *Discoteca Fim da Luna*

(☎ *266 701 719, Avenida Combatentes da Grande Guerra 56)* is near the train station.

Getting There & Away
Évora has six weekday express coach connections to Lisbon (1¼ hours) and two to Faro (four to five hours), departing from the terminal off Avenida Túlio Espanca (700m south-west of the centre). Fast trains run from Lisbon (2½ hours, three daily).

Getting Around
Bike Lab (☎ *266 735 500*) rents bikes for 250/2000$00 per hour/day. Policarpo (☎ 266

746 970, fax 266 746 984, @ viagenspol
icarpo@ip.pt), Alcárcova de Baixo 43, organises city tours and half-day jaunts to
megaliths and other nearby attractions.

MONSARAZ
pop 150

This walled village high above the plain is
well worth the trip for its medieval atmosphere, clear light and magnificent views. Of
architectural interest is the **Museu de Arte
Sacra**, probably a former tribunal, with a rare
15th-century fresco. The **castle's** parapets
have the best views.

Places to Stay & Eat

Several places along the main Rua Direita
have doubles for around 5000$00. The
tourist office (☎ 266 557 136) on the main
square has details of Turihab and other elegant places. There are several tourist-geared
restaurants and a grocery store near the
main gate. Eat before 8 pm: the town goes
to bed early.

Getting There & Away

On weekdays only, buses run to/from
Reguengos de Monsaraz (35 minutes, 17km,
two to four daily), which is connected to
Évora (one hour, six daily). The last one back
from Monsaraz leaves at 5 pm.

ESTREMOZ
pop 9000

The Estremoz region is dominated by huge
mounds of marble from its quarries. The
town's architectural appeal lies in its elegant,
gently deteriorating buildings, liberally embellished with marble.

Information

The tourist office (☎ 268 333 541, fax 268 401
089) is at Largo da República 26 just south of
the main square (known as the Rossio).

Things to See & Do

Upper Estremoz is crowned by the 14th-
century **Torre de Menagem** with fine views
of the town and countryside, and now a luxury pousada. Opposite is the **Museu Municipal**, specialising in unique Estremoz
pottery figurines, and open daily except
Monday; entry costs 180$00.

The focus of the lower town is the Rossio,
with a lively **market** on Saturday morning. The
nearby **Museu Rural**, a charming one-room
museum of rural Alentejan life, is open daily
except Sunday for 100$00. The bell-tower of
the **Museu de Arte Sacra**, open daily (admission 200$00), offers great views of the Rossio.

Vila Viçosa, another marble town 17km
from Estremoz, is centred on the **Palácio
Ducal**, ancestral home of the dukes of Bragança, and full of period furnishings and art-
work. It's open daily except Monday for a
steep 1000$00 (plus 500$00 for the armoury
museum).

Places to Stay & Eat

Friendly *Pensão-Restaurante Mateus* (☎ 268
322 226, Rua Almeida 41) has doubles for
4500/6000$00 without/with bath. Nearby
Adega do Isaias (☎ 268 223 18, Rua Almeida
21) is a popular tavern serving great grills.

Getting There & Away

On weekdays Estremoz is linked to Évora by
four local buses (1¼ hours) and two expressos (45 minutes). Daily expressos include
two to Portalegre (one hour) and five to Elvas
(50 minutes)

CASTELO DE VIDE & MARVÃO
pop 3000

From Portalegre it's a short hop to **Castelo de
Vide**, noted for its picturesque houses clustered below a castle. Highlights are the **Judi-
aria** (Old Jewish Quarter) in a well-preserved
network of medieval backstreets, and the view
from the castle. Try to spend a night here or
in **Marvão**, a mountaintop medieval walled
village (population 190) 12km from Castelo
de Vide, with grand views across large chunks
of Spain and Portugal.

Information

The tourist offices at Castelo de Vide (☎ 245
901 361, fax 245 901 827), Rua de Bartolomeu Álvares da Santa 81, and at Marvão
(☎ 245 993 886, fax 245 993 526), Largo de
Santa Maria, can help with accommodation.

Getting There & Away

On weekdays only, three buses run from Portalegre to Castelo de Vide (20 minutes) and
two to Marvão (45 minutes). One daily bus

links the two villages (with a change at Portagem, a junction 5km from Marvão).

NAZARÉ
pop 13,000

This once-peaceful 17th-century fishing village was 'discovered' by tourism in the 1970s. Fishing skills and distinctive local dress have gone overboard and in high season it's a tourist circus, but the beautiful coastline and fine seafood still make it worthwhile.

The tourist office (☎ 262 561 194), at the end of Avenida da República by the funicular, is open 10 am to 10 pm daily in high season.

Things to See & Do

Lower Nazaré's beachfront retains a core of narrow streets now catering to tourists. The cliff-top section, O Sítio, is reached by a vintage funicular railway, and the view is superb.

The beaches attract huge summer crowds. Beware of dangerous currents. The tourist office will tell you which beaches are safe.

Places to Stay & Eat

Two good campsites are the well-equipped *Vale Paraíso* (☎ 262 561 546) off the Leiria road, and an *Orbitur* (☎ 262 561 111) off the Alcobaça road, both 2.5km from Nazaré. Many townspeople rent out rooms; doubles start about 4500$00. Among budget pensões is *Residencial Marina* (☎ 262 551 541, Rua Mouzinho de Albuquerque 6), with doubles around 6000$00. Room prices rocket in August.

Seafront restaurants are expensive. For cheaper fare in simple surroundings, try *Casa Marques* (☎ 262 551 680, Rua Gil Vicente 37). Friendly *A Tasquinha* (☎ 262 551 945, Rua Adrião Batalha 54) does good *carne de porco à Alentejana* (pork and clams). Popular *Casa O Pescador* (☎ 262 553 326, Rua António Carvalho Laranjo 18-A) is also reasonably priced.

Getting There & Away

The nearest train station, 6km away at Valado, is connected to Nazaré by frequent buses. Nazaré has numerous bus connections to Lisbon, Alcobaça, Óbidos and Coimbra.

ALCOBAÇA
pop 6000

Alcobaça's attraction is the immense **Mosteiro de Santa Maria de Alcobaça,** founded in 1178. The original Gothic has undergone Manueline, Renaissance and baroque additions. Of interest are the tombs of Pedro I and Inês de Castro, the cloisters, the kings' room and the kitchens. It's open 9 am to 7 pm daily (to 5 pm in winter); entry costs 400$00 (free admission to the church).

The tourist office (☎ 262 582 377) is opposite the monastery.

Getting There & Away

There are frequent buses to/from Nazaré and Batalha. The closest train station is 5km north-west at Valado dos Frades, connected to Alcobaça by regular buses.

BATALHA

Batalha's single highlight is its monastery, the **Mosteiro de Santa Maria de Vitória,** a colossal Gothic masterpiece constructed between 1388 and 1533. Earthquakes and vandalism by French troops have taken their toll, but restoration was completed in 1965. Highlights include the Founder's Chapel (with the tomb of Henry the Navigator), the Royal Cloisters, the Chapter House and the Unfinished Chapels. It's open 9 am to 6 pm daily; entry to the Cloisters and Unfinished Chapels costs 400$00.

The tourist office (☎ 244 765 180) is next to the abbey, on Largo Paulo VI.

Getting There & Away

There are frequent bus connections to Alcobaça and Nazaré, and at least three direct buses to Lisbon daily.

ÓBIDOS
pop 500

This charming walled village is one of the prettiest (and most touristy) in Portugal. Highlights include the **Igreja de Santa Maria,** with fine azulejos, and **views** from the walls. The tourist office (☎ 262 959 231, fax 262 959 014) is on Rua Direita.

Places to Stay & Eat

Private rooms are available for around 4500$00 a double. Among several Turihab properties is romantic *Casa do Poço* (☎ 262 959 358, Travessa da Mouraria) where doubles cost around 11,500$00. *Residencial Martim de Freitas* (☎ 262 959 185, Estrada*

PORTUGAL

Nacional 8), outside the walls, has doubles from 6000$00.

Cheap cafes outside the walls include *Café Snack Bar O Aqueduto*. Inside, *Café-Restaurante 1 de Dezembro* (☎ 262 959 298), next to the Igreja de São Pedro, has pleasant outdoor seating. There's a small *grocery* just inside the town gate.

Getting There & Away
There are regular bus connections from Lisbon, directly (two hours) or via Caldas da Rainha, 10 minutes away. From the train station, outside the walls at the foot of the hill, there are five services daily to Lisbon (four with a change at Cacém).

COIMBRA
pop 150,000
Coimbra is famed for its 13th-century university, and for its traditional role as a centre of culture and art, complemented in recent times by industrial development.

The regional tourist office (☎ 239 855 930, fax 239 825 576), Largo da Portagem, has pamphlets and cultural-events information, but a municipal tourist office (☎ 239 832 591) on Praça Dom Dinis, and another (☎ 239 833 202) on Praça da República, are more useful. The Centro de Juventude (☎ 239 790 600) at Rua Pedro Monteiro 73 offers free Internet access on weekdays, with a half-hour maximum.

Coimbra's annual highlight is Queima das Fitas, a boozy week of fado and revelry beginning on the first Thursday in May, when students celebrate the end of the academic year.

Things to See
Lower Coimbra's main attraction is the **Mosteiro de Santa Cruz** with its ornate pulpit and medieval royal tombs. In the upper town, visit the **old university** with its baroque library and Manueline chapel, and the **Machado de Castro Museum**, with a fine collection of sculpture and painting. The back alleys of the university quarter are filled with student hangouts and an exuberant atmosphere.

At **Conímbriga**, 16km south of Coimbra, are the well-preserved ruins of a Roman town (open 9 am to 1 pm and 2 to 8 pm daily in summer, and to 6 pm in winter), including mosaic floors, baths and fountains. The good site museum (with a restaurant) is open 10 am to 1 pm and 2 to 6 pm except Monday. Entry costs 350$00. Frequent buses run to Condeixa, 2km from the site; direct buses depart at 9.05 or 9.35 am (only 9.35 am at weekends) from the AVIC terminal at Rua João de Ruão 18, returning at 1 and 6 pm (only 6 pm at weekends).

Activities
Daily from April to October, O Pioneiro do Mondego (☎ 239 478 385 from 8 to 10 am, 1 to 3 pm and 8 to 10 pm) rents kayaks at 3000$00 for paddling the Rio Mondego. At 10 am a free minibus collects you from Parque Dr Manuel Braga and takes you to Penacova for the 25km river journey.

Places to Stay
For Coimbra's *pousada da juventude* (☎ 239 822 955, Rua António Henriques Seco 12-14), take northbound bus No 46 from Coimbra A train station.

Near Coimbra A, *Pensão Lorvanense* (☎ 239 823 481, Rua da Sota 27) has doubles without/with bath for 4000/5000$00. Those at *Pensão Residencial Rivoli* (☎ 239 825 550, Praça do Comércio 27) cost 5500/6000$00, with shared toilets. Very central *Pensão Residencial Larbelo* (☎ 239 829 092, fax 239 829 094, Largo da Portagem 33) has doubles with bath for 6500$00.

Pensão Flôr de Coimbra (☎ 239 823 865, fax 239 821 545, Rua do Poço 5) has doubles for 5000$00 (6000/7000$00 with shower and without/with toilet), and a small daily (except Sunday) vegetarian menu. Quiet doubles with bath at *Residência Coimbra* (☎ 239 837 996, fax 239 838 124, Rua das Azeiteiras 55) start at 7000$00.

In a lane near the university, Dutch-run *Casa Pombal Guesthouse* (☎ 239 835 175, fax 239 821 548, Rua das Flores 18) has everything from 7000$00 bathless doubles to bird's-eye views at 8200$00 with bath, and a huge breakfast.

Places to Eat
The lanes west of Praça do Comércio, especially Rua das Azeiteiras, feature a concentration of good-value fare; a zero-frills eatery at No 5, *Refeição Económica* ('cheap eats'),

PORTUGAL

has hearty specials from just 600$00. *Restaurante Democrática* (☎ *239 823 784, Travessa da Rua Nova*) has Portuguese standards, with some half-portions under 900$00.

Self-service *Restaurante Jardim da Manga*, behind the fountains at the back of the Mosteiro de Santa Cruz, has a few basic dishes from 700$00; it's closed Saturday. *Zé Manel* (☎ *239 823 790, 12 Beco do Forno*) has crazy decor and huge servings; go by 8 pm to beat the crowds.

East of the university, *Bar-Restaurante ACM* (☎ *239 823 633, Rua Alexandre Herculano 21A*) has plain fare from 700$00 per dish; it's open daily except Saturday. Downstairs behind the *Centro de Juventude* (*Rua Pedro Monteiro 73*) is a clean canteen with a few main dishes under 800$00 and lots of salads.

Vaulted *Café Santa Cruz* beside the Mosteiro de Santa Cruz is great for coffee breaks.

Entertainment
Bar Diligência (☎ *239 827 667, Rua Nova 30*) and *Boémia Bar* (☎ *239 834 547, Rua do Cabido 6*) are popular casas de fado. *Café-Galeria Almedina* (☎ *239 836 192, Arco de Almedina*) offers fado and other live sounds. A good dance bar is *Aqui Há Rato* (☎ *239 824 804, Largo da Sé Velha 20*). Two popular discos are *João Ratão* (☎ *239 404 047, Avenida Afonso Henriques 43*) and *Via Latina* (☎ *239 833 034, Rua Almeida Garrett 1*).

Getting There & Away
At least a dozen buses and as many trains run daily from Lisbon and Porto, plus frequent express buses from Faro and Évora. The main long-distance train stations are Coimbra B, 2km north-west of the centre, and central Coimbra A (on timetables this is called just 'Coimbra'). Most long-distance trains call at both. Other useful connections are to Figueira da Foz and to Luso/Buçaco (from Coimbra A).

LUSO & THE BUÇACO FOREST
pop 2000

Walkers will appreciate the Buçaco Forest, chosen by 16th-century monks as a retreat, and relatively untouched ever since. It begins about 1km from the spa resort of Luso, where the tourist office (☎/fax 231 939 133) on Avenida Emídio Navarro has a general map of the forest, and leaflets about trails and over 700 tree and shrub species.

Places to Stay & Eat
The Luso tourist office has accommodation lists. *Pensão Central* (☎ *231 939 254, Avenida Emídio Navarro*) has doubles from 4500$00. Hearty meals are available at *Restaurante O Cesteiro* (☎ *231 939 360*) on the N234, 500m north from the tourist office.

The elegant five-star *Palace Hotel do Buçaco* (☎ *231 930 101, fax 231 930 509*), a former royal hunting lodge in the forest, is as fine an expression of Manueline style as any in Portugal. Singles/doubles start at 29,000/34,000$00. Figure on at least 2500$00 per dish in the restaurant or 5000$00 for the set menu.

Getting There & Away
Five buses daily go to Luso/Buçaco from Coimbra and Viseu (two at weekends). Just one train, departing around 10.30 am from Coimbra B, gives you enough time for a day trip.

SERRA DA ESTRELA
The forested Serra da Estrela is Portugal's highest mainland mountain range (topping out at the 1993m Torre), and the core of a designated *parque natural*. With its outlying ranges it stretches nearly across Portugal, and offers some of the country's best hiking.

Orientation & Information
The best place for information on the Parque Natural da Serra da Estrela is the main park office in Manteigas (☎ 275 980 060, fax 275 980 069); other offices are at Seia, Gouveia and Guarda. Other good sources for regional information are the tourist offices at Guarda (☎ 271 212 115) and Covilhã (☎ 275 319 560).

The park administration publishes *À Descoberta da Estrela*, a walking guide with maps and narratives. Park offices and some tourist offices sell an English edition (850$00), plus a detailed topographic map of the park (1100$00).

Places to Stay
The *pousada da juventude* (☎ *275 335 375, fax 275 335 109*) at Penhas da Saúde, 10km

PORTUGAL

above Covilhã, offers meals (or you can cook your own), dorms and a few functional doubles. Buses come from Covilhã twice daily in August only, and hitching is fairly safe and easy. The only other options are your feet or bike, or a taxi (about 1600$00). This makes a good base for excursions.

Guarda also has a *pousada da juventude* (☎/fax *271 224 482*), and Seia, Gouveia, Guarda and Covilhã have some modestly priced guesthouses. Manteigas, though most central of all, tends to be pricey.

Getting There & Away
Several buses run each day from Coimbra, along the park's perimeter to Seia, Gouveia, Guarda or Covilhã, plus others from Porto and Lisbon to Guarda and Covilhã. Twice-daily IC trains link Lisbon and Coimbra to Guarda, and two daily IC trains run from Lisbon to Covilhã on the Lisbon-Paris line.

Getting Around
No buses cross the park, though you can go around it: Seia-Covilhã takes two hours via Guarda. At least one or two buses link Seia, Gouveia and Guarda every day, and considerably more run between Guarda and Covilhã.

The North

Most visitors are surprised to discover Portugal's northern tier, with its wine country, great forests, mountainous Peneda-Gerês National Park and a strand of undeveloped beaches. The urban scene focuses on Porto, with its medieval centre by the Rio Douro. Within easy reach of Porto are three historical cities: Braga, the country's religious heart; finely situated Viana do Castelo; and Guimarães, which declares itself Portugal's birthplace.

PORTO
pop 270,000
Porto is Portugal's second-largest city, and the focus of the port-wine trade. Its reputation as an industrial centre belies considerable charm; indeed its old centre has been declared a Unesco World Heritage Site, and the city was, with Rotterdam, named European City of Culture for 2001.

Orientation
The city clings to the north bank of the Rio Douro, spanned here by five bridges. On the far bank is Vila Nova de Gaia and its port wine lodges, a major attraction.

Central Porto's axis is Avenida dos Aliados. Major shopping areas are eastward around the Bolhão Market and Rua Santa Catarina, and westward along Rua dos Clérigos. At the southern end of Avenida dos Aliados, Praça da Liberdade and São Bento train station are major local bus hubs. Another is Jardim da Cordoaria (called Jardim de João Chagas on some maps), about 400m westward.

The picturesque Ribeira district lies along the waterfront, in the shadow of the great Ponte de Dom Luís I bridge.

Information
Tourist Offices The main municipal tourist office (☎ 222 052 740, fax 223 323 303) at Rua Clube dos Fenianos 25 is open 9 am to 5.30 pm on weekdays. A smaller office (☎ 222 009 770) at Rua Infante Dom Henriques 63 is open during these hours and 9.30 am to 4.30 pm at weekends. From July to September both are open 9 am to 7 pm weekdays and 9.30 am to 4.30 pm at weekends.

A national (ICEP) tourist office (☎ 222 057 514, fax 222 053 212) at Praça Dom João I 43 is open 9 am to 7 pm daily in July and August, and 9 am to at least 7 pm weekdays and 9.30 am to 3.30 pm at weekends the rest of the year.

Money Banks with ATMs and exchange desks are everywhere. Better rates for travellers cheques are at the exchange bureaus Portocâmbios, Rua Rodrigues Sampaio 193, and Intercontinental, Rua de Ramalho Ortigão 8. Top Tours (☎ 222 074 020, fax 222 074 039), Rua Alferes Malheiro 96, is Porto's American Express representative.

Post & Communications The main post office (the place for poste-restante mail) is across Praça General Humberto Delgado from the main tourist office. A telephone office at Praça da Liberdade 62 is open 10 am to 10 pm daily. Faxes can be sent from the post office, and domestic ones from the telephone office.

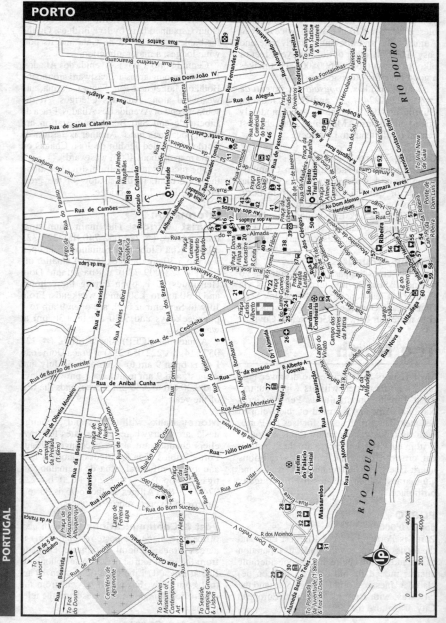

PORTO

PORTUGAL

PORTO

PLACES TO STAY		3	usit TAGUS	31	Maré Alta
6	Pensão Estoril	4	Internorte Tickets	32	Club Mau-Mau
18	Residencial Vera Cruz		and Buses	33	Mexcal
19	Pensão Pão de Açucar	5	Lavandaria Olimpica	34	Cordoaria Bus Stand
20	Pensão Porto Rico	7	Top Tours & American	35	Casa Oriental
21	Pensão São Marino		Express	36	Torre dos Clérigos
38	Residencial União	8	REDM; AV Minho; Carlos	37	Renex Tickets and Buses
42	Pensão Chique		Soares Tickets & Buses	39	Telephone Office
47	Residencial Santo André	9	Central Shopping	40	Livraria Porto Editora
48	Residencial Afonso	10	STCP Kiosk		(bookshop)
52	Pensão Astória	11	Bolhão Market	43	Portocambios Exchange
		12	Casa Januário	44	National (ICEP)
PLACES TO EAT		13	Main Post Office		Tourist Office
22	Restaurante Romão	14	Town Hall	45	Rodonorte Bus Station
23	Café Ancôra Douro	15	Main Municipal Tourist	49	Rede Expressos
25	Restaurante A Tasquinha		Office; Tourism Police		Bus Station
41	Café Embaixador	16	Portweb	50	STCP Kiosk
46	Café Majestic	17	Intercontinental Exchange	51	Sé
53	Casa Filha da Mãe Preta	24	Garrafeira do Carmo	55	Meia-Cave
54	Pub-Petisqueira O Muro	26	Santo António Hospital	56	Academia
		27	Soares dos Reis National	57	Municipal Tourist Office
OTHER			Museum	58	Arte Facto
1	STCP Kiosk	28	Solar do Vinho do Porto	59	Lavandaria São
2	Instituto Português da	29	Voice Bar		Nicolau
	Juventude	30	Tram Museum	60	Tram Terminus

Email & Internet Access The Instituto Português da Juventude (☎ 226 003 173), Rua Rodrigues Lobo 98, offers free Internet access 9 am to 8 pm weekdays. At Portweb (☎ 222 005 922), Praça General Humberto Delgado 291, access costs 100$00 per hour from 9 am to 4 pm daily, and 240$00 from then to 2 am.

Travel Agencies Two youth-oriented agencies are usit TAGUS (☎ 226 094 146, fax 226 094 141), Rua Campo Alegre 261, and Wasteels (☎ 225 370 539, fax 225 373 210), Rua Pinto Bessa 27/29 near Campanhã station. See also Top Tours under Money earlier.

Local adventure-tour operators with northern Portugal experience include Montes d'Aventura (☎ 228 305 157, fax 228 305 158) for trekking, cycling and canoeing, and Trilhos (☎/fax 225 504 604) for canyoning and hydrospeed.

Laundry Lavandaria Olimpica, Rua Miguel Bombarda, and Lavandaria 5 à Sec in the Central Shopping centre have laundry and dry-cleaning services. A cheaper municipal service, Lavandaria São Nicolau, is on Rua Infante Dom Henrique. All are closed Sunday.

Medical Services & Emergency Santo António Hospital (☎ 222 077 500), Rua Vicente José Carvalho, has English-speaking staff. Direct any request for police help to the 'tourism police' office (☎ 222 081 833) at Rua Clube dos Fenianos 11, open 8 am to 2 am daily.

Things to See & Do
The riverfront **Ribeira** district is the city's beating heart, with narrow lanes, grimy bars, good restaurants and river cruises.

The 225 steps of the **Torre dos Clérigos** on Rua dos Clérigos lead to the best panorama of the city (200$00; open 10 am to noon and 2 to 5 pm daily).

The **Sé**, the cathedral dominating central Porto, is worth a visit for its mixture of architectural styles and ornate interior (250$00; open 9 am to 12.30 pm and 2.30 to 5.30 pm except Sunday morning).

The **Soares dos Reis National Museum**, Rua Dom Manuel II 44, offers masterpieces of 19th and 20th-century Portuguese painting and sculpture (350$00; open 10 am to 12.30 pm and 2 to 6 pm, closed all day Monday and Tuesday morning).

PORTUGAL

Porto's finest new museum is the **Serralves Museum of Contemporary Art**, Rua de Serralves 947/999 (800$00; open 10 am to 7 pm, except to 10 pm Thursday, closed Monday).

The **Museu dos Carros Eléctricos** (Tram Museum), Cais do Bicalho, is a cavernous old tram warehouse with dozens of restored cars. It's open 9.30 am to 1 pm and 3 to 6 pm except Monday, for 350$00.

At the **Bolhão market**, east of Avenida dos Aliados, you can get anything from seafood to herbs and honey. It's open weekdays until 5 pm and Saturday to 1 pm.

Across the river in Vila Nova de Gaia, some two dozen **port-wine lodges** are open for tours and tastings on weekdays and Saturday, and a few on Sunday. The tourist office (☎ 223 751 902) there has details. Or select from a huge port-wine list at the **Solar do Vinho do Porto** (☎ 226 097 793), Rua Entre Quintas 220 in Porto. This bar is open 10 am to 11.45 pm weekdays and 11 am to 10.45 pm on Saturday.

Special Events

Porto's big festival is the Festa de São João (St John's Festival) in June. Also worth catching are several music festivals, including Celtic music in April-May, rock in August, and fado in October.

Places to Stay

Camping *Camping da Prelada* (☎ 228 312 616, Rua Monte dos Burgos) is 4km northwest of the centre (take bus No 6 from Praça de Liberdade or bus No 50 from Jardim da Cordoaria).

Three camping grounds near the sea in Vila Nova de Gaia are *Campismo Salgueiros* (☎ 227 810 500, fax 227 810 136, Praia de Salgueiros)*, Campismo Marisol* (☎ 227 135 942, fax 227 126 351, Praia de Canide) and *Campismo Madalena* (☎ 227 122 520, fax 227 122 534, Praia da Madalena)*. Bus No 57 runs to all of them from São Bento station.

Note that the sea at all these places is far too polluted for swimming.

Hostels The fine *pousada da juventude* (☎ 226 177 257, fax 226 177 247, Rua Paulo da Gama 551)*, 4km west of the centre, is open 24 hours a day. Doubles and dorm-style quads are available, and reservations are es-

sential. Take bus No 35 from Largo dos Lóios (a block west of Praça da Liberdade), or No 1 from São Bento station.

Guesthouses Porto's cheapest guesthouses are around Praça da Batalha, east and uphill from São Bento station. Some are dodgy, but two reliable ones where doubles with bath start at 4000$00 are *Residencial Afonso* (☎ 222 059 469, Rua Duque de Loulé 233) and *Residencial Santo André* (☎ 222 055 869, Rua Santo Ildefonso 112)*. Down towards the river, *Pensão Astória* (☎ 222 008 175, Rua Arnaldo Gama 56) has elegant old doubles, some with river views, for 5000$00 with bath and breakfast.

Plain doubles with shower at central *Residencial União* (☎ 222 003 078, Rua Conde de Vizela 62) and *Pensão Porto Rico* (☎ 223 394 690, Rua do Almada 237) start at 5000$00; the former also has cheaper rooms with shared bath. *Pensão Chique* (☎ 223 322 963, Avenida dos Aliados 206) offers small doubles for 6500$00 with breakfast. Those at *Residencial Vera Cruz* (☎ 223 323 396, fax 223 323 421, Rua Ramalho Ortigão 14) are 8000$00. *Pensão Pão de Açucar* (☎ 222 002 425, fax 222 050 239, Rua do Almada 262) has handsome doubles with shower from 9500$00; bookings are essential.

Near the university, *Pensão Estoril* (☎ 222 002 751, fax 222 082 468, Rua de Cedofeita 193) and the better-value *Pensão São Marino* (☎ 223 325 499, Praça Carlos Alberto 59) offer doubles with shower from 6500$00, with breakfast.

Places to Eat

Excellent value in the centre can be found at the self-service mezzanine at *Café Embaixador* (☎ 222 054 182, Rua Sampaio Bruno 5)*, with grills, salads and vegetables; it's open 6.30 am to 10 pm except Sunday.

Near the university, *Restaurante A Tasquinha* (☎ 223 322 145, Rua do Carmo 23) has well-prepared regional dishes for 1000$00 to 2000$00. Cheerfully downmarket *Restaurante Romão* (☎ 222 005 639, Praça Carlos Alberto 100) has northern specialities for around 900$00 per dish. A lively student haunt at lunchtime is *Café Ancôra Douro* (☎ 222 081 201, Praça de Parada Leitão 49).

An exception to the Ribeira's many overpriced, touristy eateries is *Pub-Petisqueira O*

PORTUGAL

Muro (☎ 222 083 426, *Muro dos Bacal-hoeiros 88*), with decor from dried bacalhau to Che Guevara, and good *feijoado de marisco* (a rich bean and seafood stew) for 850$00; it's open noon to 2 am daily. Congenial *Casa Filha da Mãe Preta* (☎ 222 055 515, *Cais da Ribeira 39*) has Douro views, and main dishes mostly under 2000$00.

Café Majestic (☎ 222 003 887, *Rua Santa Catarina 112*) is an extravagant Art Nouveau relic with expensive coffees and afternoon teas.

Entertainment
Lively pubs in the Ribeira include *Academia* (☎ 222 005 737, *Rua São João 80*), *Ryan's Irish Pub* (☎ 222 005 366, *Rua Infante Dom Henrique 18*) and *Meia-Cave* (☎ 223 323 214, *Praça da Ribeira 6*).

A newer generation of clubs in the riverfront area called Massarelos, 2km west of the Ribeira, includes *Mexcal* (☎ 226 009 188) and *Club Mau-Mau* (☎ 226 076 660), on Rua da Restauração; *Maré Alta* (☎ 226 162 540, *Rua do Ouro*); and *Voice* (☎ 226 067 815, *Rua do Capitão Eduardo Romero 1*). All are on the No 1 bus line from São Bento station.

Shopping
Port is, of course, a popular purchase. Shops with a broad selection include Garrafeira do Carmo, Rua do Carmo 17; Casa Januário, Rua do Bonjardim 352; and Casa Oriental, Campo dos Mártires de Pátria 111. Other good buys are shoes and gold-filigree jewellery. For handicrafts, visit Arte Facto at Rua da Reboleira 37 in the Ribeira (closed Monday).

Getting There & Away
Air Porto is connected by daily flights from Lisbon and London, and almost-daily direct links from other European centres (see the Introductory Getting There & Away and Getting Around sections of this chapter). For flight information call ☎ 229 412 141.

Bus Renex (☎ 222 003 395), with a 24-hour ticket office at Rua das Carmelitas 32, is the choice for Lisbon and the Algarve. From a terminal at Rua Alexandre Herculano 370, Rede Expressos (☎ 222 006 954) goes all over Portugal. From or near Praceto Régulo Maga-uanha, off Rua Dr Alfredo Magalhães, REDM (☎ 222 003 152) goes to Braga, AV Minho (☎ 222 006 121) to Viana do Castelo, and Carlos Soares (☎ 222 051 383) to Guimarães. Rodonorte (☎ 222 005 637) departs from its own terminal at Rua Ateneu Comércial do Porto 19, mainly to Vila Real and Bragança.

Northern Portugal's main international carrier is Internorte (see the introductory Getting There & Away section of this chapter), whose coaches depart from the booking office (☎ 226 052 420, fax 226 099 570) at Praça da Galiza 96.

Train Porto, a northern Portugal rail hub, has three stations. Most international trains, and all intercidade links, start at Campanhã, 2km east of the centre. Interregional and regional services depart from either Campanhã or the central São Bento station (bus Nos 34 and 35 run frequently between these two). For Guimarães, go to Trindade station.

At São Bento you can book tickets for services to any destination from any Porto station; for information call ☎ 225 364 141 between 8 am and 11 pm daily.

Getting Around
To/From the Airport The AeroBus (☎ 808 200 166) runs between Avenida dos Aliados and the airport via Boavista every half-hour from 7 am to 7.30 pm. The 500$00 ticket, purchased on the bus, also serves as a free bus pass until midnight of the day you buy it.

City bus Nos 56 and 87 run about every half-hour until 8.30 pm to/from Jardim da Cordoaria, and until about 12.30 am to/from Praça da Liberdade.

A taxi costs around 2500$00 plus a possible 300$00 baggage charge.

Bus Central hubs of Porto's extensive bus system include Jardim da Cordoaria, Praça da Liberdade and São Bento station (Praça Almeida Garrett). Tickets are cheapest from STCP kiosks (eg, opposite São Bento station, beside Bolhão market and at Boavista) and many newsagents and tobacconists: 90$00 for a short hop, 125$00 to outlying areas or 320$00 for an airport return trip. Tickets bought on the bus are always 180$00. Also available is a 400$00 day pass.

Tram Porto has one remaining tram, the No 1E, trundling daily from the Ribeira to the

PORTUGAL

coast at Foz do Douro and back to Boavista every half-hour all day.

Metro Work has begun on Porto's own 'underground', a combination of upgraded and new track that will reach Campanhã, Vila Nova de Gaia and several coastal resorts to the north.

Taxi To cross town, figure on about 600$00. An additional charge is made to leave the city limits, including across the Ponte Dom Luís I to Vila Nova de Gaia.

ALONG THE DOURO

The Douro Valley is one of Portugal's scenic highlights, with 200km of expansive panoramas from Porto to the Spanish border. In the upper reaches, port-wine vineyards wrap around every hillside.

The river, tamed by eight dams and locks since the late 1980s, is navigable right across Portugal. Highly recommended is the train journey from Porto to Peso da Régua (about a dozen trains daily, 2½ hours), the last 50km clinging to the river's edge; four trains continue daily to Pocinho (4½ hours). Douro Azul (☎ 223 393 950, fax 222 083 407) and other companies run one and two-day river cruises, mostly from March to October. Cyclists and drivers can choose river-hugging roads along either bank, though they're crowded at weekends.

The elegant, detailed colour map *Rio Douro* (600$00) is available from Porto bookshops.

VIANA DO CASTELO
pop 18,000

This attractive port at the mouth of the Rio Lima is renowned for its historic old town and its promotion of folk traditions. The tourist office (☎ 258 822 620, fax 258 827 873) on Rua Hospital Velho has information on festivals and the region in general.

In August Viana hosts the Festas de Nossa Senhora da Agonia (see the Facts for the Visitor section at the start of this chapter for details).

Things to See

The town's focal point is Praça da República, with its delicate fountain and el-

egant buildings, including the 16th-century **Misericórdia**.

Atop Santa Luzia Hill, the **Templo do Sagrado Coração de Jesus** offers a grand panorama across the river. A funicular railway climbs the hill from 9 am to 6 pm (hourly in the morning, every 30 minutes in the afternoon) from behind the train station.

Places to Stay

Viana's *pousada da juventude* (☎ 258 800 260, fax 258 820 870), on Rua da Argaçosa, is about 1km east of the town centre.

Pensão Vianense (☎ 258 823 118, Avenida Conde da Carreira 79) and *Casa de Hóspedes Guerreiro* (☎ 258 822 099, Rua Grande 14) have plain doubles with shared facilities from 5000$00. Doubles with bath (breakfast included) are about 6000$00 at central **Pensão Dolce Vita** (☎ 258 824 860, Rua do Poço 44) and 7500$00 at **Pensão-Restaurant Alambique** (☎ 258 821 364, Rua Manuel Espregueira 86).

The tourist office has listings of *private rooms*.

Places to Eat

Most pensões have good-value restaurants, open to nonguests too. *A Gruta Snack Bar* (☎ 258 820 214, Rua Grande 87) has lunchtime salads for under 500$00. *Adega do Padrinho* (☎ 258 826 954, Rua Gago Coutinho 162) offers traditional dishes for under 1100$00 per half-portion. Seafood is pricey, but try the cervejaria part of *Os Três Arcos* (☎ 258 824 014, Largo João Tomás da Costa 25), with half-portions from 1000$00. *Viana's Restaurante* (☎ 258 824 797, Rua Frei Bartolomeu dos Mártires 179), near the fish market, specialises in *bacalhau*, in all its forms.

Getting There & Away

Half a dozen express coaches go to Braga and to Porto every day (fewer at weekends), with daily express services on to Coimbra and Lisbon. Daily train services run north to Spain and south to Porto and Lisbon.

BRAGA
pop 80,000

Crammed with churches, Braga is considered Portugal's religious capital. During

Easter week, huge crowds attend its Holy Week Festival.

The tourist office (☎ 253 262 550) on Praça da República can help with accommodation and maps.

Things to See & Do

In the centre of Braga is the **Sé**, an elegant cathedral complex. Admission to its treasury museum and several tomb chapels costs 300$00.

At Bom Jesus do Monte, a hilltop pilgrimage site 5km from Braga, is an extraordinary stairway, the **Escadaria do Bom Jesus**, with allegorical fountains, chapels and a superb view. Buses run frequently from Braga to the site, where you can climb the steps or ascend by funicular railway.

It's an easy day trip to **Guimarães**, considered the cradle of the Portuguese nation, with a medieval town centre and a palace of the dukes of Bragança.

Places to Stay

The *pousada da juventude* (☎ 253 616 163, *Rua de Santa Margarida 6*) is a 10-minute walk from the city centre. A bargain in the centre is **Hotel Francfort** (☎ 253 262 648, *Avenida Central 7*), where well-kept old doubles start at 3500$00. *Casa Santa Zita* (☎ 253 618 331, *Rua São João 20*) is a hostel for pilgrims (and others) with doubles from 4500$00. *Grande Residência Avenida* (☎ 253 609 020, fax 253 609 028, *Avenida da Liberdade 738*) offers good value with doubles from 6000$00.

Places to Eat

Lareira do Conde (☎ 253 611 340, *Praça Conde de Agrolongo 56*) specialises in inexpensive grills. Around the corner from the bus station, *Retiro da Primavera* (☎ 253 272 482, *Rua Gabriel Pereira de Castro 100*) has good half-portions for under 900$00. *Casa Grulha* (☎ 253 262 883, *Rua dos Biscaínhos 95*) serves good-value *cabrito assado* (roast kid, a local speciality). *Taberna do Felix* (☎ 253 617 701, *Praça Velha 17*) has simple, imaginative dishes from 1000$00.

For people-watching over coffee or beer, settle down at *Café Vianna* on Praça da República.

Getting There & Away

The motorway from Porto puts Braga within easy day trip reach. Intercidade trains arrive twice daily from Lisbon, Coimbra and Porto, and there are daily connections north to Viana do Castelo and Spain. Daily bus services link Braga to Porto and Lisbon.

PENEDA-GERÊS NATIONAL PARK

This wilderness park along the Spanish border has spectacular scenery and a wide variety of fauna and flora. Portuguese daytrippers and holiday-makers tend to stick to the main villages and camping areas, leaving the rest of the park to hikers.

The park's main centre is **Vila do Gerês** (or Caldas do Gerês, or just Gerês), a sleepy, hot-spring village.

Orientation & Information

Gerês' tourist office (☎ 253 391 133, fax 253 391 282) is in the colonnade at the upper end of the village. For park information go around the corner to the park office (☎ 253 390 110).

Other park offices are at Arcos de Valdevez, Montalegre and the head office (☎ 253 203 480, fax 253 613 169) is on Avenida António Macedo in Braga. All have a map of the park (530$00) with some roads and tracks (but not trails), and a free English-language booklet on the park's features.

Activities

Hiking A long-distance footpath is being developed, mostly following traditional roads or tracks between villages where you can stop for the night. Park offices sell map-brochures (300$00) for two sections available so far.

Day hikes around Gerês are popular; at weekends and all summer the Miradouro walk at **Parque do Merendas** is crowded. A more strenuous option is the old Roman road from Mata do Albergaria (10km up-valley from Gerês by taxi or hitching), past the **Vilarinho das Furnas** reservoir to Campo do Gerês. More distant destinations include **Ermida** and **Cabril**, both with simple accommodation and cafes.

Guided walks are organised by PlanAlto (☎/fax 253 351 005) at Cerdeira camping ground in Campo do Gerês, and Trote-Gerês (☎/fax 253 659 860) at Cabril.

PORTUGAL

Cycling Mountain bikes can be hired from Água Montanha Lazer (☎ 253 391 779, fax 253 391 598, ✉ aguamontanha@mail.telepac.pt) in Rio Caldo, Pensão Carvalho Araújo (☎ 253 391 185) in Gerês, or PlanAlto.

Horse Riding The national park operates facilities (☎ 253 391 181) from beside its Vidoeiro camping ground, near Gerês. Trote-Gerês also has horses for hire.

Water Sports Rio Caldo, 8km south of Gerês, is the base for water sports on the Caniçada reservoir. Água Montanha Lazer rents canoes and other boats. For paddling the Salamonde reservoir, Trote-Gerês rents canoes from its camping ground at Cabril.

Gerês' Parque das Termas (170$00 admission) has a swimming pool, open for 700/1100$00 on weekdays/weekends.

Organised Tours
Agência no Gerês (☎ 253 391 141), at Hotel Universal in Gerês, runs two to 5½-hour minibus trips around the park in summer, for 1000$00 to 2000$00 per person.

Places to Stay
The *pousada da juventude* (☎/fax 253 351 339) and *Cerdeira Camping Ground* (☎/fax 253 351 005) at Campo do Gerês make good hiking bases. Trote-Gerês runs its own *Parque de Campismo Outeiro Alto* (☎/fax 253 659 860) at Cabril. The park runs a *camping ground* (☎ 253 391 289) 1km north of Gerês at Vidoeiro, and others at Lamas de Mouro and Entre-Ambos-os-Rios.

Gerês has plenty of pensões, though many are block-booked by spa patients in summer. Try *Pensão da Ponte* (☎ 253 391 121) beside the river, with doubles from 6000/7500$00 without/with bath. At the top of the hill, *Pensão Adelaide* (☎ 253 390 020, fax 253 390 029) provides doubles with bath from 7000$00.

Trote-Gerês runs the comfortable *Pousadinha de Paradela* (☎ 276 566 165) in Paradela, with doubles from 5000$00.

Places to Eat
Most Gerês pensões serve hearty meals, to guests and nonguests. There are several *restaurants*, plus shops in the main street for picnic provisions. The *Cerdeira Camping Ground* at Campo do Gerês has a good-value restaurant.

Getting There & Away
From Braga, 10 coaches daily run to Rio Caldo and Gerês, and seven to Campo do Gerês (fewer at weekends). Coming from Lisbon or Porto, change at Braga.

Slovenia

Little Slovenia (Slovenija) straddles Western and Eastern Europe. Many of its cities and towns bear the imprint of the Habsburg Empire and the Venetian Republic, while in the Julian Alps you'd think you were in Bavaria. The two million Slovenes were economically the most well off among the peoples of what was once Yugoslavia, and the relative affluence and orderliness of this nation is immediately apparent. Slovenia may be the gateway to the Balkans from Italy, Austria or Hungary, but it still has the feel of central Europe.

Slovenia is one of Europe's most delightful surprises for travellers. Fairy-tale Bled Castle, breathtaking Lake Bohinj, the scenic caves at Postojna and Škocjan, the lush Soča Valley, the coastal towns of Piran and Koper and thriving Ljubljana are great attractions, all accessible at much less than the cost of similar places in Western Europe. The amazing variety of settings packed into one small area makes this country truly a 'Europe in miniature'. An added bonus is that Slovenia is a nation of polyglots, and communicating with these friendly, helpful people is never difficult.

Facts about Slovenia

HISTORY

The early Slovenes settled in the river valleys of the Danube Basin and the eastern Alps in the 6th century. Slovenia was brought under Germanic rule in 748, first by the Frankish empire of the Carolingians, who converted the population to Christianity, and then as part of the Holy Roman Empire in the 9th century. The Austro-German monarchy took over in the early 14th century and continued to rule (as the Habsburg Empire from 1804) right up to the end of WWI in 1918 – with only one brief interruption. Over those six centuries, the upper classes became totally Germanised, though the peasantry retained their Slovenian identity. The Bible was translated into the vernacular during the

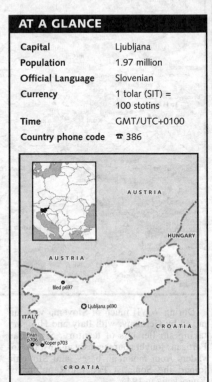

AT A GLANCE

Capital	Ljubljana
Population	1.97 million
Official Language	Slovenian
Currency	1 tolar (SIT) = 100 stotins
Time	GMT/UTC+0100
Country phone code	☎ 386

Reformation in 1584, but Slovene did not come into common use as a written language until the early 19th century.

In 1809, in a bid to isolate the Habsburg Empire from the Adriatic, Napoleon established the so-called Illyrian Provinces (Slovenia, Dalmatia and part of Croatia) with Ljubljana as the capital. Though the Habsburgs returned in 1814, French reforms in education, law and public administration endured. The democratic revolution that swept Europe in 1848 also increased political and national consciousness among Slovenes, and after WWI and the dissolution of the Austro-Hungarian Empire, Slovenia was included in the Kingdom of Serbs, Croats and Slovenes.

During WWII much of Slovenia was annexed by Germany, with Italy and Hungary taking smaller bits of territory. Slovenian Partisans fought courageously against the invaders from mountain bases, and Slovenia joined the Socialist Federal Republic of Yugoslavia in 1945.

Moves by Serbia in the late 1980s to assert its leading role culturally and economically among the Yugoslav republics was a big concern to Slovenes. When Belgrade abruptly ended the autonomy of Kosovo (where 90% of the population is ethnically Albanian) in late 1988, Slovenes feared the same could happen to them. For some years, Slovenia's interests had been shifting to the capitalist west and north; the Yugoslav connection, on the other hand, had become not only an economic burden but a political threat as well.

In the spring of 1990, Slovenia became the first Yugoslav republic to hold free elections and shed 45 years of communist rule; in December the electorate voted by 88% in favour of independence. The Slovenian government

began stockpiling weapons, and on 25 June 1991 it pulled the republic out of the Yugoslav Federation. To dramatise their bid for independence, the Slovenian leaders deliberately provoked fighting with the federal army by attempting to take control of the border crossings, and a 10-day war ensued. But resistance from the Slovenian militia was determined and, as no territorial claims or minority issues were involved, the Yugoslav government agreed to a truce brokered by the European Community (EC).

Slovenia got a new constitution in late December, and on 15 January 1992 the EC formally recognised the country. Slovenia was admitted to the United Nations in May 1992 and has now been invited to begin negotiations for full membership of the EU.

GEOGRAPHY

Slovenia is wedged between Austria and Croatia and shares much shorter borders with Italy and Hungary. Measuring just 20,256 sq km, Slovenia is the smallest country in Eastern

Europe, about the size of Wales or Israel. Much of the country is mountainous, culminating in the north-west with the Julian Alps and the nation's highest peak, Mt Triglav (2864m). From this jagged knot, the main Alpine chain continues east along the Austrian border, while the Dinaric range runs south-east along the coast into Croatia.

Below the limestone plateau of the Karst region between Ljubljana and Koper is Europe's most extensive network of karst caverns, which gave their name to other such caves around the world.

The coastal range forms a barrier isolating the Istrian Peninsula from Slovenia's corner of the Danube Basin. Much of the interior east of the Alps is drained by the Sava and Drava rivers, both of which empty into the Danube. The Soča flows through western Slovenia into the Adriatic.

CLIMATE

Slovenia is temperate with four distinct seasons, but the topography creates three individual climates. The north-west has an alpine climate with strong influences from the Atlantic as well as abundant precipitation. Temperatures in the Alpine valleys are moderate in summer but cold in winter. The coast and western Slovenia as far north as the Soča Valley has a Mediterranean climate with mild, sunny weather much of the year, though the *burja*, a cold and dry north-easterly wind from the Adriatic, can be fierce at times. Most of eastern Slovenia has a continental climate with hot summers and cold winters.

Slovenia gets most of its rain in March and April and again in October and November. January is the coldest month with an average temperature of -2°C and July the warmest (21°C).

ECOLOGY & ENVIRONMENT

Slovenia is a very green country – more than half its total area is covered in forest – and is home to 2900 plant species; Triglav National Park is especially rich in indigenous flowering plants. Common European animals (deer, boar, chamois) live here in abundance, and rare species include *Proteus anguinus*, the unique 'human fish' that inhabits pools in karst caves.

GOVERNMENT & POLITICS

Slovenia's constitution provides for a parliamentary system of government. The National Assembly, which has exclusive jurisdiction over the passing of laws, consists of 90 deputies elected for four years by proportional representation. The 40 members of the Council of State, which performs an advisory role, are elected for five-year terms by regions and special-interest groups. The head of state, the president, is elected directly for a maximum of two five-year terms. Executive power is vested in the prime minister and the 15-member cabinet.

In parliamentary elections in November 1996, a centrist alliance of the Liberal Democrats, the People's Party and the Democratic Party of Pensioners of Slovenia garnered more than 55% of the vote, seating 49 MPs. LDS leader Janez Drnovšek, prime minister from the first elections in 1992, was again named head of government. In November 1997 President Milan Kučan was returned for his second term after winning nearly 56% of the popular vote and will stand for re-election in 2002.

In April 2000 the centre-left government of Prime Minister Drnovšek collapsed when the conservative People's Party joined the opposition Christian Democrats. The newly formed coalition elected the economist, Andrej Bajuk, as Slovenia's third prime minister in May. Prime Minister Bajuk is expected to place a high priority on expediting the reforms necessary to allow Slovenia to join the EU.

ECONOMY

Slovenia has emerged as one of the strongest economies of the former socialist countries of Eastern Europe in the years since independence. Inflation has dropped, employment is on the rise and per-capita GDP – currently 72% of the EU average – is expected to surpass that of Greece and Portugal by 2002.

But for many Slovenes, the economic picture remains unclear. Real wages continue to grow – but faster than inflation, which puts Slovenia's international competitiveness at a disadvantage. Inflation rocketed up to 200% after independence and has steadily decreased since; it is currently below 5%. Unemployment is hovering around 7.4%.

POPULATION & PEOPLE

Slovenia was the most homogeneous of all the Yugoslav republics; about 87% of the population (estimated at 1,970,570 in 1999) are Slovenes. There are just over 8500 ethnic Hungarians and some 2300 Roma (Gypsies) largely in the north-east as well as 3060 Italians on the coast. 'Others', accounting for 11.5% of the population, include Croats, Serbs, ethnic Albanians and those who identify themselves simply as 'Muslims'.

ARTS

Slovenia's best loved writer is the Romantic poet France Prešeren (1800-49), whose lyric poetry set new standards for Slovenian literature and helped to raise national consciousness. Disappointed in love, Prešeren wrote sensitive love poems but also satirical verse and epic poetry.

Many notable bridges, squares and buildings in Ljubljana and elsewhere in Slovenia were designed by the architect Jože Plečnik (1872-1957), who studied under Otto Wagner in Vienna.

Postmodernist painting and sculpture has been more or less dominated since the 1980s by the multimedia group Neue Slowenische Kunst (NSK) and the five-member artists' cooperative IRWIN. Avante-garde dance is best exemplified by Betontanc, an NSK dance company that mixes live music and theatrical elements (called 'physical theatre' here) with sharp political comment.

Since WWII, many Slovenian folk traditions have been lost, but compilations by the trio Trutamora Slovenica (available at music shops in Ljubljana) examine the roots of Slovenian folk music. Folk groups – both 'pure' and popular – to watch out for include the Avseniki, Ansambel Lojzeta Slaka, the Alpski Kvintet led by Oto Pestner, and the Roma band Šukar.

Popular music runs the gamut from Slovenian *chanson* (best exemplified by Vita Mavrič) and folk to jazz and techno. Three punk groups from the late 1970s and early 1980s, Pankrti, Borghesia and Laibach, hailed from Slovenia.

LANGUAGE

Slovene is a South Slavic language written in the Roman alphabet and closely related to Croatian and Serbian. It is grammatically complex with lots of cases, genders and tenses and has something very rare in linguistics: the singular, dual and plural forms. It's one *miza* (table) and three or more *mize* (tables) but two *mizi*.

Virtually everyone in Slovenia speaks at least one other language: Croatian, Serbian, German, English and/or Italian. English is definitely the preferred language of the young. See the Language section at the end of the book for pronunciation guidelines and useful words and phrases. Lonely Planet's *Central Europe Phrasebook* contains a chapter on Slovene.

Facts for the Visitor

HIGHLIGHTS

Ljubljana, Piran and Koper have outstanding architecture; the hilltop castles at Bled and Ljubljana are impressive. The Škocjan Caves are among the foremost underground wonders of the world. The Soča Valley is indescribably beautiful in spring. The frescoed Church of St John the Baptist is in itself worth the trip to Lake Bohinj.

SUGGESTED ITINERARIES

Depending on the length of your stay, you might want to see and do the following in Slovenia:

Two days
  Visit Ljubljana
One week
  Visit Ljubljana, Bled, Bohinj, Škocjan Caves and Piran
Two weeks
  Visit all the places covered in this chapter

PLANNING
When to Go

Snow can linger in the mountains as late as June, but May and June are great months to be in the lowlands and valleys when everything is fresh and in blossom. (April can be a bit wet though.) In July and August, hotel rates are increased and there will be lots of tourists, especially on the coast. September is an excellent month to visit as the days are long and the weather still warm, and it's the best time for hiking and climbing. October and November can be rainy, and winter (December to March) is for skiers.

Maps

The Geodesic Institute of Slovenia (Geodetski Zavod Slovenije; GZS), the country's principal cartographic agency, produces national (1:300,000), regional (1:50,000) and topographical maps to the entire country (64 1:50,000-scale sheets) as well as city plans. The Alpine Association of Slovenia (Planinska Zveza Slovenije; PZS) has some 30 different hiking maps available, with scales as large as 1:25,000.

TOURIST OFFICES
Local Tourist Offices

The Slovenian Tourist Board (Center za Promocijo Turizma Slovenije; CPTS; ☎ 01-189 1840, fax 189 1841, ℮ cpts@cpts.tradepoint .si) in Ljubljana's World Trade Centre at Dunajska cesta 160 is the umbrella organisation for tourist offices in Slovenia. It can handle requests for information in writing or you can check out its excellent Web site (see Internet Resources later).

The best office for face-to-face information in Slovenia – bar none – is the Ljubljana Tourist Information Centre. Most of the places described in this chapter have some form of tourist office but if the place you're visiting doesn't, seek assistance at a branch of one of the big travel agencies (eg Kompas, Globtour or Slovenijaturist) or from hotel or museum staff.

Tourist Offices Abroad

The CPTS maintains tourist offices in the following eight countries:

Austria (☎ 01-715 4010, fax 0222-713 8177) Hilton Center, Landstrasser Hauptstrasse 2, 1030 Vienna
Germany (☎ 089-2916 1202, fax 2916 1273) Maximiliansplatz 12a, 80333 Munich
Hungary (☎ 1-269 6879, fax 156 2818) Gellérthegy utca 28, 1013 Budapest
Italy (☎ 02-2951 1187, fax 2951 4071) Via Lazzaro Palazzi 2a/III, 20124 Milan
Netherlands & Belgium (☎ 010-465 3003, fax 465 7514) Benthuizerstraat 29, 3036 CB Rotterdam

Switzerland (☎ 01-212 6394, fax 212 5266) Löwenstrasse 54, 8001 Zürich
UK (☎ 020-7287 7133, fax 7287 5476) 49 Conduit St, London W1R 9FB
USA (☎ 212-358 9686, 358 9025) 345 East 12th St, New York, NY 10003

In addition, Kompas has representative offices in many cities worldwide, including:

Australia (☎ 07-3831 4400) 323 Boundary St, Spring Hill, 4000 Queensland
Canada (☎ 514-938 4041) 4060 Ste-Catherine St West, Suite 535, Montreal, Que H3Z 2Z3
France (☎ 01 53 92 27 80) 14 Rue de la Source, 75016 Paris
USA (☎ 954 771 9200) 2826 East Commercial Blvd, Ft Lauderdale, FL 33306

VISAS & DOCUMENTS

Passport holders from Australia, Canada, Israel, Japan, New Zealand, Switzerland, USA and EU countries do not require visas for stays in Slovenia of up to 90 days; those from the EU as well as Switzerland can also enter on a national identity card for a stay of up to 30 days. Citizens of other countries requiring visas (including South Africans) can get them at any Slovenian embassy or consulate. They cost the equivalent of DM50 for single entry and DM100 for multiple entry.

EMBASSIES & CONSULATES
Slovenian Embassies & Consulates

Diplomatic representation abroad includes:

Australia (☎ 02-6243 4830) Advance Bank Centre, Level 6, 60 Marcus Clark St, Canberra, ACT 2601
Austria (☎ 01-586 1309) Nibelungengasse 13, 1010 Vienna
Canada (☎ 613-565 5781) 150 Metcalfe St, Suite 2101, Ottawa, Ont K2P 1P1
Croatia (☎ 01-631 1000) Savska cesta 41/IX, 10000 Zagreb
Hungary (☎ 1-325 9202) Cseppkő utca 68, 1025 Budapest
Italy (☎ 06-808 1272) Via Ludovico Pisano 10, 00197 Rome
UK (☎ 0171-495 7775) Cavendish Court, Suite One, 11-15 Wigmore St, London W1H 9LA
USA (☎ 202-667 5363) 1525 New Hampshire Ave NW, Washington, DC 20036

SLOVENIA

Embassies & Consulates in Slovenia

Selected countries with representation in Ljubljana (area code ☎ 01) appear in the following list. Citizens of countries not listed here should contact their embassies in Vienna or Budapest.

Albania (☎ 432 2324) Ob Ljubljanici
Australia (☎ 425 4252) Trg Republike 3/XII
Austria (☎ 479 0700) Prešernova 23
Bosnia-Hercegovina (☎ 432 4042) Likozarjeva 6
Canada (☎ 430 3570) Miklošičeva cesta 19
Croatia (☎ 425 7287) Gruberjevo nabrežje 6
France (☎ 426 2582) Barjanska 1
Germany (☎ 479 0319) Prešernova 27
Hungary (☎ 452 1882) Konrada Babnika 5
Netherlands (☎ 439 2740) Dunjaska 22
Romania (☎ 505 5432) Podlimbarskega 43
Slovakia (☎ 425 5425) Tivolska 4
South Africa (☎ 433 4180) Pražakova 4
UK (☎ 200 3910) Trg Republike 3/IV
USA (☎ 200 5500) Prešernova 31

CUSTOMS

Travellers can bring in the usual personal effects, a couple of cameras and electronic goods for their own use, 200 cigarettes, a generous 4L of spirits and 1L of wine.

MONEY
Currency

Slovenia's currency, the tolar, is abbreviated SIT. Prices in shops and restaurants, and train and bus fares are always in tolars, but a few hotels, guesthouses and even camping grounds still use Deutschmarks (though the government has asked them not to) as the tolar is linked to it.

For that reason, some forms of accommodation listed in this chapter are quoted in Deutschmarks – though you are never required to pay in the German currency.

There are coins of 50 stotin and one, two and five tolars and banknotes of 10, 20, 50, 100, 200, 500, 1000, 5000 and 10,000 tolars.

Exchange Rates

country	unit		tolar
Australia	A$1	=	136 SIT
Canada	C$1	=	156 SIT
euro	€1	=	209 SIT
France	10FF	=	319 SIT
Germany	DM1	=	107 SIT
Japan	¥100	=	212 SIT
NZ	NZ$1	=	104 SIT
UK	UK£1	=	343 SIT
USA	US$1	=	230 SIT

Exchanging Money

Cash & Travellers Cheques It is simple to change cash and travellers cheques at banks, travel agencies, any *menjalnica* (private exchange bureau) and certain post offices.

There's no black market, and exchange rates vary little, but watch out for a commission (*provizija*) of up to 3% tacked on by some tourist offices, hotels and travel agencies.

ATMs & Credit Cards Visa, MasterCard/Eurocard and American Express credit cards are widely accepted at upmarket restaurants, shops, hotels, car-rental firms and some travel agencies; Diners Club less so.

Automated teller machines (ATMs) linked to Cirrus or Plus are available in Ljubljana and some coastal towns; their locations are noted in the Information sections of the individual towns. Clients of Visa can get cash advances in tolars from any A Banka branch, MasterCard and Eurocard holders from any branch of Nova Ljubljanska Banka (☎ 01-425 0155), Trg Republike 2 in Ljubljana and American Express customers from Atlas Express (☎ 01-433 2024 or ☎ 131 9020) at Trubarjeva cesta 50 in Ljubljana.

Costs

Slovenia remains much cheaper than the neighbouring countries of Italy and Austria, but don't expect it to be a bargain basement like Hungary – everything costs about 50% more here.

If you stay in private rooms or at guesthouses, eat at medium-priced restaurants and travel 2nd class on the train or by bus, you should get by for under US$40 a day.

Those staying at hostels or college dormitories, eating takeaway for lunch and at self-service restaurants at night will cut costs considerably.

Travelling in a little more style and comfort – occasional restaurant splurges with bottles of wine, an active nightlife, staying at small hotels or guesthouses with 'character' – will cost about US$65 a day.

Taxes & Refunds

A 'circulation tax' *(prometni davek)* not unlike Value-Added Tax (VAT) covers the purchase of most goods and services here. Visitors can claim refunds on total purchases of 15,000 SIT or more (not including tobacco products or spirits) through Kompas MTS, which has offices at Brnik airport and some two dozen border crossings. Make sure you do the paperwork at the time of purchase.

Most towns and cities levy a 'tourist tax' on overnight visitors of between 120 SIT and 300 SIT per person per night (less at camping grounds) which is included in the prices listed in this chapter.

POST & COMMUNICATIONS
Post

Poste restante is sent to the main post office in a city or town (in the capital, it goes to the branch at Slovenska cesta 32, 1101 Ljubljana) where it is held for 30 days. American Express card holders can have their mail addressed c/o the Atlas Express, Trubarjeva cesta 50, 1000 Ljubljana.

Domestic mail costs 19 SIT for up to 20g and 36 SIT for up to 100g. Postcards are 18 SIT. For international mail, the base rate is 90 SIT for 20g or less, 186 SIT for up to 100g and 70 SIT to 90 SIT for a postcard, depending on the size. Then you have to add on the air-mail charge for every 10g: 20 SIT for Europe, 25 SIT for North America and 30 SIT for Australasia. An aerogramme is 120 SIT.

Telephone

The easiest place to make long-distance calls and send faxes and telegrams is from a post office or telephone centre; the one at Trg Osvobodilne Fronte (Trg OF) near the train and bus stations in Ljubljana is open 24 hours.

Public telephones on the street do not accept coins; they require a phonecard *(telefonska kartica)* available at all post offices and some newsstands.

Phonecards cost 700/1000/1700/3500 SIT for 25/50/100/300 impulses. A local one-minute call absorbs one impulse, and a three-minute call from Slovenia will cost about 277 SIT to Balkan countries, 214 SIT to Western Europe (including the UK) and the USA and 434 SIT to Australia. International rates are 20% cheaper between 7 pm and 7 am.

The international access code in Slovenia is ☎ 00. The international operator can be reached on ☎ 901 and international directory inquiries on ☎ 989. To call Slovenia from abroad dial the international access code, ☎ 386 (Slovenia's country code), the area code (without the initial zero, eg 1 in Ljubljana and 6 for mobile/cellphones) followed by the number.

Email & Internet Access

Cybercafes are a rarity in Slovenia. Currently the only public access to the Internet is at Klub K4 in Ljubljana.

INTERNET RESOURCES

The best single source of information on the Internet is the CPTS's SloWWWenia site: www.matkurja.com. It has an interactive map where you can click on to more than two dozen cities, towns, ski resorts etc as well as information on culture, history, food and wine, getting to and from Slovenia and what's on.

See the Internet Resources section in the Ljubljana section for more sites.

BOOKS

Books are very expensive in Slovenia so try to buy whatever books you can on the country before you arrive. Lonely Planet's *Slovenia* is the only complete and independent English-language guide to the country. *Discover Slovenia*, published annually by Cankarjeva Založba (3500 SIT), is a colourful and easy introduction, and Zoë Brân's *After Yugoslavia*, part of the Lonely Planet Journeys series, retraces the author's 1978 trip through the former Yugoslavia.

NEWSPAPERS & MAGAZINES

Slovenia publishes four daily newspapers, the most widely read being *Delo* (Work) and *Večer* (Evening). The magazine *Slovenia Weekly* is an English-language weekly geared to business travellers which carries economic and political news. It is available at most English-language bookshops. There are no English-language newspapers, though the *International Herald Tribune*, the *Guardian International*, the *Financial Times* and *USA Today* are available on the day of publication in the afternoon at hotels and department stores in Ljubljana.

SLOVENIA

RADIO & TV

In July and August both Radio Slovenija 1 and 2 broadcast a report on the weather, including conditions on the sea and in the mountains, in English, German and Italian at 7.15 am. News, weather, traffic and tourist information in the same languages follows on Radio 1 at 9.35 am daily except Sunday. Also during this period Radio 2 broadcasts weekend traffic conditions after each news bulletin from Friday afternoon through Sunday evening. There's a nightly news bulletin at 10.30 pm throughout the year on Radio 1.

You can listen to Radio 1 on MHz/FM frequencies 88.5, 90.0, 90.9, 91.8, 92.0, 92.9, 94.1 and 96.4 as well as AM 326.8. Radio 2 can be found on MHz/FM 87.8, 92.4, 93.5, 94.1, 95.3, 96.9, 97.6, 98.9 and 99.9.

TIME

Slovenia is one hour ahead of GMT/UTC. The country goes onto summer time (GMT/UTC plus two hours) on the last Sunday in March when clocks are advanced by one hour. On the last Sunday in October they're turned back one hour.

LAUNDRY

Commercial laundrettes are pretty much nonexistent in Slovenia. The best places to look for do-it-yourself washers and dryers are hostels, college dormitories and camping grounds, and there are a couple of places in Ljubljana that will do your laundry reasonably quickly (see Laundry under Information in the Ljubljana section).

WOMEN TRAVELLERS

Women should encounter few special problems travelling through Slovenia. Crime is low and harassment is rare. The Društvo Mesto Žensk (City of Women Association), part of the Government Office for Women's Affairs (☎ 01-438 1580), is at Kersnikova ul 4 in Ljubljana. It sponsors an international festival of contemporary arts called City of Women, usually in October. In the event of an assault, ring ☎ 080 124 or any of the following six numbers: ☎ 9780 to ☎ 9785.

GAY & LESBIAN TRAVELLERS

The gay association Roza Klub (☎ 01-430 4740), Kersnikova ul 4 in Ljubljana, organises

a disco every Sunday night at Klub K4 in Ljubljana. Magnus (☎ same as Roza Klub) is the gay branch of the Student Cultural Centre (Študentski Kulturni Center; ŠKUC).

Lesbians can contact the ŠKUC-affiliated organisation LL (☎ 01-430 4740) at Metelkova ul 6 in Ljubljana.

The GALfon (☎ 01-432 4089) is a hotline and source of general information for gays and lesbians. It operates daily from 7 to 10 pm. The Queer Resources Directory on the Internet (www.ljudmila.org/siqrd) leaves no stone unturned.

DISABLED TRAVELLERS

A group that looks after the interests and special needs of physically challenged people is the Zveza Paraplegikov Republike Slovenije (ZPRS; ☎ 01-432 7138),based at Štihova ul 14 in Ljubljana.

SENIOR TRAVELLERS

Senior citizens may be entitled to discounts in Slovenia on things like museum admission fees, provided they show proof of age.

DANGERS & ANNOYANCES

Slovenia is hardly a violent or dangerous place. Police say that 90% of all crimes reported involve theft so travellers should take the usual precautions.

EMERGENCIES

In the event of an emergency, the following numbers can be dialled nationwide:

Police	☎ 113
Fire/first aid/ambulance	☎ 112
Automobile assistance (AMZS)	☎ 987

LEGAL MATTERS

The permitted blood-alcohol level for motorists is 0.5g/kg (0.0g/kg for professional drivers) and the law is very strictly enforced. Anything over that could earn you a fine of 25,000 SIT and one to three demerit points.

BUSINESS HOURS

Shops, groceries and department stores are open from 7.30 or 8 am to 7 pm on weekdays and to 1 pm on Saturday. Bank hours are generally 8 am to 4.30 or 5 pm on weekdays (often with a lunchtime break) and till noon on Saturday. The main post office in any city or town is open 7 am to 8 pm on weekdays, till 1 pm on Saturday and occasionally 9 to 11 am on Sunday.

PUBLIC HOLIDAYS & SPECIAL EVENTS

Public holidays in Slovenia include two days at New Year (1 and 2 January), Prešeren Day (8 February), Easter Sunday and Monday (March/April), Insurrection Day (27 April), two days for Labour Day (1 and 2 May), National Day (25 June), Assumption Day (15 August), Reformation Day (31 October), All Saints' Day (1 November), Christmas (25 December) and Independence Day (26 December).

Though cultural events are scheduled year-round, the highlights of Slovenia's summer season (July and August) are the International Summer Festival in Ljubljana; the Piran Musical Evenings; the Primorska Summer Festival at Piran, Koper, Izola and Portorož; and Summer in the Old Town in Ljubljana, with three or four cultural events a week taking place.

The Cows' Ball (Kravji Bal) at Bohinj is a zany weekend of folk dance, music, eating and drinking in mid-September to mark the return of the cows to the valleys from their high pastures.

ACTIVITIES
Skiing

Skiing is by far the most popular sport in Slovenia, and every fourth Slovene is an active skier. The country has many well-equipped ski resorts in the Julian Alps, especially Vogel (skiing up to 1840m) above Lake Bohinj, Kranjska Gora (1600m), Kanin (2300m) above Bovec, and Krvavec (1970m), east of Kranj.

All these resorts have multiple chair lifts, cable cars, ski schools, equipment rentals and large resort hotels.

Hiking

Hiking is almost as popular as skiing in Slovenia, and there are approximately 7000km of marked trails and 165 mountain huts. Visitors can experience the full grandeur of the Julian Alps in the Triglav National Park at Bohinj, and for the veteran mountaineer there's the Slovenian Alpine Trail, which crosses all the highest peaks in the country.

Kayaking, Canoeing & Rafting

The best white-water rafting is on the Soča, one of only half a dozen rivers in the European Alps whose upper waters are still unspoiled. The centre is at Bovec.

Fishing

Slovenia's rivers and Alpine lakes and streams are teeming with trout, grayling, pike and other fish. The best rivers for angling are the Soča, the Krka, the Kolpa and the Sava Bohinjka near Bohinj. Lake fishing is good at Bled and Bohinj.

Cycling

Mountain bikes are available for hire at Bled and Bohinj. You can also rent bikes on the coast and in Ljubljana.

WORK

Employment of foreigners in Slovenia is among the most restricted in Europe. Even foreign businesses have difficulty obtaining working visas for their employees. It may be possible to pick up casual work teaching English for DM25 per hour, although travellers on tourist visas are forbidden to accept employment.

ACCOMMODATION
Camping

In summer, camping is the cheapest way to go, and you'll find there are conveniently located camping grounds all over the country. You don't always need a tent as some camping grounds have inexpensive bungalows or caravans, as well. Two of the best camping grounds are Zlatorog on Lake Bohinj and Jezero Fiesa near Piran, though they can be very crowded in summer. It is forbidden to camp 'rough' in Slovenia.

Hostels & Student Dormitories

Slovenia has only a handful of 'official' hostels, including two in Ljubljana and one each in Bled and Koper, but not all of them are open year-round. You'll find that some college dormitories accept travellers in the summer months.

Private Rooms & Apartments

Private rooms arranged by tourist offices and travel agencies can be inexpensive, but a surcharge of up to 50% is usually levied on stays of less than three nights. You can often bargain for rooms without the surcharge by going directly to any house with a sign reading 'sobe' (rooms).

Pensions & Guesthouses

A small guesthouse (called a penzion or gostišče) can be good value, though in July and August you may be required to take at least one meal and the rates are higher then.

Farmhouses

The agricultural cooperatives of Slovenia have organised a unique program to accommodate visitors on working farms. Prices range from 32,700 SIT per person per week for a 2nd-category room with shared bath and breakfast in the low season (from September to about mid-December and mid-January to June) to around 65,400 SIT per person per week for a 1st-category room with private bath and all meals in the high season (July and August). Bookings can be made through ABC Farm & Countryside Holidays (☎ 01-507 6127, fax 519 9876) at Ul Jožeta Jame 16 in Ljubljana or at Brnik airport (☎ 04-206 1684). Its British agent is Slovenija Pursuits (☎ 01767-631 144), Newbarn Farm, Tadlow Rd, Tadlow, Royston, Herts SG8 0EP.

Hotels

Hotel rates vary according to the time of year, with July and August the peak season and May/June and September/October the shoulder seasons. In Ljubljana, prices are constant all year. Many resort hotels, particularly on the coast, close in winter.

FOOD

Slovenian cuisine is heavily influenced by the food of its neighbours. From Austria, there's klobasa (sausage), zavitek (strudel) and Dunajski zrezek (Wiener schnitzel). Njoki (potato dumplings), rižota (risotto) and the ravioli-like žlikrofi are obviously Italian, and Hungary has contributed golaž (goulash), paprikaš (chicken or beef 'stew') and palačinke (thin pancakes filled with jam or nuts and topped with chocolate). And then there's that old Balkan stand-by, burek, a greasy, layered cheese, meat or even apple pie served at takeaway places everywhere.

No Slovenian meal can be considered complete without soup, be it the very simple goveja juha z rezanci (beef broth with little egg noodles), zelenjavna juha (vegetable soup) or gobova kremna juha (creamed mushroom soup). There are many types of Slovenian dumplings; the cheese ones called štruklji are the most popular.

Try also the baked delicacies, including potica (walnut roll) and gibanica (pastry filled with poppy seeds, walnuts, apple and/or sultanas and cheese and topped with cream). Traditional dishes are best tried at an inn (gostilna or gostišče).

DRINKS

The wine-growing regions of Slovenia are Podravje in the east, noted for such white wines as Renski Rizling (a true German Riesling), Beli Pinot (Pinot Blanc) and Traminec (Traminer); Posavje in the southeast (try the distinctly Slovenian light-red Cviček); and the area around the coast, which produces a hearty red called Teran made from Refošk grapes.

Žganje is a strong brandy or eau de vie distilled from a variety of fruits but most commonly plums. The finest brandy is Pleterska Hruška made from pears.

SPECTATOR SPORTS

For skiing enthusiasts, World Cup slalom and giant slalom events are held at Kranjska Gora in late December, and the current world ski-jumping record (200m) was set at nearby Planica in 1994.

Getting There & Away

AIR

Slovenia's national airline, Adria Airways (☎ 01-431 3000 in Ljubljana, ☎ 04-236 3462 at Brnik airport), has nonstop flights to Ljubljana from 18 cities including Amsterdam, Barcelona, Brussels, Copenhagen, Frankfurt, London (LHR), Manchester (May-October),

Moscow, Munich, Ohrid, Paris (CDG), Sarajevo, Skopje, Split, Tel Aviv, Tirana, Vienna and Zürich. You can also check out its Web site at www.adria.si for schedules.

Other airlines that provide direct flights to Ljubljana include British Airways (BA) from London, Lufthansa (LH) from Frankfurt and Swissair (SR) from Zürich.

LAND
Bus

Buses from Ljubljana serve a number of international destinations. These include the following cities and towns: Belgrade (6000 SIT, three daily); Frankfurt (14,800 SIT, six weekly); Klagenfurt (1680 SIT, Wednesday at 6.15 am); Munich (5850 SIT, six weekly); Rijeka (1870 SIT, daily at 7.40 pm); Split (5250 SIT, daily at 7.40 pm); Stuttgart (12,550 SIT, six weekly); Varaždin (3390 SIT, Saturday and Sunday at 6.35 am); and Zagreb (2570 SIT, three daily).

Italy Nova Gorica is the easiest exit/entry point between Slovenia and Italy as you can catch up to five buses a day to/from the Italian city of Gorizia or simply walk across the border at Rožna Dolina. Koper also has good connections with Italy – some 17 buses a day on weekdays go to/from Trieste, 21km to the north-east. There's also a daily bus (except Sunday) from Trieste to Ljubljana (1810 SIT).

Hungary There is no direct bus that links Ljubljana to Budapest. Instead, take one of up to five daily buses to Lendava; the Hungarian border is 5km to the north. The first Hungarian train station, Rédics, is only 2km beyond the border.

Train

The main train routes into Slovenia from Austria are Vienna to Maribor and Salzburg to Jesenice. Tickets cost 6763 SIT from Ljubljana to Salzburg (4½ hours) and 10,103 SIT to Vienna (six hours). But it's cheaper to take a local train to Maribor (1380 SIT) and buy your ticket on to Vienna from there. Similarly, from Austria you should only buy a ticket as far as Jesenice or Maribor as domestic fares are much lower than international ones.

There are three trains a day between Munich and Ljubljana (11,266 SIT, seven hours) via Salzburg. The EuroCity *Mimara* travels by day, while the *Lisinski* express goes overnight (sleeping carriage available). A 564 SIT supplement is payable on the *Mimara*. Seat reservations (200 SIT) are available on both.

Four trains a day run from Trieste to Ljubljana (3791 SIT, three hours) via the towns of Divača and Sežana. From Croatia it's Zagreb to Ljubljana (2260 SIT, 2½ hours) via Zidani Most, or Rijeka to Ljubljana (2099 SIT, 2½ hours) via Pivka. Some services between Slovenia and Croatia require a change of trains at some point, but connections are immediate. The InterCity *Drava* and *Venezia Express* trains link Ljubljana with Budapest (8833 SIT, 72½ hours) via north-west Croatia and Zagreb respectively. There is no direct train to Belgrade, but three trains daily to Zagreb will connect with Belgrade trains (6650 SIT).

Border Crossings

Slovenia maintains some 150 border crossings with Italy, Austria, Hungary and Croatia, but only 26 are considered international or inter-state crossings. The rest of these are minor crossings only open to Slovenian citizens or others with special permits.

SEA

Between early April and October on Friday, Saturday and Sunday, the *Prince of Venice*, a 39m Australian-made catamaran seating some 330 passengers, sails between Izola and Venice (8750/12,500 SIT return, 2½ hours) with an additional sailing on Tuesday from late June to early September. The price includes a sightseeing tour in Venice. From Izola there are frequent buses to Portorož, Piran and Koper. Another catamaran, the *Marconi*, links Trieste with Piran (15,000/30,000 SIT return, two hours) on Wednesday, Friday and Sunday from mid-May to September.

DEPARTURE TAX

A departure tax of 2700 SIT is levied on all passengers leaving Slovenia by air though this is almost always included in your airline ticket price.

Getting Around

BUS
Except for long journeys, the bus is preferable to the train in Slovenia and departures are frequent. In some cases you don't have much of a choice; travelling by bus is the only practical way to get to Bled and Bohinj, the Julian Alps and much of the coast from Ljubljana.

In Ljubljana you can buy your ticket with seat reservation (200 SIT, depending on the destination) the day before, but many people simply pay the driver on boarding. The one time you really might need a reservation is Friday afternoon, when many students travel from Ljubljana to their homes or people leave the city for the weekend. There is a 220 SIT charge for each bag placed underneath the bus.

Footnotes you might see on Slovenian bus schedules include: *vozi vsak dan* (runs daily); *vozi ob delavnikih* (runs on working days – Monday to Friday); *vozi ob sobotah* (runs on Saturday); and *vozi ob nedeljah in praznikih* (runs on Sunday and holidays).

TRAIN
Slovenske Železnice (SŽ; Slovenian Railways) operates on just over 1200km of track. The country's most scenic rail routes run along the Soča River from Jesenice to Nova Gorica via Bled (Bled Jezero station) and Bohinjska Bistrica (89km) and from Ljubljana to Zagreb (160km) along the Sava River.

On posted timetables in Slovenia, *odhod* or *odhodi vlakov* means 'departures' and *prihod* (or *prihodi vlakov*) is 'arrivals'. If you don't have time to buy a ticket, seek out the conductor who will sell you one for an extra charge of 200 SIT.

CAR & MOTORCYCLE
The use of seat belts in the front seats is compulsory in Slovenia, and a new law requires all vehicles to show their headlights throughout the day outside built-up areas. Speed limits for cars are 50km/h in built-up areas, 90km/h on secondary roads, 100km/h on main highways and 130km/h on motorways.

Tolls are payable on several motorways, but they're not terribly expensive; from Ljubljana to Postojna, for example, it costs 390 SIT for cars and motorcycles. Petrol remains relatively cheap: 132.30/132.80/140.30 SIT per litre for 91/95/98 octane. Diesel costs 135.30 SIT.

Slovenia's automobile club is the Avto Moto Zveza Slovenije (AMZS; ☎ 987).

Car Rental
Car rentals from international firms like National, Budget, Avis and Kompas Hertz vary widely in price, but expect to pay from around 11,100/57,700 SIT a day/week with unlimited mileage, Collision Damage Waiver, Theft Protection and Personal Accident Insurance for a Citroen AX or a Ford Fiesta. Tack on 19% VAT. Smaller agencies like ABC Rent a Car and Avtoimpex in Ljubljana (see Getting Around in that section) have more competitive rates.

Some agencies have minimum-age rules (21 or 23 years) and/or require that you've had a valid licence for one or even two years.

HITCHING
Hitchhiking is legal everywhere except on motorways and some major highways and is generally easy; even young women do it. But hitching is never a totally safe way of getting around and, although we mention it as an option, we don't recommend it.

Ljubljana

☎ 01 • pop 280,000

Ljubljana (Laibach in German) is by far Slovenia's largest and most populous city. But in many ways the city, whose name almost means 'beloved' (*ljubljena*) in Slovene, does not feel like an industrious municipality of national importance but a pleasant, self-contented town with responsibilities only to itself and its citizens. The most beautiful parts of the city are the Old Town below the castle and the embankments designed by Plečnik along the narrow Ljubljanica River.

Ljubljana began as the Roman town of Emona, and legacies of the Roman presence can still be seen throughout the city. The Habsburgs took control of Ljubljana in the 14th century and later built many of the pale-coloured churches and mansions that earned the city the nickname 'White Ljubljana'. From 1809 to 1814, Ljubljana was the capital of the Illyrian Provinces, Napoleon's short-lived springboard to the Adriatic.

Despite the patina of imperial Austria, contemporary Ljubljana has a vibrant Slavic air all its own. It's like a little Prague without the hordes of tourists but with all the facilities you'll need. More than 25,000 students attend Ljubljana University's 14 faculties and three art academies so the city always feels young.

Orientation

The tiny bus station and renovated train station are opposite one another on Trg Osvobodilne Fronte (known as Trg OF) at the northern end of town centre (called Center).

Information

Tourist Offices The Tourist Information Centre (TIC; ☎ 306 1215, fax 306 1204, e pcl.tic-lj@ljubljana.si) is in the historical Kresija building south-east of Triple Bridge at Stritarjeva ul 2. It's open from 8 am to 7 pm weekdays and 10 am to 6 pm on Saturday. The branch office (☎ 433 9475) at the train station is open from 8 am to 9 pm daily (including Sunday) June to September (10 am to 5.30 pm the rest of the year). The TIC is well worth visiting to pick up free maps and brochures.

The Cultural Information Centre (☎ 221 3025) next to Trg Francoske Revolucije 7 can answer questions about what's on in Ljubljana and has a free booklet listing all the city's museums, galleries and exhibitions.

The main office of the Alpine Association of Slovenia (☎ 434 3022) is at Dvoržakova ul 9, a small house set back from the street. Its Web site is at www.pzs.si.

Money The currency exchange office inside the train station is open 6 am to 10 pm daily. It accepts travellers cheques and charges no commission for cash exchanges but does not offer a good rate. Most branches of A Banka have ATMs that accept Visa and Plus; the closest one to the train station is at Trg Osvobodilne Fronte 2 and there's another next to the tourist office at Stritarjeva ul 2. There are three ATMs that accept MasterCard, Maestro and Cirrus as well: Banka Koper, at Cigaletova ul 4; outside the

Globtour agency in the Maximarket passageway connecting Trg Republike with Plečnikov trg; and inside Nova Ljubljanska Banka, Trg Republike 2 (open 8 am to 5 pm weekdays, and 9 am to noon on Saturday). Next to the SKB Banka on Trg Ajdovščina is a currency exchange machine that changes the banknotes of 18 countries into tolar at a good rate. The Hida exchange bureau in the Seminary building near the open-air market at Pogarčarjev trg 1 is open 7 am to 7 pm weekdays and to 2 pm on Saturday. Another Hida branch at Čopova ul 42 is open 8 am to 8 pm weekdays and to 1 pm Saturday.

Post & Communications Poste restante is held for 30 days at the post office at Slovenska cesta 32 (postal code 1101). It is open 7 am to 8 pm weekdays and to 1 pm Saturday. You can make international telephone calls or send faxes from here or the main post office at Pražakova ul 3, which keeps the same hours.

To mail a parcel you must go to the special customs post office at Trg OF 5 opposite the bus station and open round the clock. Make sure you bring your package open for inspection; the maximum weight is about 15kg, depending on the destination.

Email & Internet Access There's only one cybercafe with public access to the Internet in Ljubljana – the Klub K4 Café (☎ 431 7010) at Kersnikova ul 4.

Internet Resources Useful Web sites for Ljubljana include:

www.ljubljana.si
  City of Ljubljana
www.unl-lj.si
  Ljubljana University (check out the Welcome page with practical information in English for foreign students)

Travel Agencies Backpackers and students should head for the Erazem travel office (☎ 433 1076) at Trubarjeva cesta 7. It can provide information, make bookings and it has a message board. It also sells ISIC cards (900 SIT) and, for those under 26 but not studying, FIYTO cards (700 SIT). Mladi Turist (☎ 425 9131), at Salendrova ul 4 is the

SLOVENIA

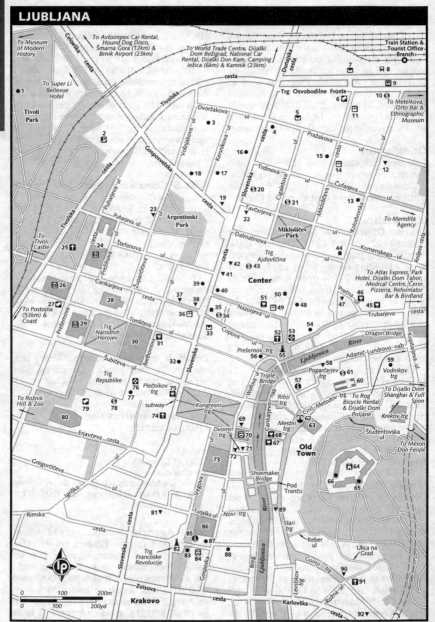

LJUBLJANA

To Museum of Modern History

To Avtoimpex Car Rental, Hound Dog Disco, Šmarna Gora (12km) & Brnik Airport (23km)

To World Trade Centre, Dijaški Dom Bežigrad, National Car Rental, Dijaški Don Kam, Camping Ježica (6km) & Kamnik (23km)

Celovška

cesta

Train Station & Tourist Office Branch

To Super Li Bellevue Hotel

Tivolska

1

Tivoli Park

Gosposvetska

Dvoržakova ul

3

Vošnjakova ul

Kersnikova ul

Dunajska cesta

Trg Osvobodilne Fronte

7

8

9

6

10

11

To Metelkova, Orto Bar & Ethnographic Museum

2

16

Slovenska cesta

5

4

Pražakova

15

14

12

18

17

Trdinova

Cigaletova ul

20

Miklošiceva

Čufarjeva

13

Kolodvorska

To Meredita Agency

Tivolska

Puharjeva ul

19

21

To Tivoli Castle

25

24

Štefanova ul

Prešernova

Župančičeva ul

cesta

23

Argentinski Park

Tavčarjeva

22

Dalmatinova

Miklošičev Park

44

Komenskega ul

Resljeva cesta

26

Cankarjeva cesta

28

Tomšičeva

37

38

39

40

35

36

34

33

Copova

Trg Ajdovščina

42

43

41

Center

51

50

52

49

48

54

To Atlas Express, Park Hotel, Dijaški Dom Tabor, Medical Centre, Cerin Pizzeria, Reformator Bar & Birdland

Prečna

46

45

47

Trubarjeva

Dragon Drive

To Postojna (53km) & Coast

27

Prešernova

29

Trg Narodnih Herojev

30

31

Beethovnova

Slovenska cesta

32

Nazorjeva ul

River

Ljubljanica

53

Prešernov trg

56

55

58

59

Vodnikov trg

To Rožnik Hill & Zoo

Šubičeva ul

Trg Republike

79

76

77

78

80

74

Erjavčeva cesta

Plečnikov trg

75

subway

Kongresni trg

Wolfova

Triple Bridge

Ribji trg

57

Cankarjevo

69

70

71

72

73

Dvorni trg

68

67

Pogarčarjev trg

61

60

Mestni trg

62

63

Ciril-Metodov trg

Old Town

64

66

65

To Rog Bicycle Rental & Dijaški Dom Poljane

Krekov trg

To Dijaški Dom Shanghai & Full Spon

Študentovska ul

To Meson Don Felipe

Gregorčičeva

Igriška

Rimska

cesta

Shoemaker Bridge

Pod Trančo

Vegova

81

86

85

82

83

84

87

88

Turjaška ul

Novi trg

89

Stari trg

Reber ul

Ulica na Grad

Trg Francoske Revolucije

Gosposka

Slovenska

Zoisova

Krakovo

Breg

Ljubljanica

River

Gornji trg

Levstikov trg

90

91

92

Rožna ul

Karlovška cesta

0   100   200m
0   100   200yd

LJUBLJANA

PLACES TO STAY
35 Slon Hotel & Cafe
44 Hotel Turist & Klub Central
50 Grand Hotel Union

PLACES TO EAT
12 Burek Stand
19 Evropa Café
22 Tav arjev Hram
23 Orient
37 Joe Pena's Cantina y Bar
38 Daj-Dam
41 Šestica
42 Super 5 Food Stand
47 Napoli Pizzeria
58 Ribca Seafood Bar
69 Delikatesa
71 Ljubljanski Dvor
72 Burja Delicatessen
81 Foculus Pizzeria
89 Pizzeria Romeo
90 Sichuan
92 Špajza

OTHER
1   Tivoli Recreation Centre, Zlati
    Klub Sauna & Klub Manhattan
2   Ilirija Swimming Pool
3   Alpine Association of
    Slovenia
4   Slovenijaturist Travel Agency
    & Burek Stand
5   Main Post Office
6   Canadian Embassy
7   Post Office (Customs)
8   City Airport Buses
9   Bus Station

10 A Banka with ATM
11 Kompas Cinema
13 Avis Car Rental
14 Kinoteka Cinema
15 Kompas Hertz Car Rental
16 City Bus Ticket Kiosks
17 Klub K4 & University Student
    Centre
18 Adria Airways Office
20 A Banka
21 Banka Koper with ATM
24 National Gallery
25 Serbian Orthodox Church
26 Museum of Modern Art
27 US Embassy
28 Opera House
29 National Museum
30 Parliament Building
31 Gajo Jazz Club
32 Mladinska Knjiga Bookshop
33 Post Office (Poste Restante)
34 Hida Exchange Bureau
36 Komuna Cinema
39 Cankarjeva Založba Bookshop
40 Kompas Travel Agency &
    Holidays' Pub
43 SKB Banka
45 TrueBar
46 Patrick's Irish Pub
48 Art Nouveau Bank Buildings
49 Union Cinema
51 Eldorado
52 Franciscan Church
53 Urbanc Building/
    Centromerkur Department
    Store
54 Erazem Travel Office

55 Prešeren Monument
56 Ura Building
57 Tourist Information Centre
    (TIC)
59 Produce Market
60 Cathedral of Saint Nicholas
61 Hida Exchange Bureau/
    Seminary
62 Robba Fountain
63 Town Hall
64 Ljubljana Castle
65 Pentagonal Tower
66 Castle Tower
67 Café Boheme
68 Maček
70 Filharmonija
73 Ljubljana University
74 Ursuline Church of the Holy
    Trinity
75 The Brewery Pub
76 Maximarket Department
    Store & Maxim Self-Service
    Restaurant
77 Globtour Agency
78 Nova Ljubljanska Banka
79 UK & Australian Embassy
80 Cankarjev Dom (Cultural
    Centre)
82 Ilirija Column
83 Križanke Booking Office
84 Križanke/Summer Festival
    Theatre
85 Cultural Information Centre
86 National & University Library
87 Kod & Kam Bookshop
88 Mladi Turist
91 Church of St Florian

office of the Slovenian Youth Hostel Association. It sells hostel cards (1800 SIT to 2200 SIT, depending on age), but you're supposed to have resided in the country for six months.

Slovenijaturist (☎ 431 5055), Slovenska cesta 58, sells BIJ international train tickets (one-third cheaper than regular fares) to those under 26 years of age.

The American Express representative is Atlas Express (☎ 433 2028) at Trubarjeva cesta 50 in Ljubljana. It will hold clients' mail but doesn't cash travellers cheques.

Bookshops Ljubljana's largest bookshop is Mladinska Knjiga at Slovenska cesta 29. It has an extensive collection of books in English and it also has a branch on Miklošičeva

cesta 40, opposite the bus station. Another good chain with a shop at Slovenska cesta 37 is Cankarjeva Založba. Kod & Kam, Trg Francoske Revolucije 7, is excellent for travel guides and maps.

The best places for English and other foreign-language newspapers and magazines are the newsstand in the lobby of the Grand Hotel Union, Miklošičeva cesta 1, and the one in the basement of the Maximarket department store on Trg Republike.

Laundry A couple of the student dormitories, including Dijaški Dom Poljane about 1.5km east of the Old Town at Potočnikova ul 3 and Dijaški Dom Kam (Building C) at Kardeljeva ploščad 14, north of the centre in

Bežigrad, have washing machines and dryers that you can use, as does the Ježica camping ground. Chemoexpress at Wolfova ul 12 near Prešernov trg is an old-style laundry and dry cleaner open 7 am to 6 pm weekdays.

Left Luggage The 24-hour left-luggage office (*garderoba*; 200 SIT per piece) at the train station is on platform No 1. A smaller garderoba (open 5.30 am to 8.15 pm) is inside the bus station.

Medical Services You can see a doctor at the medical centre (klinični center; ☎ 433 6236 or ☎ 431 3123) at Zaloška cesta 7, which is in Tabor east of the Park Hotel. The emergency unit (*urgenca*) is open 24 hours a day.

Things to See & Do

The most picturesque sights of old Ljubljana are along both banks of the Ljubljanica, a tributary of the Sava that curves around the foot of Castle Hill.

Opposite the TIC in the Kresija building is the celebrated **Triple Bridge**. In 1931, Jože Plečnik added the side bridges to the original central span dating from 1842. On the northern side of the bridge is Prešernov trg with its pink **Franciscan church** (1660), a statue (1905) of poet France Prešeren and some lovely Art Nouveau buildings. A lively pedestrian street, Čopova ul, runs to the north-west.

On the south side of the bridge in Mestni trg, the baroque **Robba Fountain** stands before the **town hall** (1718). Italian sculptor Francesco Robba designed this fountain in 1751 and modelled it after one in Rome. Enter the town hall to see the double Gothic courtyard. To the south of Mestni trg is **Stari trg**, atmospheric by day or night. North-east are the twin towers of the **Cathedral of St Nicholas** (1708), which contains impressive frescoes. Behind the cathedral is Ljubljana's colourful open-air **produce market** (closed Sunday) and a lovely **colonnade** along the riverside designed by Plečnik.

Študentovska ul, opposite the Vodnik statue in the market square, leads up to **Ljubljana Castle**. The castle has been under renovation for decades, but you can climb the 19th-century **Castle Tower** to the west

(10 am to dusk daily; 200/100 SIT adults/ children) and view the exhibits in a Gothic chapel and the **Pentagonal Tower** (closed Monday). Reber ul between Stari trg 17 and 19 also leads up to the castle.

At Gosposka ul 14 near the now-closed Municipal Museum is the **National & University Library** (1941) designed by Plečnik, and north on Gosposka ul at Kongresni trg 12 is the main building of **Ljubljana University** (1902), formerly the regional parliament. The lovely **Philharmonic Hall** (Filharmonija), at No 10 on the south-east corner of the square, is home to the Slovenian Philharmonic Orchestra. The **Ursuline Church of the Holy Trinity** (1726), with an altar by Robba, faces Kongresni trg to the west.

Walk west on Šubičeva ul to several of the city's fine museums. The **National Museum**, Muzejska ul 1 (open 10 am to 6 pm Tuesday to Sunday; 500/300 SIT), erected in 1885, has prehistory, natural history and ethnography collections. The highlight is a Celtic situla, a kind of pail, from the 6th century BC sporting a fascinating relief.

The **National Gallery**, Cankarjeva ul 20, offers Slovenian portraits and landscapes from the 17th to 19th centuries, as well as copies of medieval frescoes; the gallery's new wing to the north at Puharjeva ul 9 (separate entrance) has a permanent collection of European paintings from the Middle Ages to the 20th century and is used for temporary exhibits. It is open 10 am to 6 pm Tuesday to Sunday, and entry costs 500/300 SIT except on Saturday when it's free.

Diagonally opposite the National Gallery, at Cankarjeva ul 15, is the **Museum of Modern Art**, where the International Biennial of Graphic Arts is held every other summer in odd-numbered years. It is open 10 am to 6 pm Tuesday to Saturday and to 1 pm on Sunday. Admission costs 500/300 SIT for adults/seniors; it's free for children and on Sunday. The Serbian Orthodox **Church of Sts Cyril & Methodius** opposite the Museum of Modern Art is worth entering to see the beautiful modern frescoes (open 3 to 6 pm Tuesday to Saturday). The subway from the Museum of Modern Art leads to Ljubljana's green lung, **Tivoli Park**.

If you have time (or the inclination) for another museum or two, head for the **Museum** of **Modern History**, Celovška cesta 23 (just beyond the Tivoli Recreation Centre), which traces the history of Slovenia in the 20th century via multimedia, or the new **Slovenian Ethnographic Museum** at Metlikova ul 2. Both are open 10 am to 6 pm Tuesday to Sunday and cost 500/300 SIT.

Activities

The **Tivoli Recreation Centre**, in the Tivoli Park at Celovška cesta 25, has bowling alleys, tennis courts, an indoor swimming pool, a fitness centre and a roller-skating rink. There's even a popular sauna called **Zlati Klub** that has several saunas, a steam room, warm and cold splash pools and even a small outside pool surrounded by high walls so you can sunbathe in the nude (mixed sexes). Entry costs 1800 SIT at the weekend and 1500 SIT on weekdays and until 1 pm.

The outdoor **Ilirija pool** opposite the Tivoli hotel at Celovška cesta 3 is open in summer from 10 am to 7 pm on weekdays, 9 am to 8 pm at the weekend.

Organised Tours

From June to September, a two-hour guided tour in English (700/500 SIT adults/seniors, students and children) sponsored by the TIC departs daily at 5 pm from the town hall in Mestni trg. During the rest of the year there are tours at 11 am on Sunday only.

Places to Stay

Camping Some 6km north of Center on the Sava (bus No 6 or 8) is *Camping Ježica* (☎ 568 3913, ✉ acjezica@siol.net, Dunajska cesta 270), with a large, shady camping area (1200 SIT per person with a caravan or tent) and three dozen cramped little bungalows for two costing 8600 SIT. The camping ground is open all year.

Hostels & Student Dormitories Four student dormitories (dijaški dom) open their doors to foreign travellers in July and August. The most central by far is the *Dijaški Dom Tabor* (☎ 232 1067, ✉ ssljddta1s@guest .arnes.si, Vidovdanska ul 7), opposite the Park Hotel and affiliated with Hostelling International (HI). It charges 3100 SIT for a single room and 2300 SIT for a bed in a double or triple, including breakfast.

The *Dijaški Dom Bežigrad* (☎ 534 2867, Kardeljeva ploščad 28), another HI member, is in the Bežigrad district 2km north of the train and bus stations. It has doubles/triples with shower and toilet for 2900/2400 SIT per person and rooms with one to three beds with shared facilities for 2000 SIT per person. A HI card gets you about 10% off. The Bežigrad has 50 rooms available from late June to late August. However, this drops to 20 rooms (only available on weekends) at other times of year.

Dijaška Dom Ivana Cankarja (☎ 174 8600, Poljanska cesta 26) is just out of the town centre and has singles/doubles/triples for 3460/2800/2600 SIT including breakfast (10% less for students) for rooms with shared facilities, available in summer only.

Private Rooms & Apartments The TIC has about 40 private rooms on its list, but just a handful are in Center. Most of the others would require a bus trip up to Bežigrad. Prices range from 3500 SIT for singles and 5000 SIT for doubles. It also has eight apartments and one studio – four of which are central – for one to four people costing from 9700 SIT to 16,700 SIT. Reception is at the Meredita agency (☎ 431 1102, Kotnikova ul 5) in the Ledina shopping centre.

Hotels One of the cheapest deals in town is the 15-room *Super Li Bellevue Hotel* (☎ 433 4049, Pod Gozdom 12) on the northern edge of Tivoli Park. There are no rooms with private bath, but bright and airy singles with basins are 5300 SIT, doubles 7300 SIT.

The 122-room *Park Hotel* (☎ 433 1306, fax 433 0546, Tabor 9) is where most people usually end up as it's the city's only large budget hotel close to Center and the Old Town. It's pretty basic, but the price is right – 5800/7200 SIT for singles/doubles with breakfast and shared shower, and 6954/8880 SIT with private shower. Students with cards get a 20% discount. The staff are very helpful and friendly.

A reasonable alternative in the centre of town is the three-star *Hotel Turist* (☎ 432 2343, fax 231 9291, ✉ info@hotelturist.si, Dalmatinova 15) which has single/double rooms for 10,000/14,600 SIT (2000 SIT less off-season).

Places to Eat

Restaurants The *Tavčarjev Hram (Tavčarjev ul 4)* is a bar and restaurant with good, reasonably priced Slovenian dishes. The *Šestica (Slovenska cesta 40)* is a 200-year-old standby with a pleasant courtyard. Main courses are in the 700 SIT to 1500 SIT range and lunch menus are priced from 1000 SIT and 1200 SIT. A much more upmarket (and expensive) alternative for Slovenian specialities is the attractive *Špajza (Gornji trg 28)* in the Old Town.

The capital abounds in Italian restaurants and pizzerias. Among the best in town are *Ljubljanski Dvor (Dvorni trg 1)* on the west bank of the Ljubljanica and *Foculus (Gregorčičeva ul 3)* next to the Glej Theatre (small/large pizzas 580/880 SIT, salad bar from 380 to 450 SIT). Other pizza-pasta places include *Pizzeria Romeo (Stari trg 6)* in the Old Town opposite Cafe Julija, *Napoli (Prečna ul 7)* off Trubarjeva cesta and *Čerin (Znamenjska ul 2)* at the eastern end of Trubarjeva cesta.

Meson Don Felipe (Streliška ul 22), south-east of Krekov trg, is Ljubljana's first – and only – tapas bar (270 SIT to 890 SIT).

If you've a yen for some Chinese food, the location of *Sichuan (Gornji trg 23)* below the Church of St Florian is wonderful but the food is much more authentic at *Shanghai (Poljanska cesta 14)*. An upmarket alternative is *Orient (Župančićeva ul 9)*.

The friendly and spacious *Joe Pena's Cantina y Bar (Cankarjeva cesta 6)* serves up hearty portions of Mexican food (main courses 1500 SIT to 1900 SIT) and vegetarians will find a lot on the menu of *Full Spon (Zarnikova ul 3)*, a student hangout.

Cafes For coffee and cakes you might try the elegant *Evropa Cafe (Gosposvetska cesta 2)* on the corner of Slovenska cesta or the *Slon Cafe (Slovenska cesta 34)* in the Slon Hotel.

Self-Service & Fast Food Among the two cheapest places for lunch are the *Maxim* self-service restaurant in the basement of the Maximarket shopping arcade on Trg Republike, and *Daj-Dam (Cankarjeva ul 4)* which has a vegetarian menu (950 SIT). But don't expect Cordon Bleu food; it's real school cafeteria stuff.

For a quick and very tasty lunch, try the fried squid (670 SIT to 900 SIT) or whitebait (300 SIT to 470 SIT) at *Ribca (Pogarčarjev trg)*, a basement seafood bar below the Plečnik Colonnade.

There are *burek stands* (about 250 SIT) at several locations in Ljubljana and among the best is the one on Pražakova ul next to Slovenijaturist and the one at Kolodvorska ul 20 (open 24 hours).

If you want something more substantial, head for the outdoor *Super 5*, which faces Slovenska cesta from the shopping mall in Trg Ajdovščina. It serves cheap and cheerful Balkan grills like *čevapčiči* (600 SIT) and *pljeskavica* (500 SIT to 600 SIT) as well as *klobasa* (sausage; 750 SIT) and is open 24 hours on weekdays, from 3 pm on Saturday and 6 pm on Sunday.

Self-Catering The *supermarket* in the basement of the Maximarket shopping arcade on Trg Republike has about the largest selection in town (open 9 am to 8 pm weekdays, 8 am to 3 pm Saturday). But the best places for picnic supplies are the city's many delicatessens including *Delikatesa (Kongresni trg 9)* and *Burja (Kongresni trg 11)*.

Entertainment

Ask the TIC for its monthly program of events in English called *Where to? in Ljubljana*.

Cinema For first-run films, head for the *Komuna (Cankarjeva ul 1)*, the *Kompas (Miklošičeva cesta 38)* or the *Union (Nazorjeva ul 2)*. They generally have three screenings a day. The *Kinoteka (Miklošičeva cesta 28)* shows art and classic films. Cinema tickets generally cost around 600 SIT, and discounts are usually available at the first session on weekdays.

Clubs The most popular conventional clubs are *Eldorado (Nazorjeva ul 4)* and *Klub Central (Dalmatinova ul 15)* next to the Turist Hotel. The student *Klub K4 (Kersnikova ul 4)* has a disco on some nights. Other popular venues at present for Ljubljana's young bloods are *Hound Dog (Trg Prekomorskih Brigad 4)* in the Hotel M and *Klub Manhattan (Tivoli Recreation Centre, Celovška cesta 25)* in Tivoli Park.

Gay & Lesbian Venues A popular spot for both gays and lesbians on Sunday night is *Roza Klub* at Klub K4, open 10 pm to 4 am. At the Metelkova squat, Ljubljana's version of Christiania in Copenhagen between Metelkova ul and Maistrova ul, there's a cafe/pub for gays called *Club Tiffany*. *Monokel Club* is a popular spot for lesbians in the same building, open Thursday to Monday.

Classical Music, Opera & Dance Ljubljana is home to two orchestras. Concerts are held in various locations all over town, but the main venue – with up to 700 cultural events a year – is *Cankarjev Dom* on Trg Republike. The ticket office (☎ *252 2815*) in the basement of the nearby Maximarket mall is open 10 am to 2 pm and 4.30 to 8 pm on weekdays, 10 am to 1 pm Saturday, and an hour before performances. Tickets cost anywhere between 1500 SIT and 3000 SIT with gala performances as much as 6000 SIT. Also check for concerts at the beautiful *Filharmonija* at Kongresni trg 10.

The ticket office of the *Opera House* (☎ *425 4840, Župančičeva ul 1*), where ballets are also performed, is open 11 am to 1 pm Monday to Friday and an hour before each performance.

For tickets to the Ljubljana Summer Festival and anything else staged at the *Križanke*, go to the booking office (☎ 426 4340 or ☎ 252 6544) behind the Ilirija Column at Trg Francoske Revolucije 1-2. It is open 10 am to 2 pm and 6 to 8 pm weekdays, 10 am to 1 pm on Saturday and one hour before the performance on Sunday.

Rock & Jazz Ljubljana has a number of excellent rock clubs with canned or live music including *Orto Bar* (*Grablovičeva ul 1*) and the *Brewery Pub* (*Plečnikov trg 1*). For jazz, you can't beat the *Gajo Jazz Club* (*Beethovnova ul 8*) near the Parliament building. *Birdland* (*Trubarjeva cesta 50*) has a jam session on Wednesday night and occasional jazz concerts on the weekend.

Pubs & Bars Pleasant and congenial places for a *pivo* or glass of *vino* include *TrueBar* (*Trubarjeva cesta 53*), *Patrick's Irish Pub* (*Prečna ul 6*), *Holidays' Pub* (*Slovenska cesta 36*) next to the Kompas travel agency,

and *Reformator Bar* (*Trubarjeva cesta 18*). In good weather, locals and visitors alike head down to the adjoining *Maček* and *Café Boheme* (*Cankarjevo nabrežje 19 and 21*) for an outdoor drink along the river.

Getting There & Away

Bus You can reach virtually anywhere in the country by bus from the capital. The timetable in the shed-like bus station (☎ 434 3838) on Trg OF lists all routes and times, but here are some sample destinations and one-way fares: Bled (980 SIT, hourly); Bohinj (1480 SIT, hourly); Jesenice (1100 SIT, hourly); Koper (1900 SIT, nine to 12 a day); Maribor (2050 SIT, half-hourly); Murska Sobota (3050 SIT, nine a day); Novo Mesto (1170 SIT, hourly); Piran (2120 SIT, six to 11 a day); Postojna (900 SIT, hourly).

Train All domestic and international trains arrive at and depart from the station (☎ 231 6768) at Trg OF 6. Local trains leave Ljubljana regularly for Bled (760 SIT, 51km); Jesenice (690 SIT, 64km); Koper (1380 SIT, 153km); Maribor (1380 SIT, 156km); Murska Sobota (2080 SIT, 216km); and Novo Mesto (760 SIT, 75km).

There's a 200 SIT surcharge on the domestic InterCity train tickets. For details on international trains to/from Ljubljana, see the introductory Getting There & Away section of this chapter.

Getting Around

To/From the Airport Bus No 28 (460 SIT) makes the run between Ljubljana and Brnik airport, 23km to the north-west, hourly at 10 minutes past the hour Monday to Friday and every two hours on the weekend. A taxi will cost between 4500 SIT and 5000 SIT.

Bus Ljubljana's bus system, run by LPP (☎ 519 4114), is excellent and very user-friendly. There are 22 lines; five of them (Nos 1, 2, 3, 6 and 11) are considered main lines. These start at 3.15 am and run till midnight while the rest operate from 5 am to 10.30 pm. You can pay on board (140 SIT) or use tiny yellow plastic tokens (100 SIT) available at newsstands, tobacconists, post offices and the two kiosks on the pavement in front of Slovenska cesta 55.

Car & Motorcycle Three international car-rental chains are Kompas Hertz (☎ 231 1241), Miklošičeva ul 11; National (☎ 588 4450), Baragova 5; and Avis (☎ 430 8010), Čufarjeva ul 2. They also have counters at the airport. Two excellent smaller agencies are ABC Rent a Car (☎ 04-206 1684) at Brnik airport and Avtoimpex (☎ 505 5025), Celovška cesta 150.

Taxi You can call a taxi on one of 10 numbers: ☎ 9700 to ☎ 9709.

Bicycle Two places that visitors can rent bicycles are Rog (☎ 231 5868), next to Rozmanova ul 1 (1500 SIT per day; open 8 am to 7 pm weekdays, till noon Saturday) and Kos Damjan (☎ 505 3606) at Tugomerjeva ul 35 (1000 SIT).

Julian Alps

Slovenia shares the Julian Alps in the north-western corner of the country with Italy. Three-headed Mt Triglav (2864m), the country's highest peak, is climbed regularly by thousands of weekend warriors, but there are countless less ambitious hikes on offer in the region. Lakes Bled and Bohinj make ideal starting points – Bled with its comfortable resort facilities, Bohinj right beneath the rocky crags themselves. Most of this spectacular area falls within the boundaries of the Triglav National Park, which was established in 1924.

BLED
☎ 04 • pop 11,113
Bled, a fashionable resort at just over 501m, is set on an idyllic, 2km-long emerald-green lake with a little island and church in the centre and a dramatic castle towering overhead. Trout and carp proliferate in the clear water, which is surprisingly warm and a pleasure to swim in or go boating on. To the north-east, the highest peaks of the Karavanke range form a natural boundary with Austria, and the Julian Alps lie to the west. Bled has been a favourite destination for travellers for decades. All in all, it is beautiful but be warned that it can get very crowded – and pricey – in season.

Orientation
Bled village is at the north-eastern end of the lake below Bled Castle. The bus station is also here on Cesta Svobode, but the main Lesce-Bled train station is about 4km to the south-east. In addition there's Bled Jezero, a branch-line train station north-west of the lake, not far from the camping ground.

Information
Tourist Offices The tourist office (☎ 574 1122, fax 574 1555, ⓔ info@dzt.bled.si) is next to the Park Hotel at Cesta Svobode 15. Ask for the useful English booklet *Bled Tourist Information* which is reproduced on the town's useful Web site, www.bled.si. From April to October the office is open from 8 am to 7 pm Monday to Saturday (to 10 pm in July and August) and from 9 am to 3 pm on Sunday (to 10 pm in July and August). From November to March the hours are 9 am to 5 pm Monday to Saturday and 9 am to 2 pm on Sunday. Kompas (☎ 574 1515) in the Triglav shopping centre at Ljubljanska cesta 4 sells good hiking maps. The Triglav National Park information centre (☎ 574 1188) is at Kidričeva cesta 2 on the lake's northern shore (open from 7 am to 3 pm weekdays only).

Money Gorenjska Banka in the Park Hotel shopping complex and across from the casino on Cesta Svobode is open 9 to 11.30 am and 2 to 5 pm weekdays and 8 to 11 am Saturday. Kompas and the tourist office change money but there is no ATM in town.

Post & Communications The main post office, open 7 am to 7 pm weekdays and till noon on Saturday, is at Ljubljanska cesta 10.

Things to See
There are several trails up to **Bled Castle** (open daily, 500/250 SIT for adults/children) the easiest being the one going south from behind the hostel at Grajska cesta 17. The castle was the seat of the Bishops of Brixen (South Tirol) for over 800 years; set atop a steep cliff 100m above the lake, it offers magnificent views in clear weather. The castle's **museum** presents the history of the area and allows a peep into a small 16th-century chapel.

BLED

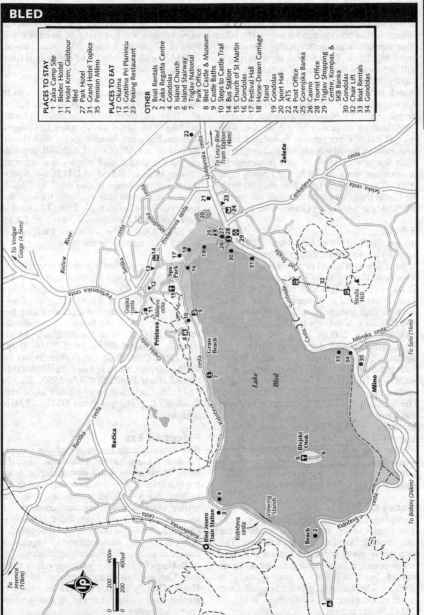

Bled's other striking feature is tiny **Bled Island** at the western end of the lake. The tolling 'bell of wishes' echoes across the lake from the tall white belfry rising above the dense vegetation. It's said that all who ring it will get their wish; naturally it chimes constantly. Underneath the present baroque church are the foundations of what was a pre-Romanesque chapel, unique in Slovenia. Most people reach the island on a *pletna*, a large gondola hand-propelled by a boatman. The price (1500 SIT per person) includes a half-hour visit to the island, church and belfry. If there are two or three of you it would be cheaper and more fun to hire a rowing boat (1000 SIT an hour for up to four people) from the Castle Baths on the shore below the castle, in Mlino or in front of the Grand Hotel Toplice.

Hiking

An excellent half-day hike from Bled features a visit to lovely **Vintgar Gorge** 4.5km to the north-west. Head north-west on Prešernova cesta then north on Partizanska cesta to Cesta v Vintgar. This will take you to Podhom, where signs point the way to the gorge entrance (open daily from May to October, 400/200 SIT). A wooden footbridge hugs the rock wall for 1600m along the Radovna River, crisscrossing the raging torrent four times over rapids, waterfalls and pools before reaching **Šum Waterfall**. From there a trail leads over Hom Hill (834m) eastward to the ancient pilgrimage **Church of St Catherine**. The trail then leads due south through Zasip and back to Bled. From late June to mid-September an Alpetour bus makes the run from Bled's bus station to Vintgar daily, or take the hourly Krnica bus to Spodnje Gorje which is a kilometre from the entrance; in summer there are two daily buses from Spodnje Gorje to the gorge entrance.

Places to Stay

Camping The *Zaka Campsite* (☎ 574 1117) is in a quiet valley at the western end of the lake about 2.5km from the bus station. The location is good and there's even a beach, tennis courts, a large restaurant and a supermarket, but Zaka fills up very quickly in summer. The camping ground is open from April to October and costs from DM9 to DM12.50 per person.

Hostels The *Bledec Hostel* (☎ 574 5250, *Grajska cesta 17)* is open year-round except in November, and has a total of 56 beds available in 13 rooms. It costs DM20 per person, or DM26 with breakfast, and check-in is from 7 am to 10 pm.

Private Rooms Finding a private room in Bled is easy. The travel agencies have extensive lists, and there are lots of houses around the lake with 'sobe' or 'Zimmer frei' signs. Kompas has single/double rooms with shared shower from DM21/30 to DM26/40, depending on the season, and singles/doubles with shower from DM25/38 to DM38/64. Apartments for two range from DM47 to DM74. Rooms and apartments available through the tourist office, Globtour Bled (☎ 574 1821) at the Krim Hotel, Ljubljanska cesta 7, and ATS (☎ 574 1736), at the Vezenine mall at Kajuhova ul 1, cost about the same.

Hotels Most of Bled's hotels are pretty expensive affairs. Among the cheapest is the 212-bed *Hotel Krim* (☎ 574 1662, fax 574 3729, ℮ hotelkrim@hotel-krim.si, Ljubljanska cesta 7) in the town centre which has singles/doubles at the height of the season for DM75/110. On the waterfront, the attractive *Pension Mlino* (☎ 574 1404, fax 574 1506, Cesta Svobode 45) has rooms for DM60/90 and, for a splurge, the old-world *Grand Hotel Toplice* (☎ 579 1000, fax 574 1841, ℮ toplice@hotel-toplice.si, Cesta Svobode 12), charges from DM132/224 in high season.

Places to Eat

Bled's best choice for an affordable meal is the homy *Gostilna Pri Planincu* (Grajska cesta 8), which is just a stone's throw from the bus station. The menu includes some excellent dishes such as mushroom soup and grilled chicken with fries and salad, which shouldn't cost much more than 1800 SIT. *Okarina* (Riklijeva cesta 9) has first-rate Indian cuisine with an assortment of vegetarian dishes as well as Slovenian specialities.

Peking (Ul Narodnih Herojev 3) is a decent Chinese restaurant opposite the Krim Hotel. There's a small *market* near the bus station and a *supermarket* in the Triglav shopping centre.

Getting There & Around

If you're coming from Ljubljana, take the bus not the train. The train from Ljubljana will leave you at the Lesce-Bled station, 4km south-east of the lake while the bus leaves you in the town centre. Buses run at least once an hour to Bohinj as far as the Zlatorog Hotel, Kranj, Ljubljana and Podhom-Zasip. One bus a day from July to mid-September goes to Bovec via Kranjska Gora and the heart-stopping Vršič Pass.

Lesce-Bled train station gets up to 15 trains a day from Ljubljana (55 minutes) via Škofja Loka, Kranj and Radovljica. They continue on to Jesenice (15 minutes), where about eight cross the Austrian border, continuing on to Germany. Up to six daily trains from Jesenice pass through Bled Jezero station on their way to Bohinjska Bistrica (20 minutes) and Nova Gorica (1¾ hours).

Kompas rents out bicycles and mountain bikes for 600/1100/1600 SIT for every hour/half-day/day.

BOHINJ
☎ 04

Bohinj is a larger and much less developed glacial lake 26km to the south-west of Bled. It is exceedingly beautiful, with high mountains rising directly from the basin-shaped valley. There are secluded beaches for swimming off the trail along the north shore and many hiking possibilities, including an ascent of Mt Triglav.

Orientation

There is no town called Bohinj; the name refers to the entire valley, its settlements and the lake. The largest town in the area is Bohinjska Bistrica (population 3080), 6km to the east of the lake. The main settlement right on the lake is Ribčev Laz at the south-eastern corner. Here, all in a row just up from the bus stop, you'll find the post office, tourist office, a supermarket, a pizzeria, and the Alpinum travel agency.

About 1km north across the Sava Bohinjka River and at the mouth of the Mostnica Canyon sits the town of Stara Fužina. The Zlatorog Hotel is situated at Ukanc at the western end of the lake near the camping ground and the cable car, which takes visitors up to Mt Vogel (1922m).

Information

Tourist Offices The helpful and very efficient tourist office (☎ 572 3370, fax 572 3330, ℮ tic@bohinj.si) at Ribčev Laz 48 is open 7.30 am to 8 pm daily from July to mid-September. During the rest of the year, the hours are 8 am to 6 pm Monday to Saturday and 9 am to 3 pm Sunday. Its Web site at www.bohinj.si contains much useful information.

Money The tourist office can change money but the rate is not very good, and there's a 3% commission. Gorenjska Banka has a branch in Bohinjska Bistrica at Trg Svobode 2b, about 100m east of the Slovenijaturist office.

Post & Communications The post office at Ribčev Laz 47 is open 8 am to 6 pm weekdays with a couple of half-hour breaks and until noon on Saturday.

Travel Agencies Alpinum travel agency (☎ 572 3441), which organises sporting activities in Bohinj, is a couple of doors down from the tourist office at Ribčev Laz 50.

Things to See & Do

The **Church of St John the Baptist**, on the northern side of the Sava Bohinjka across the stone bridge from Ribčev Laz, has exquisite 15th-century frescoes and can lay claim to being the most beautiful and evocative church in Slovenia. The **Alpine Dairy Museum** at house No 181 in Stara Fužina, about 1.5km north of Ribčev Laz, has a small but interesting collection related to Alpine dairy farming in the Bohinj Valley, once the most important such centre in Slovenia (300/160 SIT). If you have time, take a walk over to **Studor**, a village a couple of kilometres to the east renowned for its *kozolci* and *toplarji*, single and double hayracks that are unique to Slovenia.

The Alpinsport kiosk (☎ 572 3486) at Ribčev Laz 53, to the right just before you cross the stone bridge to the church, rents out equipment. **Canoes** and **kayaks** cost from 700/3000 per hour/day. It also organises guided mountain tours and kayaking trips on the Sava (3400 SIT and 3200 SIT) and 'canyoning' through the rapids of the Mostnica Gorge stuffed into a neoprene suit, life jacket and helmet for 10,400 SIT.

SLOVENIA

The **Vogel cable car**, above the camping ground at the western end of Lake Bohinj about 5km from Ribčev Laz, will whisk you 1000m up into the mountains. It runs every half-hour year round except in November, from 7.30 am to 6 pm (till 8 pm in July and August). Adults/children pay 1000/700 SIT for a return ticket. From the upper station (1540m) you can scale **Mt Vogel** in a couple of hours for a sweeping view of the region.

Places to Stay

Camping The large and beautifully situated *Zlatorog Camping Ground* (☎ 572 3441) on the lake near the Zlatorog Hotel costs 1000 SIT to 1600 SIT per person, depending on the season; it's open from May to September.

Private Rooms The tourist office can arrange private singles/doubles with shower in Ribčev Laz, Stara Fužina and neighbouring villages for 1920/3200 SIT in the low season and up to 2400/4000 SIT in July and August (though there's always a 30% surcharge for stays of less than three days).

Places to Eat

The *MK* (Ribčev Laz 50), a restaurant and pizzeria next to the Alpinum travel agency, is very popular year round. If you've got wheels of any sort, head for *Gostišče Rupa* (Srednja Vas 87), about 5km north-east of Ribčev Laz. It has some of the best home-cooking in Slovenia. For a truly different lunch, try *Planšar* (Stara Fužina 179) opposite the Alpine Dairy Museum. It specialises in home-made dairy products, and you can taste a number of local specialities for about 700 SIT. The *Mercator Supermarket* (Ribčev Laz 49) is open 7 am to 6.30 pm weekdays and to 5 pm on Saturday.

Getting There & Around

There are hourly buses between Ribčev Laz and Ljubljana via Bled, Radovljica, Kranj and Bohinjska Bistrica. There are also about six local buses a day to Bohinjska Bistrica via Stara Fužina, Studor and Srednja Vas. All of these buses stop near the post office on Triglavska cesta in Bohinjska Bistrica and in Ribčev Laz before carrying on to the Zlatorog Hotel in Ukanc. The closest train station is at Bohinjska Bistrica on the Jesenice-Nova Gorica line.

Alpinsport rents out mountain bikes and helmets for 700/2900 SIT per hour/day.

HIKING MT TRIGLAV

The Julian Alps are among the finest hiking areas in Central and Eastern Europe. A mountain hut (*planinska koča* or *planinski dom*) is normally less than five hours' walk away. The huts in the higher regions are open from July to September, and in the lower regions from June to October. You'll never be turned away if the weather looks bad, but some huts on Triglav get very crowded at weekends, especially in August and September. A bed for the night should cost about 2000 SIT per person. Meals are also available, so you don't need to carry a lot of gear. Leave most of your things below, but warm clothes, sturdy boots and good physical condition are indispensable.

The best months for hiking are August to October, though above 1500m you can encounter winter weather conditions at any time. Keep to the trails that are well marked with a red circle and a white centre, rest frequently and never *ever* try to trek alone. Before you set out, pick up a copy of the 1:20,000 *Triglav* map or the 1:50,000-scale *Julijske Alpe – Vzhodni Del* (*Julian Alps – Eastern Part*) published by the Alpine Association and available at bookshops and tourist offices.

The Route from Bohinj

An hour's hike west of the Zlatorog Hotel at Ukanc is the **Savica Waterfall** (300/150 SIT), the source of the Sava River, which gushes from a limestone cave and falls 60m into a narrow gorge.

From the waterfall a path zigzags up the steep Komarča Crag. From the top of this cliff (1340m) there's an excellent view of Lake Bohinj. Farther north, around three to four hours from the falls, is the *Koča pri Triglavskih Jezerih* (mobile/cellphone ☎ 0609-615 235), a 104-bed hut at the southern end of the fantastic Triglav Lakes Valley (1685m) where you'll spend the night. If you want a good overview of the valley and its seven permanent lakes (the others fill up in spring only), you can climb to Mt Tičarica (2091m) to the north-east in about one hour. An alternative – though longer – route from the waterfall to the Triglav Lakes Valley is via **Dom na Komni** (mobile/cellphone ☎ 0609-611 221) and the Komna Plateau.

On the second day, you hike up the valley, past the largest glacial lakes then north-east to the desert-like Hribarice Plateau (2358m). You descend to the Dolič Saddle (2164m) where the **Tržaška Koča na Doliču** (mobile/cellphone ☎ 0609-614 780) has 60 beds. You would have walked about four hours by now from the Koča pri Triglavskih Jezerih and could well carry on to **Dom Planika pod Triglavom** (mobile/cellphone ☎ 0609-614 773) about 1½ hours to the north-east, but this 80-bed hut fills up quickly.

From Dom Planika it's just over an hour to the summit of Triglav (2864m), a well trodden path indeed. Don't be surprised if you find yourself being turned over to have your bottom beaten with a birch switch. It's a long-established tradition for Triglav 'virgins'.

Soča Valley

BOVEC & KOBARID
☎ 05

The Soča Valley, defined by the bluer-than-blue Soča River, stretches from Triglav National Park to Nova Gorica and is one of the most beautiful and peaceful spots in Slovenia. Of course it wasn't always that way. During much of WWI, this was the site of the infamous Soča (or Isonzo) Front, which claimed the lives of an estimated one million people and was immortalised by the American writer Ernest Hemingway in his novel *A Farewell to Arms*. Today visitors flock to the town of Kobarid to relive these events at the award-winning **Kobarid Museum** (500/400 SIT adults/students and children) at Gregorčičeva ul 10 or, more commonly, head for Bovec, 21km to the north, to take part in some of the best white-water rafting in Europe. The season lasts from April to October.

In Bovec, the people to see for the latter are Soča Rafting (☎ 389 6200 or mobile/cellphone ☎ 041-724 472) 100m from the Alp hotel (up the hill from the main square) or Bovec Rafting Team (☎ 388 6128) in the small kiosk on Trg Golobarskih Žrtev opposite the Martinov Hram restaurant. Rafting trips on the Soča that last about 1½ hours cost 4790/5980 SIT on weekdays/weekends

(including neoprene long john, windcheater, life jacket, helmet and paddle). A kayak costs from 3230 SIT for four hours including equipment; a two-person canoe is 5380 SIT. There are kayaking courses on offer in summer (eg, a two-day intensive course for beginners costs 11,470 SIT).

In Kobarid, the tourist office in the Kobarid Museum (☎ 389 0000) and, in Bovec, the Avrigo Tours agency (☎ 388 6123) next to the Alp hotel at Trg Golobarskih Žrtev 47 can organise *private rooms* from 2410 SIT per person for a double. There are four camping grounds in Bovec, *Polovnik* (☎ 388 6069) being the closest, and there is one in Kobarid – *Koren* (☎ 388 5312) .

Getting There & Away
There are up to six daily buses between Kobarid and Bovec and to Tolmin. Other destinations include Ljubljana (two to five), Nova Gorica (four to six) and Cerkno (up to five). In July and August there's a daily bus to Ljubljana via the Vršič Pass and Kranjska Gora. From Bled there are three trains a day to Most na Soči (55 minutes) from which there are regular buses to Kobarid and Bovec (45 minutes).

Karst Region

POSTOJNA
☎ 05

Vying with Bled as the top tourist spot in Slovenia, **Postojna Cave** continues to attract the hordes, but many travellers feel they've seen Disneyland after their visit – especially if they've first been to the more natural Škocjan Caves, 33km to the south-west. Visitors get to see about 5.7km of the cave's 27km on a 1½ hour tour in their own language; about 4km are covered by an electric train that will shuttle you through colourfully lit karst formations along the so-called Old Passage and the remaining 1700m is on foot. The tour ends with a viewing of a tank full of *Proteus anguinus*, the unique salamander-like beasties inhabiting Slovenia's karst caves. Dress warmly as the cave is a constant 8°C (with 95% humidity) all year.

From May to September, tours leave on the hour between 9 am and 6 pm daily. In

March and April and again in October there are tours at 10 am, noon, 2 and 4 pm with an extra daily one at 5 pm in April and additional tours at the weekend in October at 11 am and 1, 3 and 5 pm. Between November and February, tours leave at 10 am and 2 pm on weekdays, with extra ones added at noon and 4 pm at the weekend and on public holidays. Admission costs 2100/1050 SIT for adults/students and children.

If you have some extra time on your hands, visit **Predjama Castle** (700/350 SIT), the awesome 16th-century fortress perched in the gaping mouth of a hilltop cavern 9km north-west of Postojna. As close as you'll get from Postojna by local bus (and during the school year only), though, is Bukovje, a village about 2km north of Predjama. A taxi from Postojna plus an hour's wait at the castle costs 10,000 SIT.

Orientation & Information

The cave is about 2km north-west of Postojna's bus centre and bus station while the train station is a kilometre south-east of the centre. The caves are well-signposted from the town centre and taxis are available from the bus and train stations. The unhelpful tourist office (☎ 720 1610), Tržaška cesta 4, is open 8 am to 6 pm (7 pm in summer) weekdays and till noon on Saturday. Kompas (☎ 726 4281) at Titov trg 2a has *private rooms* from 2400 SIT per person.

Getting There & Away

Postojna is a day trip from Ljubljana or a stopover on the way to/from the coast or Croatian Istria; almost all buses between the capital and the coast stop there. There are direct trains to Postojna from Ljubljana (67km, one hour) and Koper (86km, 1½ hours) but the bus station is closer to the caves.

ŠKOCJAN CAVES
☎ 05

These caves, near the village of Matavun 4km south-east of Divača (between Postojna and Koper), have been heavily promoted since 1986 when they were first entered on Unesco's World Heritage List. There are seven 1½-hour tours a day from June to September at 10 and 11.30 am and on the hour from 1 to 5 pm. In April, May and October

they leave at 10 am and at 1 and 3.30 pm. From November to March there's a daily visit at 10 am and an extra one at 3 pm on Sunday and holidays. The entry fee is 1500 SIT for adults and 700 SIT for children aged six to 12. These caves are in more natural surroundings – some consider a visit the highlight of their stay in Slovenia – than Postojna Cave but tough to reach without your own transport. From the train station at Divača (up to a dozen trains daily to/from Ljubljana), you can follow a path leading south-east through the village of Dolnje Ležeče to Matavun. The driver of any bus heading along the highway to/from the coast will let you off at the access road (there are huge signs announcing the caves) if you ask in advance. From there you can walk the remaining 1.5km to the caves' entrance.

LIPICA
☎ 05 • pop 130

The famous Lipizzaner horses of the imperial Spanish Riding School in Vienna have been bred here since the 18th century and now perform at equestrian events around the world. You can tour the 311-hectare **Lipica Stud Farm** all year round; there are between four and seven tours a day (1000 SIT). A tour combined with an exhibition performance in which the snow-white creatures go through their paces is available at 3 pm Tuesday, Friday and Sunday from May to September but Friday and Sunday only in April and October (2000 SIT). You can ride the horses all year round (one hour, 3000 SIT) or take a riding lesson (4000 SIT). There are several hotels available on the premises. Contact the farm on ☎ 739 1580, fax 734 6370 or e lipica@siol.net for further information.

Lipica is 10km south-west of Divača and 10km south of Sežana which are on the main train line from Trieste to Ljubljana. From Monday to Friday there are five buses a day from Sežana to Lipica.

The Coast

KOPER
☎ 05 • pop 24,595

Koper, only 21km south of Trieste, is the first of several quaint old coastal towns along the north side of the Istrian Peninsula. The town's Italian name, Capodistria, recalls its former status as capital of Istria under the Venetian Republic in the 15th and 16th centuries. After WWII, Koper's port was developed to provide Slovenia with an alternative to Italian Trieste and Croatian Rijeka. Once an island but now firmly connected to the mainland by a causeway, the Old Town's medieval flavour lingers despite the surrounding industry, container ports, high-rise buildings and motorways beyond its 'walls'. This administrative centre and largest town on the Slovene coast makes a good base for exploring the region.

Orientation

The bus and train stations are combined in a modern structure about a kilometre south-east of the Old Town at the end of Kolodvorska cesta. There's a left luggage facility open 5.30 am to 10 pm that costs 200 SIT.

Information

Tourist Office The tourist office (☎/fax 627 3791), opposite the marina at Ukmarjev trg 7, is open 9 am to 9 pm Monday to Saturday from June to September and 9 am to 3 pm Sunday. Hours are 9 am to 2 pm and 5 to 7 pm (until 1 pm on Saturday) the rest of the year.

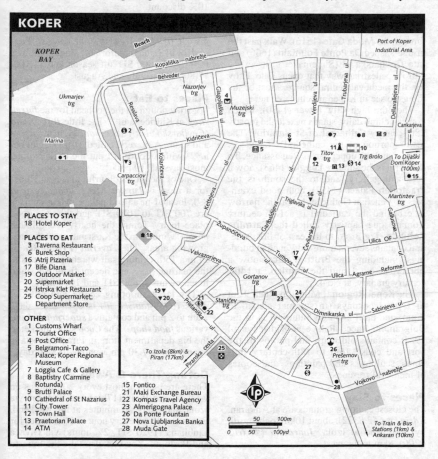

KOPER

KOPER BAY

Port of Koper Industrial Area

Beach

Ukmarjev trg

Marina

Kopališka – nabrežje

Belveder

Nazorjev trg

Glagoljaška ul

Muzejski trg

Reslava ul

Kidričeva ul

Verdijeva ul

Trubarjeva ul

Dellavallejeva ul

Cankarjeva ul

Carpacciov trg

Kolarčeva ul

Titov trg

Trg Brolo

To Dijaški Dom Koper (100m)

Martinžev trg

Gallusova ul

Župančičeva

Garibaldijeva

Triglavska ul

Cevljarska

Ulica OF

Hotel Koper

Valvazorjeva ul

Tumova ul

Ulica – Agrarne – Reforme

Gortanov trg

Staničev trg

Dimnikarska ul

Sabinjeva ul

Prešernov trg

Pristaniška

Vojkovo – nabrežje

To Izola (8km) & Piran (17km)

Pramska cesta

To Train & Bus Stations (1km) & Ankaran (10km)

PLACES TO STAY
18 Hotel Koper

PLACES TO EAT
3 Taverna Restaurant
6 Burek Shop
16 Atrij Pizzeria
17 Bife Diana
19 Outdoor Market
20 Supermarket
24 Istrska Klet Restaurant
25 Coop Supermarket; Department Store

OTHER
1 Customs Wharf
2 Tourist Office
4 Post Office
5 Belgramoni-Tacco Palace; Koper Regional Museum
7 Loggia Cafe & Gallery
8 Baptistry (Carmine Rotunda)
9 Brutti Palace
10 Cathedral of St Nazarius
11 City Tower
12 Town Hall
13 Praetorian Palace
14 ATM
15 Fontico
21 Maki Exchange Bureau
22 Kompas Travel Agency
23 Almerigogna Palace
26 Da Ponte Fountain
27 Nova Ljubljanska Banka
28 Muda Gate

0   50   100m
0   50   100yd

Money Nova Ljubljanska Banka, Pristaniška ul 45, is open 8.30 am till noon and 3.30 to 6 pm on weekdays only. There are also a couple of private exchange offices on Pristaniška ul, including Maki at No 13. Both are open 7 or 7.30 am to 7 pm weekdays and to 1 pm on Saturday. The town's only ATM is on the south-east corner of Titov trg and it accepts Visa, MasterCard, Maestro and Cirrus.

Post & Communications There's a post office at Muzejski trg 3 near the regional museum open 8 am to 7 pm weekdays and till 1 pm on Saturday.

Things to See

From the stations you enter Prešernov trg through the **Muda Gate** (1516). Walk past the bridge-shaped **Da Ponte Fountain** (1666) and into Čevljarska ul (Shoemaker's Street), a narrow pedestrian way that opens onto Titov trg, the medieval central square. Most of the things to see in Koper are clustered here.

The 36m-high **City Tower** (1480), which you can climb daily, stands next to the mostly 18th-century **Cathedral of St Nazarius**. The lower portion of the cathedral's facade is Gothic, and the upper part is Renaissance. To the north is the sublime **Loggia** (1463), now a cafe and gallery, and to the south is the **Praetorian Palace** (1452), both good examples of Venetian Gothic style. On the narrow lane behind the cathedral is a 12th-century Romanesque baptistry called the **Carmine Rotunda**. Trg Brolo to the east of the cathedral contains several more old Venetian buildings, including the **Brutti Palace**, now a library, at No 1 and the **Fontico**, a 14th-century granary, at No 4.

The **Koper Regional Museum**, open 9 am to 1 pm weekdays (in summer also 6 to 8 pm) and until noon on Saturday, is in the Belgramoni-Tacco Palace at Kidričeva ul 19. It contains old maps and photos of the port and coast, 16th to 18th-century Italianate sculptures and paintings, and copies of medieval frescoes.

Places to Stay

The closest camping grounds are at Ankaran, *Adria (☎ 652 8322),* about 10km to the north by road, and at Izola, *Jadranka (☎ 612 0200),* 8km to the west.

Both the tourist office and Kompas (☎ 627 2346) at Pristaniška ul 17 opposite the vegetable market have *private rooms* for 2000 SIT to 2500 SIT per person, depending on the category and season. Apartments for three/four people cost 6400/9400 SIT. Most of the rooms are in the new town beyond the train station.

In July and August *Dijaški Dom Koper (☎ 627 3252, Cankarjeva ul 5),* an official hostel at in the Old Town east of Trg Brolo, rents out 380 beds in triple rooms at 2300 SIT per person. The rest of the year only about 10 beds are available. An HI card will get you a 10% discount.

The only hotel in the Old Town, the recently renovated *Hotel Koper (☎ 610 0500, fax 610 0594, e koper@terme-catez.si, Pristaniška ul 3),* has comfortable singles/doubles for 9200/14,800 SIT off-season and 11,100/17,800 SIT in July and August.

Places to Eat

For fried dough on the go, head for the *burek shop* at Kidričeva ul 8. The little *Bife Diana (Čevljarska ul 36)* has čevapčiči, hamburgers and so on. A pizzeria called *Atrij (Triglavska ul 2)* with a courtyard out the back is open most days till 10 pm.

One of the most colourful places in Koper for a meal is *Istrska Klet (Župančičeva ul 39),* located in an old palace. Main courses are 700 SIT to 1000 SIT and this is a good place to try Teran, the hearty red (almost purple) wine from the Karst and coastal wine-growing areas. The *Taverna (Pristaniška ul 1)* in a 15th-century salt warehouse opposite the marina, has some decent fish dishes and lunch menus at 850 SIT and 1000 SIT.

The large shopping centre and outdoor *market (Pristaniška ul)* is open most days 7 am to 2 pm and contains a *supermarket* and various *food shops*. The *Coop* supermarket in the big department store in Piranska cesta is open 9 am to 7.30 pm Monday to Saturday.

Getting There & Away

There are buses almost every 20 minutes on weekdays to Piran (17km) and Portorož via Izola, and every 40 minutes at the weekend. Buses also leave every hour or 90 minutes for Ljubljana (1920 SIT, 2¼ hours) via Divača and Postojna. You can also take the train to

Ljubljana (1180 SIT, 2¼ hours), which is much more comfortable.

Up to 17 buses a day during the week depart for Trieste.

Destinations in Croatia include Buzet (three or four buses a day); Poreč (three or four); Pula (one or two); Rijeka (one); Rovinj (one); and Zagreb (two).

PIRAN
☎ 05 • pop 4800

Picturesque Piran (Pirano in Italian), sitting at the tip of a narrow peninsula, is everyone's favourite town on the Slovenian coast. It is a gem of Venetian Gothic architecture with narrow little streets, but it can be mobbed at the height of summer. The name derives from the Greek word for 'fire', *pyr*, referring to the ones lit at Punta, the very tip of the peninsula, to guide ships to the port at Aegida (now Koper). Piran's long history dates back to the ancient Greeks, and remnants of the medieval town walls still protect it to the east.

Orientation
Buses stop just south of Piran Harbour and next to the library on Tartinijev trg which is the heart of Piran's Old Town.

Information
Tourist Offices The tourist office (☎ 673 2507, fax 673 2509) opposite the Piran Hotel on Stjenkova ul essentially rents out rooms and keeps very brief hours. Instead head for the Maona travel agency (☎ 673 1291, ℮ maona@siol.net) at Cankarjevo nabrežje 7 whose helpful and knowledgeable staff can organise accommodation, an endless string of activities and boat cruises. The office is only open from May to September; otherwise ask at the agency in Portorož.

Money Banka Koper at Tartinijev trg 12 changes travellers cheques and cash from 8.30 am till noon and 3 to 5 pm weekdays and on Saturday morning. Outside the bank is an ATM that accepts Cirrus, Maestro, Plus, Visa and MasterCard.

Post & Communications The post office at Cankarjevo nabrežje 5 is open 8 am to 7 pm weekdays and till noon on Saturday.

Things to See
The **Maritime Museum** (9 am to noon and 3 to 6 pm Tuesday to Saturday, 500/400 SIT adults/students) in a 17th-century harbourside palace at Cankarjevo nabrežje 3 has exhibits focusing on the three 'Ss' that have been so important to Piran's development over the centuries: the sea, sailing and saltmaking (at Sečovlje south-east of Portorož). The museum's antique model ships are very fine; other rooms are filled with old figureheads, weapons and votive folk paintings placed in church for protection against shipwreck. Piran's **aquarium** (10 am to noon and 2 to 7 pm daily, 350/250 SIT) on the opposite side of the marina at Tomažičeva ul 4 may be small, but there's a tremendous variety of sea life packed into its 25 tanks.

The **town hall** and **court house** stand on Tartinijev trg, in the centre of which is a statue of the local violinist and composer Giuseppe Tartini (1692-1770). A short distance to the north-west is Prvomajski trg (also known as trg Maja) and its baroque **cistern**, used in the 18th century to store the town's fresh water.

Piran is dominated by the tall tower of the **Church of St George**, a Renaissance and baroque structure on a ridge above the sea north of Tartinijev trg. It's wonderfully decorated with frescoes and has marble altars and a large statue of the eponymous George slaying the dragon. The free-standing **bell tower** (1609) was modelled on the campanile of San Marco in Venice; the octagonal **Baptistry** from the 17th century next to it contains altars, paintings and a Roman sarcophagus from the 2nd century later used as a baptismal font.

To the east of the church is a 200m stretch of the 15th-century **town walls**, which can be climbed for superb views of Piran and the Adriatic.

Cruises
Maona and other travel agencies in Piran and Portorož can book you on any number of cruises – from a loop that takes in the towns along the coast to day-long excursions to Venice, Trieste or Brioni National Park in Croatia.

From late-May to October, the large catamaran *Marconi* goes down the Istrian coast in

PIRAN

PLACES TO STAY
4 Val Hostel
22 Giuseppe Tartini Hotel

PLACES TO EAT
3 Pizzerias & Pubs
6 Tri Vdove
7 Pavel Restaurant
8 Delfin Restaurant
25 Neptun Restaurant
27 Jestvina Supermarket
28 Surf Bar Restaurant

OTHER
1 Punta Lighthouse
2 Church of St Clement
5 Cistern
9 Market
10 Church of St George
11 Bell Tower
12 Baptistry
13 Church of St Francis & Monastery
14 Banka Koper
15 Tartini Memorial
16 Venetian House
17 Town Hall
18 Court House
19 Bus Stop
20 Tourist Office (Rooms)
21 Aquarium
23 Maritime Museum
24 Post Office
26 Maona Travel Agency
29 Customs Office
30 Bus Stop

Croatia as far as the Brioni Islands and the national park there (two hours, 8500/4250 SIT return for adults/children five to 12), with a stop at Rovinj (1¼ hours, 4000/2000 SIT return). The boat leaves at 10 am and returns at about 6.45 pm except in September when it departs and returns 20 minutes earlier. At 8.35 pm (6.50 pm in September) on the same days the *Marconi* heads for Trieste (35 minutes, 2000/4000 SIT one-way/return), returning the following morning.

The *Delfin* (mobile/cellphone ☎ 0609-628 491) sails from Piran to the marina at Portorož via the Bernadin tourist complex,

including Fiesa and Strunjan (1½ hours, 1200/600 SIT adults/children seven to 15) up to four times a day from May to October, twice a day in April.

Places to Stay

Camping The closest camping ground is *Camping Jezero Fiesa* (☎ 673 3150) at Fiesa, 4km by road from Piran (but less than a kilometre if you follow the coastal trail east of the Church of St George). It's in a quiet valley by two small, protected ponds, and close to the beach, but it gets very crowded in summer. It's open from June to September.

Private Rooms & Hostels The tourist offices in Piran and Portorož (☎ 674 7015) and the Maona travel agency can arrange *private rooms* and *apartments* throughout the year, but the biggest choice is available in summer. Single rooms are 2300 SIT to 3600 SIT, depending on the category and the season, while doubles are 3300 SIT to 5500 SIT. Apartments for two are 5200 SIT to 7200 SIT. They usually levy a 50% surcharge if you stay less then three nights.

A very central, relatively cheap place is the *Val Hostel* (☎ 674 2555, fax 674 2556, Gregorčičeva ul 38a) on the corner of Vegova ul. Open from late April to October, it has two dozen rooms with shared shower and breakfast for between 2700 SIT and 3300 SIT per person.

Hotels Though not in Piran itself one of the nicest places to stay on the coast is *Fiesa* (☎ 674 6897, fax 674 6896), a 22-room hotel overlooking the sea near the Jezero Fiesa camping ground. This pleasant four-storey hotel charges 4000/8000 SIT for singles/doubles in the low season, rising to 5200/10,400 SIT in July and August. In the town centre, the *Giuseppe Tartini Hotel* (☎ 674 3100, fax 674 3104, ✉ info@hoteli-piran.si, Tartinijev Trg 5) has decent singles/doubles for 7500/11,600 SIT.

Places to Eat

Piran has plenty of seafood restaurants along Prešernovo nabrežje but most (including *Pavel*, *Pavel 2* and *Tri Vdove*) are fairly pricey; expect to pay about 5000 SIT for two with drinks. Instead you should try the local favourites: the *Delfin* (Kosovelova ul 4) near Prvomajski trg or the more expensive *Neptun* (Župančičeva ul 7) behind the Maona travel agency.

The *Surf Bar Restaurant* (Grudnova ul 1), on a small street north-east of the bus station, is a good place for a meal or drink. It has a 'photo-album menu' with some 60 dishes and lots of pizzas. There are also several pizzerias along Prešernovo nabrežje near the Punta lighthouse including *Palma* and *Punta*. The *Jestvina* supermarket opposite Trg Bratsva 8 is open from 7 am to 8 pm Monday to Friday, to 1 pm Saturday and to 11 am Sunday.

Getting There & Away

The local bus company I&I links Piran with Portorož and Lucija (bus No 1); with Portorož and Fiesa (bus No 2; mid-June to August only); with Strunjan and Portorož (bus No 3); and with Portorož, Sečovlje and Padna (bus No 4). Schedules vary, but bus No 1 runs about every 10 to 15 minutes. The fare is 210 SIT.

Other destinations that can be reached from Piran include Ljubljana via Divača and Postojna (six to 10 a day) and Nova Gorica (one or two). Six buses head for Trieste on weekdays, and there are two daily departures for Zagreb. One bus a day heads south for Croatian Istria at 4.25 pm, stopping at the coastal towns of Umag, Poreč and Rovinj.

PORTOROŽ

☎ 05 • pop 2980

Every country with a sea coast has got to have a honky-tonk beach resort, and Portorož is Slovenia's very own Blackpool, Bondi or Atlantic City. The 'Port of Roses' is essentially a solid strip of high-rise hotels, restaurants, bars, travel agencies, shops, discos, beaches with turnstiles, parked cars and tourists, and it's not to everyone's taste. But its relatively clean, sandy beaches are the largest on the coast, there's a pleasant spa and the list of activities is endless. If you take it for what it is, Portorož can be a fun place to watch Slovenes, Italians, Austrians and others at play.

Orientation

The bus station is opposite the main beach on Postajališka pot.

Information

Tourist Offices The tourist office (☎ 674 0231, fax 674 8261) is on the ground floor of Obala 16, a short distance west of the bus station. It's open 9 am to 9 pm (earlier in the off season).

Money Banka Koper below Slovenija Hotel at Obala 33 is open 8.30 to noon and 3 to 5 pm weekdays and Saturday morning. Its ATM accepts the banknotes of 18 countries at a good rate. There's an exchange bureau at Obala 14, open 9 am to 6 pm Monday to Saturday (3 pm on Sunday), and an ATM that accepts Cirrus, Plus and Maestro at Obala 53.

Post & Communications The post office is at K Stari cesta 1 opposite the now empty Palace Hotel (1891). It is open 8 am to 7 pm weekdays and till noon on Saturday.

Activities

The beaches at Portorož, including the main one accommodating 6000 bodies, are 'managed' so you'll have to pay 500 SIT (350 SIT for children) to use them. They are open 9 am to dusk in season. Umbrellas and deck chairs are available for 600 SIT.

The Terme Palace spa complex, just beyond the post office on K Stari cesta, is famous for thalassotherapy (treatment using sea water and its by-products). It is available to the public from 1 to 9 pm Monday to Saturday. The palatial indoor swimming pool here is open 7 am to 9 pm daily. It costs 800 SIT for four hours on weekdays, 1400 SIT at the weekend, and 1000/1500 SIT from 1 to 9 pm daily.

Places to Stay

The *Lucija Camping Ground* (☎ 677 1027) has two locations. The 2nd-category site (1200 SIT to 1300 SIT per person) is southeast of the marina at the end of Cesta Solinarjev less than 2km from the bus station, and the 1st-category site (1200 SIT to 1500 SIT), 600m to the west, is on the water. Both camps are open from April to September and get very crowded in summer.

The tourist office's accommodation service (☎ 674 6199), across from the tourist office, has *private rooms* and *apartments* and is open from 9 am to 1 pm and 4 to 7 pm daily from May to September.

You can also book them through Atlas Express (☎ 674 5077) at Obala 55, just south of the bus station; Kompas (☎ 674 7032), Obala

41; and Maona (☎ 674 6423) at Obala 2. Generally singles range from 2300 SIT to 3300 SIT, depending on category and season, while doubles are 3300 SIT to 5000 SIT. Apartments for two go for a minimum of 4700 SIT to 6700 SIT. Getting a room for less than three nights (for which you must pay a 50% supplement) or a single any time is difficult.

Places to Eat

Fast-food and pizza/pasta restaurants line Obala, including *Pergola* at No 16, with pizzas costing 800 SIT to 1250 SIT. But if you want a proper sit-down meal, the terrace at the *Taverna (Obala 22)* in the sports field looks out over the marina and the bay. The *Grill Restaurant (Obala 20),* often with something large being roasted on a spit near the entrance, faces the main beach and has an attractive covered terrace and a menu starting at 1000 SIT.

The *Mercator Degro* supermarket is a few steps away from the bus station. It is open 7 am to 8 pm weekdays, to 6 pm Saturday and 8 am to 11 am Sunday.

Getting There & Away

Local I&I buses link Portorož with Piran, Strunjan, Fiesa, Lucija, Sečovlje and Podpadna; for details see Getting There & Away in the Piran section. Other destinations from Portorož include Ljubljana via Divača and Postojna (11 a day) and Nova Gorica (three a day).

International destinations include Poreč (three), Pula (one or two), Zagreb (two) and Trieste (nine a day on weekdays).

For information about boat services to Venice from Izola, see the introductory Getting There & Away section.

Spain

Spaniards approach life with such exuberance that most visitors have to stop and stare. In almost every town in the country, the nightlife will outlast the foreigners. Then just when they think they are coming to terms with the pace, they are surrounded by the beating drums of a fiesta, with day and night turning into a blur of dancing, laughing, eating and drinking. Spain also holds its own in cultural terms with formidable museums like the Prado and Thyssen-Bornemisza art galleries in Madrid, the wacky Dalí museum in Figueres, and Barcelona's Picasso and Miró museums.

Then, of course, you have the weather and the highly varied landscape. From April to October the sun shines with uncanny predictability on the Mediterranean coast and the Balearic Islands. Elsewhere you can enjoy good summer weather in the more secluded coves of Galicia, in the Pyrenees or the mountains of Andalucía, or on the surf beaches of western Andalucía or the País Vasco (Basque Country).

A wealth of history awaits the visitor to Spain: fascinating prehistoric displays at the archaeological museums in Teruel and Madrid; and from Roman times the aqueduct in Segovia, the seaside amphitheatre in Tarragona and the buried streets of Roman Barcelona made accessible via an underground walkway. After Roman times, the Moorish era left perhaps the most powerful cultural and artistic legacy, focused on Granada's Alhambra, Córdoba's mosque and Seville's *alcázar* (fortress) but evident in monuments throughout much of the country. Christian Spain also constructed hundreds of impressive castles, cathedrals, monasteries, palaces and mansions, which still stand across the length and breadth of the country.

Facts about Spain

HISTORY
Ancient History
Located at the crossroads between Europe and Africa, the Iberian Peninsula has always been a target for invading peoples and civilisations. From around 8000 to 3000 BC, people from

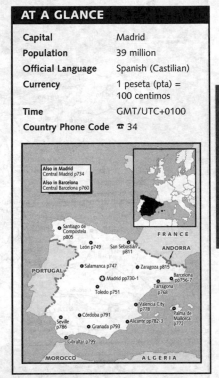

AT A GLANCE

Capital	Madrid
Population	39 million
Official Language	Spanish (Castilian)
Currency	1 peseta (pta) = 100 centimos
Time	GMT/UTC+0100
Country Phone Code	☎ 34

Also in Madrid
Central Madrid p734

Also in Barcelona
Central Barcelona p760

FRANCE
ANDORRA
PORTUGAL
Santiago de Compostela p805
León p749
San Sebastián p811
Salamanca p747
Zaragoza p815
Madrid pp730-1
Barcelona pp756-7
Toledo p751
Tarragona p768
Valencia City p778
Córdoba p791
Palma de Mallorca p772
Seville p786
Granada p793
Alicante pp782-3
Gibraltar p799
MOROCCO
ALGERIA

SPAIN

North Africa known as the Iberians crossed the Strait of Gibraltar and settled the peninsula. Around 1000 BC Celtic tribes entered northern Spain, while Phoenician merchants were establishing trading settlements along the Mediterranean coast. They were followed by Greeks and Carthaginians who arrived around 600 to 500 BC.

The Romans arrived in the 3rd century BC, but took two centuries to subdue the peninsula. Christianity came to Spain during the 1st century AD, but was initially opposed by the Romans, leading to persecution and martyrdoms. In AD 409 Roman Hispania was invaded by Germanic tribes and by 419 the Christian Visigoths, another Germanic

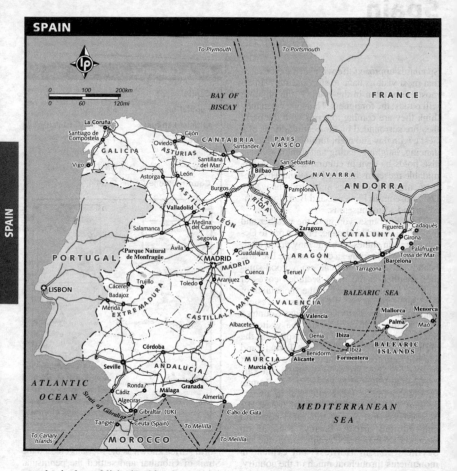

SPAIN

people, had established a kingdom which lasted until 711, when the Moors – Muslim Berbers and Arabs from North Africa – crossed the Strait of Gibraltar and defeated Roderic, the last Visigoth king.

Muslim Spain & the Reconquista

By 714, the Muslim armies had occupied the entire peninsula, apart from some northern mountain regions. Muslim dominion was to last almost 800 years in parts of Spain. In Islamic Spain – known as al-Andalus – arts and sciences prospered, new crops and agricultural techniques were introduced, and palaces,

mosques, schools, gardens and public baths were built.

In 722 a small army under the Visigothic leader Pelayo inflicted the first defeat on the Muslims (known to Christians as Moros, or Moors) at Covadonga in northern Spain. This marked the beginning of the Reconquista, the spluttering reconquest of Spain by the Christians. By the early 11th century, the frontier between Christian and Muslim Spain stretched from Barcelona to the Atlantic.

In 1085, Alfonso VI, king of León and Castile, took Toledo. This prompted the Muslim leaders to request help from northern

Africa, which arrived in the form of the Almoravids. They recaptured much territory and ruled it until the 1140s. The Almoravids were followed by the Almohads, another North African dynasty, which ruled until 1212. By the mid-13th century, the Christians had taken most of the peninsula except for the state of Granada.

In the process the kingdoms of Castile and Aragón emerged as Christian Spain's two main powers, and in 1469 they were united by the marriage of Isabel, princess of Castile, and Fernando, heir to the throne of Aragón. Known as the Catholic Monarchs, they united Spain and laid the foundations for the Spanish golden age. They also revived the notorious Inquisition, which expelled and executed thousands of Jews and other non-Christians. In 1492 the last Muslim ruler of Granada surrendered to them, marking the completion of the Reconquista.

The Golden Age

Also in 1492, while searching for an alternative passage to India, Columbus stumbled on the Bahamas and claimed the Americas for Spain. This sparked a period of exploration and exploitation that was to yield Spain enormous wealth while destroying the ancient American empires. For three centuries, gold and silver from the New World were used to finance the rapid expansion and slow decline of the Spanish empire.

In 1516, Fernando was succeeded by his grandson Carlos, of the Habsburg dynasty. Carlos was elected Holy Roman Emperor in 1519 and ruled over an empire that included Austria, southern Germany, the Netherlands, Spain and the American colonies. He and his successors were to lead Spain into a series of expensive wars that ultimately bankrupted the empire. In 1588, Sir Francis Drake's English fleet annihilated the mighty Spanish Armada. The Thirty Years' War (1618-48) saw Spain in conflict with the Netherlands, France and England. By the reign of the last Habsburg monarch, Carlos II (1655-1700), the Spanish empire was in decline.

The 18th & 19th Centuries

Carlos II died without an heir. At the end of the subsequent War of the Spanish Succession (1702-13), Felipe V, grandson of French king Louis XIV, became the first of Spain's Bourbon dynasty. A period of stability, enlightened reforms and economic growth ensued, and was ended by events after the French Revolution of 1789.

When Louis XVI was guillotined in 1793, Spain declared war on the French republic, but then turned to alliance with France and war against Britain, in which the Battle of Trafalgar (1805) ended Spanish sea power. In 1807-08 French troops entered Spain and Napoleon convinced Carlos IV, the Spanish king, to abdicate, in whose place he installed his own brother Joseph Bonaparte. The Spaniards fought a five-year war of independence. In 1815 Napoleon was defeated by Wellington and a Bourbon, Fernando VII, was restored to the Spanish throne.

Fernando's reign was a disastrous advertisement for monarchy: the Inquisition was re-established, liberals and constitutionalists were persecuted, free speech was repressed, Spain entered a severe recession and the American colonies won their independence. After his death in 1833 came the First Carlist War (1834-39), fought between conservative forces led by Don Carlos, Fernando's brother, and liberals who supported the claim of Fernando's daughter Isabel (later Isabel II) to the throne. In 1868 the monarchy was overthrown during the Septembrina Revolution and Isabel II was forced to flee. The First Republic was declared in 1873, but within 18 months the army had restored the monarchy, with Isabel's son Alfonso XII on the throne. Despite political turmoil, Spain's economy prospered in the second half of the 19th century, fuelled by industrialisation.

The disastrous Spanish-American War of 1898 marked the end of the Spanish empire. Spain was defeated by the USA and lost its last overseas possessions; Cuba won a qualified independence and Puerto Rico, Guam and the Philippines passed to the USA.

The 20th Century

The early 20th century was characterised by military disasters in Morocco and growing instability as radical forces struggled to overthrow the established order. In 1923, with Spain on the brink of civil war, Miguel Primo de Rivera made himself military dictator, ruling until 1930. In 1931 Alfonso XIII fled the country, and the Second Republic was declared.

SPAIN

SPAIN

Like its predecessor, the Second Republic fell victim to internal conflict. The 1936 elections told of a country split in two, with the Republican government (an uneasy alliance of leftist parties known as the Popular Front) and its supporters on one side, and the right-wing Nationalists (an alliance of the army, Church and the fascist-style Falange Party) on the other.

Nationalist plotters in the army rose against the government in July 1936. During the subsequent Spanish Civil War (1936-39), the Nationalists, led by General Francisco Franco, received heavy military support from Nazi Germany and fascist Italy, while the elected Republican government received support only from Russia and, to a lesser degree, from the International Brigades made up of foreign leftists.

By 1939 Franco had won and an estimated 350,000 Spaniards had died. After the war, thousands of Republicans were executed, jailed or forced into exile. Franco's 35-year dictatorship began with Spain isolated internationally and crippled by recession. It wasn't until the 1950s and 1960s, when the rise in tourism and a treaty with the USA combined to provide much needed funds, that the country began to recover. By the 1970s Spain had the fastest-growing economy in Europe.

Franco died in 1975, having named Juan Carlos, grandson of Alfonso XIII, his successor. King Juan Carlos is widely credited with having overseen Spain's transition from dictatorship to democracy. The first elections were held in 1977, a new constitution was drafted in 1978, and a failed military coup in 1981 was seen as a futile attempt to turn back the clock. Spain joined the then EC in 1986, and celebrated its return to the world stage in style in 1992, with Expo '92 in Seville and the Olympic Games in Barcelona. In 1997 it became fully integrated in the North Atlantic Treaty Organisation and in 1999 Spain met the criteria for launching the new European currency, the euro. By the time of the 2000 general election, Spain had the fastest growing economy in the EU.

GEOGRAPHY & ECOLOGY
Spain is probably Europe's most geographically diverse country, with landscapes ranging from the near-deserts of Almería to the green, Wales-like countryside and deep coastal inlets of Galicia, and from the sun-baked plains of Castilla-La Mancha to the rugged mountains of the Pyrenees.

The country covers 84% of the Iberian Peninsula and spreads over nearly 505,000 sq km, more than half of which is high tableland, the *meseta*. This is supported and divided by several mountain chains. The main ones are the Pyrenees along the border with France; the Cordillera Cantábrica backing the north coast; the Sistema Ibérico from the central north towards the middle Mediterranean coast; the Cordillera Central from north of Madrid towards the Portuguese border; and three east-west chains across Andalucía, one of which is the highest range of all, the Sierra Nevada.

The major rivers are the Ebro, Duero, Tajo (Tagus), Guadiana and Guadalquivir, each draining a different basin between the mountains and all flowing into the Atlantic Ocean, except for the Ebro which reaches the Mediterranean Sea.

CLIMATE
The meseta and the Ebro basin have a continental climate: scorching in summer, cold in winter and dry. Madrid regularly freezes in December, January and February and temperatures climb above 30°C in July and August. The Guadalquivir basin in Andalucía is only a little wetter and positively broils in high summer, with temperatures in Seville that kill people every year. This area doesn't get as cold as the meseta in winter.

The Pyrenees and the Cordillera Cantábrica backing the Bay of Biscay coast bear the brunt of cold northern and north-western airstreams. Even in high summer you never know when you might get a shower. The Mediterranean coast as a whole, and the Balearic Islands, get a little more rain than Madrid and the south can be even hotter in summer. The Mediterranean also provides Spain's warmest waters (reaching 27°C or so in August) and you *can* swim as early as April or even late March in the south-east.

In general you can rely on pleasant or hot temperatures just about everywhere from April to early November (plus March in the south, but minus a month at either end on the northern and north-western coasts). Snowfalls in the mountains start as early as October and some snow cover lasts all year on the highest peaks.

FLORA & FAUNA

The brown bear, wolf, lynx and wild boar all survive in Spain, although only the boar exists in healthy numbers. Spain's high mountains harbour the goat-like chamois and Spanish ibex (the latter is rare) and big birds of prey such as eagles, vultures and the lammergeier. The marshy Ebro delta and Guadalquivir estuary are important for waterbirds, the spectacular greater flamingo among them. Many of Spain's 5500 seed-bearing plants occur nowhere else in Europe because of the barrier of the Pyrenees. Spring wildflowers are spectacular in many country and hill areas.

The conservation picture has improved by leaps and bounds in the past 20 years and Spain now has 25,000 sq km of protected areas, including 10 national parks. But overgrazing, reservoir creation, tourism, housing developments, agricultural and industrial effluent, fires and hunting all still threaten plant and animal life.

GOVERNMENT & POLITICS

Spain is a constitutional monarchy. The 1978 constitution restored parliamentary government and grouped the country's 50 provinces into 17 autonomous communities, each with its own regional government. From 1982 to 1996 Spain was governed by the centre-left PSOE party led by Felipe González. In the 1996 election the PSOE, weakened by a series of scandals and long-term economic problems, was finally unseated by the right-of-centre Partido Popular, led by José María Aznar. Aznar was handily re-elected in 2000 in the first-ever overall parliamentary majority for a right-of-centre party in democratic Spain.

ECONOMY

Spain has experienced an amazing economic turnabout in the 20th century, raising its living standards from the lowest in Western Europe to a level comparable with the rest of the continent. Its booming economy came back to earth with a thud in the early 1990s, though an initially slow recovery sped up by the end of the decade. The official figure for those registered for unemployment benefits has dropped to 9.1%, although EU estimates put the real figure

at 15%. Either way, it is one of the higher rates in Western Europe. Service industries employ over six million people and produce close to 60% of the country's GDP. The arrival of over 50 million tourists every year brings work to around 10% of the entire labour force. Industry accounts for about one-third of both workforce and GDP, but agriculture accounts for only 4% of GDP compared to 23% in 1960, although it employs one in 10 workers.

POPULATION & PEOPLE

Spain has a population of just under 40 million, descended from all the many peoples who have settled here over the millennia, among them Iberians, Celts, Romans, Jews, Visigoths, Berbers and Arabs. The biggest cities are Madrid (3.1 million), Barcelona (1.5 million), Valencia (739,000) and Seville (701,000). Each region proudly preserves its own unique culture, and some – Catalonia and the País Vasco in particular – display a fiercely independent spirit.

ARTS
Cinema

Early Spanish cinema was hamstrung by a lack of funds and technology, and perhaps the greatest of all Spanish directors, Luis Buñuel, made his silent surrealist classics *Un Chien Andalou* (1928) and *L'Age d'Or* (1930) in France. Buñuel, however, returned to Spain to make *Tierra sin Pan* (Land without Bread, 1932), a film about rural poverty in the Las Hurdes area of Extremadura.

Under Franco there was strict censorship, but satirical and uneasy films like Juan Antonio Bardem's *Muerte de un Ciclista* (Death of a Cyclist, 1955) and Luis Berlanga's *Bienvenido Mr Marshall* (Welcome Mr Marshall, 1953) still managed to appear. Carlos Saura, with films like *Ana y los Lobos* (Anna and the Wolves, 1973), and Victor Erice, with *El Espiritu de la Colmena* (Spirit of the Beehive, 1973) and *El Sur* (The South, 1983), looked at the problems of young people scarred by the Spanish Civil War and its aftermath.

After Franco, Pedro Almodóvar broke away from this serious cinema dwelling on the past with his humorous films set amid the social and artistic revolution of the late 1970s and 1980s notably *Mujeres al Borde de un Ataque de Nervios* (Women on the Verge of

SPAIN

a Nervous Breakdown, 1988). In 1995, Ken Loach produced a moving co-production on the Spanish Civil War, *Tierra y Libertad* (Land and Freedom).

Painting

The golden age of Spanish art (1550-1650) was strongly influenced by Italy but the great Spanish artists developed their talents in unique ways. The giants were the Toledo-based El Greco (originally from Crete), and Diego Velázquez, perhaps Spain's most revered painter. Both excelled with insightful portraits. Francisco Zurbarán and Bartolomé Esteban Murillo were also prominent. The genius of the 18th and 19th centuries was Francisco Goya, whose versatility ranged from unflattering royal portraits and anguished war scenes to bullfight etchings.

Catalonia was the powerhouse of early-20th-century Spanish art, engendering the hugely prolific Pablo Picasso (born in Andalucía), the colourful symbolist Joan Miró, and Salvador Dalí, who was obsessed with the unconscious and weird. Works by these and other major Spanish artists can be found in galleries throughout the country.

Architecture

The earliest architectural relics are the prehistoric monuments on Menorca. Reminders of Roman times include the ruins of Mérida and Tarragona, and Segovia's amazing aqueduct. The Muslims left behind some of the most splendid buildings in the entire Islamic world, including Granada's Alhambra, Córdoba's mosque and Seville's alcázar – the latter an example of *mudéjar* architecture, the name given to Moorish work done throughout Christian-held territory.

The first main Christian architectural movement was Romanesque, in the north in the 11th and 12th centuries, which has left countless lovely country churches and several cathedrals, notably that of Santiago de Compostela. Later came the many great Gothic cathedrals (Toledo, Barcelona, León, Salamanca and Seville) of the 13th to 16th centuries, as well as Renaissance styles, such as the plateresque work so prominent in Salamanca and the austere work of Juan de Herrera, responsible for El Escorial. Spain then followed the usual path to baroque (17th and

18th centuries) and neoclassicism (19th century) before Catalonia produced its startling modernist (roughly Art Nouveau) movement around the turn of the 20th century, of which Antoni Gaudí's La Sagrada Família church is the most stunning example. More recent architecture is only likely to excite specialists.

Literature

One of the earliest works of Spanish literature is the *Cantar de mío Cid*, an anonymous epic poem describing the life of El Cid, an 11th-century Christian knight. Miguel de Cervantes' novel *Don Quixote de la Mancha* is the masterpiece of the literary flowering of the 16th and 17th centuries, and one of the world's great works of fiction. The playwrights Lope de Vega and Pedro Calderón de la Barca were also leading lights of the age.

The next high point, in the early 20th century, grew out of the crisis of the Spanish-American War that spawned the intellectual 'Generation of '98'. Philosophical essayist Miguel de Unamuno was prominent, but the towering figure was poet and playwright Federico García Lorca, whose tragedies *Blood Wedding* and *Yerma* won international acclaim before he was murdered in the civil war for his Republican sympathies. Camilo José Cela, author of the civil war aftermath novel *The Family of Pascal Duarte*, won the 1989 Nobel Prize for literature. Juan Goytisolo is probably the major contemporary writer; his most approachable work is his autobiography *Forbidden Territory*. There has been a proliferation of women – particularly feminist writers – in the past 25 years, among whose prominent representatives are Adelaide Morales, Ana María Matute and Rosa Montero.

SOCIETY & CONDUCT

Most Spaniards are economical with etiquette but this does not signify unfriendliness. They're gregarious people, on the whole very tolerant and easy-going towards foreigners. It's not easy to give offence. Disrespectful behaviour including excessively casual dress in churches won't go down well though.

Siesta

Contrary to popular belief, most Spaniards do not sleep in the afternoon. The siesta is generally devoted to a long leisurely lunch and lingering conversation. Then again, if you've stayed out until 5 am ...

Flamenco

Getting to see real, deeply emotional, flamenco can be hard, as it tends to happen semi-spontaneously in little bars. Andalucía is its traditional home. You'll find plenty of clubs there and elsewhere offering flamenco shows; these are generally aimed at tourists and are expensive, but some are good. Your best chance of catching the real thing is probably at one of the flamenco festivals in the south, usually held in summer.

RELIGION

Only about 20% of Spaniards are regular churchgoers, but Catholicism is deeply ingrained in the culture. As the writer Unamuno said: 'Here in Spain we are all Catholics, even the atheists'.

Many Spaniards have a deep-seated scepticism of the Church; during the civil war, churches were burnt and clerics shot because they represented repression, corruption and the old order.

LANGUAGE

Spanish, or Castilian *(castellano)* as it is often and more precisely called, is spoken by just about all Spaniards, but there are also three widely spoken regional languages: Catalan (another Romance language, closely related to Spanish and French) is spoken by about two-thirds of people in Catalonia and the Balearic Islands and half the people in the Valencia region; Galician (another Romance language that sounds like a cross between Spanish and Portuguese) is spoken by many in the northwest; and Basque (of obscure, non-Latin origin) is spoken by a minority in the País Vasco and Navarra.

English isn't as widely spoken as many travellers seem to expect. In the principal cities and tourist areas it's much easier to find people who speak at least some English, though generally you'll be better received if you at least try to communicate in Spanish.

See the Language chapter at the back of the book for pronunciation guidelines and useful words and phrases.

Facts for the Visitor

HIGHLIGHTS
Beaches

Yes, it's still possible to have a beach to yourself in Spain. In summer it may be a little tricky, but spots where things are bound to be quiet are such gems as the beaches of Cabo Favàritx in Menorca, and some of the secluded coves on Cabo de Gata in Andalucía. There are also good, relatively uncrowded beaches on the Costa de la Luz, between Tarifa and Cádiz. On the Galician coast, between Noia and Pontevedra, are literally hundreds of beaches where even in mid-August you won't feel claustrophobic.

Museums & Galleries

Spain is home to some of the finest art galleries in the world. The Prado in Madrid has few rivals, and there are outstanding art museums in Bilbao, Seville, Barcelona, Valencia and Córdoba. Fascinating smaller galleries, such as the Dalí museum in Figueres and the abstract art museum in Cuenca, also abound. Tarragona and Teruel have excellent archaeological museums.

Buildings

Try not to miss Andalucía's Muslim-era gems – the Alhambra in Granada, the alcázar in Seville and the Mezquita in Córdoba – or Barcelona's extraordinary La Sagrada Família church. The fairy-tale alcázar in Segovia has to be seen to be believed.

For even more exciting views, and loads of medieval ghosts, try to reach the ruined castle in Morella, Valencia province. Or you can fast-forward to 1997 and Bilbao's spectacular Guggenheim museum, whose wavy exterior steals the show from the contemporary art within.

Scenery

There's outstanding mountain scenery often coupled with highly picturesque villages in the Pyrenees and Picos de Europa in the north and in parts of Andalucía such as the Alpujarras. On the coasts, the rugged inlets of Galicia and stark, hilly Cabo de Gata in Andalucía stand out.

SUGGESTED ITINERARIES

If you want to whiz around as many places as possible in limited time, the following itineraries might suit you:

Two days
  Fly to Madrid, Barcelona or Seville, or nip into Barcelona or San Sebastián overland from France.
One week
  Spend two days each in Barcelona, Madrid and Seville, allowing one day for travel.
Two weeks
  As above, plus San Sebastián, Toledo, Salamanca and/or Cuenca, Córdoba and/or Granada, and maybe Cáceres and/or Trujillo.
One month
  As above, plus some of the following: side trips from the cities mentioned above; an exploration of the north, including Santiago de Compostela and the Picos de Europa; visits to Teruel, Mallorca, Formentera, Segovia, Ávila, or some smaller towns and more remote regions such as North-East Extremadura or Cabo de Gata.

PLANNING

When to Go

For most purposes the ideal months to visit Spain are May, June and September (plus April and October in the south). At these times you can rely on good weather, yet avoid the sometimes extreme heat and main crush of Spanish and foreign tourists of July and August, when temperatures may climb to 45°C in parts of Andalucía and when Madrid is unbearably hot and almost deserted.

The summer overflows with festivals, including Sanfermines, with the running of the bulls in Pamplona, and Semana Grande all along the north coast (dates vary from place to place), but there are excellent festivals during the rest of the year too.

In winter the rains never seem to stop in the north, except when they turn to snow. Madrid regularly freezes in December, January and February. At these times Andalucía is the place to be, with temperatures reaching the mid-teens in most places and good skiing in the Sierra Nevada.

Maps

Some of the best maps for travellers are published by Michelin, which produces a 1:1 million *Spain Portugal* map and six 1:400,000 regional maps. The country map doesn't show railways, but the regional maps do.

What to Bring

You can buy anything you need in Spain, but some articles, such as sun-screen lotion, are more expensive than elsewhere. Books in English tend to be expensive and are hard to find outside main cities.

A pair of strong shoes and a towel are essential. A moneybelt or shoulder wallet can be useful in big cities. Bring sunglasses if glare gets to you. If you want to blend in, don't just pack T-shirts, shorts and runners – Spaniards are quite dressy and many tourists just look like casual slobs to them.

TOURIST OFFICES

Most towns (and many villages) of any interest have a tourist office (*oficina de turismo*). These will supply you with a map and brochures with basic information on local sights, attractions, accommodation, history etc. Some can also provide information on other places too. Their staff are generally helpful and often speak some English. There is also a nationwide phone line with information in English (☎ 901-30 06 00), daily from 9 am to 6 pm.

Tourist Offices Abroad

Spain has tourist information centres in 19 countries including:

Canada (☎ 416-961-3131, @ toronto@tourspain.es) 2 Bloor St W, 34th floor, Toronto M4W 3E2
France (☎ 01 45 03 82 57, @ paris@tourspain.es) 43, rue Decamps, 75784 Paris, Cedex 16
Portugal (☎ 01-357 1992, @ lisboa@tourspain.es) Avenida Sidónio Pais 28 3 Dto, 1050 Lisbon
UK (☎ 020-7486 8077, brochure request ☎ 0891 669920 at 50p a minute, @ londres@tourspain.es) 22-23 Manchester Square, London W1M 5AP
USA (☎ 212-265 8822, @ oetny@tourspain.es) 666 Fifth Ave, 35th floor, New York, NY 10103

VISAS & DOCUMENTS

Citizens of EU countries can enter Spain with their national identity card or passport. UK citizens must have a full passport – a British visitor passport won't do. Non-EU nationals must take their passport.

SPAIN

EU, Norway and Iceland citizens require no visa. Nationals of Australia, Canada, Israel, Japan, New Zealand, Switzerland and the USA need no visa for stays of up to 90 days but must have a passport valid for the whole visit. Keep in mind this 90 day limit applies throughout the EU, so don't overstay your time in the EU even if Spain is only part of your trip. South Africans are among nationalities who do need a visa for Spain.

It's best to obtain the visa in your country of residence to avoid possible bureaucratic problems. Both 30-day and 90-day single-entry, and 90-day multiple-entry visas are available, though if you apply in a country where you're not resident the 90-day option may not be available. Multiple-entry visas will save you a lot of time and trouble if you plan to leave Spain say to Gibraltar or Morocco then re-enter it.

The Schengen System

Spain is one of the Schengen Area countries; the others are Portugal, Italy, France, Germany, Austria, the Netherlands, Belgium and Luxembourg, Sweden, Finland, Denmark and Greece. They have theoretically done away with passport control on travel between them. (In fact, checks have been known to occur at airports and on Lisbon-Madrid trains.) It is illegal to enter Spain without a visa (if you require one) and doing so can lead to deportation.

One good thing about the system is that a visa for one Schengen country is valid for others too. Compare validity periods, prices and the number of permitted entries before you apply, as these can differ between countries.

Stays of Longer than 90 Days

EU, Norway and Iceland nationals planning to stay in Spain more than 90 days are supposed to apply during their first month in the country for a residence card. This is a lengthy, complicated procedure; if you intend to subject yourself to it, consult a Spanish consulate before you go to Spain, as you'll need to take certain documents with you.

Other nationalities on a Schengen visa are flat out of luck when it comes to extensions. For stays of longer than 90 days you're supposed to get a residence card. This is a nightmarish process, starting with a residence visa issued by a Spanish consulate in your country of residence; start the process well in advance.

EMBASSIES & CONSULATES
Spanish Embassies & Consulates

Spanish embassies include:

Australia (☎ 02-6273 3555, ⊜ embespau@mail.mae.es) 15 Arkana St, Yarralumla, Canberra, ACT 2600; consulates in Brisbane, Melbourne, Perth and Sydney

Canada (☎ 613-747-2252, ⊜ spain@DocuWeb.ca) 74 Stanley Avenue, Ottawa, Ont K1M 1P4
Consulate in Toronto: (☎ 416-977-1661)
Consulate in Montreal: (☎ 514-935-5235)

France (☎ 01 44 43 18 00, ⊜ ambespfr@mail.mae.es) 22 avenue Marceau, 75008 Paris, Cedex 08

Portugal (☎ 01-347 2381, ⊜ embesppt@mail.mae.es) Rua do Salitre 1, 1250 Lisbon

UK (☎ 020-7235 5555, ⊜ espemblon@espemblon.freeserve.co.uk, 39 Chesham Place, London SW1X 8SB
Consulate: (☎ 020-7589 8989) 20 Draycott Place, London SW3 2RZ and in Edinburgh and Manchester

USA (☎ 202-452 0100) 2375 Pennsylvania Ave NW, Washington, DC 20037; consulates in Boston, Chicago, Houston, Miami, Los Angeles, New Orleans, New York and San Francisco

Embassies & Consulates in Spain

Some 70 countries have embassies in Madrid, including:

Australia (☎ 91 441 93 00) Plaza del Descubridor Diego de Ordás 3-2, Edificio Santa Engrácia 120

Canada (☎ 91 431 45 56) Calle de Núñez de Balboa 35

France (☎ 91 310 11 12) Calle del Marqués Ensenada 10

Germany (☎ 91 557 90 00) Calle de Fortuny 8

Ireland (☎ 91 436 40 95) Paseo de la Castellana 46

Japan (☎ 91 590 13 21), Calle de Serrano 109

Morocco (☎ 91 563 79 28) Calle de Serrano 179
Consulate: (☎ 91 561 21 45) Calle de Leizaran 31

New Zealand (☎ 91 523 02 26, 91 531 09 97) Plaza de la Lealtad 2

Portugal (☎ 91 561 47 23) Calle de Castelló 128
Consulate: (☎ 91 577 35 38) Calle Lagasca 88

UK (☎ 91 308 06 18) Calle de Fernando el Santo 16

SPAIN

Consulate: (☎ 91 308 53 00) Calle del Marqués Ensenada 16
USA (☎ 91 577 40 00) Calle de Serrano 75

CUSTOMS

From outside the EU you are allowed to bring in duty-free one bottle of spirits, one bottle of wine, 50ml of perfume and 200 cigarettes. From within the EU you can bring 2L of wine *and* 1L of spirits, with the same limits on the rest. Duty-free allowances for travel between EU countries were abolished in 1999.

MONEY
Currency

Spain's currency for everyday transactions until early in 2002 is the peseta (pta). The legal denominations are coins of one, five (known as a *duro*), 10, 25, 50, 100, 200 and 500 ptas. There are notes of 1000, 2000, 5000 and 10,000 ptas. Take care not to confuse the 500 ptas coin with the 100 ptas coin.

Exchange Rates

Banks mostly open 8.30 am to 2 pm Monday to Friday, 8.30 am to 1 pm Saturday and tend to give better exchange rates than currency-exchange offices. Travellers cheques attract a slightly better rate than cash. ATMs accepting a wide variety of cards are common.

country	unit		pesetas
Australia	A$1	=	106.71 ptas
Canada	C$1	=	124.16 ptas
euro	€1	=	166.38 ptas
France	1FF	=	25.36 ptas
Germany	DM1	=	85.07 ptas
Japan	¥100	=	169.5 ptas
New Zealand	NZ$1	=	82.84 ptas
UK	UK£1	=	276.89 ptas
USA	US$1	=	184.16 ptas

Costs

Spain is one of Western Europe's more affordable countries. If you are particularly frugal, it's possible to scrape by on 3000 ptas to 4000 ptas a day; this would involve staying in the cheapest possible accommodation, avoiding eating in restaurants or going to museums or bars, and not moving around too much. Places like Madrid, Barcelona, Seville and San Sebastián will place a greater strain on your moneybelt.

A more reasonable budget would be 6000 ptas a day. This could allow you 1500 ptas to 2000 ptas for accommodation; 300 ptas for breakfast (coffee and a pastry); 1000 ptas to 1500 ptas for lunch or dinner; 600 ptas to 800 ptas for another, lighter meal; 250 ptas for public transport; 500 ptas to 1000 ptas for entry fees to museum, sights or entertainment; and a bit over for a drink or two and intercity travel.

Tipping & Bargaining

In restaurants, menu prices include a service charge, and tipping is a matter of personal choice – most people leave some small change and 5% is plenty. It's common to leave small change in bars and cafes. The only places in Spain where you are likely to bargain are markets and, occasionally, cheap hotels – particularly if you're staying for a few days.

Consumer Taxes & Refunds

In Spain, VAT (value-added tax) is known as IVA *(impuesto sobre el valor añadido)*. On accommodation and restaurant prices, there's a flat rate of 7% IVA which is usually, but not always, included in quoted prices. To check, ask if the price is 'con IVA' (with VAT) or 'sin IVA' (without VAT).

On retail goods, alcohol, electrical appliances etc, IVA is 16%. Visitors are entitled to a refund of IVA on any item costing more than 15,000 ptas that they are taking out of the EU. Ask the shop for a Europe Tax-Free Shopping Cheque when you buy, then present the goods and cheque to customs when you leave. Customs stamps the cheque and you then cash it at a booth with the 'Cash Refund' sign. There are booths at all main Spanish airports, the border crossings at Algeciras, Gibraltar and Andorra, and similar refund points throughout the EU.

POST & COMMUNICATIONS
Post

Main post offices in provincial capitals are usually open about 8.30 am to 8.30 pm Monday to Friday, and about 9 am to 1.30 pm Saturday. Stamps are also sold at *estancos* (tobacconist shops with the 'Tabacos' sign in yellow letters on a maroon background). A standard airmail letter or card costs 70 ptas to Europe, 115 ptas to the

USA or Canada, and 185 ptas to Australia or New Zealand. Aerograms cost 85 ptas regardless of the destination.

Mail to/from Europe normally takes up to a week, and to North America, Australia or New Zealand around 10 days, but there may be some unaccountable long delays.

Poste-restante mail can be addressed to you at either poste restante or *lista de correos*, the Spanish name for it, in the city in question. It's a fairly reliable system, although you must be prepared for mail to arrive late. American Express card or travellers cheque holders can use the free client mail service (see the Facts for the Visitor chapter at the beginning of this book).

Common abbreviations used in Spanish addresses are 1, 2, 3 etc, which mean 1st, 2nd, 3rd floor, and s/n *(sin número)*, which means the building has no number.

Telephone & Fax

Area codes in Spain are an integral part of the phone number; all numbers are nine digits long, without area codes.

Public pay phones are blue, common and easy to use. They accept coins, phonecards *(tarjetas telefónicas)* and, in some cases, credit cards. Phonecards come in 1000 and 2000 ptas denominations and are available at main post offices and estancos. A three-minute call from a pay phone costs 25 ptas within a local area, 65 ptas to other places in the same province, 110 ptas to other provinces, or 230 ptas to another EU country. Provincial and inter-provincial calls, except those to mobile phones, are around 50% cheaper between 8 pm and 8 am and all day Saturday and Sunday; local and international calls are around 10% cheaper between 6 pm and 8 am and all day Saturday and Sunday.

International reverse-charge (collect) calls are simple to make: from a pay phone or private phone dial ☎ 900-99 00 followed by ☎ 61 for Australia, ☎ 44 for the UK, ☎ 64 for New Zealand, ☎ 15 for Canada, and for the USA ☎ 11 (AT&T) or ☎ 14 (MCI).

A three-minute call to the USA at peak rates will cost 280 ptas, and to Australia 820 ptas.

Most main post offices have a fax service, but you'll often find cheaper rates at shops or offices with 'Fax Público' signs.

INTERNET RESOURCES

Cybercafes are beginning to spring up in major Spanish cities. Charges for an hour online range anywhere from 200 ptas to 900 ptas.

An Internet search under 'Spain, Travel' will reveal dozens of sites.

BOOKS

The New Spaniards by John Hooper is a fascinating account of modern Spanish society and culture. For a readable and thorough, but not over-long, survey of Spanish history, *The Story of Spain* by Mark Williams is hard to beat.

Classic accounts of life and travel in Spain include Gerald Brenan's *South from Granada* (1920s), Laurie Lee's *As I Walked Out One Midsummer Morning* (1930s), George Orwell's *Homage to Catalonia* (the civil war), and *Iberia* by James Michener (1960s). Among the best of more recent books are *Homage to Barcelona* by Colm Toíbín, *Spanish Journeys* by Adam Hopkins and *Cities of Spain* by David Gilmour.

Of foreign literature set in Spain, Ernest Hemingway's civil war novel *For Whom the Bell Tolls* is a must.

If you're planning in-depth travels in Spain, get hold of Lonely Planet's *Spain*.

NEWSPAPERS & MAGAZINES

The major daily newspapers in Spain are the solid liberal *El País*, the conservative *ABC*, and *El Mundo*, which specialises in breaking political scandals. There's also a welter of regional dailies, some of the best being in Barcelona, the País Vasco and Andalucía.

International press such as the *International Herald Tribune*, *Time* and *Newsweek*, and daily papers from Western European countries reach major cities and elsewhere tourist areas on the day of publication; elsewhere they're harder to find and are a day or two late.

RADIO & TV

There are hundreds of radio stations, mainly on the FM band – you'll hear a substantial proportion of British and American music. The national pop/rock station, Radio 3, has admirably varied programming.

Spaniards are Europe's greatest TV watchers after the British, but do a lot of their watching in bars and cafes which makes it more of a social activity. Most TVs receive six channels: two state-run (TVE1 and La2), three privately run (Antena 3, Tele 5 and Canal+), and one regional channel. Apart from news, TV seems to consist mostly of game and talk shows, sport, soap operas, sitcoms, and English-language films dubbed into Spanish.

PHOTOGRAPHY & VIDEO

Main brands of film are widely available and processing is fast and generally efficient. A roll of print film (36 exposures, 100 ASA) costs around 700 ptas and can be processed for around 1700 ptas though there are often better deals if you have two or three rolls developed together. The equivalent in slide film is around 850 ptas plus the same for processing. Nearly all pre-recorded videos in Spain use the PAL image-registration system common to Western Europe and Australia. These won't work on many video players in France, North America and Japan.

TIME

Spain is one hour ahead of GMT/UTC during winter, and two hours ahead from the last Sunday in March to the last Sunday in September.

LAUNDRY

Self-service laundrettes are rare. Laundries (lavanderías) are common but not particularly cheap. They will usually wash, dry and fold a load for 1000 ptas to 1200 ptas.

TOILETS

Public toilets are not very common in Spain. The easiest thing to do is head for a cafe. It is polite to buy something in exchange for the toilet service.

WOMEN TRAVELLERS

The best way for women travellers to approach Spain is simply to be ready to ignore stares, cat calls and unnecessary comments. However, Spain has one of the lowest incidences of reported rape in the developed world, and even physical harassment is much less frequent than you might expect. The Asociación de Asistencia a Mujeres Violadas, at Calle de O'Donnell 42 in Madrid (☎ 91 574 01 10, Monday to Friday from 10 am to 2 pm and 4 to 7 pm; recorded message in Spanish at other times) offers advice and

help to rape victims, and can provide details of similar centres in other cities, though only limited English is spoken.

GAY & LESBIAN TRAVELLERS

Attitudes towards gays and lesbians are pretty tolerant, especially in the cities. Madrid, Barcelona, Sitges, Ibiza and Cádiz all have active gay and lesbian scenes. A good source of information on gay places and organisations throughout Spain is Coordinadora Gai-Lesbiana (☎ 93 298 00 29, fax 93 298 06 18), Carrer de Finlandia 45, 08014 Barcelona. Its Web site is www.pangea .org/org/cgl. In Madrid, the equivalent is Cogam (☎/fax 91 532 45 17), Calle del Fuencarral 37, 28004 Madrid.

DISABLED TRAVELLERS

Spanish tourist offices in other countries can provide a basic information sheet with some useful addresses, and give information on accessible accommodation in specific places. INSERSO (☎ 91 347 88 88), Calle de Ginzo de Limea 58, 28029 Madrid, is the government department for the disabled, with branches in all of Spain's 50 provinces.

You'll find some wheelchair-accessible accommodation in main centres, but it may not be in the budget category – although 25 Spanish youth hostels are classed as suitable for wheelchair users.

SENIOR TRAVELLERS

There are reduced prices for people over 60, 63 or 65 (depending on the place) at some attractions and occasionally on transport.

USEFUL ORGANISATIONS

The travel agency TIVE, with offices in major cities throughout Spain, specialises in discounted tickets and travel arrangements for students and young people. Its Madrid office (☎ 91 543 74 12, fax 91 544 00 62) is at Calle de Fernando El Católico 88.

DANGERS & ANNOYANCES

It's a good idea to take your car radio and any other valuables with you any time you leave your car. In fact it's best to leave nothing at all – certainly nothing visible – in a parked car. In youth hostels, don't leave belongings unattended as there is a high incidence of theft. Beware of pickpockets in cities and tourist resorts (Barcelona and Seville have bad reputations). There is also a relatively high incidence of mugging in such places, so keep your wits about you. Emergency numbers for the police throughout Spain are ☎ 091 (national police) and ☎ 092 (local police).

Drugs
In 1992 Spain's liberal drug laws were severely tightened. No matter what anyone tells you, it is not legal to smoke dope in public bars. There is a reasonable degree of tolerance when it comes to people having a smoke in their own home, but not in hotel rooms or guesthouses.

BUSINESS HOURS
Generally, people work Monday to Friday from 9 am to 2 pm and then again from 4.30 or 5 pm for another three hours. Shops and travel agencies are usually open these hours on Saturday too, though some may skip the evening session. Museums all have their own unique opening hours; major ones tend to open for something like normal business hours (with or without the afternoon break), but often have their weekly closing day on Monday, not Sunday.

PUBLIC HOLIDAYS & SPECIAL EVENTS
Spain has at least 14 official holidays a year, some observed nationwide, some very local. When a holiday falls close to a weekend, Spaniards like to make a *puente* (bridge) meaning they take the intervening day off too. The following holidays are observed virtually everywhere:

New Year's Day 1 January
Epiphany or Three Kings' Day (when children receive presents) 6 January
Good Friday
Labour Day 1 May
Feast of the Assumption 15 August
National Day 12 October
All Saints' Day 1 November
Feast of the Immaculate Conception 8 December
Christmas 25 December

The two main periods when Spaniards go on holiday are Semana Santa (the week leading up to Easter Sunday) and the month of August.

At these times accommodation in resorts can be scarce and transport heavily booked, but other cities are often half-empty.

Spaniards indulge their love of colour, noise, crowds and partying at innumerable local fiestas and *ferias* (fairs); even small villages will have at least one, probably several, during the year. Many fiestas are based on religion but still highly festive. Local tourist offices can always supply detailed information.

Among festivals to look out for are La Tamborada in San Sebastián on 20 January, when the whole town dresses up and goes berserk; *carnaval*, a time of fancy-dress parades and merrymaking celebrated around the country about seven weeks before Easter (wildest in Cádiz and Sitges); Valencia's week-long mid-March party, Las Fallas, with all-night dancing and drinking, first-class fireworks, and processions; Semana Santa with its parades of holy images and huge crowds, notably in Seville; Seville's Feria de Abril, a week-long party held in late April, a kind of counterbalance to the religious peak of Semana Santa; Sanfermines, with the running of the bulls, in Pamplona in July; Semana Grande, another week of heavy drinking and hangovers, all along the north coast during the first half of August; and Barcelona's week-long party, the Festes de la Mercè, around 24 September.

ACTIVITIES
Surfing & Windsurfing
The País Vasco has good surf spots – San Sebastián, Zarauz and the legendary left at Mundaca, among others. Tarifa, Spain's southernmost point, is a windsurfers' heaven, with constant breezes and long, empty beaches.

Skiing
Skiing in Spain is cheap and the facilities and conditions are good. The season runs from December to May. The most accessible resorts are in the Sierra Nevada (very close to Granada), the Pyrenees (north of Barcelona) and in the ranges north of Madrid. Contact tourist offices in these cities for information. Affordable day trips can be booked through travel agents.

Cycling
Bike touring isn't as common as in other parts of Europe because of deterrents such as the

SPAIN

often-mountainous terrain and summer heat. It's a more viable option on the Balearic Islands than on much of the mainland, although plenty of people get on their bikes in spring and autumn in the south. Mountain biking is increasingly popular and areas like Andalucía and Catalonia have many good tracks. Finding bikes to rent is a hit-and-miss affair so if you're set on the idea it's best to bring your own.

Hiking

Spain is a trekker's paradise, so much so that Lonely Planet has published a guide to some of the best treks in the country, *Walking in Spain*. See also the Mallorca and Picos de Europa sections of this chapter.

Walking country roads and paths, between settlements, can also be highly enjoyable and a great way to meet the locals.

Two organisations publish detailed close-up maps of small parts of Spain. The CNIG covers most of the country in 1:25,000 (1cm to 250m) sheets, most of which are recent. The CNIG and the Servicio Geográfico del Ejército (SGE, Army Geographic Service) each publishes a 1:50,000 series; the SGE's tends to be more up to date as the maps were published in the mid-1980s. Also useful for hiking and exploring some areas are the *Guía Cartográfica* and *Guía Excursionista y Turística* series published by Editorial Alpina. The series combines information booklets in Spanish (or sometimes Catalan) with detailed maps at scales ranging from 1:25,000 to 1:50,000, which are well worth their price (around 500 ptas). You may well find CNIG, SCE and Alpina publications in local bookshops but it's more reliable to get them in advance from specialist map or travel shops like La Tienda Verde in Madrid, and Altaïr and Quera in Barcelona.

If you fancy a really long walk, there's the Camino de Santiago. This route, which has been followed by Christian pilgrims for centuries, can be commenced at various places in France. It then crosses the Pyrenees and runs via Pamplona, Logroño and León all the way to the cathedral in Santiago de Compostela. There are numerous guidebooks explaining the route, and the best map is published by CNIG.

COURSES

The best place to take a language course in Spain is generally at a university. Those with the best reputations include Salamanca, Santiago de Compostela and Santander. It can also be fun to combine study with a stay in one of Spain's most exciting cities such as Barcelona, Madrid or Seville. There are also dozens of private language colleges throughout the country; the Instituto Cervantes (☎ 020-7235 0353), 102 Eaton Square, London SW1 W9AN, can send you lists of these and of universities that run courses. Some Spanish embassies and consulates also have information.

Other courses available in Spain include art, cookery and photography. Spanish tourist offices can help with information.

WORK

EU, Norway and Iceland nationals are allowed to work in Spain without a visa, but if they plan to stay more than three months, they are supposed to apply within the first month for a residence card (see Visas & Documents earlier in this chapter). Virtually everyone else is supposed to obtain, from a Spanish consulate in their country of residence, a work permit and, if they plan to stay more than 90 days, a residence visa. These procedures are even more difficult (see Visas & Documents). That said, quite a few people do manage to work in Spain one way or another – though with Spain's unemployment rate running at around 15%, don't rely on it. Teaching English is an obvious option – a TEFL certificate will be a big help. Another possibility is gaining summer work in a bar or restaurant in a tourist resort. Quite a lot of these are run by foreigners.

ACCOMMODATION
Camping

Spain has more than 800 camping grounds. Facilities and settings vary enormously, and grounds are officially rated from 1st class to 3rd class. You can expect to pay around 500 ptas each per person, car and tent. Tourist offices can direct you to the nearest camping ground. Many are open all year, though quite a few close from around October to Easter. With certain exceptions (such as many beaches and environmentally protected areas), it is legal to camp outside camping grounds. You'll need permission to camp on private land.

Hostels

Spain's youth hostels (*albergues juveniles*) are often the cheapest place to stay for lone travellers, but two people can usually get a double room elsewhere for a similar price. With some notable exceptions, hostels are only moderate value. Many have curfews and/or are closed during the day, or lack cooking facilities (if so they usually have a cafeteria). They can be lacking in privacy, and are often heavily booked by school groups. Most are members of the country's Hostelling International (HI) organisation, Red Española de Albergues Juveniles (REAJ), whose head office (☎ 91 347 77 00, fax 91 401 81 60) is at Calle de José Ortega y Gasset 71, 28006 Madrid.

Prices often depend on the season or whether you're under 26; typically you pay 900 ptas to 1700 ptas. Some hostels require HI membership, others don't but may charge more if you're not a member. You can buy HI cards for 1800 ptas at virtually all hostels.

Other Accommodation

Officially, all the establishments are either *hoteles* (from one to five stars), *hostales* (one to three stars) or *pensiones*. In practice, there are all sorts of overlapping categories, especially at the budget end of the market. In broad terms, the cheapest are usually *fondas* and *casas de huéspedes*, followed by pensiones. All these normally have shared bathrooms, and singles/doubles for 1250/2500 ptas to 3000/4000 ptas. Some hostales and *hostal-residencias* come in the same price range, but others have rooms with private bathroom costing anywhere up to 8000 ptas or so. Hoteles are usually beyond the means of budget travellers. The luxurious state-run *paradores*, often converted historic buildings, are prohibitively expensive.

Room rates in this chapter are generally high-season prices, which in most resorts and other heavily touristed places means July and August, Semana Santa and sometimes Christmas and New Year. At other times prices in many places go down by 5% to 25%. In many cases you have to add 7% IVA.

FOOD

It's a good idea to reset your stomach's clock in Spain, unless you want to eat alone or only with other tourists. Most Spaniards start the day with a light breakfast *(desayuno)*, perhaps coffee with a *tostada* (piece of buttered toast) or *pastel* (pastry). *Churros con chocolate* (long, deep-fried doughnuts with thick hot chocolate) are a delicious start to the day and unique to Spain. Lunch *(almuerzo* or *comida)* is usually the main meal of the day, eaten between about 1.30 and 4 pm. The evening meal *(cena)* is usually lighter and may be eaten as late as 10 or 11 pm. It's common (and a great idea!) to go to a bar or cafe for a snack around 11 am and again around 7 or 8 pm.

Spain has a huge variety of local cuisines. Seafood as well as meat is prominent almost everywhere. One of the most characteristic dishes, from the Valencia region, is *paella* – rice, seafood, the odd vegetable and often chicken or meat, all simmered up together, traditionally coloured yellow with saffron. Another dish, of Andalucían origin, is *gazpacho*, a soup made from tomatoes, breadcrumbs, cucumber and/or green peppers, eaten cold. *Tortillas* (omelettes) are an inexpensive stand-by and come in many varieties. *Jamón serrano* (cured ham) is a treat for meat-eaters.

Cafes & Bars

If you want to follow Spanish habits, you'll be spending plenty of time in cafes and bars. In almost all of them you'll find *tapas* available. These saucer-sized mini-snacks are part of the Spanish way of life and come in infinite varieties from calamari rings to potato salad to spinach with chickpeas to a small serving of tripe. A typical tapa costs 100 ptas to 250 ptas (although sometimes they will come free with your drinks), but check before you order because some are a lot dearer. A *ración* is a meal-sized serving of these snacks; a *media ración* is a half-ración.

The other popular snacks are *bocadillos*, long filled white bread rolls. Spaniards eat so many bocadillos that some cafes sell nothing else. Try not to leave Spain without sampling a *bocadillo de tortilla de patata*, a roll filled with potato omelette.

You can often save 10% to 20% by ordering and eating food at the bar rather than at a table.

Restaurants

Throughout Spain, there are plenty of restaurants serving good, simple food at affordable prices, often featuring regional specialities.

SPAIN

Many restaurants offer a *menú del día* – the budget traveller's best friend. For around 850 ptas to 1500 ptas, you typically get a starter, a main course, dessert, bread and wine – often with a choice of two or three dishes for each course. The *plato combinado* is a near relative of the *menú*. It literally translates as 'combined plate' – maybe a steak and egg with chips and salad, or fried squid with potato salad. You'll pay more for your meals if you order a la carte, but the food will be better.

Vegetarian Food

Finding vegetarian fare can be a headache. It's not uncommon for 'meatless' food to be flavoured with meat stock. But in larger cities and important student centres there's a growing awareness of vegetarianism, so that if there isn't a vegetarian restaurant, there are often vegetarian items on menus. A good vegetarian snack at almost any place with bocadillos or sandwiches is a bocadillo (or sandwich) *vegetal*, which has a filling of salad and, often, fried egg (*sin huevo* means without egg).

Self-Catering

Every town of any substance has a *mercado* (food market). These are fun and great value. Even big eaters should be able to put together a filling meal of bread, *chorizo* (spiced sausage), cheese, fruit and a drink for 500 ptas or less. If you shop carefully you can eat three healthy meals a day for as little as 700 ptas.

DRINKS

Coffee in Spain is strong. Addicts should specify how they want their fix: *café con leche* is about 50% coffee, 50% hot milk; *café solo* is a short black; *café cortado* is a short black with a little milk.

The most common way to order a beer (*cerveza*) is to ask for a *caña* (pronounced can-ya), which is a small draught beer. *Corto* and, in the País Vasco, *zurrito*, are other names for this. A larger beer (about 300ml) is often called a *tubo*, or in Catalonia a *jarra*. All these words apply to draught beer (*cerveza de barril*) – if you just ask for a cerveza you're likely to get bottled beer, which is more expensive.

Wine (*vino*) comes in white (*blanco*), red (*tinto*) or rosé (*rosado*). Tinto de verano, a

kind of wine shandy, is good in summer. There are also many regional grape specialities such as *jerez* (sherry) in Jerez de la Frontera and *cava* (like champagne) in Catalonia. *Sangría*, a sweet punch made of red wine, fruit and spirits, is refreshing and very popular with tourists.

The cheapest drink of all is, of course, water. To specify tap water (which is safe to drink almost everywhere), just ask for *agua del grifo*.

ENTERTAINMENT

Spain has some of the best nightlife in Europe; wild and *very* late nights, especially on Friday and Saturday, are an integral part of the Spain experience. Many young Spaniards don't even think about going out until midnight or so. Bars, which come in all shapes, sizes and themes, are the main attractions until around 2 or 3 am. Some play great music that will get you hopping before – if you can afford it – you move on to a disco till 5 or 6 am. Discos are generally expensive, but not to be missed if you can manage to splurge. Spain's contributions to modern dance music are *bakalao* and *makina*, kinds of frenzied (150bpm to 180bpm) techno.

The live music scene is less exciting. Spanish rock and pop tends to be imitative, though the bigger cities usually offer a reasonable choice of bands. See the earlier Society & Conduct section for information on flamenco.

Cinemas abound and are good value, though foreign films are usually dubbed into Spanish.

SPECTATOR SPORTS

The national sport is *fútbol* (soccer). The best teams to see for their crowd support as well as their play are usually Real Madrid and Barcelona, although the atmosphere can be electric anywhere. The season runs from September to May.

Bullfighting is enjoying a resurgence despite continued pressure from international animal-rights activists. It's a complex activity that's regarded as much as an art form as a sport by aficionados. If you decide to see a *corrida de toros*, the season runs from March to October. Madrid, Seville and Pamplona are among the best places to see one.

SHOPPING

Many of Spain's best handicrafts are fragile or bulky and inconvenient unless you're going straight home. Pottery comes in a great range of attractive regional varieties. Some lovely rugs and blankets are made in places like the Alpujarras and Níjar in Andalucía. There's some pleasing woodwork available too, such as Granada's marquetry boxes and chess sets. Leather jackets, bags and belts are quite good value in many places.

Getting There & Away

AIR

Spain has many international airports including Madrid, Barcelona, Bilbao, Santiago de Compostela, Seville, Málaga, Almería, Alicante, Valencia, Palma de Mallorca, Ibiza and Maó (Menorca). In general, the cheapest destinations are Málaga, the Balearic Islands, Barcelona and Madrid.

Australia

In general, the best thing to do is to fly to London, Paris, Frankfurt or Rome, and then make your way overland. Alternatively, some flight deals to these centres include a couple of short-haul flights within Europe, and Madrid or Barcelona are usually acceptable destinations for these. Some round-the-world (RTW) fares include stops in Spain. STA Travel should be able to help you out with a good price. Generally speaking, a return fare to Europe for under A$1700 is too good to pass up.

North America

Return fares to Madrid from Miami, New York, Atlanta or Chicago range from US$780 to US$830 on Iberia or Delta. From the west coast you are usually looking at about US$100 more.

The UK

Scheduled flights to Spain are generally expensive, but with the huge range of charter, discount and low-season fares, it's often cheaper to fly than to take a bus or train. Check the travel sections of *TNT* or *Time Out* magazines or the weekend newspapers. The

following are examples of short-notice low-season return fares from London:

Dest'n	Fare (UK£)	Agent Phone
Barcelona	129	Charter Flight Centre ☎ 020-7565 6755
Ibiza	119	Go ☎ 0845-605 4321
Madrid	109	EasyJet ☎ 0870-600 0000
Málaga	109	Spanish Travel Services ☎ 020-7387 5337

From Spain

For northern Europe, check the ads in local English-language papers in tourist centres like the Costa del Sol, the Costa Blanca and the Balearic Islands. You may pick up a one-way fare to London for around 12,000 ptas. The youth and student travel agency TIVE, and the general travel agency Halcón Viajes, both with branches in most main cities, have some good fares: generally you're looking at around 13,000 ptas to 15,500 ptas one way to London, Paris or Amsterdam, and at least 30,000 ptas to the USA.

LAND
Bus

There are regular bus services to Spain from all major centres in Europe, including Lisbon, London and Paris. In London, Eurolines (☎ 0870-514 3219) has services at least three times a week to Barcelona (UK£84 one way, 23 to 25 hours), Madrid (UK£77 one way, at least 27 hours) and Málaga (UK£79 one way, 34 hours). Tickets are sold by major travel agencies, and people under 26 and senior citizens qualify for a 10% discount. There are also bus services to Morocco from some Spanish cities.

Train

Reaching Spain by train is more expensive than bus unless you have a rail pass, though fares for those under 26 come close to the bus price. Normal one-way fares from London (using the ferry, not Eurostar) to Madrid (via Paris) are UK£104. For more details, contact the Rail Europe Travel Centre in London (☎ 08705-848 848) or a travel agent. See the introductory Getting Around chapter for more on rail passes and train travel through Europe.

Car & Motorcycle

If you're driving or riding to Spain from England, you'll have to choose between going through France (check visa requirements) or taking a direct ferry from England to Spain (see the following section). The cheapest way is one of the shorter ferries from England to France, then a quick drive down through France.

SEA
The UK

There are two direct ferry services. Brittany Ferries (in England ☎ 0870 536 0360) runs Plymouth-Santander ferries twice weekly from about mid-March to mid-November (24 hours), and a Portsmouth-Santander service (30 hours), usually once a week, in other months. P&O European Ferries (in England ☎ 08702 424 999) runs Portsmouth-Bilbao ferries twice weekly almost all year (35 hours). Prices on all services are similar: one-way passenger fares range from about UK£50 in winter to UK£85 in summer (cabins extra); a car and driver costs from UK£152 to UK£275, or you can take a vehicle and several passengers for UK£233 to UK£403.

Morocco

Ferry services between Spain and Morocco include Algeciras-Tangier, Algeciras-Ceuta, Gibraltar-Tangier, Málaga-Melilla, Almería-Melilla and Almería-Nador. Those to/from Algeciras are the fastest, cheapest and most frequent, with up to 20 ferries and hydrofoils a day to Ceuta (1½ hours/40 minutes) and 14 to Tangier (two hours/one hour). One-way passenger fares on the ferry/hydrofoil are 1801/2945 ptas (Ceuta) and 2960/3440 ptas (Tangier). A car to Ceuta/Tangier costs 9300/8223 ptas. You can buy tickets at Algeciras harbour, but it's more convenient to go to one of the many agencies on the waterfront. The price doesn't vary, so just look for the place with the shortest queue.

Don't buy Moroccan currency until you reach Morocco, as you will get ripped off in Algeciras.

LEAVING SPAIN

Departure taxes on flights out of Spain, which vary, are factored directly into tickets.

Getting Around

AIR

Spain has four main domestic airlines: Iberia (with subsidiary Binter Mediterráneo, both on ☎ 902-40 05 00), Air Europa (☎ 902-40 15 01) and Spanair (☎ 902-13 14 15). They and a couple of smaller airlines compete to produce some fares that can make flying worthwhile if you're in a hurry, especially for longer or return trips.

The return fare between Madrid and Barcelona can be as high as 30,000 ptas. To Palma de Mallorca, Santiago de Compostela, or Málaga you are looking at around 29,000 ptas return. All these fares can be cut in half if you comply with certain restrictions.

Among travel agencies, TIVE and Halcón Viajes are always worth checking for fares. There are some useful deals if you're under 26 (or, in some cases, over 63).

BUS

Spain's bus network is operated by dozens of independent companies and is more extensive than its train system, serving remote towns and villages as well as the major routes. The choice between bus and train depends on the particular trip you're taking; for the best value, compare fares, journey times and frequencies each time you move. Buses to/from Madrid are often cheaper than (or barely different from) cross-country routes. For instance Seville to Madrid costs 2745 ptas while the shorter Seville-Granada trip is 2700 ptas.

Many towns and cities have one main bus station where most buses arrive and depart, and these usually have an information desk giving information on all services. Tourist offices can also help with information but don't sell tickets.

TRAIN

Trains are mostly modern and comfortable, and late arrivals are now the exception rather than the rule. The main headache is deciding which compartment on which train gives you best value for money.

RENFE, the national railway company, runs numerous types of train, and travel times can vary a lot on the same route. So can fares, which may depend not just on the type of train but also the day of the week and time of day. *Regionales* are all-stops trains which are cheap and slow. *Cercanías* provide regular services from major cities to the surrounding suburbs and hinterland, sometimes even crossing regional boundaries.

Among long-distance *(largo recorrido)* trains the standard daytime train is the *diurno* (its night-time equivalent is the *estrella*). Quicker is the InterCity (mainly because it makes fewer stops), while the *Talgo* is the quickest and dearest.

Best of all is the AVE high-speed service that links Madrid and Seville in just 2½ hours. The *Talgo 200* uses part of this line to speed down to Málaga from Madrid. The *Euromed* is an AVE-style train that speeds south from Barcelona to Valencia and Alicante. A *Tren Hotel* is a 1st-class sleeper-only express.

There's also a bewildering range of accommodation types, especially on overnight trains (fares quoted in this chapter are typical 2nd-class seat fares). Fortunately ticket clerks understand the problem and are usually happy to go through a few options with you. The cheapest sleeper option is usually a *litera*, a bunk in a six-berth 2nd-class compartment.

You can buy tickets and make reservations at stations, RENFE offices in many city centres, and travel agencies that display the RENFE logo.

Train Passes

Rail passes are valid for all RENFE trains, but Inter-Rail users have to pay supplements on Talgo and InterCity services, and on the high-speed AVE service between Madrid and Seville. All pass-holders making reservations for long-distance trains pay a fee of between 500 ptas and 1500 ptas.

RENFE's Tarjeta Turística (also known as the Spain Flexipass) is a rail pass for non-Europeans, valid for three to 10 days travel in a two-month period: in 2nd class, three days costs US$155, and 10 days is US$365. It can be purchased from agents outside Europe, or a few main train stations and RENFE offices in Spain. Students and under 26s can also buy an ExploreRail card valid for seven, 15 or 30 days of unlimited travel. It's a real bargain, costing just 19,000/23,000/30,000 ptas, and available at agents such as usit UNLIMITED (☎ 902-32 52 75). Web site: www.unlimited.es.

CAR & MOTORCYCLE

If you're driving or riding around Spain, consider investing 2600 ptas in the *Michelin Atlas de Carreteras España Portugal*. It's a handy atlas with detailed road maps as well as maps of all the main towns and cities.

Spain's roads vary enormously but are generally quite good. Fastest are the *autopistas*, multilane freeways between major cities. On some, mainly in the north, you have to pay hefty tolls (from the French border to Barcelona, for example, it's 1580 ptas). Minor routes can be slow going but are usually more scenic. Petrol is relatively expensive at around 114 ptas for a litre of unleaded.

The head office of the Spanish automobile club Real Automovil Club de España (RACE; ☎ 900-20 00 93) is at Calle de José Abascal 10, 28003 Madrid. For the RACE's 24-hour, nationwide, on-road emergency service, call the toll free number ☎ 900-11 22 22.

Road Rules

Although a little hairy, driving in Spain is not too bad and locals show at least some respect for the rules. Speed limits are 120km/h on the autopistas, 90km/h or 100km/h on other country roads and 50km/h in built-up areas. The maximum allowable blood-alcohol level is 0.05%. Seat belts must be worn, and all motorcyclists must always wear a helmet and keep headlights on day and night.

Trying to find a parking spot can be a nightmare in larger towns and cities. Spanish drivers park anywhere to save themselves the hassle of a half-hour search, but *grúas* (tow trucks) will tow your car if given the chance. The cost of bailing out a car can be as high as 10,000 ptas.

Rental

Rates vary widely from place to place. The best deals tend to be in major tourist areas, including at their airports. At Málaga airport you can rent a small car for under 20,000 ptas a week. More generally, you're looking at anything up to 9000 ptas for a day with unlimited kilometres, plus insurance, damage waiver and taxes. Hiring for several days can bring the average daily cost down a great deal – a small car for a week might cost 40,000 ptas all up. Local companies often have better rates than the big firms.

BICYCLE

See Cycling in the Activities section earlier in this chapter.

HITCHING

It's still possible to thumb your way around parts of Spain, but large doses of patience and common sense are necessary. Women should avoid hitching alone. Hitching is illegal on autopistas and difficult on major highways. Your chances are better on minor roads, although the going can still be painfully slow.

BOAT

For information on ferries to, from and between the Balearic Islands, see that section of this chapter.

LOCAL TRANSPORT

In many Spanish towns you will not need to use public transport, as transport terminals and accommodation are centralised and within walking distance of most tourist attractions.

Most towns in Spain have an effective local bus system. In larger cities, these can be complicated, but tourist offices can advise on which buses you need. Barcelona and Madrid both have efficient underground systems which are faster and easier to use than the bus systems.

Taxis are still pretty cheap. If you split a cross-town fare between three or four people, it can be a decidedly good deal. Rates vary slightly from city to city: in Barcelona, they cost 295 ptas flag fall, plus about 100 ptas per kilometre; in Madrid they're a bit cheaper (190 ptas flag fall). There are supplements for luggage and airport trips.

Madrid

pop 3.1 million

Whatever apprehensions you may have about Madrid when you first arrive, Spain's capital is sure to grow on you. Madrid may lack the glamour or beauty of Barcelona and the historical richness of so many Spanish cities (it was insignificant until Felipe II made it his capital in 1561), but it more than makes up for this with a remarkable collection of museums and galleries, some lovely parks and gardens and wild nightlife.

ORIENTATION

The area of most interest to visitors lies between Parque del Buen Retiro in the east and Campo del Moro in the west. These two parks are more or less connected by Calle de Alcalá and Calle Mayor, which meet in the middle at Puerta del Sol. Calle Mayor passes the main square, Plaza Mayor, on its way from Puerta del Sol to the Palacio Real in front of Campo del Moro.

The main north-south thoroughfare is Paseo de la Castellana, which runs (changing names to Paseo de los Recoletos and finally Paseo del Prado) all the way from Chamartín train station in the north to Madrid's other big station, Atocha.

INFORMATION
Tourist Offices

The main tourist office (☎ 91 429 49 51) is at Calle del Duque de Medinaceli 2. It opens 9 am to 7 pm Monday to Friday, and 9 am to 1 pm Saturday. The office at Barajas airport (☎ 91 305 86 56) is open 8 am to 8 pm Monday to Friday and 8 am to 1 pm Saturday. The one at Chamartín train station (☎ 91 315 99 76) keeps the same hours.

Yet another Oficina de Turismo (☎ 91 364 18 76), Ronda de Toledo 1, is located in the Centro Comercial de la Puerta de Toledo. It opens 9 am to 7 pm Monday to Friday and 9.30 am to 1.30 pm Saturday.

Money

Large banks like the Caja de Madrid usually have the best rates, but check commissions first. Banking hours vary but it is generally safe to assume they will be open 9 am to 2 pm weekdays (to 1 pm Saturday). American Express (☎ 91 527 03 03 open 24 hours, ☎ 900-99 44 26 for replacing lost travellers cheques) is at Plaza de las Cortes 2 and has reasonable rates. It's open 9 am to 5.30 pm Monday to Friday and 9 am to noon Saturday.

If you're desperate there are plenty of *bureaux de change* around Puerta del Sol and Plaza Mayor, which offer appalling rates but are often open until midnight.

Post & Communications

The main post office is in the gigantic Palacio de Comunicaciones on Plaza de la Cibeles. Poste restante (lista de correos) is at windows 78 to 80 and is open 8 am to 9.30 pm weekdays and 8.30 am to 2 pm Saturday.

The Telefónica *locutorio* (phone centre) at Gran Vía 30 has phone books for the whole country and cabins where you can make calls in relative peace. It's open 9.30 am to midnight daily. Keep an eye out for private phone companies, whose offices can undercut Telefónica by 50%.

Email & Internet Access
Dozens of cafes and shops offer Internet connections, including Aroba52, on Calle de los Reyes (metro: Plaza de España) which charges 300 ptas an hour, or La Casa de Internet, Calle de Luchana 20 (metro: Bilbao) at 900 ptas an hour.

Travel Agencies
For cheap travel tickets try Viajes Zeppelin (☎ 91 542 51 54), Plaza de Santo Domingo 2; or TIVE (☎ 91 543 74 12), the student and youth travel organisation, at Calle de Fernando el Católico 88 or in the Instituto de la Juventud (☎ 91 347 77 78) at Calle de José Ortega y Gasset 71. Both open 9 am to 1 pm Monday to Friday.

Bookshops
La Casa del Libro, Gran Vía 29-31, has a broad selection of books on all subjects, including books in English and other languages. For English-language books, you could also try Booksellers, Calle de José Abascal 48. Librería de Mujeres, Calle de San Cristóbal 17, is a women's bookshop. La Tienda Verde, Calle de Maudes 38 (metro: Cuatro Caminos), specialises in walking guides and maps for many parts of Spain.

Laundry
Laundrettes include Lavandería España on Calle del Infante, Lavomatique on Calle de Cervantes, and Lavandería Alba at Calle del Barco 26.

Medical & Emergency Services
If you have medical problems pop into the nearest Insalud clinic often marked 'Centro de Salud'. A handy one in the centre is at Calle de las Navas de Tolosa 10. You can also get help at the Anglo-American Medical Unit (☎ 91 435 18 23), Calle del Conde de Aranda

1. For an ambulance call the Cruz Roja on ☎ 522 22 22 or Insalud on ☎ 061. There is a 24-hour pharmacy, Farmacia del Globo (☎ 91 369 20 00), at Plaza de Antón Martín 46.

In police emergency you can call the Policía Nacional on ☎ 091 or the Guardia Civil on ☎ 062.

THINGS TO SEE & DO
Madrid will make a lot more sense if you spend some time walking around before you get into the city's cultural delights. The following walking tour could take anywhere from a few hours to a few days – it's up to you. You'll find more detail on the major sights in following sections.

Unless you want to hit the big art galleries first, the most fitting place to begin exploring Madrid is the **Puerta del Sol**, the official city centre.

Walk up Calle de Preciados and take the second street on the left, which will bring you out to Plaza de las Descalzas. Note the **baroque doorway** in the Caja de Madrid building; it was built for King Felipe V in 1733 and faces the **Monasterio de las Descalzas Reales**.

Moving south down Calle de San Martín you come to the **Iglesia de San Ginés**, one of Madrid's oldest churches. Behind it is the wonderful **Chocolatería de San Ginés**, generally open 7 to 10 am and 1 to 7 pm.

Continue down to and cross Calle Mayor, and then into Madrid's most famous square, **Plaza Mayor**. After a coffee on the plaza, head west along Calle Mayor until you come to the historic **Plaza de la Villa**, with Madrid's 17th-century *ayuntamiento* (town hall). On the same square stand the 16th-century **Casa de Cisneros** and the Gothic-mudéjar **Torre de los Lujanes**, one of the city's oldest buildings, dating from the Middle Ages.

Take the street down the left side of the Casa de Cisneros, cross the road at the end, go down the stairs and follow the cobbled Calle del Cordón out onto Calle de Segovia. Almost directly in front of you is the mudéjar tower of the **Iglesia de San Pedro**. Proceeding down Costanilla de San Pedro you reach the **Iglesia de San Andrés**.

From here you cross Plaza de la Puerta de Moros and head south-west to the **Basílica de San Francisco El Grande**, or east past the

SPAIN

SPAIN

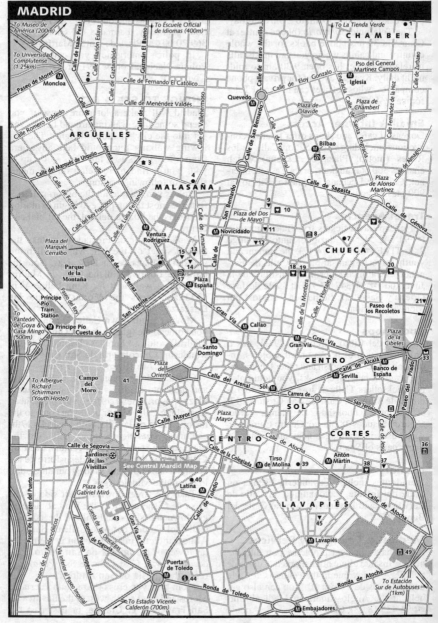

MADRID

To Museo de América (200m)

To Escuele Oficial de Idiomas (400m)

To La Tienda Verde ● 1

CHAMBERÍ

To Universidad Complutense (1.25km)

Paseo de Moret

Moncloa

Calle de Isaac Peral

Calle de Hilarión Eslava

Calle de Gaztambide

Calle de Guzmán El Bueno

2 ●

Calle de Fernando El Católico

Calle de Vallehermoso

Calle de Bravo Murillo

Calle de San Bernardo

Calle de Eloy Gonzalo

Pso del General Martínez Campos

Calle de Zurbano

Calle de Menéndez Valdés

Quevedo Ⓜ

Iglesia

Entrada Calle de Santa Engracia

Plaza de Chamberí

Calle de Santa Engracia

Calle fernández de la hoz

Plaza de Olavide

Calle de

ARGÜELLES

Calle del Marqués de Urquijo

Calle de Tutor

Calle del Rey Francisco

Calle de Luisa Fernanda

Calle de Ferraz

Pintora

Bilbao

Ⓜ 5

Plaza de Alonso Martínez

Calle de Sagasta

Calle de Almagro

3 ●

4 ●

MALASAÑA

San Bernardo

9 ▼

Plaza del Dos de Mayo

10 ▼

6 ▼

Calle de Génova

Ventura Rodríguez

15 ▼ 13 ▼

Novidicado Ⓜ

11 ▼

8 ▼

7 ●

CHUECA

Plaza del Marqués Cerralbo

16 ▼

14 ▼

12 ▼

17 ▼

18 ▼ 19 ▼

20 ▼

Parque de la Montaña

Plaza España

Calle de la Montera

Calle de Hortaleza

Paseo de los Recoletos

21 ▼

Príncipe Pío Train Station

San Vicente

Gran Vía

Callao Ⓜ

Gran Vía Ⓜ

Gran Vía

Plaza de la Cibeles

To Panteón de Goya & Casa Mingo (500m)

Ⓜ Príncipe Pío

Cuesta de

Santo Domingo Ⓜ

CENTRO

Calle de Alcalá

Banco de España

Plaza de la Cibeles

33 ▼

To Albergue Richard Schirrmann (Youth Hostel)

Campo del Moro

41

Plaza de Oriente

Calle del Arenal

Sol Ⓜ

Sevilla Ⓜ

Carrera de

San Jerónimo

34 ▼

42 ▼

Calle de Bailén

Calle Mayor

Plaza Mayor

SOL

CENTRO

Calle de Atocha

CORTES

Antón Martín Ⓜ

Calle de Jesús

36 ▼

Calle de Segovia

Jardines de las Vistillas

See Central Madrid Map

Calle de la Colegiada

Tirso de Molina Ⓜ

39 ●

38 ▼ 37 ▼

Plaza de Gabriel Miró

40 ▼

Latina Ⓜ

Calle de Toledo

LAVAPIÉS

Calle de Atocha

43 ▼

Gran Vía de San Francisco

45 ▼

Paseo de la Virgen del Puerto

Cuesta de las Descargas

Puerta de Toledo

Lavapiés Ⓜ

49 ▼

Paseo de los Melancólicos

Ronda de Segovia

44 ▼

Ronda de Toledo

To Estadio Vicente Calderón (700m)

Embajadores Ⓜ

To Estación Sur de Autobuses (1km)

Vía Inferior al Paseo Imperial

Paseo Imperial

euro currency converter €1 = 166 ptas

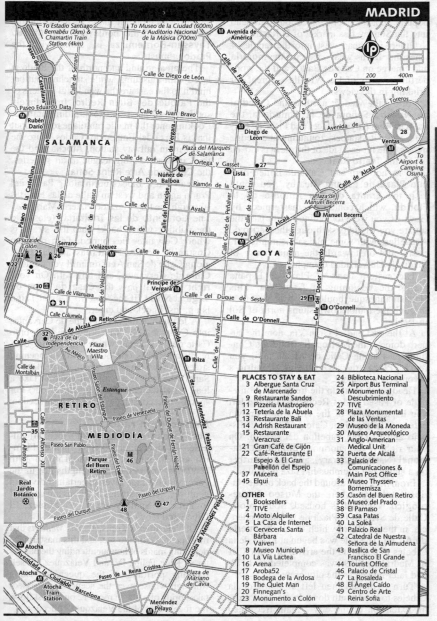

MADRID

To Estadio Santiago Bernabéu (2km) & Chamartín Train Station (4km)

To Museo de la Ciudad (600m) & Auditorio Nacional de la Música (700m)

Avenida de América

Calle de Serrano

Calle de Diego de León

Calle de Francisco Silvela

Calle de Cartagena

Paseo Eduardo Data

Rubén Darío

Calle de Juan Bravo

Avenida de

los Toreros

Ventas

SALAMANCA

Calle de la Castellana

Diego de León

Calle de José

Plaza del Marqués de Salamanca

Ortega y Gasset

To Airport & Camping Osuna

Calle de Don Balboa

Núñez de Balboa

Lista

Calle de Alcalá

Calle de Serrano

Calle de Lagasca

Calle de Don

Ramón de la Cruz

Calle de Alcántara

Plaza de Manuel Becerra

Calle del Príncipe

Ayala

Calle Conde de Peñalver

Manuel Becerra

Hermosilla

Goya

Calle de Alcalá

GOYA

Plaza de Colón

Serrano

Velázquez

Calle de Goya

Calle Fuente del Berro

Calle del Doctor Esquerdo

Calle de Vilanueva

Calle de Velázquez

Príncipe de Vergara

Calle del Duque de Sesto

O'Donnell

Calle Columela

Retiro

Calle de O'Donnell

Calle de Alcalá

Plaza de la Independencia

Av Méjico

Plaza Maestro Villa

Ibiza

Calle de Narváez

Calle de Montalbán

RETIRO

Estanque

Paseo de Venezuela

MEDIODÍA

Paseo San Pablo

Paseo del Duque de Fernán Núñez

Paseo del Uruguay

Parque del Buen Retiro

Real Jardín Botánico

Paseo del Durque

Calle de Alfonso XII

Atocha

Atocha

Avenida de la Ciudad de Barcelona

Paseo de la Reina Cristina

Atocha Train Station

Plaza de Mariano de Cávia

Menéndez Pelayo

PLACES TO STAY & EAT	
3	Albergue Santa Cruz de Marcenado
9	Restaurante Sandos
11	Pizzeria Mastropiero
12	Tetería de la Abuela
13	Restaurante Bali
14	Adrish Restaurant
15	Restaurante Veracruz
21	Gran Café de Gijón
22	Café-Restaurante El Espejo & El Gran Pabellón del Espejo
37	Maceira
45	Elqui

OTHER	
1	Booksellers
2	TIVE
4	Moto Alquiler
5	La Casa de Internet
6	Cervecería Santa Bárbara
7	Vaiven
8	Museo Municipal
10	La Vía Lactea
16	Arena
17	Aroba52
18	Bodega de la Ardosa
19	The Quiet Man
20	Finnegan's
23	Monumento a Colón

24	Biblioteca Nacional
25	Airport Bus Terminal
26	Monumento al Descubrimiento
27	TIVE
28	Plaza Monumental de las Ventas
29	Museo de la Moneda
30	Museo Arqueológico
31	Anglo-American Medical Unit
32	Puerta de Alcalá
33	Palacio de Comunicaciones & Main Post Office
34	Museo Thyssen-Bornemisza
35	Casón del Buen Retiro
36	Museo del Prado
38	El Parnaso
39	Casa Patas
40	La Soleá
41	Palacio Real
42	Catedral de Nuestra Señora de la Almudena
43	Basílica de San Francisco El Grande
44	Tourist Office
46	Palacio de Cristal
47	La Rosaleda
48	El Ángel Caído
49	Centro de Arte Reina Sofia

SPAIN

euro currency converter 100 ptas = €0.60

market along Plaza de la Cebada – once a popular spot for public executions – to head into the Sunday flea market of **El Rastro**.

Otherwise, head west into the tangle of lanes that forms what was once the **morería** and emerge on Calle de Bailén and the wonderful *terrazas* of Las Vistillas – great for drinking in the views.

Follow the viaduct north to the **Catedral de Nuestra Señora de la Almudena**, the **Palacio Real** (royal palace) and Plaza de Oriente, with its statues, fountains and hedge mazes. The far east side of the plaza is closed off by the **Teatro Real**.

At its northern end, Calle de Bailén runs into **Plaza de España**. Nearby, you could visit the **Ermita de San Antonio de la Florida**, which contains a masterpiece by Goya. If you were to continue north past the square you would pass through the Barrio de Argüelles, with some pleasant summer terrazas, and on towards the main centre of Madrid's Universidad Complutense.

The eastern flank of Plaza de España marks the beginning of **Gran Vía**. This Haussmannesque boulevard was slammed through the tumbledown slums north of Sol in 1911.

At the east end of Gran Vía, note the superb dome of the **Metropolis Building**. Continue east along Calle de Alcalá until you reach **Plaza de la Cibeles**, Madrid's favourite roundabout.

Head north (left) up the tree-lined promenade of Paseo de los Recoletos. On the left you'll pass some of the city's best known cafes, including Gran Café de Gijón, El Espejo and El Gran Pabellón del Espejo. On your right is the enormous **Biblioteca Nacional** (National Library), and a little farther on a statue of Columbus in Plaza de Colón.

From here walk around the back of the National Library, where the **Museo Arqueológico Nacional** is housed. South along Calle de Serrano is Plaza de la Independencia, in the middle of which stands the **Puerta de Alcalá**. The gate was begun at Plaza de la Cibeles to celebrate the arrival of Carlos III in Madrid in 1769, was completed in 1778, and later moved as the city grew.

Turn right and then left at Plaza de la Cibeles to head south down Paseo del Prado, an extension of the city's main tree-lined boulevard, and you'll soon reach the art gallery with which it shares its name. On the other side of the boulevard, the **Museo Thyssen-Bornemisza** is, along with the **Prado**, a must.

The area around and north of the Prado is laced with museums, while stretching out behind it to the east are the wonderful gardens of the **Parque del Buen Retiro**. Immediately south of the Prado is the **Real Jardín Botánico**. Looking onto the manic multilane roundabout that is Plaza del Emperador Carlos V are the city's main railway station, **Atocha**, and the third in Madrid's big league of art galleries, the **Centro de Arte Reina Sofía**.

Head a few blocks north along Paseo del Prado again and west up Calle de las Huertas (through the tiny Plaza de Platería Martínez). The **Convento de las Trinitarias** (closed to the public), which backs onto this street, is where Cervantes lies buried. Turn right up Costanilla de las Trinitarias and continue along Calle de San Agustín until you come to Calle de Cervantes, and turn left. On your right you will pass the **Casa de Lope de Vega** at No 11. If the '*abierto*' ('open') sign is up, just knock and enter.

A left turn at the end of Calle de Cervantes into Calle de León will bring you back onto Calle de las Huertas, which you may have already noticed is one of Madrid's happening streets. Anywhere along here or up on Plaza de Santa Ana will make a great place to take a load off at the end of this gruelling tour! For specific tips, consult the Entertainment section.

Museo del Prado

The Prado is one of the world's great art galleries. Its main emphasis is on Spanish, Flemish and Italian art from the 15th to 19th centuries, and one of its strengths lies in the generous coverage given to certain individual geniuses. Whole strings of rooms are devoted to three of Spain's greats, Velázquez, El Greco and Goya.

Of Velázquez's works, it's *Las Meninas* that most people come to see, and this masterpiece depicting maids of honour attending the daughter of King Felipe IV, and Velázquez himself painting portraits of the queen and king (through whose eyes the scene is witnessed) takes pride of place in room 12 on the 1st floor, the focal point of the Velázquez collection.

Virtually the whole south wing of the 1st floor is given over to Goya. His portraits, in rooms 34 to 38, include the pair *Maja Desnuda* and *Maja Vestida*; legend has it that the woman depicted here is the Duchess of Alba, Spain's richest woman in Goya's time. Goya was supposedly commissioned to paint her portrait for her husband and ended up having an affair with her so he painted an extra portrait for himself. In room 39 are Goya's great war masterpieces, crowned by *El Dos de Mayo 1808* (2 May 1808) and, next to it, *Los Fusilamientos de Moncloa*, also known as *El Tres de Mayo 1808* (3 May 1808), in which he recreates the pathos of the hopeless Madrid revolt against the French. There are more Goya works in rooms 66 and 67 on the ground floor.

Other well-represented artists include El Greco, the Flemish masters Hieronymus Bosch and Peter Paul Rubens, and the Italians Tintoretto, Titian and Raphael.

The Prado is open 9 am to 7 pm Tuesday to Saturday, and until 2 pm on Sunday and holidays. Tickets are 500 ptas (half-price for students) and includes the Casón del Buen Retiro, a subsidiary a short walk east that contains the collection's 19th-century works. Entry is free on Sunday and Saturday afternoon (2.30 to 7 pm), as well as on selected national holidays.

Centro de Arte Reina Sofia

At Calle de Santa Isabel 52, opposite Atocha station, the Reina Sofia museum houses a superb collection of predominantly Spanish modern art. The exhibition focuses on the period 1900 to 1940, and includes, in room 7, Picasso's famous *Guernica*, his protest at the German bombing of the Basque town of Guernica during the Spanish Civil War in 1937. The day of the bombing, 26 April, had been a typical market day in the town of 5000 people. Because of the market there were another 5000 people selling their wares or doing their weekly shopping. The bombs started to drop at 4 pm. By the time they stopped, three hours later, the town and thousands of the people in it had been annihilated.

Guernica was painted in Paris. Picasso insisted that it stay outside Spain until Franco and his cronies were gone and democracy had been restored. It was secretly brought to Spain

in 1981, and moved here from the Casón del Buen Retiro in 1992. It's displayed with a collection of preliminary sketches and paintings which Picasso put together in May 1937.

The museum also contains further works by Picasso, while room 9 is devoted to Salvador Dalí's surrealist work and room 13 contains a collection of Joan Miró's late works, characterised by their remarkable simplicity.

The gallery opens 10 am to 9 pm Monday to Saturday (except Tuesday, when it is closed), and 10 am to 2.30 pm Sunday. Entry is 500 ptas (half-price for students), but free on Sunday and Saturday afternoon (2.30 to 7 pm).

Museo Thyssen-Bornemisza

Purchased by Spain in 1993 for something over US$300 million (a snip), this extraordinary collection of 800 paintings was formerly the private collection of the German-Hungarian family of magnates, the Thyssen-Bornemiszas. Starting with medieval religious art, it moves on through Titian, El Greco and Rubens to Cézanne, Monet and Van Gogh, then from Miró, Picasso and Gris to Pollock, Dalí and Lichtenstein, thereby offering one of the best and most comprehensive art-history lessons you'll ever have. The museum is at Paseo del Prado 8, almost opposite the Prado, and opens 10 am to 7 pm Tuesday to Sunday. Entry is 700 ptas (400 ptas for students). Separate temporary exhibitions generally cost more.

Palacio Real

Madrid's 18th-century Royal Palace is a lesson in what can happen if you give your interior decorators a free hand. You'll see some of the most elaborately decorated walls and ceilings imaginable, including the sublime Throne Room (and other rooms of more dubious merit). This over-the-top palace hasn't been used as a royal residence for some time and today is only used for official receptions and, of course, tourism.

The first series of rooms you strike after buying your ticket is the Farmacia Real (Royal Pharmacy), an unending array of medicine jars and stills for mixing royal concoctions. The Armería Real (Royal Armoury) is a shiny collection of mostly 16th and 17th-century weapons and royal suits of armour. Elsewhere are a good selection of Goyas, 215 absurdly ornate clocks from the Royal Clock

SPAIN

SPAIN

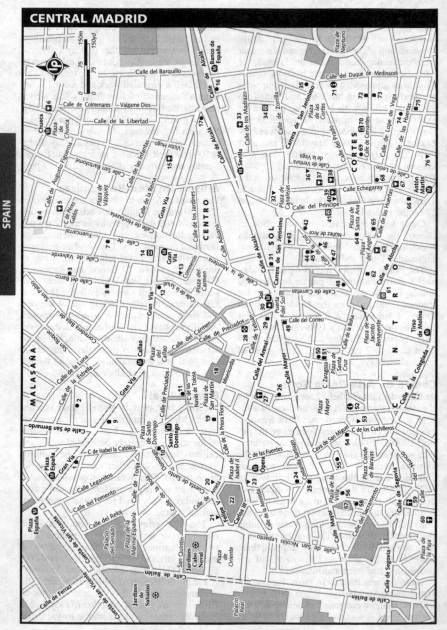

CENTRAL MADRID

euro currency converter €1 = 166 ptas

CENTRAL MADRID

PLACES TO STAY
1 Hostal Alcázar Regis
4 Hostal Medieval
7 Hostal Ginebra
8 Hotel Laris
9 Hostal Lamalonga
19 Hostal Paz
24 Hostal Mairu
25 Hostal Pinariega
29 Hostal Cosmopolitan
31 Hostal Centro Sol
44 Hostal Tineo
49 Hostal Riesco
51 Hostal Santa Cruz
54 Hostal La Macarena
62 Hostal Persal
64 Hostal Delvi
65 Hostal Vetusta
66 Hostal Matute
72 Hostal Dulcinea
73 Hostal Gonzalo
75 Hostal López

PLACES TO EAT
13 Restaurante Integral Artemisa
20 Restaurante La Paella Real
21 Taberna del Alabardero
23 Café del Real

32 La Finca de Susana
36 Restaurante Integral Artemisa
40 La Trucha
43 Museo del Jamón
45 La Casa del Abuelo
46 La Trucha
47 Las Bravas
53 Restaurante Sobrino de Botín
76 Restaurante La Sanabresa

OTHER
2 Morocco Disco
3 Lavandería Alba
5 Cruising Bar
6 Rimmel Bar
10 Viajes Zeppelin
11 Centro de Salud
12 La Casa del Libro
14 Telefónica Phone Centre
15 Cock Bar
16 RENFE Train Booking Office
17 Edificio Metropolis
18 Monasterio de las Descalzas Reales
22 Teatro Real
26 Chocolatería de San Ginés
27 Iglesia de San Ginés

28 El Corte Inglés Department Store
30 Police Station
33 Police Station
34 Teatro de la Zarzuela
35 American Express
37 La Venencia Bar
38 Carbones Bar
39 Viva Madrid
41 Teatro de la Comedia
42 Suristán
48 Torero
50 Librería de Mujeres
52 Tourist Office
55 Mercado de San Miguel
56 Torre de los Lujanes
57 Ayuntamiento
58 Casa de Cisneros
59 Iglesia de San Pedro
60 Iglesia de San Andrés
61 Teatro Calderón
63 Café Central
67 Café Populart
68 Lavandería España
69 Lavomatique
70 Casa de Lope de Vega
71 Tourist Office
74 Convento de las Trinitarias

SPAIN

Collection, and five Stradivarius violins, still used for concerts and balls. Most of the tapestries in the palace were made in the Royal Tapestry Factory. All the chandeliers are original and no two are the same.

The palace is open 9.30 am to 6 pm (5 pm October to April), Monday to Saturday, and 9 am to 2.30 pm (2 pm October to April) on Sunday and holidays. Admission costs 900 ptas (1000 ptas if you join a guided tour), or 400 ptas for students. All EU citizens get in free on Wednesday (bring your passport). The nearest metro station is Opera.

Monasterio de las Descalzas Reales

The Convent of the Barefoot Royals, on Plaza de las Descalzas, was founded in 1559 by Juana of Austria, daughter of the Spanish king Carlos I, and became one of Spain's richest religious houses thanks to gifts from noblewomen. Much of the wealth came in the form of art; on the obligatory guided tour you'll be confronted by a number of tapestries based on

works by Rubens, and a wonderful painting entitled *The Voyage of the 11,000 Virgins*. Juana of Austria is buried here. The convent is open 10.30 am to 12.45 pm Tuesday to Saturday and again (except Friday) from 4 to 5.30 pm. On Sunday and holidays it opens from 11 am to 1.45 pm. Admission costs 700 ptas (300 ptas for students), but is free on Wednesday for EU citizens.

Panteón de Goya

Also called the Ermita de San Antonio de la Florida, this little church contains not only Goya's tomb, directly in front of the altar, but also one of his greatest works – the entire ceiling and dome, beautifully painted with religious scenes (and recently restored). The scenes on the dome depict the miracle of St Anthony. The panteón is the first of two small churches 700m north-west along Paseo de la Florida from Príncipe Pío metro station. The chapel opens 10 am to 2 pm and 4 to 8 pm Tuesday to Friday (mornings only in July and August), and 10 am to 2 pm weekends.

Entry is 300 ptas, half for students (free on Wednesday and Sunday).

Museo Arqueológico

This museum on Calle de Serrano traces the history of the peninsula from the earliest prehistoric cave paintings to the Iberian, Roman, Carthaginian, Greek, Visigothic, Moorish and Christian eras. Exhibits include mosaics, pottery, fossilised bones and a partial reconstruction of the prehistoric Altamira cave paintings. It's open 9.30 am to 8.30 pm Tuesday to Saturday, and 9.30 am to 2 pm Sunday. Entry costs 500 ptas (students pay half), but is free on Sunday and from 2.30 pm on Saturday.

Other Museums

Madrid almost has more museums than the Costa del Sol has high-rise apartments. They include: the **Museo Municipal**, with assorted art including some Goyas, and some beautiful old maps, scale models, silver, porcelain and period furniture; the **Museo de la Moneda**, which follows the history of coinage in great detail and contains a mind-boggling collection of coins and paper money; the **Museo de América** with stuff brought from the Americas from the 16th to 20th centuries; and even the **Museo de la Ciudad**, perfectly described by one traveller as 'a must for infrastructure buffs!', which rather drily traces the growth of Madrid. Check the tourist office's *Enjoy Madrid* brochure for more details.

Real Jardín Botánico

The perfect answer to an overdose of art and history could be this beautiful botanic garden next door to the Prado. The eight-hectare gardens are open daily from 10 am to dark and entrance costs 250 ptas.

Parque del Buen Retiro

This is another great place to escape hustle and bustle. On a warm spring day walk between the flowerbeds and hedges or just sprawl out on one of the lawns.

Stroll along **Paseo de las Estatuas**, a path lined with statues originally from the Palacio Real. It ends at a lake overlooked by a **statue of Alfonso XII**. There are rowing boats for rent at the northern end when the weather is good.

Perhaps the most important, and certainly the most controversial, of the park's other monuments is *El Ángel Caído* (The Fallen Angel). First-prize winner at an international exhibition in Paris in 1878, this is said to be the first statue in the world dedicated to the devil.

You should also visit some of the park's gardens, such as the exquisite **La Rosaleda** (rose garden), and the **Chinese Garden** on a tiny island near the Fallen Angel. The all-glass **Palacio de Cristal** in the middle of the park occasionally stages modern-art exhibitions.

Campo del Moro

This stately garden is directly behind the Palacio Real, and the palace is visible through the trees from just about all points. A couple of fountains and statues, a thatch-roofed pagoda and a carriage museum provide artificial diversions, but nature is the real attraction.

El Rastro

If you get up early on a Sunday morning you'll find the city almost deserted, until you get to El Rastro. It is one of the biggest flea markets you're ever likely to see, and if you're prepared to hunt around, you can find almost anything. The market spreads along and between Calle de Ribera de Curtidores and Calle de los Embajadores (metro: Latina). It's said to be the place to go if you want to buy your car stereo back. Watch your pockets and bags.

ORGANISED TOURS

You can pick up a Madrid Vision bus around the centre of Madrid up to 10 times a day. There are only three on Sunday and holidays. A full round trip costs 1700 ptas and you can board the bus at any of 14 clearly marked stops. Taped commentaries in four languages, including English, are available, and the bus stops at several major monuments, including the Prado and near Plaza Mayor. If you buy the 2200 ptas ticket, you can use the buses all day to get around (2900 ptas buys you the same right for two days running).

SPECIAL EVENTS

Madrid's major fiesta celebrates its patron saint, San Isidro Labrador, throughout the third week of May. There are free music performances around the city and one of the country's top bullfight seasons at the Plaza Monumental de las Ventas. The Malasaña district, already busy enough, has its biggest party on 2 May, and the Fiesta de San Juan is held in the Parque del Buen Retiro for the seven days leading up to 24 June. The few locals who haven't left town in August will be celebrating the consecutive festivals of La Paloma, San Cayetano and San Lorenzo. The last week of September is Chamartín's Fiesta de Otoño (Autumn Festival), about the only time you would go to Chamartín other than to catch a train.

PLACES TO STAY
Finding a place to stay in Madrid is never really a problem.

Camping
There is one camping ground within striking distance of central Madrid. To reach **Camping Osuna** (☎ 91 741 05 10) on Avenida de Logroño near the airport, take metro No 5 to Canillejas (the end of the line), from where it's about 500m. It charges 660 ptas per person, car and tent.

Hostels
There are two HI youth hostels in Madrid. The **Albergue Richard Schirrman** (☎ 91 463 56 99) is in the Casa de Campo park (metro: El Lago; bus No 33 from Plaza Ópera). B&B in a room of four costs 1200 ptas (under 26) or 1700 ptas.

The **Albergue Santa Cruz de Marcenado** (☎ 91 547 45 32, Calle de Santa Cruz de Marcenado 28, metro: Argüelles; bus Nos 1, 61 and Circular), has rooms for four, six and eight people. B&B costs the same as in the other hostel. This is one of the few Spanish hostels in HI's International Booking Network.

Hostales & Pensiones
These tend to cluster in three or four parts of the city and the price-to-quality ratio is fairly standard. In summer the city is drained of people, thanks to the horrific heat, so if you are mad enough to be here then, you may well be able to make a hot deal on the price. At other times it's only worth trying to bargain if you intend to stay a while.

Around Plaza de Santa Ana Santa Ana is one of Madrid's 'in' districts – and so budget places are starting to disappear. Close to Sol and within walking distance of the Prado and

Atocha train station, it's also home to countless bars, cafes and restaurants of all classes.

On the square itself at No 15, **Hostal Delvi** (☎ 91 522 59 98, 3rd floor) is friendly enough with OK rooms, including tiny singles. You will pay from 2000/2500 ptas for its singles/doubles without bath or 4000 ptas for *en-suite* doubles.

West off the square, **Hostal Persal** (☎ 91 369 46 43, fax 91 369 19 52, Plaza del Ángel 12) is edging out of budgeteers range. Comfortable rooms with bath, TV and phone cost 5800/8700 ptas, including breakfast.

Hostal Vetusta (☎ 91 429 64 04, Calle de las Huertas 3) has small but cute rooms with own shower starting at 3000/4500 ptas; try for one looking onto the street. **Hostal Matute** (☎/fax 91 429 55 85, Plaza de Matute 11) has spacious, somewhat musty singles/doubles for 3500/5000 ptas without own bath and 4500/6000 ptas with.

Hostal Gonzalo (☎ 91 429 27 14, Calle de Cervantes 34) is in sparkling nick. Singles/doubles with private shower and TV are 5000/6200 ptas. The staff will take a few hundred pesetas off the bill if you stay at least three days. Across the road at No 19, **Hostal Dulcinea** (☎ 91 429 93 09, fax 91 369 25 69, ✆ donato@teleline.es) has well-maintained if simply furnished rooms and is often full. Rooms cost 5500/6000 ptas.

Roughly halfway between Atocha train station and Santa Ana, **Hostal López** (☎ 91 429 43 49, Calle de las Huertas 54) is a good choice. Singles/doubles start at 3600/4500 ptas without own bath, or 4200/5200 ptas with.

Around Puerta del Sol & Plaza Mayor You can't get more central than Plaza de la Puerta del Sol. This and Plaza Mayor, Madrid's true heart, are not major budget accommodation areas, but there are a few good options scattered among all the open-air cafes, tapas bars, ancient restaurants and souvenir shops.

The pick of the cheaper bunch is **Hostal Riesco** (☎ 91 522 26 92, Calle de Correo 2, 3rd floor). Singles/doubles with full bath cost 4000/5800 ptas. **Hostal Tineo** (☎ 91 521 49 43, Calle de la Victoria 6) charges a standard 3500/5500 ptas for singles/doubles with washbasin only. They range up to 5000/6500 ptas for rooms with private bathroom.

SPAIN

Hostal Santa Cruz (☎ *91 522 24 41, Plaza de Santa Cruz 6*) is in a prime location. Rooms here start from about 3600/5200 ptas. If you don't mind the traffic, *Hostal Cosmopolitan* (☎ *91 522 66 51, Puerta del Sol 9, 3rd floor*) has basic singles/doubles with washbasin for just 1800/3300 ptas.

The more upmarket *Hostal La Macarena* (☎ *91 365 92 21, fax 91 366 61 11, Cava de la Cava de San Miguel 8*) has excellent rooms with private bath, TV and phone – pricey but worth it. Singles/doubles/triples cost 6500/8500/10,500 ptas. *Hostal Centro Sol* (☎ *91 522 15 82, fax 91 522 57 78, Carrera de San Jerónimo 5*) offers smallish rooms in top order with own bath, TV, phone, heating and air-con, and mini-bar. They are good value at 6000/7500/9500 ptas for singles/doubles/triples.

Around Gran Vía The hostales on and around Gran Vía tend to be a little more expensive. All the same, it's another popular area.

Gran Vía itself is laden with accommodation. *Hostal Lamalonga* (☎ *91 547 26 31, Gran Vía 56*) is reliable. Rooms with private bath start at 4500/6500 ptas. *Hostal Alcázar Regis* (☎ *91 547 93 17, fax 91 559 07 85*), No 61, is not a bad choice at the cheaper end of the scale. Singles/doubles cost 4000/6000 ptas.

Calle de Fuencarral is similarly choked with hostales and pensiones, especially at the Gran Vía end. *Hostal Ginebra* (☎ *91 532 10 35, Calle de Fuencarral 17*) is a reliable choice not far from Gran Vía. All rooms have TV and phone; singles with washbasin only start at 3200 ptas, while singles/doubles with full bathroom cost 4200/5000 ptas. *Hostal Medieval* (☎ *91 522 25 49, Calle de Fuencarral 46*) has spacious and bright singles/doubles with shower for 3000/4500 ptas. Doubles with full private bathroom cost 5500 ptas.

Hotel Laris (☎ *91 521 46 80, fax 91 521 46 85, Calle del Barco 3*) is nudging middle range but has decent rooms with all the extras for 5800/8700 ptas.

Around Ópera The tiny *Hostal Paz* (☎ *91 547 30 47, Calle de la Priora Flora 4*) looks horrible from the outside, but the cheap rooms inside are reasonable value if a little cramped at 2600/4000 ptas. Quietly tucked away *Hostal Mairu* (☎ *91 547 30 88, Calle del Es-*

pejo 2) is a simple place with singles/doubles for 2600/4200 ptas. Doubles with own bath cost 4400 ptas. Nearby, *Hostal Pinariega* (☎*/fax 91 548 08 19, Calle de Santiago 1*) is a sunnier alternative with rooms starting at 3500/4800 ptas.

Rental
Many of the hostales mentioned above will do a deal on long stays. This may include a considerable price reduction, meals and laundry. It is simply a matter of asking. For longer stays, check the rental pages of *Segundamano* magazine or notice boards at universities, the Escuela Oficial de Idiomas and cultural institutes like the British Council or Alliance Française.

PLACES TO EAT
Around Santa Ana
There are tons of Gallego seafood restaurants in this area, but the best is the newly opened *Maceira*, away from the main tourist hubbub at Calle de Jesús 7. Splash your *pulpo a la gallega* down with a crisp white Ribeiro.

In *La Casa del Abuelo* (*Calle de la Victoria 14*), on a back street south-east of Puerta del Sol, you can sip a *chato* (small glass) of the heavy El Abuelo red wine while munching on heavenly king prawns, grilled or with garlic. Next, duck around the corner to *Las Bravas* (*Callejón de Álvarez Gato*) for a caña and the best *patatas bravas* in town. The antics of the bar staff are themselves enough to merit a minor pit stop and the distorting mirrors are a minor Madrid landmark.

La Trucha (*Calle de Núñez de Arce 6*) is one of Madrid's great bars for tapas. It's just off Plaza de Santa Ana, and there's another nearby at Calle de Manuel Fernández y González 3. You could eat your fill at the bar or sit down in the restaurant. It closes on Sunday and Monday.

Something of an institution is the *Museo del Jamón*. Walk in to one of these places and you'll understand the name. Huge clumps of every conceivable type of ham dangle all over the place. You can eat plates and plates of ham – the Spaniards' single most favoured source of nutrition. There's one at Carrera de San Jerónimo 6.

If it's just plain cheap you want, *Restaurante La Sanabresa* (*Calle del Amor de Dios 12*) has a very good *menú* for just 900 ptas.

La Finca de Susana (*Calle de Arlabán 4*) is a great new spot. Soft lighting and a veritable jungle of greenery create a soothing atmosphere for a meal that doesn't have to cost more than about 2000 ptas.

Vegetarians generally do not have an easy time of it Spain, but Madrid offers a few safe ports. *Elqui* (*Calle de Buenavista 18*) is a self-service buffet-style place open daily, but Monday for lunch (until 4 pm) and Friday and Saturday evening for dinner (a la carte). *Restaurante Integral Artemisa* (*Calle de Ventura de la Vega 4*), is excellent. A full meal will cost around 2000 ptas, and there is another branch off Gran Vía at Calle de las Tres Cruces 4.

Around Plaza Mayor

You know you're getting close to Plaza Mayor when you see signs in English saying 'Typical Spanish Restaurant' and 'Hemingway Never Ate Here'. Nevertheless, when the sun's shining (or rising) there's not a finer place to be than at one of the outdoor cafes in the plaza.

Calle de la Cava San Miguel and Calle de Cuchilleros are packed with *mesones* that aren't bad for a little tapas hopping. A cut above the rest is *Restaurante Sobrino de Botín* (*Calle de Cuchilleros 17*), one of Europe's oldest restaurants (established in 1725), where the set *menú* costs 4050 ptas – it's popular with those who can afford it.

Other Areas

Just about anywhere you go in central Madrid, you can find cheap restaurants with good food.

Casa Mingo (*Paseo de la Florida 34*), near the Panteón de Goya, is a great old place for chicken and cider. A full roast bird, salad and bottle of cider – enough for two – comes to less than 2000 ptas.

If you're after paella at all costs, head for *Restaurante La Paella Real* (*Calle de Arrieta 2*) near Plaza de Oriente, which does a whole range of rice-based dishes from 1800 ptas. For a really excellent meal in a cosy atmosphere try *Taberna del Alabardero* (*Calle de Felipe V 6*) nearby. Expect little change from 6000 ptas per person. If this is a bit steep, consider a couple of the mouthwatering tapas at the bar.

In the Malasaña area around Plaza del Dos de Mayo, *Restaurante Sandos* (*Plaza del Dos de Mayo 8*) can do you a cheap outdoor pizza and beer, or a set *menú* from 850 ptas. Better still is the crowded *Pizzeria Mastropiero* (*Calle de San Vicente Ferrer 34*) on the corner of Calle del Dos de Mayo. This is a justifiably popular Argentine-run joint where you can get pizza by the slice.

The Plaza de España area is a good hunting ground for non-Spanish food, though you're looking at 2000 ptas to 2500 ptas for a meal in the better places. *Restaurante Bali* (*Calle de San Bernardino 6*) has authentic Indonesian fare at around 6000 ptas for two. The *Adrish*, virtually across the street at No 1, is about Madrid's best Indian restaurant. The long-established *Restaurante Veracruz* (*Calle de San Leonardo de Dios 5*) has a set *menú* (including a bottle of wine) for 950 ptas. It's closed Sunday.

Cafes

Madrid has so many fine places for a coffee and a light bite that you'll certainly find your own favourites. Ours include: the historic, elegant *Café-Restaurante El Espejo* (*Paseo de Recoletos 31*) where you can also sit at the early-20th-century-style *El Gran Pabellón del Espejo* outside; the equally graceful *Gran Café de Gijón* just down the road; *Café del Real* (*Plaza de Isabel II*) with a touch of faded elegance – good for breakfast and busy at night too; or *Nuevo Café Barbieri* (*Calle del Ave María 45*), a wonderful old place, once the haunt of the artistic and hopefully artistic. An enchanting teahouse with a hint of the 1960s is the *Tetería de la Abuela* (*Calle del Espíritu Santo 19*). Along with the great range of teas you can indulge in scrummy crepes.

ENTERTAINMENT

A copy of the weekly *Guía del Ocio* (125 ptas at newsstands) will give you a good rundown of what's on in Madrid. Its comprehensive listings include music gigs, art exhibitions, cinema, TV and theatre. It's very handy even if you can't read Spanish.

Bars

The epicentres of Madrid's nightlife are the Santa Ana-Calle de las Huertas area, and the

Malasaña-Chueca zone north of Gran Vía. The latter has a decidedly lowlife element.

Any of the bars on Plaza de Santa Ana makes a pleasant stop, especially when you can sit outside in the warmer months. *Viva Madrid (Calle de Manuel Fernández y González 7)* gets hellishly crowded at weekends, but take a look at its tiles and heavy wooden ceilings. On the same street, *Carbones* is a busy place open till about 4 am with good mainstream music on the jukebox. *La Venencia (Calle de Echegaray 7)* is an ill-lit, woody place that looks as if it hasn't been cleaned in years – perfect for sampling one of its six varieties of sherry.

Café Populart (Calle de las Huertas 22) often has music, generally jazz or Celtic. For more jazz with your drinks, *Café Central (Plaza del Ángel 10)* is another good choice. Just beyond the hubbub of Huertas is *El Parnaso*, a quirky but engaging bar at Calle de Moratín 25. The area around the bar is jammed with an odd assortment of decorative paraphernalia.

In Malasaña, *Cervecería Santa Bárbara (Plaza de Santa Bárbara 8)* is a classic Madrid drinking house and a good place to kick off a night out. You can sip on a vermouth drawn from the barrel at the wonderful, dimly lit *Bodega de la Ardosa (Calle de Colón 13)*. *La Vía Láctea (Calle de Velarde 18)* is a bright place with thumping mainstream music, a young crowd and a good drinking atmosphere.

Irish pubs are very popular in Madrid: two good ones are *The Quiet Man (Calle de Valverde 44)*, and *Finnegan's (Plaza de las Salesas 9)*.

Calle de Pelayo Campoamor is lined with an assortment of bars, graduating from noisy rock bars at the north end to gay bars at the south end, where you've reached the Chueca area, the heart of Madrid's gay nightlife. *Rimmel (Calle de Luis de Góngora 4)* and *Cruising (Calle de Pérez Galdós 5)* are among the more popular gay haunts. The latter has a dark room and puts on occasional shows.

The quaintly named *Cock Bar (Calle de la Reina 16)*, once served as a discreet salon for high-class prostitution. The ladies in question have gone but this popular bar retains plenty of atmosphere.

Live Music & Discos

Latin rhythms have quite a hold in Madrid. A good place to indulge is *Vaiven (Travesía de San Mateo 1)* in Malasaña. Entry is free but a beer is about 600 ptas. *Morocco (Calle del Marqués de Leganés 7)* in Malasaña is still a popular stop on the Madrid disco circuit. It gets going about 1 am.

Near Plaza de Santa Ana, Calle de la Cruz has a couple of good dance spaces; try to pick up fliers for them before you go – they may save you queueing. *Suristán* at No 7 pulls in a wide variety of bands, from Cuban to African, usually starting at 11.30 pm, sometimes with a cover charge up to 1000 ptas. *Torero* at No 26 has Spanish music upstairs and international fare downstairs.

Arena (Calle de la Princesa 1) near Plaza de España offers music for all tastes – funky, house, techno and acid jazz – until 6.30 am from Wednesday to Sunday.

For a taste of the authentic, *La Soleá (Calle de la Cava Baja 27)* is regarded by some as the last real flamenco bar in Madrid. *Casa Patas (Calle de Cañizares 10)* hosts recognised masters of flamenco song, guitar and dance. Bigger flamenco names also play some of Madrid's theatres – check listings.

Cinemas

Cinemas are reasonably priced, with tickets around 850 ptas. Films in their original language (with Spanish subtitles) are usually marked VO *(versión original)* in listings. A good part of town for these is on and around Calle de Martín de los Heros and Calle de la Princesa, near Plaza de España. The *Renoir*, *Alphaville* and *Princesa* complexes here all screen VO movies.

Classical Music, Theatre & Opera

There's plenty happening, except in summer. The city's grandest stage, the recently reopened *Teatro Real* (☎ 91 516 06 06) is the scene for opera. If you can't get into the Teatro Real, the *Teatro Calderón* (☎ 91 369 14 34, Calle de Atocha 18) plays second fiddle. The beautiful old *Teatro de la Comedia* (☎ 91 521 49 31, Calle del Príncipe 14), home to the Compañía Nacional de Teatro Clásico, stages gems of classic Spanish and European theatre. The *Centro Cultural de la Villa* (☎ 91 575 60 80), under the waterfall at Plaza de

Colón, stages everything from classical concerts to comic theatre, opera and even classy flamenco. Also important for classical music is the **Auditorio Nacional de Música**, (☎ 91 337 01 40, Avenida del Príncipe de Vergara 146, metro: Cruz del Rayo).

SPECTATOR SPORTS

Spending an afternoon or evening at a football (soccer) match provides quite an insight into Spanish culture. Tickets can be bought on the day of the match, starting from around 2500 ptas, although big games may be sold out. Real Madrid's home is the huge Estadio Santiago Bernabéu (metro: Santiago Bernabéu). Atlético Madrid plays at Estadio Vicente Calderón (metro: Pirámides).

Bullfights take place most Sundays between March and October – more often during the festival of San Isidro Labrador in May, and in summer. Madrid has Spain's largest bullring, the Plaza Monumental de las Ventas (metro: Ventas), and a second bullring by metro Vista Alegre. Tickets are best bought in advance, from agencies or at the rings, and cost from under 2000 ptas.

SHOPPING

For general shopping needs, start at either the markets or the large department stores. The most famous market is El Rastro (see Things to See & Do earlier in this Madrid section). The largest department store chain is El Corte Inglés, with a central branch just north of Sol on Calle de Preciados.

The city's premier shopping street is Calle de Serrano, a block east of Paseo de la Castellana. Calle del Almirante off Paseo de Recoletos has a wide range of engaging, less mainstream shops. For guitars and other musical instruments, hunt around the area near the Palacio Real. For leather try the shops on Calle del Príncipe and Gran Vía, or Calle de Fuencarral for shoes. For designer clothing, try the Chueca area.

GETTING THERE & AWAY
Air
Scheduled and charter flights from all over the world arrive at Madrid's Barajas airport, 13km north-east of the city. With nowhere in Spain more than 12 hours away by bus or train, domestic flights are generally not good

value unless you're in a burning hurry. Nor is Madrid the budget international flight capital of Europe. That said, you *can* find bargains to popular destinations such as London, Paris and New York. For an idea on domestic fares, see the Getting Around section earlier in this chapter. See also Travel Agencies under Information earlier in this Madrid section.

Airline offices in Madrid include:

Air France (☎ 91 330 04 12, bookings ☎ 901-11 22 66), Torre de Madrid, Plaza de España 18
American Airlines (☎ 91 453 14 00), Calle de Orense 4
British Airways (☎ 91 387 43 00, ☎ 902-11 13 33), Calle de Serrano 60
Iberia (☎ 91 587 75 36, 902-40 05 00 for bookings), Calle de Velázquez 130
Lufthansa (☎ 902-22 01 01), Calle del Cardenal Marcelo Spinola 2

Bus
There are eight bus stations dotted around Madrid, serving many different bus companies. Tourist offices can tell you which one you need for your destination. Most buses to the south, and some to other places (including a number of international services), use the Estación Sur de Autobuses (☎ 91 468 42 00), Calle de Méndez Álvaro (metro: Méndez Álvaro). The choice between bus and train depends largely on where you're going. More detail on services to/from Madrid is given in other city sections in this chapter.

Train
Atocha station, south of the centre, is used by most trains to/from southern Spain and many destinations around Madrid. Some trains from the north also terminate here, passing through Chamartín, the other main station (in the north of the city), on the way. Chamartín (metro: Chamartín) is smaller and generally serves destinations north of Madrid, although this rule is not cast-iron; some trains to the south use Chamartín and don't pass through Atocha.

The main RENFE booking office (☎ 91 328 90 20) is at Calle de Alcalá 44 and is open 9.30 am to 8 pm Monday to Friday.

For information on fares, see the Getting There & Away section under the city you are going to.

SPAIN

Car & Motorcycle

Madrid is surrounded by two ring-road systems, the older M-30 and the M-40, considerably further out (a third, the M-50, is also planned). Roads in and out of the city can get pretty clogged at peak hours (around 8 to 10 am, 2 pm, 4 to 5 pm and 8 to 9 pm), and on Sunday night.

Car-rental companies in Madrid include Avis (☎ 91 547 20 48), Budget (☎ 91 577 63 63), Europcar (☎ 91 541 88 92) and Hertz (☎ 91 542 58 03). All these have offices at the airport, in the city centre, and often at the main train stations. Robbery on hire-cars leaving the airport is a problem, so be careful.

You can rent motorbikes from Moto Alquiler (☎ 91 542 06 57), Calle del Conde Duque 13, but it's pricey, starting at 4500 ptas plus 16% IVA per day for a 50cc Honda Sky. Rental is from 8 am to 8 pm and you have to leave a refundable deposit of 50,000 ptas on your credit card. Something like a Yamaha 650 will cost you 16,000 ptas a day plus tax and the deposit is 175,000 ptas.

GETTING AROUND
To/From the Airport

The metro runs right into town from the airport, at the upper level of the T2 terminal. Alternatively, an airport bus service runs to/from an underground terminal in Plaza de Colón every 12 to 15 minutes. The trip takes 30 minutes in average traffic and costs 385 ptas. A taxi between the airport and city centre should cost around 2000 ptas.

Bus

In general, the underground (metro) is faster and easier than city buses for getting around central Madrid. Bus route maps are available from tourist offices.

A single ride costs 135 ptas. A 10-ride *Metrobus* ticket (705 ptas) can be used on buses and metro. Night owls may find the 20 bus lines, running from midnight to 6 am, useful. They run from Puerta del Sol and Plaza de la Cibeles.

Metro

Madrid has a very efficient, safe and simple underground system. Trains run from 6.30 am to 1.30 am and the fares are the same as on buses.

Taxi

Madrid's taxis are inexpensive by European standards. They're handy late at night, although in peak hours it's quicker to walk or get the metro. Flag fall is 190 ptas, after which it's 90 ptas per kilometre (120 ptas between 10 pm and 6 am).

Car & Motorcycle

There's little point subjecting yourself to Madrid's traffic just to move from one part of the city to another, especially at peak hours. Most on-street parking space in central Madrid is designated for people with special permits, but almost everybody ignores this – ignoring the 12,000 parking tickets slapped on vehicles every day. But you risk being towed if you park in a marked no-parking or loading zone, or if you double-park. There are plenty of car parks across the city, costing about 200 ptas an hour.

Around Madrid

EL ESCORIAL

The extraordinary 16th-century monastery-palace complex of San Lorenzo de El Escorial lies one hour north-west of Madrid, just outside the town of the same name.

El Escorial was built by Felipe II, king of Spain, Naples, Sicily, Milan, the Netherlands and large parts of the Americas, to commemorate his victory over the French in the battle of St Quentin (1557) and as a mausoleum for his father Carlos I, the first of Spain's Habsburg monarchs. Felipe began searching for a site in 1558, deciding on El Escorial in 1562. The last stone was placed in 1584, and the next 11 years were spent on decoration. El Escorial's austere style, reflecting not only Felipe's wishes but also the watchful eye of architect Juan de Herrera, is loved by some, hated by others. Either way, it's a quintessential monument of Spain's golden age.

Almost all visitors to El Escorial make it a day trip from Madrid. It opens 10 am to 6 pm Tuesday to Sunday (to 5 pm from October to March); entry 900 ptas, 400 ptas for students.

Information

You can get information on El Escorial from tourist offices in Madrid, or from the tourist office (☎ 91 890 15 54) close to the monastery at Calle de Floridablanca 10. It's open 10 am to 2 pm and 3 to 5 pm Monday to Friday, and 10 am to 2 pm Saturday.

Things to See

Above the monastery's main gateway, on its west side, stands a **statue of San Lorenzo**, holding a symbolic gridiron, the instrument of his martyrdom (he was roasted alive on one). Inside, across the Patio de los Reyes, stands the restrained **basílica**, a cavernous church with a beautiful white-marble crucifixion by Benvenuto Cellini, sculpted in 1576. At either side of the altar stand bronze statues of Carlos I and his family (to the left), and Felipe II with three of his four wives and his eldest son (on the right).

From the basílica, follow signs to the ticket office *(taquilla)*, where you must pay 900 ptas (students 400 ptas) to see the other open parts of El Escorial. The price includes an optional guided tour of the *panteones* and one or two other sections.

The route you have to follow leads first to the **Museo de Arquitectura**, detailing in Spanish how El Escorial was constructed, and the **Museo de Pintura**, with 16th and 17th-century Spanish, Italian and Flemish fine art. You then head upstairs to the richly decorated **Palacio de Felipe II**, in one room of which the monarch died in 1598; his bed was positioned so that he could watch proceedings at the basílica's high altar. Next you descend to the **Panteón de los Reyes**, where almost all Spain's monarchs since Carlos I, and their spouses, lie in gilded marble coffins. Three empty sarcophagi await future arrivals. Backtracking a little, you find yourself in the **Panteón de los Infantes**, a larger series of chambers and tunnels housing the tombs of princes, princesses and other lesser royalty.

Finally, the **Salas Capitulares** in the southeast of the monastery house a minor treasure trove of El Grecos, Titians, Tintorettos and other old masters.

When you emerge, it's worth heading back to the entrance, where you can gain access to the **biblioteca** (library), once one of Europe's finest and still a haven for some 40,000 books. You can't handle them, but many historic and valuable volumes are on display.

Getting There & Away

The Herranz bus company runs up to 30 services a day from the Intercambiador de Autobuses at the Moncloa metro station in Madrid to San Lorenzo de El Escorial (405 ptas one way). Only about 10 run on Sunday and during holidays.

Up to 20 sluggish *cercanías* trains (line C-8a) serve El Escorial from Atocha station (via Chamartín) in Madrid (430 ptas). Seven of these go on to Ávila. Local buses will take you the 2km from the train station up to the monastery.

Castilla y León

The one-time centre of the mighty Christian kingdom of Castile, Castilla y León is one of Spain's most historic regions. From Segovia's Roman aqueduct to the walled city of Ávila, and from León's magnificent cathedral to the lively old centre of Salamanca, it is crowded with reminders of its prominent role in Spain's past.

SEGOVIA
pop 54,750

Segovia is justly famous for its magnificent Roman aqueduct but also has a splendid ridgetop old city worthy of more than a fleeting visit.

Originally a Celtic settlement, Segovia was conquered by the Romans around 80 BC. The Visigoths and Moors also left their mark before the city ended up in Castilian hands in the 11th century.

The main tourist office (☎ 921 46 03 34) is on Plaza Mayor, with another branch (☎ 921 46 29 06) beside the aqueduct. Both are open daily.

Things to See

You can't help but notice the 1st-century AD **aqueduct**, stretching away from the east end of the old city. It's over 800m long, up to 29m high, has 163 arches – and not a drop of mortar was used in its construction.

At the heart of the old city is the 16th-century Gothic **catedral** on the pretty Plaza Mayor. Its sombre interior is anchored by an imposing choir and enlivened by 20-odd chapels. Of these, the Capilla del Cristo del

Consuelo houses a magnificent Romanesque doorway preserved from the original church.

Rapunzel towers, turrets topped with slate witch's hats and a moat deep enough to drown Godzilla (well, almost) make the **Alcázar** a most memorable monument. A 15th-century fairy-tale castle, perched on a craggy cliff top at the west end of the old city, it was virtually destroyed by fire in 1862. What you see today is an evocative over-the-top reconstruction of the original. You can tour the inside for 400 ptas, but don't leave without climbing the Torre de Juan II for magnificent views.

Places to Stay

About 2km along the road to La Granja is *Camping Acueducto* (☎ *921 42 50 00*), open April to September.

Fonda Aragón (☎ *921 46 09 14*) and *Fonda Cubo* (☎ *921 46 09 17*), both at Plaza Mayor 4, are shabby but the cheapest accommodation in town. Both have singles only, costing 1600 ptas at the Aragón and 1300 ptas at the Cubo.

More pleasant is *Hostal Plaza* (☎ *921 46 03 03, Calle del Cronista Lecea 11*) where singles/doubles start at 3100/4500 ptas. Also central and good is *Hostal Juan Bravo* (☎ *921 46 34 13, Calle de Juan Bravo 12*), which charges 3800 ptas for doubles without or 4800 ptas for those with bath.

Outside the old town, but close to the aqueduct, is the spick-and-span *Hostal Don Jaime* (☎ *921 44 47 87, Calle de Ochoa Ondategui 8*). Doubles with private bath and TV cost 5600 ptas; singles (shared facilities only) are 3200 ptas.

Places to Eat

The simple *Bar Ratos* (*Calle de los Escuderos*) makes generously stuffed sandwiches from 350 ptas. *Cueva de San Esteban* (*Calle de Valdeláguila 15*) has delicious set lunches for 1000 ptas. Segovia's speciality is *cochinillo asado* (roast suckling pig); a good place to sample this is in the timber-laden dining room of *Mesón José María* (*Calle del Cronista Lecea 11*), a favourite among Segovians.

For meatless fare, try *La Almuzara* (*Marqués del Arco 3*), which has a warm, artsy ambience and prices that won't break the bank (closed Monday, and Tuesday lunchtime).

Getting There & Away

Up to 30 buses daily run to Madrid (825 ptas, 1½ hours), and others serve Ávila and Salamanca. The bus station is 500m south of the aqueduct, just off Paseo Ezequiel González. Trains to Madrid leave every two hours (790 ptas, 1¾ hours).

Getting Around

Bus No 2 connects the train station with the aqueduct and Plaza Mayor. Otherwise, walking is the best way to get about.

AROUND SEGOVIA

In the mountain village of San Ildefonso de la Granja, 12km south-east, you can visit the royal palace and glorious gardens of **La Granja**, a Spanish version of Versailles built by Felipe V in 1720. The 300-room Palacio Real, restored after a fire in 1918, is impressive but perhaps the lesser of La Granja's jewels. You can visit about half of the rooms, including its Museo de Tapices (Tapestry Museum; 700/300 ptas). A highlight of the gardens are its 28 fountains, some of which are switched on in summer (325 ptas).

Regular buses run from Segovia to San Ildefonso.

About 50km north-west of Segovia, **Castillo de Coca** is also well worth a visit. This beautiful all-brick castle was built in 1453 by the powerful Fonseca family and is surrounded by a deep moat. Guided tours operate daily (300 ptas). Up to five buses daily make the trip from Segovia.

ÁVILA

pop 38,200

Ávila deservedly lays claims to being one of the world's best preserved, and most impressive, walled cities. Constructed during the 11th and 12th centuries, its imposing *muralla* consists of no fewer than eight monumental gates and 88 towers.

Ávila is also distinguished by being the highest city in Spain (1130m) and the birthplace of St Teresa of Ávila, the 16th-century mystical writer and reformer of the Carmelite order. Less to be boasted about, however, is that Tomás de Torquemada orchestrated the most brutal phase of the Spanish Inquisition in Ávila, sending off 2000 people to be burnt at the stake in the late 15th century.

The tourist office (☎ 920 21 13 87), Plaza de la Catedral 4, is open daily.

Things to See & Do

Of Ávila's many convents, museums and monuments, the **catedral** (open daily) is perhaps the most interesting. Not merely a house of worship, it was also an ingenious fortress; its stout granite apse forms the central bulwark in the eastern wall of the town, the most open to attack and hence the most heavily fortified.

Around the western side, the main facade conceals the Romanesque origins of what is essentially the earliest Gothic church in Spain. You can catch a partial peek inside for free, but proceeding to the inner sanctum – plus the cloister, sacristy and small museum – costs 250 ptas.

Just outside the walls, the Romanesque **Basílica de San Vicente** (open daily; 200 ptas) is striking. Gothic modifications in granite contrast with the warm sandstone of the Romanesque original. Work started in the 11th century.

About 500m east of the old town, the **Monasterio de Santo Tomás** (open daily; 100 ptas) is thought to be Torquemada's burial place. Built hastily in 1482 as a royal residence, it is formed by three interconnecting cloisters and the church.

The **Convento de Santa Teresa** (1636) was built over the saint's birthplace. The room where she was allegedly born is now a chapel smothered in gold. The souvenir shop next door gives access to a small room crammed with Teresa relics, including her ring finger (complete with ring). Both are open daily (free).

Los Cuatro Postes, a lookout point around 1km west of the city gates on the Salamanca road, has the best view of the city and its perfectly preserved walls.

Places to Stay

Hostal Jardín (☎ 920 21 10 74, Calle de San Segundo 38) has scruffy but adequate singles/doubles from 3000/4000 ptas. Better is **Hostal El Rastro** (☎ 920 21 12 18, Plaza del Rastro 1), which is full of character and also has a good **restaurant**. Rooms start at 3880/5560 ptas. Even more comfortable is **Hostal San Juan** (☎ 920 25 14 75, Calle de los Comuneros de Castilla 3)** where rooms with telephone, TV, shower and WC cost 3800/7000 ptas.

Places to Eat

Restaurante Los Leales (Plaza de Italia 4) has a solid **menú** for 1000 ptas. Pleasant **Posada de la Fruta** (Plaza de Pedro Dávila 8) serves cheap and informal meals in its cafeteria/bar and more substantial fare in its traditional dining room.

Italiano (Calle de San Segundo 30) makes salads, pizza and pasta for under 1000 ptas, as does **Siglo Doce** just inside Puerta de los Leales. **Cafe del Adarve** (Calle de San Segundo 50) is a hip hang-out and good place for a drink, as is the wine and tapas bar **Bodeguita de San Segundo** across the street.

Gimeco (Calle Eduardo Marquina 18) is the most central supermarket.

Getting There & Away

Buses to Madrid leave up to eight times on weekdays, down to three on weekends (930 ptas, 1½ hours), while Salamanca is served four times on weekdays (700 ptas, 1½ hours) and Segovia up to seven times (550 ptas, one hour).

There are up to 30 trains a day to Madrid (865 ptas, 1½ hours); trains to Salamanca cost the same. The bus and train stations are, respectively, 700m and 1.5km east of the old town. Bus No 1 links the train station with the old town.

BURGOS

pop 161,500

A mighty chilly place in winter, Burgos is famous for being home to one of Spain's greatest Gothic cathedrals.

Just outside of town lie a couple of remarkable monasteries.

Information

The regional tourist office (☎ 947 20 31 25; closed Sunday) is on Plaza de Alonso Martínez 7. Another branch (☎/fax 947 27 87 10; closed Sunday afternoon) is inside the Teatro Principal on Paseo de Espolón. The main post office is on Plaza del Conde de Castro. The Ciber-Cafe at Calle de la Puebla 21 provides Internet access.

Things to See

It is difficult to imagine that on the site of the majestic Gothic cathedral (1261), there once stood a modest Romanesque church. Twin towers, each representing 84m of richly decorated fantasy, lord over this truly dizzying masterpiece. Inside, the highlight is the **Escalera Dorada** (gilded staircase) by Diego de Siloé. El Cid lies buried beneath the central dome, and you can visit the cloisters and church treasures for 400 ptas.

Of Burgos' two monasteries, the **Monasterio de las Huelgas** is the more interesting. About a half-hour walk west of the town centre along the south bank of the Río Arlanzón, it was founded in 1187 by Eleanor of Acquitaine and is still home to 35 Cistercian nuns. Highlights of the guided tour include Las Claustrillas, an elegant Romanesque cloister, and a museum with preserved garments once worn by Eleanor and other medieval royals (closed Monday; 700/300 ptas).

About 4km east of the centre, the **Cartuja de Miraflores** is a functioning Carthusian monastery rich in treasure. The walk along the Río Arlanzón and through a lush park is particularly pleasant.

Places to Stay & Eat

Camping Fuentes Blancas (*☎/fax 947 48 60 16*) is about 4km from the centre on the road to the Cartuja de Miraflores. It's open April to September and served by hourly bus No 26.

Beg, borrow and/or steal to secure a bed at *Pensión Peña* (*☎ 947 20 62 23, Calle de la Puebla 18*). Completely refurbished singles/doubles with washbasin cost 1700/2900 ptas. *Pensión Victoria* (*☎ 947 20 15 42, Calle de San Juan 3*) comes reader-recommended and has OK rooms with washbasin for 2800/4000 ptas. *Hostal Joma* (*☎ 947 20 33 50, Calle de San Juan 26*) is basic but in the heart of the action. Rooms go for 1750/3100 ptas.

Cervecería Morito on Calle de la Sombrerería is popular with locals for its cheap drinks and budget-friendly hot dishes. *Royal (Plaza de Huerto del Rey 23)* serves a wide range of salads, burgers and sandwiches well under 1000 ptas.

Getting There & Away

The bus station is a Calle de Miranda 3. Continental Auto runs up to 12 buses daily to

Madrid (1950 ptas). Buses also go to Santander, San Sebastián, Vitoria and Bilbao.

Trains to Madrid depart up to nine times daily (3060 ptas, four hours) and to Bilbao six times (2000 ptas, three hours). Others go to León, Salamanca and other major cities.

SALAMANCA
pop 160,500

If any major Castillian city can be said to jump with action, it's Salamanca. Year round, its countless bars, cafes and restaurants are jam-packed with students and young visitors from around the world. This is one of Spain's most inspiring cities, both in terms of the beauty of its architecture and its modern, laid-back lifestyle.

Information

The municipal tourist office (*☎ 923 21 83 42*) on Plaza Mayor, open daily, concentrates on city information. A second branch (*☎ 923 26 85 71*) in the Casa de las Conchas focuses on the wider region (closed Saturday afternoon and Sunday).

The post office is situated at Gran Vía 25. For Internet access try Campus Cibermático at Plaza Mayor 10. There's a coin-operated laundrette at Pasaje Azafranal 18.

Things to See

As in many Spanish cities, one of the joys of Salamanca is to simply wander the streets. At the heart of the old centre is the harmonious **Plaza Mayor** (1755), designed by José Churriguera, which is ringed by medallions of sundry famous figures; until the 19th century, bullfights took place here.

Salamanca's **University** was founded in 1218. Its main facade on Calle de los Libreros is a tapestry in sandstone, bursting with images of mythical and historical figures … and the famously elusive frog. Join the throngs trying to find the little creature.

Brace yourself for the **Catedral Nueva** (New Cathedral) on Rúa Mayor. This incredible Gothic structure, completed in 1733, took 220 years to build. As you try to take in the detailed relief around the entrance, you may wonder how they did it so fast. From inside the cathedral, you can enter the adjacent **Catedral Vieja** (Old Cathedral) for 300 ptas. A Romanesque construction begun in 1120, this church

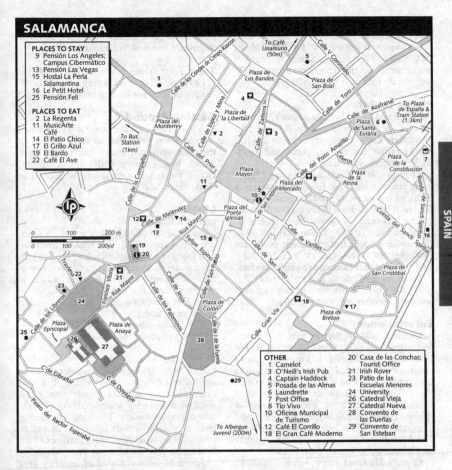

SALAMANCA

PLACES TO STAY
9 Pensión Los Angeles;
   Campus Cibermático
13 Pensión Las Vegas
15 Hostal La Perla
   Salamantina
16 Le Petit Hotel
25 Pensión Feli

PLACES TO EAT
2 La Regenta
11 MusicArte
   Café
14 El Patio Chico
17 El Grillo Azul
19 El Bardo
22 Café El Ave

OTHER
1 Camelot
3 O'Neill's Irish Pub
4 Captain Haddock
5 Posada de las Almas
6 Laundrette
7 Post Office
8 Tío Vivo
10 Oficina Municipal
   de Turismo
12 Café El Corrillo
18 El Gran Café Moderno
20 Casa de las Conchas;
   Tourist Office
21 Irish Rover
23 Patio de las
   Escuelas Menores
24 University
26 Catedral Vieja
27 Catedral Nueva
28 Convento de
   las Dueñas
29 Convento de
   San Esteban

SPAIN

is a bit of a hybrid, with some elements of Gothic; the ribbed cupola shows a Byzantine influence. Both cathedrals are open daily.

Other major sights include the **Convento de San Esteban** and the **Convento de las Dueñas**. The 15th-century **Casa de las Conchas**, named for the scallop shells clinging to its facade, is a symbol of Salamanca.

Places to Stay

Salamanca is always in season, so book ahead when possible. The central HI *Albergue Juvenil* (☎ 923 26 91 41, ✉ esterra@mmteam .disbumad.es, Calle Escoto 13-15) charges

1750 ptas per bunk, including bed linen and breakfast. Bus No 16 connects the hostel with the centre.

Pensión Los Angeles (☎ 923 21 81 66, Plaza Mayor 10) has low-frills singles/doubles with washbasin for 1900/2900 ptas. A favourite of young travellers is the tiny *Pensión Las Vegas* (☎ 923 21 87 49, Calle de Meléndez 13), where clean rooms cost 2000/3500 ptas. *Hostal La Perla Salamantina* (☎/fax 923 21 76 56, Calle de Sánchez Barbero 7) has bright rooms with washbasin for 2100/3500 ptas. Rooms at *Pensión Feli* (☎ 923 21 60 10, Calle de los Libreros 58), near the university, are cheerful and rent for 2400/3400 ptas.

For more comfort, try *Le Petit Hotel* (☎ *923 26 55 67, Ronda de Sancti-Spíritus 39)* whose small but tidy rooms with phone, TV and private bath cost 4000/6500 ptas.

Places to Eat
For good and filling breakfasts from 375 ptas, go to *Café Unamuno (Calle Zamora 55)*. *MusicArte Café (Plaza del Corrillo 22)* is a hip hang-out for coffee, pizza and sandwiches at budget prices.

El Patio Chico (Calle de Meléndez 13) is a lively place for beers and filling tapas (400 ptas each), plus a set *menú* for 1500 ptas. At *Café El Ave (Calle de los Libreros 24)* full meals can be had from 700 ptas. For more atmosphere, go to the bustling *El Bardo (Calle de la Compañia 8)*, which does decent paella for 1100 ptas. *El Grillo Azul (☎ 923 21 92 33, Calle Grillo 1)* has inexpensive vegetarian fare.

La Regenta (Calle de Espoz y Mina 19-20) is a frilly coffeehouse with velvet curtains, polished antiques and yummy cakes.

Entertainment
Salamanca, with its myriad bars, is the perfect after-dark playground. A drink at *Tío Vivo (Calle de Clavel 3)* is a must, if only to experience the whimsical decor. A long-time favourite is *El Gran Café Moderno (Gran Vía 75)*, made to resemble an early-20th-century Parisian street. *Café El Corrillo (Calle de Meléndez 8)* is great for a beer and live jazz. *O'Neill's (Calle de Zamora 14)* and *The Irish Rover* by the Casa de las Conchas are Salamanca's popular Irish pubs.

Captain Haddock is a romantic, candlelit haunt with a muted nautical theme. It's in a courtyard off Calle Consejo.

Great discos include *Camelot* inside an actual convent on Calle de la Companía, and *Posada de las Almas* on Plaza de San Boal, a fantasy world inhabited by life-sized papier-mâché figures and doll houses.

Getting There & Away
Bus Salamanca's bus station is at Avenida de Filiberto Villalobos 85, about 1km north-west of Plaza Mayor. AutoRes has frequent express service to Madrid (2250 ptas, 2½ hours), as well as a few nonexpress buses (1750 ptas, 3¾

hours). Other destinations served regularly include Santiago de Compostela, Cáceres, Ávila, Segovia, León and Valladolid.

Train Four trains leave daily for Madrid (2130 ptas, 2½ hours) via Ávila (865 ptas, 1¾ hours). A train for Lisbon leaves at 4.41 am.

Getting Around
Bus No 4 runs past the bus station and round the old town perimeter to Gran Vía. From the train station, the best bet is bus No 1, which heads down Calle de Azafranal. Going the other way, it can be picked up along Gran Vía.

LEÓN
pop 147,300
León is far too often left off travellers itineraries. For those who get here, a fresh and pleasant city awaits, with long boulevards, open squares, excellent nightlife and one of Spain's greatest cathedrals. León was at its mightiest from the 10th to 13th centuries, as capital of the expanding Christian kingdom of the same name.

The tourist office (☎ 987 23 70 82, fax 987 27 33 91), opposite the cathedral, is open daily.

Things to See
León's breathtaking 13th-century **catedral** is a wonder of Gothic architecture. It has an extraordinarily intricate facade with a rose window, three richly sculptured doorways and two muscular towers. The most outstanding feature, though, awaits inside – 128 radiant stained-glass windows (with a surface of 1800 sq metres) give the place an ethereal quality.

About 500m north-west of here is a great monument from the earlier Romanesque period – the **Real Basílica de San Isidoro**. It contains the **Panteón Real** where Leonese royalty lie buried beneath a canopy of some of the finest frescoes in all of Spain. It can only be seen on a guided tour (400 ptas).

The last in León's trio of major sights is the **Hostal de San Marcos**, at the end of the Gran Vía de San Marcos. This former pilgrim's hospital, with its golden-hued 100m-long facade (1513), now houses a parador (luxury hotel) and the Museo de León.

Also of interest is the **Casa de Botines** on Plaza de San Marcelo, designed by famed

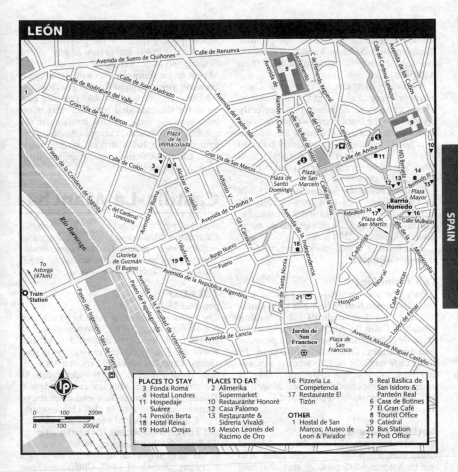

LEÓN

PLACES TO STAY
3 Fonda Roma
4 Hostal Londres
11 Hospedaje Suárez
14 Pensión Berta
18 Hotel Reina
19 Hostal Orejas

PLACES TO EAT
2 Alimerika Supermarket
10 Restaurante Honoré
12 Casa Palomo
13 Restaurante & Sidrería Vivaldi
15 Mesón Leonés del Racimo de Oro

16 Pizzeria La Competencia
17 Restaurante El Tizón

OTHER
1 Hostal de San Marcos; Museo de Leon & Parador

5 Real Basílica de San Isidoro & Panteón Real
6 Casa de Botines
7 El Gran Café
8 Tourist Office
9 Catedral
20 Bus Station
21 Post Office

Catalan architect Antoni Gaudí, although it's rather conservative by his standards.

Places to Stay

Pensión Berta (☎ *987 25 70 39, Plaza Mayor 8*) has rickety but clean doubles for 3000 ptas. The decidely no-frills *Fonda Roma* (☎ *987 22 46 63, Avenida de Roma 4*) is in an attractive old building and has rooms for 900/1500 ptas. *Hospedaje Suárez* (☎ *987 25 42 88, Calle de Ancha 7*) offers the same standard and prices.

Hotel Reina (☎ *987 20 52 12, Calle de Puerta de la Reina 2*) has rooms with wash-basin for 1870/3365 ptas and others with full bath costing 4000/5000 ptas. For more comfort, try the friendly *Hostal Londres* (☎ *987 22 22 74, Avenida de Roma 1*) where charming doubles with TV, shower and WC start at 4500 ptas. *Hostal Orejas* (☎/fax *987 25 29 09, Calle de Villafranca 8*) has rooms with similar amenities for 5500/6500 ptas; those with washbasin go for 4000/5000 ptas.

Places to Eat

Restaurante Honoré (*Calle de los Serradores 4*) has a good *menú* for 950 ptas. *Casa Palomo*, on tiny Calle de la Escalerilla, is a quality establishment with a lunch *menú* for 1300 ptas. Next door is the popular *Restaurante & Sidrería Vivaldi*, where you can wash down your meal with a cider from Asturias.

A bustling hang-out is *Pizzeria La Competencia*, wedged into tight Calle Mulhacín, whose cheap and delicious pies perfectly complement the house wine (400 ptas/bottle). *Restaurante El Tizón (Plaza de San Martín 1)* is good for big portions of meaty fare and offers an abundant set lunch for 1600 ptas. There are a few decent pizzerias and bars on the same square.

Mesón Leonés del Racimo de Oro (Calle de Caño Badillo 2) is a long-established restaurant favoured by an older crowd. Set lunches cost about 1200 ptas and mains range from 1500 ptas to 2300 ptas.

Alimerika is a well-stocked supermarket at Avenida Roma 2.

Entertainment
León's nocturnal activity flows thickest in the aptly named *Barrio Húmedo* (Wet Quarter), the crowded tangle of lanes leading south off Calle de Ancha. Its epicentre is Plaza de San Martín, a particularly pleasant spot for drinks. Outside of the Barrio, *El Gran Café* on Calle de Cervantes is a classy and popular spot, but there are plenty of other possibilities along this street as well as on Calle de Fernando Regueral and Calle de Sacramento.

Getting There & Away
Bus Alsa has up to 12 buses daily to Madrid (2665 ptas, 3½ hours). Frequent buses also run to Astorga (405 ptas, 30 minutes) and Oviedo (1015 ptas, 1¾ hours). Other destinations include Bilbao, Salamanca, Burgos and San Sebástian.

Train Up to 10 trains daily leave for Madrid (3600 ptas, 4¼ hours) and three go to Barcelona (5700 ptas, 11 hours). Plenty of trains head west to Astorga (410 ptas, 45 minutes), north to Oviedo (1700 ptas, two hours) and east to Burgos (2100 ptas, two hours).

AROUND LEÓN
A more extravagant example of Gaudí's work is in the town of **Astorga**, 47km south-

west of León. Fairy-tale turrets, frilly facades and surprising details – the playful Palacio Episcopal (1889) integrates nearly all of Gaudí's stylistic hallmarks. Inside is the Museo de los Caminos with a moderately interesting assemblage of Roman artefacts and religious art. Tickets for 400 ptas are also good for the cathedral museum next door; both have the same opening hours (with the palace closed Sunday, except in August). The cathedral itself has a striking facade, made from caramel-coloured sandstone and dripping in sculptural detail.

Castilla-La Mancha

Best known as the home of Don Quixote, Castilla-La Mancha conjures up images of endless empty plains and lonely windmills. This Spanish heartland is home to two fascinating cities, Toledo and Cuenca.

TOLEDO
pop 66,989
The history of this city stretches back into pre-Roman days. The narrow, winding streets of Toledo, perched on a small hill above the Río Tajo, are crammed with museums, churches and other monumental reminders of a splendid and turbulent past. As the main city of Muslim central Spain, Toledo was the peninsula's leading centre of learning and the arts in the 11th century. The Christians wrested control of it in 1085 and Toledo soon became the headquarters of the Spanish Church. For centuries it was one of the most important of Spain's numerous early capitals. Until 1492, Christians, Jews and Muslims coexisted peaceably here, for which Toledo still bears the label 'Ciudad de las Tres Culturas' (City of the Three Cultures). Its unique architectural combinations, with Arabic influences everywhere, are a strong reminder of Spain's mixed heritage. El Greco lived here from 1577 to 1614 and many of his works can still be seen in the city.

Toledo is quite expensive and packed with tourists and souvenir shops. Try to stay here at least overnight, since you can enjoy the street and cafe life after the tour buses have headed north in the evening.

TOLEDO

PLACES TO STAY
2 Circo Romano
5 Residencia Juvenil de San Servando
6 Pensión Segovia
11 Hotel Maravilla
15 Pensión Lumbreras
28 La Belviseña,
29 Hotel Santa Isabel

PLACES TO EAT
9 Jacaranda Bar
12 Ludeña
20 Bar La Ría
23 Osiris Bar
25 El Delfín

OTHER
1 Bus Station
3 Main Tourist Office
4 Puerta Neuva de Bisagra

7 Museo de Santa Cruz
8 Plaza de Zocodover
10 Post Office
13 Plaza de la Magdalena
14 Plaza Mayor
16 Alcázar
17 Discad Multimedia
18 Catedral
19 Plaza del Ayuntamiento
21 San Juan de los Reyes

22 Santa María La Blanca Sinagoga
24 Iglesia de Santo Tomé
26 Ayuntamiento & Tourist Office
27 Plaza de San Justo
30 Sinagoga del Tránsito & Museo Sefardí
31 Casa y Museo de El Greco
32 Plaza de Santa Isabel

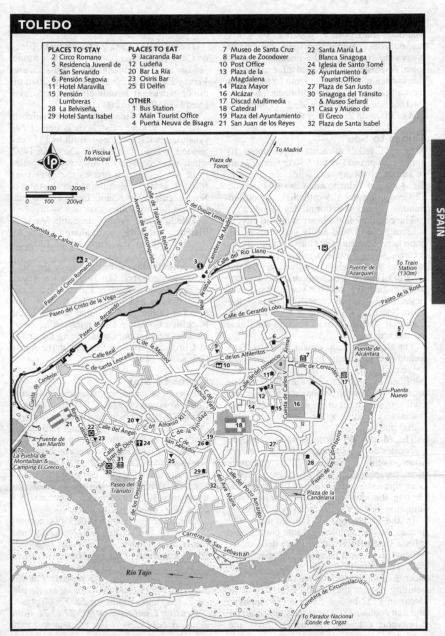

SPAIN

Information

The main tourist office (☎ 925 22 08 43) is just outside Toledo's main gate, the Puerta Nueva de Bisagra, at the northern end of town. A smaller, more helpful information office is open in the ayuntamiento (across from the cathedral). Discad Multimedia provides Internet access at Miguel de Cervantes 17, east of Plaza de Zocodover towards the river.

Things to See

Most of Toledo's attractions open about 10 am to 1.30 pm and about 3.30 to 6 pm (7 pm in summer). Many, including the alcázar, Sinagoga del Tránsito and Casa y Museo de El Greco, but not the cathedral, are closed Sunday afternoon and/or all day Monday.

The **catedral**, in the heart of the old city, is stunning. You could easily spend an afternoon here, admiring the glorious stone architecture, stained-glass windows, tombs of kings in the Capilla Mayor, and art by the likes of El Greco, Velázquez and Goya. Entry to the cathedral is free, but you have to buy a ticket (700 ptas) to enter four areas – the Coro, Sacristía, Capilla de la Torre and Sala Capitular – which contain some of the finest art and artisanry.

The **alcázar**, Toledo's main landmark, was fought over repeatedly from the Middle Ages to the civil war, when it was besieged by Republican troops. Today it's a military museum, created by the Nationalist victors of the civil war, with most of the displays which are fascinating relating to the 1936 siege. Entry is 200 ptas.

The **Museo de Santa Cruz** on Calle de Cervantes contains a large collection of furniture, fading tapestries, military and religious paraphernalia, and paintings. Upstairs is an impressive collection of El Grecos including the masterpiece *La Asunción* (Assumption of the Virgin). Entry is 200 ptas.

In the south-west of the old city, the queues outside an unremarkable church, the **Iglesia de Santo Tomé** on Plaza del Conde, indicate there must be something special inside. That something is El Greco's masterpiece *El Entierro del Conde de Orgaz*. The painting depicts the burial of the Count of Orgaz in 1322 by San Esteban (St Stephen) and San Agustín (St Augustine), observed by a heavenly entourage, including Christ, the

Virgin, John the Baptist and Noah. Entry is 200 ptas.

The so-called **Casa y Museo de El Greco** on Calle de Samuel Leví, in Toledo's former Jewish quarter, contains the artist's famous *Vista y Plano de Toledo*, plus about 20 of his minor works. It is unlikely El Greco ever lived here. Entry is 200 ptas.

Nearby, the **Sinagoga del Tránsito** on Calle de los Reyes Católicos is one of two synagogues left in Toledo. Built in 1355 and handed over to the Catholic church in 1492, when most of Spain's Jews were expelled from the country, it houses the interesting **Museo Sefardí**, examining the history of Jewish culture in Spain. Entry is 400 ptas (free on Saturday afternoon and Sunday).

Toledo's other synagogue, **Santa María La Blanca**, a short way north along Calle de los Reyes Católicos, dates back to the 12th century. Entry is 200 ptas.

A little farther north lies one of the city's most visible sights, **San Juan de los Reyes**, the Franciscan monastery and church founded by Fernando and Isabel. The prevalent late Flemish-Gothic style is tarted up with lavish Isabelline ornament and counterbalanced by mudéjar decoration. Outside hang the chains of Christian prisoners freed after the fall of Granada in 1492.

Places to Stay

The nearest camping ground is *Camping Circo Romano* (☎ 925 22 04 42, *Avenida de Carlos III 19*), but better is *Camping El Greco* (☎ 925 22 00 90), well signposted 2.5km south-west of town. Both are open all year.

Toledo's HI hostel, *Residencia Juvenil de San Servando* (☎ 925 22 45 54), is beautifully located in the Castillo de San Servando, a castle that started life as a Visigothic monastery. It's east of the Río Tajo and B&B costs 1200 ptas if you're under 26.

Cheap accommodation in the city is not easy to come by and is often full, especially from Easter to September. *La Belviseña* (☎ 925 22 00 67, *Cuesta del Can 5*), is basic but among the best value (if you can get in), with rooms at 1500 ptas per person. The pleasant *Pensión Segovia* (☎ 925 21 11 24, *Calle de los Recoletos 2*) has simple rooms for 2200/3000 ptas.

Pensión Lumbreras (☎ 925 22 15 71, *Calle de Juan Labrador 9*) has reasonable rooms and pleasant courtyard for 1700/3200/4500 ptas. *Hotel Santa Isabel* (*☎/fax 925 25 31 36, Calle de Santa Isabel 24*) is a good mid-range hotel well placed near the cathedral, yet away from the tourist hordes. Pleasant rooms with air-con are 3925/6075 ptas plus IVA. *Hotel Maravilla* (*☎ 925 22 83 17, Plaza de Barrio Rey 5*), just off the Zocodover, has rooms with private bath for 4000/6500 ptas.

Places to Eat

Among the cheap lunch spots, *El Delfin* (*Calle del Taller del Moro*) has a set *menú* for 950 ptas. For outdoor dining, the *Osiris Bar* on the shady Plaza del Barrio Nuevo is a decent choice, with set lunches from 1300 ptas.

If you just want to pick at a pâté and cheese platter over a beer, try the chilled-out *Jacaranda Bar* (*Callejón de los Dos Codos 1*). For Toledo's best seafood, the tiny *Bar La Ría* (*Callejón de los Bodegones 6*) is hard to beat at 2000 ptas for a good meal. An excellent little place for a full meal (1500 ptas *menú*) or simply a beer and tapas is *Ludeña* (*Plaza de la Magdalena 13*).

Getting There & Away

To reach most major destinations from Toledo, you need to backtrack to Madrid (or at least Aranjuez). Toledo's bus station (☎ 925 22 36 41) is on Avenida de Castilla-La Mancha. There are buses (585 ptas) every half-hour from about 6 am to 10 pm to/from Madrid (Estación Sur). The Aisa line has a service from Toledo to Cuenca at 5.30 pm, Monday to Friday.

Trains from Madrid (Atocha) are more pleasant than the bus, but there are only nine of them daily. The first from Madrid departs at 7.05 am, the last from Toledo at 8.56 pm (660 ptas one way). Toledo's train station is 400m east of the Puente de Azarquiel.

Bus No 5 links the train and bus stations with Plaza de Zocodover.

CUENCA
pop 43,733

Cuenca's setting is hard to believe. The high old town is cut off from the rest of the city by the Júcar and Huécar Rivers, sitting at the top of a deep gorge. Most of its famous monuments appear to teeter on the edge – a photographer's delight.

The Infotur office (☎ 969 23 21 19) at Calle de Alfonso VIII 2, just before the arches of Plaza Mayor, is especially helpful. La Repro, close to the train and bus stations, provides Internet access.

Things to See & Do

Cuenca's **Casas Colgadas** (Hanging Houses), originally built in the 15th century, are precariously positioned on a cliff top, their balconies literally hanging over the gorge. A footbridge across the gorge provides access to spectacular views of these buildings (and the rest of the old town) from the other side. Inside one of the Casas Colgadas is the **Museo de Arte Abstracto Español**. This exciting collection includes works by Fernando Zobel, Sempere, Millares and Chillida. Initially a private initiative of Zobel to unite works by fellow artists of the 1950s Generación Abstracta, it now holds works up to the present day. Entry is 500 ptas, and the museum opens from 11 am to 2 pm and 4 to 6 pm (to 8 pm on Saturday).

Nearby, on Calle del Obispo Valero, is the **Museo Diocesano** (200 ptas). Of the religious art and artefacts inside, the 14th-century Byzantine diptych is the jewel in the crown. Hours are the same as the Museo de Arte Abstracto Español.

South of Plaza Mayor in a former convent is the **Museo de Las Ciencias** (science museum). Displays range from a time machine to the study of the resources of Castilla-La Mancha (closed Sunday afternoon; free).

On Plaza Mayor you'll find Cuenca's strange **catedral**. The lines of the unfinished facade are Norman-Gothic and reminiscent of French cathedrals, but the stained-glass windows look like they'd be more at home in the abstract art museum.

As you wander the old town's beautiful streets, check the **Torre de Mangana**, the remains of a Moorish fortress in a square west of Calle de Alfonso VIII, overlooking the plain below.

Places to Stay & Eat

Up at the top of the *casco* is the clean and simple *Pensión La Tabanqueta* (*☎ 969 21 12 90, Calle de Trabuco 13*) costing 2000 ptas per person. Ask for a room with views of the Júcar gorge.

SPAIN

Down in the new town, there are several places on Calle de Ramón y Cajal, which runs from near the train station towards the old town. The friendly *Pensión Marín* (☎ 969 22 19 78, Calle de Ramón y Cajal 53), a short walk from the train station, has rooms for 1300/2400 ptas.

At the foot of the casco is the *Posada de San Julián* (☎ 969 21 17 04, Calle de las Torres 1), a cavernous old place with doubles for 3000 ptas (4000 ptas with own bathroom) and the *Pensión Tintes* (☎ 969 21 23 98, Calle de los Tintes 7) which has basic rooms for about 1500 ptas a head in summer.

Most restaurants and cafes around Plaza Mayor are better for a drink and people-watching than for good-value eating. A decent establishment for solid La Manchan food is the *Restaurante San Nicolás (Calle de San Pedro 15)*. Mains range between 2000 ptas and 3000 ptas.

Getting There & Away

There are up to nine buses a day to Madrid (1325 ptas to 1650 ptas, 2½ hours), and daily buses to Barcelona, Teruel and Valencia. There are five trains a day direct to Madrid (Atocha), taking 2½ hours and costing 1405 ptas one way. There are also four trains a day to Valencia.

Bus No 1 or 2 from near the bus and train stations will take you up to Plaza Mayor in the old town.

Catalunya

BARCELONA
pop 1.5 million

If you only visit one city in Spain, it probably should be Barcelona. After hosting the Olympic Games in 1992, it has finally taken its place on the list of the world's great cities. Catalonia's modernist architecture of the late 19th and early 20th centuries – a unique melting pot of Art Nouveau, Gothic, Moorish and other styles – climaxes here in the inspiring creations of Antoni Gaudí, among them La Sagrada Família church and Parc Güell. Barcelona also has world-class museums including two devoted to Picasso and Miró, a fine old quarter (the Barri Gòtic) and nightlife as good as anywhere in the country.

Orientation

Plaça de Catalunya is Barcelona's main square, and a good place to get your bearings when you arrive. The main tourist office is right here. Most travellers base themselves in Barcelona's old city (Ciutat Vella), the area bordered by the harbour Port Vell (south), Plaça de Catalunya (north), Ronda de Sant Pau (west) and Parc de la Ciutadella (east).

La Rambla, the city's best known boulevard, runs through the heart of the old city from Plaça de Catalunya down to the harbour. On the east side of La Rambla is the medieval quarter (Barri Gòtic), and on the west the seedy Barri Xinès. North of the old city is the gracious suburb L'Eixample, where you'll find the best of Barcelona's modernist architecture.

Information

Tourist Offices The main tourist office is the Centre d'Informació Turisme de Barcelona (☎ 906-30 12 82) at Plaça de Catalunya 17-S (actually underground). It opens from 9 am to 9 pm daily.

Handy offices are located at Estació Sants, the main train station, and the EU passengers arrivals hall at the airport and both open daily (mornings only on Sunday and holidays).

Money Banks usually have the best rates for both cash and travellers cheques. Banking hours are usually 8 am to 2 pm weekdays. The American Express office at Passeig de Gràcia 101 is open 9.30 am to 6 pm weekdays and 10 am to noon Saturday. There is another branch on La Rambla dels Capuxtins 74. The rates are reasonable. For after-hours emergencies, currency-exchange booths throng La Rambla.

Post & Communications The main post office is on Plaça d'Antoni López. For most services including poste restante (lista de correos), it's open Monday to Saturday from 8 am to 9.30 pm.

Email & Internet Access Among dozens of options, you can use the Internet for 600 ptas a half-hour (or 800 ptas an hour for students) upstairs at El Café de Internet (☎ 93 302 11 54), Gran Via de les Corts Catalanes 656.

Travel Agencies Usit UNLIMITED (☎ 93 412 01 04), at Ronda de l'Universitat 16, sells youth and student air, train and bus tickets. It has a branch in the Turisme Juvenil de Catalunya office at Carrer de Rocafort 116-122. Halcón Viatges (☎ 902-30 06 00) is a reliable chain of travel agents with a branch at Carrer de Pau Claris 108.

Bookshops In the Barri Gòtic, Quera, at Carrer de Petritxol 2, specialises in maps and guides. Pròleg, at Carrer de la Dagueria 13, is a good women's bookshop.

In L'Eixample, Altaïr, Carrer de Balmes 71, is a superb travel bookshop; Librería Francesa at Passeig de Gràcia 91 has French language books, and Come In, at Carrer de Provença 203, is good for novels and books on Spain, and dictionaries. The English Bookshop, Carrer d'Entença 63, has a good range of literature.

Laundry Lavomatic, at Carrer del Consolat de Mar 43-45, is a rare self-service laundrette. A 7kg load costs 575 ptas and drying costs 105 ptas for five minutes.

Emergency The Guàrdia Urbana (City Police; ☎ 092) has a station at La Rambla 43, opposite Plaça Reial. For an ambulance or emergency medical help call ☎ 061. Hospital Creu Roja (☎ 93 300 20 20), Carrer del Dos de Maig 301, has an emergency room. There's a 24-hour pharmacy at Carrer d'Aribau 62 and another at Passeig de Gràcia 26.

Dangers & Annoyances Watch your pockets, bags and cameras on the train to/from the airport, on La Rambla, in the Barri Gòtic south of Plaça Reial and in the Barri Xinès especially at night. These last two areas have been somewhat cleaned up in recent years but pickpockets, bag-snatchers and intimidating beggars still stalk the unsuspecting.

Things to See
La Rambla The best way to introduce yourself to Barcelona is by a leisurely stroll from Plaça de Catalunya down La Rambla, the magnificent boulevard of a thousand faces. This long pedestrian strip, shaded by leafy trees, is an ever-changing blur of activity, lined with newsstands, bird and flower stalls, and cafes. It's populated by artists, buskers,

human statues, shoe-shine merchants, beggars, and a constant stream of people promenading and just enjoying the sights.

About halfway down La Rambla is the wonderful **Mercat de la Boqueria**, which is worth going to just for the sights and sounds, but is also a good place to stock up on fresh fruit, vegetables, nuts, bread, pastries – everything you'll need for a park picnic. Just off La Rambla, farther south, **Plaça Reial** was, until a few years ago, a seedy square of ill repute, but it's now quite pleasant, with numerous cafes, bars and a couple of music clubs. Just off the other side of La Rambla at Carrer Nou de la Rambla 3-5 is Gaudí's moody **Palau Güell**, open 10 am to 1.30 pm and 4 to 6.30 pm daily, except Sunday (400 ptas, students 200 ptas). This is also the place to pick up **Ruta del Modernisme** tickets, which allow you to see others Gaudí efforts around the city.

Down at the end of La Rambla stands the **Monument a Colom**, a statue of Columbus atop a tall pedestal. A small lift will take you to the top of the monument (250 ptas). Just west is the **Museu Marítim**, in the beautiful 14th-century Royal Shipyards, with an impressive array of boats, models, maps and more. If you like boats and the sea, you won't be disappointed. It's open 10 am to 7 pm daily (800 ptas, 600 ptas for students and seniors).

Barri Gòtic Barcelona's serene Gothic **catedral** is open 8.30 am to 1.30 pm and 4 to 7.30 pm daily (from 5 pm on weekends). Be sure to visit the lovely cloister. Each Sunday at noon, crowds gather in front of the cathedral to dance the Catalan national dance, the *sardana*. Just east of the cathedral is the fascinating **Museu d'Història de la Ciutat** (City History Museum) composed of several buildings around **Plaça del Rei**, the palace courtyard of the medieval monarchs of Aragón. From the royal chapel, climb the multitiered Mirador del Rei Martí for good views. The museum also includes a remarkable subterranean walk through excavated portions of Roman and Visigothic Barcelona. It's all open 10 am to 2 pm and 4 to 8 pm Tuesday to Saturday, and 10 am to 2 pm Sunday. Entrance is 500 ptas.

A few minutes walk west of the cathedral, **Plaça de Sant Josep Oriol** is a hang-out for

SPAIN

SPAIN

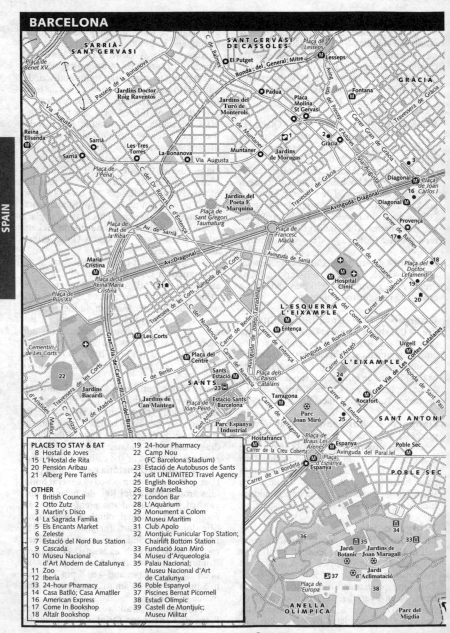

BARCELONA

PLACES TO STAY & EAT
- 8 Hostal de Joves
- 15 L'Hostal de Rita
- 20 Pensión Aribau
- 21 Alberg Pere Tarrés

OTHER
- 1 British Council
- 2 Otto Zutz
- 3 Martin's Disco
- 4 La Sagrada Família
- 5 Els Encants Market
- 6 Zeleste
- 7 Estació del Nord Bus Station
- 9 Cascada
- 10 Museu Nacional
  d'Art Modern de Catalunya
- 11 Zoo
- 12 Iberia
- 13 24-hour Pharmacy
- 14 Casa Batlló; Casa Amatller
- 16 American Express
- 17 Come In Bookshop
- 18 Altaïr Bookshop

- 19 24-hour Pharmacy
- 22 Camp Nou
  (FC Barcelona Stadium)
- 23 Estació de Autobusos de Sants
- 24 usit UNLIMITED Travel Agency
- 25 English Bookshop
- 26 Bar Marsella
- 27 London Bar
- 28 L'Aquàrium
- 29 Monument a Colom
- 30 Museu Marítim
- 31 Club Apolo
- 32 Montjuïc Funicular Top Station;
  Chairlift Bottom Station
- 33 Fundació Joan Miró
- 34 Museu d'Arqueologia
- 35 Palau Nacional;
  Museu Nacional d'Art
  de Catalunya
- 36 Poble Espanyol
- 37 Piscines Bernat Picornell
- 38 Estadi Olímpic
- 39 Castell de Montjuïc;
  Museu Militar

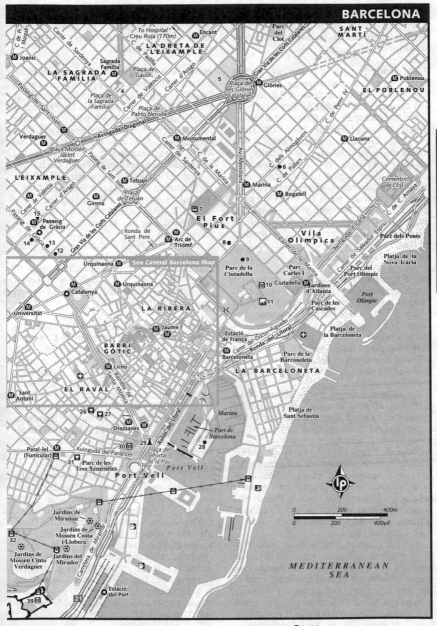

BARCELONA

SPAIN

bohemian musicians and buskers. The plaza is surrounded by cafes and towards the end of the week becomes an outdoor art and craft market.

Waterfront For a look at the new face of Barcelona, take a stroll along the once-seedy waterfront. From the bottom of La Rambla you can cross the Rambla de Mar footbridge to the **Moll d'Espanya**, a former wharf in the middle of the old harbour, Port Vell. There you'll find **L'Aquàrium**, one of Europe's best aquariums, open 9.30 am to 9 pm daily, but not cheap at 1450 ptas. North-east of Port Vell, on the far side of the drab La Barceloneta area, the city **beaches** begin. Along the beachfront, after 1.25km you'll reach the **Vila Olímpica**, site of the 1992 Olympic village, which is fronted by the impressive **Port Olímpic**, a large marina with dozens of rather touristy bars and restaurants (you won't find too many locals here).

La Sagrada Família Construction on Gaudí's principal work and Barcelona's most famous building (metro: Sagrada Família) began in 1882 and is taking a *long* time. The church is not yet half-built and it's anyone's guess whether it will be finished by 2082. Many feel that it should not be completed but left as a monument to the master, whose career was cut short when he was hit by a tram in 1926.

Today there are eight towers, all over 100m high, with 10 more to come – the total of 18 representing the 12 Apostles, the four Evangelists and the mother of God, with the tallest tower (170m) standing for her son. Although La Sagrada Família is effectively a building site, the awesome dimensions and extravagant yet careful sculpting of what has been completed make it probably Barcelona's greatest highlight. The north-east Nativity Facade was done under Gaudí's own supervision; the very different north-west Passion Facade has been built since the 1950s.

You can climb high inside some of the towers by spiral staircases for a vertiginous overview of the interior and a panorama to the sea, or you can opt out and take a lift some of the way up. Entry to La Sagrada Família, which is on Carrer de Sardenya, on the corner of Carrer de Mallorca is 800 ptas for everyone.

It's open 9 am to 8 pm daily from April to the end of August; 9 am to 7 pm in March, September and October; and 9 am to 6 pm from November to February.

More Modernism Many of the best modernist buildings are in L'Eixample, including Gaudí's beautifully coloured **Casa Batlló** at Passeig de Gràcia 43 and his **La Pedrera** at No 92, an apartment block with a grey stone facade that ripples round the corner of Carrer de Provença. Next door to Casa Batlló at No 41 is **Casa Amatller**, by another leading modernist architect, Josep Puig i Cadafalch.

Another modernist highpoint is the **Palau de la Música Catalana** concert hall at Carrer de Sant Pere mes alt 11 in the La Ribera area east of the Barri Gòtic – a marvellous concoction of tile, brick, sculpted stone and stained glass.

You can visit La Pedrera, with its giant chimney pots looking like multicoloured medieval knights, independently. It is open 10 am to 8 pm daily and entry costs 600 ptas. Guided visits take place at 6 pm; 11 am on weekends and holidays.

Museu Picasso & Around The Museu Picasso, in a medieval mansion at Carrer de Montcada 15-19 in La Ribera, houses the most important collection of Picasso's work in Spain – more than 3000 pieces, including paintings, drawings, engravings and ceramics. It concentrates on Picasso's Barcelona periods (1895-1900 and 1901-04) early in his career, and shows how the precocious Picasso learned to handle a whole spectrum of subjects and treatments before developing his own forms of expression. There are also two rooms devoted to Picasso's 1950s series of interpretations of Velázquez's masterpiece *Las Meninas*. The museum is open 10 am to 8 pm Tuesday to Saturday, and 10 am to 3 pm Sunday. Entry is 725 ptas, free on the first Sunday of each month.

The **Museu Textil i d'Indumentària** (Textile and Costume Museum), opposite the Museu Picasso, has a fascinating collection of tapestries, clothing and other textiles from centuries past and present. Opening hours are 10 am to 8 pm Tuesday to Saturday and 10 am to 3 pm Sunday. Entrance is 400 ptas (or 700 ptas if you combine it with the Museu Barbier-Mueller d'Art Precolombí next door).

The **Museu Barbier-Mueller d'Art Pre-colombí** holds one of the most prestigious collections of pre-Columbian art in the world. It opens 10 am to 8 pm Tuesday to Saturday and 10 am to 3 pm Sunday. Admission costs 500 ptas.

At the south end of Carrer de Montcada is the **Església de Santa Maria del Mar**, probably the most perfect of Barcelona's Gothic churches.

Parc de la Ciutadella As well as being ideal for a picnic or stroll, this large park east of the Ciutat Vella has some more specific attractions. Top of the list are the monumental **cascada** (waterfall), a dramatic combination of statuary, rocks, greenery and thundering water created in the 1870s with the young Gaudí lending a hand; and **Museu Nacional d'Art Modern de Catalunya**, with a good collection of 19th and early-20th-century Catalan art, open 10 am to 7 pm Tuesday to Saturday, until 2.30 pm Sunday; entry is 500 ptas. At the southern end of the park is Barcelona's **zoo**, open 10 am to 7 pm daily (1550 ptas) and famed for its albino gorilla.

Parc Güell This park, in the north of the city, is where Gaudí turned his hand to landscape gardening. It's a strange, enchanting place where Gaudí's passion for natural forms really took flight to the point where the artificial almost seems more natural than the natural.

The main, lower gate, flanked by buildings with the appearance of Hansel and Gretel's gingerbread house, sets the mood in the park, with its winding paths and carefully tended flower beds, skewed tunnels with rough stone columns resembling tree roots, and the famous dragon of broken glass and tiles. The house in which Gaudí lived most of his last 20 years has been converted into a museum, open 10 am to 8 pm daily from April to August; the rest of the year 10 am to 2 pm and 4 to 6 pm Sunday to Friday (300 ptas). The simplest way to Parc Güell is to take the metro to Lesseps then walk 10 to 15 minutes; follow the signs north-east along Travessera de Dalt then left up Carrer de Larrard. The park is open from 9 am daily: to 9 pm June to September, to 8 pm April, May and October, to 7 pm March and November, and other months to 6 pm (free).

Montjuïc This hill overlooking the city centre from the south-west is home to some of Barcelona's best museums and attractions, some fine parks, and the main 1992 Olympic sites – well worth some of your time.

On the north side of the hill, the impressive **Palau Nacional** houses the **Museu Nacional d'Art de Catalunya**, with a great collection of Romanesque frescoes, wood-carvings and sculpture from medieval Catalonia. Opening hours are 10 am to 7 pm Tuesday to Saturday (to 9 pm Thursday), 10 am to 2.30 pm Sunday and holidays. Entry is 800 ptas.

Nearby is the **Poble Espanyol** (Spanish Village), by day a tour group's paradise with its craft workshops, souvenir shops and creditable copies of famous Spanish architecture; after dark it becomes a nightlife jungle, with bars and restaurants galore. It's open from 9 am daily (to 8 pm Monday; to 2 am Tuesday to Thursday; to 4 am Friday and Saturday; to midnight Sunday). Entry is 975 ptas (students and children aged seven to 14 pay 550 ptas). After 9 pm on days other than Friday and Saturday, it's free.

Downhill east of the Palau Nacional, the **Museu d'Arqueologia** (Archaeological Museum) has a good collection from Catalonia and the Balearic Islands. Opening hours are 9.30 am to 7 pm Tuesday to Saturday, 10 am to 2.30 pm Sunday (400 ptas, free on Sunday).

Above the Palau Nacional is the **Anella Olímpica** (Olympic Ring), where you can swim in the Olympic pool, the **Piscines Bernat Picornell**, open 7 am until midnight Monday to Friday, to 9 pm Saturday, and 7.30 am to 4.30 pm Sunday for 650 ptas, and wander into the main **Estadi Olímpic** (open 10 am to 6 pm daily; admission free).

The **Fundació Joan Miró**, a short distance downhill east of the Estadi Olímpic, is one of the best modern art museums in Spain. Aside from many works by Miró, there are both permanent and changing exhibitions of other modern art. It's open 10 am to 7 pm Tuesday to Saturday (to 9.30 pm Thursday), and 10 am to 2.30 pm Sunday and holidays. Entry is 800 ptas.

At the top of Montjuïc is the **Castell de Montjuïc**, with a military museum and great views.

To get to Montjuïc you can either walk or take a bus from Plaça d'Espanya (metro:

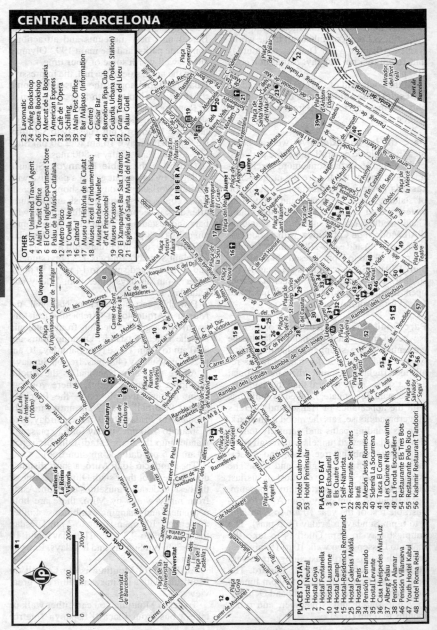

CENTRAL BARCELONA

OTHER
4 USIT Unlimited Travel Agent
5 Main Tourist Office
6 El Corte Inglés Department Store
8 Palau de la Música Catalana
12 Metro Disco
13 L'Ovella Negra
16 Catedral
17 Museu d'Història de la Ciutat
18 Museu Tèxtil d'Indumentària;
     Museu Barbier-Mueller
     d'Art Precolombí
19 Museu Picasso
20 El Xampanyet Bar Sala Tarantos
21 Església de Santa Maria del Mar
23 Lavomatic
24 Pròleg Bookshop
26 Quera Bookshop
27 Mercat de la Boqueria
31 American Express
32 Café de l'Opera
33 Schilling
39 Main Post Office
42 Bar Malpaso (Information
     Centre)
44 Glacier Bar
45 Barcelona Pipa Club
51 Guàrdia Urbana (Police Station)
52 Gran Teatre del Liceu
57 Palau Güell

PLACES TO STAY
1 Hostal Neutral
7 Hostal Goya
10 Hostal Fontanella
14 Hostal Lausanne
15 Hostal Campi
25 Hostal-Residencia Rembrandt
30 Hostal Galerias Maldà
30 Hostal París
34 Pensión Fernando
35 Hostal Levante
36 Casa Huéspedes Mari-Luz
38 Alberg Palau
38 Pensión Alamar
46 Pensión Villanueva
47 Youth Hostel Kabul
48 Hotel Roma Reial
50 Hotel Cuatro Naciones
53 Hotel Peninsular

PLACES TO EAT
3 Bar Estudiantil
9 Els Quatre Gats
11 Self-Naturista
22 Restaurante Set Portes
28 Irati
29 Mesón Jesús Romescu
40 Sidrería La Socarrena
41 Tasca El Corral
43 Les Quinze Nits Cervantes
49 La Fonda Escudellers
54 Restaurante Els Tres Bots
55 Restaurante Pollo Rico
56 Kashmir Restaurant Tandoori

Espanya). Bus No 61 from here links most of the main sights and ends at the foot of a chairlift (475 ptas) up to the castle. A funicular railway (250 ptas) from Paral.lel metro station also runs to the chairlift. From November to mid-June, the chairlift and funicular run only on weekends and holidays.

Tibidabo At 542m, this is the highest hill in the wooded range that forms the backdrop to Barcelona – a good place for a change of scene, some fresh air and, if the air's clear, 70km views. At the top are the Temple del Sagrat Cor, a church topped by a giant Christ statue, and the Parc d'Atraccions funfair. A short distance along the ridge is the 288m Torre de Collserola telecommunications tower, with a hair-raising external glass lift (it opens 11 am to 2.30 pm and 3.30 to 6 pm Wednesday to Friday, to 8 pm in summer, and weekends all day; tickets cost 500 ptas).

The fun way to Tibidabo is to take a suburban train from Plaça de Catalunya to Avinguda de Tibidabo (10 minutes), then hop on the *tramvia blau* tram (275 ptas) across the road, which will take you up to the foot of the Tibidabo funicular railway. The funicular climbs to the church at the top of the hill for 300 ptas. All these run every 10 or 15 minutes from at least 9 am to 9.30 pm.

Els Encants Market This good second-hand market by Plaça de les Glòries Catalanes, is open between 8 am and 6 pm (8 pm in summer) on Monday, Wednesday, Friday and Saturday.

Organised Tours

The Bus Turístic service covers two circuits (24 stops) linking virtually all the major tourist sights. Tourist offices and many hotels have leaflets explaining the system, or you can call ☎ 93 423 18 00. Tickets, available on the bus, are 2000 ptas for one day's unlimited rides, or 2500 ptas for two consecutive days. Service is about every 20 minutes from 9 am to 9.30 pm. Tickets entitle you to discounts of up to 300 ptas on entry fees and tickets to more than 20 sights along the route.

A walking tour of the Ciutat Vella on Saturday and Sunday mornings departs from the Oficina d'Informació de Turisme de Barcelona on Plaça de Catalunya (English at 10 am; Spanish and Catalan at noon). The price is 1000 ptas.

Special Events

Barcelona's biggest festival is the Festes de la Mercè, several days of merrymaking around 24 September including *castellers* (human-castle builders), dances of giants and *correfocs* – a parade of firework-spitting dragons and devils. There are many others – tourist offices can clue you in.

Places to Stay

Camping The closest camping ground to Barcelona is *Camping Cala Gogó* (☎ 93 379 46 00), 9km south-west, which can be reached by bus No 65 from Plaça d'Espanya. About 2km to 3km farther out in Viladecans, on Carretera C-246, *El Toro Bravo* (☎ 93 637 34 62) and *La Ballena Alegre* (☎ 93 658 05 04) are much more pleasant, and there are several more camping grounds within a few more kilometres on Carretera C-246. To get to any of these, take bus No L95 from the corner of Ronda de la Universitat and Rambla de Catalunya. All charge upwards of 3400 ptas.

Hostels A handful of places in Barcelona provide dormitory accommodation. For two people they're not great value, but they're certainly good places to meet other travellers. All require you to rent sheets, at 150 ptas to 350 ptas for your stay, if you don't have them (or a sleeping bag). Ring before you go as the hostels can get booked up.

Youth Hostel Kabul (☎ 93 318 51 90, Plaça Reial 17) is a rough-and-ready place but it has no curfew and is OK if you're looking for somewhere with a noisy party atmosphere; it has 130 places and charges 2000 ptas a night (no card needed). Security is slack but there are safes available for your valuables. Bookings are not taken.

Alberg Palau (☎ 93 412 50 80, Carrer del Palau 6) has just 40 places and is more pleasant. It charges 1600 ptas a night including breakfast and has a kitchen. It's open 7 am to midnight. No card is needed.

Hostal de Joves (☎ 93 300 31 04, Passeig de Pujades 29), near metro Arc de Triomf, is small and rather grim, with 68 beds and a kitchen, and charges 1500 ptas including breakfast; there's a 1 or 2 am curfew. A hostel

SPAIN

card is only needed during the six peak weeks in summer.

Alberg Mare de Déu de Montserrat (☎ *93 210 51 51, Passeig Mare de Déu del Coll 41-51)* is the biggest and most comfortable hostel, but is 4km north of the centre. It has 180 beds and charges 1900 ptas if you're under 25 or have an ISIC or IYTC card, 2500 ptas otherwise (breakfast included). A hostel card is needed. It's closed during the day and you can't get in after 3 am. It's a 10-minute walk from Vallcarca metro or a 20-minute ride from Plaça de Catalunya on bus No 28.

Alberg Pere Tarrés (☎ *93 410 23 09, Carrer de Numància 149)*, about a five-minute walk from Les Corts metro, has 90 beds from 1500 ptas to 2000 ptas, depending on age and whether or not you have a hostel card (rates include breakfast). It has a kitchen, and is closed during the day and you can't get in after 2 am.

Pensiones & Hostales Most of the cheaper options are scattered through the old city, on either side of La Rambla. Generally, the areas closer to the port and on the west side of La Rambla are seedier and cheaper, and as you move north towards Plaça de Catalunya standards (and prices) rise.

Hostal Galerias Maldà (☎ *93 317 30 02, Carrer del Pi 5)* is upstairs in an arcade, and about as cheap as you'll find. It's a rambling family-run establishment with basic singles/doubles for 1500/3000 ptas, and one great little single set aside in a kind of tower. The rambling ***Hostal Paris*** (☎*/fax 93 301 37 85, Carrer del Cardenal Casañas 4)* caters to backpackers, with 42 mostly large rooms for between 3000 ptas for a single and 7500 ptas a double with bath.

Casa Huéspedes Mari-Luz (☎ *93 317 34 63, Carrer del Palau 4)* is both bright and sociable, with dorms for 2000 ptas a bed and doubles 5500 ptas to 5800 ptas.

Pensión Alamar (☎ *93 302 50 12, Carrer de la Comtessa de Sobradiel 1)* has 12 singles for 2500 ptas, and one double room for 5000 ptas. ***Hostal Levante*** (☎ *93 317 95 65, Baixada de Sant Miquel 2)* is a good family-run place with singles for 3500 ptas, or doubles for 5500/6500 ptas with/without private bath. Ask about apartments for longer stays.

If you want a nice double on the square, head to ***Pension Villanueva*** (☎ *91 301 50 84,*

Plaça Reial 2). Prices start at 2500/3500 ptas for basic singles/doubles and range up to 7500 ptas for the best rooms.

Hostal Fontanella (☎*/fax 93 317 59 43, Via Laietana 71)* is a friendly, immaculate place, with 10 (in some cases smallish) rooms costing 3000/5000 ptas or 4000/6900 ptas with bathroom. An excellent deal is the friendly ***Hostal Campi*** (☎ *93 301 35 45, fax 93 301 41 33, Carrer de la Canuda 4)*. Singles/doubles without private bath cost 2700/5000 ptas, or roomy doubles with shower and toilet cost 6000 ptas.

Up near Plaça de Catalunya is the excellent ***Hostal Lausanne*** (☎ *93 302 11 39, Avinguda Portal de l'Àngel 24, 1st floor)*, with good security and rooms (mostly doubles) from 5500 ptas. ***Hostal-Residencia Rembrandt*** (☎ *93 318 10 11, Carrer Portaferrissa 23)* charges 3000/5000 ptas, or 4000/7000 ptas with shower or bath, but is often fully booked.

Once-grand ***Hotel Peninsular*** (☎ *93 302 31 38, Carrer de Sant Pau 34)* has singles/doubles from 3500/6000 ptas, although the rooms don't quite live up to the impressive foyer and central atrium. ***Pensión Fernando*** (☎ *93 301 79 93, Carrer de l'Arc del Remedio 4)* is on Carrer de Ferran, in spite of the address. Dorm beds go for 2300 ptas, and there are doubles and triples for 7000/8500 ptas. You can catch some rays on the roof.

A few cheapies are spread strategically across the upmarket L'Eixample area, north of Plaça de Catalunya. ***Hostal Goya*** (☎ *93 302 25 65, fax 93 412 04 35, Carrer de Pau Claris 74)* has 12 nice, good-sized rooms starting at 3100/4500 ptas. Doubles with private shower and toilet cost 5600 ptas. ***Pensión Aribau*** (☎ *93 453 11 06, Carrer d'Aribau 37)* offers reasonable singles/doubles for 3500/6500 ptas. The singles only have a basin but do come with a TV, while the doubles have shower, toilet, TV and even a fridge.

A leafier location is ***Hostal Neutral*** (☎ *93 487 63 90, fax 93 487 68 48, Rambla de Catalunya 42)*. En suite doubles cost 6530 ptas, rooms without are 5460 ptas. There are no singles.

Hotels Higher up the scale, but good value, is the ***Hotel Roma Reial*** (☎ *93 302 03 66, Plaça Reial 11)*. Modern singles/doubles with bath cost 6000/9000 ptas in high season.

At *Hotel Jardi* (☎ *93 301 59 00, Plaça de Sant Josep Oriol 1)* doubles with a balcony over this lovely square cost around 8000 ptas. Refurbishments underway at the time of writing should soon make this good little place even better. If you want to be right on La Rambla, *Hotel Cuatro Naciones* (☎ *93 317 36 24, fax 93 302 69 85, La Rambla 40)* has adequate rooms for 7490/10,700 ptas; a century ago this was Barcelona's top hotel.

Places to Eat

For quick food, the *Bocatta* and *Pans & Company* chains, with numerous branches around the city, do good hot and cold baguettes with a range of fillings for 360 ptas to 700 ptas.

The greatest concentration of cheaper restaurants is within walking distance of La Rambla. There are a few good-value ones on Carrer de Sant Pau, west off La Rambla. *Kashmir Restaurant Tandoori*, at No 39, does tasty curries and biryanis from around 800 ptas. *Restaurante Pollo Rico*, at No 31, has a somewhat seedy downstairs bar where you can have a quarter chicken or an omelette, with chips, bread and wine, for 500 ptas; the restaurant upstairs is more salubrious and only slightly more expensive. *Restaurante Els Tres Bots*, at No 42, is grungy but cheap, with a *menú* for 875 ptas.

There are lots more places in the Barri Gòtic. *Self-Naturista* (*Carrer de Santa Anna 13),* a self-service vegetarian restaurant, does a good lunch *menú* for 965 ptas. *Mesón Jesús Romescu* (*Carrer dels Cecs de la Boqueria 4)* is a cosy, homy place with a good lunch *menú* for 1400 ptas.

Carrer de la Mercè, running roughly west from the main Correus i Telègrafs (post office) is a good place to find little northern Spanish cider houses. *Tasca El Corral* at No 19 and *Sidrería La Socarrena* at No 21 are both worth checking, but there are many others. A Basque favourite is *Irati* (*Carrer del Cardenal Cassanyes 17)*. The set *menú* is 1500 ptas, or you can enjoy the great tapas and a zurrito of beer or six.

For something a bit more upmarket, *Les Quinze Nits Cervantes* (*Plaça Reial 6)* and *La Fonda Escudellers* (*Carrer dels Escudellers)* are two stylish bistro-like restaurants, under the same management, with a big range of good Catalan and Spanish dishes at reasonable prices, which can mean long queues in summer and at weekends. Three courses with wine and coffee will be about 2500 ptas.

Carrer dels Escudellers also has a couple of good night-time takeaway felafel joints at around 300 ptas a serve.

Or there's *Restaurante Set Portes* (☎ *93 319 30 33, Passeig d'Isabel II 14)*, a classic dating from 1836 and specialising in paella (1475 ptas to 2225 ptas). It's essential to book. Another famous institution is *Els Quatre Gats* (*Carrer Montsió 3)*, Picasso's former hang-out, and now a bit pricey.

L'Eixample has a few good restaurants to offer as well. *Bar Estudiantil* (*Plaça de la Universitat)* does economical plats combinats, eg, chicken, chips and *berenjena* (aubergine), or *botifarra*, beans and red pepper, each for around 600 ptas. This place is open until late into the night and is a genuine student hangout. *L'Hostal de Rita* (*Carrer d'Aragó 279)*, a block east of Passeig de Gràcia, is an excellent mid-range restaurant with a four-course lunch *menú* for 995 ptas, and a la carte mains for 700 ptas to 1000 ptas.

Entertainment

Barcelona's entertainment bible is the weekly *Guía del Ocio* (125 ptas at newsstands). Its excellent listings (in Spanish) include films, theatre, music and art exhibitions.

Bars Barcelona's huge variety of bars are mostly at their busiest from about 11 pm to 2 or 3 am, especially Thursday to Saturday.

Cafè de l'Òpera (*La Rambla 74)*, opposite the Liceu opera house, is the liveliest place on La Rambla. It gets packed with all and sundry at night. *Glaciar* (*Plaça Reial 3)* is busy with a young crowd of foreigners and locals. Tiny *Bar Malpaso* (*Carrer d'En Rauric 20)*, just off Plaça Reial, plays great Latin and African music. Another hip low-lit place with a more varied (including gay) clientele is *Schilling* (*Carrer de Ferran 23)*.

El Xampanyet (*Carrer de Montcada 22)*, near the Museu Picasso, is another small place, specialising in cava (Catalan champagne, around 500 ptas a bottle), with good tapas too.

West of La Rambla, *L'Ovella Negra* (*Carrer de les Sitges 5)* is a noisy, barn-like tavern

SPAIN

with a young crowd. *Bar Marsella (Carrer de Sant Pau 65)* specialises in absinthe (absenta in Catalan), a potent but mellow beverage with supposed narcotic qualities. If by 2.30 am you still need a drink and you don't want a disco, your best bet (except on Sunday) is the *London Bar (Carrer Nou de la Rambla 36)* which sometimes has live music and opens until about 5 am.

Live Music & Discos Many music places have dance space and some discos have bands on around midnight or so, to pull in some custom before the real action starts about 3 am. If you go for the band, you can normally stay for the disco at no extra cost and avoid bouncers' whims about what you're wearing etc. Women and maybe male companions may get in free at some discos if the bouncers like their looks. Count on 300 ptas to 800 ptas for a beer in any of these places. Cover charges can be anything from zero to 3000 ptas, which may include a drink.

Barcelona Pipa Club (Plaça Reial 3) has jazz Thursday to Saturday around midnight (ring the bell to get in). Entry is around 1000 ptas. *Jamboree (Plaça Reial 17)* has jazz, funk, and a disco later, from about 1.30 am. *Club Apolo (Carrer Nou de la Rambla 113)* has live world music several nights a week, followed by live salsa or a varied disco. Expect entry of around 2000 ptas for both of these.

Otto Zutz (Carrer de Lincoln 15) is for the beautiful people dressed in black. The crowd's cool and the atmosphere's great.

Zeleste (Carrer dels Almogàvers 122), in Poble Nou, is a cavernous warehouse-type club, regularly hosting visiting bands. *Mirablau*, at the foot of the Tibidabo funicular, is a bar with great views and a small disco floor; it's open till 5 am.

The two top gay discos are *Metro (Carrer de Sepúlveda 185)* and *Martin's (Passeig de Gràcia 130)*. Metro attracts some lesbians and heteros as well as gay men; Martin's is for gay men only.

Cinemas For films in their original language (with Spanish subtitles), check listings for those marked VO (versión original). A ticket is usually 600 ptas to 750 ptas but many cinemas reduce prices on Monday or Wednesday.

Classical Music & Opera The *Gran Teatre del Liceu* opera house on La Rambla, gutted by fire in 1994, reopened in October 1999. For information on opera, dance and concerts, call ☎ 93 485 99 13.

There are other fine theatres, among them the lovely *Palau de la Música Catalana (☎ 93 295 72 00, Carrer de Sant Pere més alt 11)*, the city's chief concert hall.

Getting There & Away

Air Barcelona's airport, 14km south-west of the city centre at El Prat de Llobregat, caters to international as well as domestic flights. It's not a European hub, but you can often dig up specials and cheap youth fares.

Iberia (☎ 902-40 05 00) is at Passeig de Gràcia 30; Spanair (24 hours ☎ 902-13 14 15) and Air Europa (☎ 902-40 15 01) are at the airport.

Bus The terminal for virtually all domestic and international buses is the Estació del Nord at Carrer d'Alí Bei 80 (metro: Arc de Triomf). Its information desk (☎ 93 265 65 08) is open 7 am to 9 pm daily. A few international buses go from Estació d'Autobuses de Sants beside Estació Sants train station.

Several buses a day go to most main Spanish cities. Madrid is seven or eight hours away (3400 ptas), Zaragoza 4½ hours (1655 ptas), Valencia 4½ hours (2900 ptas) and Granada 13 to 15 hours (7915 ptas). Buses run several times a week to London (14,075 ptas), Paris (11,975 ptas) and other European cities.

Train Virtually all trains travelling to/from destinations within Spain stop at Estació Sants (metro: Sants-Estació); most international trains use Estació de França (metro: Barceloneta).

For some international destinations you have to change trains at Montpellier or the French border. There are direct trains daily to Paris, Zürich and Milan.

Daily trains run to most major cities in Spain. To Madrid there are seven trains a day (5100 ptas, 6½ to 9½ hours); to San Sebastián two (4600 ptas, eight to 10 hours); to Valencia 10 (4600 ptas, as little as three hours on high-speed Euromed train) and to Granada (6400 ptas, eight hours).

Tickets and information are available at the stations or from the RENFE office in

Passeig de Gràcia metro/train station on Passeig de Gràcia, open 7 am to 10 pm daily (Sunday 9 pm).

Car & Motorcycle Tolls on the A-7 autopista to the French border are around 1500 ptas. The N-II to the French border and the N-340 southbound from Barcelona are toll-free but slower. The fastest route to Madrid is via Zaragoza on the A-2 (around 2300 ptas), which heads west off the A-7 south of Barcelona, then the toll-free N-II from Zaragoza.

Getting Around
To/From the Airport Trains link the airport to Estació Sants and Catalunya station on Plaça de Catalunya every half-hour. They take 15 to 20 minutes and a ticket is 355 ptas. The A1 Aerobús does the 40-minute run between Plaça de Catalunya and the airport every 15 minutes, or every half-hour at weekends. The fare is 500 ptas. A taxi from the airport to Plaça de Catalunya is around 2500 ptas.

Bus, Metro & Train Barcelona's metro system spreads its tentacles around the city in such a way that most places of interest are within a 10-minute walk of a station. Buses and suburban trains are only needed for a few destinations but note the Bus Turístic under Organised Tours earlier in this Barcelona section.

A single metro, bus or suburban train ride costs 150 ptas, but a T-1 ticket, valid for 10 rides, costs only 825 ptas, while a T-DIA ticket (625 ptas) gives unlimited city travel in one day.

Car & Motorcycle While traffic flows smoothly thanks to an extensive one-way system, navigating can be frustrating. Parking a car is also difficult and, if you choose a parking garage, quite expensive. It's better to ditch your car and rely on public transport.

Taxi Barcelona's black-and-yellow taxis are plentiful, reasonably priced and especially handy for late-night transport. Flagfall is 300 ptas, after which it's about 105 ptas per kilometre. From Plaça de Catalunya, it costs around 700 ptas to Estació Sants.

MONESTIR DE MONTSERRAT
Unless you are on a pilgrimage, the prime attraction of Montserrat, 50km north-west of Barcelona, is its setting. The Benedictine Monastery of Montserrat sits high on the side of an amazing 1236m mountain of truly weird rocky peaks, and is best reached by cable car. The monastery was founded in 1025 to commemorate an apparition of the Virgin Mary on this site. Pilgrims still come from all over Christendom to pay homage to its Black Virgin (La Moreneta), a 12th-century wooden sculpture of Mary, regarded as Catalonia's patroness.

Information
Montserrat's information centre (☎ 93 877 77 77), to the left along the road from the top cable-car station, is open 10 am to 6 pm daily. It has a good free leaflet/map on the mountain and monastery.

Things to See & Do
If you are making a day trip to Montserrat, come early. Apart from the monastery, exploring the mountain is a treat.

The two-part **Museu de Montserrat**, on the plaza in front of the monastery's basílica, has an excellent collection ranging from an Egyptian mummy to art by El Greco, Monet and Picasso. It's open 9.30 am to 6 pm daily, for 600 ptas (students 400 ptas).

Opening times when you can file past the image of the Black Virgin, high above the main altar of the 16th-century **basílica**, vary according to season. The Montserrat Boys' Choir (Escolania) sings in the basílica Monday to Saturday at 1 and 7 pm (1 pm only on Sunday), except in July. The church fills up quickly, so try to arrive early.

You can explore the mountain above the monastery on a web of paths leading to small chapels and some of the peaks. The Funicular de Sant Joan (580/925 ptas one way/return) will lift you up the first 250m from the monastery.

Places to Stay & Eat
There are several accommodation options (all ☎ 93 877 77 77) at the monastery. The cheapest rooms are in the *Cel.les de Montserrat*, blocks of simple apartments, with showers, for up to 10 people. A two-person apartment

SPAIN

costs up to 5990 ptas in high season. Over-looking Plaça de Santa Maria is the comfortable *Hotel Abat Cisneros*, with rooms from 6725/11,650 ptas in high season. The Cisneros has a four-course *menú* for 2700 ptas.

The *Snack Bar* near the top cable-car station has platos combinados from 875 ptas and bocadillos from about 350 ptas. *Bar de la Plaça*, in the Abat Oliva cel.les building, has similar prices. *Cafeteria Self-Service*, near the car park, has great views but is dearer.

Getting There & Away
Trains run from Plaça d'Espanya station in Barcelona to Aeri de Montserrat up to 18 times a day (most often on summer weekdays), a 1½-hour ride. Return tickets for 1905 ptas include the cable car between Aeri de Montserrat and the monastery.

There's also a daily bus to the monastery from Estació d'Autobuses de Sants in Barcelona at 9 am (plus 8 am in July and August) for a return fare of 1400 ptas. It returns at 5 pm.

COSTA BRAVA
The Costa Brava ranks with Spain's Costa Blanca and Costa del Sol among Europe's most popular holiday spots. It stands alone, however, in its spectacular scenery and proximity to northern Europe, both of which have sent prices skyrocketing in the most appealing places.

The main jumping-off points for the Costa Brava are the inland towns of Girona (Gerona in Castilian) and Figueres (Figueras). Both places are on the A-7 autopista and the toll-free N-II highway which connect Barcelona with France. Along the coast the most appealing resorts are, from north to south, Cadaqués, L'Escala (La Escala), Tamariu, Llafranc, Calella de Palafrugell and Tossa de Mar.

Tourist offices along the coast are very helpful, with information on accommodation, transport and other things; they include Girona (☎ 972 22 65 75), Figueres (☎ 972 50 31 55), Palafrugell (☎ 972 30 02 28), and Cadaqués (☎ 972 25 83 15).

Coastal Resorts
The Costa Brava (Rugged Coast) is all about picturesque inlets and coves. Some longer beaches at places like L'Estartit and Empúries

are worth visiting out of season, but there has been a tendency to build tall buildings wherever engineers think it can be done. Fortunately, in many places it just can't.

Cadaqués, about one hour's drive east of Figueres at the end of an agonising series of hairpin bends, is perhaps the most picturesque of all Spanish resorts, and haunted by the memory of the artist Salvador Dalí, who lived here. It's short on beaches, so people spend a lot of time sitting at waterfront cafes or wandering along the beautiful coast. About 10km north-east of Cadaqués is **Cap de Creus**, a rocky peninsula with a single restaurant at the top of a craggy cliff. This is paradise for anyone who likes to scramble around rocks risking life and limb with every step.

Farther down the coast, past L'Escala and L'Estartit, is Palafrugell, itself a few kilometres inland with little to offer, but near three beach towns that have to be seen to be believed. The most northerly of these, **Tamariu**, is also the smallest, least crowded and most exclusive. **Llafranc** is the biggest and busiest, and has the longest beach. **Calella de Palafrugell**, with its truly picture-postcard setting, is never overcrowded and always relaxed. If you're driving down this coast, it's worth stopping at some of these towns, particularly out of season.

Other Attractions
When you have had enough beach for a while, make sure you put the **Teatre-Museu Dalí**, on Plaça Gala i Salvador Dalí in Figueres, at the top of your list. This 19th-century theatre was converted by Dalí himself and houses a huge and fascinating collection of his strange creations. From July to September the museum is open 9 am to 7.15 pm daily. Queues are long on summer mornings. From October to June it's open 10.30 am to 5.15 pm daily (closed Monday until the end of May, and on 1 January and 25 December). Entry is 1000 ptas (800 ptas October to May).

Historical interest is provided by **Girona**, with a lovely medieval quarter centred on a Gothic cathedral, and the ruins of the Greek and Roman town of **Empúries**, 2km from L'Escala.

For a spectacular stretch of coastline, take a drive north from Tossa de Mar to San Feliu de Guíxols. There are 360 curves in this

20km stretch of road, which, with brief stops to take in the scenery, can take a good two hours.

Among the most exciting attractions on the Costa Brava are the **Illes Medes**, off the coast from the package resort of L'Estartit. These seven islets and their surrounding coral reefs, with a total land area of only 21.5 hectares, have been declared a natural park to protect their extraordinarily diverse flora and fauna. Almost 1500 different life forms have been identified on and around the islands. You can arrange glass-bottom boat trips and diving.

Places to Stay

Most visitors to the Costa Brava rent apartments. If you are interested in renting an apartment for a week or so, contact local tourist offices in advance for information.

Figueres Figueres' HI hostel, the *Alberg Tramuntana* (☎ 972 50 12 13, *Carrer Anicet Pagès 2*) is two blocks from the tourist office. It charges 1700 ptas if you're under 26 or have an ISIC or IYTC card, 2275 ptas otherwise (breakfast included). Alternatively, *Pensión Isabel II* (☎ 972 50 47 35, *Carrer de Isabel II 16*) has reasonable rooms with bath for 2800 ptas. Don't sleep in Figueres' Parc Municipal – people have been attacked here at night.

Girona *Pensión Viladomat* (☎ 972 20 31 76, *Carrer dels Ciutadans 5*) has comfortable singles/doubles starting at 2000/4000 ptas.

Cadaqués *Camping Cadaqués* (☎ 972 25 81 26) is at the top of the town as you head towards Cabo de Creus. Two adults with a tent and a car pay 2880 ptas plus IVA. At these prices, a room in town in probably a better bet. *Hostal Marina* (☎ 972 25 81 99, *Carrer de Frederico Rahola 2*) has doubles at up to 5500 ptas plus IVA, or 8000 ptas with private bath.

Near Palafrugell There are camping grounds at all three of Palafrugell's satellites, all charging similar hefty rates. In Calella de Palafrugell try *Camping Moby Dick* (☎ 972 61 43 07); in Llafranc, *Camping Kim's* (☎ 972 30 11 56); and in Tamariu, *Camping Tamariu* (☎ 972 62 04 22).

Hotel and pensión rooms are relatively thin on the ground here, as many people come on package deals and stay in apartments. In Calella de Palafrugell, the friendly *Hostería del Plancton* (☎ 972 61 50 81) is one of the best deals on the Costa Brava, with rooms at 2200 ptas per person, but it's only open from June to September. *Residencia Montaña* (☎ 972 30 04 04, *Carrer de Cesàrea 2*) in Llafranc is not a bad deal at 6300 ptas plus IVA. In Tamariu, the *Hotel Sol d'Or* (☎ 972 30 04 24, *Carrer de Riera 18*) near the beach, has doubles with bathroom for 6550 ptas.

Getting There & Away

A few buses run daily from Barcelona to Tossa del Mar, L'Estartit and Cadaqués, but for the small resorts near Palafrugell you need to get to Girona first. Girona and Figueres are both on the railway connecting Barcelona to France. The dozen or so trains daily from Barcelona to Portbou at the border all stop in Girona, and most in Figueres. The fare from Barcelona to Girona is 790 ptas to 910 ptas, to Figueres 1125 ptas to 1290 ptas.

Getting Around

There are two or three buses a day from Figueres to Cadaqués and three or four to L'Escala. Figueres bus station (☎ 972 67 42 98) is across the road from the train station.

Several buses daily run to Palafrugell from Girona (where the bus station is behind the train station), and there are buses from Palafrugell to Calella de Palafrugell, Llafranc and Tamariu. Most other coastal towns (south of Cadaqués) can be reached by bus from Girona.

TARRAGONA
pop 112,795

Tarragona makes a perfect contrast to the city life of Barcelona. Founded in 218 BC, it was for a long time the capital of much of Roman Spain, and Roman structures figure among its most important attractions. Other periods of history are also well represented, including the medieval cathedral and 17th-century British additions to the old city walls. The city's archaeological museum is one of the most interesting in Spain. Today, Tarragona is a modern city with a large student population and a lively beach scene and Spain's answer to Disneyland Paris, Port Aventura, is just a few kilometres south.

SPAIN

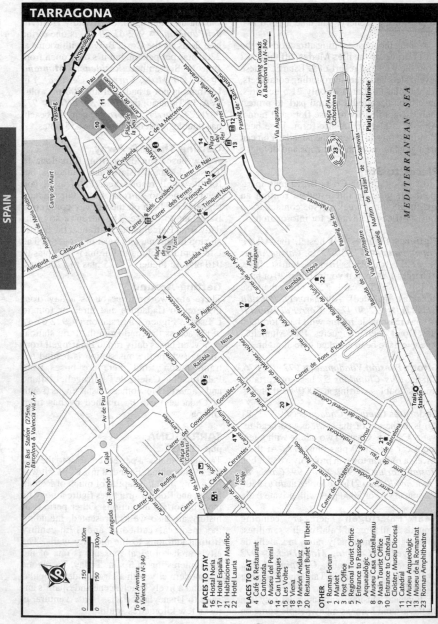

TARRAGONA

MEDITERRANEAN SEA

Platja del Miracle

PLACES TO STAY
16 Hostal Noria
17 Hotel España
21 Habitaciones Mariflor
22 Hotel Lauria

PLACES TO EAT
4 Café & Restaurant
  Cantonada
6 Museu del Pernil
14 Can Llesques
15 Les Voltes
18 Viena
19 Mesón Andaluz
20 Restaurant Bufet El Tiberi

OTHER
1 Roman Forum
2 Market
3 Post Office
5 Regional Tourist Office
7 Entrance to Passeig
  Arqueològic
8 Museu Casa Castellarnau
9 Main Tourist Office
10 Entrance to Catedral,
   Cloister; Museu Diocesà
11 Catedral
12 Museu Arqueològic
13 Museu de la Romanitat
23 Roman Amphitheatre

Orientation & Information

Tarragona's main street is Rambla Nova, which runs approximately north-west from a cliff top overlooking the Mediterranean. A couple of blocks to the east, parallel to Rambla Nova, is Rambla Vella, which marks the beginning of the old town. To the south-west, on the coast, is the train station.

Tarragona's main tourist office (☎ 977 24 50 64) is at Carrer Major 39. There is also a regional tourist office at Carrer de Fortuny 4.

Things to See & Do

The **Museu d'Història de Tarragona** comprises four separate Roman sites around the city, plus the 14th-century noble mansion now serving as the **Museu Casa Castellarnau**, Carrer dels Cavallers 14. A good site to start with is the **Museu de la Romanitat** on Plaça del Rei, which includes part of the vaults of the Roman circus, where chariot races were held. Nearby and close to the beach is the well-preserved Roman **amphitheatre**, where the gladiators battled each other, or wild animals, to the death. On Carrer de Lleida, a few blocks west of Rambla Nova, are remains of a **Roman forum**. The **Passeig Arqueològic** is a peaceful walkway along a stretch of the old city walls, which are a combination of Roman, Iberian and 17th-century British efforts.

From June to September, all these places open 9 or 10 am to 8 pm Tuesday to Saturday (the Passeig Arqueològic to midnight) and 10 am to 2 pm Sunday. In other months, they tend to open 10 am to 1.30 pm and at least two afternoon hours (10 am to 2 pm Sunday and holidays. Admission to each is 300 ptas.

Tarragona's **Museu Arqueològic** on Plaça del Rei gives further insight into the city's rich history. The carefully presented exhibits include frescoes, mosaics, sculpture and pottery dating back to the 2nd century BC. The museum is open 10 am to 1 pm and 4.30 to 7 pm Tuesday to Saturday (10 am to 8 pm in July and August), 10 am to 2 pm Sunday and holidays. Entry is 400 ptas, free on Tuesday.

The **catedral** sits grandly at the highest point of Tarragona, overlooking the old town. Some parts of the building date back to the 12th century AD. It's open for tourist visits Monday to Friday for hours that vary with the season (longest in summer) but always include 10 am to 1 pm and (except from mid-November to mid-March) 3 to 6 pm. Entrance is through the beautiful cloister with the excellent Museu Diocesà.

If you're here in summer, Platja del Miracle is the main city beach. It is reasonably clean but can get terribly crowded. Several other beaches dot the coast north of town, but in summer you will never be alone.

Port Aventura

Port Aventura (☎ 902-20 22 20), which opened in 1995 7km west of Tarragona, near Salou, is Spain's biggest and best funfair-adventure park, with a noticeable American influence. If you have 4600 ptas to spare (3400 ptas for children aged from five to 12), it makes a fun day out with never a dull moment although it only opens from Semana Santa to October. There are hair-raising experiences like a virtual submarine and the Dragon Khan, claimed to be Europe's biggest roller coaster. It is open daily during its season from 10 am to 8 pm, and from around mid-June to mid-September until midnight. Night tickets, valid from 7 pm, are 3400 ptas.

Trains run to Port Aventura's own station, about a 1km walk from the site, several times a day from Tarragona and Barcelona (1305 ptas return).

Places to Stay

Camping Tàrraco (☎ 977 23 99 89) is near Platja Arrabassada beach, off the N-340 road 2km north-east of the centre. There are more, better camping grounds on Platja Larga beach, a couple of kilometres farther on.

If you intend to spend the night in Tarragona in summer, you would be wise to call ahead to book a room. **Hostal Noria** (☎ 977 23 87 17, Plaça de la Font 53) is decent value at 2700/4600 ptas but is often full. **Habitaciones Mariflor** (☎ 977 23 82 31, Carrer del General Contreras 29) occupies a drab building near the station, but has clean rooms for 2100/4000 ptas.

Hotel España (☎ 977 23 27 12, Rambla Nova 49) is a well-positioned, but unexciting, one-star hotel where rooms with bath cost 3300/6000 ptas plus IVA. The three-star **Hotel Lauria** (☎ 977 23 67 12, Rambla Nova 20) is a worthwhile splurge at 5500/8500 ptas plus IVA, with a good location and a pool.

SPAIN

Places to Eat

For Catalan food, head for the stylish *Restaurant Bufet El Tiberi (Carrer de Martí d'Ardenya 5)*, which offers an all-you-can-eat buffet for 1450 ptas per person. Nearby *Mesón Andaluz (Carrer de Pons d'Icart 3, upstairs)*, is a backstreet local favourite, with a good three-course *menú* for 1500 ptas.

The *Museu del Pernil (Plaça de la Font 16)* is the place to dig into porcine delights. A platter of mixed meats and sausages will cost about 1700 ptas. Or if cheese is your thing, try a platter *(taula de formatges)* at *Can Llesques (Carrer de Natzaret 6)*, a pleasant spot looking onto Plaça del Rei.

Café Cantonada (Carrer de Fortuny 23) is a popular place for tapas; next door, *Restaurant Cantonada* has pizzas and pasta from around 850 ptas. Rambla Nova has several good places, either for a snack or a meal. *Viena (Rambla Nova 50)* has good croissants and a vast range of entrepans from 300 ptas.

Tucked under the vaults of the former Roman circus, *Les Voltes (Carrer de Trinquet Vell 12)* is a little overpriced, but the *menú* is not bad at 1500 ptas.

Getting There & Away

Over 20 regional trains a day run from Barcelona to Tarragona (660 ptas, one to 1½ hours). There are about 12 trains daily from Tarragona to Valencia, taking two to 3½ hours and costing 2095 ptas. To Madrid, there are four trains each day – two via Valencia – taking seven hours, and two via Zaragoza taking six hours. Fares start at 4900 ptas.

Balearic Islands

Floating out in the Mediterranean waters off the east coast of Spain, the Balearic Islands (Islas Baleares) are invaded every summer by a massive multinational force of hedonistic party animals. Not surprising really, when you consider the ingredients on offer: fine beaches, relentless sunshine and wild nightlife.

Despite all this, the islands have managed, to a degree, to maintain their individuality and strong links with their past. Beyond the bars and beaches are Gothic cathedrals, Stone Age ruins, small fishing villages, some spectacular bushwalks and endless olive groves and orange orchards.

Most place names and addresses are given in Catalan, the main language spoken in the islands. High-season prices are quoted here. Out of season, you will often find things are much cheaper and accommodation especially can be as much as half the quoted rates here.

Getting There & Away

Air Scheduled flights from the major cities on the Spanish mainland are operated by several airlines, including Iberia, Air Europa and Spanair. The cheapest and most frequent flights are from Barcelona and Valencia.

Standard one-way fares from Barcelona are not great value hovering around 10,000 ptas to Palma de Mallorca and more to the other islands. At the time of writing, however, you could get a return, valid for up to a month, for 13,000 ptas with Spanair. Booking at least four days ahead brought the price down to about 10,000 ptas return. In low season the occasionally truly silly offer, such as 4000 ptas one way, comes up. From Valencia, Ibiza is marginally cheaper by air.

When in the islands keep your eyes peeled for cheap charter flights to the mainland. At the time of writing one-way charters were going for 14,900 ptas to places like Seville and Vigo, 10,900 ptas for Málaga and 7500 ptas to Alicante.

Interisland flights are expensive (given the flying times involved), with Palma to Maó or Ibiza costing 9400 ptas (return flights cost double).

Boat Trasmediterránea (information and ticket purchases on ☎ 902-45 46 45, or www .trasmediterranea.com) is the major ferry company for the islands, with offices in (and services between) Barcelona (☎ 93 295 90 00), Valencia (☎ 96 367 65 12), Palma de Mallorca (☎ 971-40 50 14), Maó (☎ 971-36 60 50) and Ibiza city (☎ 971-31 51 00).

Scheduled services are: Barcelona-Palma (eight hours, seven to nine services weekly); Barcelona-Maó (nine hours, two to six services weekly); Barcelona-Ibiza city (9½ hours or 14½ hours via Palma, three to six services weekly); Valencia-Palma (8½ hours, six to seven services weekly); Valencia-Ibiza city

SPAIN

(seven hours, six to seven services weekly); Palma-Ibiza city (4½ hours, one or two services weekly); and Palma-Maó (6½ hours, one service weekly).

Prices quoted below are the one-way fares during summer; low and mid-season fares are considerably cheaper.

Fares from the mainland to any of the islands are 6920 ptas for a Butaca Turista (seat); a berth in a cabin ranges from 11,410 ptas (four-share) to 18,690 ptas (twin-share) per person. Taking a small car costs 19,315 ptas, or there are economy packages (Paquete Ahorro) available.

Inter-island services (Palma-Ibiza city and Palma-Maó) both cost 3540 ptas for a Butaca Turista, and 9875 ptas for a small car. Ask, too, about economy packages.

During summer, Trasmediterránea also operates the following Fast Ferry services (prices quoted are for a Butaca Turista): Barcelona-Palma (8990 ptas, 4¼ hours, up to three services a week); Valencia-Palma (6920 ptas, 6¼ hours, four services weekly); Valencia-Ibiza city (6920 ptas, 3¼ hours, four services weekly); Palma-Ibiza city (5750 ptas, 2¼ hours, four services weekly).

Another company, Balearia (☎ 902-16 01 80) operates two or three daily ferries from Denia (on the coast between Valencia and Alicante) to Sant Antoni de Portmany and one to Ibiza city (6295 ptas one way, four hours). Another service links Ibiza to Palma (3245 ptas, three hours).

Iscomar (☎ 902-11 91 28) has from one to four daily car ferries (depending on the season) between Ciutadella on Menorca and Port d'Alcúdia on Mallorca (4400 ptas one way). Cape Balear (☎ 902-10 04 44) operates up to three daily fast ferries to Ciutadella from Cala Ratjada (Mallorca) in summer for around 8000 ptas return. The crossing takes 75 minutes.

MALLORCA

Mallorca is the largest of the Balearic Islands. Most of the five million annual visitors to the island are here for the three *s* words: sun, sand and sea. There are, however, other reasons for coming. Palma, the capital, is worth exploring and the island offers a number of attractions away from the coast.

Orientation & Information

Palma de Mallorca is on the southern side of the island, on a bay famous for its brilliant sunsets. The Serra de Tramuntana mountain range, which runs parallel with the northwest coastline, is trekkers heaven. Mallorca's best beaches are along the north-east and east coasts; so are most of the big tourist resorts.

All of the major resorts have at least one tourist office. Palma has four on Plaça d'Espanya (☎ 971-75 43 29), at Carrer de Sant Domingo 11 (☎ 971-72 40 90), on Plaça de la Reina and at the airport. Palma's post office is on Carrer de la Constitució.

Things to See & Do

The enormous **catedral** on Plaça Almoina is the first landmark you will see as you approach the island by ferry. It houses an excellent museum, and some of the cathedral's interior features were designed by Antoni Gaudí; entry costs 500 ptas.

In front of the cathedral is the **Palau de l'Almudaina**, the one-time residence of the Mallorcan monarchs. Inside is a collection of tapestries and artworks, although it's not really worth the 450 ptas entry. Instead, visit the rich and varied **Museu de Mallorca** (300 ptas).

Also near the cathedral are the interesting **Museu Diocesà** and the **Banys Àrabs** (Arab baths), the only remaining monument to the Muslim domination of the island. Also worth visiting is the collection of the **Fundació Joan Miró**, housed in the artist's Palma studios at Carrer de Joan de Saridakis 29, 2km west of the centre.

Mallorca's north-west coast is a world away from the concrete jungles on the other side of the island. Dominated by the Serra de Tramuntana mountains, it's a beautiful region of olive groves, pine forests and small villages with stone buildings; it also has a rugged and rocky coastline.

There are a couple of highlights for drivers: the hair-raising road down to the small port of **Sa Calobra** and the amazing trip along the peninsula leading to the island's northern tip, **Cap Formentor**.

If you don't have your own wheels, take the **Palma to Sóller train** (see Getting Around later in this section). It's one of the most popular and spectacular excursions on the island. Sóller is also the best place to base

SPAIN

PALMA DE MALLORCA

yourself for trekking. The easy three-hour return walk from here to the beautiful village of **Deiá** is a fine introduction to trekking on Mallorca. The tourist office's *Hiking Excursions* brochure covers 20 of the island's better walks, or for more detailed information see Lonely Planet's *Walking in Spain*.

Most of Mallorca's best beaches have been consumed by tourist developments, although there are exceptions. The lovely **Cala Mondragó** on the south-east coast is backed by a solitary hostal, and a little farther south the attractive port town of **Cala Figuera** and nearby **Cala Santanyi** beach have both escaped many

of the ravages of mass tourism. There are also some good quiet beaches near the popular German resort of **Colonia San Jordi**, particularly Ses Arenes and Es Trenc, both a few kilometres back up the coast towards Palma.

Places to Stay

Palma The *Pensión Costa Brava* (☎ 971 71 17 29, *Carrer de Ca'n Martí Feliu 16*), is a backstreet cheapie with reasonable rooms from 2000/3300 ptas. The cluttered 19th-century charm of *Hostal Pons* (☎ 971 72 26 58, *Carrer del Vi 8*), overcomes its limitations (spongy beds, only one bathroom); it charges 2500 ptas

PALMA DE MALLORCA

PLACES TO STAY	13	Bon Lloc	18	Tourist Office
7 Pensión Costa Brava	14	Abaco	19	Post Office
9 Hotel Born			20	Main Tourist Office
12 Hostal Pons	**OTHER**		21	Ayuntamiento
15 Hostal Apuntadores	1	Bus Station; Airport Bus	22	Església de Santa Eulàlia
16 Hostal Ritzi	2	Tourist Office	23	Basílica de Sant Francesc
	4	Hospital	24	Palau de l'Almudaina
PLACES TO EAT	5	Església de Santa Magadalena	25	Catedral
3 Restaurant Celler Sa Premsa	6	Mercat de l'Olivar	26	Museu Diocesà
10 Celler Pagès	8	Teatro Principal	27	Museu de Mallorca
11 Bar Martín	17	American Express	28	Banys Àrabs (Arab Baths)

per person. **Hostal Apuntadores** (☎ 971 71 34 91, Carrer dels Apuntadores 8) has smartly renovated singles/doubles at 2700/4200 ptas, doubles with bathroom at 4800 ptas, or hostel beds at 1800 ptas. Next door, **Hostal Ritzi** (☎ 971 71 46 10) has good security and comfortable rooms at 3500/5000 ptas with shower, or doubles with shower/bath for 5500 ptas and 7500 ptas. It offers laundry and kitchen facilities and satellite TV in the lounge.

The superb **Hotel Born** (☎ 971 71 29 42, Carrer de Sant Jaume 3) in a restored 18th-century palace has B&B at up to 13,375/ 17,655 ptas.

Other Areas After Palma, you should head for the hills. In Deiá, the charming **Fonda Villa Verde** (☎ 971 63 90 37) charges 6000/ 8300 ptas, while **Hostal Miramar** (☎ 971 63 90 84), overlooking the town, has B&B at 4500/8500 ptas. Beside the train station in Sóller, the popular **Hotel El Guía** (☎ 971 63 02 27) has rooms for 5405/8415 ptas, or nearby (go past El Guía and turn right) the cosy **Casa de Huéspedes Margarita** (☎ 971 63 42 14) has singles/doubles/triples for 2800/ 3800/4500 ptas.

If you want to stay on the south-east coast, the large **Hostal Playa Mondragó** (☎ 971 65 77 52) at Cala Mondragó has B&B for 3800 ptas per person. At Cala Figuera, **Hostal Ca'n Jordi** (☎ 971 64 50 35) has rooms from 3200/5000 ptas.

You can also sleep cheaply at several quirky old monasteries around the island – the tourist offices have a list.

Places to Eat

For Palma's best range of eateries, wander through the maze of streets between Plaça de la Reina and the port. Carrer dels Apuntadores is lined with restaurants – seafood, Chinese, Italian and even a few Spanish restaurants! Around the corner on Carrer de Sant Joan is the amazing **Abaco**, the bar of your wildest dreams (with the drinks bill of your darkest nightmares).

For a simple cheap meal with the locals, head for **Bar Martín** (Carrer de la Santa Creu 2). It has a no-nonsense set menú for 950 ptas. You can also eat well in the tiny **Celler Pagès** (Carrer de Felip Bauçà 2) where the 1250 ptas menú sometimes includes sopa de pescado (fish soup).

The rustic **Restaurant Celler Sa Premsa** (Plaça del Bisbe Berenguer de Palou 8) is an almost obligatory stop. The hearty menú costs 1335 ptas (plus IVA). For vegetarian food, try **Bon Lloc** (Carrer de Sant Feliu 7).

Getting Around

Bus No 17 runs every half-hour between the airport and Plaça Espanya in central Palma (300 ptas, 30 minutes). Alternatively, a taxi will cost around 2000 ptas.

Most parts of the island are accessible by bus from Palma. Buses generally depart from or near the bus station at Plaça Espanya – the tourist office has details. Mallorca's two train lines also start from Plaça Espanya. One goes to the inland town of Inca and the other goes to Sóller (380 ptas one way, or 735 ptas for the 10.40 am 'Parada Turística'; both highly picturesque jaunts).

The best way to get around the island is by car – it's worth renting one just for the drive along the north-west coast. There are about 30 rental agencies in Palma (and all the big companies have reps at the airport). If you want to compare prices, then many of

SPAIN

them have harbourside offices along Passeig Marítim.

IBIZA

Ibiza (Eivissa in Catalan) is the most extreme of the Balearic Islands, both in terms of its landscape and the people it attracts. Hippies, gays, fashion victims, nudists, party animals – this is one of the world's most bizarre melting pots. The island receives over a million visitors each year. Apart from the weather and the desire to be 'seen', the main drawcards are the notorious nightlife and the many picturesque beaches.

Orientation & Information

The capital, Ibiza (Eivissa) city, is on the south-eastern side of the island. This is where most travellers arrive (by ferry or air; the airport is to the south) and it's also the best base. The next largest towns are Santa Eulària des Riu on the east coast and Sant Antoni de Portmany on the west coast. Other big resorts are scattered around the island.

In Ibiza city, the tourist office (☎ 971 30 19 00) is on Passeig des Moll opposite the Estación Marítima. The post office is at Carrer de Madrid s/n, or you can go online for 900 ptas an hour at Ibiform (☎ 971 31 58 69), Avinguda de Ignacio Wallis 8 (1st floor).

Things to See & Do

Shopping seems to be a major pastime in Ibiza city. The port area of Sa Penya is crammed with funky and trashy clothes boutiques and hippy market stalls. From here you can wander up into D'Alt Vila, the old walled town, with its upmarket restaurants, galleries and the Museu d'Art Contemporani. There are fine views from the walls and from the catedral at the top, and the Museu Arqueològic next door is worth a visit.

The heavily developed Platja de ses Figueretes beach is a 20-minute walk south of Sa Penya – you'd be better off taking the half-hour bus ride (125 ptas) south to the beaches at Ses Salines.

If you're prepared to explore, there are still numerous unspoiled and relatively undeveloped beaches around the island. On the north-east coast, Cala de Boix is the only black-sand beach in the islands, while farther north are the lovely beaches of S'Aigua Blanca. On the north coast near Portinatx, Cala Xarraca is in a picturesque, semiprotected bay, and near Port de Sant Miquel is the attractive Cala Benirras. On the south-west coast, Cala d'Hort has a spectacular setting overlooking two rugged rock-islets, Es Verda and Es Verdranell.

Places to Stay

Ibiza City There are quite a few hostales in the streets around the port, although in midsummer cheap beds are scarce. The Hostal-Residencia Ripoll (☎ 971 31 42 75, Carrer de Vicent Cuervo 14) has singles/doubles for 3800/5800 ptas. You get clean rooms and friendly hosts nearby at Hostal Sol y Brisa (☎ 971 31 08 18, Avinguda de Bartomeu Vicent Ramón 15). Singles/doubles with shared bathrooms cost from 3500/6000 ptas. On the waterfront (officially at Carrer de Barcelona 7), Hostal-Restaurante La Marina (☎ 971 31 01 72) has good doubles with harbour views for 5000 ptas to 7000 ptas. Outside peak season some rooms are let as singles for about half (back rooms are noisy).

One of the best choices is Casa de Huéspedes La Peña (☎ 971 19 02 40, Carrer de la Virgen 76) at the far end of Sa Penya. There are 13 simple and tidy doubles with shared bathrooms at rates up to 4000 ptas.

Hostal-Residencia Parque (☎ 971 30 13 58, Carrer de Vicent Cuervo 3) is quieter than most of the other hostales. Singles without private bath cost 5000 ptas, while singles/doubles with bath cost between 8000 ptas and 12,000 ptas.

Hotel Montesol (☎ 971 31 01 61, Passeig de Vara de Rey 2) is a comfortable one-star place. Singles/doubles range up to 8700/16,300 ptas. Many of the singles are too pokey for the price.

Other Areas One of the best of Ibiza's half-dozen camping grounds is Camping Cala Nova (☎ 971 33 17 74), 500m north of the resort town of Cala Nova and close to a good beach.

If you want to get away from the resort developments the following places are all worth checking. Near the Ses Salines beach (and bus stop), Hostal Mar y Sal (☎ 971 39 65 84) has doubles at 5500 ptas (plus IVA). Near the S'Aigua Blanca beaches, Pensión Sa Plana (☎ 971 33 50 73) has a pool and rooms with bath from 5000/6500 ptas, including breakfast. Or you could stay by the black-sand beach, Cala Boix, at **Hostal Cala Boix** (☎ 971 33 52 24), where B&B costs 2500 ptas per person.

Places to Eat
Bland, overpriced eateries abound in the port area, but there are a few exceptions. The no-frills **Comidas Bar San Juan** (Carrer Montgri 8) is outstanding value with main courses from 500 ptas to 850 ptas. **Ca'n Costa** (Carrer de la Cruz 19) is another family-run eating house with a menú for 900 ptas to 1100 ptas.

Moving up the ladder, **Lizarran** (Avinguda de Bartomeu Rosselló 15) is part of a Basque chain that has a firm foothold in Barcelona and has now made a hop across the sea. The tapas are good. If you're looking for somewhere intimate and romantic, head for the candle-lit **La Scala** (Carrer de sa Carrossa 6) up in D'Alt Vila.

Entertainment
Ibiza's nightlife is renowned. The gay scene is wild and the dress code expensive. Dozens of bars keep Ibiza city's port area jumping until the early hours – particularly on Carrer de Barcelona and Carrer de Garijo Cipriano. After they wind down you can continue on to one of the island's world-famous discos – if you can afford the 4000 ptas to 7000 ptas entry, that is. The big names are **Pacha**, on the north side of Ibiza city's port; **Privilege** and **Amnesia**, both 6km out on the road to Sant Antoni; **El Divino**, across the water from the town centre (hop on one of its boats); and **Space**, south of Ibiza city in Platja d'En Bossa.

Getting Around
Buses run between the airport and Ibiza city hourly (125 ptas); a taxi costs around 1800 ptas. Buses to other parts of the island leave from the series of bus stops along Avenida d'Isidoro Macabich. Pick up a copy of the timetable from the tourist office.

If you are intent on getting to some of the more secluded beaches you will need to rent wheels. In Ibiza city, Autos Isla Blanca (☎ 971 31 54 07) at Carrer de Felipe II will hire out a Renault Twingo for 18,000 ptas for three days all inclusive, or a scooter for around 1300 ptas a day.

FORMENTERA
A short boat ride south of Ibiza, Formentera is the smallest and least developed of the four main Balearic Islands. It offers fine beaches and some excellent short walking and cycling trails. A popular day trip from Ibiza, it can get pretty crowded in midsummer, but most of the time it is still possible to find a strip of sand out of earshot of other tourists.

Orientation & Information
Formentera is about 20km from east to west. Ferries arrive at La Savina on the north-west coast; the tourist office (☎ 971 32 20 57) is behind the rental agencies you'll see when you disembark. Three kilometres south is the island's pretty capital, Sant Francesc Xavier, where you'll find most of the banks. From here, the main road runs along the middle of the island before climbing to the highest point (192m). At the eastern end of the island is the Sa Mola lighthouse. Es Pujols is 3km east of La Savina and is the main tourist resort (and the only place with any nightlife to speak of).

Things to See & Do
Some of the island's best and most popular beaches are the beautiful white strips of sand along the narrow promontory which stretches north towards Ibiza. A 2km walking trail leads from the La Savina-Es Pujols road to the far end of the promontory, from where you can wade across a narrow strait to **S'Espalmador**, a tiny islet with beautiful, quiet beaches. Along Formentera's south coast, **Platja de Migjorn** is made up of numerous coves and beaches. Tracks lead down to these off the main road. On the west coast is the lovely **Cala Saona** beach.

The tourist office's Green Tours brochure outlines 19 excellent walking and cycling trails that take you through some of the island's most scenic areas.

Places to Stay
Camping is not allowed on Formentera. Sadly, the coastal accommodation places mainly cater to German and British package-tour agencies and are overpriced and/or booked out in summer. In Es Pujols you could try **Hostal Tahiti** (☎ 971 32 81 22), with B&B at 7000/10,075 ptas. If you prefer peace and quiet you are better off in Es Caló. **Fonda**

SPAIN

SPAIN

Rafalet (☎ 971 32 70 16) has good rooms on the waterfront for 5000/9000 ptas in August, or across the road the tiny and simple *Casa de Huéspedes Miramar* (☎ 971 32 70 60) charges 4000 ptas.

Perhaps the best budget bet is to base yourself in one of the small inland towns and bike it to the beaches. In Sant Ferran (1.6km south of Es Pujols), the popular *Hostal Pepe* (☎ 971 32 80 33) has B&B with bath at 3375/6090 ptas. In Sant Francesco Xavier, doubles at the amiable *Restaurant Casa Rafal* (☎ 971 32 22 05) go for 7000 ptas. La Savina isn't the most thrilling place, but *Hostal La Savina* (☎ 971 32 22 79) has rooms for up to 7500/9000 ptas, including breakfast.

Getting There & Away
There are 20 to 25 ferries daily between Ibiza city and Formentera. The trip takes about 25 minutes by jet ferry (2085 ptas one-way), or about an hour by car ferry (2300 ptas return, 9500 ptas for a small car).

Getting Around
A string of rental agencies line the harbour in La Savina. Bikes start at 650 ptas a day (900 ptas for a mountain bike). Scooters start at 1300 ptas and head up to 4000 ptas for more powerful motorbikes. Cars, though superfluous, go for 5000 ptas to 7000 ptas. A regular bus service connects all the main towns.

MENORCA
Menorca is perhaps the least overrun of the Balearics. In 1993, it was declared a Biosphere Reserve by Unesco, with the aim of preserving important environmental areas such as the Albufera d'es Grau wetlands and its unique collection of archaeological sites.

Orientation & Information
The capital, Maó (Mahón in Spanish), is at the eastern end of the island. Its busy port is the arrival point for most ferries, and Menorca's airport is 7km south-west. The main road runs down the middle of the island to Ciutadella, Menorca's second-largest town, with secondary roads leading north and south to the resorts and beaches.

The main tourist office is in Maó (☎ 971 36 37 90) at Plaça de S'Esplanada 40. During summer there are offices at the airport and in Ciutadella on Plaça des Born. Maó's post office is on Carrer del Bon Aire.

Things to See & Do
Maó and Ciutadella are both harbour towns, and from either place you'll have to commute to the beaches. Maó absorbs most of the tourist traffic. While you're here you can take a boat cruise around its impressive harbour and sample the local gin at the **Xoriguer distillery**. Ciutadella, with its smaller harbour and historic buildings, has a more distinctively Spanish feel about it.

In the centre of the island, the 357m-high **Monte Toro** has great views of the whole island, and on a clear day you can see as far as Mallorca.

With your own transport and a bit of footwork you'll be able to discover some of Menorca's off-the-beaten-track beaches. North of Maó, a drive across a lunar landscape leads to the lighthouse at **Cap de Favàritx**. If you park just before the gate to the lighthouse and climb up the rocks behind you, you'll see a couple of the eight beaches that are just waiting for scramblers like yourself to grace their sands.

On the north coast, the picturesque town of **Fornells** is on a large bay popular with windsurfers. Farther west at the beach of Binimella, you can continue (on foot) to the unspoilt Cala Pregonda.

North of Ciutadella is **La Vall**, another stretch of untouched beach backed by a private nature park (700 ptas entry per car). On the south coast are two good beaches either side of the Santa Galdana resort – Cala Mitjana to the east and Macarella to the west.

Menorca's beaches aren't its only attractions. The interior of the island is liberally sprinkled with reminders of its rich and ancient heritage. Pick up a copy of the tourist office's *Archaeological Guide to Minorca*.

Places to Stay
Menorca's two *camping grounds* are near the resorts of Santa Galdana, about 8km south of Ferreries, and Son Bou, south of Alaior. They open in summer only.

Maó and Ciutadella both have a handful of good budget options. In Maó, *Hostal Orsi* (☎ 971 36 47 51, Carrer de la Infanta 19) is run by a Glaswegian and American who are a mine of information. It's bright, clean and well located. Singles/doubles with only a washbasin cost 2600/4400 ptas. *Hostal La Isla (☎ 971 36 64 92, Carrer de Santa Catalina 4)* has excellent rooms with bath at 2300/4100 ptas plus IVA.

In Ciutadella *Hostal Oasis (☎ 971 38 21 97, Carrer de Sant Isidre 33)* is set around a spacious courtyard and has its own Italian restaurant; doubles with bath and breakfast are 5500 ptas (no singles). *Hotel Geminis (☎ 971 38 46 44, Carrer Josepa Rossinyol 4)* is a friendly and stylish two-star place with excellent rooms for 5000/8000 ptas plus IVA.

In Fornells, *Hostal La Palma (☎ 971 37 66 34, Plaça S'Algaret 3)* has singles (not available in summer) for 4000 ptas and doubles for 7250 ptas (in high season).

Places to Eat
Maó's waterfront road, Andén de Levante, is lined with restaurants with outdoor terraces. *Ristorante Roma* at No 295 is a stylish Italian eatery; it's surprisingly good value with pizzas and pastas for around 900 ptas and several set *menú* choices ranging from 1500 ptas to 2300 ptas. For a mix of dishes ranging from gazpacho to felafel, you could try the wholesome food at *La Sirena*, at No 199.

Ciutadella's port is also lined with restaurants, and you won't have any trouble finding somewhere to eat. After dinner, check *Sa Clau*, a hip little jazz and blues bar set in the old city walls.

Getting Around
From the airport, a taxi into Maó costs around 1200 ptas; there are no buses.

TMSA (☎ 971 36 03 61) runs six buses a day between Maó and Ciutadella (560 ptas), with connections to the major resorts on the south coast. In summer there are also daily bus services to most of the coastal towns from both Maó and Ciutadella.

If you're planning to hire a car, rates vary seasonally from around 3500 ptas to 8000 ptas a day; during the summer, minimum hire periods sometimes apply. In Maó, places worth trying include Autos Valls (☎ 971 36 84 65), Plaça d'Espanya 13, and Autos Isla (☎ 971 36 65 69), Avinguda de Josep Maria

Quadrado 28. Motos Menorca (☎ 971 35 47 86), at Andén de Llevant 35-36, hires out mountain bikes (1400 ptas per day), scooters and Vespas (from 3200 ptas a day).

Valencia

Although perhaps best known for the package resorts of the Costa Blanca, this region also includes Spain's lively third city, Valencia – and some rare undiscovered secrets if you penetrate inland.

VALENCIA
pop 739,000
Vibrant Valencia, birthplace of paella, is blessed with great weather and hosts the country's wildest party – Las Fallas (12-19 March), an exuberant blend of fireworks, music, all-night partying and over 350 *fallas*, giant sculptures which all go up in flames on the final night.

Orientation
The action part of the city is oval, bounded by the old course of the Turia River and the sickle-shaped inner ring road of Calles Colón, Játiva and Guillem de Castro. These trace the walls of the old city, demolished in 1865 as – believe it or not – a job-creation project which dismantled one of the Mediterranean coastline's major monuments.

Within the oval are three major squares: Plazas del Ayuntamiento, de la Reina (also known as Plaza de Zaragoza) and de la Virgen.

Many Valencian streets now have signs only in Catalan rather than Spanish, but the difference between the two is rarely confusing.

Information
The main tourist office is at Calle Paz 48 (☎ 96 398 64 22, fax 96 398 64 21). It's open 10 am to 6.30 pm weekdays (to 2 pm Saturday). Three smaller ones are at the train station, town hall and Teatro Principal. All have reams of information in English.

The imposing neobaroque main post office is on Plaza del Ayuntamiento. Poste restante is on the 1st floor.

American Express is represented by Viajes Duna (☎ 96 374 15 62, Calle Cirilo Amorós 88).

SPAIN

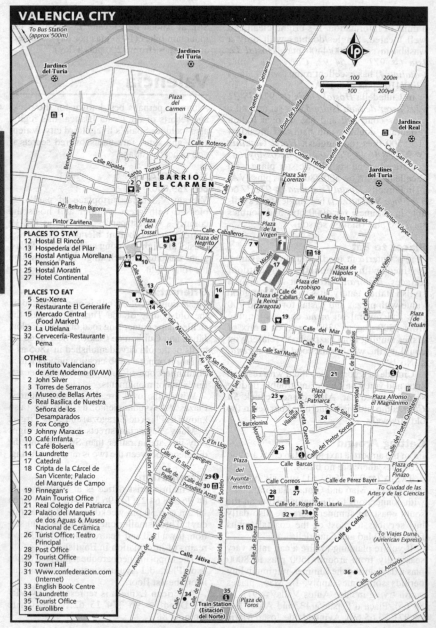

VALENCIA CITY

To Bus Station
(approx 500m)

Jardines
del Turia

Jardines
del Turia

Jardines
del Real

Jardines
del Turia

Plaza
del Carmen

Puente de Serranos

Pont de Fusta

Puente de la Trinidad

Calle del Conde Trénor

Calle San Pío V

Calle del Pintor López

BARRIO
DEL CARMEN

Calle Roteros

Calle Ripalda

Santo Tomas

Calle Alta

Beneficencia

Dtr. Beltrán Bigorra

Pintor Zariñena

Plaza
del Tossal

Calle Serranos

Calle de Samaniego

Plaza San
Lorenzo

Calle de los Trinitarios

Plaza
de la Virgen

Calle Caballeros

Plaza del
Negrito

Calle Bolsería

Plaza del Mercado

Calle Miguelete

Plaza del
Arzobispo

Plaza del
Arzobispo

Plaza de
Nápoles y
Sicilia

Calle del Gobernador Viejo

Plaza
de Cabillars

Calle de
la Reina
(Zaragoza)

Calle Milagro

Plaza
de
Tetuán

Calle del Mar

Calle del Mar

Calle San Martín

Calle San Martín

Calle de la Paz

C. de las Comedias

Av. María Cristina

Av. San Vicente Mártir

C de San Fernando

Avenida del Barón de Cárcer

Calle de Garrigues

Calle d'En Sans

Calle de
Padilla

C d'En Llop

C Barcelonina

C de Moratín

C de
Vilaragut

C de la Paz

Plaza
del
Ayunta-
miento

Plaza
de los
Pinazo

Plaza Alfonso
el Magnánimo

Plaza
del Patriarca

Calle del Pintor Sorolla

C de Salvá

C Universidad

Calle del Poeta Querol

Calle del Poeta Quintana

Calle de Correos

Calle Barcas

Calle de Pérez Bayer

Calle de Roger de Lauria

Calle de Pascual y Genis

Calle de Colón

Calle de Ribera

Calle Játiva

Calle de Pelayo

Calle de Bailén

Avenida del Marqués de Sotelo

Calle del
Periodista Azzati

Avenida de San Vicente Mártir

Calle Cirilo Amorós

To Ciudad de las
Artes y de las Ciencias

To Viajes Duna
(American Express)

Plaza
del
Toros

Train Station
(Estación
del Norte)

PLACES TO STAY
12 Hostal El Rincón
13 Hospedería del Pilar
16 Hostal Antigua Morellana
24 Pensión Paris
25 Hostal Moratín
27 Hotel Continental

PLACES TO EAT
5   Seu-Xerea
7   Restaurante El Generalife
15 Mercado Central
    (Food Market)
23 La Utielana
32 Cervecería-Restaurante
    Pema

OTHER
1   Instituto Valenciano
    de Arte Moderno (IVAM)
2   John Silver
3   Torres de Serranos
4   Museo de Bellas Artes
6   Real Basílica de Nuestra
    Señora de los
    Desamparados
8   Fox Congo
9   Johnny Maracas
10 Café Infanta
11 Café Bolsería
14 Laundrette
17 Catedral
18 Cripta de la Cárcel de
    San Vicente; Palacio
    del Marqués de Campo
19 Finnegan's
20 Main Tourist Office
21 Real Colegio del Patriarca
22 Palacio del Marqués
    de dos Aguas & Museo
    Nacional de Cerámica
26 Turist Office; Teatro
    Principal
28 Post Office
29 Tourist Office
30 Town Hall
31 Www.confederacion.com
    (Internet)
33 English Book Centre
34 Laundrette
35 Tourist Office
36 Eurollibre

0   100   200m
0   100   200yd

SPAIN

Among several cybercafes in town is the noisy, 48-terminal www.confederacion.com (yes, that's the name) at Calle Ribera 8. Just off Plaza del Ayuntamiento, it charges 500 ptas per hour.

Valencia has two good predominantly English-language bookshops: the English Book Centre, Calle Pascual y Genís 16 and Eurollibre, Calle Hernán Cortés 18.

There are two central laundrettes at Plaza del Mercado 12, close to the covered market, and Calle Pelayo 11, near the train station.

Things to See & Do

The city of Valencia merits, as a minimum, a couple of days of your life.

The aesthetically stunning, ultramodern **Ciudad de las Artes y de las Ciencias** promises to become Valencia's premier attraction. Already open to the public is the **Hemisfèric** (☎ 96 399 55 77), at once planetarium, IMAX cinema and laser show (admission to each, 1100 ptas). An interactive science museum, the **Museo de las Ciencias Príncipe Felipe**, is scheduled to open in 2001.

The **Museo de Bellas Artes** (Fine Arts Museum) ranks among Spain's best, with works by El Greco, Goya, Velázquez, Ribera, Ribalta and artists such as Sorolla and Pinazo of the Valencian impressionist school. It's open 10 am to 2.15 pm and 4 to 7.30 pm Tuesday to Saturday (continuously on Sunday). Admission is free.

The **Instituto Valenciano de Arte Moderno** (IVAM, pronounced eebam) beside Puente de las Artes, houses an impressive permanent collection of 20th-century Spanish art and hosts excellent temporary exhibitions. Admission is 350 ptas, free Sunday.

Valencia's **cathedral** boasts three magnificent portals – one Romanesque, one Gothic and one baroque. Climb the Miguelete bell tower (200 ptas) for a sweeping view of the sprawling city. The cathedral's museum also claims – among several others contenders – to be home to the Holy Grail (Santo Cáliz), which you can see in a side chapel. As for the past thousand years, the **Tribunal de las Aguas** (Water Court) meets every Thursday at noon outside the cathedral's Plaza de la Virgen doorway to resolve any irrigation disputes between farmers.

Nearby on Plaza del Arzobispo is the crypt of a Visigoth chapel, reputedly prison to the 4th-century martyr, San Vicente. It's well worth taking in the free 25-minute multimedia show, which presents Valencia's history and the saint's life. Book at the **Palacio del Marqués de Campo** just opposite and ask for a showing in English.

The baroque **Palacio del Marqués de dos Aguas**, on Calle del Poeta Querol, is fronted by an extravagantly sculpted facade. It houses the **Museo Nacional de Cerámica**, which has ceramics from around the world – and especially the renowned local production centres of Manises, Alcora and Paterna. It's open 10 am to 2 pm and 4 to 8 pm, Tuesday to Saturday plus Sunday morning (admission free).

Valencia city's beach is the broad **Playa de la Malvarrosa**, bordered by the **Paseo Marítimo** promenade and a string of restaurants. **Playa El Salér**, 10km south, is backed by shady pinewood. Autocares Herca (☎ 96 349 12 50) buses (150 ptas, 30 minutes) run hourly (every half-hour in summer) from the junction of Gran Vía de las Germanías and Calle Sueca.

Special Events

Las Fallas de San José is an exuberant, anarchic swirl of fireworks, music, festive bonfires and all-night partying. If you're in Spain from 12-19 March, head for Valencia. Accommodation is at a premium – but you can always do like thousands of others and lay your head in the old riverbed.

Places to Stay

Camping The nearest camp ground, *Devesa Gardens* (☎/fax 96 161 11 36), is 13km south of Valencia near El Saler beach. *Alberge Las Arenas* (☎/fax 96 356 42 88, Calle Eugenia Viñes 24) is a pebble's throw from Malvarrosa beach and within earshot of its wild summer nightlife. Take bus No 32 from Plaza del Ayuntamiento. Both are open year-round.

Central and near the covered market, *Hospedería del Pilar* (☎ 96 391 66 00, Plaza del Mercado 19) has clean basic singles/doubles/triples at 1600/2995/3900 ptas (2140/3850/4815 ptas with shower). Nearby, most rooms at the vast *Hostal El Rincón* (☎ 96 391 79 98, Calle de la Carda 11) are small but nicely priced at 1500/2800 ptas. It also

SPAIN

provides eight spacious renovated rooms with bathroom and air-con – excellent value at 2000/3600 ptas.

Near Plaza del Ayuntamiento, **Pensión París** (☎/fax 96 352 67 66, Calle Salvá 12) has spotless singles/doubles/triples without shower at 2500/3600/5400 ptas (doubles/triples with shower at 4200/6000 ptas). At recently renovated and welcoming **Hostal Moratín** (☎/fax 96 352 12 20, Calle Moratín 15) singles/doubles with shower are 2900/4500 ptas (3500/5500 ptas with bathroom).

Newly opened, **Hostal Antigua Morellana** (☎/fax 96 391 57 73, Calle en Bou 2) in a renovated 18th-century building has cosy singles/doubles with bathroom at 4000/6000 ptas.

Hotel Continental (☎ 96 353 52 82, Calle Correos 8) is modern and friendly, and its singles cost 7000 ptas to 9000 ptas, doubles 9000 ptas to 15,000 ptas according to season. All have air-con and satellite TV.

Places to Eat

You can eat local and well for around 1500 ptas at unpretentious **La Utielana**, tucked away off Calle Prócida, just east of Plaza del Ayuntamiento. At **Cervecería-Restaurante Pema** (Calle Mosén Femades 3) choose anything from a simple tapa to a full-blown meal. Its weekday lunch menú at 1100 ptas, including a drink and coffee, must be central Valencia's best deal.

Restaurante El Generalife (Calle Caballeros 5) has an excellent value menú for 1200 ptas. Nearby, **Seu-Xerea** (☎ 96 392 40 00, Calle del Conde de Almodóvar 4) has an inventive a la carte menu and does a warmly recommended lunchtime menú for 2200 ptas.

For authentic paella, head for Las Arenas, just north of the port, where a long line of restaurants all serve up the real stuff, and enjoy a three-course waterfront meal for around 1500 ptas.

And everyone, not only self-caterers, can have fun browsing around the bustling **Mercado Central**, Valencia's modernista covered market.

Entertainment

Valencia has four main nightlife zones, each bursting with bars: Barrio del Carmen (El Carmé), the old quarter; in vogue Mercado de Subastos on the west side of town; Plaza de Canovas for young up-and-comers; and the student haunt, Plaza de Xuquer.

In El Carmé, Calle Caballeros has swanky bars such as **Johnny Maracas**, a suave salsa place, or **Fox Congo** and others more modest in tone and price. On and around Plaza del Tosal are some of the most sophisticated bars this side of Barcelona, including **Café Infanta** and **Café Bolsería**, and cheap and cheerful places like **John Silver** on Calle Alta.

To continue partying, head for the university zone 2km east (500 ptas to 600 ptas by taxi from the centre). Along Avenida Blasco Ibáñez and particularly around Plaza de Xuquer are enough bars and discos to keep you busy beyond sunrise.

Finnegan's, an Irish pub on Plaza de la Reina, draws English-speakers.

Getting There & Away

Bus The bus station (☎ 96 349 72 22) is beside the old riverbed on Avenida de Menéndez Pidal. Bus No 8 connects it to Plaza del Ayuntamiento.

Major destinations include Madrid (2875 ptas to 3175 ptas, up to 12 daily), Barcelona (2900 ptas, up to 12 daily) and Alicante (1980 ptas, 2¼ hours).

Train Express trains run from Estación del Norte (☎ 96 352 02 02 or ☎ 902-24 02 02) to/from Madrid (5700 ptas, 3½ hours, up to 10 daily), Barcelona (mostly 4500 ptas, three to five hours, 12 daily) and Alicante (1400 ptas to 3200 ptas, 1½ to two hours, up to eight daily).

Boat In summer, Trasmediterránea (reservations ☎ 902-45 46 45) operates daily car and passenger ferries to Mallorca and Ibiza and has a weekly run to Menorca. During the rest of the year, sailings are less frequent.

Getting Around

EMT (☎ 96 352 83 99) buses run until about 10 pm with night services continuing on seven routes until around 1 am. You can pick up a route map from one of the tourist offices. Tickets cost 125 ptas, a one-day pass is 500 ptas and a 10-trip bono, 700 ptas.

The smart highspeed tram is a pleasant way to get to the beach, paella restaurants of Las Arenas and the port. Metro lines primarily serve the outer suburbs.

Ergobike (☎ 96 392 32 39, Calle Museo), just off Plaza del Carmen, rents town bikes and recumbents.

INLAND VALENCIA
Morella
pop 2850

Perched on a hill top, crowned by a castle and completely enclosed by a wall over 2km long, the fairy-tale town of Morella, in the north of the Valencia region, is one of Spain's oldest continually inhabited towns.

The tourist office (☎ 964 17 30 32, closed Sunday afternoon and Monday) is just behind the Torres de San Miguel which flank the main entrance gate.

Things to See & Do

Morella's **castle**, although in ruins, remains imposing and gives breathtaking views of the town and surrounding countryside. The castle grounds (300 ptas) are open 10.30 am until 6.30 pm daily (to 7.30 pm from May to August).

The old town itself is easily explored on foot. Three small museums, set in the towers of the ancient walls, have displays on local history, photography and the 'age of the dinosaurs'. Each costs 300 ptas or you can buy a combined ticket, including admission to the castle, for 1000 ptas.

Places to Stay & Eat

The cheapest option is friendly **Fonda Moreno** (☎ *964 16 01 05, Calle de San Nicolás 12*) which has six quaint and basic doubles at 2350 ptas. Its upstairs restaurant does a hearty *menú* for 950 ptas.

Freshly refurbished **Hostal El Cid** (☎ *964 16 01 25, Puerta de San Mateo 2*) has spruce singles/doubles with bathroom for 3400/5500 ptas.

Hotel Cardenal Ram (☎ *964 17 30 85, Cuesta de Suñer 1*), occupying a 16th-century cardinal's palace, has singles/doubles with all facilities for 5350/8550 ptas.

Restaurante Vinatea (*Calle Blasco de Alagón 17, closed Monday*) does a *menú* (1250 ptas) which is rich in local dishes. Or go a la carte and order a plateful of its scrummy *garbanzos en salsa de almendra* (chick peas in almond sauce) for 600 ptas.

Getting There & Away

On weekdays, Autos Mediterráneo (☎ 964 22 05 36) runs two buses a day to/from both Castellón and Vinarós. There's also one Saturday bus to/from Castellón.

Guadalest

A spectacular route runs west from just south of Calpe (see later in this section) to the inland town of **Alcoy**, famous for its Moros y Cristianos fiesta in April. About halfway to Alcoy, stop at the old Muslim settlement of **Guadalest**, dominated by the Castillo de San José and besieged nowadays by coach parties from the coast.

Elche (Elx)
pop 200,000

Just 20km south-west of Alicante, Elche is famed for its extensive palm groves, planted by the Muslims. Visit the **Huerto del Cura** with its tended lawns, colourful flowerbeds and a freakish eight pronged palm tree. The gardens (admission 300 ptas), opposite the hotel of the same name, are open 9 am to 6 pm daily.

The major festival is the Misteri d'Elx, a two-part medieval mystery play and lyric drama. It's performed in the Basílica de Santa María on 14 and 15 August (with public rehearsals the three previous days).

Budget accommodation options are very limited. One little gem is the friendly, spotlessly clean **Hotel Faro** (☎ *96 546 62 63*) where simple singles/doubles are 1800/3600 ptas (2000/4000 ptas from July to September).

Elche, on the Alicante-Murcia train line, has frequent services (235 ptas) to Alicante, to which AM Molla runs up to 30 buses (205 ptas) daily.

ALICANTE (ALACANT)
pop 285,000

Alicante is a dynamic town with an interesting old quarter, good beach and frenetic nightlife. It becomes even wilder for the Fiesta de Sant Joan, 24 June, when Alicante stages its own version of Las Fallas (see Special Events under Valencia city earlier in this chapter).

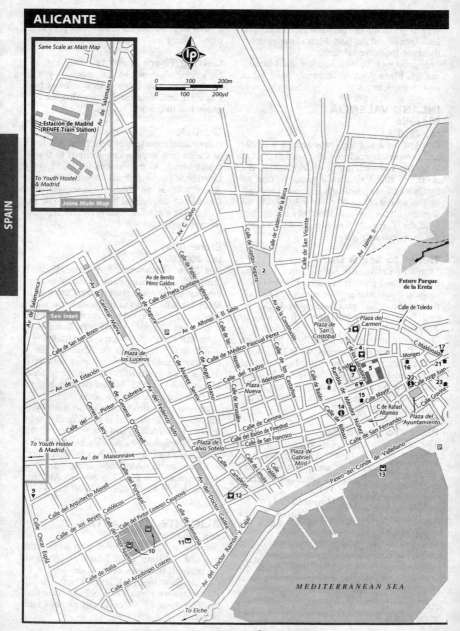

ALICANTE

Same Scale as Main Map

0   100   200m
0   100   200yd

Estación de Madrid
(RENFE Train Station)

To Youth Hostel
& Madrid

Joins Main Map

SPAIN

See Inset

Av de Salamanca

Av de General Marva

Calle de San Juan Bosco

Plaza de
los Luceros

Calle de la Estación

Av de la Estación

Calle del
General Lacy

To Youth Hostel
& Madrid

Calle del Pintor

Av de Maisonnave

Calle Oscar Esplá

Calle del Arquitecto Morell

Calle de los Reyes Católicos

Calle del Pintor Lorenzo Casanova

Calle del Pintor Agrasot

Calle de Italia

Calle del Arzobispo Loaces

9

10

11

12

Calle de Alemania

Calle del Portugal

Av del Doctor Gadea

Calle Canalejas

Calle de Anzua

Calle Vallés

Calle de San Francisco

Calle del Barón de Finestrat

Plaza de
Calvo Sotelo

Calle de Gerona

Plaza de
Gabriel
Miró

Calle de la Dionisia

Av del Doctor Ramón y Cajal

To Elche

Av de C. Calvo

Av de Benito
Pérez Galdos

Calle del Poeta Quintana

Calle de Segura

Calle de Pablo Iglesias

Av de Alfonso X El Sabio

Calle de Médico Pascual Pérez

C de Álvarez Sereix

C de Angel Lozano

Calle de Isaac Peral

Calle del Teatro

Plaza
Nueva

Calle de Jerusalén

Calle de Navas

2

Calle de Capitán Segarra

Calle de Calderón de la Barca

Calle de San Vicente

Av de la Constitución

Plaza de
San
Cristóbal

Rambla de Méndez Núñez

Calle de Bailén

Calle de los Castaños

Calle Mayor

Calle de Bilbao

Calle de San Fernando

Av Jaime II

Future Parque
de la Ereta

Calle de Toledo

Plaza del
Carmen

C Maldonado

Monges

C de los Labradores

S Isidro

3

4

7

6

5

15

8

14

16

17

21

22

23

Calle Jorge Juan

Calle Cravina

C de Rafael
Altamira

Plaza del
Ayuntamiento

Paseo del Conde de Vallellano

13

P

MEDITERRANEAN SEA

SPAIN

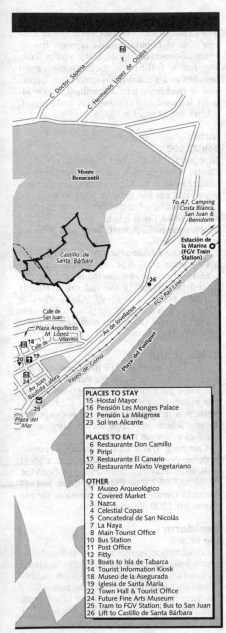

PLACES TO STAY
15 Hostal Mayor
16 Pensión Les Monges Palace
21 Pensión La Milagrosa
23 Sol Inn Alicante

PLACES TO EAT
6 Restaurante Don Camillo
9 Piripi
17 Restaurante El Canario
20 Restaurante Mixto Vegetariano

OTHER
1 Museo Arqueológico
2 Covered Market
3 Nazca
4 Celestial Copas
5 Concatedral de San Nicolás
7 La Naya
8 Main Tourist Office
10 Bus Station
11 Post Office
12 Fitty
13 Boats to Isla de Tabarca
14 Tourist Information Kiosk
16 Museo de la Asegurada
19 Iglesia de Santa María
22 Town Hall & Tourist Office
24 Future Fine Arts Museum
25 Tram to FGV Station; Bus to San Juan
26 Lift to Castillo de Santa Bárbara

Of its five tourist offices, the main one (☎ 965 20 00 00) is at Rambla de Méndez Núñez 23.

Things to See & Do
The **Castillo de Santa Bárbara**, a 16th-century fortress, overlooks the city. Take the lift (400 ptas return), reached by a footbridge opposite Playa del Postiguet, or walk via Avenida Jaime II or the new Parque de la Ereta. Admission is free.

The **Museo de la Asegurada** on Plaza Santa María houses an excellent collection of modern art, including a handful of works by Dalí, Miró and Picasso. Admission is free.

At the time of writing, the **Museo Arqueológico** was awaiting its transfer to a new permanent home off Calle Doctor Sapen. Also in preparation was the new **Museo de Bellas Artes**, Alicante's fine arts museum, which will occupy an 18th-century mansion on Calle Gravina.

Playa del Postiguet is Alicante's city beach. Larger and less crowded beaches are at **Playa de San Juan**, easily reached by buses 21 and 22.

Most days, Kontiki (☎ 96 521 63 96) runs boat trips (1800 ptas return) to the popular **Isla de Tabarca**, an island where there's good snorkelling and scuba diving from quiet beaches.

Be sure to fit in a stroll along Explanada de España, rich in cafes and running parallel to the harbour.

Places to Stay
About 10km north of Alicante, *Camping Costa Blanca*, outside Campello and 200m from the beach, has a good pool. Alicante's youth hostel, *La Florida* (☎ 96 511 30 44, *Avenida de Orihuela 59*), is 2km west of the centre and open to all only between July and September.

At the outstanding *Pensión Les Monges Palace* (☎ 96 521 50 46, *Calle de Monges 2*) rooms cost 3900/4200/5000 ptas with wash-basin/shower/full bathroom and have satellite TV and air-con (700 ptas supplement).

Pensión La Milagrosa (☎ 96 521 69 18, *Calle de Villavieja 8*) has clean, basic rooms for 1500 ptas to 2000 ptas per person according to season and a small guest kitchen. *Hostal Mayor* (☎ 96 520 13 83, *Calle Mayor 5*) has

SPAIN

pleasant singles/doubles/triples with full bathroom at 3000/6000/9000 ptas (cheaper out of season).

Sol Inn Alicante (☎ *96 521 07 00, fax 96 521 09 76,* e *sol.alicante@solmelia.es, Calle de Gravina 9*) is a modern, stylish three-star place with rooms for 9600/11,350 ptas (cheaper at weekends).

Places to Eat
Restaurante El Canario (*Calle de Maldonado 25*) is a no-frills eatery with a hearty *menú* for 950 ptas. Nearby, *Restaurante Mixto Vegetariano* (*Plaza de Santa María 2*) is a simple place with vegetarian and meat *menús* for 1000 ptas. *Restaurante Don Camillo* (*Plaza del Abad Penalva 2*) has above-average pasta dishes.

Highly regarded *Piripi* (☎ *96 522 79 40, Calle Oscar Esplá 30*) is the place for stylish tapas or fine rice and seafood dishes. Expect to pay about 3500 ptas a head.

Entertainment
Alicante's nightlife zone clusters around the cathedral – look out for *Celestial Copas*, *La Naya*, *Nazca* and *Fitty*. In summer the disco scene at Playa de San Juan is thumping. There are also dozens of discos in the coastal resorts between Alicante and Denia; FGV 'night trains' ferry partygoers along this notorious stretch.

Getting There & Away
There are daily services from the bus station on Calle de Portugal to Almería (2570 ptas, 4½ hours), Valencia (1980 ptas, 2¼ hours), Barcelona (4650 ptas, eight hours), Madrid (3345 ptas, five hours) and towns along the Costa Blanca.

From the train station on Avenida de Salamanca there's frequent service to Madrid (4700 ptas, four hours), Valencia (1400 ptas to 3200 ptas, two hours) and Barcelona (6500 ptas, around five hours).

From Estación de la Marina, the Ferrocarriles de la Generalitat Valenciana (FGV) station at the north-eastern end of Playa del Postiguet, a narrow-gauge line follows an attractive coastal route northwards as far as Denia (995 ptas) via Playa de San Juan (125 ptas), Benidorm (445 ptas) and Calpe (680 ptas).

COSTA BLANCA
The Costa Blanca (White Coast), one of Europe's most popular tourist regions, has its share of concrete jungles. But if you're looking for a full-blown social scene, good beaches and a suntan, it's unrivalled. Unless you're packing a tent, accommodation is almost impossible to find in July and August, when rates skyrocket.

Xàbia
pop 22,000
In contrast to the very Spanish resort of Denia, 10km north-west, over two-thirds of annual visitors to Xàbia (Jávea) are foreigners so it's not the greatest place to meet the locals. This laid-back resort is in three parts: the old town (3km inland), the port, and the beach zone of El Arenal, lined with pleasant bar-restaurants.

Camping El Naranjal (☎ *96 579 10 70*) is a 10-minute walk from El Arenal. The port area is pleasant and has some reasonably priced pensiones. In the old town, *Hostal Levante* (☎ *96 579 15 91, Calle Maestro Alonso 5*) has basic singles/doubles for 2700/4500 ptas (5500 ptas with shower, 6500 ptas with bathroom).

Calpe (Calp)
Calpe, 22km north-east of Benidorm, is dominated by the Gibraltaresque **Peñon de Ilfach** (332m), a giant molar protruding from the sea. The climb towards the summit is popular – while you're up there, enjoy the seascape and decide which of Calpe's two long sandy beaches you want to laze on.

Camping Ifach and *Camping Levante*, both on Avenida de la Marina, are a short walk from Playa Levante. *Pensión Céntrica* (☎ *96 583 55 28*) on Plaza de Ilfach, just off Avenida Gabriel Miró, has pleasant, simple rooms for 1500 ptas per person.

Benidorm
pop 56,500
It's dead easy to be snobbish about Benidorm, which long ago sold its birthright to cheap package tourism (nearly five million visitors annually), and indeed many of the horror tales are true. But beneath the jungle of concrete high-rises are 5km of white beaches and after dark there's a club scene to rival Ibiza's.

Almost everyone here is on a package deal and major hotels can be reasonable value out of high season, but there's no truly budget accommodation. *Hotel Nou Calpí (☎/fax 96 681 29 96, Plaza Constitución 5)* provides singles/doubles with full bathroom for 2700/5000 ptas (3000/6500 ptas, July to October), including breakfast.

Andalucía

The stronghold of the Muslims in Spain for nearly eight centuries, Andalucía is perhaps Spain's most exotic and colourful region. The home of flamenco, bullfighting and some of the country's most brilliant fiestas, it's peppered with reminders of the Muslim past from treasured monuments like the Alhambra in Granada and the Mezquita in Córdoba to the white villages clinging to its hillsides. The regional capital, Seville, is one of Spain's most exciting cities.

Away from the cities and resorts, Andalucía is surprisingly untouristed. Its scenery ranges from semideserts to lush river valleys to gorge-ridden mountains. Its long coastline stretches from the relatively remote beaches of Cabo de Gata, past the crowds of the Costa del Sol, to come within 14km of Africa at Tarifa before opening up to the Atlantic Ocean on the Costa de la Luz with its long, sandy beaches.

SEVILLE
pop 701,000
Seville (Sevilla) is one of the most exciting cities in Spain, with an atmosphere both relaxed and festive, a rich history, some great monuments, beautiful parks and gardens, and a large, lively student population. Located on the Río Guadalquivir, which is navigable to the Atlantic Ocean, Seville was the leading Muslim city in Spain in the 11th and 12th centuries. It reached its greatest heights in the 16th and 17th centuries, when it held a monopoly on Spanish trade with the Americas.

Seville is quite an expensive place, so it's worth planning your visit carefully. In July and August, the city is stiflingly hot and not a fun place to be. It's best during its unforgettable spring festivals, though rooms then (if you can get one) are expensive.

Information
The main tourist office (☎ 95 422 14 04) at Avenida de la Constitución 21 is open 9 am to 7 pm Monday to Friday, 10 am to 7 pm Saturday, 10 am to 2 pm Sunday. It's often extremely busy, so you might try the other offices at Paseo de las Delicias 9 (☎ 95 423 44 65), open 8.30 am to 2.45 pm Monday to Friday, and Calle de Arjona 28 (☎ 95 450 56 00), open 8 am to 8.45 pm Monday to Friday, 8.30 am to 2.30 pm weekends.

Seville has heaps of public Internet/email services. A typical rate is 300 ptas an hour. One good-value place is Cibercafé Torredeoro.net (☎ 95 450 28 09), Calle Núñez de Balboa 3A. Librería Beta at Avenida de la Constitución 9 and 27 has guidebooks and novels in English. Tintorería Roma, Calle de Castelar 2C, will wash, dry and fold a load of washing for 1000 ptas.

Things to See & Do
Cathedral & Giralda Seville's immense cathedral, one of the biggest in the world, was built on the site of Muslim Seville's main mosque between 1401 and 1507. The structure is primarily Gothic, though most of the internal decoration is in later styles. The adjoining tower, La Giralda, was the mosque's minaret and dates from the 12th century. The climb up La Giralda affords great views and is quite easy as there's a ramp (not stairs) all the way up inside. One highlight of the cathedral's lavish interior is Christopher Columbus' supposed tomb inside the south door (no one's 100% sure that his remains don't get mislaid somewhere in the Caribbean). The four crowned sepulchre-bearers represent the four kingdoms of Spain at the time of Columbus' sailing. The entrance to the Catedral and Giralda for nongroup visitors at our last check was the Puerta del Perdón on Calle Alemanes. Hours are 11 am to 5 pm Monday to Saturday (700 ptas; students and pensioners 200 ptas) and 2 to 7 pm Sunday (free).

Alcázar Seville's alcázar, a residence of Muslim and Christian royalty for many centuries, was founded in AD 913 as a Muslim fortress. It has been adapted by Seville's rulers in almost every century since, which makes it a mishmash of styles, but adds to its fascination. The highlights are the **Palacio de**

SPAIN

SPAIN

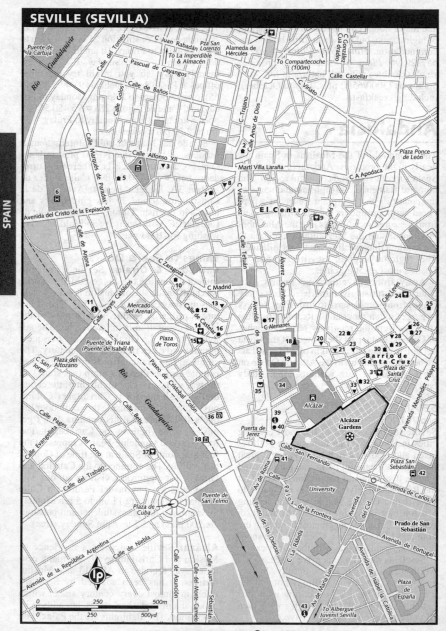

SEVILLE (SEVILLA)

SEVILLE (SEVILLA)

PLACES TO STAY	13	Bodega Paco Góngora	18	Giralda
2 Hostal Unión, Hostal Pino	20	Cervecería Giralda	19	Cathedral
5 Hostal Rmero	21	Bodega Santa Cruz	24	La Carbonería
7 Hostal Lis II	23	Pizzeria San Marco	31	Los Gallos
10 Hostal Central	28	Carmela	34	Archivo de Indias
12 Hotel La Rábida	33	Corral del Agua	35	Main Post Office
22 Hostal Goya			36	Cibercafé Torredeoro.net
25 Hostal La Montoreña	**OTHER**		37	Alambique, Mui d'Aqui &
26 Las Casas de la Judería	1	Fun Club		Big Ben
27 Hostal Bienvenido	4	Museo de Bellas Artes	38	Torre del Oro, Cruceros
29 Pensión San Pancracio	6	Plaza de Armas Bus Station		Turísticos
30 Pensión Cruces	9	El Mundo	39	Main Tourist Office
32 Hostería del Laurel	11	Tourist Office	40	Librería Beta
	14	Arena	41	Airport Bus Stop
PLACES TO EAT	15	A3	42	Prado de San Sebastián Bus
3 Bodegón Alfonso XII	16	Tintorería Roma (Laundry)		Station
8 Patio San Eloy	17	Librería Beta	43	Tourist Office

Don Pedro, exquisitely decorated by Muslim artisans for the Castilian king Pedro the Cruel in the 1360s, and the large, immaculately tended **gardens**, the perfect place to ease your body and brain after some intensive sightseeing. The Alcázar is open 9.30 am to 7 pm Tuesday to Saturday (to 5 pm from October to March), 9.30 am to 5 pm Sunday and holidays. Entry is 700 ptas (free for students and pensioners).

Walks & Parks If you're not staying in the **Barrio de Santa Cruz**, the old Jewish quarter immediately east of the cathedral and alcázar, make sure you take a stroll among its quaint streets and lovely plant-bedecked plazas. Another enjoyable walk is along the **riverbank**, where the 13th-century Torre del Oro contains a small, crowded maritime museum. Nearby is Seville's famous bullring, the **Plaza de Toros de la Real Maestranza**, one of the oldest in Spain (begun in 1758). Interesting 300-ptas tours are given in English and Spanish, about every 20 minutes from 9.30 am to 2 pm and 3 to 6 or 7 pm daily (bullfight days 10 am to 3 pm).

South of the centre, large **Parque de María Luisa** is a pleasant place to get lost in, with its maze of paths, tall trees, flowers, fountains and shaded lawns.

Museums The **Archivo de Indias**, beside the cathedral, houses over 40 million documents dating from 1492 through to the decolonisation of the Americas. There are changing displays of fascinating maps and documents, open 10 am to 1 pm Monday to Friday (free).

The **Museo de Bellas Artes**, on Plaza del Museo, has an outstanding, beautifully housed collection of Spanish art, focusing on Seville artists like Murillo and Zurbarán. It's open Tuesday to Sunday (250 ptas, free for EU citizens).

Organised Tours
One-hour river cruises (1700 ptas) by Cruceros Turísticos Torre del Oro go at least hourly from 11 am to 7 pm from the Torre del Oro.

Special Events
The first of Seville's two great festivals is Semana Santa, the week leading up to Easter Sunday. Throughout the week, long processions of religious brotherhoods (*cofradías*), dressed in strange penitents' garb with tall, pointed hoods, accompany sacred images through the city, watched by huge crowds. The Feria de Abril, a week in late April, is a kind of release after this solemnity: the festivities involve six days of music, dancing, horse riding and traditional dress on a site in the Los Remedios area west of the river, plus daily bullfights and a general city-wide party.

Places to Stay
The summer prices given here can come down substantially from October to March,

but around Semana Santa and the Feria de Abril they typically rise about 50%.

Camping Sevilla (☎ 95 451 43 79), 6km out on the N-IV towards Córdoba, charges 1790 ptas for two people with a car and tent, and runs a shuttle bus to/from Avenida de Portugal in the city.

Seville's recently-renovated HI hostel, *Albergue Juvenil Sevilla* (☎ 95 461 31 50, *Calle Isaac Peral 2*), has 277 places, all in twins or triples. It's about 10 minutes south by bus No 34 from opposite the main tourist office. Bed and breakfast is 1605/2140 ptas for under/over 26s most of the year.

The Barrio de Santa Cruz has some good-value places to stay. *Hostal Bienvenido* (☎ 95 441 36 55, *Calle Archeros 14*) provides singles/doubles from 1900/3700 ptas. Clean *Hostal La Montoreña* (☎ 95 441 24 07, *Calle San Clemente 12*) charges 2000/3000 ptas. *Pensión San Pancracio* (☎ 95 441 31 04, *Plaza de las Cruces 9*) has small singles for 2000 ptas and bigger doubles for 3400 ptas (4000 ptas with bath). *Pensión Cruces* (☎ 95 422 60 41, *Plaza de las Cruces 10*) has a few dorm beds at 1500 ptas and singles/doubles starting at 2000/4000 ptas. Sociable *Hostal Goya* (☎ 95 421 11 70, *Calle Mateos Gago 31*) has nice clean rooms with bath or shower from 4300/6000 ptas. Attractive *Hostería del Laurel* (☎ 95 422 02 95, ⓔ *host-laurel@eintec.es*, *Plaza de los Venerables 5*) charges 7000/9500 ptas plus IVA. *Las Casas de la Judería* (☎ 95 441 51 50, fax 95 442 21 70, *Callejón de Dos Hermanas 7*) is a group of charming old houses around patios and fountains, charging 12,500/18,000 ptas plus IVA.

The area north of Plaza Nueva, only a 10-minute walk from all the hustle and bustle, has some good value too. Friendly *Hostal Unión* (☎ 95 422 92 94, *Calle Tarifa 4*) has nine good clean rooms at 2000/3500 ptas (3000/4500 ptas with bath). *Hostal Pino* (☎ 95 421 28 10, *Calle Tarifa 6*), next door, is similarly priced. Little *Hostal Romero* (☎ 95 421 13 53, *Calle Gravina 21*) offers clean, bare rooms for 2000/3500 ptas. *Hostal Lis II* (☎ 95 456 02 28, ⓔ *lisII@sol.com*, *Calle Olavide 5*) in a pretty house charges 2300/4500 ptas for basic rooms or 5000 ptas for doubles with bath. *Hostal Central* (☎ 95 421 76 60, *Calle Zaragoza 18*) has well-kept rooms with bath

for 4500/6500 ptas. Impressive *Hotel La Rábida* (☎ 95 422 09 60, *Calle Castelar 24*) charges 6100/9300 ptas plus IVA.

Places to Eat
The Barrio de Santa Cruz is a good area for decent-value eating. *Hostería del Laurel* (*Plaza de los Venerables 5*) has an atmospheric old bar with good media raciónes (550 ptas to 1500 ptas) and raciónes. *Cervecería Giralda* (*Calle Mateos Gago 1*) is a good spot for breakfast. Tostadas are from 120 ptas to 480 ptas, or there's bacon and scrambled eggs for 630 ptas. *Bodega Santa Cruz* on the same street, a bar popular with visitors and locals, serves a big choice of decent-sized tapas, most at 175 ptas to 200 ptas. *Pizzeria San Marco* (*Calle Mesón del Moro 6*) does highly popular pizzas and pastas around 850 ptas (closed Monday). Calle Santa María La Blanca has several places with outdoor tables: at the *Carmela* a media ración of *tortilla Alta-Mira* (with potatoes and vegetables) is almost a meal in itself for 700 ptas. For something classier, the cool courtyard of *Corral del Agua* (*Callejón del Agua 6*) is great on a hot day, if you can get a table. Main courses (1900 ptas to 2500 ptas) include good fish choices.

West of Avenida de la Constitución, *Bodega Paco Góngora* (*Calle Padre Marchena 1*) has a huge range of good seafood at decent prices – media raciónes of fish *a la plancha* (grilled) are mostly 675 ptas. Farther north, bright, busy *Patio San Eloy* (*Calle de San Eloy 9*) serves heaps of good tapas for 175 ptas to 215 ptas. *Bodegón Alfonso XII* (*Calle Alfonso XII 33*) is excellent value with deals like scrambled eggs (*revuelto*) with cheese, ham and spinach for 550 ptas, or a bacon, eggs and coffee breakfast for 400 ptas.

Mercado del Arenal on Calle Pastor y Landero is the main food market in the central area.

Entertainment
Seville's nightlife is among the liveliest in Spain. On fine nights throngs of people block the streets outside popular bars. Seville has some great music bars, often with space for a bit of dancing. As in most places in Spain, the real action begins around midnight on Friday and Saturday.

Drinking & Dancing Until about 1 am, Plaza del Salvador is a popular spot for an open-air drink, with a studenty crowd and a couple of little bars selling carry-out drinks.

There are some hugely popular bars just north of the cathedral, but the crowds from about midnight around Calle de Adriano, west of Avenida de la Constitución, have to be seen to be believed. Busy music bars on Adriano itself include *A3* and *Arena*. Nearby on Calle de García de Vinuesa and Calle del Dos de Mayo are some quieter *bodegas* (traditional wine bars), some with good tapas, that attract a more mature crowd. Plaza de la Alfalfa is another good area; there are some great tapas bars east along Calle Alfalfa, and at least five throbbing music bars north on Calle Pérez Galdós.

The *Fun Club (Alameda de Hércules 86)* is a small, busy dance warehouse, open Thursday to Sunday – live bands play some nights. Several good pub-like bars line the same street a little farther north. The *Almacén* bar at *La Imperdible* arts centre *(Plaza San Antonio de Padua 9)* stages free music from around 11 pm Thursday to Saturday – from blues to psychedelic punk to beat-beat DJs.

In summer there's a lively scene along the east bank of the Guadalquivir, which is dotted with temporary bars. On the far bank, *Alambique*, *Mui d'Aqui* and *Big Ben*, side by side on Calle del Betis, all play good music year-round, attracting an interesting mix of students and travellers.

Flamenco Seville is arguably Spain's flamenco capital and you're most likely to catch spontaneous atmosphere (of unpredictable quality) in one of the bars staging regular nights of flamenco with no entry charge. These include the sprawling *La Carbonería (Calle Levíes 18)*, thronged nearly every night from about 11 pm to 4 am, and *El Mundo (Calle Siete Revueltas 5)*, with flamenco at 11 pm Tuesday. There are also several tourist-oriented venues with regular shows – of these, *Los Gallos (☎ 95 421 69 81, Plaza de Santa Cruz 11)* is a cut above the average, with two shows nightly (3500 ptas).

Spectator Sports
The bullfight season runs from Easter to October, with fights most Sundays about 6.30

pm, and every day during the Feria de Abril and the preceding week. The bullring is on Paseo de Cristóbal Colón. Tickets start around 1500 ptas or 3000 ptas depending on who's fighting.

Getting There & Away
Air Seville airport (☎ 95 444 90 00) has quite a range of domestic and international flights. Air Europa flies to Barcelona from 16,500 ptas.

Bus Buses to Extremadura, Madrid, Portugal and Andalucía west of Seville leave from the Plaza de Armas bus station (☎ 95 490 80 40). Numerous daily buses run to/from Madrid (2745 ptas, six hours); to/from Lisbon there are five direct buses a week (4800 ptas, eight hours). Daily buses run to/from places on the Algarve such as Faro, Albufeira and Lagos.

Buses to other parts of Andalucía and eastern Spain use Prado de San Sebastián bus station (☎ 95 441 71 11). Daily services include nine or more each to Córdoba (1225 ptas, 1¾ hours), Granada (2400 ptas, three hours) and Málaga (1900 ptas, 2½ hours).

Train Seville's Santa Justa train station is 1.5km north-east of the centre on Avenida Kansas City. To/from Madrid, there are 14 superfast AVE trains each day, covering the 471km in just 2½ hours and costing 8400 ptas to 9900 ptas in the cheapest class *(turista)*; a few other trains take 3¼ to 3¾ hours for 6600 ptas to 8300 ptas.

Other daily trains include about 20 to Córdoba (1090 ptas to 2800 ptas, 45 minutes to 1¼ hours) and three or more each to Granada (2415 ptas to 2665 ptas, three hours) and Málaga (2130 ptas, 2½ hours). For Lisbon (7000 ptas, 16 hours) you must change at Cáceres.

Car Pooling Compartecoche (☎ 95 490 75 82), Calle de González Cuadrado 49, is an intercity car-pooling service. Its service is free to drivers, while passengers pay an agreed transfer rate.

Getting Around
The airport is 7km from the centre, off the N-IV Córdoba road. Amarillos Tour (☎ 902-21 03 17) runs buses to/from Puerta de Jerez in the city at least nine times daily (350 ptas).

SPAIN

Bus No C1, in front of Santa Justa train station, follows a clockwise circuit via Avenida de Carlos V, close to Prado de San Sebastián bus station and the city centre; No C2 does the same route anticlockwise. No C4, south down Calle de Arjona from Plaza de Armas bus station, goes to Puerta de Jerez in the centre; returning, take No C3.

CÓRDOBA
pop 310,000

Roman Córdoba was the capital of Baetica province, covering most of Andalucía. Following the Muslim invasion in AD 711 it soon became the effective Muslim capital on the peninsula, a position it held until the Córdoban Caliphate broke up after the death of its ruler Al-Mansour in 1002. Muslim Córdoba at its peak was the most splendid city in Europe, and its Mezquita (Mosque) is one of the most magnificent of all Islamic buildings. From the 11th century Córdoba was overshadowed by Seville and in the 13th century both cities fell to the Christians in the Reconquista.

Córdoba is at its best from about mid-April to mid-June, when the weather is warm but not too warm and it stages most of its annual festivals.

Orientation

Immediately north of the Río Guadalquivir is the old city, a warren of narrow streets focused on the Mezquita. The main square of the modern city is Plaza de las Tendillas, 500m north of the Mezquita.

Information

The helpful regional tourist office (☎ 957 47 12 35) faces the Mezquita at Calle de Torrijos 10. It's open 10 am to 6, 7 or 8 pm (according to season) Monday to Saturday, 10 am to 2 pm on Sunday and holidays. The municipal tourist office (☎ 957 20 05 22) is on Plaza de Judá Leví, a block west of the Mezquita.

Most banks and ATMs are around Plaza de las Tendillas. One ATM handier to the old city is at the corner of Calles San Fernando and Lucano.

Things to See & Do

The inside of the famous **Mezquita**, begun by emir Abd ar-Rahman I in AD 785 and enlarged by subsequent generations, is a mesmerising sequence of two-tier arches in stripes of red brick and white stone. From 1236 the mosque was used as a church and in the 16th century a cathedral was built right in its centre – somewhat wrecking the effect of original Muslim building, in many people's opinion. Opening hours are 10 am to 7.30 pm Monday to Saturday (to 5.30 pm October to March), 3.30 to 7.30 Sunday and holidays (2 to 5.30 pm October to March). Entry is 800 ptas.

The Judería, Córdoba's medieval Jewish quarter north-west of the Mezquita, is an intriguing maze of narrow streets and small plazas. Don't miss the beautiful little **Sinagoga** on Calle Judíos, one of Spain's very few surviving medieval synagogues (open daily except Monday). Nearby are the **Casa Andalusí**, Calle Judíos 12, a 12th-century house with exhibits on Córdoba's medieval Muslim culture, and the **Museo Taurino** (Bullfighting Museum) on Plaza de Maimónides, celebrating Córdoba's legendary matadors such as El Cordobés and Manolete.

South-west of the Mezquita stands the **Alcázar de los Reyes Cristianos** (Castle of the Christian Monarchs), with large and lovely gardens. Entry is 300 ptas (free on Friday).

The **Museo Arqueólogico**, Plaza de Jerónimo Páez 7, is also worth a visit (250 ptas, free for EU citizens). On the south side of the river, across the **Puente Romano**, is the **Torre de la Calahorra** with a museum highlighting the intellectual achievements of Islamic Córdoba, with excellent models of the Mezquita and Granada's Alhambra – open daily (500 ptas).

Places to Stay

Most people look for lodgings close to the Mezquita. Córdoba's excellent youth hostel, *Albergue Juvenil Córdoba* (☎ 957 29 01 66), is perfectly positioned on Plaza de Judá Leví. It has no curfew. Most of the year, bed and breakfast is 1605/2140 ptas for under/over 26s.

Many Córdoba lodgings are built around charming patios. One such place is friendly *Huéspedes Martínez Rücker* (☎ 957 47 25 62, @ hmrucker@alcavia.net, Calle Martínez Rücker 14), a stone's throw east of the Mezquita. It has clean singles/doubles for 2000/3500 ptas. *Hostal Rey Heredia* (☎ 957

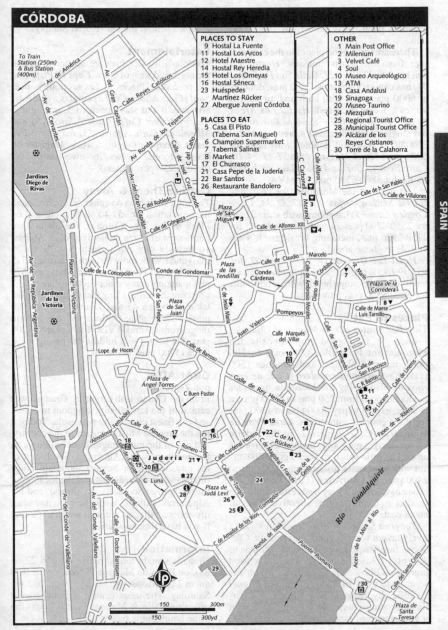

CÓRDOBA

To Train
Station (250m)
& Bus Station
(400m)

PLACES TO STAY
9 Hostal La Fuente
11 Hostal Los Arcos
12 Hotel Maestre
14 Hostal Rey Heredia
15 Hotel Los Omeyas
16 Hostal Séneca
23 Huéspedes
   Martínez Rücker
27 Albergue Juvenil Córdoba

PLACES TO EAT
5 Casa El Pisto
   (Taberna San Miguel)
6 Champion Supermarket
7 Taberna Salinas
8 Market
17 El Churrasco
21 Casa Pepe de la Judería
22 Bar Santos
26 Restaurante Bandolero

OTHER
1 Main Post Office
2 Milenium
3 Velvet Café
4 Soul
10 Museo Arqueológico
13 ATM
18 Casa Andalusí
19 Sinagoga
20 Museo Taurino
24 Mezquita
25 Regional Tourist Office
28 Municipal Tourist Office
29 Alcázar de los
   Reyes Cristianos
30 Torre de la Calahorra

Jardines
Diego de
Rivas

Jardines
de la
Victoria

Plaza de
San
Miguel

Plaza
de las
Tendillas

Plaza
de San
Juan

Plaza de
Ángel Torres

Juderia

Plaza de
Judá Levi

Río Guadalquivir

Plaza de
Santa
Teresa

0   150   300m
0   150   300yd

SPAIN

euro currency converter 100 ptas = €0.60

47 41 82, Calle Rey Heredia 26) has rooms around a plant-filled patio from 1500/3000 ptas.

There are some good places to the east, farther from the tourist masses. **Hostal La Fuente** *(☎ 957 48 78 27, Calle San Fernando 51)* has compact singles at 3500 ptas, doubles at 6000 ptas – all with bath and air-con; it serves a decent breakfast. **Hostal Los Arcos** *(☎ 957 48 56 43, Calle Romero Barros 14)* has singles/doubles around a pretty patio for 2500/4000 ptas, and doubles with bath for 5000 ptas. **Hotel Maestre** *(☎ 957 47 24 10, Calle Romero Barros 4)* has plain but bright rooms for 3800/6500 ptas plus IVA.

Just north of the Mezquita, the charming **Hostal Séneca** *(☎/fax 957 47 32 34, Calle Conde y Luque 7)* has rooms with shared bath for 2550/4700 ptas, or with attached bath for 4750/5900 ptas, including breakfast. It's advisable to phone ahead.

Hotel Los Omeyas *(☎ 957 49 22 67, fax 957 49 16 59, Calle Encarnación 17)* is an attractive middle-range hotel, with good rooms for 5000/8500 ptas plus IVA.

Places to Eat
Tiny **Bar Santos** *(Calle Magistral González Francés 3)* is a good stop opposite the Mezquita for bocadillos (200 ptas to 300 ptas), tapas (150 ptas) and raciónes (500 ptas). **Restaurante Bandolero** *(Calle de Torrijos 6)*, also facing the Mezquita, provides media raciónes from 250 ptas to 1000 ptas; a la carte, expect to pay 3000 ptas to 4000 ptas for three courses with drinks. **Casa Pepe de la Judería** *(Calle Romero 1)* in the Judería serves tasty tapas and raciónes in rooms around its little patio, and has a good restaurant with most main dishes from 1600 ptas to 2400 ptas. **El Churrasco** *(Calle Romero 16)* is one of Córdoba's very best restaurants. The food is rich and service attentive. The set *menú* costs 3500 ptas.

Taberna Salinas *(Calle Tundidores 3)* is a lively tavern serving good, inexpensive Córdoban fare. Raciónes cost around 700 ptas to 800 ptas (closed Sunday). There's a food *market* on Plaza de la Corredera, two blocks south-east. **Casa El Pisto** *(Plaza San Miguel 1)*, officially **Taberna San Miguel**, is a particularly atmospheric old watering hole with a good range of tapas, media raciónes (500

ptas to 1000 ptas) and raciónes. You can sit at tables behind the bar (closed Sunday).

Entertainment
Córdoba's livelier bars are scattered around the north and west of town. **Casa El Pisto** (see the preceding Places to Eat section) is one. **Soul** *(Calle Alfonso XIII 3)* attracts a studenty/arty crowd and stays open to 3 am nightly. Nearby **Velvet Café** *(Calle Alfaros 29)* and **Milenium** *(Calle Alfaros 33)* may have live bands a couple of nights a week. **Magister** on Calle Morería brews its own tasty beer (around 250 ptas a glass).

Getting There & Away
The train station on Avenida de América, and the bus station (☎ 957 40 40 40) behind it on Plaza de las Tres Culturas, are about 1km north-west of Plaza de las Tendillas. At least 10 buses a day run to/from Seville (1225 ptas) and five or more to/from Granada (1515 ptas), Madrid (1600 ptas) and Málaga (1570 ptas), among many other destinations.

About 20 trains a day run to/from Seville, taking between 45 and 75 minutes for 1090 ptas to 2800 ptas. Options to/from Madrid range from several AVEs (6100 ptas to 7200 ptas, 1¾ hours) to a middle-of-the-night Estrella (3700 ptas, 6¼ hours).

GRANADA
pop 241,000
From the 13th to 15th centuries, Granada was capital of the last Muslim kingdom in Spain, and the finest city on the peninsula. Today it has the greatest Muslim legacy in the country, and one of the most magnificent buildings on the continent – the Alhambra. South-east of the city, the Sierra Nevada mountain range (mainland Spain's highest and the location of Europe's most southerly ski slopes), and the Alpujarras valleys, with their picturesque, mysterious villages, are well worth exploring if you have time to spare.

Information
Granada's main tourist office (☎ 958 22 66 88), on Plaza de Mariana Pineda, opens 9.30 am to 7 pm Monday to Friday, 10 am to 2 pm Saturday. The more central regional tourist office on Calle de Mariana Pineda opens the same hours but is busier.

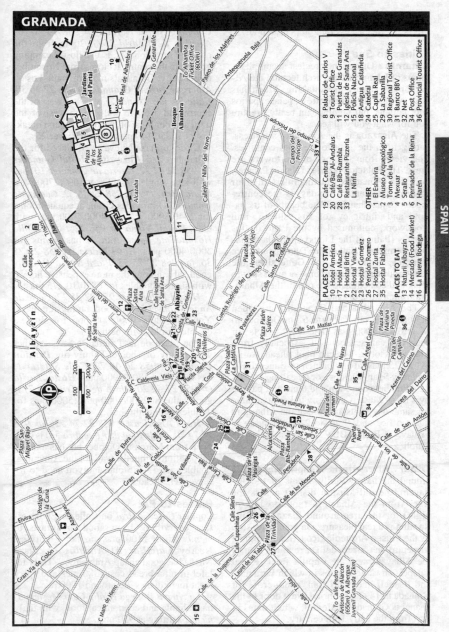

GRANADA

PLACES TO STAY
10 Hotel América
17 Hotel Macía
21 Hostal Britz
22 Hostal Viena
23 Hostal Gomérez
26 Pensión Romero
27 Hostal Zurita
35 Hostal Fabiola

PLACES TO EAT
13 Naturii Albayzín
14 Mercado (Food Market)
16 La Nueva Bodega
19 Cafe Central
20 Café/Bar Al-Andalus
28 Café Bib-Rambla
33 Restaurante Pizzería
    La Ninfa

OTHER
1 El Eshavira
2 Museo Arqueológico
3 Tome de la Vella
4 Mexuar
5 Serallo
6 Perinador de la Reina
7 Harén
8 Palacio de Carlos V
9 Tourist Office
11 Puerta de las Granadas
12 Iglesia de Santa Ana
15 Policia Nacional
18 Antigua Castañeda
24 Catedral
25 Capilla Real
29 La Sabanilla
30 Regional Tourist Office
31 Banco BBV
32 Net
34 Post Office
36 Provincial Tourist Office

euro currency converter 100 ptas = €0.60

Net, Calle Santa Escolástica 13, open daily, offers Internet access for 200 ptas an hour.

Things to See

Alhambra One of the greatest accomplishments of Islamic art and architecture, the Alhambra is simply breathtaking. Much has been written about its fortress, palace, patios and gardens, but nothing can really prepare you for what you will see.

The **Alcazaba** is the Alhambra's fortress, dating from the 11th to the 13th centuries. The views from the tops of the towers are great. The **Palacio Nazaries** (Nasrid Palace), built for Granada's Muslim rulers in their 13th to 15th-century heyday, is the centrepiece of the Alhambra. The beauty of its patios and intricacy of its stucco and woodwork, epitomised by the Patio de los Leones (Patio of the Lions) and Sala de las Dos Hermanas (Hall of the Two Sisters), are stunning. Don't miss the **Generalife**, the soul-soothing palace gardens – a great spot to relax and contemplate the rest of the Alhambra from a little distance.

The Alhambra and Generalife are open 8.30 am to 8 pm daily (to 6 pm October to March) for 1000 ptas. The 8000 tickets for each day can sell out fast, especially from May to October. You can book ahead, for an extra 125 ptas, at any branch of Banco BBV (in many Spanish cities), or by calling ☎ 902-22 44 60 between 9 am and 6 pm and paying by Visa or MasterCard. Any tickets available for same-day visits are sold at the Alhambra ticket office, and 9 am to 2 pm Monday to Friday, at Banco BBV on Plaza Isabel la Católica.

Other Attractions

Simply wandering around the narrow, hilly streets of the **Albayzín**, the old Muslim district across the river from the Alhambra (not too late at night), or the area around **Plaza de Bib-Rambla** is a real pleasure. On your way, stop by the **Museo Arqueológico** (Archaeological Museum) on Carrera del Darro at the foot of the Albayzín, and the **Capilla Real** (Royal Chapel) on Calle Oficios in which Fernando and Isabel, the Christian conquerors of Granada in 1492, are buried. Next door to the chapel is Granada's **catedral**, which dates in part from the early 16th century.

Places to Stay

Camping Sierra Nevada (☎ 958 15 00 62, Avenida de Madrid 107), 200m from the estación de autobuses, is the closest camping ground to the centre. It closes from November to February. Granada's modern youth hostel, **Albergue Juvenil Granada** (☎ 958 27 26 38, Calle Ramón y Cajal 2) is 1.7km west of the centre and a 600m walk south-west of the train station. Most of the year, bed and breakfast is 1605/2140 ptas for under/over 26s.

Close to Plaza Nueva (well placed for the Alhambra and Albayzín), **Hostal Gomérez** (☎ 958 22 44 37, Cuesta de Gomérez 10) has well-kept singles/doubles at 1600/2700 ptas. **Hostal Britz** (☎/fax 958 22 36 52, Cuesta de Gomérez 1) provides clean, adequate rooms for 2340/3900 ptas, or 4000/5400 ptas with bath. **Hostal Viena** (☎ 958 22 18 59, Calle Hospital de Santa Ana 2) has rooms for 3000/4000 ptas. **Hotel Macía** (☎ 958 22 75 36, fax 958 22 75 33, Plaza Nueva 4) offers good value among the more expensive hotels, with singles/doubles for 6820/10,275 ptas.

Hostal Fabiola (☎ 958 22 35 72, Calle de Ángel Ganivet 5) is a good, family-run place. You pay 1800/4000/5000 ptas for singles/doubles/triples with bath.

The Plaza de la Trinidad area is another with plenty of choice. Family-run **Pensión Romero** (☎ 958 26 60 79, Calle Sillería 1) has rooms for 1700/2900 ptas. **Hostal Zurita** (☎ 958 27 50 20, Plaza de la Trinidad 7) is good value at 2000/4000 ptas (5000 ptas for doubles with bathroom).

Hotel América (☎ 958 22 74 71, fax 958 22 74 70, Calle Real de Alhambra 53) is only open from March to October but has a magical position within the walls of the Alhambra; doubles are 13,375 ptas and you need to reserve well ahead.

Places to Eat

Popular **Cafe Central** on Calle de Elvira offers everything from good breakfasts to menús (from 1100 ptas) to fancy coffees. Nearby **Café/Bar Al Andalus** on Plaza Nueva has good cheap Arabic food. Tasty felafel in pitta bread costs 300 ptas and spicy meat main dishes are around 1000 ptas.

La Nueva Bodega (Calle Cetti Meriém 3) has reliable and economical food, with daily menús starting at 950 ptas.

The *teterías* (Arabic-style teahouses) on Calle Calderería Nueva, a picturesque pedestrian street west of Plaza Nueva, are expensive but can be enjoyable. *Naturii Albayzín (Calle Calderería Nueva 10)* is a good vegetarian restaurant.

Café Bib-Rambla on Plaza Bib-Rambla is great for breakfast. Coffee and toast with butter and excellent marmalade cost 400 ptas at its tables on the plaza. *Restaurante-Pizzería La Ninfa (Campo del Príncipe 14)* is an excellent Italian eatery on a plaza south of the Alhambra that buzzes at night.

For fresh fruit and vegies, the large covered *mercado* (market) is on Calle San Agustín.

In Granada's bars, tapas are often free at night.

Entertainment
The highest concentration of music bars is on and around Calle Pedro Antonio de Alarcón. To get there, walk south on Calle de las Tablas from Plaza de la Trinidad. After 11 pm at weekends, you can't miss it.

Bars in the streets west of Plaza Nueva get very lively on weekend nights. The *Antigua Castañeda* on Calle de Elvira is one of the most famous bars in Granada and an institution among locals and tourists alike, serving great tapas – which will probably come free if you're standing at the bar after 8 pm. Bars north of Plaza Nueva on Carrera del Darro and Paseo de los Tristes get fun after midnight.

Granada's oldest bar, *La Sabanilla (Calle de San Sebastián 14)*, though showing its age, is worth a visit. Don't miss *El Eshavira (Postigo de la Cuna 2)*, a roomy jazz and flamenco club down a dark alley off Calle Azacayas (open from 10 pm nightly).

In the evening some travellers go to the Sacromonte caves to see flamenco, but it's touristy and a bit of a rip-off.

Getting There & Away
Granada's bus station (☎ 958 18 54 80) is at Carretera de Jáen s/n, on the continuation of Avenida de Madrid, 3km north-west of the centre. At least nine daily buses serve Madrid (1950 ptas, five to six hours), and others run to Barcelona, Valencia and destinations across Andalucía.

The train station is about 1.5km west of the centre, on Avenida de Andaluces. Of the two

trains daily to Madrid, one takes 9½ hours overnight (3600 ptas), the other six hours (3800 ptas). To Seville, there are three trains a day (from 2415 ptas, three hours). For Málaga and Córdoba, you have to change trains in Bobadilla. There's one train daily to Valencia and Barcelona.

COSTA DE ALMERÍA
The coast east of Almería city in eastern Andalucía is perhaps the last section of Spain's Mediterranean coast where you can have a beach to yourself (not in high summer, admittedly). This is Spain's sunniest region – even in late March it can be warm enough to take in some rays and try out your new swimsuit.

The most useful tourist offices are in Almería (☎ 950 62 11 17), San José (☎ 950 38 02 99) and Mojácar (☎ 950 47 51 62).

Things to See & Do
The **Alcazaba**, an enormous 10th-century Muslim fortress, is the highlight of Almería city. In its heyday the city was more important than Granada.

The best thing about the region is the wonderful coastline and semidesert scenery of the **Cabo de Gata** promontory. All along the 50km coast from El Cabo de Gata village to Agua Amarga, some of the most beautiful and empty beaches on the Mediterranean alternate with precipitous cliffs and scattered villages. Roads or paths run along or close to this whole coastline. The main village is laid-back **San José**, with excellent beaches such as **Playa de los Genoveses** and **Playa de Mónsul** within 7km south-west.

Mojácar, 30km north of Agua Amarga, is a white town of Muslim origin, with cube-shaped houses perched on a hill 2km from the coast. Although a long resort strip, Mojácar Playa, has grown up below, Mojácar is still a pretty place and it's not hard to spend time here, especially if you fancy a livelier summer beach scene than Cabo de Gata offers.

Places to Stay & Eat
Almería Near the bus and train stations, *Hostal Americano (☎ 950 28 10 15, Avenida de la Estación 6)* offers well-kept singles/doubles from 2850/5540 ptas to 3915/6410 ptas.

SPAIN

Cabo de Gata In high summer it's a good idea to ring ahead about accommodation, as some places fill up. In San José *Camping Tau* (☎ *950 38 01 66*) and the friendly non-HI youth hostel *Albergue Juvenil de San José* (☎ *950 38 03 53, Calle Montemar s/n*), with bunks for 1300 ptas, both open from April to September. *Hostal Bahía* (☎ *950 38 03 07*) on Calle Correo has attractive singles/doubles with bathroom for 5000/7500 ptas. *Restaurante El Emigrante* across the road does good fish and meat mains around 850 ptas to 1400 ptas, and omelettes for 400 ptas to 500 ptas.

Mojácar The better-value places are mostly up in the old town. *Pensión Casa Justa* (☎ *950 47 83 72, Calle Morote 7*) is reasonable value with singles/doubles from 2500/5000 ptas. *Hostal La Esquinica* (☎ *950 47 50 09, Calle Cano 1*) charges 2500/4500 ptas. Charming *Hostal Mamabel's* (☎ *950 47 24 48, Calle Embajadores 5*) has eight big rooms with sea views and bath, for 9630 ptas a double, and a good restaurant with a three-course *menú* for 1800 ptas, plus drinks and IVA. *Restaurante El Viento del Desierto* on Plaza del Frontón is good value with main courses such as beef Bourguignon for 650 ptas to 800 ptas.

Getting There & Away
Almería has an international and domestic airport and is accessible by bus and train from Madrid, Granada and Seville, and by bus from Málaga, Valencia and Barcelona. Buses run from Almería bus station to El Cabo de Gata village and (except nonsummer Sundays) to San José. Mojácar can be reached by bus from Almería, Murcia, Granada and Madrid.

MÁLAGA
pop 528,000
The large port city of Málaga, a major entry point into Spain thanks to its international airport feeding the nearby Costa del Sol, has a bustling street life and a thumping nightlife in the narrow streets behind Plaza de la Constitución. It also boasts a 16th-century cathedral, and a Muslim palace/fortress, the Alcazaba, from which the walls of the Muslim Castillo de Gibralfaro climb to the top of the hill dominating the city. A major new museum devoted to the work of Málaga-born artist Pablo Picasso is due to open in Málaga

in late 2002. The helpful regional tourist office (☎ 95 221 34 45), in the centre at Pasaje Chinitas 4, opens daily.

The Costa del Sol, a string of tightly packed resorts running south-west from Málaga towards Gibraltar, is best avoided if you're more interested in Spain than foreign package tourists.

Places to Stay & Eat
The friendly, central *Pensión Córdoba* (☎ *95 221 44 69, Calle Bolsa 9*) has singles/doubles at 1500/3000 ptas. *Hotel Carlos V* (☎ *95 221 51 20, Calle Císter 10*) near the cathedral offers comfortable doubles for 8300 ptas.

Café Central on Plaza de la Constitución is a noisy local favourite; food prices are reasonable, with plenty of choice. A short walk north-east, *La Posada (Calle Granada 33)* is great for tapas and raciónes of *carnes a la brasa* (grilled meats). It's 1600 ptas for lamb chops.

Getting There & Away
Málaga airport has a good range of domestic as well as international flights. Trains and buses run every half-hour from the airport to the city centre The city is also linked by train and bus to all major Spanish centres. The bus and train stations are round the corner from each other, 1km west of the city centre.

RONDA
pop 34,500
One of the prettiest and most historic towns in Andalucía, Ronda is a world apart from the nearby Costa del Sol. The town straddles the savagely deep El Tajo gorge, at the heart of some lovely hill country dotted with white villages.

The regional tourist office (☎ 95 287 12 72) is at Plaza de España 1.

Things to See & Do
Ronda is a pleasure to wander around, but during the day you'll have to contend with busloads of day-trippers from the coast.

The **Plaza de Toros** (1785) is considered the home of bullfighting and is a mecca for aficionados; inside is the small but fascinating **Museo Taurino**. Entry is 400 ptas. Vertiginous cliff-top views open out from the nearby Alameda del Tajo park.

The 18th-century **Puente Nuevo** (New Bridge), an amazing feat of engineering, crosses the gorge to the originally Muslim old town (La Ciudad), which is littered with ancient churches, monuments and palaces. At the **Casa del Rey Moro**, Calle Santo Domingo 17, you can climb down a Muslim-era stairway cut inside the rock right to the bottom of the gorge (open daily, 600 ptas). Try not to miss the **Iglesia de Santa María la Mayor**, a church whose tower was once the minaret of a mosque; the **Museo del Bandolero**, Calle Armiñán 65, dedicated to the banditry for which central Andalucía was once renowned; or the beautiful **Baños Arabes** (Arab Baths), open Wednesday to Sunday.

Places to Stay & Eat
Camping El Sur (☎ *95 287 59 39*) is a good small site 2km out on the Algeciras road.

The bright *Pensión La Purísima* (☎ *95 287 10 50, Calle Sevilla 10*) has nine rooms at 2000/3000 ptas. *Hotel Morales* (☎/fax *95 287 15 38, Calle Sevilla 51*) has pleasant rooms with bath for 3500/6000 ptas and is full of information on exploring the town and surrounding country.

El Molino on Plaza del Socorro is popular for its pizzas, pasta and platos combinados from 550 ptas to 775 ptas, and varied breakfasts. *Restaurante Hermanos Macías* (*Calle Pedro Romero 3*) is a reliable mid-range eatery with meat and fish main dishes from 800 ptas to 1600 ptas.

Getting There & Away
Several buses run daily to Seville (1285 ptas, 2½ hours), Málaga (1075 ptas, two hours) and Cádiz. One goes to Algeciras (1010 ptas) Monday to Friday. The bus station is on Plaza Concepción García Redondo.

A few direct trains go to Granada (1775 ptas, 2¼ hours), Málaga (1175 ptas, two hours), Algeciras, Córdoba and Madrid. For Seville, and further trains to/from the above destinations, change at Bobadilla or Antequera. The station is on Avenida de Andalucía.

ALGECIRAS
pop 102,000
Algeciras, an unattractive industrial and fishing town between Tarifa and Gibraltar, is the major port linking Spain with Morocco. Keep your wits about you, and ignore offers from the legions of money-changers, drug-pushers and ticket-hawkers. The tourist office (☎ 956 57 26 36) on Calle Juan de la Cierva near the ferry port, opens 9 am to 2 pm Monday to Friday.

If you need a room, there's loads of budget accommodation in the streets behind Avenida de la Marina, the street the port is on. Beware early-hours market noise, though. Friendly *Hostal González* (☎ *956 65 28 43, Calle José Santacana 7*) has good, clean singles/doubles with private bath at 2000/4000 ptas.

Getting There & Away
Bus Comes, on Calle San Bernardo, about 400m inland from the port, runs frequent buses to/from La Línea, and several daily to/from Tarifa, Cádiz and Seville. Portillo, Avenida Virgen del Carmen 15, 200m north of the port, runs to/from Málaga, the Costa del Sol and Granada. Bacoma, inside the port, runs to/from Valencia, Barcelona, France, Germany and Holland.

Train Direct daily trains run to/from Madrid and Granada, passing through Ronda and through Bobadilla where you can change for Málaga, Córdoba and Seville.

Boat Trasmediterránea (☎ 902-45 46 45), EuroFerrys (☎ 956 65 11 78) and other companies operate frequent ferries to/from Tangier in Morocco and Ceuta, the Spanish enclave on the Moroccan coast. Usually at least 20 daily go to Tangier and 40 or more to Ceuta. From late June to September there are ferries almost round the clock. Buy your ticket in the port or at agencies on Avenida de la Marina – prices are the same. To Tangier, adults pay 3500 ptas one-way by ferry (2½ hours), or 4440 ptas by hydrofoil (one hour). Cars cost 10,750 ptas. To Ceuta, it's 1945 ptas by ferry (90 minutes) or 3095 ptas by 'fast ferry' (40 minutes). Cars are 8930 ptas. Buquebus (☎ 902-41 42 42) crosses to Ceuta in 30 minutes for 2945 ptas (cars 8223 ptas).

CÁDIZ, TARIFA & THE COSTA DE LA LUZ
The historic port of Cádiz is squeezed on to an island just off Andalucía's Atlantic coast, joined to the mainland by a causeway. Ninety kilometres to its south is windy Tarifa,

SPAIN

SPAIN

perched at continental Europe's most southerly point and with a lively windsurfing scene. Between the two places stretch the long, sandy beaches of the Costa de la Luz (Coast of Light), where laid-back villages such as Los Caños de Meca, Zahara de los Atunes and Bolonia have fairly plentiful middle-range accommodation – they're unfortunately a little hard to reach without your own wheels.

Things to See & Do

Cádiz Check the **Torre Tavira**, an old watchtower with a *cámara oscura* projecting moving images of the city on to a screen (open daily); the **Museo de Cádiz**, with archaeological and art collections (closed Monday); the **Castillo de Santa Catalina**, built in 1598 (open daily); and the large 18th-century **cathedral** (closed to tourist visits on Sunday). From Cádiz you can easily visit the historic sherry-making towns of El Puerto de Santa María and Jerez de la Frontera by bus or train (or boat, to El Puerto).

Tarifa A 10km-long beach beloved of windsurfers, **Playa de los Lances** stretches northwest from Tarifa. For windsurf rental and classes try places along here such as Club Mistral at the Hurricane Hotel or Spin Out in front of Camping Torre de la Peña II. In Tarifa town, enjoy exploring the winding old streets and visit the castle, **Castillo de Guzmán**, dating from the 10th century.

Places to Stay & Eat

Cádiz's excellent independent youth hostel *Quo Qádiz* (*☎/fax 956 22 19 39, Calle Diego Arias 1*) has accommodation from 1000 ptas a person including breakfast. Friendly, clean *Hostal Fantoni* (*☎ 956 28 27 04, Calle Flamenco 5*) has singles/doubles at 2000/3700 ptas. Plaza de San Juan de Dios and the Plaza de Mina area are full of varied places to eat.

In Tarifa, a good choice is *Pensión África* (*☎ 956 68 02 20, Calle María Antonia Toledo 12*) with bright, comfy rooms for 2500/4000 ptas (3500/5000 ptas with private bath). There are plenty of eating options on and near the central Calle Sancho IV El Bravo.

Getting There & Away

The Comes company (*☎ 956 21 17 63*), on Cádiz's Plaza de la Hispanidad, runs buses to/from Seville (1385 ptas, 1¾ hours), Tarifa

and Málaga. Up to 15 daily trains chuff to/from Seville (1290 ptas, two hours), with others heading for Córdoba and beyond. Comes also links Tarifa (Calle Batalla del Salado) with Algeciras, La Línea, Seville and Málaga.

Gibraltar

pop 29,000
The British colony of Gibraltar occupies a huge lump of limestone, almost 5km long and over 1km wide, near the mouth of the Mediterranean Sea. It's a curious and interesting port of call if you're in the region. Gibraltar has certainly had a rocky history: it was the bridgehead for the Muslim invasion of Spain in AD 711 and Castile didn't finally wrest it from the Muslims until 1462. In 1704 an Anglo-Dutch fleet captured Gibraltar after a one-week siege. Spain gave up military attempts to regain it from Britain after the failure of the Great Siege of 1779-83, but during the Franco period Gibraltar was an extremely sore point between Britain and Spain, and the border was closed for years.

Gibraltar is internally self-governing and an overwhelming majority of Gibraltarians – many of whom are of Genoese or Jewish ancestry – want to retain British sovereignty. Spain has offered Gibraltar autonomous-region status within Spain, but Britain and the Gibraltarians reject any compromise over sovereignty.

Information

To enter Gibraltar you need a passport or EU national identity card. EU, US, Canada, Australia, New Zealand, Israel, South Africa and Singapore passport-holders are among those who do *not* need visas for Gibraltar, but anyone who needs a visa for Spain should have at least a double-entry Spanish visa if they intend to return to Spain from Gibraltar.

Gibraltar has a helpful tourist office at the border. The main office (*☎ 45000*) is in Duke of Kent House, Cathedral Square, open 9 am to 5.30 pm Monday to Friday; another is at The Piazza (*☎ 74982*), Main St, open 9 am to 5.30 pm Monday to Friday, 10 am to 4 pm weekends.

The currency is the Gibraltar pound or pound sterling. You can use pesetas, however currency conversion rates aren't in your favour. But exchange rates for buying pesetas are a bit better than in Spain. Change any unspent Gibraltar pounds before you leave.

To phone Gibraltar from Spain, the telephone code is ☎ 9567; from other countries dial the international access code, then ☎ 350 (the code for Gibraltar) and the local number. To phone Spain from Gibraltar, just dial the nine-digit Spanish number.

Gibraltar is better than anywhere in Spain – except Palma de Mallorca – for finding (unpaid) yacht crew work. Ask around at Marina Bay harbour.

Gibraltar has lots of British high street shops, including a Safeway supermarket, in the Europort area.

Things to See & Do

Central Gibraltar is nothing special – you could almost be in Bletchley or Bradford – but the **Gibraltar Museum**, on Bomb House Lane, has a very interesting historical, architectural and military collection and includes a Muslim-era bathhouse. It's open 10 am to 6 pm Monday to Friday, 10 am to 2 pm Saturday (£2). Many graves in the **Trafalgar Cemetery** are of those who died at Gibraltar from wounds received in the Battle of Trafalgar (1805) off Los Caños de Meca.

The large **Upper Rock Nature Reserve**, covering most of the upper rock, has spectacular views and several interesting spots to visit. It's open 9.30 am to 7 pm daily. Entry, at £5 an adult and £1.50 a vehicle, includes all the following sites, which are open to 6.15 or 6.30 pm. Cable-car tickets (see Getting Around later in this section) include entry to the reserve, the Apes' Den and St Michael's Cave.

The rock's most famous inhabitants are its colony of **Barbary macaques**, the only wild primates (apart from *Homo sapiens*) in Europe. Some of these hang around the **Apes' Den** near the middle cable-car station, others can often be seen at the top station or Great Siege Tunnels.

From the top cable-car station, you can see Morocco in decent weather. **St Michael's Cave**, a 20-minute downhill walk south from here, is a big natural grotto renowned for its stalagmites and stalactites. Apart from attracting tourists in droves, it's used for concerts, plays and even fashion shows. The

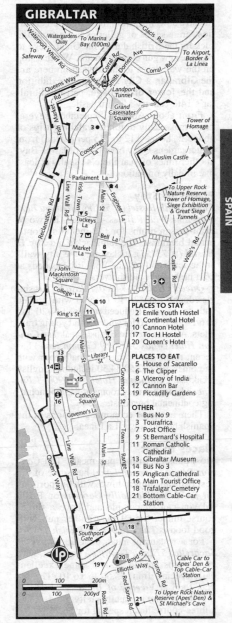

GIBRALTAR

PLACES TO STAY
2 Emile Youth Hostel
4 Continental Hotel
10 Cannon Hotel
17 Toc H Hostel
20 Queen's Hotel

PLACES TO EAT
5 House of Sacarello
6 The Clipper
8 Viceroy of India
12 Cannon Bar
19 Piccadilly Gardens

OTHER
1 Bus No 9
3 Tourafrica
7 Post Office
9 St Bernard's Hospital
11 Roman Catholic Cathedral
13 Gibraltar Museum
14 Bus No 3
15 Anglican Cathedral
16 Main Tourist Office
18 Trafalgar Cemetery
21 Bottom Cable-Car Station

Great Siege Tunnels, a 30-minute walk north (mostly downhill) from the top cable-car station, are a series of galleries hewn from the rock by the British during the Great Siege to provide new gun emplacements. Worth a stop on the way down to the town from here are the **Gibraltar, a City under Siege** exhibition and the **Tower of Homage**, part of Gibraltar's 14th-century Muslim castle.

From about April to September, several boats make daily **dolphin-watching** trips of about 2½ hours (£12 to £15 per person) from Watergardens Quay or adjacent Marina Bay; at other times of year there's usually at least one in daily operation.

Places to Stay

Emile Youth Hostel (☎ 51106, *Montagu Bastion, Line Wall Rd*) has 43 places in two to eight-person rooms for £12 including continental breakfast. The ramshackle old *Toc H Hostel* (☎ 73431), tucked into the city walls at the south end of Line Wall Rd, has beds at £6 a night and cold showers.

Queen's Hotel (☎ 74000, *1 Boyd St*) has singles/doubles at £20/30 (£36/40 with private bath or shower). Reduced rates of £14/20 and £16/24 are offered for students and young travellers. All rates include English breakfast. *Cannon Hotel* (☎/fax 51711, *9 Cannon Lane*) has decent rooms, each sharing a bathroom with one other, for £22.50/34.50 including English breakfast. *Continental Hotel* (☎ 76900, *1 Engineer Lane*) has cosy rooms at £42/55 including continental breakfast.

There are some economical options in the Spanish border town, La Línea.

Places to Eat

Most pubs do British pub meals. The *Cannon Bar* (*27 Cannon Lane*) has some of the best fish and chips in town, with big portions for £4.75. At *Piccadilly Gardens* on Rosia Rd you can sit outside and have a three-course dinner for £9.95. Another pub with good food is *The Clipper* (*78B Irish Town*).

For a restaurant meal, the chic *House of Sacarello* (*57 Irish Town*) is a good bet, with good soups around £2 and some excellent daily specials from £5.50 to £6.10. The Indian food at *Viceroy of India* (*9/11 Horse Barrack Court*) is usually pretty good. It has a three-course lunch special for £6.75.

Getting There & Away

Air GB Airways (☎ 79300, UK ☎ 0345-222111) flies daily to/from London. Return fares from London range from around £175 to £275, depending on the season. Monarch Airlines (☎ 47477, UK ☎ 08700-405040) flies daily to/from Luton, with return fares from £100 to £250. Morocco's Regional Air Lines (☎ 79300) flies Gibraltar to Casablanca most days for £104 return.

Bus There are no regular buses to Gibraltar, but La Línea bus station is only a five-minute walk from the border.

Car & Motorcycle To take a car into Gibraltar you need an insurance certificate, registration document, nationality plate and driving licence. You do *not* have to pay any fee, despite what con artists might try to tell you.

Ferry The passenger catamaran *Mons Calpe II* sails daily, except Monday and Saturday, to/from Tangier (£18/33 one way/return, 75 minutes).

There are usually two vehicle ferries a week (£18/30 one way/return per person, £40/80 per car, two hours). You can buy tickets for the catamaran at Bland Travel (☎ 77102), 81 Irish Town, and for the ferry at Tourafrica (☎ 77666), ICC Building, Main St.

Getting Around

The frequent bus Nos 3 and 9 run direct from the border into town. Few buses run after 2 pm Saturday and none on Sunday – but the 1.5km walk is quite interesting as it crosses the airport runway.

All of Gibraltar can be covered on foot, but there are other options. Weather permitting, the cable car leaves its lower station on Red Sands Rd every few minutes from 9.30 am to 5.15 pm, Monday to Saturday. The one-way/return fares are £3.65/4.90. For the Apes' Den, disembark at the middle station.

Extremadura

Extremadura, a sparsely populated tableland bordering Portugal, is far enough from the most beaten tourist trails to give you a genuine sense of exploration, something that *extremeños* themselves have a flair for. Many epic 16th-century *conquistadores* including Francisco Pizarro (who conquered the Incas) and Hernán Cortés (who did the same to the Aztecs) sprang from this land.

Trujillo and Cáceres are the two not-to-be-missed old towns, and Mérida has Spain's biggest collection of Roman ruins. A spot of hiking, or just relaxing, in the valleys of North-East Extremadura makes the perfect change from urban life. If you can, avoid June to August, when Extremadura is *uncomfortably* hot.

TRUJILLO
pop 9000
Trujillo can't be much bigger now than in 1529, when its most famous son Francisco Pizarro set off with his three brothers and a few local buddies for an expedition that culminated in the bloody conquest of the Inca empire three years later. Trujillo is blessed with a broad and fine Plaza Mayor, from which rises its remarkably preserved old town, packed with aged buildings exuding history. If you approach from the Plasencia direction you might imagine that you've driven through a time warp into the 16th century. The tourist office (☎ 927 32 26 77) is on Plaza Mayor.

Things to See
A statue of Pizarro, by American Charles Rumsey, dominates the Plaza Mayor. On the plaza's south side, the Palacio de la Conquista (closed to visitors) sports the carved images of Francisco Pizarro and the Inca princess Inés Yupanqui.

Two noble mansions you *can* visit are the 16th-century Palacio de los Duques de San Carlos, also on the Plaza Mayor (100 ptas), and Palacio de Orellana-Pizarro, through the alley in the plaza's south-west corner.

Up the hill, the Iglesia de Santa María la Mayor is an interesting hotchpotch of 13th to 16th-century styles, with some fine paintings by Fernando Gallego of the Flemish school. Higher up, the Casa-Museo de Pizarro has informative displays (in Spanish) on the lives and adventures of the Pizarro family. At the top of the hill, Trujillo's castillo is an impressive though empty structure, primarily of Moorish origin. Entry is 200 ptas for each.

Places to Stay & Eat
Camas Boni (☎ 927 32 16 04, Calle Domingo de Ramos 7) is good value with small but well-kept singles/doubles from 2000/3000 ptas, and doubles with bathroom for 4500 ptas. *Casa Roque* (☎ 927 32 23 13, Calle Domingo de Ramos 30) has rooms at 3000/3500 ptas. *Hostal Nuria* (☎ 927 32 09 07, Plaza Mayor 27) has nice rooms with bath for 3300/5500 ptas. The friendly *Hostal La Cadena* (☎ 927 32 14 63, Plaza Mayor 8) is also good, at 5500 ptas for doubles with bath.

Don't miss *Restaurante La Troya* on Plaza Mayor if you're a meat-eater. The *menú* costs 1990 ptas, but it will save you from eating much else for the next few days. Portions are gigantic and you also get a large omelette and a salad for starters, and an extra main course later on! There are great tapas here too. Elsewhere on Plaza Mayor *Cafetería Nuria* has various dishes starting at 550 ptas. *Café-Bar El Escudo* on Plaza de Santiago is also moderately priced.

Getting There & Away
The bus station (☎ 927 32 12 02) is 500m south of Plaza Mayor, on Carretera de Mérida. At least six buses run daily to/from Cáceres (390 ptas, 45 minutes), Badajoz and Madrid (2350 ptas, 2½ to four hours), and four or more to/from Mérida (1020 ptas, 1¼ hours).

CÁCERES
pop 77,768
Cáceres is larger than Trujillo and has an even bigger old town, created in the 15th and 16th centuries and so perfectly preserved that it can seem lifeless at times. The old town is worth two visits – one by day to look around and one by night to soak up the atmosphere of accumulated ages.

The tourist office (☎ 927 24 63 47) is on Plaza Mayor. Ciberjust, on Calle Diego Maria Crehuet 7, is a good Internet cafe.

Things to See
The old town is still surrounded by walls and towers raised by the Almohads in the 12th century. Entering it from Plaza Mayor, you'll see ahead the fine 15th-century Iglesia de Santa María, Cáceres' cathedral. Any time from February to September, Santa María's tower will be topped by the ungainly nests of

SPAIN

the large storks which make their homes on every worthwhile vertical protuberance in the old city.

Many of the old city's churches and imposing medieval mansions can only be admired from outside, but you *can* enter the good **Museo de Cáceres** on Plaza de Veletas, housed in a 16th-century mansion built over a 12th-century Moorish cistern *(aljibe)* the museum's prized exhibit (closed Monday, 200 ptas, free for EU citizens). Also worth a look is the **Casa-Museo Árabe Yussuf Al-Borch** at Cuesta del Marqués 4, a private house decked out with oriental and Islamic trappings to capture the feel of Moorish times (200 ptas). The **Arco del Cristo** at the bottom of this street is a Roman gate.

Places to Stay

The best area to stay is around Plaza Mayor, though it gets noisy at weekends. *Pensión Márquez* (☎ 927 24 49 60, *Calle de Gabriel y Galán 2*), just off the low end of the plaza, is a friendly place with clean rooms at 1500/3000 ptas. *Hostal Castilla* (☎ 927 24 44 04, *Calle de los Ríos Verdes 3*), one block west, has rooms for 2000/4000 ptas. *Hostal Plaza de Italia* (☎ 927 24 77 60), away from the centre at Calle Constancia 12, has clean, pleasant rooms with shower for 3500/5500 ptas.

Places to Eat

Cafetería El Puchero (*Plaza Mayor 33*) is a popular hang-out with a huge variety of eating options, from good bocadillos (around 400 ptas) and raciónes to a la carte fare. *Cafetería El Pato*, a block down the arcade, has an upstairs restaurant with good three-course *menús*, including wine, for 1200 ptas to 2000 ptas plus IVA.

Restaurante El Figón de Eustaquio (*Plaza de San Juan 12*) serves good traditional extremeño food. The three-course *menú de la casa*, with wine, is 1700 ptas plus IVA.

Getting There & Away

Bus Minimum daily services from the bus station (☎ 927 23 25 50) include at least six to Trujillo (450 ptas) and Madrid (2420 ptas, 3½ hours); five each to Mérida (675 ptas, 1¼ hours) and Plasencia; three each to Salamanca (1705 ptas, three to four hours), Zafra and

Seville (2090 ptas, four hours) and two to Badajoz.

Train Three to five trains a day run to/from Madrid (from 2385 ptas, 3½ to five hours) and Mérida (one hour) and two or three each to/from Plasencia (1¼ hours), Badajoz (two hours) and Barcelona. The single daily train to Lisbon (from 4475 ptas, six hours) leaves in the middle of the night.

MÉRIDA
pop 51,830

Once the biggest city in Roman Spain, Mérida is home to more ruins of that age than anywhere else in the country. The tourist office (☎ 924 31 53 53) is at Avenida de José Álvarez Saenz de Buruaga, by the gates to the Roman theatre. Ware Nostrum is a funky Internet cafe on Calle del Baños.

Things to See

For 800 ptas (half-price for students and EU citizens) you can get a ticket that gives you entry to the **Teatro Romano**, **Anfiteatro**, the **Casa del Anfiteatro**, the **Casa Romana del Mithraeo**, the **Alcazaba**, **Iglesia de Santa Eulalia** and the **Arqueologica de Moreria**. Entry to just the Teatro Romano and Anfiteatro is 600 ptas. The theatre was built in 15 BC and the gladiators' ring, or Anfiteatro, seven years later. Combined they could hold 20,000 spectators. Various other reminders of imperial days are scattered about town, including the **Puente Romano**, at 792m one of the longest the Romans ever built.

Places to Stay & Eat

Pensión El Arco (☎ 924 31 83 21, *Calle de Miguel de Cervantes 16*) is great value and deservedly popular with backpackers; rooms cost 1800/3500 ptas with shared bathroom. *Hostal Bueno* (☎ 924 30 29 77, *Calle Calvario 9*) is also good at 2500/4500 ptas.

Casa Benito, on Calle de San Francisco, is a great old-style wood-panelled bar and restaurant, decked with bullfighting memorabilia, serving local fare at reasonable prices.

Three good eateries line up on Calle de Felix Valverde Lillo. *Restaurante El Briz*, at No 5, does a great *montado de lomo* (pork loin sandwich) for 350 ptas and has a restaurant at the back with a *menú* for 1350 ptas.

Next door, there's the upmarket *Restaurante Nicolás* with a 2000 ptas *menú*. *Restaurante Antillano* at No 15 is popular with locals and has a *menú* for just 1200 ptas.

Getting There & Away
From the bus station (☎ 924 37 14 04) at least seven daily buses run to Badajoz (680 ptas), Seville (1550 ptas to 1590 ptas) and Madrid (from 2755 ptas), and at least four to Cáceres (675 ptas) and Trujillo (820 ptas).

At least four trains run a day to Badajoz, and two or more to Cáceres, Ciudad Real, Madrid (2945 ptas, five to six hours).

NORTH-EAST EXTREMADURA
From Plasencia, the green, almost Eden-like valleys of La Vera, Valle del Jerte and Valle del Ambroz stretch north-east into the Sierra de Gredos and its western extensions. Watered by rushing mountain streams called *gargantas*, and dotted with medieval villages, these valleys offer some excellent walking routes and attract just enough visitors to provide a good network of places to stay.

Information
The Editorial Alpina booklet *Valle del Jerte, Valle del Ambroz, La Vera* includes a 1:50,000 map of the area showing walking routes. Try to get it from a map or bookshop before you come; if not, the tourist office in Cabezuela del Valle may have copies.

There are tourist offices at Plasencia (☎ 927 42 21 59), Jaraíz de la Vera (☎ 927 17 05 87), Jarandilla de la Vera (☎ 927 56 04 60), Cabezuela del Valle (☎ 927 47 25 58) and Hervás (☎ 927 47 36 18). Most sizable villages have banks.

Things to See & Do
La Vera About halfway up the valley, **Cuacos de Yuste** has its share of narrow village streets with half-timbered houses leaning at odd angles. Up a side road, 2km north-west, is the **Monasterio de Yuste**, to which in 1557 Carlos I, once the world's most powerful man, retreated for his dying years. Guided tours of the simple royal chambers and the monastery church in Spanish are 100 ptas.

The road continues past the monastery to **Garganta la Olla**, another typically picturesque village, from where you can head

over the 1269m **Puerto del Piornal** pass into the Valle del Jerte.

Jarandilla de la Vera is a bigger village, with a 15th-century fortress-church on the main square (below the main road), and a parador occupying a castle-palace where Carlos I stayed while Yuste was being readied for him. Of the longer hikes, the Ruta de Carlos V (see the following Valle del Jerte section) is one of the most enticing. If you want to do it in reverse, ask for directions at Camping Jaranda.

Valle del Jerte This valley grows half of Spain's cherries and turns into a sea of white at blossom time in April. **Piornal**, high on the south flank, is a good base for walks along the Sierra de Tormantos. In the bottom of the valley, **Cabezuela del Valle** has a particularly medieval main street. A 35km road crosses from just north of here over the 1430m Puerto de Honduras pass to Hervás in the Valle del Ambroz. For hikers, the PR-10 trail climbs roughly parallel, to the south. From **Jerte** you can walk into the beautiful **Parque Natural de la Garganta de los Infiernos**.

Tornavacas, near the head of the valley, is the starting point of the **Ruta de Carlos V**, a 28km marked trail following the route by which Carlos I (who was also Carlos V of the Holy Roman Empire) was carried over the mountains to Jarandilla on the way to Yuste. It can be walked in one long day just as Carlos' bearers did.

Valle del Ambroz Towards the head of the valley, **Hervás**, a small pleasant town, has the best surviving 15th-century Barrio Judío (Jewish quarter) in Extremadura, where many Jews took refuge in hope of avoiding the Inquisition.

Places to Stay & Eat
There are *camping grounds* – many with fine riverside positions – in several villages including Cuacos de Yuste, Hervás, Jarandilla de la Vera and Jerte. Most are only open from March/April to September/October. There are free *zonas de acampada*, camping areas with no facilities, at Garganta la Olla and Piornal.

In Plasencia, *Hostal La Muralla* (☎ 927 41 38 74, Calle de Berrozana 6) charges from 2000/2500 ptas to 3500/4000 ptas plus IVA for a range of rooms. On the main road in Cuacos de Yuste, *Pensión Sol* (☎ 927 17 22 41) has

SPAIN

good rooms for 1900/2900 ptas, and a restaurant. In Jarandilla de la Vera, **Hostal Jaranda** (☎ 927 56 02 06, *Avenida de Soledad Vega Ortiz 101*), on the main road, has rooms with bath for 45000/7400 ptas plus IVA, and an excellent-value three-course *menú* with wine for 1200 ptas plus IVA.

In Piornal, **Pensión Los Piornos** (☎ 927 47 60 55, *Plaza de las Eras*), near the bus stop, charges 2000/4000 ptas.

In Cabezuela del Valle, the good **Hotel Aljama** (☎ 927 47 22 91, *Calle de Federico Bajo s/n*), almost touching the church across the street, has nice rooms for 3000/4900 ptas plus IVA. There are numerous places to eat and drink on nearby Calle del Hondón. **Hostal Puerto de Tornavacas** (☎ 927 19 40 97), a couple of kilometres up the N-110 from Tornavacas, is an inn-style place with rooms for 2500/4600 ptas, and a restaurant specialising in extremeño food.

Getting There & Away

Your own wheels are a big help but if you do use buses, you can walk over the mountains without worrying about how to get back to your vehicle! The following bus services run Monday to Friday, with much reduced services on weekends.

A Mirat bus from Cáceres and Plasencia to Talayuela, stopping at the villages on the C-501 in La Vera. One or two Mirat buses run from Plasencia to Garganta la Olla and Losar de la Vera. From Madrid's Estación Sur de Autobuses, Doaldi runs daily buses to La Vera.

From Plasencia, a daily bus heads for Piornal, and four a day run up the Valle del Jerte to Tornavacas.

Los Tres Pilares runs two buses between Plasencia and Hervás. Enatcar has a few services between Cáceres, Plasencia and Salamanca via the Valle del Ambroz, stopping at the Empalme de Hervás junction on the N-630, 2km from the town.

Galicia, Asturias & Cantabria

Galicia has been spared the mass tourism that has reached many other parts of Spain. Its often wild coast is indented with a series

of majestic estuaries – the Rías Altas and Rías Bajas – which hide some of the prettiest and least known beaches and coves in Spain. Inland are rolling green hills dotted with picturesque farmhouses.

In winter, Galicia can be freezing, but in summer has one of the most agreeable climates in Europe, although you must expect some rain.

The coasts of the still greener and at least as beautiful Asturias and Cantabria regions, east of Galicia, are dotted with fine sandy beaches and some picturesque villages and towns. Inland are the beautiful Picos de Europa mountains.

SANTIAGO DE COMPOSTELA
pop 87,000

This beautiful small city marks the end of the Camino de Santiago, a name given to several major medieval pilgrim routes from as far away as France, still followed today by plenty of the faithful – and plenty who just fancy a good long walk or bike ride. Thanks to its university, Santiago is a lively city almost any time, but it's at its most festive around 25 July, the Feast of Santiago (St James). Its regional tourist office (☎ 98158 40 81) at Rúa do Vilar 43 opens 10 am to 2 pm and 4 to 7 pm Monday to Friday, 11 am to 2 pm and 5 to 7 pm Saturday, and 11 am to 2 pm Sunday.

Things to See & Do

The goal of the Camino de Santiago is the **cat-edral** on magnificent **Praza do Obradoiro**. Under the main altar lies the supposed tomb of Santiago Apóstol (St James the Apostle). It's believed the saint's remains were buried here in the 1st century AD and rediscovered in 813, after which he grew into the patron saint of the Christian Reconquista, his tomb attracting streams of pilgrims from all over Western Europe. The cathedral is a superb Romanesque creation of the 11th to 13th centuries, with later decorative flourishes, and its masterpiece is the Pórtico de la Gloria inside the west facade.

Santiago's compact old town is a work of art, and a walk around the cathedral will take you through some of its most inviting squares. It's also good to stroll in the beautifully landscaped **Carballeira de Santa Susana** park

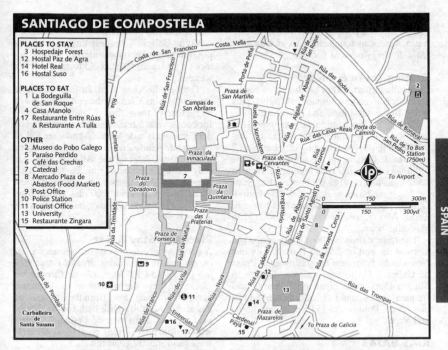

SANTIAGO DE COMPOSTELA

PLACES TO STAY
3 Hospedaje Forest
12 Hostal Paz de Agra
14 Hotel Real
16 Hostal Suso

PLACES TO EAT
1 La Bodeguilla
de San Roque
4 Casa Manolo
17 Restaurante Entre Rúas
& Restaurante A Tulla

OTHER
2 Museo do Pobo Galego
5 Paraíso Perdido
6 Café das Crechas
7 Catedral
8 Mercado Plaza de
Abastos (Food Market)
9 Post Office
10 Police Station
11 Tourist Office
13 University
15 Restaurante Zingara

SPAIN

south-west of the cathedral. Just north-east of the old city, off Porta do Camino, an impressive old convent houses the **Museo do Pobo Galego**, covering Galician life from fishing through music and crafts to traditional costume (open daily, free).

Places to Stay

Santiago is jammed with cheap pensiones, but many are full with students. A quiet central option with decent rooms is *Hospedaje Forest* (☎ 981 57 08 11, Callejón de Don Abril Ares 7) where singles/doubles start at 1600/2900 ptas. The attractive *Hostal Paz de Agra* (☎ 981 58 90 45, Rúa da Calderería 37) is a spotless old house with rooms for 2500/4000 ptas (3500/5000 ptas with private bath) – inquire at Restaurante Zingara, Rúa de Cardenal Payá. The popular little *Hostal Suso* (☎ 981 58 66 11, Rúa do Vilar 65) has comfortable modern doubles with bath for 5350 ptas. *Hotel Real* (☎ 981 56 92 90, Rúa da Calderería 49) provides good-sized singles/doubles with mod cons for 7500/10,500 ptas.

Places to Eat

Popular with readers of travel guides is *Casa Manolo (Rúa Travesa 27)*, which has a good-value set meal for 750 ptas.

A couple of medium-priced places that have some good dishes are *Restaurante Entre Rúas* and *Restaurante A Tulla*, in the tiny square on the lane Entrerúas. You should get away with having to spend around 1500 ptas.

The highly popular *La Bodeguilla de San Roque (Rúa de San Roque 13)* offers excellent, eclectic and moderately-priced fare, including enormous salads (550 ptas) and good *revoltos* (scrambled egg) concoctions.

Entertainment

For traditional Celtic music, Galician-style (sometimes live), head for *Café das Crechas (Via Sacra 3)*. *Paraíso Perdido* on the tiny square of Entrealtares is one of Santiago's oldest bars. The local drinking and dancing scene is centred in the new town, especially around Praza Roxa about 800m south-west of the cathedral. **Black** *(Avenida de Rosalía de Castro s/n)* is a popular disco. For more of a Latin American touch, look in at **Guayaba** *(Rúa de Frei Rodendo Salvado 16)*.

Getting There & Away

Lavacolla airport, 11km south-east of Santiago, caters to some international flights, plus direct flights to Madrid and Barcelona.

Santiago's bus station is just over 1km north-east of the cathedral, on Rúa de Rodriguez Viguri (connected by city bus No 10 to Praza de Galicia, on the south edge of the old town). Castromil runs regular services to La Coruña and to Vigo via Pontevedra. Enatcar has three buses to Barcelona (8½ hours). Dainco runs two to Salamanca and one to Cádiz. Alsa has one or more to Madrid (5135 ptas, nine hours).

The train station is 600m south of the old town at the end of Rúa do Horreo (city bus Nos 6 and 9 from near the station go to Praza de Galicia). Up to four trains a day run to Madrid (5900 ptas, eight to 11 hours), and frequent trains head to La Coruña (515 ptas, one hour), Pontevedra (515 ptas, one hour) and Vigo.

RÍAS BAJAS

The grandest of Galicia's estuaries are the four Rías Bajas, on its west-facing coast. From north to south these are the Ría de Muros, Ría de Arousa, Ría de Pontevedra and Ría de Vigo. All are dotted with low-key resorts, fishing villages and good beaches.

Tourist offices in the region include one at Calle del General Mola 3, Pontevedra (☎ 986 85 08 14) and another by the Estación Marítima (port) in Vigo (☎ 986 43 05 77).

Things to See & Do

On Ría de Arousa, **Isla de Arousa** is connected to the mainland by a long bridge. Its inhabitants live mainly from fishing and some of the beaches facing the mainland are very pleasant and protected, with comparatively warm water. **Cambados**, a little farther south, is a peaceful seaside town with a magnificent plaza surrounded by evocative little streets.

The small city of **Pontevedra** has managed to preserve a classic medieval centre backing on to the Río Lérez, ideal for wandering around. There are some good, tranquil beaches

around the villages of **Aldán** and **Hío**, near the south-west end of the Ría de Pontevedra.

Vigo, Galicia's biggest city, is a disappointment given its wonderful setting, although its small, tangled old town is worth a wander.

The best beaches of all in the Rías Bajas are on the **Islas Cíes** off the end of the Ría de Vigo. One of these three islands is off limits for conservation reasons. The other two, Isla del Faro and Isla de Monte Agudo, are linked by a white sandy crescent, together forming a 9km breakwater in the Atlantic. You can only visit the islands from Easter to mid-September, and numbers are strictly limited. Boats from Vigo cost 2000 ptas return; from mid-June they go every day, before that, only at weekends.

Places to Stay & Eat

A *camping ground* opens in summer on Isla de Arousa. In Cambados, **Hostal Pazos Feijoo** *(☎ 986 54 28 10, Calle de Curros Enríquez 1)*, near the waterfront in the newer part of town (one street from the bus station), has singles/doubles with bath for 4000/6000 ptas. The square Praza de Fefiñáns swarms with *restaurants* serving good local Albariño wine (and mostly good food).

In Pontevedra, **Casa Alicia** *(☎ 986 85 70 79, Avenida de Santa María 5)* and **Casa Maruja** *(☎ 986 85 49 01, Praza de Santa María 12)*, round the corner, are good. The former has homy doubles for around 3000 ptas; the latter charges 3000/4000 ptas for spotless rooms. You can eat cheaply at **O' Merlo** *(Avenida de Santa María 4)*, with an unbeatable 1000-ptas *menú*.

Hostal Stop *(☎ 986 32 94 75)* in tiny Hío has rooms for 3000/5000 ptas in summer.

In Vigo, **Hotel Pantón** *(☎ 986 22 42 70, Rúa de Lepanto 18)* has rooms with bath and TV for 3300/5900 ptas plus IVA in high summer. Old Vigo is laced with tapas bars and eateries of all descriptions. **Restaurante Fay-Bistes** *(Rúa Real 7)* has a set lunch for 1000 ptas and good tapas.

Camping is the only option to stay on the Islas Cíes. You must book (575 ptas per person and per tent, plus IVA) at the office in the *estación marítima* in Vigo. Places are limited. You can then organise a round-trip boat ticket for the days you require.

SPAIN

Getting There & Away

Pontevedra and Vigo are the area's transport hubs, with a reasonable network of local buses fanning out from them. Both are well served by buses and trains from Santiago de Compostela and La Coruña, and Vigo has services from more distant places like Madrid and Barcelona, as well as Iberia flights from those cities. Two trains a day run from Vigo to Porto in Portugal (3½ hours).

LA CORUÑA

pop 252,000

La Coruña (A Coruña in Galician) is an attractive port city with decent beaches and a wonderful seafront promenade, the Paseo Marítimo. The older part of town, the **Ciudad Vieja**, is huddled on the headland north of the port, while the most famous attraction, the **Torre de Hércules** lighthouse, originally built by the Romans (open 10 am to 6 pm or later, daily), caps the headland's northern end. The north-west side of the isthmus joining the headland to the mainland is lined with sandy **beaches**, more of which stretch along the 30km sweep of coast west of the city.

Places to Stay & Eat

Calle de Riego de Agua, a block back from the waterfront Avenida de la Marina on the southern side of the isthmus, is a good spot to find lodgings. *Pensión La Alianza (☎ 981 22 81 14, Calle de Riego de Agua 8)* charges 2200/3800 ptas for average singles/doubles. A step up is nearby *Hostal La Provinciana (☎ 981 22 04 00, Rúa Nueva 7-9)*, with rooms for 4500/6500 ptas plus IVA.

Calle de la Franja has several good places to eat. *Casa Jesusa* at No 8 offers a tasty set lunch for 1350 ptas.

Getting There & Away

Daily trains and buses run to Santiago de Compostela, Vigo, Santander, León, Madrid and Barcelona.

RÍAS ALTAS

North-east of La Coruña stretches the alternately pretty and awesome coast called the Rías Altas. This has some of the most dramatic scenery in Spain, and beaches that in good weather are every bit as inviting as those on the better known Rías Bajas. Spots to head for include the medieval towns of **Betanzos**, **Pontedeume** and **Viveiro** (all with budget accommodation), the tremendous cliffs of **Cabo Ortegal** and the **beaches** between there and Viveiro. Buses from La Coruña and Santiago de Compostela will get you into the area. After that you'll need local buses and the occasional walk or lift.

PICOS DE EUROPA

This small region straddling Asturias, Cantabria and Castilla y León has some of the finest walking country in Spain. The spectacular mountain and gorge scenery ensures a continual flow of visitors from all over Europe and beyond. The Picos begin only 20km from the coast, and are little more than 40km long and 25km wide. They comprise three limestone massifs: the eastern Macizo Ándara, with a summit of 2444m, the western Macizo El Cornión, rising to 2596m, and the central Macizo Los Urrieles, reaching 2648m.

The Picos are a national park, with its main information office (☎ 985 84 86 14) at Casa Dago, Avenida de Covadonga 43, Cangas de Onís. Plenty of information on walks is available here and at several other tourist and information offices around the Picos. Trekkers will find Lonely Planet's *Walking in Spain* useful. Good maps available locally are Adrados Ediciones' *Picos de Europa* (1:80,000) and *Picos de Europa Macizos Central y Oriental* and *Picos de Europa Macizo Occidental* (1:25,000).

The main access towns for the Picos are Cangas de Onís, Arenas de Cabrales and Potes. A good starting point for walks is **Lago Enol**, a lake 7km up from Covadonga, above Cangas de Onís in the north-west Picos. Another, though without public transport, is **Sotres** in the north-east.

Places to Stay & Eat

A few hundred metres from Lago de Enol, *Refugio Vega de Enol (☎ 985 84 85 76)* has bunks for 500 ptas and meals. You can camp free nearby. In Sotres, *Pensión La Perdiz (☎ 985 94 50 11)* charges 3100/4000 ptas for singles/doubles with private bath (less without). *Casa Cipriano (☎ 985 94 50 24)*, across the road, is a little more expensive. The good clean *Albergue Peña Castil (☎ 985 94 50 70)* offers bunks for 1100 ptas

SPAIN

to 1300 ptas and, like the Cipriano, has a restaurant.

In Espinama (for a southern approach), the attractive **Hostal Puente Deva** (☎ 942 73 66 58) has rooms for 3400/5000 ptas and a restaurant.

Cangas de Onís, Arenas de Cabrales and Potes all have a wide range of accommodation.

Getting There & Away

From the roads encircling the Picos, three main routes lead into the heart of the mountains: from Cangas de Onís to Covadonga and Lago Enol; from Arenas de Cabrales to Poncebos and Sotres; and from Potes to Espinama and Fuente Dé.

A few buses from Santander, Oviedo and León serve the three main access towns. Buses also run from Cangas de Onís to Covadonga, from Covadonga to Lago de Enol (July, August only), and (late June to mid-September) from Potes to Espinama and Fuente Dé.

SANTANDER
pop 192,000

Santander, capital of Cantabria, is a modern, cosmopolitan city with wide waterfront boulevards, leafy parks and crowded beaches. The Semana Grande fiesta in late July is a pretty wild party, but accommodation all along the north coast in the second half of July and August needs to be booked ahead.

The city tourist office (☎ 942 21 61 20) is in the harbourside Jardines de Pereda, and the regional one (☎ 942 31 07 08) is nearby at Plaza Porticada 5.

Things to See & Do

Santander's main attractions are its beaches and its bars. As you come round to the main beach, El Sardinero, on bus No 1 from the central post office, you may notice an uncanny resemblance to Bondi Beach in Australia, with surfers out in force by mid-March, despite the cold. The streets behind El Sardinero are lined with some of Spain's most expensive real estate.

Places to Stay

Camping Bellavista (☎ 942 39 15 30, Avenida del Faro s/n), out near the lighthouse about 1.5km beyond El Sardinero beach, is open all year.

The high-season rates given here fall a lot from October to May/June. **Pensión La Porticada** (☎ 942 22 78 17, Calle Méndez Núñez 6), near the train and bus stations and ferry dock, has reasonable rooms for 4000/5000 ptas. Try for one overlooking the bay. Nearby and much smarter is **Hotel México** (☎ 942 21 24 50, Calle Calderón de la Barca 3), charging 8000/12,800 ptas plus IVA.

Pensión La Corza (☎ 942 21 29 50, Calle Hernán Cortés 25) is nicely located on a pleasant square, Plaza de Pombo. Sizable, quirkily furnished rooms cost from 4750 ptas to 6000 ptas a double. Just behind Playa del Sardinero, a good-value choice is **Hostal Carlos III** (☎/fax 942 27 16 16, Avenida Reina Victoria 135), costing 6500/8500 ptas plus IVA.

Places to Eat

The older part of town has lots of highly atmospheric old mesones, which here refers to traditional wine bars also serving food. **Mesón Goya** (Calle Daóiz y Velarde 25) is typical and one of the more economical – salmon or a beef fillet *a la plancha* will cost you 800 ptas to 1000 ptas. A cavernous classic, with no name outside and more expensive, is **La Conveniente** (Calle Gómez Oreña 9). Near the latter on Plaza de Cañadio, **Bar Cañadio** serves first-class seafood and local specialities, with raciónes from 700 ptas to 1100 ptas in the bar and main dishes in its restaurant behind starting at 1500 ptas.

Near El Sardinero beach, **La Cañía** (Calle Joaquin Costa 45) has an excellent *menú* for 1400 ptas.

Entertainment

In the old town, Calle Río de la Pila – and to a marginally lesser extent Plaza de Cañadio – teem with bars of all descriptions. In summer, there's quite a good scene in El Sardinero along the main drag.

Getting There & Away

Santander is one of the major entry points to Spain, thanks to its ferry link with Plymouth, England (see Getting There & Away at the start of this chapter).

The ferry terminal and train and bus stations are all in the centre of Santander, within 300m of each other. Several daily buses head east to

Bilbao, San Sebastián (1790 ptas, 2½ hours) and Irún, and west to Oviedo (1710 ptas) and Gijón. Some stop at lesser places along the coast. Six a day go to Madrid (3300 ptas) via Burgos. Others run to Pamplona, Zaragoza, Barcelona, Salamanca and elsewhere.

Trains to Bilbao (925 ptas, 2½ hours, three daily) and Oviedo are run by FEVE, a private line which does not accept rail passes. From Oviedo FEVE continues into north-east Galicia. Trains to Madrid, Castilla y León and the rest of Galicia are run by RENFE, so rail passes are valid. To Madrid there are three trains most days (from 4300 ptas, 5½ to 8¾ hours), via Ávila.

SANTILLANA DEL MAR
pop 1030

Despite good, sandy beaches and some appealing villages along the coasts, the least missable other destination in Cantabria or Asturias is the marvellously preserved medieval village of Santillana del Mar, 30km west of Santander.

The Romanesque carvings in the cloister of the **Colegiata de Santa Julia** church are Santillana's finest works of art. There's also a **Museo de la Inquisición** (Inquisition Museum) with an alarming collection of instruments of torture and death.

Two kilometres south-west of Santillana are the world-famous **Cuevas de Altamira**, full of wonderful 14,000-year-old Stone Age animal paintings. A maximum of 20 people a day are allowed into the caves and the waiting list is three years long.

Contact the regional tourist office in Santander to find out how to join the waiting list, but for those of us who can't wait so long, a new museum at the caves, complete with full-scale replica of the caves, was due to open in 2001.

Places to Stay & Eat
Santillana has heaps of accommodation but little in the real budget range. An excellent choice is *Hospedaje Octavio* (☎ 942 81 81 99, Plaza Las Arenas 6), where charming rooms with timber-beam ceilings and private bath are 3500/5500 ptas.

Casa Cossío, about the nearest restaurant to the Colegiata, serves a good range of fare, with a *menú* for 1150 ptas.

Getting There & Away
Several daily buses call in at Santillana en route between Santander and San Vicente de la Barquera, farther west.

País Vasco, Navarra & Aragón

The Basque people have lived in Spain's País Vasco (Basque Country, or Euskadi in the Basque language), Navarra and the adjoining Pays Basque in south-western France for thousands of years. They have their own ancient language (Euskara), a distinct physical appearance, a rich culture and a proud history.

Along with this strong sense of identity has come, among a significant minority of Basques in Spain, a desire for independence. The Basque nationalist movement was born in the 19th century. During the Franco years the Basque people were brutally repressed and Euskadi ta Askatasuna (ETA), a separatist movement, began its terrorist activities. With Spain's changeover to democracy in the late 1970s, the País Vasco was granted a large degree of autonomy, but ETA has pursued its violent campaign.

ETA terrorism may be a deterrent to tourism but the País Vasco is a beautiful region. Although the Bilbao area is heavily industrialised, the region has a spectacular coastline, a green and mountainous interior and the elegance of San Sebastián and the Guggenheim museum in Bilbao itself. Another great reason to visit is to sample the delights of Basque cuisine, considered the best in Spain.

South-east of the País Vasco, the Navarra and Aragón regions reach down from the Pyrenees into drier, more southern lands. Navarra has a high Basque population and its capital is Pamplona, home of the Sanfermines festival with its running of the bulls.

The Aragón Pyrenees offer the best walking and skiing on the Spanish side of this mountain range. There are half a dozen decent ski resorts. The most spectacular walking (day hikes included) is in the Parque Nacional de Ordesa y Monte Perdido, whose main access point is the village of Torla. During Easter week and from July to September you are

SPAIN

forbidden to drive the few kilometres from Torla into the park – a shuttle bus service for a maximum 1800 people a day is provided instead (there's no limit on people walking into the park). Weatherwise the best months up there are late June to mid-September.

SAN SEBASTIÁN
pop 180,000

San Sebastián (Donostia in Basque) is a stunning city. Famed as a ritzy resort for wealthy Spaniards, it has also been a stronghold of Basque nationalist feeling since well before Franco. The surprisingly relaxed town curves round the beautiful Bahía de la Concha. Those who live here consider themselves the luckiest people in Spain, and after spending a few days on the perfect crescent-shaped beaches in preparation for the wild evenings, you may begin to understand why.

Information

The municipal tourist office (☎ 943 48 11 66) is at Boulevard Reina Regente 8 (closed Sunday afternoon). The regional tourist office (☎ 943 02 31 50) at Paseo de los Fueros 1 is open daily.

The main post office is on Calle de Urdaneta, behind the cathedral. Donosti-Net, Calle de Embeltrán 2 in the old town (*Parte Vieja*), is a good Internet cafe. Lavomatique, Calle de Iñigo 14, is a rarity in Spain – a good self-service laundrette. A full load of washing and drying costs about 1000 ptas.

Things to See

The **Playa de la Concha** and **Playa de Ondarreta** are among the most beautiful city beaches in Spain. You can reach **Isla de Santa Clara**, in the middle of the bay, by boat from the harbour. In summer, you can also swim out to rafts anchored in the bay. The Playa de la Zurriola (also known as Playa de Gros), east of the Río Urumea, is less crowded and popular with both swimmers and surfers.

San Sebástian's revamped **Aquarium** has 10 large tanks teeming with tropical fish, morays, sharks and other finned creatures. There are also exhibits on pirates, Basque explorers and related themes. It's open 10 am to 10 pm daily (to 8 pm in winter); 1100 ptas. The nearby **Museo Naval** is interesting too

but you need to read Spanish to fully appreciate the displays (200 ptas).

Museo de San Telmo, in a 16th-century monastery on Plaza de Zuloaga, has a varied collection with a heavy emphasis on Basque paintings. A highlight is the chapel whose lavish wall frescoes chronicle Basque history. Museum hours are 10.30 am to 1.30 pm and 4 to 8 pm, closed Sunday afternoon and Monday; free.

Overlooking Bahía de la Concha from the east is **Monte Urgull**, topped with a statue of Christ that enjoys sweeping views. It only takes 30 minutes to walk up – a stairway starts from Plaza de Zuloaga in the old town.

The views from the summit of Monte Igueldo are better still. You can save your legs by catching the funicular to the **Parque de Atracciones** (amusement park). At the foot of the hill, at Punta Torrepea, right in the bay, is Eduardo Chillida's abstract iron sculpture *Peine de los Vientos* (Wind Combs).

Places to Stay

As in much of northern Spain, rooms are hard to find in July and August, so arrive early or book ahead, and be aware of huge seasonal price differences. Prices given here are for peak periods.

Camping Igueldo (☎ 943 21 45 02), open year-round, is out beyond Monte Igueldo but connected to the centre by bus No 16. The HI hostel *Albergue La Sirena* (☎ 943 31 02 68, ⓔ udala-youthhostel@donostia.org, Paseo de Igueldo 25) offers bed and breakfast for 2000/2255 ptas children/adults. Curfew is midnight during the week, 2 am on weekends.

In the lively Parte Vieja, consider yourself lucky to score a room at the superfriendly *Pensión San Lorenzo* (☎ 943 42 55 16, Calle de San Lorenzo 2) whose nicely decorated doubles with bath cost 3500 ptas. Other assets include metered Internet access and kitchen use (off-season only). Also good is *Pensión Loinaz* (☎ 943 42 67 14, Calle de San Lorenzo 17), which has updated bathrooms and charges 4000/5500 ptas singles/doubles.

Pensión Aussie (☎ 943 42 28 74, Calle San Jerónimo 23) works pretty much like a hostel. Beds in two to four-bed rooms, some quite nicely decorated, are 2000 ptas. It's popular with backpackers, as is *Pensión San*

SPAIN

SAN SEBASTIÁN (DONOSTIA)

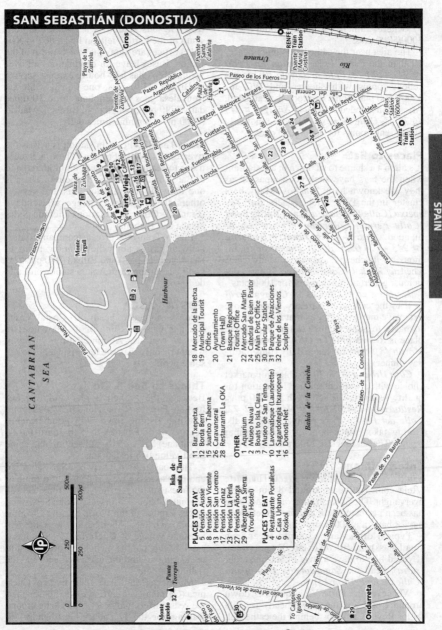

PLACES TO STAY
5 Pensión Aussie
8 Pensión San Vicente
13 Pensión San Lorenzo
17 Pensión Loinaz
23 Pensión La Perla
27 Pensión Añorga
29 Albergue La Sirena
   (Youth Hostel)

PLACES TO EAT
4 Restaurante Portaletas
6 Casa Urbano
9 Koskol

11 Bar Txepetxa
12 Borda Berri
15 Juantxo Taberna
26 Caravanserai
28 Restaurante La OKA

OTHER
1 Aquarium
2 Museo Naval
3 Boats to Isla Clara
7 Museo de San Telmo
10 Lavomatique (Laundrette)
14 Sagardotegia Itxaropena
16 Donosti-Net

18 Mercado de la Bretxa
19 Municipal Tourist
   Office
20 Ayuntamiento
   (Town Hall)
21 Basque Regional
   Tourist Office
22 Mercado San Martín
24 Catedral de Buen Pastor
25 Main Post Office
30 Funicular Station
31 Parque de Atracciones
32 Peine de los Vientos
   Sculpture

euro currency converter 100 ptas = €0.60

Vicente (☎ 943 42 29 77, Calle San Vicente 7) where rather bare-bone rooms cost 3000/5000 ptas.

The area near the cathedral is more peaceful than the Parte Vieja. *Pensión La Perla* (☎ 943 42 81 23, Calle de Loyola 10) has excellent rooms with shower and WC for 3500/5500 ptas; some overlook the cathedral. Also recommended is *Pensión Añorga* (☎ 943 46 79 45, Calle de Easo 12) whose motherly owner rents rooms for 4000/5000 ptas.

Places to Eat

It's almost a shame to sit down in a restaurant when the bars have such good tapas, or as they are known here, *pinchos*. Many bars cluster in the Parte Vieja, where *Bar Txepetxa* (Calle Pescadería 5) and *Borda Berri* (Calle Fermín Calbetrón 12) are recommended. Also here is *Juantxo Taberna* (☎ 943 42 74 05, Calle de Embeltrán 6), famous for its cheap, super-sized sandwiches. The tiny *Koskol* (Calle de Iñigo 5) has a delicious, generous lunch *menú* for 1000 ptas.

A young crowd flocks to *Caravanserai* next to the cathedral, a trendy bistro whose extensive menu runs the gamut from burgers to pasta to sandwiches. A fun vegetarian place is *Restaurante La OKA* (Calle de San Martín 43), open for lunch daily (plus Saturday dinner).

Casa Urbano at No 17 is a more upmarket choice with a well-entrenched reputation for quality seafood. The set lunch is 3000 ptas. *Restaurante Portaletas* (☎ 943 42 42 72, Calle del Puerto 8) is popular with locals. Dining takes place beneath heavy timber beams. The set lunch is 1500 ptas.

Entertainment

San Sebastián's nightlife is great. The Parte Vieja comes alive at around 8 pm nearly every night. The Spanish habit of bar-hopping has been perfected here and one street alone has 28 bars in a 300m stretch!

Typical drinks are a zurrito (beer in a small glass) and *txacolí* (a tart Basque wine). If you'd like to have a swig of Basque cider (*sidra*), head for *Sagardotegia Itxaropena* (Calle de Embeltran 16).

Whenever the Parte Vieja quietens down around 1 or 2 am, the crowd heads to Calle de los Reyes Católicos behind the cathedral.

Getting There & Away

Bus The bus station is a 20-minute walk south of the Parte Vieja on Plaza de Pío XII; ticket offices are along the streets north of the station. Buses leave for destinations all over Spain. PESA has half-hourly express service to Bilbao (1120 ptas, one hour), while La Roncalesa goes to Pamplona up to 10 times daily (790 ptas, two hours). Buses to Madrid (3800 ptas) run nine times daily.

Train The RENFE train station is across the river on Paseo de Francia. There are daily trains to Madrid (6400 ptas, eight hours) and to Barcelona (5000 ptas, 8¼ hours). There is one daily direct train to Paris and several others that require a change at Hendaye (France). Other destinations include Salamanca and Lisbon.

Eusko Tren is a private company (international passes not valid) running trains to Hendaye (115 ptas) and Bilbao (900 ptas, 2¾ hours) departing from Amara station on Calle de Easo.

COSTA VASCA

Spain's ruggedly beautiful Costa Vasca (Basque Coast) is one of its least touristy coastal regions. A combination of rainy weather, chilly seas and terrorism tends to put some people off.

Things to See & Do

Between the French border and San Sebastián, **Fuenterrabia** (Hondarribia) is a picturesque fishing town with good beaches nearby, while **Pasajes de San Juan** (Pasaia Donibane) has a pretty old section and some good-value fish restaurants.

The coastal stretch between San Sebastián and Bilbao to the west is considered some of the finest **surfing** territory in Europe. **Zarauz** (Zarautz), about 15km west of San Sebastián, stages a round of the World Surfing Championship each September. Farther west, the picturesque village of **Guetaria** (Getaria) has a small beach, but the main attraction is just in wandering around the narrow streets and the fishing harbour.

Mundaca (Mundaka), 12km north of Guernica (Gernika), is a surfing town. For much of the year, surfers and beach bums hang around waiting for the legendary 'left-hander' to break. When it does, it's one of the longest you'll ever see! The Mundaka Surf Shop rents gear and also gives surfing lessons. Food and accommodation are hopelessly overpriced in this town, even in the off-season. Your best bet is *Camping Portuondo* (☎/fax 94 687 77 01), about 1km south of town, which has lovely terraced grounds and also rents bungalows.

Getting Around

The coastal road is best explored by car. If you don't have your own transport, there are buses from San Sebastián to Zarauz and Guetaria, and from Bilbao to Guernica. From Guernica you can take a bus to Bermeo which will drop you in Mundaca. Eusko Tren from Bilbao and San Sebástian also serves a few coastal towns.

BILBAO
pop 360,000

Once the industrial heart of the north, Bilbao has spruced itself up and, since 1997, created for itself a tourist gold mine – the US$100 million **Museo Guggenheim de Arte Contemporáneo**. Designed by US architect Frank Gehry, this fantastical, swirling structure was inspired in part by the anatomy of a fish and the hull of a boat – both allusions to Bilbao's past and present economy. The interior makes wonderful use of space, with light pouring in through a central glass atrium of cathedral proportions. The permanent exhibit of modern and contemporary art is still small but choice with artists like Picasso, Mondrian and Kandinsky among those represented. All the other galleries are used for high-calibre temporary exhibits.

Museum hours are 10 am to 8 pm Tuesday to Sunday (daily in July and August); 1200/600 ptas. Arrive early and ask about free guided English-language tours.

Some 300m up the street, excellent **Museo de Bellas Artes** has works by El Greco, Velázquez and Goya, as well as 20th-century masters like Gauguin. Basque artists are shown as well (closed Monday; 600/300 ptas).

The main tourist office (☎ 94 479 57 60) is on Paseo Arenal 1 and there's also an information kiosk by the Guggenheim (closed Monday). For Internet access, go to El Señor de la Red, Calle Rodríguez Arias 69.

Places to Stay & Eat

Albergue Bilbao Aterpetxea (☎ 94 427 00 54, e aterpe@albergue.bilbao.net, Carretera Basurto-Kastrexana Errep 70) is a 10-minute direct bus ride (No 58) away from the centre and charges from 1900 ptas to 2500 ptas, including breakfast.

Pensión Méndez (☎ 94 416 03 64, Calle de Santa María 13) is central but can be a bit noisy. Singles/doubles cost 3000/4000 ptas. *Hostal La Estrella* (☎ 94 416 40 66, Calle de María Múñoz 6) is a charming, brightly painted place where rooms with washbasin cost 2700/4800 ptas and those with bath are 4000/6500 ptas.

Las Siete Calles (Seven Streets), the nucleus of Bilbao's old town, brims with tapas bars and restaurants. *Rio-Oja (Calle de Perro 6)* is among the many places for cheap food and drink. *Cafe Boulevard (Calle de Arenal 3)*, Bilbao's oldest coffeehouse (1871) nearby, has breakfasts, full meals and tapas at wallet-friendly prices. *Café Iruña (Calle de Colón Larreátegui)* is Bilbao's most celebrated cafe.

Getting There & Away

Bus Buses to Madrid (3400 ptas) and Barcelona (4850 ptas) depart from Calle de la Autonomía 17. Most other buses use the huge Termibus lot in the south-west corner of town (metro: San Mamés).

Train Four daily trains to Madrid (5800 ptas, 6¼ hours) and two to Barcelona (4900 ptas, nine hours) leave from RENFE's central Abando train station. The Eusko Tren station with regional services is about 1km south of the centre.

Boat P&O ferries leave for Portsmouth from Santurtzi, about 14km north-west of Bilbao's city centre. The voyage takes about 35 hours from England and 29 hours the other way.

PAMPLONA
pop 182,500

The madcap festivities of Sanfermines in Pamplona (Iruñea in Basque) run from 6-14 July and are characterised by nonstop partying and, of course, the running of the bulls. The safest place to watch the *encierro* (running) is on TV. If this is far too tame for you, see if you can sweet-talk your way on to a

SPAIN

balcony in one of the streets where the bulls run. The bulls are let out at 8 am, but if you want to get a good vantage point you will have to be there around 6 am.

If you visit at any other time of year, you'll find a pleasant and modern city, with lovely parks and gardens, and a compact old town with a lively bar and restaurant scene.

The tourist office (☎ 948 22 07 41) is on Plaza San Francisco and open weekdays only (plus Saturday morning in July and August).

Places to Stay & Eat

The nearest camping ground is *Camping Ezcaba* (☎ 948 33 03 15), 7km north of the city. It fills up a few days before Sanfermines. A bus service (direction Arre/Oricain) runs four times daily from Calle de Teovaldos (near the bullring).

For Sanfermines you need to book well in advance (and pay as much as triple the regular rates). During the festival, beds are also available in *casas particulares* (private houses) – check with the tourist office or haggle with the locals at the bus and train stations. Otherwise, join the many who sleep in one of the parks, plazas or shopping malls. There's a left-luggage office (*consigna*) at the bus station.

Pamplona's old centre is filled with cheap pensions renting basic singles/doubles for around 2000/3500 ptas. Contenders on the Calle San Nicolás include *Fonda Aragonesa* (☎ 948 22 34 28) at No 32, *Habitaciones San Nicolás* (☎ 948 22 13 19) at No 13 and *Habitaciones Otano* (☎ 948 22 50 95) at No 5. Near the tourist office, *Camas Escaray Lozano* (☎ 948 22 78 25, *Calle Nueva 24*) has probably the nicest rooms in this range. Right by the indoor market and next to the bull running route is *Habitaciones Redin* (☎ 948 22 21 82, *Calle de Mercado 5*).

Calle de San Nicolás is packed with tapas bars, with *Baserri* at No 32 offering the best quality. Almost as good is *Otano* (☎ 948 22 26 38) across the street.

Bar Anaitasuna (*Calle de San Gregorio 58*) has uncluttered, modern decor and is busy from breakfast to midnight. The set lunch costs 1600 ptas, platos combinados around 1000 ptas.

Getting There & Away

The bus station is on Avenida de Yangüas y Miranda, a five-minute walk south of the old town. There are 10 buses daily to San Sebastián (790 ptas) and eight to Bilbao (1580 ptas). Four daily head for Madrid (3220 ptas) and two to Barcelona (2190 ptas).

Pamplona is on the San Sebastián-Zaragoza railway line, but the station is awkwardly situated north of town. If you arrive this way, catch bus No 9 to the centre.

ZARAGOZA

pop 603,000

Zaragoza, capital of Aragón and home to half its 1.2 million people, is often said to be the most Spanish city of all. Once an important Roman city, under the name Caesaraugusta, and later a Muslim centre for four centuries, it is today primarily a hub of industry and commerce, but with a lively and interesting old heart on the south side of the Río Ebro.

The city tourist office (☎ 976 20 12 00), in a surreal-looking glass cube on Plaza del Pilar, opens 10 am to 8 pm daily.

Things to See

Zaragoza's focus is the vast 500m-long main square, **Plaza de Nuestra Señora del Pilar** (Plaza del Pilar for short). Dominating the north side is the **Basílica de Nuestra Señora del Pilar**, a 17th-century church of epic proportions. People flock to the church's Capilla Santa to kiss a piece of marble pillar believed to have been left by the Virgin Mary when she appeared to Santiago (St James) in a vision here in AD 40.

At the south-east end of the plaza is **La Seo**, Zaragoza's brooding 12th to 16th-century cathedral. Its north-west facade is a mudéjar masterpiece. The inside, reopened in 1998 after 18 years of restoration, features an impressive 15th-century main altarpiece in coloured alabaster.

The odd trapezoid structure in front of La Seo is the outside of a remarkable museum housing the **Roman forum**. Well below modern ground level you can visit the remains of shops, porticos and a great sewerage system, all brought to life by an audiovisual show. The forum is open 10 am to 2 pm and 5 to 8 pm Tuesday to Saturday, 10 am to 2 pm Sunday (300 ptas, students 200 ptas, over 65s free).

SPAIN

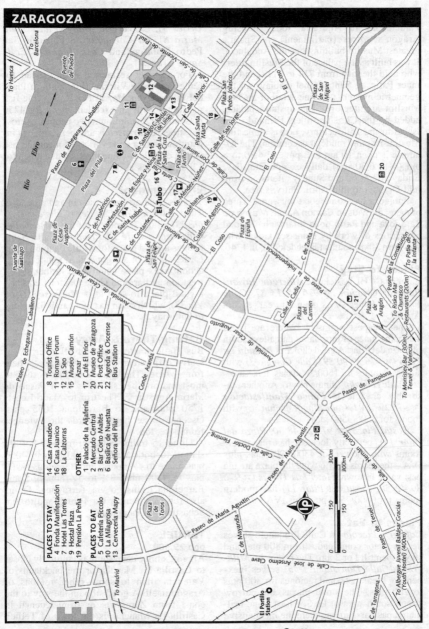

ZARAGOZA

SPAIN

PLACES TO STAY
4 Fonda Manifestación
7 Hotel Las Torres
9 Hostal Plaza
19 Pensión La Peña

PLACES TO EAT
5 Cafetería Piccolo
10 La Milagrosa
13 Cervecería Mapy

14 Casa Amadeo
16 Casa Juanico
18 La Calzorras

OTHER
1 Palacio de la Aljafería
2 Mercado Central
3 Bar Corto Maltés
6 Basílica de Nuestra Señora del Pilar

8 Tourist Office
11 Roman Forum
12 La Seo
15 Museo Camón Aznar
17 Café El Prior
20 Museo de Zaragoza
21 Post Office
22 Agreda & Oscense Bus Station

euro currency converter 100 ptas = €0.60

A little over 1km west of the plaza, the **Palacio de la Aljafería**, today housing Aragón's *cortes* (parliament), is Spain's greatest Muslim building outside Andalucía. It was built as the palace of the Muslim rulers who held the city from 714 to 1118, and the inner Patio de Santa Isabel displays all the geometric mastery and fine detail of the best Muslim architecture. The upstairs palace, added by the Christian rulers Fernando and Isabel in the 15th century, boasts some fine Muslim-inspired mudéjar decoration. The Aljafería is open 10 am to 2 pm and 4.30 to 8 pm (4 to 6.30 pm) daily except Thursday, Friday afternoon and Sunday afternoon from mid-October to mid-April. Entry is free.

Zaragoza has some good museums. Three of them, the **Museo Camón Aznar**, **Museo de Zaragoza** and **Patio de la Infanta**, have good collections of work by Francisco Goya, who was born 30km south at Fuendetodos, in 1746.

Places to Stay

Zaragoza's HI hostel, the *Albergue Juvenil Baltasar Gracián* (☎ 976 55 13 87, *Calle Franco y López 4*), is open all year, except August.

The cheapest rooms elsewhere are in El Tubo, the maze of busy lanes and alleys south of Plaza del Pilar. A good choice is *Pensión La Peña* (☎ 976 29 90 89, *Calle Cinegio 3*) with singles/doubles for 1500/3000 ptas. It has a decent little *comedor* (dining room). Another reasonable cheapie is *Fonda Manifestación* (☎ 976 29 58 21, *Calle Manifestación 36*) with rooms for 2500/3500 ptas.

Hostal Plaza (☎ 976 29 48 30, *Plaza del Pilar 14*), perfectly located, has reasonable rooms with shower for 4300/4900 ptas plus IVA – the rooms overlooking the plaza are the best value in town. *Hotel Las Torres* (☎ 976 39 42 50, *Plaza del Pilar 11*) has modern rooms for 6000/7500 ptas plus IVA.

Places to Eat

Cafetería Piccolo on Calle Prudencio serves decent platos combinados from 800 ptas and stays open till 1 or 2 am. The bright *La Milagrosa* (*Calle Don Jaime I 43*) serves inexpensive breakfasts, and raciónes for 300 ptas to 700 ptas. The small plazas and narrow streets south-west of La Seo host some brilliant tapas bars, among them the inexpensive

seafood spot **Casa Amadeo** (*Calle Jordán de Urries 3*), **Cervecería Mapy** (*Plaza Santa Marta 8*), **La Calzorras** on Plaza de San Pedro Nolasco and **Casa Juanico** (*Calle Santa Cruz 21*).

For classier restaurant eating, head for Calle Francisco Vitoria, 1km south of Plaza del Pilar. *Risko Mar* at No 16 is a fine fish restaurant with an excellent *menú* for 4250 ptas plus IVA (minimum two people). Across the street, *Churrasco* is another Zaragoza institution, with a wide variety of meat and fish and an excellent-value three-course lunch for 1300 ptas plus IVA.

Entertainment

There's no shortage of bars in and around El Tubo. At *Bar Corto Maltés* (*Calle del Temple 23*) all the barmen sport the *corto maltés* (sideburns). *Café El Prior* on Calle Santa Cruz is a good place for a little dancing in the earlier stages of a night out. Much of the bar action takes place about 1km farther southwest, on and around Calle Doctor Cerrada – a good place to start at is *Morrissey* (*Gran Vía 33*), which often has live bands Thursday to Saturday.

Getting There & Away

Bus stations are scattered all over town; tourist offices can tell you what goes where from where. The Agreda company runs to most major Spanish cities from Paseo de María Agustín 7. The trip to Madrid costs 1750 ptas and to Barcelona 1655 ptas. Oscense buses head towards the Pyrenees from here, too.

Up to 15 trains daily run from El Portillo station to both Madrid (3100 ptas to 4000 ptas, three to 4½ hours) and Barcelona (2900 ptas to 4100 ptas, 3½ to 5½ hours). Some Barcelona trains go via Tarragona. Trains also run to Valencia via Teruel, and to San Sebastián via Pamplona.

TERUEL
pop 29,300

Aragón's hilly deep south is culturally closer to Castilla-La Mancha or the backlands of Valencia than to some other regions of Aragón itself. A good stop on the way to the coast from Zaragoza, or from Cuenca in Castilla-La Mancha, is the town of Teruel, which has a flavour all its own thanks to four centuries of Muslim domination in the Middle Ages and some remarkable mudéjar architecture dating from after its capture by the Christians in 1171.

The tourist office (☎ 978 60 22 79) is at Calle Tomás Nogués 1.

Things to See
Teruel has four magnificent mudéjar towers, on the cathedral of **Santa María** (12th and 13th centuries) and the churches of **San Salvador** (13th century), **San Martín** and **San Pedro** (both 14th century). These, and the painted ceiling inside Santa María, are among Spain's best mudéjar architecture and artisanry. Note the complicated brickwork and colourful tiles on the towers, so typical of the style. The **Museo Provincial de Teruel** on Plaza Padre Polanco is well worth a visit, mainly for its fascinating archaeological section going back to *Homo erectus*.

Places to Stay & Eat
Fonda del Tozal (☎ 978 60 10 22, Calle del Rincón 5) is great value. It's an amazing rickety old house run by a friendly family, and most of the rooms have cast-iron beds, enamelled chamber pots and exposed ceiling beams. Singles/doubles cost 1500/3000 ptas. In winter, you might prefer *Hostal Aragón* (*☎ 978 60 13 87, Calle de Santa María 4*), which is also charming but has mod cons such as heating. Rooms are 2150/3200 ptas, or 3200/4860 ptas with private bath, all plus IVA. Both places are just a couple of minutes walk from the cathedral.

Teruel is famed for its ham. If you can't fit a whole leg of it in your backpack, at least sample a *tostada con jamón*, with tomato and olive oil. One of the best places for hamming up is *La Taberna de Rokelin (Calle de Tozal 33)*, a narrow bar with a beautiful rack of smoked pig hocks.

Getting There & Away
The bus station is on Ronda de Ambeles. Daily buses head to Barcelona (6½ hours), Cuenca (2¾ hours), Valencia (two hours) and Madrid (2415 ptas, 4½ hours).

By rail, Teruel is about midway between Valencia and Zaragoza, with three trains a day to both places.

Tunisia

Despite being the smallest country in North Africa, Tunisia boasts a rich cultural and social heritage – Phoenician, Roman, Byzantine, Arab, Ottoman and French empires have all come and gone in this part of the world.

Facts about Tunisia

HISTORY

Archaeological finds in the oasis towns of the south indicate that humans have lived in Tunisia for more than 200,000 years, but little is known about the country's history prior to the arrival of the Phoenicians towards the end of the second millennium BC.

The Tunisia they found was inhabited by the Berbers, a mixed-race people, the result of successive waves of immigration over the millennia; from the Levant, from southern Europe and from sub-Saharan Africa. Despite their diverse origins, they had developed a uniform language and culture right across the western half of North Africa. The Berbers were divided into a number of loose tribal confederations including the Numidians, who lived a settled existence in the fertile north of Tunisia.

The Phoenicians (from Tyre in modern Lebanon) appeared on the scene around 1100BC, establishing a series of trading posts across North Africa. They included Utica (Utique), Hippo Diarrhytus (Bizerte) and Thrabaka (Tabarka).

These early settlements found themselves playing second fiddle following the establishment of Carthage (just north of the modern capital, Tunis) at the end of the 9th century BC. Carthage quickly established itself as the leader of the western Phoenician world. While Tyre suffered at the hands of the Assyrians in the 7th and 6th centuries BC, Carthage went from strength to strength. By the end of 6th century BC, it had become the main power in the Western Mediterranean. It controlled a stretch of the North African coast from Tripolitania (western Libya) to the Atlantic and had established colonies in the Balearic Islands, Corsica, Malta, Sardinia and Sicily.

Its wealth derived from its control of trade, enforced by a powerful navy. During the 5th and 4th centuries BC, Carthage turned its attentions to expanding its empire in Africa, carving out a territory that ran from Tabarka in the north-west to Sfax in the south-east. These new lands provided both a healthy agricultural surplus for trade, and troops for Carthage's armies.

Its regional primacy brought it into inevitable conflict with the emerging Roman empire. The two fought each other almost to a standstill in the course of the 128-year Punic Wars, which began in 264 BC. Carthage's legendary general, Hannibal, appeared to

TUNISIA

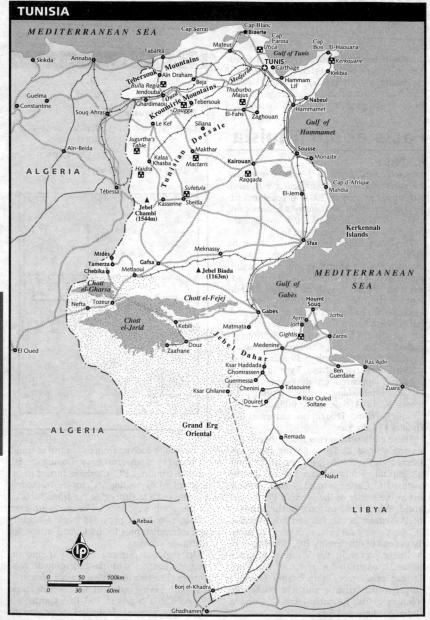

TUNISIA

MEDITERRANEAN SEA

Cap Serrat

Cap Blanc
Bizerte
Cap Farina
Cap Bon
El-Haouaria

Skikda
Annaba

Tabarka
Mateur
Utica
Gulf of Tunis
Kerkouane
Kelibia

Tebersouk Mountains
Aïn Draham
Beja
Medjerda
TUNIS
Carthage
Hammam Lif

Guelma
Constantine

Bulla Regia
Jendouba
Ghardimaou
Oued
Dougga
Thuburbo Majus
Nabeul
Hammamet

Souq Ahras
Kroumirie Mountains
Tebersouk
El-Fahs
Zaghouan

Le Kef
Siliana
Dorsale
Gulf of Hammamet

Aïn-Beida
Jugurtha's Table
Makthar

ALGERIA
Kalaa Khasba
Mactaris
Kairouan
Sousse
Monastir

Haidra
Tunisian
Raqqada
Cap d'Afrique
Mahdia

Tébessa
Sufetula
Sbeitla
El-Jem

Jebel Chambi (1544m)
Kasserine

Kerkennah Islands

Meknassy
Sfax

Midès
Tamerza
Chebika
Gafsa
Metlaoui
Jebel Biada (1163m)

MEDITERRANEAN SEA

Chott el-Gharsa
Chott el-Fejej
Gulf of Gabès
Houmt Souq

Nefta
Tozeur
Ajim
Jorf
Jerba

El Oued
Chott el-Jerid
Kebili
Matmata
Gabès
Gightis
Zarzis

Douz
Zaafrane
Medenine
Ras Ajdir

Jebel Dahar
Ksar Haddada
Ghomrassen
Ben Guerdane
Zuara

Guermessa
Chenini
Tataouine

Ksar Ghilane
Douiret
Ksar Ouled Soltane

ALGERIA
Grand Erg Oriental
Remada

LIBYA

Rebaa
Nalut

0   50   100km
0   30   60mi

Borj el-Khadra

Ghadhames

TUNISIA

have brought the Romans to their knees after his invasion of Italy in 216 BC, but the wars ended in victory for Rome. The Romans showed no mercy after the fall of Carthage in 146 BC. The city was razed and the population sold into slavery.

Carthage was rebuilt as a Roman city and it became the capital of the province of Africa, an area roughly corresponding to modern Tunisia. Africa's main attraction for the Romans was the grain-growing plains of the Medjerda valley, west of Carthage, which became known as the bread basket of Rome. It went on to become one of the wealthiest provinces in the empire, experiencing a golden age during the 2nd and 3rd centuries when wealthy citizens spent their money on construction projects like the temples of Dougga and the colosseum of El-Jem – two of modern Tunisia's best known landmarks.

The Vandals captured Carthage in 439 AD and made it the capital of their North African empire until they were ousted by the Byzantines in 533. The Byzantines never managed more than a shaky foothold, and put up little resistance when the Arabs arrived from the east in 670, ruling from the holy city of Kairouan, 150km south of Carthage. They proved to be the most influential of conquerors, introducing both Islam and the social structure which remains the basis of Tunisian life today.

After the political fragmentation of the Arab empire, Tunisia became the eastern flank of a Moroccan empire belonging to the group of Islamic Berbers known as the Almohads. The Moroccans appointed the Hafsid family as governors and they ruled, eventually as an independent monarchy, from 1207 until 1574 – a period of stability and prosperity.

The Hafsids were eventually ousted by the Ottoman Turks and Tunisia came to be ruled by a local elite of Turkish janissaries (the professional elite of the Ottoman armies). By the 18th century, this elite had merged with the local populace and produced its own national monarchy, the Husseinid beys.

After the French arrived in Algeria in the 19th century, the beys took care to avoid giving them any reason to attack. They managed to delay colonisation for some years by outlawing piracy, westernising the administration and, in 1857, adopting a constitution. However,

failure to repay foreign loans finally gave the French an excuse to invade in 1881. They established a protectorate, allowing the bey to remain head of state but transferring all effective powers to the hands of a French resident-general who ruled from the imposing French Embassy compound in Tunis. The French spent the next 50 years endeavouring to transform Tunisia into a European-style nation.

By the 1930s, colonial rule was coming under threat from the Néo-Destour movement for national liberation, led by Habib Bourguiba, a Sorbonne-educated lawyer. The French banned the movement and jailed Bourguiba. The movement flourished briefly during the German occupation of Tunis in WWII when Bourguiba was released and the beys appointed ministers from the Néo-Destour movement. This came to an end with the Allied victory in North Africa, and Bourguiba went into exile. Bourguiba orchestrated two years of guerrilla warfare against the French from Egypt, eventually forcing the French to grant autonomy in 1955. Bourguiba returned to head the new government, and Tunisia was granted independence a year later.

In 1957, the bey was deposed and Bourguiba became the first president of the new republic. In 1975, the National Assembly made him president for life. However, as the 1980s progressed, Bourguiba lost touch with his people and became isolated from the rest of the Arab world. In November 1987, the Interior Minister, Zine el-Abidine ben Ali, orchestrated Bourguiba's downfall and was installed as president. Ben Ali confirmed his hold on power at elections in 1989, 1994 and 1999. Despite criticism of his record in dealing with Islamic groups, Tunisia remains one of the most stable and moderate Arab countries. It has developed close ties with both the USA and Germany, which supply the bulk of its foreign aid.

GEOGRAPHY

Tunisia occupies an area of about 164,150 sq km, bordered by Algeria to the west, Libya to the south-east, and the Mediterranean to the east and north. The mountainous northern third of the country is dominated by the eastern extensions of the Atlas Mountains.

The north coast is Tunisia's green belt, with a fertile coastal plain backed by the

TUNISIA

densely forested Kroumirie Mountains. The country's main mountain range is the rugged Tunisian Dorsale, farther south. It runs from Kasserine in the west and peters out into Cap Bon in the east, and includes the country's highest peak, Jebel Chambi (1544m). Between these ranges lies the fertile Medjerda Valley, fed by the Oued Medjerda, the country's only permanent river. South of the Dorsale, a high plain falls away to a series of salt lakes (*chotts*) and then to a sandy desert on the edge of the Sahara known as the Grand Erg Oriental.

The east coast is remarkable for the vast areas under olive cultivation, particularly around Sfax.

CLIMATE

Northern Tunisia has a typical Mediterranean climate, with hot, dry summers and mild, wet winters. The farther south you go, the hotter and drier it gets. Some Saharan areas go without rain for years.

GOVERNMENT & POLITICS

The republic of Tunisia is governed by a president and a chamber of deputies of 163 members. Political reforms since the ousting of Bourguiba in 1987 have legalised some opposition parties, although they hold only a token number of seats. President Ben Ali claimed 99% of the vote at the presidential elections in October 1999.

ECONOMY

Tunisia's oil is running out fast in spite of new finds in the Snoussi area, west of Mahdia. The economy relies heavily on tourism to bridge the gap. Leather and textiles are the biggest income earners, followed by phosphates, olive oil, fertilisers and chemicals. Food, raw materials and capital goods are the chief imports.

The main problem is unemployment, estimated at between 15% and 20%. Living standards, however, are high compared to other developing countries.

POPULATION & PEOPLE

Tunisia has an estimated population of almost nine million, although no census has been taken since 1984. Most people are of Arab/Berber stock. The original Berbers make up only 1% of the population and are confined mainly to the south of the country. Before the creation of Israel, Tunisia had a Jewish population of around 150,000. Only 2000 remain, mainly in Tunis and on Jerba.

SOCIETY & CONDUCT

Tunisia is easy-going by Muslim standards, especially in Tunis and the major tourist areas. You'll find many western trappings, such as fast food, pop music and women dressed in the latest European fashions. However, traditional life has changed little in rural areas, where the mosque, the *hammam* (bathhouse) and the cafe remain the focal points of life.

You can avoid problems by erring on the side of modesty in what you wear. Women are advised to keep shoulders and upper arms covered and to opt for long skirts or trousers, while men should avoid shorts – which are looked on as underwear – outside resort areas.

Thanks largely to the efforts of their secular, socialist, former president, Habib Bourguiba, conditions for women in Tunisia are better than just about anywhere in the Islamic world – legally, at any rate. His 1956 Personal Status Code banned polygamy and ended divorce by renunciation. He called the *hijab* (veil) an 'odious rag', and banned it from schools as part of a campaign to phase out a garment he regarded as demeaning. He didn't quite succeed, although it is very unusual to find a woman under 30 wearing one. You will encounter some interesting mother-daughter combinations wandering around: mother wrapped in hijab, and daughter adorned in the latest western fashions.

Women make up about 20% of the paid workforce.

Always ask before taking photographs of people. Although Tunisia is a relatively liberal country, photographing women is still a no-no in parts of the country. Photographing anything to do with the military or police is forbidden – and they mean it.

ARTS

Artistic activity is heavily focused on Tunis, which has a large number of galleries – these are listed on the inside back page of the *Tunisia News*.

Tunisia has long been a popular location for international film-makers. Major films shot in Tunisia include *The Life of Brian, The English Patient, Star Wars* and *Star Wars IV*.

RELIGION
Islam is the state religion and 99.75% of the population are Sunni Muslims. There are about 20,000 Roman Catholics and 2000 Jews.

Ramadan
Ramadan is the ninth month of the Muslim calendar, when all Muslims must abstain from eating, drinking, smoking and having sex between dawn and dusk. It commemorates the month when the Koran was revealed to Mohammed.

For the traveller it can be an interesting, though frustrating, time to travel. During the day it's often difficult to find a restaurant open, although the big tourist hotels usually function normally. Be discreet about where you drink and smoke – don't do it openly during the day. When the sun goes down, things get really busy, and restaurants and shops stay open late. It's a great contrast to the normal routine, when very little happens in towns after about 9 pm.

LANGUAGE
Tunisia is virtually bilingual. Arabic is the language of education and government, but almost everyone speaks some French. You are unlikely to come across many English, German or Italian-speakers outside the main tourist centres. Tunisian Arabic is essentially the same as Moroccan Arabic (see the Language Guide at the back of the book for pronunciation guidelines and useful words and phrases).

Facts for the Visitor

HIGHLIGHTS
Most of the highlights are in the south. The oasis towns of Tozeur and Nefta are full of surprises – the *palmeraie* (palm groves) are veritable gardens of Eden. Both towns are also famous for the intricate brickwork of their traditional quarters.

Other highlights include staying in the fine old *funduqs* (caravanserai) of Houmt Souq; early morning visits to the *ksour* (traditional Berber fortified granary) around Tataouine; and camel trekking in the desert around Douz. Three Roman sites stand out among the crowd: El-Jem, Dougga and Bulla Regia.

SUGGESTED ITINERARIES
One Week
  Arrive in Tunis (one day) and visit Sousse (one day), Tozeur/Nefta (two days), Douz (one day) and Jerba (one day); fly back to Tunis.
Two Weeks
  Spend three days in Tunis, including a day trip to Dougga; then visit Sousse (two days); travel to Sfax via El-Jem (one day); visit Tozeur/Nefta (two days), Douz (two days), Jerba (two days) and Tataouine (one day); return to Tunis via Kairouan (one day).
Four Weeks
  Arrive in Tunis (three days); visit Bizerte (two days), Tabarka (two days) and Aïn Draham (one day); travel to Le Kef via Bulla Regia (two days); travel to Tunis via Dougga (one day); head south to Sousse (two days) and Mahdia (one day); travel to Sfax via El-Jem (two days); continue to Tozeur/Nefta (two days) and Douz (two days); hang out on Jerba (four days); visit Tataouine (two days); return to Tunis via Kairouan (one day).

PLANNING
When to Go
Summer is the most popular time to visit, mainly because this is the European holiday season, but it is not the ideal time because it's so hot – hovering at around 40°C for days on end. Transport during this period is also stretched to the limit and hotel rooms are hard to find after noon.

The best time to visit is in spring, when the north is still green, the south is pleasantly warm and the summer hordes have yet to arrive. Autumn is the next best time.

Maps
Tourist offices everywhere hand out a perfectly adequate road map.

What to Bring
Essential items for the summer visitor include a broad-brimmed hat, good sunglasses and sunscreen. If you're planning on visiting the Sahara, a light sweater will come in handy even in summer because it gets surprisingly cold at night. In winter, you will need a warm sweater and – in the north – a raincoat. An alarm clock is important for

TUNISIA

catching early morning buses. Unless you're happy with a diet of expensive foreign papers, bring a supply of books.

TOURIST OFFICES
Local Tourist Offices
Don't hold your breath waiting for a tidal wave of information. There are offices of the government-run Office National du Tourisme Tunisien (ONTT) in all major towns and tourist centres, as well as local offices called *syndicats d'initiative* – often a serious misnomer.

Tourist Offices Abroad
Tunisian tourist offices abroad include:

Canada (☎ 514-397 11 82) 1253 McGill College, Montreal, Quebec H3A 3B6
France (☎ 78 52 35 86) 12 Rue de Séze, 69006 Lyon
(☎ 01 47 42 72 67) 32 Ave de l'Opéra, 75002 Paris
Germany (☎ 030-885 0457) Kurfuerstendamm 171, 10707 Berlin
(☎ 0211-84 218) Steinstrasse 23, 40210 Dusseldorf
(☎ 069-23 18 91/92) Am Hauptbahnhof 6, 6329 Frankfurt Main 1
Italy (☎ 02-86 45 30 26) Via Baracchini 10, 20123 Milan
UK (☎ 0171-224 5561) 77A Wigmore St, London W1H 9LJ

VISAS
Nationals of most Western European countries can stay up to three months without a visa – you just roll up and collect a stamp in your passport. Americans, Canadians, Germans and Japanese can stay up to four months. The situation is a bit more complicated for other nationalities. Most require no visa if arriving on an organised tour.

Australians and South Africans can get a visa at the airport for TD6. New Zealanders need to get their visas in advance – they are available wherever Tunisia has diplomatic representation.

Israeli nationals are not allowed into the country.

Visa Extensions
It is unlikely that you will need to extend your visa because a month in Tunisia is ample for most people. Applications can be made only at the Interior Ministry on Ave Habib Bourguiba in Tunis. They cost TD3 (payable only in revenue stamps), take up to 10 days to issue, and require two photographs, bank receipts and a *facture* (receipt) from your hotel. It may sound simple, but the process is more hassle than it's worth.

EMBASSIES & CONSULATES
Tunisian Embassies & Consulates
Australia Honorary Consulate (☎ 02-9363 5588) GPO Box 801, Double Bay, Sydney 2028 – for visa application forms.
Canada (☎ 613-237 0330) 515 O'Connor St, Ottawa K1S 3P8
France (☎ 01-45 53 50 94) 17-19 Rue de Lubeck, 75016 Paris
(☎ 78 93 42 87) 14 Ave du Maréchal Foch, 69412 Lyon
(☎ 04-91 50 28 68) 8 Blvd d'Athènes, 13001 Marseille
Germany (☎ 030-472 20 64/7) 110 Esplanade 12, 1100 Berlin
(☎ 0211-371 007) 7-9 Graf Adolf Platz, 4000 Dusseldorf
(☎ 040-220 17 56) Overbeckstrasse 19, 2000 Hamburg 76
(☎ 089-55 45 51) Adimstrage 4, 8000 Munich 19
Greece (☎ 01-671 7590) Ethnikis Antistasseos 91, 15231 Halandri, Athens
Italy (☎ 06-860 42 82) Via Asmara 5, 00199 Rome
(☎ 091-32 89 26) 24 Piazza Ignazio Florio, 90100 Palermo
Morocco (☎ 07-73 05 76) 6 Rue de Fés, Rabat
Netherlands (☎ 070-351 22 51) Gentestraat 98, 2587 HX The Hague
South Africa (☎ 012-342 6283) 850 Church St, Arcadia, 0007 Pretoria
UK (☎ 0171-584 8117) 29 Prince's Gate, London SW7 1QG
USA (☎ 202-862 1850) 1515 Massachusetts Ave NW, Washington DC 20005

Foreign Embassies in Tunisia
Countries with diplomatic representation in Tunis include:

Australia Australian affairs are handled by the Canadian Embassy in Tunis
Canada (☎ 01-796 577) 3 Rue du Sénégal
France (☎ 01-347 838) Place de l'Indépendance, Ave Habib Bourguiba

Germany (☎ 01-786 455) 1 Rue el Hamra
Italy (☎ 01-341 811) 3 Rue de Russie
Morocco (☎ 01-782 775) 39 Rue du 1 Juin
UK (☎ 01-341 444) 5 Place de la Victoire
USA (☎ 01-782 566) 144 Ave de la Liberté

CUSTOMS

The duty-free allowance is 400 cigarettes, 2L of wine, 1L of spirits and 250mL of perfume. It is advisable to declare valuable items (such as cameras) on arrival to ensure a smooth departure.

MONEY

The Tunisian dinar is a nonconvertible currency, and it's illegal to import or export it. All the major European currencies are readily exchangeable, as well as the US and Canadian dollars and the Japanese yen. Australian and New Zealand dollars and South African rand are not accepted. It is not necessary to declare your foreign currency on arrival. Foreign currency can be exchanged at banks, post offices and major hotels.

When leaving the country, you can exchange up to 30% of the amount you changed into dinar, up to a limit of TD100. You need to produce bank receipts to prove you changed the money in the first place.

Major credit cards such as Visa, American Express and MasterCard are widely accepted throughout the country at large shops, tourist hotels, car-rental agencies and banks. Maestro-Cirrus cards can also be used, but in a limited number of places.

Cash advances are given in local currency only.

Currency

The unit of currency is the Tunisian dinar (TD), which is divided into 1000 millimes (mills). There are five, 10, 20, 50, 100 and 500-mill coins and one-dinar coins. There are five, 10, 20 and 30-dinar notes. Changing the larger notes is not a problem.

Exchange Rates

Exchange rates are regulated, so the rate is the same everywhere. Banks charge a standard 351 mills commission per travellers cheque, and the larger hotels take slightly more. Post offices will change cash only.

country	unit		Tunisian dinar
Australia	A$1	=	TD0.83
Canada	C$1	=	TD0.95
euro	€1	=	TD1.27
France	1FF	=	TD0.19
Germany	DM1	=	TD0.65
Japan	¥100	=	TD1.37
New Zealand	NZ$1	=	TD0.63
UK	UK£1	=	TD2.01
USA	US$1	=	TD1.40

Costs

Tunisia is a cheap country to travel in, especially for Europeans. It's usually possible to find a clean room for about TD5 per person, main meals in local restaurants seldom cost over TD3.500, and public transport is cheap. If you're fighting to keep costs down, you can get by on TD20 a day. You'll have more fun with a budget of about TD30 per day and you can be quite lavish for TD50.

Tipping & Bargaining

Tipping is not a requirement. Cafes and local restaurants put out a saucer for customers to throw their small change into, but this is seldom more than 50 mills. Waiters in tourist restaurants are accustomed to tips – 10% is plenty. Taxi drivers do not expect tips from locals, but they often round up the fare for foreigners.

Handicrafts are about the only items you may have to bargain for in Tunisia. To be good at bargaining, you need to enjoy the banter. If you don't, you're better off buying your souvenirs from one of the government-run craft shops (see Shopping) where prices are fixed. It's a good idea to go there anyway just to get an idea of prices.

POST & COMMUNICATIONS
Post

The Tunisian postal service is slow but reliable. Mail to Europe generally takes about a week; allow two weeks to North America and Oceania. Air-mail letters cost 650 mills to Europe, and 700 mills to Australia and the Americas; postcards cost 100 mills less.

Post office opening times are fairly complicated, with different schedules depending on the size of the town and the season. Between 1 September and 30 June, most city offices are open 8 am to noon and 3 to 6 pm

Monday to Thursday, and 8 am to 12.30 pm on Friday and Saturday. In July and August, the hours are 7.30 am to 1 pm Monday to Thursday and 7.30 am to 1.30 pm on Friday and Saturday. During Ramadan, whenever it falls, the hours are 8 am to 1.30 pm Monday to Thursday and Saturday, and 8 am to 12.30 pm Friday. The hours are similar in smaller towns, while the main post office in Tunis, on Rue Charles de Gaulle, is open seven days a week.

You can receive mail at any post office in the country. It should be addressed clearly, with your surname first in capital letters.

Parcels should be taken along unwrapped for inspection. Parcels weighing less than 2kg can be sent by ordinary mail. Larger parcels should be taken to the special parcel counter. Indicate clearly if you want to send something surface mail.

Telephone
The telephone system is efficient and modern. Public telephones, known as Taxiphones, are everywhere and it's rare to find one that doesn't work. Most places have Taxiphone offices, readily identified by the yellow sign, with about a dozen booths and attendants to give change. Local calls cost 100 mills, and long-distance calls cost a maximum of 200 mills per minute. The number for directory information is ☎ 120.

Faxes can be sent from all post offices. Most hotels have fax machines; fax numbers are listed throughout the chapter.

The same phones can also be used for international direct dialling, except that you will need to feed them one-dinar and half-dinar coins. International calls are not cheap: 980 mills per minute to most European countries, TD1.500 per minute to the USA and TD1.750 per minute to Australia and New Zealand. The international access code is ☎ 00.

To call Tunisia from abroad, the country code is ☎ 216.

Email & Internet Access
Public access to the Internet is handled by Publinet, which operates some 30 offices around the country. Addresses are listed throughout this chapter; most charge around TD3 per hour.

The Internet is still quite new in Tunisia, and few hotels or businesses have email addresses – although the number is growing fast.

INTERNET RESOURCES
The amount of information about Tunisia that can be gleaned from the Web is still fairly limited. Many of the sites turn out to little more than rehashes of official information.

The best links are to be found at: www .members.tripod.com/~Djebbana/links.html.

BOOKS
Lonely Planet's *Tunisia* provides detailed information about the country.

NEWSPAPERS & MAGAZINES
You will need to speak French or Arabic to make much sense of the Tunisian press. *La Presse* and *Le Temps* are the main French-language papers. They both have a couple of pages of international news as well as local service information such as train, bus and flight times. You can buy two-day-old European newspapers in the main centres.

RADIO & TV
There is a French-language radio station broadcasting on FM 98.2MHz. It broadcasts in English from 2 to 3 pm, German from 3 to 4 pm and Italian from 4 to 5 pm. A much better source of English-language radio is the BBC World Service, which can be picked up on 15.07MHz and 12.095MHz.

The French-language TV station has half an hour of news at 8 pm every night, which includes foreign news and sport.

TIME
Tunisia is one hour ahead of GMT/UTC from October to April, and two hours ahead of GMT/UTC from May to September.

LAUNDRY
Laundrettes don't exist in the western sense, although there is a place in Tunis (see the Tunis section) with washing machines where you can pay for washing to be done by the kilogram. You just drop off the load and collect it later. Most hotels offer a laundry service, although it tends to be expensive. Most towns have dry-cleaning shops. Typical

Facts for the Visitor – Women Travellers 827

prices are TD1.500 for a shirt, TD1.800 for jeans and TD2 for a cloth jacket.

TOILETS

Public toilets are a rarity. About the only places you'll find them are at bus and train stations. Otherwise, cafes are the best option – although you will be expected to buy a coffee or something for the privilege. Most are equipped with a hose for washing yourself; if you like to use paper, carry your own.

WOMEN TRAVELLERS

Women should encounter few problems in Tunisia, though steer clear of some of the cheap hotels (see the accommodation section following). It's advisable to dress more conservatively outside Tunis and the resort towns. A headscarf may come in handy in remote areas as proof of modesty. Cosmetics, tampons etc are widely available.

GAY & LESBIAN TRAVELLERS

While the lifestyle is liberal by Islamic standards, society has yet to come to terms with homosexuality. All forms of homosexual activity are illegal under Tunisian law.

DANGERS & ANNOYANCES

There have been isolated reports of beach thefts, but crimes such as mugging are very rare.

EMERGENCIES

The telephone number for an ambulance is ☎ 190.

BUSINESS HOURS

Government offices and businesses are open 8.30 am to 1 pm and 3 to 5.45 pm Monday to Thursday. They're also open 8.30 am to 1.30pm on Friday and Saturday. In July and August, offices don't open in the afternoon.

Banks are open 8 to 11 am and 2 to 4pm Monday to Thursday, and 8 to 11 am and 1 to 3 pm Friday. Some banks in Tunis extend opening times beyond these hours. Banks are not open in the afternoon in July and August.

Most shops are open 8 am to 12.30 pm and 2.30 to 6 pm Monday to Friday, and 8 am to noon on Saturday. Summer hours are usually 7.30 am to 1 pm.

PUBLIC HOLIDAYS & SPECIAL EVENTS

Public holidays and festivals are either religious celebrations or festivities marking the anniversary of historic events. The Islamic holidays fall 10 days earlier every western calendar year because the Gregorian (western) and Islamic calendars are of different lengths. Ramadan is the main one to watch out for, because opening hours and transport schedules are disrupted for an entire month. Avoid travel before Eid al-Fitr (celebrating the end of Ramadan) when everyone is trying to get home for the festivities.

Other major holidays in Tunisia are: New Year's Day (1 January); Independence Day (20 March); Youth Day (21 March); Martyrs' Day (9 April); Labour Day (1 May); Republic Day (25 July); and Ben Ali's Presidential Anniversary (7 November).

Festivals

The highlights of the festival calendar include events at three of the country's most celebrated ancient sites. The El-Jem Symphonic Music Festival, held every July, uses El-Jem's spectacular floodlit colosseum, while the Carthage and Dougga festivals, in July and August, feature performances of classical theatre at Carthage's Roman theatre. The Dougga Festival, also in July and August, uses the Roman theatre at Dougga.

Almost every tourist town stages an annual festival, usually a week-long line-up of parades and fairly tacky folkloric events. The main festivals are:

Hammamet Festival – Held in July/August, this festival features music and cultural events.
Tabarka Festival – This festival held in July/August features music, theatre and a coral exhibition.
Ulysses Festival – Held in July/August on Jerba, this festival is strictly for the tourists, right down to the Miss Ulysses competition.
Sahara Festival – Held in November in Douz, this festival features traditional desert sports such as camel racing and saluki dog trials as well as parades, music and dance.

ACTIVITIES
Ballooning

Tozeur-based AerOasis (☎ 06-454 577) is the only company in Tunisia offering balloon flights. It operates year-round and charges TD100 for a one hour flight, travelling as far afield as Douz in search of the right conditions.

Bird-Watching

Tunisia is a popular destination for bird-watchers. In winter, the wetlands of the World Heritage-listed Ichkeul National Park, in the north, are home to more than 200,000 migratory waterfowl from all over Europe. They include the park's emblem, the rare greylag goose. Spring and autumn are the times to see birds of prey as they migrate between Africa and Europe along the peaks of the Tunisian Dorsale.

Camel Trekking

The Saharan town of Douz is the place to go for camel trekking. You can organise anything from a one hour ride (TD2.500) to overnight treks (from TD30 per day). See the Douz section for further information.

Diving

The best place to go diving is Tabarka on the north coast. The Club de Plongèe (☎ 08-644 478), at the marina, organises trips, rents equipment and runs courses for beginners.

Golf

There are golf courses at Hammamet, Jerba, Sousse, Tabarka and Tunis. Green fees average about TD45 for 18 holes. Players need to show proof of their handicap.

ACCOMMODATION

There's accommodation to suit every budget, from camping grounds to five-star resorts.

Camping

Most official camping grounds have only basic facilities and charge about TD2.500 per person. It's technically possible to camp anywhere as long as you get the landowner's permission.

Hostels

Hostels in Tunisia fall into two categories: the government-run *maisons des jeunes* and the *auberges de jeunesse*, affiliated to Hostelling International (HI). They couldn't be more different.

The auberges de jeunesse are thoroughly recommended; most have prime locations, such as a converted palace in the Tunis medina and a fascinating old funduq at Houmt Souq, Jerba. They charge TD4.500 per night for bed and breakfast, with other meals available for TD3 each. You need an HI card to use the hostels. The address for HI in Tunisia is 25 Rue Saida Ajoula, Tunis medina (☎ 01-567 850).

Almost without exception, maisons des jeunes are characterless, concrete boxes with all the charm of army barracks. Almost every town has a maison des jeunes, normally stuck way out in the boondocks and used primarily to house visiting sporting teams and for school camps. The only reason to mention them is that sometimes they represent the only available budget accommodation. They all charge TD4 for a dormitory bed.

Hotels

Tunisian hotels also fall into two main categories: classified hotels, which have been awarded between one and five stars under the government's rating system; and non-classified hotels, which haven't.

The fact that a hotel has not been classified does not mean it is no good – the majority of the budget places recommended in this book are non-classified. You can generally find clean singles/doubles with shared bathroom for around TD8/14, sometimes less. Some of the better non-classified places also have rooms with private bathroom for a few dinars more.

Unless you're on a super tight budget, you're better off staying away from the cheap hotels in the medinas of the major cities. They are very basic, often with no showers, and charge by the bed in shared rooms. Prices range from TD2.500 to TD5 per person, depending on the level of facilities. If you want a room to yourself, you will be asked to pay for all the beds. These hotels are totally unsuitable for women travellers.

The majority of hotels are classified. The one and two star hotels tend to be smaller, older hotels, often built in colonial times. They are generally clean, if a little shabby, and are popular with local business travellers and tourists who want a decent double room with private bathroom and hot water. Expect to pay around TD25/40 for singles/doubles.

TUNISIA

A three star rating usually indicates a hotel built to cater for tour groups. Four and five star hotels are of international standard with all the usual facilities. Prices go up about TD20 per person for each star.

Hotels are required to display their tariffs by the reception desk. Prices are normally listed according to three seasons – high (*haute*), middle (*moyenne*) and low (*basse*). The high season runs from 1 July to 15 September, low season is from 1 November to 15 March, and the rest is middle season. There can be huge price differences between seasons, especially in resort areas. Non-classified hotels normally charge the same all year.

The room rates at classified hotels include breakfast; at non-classified hotels, breakfast is often quoted separately, so ask. A typical hotel breakfast consists of coffee, French bread, butter and jam.

FOOD

Tunisians love spicy food. The prime ingredient is *harissa*, a fiery chilli paste that is used to add zip to a range of stews and sauces. Locals enjoy their harissa so much that is it eaten straight as an appetiser, mopped up with fresh bread.

The national dish is *couscous* (semolina). Apparently there are more than 300 ways of preparing the stuff, sweet as well as savoury. A bowl of couscous served with some variety of stew costs about TD2.500 in local restaurants.

Bread also features prominently in the diet, and you'll find fresh French loaves everywhere. Look out for *tabouna*, the traditional flat Berber bread.

A curiosity of Tunisian cuisine is the *briq*, a crisp, very thin pastry envelope that comes with a range of fillings (always including egg).

Other dishes include:

kammounia
meat stew made with lots of cumin
lablabi
spicy chickpea broth which is doled out on a bed of broken bread
salade mechouia
spicy mixture of mashed grilled vegetables, often served as an accompaniment to dishes such as roast chicken
salade tunisienne
finely diced salad vegetables mixed with a dressing of lemon juice and olive oil

shakshuka
thick vegetable soup based on onions and green peppers; unfortunately for vegetarians, it's normally made with a meat stock
tajine
the Tunisian version is no relation to its Moroccan namesake; it's similar to an Italian frittata and is normally served cold with chips and salad

Restaurants

You'll find versions of the dishes described above in local restaurants throughout the country. Generally a main dish and salad won't cost much over TD3.500; many also serve grilled fish, lamb cutlets, *merguez* (spicy sausages) and kebabs.

If you want a drink with your meal, you'll need to eat at a licensed restaurant – known as tourist restaurants. They serve what they like to call Franco-Tunisienne cuisine, often with a strong emphasis on seafood. If you can avoid the lobster, most meals will cost under TD15, plus drinks.

Fast Food

Almost every town has a shop selling *cassecroûtes*, half a French loaf stuffed with a choice of fillings – fried egg, chips and harissa is a favourite known as *khaftegi*. *Rotisseries* specialise in spit-roast chicken. Prices start at TD1.800 for a quarter chicken with chips and salad.

Western-style fast food is also becoming popular. Pizza parlours and hamburger joints can be found in most of the major towns.

DRINKS
Nonalcoholic Drinks

Tunisians are great coffee drinkers, and good coffee is only as far away as the nearest cafe. Every cafe has an espresso machine and offers a choice of styles. The most popular is *exprès*, which equates to a short black. A *capucin* bears absolutely no resemblance to a cappuccino; it's a short black with a barely detectable dash of milk. The closest thing to a cappuccino is a *café direct*, which is served with milk frothed in the espresso machine. They also serve Turkish coffee, called *café turc*. Upmarket cafes in tourist areas also sell filtered coffee.

Green tea is also popular, but most westerners have trouble with the Tunisian way of

TUNISIA

drinking it: equal quantities of tea leaves, sugar and water are boiled up to produce something with a viscosity similar to tar. It is then sipped from very small cups. It's often served with a sprig of fresh mint, which makes it look attractive at least. English-style tea is known as an *infusion du thé* and is available only from tourist cafes and hotels.

You'll occasionally find fresh milk in supermarkets, but don't count on it. UHT milk is available everywhere. Bottled mineral water is cheap and available everywhere, as are soft drinks. Freshly squeezed orange juice is readily available in season. You can find packaged juices in supermarkets, but they are expensive.

Alcoholic Drinks

Drinking alcohol is forbidden by Islam, but that doesn't stop a lot of Tunisians from indulging in the odd tipple. There are some good local wines to sample, while Celtia is the main beer. Alcohol is sold at bars and some restaurants as well as from supermarkets. Supermarkets sell alcohol from midday to 6.30 pm only, and not on Friday.

ENTERTAINMENT

Nightlife is not promising outside Tunis and the resort areas. The favourite local entertainment is coffee and cards at the cafe, but that's strictly for the blokes. Almost every town has a cinema, although the posters don't look auspicious. If you like discos, stick to the resorts.

Bars

Bars can be found in all the major towns. They are generally hard-drinking, smoke-filled, male preserves. Most foreigners, particularly women, feel more comfortable drinking at the resort hotels.

SHOPPING

The most popular items to buy in Tunisia are rugs and carpets, jewellery, pottery, beaten copper and brass items, leather and straw goods, and *chechias* (small, red, felt hats worn by Tunisian men).

Markets

Town and village life revolves around the weekly market. Market day is a good day to be in a town because it's far livelier than

usual and the markets attract both itinerant merchants and people from outlying districts.

Getting There & Away

AIR

Tunisia has four international airports: Tunis, Jerba, Monastir and Tabarka. Tunis handles most of the scheduled flights, while Jerba and Monastir are the main charter airports.

Europe

British Airways flies to Tunis three times a week and does a 30-day return for UK£215, dropping as low as UK£160 at times. Most of the flights using Jerba and Monastir are charters. These can be incredibly cheap – as low as UK£99 return – if you don't mind minimum and maximum-stay restrictions; you get the biggest discounts at the last minute.

Overseas branches of the ONTT have lists of charter operators. In the UK, Horizon Holidays (☎ 0181-200 8733) and Thomson Holidays (same number) are the two biggest operators.

The USA & Canada

There are no direct flights between Tunisia and the USA or Canada. The cheapest way to travel between North America and Tunisia is to get a cheap fare to London and a charter flight or bucket-shop deal from there. One-month Apex fares from New York start at around US$1200.

Australia

There are no direct flights to/from Australia either, although several of the major European airlines serving Australia have good connections with Tunis.

Morocco

Royal Air Maroc and Tunis Air fly regularly between the two countries. An Apex ticket, valid for one month, costs TD360 return.

LAND
Algeria

Few tourists head this way these days, but the borders are open and busier than ever. There are *louages* (shared taxis) from Tunis to a range of destinations.

Libya

The border crossing between Tunisia and Libya is on the coast at Ras Ajdir. There is plenty of public transport, with a daily bus from Tunis to Tripoli and frequent louages. Unfortunately, tourist visas are still as scarce as hen's teeth.

SEA
Italy

There are ferries between Tunis and the Italian ports of Genoa and Trapani (Sicily). The shortest crossing is the weekly Tirrenia Lines service to Trapani (eight hours, TD65 one way). It leaves Trapani at 8 am on Monday morning and Tunis at 8 pm the same day.

Boats to Genoa are run by the Compagnie Tunisienne de Navigation (CTN). Services to Genoa vary between four a month in winter and 11 a month at the height of summer. The trip takes 24 hours and costs TD140 one way.

You can get tickets for both services from the CTN office (☎ 322 802) at 122 Rue de Yougoslavie.

France

CTN also operates regular ferries from Tunis to Marseille (24 hours, TD180 one way). There are at least seven ferries a month even in winter, and daily sailings in August. The service is packed in summer, so visitors taking cars will need to book ahead.

DEPARTURE TAX

There is no departure tax to be paid when leaving the country. A TD8 airport tax is included in the price of an air ticket, and a similar TD2 port tax is included in the price of ferry tickets.

Getting Around

Tunisia has a well-developed transport network, and just about every town in the country has daily bus connections with Tunis. For most of the year public transport copes easily with demand, but things get pretty hectic during August and September and on public holidays. Book ahead if possible.

AIR

Tunisia's domestic air network is fairly limited because it's such a small country. The main route is between Tunis and Jerba, which warrants six flights per day; two or three flights a week stop at Sfax en route. There are also up to five flights per week between Tunis and Tozeur.

BUS

SNTRI, the national bus company, operates daily air-con buses from Tunis to every town of consequence. There are also regional bus companies, which provide local services.

Most stations do not have timetables displayed; those that do have them in Arabic only. Departures tend to be early in the day. If you're seeking directions to the bus station, ask for the *gare routière*.

TRAIN

Tunisia's rail network is modern and efficient, but hardly comprehensive. The best service is on the main line south from Tunis to Sousse and Sfax. It's a good idea to travel 1st class; as well as being more comfortable, it improves your chances of getting a seat. Prices quoted in this chapter are for 1st class.

LOUAGE

Louages are long-distance taxis offering a parallel service to the buses. Whereas buses leave to a timetable, louages leave when they're full. Drivers stand by their vehicles and call out their destinations. They seldom take long to fill up. Louages are the fastest way to get around, and the fares are only slighter higher than the buses. Most louages are white with a red stripe.

In most towns, the louage 'station' is close to, or incorporated with, the bus station, enabling you to choose between the services.

CAR & MOTORCYCLE

Tunisia has an excellent road network. All but the most minor roads are tar sealed and well maintained. Potholes are almost unheard of. Many of the roads which are marked as unsealed on older maps have now been sealed.

However, there are still a lot of unsealed roads in the south. It's advisable to seek local advice about conditions. Some are graded

TUNISIA

regularly and can be negotiated easily enough with a conventional vehicle.

Road Rules

The road rules in Tunisia are basically the same as in Continental Europe. You drive on the right, and overtake on the left. The speed limits are 50km/h in built-up areas and 90km/h on the open road. The only exception is on the toll road from Tunis to Sousse, where the speed limit is 110km/h.

The regulation that causes the most problems for tourists concerns giving priority to traffic coming from the right in built-up areas. This also extends to roundabouts, where you are obliged to give way to traffic approaching from the right even if you are already on the roundabout.

Clubs

The Touring Club de Tunisie has reciprocal rights arrangements with many European automobile clubs, including Britain's Automobile Association (AA). If your car conks out, they can supply you with the name of the nearest affiliated breakdown service. The club's address is 15 Rue d'Allemagne, Tunis 1000 (☎ 01-323 114, fax 324 834).

Rental

Hiring a car can be a great way to see the country, but it's expensive. According to the advertised rates, you'll be up for at least TD500 per week for even the smallest cars (Renault Esp or Citroën 15) by the time tax and insurance have been taken into account. You can usually bargain this down to about TD350; local companies are usually more willing to negotiate than the big international operators.

Rental companies require that drivers be aged over 21 and hold a driver's licence valid for at least a year. Rental conditions are fairly straightforward. If you are paying by cash, you will be required to leave a deposit roughly equivalent to the rental charge. Credit cards don't have the same restriction.

When you hire a vehicle car, make sure there is an accident report form with the car's papers. If you have an accident, both parties involved must complete the form. If the form is not completed, you may be liable for the costs, whether you've paid for insurance or not.

BICYCLE

Cycling is an excellent way to see the country in spring or autumn. It's too hot to cycle in summer and a little bleak in winter, though it is possible to put a bike on the train if you get too exhausted or want to skip a long stretch.

A few places hire out bikes, normally for about TD8 per day.

HITCHING

The following information is intended solely as an explanation of how hitching works in Tunisia, not as a recommendation. Although many people do hitch, it is not an entirely safe method of transport, and you do so at your own risk. It is strongly recommended that women do not attempt to hitch without a male companion.

Conditions for hitching vary throughout the country. The south is the easiest because there is a great deal more tourist traffic – either people who hire cars in Jerba or overlanders heading for Tozeur and the Sahara. You shouldn't have to wait long for a lift. In the north, people seem less inclined to pick up hitchers, particularly in the summer when there are so many tourists. Between small towns in the south, hitching is a standard way of getting around, although you will normally be expected to pay the equivalent of the bus fare. See the introductory Getting Around chapter for more information on hitching.

SEA

There are two scheduled ferry services in the country. The first connects Sfax with the Kerkennah Islands. There are up to eight crossings a day in summer, dropping to four in winter. The trip takes 1½ hours and costs 570 mills. The second service runs from Jorf on the mainland to Ajim on Jerba. The crossing takes only a few minutes and the ferries run 24 hours.

LOCAL TRANSPORT

You'll find orange, metered taxis in almost every town. Flag fall is 285 mills, followed by 370 mills per kilometre. In the south, *camionnettes* (small trucks) operate between towns and outlying villages, such as Douz and Zaafrane. They charge by the seat, and leave when there are enough passengers to make it worthwhile.

Building relief in Portal de las Monjes, Mirambel, Aragón, Spain

Colourful facade, Barcelona

The windmills of Castilla-La Mancha, Spain

View from Torre de Hércules, La Coruña, Spain

The medieval city walls of Ávila, Castilla y León in Spain, are among the best preserved in the world.

Illuminated interior of the cathedral – Manacor, Mallorca, Spain

Port de Sóller, Mallorca

Orange groves, Valencia

Home in Menorca, Spain

Festes de la Mercè – Barcelona's major festival

Tunis

☎ 01 • pop 1.9 million

Tunisia's capital must be the most easy-going major city in the Islamic world. It's an easy place to spend two or three days. The main attractions are the medina, the ruins of ancient Carthage and the Bardo Museum.

Orientation

The medina, the original city of Tunis, was built on a narrow strip of land between Lake Tunis and the Sebkhet Sejoumi salt lake. When the French arrived, they built a new city, the *ville nouvelle*, on land reclaimed from Lake Tunis to the east of the medina. The main thoroughfare of the ville nouvelle is Ave Habib Bourguiba, which runs from Lake Tunis to the Bab Bhar, the medina's eastern gate – also known as the Porte de France.

Most of the budget hotels are in the area around the Bab Bhar and to the south of Ave Habib Bourguiba. A causeway at the eastern end of Ave Habib Bourguiba carries road and light-rail traffic across Lake Tunis to the port suburb of La Goulette, and north to the affluent beach suburbs of Carthage, Sidi Bou Said and La Marsa.

Information

Tourist Offices The tourist office (☎ 341 077) is on Place du 7 Novembre at the eastern end of Ave Habib Bourguiba. It has a good free map of Tunis and useful brochures on Carthage and the medina.

Money The major banks are on Ave Habib Bourguiba. The Banque de l'Habitat and the UIBC bank have 24-hour automatic exchange machines. The UIBC building also houses the offices of American Express.

Post & Communications The main post office is on Rue Charles de Gaulle. Telephone calls can be made from any of the many Taxiphone offices around the city centre (see the Central Tunis map). You can check email at the Publinet offices at 28 Ave Habib Bourguiba or at 70 Ave Jean Jaurès.

Laundry The Lavarie Tahar at 15 Rue d'Allemagne charges TD5.500 to wash and dry 5kg.

Medical & Emergency Services The telephone number for the police and fire brigade is ☎ 197 (nationwide); the number for the ambulance service is ☎ 190. There is an antipoison centre (☎ 245 075) in Tunis.

Things to See & Do

Medina The Tunis medina is a veritable treasure trove of Islamic architecture dating back to the beginning of the 8th century. The major monuments are all marked and explained in the medina brochure available from the tourist office.

The main entry to the medina is along Rue Jamaa Ez Zitouna, which runs from the Bab Bhar to the **Zitouna Mosque**, also known as the great mosque. Built by the Aghlabids at the beginning of the 8th century, it is the oldest surviving building in Tunis and features many columns salvaged from the ruins of Roman Carthage. It is open 8 am to noon daily except Friday. Admission is TD1.600.

The other major attraction is the **Dar Ben Abdallah Museum**, a splendid old Turkish palace housing traditional costumes and local artefacts. It is open 9 am to 5 pm Tuesday to Sunday. Admission is TD1.600.

Two souqs to check out are the **Souq el-Attarine** (the perfume souq) and the **Souq des Chechias**, where the traditional, red, felt caps are made. They are worn mainly by older men these days.

Bardo Museum Housed in an old palace 3km north-west of the city centre, the Bardo is home to a magnificent collection of Roman mosaics gathered from the many ancient sites around the country.

It is open 9 am to 5 pm in summer and 9.30 am to 4.30 pm in winter; closed on Monday. Entry costs TD3.150. *Métro léger* (tram) line 4 has a stop (Le Bardo) near the museum, or catch bus No 3 from opposite the Hôtel Africa Meridien on Ave Habib Bourguiba.

Carthage The ruins of Punic and Roman Carthage are spread along the coast about 10km east of the city centre. Before you head out there, stop at the tourist office in town to pick up a copy of the Carthage brochure. It has a good map of the area and information on the major sites.

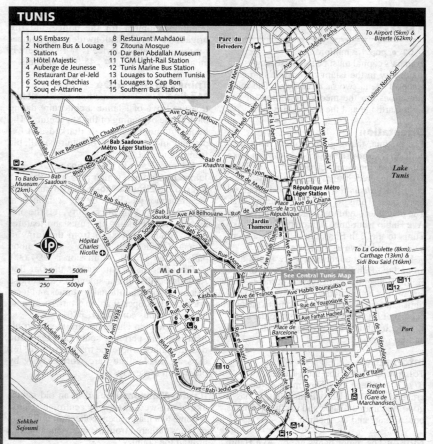

TUNIS

1 US Embassy
2 Northern Bus & Louage
   Stations
3 Hôtel Majestic
4 Auberge de Jeunesse
5 Restaurant Dar el-Jeld
6 Souq des Chechias
7 Souq el-Attarine
8 Restaurant Mahdaóui
9 Zitouna Mosque
10 Dar Ben Abdallah Museum
11 TGM Light-Rail Station
12 Tunis Marine Bus Station
13 Louages to Southern Tunisia
14 Louages to Cap Bon
15 Southern Bus Station

The Romans did such a thorough job of destroying Carthage in 146 BC that virtually nothing remains of the original city apart from the Punic ports. Excavation work has uncovered a small area of streets and houses in the grounds of the **National Museum** on top of the **Byrsa Hill**, the focal point of the ancient city.

The ruins of Roman Carthage are far more extensive. They include villas, a heavily restored **theatre** and the enormous **Antonine Baths**.

Entry to all the sites at Carthage is by a multiple ticket (TD5.200), which can be bought only at the Antonine Baths, the Roman villas and the museum. The sites are open 8.30 am to 5.30 pm every day except Monday.

The best way to visit Carthage is to take the TGM light rail from Tunis Marine bus station at the eastern end of Ave Habib Bourguiba to Carthage Hannibal station and wander from there.

Sidi Bou Said A few stops farther along the TGM line from Carthage is the beautiful, whitewashed, cliff-top village of **Sidi Bou Said**. It's really an outer suburb of Tunis, and is considered one of the city's most upmarket residential areas. Although it's on every tour group's itinerary, it remains very relaxed, especially late in the afternoon after the tour buses have left. There are no specific attractions, but it's a delight to wander through the old cobbled streets.

Places to Stay

Camping isn't really an option. The nearest camping ground is 15km south of the city near Hammam Lif.

Fortunately, Tunis has an excellent *auberge de jeunesse* (☎ 567 850, *Rue Es Saida Ajoula*). It occupies an old palace, the Dar Saida Ajoula, right in the heart of the medina. Rates range from TD5 for a dormitory bed and breakfast up to TD11 for full board. Hot showers are free.

There are dozens of cheap hotels around the medina and Place Barcelone, but nowhere that can be recommended with any confidence. It's a toss-up between *Hôtel Cirta* (☎ 321 584, *42 Rue Charles de Gaulle*) and *Hôtel Marhaba* (☎ 354 006, *5 Rue de la Commission*), just inside the medina. Both have singles/doubles for TD8/12

There are plenty of good mid-range hotels to choose from with breakfast included in the price. A favourite is *Hôtel Salammbô* (☎ 334 252, fax 337 498, ✉ hotel.salammbo@gnet.tn, *6 Rue de Grèce*). It has a choice of rooms, including singles/doubles with shower for TD17/28.

Hôtel Agriculture (☎ 326 394, fax 321 685, *25 Rue Charles de Gaulle*) is a comfortable mid-range hotel. Rooms with bathroom are TD20/30.

Hôtel Maison Doree (☎ 240 632, fax 332 401, *3 Rue el-Koufa*) is a fine old-style French hotel just north of Place de Barcelone. Rooms with shower cost TD26/29.

Hôtel Carlton (☎ 330 664, fax 338 168, ✉ carlton@planet.tn, *31 Ave Habib Bourguiba*) is a well-maintained, three-star hotel offering such comforts as satellite TV and air-con for TD47/74, including a generous buffet breakfast.

Places to Eat

There's a host of good places in the streets south of Ave Habib Bourguiba, particularly around Ave de Carthage and Rue Ibn Khaldoun. It's hard to beat *Restaurant Carcassonne* (*8 Ave de Carthage*) for value. It turns out a four-course menu for TD3.800, supplemented by as much bread as you can eat.

Restaurant Mahdaoui (*3 Rue Jamaa Ez Zitouna*), opposite the great mosque in the medina, is a good place to stop for lunch. It's the oldest restaurant in Tunis and has a daily blackboard menu featuring dishes like couscous with lamb (TD2.200).

If you want to enjoy a wine with your meal, check out the popular *Restaurant Le Cosmos* on Rue Ibn Khaldoun. A good meal for two costs around TD25, plus drinks.

For a real treat, try *Restaurant Dar el-Jeld* (☎ 560 916, *6 Rue Dar el-Jeld*), on the western side of the medina. It occupies the palatial former home of a wealthy bourgeois family, and the dining room and table settings are quite magnificent. Expect to pay about TD30 per person, plus wine. The restaurant is open Monday to Saturday for lunch and dinner. Bookings are essential.

Entertainment

There are a few restaurants that put on entertainment. *Restaurant le Bleuet* (*23 Rue de Marseille*) is something of an institution among the night owls of Tunis. It has music every night, and a belly dancer makes a brief appearance around 1 am. The action here doesn't kick off until 10 pm and then continues until about 5 am. Reckon on spending around TD25 per person.

Shopping

The SOCOPA store on the corner of Ave Habib Bourguiba and Ave de Carthage has the best selection of handicrafts in the country.

Another place worth checking out is Mains des Femmes, above the Banque de l'Habitat at 47 Ave Habib Bourguiba. It is run by Association Essalem, which promotes handicrafts produced by women in disadvantaged rural areas. It stocks some beautiful stuff – and the money goes to a good cause.

Getting There & Away

Air Domestic airline Tuninter has at least six flights a day to Jerba, via Sfax, two or three times a week and up to five flights a week to Tozeur. Tickets can be bought from the Tunis Air office (☎ 330 100) on the corner of Ave Habib Bourguiba and Rue 18 Janvier 1952.

TUNISIA

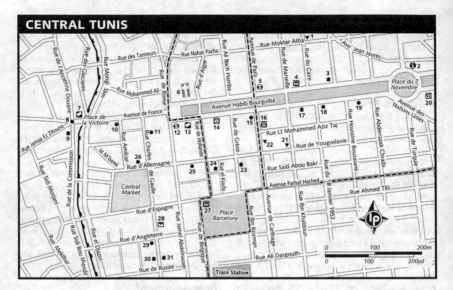

CENTRAL TUNIS

Most of the international airline offices are along Ave Habib Bourguiba and Ave de Paris.

Bus Tunis has two bus stations, one for departures to the north (Gare Routière Nord de Bab Saadoun) and the other for buses heading south or to international destinations (Gare Routière Sud de Bab el Alleoua).

The northern station is on the northwestern side of Bab Saadoun. You can get there by métro léger line Nos 3 or 4 from Place Barcelone or République stations. Get off at Bab Saadoun station and keep following the line away from Tunis for 250m.

The southern bus station is an easy 10-minute walk south of Place de Barcelone, west of the flyover at the end of Ave de la Gare. The nearest métro léger station is Bab Alleoua, the first stop south of Place de Barcelone on line No 1.

Train The train station is close to the centre of town on Place de Barcelone. There are eight trains a day to Sousse, four of which continue to El-Jem and Sfax. One train a day keeps going to the southern terminus of Gabès.

There are also useful services north to Bizerte, and west to Jendouba.

Louage Louages to the north leave from outside the northern bus station. Louages to Cap Bon leave from opposite the southern bus station, and services to other southern destinations leave from the station at the eastern end of Rue Al Aid el-Jebbari, off Ave Moncef Bey.

Car All the major car-rental companies have offices both at the airport and in town (most of them are on Ave Habib Bourguiba).

Ferry Ferries from Europe arrive in Tunis at La Goulette, at the end of the causeway that crosses Lake Tunis. The cheapest way to reach the city is by TGM light rail. From the port, walk straight out to the kasbah, turn left and walk about 500m until you come to a railway crossing; Goulette station is 100m to the right. A taxi from the port to Ave Habib Bourguiba costs about TD6.

The CTN office (☎ 322 802) at 122 Rue de Yougoslavie handles tickets for all the ferries.

Getting Around

To/From the Airport Tunis-Carthage airport is 8km north-east of the city. Yellow city bus No 35 runs to the airport from the Tunis

CENTRAL TUNIS

PLACES TO STAY & EAT	OTHER	
1 Restaurant le	2 Tourist Office	14 National Theatre
Bleuet	4 Buses to Airport; Bardo	15 SOCOPA
3 Hotel Carlton	Museum	16 Taxiphone Office
9 Hôtel Marhaba	5 Banque de l'Habitat	18 Tunis Air
17 Hôtel Africa Meridien	6 Cathedral	19 Interior Ministry
21 Restaurant Le Cosmos	7 UK Embassy	20 Publinet
22 Restaurant Carcassonne	8 Bab Bhar (Porte de France)	25 CTN Office
23 Hôtel Salammbô	10 Magasin Général	26 Lavarie Tahar
24 Hôtel Maison Doree	11 Monoprix Supermarket	27 Place Barcelone Buses &
30 Hôtel Agriculture	12 UIBC	Trams
31 Hôtel Cirta	13 French Embassy	28 Main Post Office
		29 Second-Hand Bookshop

Marine bus station every 20 minutes from 6 am to 9 pm and costs 650 mills. The bus leaves the airport from just outside the terminal building, to the right of the exit. A taxi to the city centre from the airport costs about TD5.

Bus The yellow city buses operate to all parts of the city, but apart from getting to the airport, the Bardo Museum or the northern bus station, you should have little cause to use them. Fares are cheap – 380 mills to the Bardo, for example.

There are three main bus terminals: Tunis Marine, which is next to the TGM station at the causeway end of Ave Habib Bourguiba; Place de Barcelone; and Jardin Thameur, 500m north of Ave Habib Bourguiba, off Ave Habib Thameur.

Light Rail The TGM light-rail system connects central Tunis with the beachside suburbs of La Goulette, Carthage, Sidi Bou Said and La Marsa. Trains run from 4 am until midnight.

Tram The efficient, modern métro léger has four routes. The most useful line is No 4, which has a new station right next to the Bardo Museum. Lines 3 and 4 stop at Bab Saadoun, close to the northern bus and louage stations, and Line 1 stops at Bab Alleoua, close to the southern bus station.

Taxi Taxis are a cheap and easy way to get around. Flag fall is 280 mills and the meter then ticks over at about 380 mills per kilometre.

Cap Bon Peninsula

HAMMAMET
☎ 02 • pop 20,000

The fact that a third of all Tunisia's foreign visitors wind up here doesn't make it a great place to stay. The building of more than 80 huge resort hotels has transformed this part of Tunisia into a monument to the package-tourism industry. Don't even consider coming here in summer unless you want to rub shoulders with thousands of other foreigners.

NABEUL
☎ 02 • pop 40,000

These days Nabeul has virtually merged with its boomtown southern neighbour, Hammamet, although it's not quite as over the top. Nabeul is the major service town of the Cap Bon region, and its economy is not entirely dependent on tourism.

The tourist office (☎ 286 800) is at the beach end of Ave Taieb Mehiri.

Places to Stay & Eat

Nabeul does at least have some decent budget accommodation. The *auberge de jeunesse (☎/fax 285 547)* has a great setting right by the beach at the end of Ave Mongi Slim. Dormitory accommodation and breakfast costs TD6; lunch and dinner cost an extra TD3 each. The hostel also has a camping area: TD5 per tent and TD1 per person.

Pension Les Roses (☎ 285 570) is a friendly place offering singles/doubles for TD9/16. It's right next to the main mosque in the middle of town. *Restaurant du Bonheur*, next to Pension Les Roses, specialises in

TUNISIA

couscous. Prices start at TD3 for couscous with lamb stew.

Getting There & Away

There are frequent buses from Nabeul to Tunis (one hour, TD2.800) as well as regular louages (TD3.100). The bus and louage stations are about 400m from the town centre on Ave Habib Thameur – the road to Hammamet.

Louages to Kelibia and buses to other parts of Cap Bon leave from Ave Farhat Hached, north-east of the town centre.

AROUND CAP BON

Kelibia, 58km north of Nabeul, remains relatively untouched by the ravages of mass tourism. The port is overlooked by a 16th-century **Spanish fort** which offers commanding views along the coast.

El-Haouaria, 25km farther north, sits under the mountainous northern tip of Cap Bon. The **Roman caves** near the cape were cut when stone was quarried for the building of Roman Carthage. The 3km walk from town takes about 45 minutes.

Halfway between Kelibia and El-Haouaria there's a signpost to **Kerkouane**, the country's best preserved Punic site. It's about 1.5km from the road, closed Monday.

Northern Tunisia

BIZERTE

☎ 02 • pop 135,000

Bizerte, 66km north-west of Tunis, was the scene of a post-independence conflict between the French and Tunisian governments which resulted in the death of 1000 Tunisian soldiers in the early 1960s. The French wanted to retain their naval base after independence, and didn't withdraw until 1963.

Orientation & Information

The centre of Bizerte is the ville nouvelle, built on the compact grid favoured by the French. It is flanked by a shipping canal connecting Lake Bizerte with the Mediterranean to the south-east and Ave Habib Bourguiba to the north-west. The old town – the kasbah and medina – is just north of Ave Habib Bourguiba.

The tourist office (☎ 432 897) is above the ONAT crafts shop by the old port. Most other facilities are to be found around the ville nouvelle.

Things to See & Do

The most interesting part of town is the area around the **old port**, guarded by a formidable **kasbah** (fort) on its northern side and a **ksibah** (small fort) on the southern side.

There are some reasonable **beaches** along the Corniche, which begins about 2km north-west of the city centre and runs up to Cap d'Afrique – the northernmost point of the African continent. The best beach is at **Remel Plage**, about 3km east of town off the road to Tunis.

Places to Stay & Eat

Campers can head for the *Centre de la Jeunesse* (☎ 02-440 819) at Remel Plage. Facilities are basic, but there are good shady sites beneath the pine trees and the beach is only five minutes walk away. It charges TD2 per person for camping, and TD5 for dorm beds.

Hôtel Saadi (☎ 422 528, Rue Salah ben Ali), opposite the soccer stadium, has clean singles/doubles with shared bathroom for TD7.500/13.

Restaurant La Cuisine Tunisienne (Rue du 2 Mars 1934) is the pick of the numerous cheap restaurants around the city centre. It does a spicy *chorba* (soup) for 700 mills, couscous with lamb for TD2.200 and grilled fish for TD3.

For a splurge, head out to the restaurant at *Hôtel Petite Mousse* (☎ 432 185), on the Corniche 2km west of the city centre. Reckon on spending TD30 for two, plus wine.

Getting There & Away

Public transport leaves from the south-eastern edge of town near the shipping canal.

Heading south, there are frequent buses and louages to Tunis as well as four trains (1½ hours, TD4). Heading west, SRT Jendouba operates a daily bus to Tabarka (three hours, TD5.200) and Aïn Draham (3½ hours, TD6.100) at 6 am.

Buses to Ras Jebel can drop you at the turn-off to Remel Plage.

TABARKA
☎ 08 • pop 10,000

The densely forested Kroumirie Mountains provide a dramatic backdrop to the small coastal town of Tabarka, 170km west of Tunis, near the Algerian border.

Most of the tourist development is just east of town, leaving the town itself relatively unspoiled. The small bay to the north is watched over by an impressive Genoese fort. There's not much to do except hang out at the beach, but the atmosphere is right for it.

Information
The tourist office (☎ 643 496) is housed in the old railway station on Ave 7 Novembre. There's a choice of banks along Ave Habib Bourguiba, and the post office is on Ave Hedi Chaker, diagonally opposite the Hôtel de France.

Places to Stay & Eat
The only cheap option is *Hôtel Corail* (☎ 673 082, 1 Rue de Tazerka), which charges TD7.500 per person. Most travellers head for *Pension Mamia* (☎ 671 058, 3 Rue de Tunis), which has spotless rooms built around a central courtyard. It charges TD22/30 for singles/doubles, including breakfast.

Hôtel Les Aiguilles (☎ 673 789, fax 673 604, 78 Ave Habib Bourguiba) is an old bank building which has been converted into a comfortable, modern two star hotel. Singles/doubles with breakfast are TD20/30 in low season and TD40/60 in high season.

There are lots of small restaurants around the town centre serving delicious grilled fish for TD2.500. You'll see the small *charcoal grills* out in the street around the junction of Rue du Peuple and Rue Farhat Hached.

Getting There & Away
SNTRI has nine buses a day to Tunis (3¼ hours, TD7.400), while SRT Jendouba has regular buses to Jendouba via Aïn Draham. Louages to these towns leave from the eastern end of Ave Habib Bourguiba.

AÏN DRAHAM
☎ 08 • pop 2500

Aïn Draham is Tunisia's hill station, nestled among the cork forest of the Kroumirie Mountains at an altitude of about 900m. The climate is markedly cooler than on the coast in summer, and snow is common in winter. Other than walking, there's not much to do. The 25km drive from Tabarka takes in some of the prettiest scenery in Tunisia.

Places to Stay & Eat
The pleasant *Hôtel Beauséjour* (☎ 655 0363, fax 655 527), at the top end of town on the road to Jendouba, has singles/doubles for TD23.500/36. Full board is good value: two three-course meals for an extra TD8. The porcine trophies on the walls are evidence of the hotel's popularity as a hunting lodge in colonial times.

Getting There & Away
SNTRI has three buses a day to Tunis (four hours, TD7.280) from the bus station at the foot of the hill. SRT Jendouba has regular buses to Tabarka and Jendouba, and a 6.45 am service to Le Kef.

BULLA REGIA
☎ 08

Bulla Regia, 160km west of Tunis near the town of Jendouba, is famous as the town where the Romans went underground to escape the summer heat in much the same way as the Berbers did around Matmata.

They built their villas with one level below ground, usually with a small courtyard open to the sky. They lived in some style, if the three underground homes on display are anything to go by. They are named after the mosaics that were found inside them: the Palace of Fishing; the House of Amphitrite; and the Palace of the Hunt. A few mosaics have been left *in situ*, but the best examples are now in the Bardo Museum in Tunis. The site is open from 8 am to 7 pm in summer, and 8.30 am to 5.30 pm in winter. Admission is TD2.100.

Places to Stay
There is nowhere to stay near the site. The closest accommodation is in the dull regional centre of Jendouba, 9km to the south-west, where the two-star *Hôtel Atlas* (☎ 603 217, fax 603 113, Rue 1 Juin 1955) has singles/doubles for TD22/33 with breakfast. The hotel is behind the police station, just off the main square.

Getting There & Away

The turn-off to Bulla Regia is 6km from Jendouba on the road to Aïn Draham. A taxi from Jendouba costs about TD5. You can arrange to be picked up later or take your chances; there's a fair amount of passing traffic.

Jendouba is a regional transport hub with a good range of options. Train is the most comfortable way to get to Tunis (2½ hours, TD7.050). The last of five daily services leaves at 5 pm. There are also frequent buses and louages to Tunis, as well as to Le Kef, Aïn Draham and Tabarka.

DOUGGA
☎ 08

Dougga is an excellent Roman ruin in a commanding position on the edge of the Tebersouk Mountains, 110km south-west of Tunis. The site is home to the country's most photographed Roman monument, the imposing **Capitol of Dougga**. It looks even better in situ. Next to the capitol is the **Square of the Winds**. In the centre is an enormous circular inscription listing the names of the 12 winds. On the southern edge of the site is **Trifolium House**, once the town's brothel. Dougga's well-preserved **theatre** makes a spectacular setting for performances of classical drama during the Dougga Festival in July and August. The site is open 8 am to 7 pm in summer, and 8.30 am to 5.30 pm in winter. Admission is TD2.100.

Places to Stay

Tebersouk is the closest town to the site, and the only hotel is *Hôtel Thugga* (☎ 466 647, fax 466 721). The place caters almost exclusively to tour groups and charges TD27/38 for singles/doubles with breakfast. It's easy to visit the site on a day trip from Tunis or Le Kef.

Getting There & Away

SNTRI's frequent buses between Tunis and Le Kef stop at Tebersouk, ensuring a steady flow of departures in both directions until about 6 pm. At the bus stop you'll find locals asking about TD5 to take you the remaining 7km to the site and pick you up at a time of your choice. You can also walk to the site from Nouvelle Dougga, a village on the Tunis-Le Kef road just west of Tebersouk. It's a solid 3km uphill hike.

LE KEF
☎ 08 • pop 30,000

The ancient fortress city of Le Kef, 170km south-west of Tunis, dominates the region from its spectacular setting on the slopes of Jebel Dyr. At an altitude of more than 1000m, the temperatures here are a welcome few degrees cooler than on the surrounding plains. The city centre, Place de l'Independance, is a 10-minute walk uphill from the bus and louage station.

Things to See

The city's crowning glory is its mighty **kasbah**, which overlooks the city from a spur running off Jebel Dyr. The structure that stands today is the latest of a string of fortresses that have occupied the site since the 5th century BC. It's open every day from 8 am to 5 pm, and the guardian will show you around the main points of interest.

The regional **museum** occupies a beautifully restored old *zaouia* (shrine) on the edge of the medina on Place ben Aissa – a short walk from the kasbah along Rue de la Kasbah. It has a good display on the lifestyle of the area's nomads.

Places to Stay & Eat

Hôtel Medina (☎ 204 183, 18 Rue Farhat Hached) is a safe choice with clean singles/doubles for TD10/12.

The best rooms are at *Résidence Venus* (☎/fax 204 695, Rue Mouldi Khamessi), nestled beneath the walls of the kasbah. It's a small, family-run pension with comfortable rooms for TD23/32, including breakfast.

Restaurant el-Andalous, diagonally opposite the post office on Rue Hedi Chaker, serves tasty local food.

Getting There & Away

SNTRI has regular buses to Tunis (three hours, TD7.230) via Tebersouk (1¼ hours, TD3.100). There are local buses to Jendouba.

Central Tunisia

SOUSSE
☎ 03 • pop 240,000

Sousse, 142km south of Tunis, is the country's third-largest city and a major port. It's a

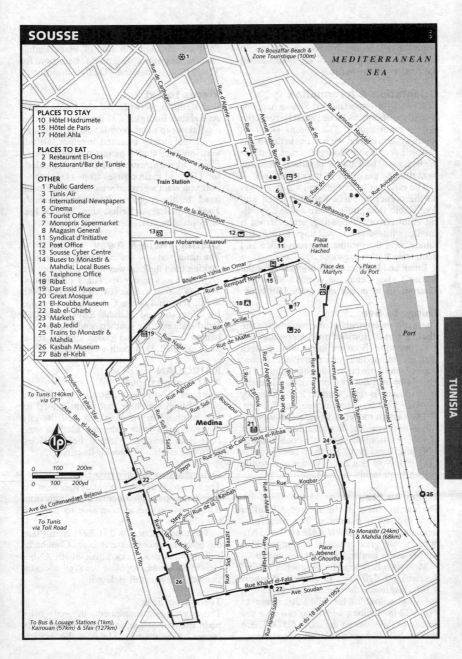

SOUSSE

To Boujaffar Beach &
Zone Touristique (100m)

MEDITERRANEAN SEA

To Tunis (140km)
via GP1

To Tunis
via Toll Road

To Bus & Louage Stations (1km),
Kairouan (57km) & Sfax (127km)

To Monastir (24km)
& Mahdia (68km)

Train Station

Medina

Port

Place
Farhat Hached

Place des
Martyrs

Place
du Port

Place Jebenet
el-Ghourba

PLACES TO STAY
10 Hôtel Hadrumete
15 Hôtel de Paris
17 Hôtel Ahla

PLACES TO EAT
2 Restaurant El-Ons
9 Restaurant/Bar de Tunisie

OTHER
1 Public Gardens
3 Tunis Air
4 International Newspapers
5 Cinema
6 Tourist Office
7 Monoprix Supermarket
8 Magasin General
11 Syndicat d'Initiative
12 Post Office
13 Sousse Cyber Centre
14 Buses to Monastir &
   Mahdia; Local Buses
16 Taxiphone Office
18 Ribat
19 Dar Essid Museum
20 Great Mosque
21 El-Koubba Museum
22 Bab el-Gharbi
23 Markets
24 Bab Jedid
25 Trains to Monastir &
   Mahdia
26 Kasbah Museum
27 Bab el-Kebli

Rue de Carthage
Rue d'Algérie
Rue Remada
Avenue Habib Bourguiba
Rue de l'Independance
Rue Laroussi Haddad
Rue du Caire
Rue Avicenne
Rue Ali Belhaouane
Ave Hasouna Ayachi
Avenue de la République
Avenue Mohamed Maarouf
Boulevard Yahia ibn Omar
Rue du Rempart Nord
Rue de Sicilie
Rue de Malte
Rue Najjar
Rue Aghlaba
Rue Sidi Said
Rue Sidi Bouraoui
Rue Zarouk
Rue d'Angleterre
Rue de Paris
Rue de France
Rue el-Aroui
Rue Souq el-Caïd
Souq el-Ribaa
Rue el-Maar
Koqbar
Rue de la Kasbah
Rue Sidi Baaziz
Rue el-Hajra
Rue Khalef el-Fata
Ave Soudan
Ave du 18 Janvier 1952
Rue Hamda Sekki
Rue Ibn-Rachid
Avenue Maréchal Tito
Avenue Mohamed V
Ave Mohamed Ali
Avenue Habib Thameur
Boulevard Tahar Sfar - Ave Ibn el-Jazzar
Ave du Commandant Bejaoui
Steps

0   100   200m
0   100   200yd

TUNISIA

lively, cosmopolitan city, centred around an imposing old medina. It's also a major tourist destination with a string of big hotels along the beaches to the north.

Orientation & Information

Everything of importance in Sousse happens around the enormous Place Farhat Hached, the town's main square. The medina is on its south-western corner, the port lies to the south-east and Ave Habib Bourguiba runs north to the beaches. The Tunis-Sfax railway line runs right through the centre of the square.

The efficient tourist office (☎ 225 157) is on the corner of Place Farhat Hached and Ave Habib Bourguiba. There's also a syndicat d'initiative, dispensing smiles from a small, white-domed building across the square, near the medina. The post office and main train station are close by.

Email and Internet access is available at the Sousse Cyber Center on Avenue Mohamed Maarouf, in the arcade next to the UIB bank.

Things to See

The main monuments of the medina are the **ribat**, a sort of fortified monastery, and the **great mosque**. Both are in the north-eastern part of the medina, close to Place Farhat Hached, and were built in the 9th century. The ribat is open 8 am to 6 pm daily, while the great mosque is open 8 am to 2.30 pm every day except Friday, when it closes at 12.30 pm.

The **kasbah museum**, at the south-western corner of the medina, houses a fine collection of mosaics from the area. It's open 8 am to 5.30 pm Tuesday to Sunday; admission is TD2.100. Note that there is no access to the kasbah from inside the medina.

Places to Stay

The cheap hotels in the medina all suffer from disastrous plumbing. The most presentable of them is *Hôtel Ahla* (☎ 220 570), opposite the great mosque. It charges TD6 per person in winter, TD7.500 in summer.

Most travellers head for the spotless *Hôtel de Paris* (☎ 220 564, 15 Rue du Rempart Nord), just inside the medina's north wall. It has singles/doubles for TD14/20, rising to TD16/22 in summer, when you can also negotiate to sleep out on the roof (TD7). There are free hot showers and laundry facilities.

Hôtel Hadrumete (☎ 226 291, fax 226 863), on the northern side of Place Farhat Hached, has rooms with private bathroom for TD13/18 in winter and TD22/36 in summer.

Places to Eat

Rue Remada, between the train station and Ave Habib Bourguiba, is the place to go for a good cheap meal. You'll find half a dozen small restaurants bunched together, all advertising very similar menus at similar prices. Places like *Restaurant el-Ons* offer salads for TD1 and main courses from TD2.200.

If you want a glass of wine with your meal, head to the popular *Restaurant/Bar de Tunisie* on Rue Ali Belhaouane. Seafood features prominently.

Getting There & Away

The train stations are conveniently central, making train the best way to travel. There are eight services a day to Tunis (2¼ hours, TD7.200), four to Sfax (two hours, TD6.500) via El-Jem, and one to Gabès. Regular trains for Monastir and Mahdia leave from Bab Jedid station at the southern end of Ave Mohamed V. The bus and louage stations are at Souq el-Ahad, 1km south-west of the medina.

KAIROUAN
☎ 07 • pop 110,000

Kairouan, 57km west of Sousse, is Tunisia's holy city. It was here that Islam gained its first foothold in the Maghreb, and the city ranks behind only Mecca, Medina and Jerusalem among Islam's holy places. Kairouan is also famous for its carpets.

Orientation & Information

The medina is the focal point of Kairouan. Its busy main street, Ave 7 Novembre, runs from Bab Tunis on the western side to Bab ech Chouhada in the south.

The tourist office (☎ 231 897) is on Place des Martyrs, opposite the Bab ech Chouhada. Travellers can check email at the Cyber Centre Kairouan, opposite the Agil fuel station on Ave Zama el-Belaoui.

Things to See

The city's main monument, the outwardly plain **great mosque**, is in the north-eastern corner of the medina. Much of the mosque

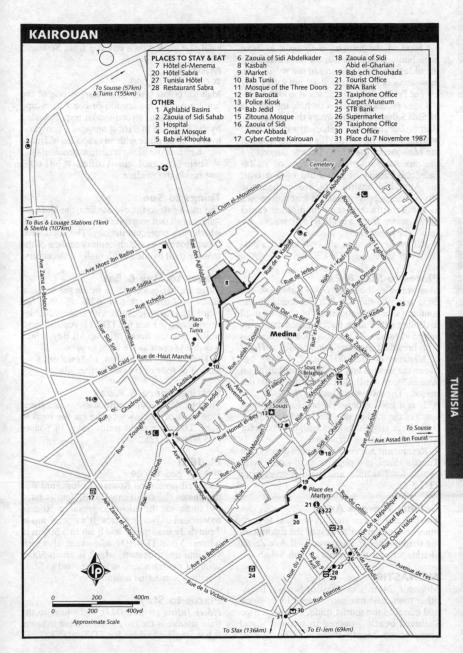

KAIROUAN

PLACES TO STAY & EAT
7   Hôtel el-Menema
20 Hôtel Sabra
27 Tunisia Hôtel
28 Restaurant Sabra

OTHER
1   Aghlabid Basins
2   Zaouia of Sidi Sahab
3   Hospital
4   Great Mosque
5   Bab el-Khouhka
6   Zaouia of Sidi Abdelkader
8   Kasbah
9   Market
10 Bab Tunis
11 Mosque of the Three Doors
12 Bir Barouta
13 Police Kiosk
14 Bab Jedid
15 Zitouna Mosque
16 Zaouia of Sidi Amor Abbada
17 Cyber Centre Kairouan
18 Zaouia of Sidi Abid el-Ghariani
19 Bab ech Chouhada
21 Tourist Office
22 BNA Bank
23 Taxiphone Office
24 Carpet Museum
25 STB Bank
26 Supermarket
29 Taxiphone Office
30 Post Office
31 Place du 7 Novembre 1987

To Sousse (57km)
& Tunis (155km)

To Bus & Louage Stations (1km)
& Sbeitla (107km)

Cemetery

Rue Sidi Abdelkader
Boulevard Brahim ben Laghed
Rue Oum el-Mouminin
Rue de la Kasbah
Rue el-Kadraoui
Rue de Jerba
Rue Sidi Bou Omrani
Rue des Aghlabites
Ave Moez ibn Badiss
Rue Sadlia
Rue Kchelfa
Rue Dar el-Bey
Rue el-Kadraoui
Rue el-Kedidi
Rue Kenahra
Rue Sidi Sfir
Place de Tunis
Medina
Rue Toukbar
Ave Zama el-Belaoui
Rue de-Haut Marché
Rue Salah Soussi
Souq el-Belaghjia
Souq el-Tailleurs
Rue de la Mosquée des trois Portes
Rue Sidi Gaïd
Boulevard Sadlika
Rue el- Chadroui
Rue Bab Jedid
Rue Sidi Gaïd
Ave 7 Novembre
Souqs
Rue Hornet el-Bey
Rue Zouaghi
Rue Sidi el-Ghariani
To Sousse
Ave de Kortoba
Ave Assad ibn Fourat
Rue des Arceaux
Rue Sidi Abdel Noumen
Ave Ali Zouaoui
Rue Ibn Macheb
Ave Zama el-Belaoui
Place des Martyrs
Rue du Gabsi
Rue de la République
Ave de la Mahdia
Ave de Mahdia
Avenue de Fes
Ave de la Victoire
Rue du 20 Mars
Rue du 9 Avril
Rue Étienne
Ave Ali Belhouane
Ave Moncef Bey
Rue Ouled Hafouz
Place de Tunis

0   200   400m
0   200   400yd
Approximate Scale

To Sfax (136km)   To El-Jem (69km)

TUNISIA

dates from the 9th century, although the lowest level of the minaret is thought to have been built early in the 8th century, making it the oldest standing minaret in the world. The mosque is open 8 am to 2.30 pm every day except Friday, when it closes at noon.

Other places of interest include the **Zaouia of Sidi Sahab**, also known as the Mosque of Barber because Sidi Sahab always carried with him three hairs from the Prophet's beard; the **Mosque of the Three Doors**, famous for the rare Arab inscriptions carved on its facade; the **Zaouia of Sidi Abid el-Ghariani**; the **Aghlabid basins**, which once held the city's water supply; and the tourist trap known as **Bir Barouta**, where a blindfolded camel draws water from a well whose waters are said to be connected to Mecca.

All the above sites are covered by a collective ticket costing TD4.200.

Places to Stay & Eat

Most travellers head for *Hôtel Sabra* (☎ 230 263), opposite the Bab ech Chouhada on the southern side of the medina. The staff are used to dealing with budget travellers and the rooms are good value at TD10/16 for singles/doubles with breakfast. Another good choice is *Hôtel el-Menema* (☎ 225 003, fax 235 033), between the medina and the Aghlabite basins on Ave el-Moez ibn Badiss. It charges TD10 per person. The two-star *Tunisia Hôtel* (☎ 231 855) is a good older-style hotel about 400m south of the medina on Ave de la République. It has large singles/doubles with bathroom for TD18/30, including breakfast.

Restaurant Sabra, a few doors down from Tunisia Hôtel, is a popular local eatery with chorba for 700 mills and main courses from TD2.500.

Getting There & Away

The bus and louage stations are next to each other about 2km north-west of the medina on the road to Sbeitla, signposted off Ave Zama el-Belaoui near the Zaouia of Sidi Sahab.

MONASTIR

Monastir, 24km south-east of Sousse, is another town that has surrendered lock, stock and barrel to the tourist trade. There's a nice sheltered **beach** – packed in summer – and scenes from Monty Python's *The Life of Brian* were shot at the **ribat**, but both can easily be visited on a day trip from Sousse.

MAHDIA

☎ 03 • pop 30,000

Mahdia, 60km south of Sousse, is one of the few towns on this section of coast to escape being turned into a total tourist trap. Founded by the Fatimids in 916, it remains a comparatively relaxed place with an unspoiled old medina stretched out along a narrow peninsula.

There is a small tourist office (☎ 681 098) just inside the medina.

Things to See

The main gate to the old medina, the **Skifa el-Kahla**, is all that remains of the 10m-thick wall which once protected the city. The unadorned **great mosque** is a 20th-century replica of the mosque built by the Mahdi in the 10th century.

Places to Stay & Eat

There are two good places inside the medina. *Hôtel el-Jazira* (☎ 681 629, 36 Rue Ibn Fourat) has a top location with singles/doubles overlooking the sea for TD7/11. Another possibility is a new *hotel*, off Rue Ali Bey, which was due to open as we went to press.

The friendly *Restaurant el-Moez* has a selection of four or five daily specials.

Getting There & Away

The bus, louage and train stations are about 1km west of the town centre on the road to Sfax. There are eight trains a day to Sousse (1½ hours, TD2).

EL-JEM

☎ 03 • pop 10,000

The well-preserved **Roman Colosseum** that dominates the small town of El-Jem is rated by some as the most impressive Roman monument in North Africa. It's open 7 am to 7 pm daily in summer and 8 am to 5.30 pm in winter. Your TD4.100 admission also gets you into the **museum**, which is about 500m south of the train station on the road to Sfax. It houses some fine mosaics.

Places to Stay

Hôtel Julius (☎ 690 044), right next to the train station, is the only hotel and bar in town. It has singles/doubles for TD21.500/30.

Getting There & Away

All forms of transport leave from around the train station, so just grab the first service that comes by – bus, louage or train.

SFAX

☎ 04 • pop 340,000

The unglamorous, eastern coastal town of Sfax is Tunisia's second-largest city. It has two big things going for it – its unspoiled old medina and the fact that there's hardly a package tourist in sight.

Orientation & Information

Sfax is a big, sprawling city. The only parts of interest to the visitor are the medina and the ville nouvelle, built on reclaimed land between the medina and the port.

The tourist office (☎ 211 040) is out by the port on Ave Mohammed Hedi Khefecha. The post office occupies most of a block at the north-eastern end of Ave Habib Bourguiba, near the train station. There are plenty of banks, mostly along Ave Habib Bourguiba and Ave Hedi Chaker.

You can check your emails at the Publinet office at 7 Ave Ali Bach Hamba.

Things to See & Do

It's easy to spend hours wandering around the medina's maze of narrow streets. This is still a working medina, without the glitz and wall-to-wall tourist shops of the medinas in Tunis and Sousse. Highlights include the atmospheric old **covered souqs**, just north of the 9th-century **Great Mosque**, and the **Dar Jellouli Museum of Popular Traditions**, housed in a beautiful 17th-century mansion.

Places to Stay

The cheap hotels are in the medina. The only place worth considering is *Hôtel Medina* (☎ 220 354, 51 Rue Mongi Slim). It charges TD4 per person.

Most travellers prefer the comforts of the ville nouvelle. *Hôtel de la Paix* (☎ 296 437, 10 Rue Alexandre Dumas) has singles/doubles with private bathroom for TD10/12. *Hôtel Alexander* (☎ 221 613, 16 Rue Alexandre Dumas), a few doors away, is a popular old-style French place with larger, more comfortable rooms for TD15/20.

Seafood is Sfax's speciality. Try *Restaurant au Bec Fin* (Place 2 Mars) where waiters clad in snappy bow ties dole out a delicious fish chorba (TD1.200) and spaghetti aux fruits de mer (TD4).

Getting There & Away

You'd have to be in a mad rush to fly, but Tuninter stops at Sfax twice a week on the route between Tunis and Jerba.

The trains are fine for most people. The station is conveniently central, and there are two trains a day to Gabès and four to Tunis via El-Jem and Sousse.

The SNTRI bus station is opposite the train station on Rue Tazarka, although there are plans to move to a new bus complex on Rue Commandant Bejaoui, presently the base of local company Soretras. SNTRI has regular buses to Tunis (four hours, TD10.260) via Sousse (two hours, TD5.560). Other destinations include Douz, Gabès, Jerba and Tataouine. The louage station is 300m further east on Rue Commandant Bejaoui.

Southern Tunisia

TOZEUR

☎ 06 • pop 22,000

Tozeur is a thriving oasis town on the edge of the Chott el-Jerid, the largest of Tunisia's salt lakes. Tourism is big business here, with a rapidly-expanding band of big hotels in the zone touristique south-west of town. It's also well set up for travellers.

Information

The ONTT tourist office is on Ave Abdulkacem Chebbi (☎ 454 088). You'll find branches of all the major banks around the town centre, as well as numerous tour agencies. Internet access is available at Publinet, near the tourist office on Ave 7 Novembre.

Things to See & Do

The **Ouled el-Hadef**, the town's labyrinthine old quarter, is well worth exploring for its striking architecture and brickwork; enter by the road past Hôtel Splendid.

The enormous **palmeraie** (palm grove) is best explored by bicycle, which can be hired opposite the Museum Dar Charait. The **Zoo du**

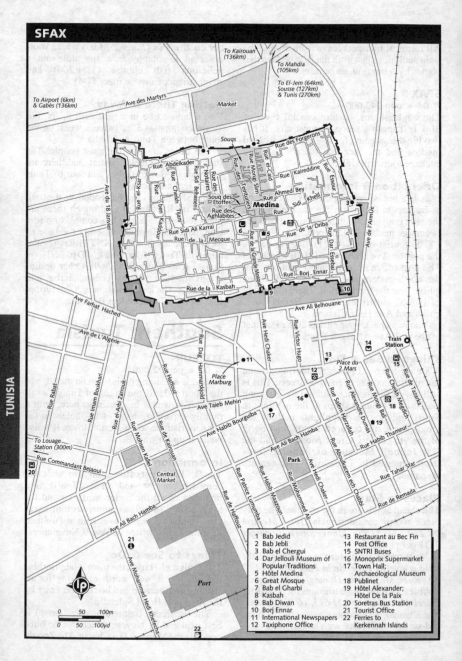

SFAX

To Kairouan
(136km)

To Mahdia
(105km)

To El-Jem (64km),
Sousse (127km)
& Tunis (270km)

To Airport (6km)
& Gabès (136km)

Ave des Martyrs

Market

Souqs

Rue des Forgerons

Rue el-Caïd

Rue Mong Slim

Rue des Teinturiers

Rue Abdelkader

Rue Kaireddine

Rue Sidi Belhassen

Rue Essour

Rue Ahmed Bey

Rue Cheikh Tijani

Rue des Notaires

Sidi Khelil

Souq des Etoffes

Medina

Rue Aghlabites

Rue Ben Kaddour

Rue de la Driba

Rue Sidi Ali Karrai

Rue de la Mecque

Rue Dar Essebai

Rue de la Grande Mosquée

Rue Borj Ennar

Rue de la Kasbah

Ave de l'Armi'le

Ave du 18 Janvier

Ave el-Kaïa

Ave Farhat Hached

Ave Ali Belhouane

Ave de L'Algérie

Ave Victor Hugo

Train
Station

Rue Dag Hammarskjöld

Rue Hafouz

Place du
2 Mars

Place
Marburg

Rue Hedi Chaker

Rue de Tazarka

Rue Rabat

Rue Imam Boukhari

Rue el-Arbi Zarrouk

Ave Taieb Mehiri

Rue Alexander Dumas

Rue Cheikh Megdich

Rue Mong Bali

Rue Salem Harzallah

Ave Habib Bourguiba

Rue Mohsen Kallel

Rue de Kairouan

Rue Habib Thameur

To Louage
Station (300m)

Rue Commandant Bejaoui

Ave Ali Bach Hamba

Central
Market

Rue Patrice Lumumba

Rue Habib Maazoun

Ave Ali Bach Hamba

Rue Aboulkacem ech Chabbi

Ave Hedi Chaker

Park

Rue Tahar Sfar

Rue de Remada

Rue de Hafouz

Rue Mohammed Ali

Port

To Louage
Station

Ave Mohammed Hedi Khefacha

0   50   100m
0   50   100yd

1	Bab Jedid	13	Restaurant au Bec Fin
2	Bab Jebli	14	Post Office
3	Bab el Chergui	15	SNTRI Buses
4	Dar Jellouli Museum of	16	Monoprix Supermarket
	Popular Traditions	17	Town Hall;
5	Hôtel Medina		Archaeological Museum
6	Great Mosque	18	Publinet
7	Bab el Gharbi	19	Hôtel Alexander;
8	Kasbah		Hôtel De la Paix
9	Bab Diwan	20	Soretras Bus Station
10	Borj Ennar	21	Tourist Office
11	International Newspapers	22	Ferries to
12	Taxiphone Office		Kerkennah Islands

TUNISIA

Paradis, on the southern side of the palmaraie, is home to a Coca Cola-drinking camel.

The impressive **Museum Dar Charait** is 1km beyond the tourist office at the western end of Ave Abdulkacem Chebbi. It's open 8 am until midnight daily; admission is TD3.

Places to Stay
Camping Les Beaux Rêves (☎ 453 331), west of the tourist office on Ave Abdulkacem Chebbi, is a good, shady site that backs onto the palmeraie. It charges TD4 per person, either in your own tent or one of the communal nomad-style tents.

The cheap hotels aren't worth knowing about, but there are some very good mid-range places on Ave Chebbi. *Residence Warda* (☎ 452 597, 29 Ave Abdulkacem Chebbi), and *Hôtel Karim* (☎ 454 574, 150 Ave Abdulkacem Chebbi) – opposite the calèche waiting area, are both top value at TD12/19 for singles/doubles with private bathroom. Smarter still is the brand new *Pension el-Arich* (☎ 462 644, c arich@xoommail.com, 93 Ave Abdulkacem Chebbi), next to the tourist office, where rooms are TD13/22. All these prices include breakfast.

Places to Eat
Ave Chebbi is well served for restaurants as well as hotels, starting with the popular *Restaurant du Soleil*, opposite Residence Warda. It has a good choice of main meals from TD3, and is one of the few places in the country to acknowledge the existence of vegetarians.

Restaurant de la République, off Ave Habib Bourguiba near the mosque, is another favourite.

Shopping
Ave Habib Bourguiba is lined with souvenir shops selling the area's famous rugs. Bargain hard if you're buying.

Getting There & Away
Tozeur has at least three flights a week to Tunis (70 minutes, TD48.500 one way).

SNTRI has five buses a day to Tunis (seven hours, TD16.550), and there are frequent local buses to Nefta (30 minutes, 950 mills). Services east to Douz and Gabès are very sketchy; it's best to catch a louage to Kebili and change.

Getting Around
Calèches (horse-drawn carriages) can be hired from opposite the Hôtel Karim for TD10 per hour.

AROUND TOZEUR
The beautiful old Berber villages of **Tamerza, Midès** and **Chebika** lie close to the Algerian border in the rugged Jebel en-Negeb ranges, about 60km north of Tozeur.

The original mudbrick villages, which had existed since Roman times, were abandoned after the region was hit by 22 days of torrential rain in 1969. The freak rains turned the houses into mud, and the villagers moved to new settlements that were hastily constructed nearby. The original villages are now 'ghost villages', and they are fascinating places to explore.

The biggest of them is Tamerza, which is large enough to warrant two SNTRI buses a day to Tunis, and two to Tozeur. Most people visit on organised tours. The agencies in Tozeur charge about TD30 for a half-day tour that calls at all three villages.

Tamerza also has accommodation at *Hôtel Les Cascades* (☎ 06-485 322), which charges over the odds at TD20/25 for singles/doubles with breakfast – but it does have a great setting.

DOUZ
☎ 05 • pop 12,000
Perched right on the fringe of the Grand Erg Oriental (Great Eastern Desert), the oasis town of Douz promotes itself as the 'gateway to the Sahara'.

It remains pretty laid-back in spite of the huge numbers of 4WDs that pass through town. Most of them head straight for the hotels of the small *zone touristique* (tourist strip), which faces the desert on the southern edge of the enormous palmeraie.

The town centre is probably the most backpacker friendly place in Tunisia, with some great budget accommodation and plenty of small restaurants.

Orientation & Information
Douz isn't big enough to get lost in. The town centre has all the facilities of importance to travellers, including banks and Internet access. Everyone in town claims to be a cameltrekking guide, but it's safer to use one of the

TUNISIA

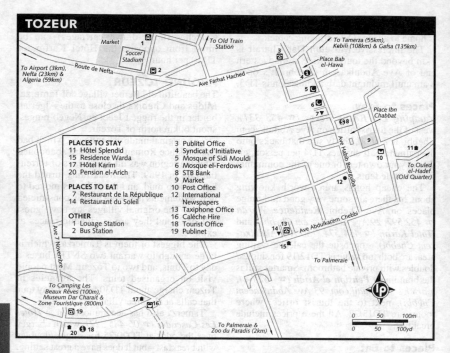

TOZEUR

To Airport (3km),
Nefta (23km) &
Algeria (59km)

Route de Nefta

Market

Soccer
Stadium

To Old Train
Station

Ave Farhat Hached

To Tamerza (55km),
Kebili (108km) & Gafsa (135km)

Place Bab
el-Hawa

Place Ibn
Chabbat

Ave Habib Bourguiba

Ave 7 Novembre

To Ouled
el-Hadef
(Old Quarter)

Ave Abdulkacem Chebbi

To Palmeraie

To Camping Les
Beaux Rêves (100m),
Museum Dar Charait &
Zone Touristique (800m)

To Palmeraie &
Zoo du Paradis (2km)

PLACES TO STAY		3 Publitel Office
11 Hôtel Splendid		4 Syndicat d'Initiative
15 Residence Warda		5 Mosque of Sidi Mouldi
17 Hôtel Karim		6 Mosque el-Ferdows
20 Pension el-Arich		8 STB Bank
		9 Market
PLACES TO EAT		10 Post Office
7 Restaurant de la République		12 International
14 Restaurant du Soleil		Newspapers
		13 Taxiphone Office
OTHER		16 Calèche Hire
1 Louage Station		18 Tourist Office
2 Bus Station		19 Publinet

0   50   100m
0   50   100yd

nine tour agencies or seek advice from the
ONTT tourist office (☎ 470 351).

Camel Trekking

Most people come to Douz to organise camel
trekking. If you just want to sit on a camel,
you'll find plenty at the zone touristique;
you'll probably have to bargain hard to get
the official rate of TD2.50 per hour.
Overnight trips cost from TD25 per day.

The desert immediately south of Douz
isn't very interesting, and is crawling with
package groups on one-hour treks. You'll
find more interesting country around **Zaafrane**, 14km south-west of Douz, as well as
lots of camels and similar prices.

The giant dunes of the **Grand Erg Oriental** lie a long way farther south. Tour agencies
use 4WDs to transfer clients to desert bases
for the start of treks.

Things to See

Try to time your visit so that you're in town
for the famous **Thursday market**, still an

authentic market in spite of all the tour buses.
Don't miss the livestock markets, where the
last of Tunisia's nomadic camel herdsmen
come to trade.

The **palmaraie** is a wonderful, cool place
for a stroll. It's the largest in the country with
more than 400,000 trees.

Special Events

The Sahara Festival, usually staged in November, features displays of traditional desert
sports as well as colourful parades and music.

Places to Stay

Douz has good budget accommodation, starting with the **Desert Club** camping ground
(☎ 495 595), in the palmeraie at the southern
end of Ave 7 Novembre.

The best of the budget hotels is the very
friendly **Hôtel 20 Mars** (☎ 470 269), which
has rooms around a small courtyard. Rates
start at TD5 per person with shared bathroom. It also has a good restaurant with meals
for TD3.500.

Getting There & Away

All public transport leaves from the bus and louage station on the northern edge of town. SNTRI has two buses a day to Tunis (nine hours, TD19.640). There are lots of services to the regional centre of Kebili, 40km to the north, and daily buses to Gabès and Tozeur. There also are regular buses and camionettes to Zaafrane.

GABÈS

☎ 05 • pop 90,000

There is little reason to stay in this industrial city on the Gulf of Gabès. If you get stuck overnight, *Hôtel Ben Nejima (☎ 271 591)* is a clean place charging TD6 per person. It's close to the bus station at the junction of Ave Farhat Hached and Rue Haj Djilani Lahbib.

The bus and louage stations are at the western end of Ave Farhat Hached. Three bus companies operate from here and can take you just about anywhere in Tunisia. SNTRI has regular departures to Tunis for TD14.700. There are two trains a day to Sfax.

MATMATA

☎ 05 • population 1000

It's easy to work out why the makers of *Star Wars* picked Matmata, 45km south-west of Gabès, as the home planet of Luke Skywalker. Set amid a bizarre lunar landscape, the Berbers of Matmata went underground centuries ago to escape the summer heat.

Although conventional modern buildings are now in the majority, the town still boasts dozens of the troglodyte pit homes that are its main attraction. Each of the many mounds represents a home. They are all built along the same lines: a large central courtyard, usually circular, is dug out of the soft sandstone, and the rooms are then tunnelled off the perimeter.

Not surprisingly, Matmata gets more than it's fair share of tour groups. Most head back to the coastal resorts in the evening, so aim to arrive after 5pm.

Places to Stay

Three troglodyte homes have been transformed into interesting budget hotels. *Sidi Driss (☎ 230 005)*, setting for the bar scene in *Star Wars*, is the best of them – and good value at TD13 for dinner, bed and breakfast or 7.200 per person for B&B.

MEDENINE

☎ 05 • pop 20,000

Medenine, 75km south-east of Gabès, is the main town of the ksour (plural of *ksar*, a fortified Berber granary) area of the country's south. Medenine itself has a small ksar, which is something of a tourist trap, but the best examples are farther south, near Tataouine.

There's no reason to stay in Medenine, but *Hôtel Essaada (☎ 640 300)* on Ave Habib Bourguiba is OK if you get stuck. It asks TD4.500/7 for singles/doubles.

The bus station and main louage station is about 2km north of town on the road to Gabès. Louages to Jerba and Tataouine leave from Rue 18 Janvier in the centre of town.

TATAOUINE

☎ 05 • pop 8000

Tataouine, 124km south-east of Gabès, lies at the heart of the fascinating ksour district, famous for its spectacular Berber villages. The town itself is no more than a modern administrative centre, but it has all the facilities a traveller needs – including a Publinet office, an ONTT tourist office (☎ 850 686), hotels and restaurants.

Places to Stay & Eat

The best budget rooms are at the tiny *Hôtel Residence Hamza (☎ 863 506, Ave Hedi Chaker)*, which charges TD8.500 per person for B&B. If it's full, try *Hôtel Essour (☎ 860 104, Rue 18 Janvier)*. The rooms are basic but cheap at TD6 per person with hot shower and breakfast. *Hôtel Medina*, opposite, has a good restaurant on the first floor.

Getting There & Away

Buses and louages leave from a range of locations around the town centre. The main destination is the regional centre of Medenine, 49km to the north. There are occasional buses to Jerba, Gabès and Tunis (nine hours, TD19.380).

AROUND TATAOUINE

The most impressive of the ksour is **Ksar Ouled Soltane**, 24km south-east of Tataouine, where the *ghorfas* rise a dizzying four stories. **Ksar Haddada**, 26km north-west of Tataouine, was used as a location for Star Wars during its time as a hotel – which are now over.

TUNISIA

Equally as impressive are the region's ancient hilltop villages. **Chenini**, 18km west of Tataouine, is the best known and gets all the crowds. **Douiret** and **Guermessa** are every bit as spectacular and much less visited.

Getting Around

Public transport isn't really an option. It costs about TD25 to charter a taxi from Tataouine to any of these sites, which includes adequate waiting time.

Jerba

Jerbans, especially those involved in the tourist industry, like to claim that their island is the legendary Land of the Lotus Eaters visited by Ulysses in the course of Homer's *Odyssey*.

These days it's beaches, not lotus fruit, that are the prime attraction – as well as winter temperatures that seldom fall below 15°C.

The island's main town and transport hub is Houmt Souq, in the middle of the north coast. Tourist development is concentrated on the beaches of the north-east. The island is linked to the mainland by a causeway built in Roman times, and by 24-hour car ferries between Ajim and Jorf.

HOUMT SOUQ
☎ 05 • pop 65,000

Jerba's main town is a tangle of whitewashed houses, narrow alleys and attractive cafe-lined squares. There are a couple of tourist offices, but the syndicat d'initiative (☎ 650 915) in the middle of town is the only one worth visiting. There are several banks, a post office and countless souvenir shops.

Internet access is available at Djerba Cyber Espace, 135 Ave Habib Bourguiba. Walk through the archway at No 135, and the office is up the steps to the left.

Places to Stay

Houmt Souq has some of the most interesting places to stay in the country – old funduqs that have been converted into a range of accommodation to suit every budget.

They start with the excellent *auberge de jeunesse* (☎ 650 619, 11 Rue Moncef Bey). It's great value at TD4.500 for a dorm bed and breakfast, or TD7.500 with dinner as

well. The popular *Hôtel Arischa* (☎ 650 384, 38 Rue Ghazi Mustapha), has singles/doubles for TD11/16.

The best of the funduqs is *Hôtel Erriadh* (☎ 650 756, 10 Rue Mohammed Ferjani), which charges TD17.500/26 for large comfortable rooms with private bathroom. Another excellent option is the nearby *Hôtel Sables d'Or* (☎ 650 423, 30 Rue Mohammed Ferjani).

Places to Eat

For cheap local eats, head for the tiny *Restaurant La Mamma* on Rue Habib Bougatfa. For a bit more style, try *Restaurant Les Palmiers*, nearby on Place d'Algérie.

Getting There & Away

Tuninter flies to Tunis (one hour, TD50.500 one way) up to six times a day, depending on the season. The airport is 8km from Houmt Souq – about TD4 by taxi.

The bus and louage stations are side by side at the southern end of the main street. There are frequent services to Medenine as well as to Gabès and points north. SNTRI has four buses a day to Tunis; services via Kairouan are cheaper and faster than those via Sfax and Sousse.

JERBA ISLAND
☎ 05

Jerba's star attraction is **Sidi Mahres Beach**, which begins 10km east of Houmt Souq and continues all the way to **Ras Taguermes** at the north-eastern tip of the island. It's monopolised by the residents of the big hotels. There's nothing to prevent nonresidents from using them, and you'll find every conceivable form of water sports, from windsurfing to parasailing.

Places to Stay

There is camping on the east coast at *Auberge Centre Aghir* (☎ 657 366). Bus No 11 from Houmt Souq goes past the site.

The hotels of the zone touristique are priced beyond the means of most backpackers, but there are some good mid-range places. Try *Hôtel Dar Salem* (☎/fax 757 667), signposted off the main road about 12km east of Houmt Souq. It charges TD21/32 for singles/doubles with breakfast.

TUNISIA

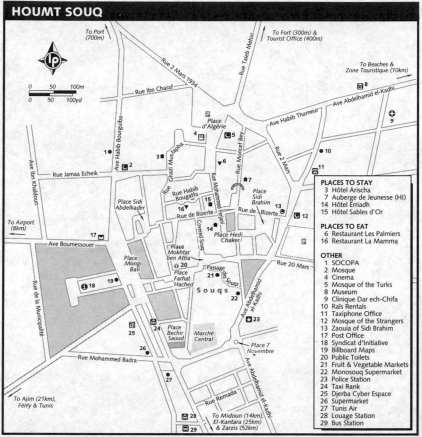

HOUMT SOUQ

PLACES TO STAY
3 Hôtel Arischa
7 Auberge de Jeunesse (HI)
14 Hôtel Erriadh
15 Hôtel Sables d'Or

PLACES TO EAT
6 Restaurant Les Palmiers
16 Restaurant La Mamma

OTHER
1 SOCOPA
2 Mosque
4 Cinema
5 Mosque of the Turks
8 Museum
9 Clinique Dar ech-Chifa
10 Raïs Rentals
11 Taxiphone Office
12 Mosque of the Strangers
13 Zaouia of Sidi Brahim
17 Post Office
18 Syndicat d'Initiative
19 Billboard Maps
20 Public Toilets
21 Fruit & Vegetable Markets
22 Monosouq Supermarket
23 Police Station
24 Taxi Rank
25 Djerba Cyber Espace
26 Supermarket
27 Tunis Air
28 Louage Station
29 Bus Station

TUNISIA

Getting Around

Most of Jerba is flat, which makes it a good place to explore either by bicycle or moped, both of which can be hired from Raïs Rentals (☎ 650 303) on Ave Abdelhamid el-Kadhi in Houmt Souq. The island's bus network is centred on the main town of Houmt Souq.

Turkey

Turkey is Asia's foothold in Europe, the country that bridges two continents. With over 4000km of warm-water coastline, it's certainly fair to call it a Mediterranean country and the tourism boom of the 1990s put it on the travel map for everyone from package holiday-makers to villa-renters. The hundreds of ruined Greek and Roman cities now have to share shore space with hundreds of holiday villages, not all of them lovely to look at.

The Turks are mostly very friendly, especially when you escape the resorts and head into the heartland, and prices remain fairly low compared to Western Europe. Prices are highest along the coast.

Facts about Turkey

HISTORY
By 7000 BC a Neolithic city, one of the oldest ever recorded, was already established at Çatal Höyük, near Konya. The greatest of the early civilisations of Anatolia (Asian Turkey) was that of the Hittites, a force to be reckoned with from 2000 to 1200 BC with their capital at Hattuşa, north of Ankara.

After the collapse of the Hittite empire, Anatolia splintered into a number of small states, and it wasn't until the Graeco-Roman period that parts of the country were reunited. Later, Christianity spread through Anatolia, carried by the apostle Paul, a native of Tarsus (near Adana).

Byzantine Empire
In 330 AD the Roman emperor Constantine founded a new imperial city at Byzantium (modern İstanbul). Renamed Constantinople, this strategic city became the capital of the Eastern Roman Empire and was the centre of the Byzantine Empire for 1000 years. During the European Dark Ages, when the glories of Greece were just a memory and Rome had been overrun by barbarians, the Byzantine Empire kept alive the flame of western culture. Over the centuries it was threatened by the powerful empires of the east (Persians,

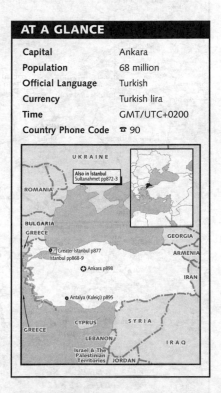

AT A GLANCE

Capital	Ankara
Population	68 million
Official Language	Turkish
Currency	Turkish lira
Time	GMT/UTC+0200
Country Phone Code	☎ 90

Arabs, Turks) and west (the Christian powers of Europe).

The beginning of the Byzantine Empire's decline came with the arrival of the Seljuk Turks and their defeat of the Byzantine forces at Manzikert, near Lake Van, in August 1071. The Seljuks overran most of Anatolia, and established a provincial capital at Konya. Their domains included today's Turkey, Iran and Iraq.

The Crusades
With significantly reduced territory, the Byzantines endeavoured to protect Constantinople and reclaim Anatolia. In 1095 Pope Urban II called for crusaders to fight a holy war. To reach the Holy Land it was necessary

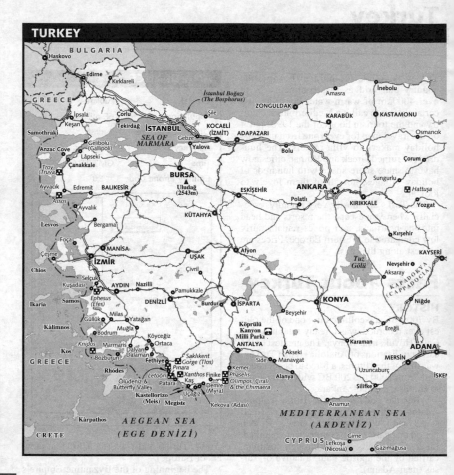

TURKEY

for the First Crusade to pass through Constantinople. In return for this right of passage, the Emperor Alexius Comnenus struck a deal with the crusade leaders, demanding that any territories won from the Turks by the crusaders be returned to the Byzantines. The crusaders quickly reneged on the deal but in 1097 the Byzantines still won back the city of Nicaea from the Seljuks and reoccupied western Anatolia; the Seljuks maintained their power in the rest of Anatolia. The Fourth Crusade (1202–04) proved disastrous for the Byzantines, with a combined Venetian and crusader force taking and plundering the city

of Constantinople. The Byzantines eventually regained the ravaged city in 1261.

Ottoman Empire

A Mongol invasion of the late 1200s put an end to Seljuk power, but new small Turkish states soon arose in western Anatolia. One, headed by Osman (1258–1326), grew into the Ottoman Empire, and in 1453 Constantinople finally fell to the Ottoman sultan Mehmet II (the Conqueror).

A century later, under Süleyman the Magnificent, the Ottoman Empire reached the peak of its cultural brilliance and power,

TURKEY

spreading deep into Europe, Asia and North Africa. The janissaries, the first modern standing army, gave the Turks an advantage, as the European nations had to raise fresh armies for each war. The Turks tolerated minority groups, including Christians and Jews.

Ottoman success was based on military expansion. When the march westwards was stalled at Vienna in 1683, the rot started. A succession of incompetent sultans hardly helped, and the discontented janissaries became totally unreliable.

By the 19th century the great European powers had begun to covet the sultan's vast domains. Nationalist ideas swept through Europe after the French Revolution, and Turkey found itself with unruly subject populations in the Balkans. In 1829 the Greeks won their independence, followed by the Serbs, the Romanians and, in 1878, the Bulgarians. Italy took Tripolitania in North Africa from Turkey in 1911, and after the 1912–13 Balkan War the Ottomans lost Albania and Macedonia.

Finally, the unfortunate Turks emerged from WWI stripped of their last non-Turkish provinces – Syria, Palestine, Mesopotamia (Iraq) and Arabia. Most of Anatolia itself was to be parcelled out to the victorious Greeks, Italians, French and Russians, leaving the Turks virtually nothing.

Mustafa Kemal Atatürk

At this low point in Turkish history, Mustafa Kemal, the father of modern Turkey, took over. Atatürk, as he was later called, made his name by repelling the Anzacs in their heroic but futile attempt to capture Gallipoli. Rallying the tattered remnants of the Turkish army, he pushed the last of the weak Ottoman rulers aside and out-manoeuvred the Allied forces in the War of Independence.

The Turks finally won the War of Independence in 1923 when the invading Greeks were literally pushed into the sea at Smyrna (modern İzmir), a city with a large Greek population. There followed an exchange of populations similar to that which took place in India at the time of the India-Pakistan partition. Well over a million Greeks left Turkey and nearly half a million Turks moved in.

With Turkey reduced to smaller but more secure boundaries, Atatürk embarked on a rapid modernisation program centred on establishing a secular democracy, de-emphasising religion, introducing the Roman alphabet and European dress, and moving towards equal rights for women. In 1923 the country's capital was moved from 'decadent' İstanbul to Ankara. Naturally, such sweeping changes did not come easily, but Turkey is certainly more progressive in these areas than most of its neighbours.

Relations with Greece improved in 1930 but were soured again after WWII by the conflict over Cyprus, particularly after the Greek-led anti-Makarios coup and subsequent Turkish invasion of the island in 1974.

Modern Turkey

In 1960, 1970 and 1980, the army stepped in to 'correct' what it saw as an undemocratic drift away from the principles set forth by Atatürk. Since the return to democratic government there has been rapid economic development, at least in western Turkey.

In 1999 the leader of the Kurdistan Workers' Party (PKK) Abdullah Ocalan was captured, signalling the probable end of a struggle for an independent Kurdish homeland that had

devastated eastern Turkey since 1985, claiming 30,000 lives.

Also in 1999 two earthquakes hit northwestern Turkey, causing enormous social, economic and political problems.

GEOGRAPHY

Turkey is divided into Asian and European parts by the Dardanelles, the Sea of Marmara and the Bosphorus. Thrace (European Turkey) comprises only 3% of the total 780,580 sq km land area. The remaining 97% is Anatolia, a vast plateau rising eastward towards the Caucasus Mountains. Turkey's coastline is over 6000km long and includes many popular resort areas.

CLIMATE

The Aegean and Mediterranean coasts have mild, rainy winters and hot, dry summers. In İstanbul, summer temperatures average around 28° to 30°C; the winters are chilly but usually above freezing, with rain and perhaps a dusting of snow. The Anatolian plateau is baking hot in summer and very cold in winter. The Black Sea coast is mild and rainy in summer, and chilly and rainy in winter.

Mountainous eastern Turkey is very cold and snowy in winter, and only pleasantly warm in high summer. The south-east is dry and mild in winter and very hot in summer, with temperatures above 45°C not unusual.

ECOLOGY & ENVIRONMENT

In theory Turkey is ecologically conscious with admirable environmental protection laws. Unfortunately, weak government enforcement and strong commercial pressures often retard ecological progress, as was made painfully obvious when many of the deaths from the 1999 earthquakes were attributed to poor construction work rather than the quakes themselves.

Despite this, Turkey is still proposing to build a nuclear power station on the coast near Adana, close to a known fault line.

FLORA & FAUNA

Turkey has a network of national parks protecting some of its most spectacular scenery and, with it, the bird and animal life. But the speed of development in the west is rapidly eliminating all the remaining wildlife; you'll see many more birds, for example, in eastern Turkey than in the west.

GOVERNMENT & POLITICS

Turkey is a multi-party parliamentary democracy, with the army acting as a behind-the-scenes guarantor of democracy and secularism. The president is the head of state, with limited constitutional powers. The prime minister is the head of government.

Elections in 1999 led to the forming of a tripartite coalition government in which, for the first time, the nationalist MHP (National Action Party) played a major role even though the prime minister is veteran leftist politician Bulent Ecevit. In 2000 the equally veteran Suleyman Demirel was finally replaced as president by the high court judge Ahmet Necdet Sezer.

Turkey's recent acceptance as a candidate for EU membership has given added urgency to discussions about how Turkey can be turned into a fully-fledged western-style democracy with more concern for human rights.

ECONOMY

Until 1999 Turkey's economy had been following a steady upward growth curve. However, the twin earthquakes that hit the north-western industrial heartlands combined with a collapse of tourism caused the economy to contract sharply. The government is now following IMF advice on how to restructure, and hopefully strengthen, an economy that is still rooted in agriculture but has a strong manufacturing sector, producing motor vehicles, appliances and consumer goods.

In a normal year tourism brings in billions of dollars. Many Turks also send home money from jobs in Europe, particularly from Germany.

POPULATION & PEOPLE

Turkey's population of 68 million is made up predominantly of Muslim Turks, although Muslim Kurds are a significant minority (perhaps 12 million). There are also small groups of Jews, Greeks, Armenians, Laz and Hemşins (Black Sea peoples) and Arabs. The five biggest cities are İstanbul (16 million people), Ankara (3.2 million), İzmir (2.7 million), Adana (1.9 million) and Bursa (1.6 million).

ARTS

Islam discourages images of any being 'with a soul' (ie animal or human), so the Ottomans produced little sculpture or portraiture. Instead Turkish artists concentrated on calligraphy, architecture, carpet-making, textile design, jewellery, faïence and glass-making.

Ottoman literature and court music were mostly religious, and both sound pompous and lugubrious to western ears. Folk music was (and still is) sprightly; troubadours were highly skilled and very popular, although TV and cassettes have largely seen them off.

As with all else, Atatürk changed Turkey's cultural picture, encouraging painting, sculpture, western music (he loved opera), dance and drama. Recently Ottoman arts like paper-marbling and Karagöz shadow-puppet plays have been enjoying a resurgence, seen as traditions worthy of preservation. Carpet-weaving is, was and always will be a Turkish passion.

SOCIETY & CONDUCT
Traditional Culture

Republican Turkey has largely adapted to a modern, Westernised lifestyle. Although many Turks drink alcohol and behave much like westerners, it's still important to remember that they revere the moral and spiritual teachings of their religion and observe many of its customs, especially during *Ramazan* (Ramadan), the holy month of fasting.

Liberal western attitudes born of Atatürk's reforms are strongest in the urban centres of the west and along the coasts, especially among the middle and upper classes. The working and farming classes, particularly in the east, tend to be more conservative, traditional and religious.

Dos & Don'ts

When visiting mosques you should take particular care not to give offence. Both sexes should remove their shoes before entering and wear long trousers instead of shorts. Women should cover their heads, arms and shoulders.

Don't photograph anything military. In areas off the tourist track, it's polite to ask '*Foto/video çekebilir miyim?*' (May I take a photo/video?) before shooting close-ups of people.

RELIGION

Turkey is 99% Muslim, predominantly Sunni, with Shias in the east and south-east. A small but growing band of 'born-again' Muslims are fervent and strict in their religion. They're unlikely to press you to convert but may treat you with caution bordering on hostility.

LANGUAGE

Ottoman Turkish was written in Arabic script until Atatürk decreed a change to Roman script in 1928. In big cities and tourist areas, many locals know at least some English and/or German. See the Language Guide at the back of this book for pronunciation guidelines and useful words and phrases.

Facts for the Visitor

HIGHLIGHTS

The must-sees of İstanbul include Topkapı Palace, Aya Sofya (Hagia Sofia), the Blue Mosque, the Turkish and Islamic Arts Museum, the Yerebatan Sarnıçı (cistern) and the Kariye (Chora) Museum. The battlefields of Gallipoli on the Dardanelles are particularly moving although many visitors find nearby Troy disappointing. Ephesus is the best-preserved classical city on the Mediterranean.

There are fine examples of Seljuk Turkish architecture in Alanya, Konya, and Erzurum. The Black Sea coastal town of Trabzon gives you a taster of a Turkey that is increasingly influenced by Russia.

Turkey's best beaches are at Pamucak (near Ephesus), Ölüdeniz, Bodrum, Patara, Antalya, Side and Alanya. The improbable 'lunar' landscapes of Cappadocia are perhaps the single most visually impressive feature in all Turkey. Farther east near Malatya, the great Commagenian heads on Nemrut Dağı certainly repay a long drive and an early start to the day.

SUGGESTED ITINERARIES

Most people come primarily to see İstanbul, the Aegean and Mediterranean coasts and Cappadocia. The Black Sea coast can be travelled in a day or a week, as time allows. With limited time, consider these itineraries:

Two days
  Explore İstanbul or Selçuk/Ephesus.
One week
  See İstanbul and the Aegean coast to Bodrum or Marmaris.
Two weeks
  Travel from İstanbul south and east along the coasts to Antalya or Alanya, then return to İstanbul via Cappadocia.
Three weeks or more
  Travel from İstanbul to Bursa and then down the Aegean and Mediterranean coasts to Silifke, before cutting inland to Konya, Cappadocia and Ankara, and then back to İstanbul.

PLANNING
When to Go

In general, spring (April/May) and autumn (September/October) have the most pleasant weather. The heat and crowds of July and August can be pretty unbearable, especially in İstanbul.

WHAT KIND OF TRIP

Turkey's excellent bus network makes it extremely easy for travellers to get around without taking a tour. For more information, see Organised Tours in the Getting Around section below.

Maps

Lonely Planet publishes a detailed *Turkey Travel Atlas*.

The free tourist-office-produced maps of İstanbul, İzmir, Ankara, Antalya and Adana are excellent. Otherwise inspect all locally produced maps carefully before buying; many are little more than sketches.

What to Bring

You'll find the following items useful in Turkey: prescription medicines (refills are sometimes available), mosquito repellent (from April to September), sunscreen (it's expensive here), a universal sink plug, a towel and reading matter. Women should bring favoured tampons.

TOURIST OFFICES
Local Tourist Offices

Government tourist offices exist in every tourist-oriented town but they can rarely do much more than hand out glossy brochures.

TURKEY

Ask for the *Youth Travel Guide Book*, which has lots of advice for budget travellers.

Tourist Offices Abroad
Turkey has tourist offices in the following countries:

Australia (☎ 02-9223 3055, fax 9223 3204, ✉ turkish@ozemail.com.au) Room 17, Level 3, 428 George St, Sydney NSW 2000
Canada (☎ 613-230 8654, fax 230 3683) Suite 801, Constitution Square, 360 Albert St, Ottawa Ontario K1R 7X7
UK (☎ 020-7629 7771, fax 7491 0773, ✉ TTO@cityscape.co.uk) 1st floor, 170-173 Piccadilly, London W1V 9DD
USA (☎ 212-687 2194, fax 599 7568, ✉ tourny@idt.net) 821 UN Plaza, New York, NY 10017

VISAS & DOCUMENTS
Passport
Make sure your passport is valid for at least three months beyond your date of entry into Turkey.

Visas
Nationals of most Western European countries may enter free for visits of up to three months (90 days) but others must pay a visa fee on arrival: UK subjects pay UK£10, Australians US$20, US citizens US$45.

EMBASSIES & CONSULATES
The embassies are in Ankara but many nations also have consulates in İstanbul, and some have them in İzmir and resort towns too.

Turkish Embassies & Consulates
Turkey has embassies in the following countries:

Australia (☎ 02-6295 0227, fax 6239 6592) 60 Mugga Way, Red Hill 2603 ACT
Bulgaria (☎ 02-980 2270, fax 981 9358) Blvd Vasil Levski No 80, 1000 Sofia
Canada (☎ 613-789 4044, fax 781 3442) 197 Wurtemburg St, Ottawa, Ontario K1N 8L9
Greece (☎ 01-724 5915, fax 722 9597) Vasilissis Georgiou B 8, 10674 Athens
UK (☎ 020-7393 0202, fax 7393 0066) 43 Belgrave Square, London SW1X 8PA
USA (☎ 202-659 8200, fax 659 0744) 1714 Massachusetts Ave NW, Washington, DC, 20036

Embassies & Consulates in Turkey
Countries with diplomatic representation in İstanbul include:

Australia (☎ 212-257 7050, fax 257 7054) Tepecik Yolu 58, 80630 Etiler
Canada (☎ 212-272 5174) 3rd floor, Büyükdere Caddesi 107/3, Bengün Han, Gayrettepe
France (☎ 212-243 1852, fax 249 9168) İstiklal Caddesi 8, Taksim
Greece (☎ 212-245 0596, fax 252 1365) Turnacıbaşı Sokak 32, Ağahamam, Beyoğlu
New Zealand (☎ 212-275 2989, fax 275 5008) Maya Akar Center, 24th floor, Büyükdere Caddesi 100/102, Esentepe 80280
UK (☎ 212-293 7545, fax 245 4989) Meşrutiyet Caddesi 34, Tepebaşı, Beyoğlu
USA (☎ 212-251 3602, fax 267 0057) Meşrutiyet Caddesi 104-108, Tepebaşı, Beyoğlu

CUSTOMS
You may import, duty-free, two cartons (400) of cigarettes, 50 cigars or 200g of smoking tobacco, and 5L of liquor. Duty-free items are sold in both arrival and departure areas of Turkey's international airports.

Turkey is full of antiquities but it's strictly illegal to buy, sell or export any of them. Penalties are severe – if caught, *you may go to jail*. Customs officers spot-check the luggage of departing passengers.

For information on bringing a motor vehicle into Turkey, see Car & Motorcycle in the Getting Around section of this chapter.

MONEY
Currency
The Turkish lira (TL) comes in coins of 10,000, 25,000, 50,000 and 100,000 liras, and notes (bills) of 100,000, 250,000, 500,000, one million, five million and ten million liras. The Central Bank has suggested that in 2001 or 2002, the mind-boggling six zeros will be knocked off the currency, a great idea but likely to prove chaotic in the short term.

Turkey has no black market but you can often spend US dollars or Deutschmarks in place of liras.

Exchange Rates
Although the government has partially pegged exchange rates in an effort to curb inflation, prices in this chapter are quoted in US dollars for greater stability. At the time of

TURKEY

writing Turkey still had 50% inflation/ devaluation – an exchange table has not been provided as it would be prehistoric by the time you arrive.

Exchanging Money

Exchanging cash in major currencies is fast and easy in most banks, exchange offices, post offices, shops and hotels. Cashing even major travellers cheques is less easy and the exchange rate is usually slightly lower. Many places charge a commission (*komisyon*); ask first.

ATMs & Credit Cards

Turkey has an extensive, reliable network of ATMs linked to the MasterCard, Visa, Cirrus and Plus networks – by far the easiest way to handle your money is to bring your normal cashcard from home. The keypads only accept numeric PINs.

Credit cards are readily accepted by luxury hotels, airlines and some shops but don't expect to depend on them off-the-beaten track.

Security

Although Turkey is considered one of Europe's safest countries, you must still take precautions. Wear a money belt under your clothing and beware of pickpockets and purse-snatchers in buses, markets and other crowded places. Be especially careful in İstanbul and when staying in hostels.

Costs

Turkey is Europe's bargain-basement destination and although prices may be steadily rising you can still travel on as little as US$15 to US$20 per person per day using buses, staying in pensions, and eating one restaurant meal daily. For US$20 to US$35 per day you can stay in one and two-star hotels with private bath, and eat most meals in average restaurants. For US$35 to US$70 per person per day you can move up to three and four-star hotels, take the occasional airline flight and dine in restaurants all the time. Costs are highest in İstanbul and the big coastal resorts.

Tipping & Bargaining

In mid-range restaurants, waiters appreciate a tip of 5% to 10%; barbers, hairdressers and Turkish-bath attendants expect 10% to 15%. It's normal to round taxi fares up rather than actually tipping but you never need to tip *dolmuş* (minibus) drivers.

It's wise to bargain for souvenirs. Even if the establishment has set prices, it's still worth trying if you're buying several items or shopping in the low season. In tourist areas hotel prices tend to be fixed; elsewhere it's worth bargaining if you visit between October and late May or plan to stay more than one night.

Taxes & Refunds

A value-added tax (KDV, Katma Değer Vergisi) of 15% to 20% is included (KDV *dahil*) in the price of most items and services. A few hotels and shops give discounts if you don't want an official receipt (*fatura*); this way you both avoid paying tax. It's illegal but hardly unusual.

If you buy an expensive item (eg carpet, leather apparel) for export, ask the shopkeeper for a KDV *iade özel fatura* (special VAT refund receipt). Get this stamped as you clear customs, then get your refund at a bank branch in the airport departure lounge; or you can mail the receipt and be sent a cheque.

POST & COMMUNICATIONS
Post

Turkish post offices are called 'Posta Telgraf' or 'PTT'; look for the black-on-yellow signs or ask for the *postane*. If you have mail addressed to you care of poste restante in a major city, the address should include Merkez Postane (central post office) or the name of the neighbourhood post office at which you wish to retrieve it.

Telephone

Turkey's pricey public telephones, now separated from the PTT and operated by Türk Telekom, take a *telekart* (phonecard), sold at telephone centres, at shops and by street vendors. A few older phones use *jetons* (tokens). Turkey's country code is ☎ 90.

To call from one city to another, dial ☎ 0 (zero), then the city code and number. To call abroad, dial ☎ 00, then the country and area codes, and number. A three-minute telekart call to the USA costs US$6 peak, US$4.50 off peak (ie, in the evening or at weekends).

In theory, you can call one of the numbers below toll-free from Turkey to access your home telephone company, which may have cheaper rates. In practice, the call often doesn't go through:

Australia	☎ (00-800) 61 1177
Canada (Teleglobe)	☎ (00-800) 1 6677
France (Telecom)	☎ (00-800) 33 1177
Germany (PTT)	☎ (00-800) 49 1149
Ireland	☎ (00-800) 353 1177
Italy	☎ (00-800) 39 1177
Japan (IDC Direct)	☎ (00-800) 81 0086
(IDC)	☎ (00-800) 81 0080
(KDD)	☎ (00-800) 81 1177
Netherlands (PTT)	☎ (00-800) 31 1177
UK (BTI)	☎ (00-800) 44 1177
USA(AT&T)	☎ (00-800) 1 2277
(MCI)	☎ (00-800) 1 1177
(SPRINT)	☎ (00-800) 1 4477

Note that you cannot make a collect call to New Zealand from Turkey.

Fax
It's easiest and cheapest to send and receive faxes at your hotel. Türk Telekom telephone centres have faxes but will tie you up in paperwork.

Email & Internet Access
Turkish post offices offer Internet access but you're better off using one of the Internet cafes which are popping up all over Turkey even as you read this. Many small hotels and pensions will also let you use their Internet service for a small fee.

INTERNET RESOURCES
The Turkey Home Page (www.turkey.org/) has news, arts and cultural features, lists of coming events and links to dozens of Turkey-related websites. The *Turkish Daily News* site (www.turkishdailynews.com) is also useful. For details on getting about, try: www .neredennereye.com.

BOOKS
Lonely Planet
Lonely Planet's *Turkey* is a detailed guide to the entire country. LP also publishes a *Turkish phrasebook* and a Turkey *World Food* guide.

Travel
Jeremy Seal's *A Fez of the Heart* and Tim Kelsey's *Dervish* are very readable accounts of recent travels in Turkey.

History & Politics
For a good factual account of the making of modern Turkey look for *Turkey Unveiled* by Nicole and Hugh Pope.

NEWSPAPERS & MAGAZINES
The dull-as-ditchwater *Turkish Daily News* is the local English-language paper. In major tourist areas you'll find many day-old European and US newspapers and magazines.

RADIO & TV
The government-funded TRT (Turkish Radio & Television) offers short news broadcasts in English each morning and evening on radio, and late each evening on TV.

Independent TV channels are a thriving Turkish industry although their quality is often lamentable – flick through the channels in a hotel bedroom and you may well think the only thing they broadcast is adverts!

TIME
Turkey is on Eastern European Time, two hours ahead of GMT/UTC. When it's noon in Turkey, it's 11 am in Paris and Frankfurt, 10 am in London, 5 am in New York and 2 am in Los Angeles. In summer/winter it's 5/7 pm in Perth and Hong Kong, 7/9 pm in Sydney and 9/11 pm in Auckland. From late March to late September, Turkey observes daylight-saving time when clocks are turned ahead one hour.

LAUNDRY
Laundrettes are beginning to appear in the larger cities, but most people get their washing done in their hotel or pension for around US$5 a load.

TOILETS
Though most hotels and many public toilets (*tuvalet*) have the familiar raised bowl commode, Turkey also has hole-in-the-ground squat toilets. Traditionally, one cleans up not with toilet paper but with water (from a jug or a little pipe attached to the toilet), using the left hand. When not in your hotel, always carry toilet paper with you. Since the toilets can't swallow paper, always throw it in the bin provided.

All mosques have toilets, usually basic and smelly. Major tourist sites have better ones. Almost all public toilets require payment of a small fee (US$0.15).

TURKEY

WOMEN TRAVELLERS

Things may be slowly changing but Turkish society is still basically sexually segregated, especially once you get away from the big cities and tourist resorts. Although younger Turks are questioning the old ways and some women now hold positions of authority (there's even been a woman prime minister), foreign women still find themselves being hassled, supposedly because Turkish men are unaccustomed to brazen western ways. Mostly it's just silliness but serious assaults do occasionally occur. Travelling with a male usually improves matters, as does travelling with another female.

Turkish women completely ignore men who speak to them in the street. Wearing a headscarf, a skirt that comes below the knees, a wedding ring and sunglasses makes you less conspicuous. Away from beach resorts you should certainly avoid skimpy tops and brief shorts.

GAY & LESBIAN TRAVELLERS

Although not illegal, homosexuality is not widely accepted in Turkey. It may exist openly at a small number of gay bars and clubs in major cities and resorts but you should still be discreet. For more information, surf to www.qrd.org/qrd/world/europe/turkey

DISABLED TRAVELLERS

Turkey must be a nightmare for a disabled traveller. Steps and obstacles are everywhere; ramps, wide doorways and properly equipped toilets almost unheard-of. Crossing most streets is for the young and agile; all others do so at their peril. You must plan each hour of your trip carefully and, sadly, budget to patronise luxury hotels, restaurants and transport.

TRAVEL WITH CHILDREN

Turks just adore children so bringing yours along should prove a bonus provided you're especially careful over hygiene. Disposable nappies are readily available; not so pre-prepared baby food. Cappadocia, in particular, has been recommended as a paradise for children of all ages who generally love the opportunities offered by the troglodyte lifestyle.

USEFUL ORGANISATIONS

The International Student Identity Card (ISIC) gets you reductions at some museums and archaeological sites (20% to 50%), on trains (20%), on Turkish Maritime Lines ships (10%) and sometimes on private buses and Turkish Airlines.

DANGERS & ANNOYANCES

Single men in İstanbul need to be particularly wary of new Turkish 'friends' who lure them to a bar or nightclub (often near İstiklal Caddesi) where the man is forced to pay an outrageous bar bill regardless of whether he drank anything or not.

On intercity buses, there have been isolated incidents of theft by drugging: a person (or persons) who has befriended you buys you a beverage (often *ayran*) at a rest stop, injects a drug into it and, as you sleep, makes off with your luggage.

More commonly, the hard-sell tactics of carpet sellers can drive you to distraction; be warned that 'free' lifts and suspiciously cheap accommodation often come attached to near-compulsory visits to carpet showrooms.

BUSINESS HOURS

Most banks, museums and offices are open 8.30 am to noon and 1.30 to 5 pm weekdays. In tourist areas food and souvenir shops are often open virtually round the clock.

PUBLIC HOLIDAYS & SPECIAL EVENTS

National public holidays include: 1 January; 23 April (National Sovereignty and Children's Day); 19 May (Youth & Sports Day); 30 August (Victory Day) and 29 October (Republic Day).

The official Turkish calendar is the western Gregorian one used in Europe, but religious festivals are celebrated according to the Muslim Hijri lunar calendar which is 11 days shorter than the Gregorian. Thus Muslim festivals take place around 11 days earlier each year.

Kurban Bayramı (Sacrifice Holiday) This four-day holiday, commemorating Abraham's near-sacrifice of Isaac, is the most important religious holiday of the year. Millions of families sacrifice rams and have a feast, donating most of the meat to charity. It starts on 22 February 2002 and 11

February 2003. Plan ahead – almost everything closes.

Kırkpınar Oiled Wrestling Competition In late June or early July, huge men clad only in leather breeches gather in Edirne to slather themselves with olive oil and wrestle Turkish-style for three days (Friday to Sunday).

International İstanbul Music Festival From early June to early July, world-class musicians gather in İstanbul. A highlight is the performance of Mozart's Abduction from the Seraglio staged inside Topkapı Palace.

Anniversary of Atatürk's Death Although not a public holiday, the national hero's death on 10 November 1938 is commemorated with special ceremonies.

Mevlana Festival The Mevlevi dervishes whirl in Konya from 10 to 17 December to commemorate their spiritual leader, the great mystic poet and philosopher Mevlana. Celebrations culminate on the 17th, the anniversary of Mevlana's death, or 'wedding night with God'. Reserve your hotel room well in advance.

Ramazan (Ramadan) During the holy month of Ramazan, observant Muslims fast during daylight hours, then after sunset and go to mosque often. The month-long observance is followed by the three-day Şeker Bayramı (Sweets Holiday), a public holiday when children go door-to-door requesting treats. Ramazan runs from 27 November to 26 December 2001, 16 November to 15 December 2002 and from 5 November to 4 December 2003.

ACTIVITIES
Cycling
Although a lot of people do choose to cycle in Turkey it is not an especially cycle-friendly country, with a high road accident rate and few designated cycle paths. On back roads you must watch out for stone-throwing children and rampaging sheepdogs.

Skiing
There are ski resorts on Uludağ, near Bursa, on Erciyes, near Kayseri, and at Palendöken, near Erzurum, but facilities are rudimentary compared with those in western Europe.

Hiking
Turkey has some excellent hiking country, especially in the Kaçkar Mountains of the north-east and the Taurus Mountains of the south. More casual hiking is possible around Cappadocia. Turkey's first waymarked long-distance footpath, the Lycian Way, runs from near Fethiye to just outside Antalya.

Water Sports
The Aegean and Mediterranean coasts are the places to go and many big resort hotels have windsurfing, snorkelling, scuba-diving and rowing gear for hire.

You can also cruise on a traditional wooden yacht *(gulet)* for anything from one day to two weeks. Antalya, Bodrum, Fethiye, Kuşadası and Marmaris are the main centres. Ask near the docks for information.

Turkish Baths (Hamams)
The pleasures of the Turkish bath are famous: soaking in the steamy heat, being kneaded and pummelled by a masseur, then being scrubbed squeaky clean and lathered all over by a bath attendant before emerging swaddled in puffy Turkish towels for a bracing glass of tea.

Traditionally, men and women bathe separately, but in popular tourist areas baths often accept foreign men and women at the same time for higher than usual prices. For safety's sake, women should know at least some of the men in the bath with them, and females might want to avoid male masseurs (a Turkish woman would only accept a masseuse). Not all baths accept women.

COURSES
Several schools in İstanbul offer Turkish-language courses lasting for anything from one month to a year; Taksim Dilmer, İnönü Caddesi, Profesor Dr Tarık Zafer Tunaya Sokak 18 (☎ 212-292 9696, fax 292 9693, ✉ taksi mdilmer@turk.net) is one reliable, centrally-positioned school. It's Web site is at www.dilmer.com. Private tutors advertise in the *Turkish Daily News* and in the İstanbul freebie *İstanbull...* which can be picked up in cafes along İstiklal Caddesi.

WORK
Your employer should be able to help you organise the residence and work permits without which it's illegal to work in Turkey. Some people do work illegally (as waiters, English teachers or nannies) and travel to Greece every three months to get a new visa. Job opportunities for English-speakers are listed in the classifieds of the *Turkish Daily News*.

ACCOMMODATION
Camping

Camping facilities are dotted about Turkey and some hotels and pensions will let you camp in their grounds and use their toilets and washrooms for a small fee. Well-equipped European-style camp sites are rare.

Hostels & University Accommodation

Outside İstanbul true hostels are thin on the ground; the few accredited Hostelling International (HI) youth hostels differ little from cheap hotels. A few very basic student hostels are available also in summer but they're rarely conveniently positioned for travellers.

Hotels & Pensions

Turkey has plenty of cheap hotels, although the very cheapest are basically dormitories where you're crammed into a room with whoever else fronts up. They'll be too basic for many tastes and not really suitable for lone women.

Tourist areas usually boast lots of small family-run pensions, some of them offering self-catering facilities.

The price of most hotels is decided by the local authorities and should be on display in the reception although often you'll find the price you're quoted is cheaper than the one on display (it should never be more). One and two-star hotels (US$20 to US$45 a double) offer reasonable comfort and private bathrooms at excellent prices; three-star places can be quite luxurious.

FOOD

Turkish food is similar to Greek but more refined. *Şiş kebap* (shish kebab), lamb grilled on a skewer, is a Turkish invention. You'll find the *kebapçı*, a cheap eatery specialising in roast lamb, everywhere. Try the ubiquitous *döner kebap* – lamb packed onto a vertical revolving spit and sliced off when done.

The best cheap and tasty meal is *pide*, Turkish pizza. Fish, though excellent, is often expensive – be sure to ask the price before you order.

A proper meal consists of a long procession of dishes. First come the *meze* (hors d'oeuvres), such as:

beyaz peynir – white sheep's-milk cheese
börek – flaky pastry stuffed with white cheese and parsley
cacık – yoghurt, cucumber and garlic
(*kuru*) *fasulye* – (dried) beans
kabak dolması – stuffed zucchini
patlıcan salatası – puréed aubergine salad
patlıcan tava – fried aubergine
taramasalata – fish-roe dip

Dolma are vegetables (aubergine, zucchini, peppers, cabbage or vine leaves) stuffed with rice, currants and pine nuts, and served cold, or hot with lamb. The aubergine (eggplant) is the number one vegetable to the Turks. It can be stuffed as a dolma (patlıcan dolması), served puréed with lamb (hünkar beğendi), stuffed with minced meat (karnıyarık) or appear with exotic names like imam bayıldı – 'the imam fainted' – which means stuffed with ground lamb, tomatoes, onions and garlic. Well might he!

For dessert, try *fırın sütlaç* (baked rice pudding), *kazandibi* (caramelised pudding), *aşure* (fruit and nut pudding), baklava (flaky pastry stuffed with walnuts or pistachios, soaked in honey), or *kadayıf* or *burma kadayıf* (shredded wheat with nuts in honey).

DRINKS

Good bottled water is sold everywhere. Beers, such as Tuborg lager or Efes Pilsen, the sturdy Turkish pilsener, supplement the familiar soft drinks. There's also good Turkish wine – red or white – and fierce aniseed *rakı*, which is like Greek ouzo (the Turks usually cut it half-and-half with water). Turkish coffee *(kahve)* is legendary; order your first cup *orta* (with middling sugar). Turkish tea *(çay)*, grown on the eastern Black Sea coast, is served in tiny glasses, sweet and without milk. A milder, wholly chemical alternative is apple tea *(elma çay)*.

ENTERTAINMENT

İstanbul, Ankara and İzmir have opera, symphony, ballet and theatre. Many smaller towns have folk-dance troupes. Most Turkish towns have at least one cinema, often showing films in the original language, and one nightclub with live entertainment. In summer, resorts like Bodrum throb to the sound of innumerable clubs and discos.

TURKEY

Troglodyte dwellings in the bizarre lunar landscape of Matmata, Tunisia, location of the movie *Star Wars*.

View of Bodrum from the Castle of St Peter, the South Aegean's most picturesque resort, Turkey

Şanliurfa, Anatolia, Turkey

Cap off a trip to Turkey...

İshak Paşa Sarayı, Doğubayazıt

The town of Prizren, Kosovo

A harbour in Montenegro, Yugoslavia

SPECTATOR SPORTS

Turks are mad keen football-lovers and if you can get to a match – especially, perhaps, with one of İstanbul's biggies, Galatasaray, Fenerbahçe or Beşiktaş – you're pretty much guaranteed a good time.

SHOPPING

Clothes, jewellery, handicrafts, leather apparel, carpets, coloured tiles, woollen socks, meerschaum pipes, brass and copperware can all be good buys. Bargaining usually pays off.

Getting There & Away

You can get in and out of Turkey by air, sea, rail and bus, across the borders of seven countries.

AIR

There are international airports at Adana, Ankara, Antalya, Bodrum, Dalaman, İstanbul and İzmir. Turkish Airlines has direct flights from İstanbul to two dozen European cities, New York and Chicago, the Middle East, North and South Africa, Central Asia, Bangkok, Karachi, Singapore, Tokyo and Osaka.

Major European airlines such as Aeroflot, Air France, Alitalia, Austrian Airlines, British Airways, Finnair, KLM, Lufthansa, SAS and Swissair fly to İstanbul; British Airways, Lufthansa and the independent airline İstanbul Airlines have flights to Ankara, Antalya, Dalaman and İzmir as well. One-way full-fare tickets from London to İstanbul can cost as much as US$450, so it's usually advisable to buy an excursion ticket for around US$300 even if you don't plan to use the return portion.

Turkish Airlines flies nonstop to İstanbul from New York and Chicago, Delta flies nonstop from New York. The European airlines also fly one-stop services from many North American cities to İstanbul. Return fares range from US$500 to US$1200.

There are no direct flights from Australia or New Zealand to Turkey, but you can fly Qantas or British Airways to London, or Olympic to Athens, and get a connecting flight from these cities. You can also fly Qantas or Singapore Airlines from most Australian cities, or from Kuala Lumpur, to Singapore to connect with Turkish Airlines' thrice-weekly flights to İstanbul. Excursion fares start from around US$2200, which is almost as much as you would pay for a more versatile round-the-world (RTW) ticket.

LAND

Europe

The daily *Balkan Express* train links Budapest and İstanbul (31 hours), while the *Bucharest-İstanbul Express* links Bucharest and İstanbul (17 hours). Neither service is speedy, the trains are barely comfortable and theft is a problem.

Several Turkish bus lines, including Ulusoy and Varan/Bosfor, offer services between İstanbul and European cities such as Athens, Frankfurt, Munich and Vienna. A one-way ticket to Sofia costs just US$30, a ticket to Moscow US$90.

Greece There are daily bus connections (Varan charges US$65) between Athens and İstanbul via Thessaloniki. There's also a daily train from İstanbul to Athens and vice-versa but it takes much longer than the bus to cover the same distance.

SEA

Turkish Maritime Lines (TML) runs car ferries between İzmir and Venice weekly year-round. The one-way fare with reclining seat is US$215; or US$390 per person in a mid-price cabin.

There are daily services to Turkish Cyprus from Taşucu (near Silifke), and less frequent services from Antalya and Alanya.

Private ferries run between Turkey's Aegean coast and the Greek islands, which are in turn linked by air or boat to Athens. Services are frequent (usually daily) in summer, several times weekly in spring and autumn, and infrequent (perhaps once a week) in winter. The most reliable winter services are Chios-Çeşme, Rhodes-Marmaris and Samos-Kuşadası; other in-season services include Lesvos-Ayvalık, Lesvos-Dikili, Kos-Bodrum, Rhodes-Bodrum and Kastellorizo-Kaş.

DEPARTURE TAX

The US$12 departure tax is included in the price of your air ticket.

TURKEY

Getting Around

AIR

Turkish Airlines (Türk Hava Yolları, THY) links all the country's major cities, including the busy İstanbul-Ankara corridor (50 minutes, US$90). Domestic flights tend to fill up fast, so try and book a few days ahead. On a few routes İstanbul Airlines offers cheaper flights with lower fares but less frequently. Smoking is prohibited on all domestic flights.

The network of domestic airports is growing fast and although flying is relatively expensive, given the size of Turkey taking one internal flight can be a good way to cut down the time spent in buses.

BUS

Comfortable modern buses go everywhere frequently and cheaply (around US$3 to US$4 per hour or 100km). Kamil Koç, Metro, Ulusoy and Varan cost a bit more but have better safety records than most. Traffic accidents claim thousands of Turkish lives every year.

The bus station (otogar) is often on the outskirts of town, but the bigger bus companies usually offer free servises (minibuses) between the city-centre ticket office and the otogar. Many of the larger otogars have left-luggage rooms or emanets with a small charge. Don't leave valuables in unlocked luggage. If there's no emanet, leave luggage at the bus ticket office.

No smoking is allowed on the buses although the driver may (and usually does) smoke.

TRAIN

The Turkish State Railways' ageing rolling stock has a hard time competing with the long-distance buses for speed or comfort. Only on the special İstanbul-Ankara express trains such as the Fatih and Başkent can you get somewhere faster and more comfortably than by bus, at a comparable price.

Slower Ekspres and mototren services sometimes have one class only and are cheaper than the buses. If they have 2nd class it costs 30% less than 1st. Student fares are 20% cheaper, as are return fares. On yolcu and posta trains you could grow old and die before reaching your destination. Trains east of Ankara are not as punctual or comfortable as those to the west.

Sleeping-car trains linking İstanbul and Ankara (US$25 a single, US$35 a double, all in) are good value; the cheaper örtülü kuşetli carriages have four simple beds per compartment.

Major stations have emanet (left-luggage rooms).

CAR & MOTORCYCLE

Turkey has a very high motor vehicle accident rate. Drive defensively, avoid driving at night, don't drink and drive, and never let emotion affect your driving.

An International Driving Permit may be handy if your licence is from a country likely to seem obscure to a Turkish police officer.

Türkiye Turing ve Otomobil Kurumu (TTOK), the Turkish Touring & Automobile Association (☎ 212-282 8140, fax 282 8042), Oto Sanayi Sitesi Yanı, 4 Levent, İstanbul, can help with questions and problems.

Carnets are not required if you're staying for less than three months, but details of your car are stamped in your passport to ensure it leaves the country with you.

Mechanical services are easy to find, reasonably competent and cheap. The most easily serviced cars are Fiat, Mercedes, Renault and Toyota.

If you plan to spend time in a major city, park your car and use public transport: traffic is terrible and parking impossible. Your hotel will advise you on parking. Multilevel car parks are called katotopark.

BICYCLE

The countryside is varied and beautiful, and road surfaces acceptable if a bit rough (though often narrow). Turkish drivers regard cyclists as a curiosity and/or a nuisance.

HITCHING

Because of the extensive, cheap bus system, hitching is not normal in Turkey. If you ask for a ride, the driver will expect you to offer the bus fare for the privilege. They may refuse to accept it, but if you don't offer you will be considered a freeloader.

Women should never hitchhike, especially alone; if you absolutely must do it, do it with another woman or (preferably) a man, don't accept a ride in a vehicle that has only men in it, and expect some hassles.

BOAT

Car ferries depart from İstanbul on Friday year-round and arrive the next morning in İzmir. From İzmir departures are on Sunday afternoon. Fares, including meals, are US$16 (reclining seat) to US$100 (luxury cabin bed), and US$60 for a car.

In summer a ferry leaves İstanbul for Trabzon at 2 pm every Monday, returning from Trabzon on Wednesday at 8 pm. A Pullman seat costs US$17.50 or there are shared cabins starting from US$35 a berth.

Fast ferries from İstanbul to Bandırma (US$3) also connect with a daily train service to İzmir (the *Marmara Ekspresi*). Heading to İzmir the train leaves Bandırma at 3 pm daily; returning to İstanbul it leaves Bandırma at 2.12 pm daily.

LOCAL TRANSPORT

The big towns all have local bus services and private dolmuş (shared taxi or minibus) services. İstanbul has a growing metro system of overground and underground trains and trams. Ankara has an excellent if limited metro.

In the big cities, taxis are required by law to run their digital meters. The greatest risk of taxi rip-offs (drivers refusing to run the meter, taking the long way etc) is in İstanbul; drivers are usually fairly honest in the other big cities. In smaller places, where taxis have no meters, agree a fare before starting out to avoid arguments later.

ORGANISED TOURS

Most independent travellers find organised tours expensive, not least because many park you in a carpet shop for an hour or two so the guide can get a kickback of up to 30%. Always ask about shopping before signing up for a tour.

Most people only need consider a tour if, for example, they want to visit the Gallipoli battlefields, Sumela monastery or the scattered sites of Cappadocia and have limited time.

Some people, especially lone women, like to travel with the Fez Bus, a hop-on, hop-off bus service operating out of İstanbul (☎ 212-516 9024, fax 517 1626, Akbıyık Caddesi,

Sultanahmet), but before signing up check that it won't cost you more than travelling by yourself.

İstanbul

☎ 212

With 3000 years of colourful history, İstanbul, formerly Constantinople, has plenty to show for itself. This city is more than a step back in time; after dark, a plethora of bars and fine restaurants will satiate the most energetic of souls, İstanbul has theatre, galleries – and is a shopper's paradise.

History

In the late 2nd century AD, Rome conquered the small city of Byzantium. In 330, Emperor Constantine moved the capital of his empire there from Rome and renamed the city Constantinople.

The city walls kept out barbarians for centuries as the western part of the Roman Empire collapsed before Goths, Vandals and Huns. When Constantinople fell for the first time it was to the misguided Fourth Crusade in 1204. Bent on pillage, the crusaders abandoned their dreams of Jerusalem and ravaged Constantinople's churches, shipping out the art and melting down the silver and gold. When the Byzantines regained the city in 1261 it was a shadow of its former glory.

The Ottoman Turks' first attempt to take Constantinople was in 1314. Finally, in 1453, after a long and bitter siege, the walls were breached near Topkapı Gate on the western side of the city. Mehmet the Conqueror marched to Hagia Sofia (Aya Sofya) and converted the church to a mosque. The Byzantine Empire had ended.

As capital of the Ottoman Empire, the city entered a new golden age. During the glittering reign of Süleyman the Magnificent (1520-66), the city was graced with many new buildings of great beauty. The empire's long and celebrated decline was accelerated by the capital's occupation by Allied forces after WWI. İstanbul's final conquest was a catalyst for Atatürk's armies to shape a new, republican state.

The Turkish Republic was proclaimed in 1923, with Ankara as its capital. But İstanbul,

TURKEY

İSTANBUL

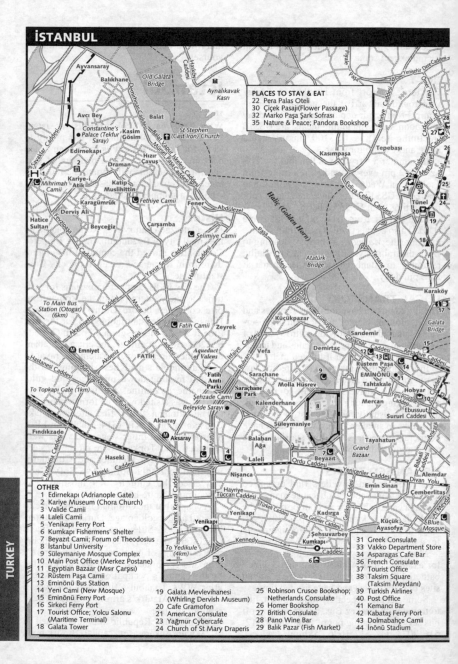

PLACES TO STAY & EAT
22 Pera Palas Oteli
30 Çiçek Pasajı(Flower Passage)
32 Marko Paşa Şark Sofrası
35 Nature & Peace; Pandora Bookshop

OTHER
1 Edirnekapı (Adrianople Gate)
2 Kariye Museum (Chora Church)
3 Valide Camii
4 Laleli Camii
5 Yenikapı Ferry Port
6 Kumkapı Fishermens' Shelter
7 Beyazıt Camii; Forum of Theodosius
8 İstanbul University
9 Süleymaniye Mosque Complex
10 Main Post Office (Merkez Postane)
11 Egyptian Bazaar (Mısır Çarşısı)
12 Rüstem Paşa Camii
13 Eminönü Bus Station
14 Yeni Cami (New Mosque)
15 Eminönü Ferry Port
16 Sirkeci Ferry Port
17 Tourist Office; Yolcu Salonu
    (Maritime Terminal)
18 Galata Tower

19 Galata Mevlevihanesi
    (Whirling Dervish Museum)
20 Cafe Gramofon
21 American Consulate
23 Yağmur Cybercafé
24 Church of St Mary Draperis

25 Robinson Crusoe Bookshop;
    Netherlands Consulate
26 Homer Bookshop
27 British Consulate
28 Pano Wine Bar
29 Balık Pazar (Fish Market)

31 Greek Consulate
33 Vakko Department Store
34 Asparagas Cafe Bar
36 French Consulate
37 Tourist Office
38 Taksim Square
    (Taksim Meydanı)
39 Turkish Airlines
40 Post Office
41 Kemancı Bar
42 Kabataş Ferry Port
43 Dolmabahçe Camii
44 İnönü Stadium

TURKEY

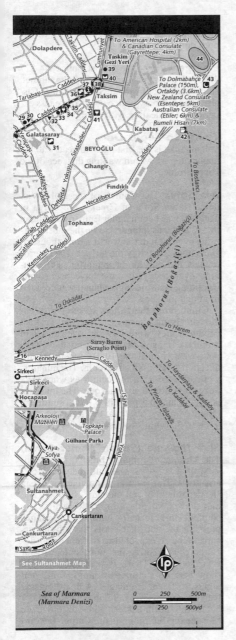

the much beloved metropolis, is still the centre of business, finance, journalism and the arts.

Orientation

The Bosphorus strait, between the Black and Marmara seas, divides Europe from Asia. European İstanbul is divided by the Haliç (Golden Horn) estuary into the 'newer' quarter of Beyoğlu in the north and Old İstanbul in the south; the Galata Bridge spans the two.

Sultanahmet, the heart of Old İstanbul, has many tourist sites, cheap hotels and restaurants. The boulevard Divan Yolu, runs west, through Sultanahmet, past the Grand Bazaar (Kapalı Çarşı) and İstanbul University to Aksaray, a major traffic intersection.

Eminönü, north of Sultanahmet at the southern end of Galata Bridge, is the terminus of a tram and many bus lines and ferries. Sirkeci train station, the terminus for the European train line, is 100m east of Eminönü.

Karaköy, at the northern end of Galata Bridge, is another ferry terminus. Up the hill from Karaköy is the southern end of Beyoğlu's pedestrian mall, İstiklal Caddesi. At the northern end of the street is Taksim Square (Taksim Meydanı), heart of 'modern' İstanbul with its fancy hotels and airline offices.

Maps

The free map given out by the tourist office should be all you need. If you want more detail, pick up *İstanbul* from Lonely Planet's City Map series.

Information

Tourist Offices There are tourist offices in the international arrivals hall at Atatürk airport (☎ 573 4136); in the *yolcu salonu* (maritime terminal; ☎ 249 5776) at Karaköy; in Sirkeci train station (☎ 511 5888); at the north-eastern end of the Hippodrome in Sultanahmet (☎ 518 8754); and on İstiklal Caddesi (☎ 245 6876), near Taksim Square.

Money Ubiquitous ATMs spit out Turkish liras upon insertion of your credit or bank cash card; Yapı Kredi seems best, İs Bankası least good because it lets you remove so little at a time. Exchange offices are cheapest outside the Kapalı Çarşı (Grand Bazaar), but are also plentiful in Sultanahmet, Sirkeci and Taksim. Most are open 9 am to 9 pm.

TURKEY

Post & Communications The main post office *(merkez postane)* is just south-west of Sirkeci train station. Go there for poste-restante mail. Other post offices are in the law courts near the Hippodrome, in Sultanahmet; beside the Grand Bazaar; on Taksim Square; and in the departure areas at the airport.

İstanbul has two telephone codes: ☎ 212 for the European side and ☎ 216 for the Asian. Assume phone numbers given here are ☎ 212 unless stated otherwise.

Internet cafes are popping up everywhere; many places to stay also have facilities. In Sultanahmet try the Backpackers Internet Cafe opposite the Orient Youth Hostel. In Beyoğlu, sniff out the waffles at Yağmur Cybercafe, Şeyh Bender Sokak 18, near Pera Palas Oteli.

Internet Resources The freebie magazine *İstanbull...* is available on www.beyogluweb.com/istanbullshit

Travel Agencies Sultanahmet has many small travel agencies, all of them selling transport tickets and tours, some offering foreign exchange; shop around for the best deals. Midillis (☎ 458 0800, ✉ midillis@fornet.net.tr), at Küçük Ayasofya Caddesi 21, has a good reputation.

Bookshops Aypa (☎ 516 0100), Mimar Mehmetağa Caddesi 19, Sultanahmet, just down the hill from the Blue Mosque, has a good selection.

The best shops are on or near İstiklal Caddesi, including Robinson Crusoe (☎ 293 6968), İstiklal Caddesi 389; Homer (☎ 249 5902), Yeni Çarşı Caddesi 28; and Pandora (☎ 243 3503), Büyükparmakkapı Sokak 3.

Laundry Laundry costs around US$1.50 per kg (wash and dry). In Sultanahmet, dump your crusty clothes at the Hobby Laundry (☎ 513 6150) in the Yücelt Interyouth Hostel or the cheaper Star Laundry (☎ 638 2302), Akbıyık Caddesi 18, opposite the Orient Youth Hostel. Your hotel may also have laundry facilities.

Medical Services Both the American Hospital (☎ 311 2000), at Güzelbahçe Sokak 20, Nişantaşı (2km north-east of Taksim Square),

and the International Hospital (☎ 663 3000), İstanbul Caddesi 82, in Yeşilköy near the airport, do good work.

Emergency Try the tourist police (☎ 527 4503), Yerebatan Caddesi 6, Sultanahmet, across the street from the Sunken Palace Cistern. The ordinary police (☎ 155) are less experienced in dealing with foreigners.

Things to See & Do

Sultanahmet is the first place to head – all the major sites are within walking distance of the Hippodrome.

Aya Sofya The Church of the Holy Wisdom (Hagia Sofia in Greek, Aya Sofya in Turkish) was begun under Emperor Justinian in 532 and was intended to be the most magnificent church in the world – for a thousand years it was certainly the largest. The interior reveals the building's magnificence; stunning even today, it must have been overwhelming centuries ago when it was covered in gilded mosaics.

Climb up to the gallery to see the splendid surviving mosaics; after the Turkish conquest they were covered over as Islam prohibits images of beings and they were not revealed until the 1930s, when Atatürk declared Aya Sofya a museum. The minarets were added during the centuries when Aya Sofya functioned as a mosque. The museum is open 9 am to 4 pm (till 5 pm in summer), closed Monday; note that the gallery is open 9 am to 3.30 pm. Admission is US$5.

Blue Mosque (Sultan Ahmet Camii) The Mosque of Sultan Ahmet I, just southwest of Aya Sofya, was built between 1609 and 1619. The exterior is notable for its six slender minarets and cascade of domes and half-domes. Inside, the tiled walls and painted dome create the luminous overall impression of blue that earns the mosque its name. You're expected to make a small donation when visiting the mosque; leave your shoes outside. There is a sound-and-light show here on summer evenings – different nights, different languages. A board outside lists which languages are on which night.

On the north-eastern side of the Blue Mosque, up the ramp, is the **Carpet & Kilim**

Museum (open 9 am to 4 pm, closed Sunday and Monday; entry costs US$1.30).

Rent earned from the **Arasta** (row of shops), on the street to the east of the Blue Mosque, provide support for the mosque's upkeep. In the Arasta you'll find – between the carpet touts – the entrance to the **Great Palace Mosaic Museum** with exquisite portions of Byzantine pavements showing scenes from nature. It's open 9 am to 4 pm, closed Monday; entry is US$1.30.

Topkapı Palace Just north-east of Aya Sofya is the fortified, sprawling Topkapı Sarayı, the opulent palace of the sultans from 1462 until they moved to Dolmabahçe Palace in the 19th century. Topkapı is not just a palace but a collection of courtyards, houses and libraries, with an intriguing 400-room harem. In the vast First Court, where the crack troops known as janissaries once gathered, is **Aya İrini** or the Church of Divine Peace, dating from around 540.

Buy your ticket at the Ortakapı (middle gate) to the Second Court.

Within the Second Court are exhibits of priceless porcelain (in the former palace kitchens), silverware and crystal, arms and calligraphy. Right beside the Kubbealtı, or Imperial Council Chamber, is the entrance to the **harem**, a succession of sumptuously decorated rooms which served as the sultan's family quarters.

In the Third Court are the sultan's ceremonial robes and the fabulous **treasury**, which contains an incredible wealth of gold and gems. The **Shrine of the Holy Relics** holds a solid-gold casket containing the Prophet Mohammed's cloak and other Islamic relics.

In the Fourth Court, beautiful tiled kiosks have fine views of the city.

Topkapı is open 9 am to 4.30 pm, closed Tuesday; admission costs US$6, with an extra US$2.50 to visit the harem, which is open 9.30 am to 3.30 pm.

Sunken Palace Cistern Across Divan Yolu, from the north-eastern end of the Hippodrome, is the entrance to the beautiful Yerebatan Sarnıcı. Built by Constantine and later enlarged by Justinian, this vast, columned cistern held water not only for summer use but also for times of siege. It's open 9 am to 4.30 pm (5.30 pm in summer); admission is US$4.50.

Grand Bazaar (Kapalı Çarşı) Built during Mehmet the Conqueror's reign, this labyrinthine bazaar has a long history of selling. Only in the last few decades has it turned its focus on tourists; many of the old stalls have been converted into modern glassed-in shops. Some streets are given over to selling one type of touristy item: carpets for example, or jewellery, clothing or silverware and so on. Still, 65 streets and a tempting 4400 shops, make it a great place to get lost – which you certainly will. The bazaar is open 8.30 am to 7 pm, closed Sunday.

The Hippodrome In front of the Blue Mosque is the Hippodrome, where chariot races and the Byzantine riots took place. Construction started in 203 AD and it was later enlarged by Constantine. Today, three ancient monuments remain. The **Obelisk of Theodosius** is an Egyptian column from the temple of Karnak resting on a Byzantine base, with pristine 3500-year-old hieroglyphs. The 10m-high **Obelisk of Constantine Porphyrogenitus** was covered in bronze plates (until the crusaders spotted them). The base rests at the former level of the Hippodrome, now several metres below the ground. Between these two monuments are the remains of the **Spiral Column**, erected at Delphi by the Greeks to celebrate their victory over the Persians. The bronze sculpture of three intertwined snakes was later transported to the Hippodrome and the snakes' heads disappeared (not the crusaders this time!).

At the north-eastern end of the Hippodrome is a ceremonial fountain built to commemorate Kaiser Wilhelm's visit in 1901.

Turkish & Islamic Arts Museum On the western side of the Hippodrome, the Türk ve İslam Eserleri Müzesi is housed in the former palace of İbrahim Pasha, grand vizier and son-in-law of Süleyman the Magnificent. The exhibits run the gamut of Islamic history, from beautifully illuminated Korans to exquisite carpets and mosque furniture. The museum is open 9 am to 4.30 pm, closed Monday; entry is US$2.50.

Archaeological Museums Down the hill from the outer courtyard of Topkapı Palace, are the Arkeoloji Müzeleri, a complex of three museums. The **Archaeological Museum** has an outstanding collection of Greek and Roman statuary, and what was once thought to be Alexander the Great's sarcophagus (stone coffin). The **Museum of the Ancient Orient** (Eski Şark Eserleri Müzesi) is dedicated to the pre-Islamic and pre-Byzantine civilisations. The **Çinili Köşk** (Tiled Pavilion), built by order of Mehmet the Conqueror in 1472, is among the oldest Turkish buildings in the city. It is now a museum of Turkish tile work.

The museums are open 9 am to 4.30 pm (they're all closed on Monday; the Museum of the Ancient Orient only opens Tuesday to Friday, and the Tiled Pavilion opens on Tuesday afternoon); admission to all three costs US$4.

Beyazıt & Süleymaniye Beyazıt takes its name from the graceful mosque, the **Beyazıt Camii**, built in 1506 on the orders of Sultan Beyazıt II, son of Mehmet the Conqueror. In Byzantine times this plaza was the **Forum of Theodosius**, laid out in 393 AD. The great portal on the north side of the square is that of **İstanbul University**. The portal, enclosure and buildings behind it date mostly from Ottoman times when this was the Ministry of War.

Behind the university, to the north, rises (architect) Mimar Sinan's magnificent **Süleymaniye** mosque complex. Sinan was responsible for many fine buildings during Süleyman the Magnificent's reign; this one, second-best to his Selimiye Camii (in Edirne), was completed in 1557. Süleyman and his foreign-born wife Roxelana (Haseki Hürrem) are buried in **mausolea** behind the mosque to the south-east. The buildings surrounding the mosque were originally seminaries, a hospital, soup kitchen, baths and hospice.

Byzantine Walls Stretching for 7km from the Golden Horn to the Sea of Marmara, the walls date back to Theodosius II's reign (about 420 AD) but many parts have been restored recently.

Near the **Edirnekapı** (Adrianople Gate) is the marvellous **Kariye Museum** (Chora

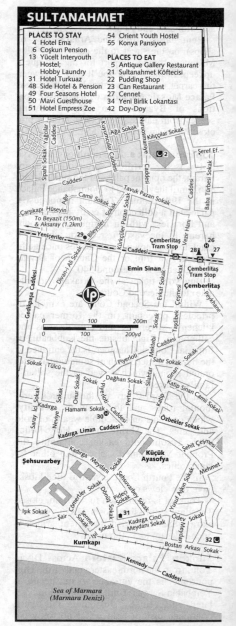

SULTANAHMET

PLACES TO STAY
- 4 Hotel Ema
- 6 Coşkun Pension
- 13 Yücelt Interyouth Hostel; Hobby Laundry
- 31 Hotel Turkuaz
- 48 Side Hotel & Pension
- 49 Four Seasons Hotel
- 50 Mavi Guesthouse
- 51 Hotel Empress Zoe
- 54 Orient Youth Hostel
- 55 Konya Pansiyon

PLACES TO EAT
- 5 Antique Gallery Restaurant
- 21 Sultanahmet Köftecisi
- 22 Pudding Shop
- 23 Can Restaurant
- 27 Cennet
- 34 Yeni Birlik Lokantası
- 42 Doy-Doy

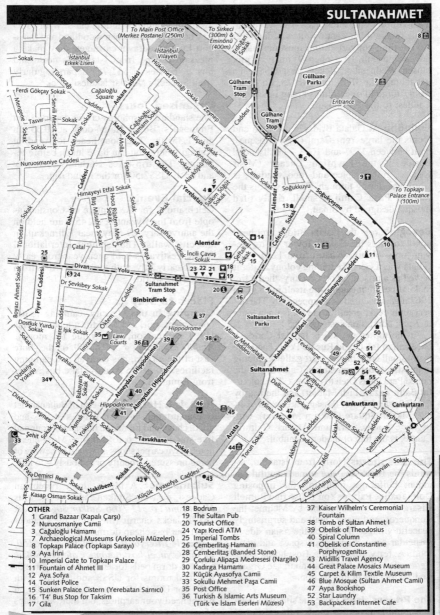

SULTANAHMET

OTHER
1 Grand Bazaar (Kapalı Çarşı)
2 Nuruosmaniye Camii
3 Cağaloğlu Hamamı
7 Archaeological Museums (Arkeoloji Müzeleri)
8 Topkapı Palace (Topkapı Sarayı)
9 Aya İrini
10 Imperial Gate to Topkapı Palace
11 Fountain of Ahmet III
12 Aya Sofya
14 Tourist Police
15 Sunken Palace Cistern (Yerebatan Sarnıcı)
16 'T4' Bus Stop for Taksim
17 Gila

18 Bodrum
19 The Sultan Pub
20 Tourist Office
24 Yapı Kredi ATM
25 Imperial Tombs
26 Çemberlitaş Hamamı
28 Çemberlitaş (Banded Stone)
29 Çorlulu Alipaşa Medresesi (Nargile)
30 Kadırga Hamamı
32 Küçük Ayasofya Camii
33 Sokullu Mehmet Paşa Camii
35 Post Office
36 Turkish & Islamic Arts Museum
   (Türk ve İslam Eserleri Müzesi)

37 Kaiser Wilhelm's Ceremonial
   Fountain
38 Tomb of Sultan Ahmet I
39 Obelisk of Theodosius
40 Spiral Column
41 Obelisk of Constantine
   Porphyrogenitus
43 Midillis Travel Agency
44 Great Palace Mosaics Museum
45 Carpet & Kilim Textile Museum
46 Blue Mosque (Sultan Ahmet Camii)
49 Aypa Bookshop
52 Star Laundry
53 Backpackers Internet Cafe

TURKEY

Church), a Byzantine building with the best 14th-century mosaics east of Ravenna. Built in the 11th century, it was later restored, then converted to a mosque, and is now a museum. It's open 9 am to 4 pm, closed Wednesday; tickets cost US$3. To get there, take İETT bus No 28, 86 or 91 from Eminönü or a dolmuş along Fevzipaşa Caddesi to the Edirnekapı.

Eminönü At Galata Bridge's southern end looms the large **Yeni Cami** (New Mosque), built between 1597 and 1663 – hardly new! Beside it the **Egyptian Bazaar** (Mısır Çarşısı), full of spice and food vendors, is worth wandering through. To the west is the **Rüstem Paşa Camii**, a small, richly tiled mosque designed by Sinan.

Beyoğlu Cross the Galata Bridge and head uphill towards the **Galata Tower**. In its present form this tower dates from 1216 when Galata was a Genoese trading colony. Later it served as a prison, an observatory, then a fire lookout before it caught fire itself in 1835. In 1967 it was restored as a supper club. The observation deck, great for views, is open 9 am to 7 pm; admission costs US$2.50.

At the top of the hill is **İstiklal Caddesi**, once called the Grand Rue de Péra. There are many small contemporary **art galleries** hiding in the streets between İstiklal Caddesi and the famed Pera Palas Oteli to the west. The colourful **Balık Pazar** (Fish Market) and the nearby **Çiçek Pasajı** (Flower Passage) are worth visiting. **Taksim Square** (Taksim Meydanı), with its huge hotels, park and Atatürk Cultural Centre, is the hub of modern İstanbul.

The Bosphorus North from İstanbul, towards the Black Sea, are some beautiful Ottoman buildings, including the imposing **Dolmabahçe Palace**. You'll also find **Rumeli Hisarı**, the huge castle built by Mehmet the Conqueror, and many small and surprisingly peaceful villages. Towns on the Asian side in particular have charm, open space and good food. A ferry ride up the Bosphorus is *de rigueur* for all visitors to İstanbul; see Organised Tours later in this section.

The Princes' Isles Once the site of monasteries and a haven for pirates, this string of nine small islands is a popular summer getaway for İstanbul's middle class. With a few tiny beaches, some open woodland and transport by horse-drawn carriages, they make a pleasant escape from İstanbul's noise and hustle. Ferries (US$1.75) depart regularly from Sirkeci's 'Adalar İskelesi' dock.

Organised Tours
The standard Bosphorus cruise departs from Eminönü's 'Boğaz Hattı' dock at 10.35 am and 1.35 pm. The boat heads to Anadolu Kavağı where you can have lunch before returning. The trip takes 1½ hours each way and costs US$2.50 for the round trip.

Special Events
Celebrations for the capture of Constantinople from the Byzantines (1453) are held on the anniversary, 29 May, near Edirnekapı in the city walls. The İstanbul International Music Festival is held each year from early June to early July, with top-name artists from around the world.

Places to Stay
Camping In this big city, camping is not convenient, nor, at US$3 for a tent site plus US$4 per person, is it value for money. *Ataköy Mocamp* (☎ 559 6000), on the shore east of the airport, has caravan and camping facilities. To get to Ataköy, take bus No 81 from Eminönü.

Hostels & Hotels South-east of Sultanahmet is Cankurtaran, an area of quiet streets and good, cheap and moderate hotels. For four and five-star hotels, go to Taksim. Most cheap hotels have carpet shops attached, so beware of being pressured – gently or tediously – to buy.

Sultanahmet A block along Yerebatan Caddesi, past the Sunken Palace Cistern, is *Hotel Ema* (☎ 511 7166, Salkım Söğüt Sokak 18). It lacks charm (including the chandeliers), but has cheap dorm beds (US$5).

Yücelt Interyouth Hostel (☎ 513 6150, ✉ info@yucelthostel.com, Caferiye Sokak 6/1) has dorm beds for US$6, beds in three or four-bed rooms for US$8 and doubles with toilet for US$18. Rooms are bland and you might need your earplugs, but there are heaps of services on offer.

TURKEY

Nestled against the Topkapı Palace walls, quaint *Coşkun Pension* (☎ 526 9854, ✉ chie ko@atlas.net.tr, Soğukçeşme Sokak 40) has clean singles/doubles (with bathroom) for US$20 to US$45 depending on the room; book ahead.

Cankurtaran Many budget hotels are clustered around the out-of-our-league Four Seasons Hotel (US$320+/double, south-east of the fountain park between Aya Sofya and the Blue Mosque. Dry your tears and continue around the corner to Kutlugün Sokak. *Mavi Guesthouse* (☎ 516 5878, ✉mavi pans@ho tmail .com), at No 3, has basic dorm beds for US$8, doubles for US$18; both prices include breakfast. Continue down the hill and around the corner to Akbıyık Caddesi where, at No 13, you can't miss *Orient Youth Hostel* (☎ 518 0789, ✉ orienthostel@superonline.com). Dorm beds cost US$6, doubles US$14. The top-floor cafe has marvellous Bosphorus views and decent food. In high season, both these places offer rooftop mattresses for a dirt-cheap US$4.

Another option farther downhill is the friendly *Konya Pansiyon* (☎ 638 3638, ✉ aytekinelif@hotmail.com, Terbıyık Sokak 15), with dorm beds for US$5 and doubles for US$14. There's a shabby kitchen you can use.

Near the Four Seasons, *Side Hotel & Pension* (☎ 517 6590, ✉ info@sidehotel.com, Utangaç Sokak 20) is good value. The pension rooms cost US$20/25 per single/double, US$30/35 with bathroom; the adjoining newer building has squeaky-clean rooms for US$40/50 with bathroom. The terrace has awesome Bosphorus views.

The Ottoman-styled *Hotel Empress Zoe* (☎ 518 2504, ✉ emzoe@ibm.net, Adliye Sokak 10) is worth the US$55/75, with breakfast and spotless bathrooms. There's a garden, and a bar upstairs with stunning views. It's a good choice for single women.

Craving authentic Ottoman ambience? Don't miss *Hotel Turkuaz* (☎ 516 0862, ✉ hotelturkuaz@garanti.net.tr, Kadırga Cinci Meydanı 36, Kumkapı), at the bottom of the hill from the south-western corner of the Hippodrome. It's a bit out of the way, but here the rooms, furnishings, Turkish bath

and Turkish folk-art lounge are the real thing. Doubles (with bathroom) cost between US$40 and US$80, breakfast included.

Places to Eat
Sultanahmet For a cheap lunch, buy a filling fish sandwich from one of the boats near the Galata Bridge for just US$1.

At *Cennet (Divan Yolu 90)* you can watch *gözleme* (Turkish crepe) being made, try on Turkish traditional dress, or recline 'Ottoman-style' and listen to live musicians. It's as cheesy as it sounds. You'll pay about US$2 per *gözleme*.

Get a bargain feed at *Doy-Doy (Şifa Hamam Sokak 13)*, downhill from the south-western end of the Hippodrome. Pides and kebabs will set you back US$2 to US$3. Head north-west to *Yeni Birlik Lokantası (Peykhane Sokak 46)*, a restaurant serving delicious ready-made food (some vegetarian) and favoured by attorneys from the nearby law courts. Meals cost around US$5; open 11 am to 4 pm Monday to Friday.

Once a legend amongst travellers, the *Pudding Shop* (or Lale Restaurant) is just one of a string of medium-priced restaurants along Divan Yolu – typical meals cost US$5 to US$7. Try *Can Restaurant*, a brightly lit, hyperactive place or the *Sultanahmet Köftecisi* for delicious grilled lamb meatballs (*köfte*).

Beside Hotel Ema, the Ottoman-styled *Antique Gallery Restaurant (Salkım Söğüt Sokak 18)* has live classical music every night. What the food lacks is made up for by the service and ambience. You'll pay around US$12 for a full meal with drinks.

Beyoğlu Try out some of the restaurants just off İstiklal Caddesi. South of Vakko Department Store (İstiklal Caddesi 123-5), along Sadri Alışık Sokak you can't miss the stuffed goats outside *Marko Paşa Şark Sofrası*. If you thought Cennet restaurant was in dubious taste, you haven't seen anything yet. Meals go for around US$3. North of Vakko, Büyükparmakkapı Sokak has bars and restaurants. At 21, *Nature & Peace* offers what you may have been craving – vegetarian food. You'll pay for the privilege (US$6 per main), but the decor is

TURKEY

stylish and the food's tasty. Scan your bill carefully at the pricier **Çiçek Pasajı** *(İstiklal Caddesi 172)*.

Self Catering Pop into one of the *halk pazarı* (people's markets) and you'll find most things you're after. Akbıyık Caddesi, in Cankurtaran, has a fruit and vegetable market on Wednesday. In Eminönü, the Egyptian Bazaar and surrounding streets have dried fruit, pulses, fish and more.

Entertainment

Turkish Baths İstanbul's historical baths are worth visiting, but they're also very touristy. A basic option is the **Kadırga Hamamı** (Kadırga Hamamı Sokak), in Küçük Ayasofya; it costs US$8 for the works. The **Çemberlitaş Hamamı**, off Divan Yolu, was designed by Sinan in 1584. It charges a whopping US$15 for all services. The famous and attractive **Cağaloğlu Hamamı**, Kazım İsmail Gürkan Caddesi 34, costs a crazy US$20 for a bath and massage.

Bars & Clubs There are heaps of touristy bars in Sultanahmet and Cankurtaran; you'll pay around US$1 for a beer. Near the Sunken Palace Cistern you'll find a group of bars. Bunker-style ***Bodrum*** really fires up, ***Gila*** attracts *some* locals and has awesome views of Aya Sofya and ***The Sultan Pub*** is better for a quiet drink (and good for women travellers). The Orient and Yücelt hostels have popular, smoky ***bars*** frequented by the 'best belly dancer in İstanbul' – don't be fooled.

In Beyoğlu you'll see how some Turks spend their time and money (and at US$4 to US$6 per beer, they have plenty of it). Ritzy ***Cafe Gramofon***, at the southern end of İstiklal Caddesi, has live jazz (it's also a comfortable environment for women). Dig out the buzzing ***Pano*** wine bar, opposite the British Consulate (ask for İngiliz Konsolosluğu Karşısı), approximately half way up İstiklal Caddesi. This place really knows how to wine and dine. Opposite the Nature & Peace restaurant, ***Asparagas Cafe Bar*** has live Turkish rock every night while up the northern end of İstiklal Caddesi, ***Kemancı*** *(Sıraselviler Caddesi 69)* will satiate the headbangers amongst you.

Beyoğlu can be seedy. Ignore touts who try to encourage you into their bar/club – it'll only end in tears.

Nargiles The Orient and Yücelt hostels offer the use of *nargiles* (water pipes). However you'll have a more authentic experience at **Çorlulu Alipaşa Medresesi**, on Divan Yolu, 250m west of the Çemberlitaş Hamamı. You'll pay US$2 per session.

Shopping Tea is a Turkish salesperson's lubricant – resign yourself to drinking a lot of it. Your shopping day may go along these lines: start at Arasta (near the Blue Mosque) for wall-to-wall carpets and kilims, tea, head to the Egyptian Bazaar for tea, spices and *lokum* (Turkish Delight) over to Beyoğlu for clothing and antiques, tea, and finish at the Grand Bazaar sipping tea and sifting through leather, jewellery and ceramic wares.

Ferry Cruising Enjoy İstanbul, by water, on a 'budget cruise' across the Bosphorus. Board a ferry from Eminönü for Üsküdar or Kadıköy, or from Karaköy for Haydarpaşa or Kadıköy (US$0.50).

Getting There & Away

Air İstanbul is Turkey's airline hub. Most foreign airlines have offices around Taksim Square. You can buy Turkish Airlines tickets in Taksim (☎ 663 6363, Cumhuriyet Caddesi 10), or at any travel agency. Most domestic flights cost around US$100.

İstanbul Airlines (☎ 423 7100) fly to many Turkish and European cities. Most domestic flights cost US$65 to US$90.

Bus İstanbul's main bus station (☎ 658 0037) is at Esenler, about 10km north-west of Sultanahmet. Buses depart from here to all parts of Turkey and beyond. To get to it take the light railway from Aksaray to Otogar.

Buses depart for Ankara (US$15 to US$24, seven hours) roughly every 15 minutes, day and night, and to most other cities at least every hour. Heading to Anatolia, you'll save time if you board at the smaller otogar at Harem (☎ 216-333 3763) on the Asian shore, served by car ferry from Sirkeci. Let the bus company know you plan to do this when you buy your ticket. For

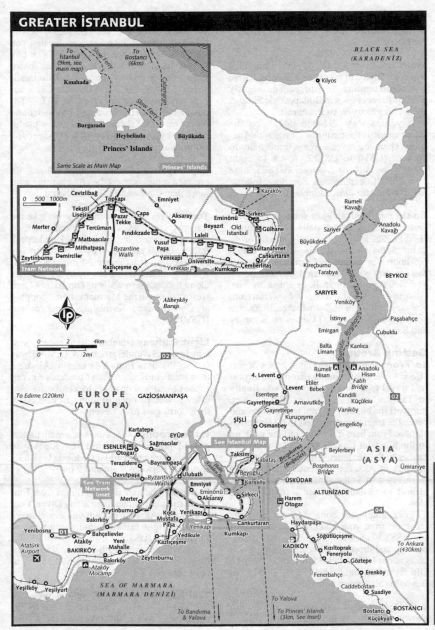

GREATER İSTANBUL

To İstanbul (9km, see main map) — Slow Ferry — *To Bostancı (6km)* — Çakmakçılar

BLACK SEA (KARADENİZ)

Kınalıada

Burgazada

Heybeliada   Büyükada

Slow Ferry

Princes' Islands

Same Scale as Main Map   Princes' Islands

0   500   1000m

Karaköy

Cevizlibağ   Topkapı   Emniyet
Tekstil Lisesi   Çapa   Aksaray   Eminönü   Sirkeci
Merter   Pazar Tekke   Beyazıt   Gülhane
Tercüman   Fındıkzade   Laleli   Old İstanbul
Matbaacılar   Yusuf Paşa   Sultanahmet
Mithatpaşa   *Byzantine Walls*   Üniversite   Çankurtaran
Zeytinburnu   Demirciler   Yenikapı   Kumkapı   Çemberlitaş
Kazlıçeşme   Yenikapı

Tram Network

Kilyos

Rumeli Kavağı
Anadolu Kavağı
Sarıyer
Büyükdere
SARIYER   Yeniköy   Paşabahçe
İstinye   Çubuklu
Emirgan   Kanlıca
Balta Limanı   Kandilli Küçüksu
4. Levent   Rumeli Hisarı   Anadolu Hisarı   *Fatih Bridge*
Etiler   Vaniköy
Esentepe   Levent   Bebek
Gayrettepe   Arnavutköy   Çengelköy
Gayrettepe   Kuruçeşme
ŞİŞLİ   Osmanbey   Ortaköy   Beylerbeyi
Taksim   Kabataş   *Bosphorus (Boğaziçi)*   ASIA (ASYA)
Beyoğlu   *Bosphorus Bridge*
ÜSKÜDAR
Ümraniye
ALTUNİZADE

To Edirne (220km)

EUROPE (AVRUPA)   GAZİOSMANPAŞA

02

Alibeyköy Barajı

0   2   4km
0   1   2mi

Kartatepe
EYÜP
ESENLER   Sağmacılar
Otogar   Bayrampaşa
Terazidere   Davutpaşa   *Byzantine Walls*   Ulubatlı
See Tram Network Inset   Emniyet   Karaköy
Merter   Eminönü   Sirkeci
Zeytinburnu   Koca Mustafa Paşa   Aksaray
Bakırköy   Yenikapı   Cankurtaran
Yedikule   Kumkapı
Yenibosna   Bahçelievler   Yeni Mahalle   Kazlıçeşme
Ataköy   Bakırköy   Zeytinburnu
BAKIRKÖY   Ataköy Mocamp
Yeşilköy   Yeşilyurt

See İstanbul Map

Golden Horn (Haliç)

Harem Otogar

Haydarpaşa
Söğütlüçeşme
KADIKÖY   Kızıltoprak Feneryolu
Moda   Göztepe
Fenerbahçe   Erenköy
Caddebostan   Suadiye
Bostancı   BOSTANCI
Küçükyalı

To Ankara (430km)

SEA OF MARMARA (MARMARA DENİZİ)

To Bandırma & Yalova   *To Yalova*   *To Princes' Islands (3km, See inset)*

Atatürk Airport

01

02

04

TURKEY

Cappadocia you can usually pick up the night bus direct from around the Hippodrome.

Train Sirkeci (☎ 527 0050) is the station for trains to Thrace (Trakya) and Europe. There are regular trains to Edirne. The nightly *Balkan Express* goes to Budapest via Skopje, the *Bukreş Ekspresi* to Bucharest.

Haydarpaşa (☎ 216-336 0475), on the Asian shore, is the terminus for trains to Anatolia. There are seven express trains daily to Ankara (US$6 to US$12, seven to eight hours); the *Ankara Ekspresi* (US$25, nine hours) is all sleeping cars. See Boat, following, for the *Marmara Ekspresi* to İzmir.

Boat From Yenikapı, just south of Aksaray, fast car ferries depart daily for Bandırma (US$11, 2½ hours); you can continue on to İzmir on the *Marmara Ekspresi* train (US$5, 6½ hours), or by bus to Çanakkale. Another fast car ferry goes to Yalova (US$7, one hour); you can continue to İznik or Bursa by bus. Also, fast catamarans *(deniz otobüsü)* run from Kabataş, just south of Dolmabahçe, to Yalova six times on weekdays, 11 times on Saturday and Sunday.

Getting Around
To/From the Airport Havaş buses depart (US$3, every 30 minutes) from the airport and travel to Bakırköy, Aksaray and finally to Taksim Square. To get to Sultanahmet, jump off the bus at Yenikapı train station and catch the train two stops east to Cankurtaran station. From here it's a five-minute walk up to the hotels at Cankurtaran, a few minutes farther to Sultanahmet. Alternatively, stay on the bus to Aksaray and catch the tramvay (tram) east to Sultanahmet. Buses from the airport to Sultanahmet are infrequent and slow.

Your hotel can book 24-hour minibus transport from your hotel door to the airport for US$3.50. Some hotels also offer a free pick-up and drop off service. An airport taxi costs about US$11 to US$14 for the 23km to Old İstanbul, and US$13 to US$15 to Beyoğlu (50% more at night).

Bus Destinations on city bus routes are shown on signs on the right (kerb) side of the bus. İETT buses are run by the city, and you must have a ticket (US$0.50) before boarding; some long routes require that you stuff two tickets into the box. You can buy tickets from the white booths near major stops or from nearby shops. Stock up in advance. Private *Özel Halk Otobüsü* buses accept city bus tickets or cash. An İETT 'T4' bus passes the Hippodrome in Sultanahmet on its way to Taksim Square. It's a useful service but waiting for it will have you frothing at the mouth.

Dolmuş Cute minibuses called dolmuş run on fixed routes around the city charging a bit more than the bus fare. Pay on board.

Train To get to Sirkeci train station, take the tramvay from Aksaray or Sultanahmet, or any bus signed for Eminönü. Haydarpaşa train station is connected by ferry to Karaköy (US$0.60, at least every 30 minutes). Banliyö (suburban) trains run every 20 minutes along the southern walls of Old İstanbul and westward along the Marmara shore, stopping at Cankurtaran, Kumkapı, Yenikapı etc (US$0.50).

Light Railway İstanbul's light railway system is largely underground. A light railway (US$0.45) runs from Yenikapı to Aksaray, then westwards via Adnan Menderes Bulvarı to the otogar and onwards to Yenibosna. Another is due to open, running from Taksim then north-east to 4. Levent.

Underground The Tünel, a small underground train, climbs the hill from Karaköy to Tünel Square and İstiklal Caddesi (US$0.35, regularly between 7 am and 9 pm).

Tramvay The tramvay (tram) runs from Eminönü to Sultanahmet, then along Divan Yolu to Beyazıt, Aksaray (where you can connect with the light railway) and south-west to Zeytinburnu (US$0.45).

A restored early-19th-century tram trundles along İstiklal Caddesi (US$0.35, regularly between 7 am and 9 pm).

Taxi İstanbul has 60,000 yellow taxis, all with digital meters; some are driven by lunatics who will really take you for a ride.

From Sultanahmet to Taksim costs US$3 to US$4; to the otogar costs around US$9.

Around İstanbul

EDİRNE
☎ 284

European Turkey is known as Thrace (Trakya). Close to the border crossings to Greece and Bulgaria you'll find the pleasant, under-visited town of Edirne. It's an oil-wrestler's heaven (see the Public Holidays & Special Events section earlier in this chapter), offering everyone's favourite – *ciğer* (deep-fried liver), crumbling Ottoman houses and several striking mosques. The best is the **Selimiye Camii**, the finest work of Süleyman the Magnificent's master architect Sinan. The impressive **Beyazıt II Camii** is well worth a walk across the river. Both the **Üçşerefeli Cami** and the **Eski Cami** are undergoing restoration, but are still impressive. The tourist office (☎/fax 213 9208), Hürriyet Meydanı 17, is in the town centre. The otogar is 2km south-east of Eski Cami.

Fifi Mocamp (☎ 212 0101) is open in summer for campers. Head south from the tourist office along Maarif Caddesi to the quaint *Hotel Aksaray (☎ 212 6035, Alipaşa Ortakapı Caddesi 8)*. Basic rooms cost US$7/12 for singles/doubles. The spotless *Efe Hotel (☎ 213 6166)*, next door, has beds for US$25/42 and two bars. It's a good, though pricey, option for women travellers. Near Eski Cami, *Otel Şaban Açıkgöz (☎ 213 1404, Çilingirler Caddesi 9)* is good value at US$16/23. The nearby Ottoman caravanserai *Hotel Rüstempaşa Kervansaray (☎ 225 2195, İki Kapılıhan 57)* has rustic rooms for US$18/36.

Try *Serhad Köftecisi* on Saraçlar Caddesi, just off Hürriyet Meydanı, for scrumptious meals and ciğer for US$4.

Buses run frequently to İstanbul (US$8, 2½ hours) and five times daily south to Çanakkale (US$6, 3½ hours).

BURSA
☎ 224

Sprawled at the base of Uludağ mountain (Turkey's biggest winter sports centre), Bursa was the first Ottoman capital city. It retains several fine mosques and pretty neighbourhoods from early Ottoman times, but Bursa's big attraction, now and historically, is its mineral springs. Besides healthy hot water, Bursa produces succulent fruit and most of the cars made in Turkey. It's also home to the famous Karagöz shadow puppets and delicious *İskender kebap* (döner kebap topped with savoury tomato sauce and browned butter).

Orientation & Information
The city centre is along Atatürk Caddesi between the Ulu Cami (Grand Mosque) to the west and the main square, Cumhuriyet Alanı, commonly called Heykel (statue), to the east. The post office is opposite Ulu Cami. Çekirge, with its mineral baths, is about 6km west of Heykel. Bursa's bus station ('terminal') is 10km north on the Yalova road.

Grab a map at the tourist office (☎ 220 1848) in the Orhangazi Altgeçidi subway, Ulu Cami Parkı 1, beside the belediye (town hall).

Things to See & Do
The largest of Bursa's beautiful mosques is the 20-domed **Ulu Cami** (Grand Mosque), built in 1399; it's on Atatürk Caddesi in the city centre. North-east of Ulu Cami is the **bedesten** or covered bazaar. Here you'll find the **Karagöz** shop (☎ 221 8727) with details about the puppet shows. The **Koza Han** (silk market) is worth wandering through too.

North-west of Ulu Cami is the **Muradiye Complex**, with decorated tombs dating from the 14th and 15th centuries. Continue on to the **mineral baths** in the suburb of Çekirge. To rejuvenate at **Eski Kaplıca**, beside the Kervansaray Termal Hotel, will set you back US$5; another US$5 for a scrub or a limp-wristed massage. The women's part of the baths is nothing special; keep your underwear on!

About 1km east of Heykel in a pretty pedestrian zone you'll find the early-Ottoman **Yeşil Cami** (Green Mosque; built in 1424) and its beautifully tiled **Yeşil Türbe** (Green Tomb; open 8.30 am to 5.30 pm; free entry). The nearby **Turkish & Islamic Arts Museum**, or Türk İslam Eserleri Müzesi, is open 8.30 am to noon and 1 to 5 pm, closed Monday; entry is US$1.70. A few hundred metres farther east is the **Emir Sultan Camii** (1805).

TURKEY

On a clear day it's worth going up **Uludağ**. From Heykel take bus 3/B, 3/C or a dolmuş east to the *teleferik* (cable car) up the mountain (US$6 one way).

Places to Stay

You can camp at *Çeltik Köyü Kamp* (☎ 253 0282) on the road to Yalova.

The centre of town has a motley bunch of places to stay. You're better off forking about a bit more and staying in Çekirge where you'll also get free mineral baths. The *Öz Yeşil Yayla Termal Otel* (☎ 239 6496, Selvi Sokak 6) is straight from the 1950s, with matching prices: US$24 a double. The *Boyugüzel* (☎ 239 9999) next door is pricier but includes breakfast. Four and five-star hotels abound.

If you stay in the centre, *Otel Güneş* (☎ 222 1404, İnebey Caddesi 75) in Tahtakale, south-west of Ulu Cami, is the best option. It's clean, friendly and has rooms for US$9/14; book ahead. If you're desperate, the neighbouring *Otel Çamlıbel* (☎ 221 2565, İnebey Caddesi 71) will happily rip you off for US$16/27 a single/double. The prissy *Hotel Çeşmeli* (☎ 224 1511, Gümüşçeken Caddesi 6), just north-west of Heykel, is good but pricey at US$33/50, with breakfast.

Places to Eat

For cheap eats, head to Tahtakale. The *Şehir* and *Ümit* restaurants along İnebey Caddesi will fill you up for around US$3. Head 100m west to the Hacı Sevinç Camii to find *Yeşil İnci Lokantası* – great food and it's also comfy for women travellers.

Bursa's İskender kebap will send your cholesterol levels rocketing and it's worth every sinful mouthful. *Adanur Hacıbey (Ünlü Caddesi 4)*, just east of Heykel, is tacky but will grease you up with İskender for US$5. You'll pay the same at gaudy *Kebapçı İskender*, opposite, which dates back to 1867.

Çiçek Izgara (Belediye Caddesi 15), just north of the belediye, has decently priced food (around US$4 for meats) despite its ritzy facade.

Getting There & Away

The fastest way to/from İstanbul is to take the bus to Yalova (US$3, 70 minutes, every half-

hour), then catch the fast Yalova-İstanbul (Yenikapı) deniz otobüsü (catamaran; one hour, five a day), or the 'jet feribot' to Yenikapı; both cost US$6. You can also book a designated *feribot ile* bus through to İstanbul. These buses use the Topçular-Eskihisar ferry and are quicker (US$7, 2½ hours) than the land route *(karayolu ile)* around the Marmara (US$9, four hours).

Buses leave frequently for Çanakkale (US$7, five hours), İzmir (US$7, six hours) and Ankara (US$12, 5½ hours).

Getting Around

Most buses stop outside the post office on Atatürk Caddesi. For the otogar, catch the grey buses marked 'Terminal' which leave every half-hour from outside the Emlak Bankası beside the post office.

Catch dolmuş in two streets (west of Heykel) which run off Atatürk Caddesi: along Tuz Pazarı Sokak, dolmuş head westward to Çekirge, along Kültür Sokak they go to Emir Sultan Camii, the Muradiye Complex and the *teleferik* (for Uludağ).

Dolmuş and buses charge the same set fee (US$0.45).

The Aegean Coast

Olive groves and a unique history distinguish this gorgeous but rapidly developing coast. Gallipoli, Troy and Pergamum are only a few of the famous places to be visited.

ÇANAKKALE
☎ 286

Laid-back Çanakkale is a hub for transport to Troy and across the Dardanelles to Gallipoli. It was here that Leander swam across what was then called the Hellespont to his lover Hero, and here too that Lord Byron did his romantic bit and duplicated the feat. The defence of the straits during WWI led to a Turkish victory over Anzac forces, placing this area on the map as a pilgrimage site for many Australians and New Zealanders.

The helpful tourist office (☎/fax 217 1187) and many cheap hotels are within a few blocks of the ferry pier, near the landmark clock tower. Micronet Internet Cafe is also near the tower.

The Ottoman **castle** built by Mehmet the Conqueror is now the **Army & Navy Museum**. Just over 2km south of the ferry pier, the **Archaeological Museum** holds artefacts found at Troy and Assos.

Places to Stay

Most accommodation is heavily booked in summer and the town is insanely crowded around Anzac Day, 25 April.

You can camp at Güzelyalı Beach, 15km south by dolmuş off the road to Troy; try *Mocamp Trova* (☎ 283 0061).

Near the clock tower, *Kervansaray* (☎ 217 8192, Fetvane Sokak 13) has a gorgeous garden. You'll pay US$5/9 for singles/doubles with charm, not cleanliness. Crazy-paved *Yellow Rose Pension* (☎ 217 3343, @ yell owrose1@mailexcite.com, Yeni Sokak 5), nearby, has dorm beds for US$3, rooms for US$6/12. It gets mixed reviews from readers. *Hotel Efes* (☎ 217 3256, Aralık Sokak 6), behind the clock tower, is run by a Turkish woman; beds go for US$8/14. Popular *Anzac House* (☎ 213 5969, @ hasslefree@anzach ouse.com, Cumhuriyet Meydanı 61) offers dorm beds for US$5, sterile rooms for US$9/14 and heaps of services.

Ugly *Otel Anafartalar* (☎ 217 4454, fax 217 4457, İskele Meydanı), right on the waterfront, is decent value at US$25/37 for views and breakfast.

Places to Eat

Gaziantep Aile Kebap ve Pide Salonu, behind the clock tower, serves excellent, cheap pide and kebabs. *Trakya Restaurant*, on the main square, has similar prices with a greater selection. *Aussie & Kiwi Restaurant (Yalı Caddesi 32)*, closer to the Army & Navy Museum, has delicious meals for around US$4 if you're willing to brave the dated antipodean decor and music.

Women travellers should feel comfortable drinking at the jumping *TNT* by the clock tower, or the quieter *Yalı Hanı (Fetvane Sokak 28)*. Out on the waterfront, near Otel Anafartalar, is the decently priced *Yacht Club*.

GALLIPOLI

Although the Dardanelles had always been İstanbul's first line of defence, it was in WWI that they proved their worth. After an unsuccessful naval attempt on the strait by the British, on 25 April 1915, allied forces were sent in to take Gallipoli peninsula. The Anzacs miscalculated and landed at Ari Burnu, a desolate beach lined by towering slopes. Mustafa Kemal (Atatürk) and his troops were soon waiting at the top – the Anzacs didn't stand a chance.

As a reminder of nine months of bloodshed the Gallipoli (Gelibolu) peninsula now has many sombre exhibits – gravesites, trenches, shrapnel and bones. It's a testament to the horrors of war, the waste of young lives and the bravery and sacrifice shown by the soldiers on both sides.

The easiest way to visit Gallipoli is to take one of the decent tours on offer. Several companies run six-hour minibus tours (around US$19) from Çanakkale, Eceabat and Gelibolu. Try Hassle Free (@ hasslefree@anzach ouse.com) at Anzac House, Çanakkale, or TJs Tours (@ TJs–TOURS@excite.com). If you're a hiker, take a ferry from Çanakkale to Eceabat and a dolmuş to Kabatepe, and follow the trail around the sites described in a booklet sold at the visitor centre (Kabatepe Tanıtma Merkezi) there.

Turkish Maritime Lines' car ferries cross the straits hourly from Lapseki to Gelibolu and from Çanakkale to Eceabat (US$0.70 per person). Small private ferries cross from Çanakkale (in front of Hotel Bakır) to Kilitbahir.

TROY

Don't get excited – there's little of Troy (Truva) to be seen and most people aren't thrilled with the tacky 'Trojan Horse'. It's estimated that nine successive cities have been built on this same site: Troy I goes right back to the Bronze Age; legendary Troy is thought to be Troy VI; most of the ruins you see are Roman ones from Troy IX. You may want to take one of the tours (around US$17) offered in Çanakkale to get more out of Troy.

Troy is open 9 am to 5 pm daily; admission is US$2.50.

Dolmuş run the 30km from Çanakkale frequently for US$1.50. Walk straight inland from the ferry pier to Atatürk Caddesi, and turn right towards Troy; the dolmuş stop is at the bridge.

TURKEY

BEHRAMKALE (ASSOS)
☎ 286

Nineteen kilometres west of Ayvacık, Behramkale, once known as Assos, has the hill-top **Temple of Athena** looking across the water to Lesvos (Greece), and was considered one of the most beautiful cities of its time. It's still stunning, particularly the tiny port *(iskele)* 2km beyond the village. Offseason Assos is a nightmare to get to; you may have to hitch.

Accommodation prices at the port include two meals; bargain hard if you don't want the feed. *Plaj Camping* provides tent sites (US$7 per tent) and bungalows (US$30 for two) beside the water. On the heights, *Timur Pansiyon* (☎ 721 7449), near the top entrance to the Temple, has awesome views for US$25 per couple; the *Kale Restaurant* will feed you. You pay for location at the port hotels *Şen* (☎ 721 7076), *Behram* (☎ 721 7016) and *Yıldızsaray* (☎ 721 7025) which charge US$40 to US$50 per couple. Visit in low season (US$25 a double) if you can.

AYVALIK
☎ 266

Beautiful Ayvalık has winding cobbled streets, terracotta-tiled roofs and Greek Orthodox churches (now converted to mosques) from its time as an Ottoman Greek village. It's hectic with Turkish tourists in summer but is worth a short visit. The main street, İnönü Caddesi, links the otogar, 1.5km north of the town centre, and the tourist office (☎ 312 2122), 1km south, opposite the yacht marina.

Offshore is **Alibey Adası** (island), with open-air restaurants, linked by ferries and a causeway to the mainland (take the red 'Ayvalık Belediyesi' bus north). Six kilometres south on a blue 'Sarımsaklı Belediyesi' bus is the 12km-long **Sarımsaklı Plaj** (beach), also called Plajlar.

Turkish boats make the two-hour trip to Lesvos in the morning, Greek boats in the evening, for an outrageous US$50 one way and US$65 same-day return (including taxes). Boats operate at least three days per week from early July to late September.

Places to Stay & Eat

Several camping grounds are on Alibey Adası outside the village. Down on the waterfront, on the street directly behind the post office, is *Yalı Pansiyon* (☎ 312 2423), a grand old house. Rooms are fairly basic but the house has a large garden lit with coloured lights, and its own jetty. Dorms go for US$5, doubles/triples/quads cost US$30/35/40 with breakfast. Don't miss the stunning *Taksiyarhis Pansiyon* (☎ 312 1494, Maraşal Çakmak Caddesi 71), which charges US$8 per bed; book ahead. *Kıyı Motel* (☎ 312 6677, Gümrük Meydanı 18), with car parking, charges the same for small rooms with shower.

Anadolu Pide ve Kebap Salonu on İnönü Caddesi and *Yeni Bahar Lokantası* just off it, have decent cheap meals. *Öz Canlı Balık Restaurant* on the waterfront is pricier but good for seafood or a drink in the evening.

Getting There & Away

Coming from the north or south you may get dropped at the highway; a free dolmuş *should* be waiting to take you into town. Going north you'll need to catch a dolmuş to Edremit or the OPET petrol station along the highway and change buses.

BERGAMA
☎ 232

From the 4th to the 2nd centuries BC, Bergama (Pergamum) was a powerful and cultured kingdom. A line of rulers beginning with a general under Alexander the Great ruled over this small but wealthy kingdom, whose **asclepion** (medical school; 2.5km from the city centre; entry US$2.50) grew famous and whose library rivalled that of Alexandria in Egypt. The star attractions here are the city's ruins, especially the **acropolis** (a hill-top site 6km from the city centre; entry US$2), and an excellent **archaeology & ethnography museum** in the city centre (entry US$2).

The tourist office (☎ 633 1862) is at İzmir Caddesi 54. Taxis wait here and charge US$5 to the acropolis, US$12 total if they wait an hour and bring you back down. If you're feeling fit, follow the path down through the ruins instead. A tour of the acropolis, the asclepion and the museum costs US$22.

Köse Internet is on the street, north of the tourist office that heads up to the asclepion.

Places to Stay & Eat

Camp at *Hotel Berksoy* (☎ 633 2595), 2km south-west of town on the main road to the highway to İzmir.

The friendly *Pension Athena* (☎ 633 3420, ✉ aydinathena@hotmail.com, İmam Çıkmazı 5), in the north-eastern part of town, is in a 160-year-old stone house. Rooms with/without shower cost US$7/5 per person, delicious breakfast another US$2. Cross the nearby bridge and turn left to find *Nike Pension* (☎ 633 3901, Tabak Köprü Çıkmazı 2), a gorgeous 300-year-old Ottoman Greek house offering doubles for US$17, including breakfast.

South of the otogar, you'll find the spotless, family-run *Böblingen Pension* (☎ 633 2153, Asklepion Caddesi 2), offering rooms with bathroom and breakfast for US$13/16. Continue out of town, along İzmir Caddesi towards the İzmir highway, to the fancy *Hotel Berksoy* (☎ 633 2595), which charges US$45/65 per room amid well-kept gardens with a pool.

Just south-west of the red basilica is a small square, on the main drag, where you'll find the *Meydan Restaurant* charging about US$5 for a delicious feed. The nearby *Sarmaşık Lokantası* has no outdoor seating, but is cheaper, as is the *Çiçeksever Kebap Salonu* on the way to the museum.

Try your hand at *tavla* (backgammon) in one of the outdoor *tea gardens* opposite the museum.

Getting There & Away

Whether you approach Bergama from the north or south, check to see your bus drops you *in* Bergama or you may find yourself twiddling your thumbs beside the highway. Buses to İzmir go every half-hour in summer (US$4, 1¾ hours). Five buses go to Ayvalık daily (US$2, 45 minutes), or you can hitch out to the highway and flag a bus.

İZMİR
☎ 232

Turkey's third-largest city, once named Smyrna, is said to be the place where Homer was born in 700 BC. Today it's a transport hub and a good place to dodge. If you do stay, İzmir does have some pluses: few tourists, the interesting **bazaar**, the 2nd-century Roman

agora, the hill-top Kadifekale **fortress**, and the **archaeological** and **ethnographic museums**. You can get to the Greek island of Chios from Çeşme, 90km (two hours) west of İzmir.

Orientation & Information

Budget hotels are along Anafartalar Caddesi which twists through the labyrinthine bazaar towards the waterfront at Konak, the commercial and government centre. Atatürk Caddesi, also called Birinci Kordon, runs north-east from Konak along the waterfront 1km to Cumhuriyet Meydanı (and its equestrian statue of Atatürk). Here you'll find the main post office, the Büyük Efes Oteli, the tourist office and airline offices. İzmir's otogar is 3km north-east of the city centre.

Grab a map at the tourist office (☎ 445 7390) beneath the Büyük Efes Oteli at Gaziosmanpaşa Bulvarı 1/1D, Cumhuriyet Meydanı. There's also a good information desk (☎ 489 0500) in the belediye (town hall) in Konak.

Places to Stay

You can camp at *Oba Camping* (☎ 234 2015), in Güzelbahçe, 15km south-west of İzmir.

Decent mid-range places are scarce in İzmir and it has more than its fair share of seedy dives. Still keen? Head to Anafartalar Caddesi (south-west of Basmane train station). Women may not feel comfortable in this area at night, but the three hotels recommended are suitable for women travellers.

Near the Hatuniye (or Kuşlu) Camii (mosque) is *Otel Saray* (☎ 483 6946, Anafartalar Caddesi 635), which has been popular with backpackers for years and looks it. Rooms go for US$4 per person. If the 'Saturday Night Fever' foyer doesn't scare you off, the nearby *Otel Hikmet* (☎ 484 2672, 945 Sokak No 26) is better and charges US$7/13 for rooms with a shower. The clean *Otel Antik Han* (☎ 489 2750, Anafartalar Caddesi 600), set around a pretty courtyard, charges US$20/30 with bathroom and breakfast.

Places to Eat & Drink

Immediately opposite Basmane station, the *Ankara*, *Ödemis Azim* and *Aydın-Denizli-Nazili* restaurants offer quick, cheap meals.

On 1296 Sokak you'll find the good value *Güneydoğu Kebap Salonu*, where a kebab and a drink costs around US$3. At *Dört Mevsim Et*

Lokantası (*1369 Sokak No 51/A*), watch your meat cook on the *ocakbaşı* (fireside) grill. You'll be stuffed with food for US$5.

Try *Gemi Restoran*, a floating fish restaurant, moored along the waterfront south-west of Cumhuriyet Meydanı. You'll pay around US$6 per meal. Sway to the *Anchor Rock Cafe* boat, next door, where you can have a beer while the motion rocks down (or up) your meal.

Getting There & Away
Air İstanbul Airlines (☎ 489 0541), Gaziosmanpaşa Bulvarı 2/E, opposite the Büyük Efes Oteli, has flights to İstanbul (US$70, 50 minutes), and numerous flights to Europe. Turkish Airlines (☎ 489 0541) is beneath the Büyük Efes Oteli.

Bus Many bus companies have ticket offices around Dokuz Eylül Meydanı, just north of Basmane train station. Ask about the free minibus to the otogar.

Train The evening *mavi tren* hauls sleeping and dining cars from Basmane station to Ankara (US$18, 14 hours). The evening *İzmir Ekspresi* to Ankara (15 hours) has 1st/2nd-class carriages for US$9/6.

For İstanbul, take the *Marmara Ekspresi* to Bandırma, then a car ferry to Yenikapı; in total the journey costs US$11. Four pokey cheap trains go from Basmane to Selçuk/Ephesus (US$1.50, 2½ hours); three continue to Denizli (for Pamukkale, US$4, six hours).

Boat The Getting There & Away and Getting Around sections earlier in this chapter have information on ferries to the Greek Islands and Venice. Ferries to Chios depart from Çeşme, west of İzmir, daily in summer (US$30 one-way, including taxes). Catch any Güzelyalı, Altay Meydanı or Balçova bus or dolmuş from Konak and get out at Güzelyalı (Fahrettin)/Altay Meydanı to board a Çeşme-bound bus (US$3, 1½ hours).

Getting Around
To/From the Airport A Havaş bus (US$3.50, 45 minutes) departs from the Turkish Airlines office under the Büyük Efes Oteli many times daily for the 25km trip to Adnan Menderes airport. A taxi costs around US$18.

To/From the Otogar If you crawled into town you would arrive before the city buses (look for 'Basmane' signs on the bus; US$0.50) which go from the otogar to Konak via the Basmane train station. Save your sanity and jump on the free minibus services (*şehir-içi servis*) to/from İzmir's otogar. A taxi from the city centre to the otogar costs about US$5.

SELÇUK & EPHESUS
☎ 232

Selçuk has ruins, resident storks and an annual camel wrestling festival to entice visitors, but this quaint town lives in the shadow of its neighbour – the splendid Roman ruins of Ephesus (Efes). In its Ionian heyday only Athens was more magnificent, and in Roman times this was Asia's capital.

Orientation & Information
On the eastern side of the main road (Atatürk Caddesi) are the otogar, restaurants, some hotels and the train station; on the western side, behind the museum, are many pensions. The tourist office (☎ 892 6328) is in the park opposite the otogar. Namel Internet Cafe is on Siegburg Caddesi.

Ephesus is 3.5km west from the centre of Selçuk.

Things to See
Ephesus flourished as the centre for worship of the Anatolian goddess later identified with Diana/Artemis. The **Arcadian Way** through Ephesus was the main street to the port, which has long been silted up. The immense **Great Theatre** holds 24,000 people. The **Temple of Hadrian**, the **Celsus Library**, the **Marble Way** (where the rich lived) and the **Fountain of Trajan** are still in amazingly good shape, or under painstaking restoration. Ephesus was also a centre of early Christianity; it was visited by St Paul.

The site, permanently swamped with coach groups, is open from 8 am to 5.30 pm (7 pm in summer). Admission costs US$5. Ephesus is a 3km, 35-minute walk west from Selçuk's otogar along a shady road – turn left (south) at the Tusan Motel. Frequent dolmuş to Pamucak and Kuşadası pass the Ephesus turn-off (US$0.50, five minutes).

Selçuk's main site is the excellent **Ephesus Museum** with its striking collection of artefacts from the Roman period. It's open 8.30 am to noon and 1 to 5.30 pm; tickets cost $3.50. Above Selçuk, visit the **Basilica of St John**, said to be built over his tomb. Between Ephesus and Selçuk, the foundations of the **Temple of Artemis** are all that are left of one of the Seven Wonders of the World. At the hill-top site of **Meryemana**, south of town, the Virgin Mary is alleged to have lived her last years.

Places to Stay

Garden Motel & Camping (☎ 892 2489) is west of Ayasoluk, the hill bearing the Basilica of St John; walk past the basilica, down the hill, then turn right at the İsabey Camii. Tent and caravan sites amidst orchards cost US$4 per person.

There are many pensions up the hill behind the Ephesus Museum, all charging about US$4 to US$8 per person. A good choice is *Barım* (☎ 892 6923, *Turgutreis Sokak 34*), on the first street back from the museum. The popular *Australia & New Zealand Pension* (☎ 892 6050, ✉ oznzpension@superonline.com, 1064 Sokak No 12), on the second street back, has dorm beds (US$4) in the 'dungeon'. Also worth seeking out is the friendly *Homeros* (☎ 892 3995, ✉ homerospension@yahoo.com, Asmalı Sokak 17). Over near the train station *Artemis Guest House,* or 'Jimmy's' (☎ 892 6191, ✉ jimmy@egenet.com.tr, 1012 Sokak No 2), has similar prices and many services.

Yearning for luxury? Splash in the pool at the atmospheric *Hotel Kale Han* (☎ 892 6154, ✉ ergirh@superonline.com), on Atatürk Caddesi in the northern reaches of town. Sumptuous rooms with showers and air-con cost US$42/60 a single/double with breakfast.

Places to Eat & Drink

For cheap eats (around US$2), try *Artemis Pide Salonu*, near 'Jimmy's'; *Hünkarım Pide Salonu* (*Kızılay Caddesi 16*) is similar. If you crave a change the *Çin Lokantası*, behind the tourist office, has tasty Chinese food for around US$6 a meal. *Pink Bistro Cafe Bar* (*Siegburg Caddesi 24/A*) livens up after dark.

Getting There & Away

Minibuses leave frequently for Kuşadası (US$1, 30 minutes) and Pamucak (US$0.80, 10 minutes).

You can make a day trip to Pamukkale (US$7 one-way, three hours) on direct buses leaving before 9 am and returning by 5 pm. Frequent buses and three cheap trains (US$3) go daily to Denizli, where you can get a dolmuş to Pamukkale. Buses leave regularly for İzmir (US$2, 1¼ hours), Bodrum (US$5.50, three hours) and Marmaris (US$10, 6½ hours).

KUŞADASI
☎ 256

Welcome to this cruise-ship port and cheerfully sleazy tourist trap. The main reason to visit is to catch a boat to the Greek island of Samos, though Kuşadası does have a pretty kaleiçi (old town) worth strolling through and decent accommodation. It's also a good base for visits to **Priene**, **Miletus** and **Didyma** to the south. There are OK beaches: Kadinlar Denizi and Pamucak.

The tourist office (☎ 614 1103) is in the middle of town, right by the pier. The dolmuş station is on Adnan Menderes Bulvarı, 1km south-east of the tourist office; continue 500m to the otogar out on the highway. Kismet Internet Café is near the pier.

Boats to Samos (Sisam) sail daily in summer for US$30 one way, US$35 same-day return, or US$63 open return, including Turkish and Greek port taxes; call Azim Tour (☎ 614 1553) or Diana Travel (☎ 614 3859) for details.

Places to Stay

Camping at *Önder* (☎ 614 2413), north of town near the marina, costs US$9 for two.

Some good, cheap lodgings are uphill behind the tourist office near or along Aslanlar Caddesi. The pension-with-the-best-views award goes to the clean *Pension Golden Bed* (☎ 614 8708, *Uğurlu 1 Çıkmazı 4*) off Aslanlar Caddesi. Dorm beds cost US$4, rooms US$10/16. Strongly contesting the title is *Liman Otel* (☎ 614 7770, *Buyral Sokak 4*), near the waterfront, with similar prices.

Hotel Sammy's Palace (☎ 612 2588, ✉ sammy@superonline.com, *Kıbrıs Caddesi 14*), gets mixed reviews from readers. The services – daily room cleaning, free belly-dance shows and bed/food deals – are OK value for US$5 for dorm beds, US$12/16 for singles/doubles. Opposite, at *Özhan Pansiyon*

TURKEY

(☎ *614 2932*), you'll pay a few dollars less to feel like you're sleeping in a quaint village bedroom.

The historic **Hotel Kervansaray** (☎ *614 4115)* in the centre of town costs US$50/80, with breakfast; it can be noisy so you may just want to enjoy a drink in the courtyard.

Places to Eat & Drink

Avlu Restaurant (*Cephane Sokak 15)* has delicious, dirt-cheap food and the best *firin sütlaç* (baked rice pudding) tasted by our sütlaç connoisseurs. Cheap meals (US$2 to US$6) are also served on Sağlık Caddesi. Good seafood places along the waterfront charge around US$15 for a feed.

In the late arvo grab first-rate views and a coffee at *Ada Cafe* on Güvercin Adası (the little fort-topped island). After dark head to *İstanbul Meyhanesi* (*Kısla Sokak 7)* in the kaleiçi district, where punters scrawl their name on the walls while listening to live music. Meals cost US$5 to US$10; no cover charge. If you're desperate head to Pub Lane with its seedy 'Irish' pubs.

Getting There & Away

Dolmuş leave frequently for Selçuk (US$1, 30 minutes), via Pamucak from Adnan Menderes Bulvarı. Head to the otogar for far-flung destinations such as İzmir (US$3, 1¾ hours), Bodrum (US$6.50, 3½ hours) and Marmaris (US$11, seven hours).

PAMUKKALE
☎ 258

Three hours east of Selçuk, you'll find the Unesco World Heritage Site of Pamukkale. It's famous for the hot, calcium-rich waters that flowed over a plateau edge and cooled to form brilliant white ledges. Today some visitors are disappointed: much of the water has been diverted, most of the terraces are dry and the days of wallowing in the water-filled ledges are (thankfully) over. You can still swim in the calcium-rich waters at Pamukkale Motel at the top of the ridge (US$5 for two hours).

A ticket (US$4.50) to the site will give you two entries over 24 hours.

Above and behind this natural wonder lie the extensive ruins of the Roman city of **Hierapolis** (entry US$5), an ancient spa.

There's a tourist office on the ridge at Pamukkale (☎ 272 2077) and one in Denizli train station.

If you're heading west, a worthwhile but time-consuming detour would be to the beautiful ruined city of **Aphrodisias**, south of Nazilli near Karacasu. Many think it rivals Ephesus.

Places to Stay & Eat

Beds at **Meltem Motel Backpackers Inn** (☎ *272 2413,* ✉ *meltemmotel@superonline .com.tr)* cost US$4 for dorms, US$5/10 for a single/double. There are videos and a comfy lounge but some of the rooms are dark. For super-friendly service and decent rooms, try the family-run *Kervansaray Pension (*☎ *272 2209)* for US$12/18 a single/double with breakfast and a pool. The nearby *Aspawa* (☎ *272 2094)* is similar. *Koray Otel* (☎ *272 2300),* a few streets south, has a pretty garden, pool and basic rooms for US$15/20, including breakfast.

Taking meals in your pension or hotel is usually best here. Venture out and you'll pay only US$3 per meal to be offended at *Mustafa's*, on the main drag. Munch on tasty food (some vegetarian) while he mimics foreigners; tally your bill. Maintain your dignity at *Han 2*, opposite the calcium ledges, and grab great views for a similar price.

Getting There & Away

Heading to Pamukkale you might get dropped in Denizli otogar; you'll need to jump on one of the dolmuş (US$0.70, 30 minutes) that shuttle to and from Pamukkale.

BODRUM
☎ 252

Don your 'designer' sunglasses, stuff tissues in your wallet and take a stroll through the dazzling white laneways of this postcard-perfect yachting town. After dark Bodrum has a thumping nightlife. Come morning, revellers hide in the restaurants lining the bays; during the day they shop. But this town has more than hedonistic pursuits; formerly Halicarnassus, Bodrum is the site of the **Mausoleum**, the monumental tomb of King Mausolus, another of the Seven Wonders of the World. Little remains of the Mausoleum, which was probably partially destroyed by an earthquake and finished off by the Knights of St John. It's open 8 am to noon and 1 to 5 pm, closed Monday; admission is US$2.50.

Placed between Bodrum's perfect twin bays is the medieval **Castle of St Peter**, built in 1402 and rebuilt in 1522 by the knights, using stones from the Mausoleum. It's now a **museum of underwater archaeology** and contains finds from the oldest shipwreck ever discovered. The museum is open 8.30 am to noon and 1 to 5 pm, closed Monday; entry is US$4.50. It's another US$2 each to visit the ancient wreck and a model of a Carian princess' tomb; both are closed weekends.

Gümüşlük, to the far west of the Bodrum peninsula, is the best of the many smaller villages nearby. Dolmuş run there every hour (US$1).

Orientation & Information
Bodrum lines two bays divided by the castle-topped peninsula. Below the castle lies the centre of town where you'll find the tourist office (☎ 316 1091) and Adliye Camii. Cevat Şakir Caddesi runs from Adliye Camii 500m inland to the otogar; along this street are the post office and several banks. Head north of Adliye Camii up Türkkuyusu Sokak where you'll find the Neşe-i Muhabbet Internet Cafe and much of the accommodation; more is behind Cumhuriyet Caddesi around the east bay.

Places to Stay
Some villages on the peninsula, such as Bitez Yalısı and Ortakent Yalısı, have camp sites.

Head up Türkkuyusu Sokak to the friendly **Şenlik Pansiyon** (☎ 316 6382) at No 115, charging US$7/12 for singles/doubles. Behind, at the family-run **Sedan** (☎ 316 0355, *Türkkuyusu Sokak 121*), you'll pay a few dollars more for the bonuses of car spaces and a large garden.

Closer to the action (read: dust out the earplugs), behind Cumhuriyet Caddesi, you'll find **Durak Villa** (☎ 316 4053, *Rasathane Sokak 16*) with clean rooms and superb terrace views for US$8/15 with breakfast. Nearby **Evin Pansiyon** (☎ 316 1312, *Ortanca Sokak 7*) charges a bit more for its rooms (with balconies).

Gurup Otel (☎ 316 1140, Karantina Sokak 3) charges US$15 per person, with breakfast, for rooms with balconies overlooking the marina; check there's hot water.

The colourful **Su Otel** (☎ 316 6906, ✉ *suo tel@superonline.com, Turgutreis Caddesi 1201 Sokak, Tepecik Mahallesi*) has a charming courtyard and a pool. Doubles with bathroom cost US$70.

Places to Eat
Between the cane-chair-swamped eateries along Cumhuriyet Caddesi you'll find a few gems. Up the western end, the cheapest feed is at No 96, the **Meşhur Karadeniz Börek ve Pide Salonu**. Up the other end, the unpretentious **Berk Balık Restaurant** (*Kumbahçe Parkı Karşısı*) is well worth the US$6 to US$8 you'll pay for a superb meal; the place is packed with locals. About halfway along, **Cafe Penguen**, right by the water, has pricey but delicious breakfasts.

In the grid of small market streets just east of the Adliye Camii are several restaurants. One of the best is **Kardeşler Restaurant** (*Yeni Çarşı, 6 Sokak 10*), with tasty meat dishes for about US$5; beer costs US$1.

Entertainment
Too many bars await you along, and around, Dr Alim Bey Caddesi and its continuation, Cumhuriyet Caddesi. Try **Seyfi Bar Restaurant**, the feisty live music joint; grin and bear the hefty prices (US$8 for your first drink). **Cafe-In Bar** (*Cumhuriyet Caddesi 84*) opens onto the bay. Turkish cover songs are played here every night; it's a good spot for women travellers. Quaint **Mavi**, near the end of Cumhuriyet Caddesi, has live flamenco on Friday and Saturday nights. Join the queue, open the purse strings and release the ridiculous sum of US$17 to enter the noisy, brash and mega-fun **Halikarnas Night Club**.

Getting There & Away
Bodrum is a well connected town. Some bus services include İzmir (US$12, four hours), Selçuk (US$5.50, three hours) and Marmaris (US$6, three hours). Catch the Havaş bus (US$4) from the otogar to the Milas airport.

Boats go to Kos (İstanköy) frequently in summer for US$16 one-way, US$20 same-day and US$30 open return; these prices include port taxes. In summer there are also boats to Datça, Dalyan, Didyma, Marmaris and Rhodes.

TURKEY

The Mediterranean Coast

Turkey's Mediterranean coastline winds eastward for more than 1200km from Marmaris to Antakya on the Syrian border. East of Marmaris, the 'Turquoise Coast' is perfect for boat excursions, with many secluded coves and quiet bays all the way to Fethiye. The rugged coastline from Fethiye east to Antalya – immortalized by Homer as Lycia – and the Taurus Mountains east of Antalya are wild and beautiful. The entire coast is liberally sprinkled with impressive ruins, studded with beautiful beaches and washed by clear water, ideal for sports.

MARMARİS
☎ 252

Primed for the package holiday set, Marmaris has decent food, innumerable souvenirs and lascivious living after dark. If you're after something else it's time to move on – this bustling town has limited offerings. Still, it's a pretty setting, the best spot to head to the Greek island of Rhodes (Rodos) and a good place to pick up a boat or *gulet* (a Turkish wooden yacht) trip.

Orientation & Information
Marmaris has a small castle overlooking the town centre. Barbaros Caddesi, with its many restaurants, curls south, around the castle and heads east to Netsel marina. İskele Meydanı (the main square) and the tourist office (☎ 412 1035) are just north of the castle. Hacı Mustafa Sokak (or Bar Street) runs east from İskele Meydanı; the bazaar spreads northwards. Beside Netsel marina is the homely Marmaris Internet Cafe-Bar.

The otogar is 1.5km north-east of the centre of town, on the way to Muğla.

Things to See & Do
The **castle** offers unexciting exhibitions (ho-hum), resident peacocks and fine views of Marmaris. It's open from 8 am to noon and 1 to 5.30 pm, closed Monday; entry costs US$2.

There are daily boat trips in summer to **Paradise Island** (about US$15 a head) and farther afield to **Dalyan** and **Kaunos** (US$20 to US$30 a head). The beach at **İçmeler**, 10km away by minibus, is marginally better than that at Marmaris. **Datça**, a village on the peninsula, has been 'discovered' but is still a great place to visit; less spoilt are **Bozburun**, not as far west, and **Aktaş**, 4km east of Marmaris. At the tip of the peninsula are the ruins of the ancient port of **Knidos**.

You can hook up with a gulet by contacting Marmaris International Yacht Club (☎ 412 3835), PO Box 132, 48700, Marmaris. Scuba dive with the Marmaris Diving Centre (☎ 411 1341, around US$35 per day) moored near the tourist office. There are several other outfits nearby.

Places to Stay
About 1km east of Marmaris is the Günlücek Reserve and basic *Dimet Camping* (☎ 412 5601).

The quaint *Yılmaz Pansiyon* (☎ 412 3754, *K.altı Mahallesi, 7 Sokak No 33)* is just inland from the little park near the Turkish Airlines office on Atatürk Caddesi. Doubles/triples cost US$9/13. The spartan, but clean, *Interyouth Hostel* (☎ 412 3687, **☻** *inter youth@turk.net, Tepe Mahallesi, 42 Sokak No 45)*, in the bazaar, charges US$4.50 for a dorm bed, US$6/12 for singles/doubles. In the same price range are the *İmbat Otel* (☎ 412 1413) and *Otel Karaaslan* (☎ 412 1867), close to the tourist office, have sea view balconies but can be noisy.

Wallow in the pool set amongst pretty gardens at *Hotel Halıcı* (☎ 412 1683, *Hacı Cem Sokak 1)*, inland from Abdi İpekçi Park. Doubles with breakfast cost US$40.

Places to Eat & Drink
Head to the open-air restaurants along 51 Sokak (the street with the post office). Try *Marmaris Lokantası* for a US$4 feed or the better (and pricier) *Yeni Liman Restaurant* (*İsmetpaşa Caddesi)* around the corner.

South of the castle along Barbaros Caddesi, posh restaurants come from the same bland mould; *Birtat Restaurant* is popular. Squeezing between these restaurants, quaint *Barış Cafe* will let you enjoy the same views for half the price.

For sundowners head to the aptly named *Panorama Bar*; follow the signs from the castle end of the bazaar.

TURKEY

Spruce up and brave the snobby bar staff at the drinking dens on Bar Street. You could be in for a long (and expensive) night. **Down Town** is decked out with windmills; you'll get lost in **Greenhouse**. **Le Petit Cafe** offers respite and jazz (and is a haven for women travellers) while **Sıla Türkü Bar** has live, traditional music.

Getting There & Away
To get to the otogar, catch a dolmuş outside the Tansaş shopping centre, north of the Atatürk statue; arriving in town you may get dropped here instead of the otogar.

Marmaris has frequent direct bus services to all places in the region, including Antalya (US$12, seven hours), Bodrum (US$6, three hours), Köyceğiz (US$3, one hour), Datça (US$4, 1¾ hours) and Bozburun (US$2, 1½ hours).

Small car ferries run to Rhodes daily in summer (less frequently in the off season) for US$35 one-way, US$40 same-day, or US$70 open return; these fares include port taxes. Ask the tourist office for details.

KÖYCEĞİZ
☎ 252
Köyceğiz, 75km east of Marmaris, nestles beside the enormous Köyceğiz Gölü (lake) surrounded by hills. It's becoming a popular choice with backpackers for good reasons: it has decent places to stay, plenty of things to do, and (so far) it's relatively untouched by tourism.

The otogar is 2km north of the town centre. On the main square, right by the water, is the tourist office (☎ 262 4703).

Everything you can do at Dalyan you can do from Köyceğiz. A day boat tour to 'turtle' beach and the mud baths will set you back US$10. Visit the **hot springs** at Sultaniye Kaplıcaları and swim at Köyceğiz's nearby waterfall.

Places to Stay & Eat
There's camping at **Anatolia Camping** (☎ 262 2752), near the water.

Tango Pension (☎ 262 2501, ✉ tangopension@superonline.com,), on Alihsan Kalmaz Caddesi, gets rave reviews. Beds under the stars cost US$2.50, dorm beds US$5 and singles/doubles go for US$7/14. They also

serve good, cheap meals. Hoping the success of a peach-coloured paint scheme will rub off, the nearby **Fulya Pension** (☎ 262 2301) has fewer services but similar prices and a shady rooftop terrace.

Posh **Panorama Plaza** (☎ 262 3773, ✉ info@panorama-plaza.de, Cengiz Topel Caddesi 69), has spotless rooms with lakeside views. You'll pay US$25/40, with breakfast and dinner.

Köyceğiz has limited eating options. There are **cafes** on the waterfront; **Çiçek Restaurant** on the main square will feed you for US$2 to US$5.

Getting There & Away
Regular buses go to Marmaris (US$3, one hour). You can catch a minibus to Dalyan via Ortaca (US$1.50, 40 minutes) or take the scenic (and pricier) option of a boat (US$6 one way).

DALYAN
☎ 252
Set in lush river-delta farming country, Dalyan has it all: fertile soil, a river meandering by, excellent fishing and, to the south at İztuzu, a beautiful **beach** which is the nesting ground of the *Carretta carretta*, or ancient sea turtle. As if that were not enough, Dalyan has ruins: dramatic rock-cut **Lycian tombs** overlooking the town, and the ruined city of **Kaunos** easily visited by boat excursion downriver. Upriver there are **mud baths**; there are **hot springs** at Sultaniye Kaplıcaları, on the shores of Köyceğiz Lake.

The local boaters' cooperative sets rates for river excursions. Daily tours taking in the mud baths, the ruins at Kaunos and 'turtle' beach cost about US$5 a head. Forty-minute (one way) runs just to the beach cost US$2.50.

The town surrounds a square and mosque; here you'll find the bus stop, post office and the tourist office (☎ 284 4235). On the same street as the belediye (town hall) is Perfect Net, an Internet cafe.

Places to Stay & Eat
South of Dalyan's centre, along Maraş Mahallesi, you'll be spoilt with too-good-to-be-true riverside views coupled with decent

prices. *Dalyan Camping* has tent sites for US$4. The family-run *Önder Pansiyon* (☎ 284 2605) charges US$12/17 for singles/doubles, including their divine breakfast. With similar prices, *Sahil Pansiyon* (☎ 284 2187), close by, has a building beside the river and another inland; ask to pay less for their rooms inland. Just north of the centre of town, *Hotel Göl* (☎ 284 2096, fax 284 2555, Gülpınar Mahallesi) charges US$12/20 with breakfast, a pool and great riverside views.

There are heaps of pricey (US$10 for fish) restaurants lining the river. Inland, near the tourist office, *Narin* has good food for around US$4. For a drink the *Sofra* cafe-bar has been well tested; the *Albatros* is good for dancing.

Getting There & Away

Getting to Dalyan you'll most probably get dropped off the bus at Ortaca. Between 7 am and 8 pm you'll need to change to a dolmuş (US$0.50); at other times catch a taxi (US$9). In summer there are morning buses from Dalyan to Marmaris, Fethiye and Muğla; if not, catch a dolmuş to Ortaca and change.

FETHİYE
☎ 252

Fethiye has superb beaches, cheap lodgings and plenty of nightlife; it's crowded in summer but worth the diversion off the road. This is the site of ancient **Telmessos**, with giant Lycian stone **sarcophagi** from 400 BC littered about.

Orientation & Information

The tourist office (☎ 614 1527), next to the Dedeoğlu Otel, is near the yacht marina on the western side of town. Restaurants and bars are in, or around, the bazaar area, east of the tourist office. The otogar is 2km east of the town centre.

Things to See & Do

Check out the rock-cut **Tomb of Amyntas** (US$1.50), looming from a cliff above the town. There's also a marked hiking trail over the hills to the beautiful Ottoman Greek ghost town of **Kayaköy** or you can catch the dolmuş (marked 'Kaya'; entry to the town costs US$1; dolmuş costs US$1.50). Working up a sweat? Head to the beach at **Çalış**, or the gorgeous

Saklıkent Gorge, which cuts 18km into the Akdağlar mountains. Next stop could be the hamam in the bazaar back in town. It's open from 7 am to midnight; the full treatment costs US$11. There's no masseuse; women, you might want to forgo the massage!

A '12 Island Tour' boat excursion is a must. With its swimming, cruising and sightseeing, it may be your best day in Fethiye. Prices average around US$12 per person.

Places to Stay

Close to the otogar is *Göreme Pansiyon* (☎ 614 6944, Dolgu Sahası, Stadyum Yanı 25), just north of the stadium, 450m off Atatürk Caddesi. It has clean singles/doubles for US$6/12, and is run by a woman who lived in London.

Far better options are up the hill, off Fevzi Çakmak Caddesi, west of the tourist office. The family-run *Tan Pansiyon* (☎ 614 1584, Eski Karagözler Caddesi 89) has clean rooms for US$5/10 and a huge tiled terrace. Next door *Yeşilcam Pansiyon* (☎ 612 3518) is similar, but has better views from its monstrous terrace.

Farther up the hill, the popular *İdeal Pension* (☎/fax 614 1981, Zafer Caddesi 1) costs a few dollars more, but has a great terrace and muesli for breakfast.

Otel Mara (☎ 614 9307, fax 614 8039, Kral Caddesi, Yalı Sokak 2), north-west of the hospital, offers fine comfort for US$20/40, with air-con, private bathroom and breakfast.

Places to Eat & Drink

The bazaar is packed with open-air restaurants, where you should watch out for bill fiddling. *Özlem Kebap Salonu* on Çarşı Caddesi (the main market street) will fill you up for around US$2. Cross the road to find Tütün Sokak where *Sedir Restaurant* serves pizzas (around US$2.50), mezes (US$1.25), and main courses (US$3 to US$4), including a 'vegetarian surprise'. *The Duck Pond* (guess the gimmick) has similar fare.

Pricier, but with a wonderful choice of appetisers, is *Meğri Restaurant* (Likya Caddesi 8-9) in the bazaar. A good meat-based meal should cost between US$7 and US$10; fish is more expensive.

In the bazaar the *Car Cemetery Bar* and *Club Bananas* should get you dancing. Beside the Roman theatre, **Zeytin Cafe Bar** has live traditional music every night in summer. Nearby, the mock classical decorating alone makes **Yasmin Bar** worth a visit.

Getting There & Away

The coastal mountains force long-haul bus services to travel east and west – to Marmaris, Muğla and Antalya – before going anywhere else. If you're heading directly for Antalya, note that the *yayla* (inland) route is shorter (3½ hours) and cheaper (US$6) than the *sahil* (coastal) route (US$8, eight hours).

Buses from the otogar also serve Kalkan (US$3.50, two hours) and Kaş (US$4.50, 2½ hours). Minibuses depart from their own terminal, 600m west of the otogar toward the centre, on short hops to other points along the coast, like Patara (US$2.50, 1½ hours), Kınık (for Xanthos, US$2, 1½ hours) and Ölüdeniz (US$1.50, 15 minutes).

ÖLÜDENİZ & BUTTERFLY VALLEY
☎ 252

As you dolmuş through Hisarönü, the bland tourist-metropolis spreading from Fethiye to Ölüdeniz, you're probably wishing you could wrench the steering wheel out of the driver's hand and turn the bus around. Fear not, Ölüdeniz has (mostly) hidden from the monstrous hotels on the hills and is still a beautiful beach spot. There are moderately priced bungalows and camping areas; book ahead.

Nestling beside Ölüdeniz Lagoon, *Ölüdeniz Camping* (☎ 617 0048, fax 617 0181) has bungalows with/without bathroom for US$13/10 a double; camp for US$2 per person. Right in the centre of town at *Deniz Camp* (☎ 617 0450, ✉ info@gurkanlar.com), beside Belcekız Plajı, you'll pay a little more for the same facilities. Both places have restaurants and buzzing bars.

A boat ride (US$7 per person) away from Ölüdeniz is stunning **Butterfly Valley**, where you'll find serenity, your sanity, and butterflies (if you're there between May and September). Visit the waterfall or brave the hike (45 minutes) to the village above and *George's Place* (☎ 642 1102). George offers no frills bed, breakfast and dinner for US$6. Alternatively, you can doss in basic *treehouses* near the beach for US$10, all meals included.

RUINS NEAR FETHİYE

Lycia was heavily populated in ancient times, as shown by the large number of wonderful old cities that can be reached by minibus from Fethiye.

Tlos is 40km up into the mountains near Kemer on the way to Saklıkent Gorge. **Pınara**, south-east of Fethiye, is an under-visited mountainous site.

Letoön, 4km off the highway in a fertile valley filled with tomato greenhouses, has excellent mosaics, a good theatre and a pool sacred as the place of worship of the goddess Leto. **Xanthos**, a few kilometres north-east of Letoön above the village of Kınık, is among the most impressive sites along this part of the coast, with its Roman theatre and Lycian pillar tombs.

At **Patara**, 7km farther south (turn at Ovaköy), the attraction is not so much the ruins as the incredible 20km-long beach. Lodgings in Patara village, 2.5km inland from the beach, range from camping through to cheap pensions and hotels.

KALKAN
☎ 242

Kalkan, everybody's idea of what a small Turkish fishing village should be, is 11km east of the Patara turn-off and 27km from Kaş. It tumbles down a steep hillside to a yacht marina (in ancient times, the port). Peak season can be hell on earth, at other times it's a gorgeous sleepy town.

Kalkan's old stone and wood houses have been restored as lodgings – some expensive, some moderate, some still fairly cheap. The streets above the marina are chock-a-block with atmospheric open-air restaurants. There are no good beaches to speak of, but the inevitable excursion boat tours (or minibuses) can take you to Patara Beach and secluded coves along the coast.

Dolmuş from Kaş (US$1.50, 35 minutes) or Fethiye (US$3.50, two hours) will offload you near the post office, a short walk north of the marina. Kalkan doesn't have a tourist office but it has a Web site (www.kalkan.org.tr). Adda Tours has Internet facilities.

Places to Stay

Overlooking the harbour are two pansiyons. The pretty *Akın* (☎ 844 3025) has waterless rooms on the top floor (US$12 a double) and rooms lower down with private showers (US$16). *Ay* (☎ *844 3058*), overlooking the harbour, oozes charm and charges US$8 to US$14 per double.

Inland from the harbour, the atmospheric *Pasha's Inn* (☎ *844 3666*, ✉ *fbalaban@ superonline.com, 10 Sokak 8*), run by an English woman, has comfy double beds for US$25. It's a couples kind of place; breakfast, my darling, is on the terrace.

Ritzy and clean, *Zinbad Hotel* (☎ *844 3404, Yalıboyu Mahallesi 18*) is north-west of the mosque. For fine sea views you'll pay US$20/35 a single/double, breakfast included.

Places to Eat & Drink

Near the post office are plenty of decent, cheapish (US$6 per feed) restaurants; *Ali Baba* is good, but *Doyum Restaurant* wins the prize for gaudiest decor. For fancier meals, head down to the harbour where *Pala'nın Yeri* and *Yakamoz* offer tasty meals for US$8 to US$12, more for fish.

Kalkan has plenty of bars sprinkled throughout. Both *Yalı* and *Moonlight Café & Bar* liven up after dark.

KAŞ
☎ 242

Kaş has a picturesque quayside square, a big Friday market, Lycian stone sarcophagi, and rock-cut tombs in the cliffs above the town – it's a fine, laid-back place. Aside from enjoying the town's ambience and a few small pebble beaches, you can walk to the well preserved theatre. Or you can take one of the boat excursions to Kalkan, Patara, the Blue Cave, Saklıkent Gorge, Üçağız (see the Kekova & Üçağız section later in this chapter) or Demre.

The Greek island of Kastellorizo (Meis in Turkish) is visible just a short distance across the water and can be reached by daily boat in summer (US$30 one way).

The otogar is 400m north-west of the main square and marina. The tourist office (☎ 836 1238) is on the main square; the post office and Net-House Internet Cafe are a short walk north.

Places to Stay

Kaş Camping (☎ *836 1050*), in an olive grove 1km west of town past the theatre, has tent sites and simple bungalows.

At the otogar you'll be accosted by pension-pushers. Yenicami Caddesi (or Recep Bilgin Caddesi), just south of the otogar, has lots of standard, clean places charging US$10/15 for singles/doubles, with breakfast. Try *Anı Motel* (☎ *836 1791*) or the *Melisa* (☎ *836 1068*). At the southern end of the street near the mosque is *Ay Pansiyon* (☎ *836 1562*), where the front rooms have sea views. Head down the hill to find even better views at the friendly *Yalı Pansion* (☎ *836 1132*), stylishly decorated like your grandmother's.

For more comforts and services, try the two-star *Hotel Kayahan* (☎ *836 1313*, ✉ *hotelkay ahan@superonline.com*), north-east of Küçük Çakıl Plaj. Rooms with wonderful sea views cost US$20/35, with breakfast.

Places to Eat & Drink

Corner Café, at the post office end of İbrahim Serin Caddesi, serves juices or a vegetable omelette for US$1.50, and yogurt with fruit and honey for US$2. *Café Merhaba* across the street is good for cakes.

The *Eriş*, behind the tourist office, is a favourite, as much for its setting as for its food. Also popular is *Smiley's Restaurant* next door, where pizza or mains cost around US$4. *Bahçe Restaurant*, farther inland, is even better. The *Dolphin* (*Sandıkçı Sokak 18*) has superb views. A delicious fish meal will set you back around US$12.

On the main square, *Noel Baba* is well placed to 'people watch' or, right on the water, *Sahil Çay Bahçesi* is a great place for a sundowner. Lift the pace at trendy *Redpoint* or the outdoors *Full Moon Club*, a little out of town, but right on the waterfront.

Getting There & Away

Regular buses go from the otogar to Kalkan (US$1.50, 35 minutes), Demre (US$2.50, one hour), Patara (US$3, one hour), Fethiye (US$4.50, 2½ hours), Antalya (US$5, four hours) and İstanbul (US$25, 12 hours).

KEKOVA ADASI & ÜÇAĞIZ

Up in the hills 14km east of Kaş, a road goes south to Kekova and Üçağız, two villages amid partly sunken ancient ruins. Üçağız, 20km from the highway, is a farming and fishing hamlet with a handful of very basic pensions and a few simple waterfront restaurants built on top of the ruins of ancient Teimiussa.

Boat owners will try to cajole you into taking a tour (US$12 to US$18 per person) of the bay, including a look at the picturesque little village of **Kale** (not to be confused with the other Kale, which is also known as Demre/Myra), and the sunken ruins (Batık Şehir) on **Kekova Adası** (island). A swim near the ruins is included.

KAŞ TO ANTALYA

Hugging a coast backed by pine-clad mountains, the main road goes east from Kaş and then north to Antalya, passing a dozen ruined cities. From ancient times until the 1970s, virtually all transport to this region was by sea. The modern towns built over or near the ancient ones are still deeply involved in maritime life.

Demre
☎ 242

Demre (ancient Myra, also known as Kale), set in a rich alluvial plain covered in greenhouses, is interesting because of its generous 4th-century bishop, later canonised as St Nicholas, and believed to be the original Father Christmas or Santa Claus.

For a lofty US$3 you can visit the restored 12th-century **Church of St Nicholas** (Noel Baba), which was built to hold his tomb. Save your money; there's little to see inside. Two kilometres inland from the church are the ruins of Myra. Here you'll find a rock face honeycombed with ancient **tombs**, right next to a large **Roman theatre**. Both are open 8 am to 7.30 pm in summer; entry won't break you at US$1.30.

Few people stay overnight here, but if you do there are a bunch of places to stay (rates include breakfast) near the junction with the highway to Antalya. Try *Kekova Pansiyon* (☎ 871 2186) for basic singles/doubles for US$5/11. The quieter *Hotel Kıyak* (☎ 871 2092) charges US$12/17. Across the highway, *Hotel Andriake* (☎ 871 4640) is worth the few extra dollars, despite their scary choice of paint colours.

As for meals, near Santa's church you'll find heaps of overpriced eateries. Between the Santa-sized tourists you'll find locals

eating at *İpek Restaurant*, paying US$3 for their tasty feast. *İnci Pastanesi* close-by, will service the sweet-toothed. In summer, try dining 5km west at **Çayağzı**, the ancient Andriake, Demre's harbour, where the beach, the views and the food are fine.

Olimpos, Çıralı & the Chimaera
☎ 242

There are two roads off the main Kaş-Antalya highway to Olimpos. One you'll reach coming from Kumluca (from the west); the other as you come from Tekirova (from the east). The bus will drop you off at the top of the eastern road. From here it's a dolmuş ride just over 8km down a winding road to the first of the string of pensions, and a farther 3.5km to the site of ancient Olimpos. Wild and abandoned, the Olimpos ruins peek out from forest copses and river banks. The pebble beach is magnificent.

Olimpos's accommodation has had its fair share of criticism (and praise). Be mindful of what you're after: boozy, thigh-slapping dens where you may catch a whiff of 'puff', or low-key, BYO personality places. Both outfits offer bungalow beds or a mattress on the floor in a treehouse; rates include breakfast and dinner. Security has been a big issue around here – none of the treehouses have locks but most of the pensions have safes you can use.

The following two places can both be a little wild. You'll be 'gone' after a mere stroll through the thick air of the dark, friendly *Gypsy Pansiyon* (☎ 892 1223). After a session in the bar downstairs crawl up to your shabby mattress on the rooftop (US$3.50) or ask for the pink psychedelic back bedroom (US$8 per double) if you dare. The toilets are not for the faint hearted. You must have heard the good (and bad) hype about *Kadir's* (☎ 892 1250, ✉ treehouse@superonline.com) – it's *the* place to stay. It has Internet access, a bar, vegetarian food and the highest treehouses – bungalows will set you back US$12 per person, treehouses US$7.

Quieter places include local personality *Sheriff* (☎ 892 1301) with good value, clean treehouses/bungalows for US$4/6 per person and family-run *Şaban's* (☎ 892 1265) with a pretty setting against a hill (US$7/10). You'll pay the same at friendly *Bayram's* (☎ 892

TURKEY

1243), set in an orange grove. *Orange Pansiyon (☎ 892 1242)* gets good reviews from readers and charges US$7/12, but has identical facilities to the others.

Çıralı and Olimpos face onto the same beach and cove. The turn off to Çıralı from the highway is less than 1km east of the eastern Olimpos turn-off. There's no dolmuş service to Çıralı, so you'll need to hitch or take the 20 minute walk along the beach from Olimpos.

If you prefer your comforts, Çıralı has clean, quiet accommodation. At the northern end of the beach, pretty *Green Point (☎ 825 7182)* charges US$2 per tent plus US$2 for each person. Missing Olimpos already? Doss for US$10 (with breakfast and dinner) in an overgrown shower-cap at *Off Road House (☎ 0532 552 2388)*; you must book ahead, this place fires up after dark. Inland from the beach, family-run *Aygün Pansiyon (☎ 825 7146)* and *Çıralı Pansiyon (☎ 825 7175)*, charge US$20 for comfy doubles with breakfast.

According to legend, the **Chimaera** (Yanartaş), a natural eternal flame, was the hot breath of a subterranean monster. Easily sighted by mariners in ancient times, it's a mere glimmer of its former self now. To see the Chimaera – best visited at night – go 3km east from Çıralı down a neighbouring valley. It's a half-hour climb to the flame. Most of the pensions organise night-time 'romantic flame' tours.

Phaselis

Two kilometres from the highway, Phaselis is a collection of ruins framing three small, perfect bays. It's a good place for a swim and a picnic. The ruins are open 7.30 am to 7 pm in summer; entry costs US$1.50.

ANTALYA
☎ 242

The main town along the coast, set against the Taurus mountains, Antalya has one of the most attractive harbour settings in the Mediterranean. Much of Antalya is ugly apartment blocks – its saving grace is kaleiçi, the restored Ottoman town by the Roman harbour (now the yacht marina). The beaches are out of town: Konyaaltı Plajı, a long pebble beach, to the west, and Lara Plajı, a sand beach, to the east. Antalya's archaeological museum is outstanding.

Orientation & Information

The otogar is 4km north of the centre on the D650 highway to Burdur, reached by dolmuş along Güllük (Anafartalar) Caddesi. The city centre is at Kalekapısı, near Cumhuriyet Meydanı, with its dramatic equestrian statue of Atatürk. Kaleiçi, the old town, is south of Kalekapısı down the hill.

Atatürk Caddesi, 100m east of Kalekapısı, goes south past Hadriyanüs Kapısı (Hadrian's Gate). A bit farther along is the pleasant Karaalioğlu Park.

The tourist office (☎ 241 1747, Cumhuriyet Caddesi 2) is 500m west of Kalekapısı (look for the sign 'Antalya Devlet Tiyatrosu' on the right-hand side; it's in this building). The Turkish Airlines office (☎ 243 4383) is in the same building. The central post office is around the corner on Güllük Caddesi. Sanal Alem Net Cafe, 260m north of Kalekapısı, has Internet access.

Be careful after dark – kaleiçi and around Kalekapısı can be sleazy.

Things to See & Do

Don't miss the **Antalya Museum** (catch the tram, west along Cumhuriyet Caddesi); it houses finds from Perge and some wonderful ethnographical exhibits. It's open 9 am to 6 pm, closed Monday; entry costs US$4.

Some of the ancient monuments scattered in and around kaleiçi are worth hunting out. **Hadriyanüs Kapısı** (Hadrian's Gate) was built for the Roman emperor's visit in 130 AD. Near the clock tower is Antalya's graceful symbol, the **Yivli Minare** (Grooved Minaret), which rises above an old building, once a mosque and now a fine-arts gallery. In kaleiçi, the **Kesik Minare** (Truncated Minaret) marks a ruined Roman temple.

At the marina there are plenty of yacht cruises (US$10 for two hours) on offer or you could soak your sunspots at Konyaaltı Plajı (catch tram to 'Müze' and walk down the hill).

From Antalya you can also visit Termessos, Perge and Aspendos.

Places to Stay

The small, shady *Bambus Motel, Restaurant & Camping (☎ 321 5263)*, 300m west of Hotel Dedeman on the one-way (eastbound) coast road to Lara Plajı, has tent and caravan facilities.

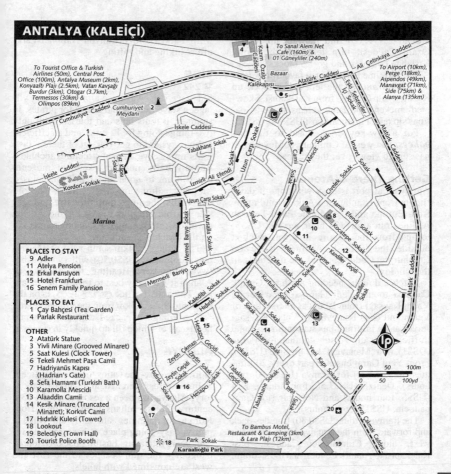

ANTALYA (KALEİÇİ)

PLACES TO STAY
9 Adler
11 Atelya Pension
12 Erkal Pansiyon
15 Hotel Frankfurt
16 Senem Family Pansion

PLACES TO EAT
1 Çay Bahçesi (Tea Garden)
4 Parlak Restaurant

OTHER
2 Atatürk Statue
3 Yivli Minare (Grooved Minaret)
5 Saat Kulesi (Clock Tower)
6 Tekeli Mehmet Paşa Camii
7 Hadriyanüs Kapısı (Hadrian's Gate)
8 Sefa Hamamı (Turkish Bath)
10 Karamolla Mescidi
13 Alaaddin Camii
14 Kesik Minare (Truncated Minaret); Korkut Camii
17 Hıdırlık Kulesi (Tower)
18 Lookout
19 Belediye (Town Hall)
20 Tourist Police Booth

Kaleiçi is crawling with pensions; find yours by following the signs.

Adler (☎ 241 7818, *Civelek Sokak 16*) is grim but friendly; beds are US$5 a night. *Erkal Pansiyon* (☎ 244 0159, *Kandiller Geçidi 5*) is good value, for a few dollars more. A good choice for women travellers is *Senem Family Pansion* (☎ 247 1752, *Zeytin Geçidi Sokak 9*). You'll pay US$12/18 for singles/doubles with the bonus of a terrace with views.

Feeling lazy? Recline in the leafy garden at the gorgeous *Atelya Pension* (☎ 241 6416, *Civelek Sokak 21*), or soak your bones in the pool at the squeaky-clean, soulless *Hotel Frankfurt* (☎ 247 6224, *Hıdırlık Sokak 17*). Both charge US$20/30 with breakfast.

Places to Eat & Drink

Eski Sebzeciler İçi Sokak, a short street just south-west of the junction of Cumhuriyet and Atatürk caddesis, is filled with *open-air restaurants* where a kebab, salad and drink can cost as little as US$4. Try Antalya's own *tandır kebap* (mutton cooked in an earthenware pot).

Antalya's most popular kebapçı is *01 Güneyliler* (*Elmalı Mahallesi, 4 Sokak 12/A*),

TURKEY

with fresh flat bread and tasty full meals for around US$4. To find it, walk up Kazım Özalp Caddesi, turn left past the Hotel Kışlahan complex and go 1½ blocks.

The old-time bar-and-grill favourite is *Parlak Restaurant*, on the left, half a block up Kazım Özalp Caddesi from Kalekapısı. Skewered chickens and lamb kebabs sizzle as patrons sip rakı. Full meals cost US$8 to US$12.

For a low-key drink, head to the *çay bahçesi* just west of Cumhuriyet Meydanı. It has superb views over the marina.

Getting There & Around

Antalya's airport is busy with lots of daily flights from İstanbul and Ankara, and many from Europe and the Middle East. Turkish Airlines run a bus (24 hour service; US$3) to and from the airport. In town, catch it outside the Turkish Airlines office on Cumhuriyet Caddesi; check the timetable in the window.

Catch a dolmuş heading north on Güllük Caddesi to the Yeni Garaj (otogar) or to Vatan Kavşağı (roundabout at intersection of Vatan and Gazi boulevards). Vatan Kavşağı serves as an informal bus station for regional traffic; take an 'Aksu' dolmuş for Perge (US$1), or a 'Manavgat' bus for Side (US$2). From Yeni Garaj buses depart every 20 minutes (in summer) for Alanya (US$3.50, two hours), Denizli (US$7.50, four hours), Kaş (US$5, four hours) and Nevşehir (for Cappadocia, US$12, eight hours).

The tramvay (tram; US$0.30) trundles back and forward from the Antalya Museum in the west, along Cumhuriyet Caddesi, past Kalekapısı to Atatürk Caddesi and the stadium.

AROUND ANTALYA

This stretch of coast has plenty more Greek and Roman ruins if you can take them. **Perge**, 15km east of Antalya, just north of Aksu, includes a 12,000-seat stadium and a theatre for 15,000. **Aspendos**, 47km east of Antalya, has Turkey's best-preserved ancient theatre, dating from the 2nd century AD; it is still used for performances during the Antalya Festival in September. **Termessos**, high in the mountains off the road to Korkuteli, has a spectacular setting and demands some vigorous walking and climbing if you want to see it all.

North-east of Antalya, Köprülü Kanyon Milli Parkı (Bridge Canyon National Park) offers hiking and rafting.

SİDE
☎ 242

Side (see-deh) was once a pretty fishing village, a slave market and a base for pirates. In summer, it touts tans and tourists with only two things going for it: ruins, and an efficient dolmuş system to get you out of there – fast.

Its impressive ancient structures include a **Roman bath**, now an excellent museum (open 8 am to noon and 1 to 5 pm, closed Monday; admission costs US$3). The old **city walls**, the huge **amphitheatre** and seaside marble **temples** to Apollo and Athena are also worth seeing. It's standing room only on the beaches in summer.

The village is 4km south-west of Manavgat; minibuses (US$0.70) will run you between the two. Heading for Antalya or Alanya it's usually best to travel via Manavgat. The tourist office (☎ 753 1265) is on the road into Side, 1.5km from the village centre.

The village is packed with pensions and hotels, all of which fill up quickly in summer.

ALANYA
☎ 242

Dominated by the ruins of a magnificent Seljuk fortress perched high on a promontory, Alanya has been a resort since the 13th century. Seljuk sultans used to come from Konya for summer sun and fun. Once a pretty, easy-going place, it has grown in recent years into a big, bustling package tourist hangout – the thin beaches to the east and west are now lined with hotels.

The otogar is 3km west of the centre; you can get into town by dolmuş or bus. Buses from Side or Manavgat stop at the dolmuş station, five minutes north of the town centre. The waterfront area has tourist shops and good food; to the west is İskele Caddesi with cheap hotels and plenty of Internet cafes. The tourist office (☎ 513 1240), Damlataş Caddesi 1, is beside the roundabout on the western side of the promontory.

Things to See & Do

Visit the Seljuk Kızıl Kule (Red Tower), built in 1226, down by the harbour. It's open 8 am to noon and 1.30 to 5.30 pm, closed Monday; tickets cost US$2. At the entrance of Kızıl Kule, a path winds up past ancient houses and gardens to the **fortress** (*kale*), also built in 1226, atop the promontory. Feeling lazy? Near the tourist office there are regular buses to take you up (US$1). The fortress is open 9 am to 7 pm; you'll pay US$4 for the sublime views.

The hyper-touristy **Damlataş Mağarası** (Dripping Stones Cave, US$2), supposedly good for asthma sufferers, is on the western side of the promontory, near the tourist office and the museum. Take a **boat excursion** (around US$7 per person) from the marina to other caves beneath the promontory.

Places to Stay & Eat

You can camp at *İncekum* (19km west of town, on the way to Side).

Along İskele Caddesi, *Yayla Palas Oteli* (☎ 513 1017), at No 24, has scary carpet, cheap-as-chips prices (US$5 per person) and excellent views. Hot water? Who needs it! *Baba Hotel* (☎ 513 1032), at No 6, is a fancier option at US$7/14 per single/double. *Hotel Temiz* (☎ 513 1016), at No 12, has comfy, clean rooms with balconies for US$12/20, with breakfast.

Well worth a splurge, *Club Hotel Bedestan* (☎ 512 1234, fax 513 7934), hiding within the fortress walls, has a pool and wonderful views. Lush rooms go for US$55 per double.

The best area for cheap food is between the first two waterfront streets. Look for signs saying 'İnegöl Köftecisi', and snap up grilled meatballs and salad for around US$4. Restaurants along the waterfront charge around US$8 to US$12 per full meal.

Central Anatolia

İstanbul may be exotic and intriguing, the coasts pretty and relaxing, but it's the Anatolian plateau which is Turkey's heartland, as Atatürk acknowledged when he moved the capital to Ankara in 1923.

ANKARA
☎ 312

Despite its being the capital of Turkey, no one could call Ankara an exciting city. Nevertheless, due to its central location, and because most of the embassies are here, there's a good chance you'll at least pass through.

Orientation

Atatürk Bulvarı is the city's north-south axis. AŞTİ, Ankara's mammoth otogar, is 6.5km south-west of Ulus, the historic centre, and 6km west of Kızılay, the modern centre. Turkish Airlines city buses stop at the train station (*gar*), 1.4km south-west of Ulus, and at AŞTİ otogar.

The Ankara underground train network has two lines: the Ankaray running between AŞTİ otogar in the west through Kızılay to Dikimevi in the east; and the Metro running from Kızılay north-west via Sıhhiye, Maltepe and Ulus to Batıkent. The two lines interconnect at Kızılay.

Most of the embassies are in Çankaya, 5km south of Kızılay, and the adjoining districts of Gaziosmanpaşa and Kavaklıdere.

Information

The tourist office (☎ 231 5572) is at Gazi Mustafa Kemal Bulvarı 121, opposite the Maltepe Ankaray station. The main post office is on Atatürk Bulvarı just south of Ulus, although there's a handy branch beside the train station where you can also change cash and travellers cheques.

Things to See

The **Anatolian Civilisations Museum** (Anadolu Medeniyetleri Müzesi), on Hisarparkı Caddesi, is Ankara's most worthwhile attraction. With the world's richest collection of Hittite artefacts, it's an essential supplement to visiting central Turkey's Hittite sites. It's uphill (south-west) from Ulus, and is open 8.30 am to 5 pm, 'closed' on Monday in winter unless you pay twice the US$3 entry fee. When you're done at the museum, go to the top of the hill and wander among the castle's old streets.

North of Ulus and east of Çankırı Caddesi (the continuation of Atatürk Bulvarı north of Ulus) are some fine Roman ruins, including **Julian's Column**, erected in 363 AD, and the **Temple of Augustus & Rome**. Next to the temple is the **Hacı Bayram Camii**, a sacred mosque commemorating the founder of a dervish order established in 1400. On the western side of Çankırı Caddesi are the **Roma Hamamları** (Roman Baths).

TURKEY

ANKARA

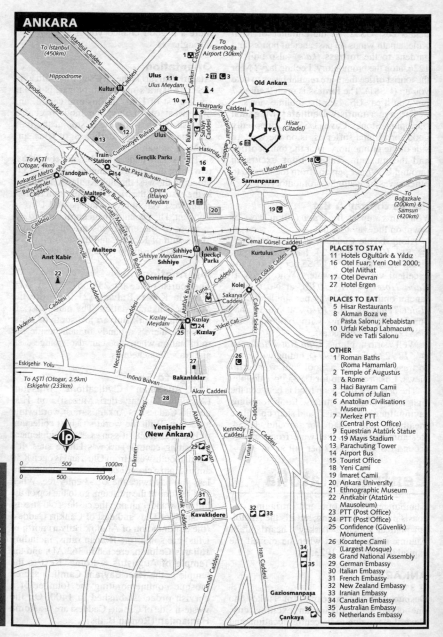

To İstanbul
(450km)

İstanbul Caddesi

To
Esenboğa
Airport (30km)

Hippodrome

Hipodrom Caddesi

Kültür

Ulus
Ulus Meydanı

11

Kazım Karabekir

Çankırı Caddesi

1

2 3

4

Old Ankara

10

Hisarparkı   Caddesi

9

Anafartalar Caddesi

Hisar
(Citadel)

8

7

Sanayi Caddesi

Çankırı Sok.

5

6

12

Cumhuriyet Bulvarı

Ulus

Atatürk Bulvarı

To AŞTİ
(Otogar, 4km)

13

Gençlik Parkı

Hasırcılar Cad.

18

Train
Station

Ankaray Metro

Do Gol

Talat Paşa Bulvarı

14

16

Ulucanlar

To
Boğazkale
(200km) &
Samsun
(420km)

Tandoğan

Celal Bayar Bulvarı

17

Samanpazarı

Bahçelievler
Caddesi

Maltepe

Gazi Mustafa Kemal Bulvarı

Opera
(İtfaiye)
Meydanı

15

21

20

19

Anıt
Caddesi

Cemal Gürsel Caddesi

Gençlik

PLACES TO STAY
11 Hotels Oğultürk & Yıldız
16 Otel Fuar; Yeni Otel 2000;
   Otel Mithat
17 Otel Devran
27 Hotel Ergen

Anıt Kabir

Maltepe

Akdeniz Caddesi

22

Sıhhiye
Meydanı

Sıhhiye

Sıhhiye

Abdi
İpekçci
Parkı

Kurtulus

Ziya Gökalp Caddesi

PLACES TO EAT
5 Hisar Restaurants
8 Akman Boza ve
   Pasta Salonu; Kebabistan
10 Urfalı Kebap Lahmacum,
   Pide ve Tatlı Salonu

Demirtepe

Atatürk Bulvarı

Tuna Caddesi

Kolej

Sakarya
Caddesi

23

Çaldıran Sokak

OTHER
1 Roman Baths
   (Roma Hamamları)
2 Temple of Augustus
   & Rome
3 Hacı Bayram Camii
4 Column of Julian
6 Anatolian Civilisations
   Museum
7 Merkez PTT
   (Central Post Office)
9 Equestrian Atatürk Statue
12 19 Mayıs Stadium
13 Parachuting Tower
14 Airport Bus
15 Tourist Office
18 Yeni Cami
19 İmaret Camii
20 Ankara University
21 Ethnographic Museum
22 Anıtkabir (Atatürk
   Mausoleum)
23 PTT (Post Office)
24 PTT (Post Office)
25 Confidence (Güvenlik)
   Monument
26 Kocatepe Camii
   (Largest Mosque)
28 Grand National Assembly
29 German Embassy
30 Italian Embassy
31 French Embassy
32 New Zealand Embassy
33 Iranian Embassy
34 Canadian Embassy
35 Australian Embassy
36 Netherlands Embassy

Kızılay
Meydanı

Kızılay

Yüksel Cad.

24

25

Kızılay

Necatibey Caddesi

Eskişehir Yolu

To AŞTİ (Otogar, 2.5km)
Eskişehir (233km)

İnönü Bulvarı

27

Bakanlıklar

26

28

Atatürk Bulvarı

Esat Caddesi

Yenişehir
(New Ankara)

Akay Caddesi

Kennedy Caddesi

Tunalı Hilmi Caddesi

29

30

Dikmen Caddesi

Güvenlik Caddesi

Kavaklıdere

31

32 33

34

35

Cinnah Caddesi

İran Caddesi

Gaziosmanpaşa

36

Çankaya

0   500   1000m
0   500   1000yd

TURKEY

The **Anıt kabir** (Mausoleum of Atatürk), 2km west of Kızılay, is a monumental memorial to the founder of modern Turkey. It's open daily 9 am to 5 pm, free.

Places to Stay

Along the seedy eastern side of Opera (or İtfaiye) Meydanı, on Kosova Sokak and Tavus Sokak near the Gazi Lisesi high school, try *Otel Devran* (*☎ 311 0485, Tavus Sokak 8*), *Otel Mithat* (*☎ 311 5410, Tavus Sokak 2*) or the newer *Otel Yeni 2000* (*☎ 324 6995, Kosova Sokak 3*), all with singles/doubles for US\$12/19. *Otel Fuar* (*☎ 312 3288, Kosova Sokak 11*) charges US\$6/10 for very grungy singles/doubles with showers down the hall.

For more comfort, *Otel Akman* (*☎ 324 4140, Tavus Sokak 6*) charges only marginally more.

North of Ulus and one street west of Çankırı Caddesi, the three-star *Hotel Oğultürk* (*☎ 309 2900, Rüzgarlı Eşdost Sokak 6*) has singles/doubles with TV and minibar for US\$40/60 negotiable, breakfast included. The nearby *Yıldız* (*☎ 312 7581*) is around US\$5 cheaper.

In 'new' Ankara, south of Kızılay, the one-star *Hotel Ergen* (*☎ 417 5906, Karanfil Sokak 48*) charges US\$35/47 a single/double with bath.

Places to Eat

At the south-eastern corner of Ulus at Atatürk Bulvarı 3 is *Akman Boza ve Pasta Salonu*, in the courtyard of a huge block of offices and shops. Order a pastry, omelette, sandwich or snack, and consume it at terrace tables around a fountain. On the upper storey is *Kebabistan*, a kebab place with good food and low prices – about US\$3 to US\$5 for a full meal of roast lamb, less for just pide.

In Ruzgarlı Sokak *Urfalı Kebap, Lahmacun, Pide ve Tatlı Salonu* is an all-in-one restaurant with a family atmosphere and good, cheap food.

For a memorable meal at a very reasonable price (US\$9 to US\$16 per person), try the *Zenger Paşa Konağı* (*☎ 311 7070, Doyran Sokak 13*) in Ankara's *hisar* (castle). It's an old house with wonderful crafts and ethnographic displays, as well as good Ottoman-style food. *Kınacılar Evi* (*☎ 312 5601, Kalekapısı Sokak 28*), straight uphill from the castle entrance, is an imposing place with airy rooms and some traditional dishes like mantı (Turkish ravioli).

Getting There & Away

Air Turkish Airlines (*☎ 309 0400*), at Atatürk Bulvarı 154, Kavaklıdere, has flights daily to most Turkish cities. Most international routes require a connection in İstanbul. İstanbul Airlines (*☎ 432 2234*), Atatürk Bulvarı 64/1, Kızılay, mainly serves international airports but there's the odd domestic flight too.

Bus Ankara's huge otogar (AŞTİ) is the vehicular heart of the nation, with buses to all places day and night. For İstanbul (from US\$10, six hours) they go at least every 15 minutes. Other coaches go to Nevşehir/Cappadocia (US\$8, five hours), İzmir (US\$10, eight hours), Antalya (US\$12, eight hours), Bodrum (US\$12, 10 hours) and Erzurum (US\$18, 13 hours).

Train Seven express trains, two of them with sleeping cars, connect Ankara and İstanbul (US\$12 to US\$15, 7½ to 11 hours). The *Fatih* and *Başkent* express trains are the fastest and most expensive.

The *İzmir Mavi Tren* (14 hours) hauls sleeping (US\$24) and dining cars. The evening *İzmir Ekspresi* (15 hours) has 1st/2nd-class carriages (US\$9/7) and couchettes (US\$11).

Trains heading east of Ankara are not as comfortable or punctual as those travelling westward. The *Yeni Doğu Ekspresi* to Erzurum and Kars (21 hours, US\$11, or US\$19 in a sleeper) is faster and better than the *Doğu Ekspresi*.

Getting Around

To/From the Airport Ankara's Esenboğa airport is 33km north of the city centre. Havaş buses (US\$3.50) depart about every 30 minutes from AŞTİ otogar, stopping at Ankara Garı train station; allow two hours to reach the airport. A taxi is likely to cost about US\$25. Cheaper shared taxis run from the train station to the airport as well.

To/From the Otogar The easiest way to get to or from the otogar is to take the metro from immediately outside to Ulus or Kızılay.

TURKEY

Local Transport The Ankaray underground train is useful (see Orientation). For the train station, use the Maltepe Ankaray station and the long underground walkway. Many city buses run the length of Atatürk Bulvarı. Buy a *bilet* (ticket, US$0.50) from kiosks by bus stops, or from a shop with the sign 'EGO Bilet(i)'.

City bus No 198 runs from the otogar to the train station and Ulus; bus No 623 goes via Kızılay to Gaziler.

An average taxi ride should cost around US$4.

BOĞAZKALE
☎ 364

The Hittites ruled central Anatolia from about 2000 to 1180 BC. To see where they lived, visit Boğazkale, 29km off the Ankara-Samsun road. The Hattuşa of the Hittites, this was their ancient capital until it was destroyed by the Phrygians.

Today there's little left apart from the foundations of buildings and great crumbling walls which stretch for over 10km. There are five entrances, including the **Kral Kapı** (King's Gate), the **Aslanlı Kapı** (Lion Gate) and an underground tunnel, **Yer Kapı**.

The massive foundations are also inspiring. Largest is the site of the **Büyük Mabed** (Great Temple of the Storm God), which has no fewer than 70 storerooms. The natural rock temple of **Yazılıkaya**, 2km from the main site, has bas-reliefs of Hittite deities carved into the rock face.

Alacahöyük, 36km from Boğazkale near the main road, is a pre-Hittite site, probably 6000 years old. However, the remains, including the **Sphinx Gate**, are Hittite.

Buses run to Boğazkale from Ankara, or take a bus to Sungurlu, from where there should be minibuses to Boğazkale and Alacahöyük.

All Boğazkale's small hotels – the *Hattuşaş* (☎ 452 2013), *Başkent* (☎ 452 2037) and *Aşikoğlu* (☎ 452 2004) – can fill up in summer, but they all have camping grounds.

KONYA
☎ 332

Known as Iconium in Roman times, Konya may be a religiously conservative town but it's also one of the oldest continually occupied cities in the world, and a showplace for some striking Seljuk architecture. This was the capital of the Seljuk Turks, and it was here, in the 13th century, that the poet Celaleddin Rumi (Mevlana) founded the whirling dervishes, one of Islam's major mystical orders. Atatürk put a stop to the whirling except as 'folk dance'; you can see it here during the **Mevlana Festival** every December.

Mevlana's **tomb** is topped by the brilliant turquoise-tiled tower near the tourist office (☎ 351 1074) and hotel area; it's now the **Mevlana Müzesi**, open 9 am to 5.30 pm daily (10 am to 5 pm Monday), for US$2.50. Other fine Seljuk buildings include the **Karatay Müzesi**, once a Muslim theological seminary and now a ceramics museum, and the **İnce Minare Medresesi**, now a wood and stone-carving museum.

If you're staying, the cheapest place is *Hotel Ulusan* (☎ 351 5004), behind the post office, where beds in waterless rooms cost just US$6. For more comfort, *Yeni Köşk Otel* (☎ 352 0671, Yeni Aziziye Caddesi, Kadılar Sokak 28) has singles/doubles with private bath for US$14/20. For food, try the *Şifa Lokantası* (Mevlana Caddesi 30).

The otogar is 3.5km north of the city centre, linked by the Konak-Otogar minibus (US$0.30).

CAPPADOCIA (KAPADOKYA)

South-east of Ankara, almost in the centre of the country, the Cappadocia region is famous for the fantastic natural **rock formations** of its valleys. Over the centuries people have carved houses, churches, fortresses and even complete underground cities into the soft, eerily eroded volcanic stone.

Attractions include the Göreme, Zelve and Soğanlı valleys with their scores of rock-cut churches; the fortress towns of Uçhisar and Ortahisar; and rugged Ihlara Valley (south of Aksaray), dotted with ancient churches.

Nevşehir
☎ 384

The unattractive provincial capital Nevşehir is good only for transport connections. Catch buses here for the astonishing underground cities of **Derinkuyu** and **Kaymaklı** (open 8 am to 5 pm, to 6.30 pm in summer; US$1.75 entry), and for the rock-carved Eski Gümüşler

TURKEY

monastery and interesting mosques much farther south at **Niğde**.

Nevşehir's tourist office (☎ 213 3659) is sympathetic to budget travellers.

Göreme
☎ 384

The Göreme Valley is one of the most amazing sights in Turkey. Over the centuries a thick layer of volcanic tuff has eroded into fantastic shapes. Early Christians carved cross-shaped churches, stables and homes into the cliffs and cones. Painted **church murals** date from as early as the 8th century, though the best are from the 10th to 13th centuries; unlit for many centuries, they've hardly faded at all, although vandals have left their indelible mark. The best are those in the **Göreme Open-Air Museum**, which is open 8 am to 5.30 pm (4.30 pm in winter) daily; entry is US$5, plus an extra US$7 to see the newly restored Karanlık church.

If time is tight, Göreme travel agents can sell you a day tour which takes in the main sites, including one of the underground cities and a stretch of the Ihlara Gorge, for about US$30.

Places to Stay You can camp in the gardens of many pensions, or at the *Dilek* or *Berlin* camping grounds, side by side amid wonderful rock formations on the road leading from Göreme village to the open-air museum. *Kaya Camping*, off the road to Ortahisar, is even better.

Pensions in Göreme village charge similar rates: around US$4 for a dorm bed, US$5.50 in a waterless private room, and US$7 to US$10 per bed in a private room with bath and/or toilet.

Favourites include *Köse* (☎ 271 2294), near the post office, with a swimming pool and good meals; *Kelebek* (☎ 271 2531), with cave rooms and spectacular views; *Flintstones* (☎ 271 2555) with a swimming pool; *Paradise* (☎ 271 2248); and *Peri* (☎ 271 2136), with an inviting cave bar.

Cave Hotel Melek (☎ 271 2463), high on the valley wall, has rock-cut double rooms with private bath and breakfast for US$25. The newer *Ottoman House* (☎ 271 2616) offers luxury rooms for US$15/30, plus US$5 for an excellent buffet breakfast and US$10 for a set dinner menu.

Places to Eat Several of the pensions serve good-value evening meals. Of the restaurants along the main road, *SOS* tends to be cheapest but *Sultan*, *Sedef* and *Tardelli* all serve up good standard Turkish fare. *Orient,* on the road heading for Üçhisar, serves a filling set dinner menu for US$4.75 in pleasing surroundings. Across the road *Cafedoci@* serves a more Westernised menu – big portions of burgers etc.

Üçhisar
☎ 384

Three kilometres south-west of Göreme village is picturesque Üçhisar, a town built around, and into, a prominent peak. A room-to-room scramble through its rock citadel (US$1.25) leads to fine views from the summit. Üçhisar makes a great alternative base to Göreme. The clean, simple *Kilim Pansiyon* (☎ 384-219 2774) offers beds in arched rooms with great views for US$20 a double including breakfast but there are plenty of other choices too.

Avanos
☎ 384

On the northern bank of the Kızılırmak (Red River), Avanos is known particularly for its pottery. Of the pensions, best value are *Kirkit Pansiyon* (☎ 511 3148), where beds in rooms with shower cost US$10 each, breakfast included; or for the same price, the new *Venessa Pension* (☎ 511 3840), just north of the high street and boasting its very own underground city.

Moving up the price and comfort scale, *Sofa Motel* (☎ 511 5186), just across the bridge, has tastefully decorated rooms in a group of old houses for US$30/50 a single/double with private bath.

Ürgüp
☎ 384

Bigger than Göreme, this low-rise town is still very appealing, with its old sandstone buildings, cobbled streets and a stone hill carved full of rooms and passages. The Turasan factory at the top of the hill heading out to Nevşehir offers **wine-tasting**.

TURKEY

The helpful tourist office (☎ 341 4059) is in the park, downhill from the main square.

Places to Stay & Eat Bahçe Hostel
(☎ 341 3314), across the road from the hamam, charges just US$4 for a dorm bed, slightly more for a basic pension room. *Hotel Kilim* (☎ 341 3131), a block from the otogar at Dumlupınar Caddesi 47, charges US$12/20 a single/double with shower. *Elvan* (☎ 341 4191), west of the otogar past the Dutlu Cami, has great rooms with shower for US$15/25.

Asia Minor Hotel (☎ 341 4645), on İstiklal Caddesi, has beautifully decorated cave and stone-arched rooms for US$30/40 with private bath and breakfast.

Şölen and *Kardeşler* restaurants behind the otogar have good, cheap food. *Şömine*, right in the centre, has a wide range of salads, mezes and interesting kebabs. Across the road *Prokopi Bar* is *the* place to wind up the evening over a drink before hitting *Armağan Disco*.

Ihlara Valley
☎ 382

Ihlara is a remote canyon full of carved and painted Byzantine churches – a must for walkers.

The village of Ihlara Köyü is 85km southwest of Nevşehir and 40km south-east of Aksaray. The simple *Akar Pansiyon* (☎ 453 7018), on the Aksaray road, offers doubles with shower for US$15, breakfast included. The similar *Anatolia Pansiyon* (☎ 453 7440) has basic rooms with showers for US$18, or camping for US$3. There are more pensions and a camp site in the gorge itself at the village of Belisırma.

Ihlara Belediyesi buses run several times daily from Aksaray's otogar and charge US$0.75 one way.

Kayseri
☎ 352

Sitting in the shadow of snowy Mt Erciyes, Kayseri, known as Caesarea in Roman times, was the provincial capital of Cappadocia. A religiously conservative town, it's full of mosques, tombs and old seminaries (*medrese*). Near the tourist office (☎ 222 3903) is the beautiful Hunat Hatun mosque, tomb and

seminary. Right behind it is Kayseri's best cheap hotel, *Hunat Oteli* (☎ 232 4319), with waterless rooms for US$7 per person. The Güpgüpoğlu Konağı is a 19th-century mansion which now serves as the Ethnography Museum.

Behind the massive 6th-century city walls are the bazaar and the Ulu Cami (Great Mosque), begun by the Seljuks in 1136. Look out for the fine decorations on the Döner Kümbet (Revolving Tomb), 1km south of the tourist office on Talas Caddesi.

The Black Sea Coast

This region is dramatically different from the rest of Turkey – steep and craggy, damp and lush, and isolated by the Pontic Mountains along most of its length. It's the country's dairy belt, and the area's hazelnuts make Turkey the world's biggest exporter of them. The tea you drink in İstanbul probably comes from east of Trabzon; the cigarette smoke you endure probably comes from tobacco grown west of Samsun.

Partly because of heavy industry around Zonguldak, the western Black Sea coast is almost unknown to tourists, though the fishing port of Amasra, with its Roman and Byzantine ruins, is worth a look. Sinop is a fishing and boat-building town with good beaches on both sides of the peninsula.

There's little of interest in Samsun, but as a port of call for the ferry from İstanbul it makes a good starting point for travel along the coast.

On your way to the coast, stop at Amasya, a lovely old Ottoman town in a dramatic mountain setting, and Safranbolu, a beautiful town of traditional timber houses, listed as a world heritage site by Unesco.

TRABZON
☎ 462

Trabzon is certainly the most interesting town on the Black Sea coast, with mild weather, Byzantine architecture, beaches and the amazing Sumela Monastery nearby. Known as Trebizond in Byzantine times, this town was a stronghold against the Seljuks and Mongols, and was the last to fall to the Ottoman Turks as well.

Orientation & Information

Modern Trabzon is centred on Atatürk Alanı (Atatürk Square), on a steep hill above the harbour. Uphill from it are Ulusoy and Metro bus ticket offices. Turkish Airlines is on the western side of the square. The long-distance otogar is 3km east of the port. The tourist office (☎ 321 4659) is behind the belediye (town hall), between the Beldi and Nur hotels.

Things to See

The dark walls of the Byzantine city are a half-hour walk west from Atatürk Alanı. The **old town**, with its timber houses and stone bridges, still looks medieval.

Of Trabzon's several **Byzantine churches**, best-preserved is the 13th-century Aya Sofya, now a museum (open 8.30 am to 5 pm daily but closed on winter Mondays; entry US$1.25); take a dolmuş from Atatürk Alanı. Among its more beautiful Ottoman mosques are the **Gülbahar Hatun Camii** west of the city walls and the **Çarşı Camii** (or Osmanpaşa Camii) in the bazaar. For a look at a beautiful 19th-century villa, visit the **Atatürk Köşkü** high above the town.

Some travellers come to Trabzon just to visit the 14th-century **Sumela Monastery**, built into a cliff-face like a swallow's nest. It was inhabited until 1923 and has many fine murals (much damaged by vandals but under restoration) and amazing views. In summer, Ulusoy runs a 10 am bus (returning at 2 and 3 pm) from the town-centre terminal just uphill from Atatürk Alanı. The 40-minute trip costs US$7. Local travel agents also offer daily trips to Sumela.

Taxis depart from Atatürk Alanı and charge around US$35 to take a carload to the monastery, wait two hours and come back again. Entry to Sumela National Park costs US$1.25.

Places to Stay

Many of the hotels east of Atatürk Alanı on Güzelhisar Caddesi and adjacent streets are filled with traders and prostitutes, known locally as 'Natashas', from the former Soviet states. The following seemed thankfully Natasha-free at the time of writing.

Anıl (☎ 326 7282, *Güzelhisar Caddesi 10*) has a flashy lobby and fairly clean rooms with bath and TV for US$12/20 a single/double. *Gözde* (☎ 321 9579), just off Güzelhisar Caddesi, is much dingier but the beds cost only US$4.50 each.

Rooms at *Hotel Benli* (☎ 321 1022, *Cami Çıkmazı Sokak 5*), behind the belediye, are old and drab but beds cost only US$3.50 plus another US$1 for a shower. The newer *Nur* (☎ 321 2798), opposite, has clean, comfortable rooms with sinks for US$12/20.

Sankta Maria Katolik Kilisesi Hostel (☎ 321 2192, *Sümer Sokak 26*) was built by French Capuchins in 1869 when Trabzon was a cosmopolitan trading port. It offers clean, simple rooms and the use of hot showers in exchange for a (realistic) donation. You needn't be Catholic to stay here.

Probably the best bet, if you can afford it, is *Otel Horon* (☎ 326 6455, *Sıramağazalar 125*), where clean rooms with shower cost US$50/65, breakfast included.

Places to Eat

Derya Restaurant, across from the belediye on the north-eastern corner of Atatürk Alanı, has a good selection of ready-made food and serves a tasty İskender kebap for US$3. *Volkan 2*, a few steps to the west, and *Murat Balık Salonu* offer a range of fish dishes.

Çardak Pide Salonu, behind the Turkish Airlines office (enter from Uzun Sokak), serves fresh, cheap Turkish pizza for US$1.50 to US$2.

On the southern side of Atatürk Alanı is *Çınar Lokantası*, with a good selection of ready-made meals, best eaten fresh at lunchtime.

Upstairs at *Kıbrıs Restaurant* on the eastern side of the square you can get alcoholic drinks with your meal (US$6 to US$10).

Getting There & Away

Air Turkish Airlines (☎ 321 1680), on the south-western corner of Atatürk Alanı, has daily flights to Ankara and İstanbul. İstanbul Airlines (☎ 322 3806), Kazazoğlu Sokak 9, Sanat İşhanı, on the north-western corner of Atatürk Alanı, also flies daily to İstanbul for slightly less. Dolmuş to the airport leave from near Hotel Toros.

TURKEY

Bus Dolmuş taxis to the otogar (Garajlar or K.T.U.) leave from Atatürk Alanı, near Volkan 2 restaurant.

From the otogar, half-hourly minibuses go to Rize (US$2.50, 1½ hours), Hopa (US$4.50, three hours) and Artvin (US$7, five hours). A dozen buses a day head for Erzurum (US$10, six hours), a beautiful but slow ride via Gümüşhane or Artvin.

Boat See the Getting Around section at the beginning of this chapter for information about car ferries to and from İstanbul.

KAÇKAR MOUNTAINS
The eastern end of the coastal mountain range is dominated by Kaçkar Dağı (3937m), inland from Rize. Around it are excellent opportunities for camping and wilderness treks, and even white-water rafting on the Çoruh River. The many small villages offer cheap, simple hikers' accommodation.

At **Uzungöl**, 50km east of Trabzon and 50km inland, an alpine lake offers camping, bungalows and a few small hotels. A good base for day hikes and trekking towards Kaçkar Dağı is **Ayder**, 40km east of Rize and 40km inland, with hot springs as a bonus.

Eastern Turkey

Turkey's eastern region is the harshest and hardest part of the country but rewards visitors who venture this far with dramatic landscapes like the majestic views of the 5165m Mt Ararat (believed to be the resting place of the legendary Noah's Ark). In winter, bitterly cold weather is imported direct from the Russian steppes, so unless you're well equipped and something of a masochist, avoid travelling here from October to April. For full coverage of this region see Lonely Planet's *Turkey* guide.

ERZURUM
☎ 442
Eastern Turkey's main transport hub and a military centre, Erzurum is a fairly drab town famous for its harsh climate, although it has some striking Seljuk buildings that justify staying for a day or so.

Orientation & Information
The tourist office (☎ 218 5697) is on Cemal Gürsel Caddesi, the main street, just west of the Atatürk statue. The otogar is inconveniently located 3km north-east of the town centre on the airport road, but the town centre itself is compact, with all the main sites within walking distance.

Things to See & Do
From the well-preserved walls of a 5th-century **Byzantine fortress**, you get a good view of the town's layout and the bleak plains that surround it. The beautifully symmetrical **Çifte Minareli Medrese** (built in 1253) is a seminary famous for its Seljuk architecture, with a classic carved portal flanked by twin minarets. Next door is the oldest mosque, the **Ulu Cami**, built in 1179. Farther west along Cumhuriyet Caddesi, an open square marks the centre of town, with an Ottoman mosque and another seminary, the **Yakutiye Medresesi**, built by the local Mongol emir in 1310. It's now the Turkish and Islamic Arts and Ethnography Museum (open 8 am to noon and 12.30 to 5 pm daily except Monday; entry costs US$1.25).

To go white-water rafting on the Çoruh River, take an excursion to **Yusufeli**, north of Erzurum, bearing in mind that accommodation there is extremely basic.

Places to Stay
Erzurum has lots of cheapies, although some of them are pretty dismal. *Örnek Otel* (☎ 218 1204, Kazım Karabekir Caddesi 8) has basic singles/doubles for US$9/12. Nearby *Otel Polat* (☎ 218 1623, Kazım Karabekir Caddesi 3) is much better, with rooms from US$13/21. Around the corner, Hotel Sefer (☎ 218 6714, İstasyon Caddesi) charges US$15/25 for rooms with bath and TV, including breakfast. All three are handily situated between the train station and the town centre.

Highly recommended by readers is *Yeni Hotel Çınar* (☎ 213 1050, Ayazpaşa Caddesi 18), which charges about the same as the Örnek. To find it, look for the Gürpınar Sineması (cinema) in the bazaar. The street opposite site leads to the Çınar.

Places to Eat
Cheap *kebapcıs* line Cumhuriyet Caddesi near the Yakutiye Medresesi; try *Salon*

Çağın and *Salon Asya* for starters. The nearby *Güzelyurt Restorant* looks more expensive than it is; try the house speciality *mantarlı güveç*, a delicious mushroom stew. *Sultan Sekisi Şark Sofrası*, opposite the Çifte Minareli Medrese, serves local fare amid traditional decor for US$3 to US$5.

Getting There & Away
Air Turkish Airlines (☎ 234 1516), Kazım Karabekir Caddesi, has two flights daily to Ankara (US$65), with connections to İstanbul and İzmir. A taxi to the airport costs US$3.50.

Bus If there's no *servis* bus, Bus No 2 runs into town from the otogar.

KARS
☎ 474
About 260km north-east of Erzurum, this frontier town was much fought over and has a suitably massive fortress. The main reasons to come here now are to see the ruins of ancient Ani and look across the border at Armenia.

The tourist office (☎ 223 2300) is on Atatürk Caddesi. There's not much to do in Kars itself, although the **museum**, north-east of the train station on Cumhuriyet Caddesi, has exhibits dating from the Bronze Age (admission US$1.25).

The best value place to stay is the *Güngören Oteli* (☎ 212 5630, fax 223 4821, Halit Paşa Caddesi, Millet Sokak 4) where spacious rooms cost US$15/25 a single/double.

Ani, 44km east of Kars, was completely deserted in 1239 after a Mongol invasion but before that had been a major city and a capital of both the Urartian and Armenian kingdoms. Surrounded by huge walls, the ruins lie in fields overlooking the Arpaçay River, which forms the border with Armenia. The ghost city is extremely dramatic and there are several notable churches, including a cathedral built between 989 and 1010 that was the seat of the Armenian prelate.

To get permission to go to Ani, first go to the Kars tourist office and fill out a form. Then take the form to the Emniyet Müdürglü for approval. Then go to Kars museum and buy your ticket. Taxi drivers know the procedure only too well and charge around US$30 for arranging the entire trip.

DOĞUBAYAZIT
☎ 472
This drab frontier town, dramatically situated at the far side of a sweeping grass plain that runs to the foot of Mt Ararat, is where you come to cross into Iran. It doesn't take long to find your bearings, as everything is within a five-minute walk. Apart from spectacular views of **Mt Ararat**, there's an interesting palace-fort, the **İshak Paşa Sarayı** (open from 8 am to 5 pm; entry US$2), perched romantically among rocky crags 5km east of town. The occasional dolmuş passes nearby, but unless you want to walk you'll probably have to negotiate for a taxi (about US$5 there and back).

Getting permission to climb Mt Ararat can be time consuming. Otherwise, there are excursions to a giant **meteor crater**, **Diyadin hot springs** and the supposed resting-place of **Noah's Ark**.

If you decide to stay, a good choice is *Hotel Ararat* (☎ 312 4988) right beside the bazaar and with doubles with views for US$15. *Hotel İsfahan* (☎ 311 5159, Emniyet Caddesi 26) also has serviceable rooms for US$25/38 a single/double. Smaller hotels, like the nearby *Hotel Erzurum* (☎ 312 5080, Belediye Caddesi), provide beds for US$5 to US$7.

SOUTH-EASTERN TURKEY
Turkey's south-eastern corner, along the border with Syria and Iraq and drained by the Tigris (Dicle) and Euphrates (Fırat) rivers, was once known as Upper Mesopotamia. The area has the largest Kurdish population in Turkey and so was the worst affected by PKK terrorism and government reprisals.

Warning

For the last 16 years, the Kurdistan Workers' Party (PKK) had been fighting for an independent Kurdistan in south-eastern Turkey. At the time of writing, a ceasefire was in effect but it's still wise to read your government's advice to travellers before venturing to the south-east of the country, especially if you're heading to Diyarbakır, Mardin or points east of them.

TURKEY

Nemrut Dağı

North of Şanlıurfa and south of Malatya, pretty much in the middle of nowhere, stands Nemrut Dağı (Mt Nimrod), surmounted by a 2000-year-old **memorial sanctuary** to an obscure Commagene king. The heads of huge statues of gods and kings lie toppled by earthquakes and scattered on the ground. Most people approach from the southern side of the mountain where the **Kahta** tourist office (☎ 416-725 5007) is particularly helpful. All Kahta's hotels, including the *Kommagene* (☎ 416-715 1092), *Mezopotamya* (☎ 416-725 5112) and *Zeus Camping* (☎ 416-725 5695), arrange tours to see the heads. Three-day trips to Nemrut are also available from Göreme; they costs US$150 per person and take in lots of other sites along the way.

VAN
☎ 432

The town of Van, on the south-eastern shore of the vast salt lake of the same name, has a 3000-year-old **citadel** at Van Kalesi (Rock of Van) and a small **museum**.

The tourist office (☎ 216 2018) is at Cumhuriyet Caddesi 19. The otogar is several kilometres north-west of the centre.

The 10th-century church on **Akdamar Island** is a fascinating piece of Armenian architecture, with frescoes inside and reliefs outside depicting biblical scenes. It has a beautiful setting right in the middle of Lake Van.

Dolmuş (US$1) from Beş Yol in Van take you to the dock for boats to Akdamar but unless you can rustle up a group to share costs, expect to pay US$18 to US$20 for a boat.

Places to Stay

Cheap hotels in the **bazaar** (çarşı) charge US$4.50 per person in rooms with sink and/or private shower. Among the better ones are *Otel İpek* (☎ 216 3033) and the more basic *Aslan Oteli* (☎ 216 2469, *Eski Hal Civarı*).

For more comfort, try the two-star *Büyük Asur Oteli* (☎ 216 8792, *Cumhuriyet Caddesi, Turizm Sokak 5*) which has comfortable, clean rooms with shower for US$18/25 a single/double with plentiful hot water.

Erzurum's best is the three-star *Büyük Urartu Oteli* (☎ 212 0660), near the Devlet Hastanesi hospital, overpriced at US$65/78 a single/double, although they'll come down if you bargain.

Yugoslavia (Југославија)

The Federal Republic of Yugoslavia, consisting of Serbia and Montenegro, occupies the heart of the Balkans astride the main land and river routes from Western Europe to Asia Minor. It is a region with a tumultuous history.

Since June 1999 Kosovo, previously an annexed part of Serbia, has been a UN-NATO protectorate. The UN still recognises the region as part of Yugoslavia until its future is decided. For this reason it is included in this chapter.

Facts about Yugoslavia

HISTORY
The original inhabitants of this region were the Illyrians, followed by the Celts, who arrived in the 4th century BC. The Roman conquest of Moesia Superior (Serbia) began in the 3rd century BC and under Augustus the empire extended to Singidunum (Belgrade) on the Danube. In AD 395 Theodosius I divided the empire and what is now Serbia passed to the Byzantine Empire, while Croatia remained part of the Western Roman Empire.

During the middle of the 6th century, Slavic tribes (Serbs, Croats and Slovenes) crossed the Danube and occupied much of the Balkan Peninsula. In 879 Sts Cyril and Methodius converted the Serbs to the Orthodox Church.

An independent Serbian kingdom appeared in 1217 with a 'Golden Age' during the reign of Stefan Dušan (1346-55), who built many frescoed Orthodox monasteries. After Stefan's death Serbia declined, and at the Battle of Kosovo on 28 June 1389 the Serbian army was defeated by the Ottoman Turks, ushering in 500 years of Islamic rule. Despite the heavy defeat, this battle is viewed as a moment of national pride by Serbians.

A revolt in 1815 led to de facto Serbian independence from the Turks. Autonomy was recognised in 1829 and complete Serbian independence was achieved in 1878.

AT A GLANCE

Capital	Belgrade
Population	11.21 million (1999 est.)
Language	Serbia and Montenegro – Serbian (Serbo-Croatian) Kosovo – Albanian
Currency	1 Yugoslav novi dinar (DIN) = 100 paras
Time	GMT/UTC+0100
Country Code	☎ 381

On 28 June 1914, Austria-Hungary used the assassination of Archduke Ferdinand by a Serb nationalist as an excuse to invade Serbia, thus sparking WWI. After the war, Croatia, Slovenia and Vojvodina were united with Serbia, Montenegro and Macedonia to form the Kingdom of Serbs, Croats and Slovenes under the king of Serbia. In 1929 the name was changed to Yugoslavia.

On 25 March 1941, Yugoslavia joined the Tripartite Alliance, a fascist military pact supported by the Nazis. This sparked a military coup that installed Peter II as king, and Yugoslavia abruptly withdrew from the alliance.

The Effects of War

NATO bombing and sanctions have affected travel, but new bridges have made road and rail communications over the Danube possible again. Travellers using the new railway bridge can feel spiritually elevated knowing that Serbian leader Slobodan Milošević has described it as a 'morally superior bridge'. However, there are fewer international trains and none run in Kosovo. Sanctions and the breakdown of economic ties have affected the acceptance of travellers cheques and credit cards. In Kosovo and Montenegro the currency is now effectively the Deutschmark. Travellers should bring cash. Accommodation has become much more expensive, especially in Kosovo. Travel in Kosovo, formerly unadvisable, is now easy and reasonably safe in the main towns. Some NATO countries' institutions, such as embassies and cultural centres are closed. Visas for Yugoslavia (Serbia) have become difficult to obtain. See the appropriate sections for further information. Western travellers are treated well in Kosovo and Montenegro and there seem to be no problems in Belgrade.

Livid, Hitler ordered an immediate invasion and the country was carved up between Germany, Italy, Hungary and Bulgaria.

Almost immediately the Communist Party, under Josip Broz Tito, declared an armed uprising, laying the basis for a future communist-led Yugoslavia under Tito.

In 1945 the Communist Party (officially banned since 1920) won control of the national assembly, which in November abolished the monarchy and declared Yugoslavia a federal republic. Serbia's size was then greatly reduced when Bosnia-Hercegovina, Montenegro and Macedonia were granted republic status within this 'second' Yugoslavia. The Albanians of Kosovo and Hungarians of Vojvodina were denied republics of their own, however, on the pretext that they were not nations because their national homelands were outside the boundaries of Yugoslavia.

Tito broke with Stalin in 1948 and, as a reward, received US$2 billion in economic and military aid from the USA and UK between 1950 and 1960. Growing regional inequalities led, however, to increased tension as Slovenia, Croatia and Kosovo demanded greater autonomy within the Yugoslav federation.

In 1986 the Serbian Academy of Sciences prepared a memorandum calling on Serbia to reassert its hegemony in Yugoslavia. A year later Slobodan Milošević took over as Communist Party leader in Serbia, espousing a vision of a 'Greater Serbia' that horrified residents of Slovenia and Croatia. As a result, on 25 June 1991, Slovenia and Croatia declared their independence, leading to an invasion of Slovenia by the Yugoslav federal army. As punishment the European Community (EC), now the European Union (EU), imposed a weapons embargo on Yugoslavia.

On 15 January 1992, the EC recognised the independence of Croatia and Slovenia, prompting Macedonia and Bosnia-Hercegovina to demand recognition of their own independence. Montenegro alone voted to remain in Yugoslavia.

On 27 April 1992 a 'third' Yugoslav federation was declared by Serbia and Montenegro. The new Yugoslav constitution made no mention of 'autonomous provinces', infuriating the Albanian majority in the province of Kosovo, long brutally repressed by Serbia. Violence in Kosovo erupted in January 1998, largely provoked by the Yugoslav federal army.

The West provided a storm of protest but little else other than a reimposition of an arms embargo. In March 1999, peace talks in Paris failed when Serbia rejected a US-brokered peace plan. In a reply to resistance in Kosovo, Serbian forces moved to clear the country of its Albanian population. Hundreds of thousands fleeing into Macedonia and Albania, robbed of their possessions, galvanised the USA and NATO into action. Not wishing to enter into a potentially disastrous land war, their forces embarked on a 78-day bombing campaign. On 12 June 1999 Serbian forces withdrew from Kosovo.

GEOGRAPHY

Mountains and plateaus account for the lower half of this 102,350-sq-km country. Serbia covers 77,651 sq km, Montenegro accounts for 13,812 sq km, and Kosovo is 10,887 sq km. Yugoslavia's interior and southern mountains belong to the Balkan range while the

YUGOSLAVIA

Note: At the time of publication the railway network in Kosovo was not operating

HUNGARY

Pécs
Baja
Horgoš
Szeged
Subotica
Srpska Crnja
Timişoara

CROATIA

Danube River
Tisa River
Novi Sad
Vojvodina
Vatin
Vršac

ROMANIA

Sava River
Bijeljina
Drina River
Zvornik

BELGRADE
Smederevo
Golubac
Kladovo

BOSNIA-HERCEGOVINA

Sandžak

SERBIA

Negotin
Vidin

Danube River

Manasija
Zaječar

Čačak
Čuprija
Morava River

Požega
Kraljevo
Kruševac
E75

Tara River
Ušče
Studenica
Brus
Ibar River
Niš

Pljevlja
Raška
Kapaonik (2017m)

Žabljak
Đurđevića Tara
Durmitor National Park
Bijelo Polje
Novi Pazar
Leskovac
Dimitrovgrad

MONTENEGRO
Mojkovac
Berane
Rožaje
Mitrovica (Titova Mitrovica)

Nikšić
Kolašin
Klina (Metohija Junction)
Klisura

Herceg-Novi
Kotor
Cetinje
Peja (Péc)
Prishtina (Priština)
BULGARIA

Tivat
Podgorica
Dečani (Dečani)
Kosovo Polje

Bay of Kotor
Budva
Sveti Stefan
Lake Skadar
KOSOVO

To Ancona, Italy
Bar
Shkodra
Hani Elezit (Đeneral Janković)
Preševo

To Bari, Italy
Ulcinj
ALBANIA
Prizren
Kumanovo

Kukës
Šar Planina
SKOPJE

ADRIATIC SEA
MACEDONIA

coastal range is an arm of the Dinaric Alps. Most of the rivers flow north into the Danube, which runs through Yugoslavia for 588km. In the south, rivers have cut deep canyons into the plateau.

Yugoslavia's only coast is the scenically superb 150km Montenegrin coast. The Bay of Kotor here is the only real fjord in southern Europe and Montenegro's Durmitor National Park has Europe's largest canyon.

CLIMATE

The north has a continental climate with cold winters and hot, humid summers. The coastal region has hot, dry summers and relatively cold winters with heavy snowfall inland.

GOVERNMENT & POLITICS

Nominally, Yugoslavia has a presidential parliamentarian system. At the time of writing, power was in the hands of Slobodan Milošević, two-term president of Serbia and now president of Yugoslavia. However, with an election due in late 2000, there have been forecasts of a strong showing by the opposition parties.

ECONOMY

Yugoslavia has not successfully restructured its state socialist economy like other former Eastern bloc countries such as Hungary and the Czech Republic. Conflict and the disruption of trade links have devastated the economy over the last 20 years. Hyperinflation, the highest in European history, has been a constant problem. At one point, it was cheaper to use banknotes as wallpaper than buy it. The dinar continues to lose value against hard currencies.

Agricultural production is mainly on the northern plain. Vojvodina and Kosovo have most of the mineral resources, including coal and petroleum, hence the strategic importance of those former autonomous regions to Serbia. Yugoslavia is largely self-sufficient in fuel.

POPULATION & PEOPLE

There have been no official revisions to the population total of 11 million since the 1991 census (1999 estimate 11.21 million). Then the ethnic proportions were Serbs (including Montenegrins; 67.3%), Albanians (16.6%), Hungarians (3.3%) and Slavic Muslims (3.1%),

plus a smattering of Croats, Romas, Slovaks, Macedonians, Romanians, Bulgarians, Turks and Ukrainians. War will have altered those figures especially as there are now some 600,000 refugees in Serbia and Montenegro.

Nearly a quarter of Vojvodina's population is Hungarian and there are large Slavic Muslim and Albanian minorities in Montenegro and southern Serbia.

ARTS
Literature

Bosnian-born Nobel Prize winner Ivo Andrić is Serbia's most respected writer. His novel *Bridge over the Drina* accurately foresaw the region's disasters of the early 1990s. Respected writer Milorad Pavić's novel *Hazar Dictionary*, a historical narrative, has been translated into English. An excellent source of books on the region is Eastern Books (☎/fax 020-8871 0880, ✉ info@easternbooks.com) in London.

Cinema

The award-winning film *Underground*, by Sarajevo-born director Emil Kusturica, is worth seeing. Told in a chaotic, colourful style, the film deals with Yugoslav history over the last 50 years.

Music

Serbia's vibrant dances are similar to those of Bulgaria with musicians using bagpipes, flutes and fiddles.

The music of Kosovo bears the deep imprint of five centuries of Turkish rule with the high whine flute carrying the tune above the beat of a goatskin drum.

Blehmuzika, or brass music influenced by Turkish and Austrian military music has become the national music of Serbia.

Popular with the younger generation is Momčilo Bajagić whose music fuses traditional elements with street poetry and jazz. Đorđe Balašević appeals to a wider listening audience, again combining traditional elements with modern motifs.

SOCIETY & CONDUCT

The Serbs are a proud people, and very hospitable to visitors despite their country's reputation. Respect should be shown for all religious establishments and customs.

Dress appropriately at all times and bear in mind that learning some basic words will open doors and create smiles.

RELIGION
The Serbs and Montenegrins are Orthodox, the Hungarians are Roman Catholic and the Albanians are predominantly Muslim.

LANGUAGE
Serbian is the common language, with Albanian spoken in Kosovo. Through working abroad, many Yugoslavs know German as a second language and educated people often know French.

Hungarians in Vojvodina use the Latin alphabet, Montenegrins use both Latin and Cyrillic, but in Serbia most things are in Cyrillic. (See the Macedonian language section at the back of this book for the alphabet.)

Facts for the Visitor

HIGHLIGHTS
Yugoslavia has a wealth of castles, including the baroque fortress of Petrovaradin Citadel at Novi Sad and Belgrade's Kalemegdan Citadel. Kosovo has the Turkish architecture and street cafes of Prizren, and the old Montenegrin capital of Cetinje will please romantics. Of the beach resorts, Budva is chic but Kotor is more impressive, with its fjord and medieval walled town. Montenegro's Tara Canyon and Durmitor National Park are on a par with any similar sights in the world.

SUGGESTED ITINERARIES
Due to visa restrictions always visit Serbia first if you intend to go to Kosovo. Depending on the length of your stay and where you arrive you might want to visit the following:

Two days
  Visit either Serbia (Belgrade and Novi Sad) or Montenegro (Budva, Cetinje and Kotor) or Kosovo (Prizren)
One week
  Visit two of the above
Two weeks
  Visit all areas covered in this chapter for two of the above
One month
  Visit all areas covered in this chapter

PLANNING
When to Go
The Montenegrin coast should be avoided during the months of July and August. Accommodation is more expensive, difficult to find and transport crowded. For skiers the season in Mount Durmitor National Park is December to March.

Maps
The Freytag & Berndt map *Yugoslavia, Slovenia, Croatia* shows former Yugoslavia with the new countries. The *Savezna Republika Jugoslavija Autokarta* map shows the new borders and some town maps. *Plan Grada Beograd* is a detailed Belgrade city map. These two are free from the Tourist Organisation of Belgrade. A Kosovo map is available from bookshops in Prishtina.

TOURIST OFFICES
There are tourist offices in Belgrade, Novi Sad, Prishtina and Prizren. Elsewhere, travel agencies will often help with information.

VISAS & DOCUMENTS
Allow at least six weeks to get a visa for Yugoslavia (Serbia); you don't need one for Montenegro or Kosovo. Visitors to Yugoslavia (Serbia) need either an invitation from an official body or a pre-arranged itinerary with booked hotels – all in writing.

If you intend entering Yugoslavia more than once, ask for a double- or triple-entry visa. Otherwise, you'll find it's another impossible process.

EMBASSIES & CONSULATES
Yugoslav Embassies & Consulates
In addition to those listed, Yugoslav consulates or embassies can also be found in its neighbours' capitals.

Australia (☎ 02-9362 3003, fax 9362 4555, ⓔ yugcon@rosebay.matra.com.au)
  12 Trelawney St, Woollahra, NSW 2025
Canada (☎ 613-233 6289) 17 Blackburn Ave, Ottawa, Ontario, K1N 8A2
France (☎ 01 40 72 24 24, fax 01 40 72 24 11)
  54 rue Faisanderie 16e, Paris
UK (☎ 0171-370 6105, fax 0171-370 3838)
  5 Lexham Gardens, London, W8 5JJ
USA (☎ 202-462 6566) 2410 California St NW, Washington DC, 20008

Embassies & Consulates in Yugoslavia

Most consulates and embassies are on or near Belgrade's Kneza Miloša. Visas are payable in US$ or DM, cash only. The Canadian, UK and US embassies are closed.

Australia
Embassy: (☎ 011-624 655, fax 628 189) Cika Ljubina 13

MONEY
Currency

Kosovo has adopted the Deutschmark as its currency. It's also the de facto currency of Montenegro where prices are quoted in Deutschmarks, and dinar is only used for small transactions or small change. Shops and businesses advertise the exchange rate in their windows. Serbia clings to the dinar but people favour the Deutschmark as a hard currency. However, this situation will inevitably change when the euro is introduced in 2002.

Exchange Rates

country	unit		Deutschmark		dinar
Australia	A$1	=	DM1.27	=	6.88DIN
Canada	C$1	=	DM1.46	=	7.91DIN
euro	€1	=	DM1.96	=	10.59DIN
France	10FF	=	DM2.98	=	16.14DIN
Germany	DM1	=	–	=	5.41DIN
Japan	¥100	=	DM1.99	=	10.76DIN
NZ	NZ$1	=	DM0.97	=	5.25DIN
UK	£1	=	DM3.21	=	17.37DIN
USA	US$1	=	DM2.15	=	11.66DIN

Exchanging Money

Bring Deutschmarks in cash as few banks will change travellers cheques. For exchange places, see the later Belgrade Information section. Banks in Serbia will change Deutschmarks at the unofficial street exchange rate of 22.5 DIN for DM1, although your receipt will only show the official rate of six for one. The newspapers give the current rate in a table printed in the Latin alphabet. In Montenegro the unofficial rate is 26 DIN for DM1. There are no ATMs for non-Yugoslav cards.

Tipping

It is common practice to round up restaurant bills to the nearest convenient figure. Taxi drivers will also expect the same.

POST & COMMUNICATIONS
Post

To mail a parcel, take it unsealed to a main post office for inspection. Allow plenty of time to check the repacking and complete the transaction.

You can receive mail addressed poste restante in all towns for a small charge.

Telephone

For long-distance calls it's best to use the main post office. The international access code for outgoing calls is ☎ 99. To call another town within Yugoslavia dial the area code with the initial zero and the number.

International calls from post offices cost 42 DIN a minute to the USA and Australia. International calls from card phones in Belgrade are possible but the limited value of the phone cards, 50 or 90 DIN, gives only a short call.

To call Yugoslavia from outside dial the international access code, ☎ 381 (country code), area code (without the initial zero) and the number.

Fax

Faxes can be sent from any large hotel or post offices that will charge 139 DIN per page to Australia or the USA and 101 DIN to Europe.

Email & Internet Access

There are Internet cafes in most towns. See the Information section for the appropriate town.

INTERNET RESOURCES

The Tourist Organisation of Belgrade has a useful Web site (www.belgradetourism.org .yu). Check out www.montenet.org for Montenegro news. With both sites some information is out of date.

BOOKS

Rebecca West's *Black Lamb & Grey Falcon* is a classic portrait of prewar Yugoslavia. Former partisan and leading dissident Milovan Djilas' fascinating books about Yugoslav history and politics are published in English.

Titles dealing with the turbulence of the 1990s include *The Death of Yugoslavia* by Laura Silber and Allan Little, Misha Glenny's 1992 book *The Fall of Yugoslavia* and *Yugoslavia's Bloody Collapse* by Christopher

Bennett (1996). Zoë Brân's *After Yugoslavia*, part of the Lonely Planet Journeys series, re-traces the author's 1978 trip through the for-mer Yugoslavia.

NEWSPAPERS & MAGAZINES
Some foreign-language magazines are avail-able in Yugoslavia, but not many foreign-language newspapers.

RADIO & TV
Studio B, the independent radio and TV sta-tion, was closed in May 2000 on the pretext that it was undermining state security. This was not the first time and it usually manages to resurface with a new identity. There are also a number of state-owned TV stations. Montenegrin media is less controlled. CNN, Eurosport and MTV are also available with the right equipment. Many FM and AM radio stations cater to all tastes.

TOILETS
Restaurant and hotel toilets are a cleaner op-tion than public toilets, which usually charge 2 or 3 DIN in Belgrade.

WOMEN TRAVELLERS
Other than cursory interest shown by men to-wards solo women travellers, travel is hassle-free and easy. Dress more conservatively than usual in Muslim areas of Kosovo.

GAY & LESBIAN TRAVELLERS
Homosexuality has been legal in Yugoslavia since 1932. For more information, contact Arkadia, Brace Baruh 11, 11000 Belgrade.

DISABLED TRAVELLERS
Few public buildings or streets have facilities for wheelchairs. Access could be problematic in Belgrade with its numerous inclines.

DANGERS & ANNOYANCES
Travel in northern Serbia and Montenegro is safe but south-eastern Serbia around the Kosovo border should be avoided. Travel in the Albanian parts of Kosovo is reasonably safe but there are many landmines and unex-ploded bombs in the countryside. Don't go to areas like Mitrovica where there is Albanian-Serb tension; see 'The Current Situation' boxed text later in this chapter for more detail.

Belgrade is a remarkably safe city per-haps because of the heavy police presence. Throughout Yugoslavia theft is rare.

Many Yugoslavs are chain-smokers who can't imagine that they might inconvenience nonsmokers, so choose your seat in public places carefully. 'No smoking' signs are often ignored.

It's wise to avoid political discussions and don't give police the impression you are anything but a tourist. Otherwise they'll start to investigate. Don't photograph police or military-guarded buildings.

LEGAL MATTERS
If you are visiting Serbia it is sensible to register with your embassy in Belgrade in case of problems. Citizens of Canada, the UK and USA, whose Belgrade embassies are closed, should check about registration with their governments.

BUSINESS HOURS
Banks keep long hours, often from 7 am to 7 pm weekdays and 7 am to noon on Satur-day. On weekdays many shops open from 7 am, close from noon to 4 pm but reopen until 8 pm. Department stores, supermarkets and some restaurants generally stay open all day. Most government offices are closed on Saturday; although shops stay open until 2 pm many other businesses close at 3 pm.

PUBLIC HOLIDAYS & SPECIAL EVENTS
Public holidays include:

New Year	1 & 2 January
Orthodox Christmas	6 & 7 January
Day of the FR of Yugoslavia	27 April
International Labour Days	1 & 2 May
Victory Day	9 May
Republic Days	29 & 30 November

Constitution Day (28 March) and Uprising Day (7 July) are holidays in Serbia and 13 July is a holiday in Montenegro. If these fall on a Sunday, then the following Monday or Tuesday is a holiday.

Orthodox Easter is between one and three weeks later than regular Easter. Most institu-tions close down at this time, so check the dates before you travel.

Belgrade hosts a film festival in February, a jazz festival in August, an international theatre festival in mid-September and a festival of classical music in October. Budva has a summer festival in July and August.

ACTIVITIES
Skiing
Serbia and Kosovo's skiing resorts were closed at the time of writing due to the war. Montenegro's main ski resort is at Žabljak. The ski season is from about December to March.

White-Water Rafting & Hiking
White-water rafting is offered on the Tara River in Montenegro's Durmitor National Park. The same region is also a popular hiking area.

ACCOMMODATION
Hotels in Yugoslavia are not cheap and foreigners often have to pay up to twice what a local would pay. In Kosovo accommodation is even more expensive due to the shortage of hotels.

In summer you can camp along the Montenegrin coast; organised camping grounds are few and many of those that do exist are closed due to the absence of tourists. There's a hostel in Belgrade but it's far from the centre (see the later Belgrade Places to Stay section for contact details). HI hostels exist at Kopaonik and Ulcinj (summer only).

Private rooms are usually available along the coast, seldom inland and not in Belgrade. An overnight bus or train can sometimes get you out of an accommodation jam.

FOOD
The cheapest snack is *burek*, a greasy layered pie made with cheese *(sir)*, meat *(meso)* or potato *(Krompirusa)*. Grilled meats *(čevapčići)* are popular everywhere, as is the universal pizza.

Regional Dishes
Yugoslavia's regional cuisines range from spicy Hungarian goulash in Vojvodina to Turkish kebab in Serbia and Kosovo. A speciality of Vojvodina is *alaska čorba* (fiery riverfish stew). In Montenegro, try boiled lamb or *kajmak* (cream from boiled milk which is salted and turned into cheese).

Serbia is famous for grilled meats such as *čevapčići* (kebabs of spiced, minced meat, grilled), *pljeskavica* (a large, spicy hamburger steak) and *razvnjići* (a pork or veal shish kebab with onions and peppers). If you want to try them all at once, order a *mešano meso* (mixed grill). Serbian *duveč* is grilled pork cutlets with spiced stewed peppers, zucchini and tomatoes in rice cooked in an oven – delicious.

Other popular dishes are *musaka* (aubergine and potato baked in layers with minced meat), *sarma* (cabbage stuffed with minced meat and rice), *kapama* (stewed lamb, onions and spinach served with yoghurt), *punjena tikvica* (zucchini stuffed with minced meat and rice) and peppers stuffed with minced meat, rice and spices, cooked in tomato sauce.

Most traditional Yugoslav dishes are based on meat, so vegetarians will have problems, but there's the ubiquitous pizza or a Serbian salad *(Srpska salata)* of raw peppers, onions and tomatoes, seasoned with oil, vinegar and chilli. Also ask for *gibanica* (a layered cheese pie) and *zeljanica* (cheese pie with spinach). *Švopska salata* is also very popular, consisting of chopped tomatoes, cucumber and onion, topped with grated soft white cheese.

DRINKS
Beer *(pivo)* is universally available. Nikšićko pivo brewed at Nikšić in Montenegro is terribly good when imbibed ice-cold at the beach on a hot summer day.

Yugoslav cognac (grape brandy) is called *vinjak*. Coffee is usually served Turkish-style, boiled in a small individual pot, 'black as hell, strong as death and sweet as love'. Superb espresso and cappuccino, however, can be found in many cafes.

Getting There & Away

There is a currency declaration form that visitors should fill out on arrival and show on departure.

AIR
JAT Yugoslav Airlines has domestic and regional services. Other international airlines

fly to Belgrade and many European airlines fly to Prishtina.

LAND

All borders are open except the one between Serbia and Kosovo. Due to banditry it is not safe to cross into northern Albania.

Bus

There are daily international buses from Belgrade, Podgorica and Prishtina. Buses to/from Croatia require a change of bus at the border.

In Belgrade, travel agencies Basturist, Turist Biro Lasta and BS Tours all sell tickets for international buses (see Travel Agencies in the Belgrade section for addresses and contact numbers). Sample fares from Belgrade, payable in Deutschmarks only, are:

Destination	Cost
Munich	DM104
Paris	DM180
Vienna	DM76
Zagreb	DM40
Zürich	DM85

In Kosovo check with any travel agency in Prizren or Prishtina. In Montenegro approach travel agencies in Podgorica and Budva.

Train

Coming into Yugoslavia you can save money by breaking your journey at the first Yugoslav station, as domestic fares are much cheaper. Reservations are recommended and a student card will get you a reduction on train fares from Yugoslavia to other Eastern European countries.

All international trains run daily and leave from Belgrade. There are no train services at present into or out of Kosovo.

Bulgaria There are two trains daily to Sofia (690 DIN, nine hours, 417km).

Croatia Trains to Vienna, Venice and Munich all run through Zagreb. The cost for the 12½-hour journey is 720 DIN.

Greece There's only the daily train to Thessaloniki that takes 16 hours and costs 1100 DIN.

Hungary & Beyond Five trains a day travel to Budapest (1400 DIN, six hours, 354km) and two to Vienna (Beč; 2200 DIN, 11 hours, 627km).

Romania The fare for the overnight train to Bucharest is 1600 DIN.

SEA

A ferry service operates between Bar and Italy. (See the Bar section later in this chapter).

DEPARTURE TAX

The airport departure tax on international flights is 80 DIN.

Getting Around

AIR

JAT domestic flights operate from Belgrade to Tivat (Montenegro) four to six times daily, and to Podgorica (Montenegro) twice daily. JAT runs inexpensive buses between airports and city centres.

BUS

Buses are necessary for getting around in Kosovo and to Rožaje (Montenegro), the gateway to Kosovo. You'll also need buses for travelling along the Montenegrin coast between Ulcinj and Kotor and getting to Durmitor National Park. On long hauls, overnight buses can be exhausting but they do save time and money.

TRAIN

Jugoslovenske Železnice (JŽ) provides adequate railway services along the main line from Subotica to Novi Sad, Belgrade and Niš, and the highly scenic line down to the coast at Bar. There are four classes of train: *ekspresni* (express), *poslovni* (rapid), *brzi* (fast) and *putnicki* (slow) so make sure you have the right ticket for your train.

Inter-Rail passes are valid in Yugoslavia but Eurail passes are not. All train stations have left-luggage offices where you can dump your bag (passport required).

CAR & MOTORCYCLE

Given the overt police presence in Serbia, it's probably best to stick to public transport.

Serbia

BELGRADE (БЕОГРАД)
☎ 011 • pop 2 million (est. 2000)

The dominant role of Serbia (Srbija) in Yugoslavia was underlined by its control of two formerly autonomous provinces, Vojvodina and Kosovo, and the federal capital being Belgrade. Belgrade (Beograd) is strategically situated on the southern edge of the Carpathian basin where the Sava River joins the Danube. Destroyed and rebuilt 40 times in its 2300-year history, Belgrade has never quite managed to pick up all the pieces. It is nonetheless a lively, vibrant city with fine restaurants and street cafes, and a rhythm more like northern Europe than the Balkans.

History
The Celtic settlement of Singidunum was founded in the 3rd century BC on a bluff overlooking the confluence of the Sava and Danube rivers. The Romans arrived in the 1st century AD and stayed until the 5th century. The Slavic name Beograd (White City) first appeared in a papal letter in 878.

The Serbs made Belgrade their capital in 1403 after being pushed north by Turks who captured the city in 1521. In 1842 the city became the Serbian capital and in 1918 the capital of the Kingdom of Serbs, Croats and Slovenes, later Yugoslavia. The population is estimated to be approaching two million.

Orientation
The train station and adjacent bus station are on the south side of the city. From the train station, travel east along Milovana Milovanovića and up Balkanska to Terazije, the heart of modern Belgrade. Kneza Mihaila, Belgrade's lively pedestrian boulevard, runs north-west through Stari Grad (the old town) from Terazije to the citadel. The crowds are surprisingly chic, cafes well patronised and the atmosphere bustling and businesslike.

Information
Tourist Offices The friendly, helpful Tourist Organisation of Belgrade (☎/fax 635 343), open 9 am to 8 pm weekdays and 9 am to 4 pm Saturday, is in the underpass at Terazije on the corner of Kneza Mihaila. (Note the public toilets for future reference.) The airport tourist office is open 8 am to 8 pm daily.

Information on HI hostels is available from Ferijalni Savez Beograd (☎ 324 8550, fax 322 0762), Makedonska 22.

Money The JIK Banka is across the park from the train station; it's open 8 am to 8 pm weekdays and 8 am to 3 pm Saturday. The National Bank will change Deutschmarks at the unofficial rate.

American Express travellers cheques can only be changed at the Astral (formerly Karić) Banka on the corner of Maršala Birjuzova and Pop Lukina; at the airport branch (also open on weekends); and at the Komercijalna Banka on trg Nikole Pašića. Except for a few high class hotels and restaurants, credit cards are not accepted.

There are a few private exchange offices in Belgrade. One very central office is VODR; it's open weekdays from 9 am to 7 pm and Saturday from 9 am to 3 pm. Another is near Zeleni Venac market, 300m north of the train station. Private kiosks (except those with Politika or Duvan signs, which are state owned) will change money.

There are no ATM machines for foreign-issued cards in Belgrade. Come prepared with cash in Deutschmarks.

Post & Communications The main post office, at Takovska 2, holds poste-restante mail at window No 2 for one month.

You can make international telephone calls between 7 am and 10 pm daily. A more convenient telephone centre (open 24 hours a day) is in the central post office at Zmaj Jovina 17. The telephone centre in the large post office by the train station opens 7 am to midnight weekdays and 7 am to 10 pm weekends.

Belgrade is still introducing seven-digit phone numbers, so be aware of probable changes to numbers listed in this section.

Most post offices will send a fax (see the earlier Facts for the Visitor section for prices).

Email & Internet Access Café Sezam (☎ 322 7231, ⓔ info@sezampro.yu), Skadarska 40c, is open 10 am to 11 pm. Five minutes away there's another on the ground floor of the Bioskop Doma Omladine cinema on the corner of Makedonska and Moše Pijade.

BELGRADE

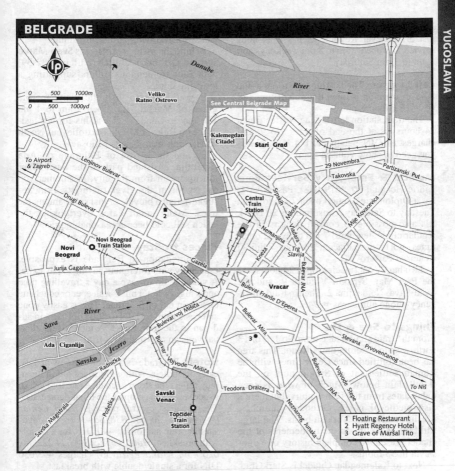

1 Floating Restaurant
2 Hyatt Regency Hotel
3 Grave of Maršal Tito

Travel Agencies Putnik Travel Agency
(☎ 330 669, fax 334 505), Terazije 27, offers
a wide range of services both domestically
and internationally. BS Tours (☎ 3619 616),
Gavril Principa 46, also runs buses to Croatia.

Basturist (office with the JAT sign in the
window between the bus and train stations),
Turist Biro Lasta (☎ 641 251, fax 642 473)
and the adjacent Putnik office on Milovana
Milovanovića all sell tickets for international
buses (see Getting There & Away earlier in
this chapter for fares).

Beograd Tours (☎ 641 258, fax 687 447),
Milovana Milovanovića 5, has reliable train

information and tickets at train station prices
but without the crowds.

Bookshops A good place to buy your
magazines and newspapers is the Plato
Bookshop, Vasina 17. The International
Press Service Bookshop in the basement of
Bilet Servis in the centre of Trg Republike is
another option.

Libraries The City Library is at the Kalemegdan end of Kneza Mihaila. Here you can
do some photocopying or have a coffee or a
beer in the snack bar.

Laundry The dry cleaners at Resavska 6, just off Bulevar Revolucije, has a 24-hour service. It's open 7 am to 8 pm weekdays and 8 am to 3 pm Saturday.

Left Luggage The left-luggage room at the BAS bus station is open 6 am to 10 pm and costs 15 DIN per piece.

The train station left-luggage office (open 24 hours) is at the end of track No 9, and charges 10 DIN per piece. For both places you need to show your passport.

Medical & Emergency Services Boris Kidrič Hospital (☎ 3619 088), Pasterova 1, has a Diplomatic Section open 7 am to 1 pm Tuesday to Saturday (consultations 20 DIN). It's also possible to consult doctors in the regular clinic here until 7 pm daily. At other times, go to the adjacent 24-hour Klinički Centar at Pasterova 2.

Two handy pharmacies, open 24 hours, are the Prvi Maj, Srpskih Vladara 9; and the Sveti Sava, Nemanjina 2. The first-aid emergency phone number is ☎ 94.

Things to See & Do
From the train station take tram No 1, 2 or 13 north-west to **Kalemegdan Citadel**. This area has been fortified since Celtic times with the Roman settlement of Singidunum on the flood plain below. Much of what is seen today dates from the 17th century, but there's also medieval gates, Orthodox churches, Muslim tombs and Turkish baths. The large **Military Museum** on the battlements of the citadel presents a complete history of Yugoslavia in 53 rooms.

Next to Kalemegdan Citadel is Stari Grad, the oldest part of Belgrade. The best museums are here, especially the **National Museum** on Trg Republike, with archaeological exhibits and a good collection of European art. A few blocks away at Studentski trg 13 is the **Ethnographical Museum** with an excellent collection of Serbian costumes and folk art. Detailed explanations are provided in English. Nearby at Cara Uroša 20 is the **Gallery of Frescoes** with full-size replicas of paintings from remote churches in Serbia and Macedonia. Belgrade's most memorable museum is the **Palace of Princess Ljubice** on the corner of Kneza Svetozara Markovića and Kralja Petra, a Balkan-style palace (1831) with period furnishings.

Behind the main post office is **Sveti Marko Serbian Orthodox Church** (built in 1932-39) with four tremendous pillars supporting a towering dome.

If you'd like to visit the white marble **grave of Maršal Tito** (open 9 am to 4 pm Tuesday to Sunday), it's at his former residence on Bulevar Mira; take trolleybus No 40 or 41 south from Kneza Miloša 64.

Escape the bustle of Belgrade on **Ada Ciganlija**, an island park in the Sava River just upstream from the city. In summer you can swim in the river (naturists 1km upstream), rent a bicycle or just stroll among the trees. Many small cafes overlooking the beach sell cold beer at reasonable prices.

Places to Stay
Accommodation in Belgrade is expensive, especially with foreigners having to pay extra. A valuable tip to save a day's travelling time and a night's hotel bill is a sleeper or couchette on a train out of Belgrade. This is easily done and costs from 80 DIN to 560 DIN extra in addition to the train ticket. A more tiring alternative is an overnight bus trip.

Hotels Belgrade is full of state-owned B-category hotels. Although prices are in dinar, they reflect the street exchange rate for DM, so expect prices to go up as the dinar depreciates. The cheapest central place is *Hotel Centar* (☎ 644 055, fax 657 838, Savski trg 7), opposite the train station, at 440 DIN for a double with breakfast. *Hotel Toplice* (☎ 634 222, fax 626 459, Kralja Petra 56) charges 443/636 DIN for a single/double with breakfast.

Hotel Beograd (☎ 645 199, fax 643 746, Nemanjina 6), visible from the train station, has time-worn rooms for 458/716 DIN including breakfast. *Hotel Astorija* (☎ 645 422, fax 686 437, Milovana Milovanovića 1) has rooms with breakfast for 520/790 DIN.

Balkan Hotel (☎ 687 466, fax 687 543), on the corner of Terazije and Prizrenska, is very central and fine if you want to pay around US$50/65 for a single/double for that extra bit of comfort. If you want to go overboard, the *Hyatt Regency* (☎ 311 1234) in dull Novi Beograd will charge you US$220 for the privilege of sleeping there.

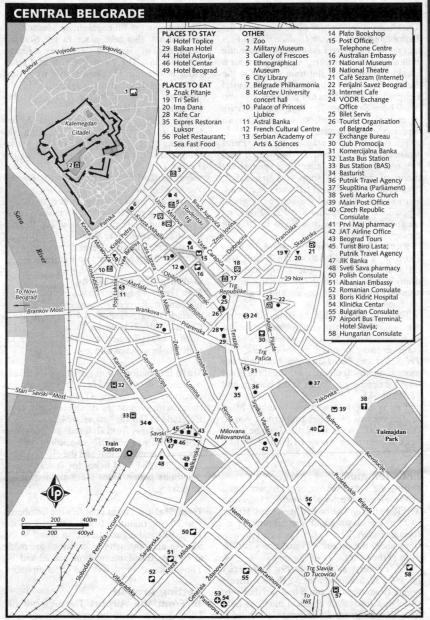

CENTRAL BELGRADE

PLACES TO STAY
4 Hotel Toplice
29 Balkan Hotel
44 Hotel Astorija
46 Hotel Centar
49 Hotel Beograd

PLACES TO EAT
9 Znak Pitanje
19 Tri Šeširi
20 Ima Dana
28 Kafe Car
35 Expres Restoran Luksor
56 Polet Restaurant; Sea Fast Food

OTHER
1 Zoo
2 Military Museum
3 Gallery of Frescoes
5 Ethnographical Museum
6 City Library
7 Belgrade Philharmonia
8 Kolarčev University concert hall
10 Palace of Princess Ljubice
11 Astral Banka
12 French Cultural Centre
13 Serbian Academy of Arts & Sciences

14 Plato Bookshop
15 Post Office; Telephone Centre
16 Australian Embassy
17 National Museum
18 National Theatre
21 Café Sezam (Internet)
22 Ferijalni Savez Beograd
23 Internet Cafe
24 VODR Exchange Office
25 Bilet Servis
26 Tourist Organisation of Belgrade
27 Exchange Bureau
30 Club Promocija
31 Komercijalna Banka
32 Lasta Bus Station
33 Bus Station (BAS)
34 Basturist
36 Putnik Travel Agency
37 Skupština (Parliament)
38 Sveti Marko Church
39 Main Post Office
40 Czech Republic Consulate
41 Prvi Maj pharmacy
42 JAT Airline Office
43 Beograd Tours
45 Turist Biro Lasta; Putnik Travel Agency
47 JIK Banka
48 Sveti Sava pharmacy
50 Polish Consulate
51 Albanian Embassy
52 Romanian Consulate
53 Boris Kidrič Hospital
54 Klinička Centar
55 Bulgarian Consulate
57 Airport Bus Terminal; Hotel Slavija;
58 Hungarian Consulate

Places to Eat

The cheapest self-service place in town is the *Expres Restoran Luksor (Balkanska 7)*. Farther up the street, the *Leskovac* sells authentic Balkan-style hamburgers. A great place for a breakfast burek near the train station is the *Burek i Pecivo (Nemanjina 5)*, near the Hotel Beograd. It's open 5 am to 1 pm weekdays and 5 to 11 am Saturday. The *Kafe Car (Terazije 4)* near the tourist office is perfect for an espresso and a croissant.

For inexpensive seafood try the *Polet Restaurant (Njegoševa 1)*. Between 1 and 6 pm on weekdays, there's a special set menu of spicy fish soup *(čorba)*, salad, bread and a main dish of fish and vegetables. Portions are large and the service is good. Opposite you'll find the *Sea Fast Food*, an inexpensive place with a good reputation among locals.

Znak Pitanje (Question Mark; Kralja Petra 6) is in an old Balkan inn serving traditional meat dishes, side salads and flat draught beer. Look for the question-mark sign above the door. Prices are mid-range and the food is very good.

For local colour visit the Bohemian quarter along the atmospheric cobbled street of Skadarska where folkloric restaurants often stage evening open-air performances. The *Tri Šeširi* and *Ima Dana* stand out, but for more economical dining there are three good outdoor hamburger stands at the bottom end of Skadarska.

Taking a walk across the Brankov Most bridge towards Novi Beograd brings you to floating restaurants along the Danube river bank opposite the wooded island of Veliko Ratno Ostrovo.

Entertainment

During the winter season, opera is performed at the elegant *National Theatre* (1869) on Trg Republike. The box office opens 10 am to 2 pm Tuesday to Sunday and 3 pm on performance days. The Yugoslavs aren't pretentious about the theatre – casual dress is OK, even at the opera.

For concerts at the *Kolarčev University* (☎ 630 550, Studentski trg 5), the box office opens 10 am to noon and 6 to 8 pm daily. In October a festival of classical music is held here. The *Belgrade Philharmonia* is hidden at the end of the passageway at Studentski trg 11, opposite the Ethnographical Museum.

Concerts also take place in the *Serbian Academy of Arts & Sciences (Kneza Mihaila 35)*. The *French Cultural Centre (Kneza Mihaila 31)* often shows free films and videos (closed on weekends). In the evening throngs of street musicians play along Kneza Mihaila.

The Bilet Servis, Trg Republike 5, has tickets to many events and the English-speaking staff will happily search for something musical for you. Ask them about the *Teatar T (Bulevard Revolucije 77a)*, which stages musicals several times a week (closed Wednesday and Thursday).

Belgrade has a growing number of discos, though most people do their socialising in the many fashionable cafes around Trg Republike. *Club Promocija (Nušićeva 8)* is through a dark lane just off Terazije, and is open 11 pm to 5 am Monday to Saturday.

Getting There & Away

Bus The two bus stations have computerised ticketing with overnight buses to many places around Yugoslavia. Posted destinations are in Cyrillic only. It is easier to buy your ticket from a ticket agency and book well in advance to be assured of a good seat.

Train International trains on these routes are covered in the Getting There & Away section earlier in this chapter. Overnight domestic trains with couchettes or sleepers run from Belgrade to Bar (8½ hours, 524km).

Sleeper fares from Belgrade to Bar range from 80 DIN to 560 DIN depending on how many in a compartment and the class. Add to that a 200/284 DIN ticket for 2nd/1st class. All trains depart from the main station on Savski trg.

Train Station Ticket counters are numbered 1 to 26. International tickets are sold at Nos 11 and 12 and regular tickets at Nos 7 to 20. Sleeper and couchette reservations are made at 19 and 20 and information is at 23 and 24. Timetables are posted in the Latin alphabet.

Getting Around

To/From the Airport The JAT bus (30 DIN) departs from the street next to Hotel

Slavija, Trg Slavija (D Tucovića), roughly every hour. This bus also picks up from the main train station. Surčin airport is 18km west of the city. If you've got time at the airport visit the nearby Yugoslav Aviation Museum (closed Monday).

Public Transport Private buses have joined the state-owned buses, trams and trolleybuses and you can now pay your 3 DIN to the conductor on board.

Taxi Belgrade's taxis are in plentiful supply, a motley bunch of old and new vehicles all in different colours. Flag fall is 10 DIN. A trip around the centre of town should cost between 50 DIN and 60 DIN. Check that the taxi meter is running. If not, point it out to the driver.

VOJVODINA (ВОЈВОДИНА)

Vojvodina (21,506 sq km) was an autonomous province until annexed by Serbia in 1990. Slavs settled here in the 6th century, Hungarians in the 10th century and Serbs in 1389 following their defeat by the Turks. The region was under Turkish rule from the 16th century until the Habsburgs cleared them out in the late 17th century. Again, it became a refuge for Serbs leaving the Turkish-controlled lands farther south. The region remained a part of Hungary until 1918. Today Serbs make up most of the population with Hungarians at about 25%.

This low-lying land of many rivers merges imperceptibly into the Great Hungarian Plain and Romania's Banat. Numerous canals crisscross this fertile plain that provides much of Yugoslavia's wheat, corn and crude oil.

Novi Sad (Нови Сад)
☎ 021 • pop 250,000 (est. 2000)

Novi Sad, capital of Vojvodina, is a friendly, modern city situated at a strategic bend of the Danube. The city developed in the 18th century when a powerful fortress was constructed on a hill-top overlooking the river to hold the area for the Habsburgs.

Novi Sad's attractions are simply wandering the pedestrian streets with their smart boutiques and outdoor cafes, and visiting the Petrovaradin Citadel.

Orientation & Information The adjacent train and bus stations are at the end of Bulevar Oslobođenja, on the north-west side of the city centre. There is a tourist agency by the train station.

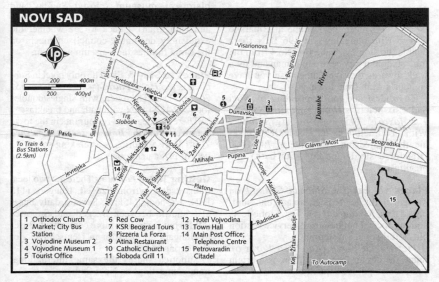

NOVI SAD

1 Orthodox Church	6 Red Cow	12 Hotel Vojvodina
2 Market; City Bus Station	7 KSR Beograd Tours	13 Town Hall
3 Vojvodine Museum 2	8 Pizzeria La Forza	14 Main Post Office; Telephone Centre
4 Vojvodine Museum 1	9 Atina Restaurant	15 Petrovaradin Citadel
5 Tourist Office	10 Catholic Church	
	11 Sloboda Grill 11	

It's a 20-minute walk from the train station to the city centre, otherwise catch bus No 4 from the station to Bulevar Mihajla Pupina. Then ask directions to the tourist office at Dunavska 27 in a quaint old part of town. It has brochures and maps of Novi Sad.

The telephone centre next to the main post office is open 24 hours.

It's easier to buy domestic and international train tickets from KSR Beograd Tours on Svetozara Miletića than at the train station.

Things to See There are two **museums** (at Dunavska 35 and 39) that are part of the **Muzej Vojvodine**. They have interesting exhibits on Vojvodina and are open 9 am to 7 pm Tuesday to Saturday and 9 am to 2 pm on Sunday. Entry is 3 DIN.

Walk across the old bridge to majestic **Petrovaradin Citadel** (built 1699-1780), the 'Gibraltar of the Danube', designed by French architect Vauban. Stairs beside the large church in the lower town lead up to the fortress. The citadel contains two small museums (closed Monday), but the chief pleasure is simply to walk along the walls and enjoy the splendid view. The vista also includes the damage that NATO bombing did to the Danube bridges.

Places to Stay There's a large *autocamp* (☎ 368 400) near the Danube at Ribarsko Ostrvo with bungalows at 496 DIN for a double (no singles). Take Bus No 4 from the train station or city centre to Liman and then walk towards the river, otherwise you have an hour's walk from town.

The oldest and most appealing of Novi Sad's six hotels is *Hotel Vojvodina* (☎ 622 122, fax 615 445) right on Trg Slobode. With an attractive pastel facade, it's conveniently located but expensive at 700/1000 DIN for a single/double (with bath) and breakfast.

Places to Eat The *Sloboda Grill 11* on Modene in the centre is cheap and unassuming. *Atina Restaurant* on Trg Slobode is nothing special but has a self-service section plus a full-service restaurant.

Pizzeria La Forza (*Katolička Porta 6*), round the corner from the Atina, is a bright and cheery spot for a quick bite.

Entertainment The *Red Cow* Irish pub off Zmaj Jovina is a trendy spot for Guinness (cans only) and for an evening out.

Getting There & Away Novi Sad is on the railway line from Belgrade and is served by international and national trains. See the Getting There & Away section earlier in the Yugoslavia section.

Subotica (Суботица)
☎ 024 • pop 160,000 (est. 2000)

At 10km from the border at Kelebija, Subotica is a useful transit point to/from Szeged (Hungary). The train station is just a short walk from the centre of town.

The left-luggage office at the train station is open 24 hours (passport required and 10 DIN per item).

Vojvođanska Banka has a currency exchange office in the old town hall (open 7.30 am to 7 pm weekdays and 7.30 am to 1 pm Saturday). Other exchange offices are at the train station and at the Hotel Patria.

Putnik (☎ 525 400), Borisa Kidriča 4, is helpful with information and sells train tickets.

Things to See The imposing Art Nouveau **town hall** (1910) contains an excellent **historical museum** (closed Sunday and Monday) on the 1st floor (captions in Serbian and Hungarian). Check to see whether the exquisitely decorated council chambers on the same floor as the museum are open.

Places to Stay & Eat The only hotel in Subotica is the *Hotel Patria* (☎ 554 500, fax 551 762) on Đure Đakovića, with singles/doubles for 1212/1824 DIN with bath and breakfast.

There is a dearth of restaurants in the town centre area but the *Boss Pizzeria* (*Engelsova 7*) off Borisa Kidriča is a relaxing spot for a decent pizza and a beer.

Getting There & Away There are two local trains a day to/from Szeged, Hungary (115 DIN, 1¾ hours, 45km). Several daily buses also shuttle between Szeged and Subotica (DM5) but the train is more convenient. Buses to Hungary are paid for in Deutschmarks or Hungarian forints.

Subotica shares the same international train connections as Novi Sad.

Montenegro
(Црна Гора)

The 13,812-sq-km Republic of Montenegro (Crna Gora) has impressive bare limestone mountains plummeting down to an Adriatic coastline. This is a very popular holiday spot with the rest of Yugoslavia, and July and August are the high season.

North of Podgorica, both railway and road run through the Morača Canyon giving fantastic views of canyon walls and clear emerald waters, while 40km west of Mojkovac is the 1.3km deep Tara Canyon. Other striking features are the winding Bay of Kotor and the vast Lake Skadar shared with Albania. Of historical interest are the old towns of Budva, Cetinje and Kotor.

History

Only tiny Montenegro kept its head above the Turkish tide which engulfed the Balkans for over four centuries from the 14th century. From 1482 Montenegro was ruled from Cetinje by *vladike* (bishops).

With the defeat of the Turks in 1878, Montenegrin independence was assured and later recognised by the Congress of Berlin. Nicola I Petrović, Montenegro's ruler, declared himself king in 1910 but was evicted by the Austrians in 1916; following WWI Montenegro was incorporated into Serbia. During WWII Montenegrins fought valiantly in Tito's partisan army and after the war the region was rewarded with republic status within Yugoslavia.

Montenegro has been in the Yugoslav federation through its several incarnations. At the time of writing, only it and Serbia remained. Some Montenegrins wish for independence. Whether that happens without bloodshed will be a test of Montenegrin democracy and the skills of its leaders.

Getting There & Away

You can enter Montenegro by road from Croatia, Serbia and Kosovo. Entry is not recommended from northern Albania due to the banditry in that area. A main rail line runs from Belgrade to Bar where ferries connect with Italy and shortly Corfu.

PODGORICA
☎ 081 • pop 159,000 (est. 2000)

Podgorica is a place to arrive in, do your business and leave. There's little of interest to see.

The bus and train station are adjacent in the east of the town. The hub of the town centres around Slobode to the west.

Information

The Gorbis Travel Service (☎/fax 230 624, Ⓔ gorbis@cg.yu), Slobode 47, and MCM Travel (☎/fax 613 088, Ⓔ McmBravo@cg.yu), Balšićeva 4, are helpful with queries. You'll find an Internet cafe at Bokeška 20 called Internet cg.

Places to Stay & Eat

Plan your travel so that you don't have to stay overnight as hotels are expensive. You should be able to find a *private room* with the aid of a taxi driver, but make sure you check prices beforehand.

There are a number of cheap eating places around the bus and train stations, and some pleasant cafes in Bokeška.

Getting There & Away

There are five buses to Belgrade (DM15), many to Cetinje and four to Žabljak (Durmitor National Park). If you're in a hurry you can fly to Belgrade for DM43 or take the scenic train route for DM8. There are 12 trains to Bar. See the Bar Getting There & Away section for Belgrade train details.

BAR (БАР)
☎ 085

Backed by a barren coastal range, Bar is a would-be modern city whose architects seemed to have graduated from the socialist cement school of thought. However, it's a strategically important city as it's Yugoslavia's only port.

Bar is a convenient transport centre and if you find a cheap private room it makes a good base for day trips to Ulcinj, Cetinje, Kotor and Budva.

Orientation

The ferry terminal in Bar is only a few hundred metres from the centre of town, but the bus and train stations are about 2km southeast of the centre.

Information

Tourist information is very limited and your best bet is to try Montenegro Tourist by the ferry terminal. Ask for directions to the Internet cafe, which is opposite the Lunar Café.

Left-luggage at the train station is open 7 am to 8 pm and at the bus station 6 am to 10 pm.

Places to Stay & Eat

Visitors with time or their own transport will be able to choose from a whole range of places with 'sobe', 'zimmer' or 'private room' signs all along the coast. Putnik Turist Biro (☎/fax 313 621) has *private rooms* for DM10/20 for a single/double, but its opening hours are limited. Adria Tours (☎ 313 621), a couple of kilometres north-west at Šušanj, has rooms for DM8/16.

Hotel Topolica (☎ 311 244, fax 312 731, ℮ htpkorali@cg.yu), a four-storey socialist relic, is the only hotel in town. With rooms for DM33/50 in its B grade section, it's the best place if you have money or are desperate.

Places to eat are limited with drinks-only cafes and bars outnumbering restaurants. *Pizzeria Napoletana* just up the street from the ferry terminal is reasonable and if you're at the train station, the *Grill Holiday* is convenient for a tasty hamburger while waiting for a bus or train.

Getting There & Away

Four trains a day travel to/from Belgrade (DM9.5, nine hours, 524km). At DM13, first class is a comfier option. The couchette supplement is DM2, making this cheap accommodation plus transport.

There are frequent buses to all destinations along the coast.

Depending on the season there are a number of ferries each week to Bari and Ancona in Italy, and a service to Corfu. Contact Martina Ltd (☎ 311 181, fax 312 330, ℮ martina@cg.yu) for details. In midsummer, transport to/from Bar is very crowded as all of Serbia heads for the beach.

ULCINJ (УЛЦИЊ)
☎ 085

Founded by the Greeks, Ulcinj gained notoriety as a base for North African pirates between 1571 and 1878. There was even a market for slaves from whom the few resident black families are descended. The Turks held Bar and Ulcinj for over 300 years.

Orientation

Buses from Bar stop about 2km from Mala Plaža, the small beach below the old town. Walk into town by turning right onto 26 Novembar at the first major junction. Along the route you'll find many buildings and travel agencies with 'sobe' and 'zimmer' signs where you can rent a room. Velika Plaža (Great Beach), Ulcinj's famous 12km stretch of unbroken sand, begins about 5km southeast of town (take the bus to Ada).

Information

Any of the travel agencies can help you with information.

Things to See

The ancient **ramparts** of old Ulcinj overlook the sea, but most of the buildings inside were shattered by earthquakes in 1979 and later reconstructed. The **museum** (closed Monday) is by the upper gate. You can walk among the houses and along the wall for the view.

Places to Stay

Camping There are two camping grounds on the Ada road after Milena and adjacent to Velika Plaža. The first is called *Tomi*, while the second *autocamp* 100m on is marked by a road sign showing a tent. These camp sites may only be open in the season from July to August. About 15km farther, on Ada Island is *Camping Ada Bojana FKK*, a nudist camping ground accessible by bus (guests only).

Private Rooms Travel Agencies seem to come and go but try the Montenegro Travel Agency (☎/fax 51 522), Bratstva Jedinstva, a few hundred metres from the bus stop. This agency has rooms from DM4/8 for a single/double depending on the class of accommodation and time of year.

If you continue into town along 26 Novembar, you'll pass the Real Estate Tourist Agency (☎ 51 081, fax 51 509, ℮ RGANO@cg.yu), which has apartments available with bedrooms, bathroom and kitchen. For one or two people the cost is DM48 to DM58 depending on the season. For six people the cost is DM102 to DM123.

Hotels The *Albatros* (☎ *51 188, fax 81 910),* is a pleasant modern hotel five minutes' walk uphill from Mala Plaža. Singles costing DM35 to DM48, and doubles from DM46 to DM125 (depending on season) have private bathrooms, and the price includes full board.

Places to Eat
There are some chic eating places like the *Restaurant Teuta* in the old town if your budget can stand it. There are also numerous inexpensive restaurants around town offering *ćevapčići*. For seafood try the *Amfora* at the end of 26 Novembar at the Mala Plaža.

Getting There & Away
Buses to/from Bar (DM2, 26km) run every couple of hours.

BUDVA (БУДВА)
☎ 086
Budva is Yugoslavia's top beach resort. A series of fine beaches punctuate the coastline all the way to Sveti Stefan with the high coastal mountains forming a magnificent backdrop. Although Bar has more transport options as a base, Budva is more beautiful and worth the extra effort and expense.

Orientation & Information
The modern bus station is about 1km from the old town. The main square is at the end of Mediteranska by the harbour and old town. There's no left-luggage office at Budva bus station.

Things to See
Budva's big tourist-puller is its old **walled town**. Levelled by two earthquakes in 1979, it has since been completely rebuilt as a tourist attraction. It's so picturesque it seems almost contrived. Budva's main beach is pebbly and average. Better is **Mogren Beach**, reached by following a coastal path northwards for 500m from the Grand Hotel Avala.

About 5km south-east of Budva is the former village of **Sveti Stefan**, an island now linked to the mainland and a luxury hotel complex. You will be charged admission during the summer months so settle for the long-range picture-postcard view and keep your money.

Places to Stay
Camping If you have a tent, try *Autocamp Avala* (☎ *51 205)* at Boreti, 2km on the road to Bar. It's crowded with caravans, but at least it's near the beach. No bungalows are available but the manager may help you find a private room nearby. Avala is open from June to September.

Private Rooms Helpful Emona Globtour (☎ 51 020, fax 52 827, @ mpalic@cg.yu), Mediteranska 23, can arrange private rooms, or just look out for signs that say sobe, zimmer or rooms.

Hotels The most convenient option is the modern *Hotel Mogren* (☎ *51 780, fax 51 750)* just outside the north gate of the old town. Rates are a very pricey DM80/130 for singles/doubles in July and August; out of season prices are DM60/90.

The pleasant *Hotel Mediteran* (☎ *51 423, fax 51 634),* about 2km south along the coast at Bečići has rooms for DM26/49 to DM42/66 depending on the season.

Places to Eat
For a cheap feed without the frills, *Restoran Centar* is upstairs above the supermarket (by the vegetable market) just inland from the post office. At the bus station there is a reasonable *restaurant* if you are in transit or waiting for a bus.

Budva has no shortage of expensive bars and restaurants. Locals go for places with fish dishes at quite affordable prices like the *Restaurant Jadran* about 800m along the waterfront from the old town.

Getting There & Away
There are 24 buses daily to Podgorica (74km) via Cetinje (31km), 13 to Kotor and seven a day to Bar (38km). There are also eight buses daily to Belgrade and one to Žabljak.

If coming by train from Belgrade, get off at Podgorica and catch a bus. When returning, however, it's probably best to take the bus to Bar and catch the Belgrade train there, since many people board at Podgorica.

If you fly to Tivat on the coast, a JAT bus (DM2) will take you to their Budva office at the end of Mediteranska.

KOTOR
☎ 082

Kotor is something of a secret. Not only is the town at the head of southern Europe's deepest fjord, but it also has a walled medieval city that is UNESCO listed.

There are frequent buses from Budva but it's enjoyable to stay within the old town. The Meridian Travel Agency (☎ 11 188, fax 11 226, e travel@cg.yu) can arrange private rooms from DM10/20 for a single/double in the low season and DM15/30 in the high season.

CETINJE (ЦЕТИЊЕ)
☎ 086

Cetinje, perched on a high plateau above Budva, is the old capital of Montenegro, subject of songs and epic poems. Much remains of old Cetinje, from museums to palaces, mansions and monasteries. At the turn of the 20th century all the large states of Europe had embassies here. Short hikes can be made in the hills behind Cetinje Monastery.

Orientation & Information
The bus station is 500m from the main square, Balšića Pazar. From the station turn left and then right and you will find it easily. There is a big wall map in the square to help you get oriented.

Things to See
The most imposing building in Cetinje is the State Museum, the former palace (1871) of Nicola I Petrović, the last king. Looted during WWII, only a few furnishings remain but the many portraits and period weapons give a representative picture of the times.

Adjacent is the 1832 residence of the prince-bishop Petar II Petrović Njegoš. This building, now a museum, is also known as Biljarda Hall because of the billiard table installed in 1840. The Hall houses a fascinating relief map of Montenegro created by the Austrians in 1917 for tactical planning purposes. Ask an attendant for access.

Cetinje Monastery, founded in 1484 but rebuilt in 1785, contains a copy of the Oktoih or Octoechos (Book of the Eight Voices),

printed near here in 1494 – it's one of the oldest collections of liturgical songs in a Slavic language.

Twenty kilometres away on the summit of Mt Lovčen (1749m), the 'Black Mountain' which gave Montenegro its Italian name, is the mausoleum of Petar II Petrović Njegoš, a revered poet as well as ruler. Access to Lovčen is by taxi and then 461 steps to the mausoleum, with its sweeping view of the Bay of Kotor, mountains, the coast and on a clear morning, Italy.

Places to Stay & Eat
For a *private room* ask at Intours (☎ 31 157), next to the post office, or go to Petar Martinović, a block away at Bajova Pivljanina 50. He charges DM10 per person a night, which doesn't include breakfast.

Otherwise the only hotel is the *Grand Hotel* (☎ 31 104, fax 31 213), a modern overrated 'five-star'. Singles/doubles are DM80/170 with bath and breakfast. It's a five-minute walk from the centre.

There is not a glut of eating places in Cetinje. The *Restoran Korzo* next to the post office and the *Spoleto* pizzeria farther down from the post office have reasonable food.

Getting There & Away
There are many buses between Cetinje and Podgorica (45km) and to Budva (31km). Cetinje can be a day trip from Bar by catching an early train to Podgorica and then a bus to Cetinje. Then an afternoon bus to Budva will give you time to wander around before taking a late bus back to Bar.

DURMITOR NATIONAL PARK
☎ 0872

Durmitor National Park is a popular hiking and mountaineering area just west of Žabljak, a ski resort that's also the highest town in Yugoslavia (1450m).

Some 18 mountain lakes dot the slopes of the Durmitor Range; you can walk around the largest, Crno jezero (Black Lake), 3km from Žabljak, in an hour or two and swim in its waters in summer. The rounded mass of Međed (2287m) rises directly behind the lake surrounded by a backdrop of other peaks, including Savin kuk (2313m) which can be climbed in eight hours there and back.

The national park office next to Hotel Durmitor sells good maps of the park. Be prepared as the weather is very changeable, even in summer.

Durmitor's claim to fame is the 1.3km-deep **Tara Canyon** that cuts dramatically into the mountain slopes and plateau for about 80km. A good place to see the canyon is from a rock promontory at Ćurevac, a 17km round-trip hike from Žabljak, or a DM7 taxi ride.

White-Water Rafting

There are rafting trips down the steep forested Tara Gorge and over countless foaming rapids. These begin at Splavište near the Đurđevića Tara bridge.

For information on white-water rafting on the Tara River, contact Ski Centar Durmitor (☎ 61 144, fax 61 579) in Žabljak or the same organisation in Podgorica (☎/fax 81 242 387). One and two-day raft trips depart from Žabljak every Tuesday and Friday from June to September.

Places to Stay

The Sveti Đorđije (☎/fax 61 367), just opposite the turn-off to Hotel Jezera, is a tourist agency run by Milanka who speaks English. She can arrange private rooms for DM10 a person, sharing bathrooms. The log cabin tourist bureau in the centre of Žabljak is run by her husband, the local artist, who doesn't speak English.

Žabljak has four hotels owned by Montenegroturist. *Planinka* (☎ 61 304) and *Jezera* (☎ 61 144, fax 61 579) are modern ski hotels charging DM72/120 for a single/double with half-board in summer. *Hotel Žabljak* (☎ 88 300), right in the centre of town, also offers rooms with breakfast for DM49 per person.

The cheapest is the shabby four-storey wooden *Hotel Durmitor* (☎ 61 278) past Hotel Jezera at the entrance to the national park, a 15-minute walk from town. Singles/doubles with shared bath are DM24/36 with half-board. The good news is that some rooms face the mountains: the bad news is that there's no hot water or showers.

On a hill-top five minutes' walk beyond the national park office is *Autocamp Ivan-do* which is little more than a fenced-off field. People around here rent *private rooms* at about DM10 per person but it's advisable to

bring your own sleeping bag or sheet. Set right in the middle of the forest, Ivan-do is a perfect base for hikers.

Places to Eat

The *Pizzeria*, about 200m down the road towards the bus station, is the only place apart from the hotels that serves meals.

Getting There & Away

From the North The easiest way is to take a bus from Belgrade to Pljevlja (334km) and then one of the two daily buses to Žabljak (57km). On the return journey, these buses leave for Pljevlja at 4.30 am and 5 pm, connecting for Mojkovac and Podgorica at Đurđevića Tara, where there's a spectacular bridge over the canyon.

From the South You can catch a direct bus from Budva or Podgorica which may involve changing buses at Đurđevića Tara. Catching the mid-morning train to Mojkovac from Bar (stopping Podgorica) involves many hours of waiting for connecting buses.

KOSOVO

Since June 1999, Kosovo has been administered as a UN-NATO protectorate. Before ethnic cleansing, some two million people occupied Kosovo's 10,887 sq km, making it a densely populated region with a high birth rate. Today it is a divided region with the remaining Serbs living in ghettos. The majority of the Albanian refugees have returned, but many Serbs have fled.

The Albanians adopted Islam after the Turkish conquest and today the region has a definite Muslim air, from food and dress to the ubiquitous mosques.

History

Following their defeat in 1389 by the Turks, the Serbs abandoned the region to the Albanians, descendants of the Illyrians, the original inhabitants.

When the Turks left in 1913 Serbia regained control. In the ensuing years half a million Albanians emigrated and Serb families were brought in to settle the vacated lands. During WWII, Kosovo was incorporated into

The Current Situation

As an emerging entity, Kosovo is in a state of flux. Divorced from the Yugoslav administrative machine, Kosovo under the United Nations Mission in Kosovo (UNMIK) is starting from scratch. The information in this section will change rapidly.

The railway is not operating and there's no postal system. The only functioning bank, the German Micro Enterprise Bank, has branches in Prishtina, Prizren and Peja. Bring sufficient cash in Deutschmarks, the new currency, for your stay.

In a process of 'Albanianisation', Serbian place names have been painted out on route signs, street names in Cyrillic have been removed, and generally Serbian names are no longer used. Many streets now have no names. In this section Albanian names are used with the Serbian ones (in brackets).

Despite the recent conflict there are no shortages of food or basic consumer goods, which are mostly imported.

Warning!

Despite the presence of KFOR troops in Kosovo there are still dangers. Be aware that there are many landmines and unexploded bombs left in this recent war zone and avoid any places like Mitrovica where there are Albanian-Serb tensions. The main towns of Prishtina, Peja and Prizren and the roads between are relatively safe but it is essential to check with KFOR or the UN administration about travelling elsewhere and especially into the countryside.

Italian-controlled Albania, and in October 1944 the region was liberated by Albanian communist partisans.

Tito wanted Albania united with Kosovo in the new Yugoslavia. This never happened and two decades of pernicious neglect ensued until an autonomous province was created in 1974 and economic aid increased. Little changed, however, and the standard of living in Kosovo remained a quarter of the Yugoslav average. In 1981 demonstrations calling for full republic status were put down by military force, resulting in 300 deaths and the imprisonment of 700 Albanians.

State of Emergency Trouble began anew in November 1988 with demonstrations against the sacking of local officials and president Azem Vllasi. Further unrest and a coal miners' strike in February 1989 led to the suspension of Kosovo's autonomy and a state of emergency. Serious rioting followed and 24 unarmed Albanian civilians were shot dead.

On 5 July 1990 the Serbian parliament cancelled Kosovo's autonomy, broadcasts in Albanian ceased, and the only Albanian-language newspaper was banned. Some 115,000 Albanians lost their jobs and were replaced by loyalist Serbs. Despite Serbian opposition, a referendum with a 90% turnout produced a 98% vote for independence.

The Spectre of War The Kosovo Liberation Army (KLA) was formed in 1997 out of frustrated attempts to negotiate autonomy. About 40,000 Yugoslav troops and police were stationed in Kosovo to protect Serbia's 'historic right' to Kosovo. Early in 1998 the Yugoslav army attacked the village of Deçani (Dečani) near Peja. Officially, 40 people were killed, including women and children, but the true number is unknown. Condemned widely by most international governments, the Milošević regime continued the clampdown, attracting a US-led arms embargo.

In March 1999, during talks in Paris between Serb and Kosovo representatives, a US-backed plan to return Kosovo's autonomy was rejected by Serbia. Stepping up their attacks on the KLA, they moved to empty the country of its Albanian population.

Nearly 850,000 Albanian Kosovars fled into Albania and Macedonia. Serbia ignored demands to desist and NATO unleashed a bombing campaign on 24 March 1999 in preference to a politically unpalatable invasion. It looked as if Milošević would stand his ground but on 2 June he acquiesced to a UN settlement. Ten days later Serb forces withdrew and the Kosovo Force (KFOR), comprising of NATO and Russian forces, took over.

Peace has not been easy. KFOR had to persuade the KLA to demilitarise and the Serb population to return. Some 230,000 Serbs and Roma had fled with the departing Serb forces. Continuing revenge attacks on the remaining Serbs have made them isolated communities protected by KFOR. Many Serb properties have been destroyed and Orthodox churches and monasteries are guarded to prevent their destruction.

Getting There & Away

Several direct buses travel from Skopje in Macedonia to Prishtina (DM10) and Prizren (DM15) daily. Alternatively, a taxi to the border costs DM30 and from there to Prizren or Prishtina costs DM40, but you'll need to bargain hard.

There are direct buses from Prishtina and Prizren to major cities such as Istanbul, Sofia, Rome and Paris. From Montenegro or Serbia you can catch a bus stopping at Rožaje. From there a minibus (DM10) or taxi (DM50) hanging around the bus station can take you direct to Peja.

If you have to stay at Rožaje there's the reportedly dreadful *Rožaje Hotel* (☎ 0871-71 335) that charges DM50 for a single room with breakfast.

Getting Around

There are many buses that link Prizren, Prishtina and Peja with minibuses travelling to smaller towns. Fares are cheap and the service good.

PRISHTINA (PRIŠTINA)

☎ 038

The capital has all the beauty and grace that Soviet-style excesses in concrete could bestow. Prishtina has little to offer and can be considered a jumping-off point to the more interesting towns of Peja and Prizren.

Orientation

Central Prishtina focuses on Mother Theresa and Ramiz Sadiku Sts that run in a general south to north direction converging near the National Theatre at the northern end. The bus station is in the south-western outskirts of Prishtina, off Kral Petri St on the Peja road. The airport is 17km to the south-west.

Maps of Prishtina can sometimes be difficult to find but ask at kiosks or bookshops along Mother Theresa.

Information

Tourist Offices The Tourist Office just north of the Grand Hotel has minimal written information but staff can answer questions in English. Several travel agencies on the same street can be useful sources of information.

Money Unfortunately, there's nowhere to change money at the airport. The Micro Enterprise Bank, off Mother Theresa, cashes DM travellers cheques and can receive money transferred through Western Union. It's open 9 am to 4 pm Monday to Friday.

Post & Communications The telephone exchange is in the stylish coppered-roof building next to the National Theatre.

Email & Internet access The Internet@ Click! Café, open 8.30 am to midnight (DM6 per hour), is in a long arcade in the district of Dardania. Turn south from Kral Petri St under the clock on the archway that is the entrance to Dardania.

Things to See

The **Kosovo Museum** building has been appropriated by the EU, but the artefacts are crowded onto the 1st floor. Most of the best exhibits were removed to Belgrade but there are new items covering the KLA campaign – see the clothes of their gun runners. Behind are two mosques: **Sultan Fatih** (the larger) and **Jashar Pasha** with some nice decorative work.

Places to Stay

There are only four hotels in the city, with two more under construction. With the influx of foreign government agencies, rooms and prices are at a premium. The *Grand Hotel* (☎ 590 001, fax 521 833, Mother Theresa) charges DM150/220 for a single/double including breakfast. Farther north on Mother Theresa is the *Iliria* (☎ 24 042), the cheapest in town at DM70/140 including breakfast. The *Park Hotel* (☎ 526 946, Shar Pllanina St), overlooking the small and rather scruffy Central Park, charges DM150/220 including breakfast. Reception can direct you to a nearby *private room* costing DM50 (no breakfast). If you're desperate, you might just suffer the *Hotel Dea*, which charges DM154/200 including breakfast. It's in the eastern suburbs overlooking the power station and city rubbish dump.

Places to Eat

There are many places to eat along Mother Theresa and Ramiz Sadiku Sts. Cafes in side streets abound, selling burek and hamburgers for DM2 to DM3. Pasta and pizza cafes charge up to DM5. Breakfast at *Restaurant America (Mother Theresa St)*, under the trees on the pavement, is a pleasant experience first thing in the morning. Morning or afternoon coffee can be taken on the steps of the National Theatre. The *Pini (☎ 41 136, Kurrizi 42)* in Dardania is a favourite among locals.

Getting Around

Numbered Kombis (minibuses) roam the streets. Bus Nos 1 and 2 go down Kral Petri St, from where it's a short walk through a housing estate to the bus station. The fare is 50 pfennig.

There is no public bus to the airport. The cheapest way is a Kombi to Slatina and a taxi from there. There are occasional airline minibuses but ask at a travel agent for details. Radio Taxi Victory (☎ 044 111 222) charges DM20 to the airport.

PEJA (PEŽ)
☎ 039

Peja was badly damaged by departing Yugoslav forces and many picturesque buildings are rubble. Roads are bad because of neglect and heavy military traffic. Traffic volumes (all those NGO four-wheel drive vehicles) are too great for the narrow roads. Add to that the replacement of all (Serbian) street names with numbers and there's a sense of chaos in Peja. However, the backdrop is superb with 2000m-plus mountains towering over the town.

Orientation

Both road and railway from Prishtina run into the northern part of town. Striking south, and into town, is former Maršal Tito St which currently has no name. The bus station is at the intersection of these two routes.

Information

The UNMIK police station is on the former Maršal Tito St and is a useful source of information. The former Yugoslav-run travel agencies have left town and their replacements are still finding their feet – but give them a try.

Post & Communications Peja is blessed with several private telephone centres. Look for the big yellow 'Telefon' sign; there's even one in the bus station.

Email & Internet Access Between the bazaar and the (closed) Hotel Korzo is the Internet Caffe, open 8 am to 11 pm daily and charging DM10 per hour.

Things to See

Peja's mosques have been severely damaged and are locked awaiting restoration. However, the imposing dome of the 15th-century **Bajrakli Mosque** rising above the colourful **bazaar**, gives Peja an authentic Oriental air.

Two kilometres west is the **Patrijaršija Monastery**, seat of the Serbian Orthodox patriarchate. The monastery is closed to visitors but you may be able to wangle a pass from KFOR. If you do you'll be rewarded with three mid-13th-century churches with glorious medieval frescoes.

Two kilometres farther along is the start of the magnificent **Rugovo Gorge** which is an excellent hiking area. Although there should be no problem, check with KFOR before doing anything adventurous.

Another site needing KFOR's OK is Peja's most impressive **Visoki Dečani Monastery** (1335). It's 15km south, but accessible by frequent local buses and a 2km walk.

Places to Stay & Eat

With *Kamp Karagač*, *Hotel Park* and the *Hotel Korzo* closed at present, and the best in town, the *Metohija Hotel*, commandeered by the Italian KFOR command, the private *Hotel Dypon (☎/fax 31 593)* has got it made as the only hotel in town. Prices of DM100/170 for a single/double including breakfast show what you can do with a monopoly. Check whether any of the opposition have reopened before going to the Dypon.

There are plenty of cheap burek and hamburger joints near the bus station. For a little more, the *Zogza* restaurant opposite the market on the Prishtina road is a speciality grill.

PRIZREN

☎ 029

Prizren was once the medieval capital of 'Old Serbia' but the architectural influence is Turkish. Now that Serbian oppression has come to an end, the place seems like a party town as people throng the many bars and cafes along the river and in Shadrvan. Strengthening this impression is the large number of UN and NGO personnel and the fact that there are no alternative activities for the younger population.

Warning Prizren has a curfew, so be off the streets between 1 and 4 am.

Orientation

Most of the (Serbian) road names have been removed and until new ones have been conjured up there are very few street names. The town revolves around the river and Shadrvan, a cobblestoned plaza with a fountain in the middle. The bus station is on the north-west side of town. Crossing the river just west of the main bridge is a 'new' medieval bridge built to replace the old one destroyed by floods in 1979.

Information

Tourist Offices Try the Tourist Association of Prizren (☎ 32 843) for a city map. The office is behind the Turkish restaurant a few metres south-east of the main bridge.

Post & Communications The main post office, adjacent to the Theranda Hotel, is currently just a telephone centre. It's open 7 am to 9 pm Monday to Saturday.

Email & Internet Access UNMIK runs a free Internet centre behind the post office, open to visitors 8 am to 10 pm Monday to Saturday. Book in advance.

Things to See

The Orthodox **Church of Bogorodica Ljeviška** (1307) and **Sveti Georgi** (1856) are closed and protected by soldiers and barbed wire. You cannot enter, but it's worth a look at their current fortifications and a chat to the soldiers. **Sveti Spas** above the town is an observation post with barbed wire blocking access.

The **Sinan Pasha Mosque** (1561) beside the river dominates the centre and has a fine decorated high-dome ceiling. Up the road from the Theranda Hotel are the **Gazi Mehmed Pasha Baths** (1563), now being restored.

Places to Stay & Eat

Accommodation in Prizren is limited. The faded *Theranda Hotel* (☎ *22 292*), in the centre of town, charges DM70/90 for a single/double with private bath and breakfast.

Hotel Prizren (☎ *41 552, fax 43 107*), about a kilometre north-west of the centre, charges DM50/70 for rooms with bath and breakfast.

There is an abundance of cafes, bars and restaurants around the central area. Many have menus in German and English. Down by the 'new' medieval bridge is the restaurant *Holiday* that has excellent fish courses for between DM5 and DM10. Next door is the bar *Tomleys*, one of two discos in town. The other, *Red Bull*, is behind. A Turkish restaurant *Gani Cavdarbushi ve Sanat '94*, down a side street at the back of the Theranda Hotel, receives good reports from aid workers.

Appendix I – Climate Charts

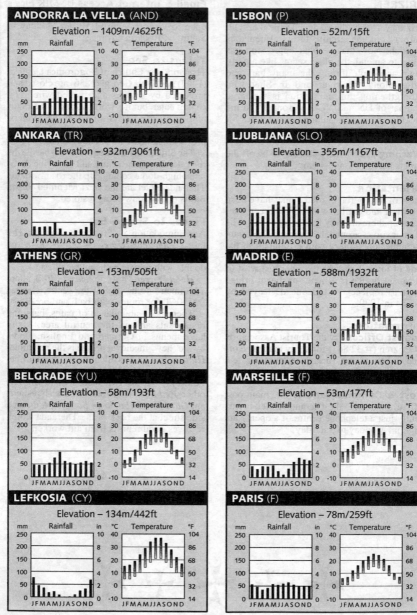

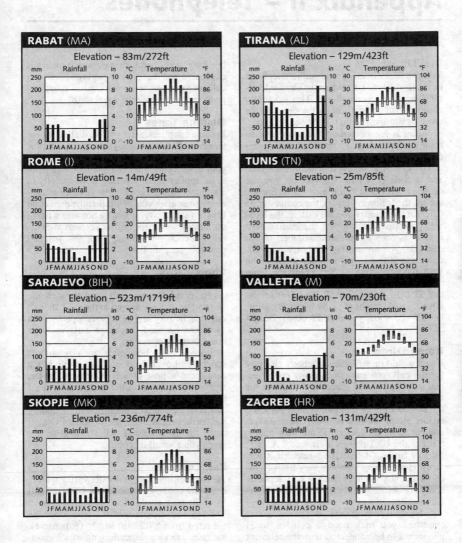

Appendix II – Telephones

Dial Direct

You can dial directly from public telephone boxes from almost anywhere in Europe to almost anywhere in the world. This is usually cheaper than going through the operator. In much of Europe, public telephones accepting phonecards are becoming the norm and in some countries coin-operated phones are difficult to find.

To call abroad simply dial the international access code (IAC) for the country you are calling from (most commonly 00 in Europe but see the following table), the country code (CC) for the country you are calling, the local area code (usually dropping the leading zero if there is one) and then the number. If, for example, you are in Italy (international access code 00) and want to make a call to the USA (country code 1), San Francisco (area code 212), number ☎ 123 4567, then you dial ☎ 00-1-212-123 4567. To call from the UK (00) to Australia (61), Sydney (02), number ☎ 123 4567, you dial ☎ 00-61-2-1234 5678.

Home Direct

If you would rather have somebody else pay for the call, you can, from many countries, dial directly to your home country operator and then reverse charges; you can also charge the call to a phone company credit card. To do this, simply dial the relevant 'home direct' number to be connected to your own operator. For the USA there's a choice of AT&T, MCI or Sprint Global One home direct services. Home direct numbers vary from country to country – check with your telephone company before you leave, or with the international operator in the country you're ringing from. From phone boxes in some countries you may need a coin or local phonecard to be connected with the relevant home direct operator.

In some places (particularly airports), you may find dedicated home direct phones where you simply press the button labelled USA, Australia, Hong Kong or whatever for direct connection to the operator. Note that the home direct service does not operate to and from all countries, and that the call could be charged at operator rates, which makes it expensive for the person paying. Placing a call on your phone credit card is more expensive than paying the local tariff.

Dialling Tones

In some countries, after you've dialled the international access code, you have to wait for a second dial tone before dialing the code for your target country and the number. Often the same applies when you ring from one city to another within these countries: wait for a dialling tone after you've dialled the area code for your target city. If you're not sure what to do, simply wait three or four seconds after dialling a code – if nothing happens, you can probably keep dialling.

Phonecards

In major locations phones may accept credit cards: simply swipe your card through the slot and the call is charged to the card, though rates can be very high. Phone-company credit cards can be used to charge calls via your home country operator.

Stored-value phonecards are now almost standard all over Europe. You usually buy a card from a post office, telephone centre, newsstand or retail outlet and simply insert the card into the phone each time you make a call. The card solves the problem of finding the correct coins for calls (or lots of correct coins for international calls) and generally gives you a small discount.

Call Costs

The cost of international calls varies widely from one country to another: a US$1.20 call from Britain could cost you US$6 from Turkey. The countries in the table opposite are rated from * (cheap) to *** (expensive), but rates can vary depending on which country you are calling to (for example, from Italy it's relatively cheap to call North America, but more expensive to call Australia). Reduced rates are available at certain times, usually from mid-evening to early morning, though it varies from country to country – check the local phone book or ask the operator. Calling from hotel rooms can be very

Telephone Codes & Costs

	CC	cost (see text)	IAC	IO
Albania	355	***		
Andorra	376	**	00	821111
Austria	43	*	00	09
Belgium	32	**	00	1224 (private phone)
				1223 (public phone)
Bosnia	387	**	00	901
Bulgaria	359	***	00	
Croatia	385	**	00	901
Cyprus	357	***	00	
Cyprus (Turkish)	90+392		00	
Czech Republic	420	***	00	0149
Denmark	45	**	00	141
Estonia	372	***	00	165
Finland	358	**	00, 990, 994, 999	020222
France	33	*	00(w)	12
Germany	49	*	00	11834
Gibraltar	350	***	00	100
Greece	30	*	00	161
Hungary	36	*	00(w)	199
Iceland	354	***	00	5335010
Ireland	353	*	00	114
Northern Ireland	44+28	*	00	155
Italy	39	**	00	15
Latvia	371	***	1 (w) 00	1 (w) 115
Liechtenstein	423	***	00	114
Lithuania	370	***	8(w)10	194/195
Luxembourg	352	**	00	0010
Macedonia	389	***	99	
Malta	356	**	00	194
Morocco	212	***	00(w)	12
Netherlands	31	**	00	0800-0410
Norway	47	**	00	181
Poland	48	**	0(w)0	901
Portugal	351	*	00	099
Romania	40	***	00	071
Russia	7	***	8(w)10	
Slovakia	421	**	00	0149/0139
Slovenia	386	**	00	901
Spain	34	**	00(w)	025
Sweden	46	**	00	0018
Switzerland	41	**	00	114
Tunisia	216	**	00	
Turkey	90	***	00	115
UK	44	*	00	155
Yugoslavia	381	***	99	901

CC – Country Code (to call into that country)
IAC – International Access Code (to call abroad from that country)
IO – International Operator (to make enquiries)
(w) – wait for dialling tone

Other country codes include: Australia 61, Canada 1, Hong Kong 852, India 91, Indonesia 62, Israel 972, Japan 81, Macau 853, Malaysia 60, New Zealand 64, Singapore 65, South Africa 27, Thailand 66, USA 1

Appendix III – European Organisations

Membership of Political & Economic Organisations

	Council of Europe	EU	EFTA	NATO	Nordic Council	OECD
Albania	✓	–	–	–	–	–
Andorra	✓	–	–	–	–	–
Austria	✓	✓	–	–	–	✓
Belgium	✓	✓	–	✓	–	✓
Bosnia-Hercegovina	✦	–	–	–	–	–
Bulgaria	✓	–	–	–	–	–
Croatia	✓	–	–	–	–	–
Cyprus	✓	–	–	–	–	–
Czech Republic	✓	–	–	✓	–	✓
Denmark	✓	✓	–	✓	✓	✓
Estonia	✓	–	–	–	–	–
Finland	✓	✓	–	–	✓	✓
France	✓	✓	–	✓	–	✓
Georgia	✓	–	–	–	–	–
Germany	✓	✓	–	✓	–	✓
Greece	✓	✓	–	✓	–	✓
Hungary	✓	–	–	✓	–	✓
Iceland	✓	–	✓	✓	✓	✓
Ireland	✓	✓	–	–	–	✓
Italy	✓	✓	–	✓	–	✓
Latvia	✓	–	–	–	–	–
Liechtenstein	✓	–	✓	–	–	–
Lithuania	✓	–	–	–	–	–
Luxembourg	✓	✓	–	✓	–	✓
Macedonia	✓	–	–	–	–	–
Malta	✓	–	–	–	–	–
Netherlands	✓	✓	–	✓	–	✓
Norway	✓	–	✓	✓	✓	✓
Poland	✓	–	–	✓	–	✓
Portugal	✓	✓	–	✓	–	✓
Romania	✓	–	–	–	–	–
Russian Federation	✓	–	–	–	–	–
Slovakia	✓	–	–	–	–	–
Slovenia	✓	–	–	–	–	–
Spain	✓	✓	–	✓	–	✓
Sweden	✓	✓	–	–	✓	✓
Switzerland	✓	–	✓	–	–	✓
Turkey	✓	–	–	✓	–	✓
UK	✓	✓	–	✓	–	✓
Ukraine	✓	–	–	–	–	–
Yugoslavia	–	–	–	–	–	–

✓ full member   ✦ special guest status

Council of Europe

Established in 1949, the Council of Europe is the oldest of Europe's political institutions. It aims to promote European unity, protect human rights and assist in the cultural, social and economic development of its member states, but its powers are purely advisory. Founding states were Belgium, Denmark, France, Ireland, Italy, Luxembourg, the Netherlands, Norway, Sweden and the UK. It now counts 41 members. Its headquarters are in Strasbourg.

European Union (EU)

Founded by the Treaty of Rome in 1957, the European Economic Community, or Common Market as it was once known, broadened its scope far beyond economic measures as it developed into the European Community (1967) and finally the European Union (1993). Its original aims were to develop and expand the economies of its member states by abolishing customs tariffs, coordinating transportation systems and general economic policies, establishing a common economic policy towards nonmember states, and promoting the free movement of labour and capital within its borders. Further measures included the abolition of border controls and the linking of currency exchange rates. Since the 1991 Maastricht treaty, the EU is committed to establishing a common foreign and security policy and close cooperation in home affairs and the judiciary. A single European currency called the euro came into effect in January 1999.

The EEC's founding states were Belgium, France, West Germany, Italy, Luxembourg and the Netherlands – the Treaty of Rome was an extension of the European Coal and Steel Community (ECSC) founded by these six states in 1952. Denmark, Ireland and the UK joined in 1973, Greece in 1981, Spain and Portugal in 1986 and Austria, Finland and Sweden in 1995. In 1998, membership negotiations opened with Cyprus, Czech Republic, Estonia, Hungary, Poland and Slovenia, with full membership expected to be granted in 2002. Bulgaria, Latvia, Lithuania, Malta, Ro-

mania and Slovakia joined accession talks in 2000. The main EU organisations are the European Parliament (elected by direct universal suffrage, with growing powers), the European Commission (the daily government), the Council of Ministers (ministers of member states who make the important decisions) and the Court of Justice. The European Parliament meets in Strasbourg; Luxembourg is home to the Court of Justice. Other EU organisations are based in Brussels.

North Atlantic Treaty Organisation (NATO)

The document creating this defence alliance was signed in 1949 by the USA, Canada and 10 European countries to safeguard their common political, social and economic systems against external threats (read: against the powerful Soviet military presence in Europe after WWII). An attack against any member state would be considered an attack against them all. Greece and Turkey joined in 1952, West Germany in 1955, and Spain in 1982; France withdrew from NATO's integrated military command in 1966 and Greece did likewise in 1974, though both remain members. NATO's Soviet counterpart, the Warsaw Pact founded in 1955, collapsed with the democratic revolutions of 1989 and the subsequent disintegration of the Soviet Union; most of its former members are now NATO associates. NATO's headquarters are in Brussels.

Organisation for Economic Cooperation & Development (OECD)

The OECD was set up in 1961 to supersede the Organisation for European Economic Cooperation, which allocated US aid under the Marshall Plan and coordinated the reconstruction of postwar Europe. Sometimes seen as the club of the world's rich countries, the OECD aims to encourage economic growth and world trade. Its member states include most of Europe, as well as Australia, Canada, Japan, Mexico, New Zealand and the USA. Its headquarters are in Paris.

Appendix IV – Alternative Place Names

The following abbreviations are used:

(A) Albanian	(Gr) Greek
(Ar) Arabic	(I) Italian
(B) Basque	(P) Portuguese
(C) Catalan	(S) Serbian
(Cr) Croatian	(Sle) Slovene
(E) English	(S) Spanish
(F) French	(T) Turkish
(G) German	

ALBANIA
Shgipëi
Durrës (A) – Durazzo
Korça (A) – Koritsa (Gr)
Lezha (A) – Allessio (I)
Saranda (E) – Sarandë (A)
Shkodra (E) – Shkodër (A), Scutari (I)
Tirana (E) – Tiranë (A)

CYPRUS
Kípros (Gr)
Kibris (T)
Gazimağusa (T) – Famagusta (Gr),
  Ammochostos (Gr)
Girne (T) – Kyrenia (Gr), Keryneia (Gr)
Lefkoşa (T) – Nicosia (Gr)
Limassol (Gr) – Lemessos (Gr)

CROATIA
Hrvatska
Brač (Cr) – Brazza (I)
Brijuni (Cr) – Brioni (I)
Cres (Cr) – Cherso (I)
Dalmatia (E) – Dalmacija (Cr)
Dubrovnik (Cr) – Ragusa (I)
Hvar (Cr) – Lesina (I)
Korčula – Curzola (I)
Krk (Cr) – Veglia (I)
Kvarner (Cr) – Quarnero (I)
Losinj (Cr) – Lussino (I)
Mljet Island (Cr) – Melita (I)
Poreč (Cr) – Parenzo (I)
Rab (Cr) – Arbe (G)
Rijeka (Cr) – Fiume (I)
Rovinj (Cr) – Rovigno (I)
Split (Cr) – Spalato (I)
Trogir (Cr) – Trau (G)

Zadar (Cr) – Zara (I)
Zagreb (Cr) – Agram (G)

FRANCE
Bayonne (F, E) – Baiona (B)
Basque Country (E) – Euskadi (B),
  Pays Basque (F)
Burgundy (E) – Bourgogne (F)
Brittany (E) – Bretagne (F)
Corsica (E) – Corse (F)
French Riviera (E) – Côte d'Azur (F)
Dunkirk (E) – Dunkerque (F)
Channel Islands (E) – Îles Anglo-Normandes (F)
English Channel (E) – La Manche (F)
Lake Geneva (E) – Lac Léman (F)
Lyons (E) – Lyon (F)
Marseilles (E) – Marseille (F)
Normandy (E) – Normandie (F)
Rheims (E) – Reims (F)
Rhine (River) (E) – Rhin (F), Rhein (G)
Saint Jean de Luz (F) – Donibane Lohizune (B)
Saint Jean Pied de Port (F) – Donibane Garazi (B)
Sark (Channel Islands; E) – Sercq (F)

GREECE
Hellas (or Ελλας)
Athens (E) – Athina (Gr)
Corfu (E) – Kerkyra (Gr)
Crete (E) – Kriti (Gr)
Patras (E) – Patra (Gr)
Rhodes (E) – Rodos (Gr)
Salonica (E) – Thessaloniki (Gr)
Samothrace (E) – Samothraki (Gr)
Santorini (E, Gr, I) – Thira (Gr)

ITALY
Italia
Aeolian Islands (E) – Isole Eolie (I)
Apulia (E) – Puglia (I)
Florence (E) – Firenze (I)
Genoa (E) – Genova (I)
Herculaneum (E) – Ercolano (I)
Lombardy (E) – Lombardia (I)
Mantua (E) – Mantova (I)
Milan (E) – Milano (I)
Naples (E) – Napoli (I)
Padua (E) – Padova (I)
Rome (E) – Roma (I)

Sicily (E) – Sicilia (I)
Sardinia (E) – Sardegna (I)
Syracuse (E) – Siracusa (I)
Tiber (River) (E) – Tevere (I)
Venice (E) – Venezia (I)

MOROCCO

Ceuta (S) – Sebta (Ar)
Casablanca (F) – Dar al-Beida (Ar)
Marrakesh (E) – Marrakech (F)
Tangier (E) – Tanger (F), Tanja (Ar)

PORTUGAL

Cape St Vincent (E) – Cabo de São Vicente (P)
Lisbon (E) – Lisboa (P)
Oporto (E) – Porto (P)

SLOVENIA

Slovenija
Koper (Sle) – Capodistria (I)
Ljubljana (Sle) – Laibach (G)
Piran (Sle) – Pireos (Gk)
Postiojna Caves (Sle) – Adelsberger Grotten (G)
Vintgar Gorge (E) – Soteska Vintgar (Sle)

SPAIN

España
Andalusia (E) – Andalucía (S)
Balearic Islands (E) – Islas Baleares (S)
Basque Country (E) – Euskadi (B), País Vasco (S)
Catalonia (E) – Catalunya (C), Cataluña (S)
Cordova (E) – Córdoba (S)
Corunna (E) – La Coruña (S)

Majorca (E) – Mallorca (S)
Minorca (E) – Menorca (S)
Navarre (E) – Navarra (S)
San Sebastián (E, S) – Donostia (B)
Saragossa (E) – Zaragoza (S)
Seville (E) – Sevilla (S)

TURKEY

Türkiye
Cappadocia (E) – Kapadokya (T)
Ephesus (E) – Efes (T)
Euphrates River (E) – Firat (T)
Gallipoli (E) – Gelibolu (T)
İzmir (T) – Smyrna (G)
Mt Ararat (E) – Ağri Daği (T)
Mt Nimrod (E) – Nemrut Daği (T)
Thrace (E) – Trakya (T)
Tigris River (E) – Dicle (T)
Trebizond (E) – Trabzon (T)
Troy (E) – Truva (T)

YUGOSLAVIA

Jugoslavija
Bar (Se) – Antivari (I)
Belgrade (E) – Beograd (Se)
Deçan (A) – Dećani (Se)
Kotor (Se) – Cattaro (I)
Montenegro (E) – Crna Gora (Se)
Novi Sad (Se) – Neusatz (G)
Peć (Se) – Pejë (A)
Priština (Se) – Prishtinë
Serbia (E) – Serbija (Se)
Ulcinj (Se) – Ulqin (A), Dulcigno (I)

Appendix V – International Country Abbreviations

The following is a list of official abbreviations that you may encounter on motor vehicles in Europe. Other abbreviations are likely to be unofficial ones, often referring to a particular region, province or even city. A vehicle entering a foreign country must carry a sticker identifying its country of registration, though this rule is not always enforced.

A	–	Austria
AL	–	Albania
AND	–	Andorra
B	–	Belgium
BG	–	Bulgaria
BIH	–	Bosnia-Hercegovina
BY	–	Belarus
CDN	–	Canada
CH	–	Switzerland
CY	–	Cyprus
CZ	–	Czech Republic
D	–	Germany
DK	–	Denmark
DZ	–	Algeria
E	–	Spain
EST	–	Estonia
ET	–	Egypt
F	–	France
FIN	–	Finland
FL	–	Liechtenstein
FR	–	Faroe Islands
GB	–	Great Britain
GE	–	Georgia
GR	–	Greece
H	–	Hungary
HKJ	–	Jordan
HR	–	Croatia
I	–	Italy
IL	–	Israel
IRL	–	Ireland
IS	–	Iceland
L	–	Luxembourg
LAR	–	Libya
LT	–	Lithuania
LV	–	Latvia
M	–	Malta
MA	–	Morocco
MC	–	Monaco
MD	–	Moldavia
MK	–	Macedonia
N	–	Norway
NGR	–	Nigeria
NL	–	Netherlands
NZ	–	New Zealand
P	–	Portugal
PL	–	Poland
RL	–	Lebanon
RO	–	Romania
RSM	–	San Marino
RUS	–	Russia
S	–	Sweden
SK	–	Slovakia
SLO	–	Slovenia
SYR	–	Syria
TN	–	Tunisia
TR	–	Turkey
UA	–	Ukraine
USA	–	United States of America
V	–	Vatican City
YU	–	Yugoslavia
ZA	–	South Africa

OTHER

CC	–	Consular Corps
CD	–	Diplomatic Corps
GBA	–	Alderney
GBG	–	Guernsey
GBJ	–	Jersey
GBM	–	Isle of Man
GBZ	–	Gibraltar

Language

This language guide contains pronunciation tips and basic vocabulary to help you get around Mediterranean Europe. For background information about each language see the individual country chapters. For more extensive coverage of the languages included here, see Lonely Planet's *Europe* and *Eastern Europe* phrasebooks.

Albanian

Pronunciation

Written Albanian is phonetically consistent and pronunciation shouldn't pose too many problems for English speakers. The Albanian 'rr' is trilled and each vowel in a diphthong is pronounced. However, Albanian possesses certain letters that are present in English but rendered differently. These include:

ë	often silent; at the beginning af a word it's like the 'a' in 'ago'
c	as the 'ts' in 'bits'
ç	as the 'ch' in 'church'
dh	as the 'th' in 'this'
gj	as the 'gy' in 'hogyard'
j	as the 'y' in 'yellow'
q	between 'ch' and 'ky', similar to the 'cu' in 'cure'
th	as in 'thistle'
x	as the 'dz' in 'adze'
xh	as the 'j' in 'jewel'
zh	as the 's' in 'pleasure'

Basics

Hello.	*Tungjatjeta/Allo.*
Goodbye.	*Lamtumirë.*
	Mirupafshim. (informal)
Yes.	*Po.*
No.	*Jo.*
Please.	*Ju lutem.*
Thank you.	*Ju falem nderit.*
That's fine.	*Eshtë e mirë.*
You're welcome.	*S'ka përse.*
Excuse me.	*Me falni.*
Sorry. (excuse me, forgive me)	*Më vjen keq.* or *Më falni, ju lutem)*
Do you speak English?	*A flisni anglisht?*

How much is it?	*Sa kushton?*
What's your name?	*Si quheni ju lutem?*
My name is ...	*Unë quhem ...* or *Mua më quajnë ...*

Getting Around

What time does the ... leave/arrive?	*Në ç'orë niset /arrin ...?*
boat	*barka/lundra*
bus	*autobusi*
tram	*tramvaji*
train	*treni*

I'd like ...	*Dëshiroj ...*
a one-way ticket	*një biletë vajtje*
a return ticket	*një biletë kthimi*

1st/2nd class	*klas i parë/i dytë*
timetable	*orar*
bus stop	*stacion autobusi*

Where is ...?	*Ku është ...?*
Go straight ahead.	*Shko drejt.*
Turn left.	*Kthehu majtas.*
Turn right.	*Kthehu djathtas.*
near/far	*afër/larg*

Around Town

a bank	*një bankë*
chemist/pharmacy	*farmaci*
the ... embassy	*... ambasadën*
my hotel	*hotelin tim*
the market	*pazarin*
newsagents	*agjensia e lajmeve*
the post office	*postën*

Signs – Albanian

Hyrje	**Entrance**
Dalje	**Exit**
Informim	**Information**
Hapur	**Open**
Mbyllur	**Closed**
E Ndaluar	**Prohibited**
Policia	**Police**
Stacioni I Policisë	**Police Station**
Nevojtorja	**Toilets**
Burra	**Men**
Gra	**Women**

Emergencies – Albanian

Help!	Ndihmë!
Call a doctor!	Thirrni doktorin!
Call the police!	Thirrni policinë!
Go away!	Zhduku!/Largohuni!
I'm lost.	Kam humbur rrugë

the telephone centre	centralin telefonik
the tourist office	zyrën e informimeve turistike
What time does it open/close?	Në ç'ore hapet/ mbyllet?

Accommodation

hotel	hotel
camping ground	kamp pushimi
Do you have any rooms available?	A keni ndonjë dhomë të lirë?
a single room	një dhomë më një krevat
a double room	një dhomë më dy krevat
How much is it per night/per person?	Sa kushton për një natë/ për një njeri?
Does it include breakfast?	A e përfshin edhe mëngjesin?

Time, Days & Numbers

What time is it?	Sa është ora?
today	sot
tomorrow	nesër
yesterday	dje
in the morning	në mëngjes
in the afternoon	pas dreke

Monday	e hënë
Tuesday	e martë
Wednesday	e mërkurë
Thursday	e ënjte
Friday	e premte
Saturday	e shtunë
Sunday	e diel

1	një
2	dy
3	tre
4	katër
5	pesë
6	gjashtë
7	shtatë
8	tetë
9	nëntë
10	dhjetë
100	njëqind
1000	njëmijë

one million	një milion

Bosnian, Croatian & Serbian

Pronunciation

The writing systems of Bosnian, Croatian and Serbian are phonetically consistent: every letter is pronounced and its sound will not vary from word to word. With regard to the position of stress, only one rule can be given: the last syllable of a word is never stressed. In most cases the accent falls on the first vowel in the word.

Serbian uses the Cyrillic alphabet so it's worth familiarising yourself with it (see the Macedonian section in this chapter). Bosnian and Croatian use a Roman alphabet; many letters are pronounced as in English – the following are some specific pronunciations.

c	as the 'ts' in 'cats'
ć	as the 'tch' sound in 'future'
č	as the 'ch' in 'chop'
đ	as the 'dy' sound in 'verdure'
dž	as the 'j' in 'just'
j	as the 'y' in 'young'
lj	as the 'lli' in 'million'
nj	as the 'ny' in 'canyon'
š	as the 'sh' in 'hush'
ž	as the 's' in 'pleasure'

The principal difference between Serbian and Croatian is in the pronunciation of the vowel 'e' in certain words. A long 'e' in Serbian becomes 'ije' in Croatian (eg, reka, rijeka, 'river'), and a short 'e' in Serbian becomes 'je' in Croatian (eg, pesma, pjesma, 'song'). Sometimes, however, the vowel 'e' is the same in both languages, as in selo, 'village'. Bosnian shares some of its vocab with both Serbian and Croatian, but there are also a number of variations in vocabulary between all three languages. In the following phraselist these are indicated with 'B' for Bosnian, 'C' for Croatian and 'S' for Serbian.

Basics

Hello.
Zdravo.	Здраво.

Goodbye.
Doviđenja.	Довиђења.

Yes.
Da.	Да.

No.
Ne.	Не.

Please.
Molim.	Молим.

Thank you.
Hvala.	Хвала.

That's fine/
You're welcome.
U redu je/	У реду је/
Nema na čemu.	Нема на чему.

Excuse me.
Oprostite.	Опростите.

Sorry. (excuse me, forgive me)
Pardon.	Пардон.

Do you speak English?
Govorite li	Говорите ли
engleski?	енглески?

How much is it ...?
Koliko košta ...?	Колико кошта ...?

What's your name?
Kako se zovete?	Како се зовете?

My name is ...
Zovem se ...	Зовем се ...

Getting Around

What time does
the ... leave/arrive?
Kada ...	Када ...
polazi/dolazi?	полази/долази?

boat
brod	брод

bus (city)
autobus	аутобус
(gradski)	(градски)

bus (intercity)
autobus	аутобус
(međugradski)	(међуградски)

train
voz (S, B)/	воз
vlak (C)	

tram
tramvaj	трамвај

one-way ticket
kartu u jednom	карту у једном
pravcu	правцу

return ticket
povratnu kartu	повратну карту

1st class
prvu klasu	прву класу

2nd class
drugu klasu	другу класу

Where is the bus/tram stop?
Gde je autobuska/tramvajska stanica? (S)
Gdje je autobuska/tramvajska postaja? (C)
Где је аутобуска/трамвајска станица?
Can you show me (on the map)?
Možete li mi pokazati (na karti)?
Можете ли ми показати (на карти)?
Go straight ahead.
Idite pravo napred (S)/*naprijed.* (B, C)
Идите право напред.
Turn left.
Skrenite lijevo (B, C)/*levo.* (S)
Скрените лево.

Signs

Entrance/Exit
Улаз/Излаз
Ulaz/Izlaz

Open/Closed
Отворено/Затворено
Otvoreno/Zatvoreno

Information
Информације
Informacije

Rooms Available
Слободне Собе
Slobodne Sobe

Full/No Vacancies
Нема Слободне Собе
Nema Slobodne Sobe

Police
Милиција
Milicija (S)/*Policija* (B, C)

Police Station
Станица Милиције
Stanica Milicije (S)/*Policija* (B, C)

Prohibited
Забрањено
Zabranjeno

Toilets
Тоалети
Toaleti (S, B)/*Zahodi* (C)

LANGUAGE

Turn right.
Skrenite desno.
Скрените десно.
near
blizu
близу
far
daleko
далеку

Around Town
I'm looking for ...
Tražim ...   Тражим ...
a bank
banku   банку
the ... embassy
... ambasadu   ... амбасаду
my hotel
moj hotel   мој хотел
the market
pijacu   пијацу
the post office
poštu   пошту
the telephone centre
telefonsku   телефонску централу
centralu
the tourist office
turistički biro   туристички биро

Accommodation
hotel
hotel   хотел
guesthouse
privatno   приватно
prenoćište   преноћиште
youth hostel
omladinsko   омладинско
prenoćište   преноћиште
camping ground
kamping   кампинг

Do you have any rooms available?
Imate li slobodne sobe?
Имате ли слободне собе?
How much is it per night/per person?
Koliko košta za jednu noć/po osobi?
Колико кошта за једну ноћ/по особи?
Does it include breakfast?
Dali je u cenu (S)/*cijenu* (B, C)
uključen i doručak?
Дали је у цену укључен и доручак?
I'd like ...
Želim ...
Желим ...

Emergencies

Help!
Upomoć!
Упомоћ!
Call a doctor!
Pozovite lekara! (B, S)
Pozovite liječnika! (C)
Позовите лекара!
Call the police!
Pozovite miliciju! (S)
Pozovite policiju! (C)
Позовите милицију!
Go away!
Idite!
Идите!
I'm lost.
Izgubio/Izgubila sam se. (m/f) (B, S)
Izgubljen/Izgubljena sam. (m/f) (C)
Изгубио сам се/Изгубила сам се.

a single room
sobu sa jednim krevetom
собу са једним креветом
a double room
sobu sa duplim krevetom
собу са дуплим креветом

Time, Days & Numbers
What time is it?
Koliko je sati?   Колико је сати?
today
danas   данас
tomorrow
sutra   сутра
yesterday
juče (S, B)   јуче
jučer (C)
in the morning
ujutro   ујутро
in the afternoon
popodne   поподне

Monday
ponedeljak   понедељак
Tuesday
utorak   уторак
Wednesday
sreda (S)   среда
srijeda (B, C)
Thursday
četvrtak   четвртак

Friday
   petak   петак
Saturday
   subota   субота
Sunday
   nedelja (S)   недеља
   nedjelja (B, C)

1	*jedan*	један
2	*dva*	два
3	*tri*	три
4	*četiri*	четири
5	*pet*	пет
6	*šest*	шест
7	*sedam*	седам
8	*osam*	осам
9	*devet*	девет
10	*deset*	десет
100	*sto*	сто
1000	*hiljada* (B, S)	иљада
	tisuću (C)	

one million *jedan milion* (S)   један милион
         jedan milijun (B, C)

French

Pronunciation

French has a number of sounds which are difficult for Anglophones to produce. These include:

- The distinction between the 'u' sound (as in *tu*) and 'oo' sound (as in *tout*). For both sounds, the lips are rounded and projected forward, but for the 'u' the tongue is towards the front of the mouth, its tip against the lower front teeth, whereas for the 'oo' the tongue is towards the back of the mouth, its tip behind the gums of the lower front teeth.
- The nasal vowels. During the production of nasal vowels the breath partly escapes partly through the nose and partly through the mouth. There are no nasal vowels in English; in French there are three, as in *bon vin blanc*, 'good white wine'. These sounds occur where a syllable ends in a single 'n' or 'm'; the 'n' or 'm' is silent but indicates the nasalisation of the preceding vowel.
- The 'r'. The standard 'r' of Parisian French is produced by moving the bulk of the tongue backwards to constrict the air flow in the pharynx while the tip of the tongue rests behind the lower front teeth. It's similar to the noise made by some people before spitting, but with much less friction.

Basics

Hello.	*Bonjour.*
Goodbye.	*Au revoir.*
Yes.	*Oui.*
No.	*Non.*
Please.	*S'il vous plaît.*
Thank you.	*Merci.*
That's fine, you're welcome.	*Je vous en prie.*
Excuse me.	*Excusez-moi.*
I'm sorry.	*Pardon*
Do you speak English?	*Parlez-vous anglais?*
How much is it?	*C'est combien?*
What's your name?	*Comment vous appelez-vous?*
My name is ...	*Je m'appelle ...*

Getting Around

When does the next ... leave/arrive?	*À quelle heure part/ arrive le prochain ...?*
boat	*bateau*
bus (city)	*bus*
bus (intercity)	*car*
tram	*tramway*
train	*train*

I'd like a ... ticket.	*Je voudrais un billet ...*
one-way	*aller simple*
return	*aller retour*
1st class	*de première classe*
2nd class	*de deuxième classe*

Signs – French	
Entrée	**Entrance**
Sortie	**Exit**
Chambres Libres	**Rooms Available**
Complet	**Full/No Vacancies**
Renseignements	**Information**
Ouvert/Fermée	**Open/Closed**
Interdit	**Prohibited**
(Commissariat de) Police	**Police Station**
Toilettes, WC	**Toilets**
Hommes	**Men**
Femmes	**Women**

Emergencies – French

Help!	*Au secours!*
Call a doctor!	*Appelez un médecin!*
Call the police!	*Appelez la police!*
Leave me alone!	*Fichez-moi la paix!*
I'm lost.	*Je me suis égaré/e.*

left luggage (office)	*consigne*
timetable	*horaire*
bus/tram stop	*arrêt d'autobus/ de tramway*
train station/ ferry terminal	*gare/gare maritime*
I'd like to hire a car/bicycle.	*Je voudrais louer une voiture/un vélo.*
Where is ...?	*Où est ...?*
Go straight ahead.	*Continuez tout droit.*
Turn left.	*Tournez à gauche.*
Turn right.	*Tournez à droite.*
near/far	*proche/loin*

Around Town

a bank	*une banque*
the ... embassy	*l'ambassade de ...*
my hotel	*mon hôtel*
post office	*le bureau de poste*
market	*le marché*
chemist/pharmacy	*la pharmacie*
newsagents/ stationers	*l'agence de presse/ la papeterie*
a public telephone	*une cabine téléphonique*
the tourist office	*l'office de tourisme/ le syndicat d'initiative*
What time does it open/close?	*Quelle est l' heure de ouverture/fermeture?*

Accommodation

the hotel	*l'hôtel*
the youth hostel	*l'auberge de jeunesse*
the camping ground	*le camping*
Do you have any rooms available?	*Est-ce que vous avez des chambres libres?*
How much is it per night/ per person?	*Quel est le prix par nuit/ par personne?*
Is breakfast included?	*Est-ce que le petit dé- jeuner est compris?*
for one person	*pour une personne*
for two people	*deux personnes*

Time, Days & Numbers

What time is it?	*Quelle heure est-il?*
today	*aujourd'hui*
tomorrow	*demain*
yesterday	*hier*
morning/afternoon	*matin/après-midi*

Monday	*lundi*
Tuesday	*mardi*
Wednesday	*mercredi*
Thursday	*jeudi*
Friday	*vendredi*
Saturday	*samedi*
Sunday	*dimanche*

1	*un*
2	*deux*
3	*trois*
4	*quatre*
5	*cinq*
6	*six*
7	*sept*
8	*huit*
9	*neuf*
10	*dix*
100	*cent*
1000	*mille*

one million	*un million*

Greek

Alphabet & Pronunciation

Pronunciation of Greek letters is shown using the closest-sounding English letter.

Greek	English	Pronunciation
Α α	a	as in 'father'
Β β	v	as the 'v' in 'vine'
Γ γ	gh, y	like a rough 'g', or as the 'y' in 'yes'
Δ δ	dh	as the 'th' in 'then'
Ε ε	e	as in 'egg'
Ζ ζ	z	as in 'zoo'
Η η	i	as the 'ee' in 'feet'
Θ θ	th	as the 'th' in 'throw'
Ι ι	i	as the 'ee' in 'feet'
Κ κ	k	as in 'kite'
Λ λ	l	as in 'leg'
Μ μ	m	as in 'man'
Ν ν	n	as in 'net'
Ξ ξ	x	as the 'ks' in 'looks'
Ο ο	o	as in 'hot'

Π π	p	as in 'pup'
Ρ ρ	r	slightly trilled 'r'
Σ σ	s	as in 'sand' ('ς' at the end of a word)
Τ τ	t	as in 'to'
Υ υ	i	as the 'ee' in 'feet'
Φ φ	f	as in 'fee'
Χ χ	kh, h	as the 'ch' in Scottish *loch*, or as a rough 'h'
Ψ ψ	ps	as the 'ps' in 'lapse'
Ω ω	o	as in 'lot'

Letter Combinations

ει, οι	i	as the 'ee' in 'feet'
αι	e	as in 'bet'
ου	u	as the 'oo' in 'mood'
μπ	b	as in 'be'
	mb	as in 'amber' (or as the 'mp' in 'ample')
ντ	d	as in 'do'
	nd	as in 'bend' (or as the 'nt' in 'sent')
γκ	g	as in 'go'
γγ	ng	as the 'ng' in 'angle'
γξ	ks	as in 'yaks'
τζ	dz	as the 'ds' in 'suds'

Certain pairs of vowels are pronounced separately if the first has an acute accent (eg, ά), or the second has a dieresis (eg, ϊ).

All Greek words of two or more syllables have an acute accent which indicates where the stress falls. The suffix of some Greek words depends on the gender of the speaker, eg, *asthmatikos* (m) and *asthmatikya* (f).

Basics

Hello.	*yasu* (inf)/ *yasas* (polite, plural)
Goodbye.	*andio*
Yes.	*ne*
No.	*okhi*
Please.	*sas parakalo*
Thank you.	*sas efkharisto*
That's fine/ You're welcome.	*ine endaksi/parakalo*
Excuse me. (forgive me)	*signomi*
Do you speak English?	*milate anglika?*
How much is it?	*poso kani?*
What's your name?	*pos sas lene/ pos legeste?*
My name is ...	*me lene ...*

Getting Around

What time does the ... leave/arrive?	*ti ora fevyi/apo horito ...?*
boat	*to plio*
bus (city)	*to leoforio (ya tin boli)*
bus (intercity)	*to leoforio (ya ta proastia)*
train	*to treno*

I'd like a ... ticket.	*tha ithela isitirio ...*
one-way	*horis epistrofi*
return	*met epistrois*

1st class	*proti thesi*
2nd class	*dhefteri thesi*
left luggage	*horos aspokevon*
timetable	*dhromologhio*
bus stop	*i stasi tu leoforiu*

Go straight ahead.	*pighenete efthia*
Turn left.	*stripste aristera*
Turn right.	*stripste dheksya*
near/far	*konda/makria*

Around Town

the bank	*i trapeza*
the ... embassy	*i ... presvia*
the hotel	*to ksenodho khio*
the market	*i aghora*
the newsagents	*to efimeridhon*
the pharmacy	*to farmakio*
the post office	*to takhidhromio*
the telephone centre	*to tilefoniko kentro*
the tourist office	*to ghrafio turistikon pliroforion*

| What time does it open/close? | *ti ora aniyi/klini?* |

Signs – Greek

Εισοδοσ	Entrance
Εξοδοσ	Exit
Πληροφοριεσ	Information
Ανοικτο	Open
Κλειστο	Closed
Αστυνομικοσ Σταθμοσ	Police Station
Απαγορευεται	Prohibited
Τουαλετεσ	Toilets
Ανδρων	Men
Γυναικων	Women

Emergencies – Greek

Help!	voithia!
Call a doctor!	fona kste ena yatro!
Call the police!	tilefoniste stin astinomia!
Go away!	fighe/dhromo!
I'm lost.	eho hathi

Accommodation

a camp site	ena kamping
a hotel	ena xenothohio
a youth hostel	enas xenonas neoitos

I'd like a ... room.	thelo ena dhomatio ...
single	ya ena atomo
double	ya dhio atoma

How much is it ...?	poso kostizi ...?
per night	ya ena vradhi
per person	ya ena atomo

Time, Days & Numbers

What time is it?	ti ora ine?
today	simera
tomorrow	avrio
yesterday	hthes
in the morning	to proi
in the afternoon	to apoyevma

Monday	dheftera
Tuesday	triti
Wednesday	tetarti
Thursday	pempti
Friday	paraskevi
Saturday	savato
Sunday	kiryaki

1	ena
2	dhio
3	tria
4	tesera
5	pende
6	eksi
7	epta
8	okhto
9	enea
10	dheka
100	ekato
1000	khilya

one million	ena ekatomirio

Italian

Pronunciation

Italian pronunciation isn't difficult once you learn a few basic rules. Although some of the more clipped vowels and stress on double letters require careful practice for English speakers, it's easy enough to make yourself understood.

Vowels Vowels are generally more clipped than in English.

a	as the second 'a' in 'camera'
e	as the 'ay' in 'day', but without the 'i' sound
i	as the 'ee' in 'see'
o	as in 'dot'
u	as the 'oo' in 'too'

Consonants The pronunciation of many Italian consonants is similar to that of English. The following sounds depend on certain rules:

c	as 'k' before a, o and u; as the 'ch' in 'choose' before e and i
ch	a hard 'k' sound
g	as in 'get' before a, o
gh	as in 'get'
gli	as the 'lli' in 'million'
gn	as the 'ny' in 'canyon'
h	always silent
r	a rolled 'rrr' sound
sc	as the 'sh' in 'sheep' before e and i; a hard sound as in 'school' before h, a, o and u
z	as the 'ts' in 'lights' or as the 'ds' in 'beds'

Note that, unless it's accented, the i in 'ci', 'gi' and 'sci' isn't pronounced when followed by a, o or u. Thus the name 'Giovanni' is pronounced 'joh-VAHN-nee' – the 'i' sound after the initial 'g' isn't pronounced.

Stress Stress often falls on the next to last syllable, as in 'spaghetti'. When a word has an accent, the stress is on that syllable, as in città (city). Double consonants are pronounced as a longer, often more forceful sound than a single consonant.

Basics

Hello.	*Buongiorno.* (polite)/ *Ciao.* (informal)
Goodbye.	*Arrivederci.* (polite)/ *Ciao.* (informal)
Yes.	*Sì.*
No.	*No.*
Please.	*Per favore/Per piacere.*
Thank you.	*Grazie.*
You're welcome.	*Prego.*
Excuse me.	*Mi scusi.*
Sorry. (forgive me)	*Mi scusi/Mi perdoni.*
Do you speak English?	*Parla inglese?*
How much is it?	*Quanto costa?*
What's your name?	*Come si chiama?*
My name is ...	*Mi chiamo ...*

Getting Around

What time does the ... leave/arrive?	*A che ora parte/ arriva ...?*
boat	*la barca*
bus	*l'autobus*
ferry	*il traghetto*
train	*il treno*
tram	*il tram*

I'd like a ... ticket.	*Vorrei un biglietto ...*
one-way	*di solo andata*
return	*di andata e ritorno*
1st class	*di prima classe*
2nd class	*di seconda classe*

bus stop	*fermata dell'autobus*
ferry terminal	*stazione marittima*
train station	*stazione*
left luggage	*deposito bagagli*

Signs – Italian

Ingresso/Entrata	**Entrance**
Uscita	**Exit**
Camere Libere	**Rooms Available**
Completo	**Full/No Vacancies**
Informazione	**Information**
Aperto	**Open**
Chiuso	**Closed**
Proibito/Vietato	**Prohibited**
Polizia/Carabinieri	**Police**
Questura	**Police Station**
Gabinetti/Bagni	**Toilets**
Uomini	**Men**
Donne	**Women**

Emergencies – Italian

Help!	*Aiuto!*
Call a doctor!	*Chiama un dottore/ un medico!*
Call the police!	*Chiama la polizia!*
Go away!	*Vai via!*
I'm lost.	*Mi sono perso.* (m) *Mi sono persa.* (f)

timetable	*orario*
I'd like to hire a car/bicycle.	*Vorrei noleggiare una macchina/bicicletta.*
Where is ...?	*Dov'è ...?*
Go straight ahead.	*Si va sempre diritto.*
Turn left.	*Giri a sinistra.*
Turn right.	*Giri a destra.*
near/far	*vicino/lontano*

Around Town

a bank	*una banca*
chemist/pharmacy	*la farmacia*
the ... embassy	*l'ambasciata di ...*
my hotel	*il mio albergo*
market	*il mercato*
newsagents	*l'edicola*
post office	*la posta*
stationers	*il cartolaio*
telephone centre	*il centro telefonico*
the tourist office	*l'ufficio di turismo*

What time does it open/close?	*A che ora (si) apre/chiude?*

Accommodation

hotel	*albergo*
guesthouse	*pensione*
youth hostel	*ostello per la gioventù*
camping ground	*campeggio*

Do you have any rooms available?	*Ha delle camere libere/ C'è una camera libera?*
How much is it per night/per person?	*Quanto costa per la notte/ciascuno?*
Is breakfast included?	*È compresa la colazione?*

a single room	*una camera singola*
a double/twin room	*una camera matrimoniale/doppia*
for one night	*per una notte*
for two nights	*per due notti*

Time, Days & Numbers

What time is it?	*Che ora è?/*
	Che ore sono?
today	*oggi*
tomorrow	*domani*
yesterday	*ieri*
morning	*mattina*
afternoon	*pomeriggio*
Monday	*lunedì*
Tuesday	*martedì*
Wednesday	*mercoledì*
Thursday	*giovedì*
Friday	*venerdì*
Saturday	*sabato*
Sunday	*domenica*

1	*uno*
2	*due*
3	*tre*
4	*quattro*
5	*cinque*
6	*sei*
7	*sette*
8	*otto*
9	*nove*
10	*dieci*
100	*cento*
1000	*mille*

one million   *un milione*

Macedonian

Pronunciation

The spelling of Macedonian is more or less phonetic: almost every word is written exactly the way it's pronounced and every letter is pronounced. With regard to the position of word stress, only one rule can be given: the last syllable of a word is never stressed. There are 31 letters in the Cyrillic alphabet. The pronunciation of the Roman or Cyrillic letter is given to the nearest English equivalent.

Basics

Hello.		
	Zdravo.	Здраво.
Goodbye.		
	Priatno.	Приатно.
Yes.		
	Da.	Да.
No.		
	Ne.	Не.

The Cyrillic Alphabet

Cyrillic	Roman	English Pronunciation
А а	a	as in 'rather'
Б б	b	as in 'be'
В в	v	as in 'vodka'
Г г	g	as in 'go'
Д д	d	as in 'do'
Ѓ ѓ	gj	as the 'gu' in 'legume'
Е е	e	as the 'e' in 'bear'
Ж ж	zh	as the 's' in 'pleasure'
З з	z	as in 'zero'
Ѕ ѕ	zj	as the 'ds' in suds
И и	i	as the 'i' in 'machine'
Ј ј	j	as the 'y' in 'young'
К к	k	as in 'keg'
Л л	l	as in 'let'
Љ љ	lj	as the 'lli' in 'million'
М м	m	as in 'map'
Н н	n	as in 'no'
Њ њ	nj	as the 'ny' in 'canyon'
О о	o	as the 'aw' in 'shawl'
П п	p	as in 'pop'
Р р	r	as in 'rock'
С с	s	as in 'safe'
Т т	t	as in 'too'
Ќ ќ	ć	as the 'cu' in 'cure'
У у	u	as the 'oo' in 'room'
Ф ф	f	as in 'fat'
Х х	h	as in 'hot'
Ц ц	c	as the 'ts' in 'cats'
Ч ч	č	as the 'ch' in 'chop'
Џ џ	dz	as the 'j' in 'judge'
Ш ш	š	as the 'sh' in 'shoe'

Please.		
	Molam.	Молам.
Thank you.		
	Blagodaram.	Благодарам.
You're welcome.		
	Nema zošto/	Нема зошто/
	Milo mi e.	Мило ми е.
Excuse me.		
	Izvinete.	Извинете.
Sorry. (forgive me)		
	Oprostete ve molam.	Опростете ве молам.
Do you speak English?		
	Zboruvate li angliski?	Зборувате ли англиски?

What's your name?
Kako se vikate? Како се викате?
My name is ...
Jas se vikam ... Јас се викам ...
How much is it?
Kolku čini toa? Колку чини тоа?

Getting Around

What time does the next ... leave/arrive?
Koga doagja/zaminuva idniot ...?
Кога доаѓа/заминува идниот ...?

boat
brod брод
bus (city)
avtobus (gradski) автобус (градски)
bus (intercity)
avtobus автобус
(megjugradski) (меѓуградски)
train
voz воз
tram
tramvaj трамвај

I'd like ...
Sakam ... Сакам ...
a one-way ticket
bilet vo eden билет во еден правец
pravec
a return ticket
povraten bilet повратен билет
1st class
prva klasa прва класа
2nd class
vtora klasa втора класа
timetable
vozen red возен ред
bus stop
avtobuska stanica автобуска станица
train station
zheleznička железничка станица
stanica

Where is ...?
Kade je ...? Каде је ...?
Go straight ahead.
Odete pravo Одете право напред.
napred.
Turn left/right.
Svrtete levo/desno. Свртете лево/десно.
near/far
blisku/daleku блиску/далеку

Signs – Macedonian

Entrance
Влез
Vlez
Exit
Излез
Izlez
Open
Отворено
Otvoreno
Closed
Затворено
Zatvoreno
Information
Информации
Informacii
Rooms Available
Сози За Издавање
Sobi Za Izdavanje
Full/No Vacancies
Полно/Нема Место
Polno/Nema Mesto
Police
Полиција
Policija
Police Station
Полициска Станица
Policiska Stanica
Prohibited
Забането
Zabraneto
Toilets (Men/Women)
Клозети (Машки/Женски)
Klozeti (Maški/Enski)

I'd like to hire a car/bicycle.
Sakam da iznajmam kola/točak.
Сакам ла изнајмам кола/точак.

Around Town

bank
banka банка
chemist/pharmacy
apteka аптека
the embassy
ambasadata амбасадата
my hotel
mojot hotel мојот хотел
the market
pazarot пазарот

LANGUAGE

newsagents
  kiosk za vesnici киоск за весници
the post office
  poštata поштата
stationers
  knižarnica книжарница
the telephone centre
  telefonskata телефонската
  centrala централа
the tourist office
  turističkoto biro туристичкото биро

What time does it open/close?
  Koga se otvora/zatvora?
  Кога се отвора/затвора?

Accommodation

Do you have any rooms available?
  Dali imate slobodni sobi?
  Дали имате слободни соби?
How much is it per night/per person?
  Koja e cenata po noć/po osoba?
  Која е цената по ноќ/по особа?
Does it include breakfast?
  Dali e vključen pojadok?
  Дали е вклучен ројадок?

hotel
  hotel
  хотел
guesthouse
  privatno smetuvanje
  приватно сметување
youth hostel
  mladinsko prenoćište
  младинско преноќиште
camping ground
  kamping
  кампинг

a single room
  soba so eden krevet
  соба со еден кревет
a double room
  soba so braćen krevet
  соба со брачен кревет
for one/two nights
  za edna/dva večeri
  за една/два вечери

Time, Days & Numbers

What time is it?
  Kolku e časot?
  Колку е часот?

today
  denes денес
tomorrow
  utre утре
yesterday
  včera вчера
morning
  utro утро
afternoon
  popladne попладне

Monday
  ponedelnik понеделник
Tuesday
  vtornik вторник
Wednesday
  sreda среда
Thursday
  četvrtok четврток
Friday
  petok петок
Saturday
  sabota сабота
Sunday
  nedela недела

1	*eden*	еден
2	*dva*	два
3	*tri*	три
4	*četiri*	четири
5	*pet*	пет
6	*šest*	шест
7	*sedum*	седум
8	*osum*	осум
9	*devet*	девет
10	*deset*	десет
100	*sto*	сто

one million *eden milion* еден милион

Emergencies – Macedonian

Help!
  Pomoš! Помош!
Call a doctor!
  Povikajte lekar! Повикајте лекар!
Call the police!
  Viknete policija! Викнете полиција!
Go away!
  Odete si! Одете си!
I'm lost.
  Jas zaginav. Јас загинав.

Maltese

The following is a brief guide to Maltese pronunciation, and includes a few useful words and phrases.

Pronunciation

ċ	as the 'ch' in child
g	as in good
ġ	'soft' as the 'j' in job
għ	silent; lengthens the preceding or following vowel
h	silent, as in 'hour'
ħ	as the 'h' in 'hand'
j	as the 'y' in 'yellow'
ij	as the 'igh' in 'high'
ej	as the 'ay' in 'day'
q	a glottal stop; like the missing 't' between the two syllables in 'bottle'
x	as the 'sh' in shop
z	as the 'ts' in 'bits'
ż	soft as in 'buzz'

Basics

Hello.	Merħba
Good morning/ Good day.	Bonġu.
Goodbye.	Saħħa.
Yes.	Iva.
No.	Le.
Please.	Jekk jogħġbok.
Thank you.	Grazzi.
Excuse me.	Skużani.
Do you speak English?	Titkellem bl-ingliż? (informal)
How much is it?	Kemm?
What's your name?	X'ismek?
My name is ...	Jisimni ...

Getting Around

When does the boat leave/arrive?	Meta jitlaq/jasal il-vapur?
When does the bus leave/arrive?	Meta titlaq/jasal il-karozza?
I'd like a ... ticket.	Nixtieq biljett ...
one-way/return	'one-way/return'
1st/2nd class	'1st/2nd class'
left luggage	ħallejt il-bagalji
bus/trolleybus stop	xarabank/coach
I'd like to hire a car/bicycle.	Nixtieq nikri karozza/rota.

Signs – Maltese

Dhul	Entrance
Hrug	Exit
Informazjoni	Information
Miftuħ	Open
Magħluq	Closed
Tidholx	No Entry
Pulizija	Police
Toilets	Toilets
Rġiel	Men
Nisa	Women

Where is a/the ...?	Fejn hu ...?
Go straight ahead.	Mur dritt.
Turn left.	Dur fuq il-lemin.
Turn right.	Dur fuq il-ix-xellug.
near/far	il-viċin/-bogħod

Around Town

the bank	il-bank
chemist/pharmacy	l-ispiżerija
the ... embassy	l'ambaxxata ...
the hotel	hotel/il-lakanda
the market	is-suq
the post office	il-posta
a public telephone	telefon pubbliku
shop	ħanut
stamp	timbru
What time does it open/close?	Fix'ħin jiftaħ/jagħlaq?

Accommodation

Do you have a room available?	Għandek kamra jekk jogħġbok?
Do you have a room for one person/ two people?	Għandek kamra għal wieħed/ tnejn?
Do you have a room for one/two nights?	Għandek kamra għal lejl/żewgt iljieli?
Is breakfast included?	Il-breakfast inkluż?

Time, Days & Numbers

What's the time?	X'ħin hu?
today	illum
tomorrow	għada
yesterday	il-bieraħ
morning	fil-għodu
afternoon	nofs in-nhar

Emergencies – Maltese

Help!	Ajjut!
Call a doctor.	Qibgħad ghat-tabib.
Police!	Pulizija!
I'm lost.	Ninsab mitluf.
hospital	sptar
ambulance	ambulans

Monday	it-tnejn
Tuesday	it-tlieta
Wednesday	l-erbgħa
Thursday	il-hamis
Friday	il-gimgha
Saturday	is-sibt
Sunday	il-hadd

0	xejn
1	wiehed
2	tnejn
3	tlieta
4	erbgha
5	hamsa
6	sitta
7	sebgha
8	tmienja
9	disgha
10	ghaxra
11	hdax
100	mija
1000	elf

one million	miljun

Moroccan Arabic

Pronunciation

Arabic is a difficult language to learn, but even knowing a few words can win you a friendly smile from the locals.

Vowels There are at least five basic vowel sounds that can be distinguished:

a	as in 'had' (sometimes very short)
e	as in 'bet' (sometimes very short)
i	as in 'hit'
o	as in 'hot'
u	as the 'oo' in 'book'

A stroke over a vowel ('macron') gives it a long sound. For example:

ā	as in 'far'
ē	as in 'ten', but lengthened
ī	as the 'e' in 'ear', only softer (often written as 'ee')
ō	as in 'for'
ū	as the 'oo' in 'food'

Combinations Certain combinations of vowels with vowels or consonants form other vowel sounds (diphthongs):

aw	as the 'ow' in 'how'
ai	as the 'i' in 'high'
ei, ay	as the 'a' in 'cake'

Consonants Many consonants are the same as in English, but there are some tricky ones:

j	more or less as the 'j' in 'John'
H	a strongly whispered 'h', almost like a sigh of relief
q	a strong guttural 'k' sound
kh	a slightly gurgling sound, like the 'ch' in Scottish 'loch'
r	a rolled 'r' sound
s	as in 'sit', never as in 'wisdom'
sh	as in 'she'
z	as the 's' in pleasure
gh	called 'ghayn', similar to the French 'r', but more guttural

Glottal Stop (') The glottal stop is the sound you hear between the vowels in the expression 'oh oh!'. In Arabic it can occur anywhere in a word – at the beginning, middle or end. When the (') occurs before a vowel (eg, 'ayn), the vowel is 'growled' from the back of the throat. If it's before a consonant or at the end of a word, it sounds like a glottal stop.

Basics

Hello.	as-salām 'alaykum
Goodbye.	ma' as-salāma
Yes.	īyeh
No.	la
Please.	'afak
Thank you (very much).	shukran (jazilan)
You're welcome.	la shukran, 'ala wajib
Excuse me.	smeH līya
Do you speak English?	wash kat'ref neglīzīya?
I understand.	fhemt

Emergencies – Moroccan Arabic	
Help!	*'teqnī!*
Call a doctor!	*'eyyet at-tabīb!*
Call the police!	*'eyyet al-bolīs!*
Go away!	*sīr fHalek!*

I don't understand.	*mafhemtsh*
How much (is it)?	*bish-hal?*
What's your name?	*asmītak?*
My name is ...	*smītī ...*

Getting Around

What time does the ... leave/arrive?	*emta qiyam/wusūl ...*
boat	*al-babūr*
bus (city)	*al-otobīs*
bus (intercity)	*al-kar*
train	*al-mashīna*

1st/2nd class	*ddarazha llūla/ttanīya*
train station	*maHattat al-mashīna/ al-qitar*
bus stop	*mawqif al-otobis*
Where can I hire a car/bicycle?	*fein yimkin ana akra tomobīl/beshklīta?*
Where is (the) ...?	*fein ...?*
Go straight ahead.	*sīr nīshan*
Turn right.	*dor 'al līmen*
Turn left.	*dor 'al līser*

Around Town

the bank	*al-banka*
the embassy	*as-sifāra*
the market	*as-sūq*
the police station	*al-bolīs*
the post office	*al-bōsta, maktab al-barīd*
a toilet	*bayt al-ma, mirHad*

Accommodation

hotel	*al-otēl*
youth hostel	*dar shabbab*
camp site	*mukhaym*

Is there a room available?	*wash kayn shī bīt xawīya?*
How much is this room per night?	*bshaHal al-bayt liyal?*
Is breakfast included?	*wash lftor mHsūb m'a lbīt?*

Time, Dates & Numbers

What time is it?	*shHal fessa'a?*
today	*al-yūm*
tomorrow	*ghaddan*
yesterday	*al-bareh*
in the morning	*fis-sabaH*
in the evening	*fil-masa'*

Monday	*(nhar) al-itnēn*
Tuesday	*(nhar) at-talata*
Wednesday	*(nhar) al-arba'*
Thursday	*(nhar) al-khamīs*
Friday	*(nhar) al-juma'*
Saturday	*(nhar) as-sabt*
Sunday	*(nhar) al-ahad*

Arabic numerals are simple enough to learn and, unlike the written language, run from left to right. In Morocco, European numerals are also often used.

1	*wāHid*
2	*jūj* or *itnīn*
3	*talata*
4	*arba'a*
5	*khamsa*
6	*sitta*
7	*saba'a*
8	*tamanya*
9	*tissa'*
10	*'ashara*
100	*miyya*
1000	*alf*

one million	*melyūn*

Portuguese

Portuguese pronunciation can be tricky for the uninitiated; like English, vowels and consonants have more than one possible sound depending on position and stress. Moreover, there are nasal vowels and diphthongs in Portuguese with no English equivalents.

ã	as the 'an' in 'fan' plus the '-ng' sound at the end of the word 'sing'
ão	as the 'ow' in 'how'
é	as the 'e' in 'whey'
ç	as the 'c' in 'celery'
c	as the 'k' in 'kit' before 'a', 'o' and 'u'; as the 's' in 'sin' before 'e' and 'i'
ch	as the 'sh' in 'shake'

h	usually silent; sometimes as in 'hot'
m	often silent; nasalises the preceding vowel
s	as in 'sun' when word-initial; as 'sh' before c, f, p, q or t; as in 'pleasure' before b, d, g, l, m, n, r and v
qu	as the 'k' in 'kiosk' before 'e' or 'i'; elsewhere as in 'queen'
x	as the 'sh' in 'shake'
z	as 'jz' when word-final; elsewhere as 'sz'

Word stress is important in Portuguese, as it can affect meaning. In words with a written accent, the stress always falls on the accented syllable. Note also that Portugese uses masculine and feminine word endings, usually '-o' and '-a' respectively – to say 'thank you', a man will therefore use *obrigado*, a woman, *obrigada*.

Basics

Hello/Goodbye.	*Bom dia/Adeus.*
Yes.	*Sim.*
No.	*Não.*
Please.	*Se faz favor.*
Thank you.	*Obrigado/a.* (m/f)
You're welcome.	*De nada.*
Excuse me.	*Com licença.*
Sorry. (forgive me)	*Desculpe.*
Do you speak English?	*Fala Inglês?*
How much is it?	*Quanto custa?*
What's your name?	*Como se chama?*
My name is ...	*Chamo-me ...*

Getting Around

What time does the ... leave/arrive?	*A que horas parte/ chega ...?*
boat	*o barco*
bus (city)	*o autocarro*
bus (intercity)	*a camioneta*
tram	*o eléctrico*
train	*o combóio*

I'd like a ... ticket.	*Queria um bilhete ...*
one-way	*simples/de ida*
return	*de ida e volta*
1st class	*de primeira classe*
2nd class	*de segunda classe*

I'd like to hire ...	*Queria alugar ...*
a car	*um carro*
a bicycle	*uma bicicleta*

timetable	*horário*
bus stop	*paragem de autocarro*
train station	*estação ferroviária*

Where is ...?	*Onde é ...?*
Go straight ahead.	*Siga sempre a direito/ Siga sempre em frente.*
Turn left.	*Vire à esquerda.*
Turn right.	*Vire à direita.*
near/far	*perto/longe*

Around Town

a bank	*um banco*
the chemist/ pharmacy	*a farmácia*
the ... embassy	*a embaixada de ...*
my hotel	*o meu hotel*
the market	*o mercado*
the newsagents	*a papelaria*
the post office	*os correios*
the stationers	*a tabacaria*
the telephone centre	*a central de telefones*
the tourist office	*o turismo/o posto de turismo*

What time does it open/close?	*A que horas abre/ fecha?*

Accommodation

hotel	*hotel*
guesthouse	*pensão*
youth hostel	*pousada da juventude*
camping ground	*parque de campismo*
Do you have any rooms available?	*Tem quartos livres?*
How much is it per night/per person?	*Quanto é por noite/ por pessoa?*

Emergencies – Portuguese

Help!	Socorro!
Call a doctor!	Chame um médico!
Call the police!	Chame a polícia!
Go away!	Deixe-me em paz!/
	Vai-te embora! (inf)
I'm lost.	Estou perdido/a. (m/f)

Is breakfast included?	O pequeno almoço está incluído?
a single room	um quarto individual
a double room	um quarto duplo/de casal
for one/two night/s	para uma/duas noite/s

Time, Days & Numbers

What time is it?	Que horas são?
today	hoje
tomorrow	amanhã
yesterday	ontem
morning	manhã
afternoon	tarde
Monday	segunda-feira
Tuesday	terça-feira
Wednesday	quarta-feira
Thursday	quinta-feira
Friday	sexta-feira
Saturday	sábado
Sunday	domingo

1	um/uma
2	dois/duas
3	três
4	quatro
5	cinco
6	seis
7	sete
8	oito
9	nove
10	dez
11	onze
20	vinte
21	vinte e um/uma
30	trinta
40	quarenta
100	cem
1000	mil

one million	um milhão

Slovene

Pronunciation

Slovene pronunciation isn't difficult. The alphabet consists of 25 letters, most of which are very similar to English. It doesn't have the letters 'q', 'w', 'x' and 'y', but the following letters are added: ê, é, ó, ò, č, š and ž. Each letter represents only one sound, with very few exceptions, and the sounds are pure and not diphthongal. The letters l and v are both pronounced like the English 'w' when they occur at the end of syllables and before vowels. Though words like *trn* (thorn) look unpronounceable, most Slovenes add a short vowel like an 'a' or the German 'ö' (depending on dialect) in front of the 'r' to give a Scot's pronunciation of 'tern' or 'tarn'. Here is a list of letters specific to Slovene.

c	as the 'ts' in 'its'
č	as the 'ch' in 'church'
ê	as the 'a' in 'apple'
e	as the 'er' in 'opera' (when unstressed)
é	as the 'ay' in 'day'
j	as the 'y' in 'yellow'
ó	as the 'o' in 'more'
ò	as the 'o' in 'soft'
r	a rolled 'r' sound
š	as the 'sh' in 'ship'
u	as the 'oo' in 'good'
ž	as the 's' in 'treasure'

Basics

Hello.	Pozdravljeni. (formal)
	Zdravo or Žvivio. (informal)
Good day.	Dober dan!
Goodbye.	Nasvidenje!
Yes.	Da. or Ja. (informal)
No.	Ne.
Please.	Prosim.
Thank you (very much).	Hvala (lepa).
You're welcome.	Prosim/Ni za kaj!
Excuse me.	Oprostite.
What's your name?	Kako vam je ime?
My name is ...	Jaz sem ...
Where are you from?	Od kod ste?
I'm from ...	Sem iz ...

Getting Around

What time does ... leave/arrive?	Kdaj odpelje/ pripelje ...?
boat/ferry	ladja/trajekt
bus	avtobus
train	vlak

one-way (ticket)	enosmerna (vozovnica)
return (ticket)	povratna (vozovnica)

Around Town

Where is the/a ...?	Kje je ...?
bank/exchange	banka/menjalnica
embassy	konzulat/ambasada
post office	pošta
telephone centre	telefonska centrala
tourist office	turistični informa- cijski urad

Accommodation

hotel	hotel
guesthouse	gostišče
camping ground	kamping

Do you have a ...?	Ali imate prosto ...?
bed	posteljo
cheap room	poceni sobo
single room	enoposteljno sobo
double room	dvoposteljno sobo

How much is it per night?	Koliko stane za eno noč?
How much is it per person?	Koliko stane za eno osebo?
for one/two nights	za eno noč/za dve noči
Is breakfast included?	Ali je zajtrk vključen?

Time, Days & Numbers

today	danes
tonight	nocoj
tomorrow	jutri

in the morning	zjutraj
in the evening	zvečer

Monday	ponedeljek
Tuesday	torek
Wednesday	sreda
Thursday	četrtek
Friday	petek
Saturday	sobota
Sunday	nedelja

1	ena
2	dve
3	tri
4	štiri
5	pet
6	šest
7	sedem
8	osem
9	devet
10	deset
100	sto
1000	tisoč

one million	milijon

Spanish

Pronunciation

Spanish pronunciation isn't difficult, given that many Spanish sounds are similar to their English counterparts and there's a clear and consistent relationship between pronunciation and spelling. If you stick to the following rules you should have very few problems making yourself understood.

Vowels Unlike English, each of the vowels in Spanish has a uniform pronunciation which doesn't vary. For example, the Spanish 'a' has one pronunciation rather than the numerous pronunciations we find in English, such as 'cat', 'cake', 'cart', 'care', 'call'. Many Spanish words have a written accent. The acute accent (as in días) generally indicates a stressed syllable and doesn't change the sound of the vowel. Vowels are pronounced clearly even if they are in unstressed positions or at the end of a word.

a	as the 'u' in 'nut', or a shorter sound than the 'a' in 'art'
e	as in 'met'
i	somewhere between the 'i' in 'marine' and the 'i' in 'flip'
o	similar to the 'o' in 'hot'
u	as the 'oo' in 'hoof'

Consonants Some Spanish consonants are the same as their English counterparts. The pronunciation of other consonants varies according to which vowel follows and also according to which part of Spain you happen to be in. The Spanish alphabet also contains three consonants that are not found within the English alphabet: **ch**, **ll** and **ñ**.

b	softer than in English; sometimes as in 'be' when word-initial or preceded by a nasal
c	a hard 'c' as in 'cat' when followed by **a**, **o**, **u** or a consonant; as the 'th' in 'thin' before **e** and **i**
ch	as in 'church'
d	as in 'do' when initial; elsewhere as the 'th' in 'then'
g	as in 'get' when initial and before **a**, **o** and **u**; elsewhere much softer. Before **e** or **i** it's a harsh, breathy sound, similar to the 'h' in 'hit'
h	silent
j	a harsh, guttural sound similar to the 'ch' in Scottish 'loch'
ll	as the 'lli' in 'million'; some pronounce it rather like the 'y' in 'yellow'
ñ	a nasal sound, as the 'nl' in 'onion'
q	as the 'k' in 'kick'; **q** is always followed by a silent **u** and is combined only with the vowels **e** (as in *que*) and **i** (as in *qui*)
r	a rolled 'r' sound; longer and stronger when initial or doubled
s	as in 'see'
v	the same sound as **b**
x	as the 'ks' sound in 'taxi' when between two vowels; as the 's' in 'see' when preceding a consonant
z	as the 'th' in 'thin'

Signs – Spanish

Entrada	**Entrance**
Salida	**Exit**
Habtaciones	**Rooms Available**
Libres	
Completo	**Full/No Vacancies**
Información	**Information**
Abierto	**Open**
Cerrado	**Closed**
Prohibido	**Prohibited**
Comisaría	**Police Station**
Servicios/Aseos	**Toilets**
Hombres	**Men**
Mujeres	**Women**

Semiconsonant Spanish also has the semiconsonant **y**. When at the end of a word or when standing alone as a conjunction it's pronounced like the Spanish **i**. As a consonant, it's somewhere between the 'y' in 'yonder' and the 'g' in 'beige', depending on the region.

Basics

Hello.	*¡Hola!*
Goodbye.	*¡Adiós!*
Yes.	*Sí.*
No.	*No.*
Please.	*Por favor.*
Thank you.	*Gracias.*
You're welcome.	*De nada.*
Excuse me.	*Perdón/Perdoneme.*
I'm sorry. (forgive me)	*Lo siento/Discúlpeme.*
Do you speak English?	*¿Habla inglés?*
How much is it?	*¿Cuánto cuesta?/ ¿Cuánto vale?*
What's your name?	*¿Cómo se llama?*
My name is ...	*Me llamo ...*

Getting Around

What time does the next ... leave/arrive?	*¿A qué hora sale/ llega el próximo ...?*
boat	*barco*
bus (city)	*autobús, bus*
bus (intercity)	*autocar*
train	*tranvía*
I'd like a ... ticket.	*Quisiera un billete ...*
one-way	*sencillo/de sólo ida*
return	*de ida y vuelta*

Emergencies – Spanish

Help!	¡Socorro!/¡Auxilio!
Call a doctor!	¡Llame a un doctor!
Call the police!	¡Llame a la policía!
Go away!	¡Váyase!
I'm lost.	Estoy perdido/a. (m/f)

1st/2nd class	primera/segunda clase
left luggage	consigna
timetable	horario
bus stop	parada de autobus
train station	estación de ferrocarril

I'd like to hire ...	Quisiera alquilar ...
a car	un coche
a bicycle	una bicicleta

Where is ...?	¿Dónde está ...?
Go straight ahead.	Siga/Vaya todo derecho.
Turn left.	Gire a la izquierda.
Turn right.	Gire a la derecha/recto.
near/far	cerca/lejos

Around Town

a bank	un banco
chemist/pharmacy	la farmacia
the ... embassy	la embajada ...
my hotel	mi hotel
the market	el mercado
newsagents/	papelería
stationers	
the post office	los correos
the telephone centre	el locutorio
the tourist office	la oficina de turismo

What time does it open/close?	¿A qué hora abren/ cierran?

Accommodation

camping ground	camping
guesthouse	pensión/casa de huéspedes
hotel	hotel
youth hostel	albergue juvenil

Do you have any rooms available?	¿Tiene habitaciones libres?
How much is it per night/per person?	¿Cuánto cuesta por noche/por persona?
Is breakfast included?	¿Incluye el desayuno?

a single room	una habitación individual
a double room	una habitación doble
for one/two night/s	para una/dos noche/s

Time, Days & Numbers

What time is it?	¿Qué hora es?
today	hoy
tomorrow	mañana
yesterday	ayer
morning	mañana
afternoon	tarde

Monday	lunes
Tuesday	martes
Wednesday	miércoles
Thursday	jueves
Friday	viernes
Saturday	sábado
Sunday	domingo

1	uno, una
2	dos
3	tres
4	cuatro
5	cinco
6	seis
7	siete
8	ocho
9	nueve
10	diez
11	once
12	doce
13	trece
14	catorce
15	quince
16	dieciéis
100	cien/ciento
1000	mil

one million	un millón

Turkish

Pronunciation

The new Turkish alphabet is phonetic and thus reasonably easy to pronounce, once you've learned a few basic rules. Each Turkish letter is pronounced, there are no diphthongs, and the only silent letter is ğ.

Vowels Turkish vowels are pronounced as follows:

A, a	as the 'ar' in 'art' or 'bar'
E, e	as in 'fell'
İ, i	as 'ee'
I, ı	as 'uh'
O, o	as in 'hot'
U, u	as the 'oo' in 'moo'
Ö, ö	as the 'ur' in 'fur'
Ü, ü	as the 'ew' in 'few'

Note that both ö and ü are pronounced with pursed lips.

Consonants Most consonants are pronounced as in English, with a few exceptions:

Ç, ç	as the 'ch' in 'church'
C, c	as English 'j'
Ğ, ğ	not pronounced; draws out the preceding vowel a bit – ignore it!
G, g	hard, as in 'gun'
H, h	as the 'h' in 'half'
J, j	as the 's' in 'treasure'
S, s	hard, as in 'stress'
Ş, ş	as the 'sh' in 'shoe'
V, v	as the 'w' in 'weather'

Basics

Hello.	Merhaba.
Goodbye.	Allahaısmarladık/ Güle güle.
Yes.	Evet.
No.	Hayır.
Please.	Lütfen.
Thank you.	Teşekkür ederim.
That's fine/ You're welcome.	Bir şey değil.
Excuse me.	Affedersiniz.
Sorry/Pardon.	Pardon.
Do you speak English?	İngilizce biliyor musunuz?
How much is it?	Ne kadar?
What's your name?	Adınız ne?
My name is ...	Adım ...

Getting Around

What time does the next ... leave/arrive?	Gelecek ... ne zaman kalkar/gelir?
ferry/boat	feribot/vapur
bus (city)	şehir otobüsü
bus (intercity)	otobüs
tram	tramvay
train	tren

Signs – Turkish

Giriş	Entrance
Çikiş	Exit
Açık/Kapali	Open/Closed
Danişma	Information
Boş Oda Var	Rooms Available
Dolu	Full/No Vacancies
Polis/Emniyet	Police
Polis Karakolu/ Emniyet Müdürlüğü	Police Station
Yasak(tir)	Prohibited
Tuvalet	Toilets

I'd like ...	... istiyorum
a one-way ticket	gidiş bileti
a return ticket	gidiş-dönüş bileti
1st/2nd class	birinci/ikinci mevkii

left luggage	emanetçi
timetable	tarife
bus/tram stop	otobüs/tramvay durağı
train station	gar/istasyon
boat/ship dock	iskele

I'd like to hire a car/bicycle.	Araba/bisiklet kirala mak istiyorum.
Where is a/the ...?	... nerede?
Go straight ahead.	Doğru gidin.
Turn left.	Sola dönün.
Turn right.	Sağa dönün.
near/far	yakın/uzak

Around Town

a bank	bir banka
the ... embassy	... büyükelçiliği
my hotel	otelimi
the post office	postane
the market	çarşı
a chemist/pharmacy	bir eczane
the telephone centre	telefon merkezi
the tourist office	turizm danışma bürosu

| What time does it open/close? | Ne zamam açılır/kapanır? |

Accommodation

hotel	otel(i)
guesthouse	pansiyon
student hostel	öğrenci yurdu
camping ground	kampink

Emergencies – Turkish

Help!/Emergency!	İmdat!
There's been an accident!	Bir kaza oldu!
(There's a) fire!	Yangın var!
Call a doctor!	Doktor çağırın!
Call the police!	Polis çağırın!
Could you help us please?	Bize yardım edebilirmisiniz lütfen?
Go away!	Gidin/Git!/Defol!
I'm lost.	Kayboldum.

Do you have any rooms available?	Boş oda var mı?
How much is it per night/per person?	Bir gecelik/Kişibaşına kaç para?
Is breakfast included?	Kahvaltı dahil mi?
a single room	tek kişilik oda
a double room	iki kişilik oda

Time, Days & Numbers

What time is it?	Saat kaç?
today	bugün
tomorrow	yarın
yesterday	dün
morning	sabah
afternoon	öğleden sonra
Monday	Pazartesi
Tuesday	Salı
Wednesday	Çarşamba
Thursday	Perşembe
Friday	Cuma
Saturday	Cumartesi
Sunday	Pazar
January	Ocak
February	Şubat
March	Mart
April	Nisan
May	Mayıs
June	Haziran
July	Temmuz
August	Ağustos
September	Eylül
October	Ekim
November	Kasım
December	Aralık

1	bir
2	iki
3	üç
4	dört
5	beş
6	altı
7	yedi
8	sekiz
9	dokuz
10	on
11	on bir
12	on iki
13	on üç
100	yüz
1000	bin
one million	bir milyon

Acknowledgements

THANKS FROM THE AUTHORS

Janet Austin Thanks to the extremely helpful staff at the various tourist information offices I visited, and to Giancarlo and Christina in Liguria. Special thanks go to Alice in Rome, Alex in La Spezia, Maria in Melbourne, Riddle and George, Beck and Moby, and last but not least to Dave who came along for the slog.

Carolyn Bain Firstly, thanks to those at LP who got me involved in this project, to David Willett, co-author of this Greece chapter, Ian Madanis for the (attempted) Greek lessons, and Dierdre Roberts for invaluable insights into all things Cretan.

A heartfelt *efharisto* to the many locals who helped me out in Greece. Special mention goes to Evangelos for playing impromptu tour guide in Mykonos; Francesco for demonstrating the calmer side of Ios; Petros and his family in Fira for letting me share in an authentic Greek Easter; Alexis and his family in Kos for treating me as one of their own; and Alex of Chios for helping me discover the best grilled octopus in the country. Cheers also to the expats and travellers I met, including Theo in Mykonos, Sara and the crew from Kafe Besara in Rhodes, and especially Rosa Fernandez and Lars Hedegaard.

Boundless gratitude to my sister Jules and her partner John for allowing me free run of their home in London, to my parents for their support, and to my friends for following my adventures with just the right amount of interest, encouragement and envy!

Neal Bedford Thanks firstly goes to Ryan Ver Berkmoes and Steve Fallon for setting me off on the right track and Damien Simonis and John Noble for their invaluable advice on Spain. A special thanks goes to the whole London LP office for the support I received, in particular for their extra special effort (which you had no choice in giving!) – Paul Bloomfield, Katrina Browning, Imogen Franks, Tom Hall, Howard Ralley, Tim Ryder, Sam Trafford, Angie Watts and Dave Wenk. And also to the ex LPers – Tom Bevan, Nicky Robinson and Anna Sutton. My gratitude and sympathy goes out to those who had to put up with me on the road, the Bevans, John Richards, Robert Box, Claire Delamey, Nik Pickard and Rachel Parker. And a big bussi to Christina Tlustos for all the support and guidance.

Verity Campbell Thanks to Rachel, Katie, Caro & Gabi for making it happen; Michelle, Geoff & Brett for holding the fort while I gallivanted (Oh, I had a terrible time!); Johnny 'BOS' for your emails; Kirst and Steven for mopping the tears; Max for being a forgiving dog – Danny & Steven for putting up with him; and, of course, my beloved tease of a mother. In Turkey a huge thanks to the Coşkuns for remembering me (or politely pretending to). Thanks to Kay and Janet in İstanbul, Karin in Antalya. Merhaba to the Olimpos gang, 'daat' Ben, Osman, Ross, Matt, Julie, Craig and Marie. *Ta Etienne,* for your dedication to your job (ra, ra). A tipped Fez to fellow authors Joyce, Simon, Richard, Matt and especially to Pat Yale. *Teşekkürler* to all the tourist officials (especially in İzmir, Dalyan, Bursa and Çanakkale) who were incredibly helpful. Thanks to the travellers I met (and letters you sent) – your contributions were invaluable – and lastly *çok teşekkür ederim* to the Turkish people whose generosity, patience and ability at backgammon never ceases to amaze me.

Joyce Connolly Thanks to following travellers, moroccans and coworkers: Jason Rankin (aka Cowboy Surfer); Benjamin Villand; Joanne Vella; Clare Irvin; to Matt Fletcher for all the words of encouragement; my mum (Mary Leggat); Alan Campbell; Verity Campbell; Jan Campbell & Josef; Bob O'Sullivan; Paul Maxwell & James Schultz; Angelina & Amy; Esteban; Frankie & Abby; Christoff Reinecke; Angela Pugh & Steven Buckler; Elly Fattore; Agnes Pottier; Didier Heberli; Hartley Wynberg; Matt Hargest & Marcel Mettelseifen; Monique & Bas; Michael & Justine; Daniella & David; Brahim Bahri; and Phil; Clive & Justin; the Bazar Zougagh Fatima family; Nemri Sala Heddine; Malek in Safi; Ben Zitoun Youness; Fiona Cameron & Preben Kristensen; Aziz Mnii; Youssef Lafquih; Amina Zakkari Fés; Geoff Stringer; Lucienne Cooper and Jennifer Smith – thanks, I couldn't have done it without you.

Fionn Davenport For the Italian section, my deepest thanks to Sandra, Giorgia and Luigi Sabarini for their hospitality and help. I couldn't have done it without you. Thanks also to the various tourist offices, particularly Rome, Naples and Cagliari, who went beyond the call of duty to facilitate my research. For the Britain section, I would like to express my gratitude to all in Cambridge for pointing me in the right direction.

Matt Fletcher Thanks firstly to Clare Irvin (again), to Dr Jaouad Berrada for the welcome in Rabat and Joyce for her hard work in Morocco. Thanks also to Lorna and Akim in Mohammedia, Harvey Palmer, Cathy Myers and Robert Drechsler (thanks for the laughs at the mort de mouton), Azi Mnii at the London Moroccan tourist office, Adel Nouayba the genial director of Centre de Hassan II in Asilah, Harrak Abdeslm in Tetouan, Abdel Aziz el Mouden and his very knowledgeable big brother Abdeslam. Thanks also to the staff at the British Embassy, plus Leila Mourad and John Shackleton at the British Council. In Tangier Debbi Hamida, Stephanie Sweet, Matt Schofield and Thor Kuniholm were a great help.

Kate Galbraith In Macedonia great thanks to Goce Bozinovski from the tourist office for driving me around the country, rakija and all. Thanks to Keith Brown of the US Institute for Peace for sharing his historical and cultural expertise. In Albania a million thanks to Gazmend Haxia for orienting me in Tirana, and to Stacy Sullivan for the link and for loving Albania. Thanks to Abe Sutherland for braving Albania before me and living to tell. Also thanks to the Thorn Tree contributor on Albania. Many thanks to the OSCE in both countries – Harald Schenker in Skopje, Tim Bittiger in Tirana, the OSCE crew in Durrës, Christian Bodewig for putting me in touch, to Tim's friends Bjorn Kuhne and Nicola Schmidt, and to Michela Johnson.

Jeremy Gray The utterly lovely, charitable staff in the French tourist offices I visited deserve my boundless gratitude. Isabelle at Le Conquet (Brittany) deserves a very special mention – I never would have found those secret treasures without her. Thanks, too, to Jen Wabisabi for getting lost with me at all those confusing roundabouts, and to Jacques and Gi Veit for being the consummate

hosts (I'll never forget the truffle-scented eggs). Fellow authors Steve Fallon, Paul Hellander, Daniel Robinson, Miles Roddis and Nicola Williams all earn a *palme d'or* for being sooo professional and for infusing the France chapter with so much character.

Paul Hellander Certain people and organisations who contributed to my work in one way or another deserve a mention. Thanks to the very co-operative *Offices de Tourisme* that plied me with excellent data and to SNCM for transport to and from Corsica. Thanks to my wife Stella for her assistance for her excellent photography. Special mention also to the following individuals: Louiza Maragozidis; Nicola Williams and Matthias Lüftkens; Stéphanie 4; Michel, Stella & Véronique le Petit; Iain & Liz Purce; Jean-Marie & Irène Casta and Deborah Palmer. To sons Byron and Marcus in Greece – another title bites the dust for you.

Mark Honan As usual, many thanks are due to staff in the press/media section of Switzerland Tourism and the Austrian National Tourist Office. Much credit to those who answered my diverse inquiries (most notably Charles Page in Rail Europe, Kathrin Rohrbach in the Bern tourist office and my fellow authors on these Europe guidebooks); much discredit to those who didn't (the AA – I'm still waiting). Thanks also to Sue in Geneva and Irmgard in Vienna.

Patrick Horton My special thanks go to Zarko Tankosic for his great help in putting the Serbian section together. In Montenegro I would like to thank Vesna Sekulić & Čelko Krgovic for their assistance in making my work easier. In Kosovo I would like to thank Naim Shala for his help and hospitality, and the manager and staff of the Hotel Dypon, who despite charging two arms and a leg, went out of their way to show me around. Lastly I would like to acknowledge the hospitality and interest shown by all the people I met and their willingness to converse with a visitor.

Jeanne Oliver In Croatia, I would like to thank Vesna Jovićić in Pula, Gordana Perić and Xenia Kardun in Zadar, Ankica Bokšić in Split, Stanka Kraljević and Aljoša Milat in Korčula. I would also like to thank the National Tourist Board, and the Tourist Boards of Istria, Kvarner, Zadar, Split-Dalmatia, Dubrovnik and Zagreb.

In Slovenia, thanks to Rok Klančnik for his invaluable support as well as the tourist offices of Ljubljana, Bled, Bohinj, Koper, Piran and Portorož.

Daniel Robinson My work in Strasbourg would not have been anywhere near as much fun were it not for my parents, Bernie and Yetta Robinson, who came to visit; and Corrine and Rachel of Radio Judaica, who helped me track down Salim Halali's unique Arabic version of the Yiddish classic *Œma Yiddische Mama'*. In Dijon, warmth and hominess were contributed by Professor Bob Wiener, Albert and Myrna Huberfel, and the Tenenbaum family: Françoise, Denis, Charles, Annabelle and Nathalie. Paris' relentness urbanness was softened by the staff of Lonely Planet's Paris bureau, including Arnot, Benjamin, Caroline, Didier, Rob and Zahia; Rabbis Pauline Bebe and Tom Cohen; Diane Holt and Michael Feldman, who are always up for a weekend away from Naples; David Saliamonis, whom life's journey has taken all the way from Glen Ellyn, Illinois to Paris; my almost-cousin Miel de Botton; Eliane Bebe; Antoine Bebe; and Kamal, Karim, Madame Sadou and the inimitable staff of the Hôtel Rivoli.

Miles Roddis To Ingrid for sharing it all, both the excitement and the tedium.

David Rowson & Keti Japaridze We are very grateful to Mike Solly and Duncan Still, who generously shared their knowledge and understanding of Bosnia-Hercegovina, and whose enthusiasm was contagious. Also our appreciation to Mlhajlo, our host in Sarajevo, and thanks to Aisa Telalovic and Noreen Skillet for the insights they gave us.

Andrea Schulte-Peevers People throughout my area of coverage were generous in answering questions and patient in putting up with my rusty Spanish. Those who stand out for going beyond the call of duty are: Jasone Aretxabaleta of the Dirección General de Turismo del País Vasco; Visi Urtiaga in Bilbao; Diana Draper in San Sebastián; Jason Kykendall and Mar Martín Alonso in Salamanca; Belén Cubo Alias in Segovia; Mónica Garcia Hernando in Valladolid; and Alberto Abad Pérez, Margarita and her parents in Soria.

The biggest round of applause, though, belongs to my husband David Peevers for keeping me company – and sane – on the road. Thanks for your good humor and patience in checking out Castilia's countless churches, castles and shower curtains.

Rachel Suddart Thanks to: the BBC and Lonely Planet Publications for allowing me the chance to get a 'foot in the door'; the Lonely Planet staff for all their help and guidance; the Cyprus Tourist Organisation and the TRNC Tourist Organisation for all their vital information and literature; Jay and Karl for letting me constantly abuse their sofa bed; Kelly, Christine and Tim for not letting me quit when times were hard; Mr. Alan Daltrey for teaching me to stand up and be counted; and finally, my mum and dad for their continual love and support. Cheers!

Julia Wilkinson & John King Special thanks go to the following dedicated tourist officers: Miguel Gonzaga (Turismo de Lisboa), Anabela Pereira (Bragança), Marla do Rosário Graça (Vila Real) and Carla Basílio (Covilhã), along with long-suffering turismo staff at Beja, Braga, Portalegre and Sintra. Thanks also to Clara and Dionisio Vitorino, Michael Collins (Portuguese Arts Trust), Miranda Jessop (KTA International), Geraldine Ahearn (TAP Air Portugal), Anabela Esteves (ADERE), John Fisher (Connex South Eastern) and Peter Mills (Rail Europe). John Noble provided frequent, detailed help with Spain information.

David Willett My thanks go first to my partner, Rowan, and our son, Tom, for holding the fort at home during another extended stay away. Athens feels almost like home these days. I look forward to catching up with my friends (and guides) Yiannis and Katerina, Maria, Anna, Jarek and Tolis.

Nicola Williams *Un grand merci* in no particular order to Catherine Moulé at Saumur's École Nationale d'Équitation, Laurent de Froberville at Château de Cheverny, Christa Lüfkens, Monsieur and Madame Gaultier, and the myriad friends and acquaintances in Lyon for the feast of restaurant recommendations over the years. Oh, and to husband Matthias for being that perfect dining partner.

Neil Wilson Thanks to Claude Muscat Doublesin, Sandra Aquilina and Joanna Dowling at NSTS in Valletta; and to James Azzopardi of the

Malta Tourist Authority. Thanks also to Carol Downie for dedicated restaurant research. Many thanks to the readers who wrote in with helpful hints, useful advice and interesting anecdotes: Muireann Cullen, John Deacon, Barbara Foster, Sonja Sun Johnsen, Mackay Smith and Anthony Thompson.

Pat Yale Thanks: As ever I have been overwhelmed by the help and hospitality of the Turkish people, but special thanks must go to: Adnan Pirioğulu in Ayder; Volkan in Erzurum; Ahmet Baykal in Hattuşa; Roni Askey-Doran and Ken in İstanbul; Hüseyn Kaplan and Ahmet Bilge in Konya; Özcan Arslan in Şanlıurfa; Suha Ersoz in Ürgüp; and Remzi Bozbay in Van. I might still be battling with the technology required to see this book to the publishers were it not for Mustafa Güney at Göreme's Nese Internet Café. In Göreme, too, I'm especially grateful to Maggie Cassidy, Idris Demir, Dawn Köse, Nico Leyssen, Ruth Lockwood, Kylie Warner, Ali Yavuz and all my lovely neighbours for answering my endless queries, feeding my cat and generally keeping the home fires burning. Finally, for support and encouragement in the last stressful days before the deadline, warm thanks to Paul Harding, Yilmaz Özlük and all the Kiğuili family at the Side Pension in İstanbul, in particular to Mahmoud.

THANKS
Many thanks to the travellers who used the last edition and wrote to us with helpful hints, useful advice and interesting anecdotes:

Alan Bartlett, Alexander Winter, Allan M Healy, Anita J Cunningham, Barbara Foster, Berny Lottner, Betty Marriott, Betty Wilson, Brends McIntyre, Cathy Downes, Chantel Benoit, Chris Munro, Con Vaitsas, Craig Baron, Daniel Lawson, Dayna Carson, Frantisek Sistek, Georgie Plain, Helen Myers, HG Burnab, Huw Roberts, Janet Townsend, Jeannie Randall, Joe Lewardowski, John Dunkelberger, Julie Kuppers, K Gorringe, Kevin & Beth Salt, Kevin Micallef, Kim Sowman, Lisa & Steve Kingston, Maggie Carter, Martin & Phyllis Schulmeister, Massimo Bisiachi, Massoud Javadi, Matt Huddleston, Melissa Anderson, Melissa Rymer, N Arulraj, Nardia Haigh, Nicole Peel, Norwood Price, Paula Huber, Peter & Gail Kirby, Peter Adams, Piper & Andrea Roelen, Ragnar Aschim, Rebecca Skinner, Richard Cousineau de la Mirande, Richard Maurice, Richard Runcie, Rita Portelli, Rosario Di Fresco, Sacha Lethborg, Sophie Spartalis, Stephen & Annie Faustino, Stephen Wahl, Tania Daniels, Tom Jansing , Travis Swenson, Zach Rohaizad Roj Haron, Zoran Zinzovski

LONELY PLANET

You already know that Lonely Planet produces more than this one guidebook, but you might not be aware of the other products we have on this region. Here is a selection of titles that you may want to check out as well:

Europe on a shoestring

Mediterranean Europe phrasebook

CitySync: Paris
Rome

Read this First: Europe

Europe phrasebook

Condensed Guides:
Crete
Paris

Cycling France

World Food:
Italy
France
Spain

Walking Guides:
Spain
France
Italy

City Maps: Rome
Barcelona
Paris

Portugal Travel Atlas

Available wherever books are sold

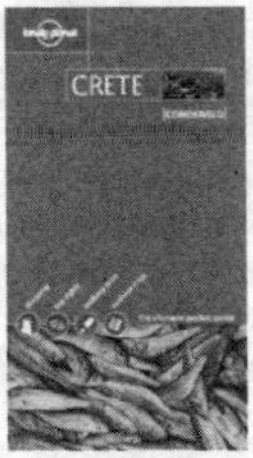

LONELY PLANET

ON THE ROAD

Travel Guides explore cities, regions and countries, and supply information on transport, restaurants and accommodation, covering all
budgets. They come with reliable, easy-to-use maps, practical advice,
cultural and historical facts and a rundown on attractions both on and
off the beaten track. There are over 200 titles in this classic series, covering nearly every country in the world.

 Lonely Planet Upgrades extend the shelf life of existing travel
guides by detailing any changes that may affect travel in a
region since a book has been published. Upgrades can be
downloaded for free from **www.lonelyplanet.com/upgrades**

For travellers with more time than money, **Shoestring** guides offer dependable, first-hand information with hundreds of detailed maps, plus
insider tips for stretching money as far as possible. Covering entire
continents in most cases, the six-volume shoestring guides are known
around the world as 'backpackers bibles'.

For the discerning short-term visitor, **Condensed** guides highlight the
best a destination has to offer in a full-colour, pocket-sized format
designed for quick access. They include everything from top sights and
walking tours to opinionated reviews of where to eat, stay, shop and
have fun.

CitySync lets travellers use their Palm™ or Visor™ hand-held computers to guide them through a city with handy tips on transport, history,
cultural life, major sights, and shopping and entertainment options.
It can also quickly search and sort hundreds of reviews of hotels,
restaurants and attractions, and pinpoint their location on scrollable
street maps. CitySync can be downloaded from **www.citysync.com**

MAPS & ATLASES

Lonely Planet's **City Maps** feature downtown and metropolitan maps,
as well as transit routes and walking tours. The maps come complete
with an index of streets, a listing of sights and a plastic coat for extra
durability.

Road Atlases are an essential navigation tool for serious travellers.
Cross-referenced with the guidebooks, they also feature distance and
climate charts and a complete site index.

LONELY PLANET

ESSENTIALS

Read This First books help new travellers to hit the road with confidence. These invaluable predeparture guides give step-by-step advice on preparing for a trip, budgeting, arranging a visa, planning an itinerary and staying safe while still getting off the beaten track.

Healthy Travel pocket guides offer a regional rundown on disease hot spots and practical advice on predeparture health measures, staying well on the road and what to do in emergencies. The guides come with a user-friendly design and helpful diagrams and tables.

Lonely Planet's **Phrasebooks** cover the essential words and phrases travellers need when they're strangers in a strange land. They come in a pocket-sized format with colour tabs for quick reference, extensive vocabulary lists, easy-to-follow pronunciation keys and two-way dictionaries.

Miffed by blurry photos of the Taj Mahal? Tired of the classic 'top of the head cut off' shot? **Travel Photography: A Guide to Taking Better Pictures** will help you turn ordinary holiday snaps into striking images and give you the know-how to capture every scene, from frenetic festivals to peaceful beach sunrises.

Lonely Planet's **Travel Journal** is a lightweight but sturdy travel diary for jotting down all those on-the-road observations and significant travel moments. It comes with a handy time-zone wheel, world maps and useful travel information.

Lonely Planet's eKno is an all-in-one communication service developed especially for travellers. It offers low-cost international calls and free email and voicemail so that you can keep in touch while on the road. Check it out on **www.ekno.lonelyplanet.com**

FOOD & RESTAURANT GUIDES

Lonely Planet's **Out to Eat** guides recommend the brightest and best places to eat and drink in top international cities. These gourmet companions are arranged by neighbourhood, packed with dependable maps, garnished with scene-setting photos and served with quirky features.

For people who live to eat, drink and travel, **World Food** guides explore the culinary culture of each country. Entertaining and adventurous, each guide is packed with detail on staples and specialities, regional cuisine and local markets, as well as sumptuous recipes, comprehensive culinary dictionaries and lavish photos good enough to eat.

LONELY PLANET

OUTDOOR GUIDES

For those who believe the best way to see the world is on foot, Lonely Planet's **Walking Guides** detail everything from family strolls to difficult treks, with 'when to go and how to do it' advice supplemented by reliable maps and essential travel information.

Cycling Guides map a destination's best bike tours, long and short, in day-by-day detail. They contain all the information a cyclist needs, including advice on bike maintenance, places to eat and stay, innovative maps with detailed cues to the rides, and elevation charts.

The **Watching Wildlife** series is perfect for travellers who want authoritative information but don't want to tote a heavy field guide. Packed with advice on where, when and how to view a region's wildlife, each title features photos of over 300 species and contains engaging comments on the local flora and fauna.

With underwater colour photos throughout, **Pisces Books** explore the world's best diving and snorkelling areas. Each book contains listings of diving services and dive resorts, detailed information on depth, visibility and difficulty of dives, and a roundup of the marine life you're likely to see through your mask.

LONELY PLANET

OFF THE ROAD

Journeys, the travel literature series written by renowned travel authors, capture the spirit of a place or illuminate a culture with a journalist's attention to detail and a novelist's flair for words. These are tales to soak up while you're actually on the road or dip into as an at-home armchair indulgence.

The new range of lavishly illustrated **Pictorial** books is just the ticket for both travellers and dreamers. Off-beat tales and vivid photographs bring the adventure of travel to your doorstep long before the journey begins and long after it is over.

Lonely Planet **Videos** encourage the same independent, tough-minded approach as the guidebooks. Currently airing throughout the world, this award-winning series features innovative footage and an original soundtrack.

Yes, we know, work is tough, so do a little bit of deskside dreaming with the spiral-bound Lonely Planet **Diary**, the tearaway page-a-day **Day-to-Day Calendar** or a Lonely Planet **Wall Calendar**, filled with great photos from around the world.

TRAVELLERS NETWORK

Lonely Planet Online. Lonely Planet's award-winning Web site has insider information on hundreds of destinations, from Amsterdam to Zimbabwe, complete with interactive maps and relevant links. The site also offers the latest travel news, recent reports from travellers on the road, guidebook upgrades, a travel links site, an online book-buying option and a lively traveller's bulletin board. It can be viewed at **www.lonelyplanet.com** or AOL keyword: lp.

Planet Talk is a quarterly print newsletter, full of gossip, advice, anecdotes and author articles. It provides an antidote to the being-at-home blues and lets you plan and dream for the next trip. Contact the nearest Lonely Planet office for your free copy.

Comet, the free Lonely Planet newsletter, comes via email once a month. It's loaded with travel news, advice, dispatches from authors, travel competitions and letters from readers. To subscribe, click on the Comet subscription link on the front page of the Web site.

Guides by Region

Lonely Planet is known worldwide for publishing practical, reliable and no-nonsense travel information in our guides and on our Web site. The Lonely Planet list covers just about every accessible part of the world. Currently there are 16 series: Travel guides, Shoestring guides, Condensed guides, Phrasebooks, Read This First, Healthy Travel, Walking guides, Cycling guides, Watching Wildlife guides, Pisces Diving & Snorkeling guides, City Maps, Road Atlases, Out to Eat, World Food, Journeys travel literature and Pictorials.

AFRICA Africa on a shoestring • Cairo • Cairo City Map • Cape Town • Cape Town City Map • East Africa • Egypt • Egyptian Arabic phrasebook • Ethiopia, Eritrea & Djibouti • Ethiopian (Amharic) phrasebook • The Gambia & Senegal • Healthy Travel Africa • Kenya • Malawi • Morocco • Moroccan Arabic phrasebook • Mozambique • Read This First: Africa • South Africa, Lesotho & Swaziland • Southern Africa • Southern Africa Road Atlas • Swahili phrasebook • Tanzania, Zanzibar & Pemba • Trekking in East Africa • Tunisia • Watching Wildlife East Africa •   Watching Wildlife Southern Africa • West Africa • World Food Morocco • Zimbabwe, Botswana & Namibia
Travel Literature: Mali Blues: Traveling to an African Beat • The Rainbird: A Central African Journey • Songs to an African Sunset: A Zimbabwean Story

AUSTRALIA & THE PACIFIC Auckland • Australia • Australian phrasebook • Australia Road Atlas • Bushwalking in Australia •Cycling New Zealand • Fiji • Fijian phrasebook • Healthy Travel Australia, NZ and the Pacific • Islands of Australia's Great Barrier Reef • Melbourne • Melbourne City Map • Micronesia • New Caledonia • New South Wales & the ACT • New Zealand • Northern Territory • Outback Australia • Out to Eat – Melbourne • Out to Eat – Sydney • Papua New Guinea • Pidgin phrasebook • Queensland • Rarotonga & the Cook Islands • Samoa • Solomon Islands • South Australia • South Pacific • South Pacific phrasebook • Sydney • Sydney City Map • Sydney Condensed • Tahiti & French Polynesia • Tasmania • Tonga • Tramping in New Zealand • Vanuatu • Victoria • Walking in Australia • Watching Wildlife Australia • Western Australia
Travel Literature: Islands in the Clouds: Travels in the Highlands of New Guinea • Kiwi Tracks: A New Zealand Journey • Sean & David's Long Drive

CENTRAL AMERICA & THE CARIBBEAN Bahamas, Turks & Caicos • Baja California • Bermuda • Central America on a shoestring • Costa Rica • Costa Rica Spanish phrasebook • Cuba • Dominican Republic & Haiti • Eastern Caribbean • Guatemala • Guatemala, Belize & Yucatán: La Ruta Maya • Healthy Travel Central & South America • Jamaica • Mexico • Mexico City • Panama • Puerto Rico • Read This First: Central & South America • World Food Mexico • Yucatán
Travel Literature: Green Dreams: Travels in Central America

EUROPE Amsterdam • Amsterdam City Map • Amsterdam Condensed • Andalucía • Austria • Baltic States phrasebook • Barcelona • Barcelona City Map • Berlin • Berlin City Map • Britain • British phrasebook • Brussels, Bruges & Antwerp • Brussels City Map • Budapest • Budapest City Map • Canary Islands • Central Europe • Central Europe phrasebook • Corfu & the Ionians • Corsica • Crete • Crete Condensed • Croatia • Cycling Britain • Cycling France • Cyprus • Czech & Slovak Republics • Denmark • Dublin • Dublin City Map • Eastern Europe • Eastern Europe phrasebook • Edinburgh • Estonia, Latvia & Lithuania • Europe on a shoestring • Finland • Florence • France • Frankfurt Condensed • French phrasebook • Georgia, Armenia & Azerbaijan • Germany • German phrasebook • Greece • Greek Islands • Greek phrasebook • Hungary • Iceland, Greenland & the Faroe Islands • Ireland • Istanbul • Italian phrasebook • Italy • Krakow • Lisbon • The Loire • London • London City Map • London Condensed • Madrid • Malta • Mediterranean Europe • Mediterranean Europe phrasebook • Moscow • Mozambique • Munich • the Netherlands • Norway • Out to Eat – London • Paris • Paris City Map • Paris Condensed • Poland • Portugal • Portuguese phrasebook • Prague • Prague City Map • Provence & the Côte d'Azur • Read This First: Europe • Romania & Moldova • Rome • Rome City Map • Russia, Ukraine & Belarus • Russian phrasebook • Scandinavian & Baltic Europe • Scandinavian Europe phrasebook • Scotland • Sicily • Slovenia • South-West France • Spain • Spanish phrasebook • St Petersburg • St Petersburg City Map • Sweden • Switzerland • Trekking in Spain • Tuscany • Ukrainian phrasebook • Venice • Vienna • Walking in Britain • Walking in France • Walking in Ireland • Walking in Italy • Walking in Spain • Walking in Switzerland • Western Europe • Western Europe phrasebook • World Food France • World Food Italy • World Food Spain
Travel Literature: Love and War in the Apennines • The Olive Grove: Travels in Greece • On the Shores of the Mediterranean • Round Ireland in Low Gear • A Small Place in Italy • After Yugoslavia

LONELY PLANET

Mail Order

Lonely Planet products are distributed worldwide. They are also available by mail order from Lonely Planet, so if you have difficulty finding a title please write to us. North and South American residents should write to 150 Linden St, Oakland, CA 94607, USA; European and African residents should write to 10a Spring Place, London NW5 3BH, UK; and residents of other countries to Locked Bag 1, Footscray, Victoria 3011, Australia.

INDIAN SUBCONTINENT Bangladesh • Bengali phrasebook • Bhutan • Delhi • Goa • Healthy Travel Asia & India • Hindi & Urdu phrasebook • India • Indian Himalaya • Karakoram Highway • Kerala • Mumbai (Bombay) • Nepal • Nepali phrasebook • Pakistan • Rajasthan • Read This First: Asia & India • South India • Sri Lanka • Sri Lanka phrasebook • Tibet • Tibetan phrasebook • Trekking in the Indian Himalaya • Trekking in the Karakoram & Hindukush • Trekking in the Nepal Himalaya
Travel Literature: The Age of Kali: Indian Travels and Encounters • Hello Goodnight: A Life of Goa • In Rajasthan • A Season in Heaven: True Tales from the Road to Kathmandu • Shopping for Buddhas • A Short Walk in the Hindu Kush • Slowly Down the Ganges

ISLANDS OF THE INDIAN OCEAN Madagascar & Comoros • Maldives • Mauritius, Réunion & Seychelles

MIDDLE EAST & CENTRAL ASIA Bahrain, Kuwait & Qatar • Central Asia • Central Asia phrasebook • Dubai • Hebrew phrasebook • Iran • Israel & the Palestinian Territories • Istanbul • Istanbul City Map • Istanbul to Cairo on a shoestring • Jerusalem • Jerusalem City Map • Jordan • Lebanon • Middle East • Oman & the United Arab Emirates • Syria • Turkey • Turkish phrasebook • World Food Turkey • Yemen
Travel Literature: Black on Black: Iran Revisited • The Gates of Damascus • Kingdom of the Film Stars: Journey into Jordan

NORTH AMERICA Alaska • Boston • Boston City Map • California & Nevada • California Condensed • Canada • Chicago • Chicago City Map • Deep South • Florida • Great Lakes • Hawaii • Hiking in Alaska • Hiking in the USA • Honolulu • Las Vegas • Los Angeles • Los Angeles City Map • Louisiana & The Deep South • Miami • Miami City Map • New England • New Orleans • New York City • New York City City Map • New York City Condensed • New York, New Jersey & Pennsylvania • Oahu • Out to Eat – San Francisco • Pacific Northwest • Puerto Rico • Rocky Mountains • San Francisco • San Francisco City Map • Seattle • Southwest • Texas • USA • USA phrasebook • Vancouver • Virginia & the Capital Region • Washington DC • Washington, DC City Map • World Food Deep South, USA • World Food New Orleans
Travel Literature: Caught Inside: A Surfer's Year on the California Coast • Drive Thru America

NORTH-EAST ASIA Beijing • Beijing City Map • Cantonese phrasebook • China • Hiking in Japan • Hong Kong • Hong Kong City Map • Hong Kong Condensed • Hong Kong, Macau & Guangzhou • Japan • Japanese phrasebook • Korea • Korean phrasebook • Kyoto • Mandarin phrasebook • Mongolia • Mongolian phrasebook • Seoul • Shanghai • South-West China • Taiwan • Tokyo
Travel Literature: In Xanadu: A Quest • Lost Japan

SOUTH AMERICA Argentina, Uruguay & Paraguay • Bolivia • Brazil • Brazilian phrasebook • Buenos Aires • Chile & Easter Island • Colombia • Ecuador & the Galapagos Islands • Healthy Travel Central & South America • Latin American Spanish phrasebook • Peru • Quechua phrasebook • Read This First: Central & South America • Rio de Janeiro • Rio de Janeiro City Map • Santiago • South America on a shoestring • Santiago • Trekking in the Patagonian Andes • Venezuela
Travel Literature: Full Circle: A South American Journey

SOUTH-EAST ASIA Bali & Lombok • Bangkok • Bangkok City Map • Burmese phrasebook • Cambodia • Hanoi • Healthy Travel Asia & India • Hill Tribes phrasebook • Ho Chi Minh City • Indonesia • Indonesian phrasebook • Indonesia's Eastern Islands • Jakarta • Java • Lao phrasebook • Laos • Malay phrasebook • Malaysia, Singapore & Brunei • Myanmar (Burma) • Philippines • Pilipino (Tagalog) phrasebook • Read This First: Asia & India • Singapore • Singapore City Map • South-East Asia on a shoestring • South-East Asia phrasebook • Thailand • Thailand's Islands & Beaches • Thailand, Vietnam, Laos & Cambodia Road Atlas • Thai phrasebook • Vietnam • Vietnamese phrasebook • World Food Thailand • World Food Vietnam

ALSO AVAILABLE: Antarctica • The Arctic • The Blue Man: Tales of Travel, Love and Coffee • Brief Encounters: Stories of Love, Sex & Travel • Chasing Rickshaws • The Last Grain Race • Lonely Planet Unpacked • Not the Only Planet: Science Fiction Travel Stories • Lonely Planet On the Edge • Sacred India • Travel with Children • Travel Photography: A Guide to Taking Better Pictures

Index

Abbreviations

AL – Albania
AND – Andorra
BIH – Bosnia-Hercegovina
HR – Croatia
CY – Cyprus
F – France

GR – Greece
I – Italy
MK – Macedonia
M – Malta
MA – Morocco
P – Portugal

SLO – Slovenia
E – Spain
TN – Tunisia
TR – Turkey
YU – Yugoslavia

Text

Bold indicates maps.

Bold indicates maps.

MAP LEGEND

CITY ROUTES

Freeway .... Freeway	══ ══ ══ .... Unsealed Road
Highway .... Primary Road	══➤══ .... One Way Street
Road .... Secondary Road	═══════ .... Pedestrian Street
Street .... Street	▢▢▢▢▢▢ .... Stepped Street
Lane .... Lane	⟩══ ══ .... Tunnel
══════ .... On/Off Ramp	══════ .... Footbridge

HYDROGRAPHY

.... River, Creek	◯ ◯ .. Dry Lake; Salt Lake
.... Canal	⊙ ⟿ .... Spring; Rapids
◯ .... Lake	◯ ⥿ ◁ .... Waterfalls

REGIONAL ROUTES

══════ .... Tollway, Freeway	
══════ .... Primary Road	
══════ .... Secondary Road	
═════ .... Minor Road	

TRANSPORT ROUTES & STATIONS

├─●─ .... Train	─────▢ .... Ferry
├ + + + ─. Underground Train	───────── .... Walking Trail
──Ⓜ── .... Metro	· · · · · · · · ─ .... Walking Tour
═ ═ ═ ═ .... Tramway	═══════ .... Path
─∥─∥─∥─ ... Cable Car, Chairlift	─────── .... Pier or Jetty

BOUNDARIES

─·─··─·─ .... International
─··─··─ .... State
── ── ── .... Disputed
▬▬▬ .... Fortified Wall

AREA FEATURES

▬▬ .... Building	◯ .... Market	.... Forest
❀ .... Park, Gardens	◯ ... Sports Ground	+ + ... Cemetery

.... Campus
.... Plaza

POPULATION SYMBOLS

✪ CAPITAL .... National Capital	● CITY .... City	● Village .... Village
◉ CAPITAL .... State Capital	● Town .... Town	▬▬ .... Urban Area

MAP SYMBOLS

♠ .... Place to Stay	▼ .... Place to Eat	● .... Point of Interest

✈	.... Airport	▢	.. Embassy, Consulate	▢	.... National Park	▣	.... Swimming Pool
⑤	.... Bank	⚓	.... Fountain	▣	.... Parking	▢	.... Synagogue
▢	.... Bus Terminal	✚	.... Hospital	)(	.... Pass	▢	.... Telephone
▣	.. Cable Car, Funicular	▣	.... Internet Cafe	▣	.... Police Station	▢	.... Theatre
▣	.... Castle, Château	※	.... Lookout	▭	.... Post Office	❶	... Tourist Information
✚ ▢	.... Church	▲	.... Monument	▢	.... Pub or Bar	♨	.... Winery
▣	.... Cinema	▥	.... Museum	✖	.... Shopping Centre	▢	.... Zoo

Note: not all symbols displayed above appear in this book

LONELY PLANET OFFICES

Australia
Locked Bag 1, Footscray, Victoria 3011
☎ 03 9689 4666 fax 03 9689 6833
email: talk2us@lonelyplanet.com.au

USA
150 Linden St, Oakland, CA 94607
☎ 510 893 8555 TOLL FREE: 800 275 8555
fax 510 893 8572
email: info@lonelyplanet.com

UK
10a Spring Place, London NW5 3BH
☎ 020 7428 4800 fax 020 7428 4828
email: go@lonelyplanet.co.uk

France
1 rue du Dahomey, 75011 Paris
☎ 01 55 25 33 00 fax 01 55 25 33 01
email: bip@lonelyplanet.fr
www.lonelyplanet.fr

**World Wide Web: www.lonelyplanet.com or AOL keyword: lp
Lonely Planet Images: lpi@lonelyplanet.com.au**